C288285400

WITHDRAWN FROM
NEWCASTLE UPON TYNE
CITY LIBRARIES

GALAXY
2000

D1612367

ENGLISH GOLDSMITHS

AND

THEIR MARKS

Standing Salt   Hall-marked London 1569
Height 12 inches
The property of the Vintners Company

ENGLISH GOLDSMITHS

AND

THEIR MARKS

A HISTORY OF
THE GOLDSMITHS AND PLATE WORKERS OF
ENGLAND, SCOTLAND, AND IRELAND

WITH OVER THIRTEEN THOUSAND MARKS

REPRODUCED IN FACSIMILE
FROM AUTHENTIC EXAMPLES OF PLATE

AND

TABLES OF DATE-LETTERS AND OTHER HALL-MARKS

USED IN
THE ASSAY OFFICES OF THE UNITED KINGDOM

BY

SIR CHARLES JAMES JACKSON, F.S.A.

OF THE MIDDLE TEMPLE, BARRISTER-AT-LAW
AUTHOR OF "AN ILLUSTRATED HISTORY OF ENGLISH PLATE"

SECOND EDITION, REVISED AND ENLARGED

DOVER PUBLICATIONS, INC.
NEW YORK   NEW YORK

NEWCASTLE UPON TYNE
REFERENCE   LIBRARY

Copyright © 1921 by Philip Gordon Dunn, Derek Ainslie Jackson, and John Emlyn Victor Mason.

All rights reserved under Pan American and International Copyright Conventions.

Published in the United Kingdom by Constable & Company, Ltd., 10 Orange Street, London W. C. 2.

This Dover edition, first published in 1964, is an unabridged and unaltered republication of the work first published by Macmillan and Co. in 1921.

NEWCASTLE UPON TYNE CITY LIBRARIES	
Class No.	Acc. No. G
739.1	267012 SR
Checked SV	Issued 14·9·65

Library of Congress Catalog Card Number: 64-18852

Manufactured in the United States of America

Dover Publications, Inc.
180 Varick Street
New York 14, N. Y.

To

The Worshipful Company of Goldsmiths of London,

TO WHOM THE AUTHOR IS INDEBTED FOR MUCH OF WHAT IS

CONTAINED HEREIN, THIS SECOND EDITION OF

ENGLISH GOLDSMITHS AND THEIR MARKS

IS, WITH THE EXPRESS PERMISSION OF

THE WARDENS AND COURT OF ASSISTANTS,

RESPECTFULLY DEDICATED.

PREFACE TO THE SECOND EDITION

IN submitting to readers a second edition of *English Goldsmiths and their Marks*, the Author feels obliged to express his gratification with the appreciative reception accorded to the first edition of this work.

Since the publication of the first edition, the further researches of the Author and his friends have resulted in the discovery of more than two thousand additional marks, which have been classified in their proper order and represented in *facsimile*. There has also been a considerable amount of emendation, rendered necessary in connection with the additional particulars which have been brought to light.

In addition to bringing up to the present time the Tables of Date-Letters, &c., relating to the Assay Offices still in active existence, the Author has devoted a great deal of attention to increasing his records of makers' marks, over six hundred of which have been added to the chronological list of London goldsmiths' marks alone.

By the cordial assistance of the Rev. J. F. Chanter, M.A., and the Rev. Canon Mills, the Exeter and Barnstaple records have been extended, and lists of other Devon and Cornwall marks compiled.

Groups of marks pertaining to Lewes, Colchester, Salisbury, Poole, the Channel Islands, Calcutta, and Jamaica have also been arranged by the Author, while the lists of Unascribed marks have been largely increased. In many of the tables the number of marks has been doubled, and some lists of goldsmiths' names are given which were not recorded in the first edition.

The Author is pleased to mention the able treatment which the late Mr. W. J. Cripps devoted to the subject of Old English Plate, and the marks thereon, his work having been much superior to that of the late Mr. W. Chaffers, which was published at an earlier date.

Mr. Dudley Westropp, M.R.I.A., has very kindly supplied the Author with numerous impressions of marks, and has perused the proofs of the Chapters comprised in the Irish section.   Mr. Llewellyn Davies, the Author's Estate Manager, has also rendered valuable assistance in the perusal of the representations of marks and all the proof sheets as received from the Printers.

Reference has been made in the first edition of this work to the enthusiastic assistance rendered to the Author by goldsmiths and dealers in plate in the United Kingdom.   In addition thereto great assistance has been received from Mr. Frederick Bradbury, Messrs. Carrington, Messrs. Comyns, Mr. Harry Alston, Mr. W. H. Willson, and particularly the individual partners of Messrs. Crichton Bros., who have supplied the Author with more notes and impressions of marks than any other members of their trade.

CHARLES J. JACKSON.

6 ENNISMORE GARDENS,
LONDON, S.W.,
October, 1921.

PREFACE TO THE FIRST EDITION

(WHICH WAS DEDICATED TO THE MOST HONOURABLE THE MARQUESS OF BREADALBANE, K.G., TO WHOM THE AUTHOR IS INDEBTED FOR MUCH CORDIAL ASSISTANCE IN THE COMPOSITION OF THE CHAPTER ON THE SCOTTISH PROVINCIAL GOLDSMITHS AND THEIR MARKS).

THE work comprised in the following pages has engaged my attention for no less than seventeen years. It was commenced in the year 1887, in connection with the composition of a monograph on *The Spoon and its History*, read at a meeting of the Society of Antiquaries and published in *Archæologia*, LIII. I intended to incorporate the history of the spoon in a more comprehensive work under the title of *An Illustrated History of English Plate, Ecclesiastical and Secular*, to the preparation of which I had devoted a considerable amount of time.

In the course of my studies, however, I found that in no obtainable work were the marks on English plate represented with as much accuracy as might reasonably have been expected, and that no published tables of Irish marks were even approximately accurate. I decided, therefore, to construct tables of date-letters and other hall-marks, for insertion in an appendix to my history of plate. I obtained access to many important collections, and prepared a number of engravings in the style of the frontispiece of this book, and a great many half-tone illustrations similar to that of the "Bekegle Cup," and I proceeded with the compilation of the tables of marks concurrently with the composition and illustration of the history. I had not, however, proceeded very far, before I found that "Marks on plate of English* manufacture" was too large a subject for an appendix, and that in connection with the marks on English* plate it was necessary, or at the least expedient, to refer to the goldsmiths† who employed those marks to indicate the quality of the plate and the identity of the maker. Here, then, was a subject large enough for a volume to itself, and being of opinion that it had not theretofore been dealt with as fully as it deserved, and influenced by the impression that the need for a work on "English goldsmiths and their marks"

* The term "English" is used here, as in the title of the book, comprehensively, and includes both Scotch and Irish.
† The term "goldsmiths" is also used comprehensively, and includes silversmiths.

was more urgent than for a history of plate, I resolved to set aside the latter until I had completed the former.

Year after year I have proceeded with the collection and reproduction in *fac-simile* of marks which are here tabulated under their respective headings, but, notwithstanding my close application to it, the book would not have been ready for publication even now, without the cordial assistance which I have received from the numerous friends whose names are mentioned in its pages. Yet while the composition of this book has required so many years, other authors have been able to produce works on the same subject in about as many months. For example, a Mr. Montagu Howard, of New York, has published a massive book, entitled, *Old London Silver*, in which a great number of marks are illustrated by the simple process of reproduction from the works of Mr. Cripps and Mr. Chaffers.

The way in which I have reproduced the marks in my tables is explained in the pages. The plan is both laborious and costly, but I have spent time and money ungrudgingly in the production of the work, and although the sale of the entire edition may not recoup my expenditure, I shall not be disappointed, because the work was undertaken for pleasure and not for profit.

To me the most satisfactory part of the book is contained in Chapters XXII. to XXV. inclusive, which have reference to "The Irish Goldsmiths and their Marks," a topic which hitherto has been the subject of but little research. The help which I have received in the composition of those chapters from the gentlemen named therein has been invaluable. The assistance rendered by Mr. Garstin and Mr. Westropp has not been confined to the Irish section; they have read every proof-sheet as it has come from the printers, and without their co-operation the lines of *corrigenda* would have been more numerous, and some of the printers' errors there mentioned might have escaped my notice.

It remains for me to express my thanks to the clergy of England and Ireland generally, and to custodians of communion plate in Scotland, for the opportunity of reproducing marks on ecclesiastical plate which are tabulated in the following pages; to the Assay Masters of Chester, Birmingham, Sheffield, Edinburgh, Glasgow and Dublin for cordial assistance; to Mr. W. H. St. John Hope, M.A.; Mr. R. C. Hope, F.S.A.*; Mr. R. Day, F.S.A.; Mr. J. H. Walter, and Mr. H. D. Ellis, for many valuable suggestions; and to Mr. Arthur Irwin Dasent for kindly compiling the index as "a labour of love".

Thanks have also to be expressed to the authorities of the British Museum, the Victoria and Albert Museum (South Kensington), the Museums of Edinburgh,

---

* I am indebted to Mr. R. C. Hope for permission to reprint the names of many London and provincial goldsmiths collected by him.

Dublin, Bath, Croydon, Reading, and other towns; to the Corporations of London, Dublin, York, Chester, Gloucester, Hull and other towns for access to their collections of plate; to the Benchers of the Inner Temple, the Middle Temple and Gray's Inn; and to the following City Companies :—the Mercers, the Merchant Taylors, the Armourers and Braziers, the Ironmongers and the Innholders, for similar courtesies; and to Messrs. Christie, Manson and Woods, and other auctioneers for opportunities for the examination of many fine collections of plate entrusted to them for sale.

Goldsmiths and dealers in plate throughout the United Kingdom have enthusiastically assisted me in my efforts to accurately construct my tables of marks by giving me every possible facility for transcribing marks from plate in their possession; those of them who have rendered the greatest assistance, and who must not be passed over unnoticed, are : Messrs. Garrard, Messrs. Crichton, Messrs. Spink, Messrs. Dobson, Messrs. Hancock, Messrs. M. and S. Lyon, Mr. S. J. Phillips, and the late Mr. W. Boore, of London ; Mr. Rossi, of Norwich ; Mr. Depree and Mr. Lake, of Exeter ; Mr. A. J. S. Brook, Mr. Chisholm, and Messrs. Hamilton and Inches, of Edinburgh ; Messrs. Sorley, and Messrs. Smith and Rait, of Glasgow ; and Messrs. West and Son, of Dublin.

Collectors and dealers will by the aid of this work be enabled to locate and fix the date of much English, Scotch and Irish plate, and to identify many marks which have been hitherto unknown or regarded as doubtful or uncertain.

Should any marks on English plate not represented in this work, or appearing to be different from any illustrated herein, be found by a reader I shall be grateful for information concerning them.

Notwithstanding the care which has been taken in its preparation, the work is still far from being perfect, and is greatly inferior to what I wished it to be ; but I have done my best to place the subject upon a clearer and more definite footing than it has heretofore rested. Those who have already attempted work of a similar nature will appreciate its attendant difficulties, and will, I have no doubt, make allowances in respect of them.

C. J. JACKSON.

LONDON, *June*, 1905.

TABLE OF CONTENTS

Contents

Contents

LIST OF ILLUSTRATIONS

ENGLISH GOLDSMITHS

AND

THEIR MARKS

CHAPTER I.

INTRODUCTION.

In these pages the term "Goldsmith" is used, as it formerly was, not only with reference to the worker in gold, but as comprising the Silversmith and the worker in both gold and silver. So, too, in many cases where vessels are described in inventories as "gold cups," they are seldom wholly of gold but are for the most part silver-gilt, cups and the like entirely of gold being extremely rare. In the same way the word "English" is here used not merely with reference to the goldsmiths of England and Wales but to those of Scotland and Ireland also.

"Goldsmith" includes Silversmith.

"Gold" often means Silver-gilt.

The Craft or "Mystery" (as it was called in early times) of the Goldsmith is a very ancient one, and was practised in England at a very remote period. In the year 1180 an association or "guild" of gold-smiths was, with other guilds, fined for being irregularly established without the King's licence (*adulterine*), and in the year 1238, by reason of numerous frauds having been perpetrated by certain goldsmiths, an order was made by the King (Henry III.), in council, commanding the Mayor and Aldermen of London to choose six of the most discreet gold-smiths of the city to superintend the "craft". This order was duly obeyed, and the six "discreet goldsmiths" were succeeded by others in the office of superintendents or wardens of the craft. In the 28 Edw. I. c. 20, of the year 1300, we find them recognised and referred to as such under the style of "gardiens," a part of whose duties was to assay every vessel of silver before it passed from the hands of the workers, and mark it with a *leopard's head*.

Guild of London Goldsmiths, 1180.

Mark of the leopard's head first mentioned in 1300.

The goldsmiths of London were a numerous and powerful, not to say truculent, body in the thirteenth century, for we find in the chronicles of the city reference to numerous affrays in which they engaged, and to one in particular which was fought in 1267 between them and the "Taylors," in which 500 men were engaged on each side, many of whom were killed and their bodies thrown into the Thames.

Guild of London
Goldsmiths
incorporated
in 1327.

The Guild of London Goldsmiths became regularly incorporated in 1327 by Royal Charter (1 Edw. III.), under the title of "The Wardens and Commonalty of the Mystery of Goldsmiths of the City of London". They are referred to in an Act of the year 1363 (37 Edw. III. cap. 7)

1363 the Maker's
mark first
mentioned.

—set out (*infra*) in the chapter on legislation concerning goldsmiths— whereby, amongst other things, *every master goldsmith was required to have a mark*, and in February, 139⅔, they were re-incorporated by charter (16 Ric. II.) with extended powers. In 1462, by charter of Edward IV.

London
Goldsmiths'
Company
constituted a
corporate body
with perpetual
succession, 1462.

the Goldsmiths' Company were constituted a corporate body with perpetual succession, their powers were further extended, and they were enabled to use a common seal and given various privileges and duties.

The powers, duties, and privileges conferred as above were re-affirmed and enlarged by other charters from time to time, down to the reign of Charles II., a charter of which reign recites and confirms all those previously granted.

While there is evidence that in these early times the goldsmiths of London were controlled by a guild or company composed of wardens and other officers of their own calling, there is also evidence of the

Early
Provincial
Goldsmiths.

existence of similar guilds or companies in the provinces at a period but little less early, for in 1423, by a statute (2 Hen. VI. c. 14), "York, Newcastle-upon-Tine, Lincoln, Norwich, Bristow, Salisbury, and Coventry," were appointed "to have divers Touches" for silver wares. There are records of goldsmiths working at Lincoln in 1155-63, Chester in 1225, Norwich as early as 1285, York in 1313, Shrewsbury in 1482, Hull in 1499, and in other provincial towns but little less early.

Early
Scottish
Goldsmiths.

In Scotland there were goldsmiths working at a date in all probability as early, or nearly as early, as in England, for we find an Act of James II. of Scotland of 1457 "anent the reformation of gold and silver wrought be goldsmiths".

Early Irish
Goldsmiths.

In Ireland, apart from the gold ornaments of the Celtic period which have been found there, the Chalice of Ardagh proves the existence of highly skilled Irish goldsmiths at a period earlier than the date of the Norman Conquest, although the date of the earliest existing Charter of Incorporation of the Dublin Goldsmiths' Company is no earlier than December, 1637.*

English goldsmiths now mainly depend on Australia, South Africa, and North America for their supplies of gold, and on North and South America for silver. It, was, however, not always so, for in the past gold was found in considerable quantities in the British Isles. Gold is still found in the United Kingdom, but not in very large quantities, and where English gold mining has been resorted to in recent years, as in North Wales, Scotland, and Ireland, the operations do not appear to have been carried on with great financial success. The home production of silver is now limited to such as is found combined with lead, and the silver is separated from the latter in the process of manufacture. Gold and Silver, where found.

Although silver is now everywhere found, and used, in immensely greater quantities than gold, it does not appear to have been always thus in all parts of the British Isles, for in Ireland there are numerous examples of wrought gold of the Celtic period in the shape of objects for personal use and ornament, while the finding of similar articles of silver cf the same period has been extremely rare.

Gold and silver, by reason of their natural properties, have for ages been the materials most favoured for articles of ornament and use, whether personal or ceremonial, their extreme ductility and malleability lending themselves to the hammerman in the construction of forms both simple and complex ; and by reason of the high polish which they are capable of receiving, and the beauty of their colours, effects are obtained in these metals which are unattainable in any other material. Gold can be beaten so thin that a quarter of a million leaves will measure no more than an inch in thickness, and can be drawn into wire so fine as to be almost invisible to the average sight. Silver, while not so extremely malleable as gold, still possesses this quality in a marked degree. It may be beaten into leaves one thousand to the inch, and drawn into wire correspondingly fine. The one great objection to the use of gold is its weight, which is between nineteen and twenty times that of water ; silver being only about half the weight of gold. In other words, while the specific gravity of pure gold varies from 19·25 to 19·40, that of pure silver is 10·40 to 10·60, according to whether it has been merely cast, Natural properties of Gold and Silver. Their beauty, malleability, and ductility.

---

* The records of the Dublin Corporation contain a reference to a Charter of earlier date than the reign of Queen Mary. That Charter was, however, accidentally burnt.

or compressed by rolling or hammering. It is, perhaps, due to the greater weight of gold, almost as much as to its greater scarcity, that the work of the goldsmith has been mainly confined to silver, and that where gold has been used, it has been applied to the surface, either all over or in parts, and is then technically described as either " wholly " or " parcel " gilt-*plate.**

"Alloy"
necessary for
gold and silver.

Neither pure gold nor pure silver is ever used by the goldsmith for his wares, nor has it been used since the reign of Edward III. by the Mint for coinage. The pure metal is much too soft for either purpose. The required hardness is obtained by the mixture of some other metal of less value called alloy.† In the case of gold the alloy used is either silver or copper or an admixture of both, and on the nature of the alloy the ultimate colour of the manufactured gold depends. The bright yellow of pure gold partakes of a greenish tinge when alloyed with silver, of a reddish hue when alloyed with copper, and of a paler yellow when alloyed with both silver and copper. Until about 1829 the standard gold of the English coinage was alloyed with both silver and copper, which accounts for the pale colour of the old guineas. At the Sydney Mint silver was used, which accounts for the pale greenish hue of the sovereigns coined there. Since about 1829 copper only has been used as an alloy at the London Mint, and the specific gravity of standard gold has been thereby reduced from about 17·82 to 17·57. In the reign of Queen Victoria a process of passing a stream of chlorine gas through the molten gold was adopted, whereby even the traces of silver and other impurities—likely to cause defects in the coinage—existing in the natural gold are removed, and the gold remaining is rendered less brittle.

Description of
alloy used.

For silver, the alloy used is always copper ; the use of any other base metal with silver makes it brittle and difficult to work. By the proper admixture of copper alloy with pure gold, as performed at the English Mint, the metal formed is practically homogeneous, every part

---

* The term " Plate " (from Old French *plate, platte, plette;* Spanish, *plata*—silver), although, strictly speaking, used with reference to articles of silver, is frequently found in Acts of Parliament and elsewhere more comprehensively employed to describe ornaments, utensils, &c., made either of gold or silver, and is then called respectively " gold plate " and " silver plate ". Throughout this book the use of the term " plate " will be limited as much as possible (or at any rate expedient) to articles of silver.

† " Alloy " (from the French " *à la loi* "—according to law), the amount of base metal which may be added to pure gold or pure silver by permission of the law. The amount of added base metal is frequently (for fraudulent purposes) in excess of what the law allows, but is still called " alloy ". The word is frequently used to describe the mixture of pure and base metal, which, when of standard quality, is described as the " true alloy," and for this reason the term is considered by some to have been derived from *allier*—to mix.

being of very nearly the same quality. In the case of silver similarly alloyed the result is not so satisfactory, and portions taken from different parts of a trial plate are found to vary much more than in the case of gold.

Before the reign of Henry VIII. silver money and plate were computed by the medieval or " Tower " pound sterling, which was the equivalent of 5,400 grains (Troy), and in the old inventories the weights of the various articles of plate are recorded in pounds, shillings, and pence, with (sometimes) an additional fraction of a pound called a mark. The shilling was one-twentieth of a pound, the pennyweight one-twelfth of a shilling, and the mark two-thirds of a pound, or one hundred and sixty pennyweights. The table is as follows :—

"Tower" pound.

POUND.		MARKS.		SHILLINGS.		PENCE OR PENNYWEIGHTS.		GRAINS (TROY).
I	=	$1\frac{1}{2}$	=	20	=	240	=	5,400
		I	=	$13\frac{1}{3}$	=	160	=	3,600
				I	=	12	=	270
						I	=	$22\frac{1}{2}$

Medieval Goldsmiths' weights.

In 152$\frac{6}{7}$ the old Tower pound was abolished by Royal Proclamation, and Troy weight (which had been introduced into England from Troyes, in France, about a century earlier) was substituted for it. The weight of gold and silver is usually expressed in ounces and pennyweights, and, for exactitude, grains, but not in pounds, however great the amount may be.[*]

The ounce (Troy) was originally divided into twenty-four parts called "*carats*," and each carat into four grains ; a carat grain is therefore equivalent to five grains (Troy), or a quarter of a pennyweight, and when gold is described as so many carats fine what is meant is, that the number of carats mentioned is pure gold : " 18-*carat gold*" meaning a metal composed of 18 parts of pure gold and 6 parts alloy.

The table of Troy weight is as follows :—

POUNDS.		OUNCES.		PENNYWEIGHTS.		GRAINS.
I	=	12	=	240	=	5,760
		I	=	20	=	480
				I	=	24

Troy weight.

The pound, ounce, and grain are the same in Apothecaries' weight.

[*] In some of the records of the Goldsmiths' Company of Dublin the weight of plate assayed is stated in pounds, but that is unusual.

The table of carat weight for gold is as follows :—

OUNCE (TROY).		CARATS (GOLD).		CARAT GRAINS.
1	=	24	=	96
		1	=	4

A pound (Troy) of standard gold (22 carats fine) is coined into $46\frac{29}{40}$ sovereigns, the weight of a sovereign being 123·27447 grains (Troy). The value, therefore, of such gold is (in gold coinage) £3 17s. 10½d. per ounce, and the value of pure gold £4 5s. 0d. per ounce. The value per ounce of 18 carat gold is £3 3s. 8½d., of 15 carat £2 13s. 1d., of 12 carat £2 2s. 6d., and of 9 carat £1 11s. 10½d.

The pound (Avoirdupois) is equal to 7,000 grains (Troy).

One hundred and ninety-two ounces (Avoirdupois) are equal to 175 ounces (Troy). A pound (Troy) of silver is coined into 66 shillings or 132 sixpences, the weight of a shilling being 87·27· grains. Unworn silver coins, therefore, to the value of 5s. 6d. will weigh an ounce.

These facts may be worth remembering in case it may be necessary to ascertain the approximate weight of silver or gold when Troy weights are not accessible.

The present * value of silver in ingots is about 4s. 4d. per ounce; in 1894 it was about 2s. 6d.

* July, 1920.

CHAPTER II.

LEGISLATION CONCERNING GOLDSMITHS.

(THE STATUTES CHRONOLOGICALLY ARRANGED.)

As early as the year 1238 an ordinance (22 Henry III.) was issued concerning the work of English goldsmiths, entitled, "*De auro fabricando in Civitate Londoniarum*," by reason of the fraudulent use of more than the proper quantity of alloy in the manufacture of gold and silver wares. This ordinance provided that no one should use any gold of which the mark was not worth one hundred shillings at the least, nor any silver worse than the standard of the silver coinage. It is evident from the earliest records concerning goldsmiths that the main object of nearly every statute and ordinance affecting them in their work has been the maintenance of uniformity in the standards of wrought gold and silver, and the protection of the public against the fraudulent use of inferior metal by the dishonest worker. *[margin: 22 Henry III. (1238). De auro fabricando.]*

In 1292 the Act 20 Edward I. stat. 4 (*Statutum de Moneta*) proscribed the importation and use of foreign money (the quality of which was unknown), and restricted the circulating medium to home-struck coins, the quality of which was the care of the Sovereign. *[margin: 20 Edw. I. stat. 4 (1292). Statutum de Moneta.]*

The Act 28 Edward I. c. 20, which became law in 1300, provided that no gold or silver wares should be sold until they had been assayed by persons duly authorised to perform that duty. It runs as follows :—* *[margin: 28 Edw. I. stat. 3, c. 20 (1300).]*

"It is ordained, that no goldsmith of England, nor none otherwise within the King's dominion, shall from henceforth make or cause to be made any manner of vessel, jewel, or any other thing of gold or silver, except it be good and true allay,† that is to say, gold of a certain touch, and silver of the sterling‡ allay or of better, at the pleasure of him to whom the work belongeth; and that none work worse silver than money; and that no manner of vessel of silver depart out of the hands of the workers until it be essayed by the Wardens (Gardiens) of the craft, and further that it be marked with a Leopard's Head, and that they work no worse gold than of the Touch of Paris; and that the *[margin: Wrought gold to be of the true alloy, and wrought silver to be of the "sterling" alloy. All to be marked with a leopard's head.]*

---

* The original is in Old French.

† Allay = alloy. Here, as often occurs, the term is used with reference to gold and silver of standard quality, that is, pure gold or silver with the allowed addition of inferior metal, although, properly speaking, the meaning is restricted to the added base metal.

‡ Sterling is "esterling" in the original. The meaning and derivation of the word are explained in the chapter on The Standards.

Wardens of the craft shall go from shop to shop among the goldsmiths to essay if their gold be of the same Touch that is spoken of before, and if they find any other than of the Touch aforesaid, the gold shall be forfeit to the King. And that none shall make rings, crosses, nor locks, and that none shall set any stone in gold except it be natural. And that gravers, cutters of stones and of seals, shall give to each their weight of silver and gold (as near as they can) upon their fidelity; and the jewels of base gold which they have on their hands they shall utter as fast as they can; and from thenceforth, if they buy any of the same work, they shall buy it to work upon, and not to sell again; *and that all the good towns of England, where any goldsmith be dwelling, shall be ordered according to this statute as they of London be; and that one shall come from every good town for all the residue that be dwelling in the same unto London, for to be ascertained of their Touch.* And if any goldsmith be attainted hereafter because that he hath done otherwise than before is ordained, he shall be punished by imprisonment, and by ransom at the King's pleasure. And notwithstanding all these things before-mentioned, or any point of them, both the King and his Council, and all they that were present at the making of this ordinance will and intend that the right and prerogative of his crown shall be saved to him in all things."

9 Edw. III. c. 1 (1335). No gold or silver to be exported without license.

In 1335 a second *Statutum de Moneta* (9 Edward III. c. 1) recites that counterfeit money had been introduced by foreigners, and enacts that, in order to provide convenient remedy, and "so that our money be increased in our realm," plate shall not be exported without licence, nor goldsmiths melt down certain sterling money, nor any person leave the kingdom except at Dover, and there to be searched, and that innkeepers in every port shall be sworn to search their guests in the same manner as searchers do, "so that no man of whatsoever state or condition he be shall carry out of our realm sterling money, silver or plate, neither in vessel of gold or of silver without our leave".

37 Edw. III. c. 7 (1363). No gold or silver but good sterling to be worked.

In the year 1363 it was enacted by the Statute 37 Edward III. c. 7, that no goldsmith, as well in London as elsewhere within the realm, should work any gold or silver but of the alloy of good sterling (*de bon esterlyng*), that every master goldsmith should "*have a mark by himself, which mark shall be known by them assigned by the King to survey their work and allay,*" that the goldsmiths should not set their mark till their work

All work to be assayed and stamped with King's mark.

Then maker to set his own mark on it.

was assayed: and that *after the assay made the surveyor should set the King's mark upon it, and then the goldsmith his mark,* for which he should answer; that no goldsmith should charge for silver vessel but 1s. 6d. for the pound of two marks, as at Paris; that no silversmith should meddle with gilding; and that no gilder should work in silver.

In the following year the 38 Edw. III. c. 2 renewed the prohibition against the exportation of gold or silver in plate or money.

2 Rich. II. (1378).

In 1378 it was enacted (2 Richard II.) that "because gold and silver, which is wrought by goldsmiths in England, is oftentimes less fine than it ought to be, because the goldsmiths are their own judges, be it ordained that henceforth *every goldsmith puts his own mark upon his work ; and the assay of the touch belongs to the Mayors and Governors of the cities and boroughs, with the aid of the Master of the Mint, if there be such, putting the mark of the city or borough where the assay is."* *

The assay of the touch belongs to the Mayors and Governors of the Cities and Boroughs where the assay is.

In the same Roll (2 Richard II.) the following Act is also to be found :—

"It is further ordained that every goldsmith shall have his own mark by himself, and if any vessel which has been made is found within the realm after the Nativity of St. John next coming, not marked with the mark of the goldsmith who made it, or shall be of worse alloy than the sterling, then the same goldsmith shall pay to the party complaining double the value of the vessel, and be put in prison, and pay a fine according to the extent of the trespass. And our Lord the King shall appoint such as he thinks proper to make the said assay as well in London as elsewhere, at all such times as shall be necessary, and after the assay made, to mark the said work with another mark, appointed therefor by our said Lord the King. And it is assented that this ordinance shall begin from the said Feast of St. John, and shall last as long as the next Parliament, to try within that time whether it be useful or no." *

Penalty of double value on goldsmith for not marking with his mark or for making any vessel worse than sterling.

This Act appears not to have been renewed at the end of the term for which it was enacted, but similar provisions are to be found in statutes of the following reign.

The Statute 5 Richard II. c. 2 (1381) enacted that none shall transport gold or silver without licence : " For the great mischief which the realm suffereth and long hath done, for that gold and silver as well in money as in plate and jewels as otherwise by exchanges made in divers manners is carried out of the realm so that in effect there is none left, which thing, if it should be longer suffered, would shortly be the destruction of the same realm, which God forbid".

5 Rich. II. c. 2 (1381). No gold or silver to be exported without license.

In 1392 the Charter incorporating the London goldsmiths, which had been granted by Edward III., was renewed by a Charter of Richard II., bearing date 6 February, 16 Ric. II. Their first Charter was thereby confirmed and powers were given them to choose Wardens and other officers.

Renewal of Charter to London Goldsmiths Company 16 Rich. II. (1392).

The statute 5 Henry IV. c. 4 (1403), enacted "That none from henceforth shall use to multiply † gold or silver, nor use the craft of multiplication, and if any the same do and be thereof attaint that he incur the pain of felony in this case ".

5 Hen. IV. c. 4 (1403). Multiplication of Gold or Silver prohibited.

In 140$\frac{3}{4}$ was also enacted the Statute 5 Hen. IV. c. 13, entitled, " What things may be plated with gold or silver and what not "; which, after

5 Hen. IV. c. 13 (1403-4). Gilding and Silvering of base metal prohibited unless for the Church.

* Roll of Parliament, 2 Rich. II., No. 30.
† " Multiply " seems here to have meant to increase either by refining ores or by adulterating fine silver, or possibly by the trickery of an alchemist.

reciting that "fraudulent artificers, imagining to deceive the common people, do daily make locks, rings, beads, candlesticks, harness * for girdles, hilts, chalices, and sword pomels, powder boxes, and covers for cups, of copper and of latten, and the same overgild and silver, like to gold or silver, and the same sell and put to gage to many men not having full knowledge thereof for whole gold and whole silver, to the great deceit, loss and hindrance of the common people, and the wasting of gold and silver," made it a penal offence to gild or silver any of the articles mentioned in the recital, made of copper or latten, with an exception that ornaments for the Church might be made of copper or latten, provided that in the foot or some other part of the ornament the copper was left bare : so "that a man may see whereof the thing is made, for to eschew the deceit aforesaid".

In the same year (1404), the Charter of Edward III. was confirmed by Henry IV., and the London goldsmiths were given jurisdiction in respect of gold and silver work used by the cutlers.

2 Hen. V. c. 4 (1414). Price of Silver-gilt regulated.

In the year 1414, by the 2 Hen. V. c. 4, the selling price of silver gilt was regulated, "for that the goldsmiths of England of their covin and ordinances will not sell the wares of their mystery gilt but at the double price of the weight of silver of the same, which seemeth to the King very outrageous and too excessive a price ; the King for the ease of his people hath ordained that all goldsmiths of England shall gild no silver wares worse than the alloy of the English sterling ; and that they take for a pound of troy gilt but forty-six shillings and eight-pence at the most, and of greater weight or less, according to the quantity and weight of the same, and that which shall be by them gilt from henceforth shall be of a reasonable price, and not excessive ; and if any goldsmith do contrary to this statute, he shall forfeit to the King the value of the thing sold."

8 Hen. V. c. 3 (1420). Spurs of Nobles and Knights allowed to be silvered.

By a later statute of the same reign the nobles and knights of the realm obtained an amendment of the statute 5 Hen. IV. (*supra*), prohibiting the gilding of base metal except for the Church : the provisions of the 8 Hen. V. c. 3 being that no other metal than silver shall be gilt except "the ornaments of Holy Church" ; and no metal shall be silvered except "knights' spurs and all the apparel that pertaineth to a baron and above that estate".

2 Hen. VI. c. 12 (1423). Master of the Mint to give full value for silver.

In 1423, by the Act 2 Henry VI. c. 12, "to the intent that the more bullion may be brought to the Mint and the greater plenty of white money be made and current within the realm, for the ease and profit of the commonalty of the same," the Master of the Mint was required to keep his allay ; to bring to every person bringing silver its true value ; the King's Assayer, "which is a person indifferent betwixt the Master of the Mint and the Merchant ; and also the Controller," is to be present when

---

* "Harness" originally comprised all the accoutrements of an armed horseman; it appears to be here limited to the studs and buckles of girdles.

any bullion is brought to the Mint, and affix its true value in case of difference; the Assayer and Controller to be credible, substantial and expert men, having perfect knowledge of the mystery of goldsmiths and of the Mint; the Master of the Mint to convert into coin all gold and silver, wrought or unwrought, coined or uncoined.

The Act 2 Henry VI. c. 13 fixed the price of a pound weight of silver "(forasmuch as great scarcity of white money is within the realms, because that silver is bought and sold, not coined) at 22s. the lb.".

2 Hen. VI. c. 13. Price of Silver fixed at 22s. the pound.

In the same year, by the Act 2 Hen. VI. c. 14, the provisions of former statutes as to the quality of wrought silver and as to its being touched and stamped with the leopard's head and maker's mark before being set for sale, under a penalty of double the value, were re-enacted with additions directing that the mark or sign of every goldsmith be known to the Wardens of the same craft, and that an allowance be made for such "souder" as may be necessary, and imposing a penalty of double value on "the keeper of the touch for every 'harness of silver'* which he shall touch that is worse than sterling". It was by this statute that "York, Newcastle-upon-Tine, Lincoln, Norwich, Bristow, Salisbury, and Coventry," were appointed "to have divers touches". Except, however, for the appointment of "touches" in these provincial towns the operation of this Act is confined to the City of London.

2 Hen. VI. c. 14. Penalty of double value on the Keeper of the Touch for "touching" silver worse than sterling.

"Touches" appointed to York, Newcastle, Lincoln, Norwich, Bristol, Salisbury, and Coventry (1423).

In 1462 the succeeding monarch, Edward IV., within twelve months of his having supplanted Henry VI. on the throne, granted to the London Goldsmiths' Company a new charter dated 30 May, 2 Ed. IV., whereby the charter of Richard II. was confirmed, and they were for the first time constituted a body corporate and politic with power to use a common seal and hold lands in perpetual succession. They were also invested with additional powers enabling them to search for, inspect, test and regulate the working of all gold and silver wares in the city of London and its suburbs, in all fairs and markets, and in all cities, towns and boroughs, and all other places whatsoever throughout England, with power to punish those who worked gold or silver below standard.

London Goldsmiths Company's third Charter (1462), constituted a corporate Body with large powers.

In 1477 by the Statute 17 Edward IV. c. 1, the gold standard was more strictly defined, and provisions were made with reference to the assaying of all gold and silver wares which will be seen to have had a very important effect and to lead up to the system of marking by which,

17 Edw. IV. c. 1. (1477).

* "Harness of Silver"; the term here appears to be used in the wider sense of a general equipment.

from 1478 onwards, the exact year in which any fully marked example of London-made plate was wrought can be determined by the Hall-marks stamped on it. The Act provides that :—

Reciting the provisions of the Act 2 Hen. VI. c. 14 (*supra.*)

Reciting that the Act of Hen. VI. as to the quality of silver is daily broken.

The "touch" of the Leopard's Head being often set to things worse than standard.

And that oftentimes the sign of the worker is not set as ordained, whereby the purchaser is deprived of his remedy.

Provides that no gold shall be wrought, sold, or set to sale under the fineness of 18 carats.

And no silver unless it be as fine as "sterling".

So much solder as is necessary only to be allowed.

And none to be set to sale in London or within two miles of London before it be "touched" with a touch of the Leopard's Head crowned.

[First mention of the *crowned* Leopard's Head.]

And also to be marked with the worker's mark.

" Whereas in the Parliament holden the second year of the usurped reign of Henry the Sixth, late in deed and not of right King of England, amongst other it was ordained, that no goldsmith nor worker of silver within the City of London should sell anything wrought of silver, unless it be as fine as the sterling, except that, that needeth solder in the making, which shall be allowed according as the solder shall be necessary to be wrought in the same. And that no goldsmith, nor jeweller, nor other man that worketh harness of silver, shall put any of the same to sale in the same city, before it be touched with the touch of the Leopard's Head, that which may reasonably bear the same touch; and also with the mark or sign of the worker of the same, upon pain of forfeiture of the double. And that the mark or sign of every goldsmith shall be committed to the Wardens of the same mystery. And if it may be found, that the Keeper of the Touch aforesaid do touch any such harness with the Leopard's Head, which is not as fine in allay as the sterling, that then the Keeper of the Touch for everything so proved not so good in allay as the sterling, shall forfeit the double value to our Sovereign Lord the King and to the party, which statute is daily broken by the goldsmiths and other workers of silver, inhabiting as well in the city of London as elsewhere, within this realm and Wales; and our Sovereign Lord the King in effect nothing answered of any forfeiture comprised in the same statute, albeit that the King's liege people daily buying things wrought by the said goldsmiths or workers, as fine gold or fine silver, supposing it to be the same, when in deed it is not so, be grieviously deceived, because the said touch of the Leopard's Head is oftentimes set to such things by the said Keeper of the said touch of London and other places, as though the thing were fine and not defective. And oftentimes the sign of the worker of the same is not set thereto according to the statute aforesaid, nor the action given in the same statute is no perfect remedy to the persons grieved in this behalf. It is ordained by authority of this present parliament, for the better execution of the said statute, and for to eschew the deceit daily done by the said goldsmiths and workers of gold and silver in the said city of London and elsewhere, within this realm and Wales, that no goldsmith nor other worker of gold or silver, or either of the same metals, from the said feast of Easter shall work, sell, or set to sale any manner of base gold under the fineness of eighteen carats, otherwise called crates, nor no silver, unless it be as fine as the sterling; except such thing as required solder in making of the same, which shall be allowed according to the solder necessary to the making of the same, upon pain of forfeiture of the double value of any such gold or silver wrought or sold to the contrary. Nor that no goldsmith, jeweller, nor other worker of harness of silver shall set no harness of silver plate, nor jewel of silver to sale, from the said feast of Easter, within the said city of London, or within two miles of London, before it be touched with a touch of the Leopard's Head crowned, such as may bear the same touch; and also with a mark or sign of the worker of the same, so wrought within the city of London, or two miles of the same, upon pain of forfeiture of the double value of any such silver wrought and sold to the contrary. And that the mark or sign of every goldsmith be committed to the Wardens of the same mystery. And if it may be found that the said Keeper of the Touch of the Leopard's Head crowned aforesaid, do mark or touch any such harness with the Leopard's Head, if it be not as fine in allay as the sterling, then the said Keeper of the said Touch for everything proved not of as good allay as the sterling, shall forfeit the double value: the same forfeitures to be divided in two parts, the one half to be applied to the use of the King's house, and the other half thereof to the party grieved or hurt, in this behalf; or in his default, any other person which will pursue and prove such forfeiture shall be thereto received, and have in this behalf an action of debt or at the common law at his election, or before the justices of the peace of the county out of the city or town corporate where such forfeiture shall happen, to pursue as well for the King as for himself; and if it happen in city, borough, or town corporate, then before the mayor, sheriff or sheriffs, bailiff or bailiffs, or other chief governor there, by bill or bills in this party. In which action of debt, and in the bill or bills to be pursued, like disposition, demean, behaviour, judgment and execution in this party shall be had, according as in the said article concerning the money of Ireland is comprised, any charter, grant, corporation, or act made to the contrary notwithstanding. And because there be divers goldsmiths and other workers of gold and silver, aliens and strangers inhabiting in the city of London, and other places nigh thereabout, working their works in secret places and privileged, and eloin the same, and will not be searched by the said Wardens of the said Goldsmiths of London for the time being, nor will not be obedient and governed by them: therefore it is hereby ordained, that from the said feast of Easter, every such alien and stranger goldsmith and worker of gold and silver, inhabiting or to inhabit in the said city of London, and other places within two miles of the same city, shall be obedient and ruled by the said Wardens of the said Goldsmiths, in all things lawful and reasonable, and suffer the stuff of gold and silver by them wrought to be searched and marked after the rule of the said city, upon pain to be punished in manner and form as goldsmiths and workers of gold and silver of England, inhabiting within the said city, by the rules of the said craft of goldsmiths ought to be ruled. So always that the said aliens and strangers be not evil entreated, nor otherwise charged by any manner imposition other than the said English goldsmiths be, shall be and ought to be. And for the better surveying of the said aliens and strangers in time to come to be had, it is ordained by the authority aforesaid, that the same aliens and strangers, goldsmiths and workers of gold and silver, inhabiting within the said city, and every of them, from the feast of Saint Michael the archangel next coming, shall inhabit them in the open streets of the said city, and where better and more open showing is of their craft. *And it is ordained by the said authority that if the aforesaid Keeper of the said Touch, or worker of harness or other thing of gold or silver not made of the said fineness, do touch or mark the same harness or other thing as fine and able, that then for non-sufficiency of the said Keeper and Worker, the persons of the said craft of goldsmiths of the said city of London, by whatsoever name or names they be corporate, shall be chargeable and charged of the forfeitures by like action or actions of debt as is aforesaid in like manner and form as immediately before is specified.*"

It is remarkable that, while the Act of 1300 and that of 1477 last quoted both provide that no wrought silver shall be sold before it be marked with the leopard's head, there is no such provision in express

The mark of every goldsmith to be committed to the Warden of the mystery.

The Keeper of the Touch to forfeit double value for marking with the Leopard's Head anything below standard.

Half the penalty to the use of the King's house and half to the party grieved.

The penalty to be recoverable before the justices in a county or the mayor or other chief governor in a borough.

Strangers working gold and silver in secret places to be subject to search and shall inhabit them in the open streets where better and more open showing is of their craft, on pain of punishment, as if they were goldsmiths of England.

If the Keeper of the Touch do mark anything of gold or silver as fine then in case of non-sufficiency the persons of the craft of goldsmiths of London shall be chargeable therewith.

terms in either Act with regard to the mark of the leopard's head being set on gold. There is, however, the express provision that if the keeper of the touch, or worker of *gold or silver*, do touch or mark the same as fine and able, that then the craft of goldsmiths of London, by whatsoever name or names they be corporate, shall be chargeable. It would seem, therefore, that except by implication there was no statutory provision requiring the leopard's head mark to be struck on gold.

The facts that in the Act of 1477 the leopard's head is for the first time described as "*crowned,*" and that the persons of the craft of goldsmiths of London, by whatever name incorporated, are made liable in case the keeper of the touch should mark inferior metal as fine gold or fine silver, will be found considered in Chapter VI.

It was provided by the Act of 1477 that its provisions should continue in force for seven years, which was re-enacted in $148\frac{8}{9}$ for a term of twenty years, and in $155\frac{2}{3}$ for a further twenty years.

4 Hen. VII. c. 2 (1488-9).

In the year $148\frac{8}{9}$ the Act 4 Hen. VII. c. 2 was passed, from the preamble of which it appears that in previous years all gold and silver required, as well by the Mints as by goldsmiths, had been refined by "finers and parters"[*] under "a rule or order of the mints of London, Calais, Canterbury, York, and Durham, for the amendment of money and plate . . . that everything might be reformed to the right standard," but that now they (the finers and parters) dwelt abroad [†] in every part of the realm and out of the (operation of the) rules beforementioned, and that a practice had grown up in certain places distant from those towns, where mints were established, of buying "gilt silver" and "parting and fining it," and of alloying the silver so obtained without regard to the sterling alloy, and so causing "money and plate in divers places of the realm to be worse in fineness than it should be," so that men could get no fine silver. It was therefore enacted that "*no finer of gold or silver,*" nor any "*parter of the same by fire or water,*" should alloy *fine gold or silver, nor sell any except to the "officers of the mints, changes, and goldsmiths,*" that every finer should put his mark on the silver parted by him, and that no silver should be sold "molten into mass".

No Refiner to alloy silver or gold, or sell either except to the mint, changes, and goldsmiths.

18 Hen. VIII. (1526-7). Old "Tower" pound abolished.

In $152\frac{6}{7}$ (18 Hen. VIII.) the old "Tower" pound, by which silver had been formerly weighed,[‡] was abolished by Royal Proclamation.

---

[*] A "parter" was one who separated gold and silver from the ore; another word for refiner.
[†] "Abroad"; not necessarily out of the country, but at some distance away.
[‡] See Tables of Goldsmiths' Weights in Chapter I. (*supra*).

The silver coinage, which had been scandalously debased in the reigns of Henry VIII. and Edward VI.,* to the extent that in 1551 the issue consisted of only three ounces of silver in every pound weight of coins, was raised to 11-oz. 1-dwt. fine in the following year, and lowered again by Queen Mary in 1553 to 11 ounces, but was restored in 1560 by an Act of the 2 Eliz. to the old Sterling Standard of 11-oz. 2-dwts. fine, and on the 19 February, 156⁰⁄₁, the base money was called in by Royal proclamation. From that time to the present day (except from 25 March, 1697, to 1719) the standard for silver money and manufactured plate has been identical.

2 Eliz. (1560). Silver coinage restored to old sterling.

In 1576, by reason of the number of complaints which had been made against goldsmiths generally of making gold and silver wares below the standard of fineness and of using more solder than was necessary, for the purpose of increasing the weight and selling the same at high prices—many of the leading members of the craft being amongst the offenders—it was enacted by the 18 Eliz. c. 15, on the 8 February, 157⁵⁄₆, that "after the 20th April, 1576, no goldsmith should work, sell, or exchange any wares of gold less in fineness than 22 carats, and that he should use *no sother, amel, or other stuffing* more than was necessary for finishing the same, nor make, sell, nor exhange any wares of silver less in fineness than 11 ounces 2 pennyweights, nor take above twelve pence for the ounce of gold or pound of silver, for the fashioning, more than the buyer should or might be allowed for the same at the Queen's Exchange or Mint, nor put to sale any ware before he had set his own mark on so much thereof as might conveniently bear the same, and if after the above day any gold or silver wares should be touched (as and) for good by the Wardens or Masters of the Mystery and there should afterwards be found fraud or deceit therein, the wardens shall pay forfeit, the value of the thing so marked."

18 Eliz. c. 15 (1575-6). Gold standard fixed at 22 carats and Silver at 11-oz. 2-dwts fine.

No unnecessary solder to be used.

Goldsmiths' charges fixed at 12d. per ounce for "fashion".

Goldsmith to set his own mark on all his wares before sale.

Wardens to pay forfeit the value, for "touching" gold or silver wares worse than standard.

It is remarkable that in this statute, while it requires the goldsmith to set his own mark on all wares before sale, and imposes a penalty of the value of the thing upon the master and wardens (of the Goldsmiths' Company) for touching as "good" any gold or silver wares in which fraud or deceit should afterwards be found, no mention is made of the mark of the leopard's head (as in former statutes) nor of the date letter or lion passant, which long before this had become the distinguishing

Possible explanation of absence of Hall Marks from much plate of the period 1575 to 1675 (Feb. 23), when Goldsmiths'Company issued notice on subject.†

---

* See the Table of Silver Standards in Chapter III. (*infra*).
† A copy of this notice is set forth in Chapter V.

Cf. the reference to Wm. Cater in chap. V., p. 44, *infra.*

marks of gold and silver wares touched as "good" at Goldsmiths' Hall. It is remarkable, also, that no reference is made to the Act of 17 Edward IV. (1477) which fixed the standard for gold wares at 18 carats fine. Possibly the omission of any mention in this Act of Elizabeth of any marks other than the maker's mark being required to be stamped on gold or plate may account for the number of pieces of plate which are found bearing the marks of London makers and provincial makers of the 16th and 17th centuries and no other marks.

Few enactments concerning Goldsmiths in 17th century.

No enactment upon this subject appears in the statute books for a long period after the passing of the Act of 1576; in fact, with the exception of the Act 21. Jac. I. c. 28, 162¾ (which repealed the restrictions contained in the Act 37 Edward III. c. 7, against silversmiths meddling with gilding, and against gilders working in silver) and the three Acts of Wm. & Mary and Wm. III. (*infra*), which were passed with the object of obtaining silver for the mint and preventing the melting down of coin, no statute concerning English goldsmiths, their work, or marks appears to have been enacted by the Legislature between 1576 and 1696, a period of one hundred and twenty years, during the greater part of which the goldsmiths of England appear to have been allowed to conduct their business very much in their own way without interference.

The fact that the forces of the country were, during the reign of Charles I., more busily engaged in the confiscation and melting down of plate than in its manufacture, would probably account both for the scarcity of plate made during that period and for the absence of legislation on the subject. However that may be, very little seems to have been done to prevent irregularities in the trade during that reign, or until fifteen years after the Restoration, and even then it appears to have been left entirely to the Goldsmiths' Company to enforce the old laws with reference to the fineness and Hall-marking of plate, without any fresh statutory aid. Meanwhile, the country had recovered from the consequences of the wars, and with restored means the people had abandoned the frugal simplicity of the Puritanical life and had adopted a more luxurious style requiring more costly equipments. There was consequently a greater demand for wrought silver then, so that, instead of plate being melted

Silver coinage melted down and used for plate.

down for coinage, as had been the case half a century before, time's revenge had wrought a contrary result, and the silver coin of the realm was freely resorted to as material for the plateworker. To such an extent was coin used for this purpose, not only by the nobility and wealthy commoners, but by the keepers of inns and taverns for drinking vessels in common use, that the amount of silver coin left in circulation became insufficient for the requirements of the public, and great difficulty was experienced in providing sufficient silver for the Mint. Moreover, the fact of this common use of plate in public houses, and places where formerly pewter had been found sufficient, occasioned, it was alleged, many burglaries and murders, and the inconvenience to the community from these causes had become so accentuated by the year 1695 that the Grand Jury of Middlesex made a presentment on the subject to His Majesty's judges, praying them to make application to His Majesty's Council or Parliament to discover means for preventing the common use of silver in such places. Scarcity of silver coins. Common use of silver vessels in 1695.

The first statute which had been passed since the reign of James I. up to this time, with reference to gold and silver, was : 1 William and Mary, c. 30 (1689), repealing the 5 Henry IV. c. 4, because great advances had been made by divers persons in the art of refining metals "which abound in this realm," and extracting gold and silver out of the same, "who dare not exercise their skill within the realm for fear of falling under the penalty of the said statute but exercise the said art in foreign parts". This repeal of the statute restricting the "multi-plication" of gold and silver was subject to the proviso "that all gold and silver that shall be extracted . . . shall be employed for no other use or uses whatsoever but for the increase of moneys," and are to be taken to the Mint, in London, where the full value is to be given. 1 Wm. & My. c. 30 (1689). Repeals restrictions against multiplying gold and silver. Efforts to procure silver for the Mint.

The Act 6 and 7 William III. c. 17 (169⁴⁄₅), provided that no person should export bullion unless stamped at Goldsmiths' Hall, and the Wardens were not to stamp it without proof that no part of it, before it was molten, was coin. 6 & 7 Wm. III. c. 17 (1694-5). Restriction on exportation of bullion.

With the object therefore of preventing the silver coin of the realm from being melted down and converted into "monteaths," tankards, cups, bowls, and the like, for use in public places, it was enacted by the statute 7 and 8 William III. c. 19 (169⁵⁄₆) entitled "An Act to encourage bringing of plate to the mint to be coined and for remedying the ill state of the coin of this realm," that no person keeping an inn or tavern, or selling wine, should expose in his house any plate, except spoons, under the penalty of forfeiting the same, and that no silver should be exported without a certificate from the Court of the Lord Mayor and Alderman that it was foreign bullion before it was molten. 7 & 8 Wm. III. c. 19 (1695-6). To encourage bringing of plate to the Mint.

But these provisions being insufficient, a further statute was enacted in 169⁶⁄₇ (8 Wm. III. c. 8)* whereby the standard for wrought plate was, on the 25 March, 1697, raised to 11 oz. 10 dwts. fine, as set forth in the chapter on the Standards for Gold and Silver; and in order to replenish the stock of silver for coinage, the Act also provided for the purchase by the Mint of any wrought plate bearing the stamps of the London Goldsmiths' Company at 5s. 4d. per ounce. This Act further provided that plate should be stamped with marks of a kind different from those which had been used previously. These marks will be found referred to in Chapter VI., which deals with the subject. In this Act also an express exemption is made for the first time from the control of the assay office of silver wire and articles which by reason of their smallness were incapable of being stamped with the prescribed marks. The Act imposed a penalty of £500 for counterfeiting marks on wrought plate, and re-enacted the provision for a penalty being imposed upon the Goldsmiths' Company in respect of every article marked by them in which it might appear that there was fraud or deceit.

The provisions of this Act were continued for twenty-one years, the stocks of silver having been in the meantime to some extent replenished by capture from the Spaniards, although large quantities had been exported to the East Indies and other parts—not without complaints in the country and Parliament as to continued scarcity. In 1719 the provisions of the Act of 1696 making compulsory the use of the extra fine or Britannia standard for wrought plate (which had been found to be too soft for hard wear) were repealed. Meanwhile the restrictions against the exportation of silver had been to a slight extent removed by the 9 and 10 William III. c. 28, which permitted the exportation of watches and other manufactured articles of silver, with the proviso that no watch-cases were to be exported without movements and that the maker's name was to be engraved on all watches made.

An omission (probably unintentional) from the Act of 1696 of any mention of the provincial assay offices appears to have caused them great hardship for the reason that while the standard for plate was raised throughout England the provincial offices were not empowered to use the marks with which such higher standard plate was to be stamped. They were, therefore, practically deprived of all their business until in the

---

* This Act did not extend to Scotland or Ireland.

8 Wm. III. c. 8 (1696-7).

Silver standard raised to 11 oz. 10 dwts. fine.

Exemption of silver wire and very small articles from being Hall-marked.

12 & 13 W. III. c. 4 (1700-1). Re-establishment of Provincial Assay Offices.

year 170$^{0}_{1}$, the statute 12 & 13 Wm. III. c. 4, reciting the difficulties and hardships which had been endured, appointed Wardens and Assay Masters in the Cities of York, Exeter, Bristol, Chester and Norwich,* to assay and touch wrought plate of the new standard. The provisions of this statute will be found more fully dealt with in the chapters on the Provincial Assay Offices. This statute also imposed a penalty of £500 for counterfeiting marks on wrought plate.

Penalty of £500 imposed for counterfeiting marks on wrought plate.

By the Act 6 Geo. I. c. 11 (1719), the old standard of 11 oz. 2 dwts. for silver was revived for the reason (as stated in the preamble) that silver wares of that standard were more serviceable and durable than those made of the standard of 11 oz. 10 dwts. fine. The higher (or Britannia) standard was, however, not abolished, its use being left to the option of the goldsmith concurrently with the lower standard. The same Act imposed a tax of sixpence per ounce on all silver plate wrought in Great Britain which "should or ought to be touched, assayed, or marked". This was the first imposition of duty on plate, and it was collected by the Officers of Excise, but, owing to the provisions for ascertaining and collecting the duty having been found ineffectual, the Act was repealed thirty-eight years afterwards, and a duty for licences to deal in plate was substituted therefor.

6 Geo. I. c. 11 (1719). Duty 6d. per oz. on Plate first imposed.

In 1738, by reason of the number of charges of dishonest practices which had been brought against goldsmiths and plate workers, it became necessary to promote further legislation on the subject, and the important statute, 12 Geo. II. c. 26, entitled: "An Act for the better preventing Frauds and Abuses in Gold and Silver Wares" was passed, reciting that the standards of the "plate of this Kingdom are both for the honour and riches of the realm, and so highly concern His Majesty's subjects that the same ought to be most carefully observed and all deceits therein to be prevented as much as possible," and that great frauds are committed daily for the lack of power to effectually prevent them. The frauds referred to being chiefly that gold and silver wares had been wrought below the standard, and in particular that excessive quantities of solder had been used in the manufacture and sold as standard metal—the Act again fixed the standard for gold at 22 carats, and for silver at 11 oz. 2 dwts. (the old standard) without abolishing the higher standard of 11 oz. 10 dwt.; and it imposed new penalties with imprisonment in default of payment for selling gold and silver wares below standard and without the proper

12 Geo. II. c. 26 (1738-9), for preventing frauds and abuses.

New penalties for selling gold and silver wares below standard and without the proper assay marks and for forging marks.

---

* Bristol and Norwich do not appear to have taken advantage of this Act. Newcastle was given similar privileges by an Act of the following year.

assay marks, and for forging marks. Certain gold and silver wares, mostly small articles, were excepted from the operation of the Act.*
Workers were required to send particular information to the assay offices with the wares of gold or silver sent to be assayed, in order to check frauds in regard to the duty by the "private making and manufacturing of silver plate". The duties of the wardens were in some respects defined, regulations were made for the London Assay

New form for makers' marks ordered, and old marks to be destroyed.

Office, the charges to be made for assays were limited, and a new form was defined for makers' marks, and the old marks were ordered to be destroyed, particulars respecting which will be found set forth in Chapter VI., in which the subject of Marks on Plate is dealt with.

31 Geo. II. c. 32 (1757-8).
Annual License Tax to be paid by dealers in lieu of duty.
Death penalty for counterfeiting marks.

The Act 31 Geo. II. c. 32 (1757-8) repealing the 6 Geo. I. c. 11, whereby 6d. per oz. duty had been made payable on plate from 1720, substituted a licence tax of 40s. per annum, payable by every dealer in gold and silver wares, and for the first time declared the counterfeiting of dies and marks used at the assay offices, and the fraudulent transposing of genuine marks, to be felony punishable by death.

That Act was amended by another Act of the following year (32 Geo. II.) which provided that from and after the 5th of July, 1759, no person should be subject or liable to take out a licence for selling any gold not exceeding two pennyweights in one separate and distinct piece or any quantity of silver not exceeding five pennyweights in one separate piece, and in order to make good any deficiency in the produce of the said duty, there should from and after the said 5th July, 1759, be paid a duty of five pounds for every licence to be taken out by each trader in or seller of gold or silver plate, or goods in which any gold or silver is manufactured and all refiners of gold or silver in which the quantity of gold should be of the weight of two ounces or upwards or in which the quantity of silver should be of the weight of thirty ounces or upwards and such licence should be taken out each year by every person trading in or offering to trade in or sell any such plate or goods under a penalty of twenty pounds for every offence of omitting to take out such licence, and no pawnbroker or refiner of gold or silver was allowed to trade in or sell any gold or silver ware without taking out such licence each year under a like penalty.

Establishment of Assay Offices at Birmingham and Sheffield (772-3).

The Statute 13 Geo. III. c. 52 (1772-3) is the local Act establishing

---

* A list of these will be found in Chapter VI. at the conclusion of the remarks on the Sovereign's head.

the assay offices of Birmingham and Sheffield, which will be found mentioned in the chapter on Provincial Assay Offices.

The 13 Geo. III. c. 59, substituted transportation for fourteen years for the death penalty under the 31 George II. c. 32.

Death penalty reduced to transportation for fourteen years (1772-3)

In 1784, the duty on plate (which had been repealed by 31 Geo. II. c. 32) was re-imposed and extended to gold by the Statute 24 Geo. III. c. 53. The duty imposed by this Act was 8s. per ounce on gold and 6d. per oz. on silver, payable on and after 1 December, 1784. The amount of the duty was increased from time to time, but the provisions of the Act requiring that the duty should be paid to the Assayers at the various assay offices, and by them paid each day to the Accountant, continued in force until the duty was repealed in 1890. Every worker was required under a penalty to deliver at the assay office a ticket or note containing his name, place of abode, and an account of the wares and duty, with every parcel of work. These notes were filed by the Accountant, who was obliged to deliver to an officer of the Inland Revenue, within two months after the end of every quarter, a copy of his account, and at the same time pay over the duty received, less $2\frac{1}{2}$ per cent. commission, which was reduced to 1 per cent. by the 12 and 13 Vic. c. 80. Forging the duty mark was made a capital felony punishable with death.

24 Geo. III. c. 53 (1784). Duty 8s. per oz. on gold and 6d. per oz. on silver re-imposed.

By the Act 37 Geo. III. c. 90 (1796-7), the duty on gold was continued at eight shillings per ounce, but the duty on silver plate was increased to one shilling per ounce.

The Act 25 Geo. III. c. 64 (1785), required every dealer in gold and silver plate to take out a licence annually at the cost of £2 6s. or £2 15s., according to the description of the articles in which he dealt, and this licence was an addition to the duty payable at the assay offices on manufactured gold and silver. This Act gave relief to manufacturers in the shape of drawback on exported goods, but exporters were required to stamp or engrave on the inside of every watch-case a number corresponding with the number upon the works of the watch.

25 Geo. III. c. 64 (1785). Scale for dealers' licences.

In 1797-8, by the Act 38 Geo. III. c. 24, watch-cases both of gold and silver were exempted from the duty which had been payable since 1784, and this exemption was continued thenceforward until the repeal of the duty on plate.

38 George III. c. 24 (1797-8). Watch-cases exempted from duty.

By a later statute of the same year (38 Geo. III. c. 69) the additional standard of 18 carats fine was added to the single standard of

38 Geo. III. c. 69. New standard of 18 carats added for gold, and change of mark ordered.

22 carats previously in use, as mentioned in the chapter on the Standards, and it was provided that this additional standard should be marked with a crown and the figures 18, and that the lion passant should not be struck on it. This Act also provided that if any ware after being duly assayed should be altered so that its character was changed, or should have an addition made to it bearing a greater proportion to its original weight than four ounces to every pound Troy, then it should be assayed as a new ware and the duty paid on the whole weight. In the case of an addition of a less proportion than four ounces to the pound, then the addition only should be assayed and marked, and the duty paid on such addition only, provided that the worker had, previously to making it, submitted the original ware with a description of the proposed addition to the assay office and obtained the sanction of the Authorities to the addition being made. This statute clearly defines the offences of forging dies and marks, and makes the offence of forging the mark denoting the gold standard then established a felony punishable by transportation for seven years.

By the Act 44 Geo. III. c. 98 (1803-4) the duty on gold was increased to sixteen shillings per ounce, and that on silver plate to one shilling and three pence per ounce.

In 1814-5 by the Act 55 Geo. III. c. 185, the duty on manufactured gold was increased to seventeen shillings per ounce, and on silver to eighteen pence per ounce.

The Statutes 52 Geo. III. c. 59 (1812), 1 Geo. IV. c. 14 (1820), and the 3 & 4 Wm. IV. c. 97 (1833), provided for allowance of drawback of duty on exported gold wares and plate—excepting gold rings and small wares under two ounces—upon the Officers of Customs being satisfied that the duty had been paid, and that the plate was new and had not been used, and upon the owner giving security that it should not be reimported.

The Act 1 Wm. IV. c. 66 (1830), substituted transportation for death as the punishment for the forgery of assay office marks, and the Act 4 and 5 Vic. c. 56 (1841) abolished the death punishment and substituted transportation for forging the duty mark.

The Act 5 and 6 Vic. c. 46 (1842) provided that all gold and silver plate not being battered, which should be imported from Foreign parts to be sold or exchanged or exposed to sale, should be of the respective standards now applicable to English-made plate, and that none should

Margin notes:

Additions to finished plate prohibited.

Punishment for forging marks, Seven years' transportation.

52 Geo. III. c. 59 (1812).

1 Geo. IV. c. 14 (1820).

3 & 4 Wm. IV. c. 97 (1833). Allowing drawback on exported plate.

1 Wm. IV. c. 66 (1830). Transportation substituted for the death penalty for forging marks.

be sold until it had been assayed and marked in England, Scotland, or Ireland. An exception was made in favour of such as had been wrought previous to the year 1800: the onus of proving the date of the manufacture being on the party selling or offering such plate.

The Act 7 & 8 Vic. c. 22 (1844) repealed the 13 Geo. III. c. 59 as to the punishment for certain frauds and offences, and codified the offences. The statute declares each of the following offences to be felony, and punishable with transportation (now penal servitude) or imprisonment :—

7 & 8 Vic. c. 22 (1844). Codified offences and ordered new mark for 22 carat gold.

Forging or counterfeiting any die used by any of the companies of goldsmiths or guardians of the standard of wrought plate.

Marking wares with a forged die.

Counterfeiting marks of any die.

Transposing marks from one article of gold or silver to another, or to an article of base metal.

Having possession without lawful excuse, and knowingly, of a forged die, or of any article bearing the mark of a forged die or a transposed mark.

Cutting off marks with intent to affix them to other wares.

Affixing to any ware a mark cut from another ware.

Fraudulently using genuine dies.

This Act also provided that 22 carat gold should not continue to be marked as theretofore with the lion passant to indicate the standard but should be marked with a crown and 22.

In 1854, effect was given to representations which had been made from time to time to the Board of Trade, that there was a great demand in the United States of America and other parts for English watches, but that English gold cases, by reason of the high quality of the gold compulsorily used, were too costly for those markets. It was further alleged that the Americans imported English movements without cases, which they put into cases of about 10 carat standard and sold in South America and other parts at lower prices than articles of the same appearance could be made for in England, much to the detriment of English trade. The Act 17 & 18 Vic. c. 96, was consequently passed, permitting the adoption of any gold standard not being less than one-third of fine gold to be approved by Her Majesty in Council. In pursuance of this enactment, three lower standards of 15 carat, 12 carat and 9 carat respectively were added to the standards of 22 carat and 18

17 & 18 Vic. c. 96 (1854). New standards of 15, 12, and 9 carats fine for gold established.

carat previously sanctioned, and it was provided that the marks denoting each standard should be the figures : " 15 " and " ·625 " for 15 carat ; " 12 " and " ·5 " for 12 carat, and " 9 " and " ·375 " for 9 carat. The decimal fraction in each case representing the proportion of fine gold in the alloyed metal.

30 & 31 Vic.
c. 90 (1867).
New scale for
dealers' licences.

The Act 30 & 31 Vic. c. 90 (1867) rearranged the duty payable by dealers in gold and silver, the scale being :—

Dealers in gold exceeding	2 dwts.	and	under	2 oz.			£2 6s. per	
„ „ silver	„	5	„	„	„	30 „	annum.	
Dealers in gold exceeding	2 oz.	up to any weight					£5 15s. per	
„ „ silver	„	30 „	„	„			annum.	

46 & 47 Vic.
c. 55 (1883).
Compulsory
assay of foreign
plate. To be
marked in same
manner as
English, with
the addition of
letter F. Excep-
tion in case of
plate not for sale
or exchange, and
plate incapable
of being stamped
without injury.

The Act 46 & 47 Vic. c. 55 (1883) provides, under a penalty of £50 and forfeiture of the goods, that Foreign plate shall be assayed and Hall-marked in the same manner as if it were English, but with the addition of the letter **F**—exception being made in favour of goods imported solely for private use and not for sale or exchange—and that on being imported it shall be taken into the custody of the Revenue Officers until the Act is complied with.

This Act, which was passed in connection with the collection of duty, is still in force as to assaying and marking, and the penalty for attempted evasion is also still in force.   The Act 47 & 48 Vic. c. 62 (1884), however, excepted from compulsory assay imported Foreign plate and filigree work so ornamental as to be incapable of being marked without damage.

53 Vic. c. 8
(1890).
Abolition of
duty on gold and
silver plate.

The Act 53 Vic. c. 8 (1890) provided that " on and after 1st May, 1890, the duties on 'plate of gold and plate of silver' shall cease to be payable, and the drawback upon the exportation of plate shall cease to be allowed," and that an allowance by way of drawback according to weight should be paid to every licensed dealer in plate who had, on or before 7 May, 1890, given notice to the Commissioners of Inland Revenue of his intention to claim the allowance in respect of articles of plate of silver manufactured in the United Kingdom which had not left the stock of any manufacturer or dealer, provided that such articles should have been produced and taken account of by the proper officer of Inland Revenue and the weight ascertained in the month of June in the same year. The Act contains further provisions as to drawback in respect of duty which had been paid on new plate in the stock of manufacturers and dealers ; but these are mere details, the main provisions of the Act being that the duties on "gold and silver plate" ceased on 1 May, 1890, from which date the use of the duty stamp —a representation of the Sovereign's head—was also discontinued.

THE HALL-MARKING OF FOREIGN PLATE ACT, 1904.

While the first edition of this work was being printed, the above Act entitled " The Hall-Marking of Foreign Plate Act 1904" (4 Ed. VII. c. 6) was passed.   It provides that :— 4 Ed. VII. c. 6. Hall-Marking of Foreign Plate Act, 1904.

(Sec. 1.).   " Where for the purpose of complying with Sections fifty-nine and sixty of the Customs Act, 1842, or Section ten of the Revenue Act, 1883, any plate has to be assayed, stamped, and marked, or where for any other purpose any plate or article imported from a foreign port is brought to an Assay Office in the United Kingdom to be assayed, stamped, or marked, the plate or article shall be marked in such manner as His Majesty may determine by Order in Council, so as readily to distinguish whether the plate or other article was wrought or made in England, Scotland, or Ireland, or was imported from foreign parts, and such mark or marks shall be deemed to be a compliance with the said Acts."

(Sec. 2.)   " Any person, who, after a date fixed by His Majesty by Order in Council, brings or causes to be brought any plate or other article to be assayed, stamped, and marked, at an Assay Office, shall state in writing, in manner provided by His Majesty by Order in Council, whether the plate or article was wrought or made in England, Scotland, or Ireland, or was imported from foreign parts, but it shall not be necessary to make such statement in writing where any plate or other article is brought to an Assay Office in charge of an Officer of Customs under the provisions of the Revenue Act, 1883, for the purpose of being assayed, stamped, or marked, as having been imported from foreign parts."

(Sec. 3).   " Where any person, who, after the date fixed as aforesaid, brings or causes to be brought, any plate or other article to be assayed, stamped, and marked at an Assay Office, does not know and is not able to state, whether the plate or other article was wrought or made in England, Scotland, or Ireland, or was imported from foreign parts, such person shall make a statement in writing to that effect in the manner prescribed in this Section, and the plate or other article referred to in the said statement shall be stamped and marked as if it were imported from foreign parts."

(Sec. 4.)   " If any person knowingly makes a false statement under this Section he shall be liable, on summary conviction, under the Summary Jurisdiction Acts to a fine not exceeding five pounds for every article in respect of which the false statement is made."

(Sec. 5.)   " The Customs Act, 1842, shall apply as if a reference to the mode of marking required under this Act were substituted for a reference to the mode of marking under that Act."

(Sec. 6.)   " His Majesty may, by Order in Council, revoke, vary, or add to any Order in Council made under this Act."

THE HALL-MARKING OF FOREIGN PLATE ACT, 1904—*continued.*

ORDER IN COUNCIL.

The King, in exercise of the powers vested in His Majesty by the above provisions, on the 24th of October, 1904, determined that :—

(1.) The mark or marks to be stamped or marked upon any plate or article imported from foreign parts brought to an Assay Office in the United Kingdom to be assayed, stamped, or marked, shall be the mark or marks described in the First Part of the Schedule hereto.

(2.) The statement in writing to be made by any person, other than an Officer of Customs, who after the 31st day of October, 1904, brings or causes to be brought any plate or article to be assayed, stamped, and marked at an Assay Office, shall be in the form set out in the Second Part of the Schedule hereto.

SCHEDULE.

PART I.

ON FOREIGN GOLD PLATE.

The Hall-mark particular to each Assay Office as shewn in Figure 1 of the Appendix hereto ; the carat value of the gold, together with the decimal equivalent of the carat value, as shewn in Figure 2 of the Appendix.

ON FOREIGN SILVER PLATE.

The Hall-mark particular to each Assay Office, as shewn in Figure 1 of the Appendix hereto, together with the decimal equivalent of the standard value of the silver, as shewn in Figure 2 of the appendix.

The mark for the annual date-letter is to be added by each Assay Office after the mark for the particular Hall and the mark for standard.

PART II.

HALL-MARKING OF PLATE.

Statement to be made in writing by manufacturers, dealers, and others bringing or sending gold and silver plate to be assayed and marked.

A list of the articles brought or sent to be assayed and marked to be set out above the declaration.

I hereby certify and declare that all the above-mentioned articles were..

Here set out whether wrought or made in England, Scotland or Ireland, or whether imported from foreign parts.

....

....

or

I hereby certify and declare that the place of manufacture of the above-mentioned articles is unknown to me.

To be signed by a member of the Firm, or in the case of a Company, by the Managing Director.   ....

THE HALL-MARKING OF FOREIGN PLATE ACT, 1904—*continued.*

APPENDIX.

FIGURE 1.

PARTICULAR MARK FOR EACH ASSAY AUTHORITY.

GOLD.

LONDON	BIRMINGHAM	CHESTER	SHEFFIELD	EDINBURGH	GLASGOW	DUBLIN
(PHŒBUS).	(EQUILATERAL TRIANGLE).	(ACORN AND TWO LEAVES).	(CROSSED ARROWS).	(ST. ANDREW'S CROSS).	(BISHOP'S MITRE).	(SHAMROCK)

SILVER.

FIGURE 2.

REPRESENTATION OF STANDARD MARKS.

GOLD.　　　　　　　　　　SILVER.

22 ·916　　20 ·833　　18 ·75　　　　·925　　·9584

15 ·625　　12 ·5　　9 ·375

The annual date-letter is to be added by the Assay Office.

The above-mentioned Act was amended by an Order in Council dated 11th day of May, 1906, as follows :—

GOLD.

LONDON	SHEFFIELD	GLASGOW	DUBLIN
(SIGN OF CONSTELLATION LEO).	(LIBRA).	(DOUBLE BLOCK LETTER F INVERTED).	(BOUJET).

SILVER.

The marks of BIRMINGHAM, CHESTER, and EDINBURGH were not altered by the above Order in Council.

CHAPTER III.

THE STANDARDS FOR GOLD AND SILVER WARES.

"Standards" for Gold and Silver. The first introduction of a Standard for gold wares in England was by the Statute 28 Edw. I. c. 20 (1300) which provided that no goldsmith should make any wares of gold worse than the Touch of Paris (which was $19\frac{1}{5}$ carats fine), or of silver except of the "esterling allay" (sterling alloy).* This standard for gold continued in force until 1477, when by the 17 Edw. IV. c. 1, it was fixed at 18 carats. In 1576, by the 18 Eliz. c. 15, it was raised to 22 carats. In 1798 the Act 38 Geo. III. c. 69 established two distinct standards of 22 carats and 18 carats, which have been in force ever since, and in 1854—by the Act 17 and 18 Vic. c. 96—three lower standards of 15, 12, and 9 carats respectively were added.

Proportion of Alloy to fine metal. The smallest proportion of alloy which has been found sufficient to give the necessary degree of hardness to gold is 2 parts of alloy to 22 parts of pure gold, whereby gold 22 carats fine is obtained, which now is, and has been ever since the year 1660, the *standard* of the English gold coinage. In Ireland, gold 20 carats fine (for which there is a particular stamp) is occasionally, but very rarely, used. The standard for the silver coinage, established in 1300 by Edward I. was 11 oz. 2 dwts. of pure silver and 18 dwts. of copper to the pound (Troy). This standard continued in force until the year 1542, from which year the coinage was debased more or less till 1559-60 when the old standard of 11 oz. 2 dwts. was restored, and it has been retained as the standard for Meaning of "Sterling". the silver coinage ever since. Silver of this standard is called "sterling," derived, it is supposed, "from the Germans, who were termed Easterlings by the English, from their living Eastward; and who were first called in by King John to reduce the silver to its due fineness, and such (silver) money in ancient writings is called "Easterlings".† In the course of years the first two letters were dropped, and in a statute of 1343 (17 Edw. III.) it is ordained that "good *sterling* money should be made in

---

* "Alloy" is here used with reference to the mixture of pure silver and alloy.
† Camden *Britannia*.

England". Whenever, therefore, the term "sterling" is used with reference to silver, it must be understood as being at least 11 oz. 2 dwts. fine with no more than 18 dwts. of alloy in every 12 oz. gross.

The standard for silver wares was established in the year 1300, and remained as then established until 1696.

In the year 1696 an Act of Parliament (8 & 9 Wm. III. c. 8) was passed providing that on and after 25 March, 1697, no plate-worker in England should make any article of silver of less fineness than 11 oz. 10 dwts. of fine silver in every pound (Troy), nor offer for sale, exchange or sell any article made after that day but of that standard, nor until it had been marked with the marks appointed to distinguish plate of this new standard. The marks being : the worker's mark, to be expressed by the first two letters of his surname ; the marks of the goldsmiths' craft, which (instead of the leopard's head and lion as formerly) were to be the figure of a lion's head erased, and the figure of a woman commonly called Britannia ; and a distinct and variable mark to denote the year in which such plate was made. The reason for this alteration of the standard for silver was that, large quantities of plate having been sacrificed or confiscated by Royalists and Parliamentarians, the stores of plate throughout the country had become depleted by the middle of the 17th century, and on peace being restored the silver coin of the realm was resorted to for conversion by the goldsmith into all kinds of vessels for daily use. Silver coin thus became scarce, and this scarcity became so accentuated in 1695 that Parliament was petitioned to prevent such use of the silver coinage, and the Act above cited, making the standard for plate 8 dwts finer than the silver coinage, was the result, and plate of this extra fineness is commonly known as of the "Britannia standard". This standard was, however, compulsory for twenty-three years only, it being found too soft for general use, and the old "sterling" standard was restored by the 6 Geo. I. c. 11, which took effect on 1 June, 1720, since which date the use of both standards is permitted at the option of the goldsmith. This option will be found referred to further on.

Britannia standard for silver.

It being found impossible in practice to mix alloy and pure metal with such absolute exactness that every part of the mixture shall have exactly the same proportions of pure metal and alloy, a very slight divergence from standard is allowed. This permitted divergence from standard, technically called the "remedy," has varied from time to time. The earliest recorded for gold coin was $\frac{1}{8}$th of a carat, allowed by

Permitted divergence from standard particularly small.

Edw. III. in 1345, when the standard was 23 carats $3\frac{1}{2}$ grains fine. This "remedy" continued to be the allowance until 1649, thenceforward $\frac{1}{6}$th of a carat was allowed until 1817, when it was reduced to $\frac{1}{16}$th of a carat. It was further reduced in the reign of Queen Victoria by about 25 per cent. of the old allowance to ·002, or $\frac{1}{500}$th, less than a halfpenny in the pound. The silver "remedy" was 2 dwts. per pound from 1601 to 1817, when it was reduced by half, and this was further reduced in the reign of Queen Victoria to ·004, or $\frac{1}{250}$th, exactly double the variation which is allowed in the case of gold, or, in other words, an allowance of a little less than a pennyworth in a pound's worth of silver.

The following tables show the standards in force for gold and silver money and for gold and silver wares from the year 1300, it being understood that the standard shown as fixed at any particular date remained in force until the date of the succeeding entry :—

TABLE OF GOLD STANDARDS.

A.D.	Reigns.	Standard for Gold Money. Per oz. of Gold Coin.		Standard for Gold Wares. Per oz. of Wrought Gold.	
		Pure Gold.	Alloy.	Pure Gold.	Alloy.
1300	28 Edward I.	24 carats ...	none ...	$19\frac{1}{5}$ carats +	$4\frac{4}{5}$ carats*
1344	18 Edward III.	23 carats $3\frac{1}{2}$ grains +	... $\frac{1}{2}$ grain	,, ,, +	,, ,,
1477	17 Edward IV.	,, ,, ,, ,, +	... ,, ,,	18 ,, +	6 ,,
1509	1 Henry VIII.	22 carats ...	+ 2 carats ...	,, ,, +	,, ,,
1542	34 ,, ,,	23 ,, ...	+ 1 ,, ...	,, ,, +	,, ,,
1544	36 ,, ,,	22 ,, ...	+ 2 ,, ...	,, ,, +	,, ,,
1545	37 ,, ,,	20 ,, ...	+ 4 ,, ...	,, ,, +	,, ,,
1549	3 Edward VI.	22 ,, ...	+ 2 ,, ...	,, ,, +	,, ,,
1550	4 ,, ,,	23 ,, $3\frac{1}{2}$ grains +	... $\frac{1}{2}$ grain	,, ,, +	,, ,,
1575	18 Elizabeth	,, ,, ,, ,, +	... ,,	22 ,, +	2 ,,
1592	35 ,,	22 ,, ...	+ 2 carats ...	,, ,, +	,, ,,
1600	43 ,,	23 ,, $3\frac{1}{2}$ grains +	... $\frac{1}{2}$ grain	,, ,, +	,, ,,
1604	2 James I.	22 ,, ...	+ 2 carats ...	,, ,, +	,, ,,
1605	3 , ,,	23 ,, $3\frac{1}{2}$ grains +	... $\frac{1}{2}$ grain	,, ,, +	,, ,,
1626	2 Charles I.	22 ,, ...	+ 2 carats ...	,, ,, +	,, ,,
1798	38 George III.	,, ,, ,, ,, +	,, ,, ...	{ ,, ,, + 18 ,, (an additional standard)	,, ,,
1854	17 & 18 Vict.	,, ,, ,, ,, +	,, ,, ..	Three additional standards of 15, 12 and 9 carats respectively added, the two old standards of 22 and 18 carats being continued.	

* The "Touch of Paris".

TABLE OF SILVER STANDARDS.

(THE STANDARD FIXED AT ANY PARTICULAR DATE REMAINED IN FORCE UNTIL THE DATE OF THE SUCCEEDING ENTRY.)

A.D.	REIGNS.	SILVER MONEY. Per 12 oz. of Silver Coin.		SILVER WARES (PLATE). Per 12 oz. of Plate.	
		PURE SILVER.	ALLOY.	PURE SILVER.	ALLOY.
1300	28 Edward I.	11 oz. 2 dwts. +	18 dwts. (Sterling)	11 oz. 2 dwts. +	18 dwts.*
1542	34 Henry VIII.	10 ,, 0 ,, + 2 oz. 0 ,, (Debased)		,, ,, ,, ,, + ,, ,,	
1544	36 ,, ,,	6 ,, 0 ,, + 6 ,, 0 ,, ,,		,, ,, ,, ,, + ,, ,,	
1545	37 ,, ,,	4 ,, 0 ,, + 8 ,, 0 ,, ,,		,, ,, ,, ,, + ,, ,,	
1549	3 Edward VI.	6 ,, 0 ,, + 6 ,, 0 ,, ,,		,, ,, ,, ,, + ,, ,,	
1551	5 ,, ,,	3 ,, 0 ,, + 9 ,, 0 ,, ,,		,, ,, ,, ,, + ,, ,,	
1552	6 ,, ,,	11 ,, 1 ,, + 0 ,, 19 ,, (Restored)		,, ,, ,, ,, + ,, ,,	
1553	1 Mary	11 ,, 0 ,, + 1 ,, 0 ,, ,,		,, ,, ,, ,, + ,, ,,	
1560	2 Elizabeth	11 ,, 2 ,, + 0 ,, 18 ,, (Sterling)		,, ,, ,, ,, + ,, ,,	
1696	8 & 9 Willm. III.	,, ,, ,, ,, + ,, ,, ,, ,, ,		11 ,, 10 ,, + 10 ,, †	
1719	6 George I.	,, ,, ,, ,, + ,, ,, ,, ,, ,,		11 ,, 2 ,, + 18 ,, §	

* " As good as Sterling." + " Britannia " Standard. § Old " Sterling " Standard restored.

From 1720 to the present day—the operation of the Act of 1719 having been deferred till 1 June, 1920—the standards for silver money and plate have been the same, with the addition that goldsmiths have had, and still have, the option of making plate of the higher or Britannia standard and of having such plate stamped with the " Britannia " marks at Goldsmiths' Hall, London or one of the other assay offices.

It does not appear that the Britannia standard was ever adopted in Scotland or in Ireland, but there is nothing to prevent the higher standard being used if desired.

It is remarkable that notwithstanding the debasement of silver money from the time of Henry VIII. to nearly the end of the reign of Edward VI. (when in 1551 it was so bad that there was only one-fourth pure silver to three-fourths alloy, and the coins made of such base metal could but be regarded as mere tokens), still all through these years the standard for wrought plate was maintained at 11 oz. 2 dwts of pure silver and 18 dwts of alloy to each pound weight.

CHAPTER IV.

THE ASSAY.

Meaning of Assay.

Assay (from the Old French *assai*, assay, essay = examination, trial, essay) is the operation of testing the purity of metals, and has from the earliest period in the history of English goldsmiths been resorted to in some mode or other for ascertaining—at any rate approximately—the amount of pure gold or pure silver contained in any object described as or represented to be "gold" or "silver".

Technical Terms.

The following technical terms used with reference to the operation of assaying gold and silver should be borne in mind in reading the following pages :—

"Touch."

The "Touch" is the operation of testing gold or silver by the early method of rubbing it on a "touch-stone". This term continued to be used with reference to the assay by crucible after the latter method had superseded the former, except for rough and ready tests.

"Touch-stone."

The "Touch-stone" is the stone on which the gold and silver is rubbed to ascertain its quality.

"Touch-penny." "Touch-money."

"Touch-penny," "Touch-money," is the money payable for the compulsory assaying of gold and silver wares, the ancient charge for which was a penny per pound.

In old times the word "Touch" was used not only with reference to the trial or testing, but also to the quality of the metal. as the "Touch of Paris," and sometimes to the mark of the Assay Office impressed on it. As for example, in the State Papers (Domestic) Henry VIII. (1536), mention is made that a report was widely spread in the North Country that everybody was to bring in his plate in order that it might have the "Touch of the Tower" struck on it.

"Partings."

"Partings" are the assays of metal which are composed of gold and silver only ; when gold predominates it is called a "gold parting," and when silver predominates a "silver parting".

"Diet."

"The Diet"—Medieval Latin *dieta*, from *dies*, a day, an assembly held on a set day—is the term used to denote the scrapings taken from wares sent to be assayed, and was so called because assays were made periodically on certain fixed days.

It has been the avowed object of nearly every statute affecting gold- smiths to prevent the use of too much alloy, whereby the public may be defrauded by a dishonest dealer. No fraud could be practised more profitably or with greater impunity than the sale of adulterated gold and silver wares, were it not for the assistance which the law renders to purchasers in the prevention of such offences and the detection and punishment of offenders; for gold may be alloyed considerably below standard without detection, except by a special test, and in the case of silver an amount of alloy almost equal to the weight of the silver may be added without the colour being appreciably impaired. The means taken for the prevention of such frauds were the establishment of assay offices in the Metropolis and other parts of the Kingdom for the purpose of testing gold and silver wares, and the incorporation of guilds or companies of goldsmiths entrusted with the conduct of the assay offices and empowered to deal with offenders and bring them to justice.

Compulsory assay for the prevention of adulteration.

In all parts within the jurisdiction of these bodies, a goldsmith or silversmith, before he commenced working, must have entered his name and residence or place of business at one of these assay offices, and have registered his mark in the form of a distinctive stamp or punch-mark to be struck on every piece of gold or silver work manufactured by him.* Having prepared his metal, taking care that its fineness is equal to the required standard, he shapes it into the form in which it is intended to be made, and before finishing it, lest it should be damaged by the assayer, he stamps it with his own punch-mark and sends it to the assay office in which his mark is registered (usually by being struck on a copper plate). It is here examined by the assayers $^{and}_{or}$ other officers of the Cor- poration, in order to ascertain if it bear the maker's registered mark, whether all the parts of which it is intended to be made are permanently fixed together, and whether the weight is increased by any unnecessary solder. If the result of this examination is unsatisfactory, it is returned to the maker; but if satisfactory, then a scraping is taken from it— from its several parts, if made of more than one piece—and the scrapings are subjected to analysis to ascertain the quality of the metal. If it be found deficient, then two other assays are made, and if still found deficient

The methods of Assayers.

---

* A list of some very small articles of gold and silver exempt from this rule will be found further on.

the work is cut through and the article is returned to the worker. If it be suspected that base metal has been fraudulently introduced within the work from which a scraping could not be taken, the assayer is authorised to cut the work through, and if the fraudulent introduction of base metal is discovered, the entire work is confiscated ; but if no fraud be discovered, compensation is made to the owner for the destruction of his work. But the plate-worker generally takes care to be on the safe side, and as a rule the assayer finds the plate as good or slightly better than standard. It is then stamped with the official stamps of the assay office and returned to the worker, who finishes it for sale.*

One of the earliest modes of ascertaining the quality of gold and silver in England was *by touch*. The metal to be tested was rubbed on the "touch-stone,"† and the quality of the metal was ascertained by comparing its rubbings with rubbings of pure gold and pure silver. In a small book on this subject, entitled *A New Touchstone for Gold and Silver Wares*,‡ the following paragraph occurs :—

> " To know a good touchstone, you must observe that the best sort are very black and of a very fine grain, polished very smooth and without any spongy or grain holes, and near the hardness of a flint, but yet with such a sharp cutting greet (grit) that it will cut or wear the silver or gold when rubbed thereon. The way to make a true touch on the touchstone is thus : When your touchstone is very clean (which if foul or soily it may be taken off by wetting and then rubbing it dry with a clean woollen cloth ; or if filled with touches of gold or silver, &c., it may be taken off by rubbing the touchstone with a pumice-stone in water, and it will make it very clean), then your silver being filed, rub it steadily and very hard on the stone, not spreading your touch above a quarter of an inch long, and no broader than the thickness of a five shilling piece of silver, and so continue rubbing it until the place of the stone whereon you rub be like the metal itself ; and when every sort is rubbed on that you intend at that time, wet all the touched places with your tongue, and it will show itself in its own countenance."

The use of the "touchstone".

Any hard, black silicious stone or earthenware will serve for a touchstone, and in the latter half of the 18th century touchstones were made of black pottery at Etruria by Josiah Wedgwood, stamped with the factory mark, and supplied to goldsmiths and assayers. For "touching" gold, strips of metal called "touch-needles" were used in three sets. One set was composed of gold alloyed with silver, another was alloyed with copper, and a third was alloyed

The use of the touchstone explained.

* See Watherston's *Art of Assaying*.
† A piece of black flinty slate or imperfect jasper, found in Lydia, and sometimes called *Lapis Lydiæ*.
‡ By " W.B. of London, Goldsmith ; London, 1667 ".

with a mixture of silver and copper. There were twenty-four needles in each set, varying from one to twenty-four carats fine. The streak of metal left on the touchstone was compared with the streaks made by the needles, all being washed with nitric acid, which, dissolving the alloy, left only pure gold on the stone, and, by comparison of the quantity of gold so left, the fineness of the metal tested was determined. Sets of touch-needles were used in a somewhat similar way for silver, but with less satisfactory results, and the use of the touchstone for silver is seldom resorted to for several reasons, amongst others that acid used in dissolving the alloy corrodes the silver; moreover, as so much copper could be added to silver without materially affecting its colour, but little assistance was obtained from the appearance of the rubbings. Doubtless, the expert assayer could tell, with some approximation to accuracy, from the sensations of roughness or the reverse, or the greasiness or dryness imparted by the " touch," the quality of the metal " touched," but, for the above reasons, this mode of assaying silver was discarded in favour of the crucible at an early period. As a rough-and-ready means of approximately ascertaining the fineness of gold, however, the touchstone has continued in use by goldsmiths down to the present day.

No record of the date when the assay by crucible was first introduced has been brought to light, but we find in the earliest statute on the subject,* which became law in 1300, a provision that "no vessel of silver should depart out of the hands of the worker until it be assayed by the wardens of the craft," and this probably had reference to the assay by crucible, which is performed in this manner: For gold, a small quantity of the metal is scraped from the article to be assayed (eight grains for every pound Troy is allowed), which is carefully weighed, and silver is added to the amount of about three times the weight of the gold contained in the sample, e.g. the silver added to a sample of nine carat gold weighing eight grains would be nine grains; but for a sample of eighteen carat gold the silver to be added would be double the amount, i.e. eighteen grains; and the whole wrapped in a thin sheet of lead, is placed in a small shallow porous crucible made of bone ashes, and called a "cupel". This is put into a furnace and exposed to incandescent heat, whereby the base metals become oxydised and are absorbed by the cupel while the gold and silver combine in a globule or pellet at the bottom of the cupel. This pellet when

Assay by crucible.

---

* 28 *Edw. I. cap.* 20.

cool is rolled or hammered out into a thin strip and is coiled into a spiral cone called a cornet, which is placed in a bath of hot diluted nitric acid whereby the silver is dissolved. The cornet is then bathed in stronger nitric acid, washed, and afterwards made red hot. Nothing is then left but pure gold, the weight of which in proportion to the original weight of the scrapings determines the fineness of the metal assayed.

The process for silver is somewhat similar : a scraping is taken from each part of the article to be assayed, weighed, wrapped in lead of proportionate weight, and the whole is heated in the cupel as for gold. In the result, all the alloying metal is absorbed and a pellet of pure silver remains, the weight of which in proportion to the original weight of the scrapings determines the fineness of the silver assayed.

Another method of testing the quality of silver by the use of sulpho-cyanide of ammonium has been described by Mr. Arthur Westwood, the Birmingham Assay Master, in the following terms :—

The assay of
silver by the
" wet " process.
" A sample of definite weight, obtained by cutting or scraping pieces from the different parts of the silver ware, is put into a glass flask and dissolved, with the aid of a gentle heat, in nitric acid.

" To the dissolved sample a measured volume of a dilute solution of a salt of iron is added. This completes the preliminary operations.

" A standard solution of sulphocyanide of ammonium, a measured volume of which is capable of combining with and precipitating from solution a known weight of silver, is then slowly run into the glass flask containing the dissolved sample, which is shaken in order to thoroughly mix the two liquids.

" The silver precipitate sinks to the bottom of the clear liquid as a white powder.

" When the whole of the silver contained in the dissolved sample has been precipitated, the addition of a single drop of sulphocyanide has the visible effect of causing the clear liquid to become coloured a light brown tint. At this point the volume of the sulphocyanide solution used is ascertained, which gives directly the weight of silver in the sample and its proportion to the other metals in the alloy.

" The colour is due to the interaction of the sulphocyanide with the solution of iron introduced in the preliminary operations ; this inter-action cannot take place until the whole of the silver is precipitated."

Not applicable
to gold
The sulphocyanide method is not applicable to gold.

The electrolytic methods of assay of gold and silver do not give such accurate results as the ordinary methods, and are practically never used.

Every duly appointed assayer, whether engaged at Goldsmiths' Hall, London, or at any provincial assay office, on his appointment undertakes that he will faithfully perform his duties, that he will make no undue profit, that he will take no more than four grains from every pound of wrought plate to be put into the diet-box, and four grains allowed for waste in making the assays ; that he will "touch" no gold or silver except such as shall have been ascertained by him to be equal to standard, that he will keep an account of all gold and silver brought to be assayed, and return all to the owner except the allowance of eight grains to the pound ; that he will not assay anything unless it be marked with the mark of the maker or owner, and that he will put into the diet-box only such metal as he shall have taken from plate which he shall have assayed and passed for standard. The Assay Masters of Birmingham and Sheffield are required by Act of Parliament to take an oath to that effect.

The diet-box is kept with the greatest possible care, secured with several locks, the keys of which are kept by different officers, so that it may not be opened by one except in the presence of the others, and the diet is tested in the same manner " as the pyx of the coin of this kingdom is tried ". *

* " Pyx " (L. *pyxis*), a box. " The trial of the pyx," so called because of the practice of taking several coins from a certain quantity, called a "journee" (a day's work), and depositing them in a safely-kept box until the purity of the metal of which they were made had been tested, is a highly important proceeding, instituted and continued for the purpose of maintaining the purity of the coinage. The trial formerly took place before the Privy Council at Westminster, the Lord Chancellor presiding, but since the Coinage Act of 1870 the test, which now is made at Goldsmiths' Hall, has been deprived of much of its pomp and ceremony. The practice now followed is to take a sample from each melting of gold and silver at the Mint. The sample coins are placed in the " Pyx," and kept until tested. For the trial a jury of the Goldsmiths' Company is summoned to appear before the King's Remembrancer, who, after the jurors have been sworn, charges them with reference to the performance of their duty. The coins found in the Pyx are then assayed and compared with the standard trial plates kept by the Warden of the Standards. On the verdict of the jury depends the acquittal of the authorities of the Mint, who during the trial "stand upon their deliverance".

CHAPTER V.

THE LONDON GOLDSMITHS.

We have seen (Chapter I.) that there was in London, as early as 1180, a guild or association of goldsmiths, although not legally recognised as such. In the year 1327 " The Wardens and Commonalty of the Mystery of Goldsmiths of the City of London," as they were then designated, having presented a petition to the King and his Council in Parliament, their first charter, bearing date 30 May, 1 Edward III. (1327), was granted to them as follows :—

30 May
I Edw. III (1327)
London
Goldsmiths'
FIRST CHARTER.

" That the goldsmiths of our City of London had by their petition, exhibited to the King and Council in Parliament holden at Westminster, shown that theretofore no private merchants or strangers were wont to bring into this land any money coined but plate of silver to exchange for our coin; that it had been ordained that all of the trade of goldsmiths were to sit in their shops in the High Street Cheap and that no silver or gold plate ought to be sold in the city of London except in the King's Exchange or in Cheap, among the goldsmiths, and that publicly, to the end that persons in the trade might inform themselves whether the seller came lawfully by it: but that of late both private merchants and strangers bring from foreign lands counterfeit sterling whereof the pound is not worth sixteen sols of the right sterling, and of this money none can know the right value but by melting it down; and that many of the trade of goldsmiths do keep shops in obscure streets, and do buy vessels of gold and silver secretly

The making of
counterfeit
jewels and
plate prohibited.

without inquiring whether such vessels were stolen or come lawfully by, and immediately melting it down, make it into plate, and sell it to merchants trading beyond sea, and so make false work of gold, silver, and jewels, in which they set glass of divers colours, counterfeiting right stones, and put more alloy in their silver than they ought which they sell to such as have no skill in such things; and that the cutlers cover tin with silver so subtiley and with such sleight, that the same cannot be discovered nor separated, and so sell the tin for fine silver, to the great damage and deceit of us and our people: We, with the assent of our lords spiritual and temporal and the commons of our realme, will and grant for us and our heirs, that henceforth no one shall bring into this land any sort of money, but only plate of fine silver, and that no plate of gold or silver be sold to sell again, or be carried out of the Kingdom, but shall be sold openly for private

No goldsmith
to keep any
shop except in
Cheap.

use; that none of the trade shall keep any shop except in Cheap, that it may be seen that their work be good; that those of the trade may by virtue of these presents, elect honest and sufficient men, best skilled in the trade, to inquire of the matters aforesaid, and that they who are so chosen reform what defects they shall find, and inflict punishment on the offenders, and that by the help of the Mayor and Sheriffs, if need be; that in all trading cities in England where goldsmiths reside, the same ordinance be observed as in London, and that one or two of every such city or town for the rest of the trade shall come to London to be ascertained of their touch of gold, *and there to have a stamp of a punchion of a leopard's head marked upon their work as it was anciently ordained."* *

Mark of leopard's head again mentioned.

In 1392-3 the London goldsmiths obtained a second charter, dated 6 February, 16 Richard II., whereby they were re-incorporated : all the powers and privileges conferred on them by their original charter were confirmed, and they were given additional powers enabling them to choose four wardens from amongst themselves to govern the commonalty and administer its business.

16 Ric. II. London Goldsmiths' second Charter (1392-3).

It is interesting to note some of the modes of procedure of this great company in the management of its affairs, and in particular with reference to the acquisition of the powers with which they have from time to time been entrusted by the legislature.

In the year 1404 (5 Hen. IV.), by reason of a dispute with the cutlers, the goldsmiths presented to Parliament a petition in the following terms :—

Petition of the London Goldsmiths to Henry IV. (1404).

"To our very redoubtable and very sovereign Lord the King, and to the very wise Lords of the present Parliament : Pray your humble lieges, Willliam Grantham, Salamon Oxeneye, Thomas Senycle, and Robert Hall, citizens and goldsmiths of your city of London, and Wardens of the Mystery of Goldsmiths of your said city, and all the Commonalty of the same Mystery. Whereas the said wardens and all others who have been wardens of the said Mystery in the said city, from time whereof memory runneth not, have had and used to have the search, survey, assay, and government of all manner of gold and of silver works, as well in the city as elsewhere in your Kingdom of England. And whereas the very noble King Edward, your ancestor, whom God assoil, upon certain defaults shewn to him and to his Council in his parliament held at Westminster in the first year of his reign, touching works of silver by the cutlers done in the said city upon cutlery, granted to the goldsmiths of the same city, that they might choose good people, and sufficient, of their Mystery of Goldsmiths, to inquire and search into the said defaults, and to amend and redress the faults found in the said Mystery, and due punishment to give to the wrong-doers, by aid of The Mayor and Sheriffs of the said city, and now the said cutlers are wont to work in gold and in silver in a different manner to what they did in the times aforesaid, through which, by the defaults and subtilties in the work of the said cutlers, great scandal and drawbacks will come to the said Mystery of Goldsmiths if remedy be not applied. May it please your Royal Majesty to grant to the said suppliants, that neither the said cutlers nor any other artificers whatsoever, may execute in any other manner workmanship of gold or of silver than they were wont at the time of the grant by your very noble ancestor aforesaid, and, besides that, of your more abundant grace, to grant to the said Wardens that they and their successors, Wardens of the said Mystery of Goldsmith-work may always

* See Herbert's *History of the London Livery Companies* where the Charter is set forth in French (as in the original) and in English.

have the search, survey, assay, and governance of all kinds of work done, and to be done, of gold and silver, by any person, of any mystery, as well in the said city as elsewhere in your said kingdom, and by them to put due punishment and redress for works defective and deceptive as well by aid of the Mayor and Sheriffs of the said city, as and shall be, as by aid of the Mayors, Sheriffs, Bailiffs, or any other officers elsewhere through the kingdom for the time being, as need may be, in the same way the goldsmiths have used always before now; reserving to the lords of Franchises the profits which to them may belong on account of such false works as shall be found and proven in the Franchises by the Wardens of the aforesaid Mystery: for Love of God and of Charity."

Which petition, having been read before the King and the lords in Parliament and by them fully considered, was answered in the following manner :—

Writ to the Lord Mayor of London to take evidence as to usages.

"Let a Writ containing the purport of this Petition, as well as that of the Cutlers now before Parliament, be sent to the Mayor of the City of London: and let the Mayor be empowered, by the Authority of Parliament, to cause to come before him both the men of the Mystery of the Goldsmiths in London and the men of the Cutlers Mystery, and let them show before the said Mayor the evidences and usages past and present, as well on the one side as the other, in the said city, from old times past: and let inquisition be made, if need be: and let the said Mayor certify to the King and his Council in this present Parliament without delay, what shall be found concerning this matter: to the end that the King, having had the counsel and advice of Parliament, may be able to do that which shall seem best in the matter."

Petition of the cutlers to King Henry IV. (1404).

The cutlers of London also on their side presented a petition to Parliament in the following terms :—

"To the very honourable and very wise lords of the present Parliament.— The citizens of London of the Craft of Cutlers humbly supplicate your aid that, as they and their predecessors from all times have worked gold and silver upon cutlery, &c., in their said craft, and have had four Wardens of their own elected before the Mayor of the said city, and sworn before him to amend all defaults in the same craft; and now lately the goldsmiths of the said city have made a suggestion to you, not at all true as they are informed, saying that the said cutlers have worked in gold and silver not according to agreement, to the intent that the said goldsmiths should have the government of the said cutlers, which would be the destruction and ruin of your petitioners. May it please your very gracious Lords to aid your said petitioners, that their rights and franchises may be saved, that they may have and enjoy their franchises in the same manner that they and their predecessors have had them before now: and that no charter be granted to the contrary: for the love of God and of charity."

Writs, accompanied by the petitions, addressed to the Lord Mayor of London and returned by him to Parliament.

The answer to this petition was similar to that given to the goldsmiths. Writs were addressed to the Lord Mayor of London, accompanied by both petitions with the answers (as above) endorsed thereon, desiring him to take such steps in the matter as seemed to him best and to make return thereto forthwith to Parliament: which writs were returned to the same Parliament and were answered by the Lord Mayor in the following manner :—

"By virtue of two writs of our Lord the King to me, William Askham, Mayor of London, directed and hereunto attached, the tenour of two petitions to our Lord the King, in the present Parliament, presented by the Cutlers and Goldsmiths of the said City, together with the endorsements thereupon, having been inspected, I caused to come before me, the aforesaid Mayor, at the Guildhall of the said City, as well good men of the said mysteries as many other good and sufficient ancient men from all the Wards of the said City : and the Charters, rolls, and evidences, as well written as not written, being there shown before me, by the said mysteries, touching and concerning the rule, custom, assay, and government of the said mysteries, it was determined before me,* the said Mayor, that the cutlers, citizens of the said City, have been accustomed from ancient times to work gold and silver within the liberty of the said City, as fashion and their skill dictated, and still the same cutlers work gold and silver in the said City, as fashion and their skill, according to the change of times, dictate and require ; and that the Wardens of the Mystery of the Art of the said Goldsmiths for the time being, subject to the Mayor and Aldermen of the said City for the time being, have been accustomed from ancient times to have the assay of the gold and silver wrought by the said cutlers within the liberty of the said City."

The Lord Mayor's answer to the writs.

Whereupon the King, having advised with the lords in the same Parliament, granted to the goldsmiths a confirmation of the Charter granted to them by Edward III. in the first year of his reign.

The King (Henry IV.) confirms the Charter of Edw. III.

It is recorded that in 1442 the wardens went to a Prior of St. Bartholomew to complain of "some untrue workers" in the precincts of the priory ; that the Prior accompanied the wardens to the shop of one Tomkins, and that having obtained admission they found there "a pan which was copper and silver above, the which was likely for to have be sold for good silver," and that whilst the search was being effected the delinquent stole away, "or else he had be set in the stokkis". In 1444 a member of the craft was fined 6s. 8d. for "withstanding the Wardens in making the assay," and in 1452 one German Lyas was fined "for selling a tablet of gold dishonestly wrought, being two parts silver". The fine was a gilt cup of 24 oz. to the fraternity.

In 1462 the London goldsmiths were granted a further charter, dated 30 May, 2 Edward IV., whereby they were not only confirmed in the enjoyment of the powers and privileges granted by their former charter, but were constituted a body corporate and politic, with

Further Charter to the London Goldsmiths by Edw. IV. (1462).

* "*Coram*," not *per*.

perpetual succession and larger and more extensive powers and privileges, including the right to use a common seal wherewith their elected wardens might execute formal documents in the name of the commonalty, and the power to search, inspect, assay and regulate the working of all gold and silver wares in the City of London, and in all fairs, markets, and exchanges, and in all cities, towns and boroughs, and all other places whatsoever throughout this realm, and to punish offenders for making wares of gold and silver worse than standard.

Goldsmiths' exercise of powers.

That the powers conferred by these charters were constantly exercised, and that progresses were made through the kingdom and searches effected in various parts in the exercise of such powers, the old accounts of the Company, from which the above instances have been taken, furnish abundant evidence. The following extracts are given as additional examples :—

46 Edward III. (1372). Thomas Lauleye, for having sold and exposed for sale divers cups (mazers) bound with circlets of "latone" (*latten*, a base metal like brass), as well in the city as without, pretending that they were of silver gilt, was put in the pillory with the cups hung round his neck.

50 Edward III. (1376). Peter Randolfe was proceeded against for having wrought cuppebondes (circlets for mazers) of silver worse than standard.

2 Henry V. (1414). "John of Rochester," for having made cupbands of base metal, silver and gilt, in the City of Rochester, was taken by the master of the trade of that city to London to answer for the offence.

38 Henry VI. (1460). Expensis don vpon John Brooking, of Bridgwater, for disobeying and rebukying of the Wardeyns in time of serche ... iiij$^{li \cdot}$ xij$^{s \cdot}$ i$^{d \cdot}$

8 Edward IV. (1469). For boat hire to Westminster and home again, for the suit in Chancery begun in Ye Olde Wardeyns time, for the recovery of a counterfeit dyamond set in a ring of gold ... ... vi$^{d \cdot}$

For a breakfast at Westminster spent on our counsel ... ... i$^{s \cdot}$ vi$^{d \cdot}$

To W. Catesby, Sergeant-at-law, to plead for the same ... ... iii$^{s \cdot}$ iiij$^{d \cdot}$

1470. The following items occur in the "expenses necessarie":—

For engraving the punches ... ... ij$^{s \cdot}$ o

For costs done in taking of assays ... i$^{l \cdot}$ vj$^{s \cdot}$ viij$^{d \cdot}$

In pursuance of their charters the London Goldsmiths' Company issued as occasion arose ordinances or bye-laws for the government of the craft, and these run from 1478 downwards. Amongst the earliest are the following :—

" That no goldsmiths of England nor nowhere else within the realme, work Goldsmiths' Ordinances. no manner of vessel nor any other thing of gold nor silver, but if it be of the very alloy according to the Standard of England, called sterling money, or better."

" That no manner of vessel or any other thing . . . . be sold till it be Plate to be assayed and marked before sale. assayed by the Wardens of the Craft or their Deputy, the Assayer ordained therefor, and *that it be marked with the lyperde's head crowned,* according to the Acts of divers Parliaments, *and the mark of the maker thereof.*"

An ordinance of the Company dated 5 Henry VIII. (1513) provides First mention of the " Assayer's mark " in addition to the leopard's head and maker's mark. that " before any work of gold or silver is put to sale the maker shall set on it his own mark, that it *shall* (then) *be assayed by the assayer, who* (if it be found of the true alloy) *shall set on it his mark, and that the Wardens shall mark it with the leopard's head crowned*".

Notwithstanding these ordinances it seems that plate was occasionally sold without being assayed and marked, as shown by the following entries in the Company's books :—

" Friday, 12 February, 1562. At this court William Cater promised to bring Wm. Cater before the Goldsmiths for selling a cup " untouched," 1562. in within this month a Communion cup which he made and sold into the country untouched."

" Friday, 26 February, 1562. At this court William Cater brought in a Communion cup according to his promise here made the 12th day of this month, which cup he sold into Kent untouched, and the same at the assay was found good and so delivered to the said Cater again." *

In this case, at any rate, the reason for the cup not having been taken to the assayer to be touched was not that it was below standard. Possibly the reason might have been found in the prejudice or venality of the Assay Master, for we find that in 1583 a complaint was carried to the Complaints respecting the assayer's conduct in 1583. Master of the Mint by Richard Mathews and Henry Colley concerning "the grefes of us poor goldsmiths" by reason of the unfair treatment accorded to them by Thomas Kelynge, then the Assay Master at Goldsmith's Hall. They alleged that he had broken their plate unjustly, and that when they had refashioned part of the broken plate and sent it in again bearing another maker's mark, it had passed, and that part of a condemned platter had been converted into a taster and had passed. They also complained that from a nest of bowls or a tankard weighing not more than thirty ounces he had taken as much as a quarter of an ounce for himself.†

These complaints against their Assay Master, although apparently borne out by evidence, do not seem to have deterred the Goldsmiths' Company from prosecuting offenders, for they appear to have invoked

* Communicated by Mr. H. D. Ellis. See Cater's mark of 1562 on page 98.
† *Mint Miscellanies—Exchequer, Q.R. Temp. Eliz.* Public Record Office.

the aid of the Treasury not many years afterwards in bringing to justice two goldsmiths accused of gross fraud, as testified by the following entry :—

4 May, 1597. John Moore and Robt. Thomas indicted for working and selling debased plate and counterfeiting the marks of Her Majesty's lion, the leopard's head, and the alphabetical marks thereon.

"4th May, 1597. Edward Cole, Attorney General, filed an information against John Moore and Robert Thomas, that whereas it had been heretofore of long time provided by divers laws and statutes for the avoiding of deceit and fraud in the making of plate, that every goldsmith should before the sale of any plate by him made, bring the same first to the Goldsmiths' Hall for trial by assay, to be touched or marked and allowed by the wardens of the said company of Goldsmiths, the which wardens did by their indenture in their search, find out the aforesaid deceitful workmanship and counterfeit also of plate and puncheons ; yet the said John Moore and R. Thomas, being lately made free of the Goldsmiths' Company, did about three months past make divers parcels of counterfeit plate debased and worse than her Majesty's standard 12d. and more in the oz. ; and to give appearance to the said counterfeit plate being good and lawful, did thereto counterfeit and put the marks of her Majesty's Lion, the leopard's head, limited by statute, *and the alphabetical mark* approved by ordinance amongst themselves, which are the private marks of the Goldsmiths' Hall, and be and remain in the custody of the said wardens and puncheons to be worked and imprinted thereon, and the said John Moore did afterwards sell the same for good and sufficient plate to the defrauding of her Majesty's subjects, &c."

First mention of the lion, and second mention of the alphabetical mark.

Conviction of Moore and Thomas.

Moore and Thomas were convicted of the offences charged against them and were sentenced to be put in the pillory with their ears nailed to it, with papers affixed above their heads stating their offence to have been "for making false plate and counterfeiting her Majesty's touch". It is recorded that the sentence was carried out, that each of the offenders had an ear cut off, that they were taken through Foster Lane to Fleet Prison, and that they were each fined ten marks in addition to the exemplary punishment which they suffered.

Between 1597 and 1675, probably much plate wrought and sold untouched by the assayer and marked only with maker's mark.

From 1597 until 1675 there appears very little of interest to relate concerning the London Goldsmiths' Company. There is not much evidence of any efforts having been made to enforce the old-time laws and ordinances with reference to the obligation to submit all gold and silver wares to their assayer's "touch," and it seems probable that a large number of goldsmiths in London and the provinces followed the example set by William Cater in 1562 and sold wrought plate without being either assayed or marked other than with their own stamp. Indeed, the notice which was issued by the London Goldsmiths' Company on 23 February, 1675, can have no other reference, and points quite obviously to that conclusion. The order in question is thus set forth in the *Touchstone* :—

THE GOLDSMITHS' ORDER,

Lately made and set forth for Prevention and Redress of the Great Abuses committed in the several Wares aforementioned.

GOLDSMITHS' HALL,

THE 23RD DAY OF FEBRUARY, 1675.

Whereas complaint hath been made to the Wardens of the Company of *Goldsmiths, London*, that divers small works, as buckles for belts, silver hilts, and the pieces thereto belonging, with divers other small wares, both of gold and silver, are frequently wrought and put to sale by divers goldsmiths and others, worse than standard, to the abuse of his Majesty's good subjects, and great discredit of that manufacture ; and that there are also divers pieces of silver plate sold, not being assayed at *Goldsmiths' Hall*, and so not marked with the *Leopard's Head crowned*, as by law the same ought to be : And whereas the Wardens of the said Company, to prevent the said frauds, have formally required all persons to forbear putting to sale any adulterate wares either of gold or silver, but that they cause the same forthwith to be defaced ; and that as well plate-workers as small-workers should cause their respective marks to be brought to Goldsmiths' Hall, and there strike the same in a table kept in the Assay Office, and likewise enter their names and places of habitation in a book there kept for that purpose, whereby the persons and their marks might be known unto the Wardens of the said Company, which having not hitherto been duly observed, these are therefore to give notice to, and to require again all those who exercise the said art or mystery of goldsmiths in or about the Cities of *London* and Westminster, and the suburbs of the same ; that they forthwith repair to *Goldsmiths' Hall* and there strike their marks in a table appointed for that purpose, and likewise enter their names with the places of their respective dwellings, in a book remaining in the *Assay Office* there. And that as well the worker as shop-keeper, and all others working and trading in gold or silver wares of what kind or quality soever they be, forbear putting to sale any of the said works, not being agreeable to standard, that is to say, gold not less in fineness than two and twenty carats, and silver not less in fineness than eleven ounces two pennyweights : and that no person or persons do from henceforth put to sale any of the said wares either small or great, before the workman's mark be struck thereon, and the same assayed at *Goldsmiths' Hall*, and there approved for standard, by striking thereon the *Lyon* and *Leopard's Head crowned*, or one of them, if the said works will conveniently bear the same : and hereof all persons concerned are desired to take notice, and demean themselves accordingly : otherwise the Wardens will make it their care to procure them to be proceeded against according to law.

This order seems to have had the desired effect ; the result being that after its issue the table referred to in the order soon became impressed with the marks of some hundreds of makers "*of which not any other entry is to be found*". It is, therefore, not surprising that very much more London Hall-marked plate is to be found with the marks of 1675 and the following nine years than in the period reckoned backwards from 1675 to the time of the Great Fire, and this is probably attributable

23 Feb., 1675. Goldsmiths' Order requiring workers to bring in their marks, and to sell no wares worse than standard, nor before being assayed at Goldsmiths' Hall.

to the fact recited in the Goldsmiths' Order that "divers pieces of silver plate were sold" prior to 1675 which had not been assayed at Goldsmiths' Hall. The "table" referred to in the "order" is a copper plate, which is preserved by the Goldsmiths' Company as one of its valued possessions.

In 1677, when *The Touchstone* was published, a record of the names of makers written on vellum was preserved, but this record has long since disappeared, so that makers' marks struck before 1697 can now only in rare instances be with absolute certainty identified with the names.

Makers' marks and names preserved at Goldsmiths' Hall from 1697.

From April, 1697, however, by means of the entries in the Company's books (except in a few cases where a leaf is missing) identification is quite simple.

The ordinances of the London Goldsmiths' Company, other than those which have already been referred to, concern mainly—after the ascertaining of the quality of gold and silver wares and the prevention of fraud—the subject of marking those wares with the proper marks, and these will be found dealt with in the following chapter. A few observations, however, remain to be made concerning the personality of the London goldsmiths before concluding this.

Reference has been made to disreputable goldsmiths who had been found guilty of fraudulent practices. These, happily, have been but the dregs of that fraternity which has for centuries maintained an exalted character for honour and integrity, and their history shows that from their trade as much as, if not more than, from any other have members been raised to noble rank. It is needless here to dwell on the well-worn theme that "goldsmith" and "banker" were in former times synonymous terms, and that as late as the 18th century well-known banking firms were styled "Goldsmiths of London," but it may not be out of place to mention a few London goldsmiths of the past who figured as men of eminence amongst their contemporaries.

Renowned London goldsmiths.

Ralph Flael, a goldsmith and alderman of the city of London, is mentioned in 1180 as one of the members of the guild fined for having been established without the King's licence.

Henry FitzAlwyn was chosen as the first Mayor of London in 1189, and continued in office till 1213.

William Fitzwilliam (son of William the Goldsmith), from whom Earl Fitzwilliam is said to be descended, was an eminent London goldsmith in 1212.

Ralph Essory was one of the sheriffs of London in 1242 and Mayor in 1243.

Gregory de Rokesley, goldsmith, was keeper of the King's Exchange and Chief Assay Master of all the King's Mints in England, and he was eight times Mayor. In 1285, in maintaining the dignity of his office, as he appeared to think, he refused to appear before the King's justices as Mayor, but disrobed and attended as a private person, for which contempt of court the office of Mayor was suspended, but it was afterwards restored.

Sir John de Chichester, goldsmith, whose shop was at the corner of Friday Street in the Chepe, was Sheriff in 1359, Master of the King's Mint in 1365, and Lord Mayor 1369-70.*

Sir Nicholas Twyford was goldsmith to Edward III., and was knighted in 1388, during his mayoralty of the city.

Adam Browne, a goldsmith, was Lord Mayor in 1397.

Solomon Oxeneye, one of the wardens of the Goldsmiths' Company in 1403, was a member of Parliament for the city in 1419.

Sir John Pattesley was a celebrated goldsmith in the time of Henry VI. He was Sheriff in 1432, and Lord Mayor, 1440-1.

Sir Mathew Philip, goldsmith (Lord Mayor, 1463-4), was made a Knight of the Bath by Edward IV. for bravery in battle, having taken a prominent part in the rout of Falconbridge and his rebel army in their attempt to take the city.

Sir Edmund Shaw was goldsmith to the King; engraver to the Mint in 1462; warden of the Company and Sheriff of the city, 1474; Lord Mayor, 1482-3. During his year of office his claim to be Cup-bearer to the King was allowed, and he attended the coronation of Richard III in that capacity.

Sir John Shaw, goldsmith, engraver to the Mint in 1483, was knighted on the field of Bosworth 1485, and was Lord Mayor in 1501-2.

Sir Martin Bowes, goldsmith and banker, was Sheriff 1540; Lord Mayor, 1545-6; Master of the Mint, 1546, and member of Parliament for London, 1546 to 1555. He was butler at Queen Elizabeth's coronation.

To these goldsmith-bankers might be added the names of Viner, Child, Coutts, Drummond, Fowler, Hankey, and others, but they were for the most part dealers in money rather than makers of plate. It is the purpose of this book rather to direct attention to those names which represent the actual workers in the precious metals—

* The first *Lord* Mayor was Sir Thomas Legge in 1354.

goldsmiths who wrought plate which has endured long after their lives have ceased, and who have left behind them something more than a mere record—objects of art in silver and gold, whereby they have earned a lasting fame. Of these, the names, beyond those already mentioned, which appear the most prominent in the time of Charles II. are Ralph Leake, Pierre Harache, William Gamble, Anthony Fickets, George Garthorne, William Gamble, Anthony Nelme, and Lawrence Coles, the majority of whom continued working until the end of the century and registered their marks at Goldsmiths' Hall in 1697. Of the goldsmiths of Queen Anne's time we have Pierre Platel, David Willaume, Daniel Garnier, Mark Paillet, Lewis Mettayer, Augustin Courtauld, Humphrey Payne, John Bodington, Simon Pantin, Louys Cuny, Jean Petrij, Pierre Le Chaube, Philip Rainaud, and (about the end of that reign) Paul Lamerie, looming large as actual plate-workers.

Immigration of French refugee goldsmiths, 1685 to 1700.

It will be observed that a large proportion of these names are those of French Protestants who, for the most part, quitted France to escape the persecution consequent upon the revocation of the Edict of Nantes in 1685, and to the immigration of these excellent workmen may be attributed the introduction of French "feeling" into the art of the English goldsmith of this period.

It is unnecessary here to extend these references to individuals, there being a list of the London goldsmiths from 1090 to 1850 in Chapter VIII.

Down to the 18th century it was the practice for goldsmiths to carry on their business under a sign such as the lion, the bear, the spreadeagle, the swan, the fox, the squirrel, the griffon, the falcon, the unicorn, the sun, the half-moon, the harp, an angel, a saint's head, a sprig, a flower, or other symbol, whereby the unlettered public might distinguish their shops. Signs or symbols such as these on a small scale were used also as makers' marks from 1363, the date when goldsmiths were first required to use a mark, until initial letters were by degrees adopted in place of symbols in the 16th and 17th centuries. In some cases the names of the makers may be identified by reason of these marks being miniature reproductions of their signs.*

---

* For further particulars concerning the lives of Early English goldsmiths and bankers the reader is referred to the interesting paper of Mr. F. G. Hilton Price, F.S.A., *Proc. Lond. and Mid. Archl. Socy.*, and to the following works : Herbert's *History of the London Livery Companies;* Riley's *Memorials of London and London Life in the XIII., XIV., and XV. Centuries; Chronicles of the Mayors and Sheriffs of London,* by the same author; and to the *Mint Miscellanies* at the Public Record Office.

CHAPTER VI.

THE MARKS ON LONDON PLATE.

On every article of gold or silver subsequent to 1300—except Royal Plate, articles made of silver supplied by the person or persons requiring it to be wrought, or some very small objects enumerated in the list of exceptions—there is, or ought to be, a mark, or group of marks, generally indicative of the quality of the metal of which it is made. These marks vary in character according to the rule of the office where the article has been assayed. The distinguishing marks of each provincial assay office will be found dealt with in later chapters.

The marks on plate, devised to prevent fraud, and indicate quality.

Although the law required that from the year 1300 a certain mark or marks should be impressed on all English-wrought silver, yet, for a long period in our history, this law was much "honoured in the breach," and much plate was disposed of either unmarked or marked with the maker's mark only. For that reason, it should be borne in mind that a piece of English plate purporting to have been made at a particular period may possibly be a perfectly genuine example of that period although devoid of the Hall marks establishing its authenticity.

Many early examples of plate unmarked, or bearing maker's mark only.

We have seen in a previous chapter that the marks now being considered were not devised for the purpose of enabling the modern plate-collector to ascertain the year when such marks were impressed, but solely with the object of preventing fraud, and detecting the offenders in case of fraud being practised ; but by reason of the changes which were annually made in one of these marks, we are in fact enabled to determine the exact year when a fully-marked example of London plate was assayed.

Marks devised for prevention of fraud, and not for determining date of fabrication, but incidentally serve the latter purpose.

The marks which are, or ought to be, found on plate assayed in London are in their chronological order as follows :—

1. The leopard's head.
2. The worker's or maker's mark.
3. The annual letter.
4. The lion passant.
5. { The lion's head erased, and
   { The figure of Britannia.
6. The Sovereign's head.

Marks found on London Plate.

Mr. Octavius
Morgan, F.S.A.,
the first to
compile tables
of London
date-letters.

The late Mr. Octavius Morgan, F.S.A., devoted a considerable amount of time and care to the evolution of a system whereby the marks on old London plate might be identified and their meaning made clear, and at a meeting of the Archæological Institute held at Bristol on 1st August, 1851, he offered some interesting remarks upon the assay and year marks used by goldsmiths in England, and stated that he had been able to carry back the latter to a much more distant period than was comprised in the lists of the Goldsmiths' Company, thus affording the means of precisely ascertaining the date of fabrication of ancient English plate.*

Up to that time all that had been published concerning this subject was what was contained in *The Touchstone* (printed in 1677), which, amongst other interesting matter, gave the date-letter in use for 1676-7, followed by the publication of the various alphabets used at Goldsmiths' Hall from 1696 downwards. With the exception of these and the entries in the minutes of the Goldsmiths' Company, where many of the date-letters used between 1618 and 1696 are sketched with more or less resemblance to the actual stamps, the marks used prior to 1696 and their exact meaning were unknown. This was the state of the matter when Mr. Morgan set about his task of finding a way back to the Medieval starting point, and clearing away from the landmarks the entanglements which in the course of centuries had grown around them.

In 1852 Mr. Morgan published the results of his labours,† which gave to his fellow antiquaries and all others whom it might concern the means of ascertaining the exact year (from 1478‡ downwards) when any fully marked piece of London plate was made, and as the work of that learned antiquary has been the basis upon which every series of tables of London Hall Marks has been constructed by every writer who has subsequently pursued the subject (in many cases with but slight, if any, acknowledgment) it is due to his memory that the services which he so generously rendered to every one interested in Old English Plate should be fully and freely recognised.

The earliest known record of any authorised mark on plate is that referring to the fact that in 1275 Philip le Hardi, King of France,

---

* *Archæological Journal*, Vol. VIII. 330 (1851).

† *Archæological Journal*, Vol. IX. 126, 231, 313 (1852); Vol. X. 33 (1853).

‡ Misled by a tradition in connection with the Pudsey spoon, Mr. Morgan ascribed the Lombardic H stamped on its stem to 1445 instead of to 1525, the year to which it rightly belongs. With that single exception the arrangement of Mr. Morgan's tables of London date-letters (framed amidst difficulties such as always beset a pioneer) is absolutely correct.

ordained that each city should have a particular mark of its own for wrought silver. The next in order is our own statute of the year 1300 previously referred to, with which our own marks begin, the first in order being

THE LEOPARD'S HEAD.

This mark, as we have seen, was first established by statute in 1300, and in the statute of 1363 it is called the King's Mark. In the translation of the original Norman French given in the statutes at large, the words used are "*the* Leopard's head," as if it had been some long known and recognised symbol; but in the original, the words are "*une* Teste de Leopart," and from the use of the article "une," and from the fact that plate of earlier date has not been so marked, it was probably a new mark then devised and established for the express purpose of marking plate. Some confusion and error appear to have existed with regard to the term "*Leopard's* head," it being, in fact, a lion's head. The error, said Mr. Morgan, "has arisen from the fact not being known or understood that in the Old French language (the language of our early statutes), the heraldic term 'Leopart' means a lion passant guardant. The arms of England from the time of Henry III. have been three lions passant guardant, and in the Old French heraldic words are described as 'three Leoparts,' or Lions Leopardes. The leopard's head, therefore, is properly the head of a lion passant guardant, which, in fact, is a lion's front face, as is this mark, and it was most probably taken from the arms of the sovereign."

Earliest English plate mark: the Leopard's head (1300).

"Leopard's head" really a lion's face.

All the early examples of this mark show a fine bold lion's face, having on the head a ducal crown or coronet. In the reign of George II., however, the size of the head was diminished; and in 1821, from the fact, as Mr. Morgan was informed, that in some document the simple "Leopard's head" was found mentioned without being followed by the word "crown," and the parties employed probably not being aware of the circumstances above related, the form of the stamp was altogether changed when the new punches were engraved; the lion's head was deprived of his crown, and shorn of his mane and beard; and it has ever since then presented an object far more resembling the head of a cat than the fine bold lion's head of former days.

It must be here observed that all the examples of the mark of the leopard's head stamped on plate of a date anterior to the introduction of the date-letter which have been as yet discovered are without the crown,

Leopard's head without a crown before 1478.

which, while being perfectly consistent with the Act of 1300, ordaining that all articles of gold and silver should be marked with a "leopard's head" (no mention being made of a crown), is consistent also with the suggestion now made, that the crown was first put on the leopard's head at or about the time (1478) when the date-letter was first adopted.* It remains also to be observed that the form of the leopard's head crowned differed very appreciably at different times between 1478 and 1821. Prior to 1478 the uncrowned leopard's head is also found to vary somewhat in appearance, sometimes presenting a broad, chubby-looking face, at others more elongated and with the tongue extended, but generally without mane and beard, and mostly within a ring of pellets in a circular stamp. From 1478, or rather 1479 —the earliest noted example with a date-letter being the Nettlecombe chalice with the Lombardic B of 1479-80—until 1482, the leopard's head, ducally crowned, but without mane and beard, is within a depression or field, the outline of which follows the outline of the head and crown; in other words, the marks have been struck by a stamp of irregular shape. From 1488 to 1497 the crowned head is still not bearded, but is within a circular field. In 1498 the mane and beard appear on the face for the first time—still in a circular field—and the mark presents unmistakably the appearance of a lion's face, which appearance is subsequently preserved in this mark for more than two centuries. In 1515 a change was made in the shape of the crown, which, instead of being a fine, bold ducal crown, as it is seen to have been from 1479, is diminished in size to little more than an invected band, or fillet, with four small arches and three spikes, an unimposing and somewhat mean-looking substitute for the bold ducal crown which it superseded. This change in the form of the crown over the leopard's head was noticed by the late Mr. W. H. St. John Hope, M.A. (Sec. Soc. Antiq.) in the year 1887 †, and is of the greatest importance in distinguishing the date letters of 1518 to 1543 from those of the first alphabet 1478-97, as some of the later letters bear a very close resemblance to some of the earlier and are scarcely distinguishable without the aid of the leopard's head.

This change in the form of the crown of the leopard's head was pointed out to the late Mr. Wilfred Cripps, C.B., and was referred to in

Leopard's head different in design from time to time.

Various forms of the leopard's head crowned.

---

* It had been stated in several successive editions of *Old English Plate* that "the leopard's head was crowned from the first". The author directed attention to this error in 1889 when writing a monograph on *The Spoon and its History*, printed in *The Archæologia*, Vol. LIII.
† *Soc. Antiq. Proc.*, 2nd Series, XI., 426.

Old English Plate at the foot of the table of London date-letters 1478-1557 "*as occasionally found, e g., 1515 and 1521, etc.*," but its value appears not to have been fully appreciated, inasmuch as the changed form is regularly found from 1515 to 1543. As a result Mr. Stanyforth's spoon with "writhen" or "spirally fluted" knob was assigned in *Old English Plate* to the year 1528 instead of to 1488-9, which is its true date.

In 1531-2 the outline of the punch with which the leopard's head mark was struck was no longer quite circular, but was contracted in width towards the chin. In 1539-40 the outline, instead of being smooth and regular, follows the indentations of the head and crown, and the face presents a more archaic appearance than in the few preceding years, and in 1544-5 it appears still more archaic, and the old form of ducal coronet is resumed.* In 1545-6 an almost regular outline somewhat similar to that of 1531-8, but slightly more elliptical, was resorted to. A punch with this kind of outline was used until 1551, when the face, crown, and outline of punch are all changed; the face is bolder, the mane more noticeable, and the crown completely transformed, is now composed of the cross *patée* and *fleur-de-lys*, while the outline of the field is in form almost hexagonal. In the three following years (1552-5) the face and crown are unaltered, but the outline of the field is invected, following the lines of the head and crown. In 1555-6 the crowned leopard's head (still resembling that of the four preceding years) is, for the first time, set in an angular heraldic shield of pentagonal form, but in the following year (1556-7) the invected or wavy outline is again reverted to, and thence continued for more than a hundred and twenty years with only such slight variations in the crowned leopard's head as might be expected from the fact that the punches used during such a long period must of necessity have been cut by different hands while working, broadly speaking, "to the same design". The slight variations now referred to are shown in the tables at the dates when they occur, and it is, therefore, unnecessary to describe them more fully here, but it must be mentioned that the practice of indenting the punch to the line of the crowned head was abandoned in 1680, and has never since been resumed. The punch then adopted was of about the same size as before, but gibbous in outline as appears in the tables. The bold character of the head is still preserved, but the

Archaic form of leopard's head crowned reverted to in 1544-5.

Various forms of the leopard's head stamp from 1545 to 1697.

---

* This may have been for the same object as appears to have occasioned the adoption of the lion in the same year, viz., to mark the fact that, although the silver coinage was then debased, the old " sterling " standard was maintained for plate. (See page 69, *infra*.)

face is somewhat smaller, with more mane and beard displayed, and a little more space between the head and the outline of the punch. This form continued in use until 27 March, 1697, when the mark of the "leopard's head crowned" was proscribed, by reason of the alteration of the standard, but the old punches which had been in use from 1680 to 1697, or new punches resembling them, were resorted to on the restoration of the old standard in 1719-20. Between 1720 and 1729 we find that a new form of punch was also used for this mark: a leopard's head crowned with a ducal coronet in an angular shield, pentagonal in form, of smaller size and less bold design than that of the old head which is found to have been still occasionally used. The result of the use of punches of the old form being that, when the date-letter is indistinct, the marks might easily be mistaken for those of the period 1680-97. In 1729 the, stamp, still pentagonal in outline, is reduced in size, and very little of either mane or beard is left; the crown or coronet has two pearls introduced into it, giving it the appearance of a marquisal coronet heightened and laterally compressed. In 1739 the form is again altered; the mane and beard are found to have entirely disappeared, the width of the jaws is much contracted, and a few straight hairs or "whiskers" are substituted for the beard. This head, in a somewhat attenuated stamp, formed of a series of ogees or waved lines, presents an appearance somewhat mean and unimportant as compared with its predecessors. From 1756 to 1776 the head is a little fuller in the jowl, and the containing shield is not shaped, but a plain oblong, with the bottom corners rounded; and except that from 1776 the top corners of the shield are clipped off, this mark remains of the same form until 1821-2, when the crown disappears and the containing shield is brought to a point at the base. The absence of the crown from the leopard's head affords the principal means of distinguishing the marks of the years 1826 to 1831 from those of 1786 to 1791. There is very little difference in the form of this mark during the following fifty-five years—the slight changes are however shown in the following tables; but in 1896, while the head remains unaltered, the top of the containing shield is invected, and three lobes take the place of the straight top with clipped corners which had preceded it.

Marginal note: Use of leopard's head crowned discontinued in 1697, resumed in 1719-20.

Marginal note: Crown disappears from leopard's head in 1821-2.

THE WORKER'S OR MAKER'S MARK.

The mark which in chronological order has next to be considered, is the Maker's Mark, first instituted in England by the Statute of

1363, which ordained that every Master Goldsmith should have a mark of his own, known to those appointed by the King to survey their work, which mark should be set on their works after they had been assayed. This requirement was repeated in almost every subsequent statute, and it is frequently styled the " Mark or *Sign* " of the worker. These makers' marks were at first emblems or symbols, as a fish, a bird a horse or other animal, a heart, a cross, a rose or other flower ; probably often selected in allusion to the name of the maker. In early times, when the majority of the people were unlettered, goldsmiths, like other shop-keepers, had signs by which their shops were known, and some retained the custom down to quite recent times. The written name would have been of little use when few could read, whereas the setting up of a sign which was easily understood afforded a convenient means of distinguishing the shop ; it is, therefore, not improbable that goldsmiths took for their mark the sign of their shop. After a time, however, as may be seen in the tables, letters were used as the worker's mark.

Signs or Symbols used as makers' marks.

The custom of using signs or symbols for makers' marks gradually fell into disuse in the 17th century, and (except in conjunction with initial letters) by the time of Charles II. we find but very few marks consisting of symbols. A rose in a pentagon, an escallop, a goose, three storks and very few others comprise all that are used without letters accompanying them. But symbols with letters either above, below, or between them, were used in plenty down to the middle of the 18th century, the most favoured device being a crown or coronet placed over two letters, and this is found in use as late as the last quarter of the 19th century.

Discontinued in 17th century.

The *Touchstone for Gold and Silver Wares*, printed in 1677, contains the following reference to makers' marks. After describing the assay office, the author proceeds :

" In this office is likewise kept for publique view a table or tables artificially made of columns of parchment or velom, and several of the same sorts ; in the lead are struck or entered the workers' marks (*which are generally the first letters of their Christian and Sirnames*), and right against them in the parchment or velom columns, are writ and entered the owners' names ; This is that which is meant in the before-recited statutes by the expression of *making the workers' marks known to the Surveyors or Wardens of the Craft ;* which said wardens' duty is to see that the marks be plain and of a fit size, and not one like another, and to require the thus entering the said marks, and also the setting them clear and visible on all gold and silver work, not only on every work, but also on every

Records of maker's marks preserved in the time of Charles II.

part thereof that is wrought apart and afterwards soddered, or made fast thereto in finishing the same."

"Our law makers (as I conceive) did think the thus setting the marks on the work to be the securest way to prevent fraud in this kind; for if it would not deter from the working and selling coarse silver and gold wares, yet would it be a sure way to find out the offenders, and to have the injured righted. But if the marks might be omitted, and the works should pass but into a third owner's hand, for the most part it would be impossible to discern one man's work from another, by reason that divers workers made all sorts of work in shapes so near alike."

Their subsequent disappearance.

The records mentioned in *The Touchstone* are unfortunately not now to be found, and as they were in existence after the Fire of London they were in all probability deliberately destroyed. The only official records now in existence are those previously mentioned, viz., the copper plates in which are struck the makers' marks in use when the order of the Goldsmiths' Company of 1675 was enforced, and the books in which the goldsmiths' names and their marks from 1697 are registered. It is, therefore, extremely difficult to assign the name of the worker to any particular maker's mark prior to that date, and it can only be done with certainty when it is fixed by an entry in some contemporaneous account or inventory. There are, however, some few marks, *e.g.*, those of W. Cater * (1562), T. Maundy, R. Timbrell (1690), and Benjamin Pyne, William Scarlett, Peter Harache, and Timothy Ley before and after 1697, about which there can be no doubt.

The Statute 8 Wm. III. c. 8 (1696-7) which raised the standard for silver plate from 11 oz. 2 dwts. to 11 oz. 10 dwts. fine, provided that from the 25 March, 1697 (O.S. 25 March (169$\frac{6}{7}$), the worker's or maker's mark should be *the first two letters of his surname*, and this provision applied as well to gold as silver. Probably either no plate was assayed from the 25th to the 27th of the month, or the intervening days were occupied in assaying and marking plate sent to Goldsmiths' Hall before the 25th, for the Act does not appear to have been enforced until

Alteration of makers' marks 1697.

the 27th, when a general change of marks was made, and the use of all the old marks discontinued. On the 15 April, 1697, all the new marks which had by that date been adopted were recorded in the book then opened at Goldsmiths' Hall for the purpose of registering the marks and names of workers, and their names, addresses, and date of entry were in each case written opposite their marks in this book. From that time forth this practice was continued, but a leaf or two of the first

* See page 43.

book and some of the books containing entries from 1758 to 1783 are missing. This form of mark, consisting of the first two letters of the surname, was compulsorily in use for twenty-three years only, for with the passing of the Act 6 Geo. I. c. 11 in 1719, which restored the old standard of 11 oz. 2 dwts. fine, the use of the old form of maker's mark was revived, and from that time each maker who worked in both standards used for the new or Britannia standard the mark composed of *Re-use of old makers' marks 1719-20.* the first two letters of his surname, and for the lower or old standard the initials of his Christian and surname, or (as the mark of Benjamin Pyne, which was the letter P surmounted by a Crown) otherwise the mark in use by him prior to 25 March, 1697. This practice of using marks of two kinds was continued until 1739, when, because of the confusion which had arisen by reason of different sets of marks being used by the same makers at the same time, it was by the Act 12 Geo. II. c. 26, which came into operation on 28 May, 1739, ordered that plate workers should destroy their existing marks and substitute others with *the initials of their Christian names and surnames* in letters of a different character from those used previously.* The form of mark consisting *New makers' marks ordered in 1739.* of the initials of the Christian name and the surname has been in use from May, 1739, to the present day.

THE DATE-LETTER.

The next in order of the series of marks found on London plate is the date-letter: *the alphabetical mark approved by ordinance*, which is regularly changed in the month of May in each year, and has been variously styled "the date mark," "the alphabetical mark" and "the assayer's or warden's mark".

This mark is, as Mr. Octavius Morgan remarked, "perhaps the most *The date-letter.* interesting of the entire series, for it enables us to ascertain the precise *Earliest reference to it as "The letter of the year" occurs in 1560.* year in which any piece of plate was made". The earliest reference to it as a date-letter or "letter of the year" occurs in a Minute of the Goldsmiths' Company of 1560. In the indictment of John Moore and Robert Thomas for working fraudulent plate and counterfeiting the marks in 1597 † it is described as "the alphabetical mark approved by ordinance amongst the goldsmiths," although the ordinance by which it was "approved" is not to be found. It had, however, most certainly

---

* Notwithstanding this order, marks are occasionally found which do not comply with it.
† See Chapter V. *ante.*

Earliest letter
named in the
Goldsmiths'
Minutes is the
" m " for
1629-30.

been in use for more than a century before 1597.   No mention is made
in the Company's Minutes of the denomination of any particular year-
letter until the occurrence of some dispute with the officers of the
assay, after which the letters are mentioned in the minutes, the earliest
described being the letter m for 1629-30.   From that date they are
mentioned with sufficient regularity to enable one to construct the
successive alphabets, but as regards the earlier cycles it is only by the
examination of a large number of pieces of antique plate, for the most
part belonging to churches, public companies, colleges and corporations,
of which the histories are known, that it has been possible to collect the
information necessary for the construction of the tables of marks from
the commencement of the use of the date-letter down to 1629.

The use of this mark was arranged in cycles of twenty years each,
twenty letters of an alphabet—A to U or V, excluding J—being used
for each cycle, and at the end of each of the years in which U or V had
been used a new alphabet was adopted for the next succeeding cycle.
As a rule, therefore, when any letter is found, its character and its
accompanying marks at once indicate whether it belongs to a cycle
earlier or later than that in which the letter m of 1629 occurs.   If it
belongs to the cycle 1618-38 or later, the goldsmith's records, before-
mentioned, fix its exact position ; if, however, the letter should not agree
in character with any of the letters from 1618 downwards, its position
has to be ascertained by other means, and this was where Mr. Morgan
experienced the difficulty of framing the earlier tables.   The course he
adopted was to select pieces of plate which were believed to have
belonged to churches or corporate bodies from the time when they were
made, with respect to which some evidence was obtainable, and which
from their design and workmanship might well belong to the date
ascribed to them.   The marks found on such examples were set in their
respective cycles.   A certain letter having been found in this way to
belong to a particular year, and that year its proper one in the order
of the particular cycle of twenty years to which it belonged, the
character of the alphabet used throughout that cycle was as a rule
ascertained, the exceptions being in the cases of those alphabets which
resembled each other, and in that cycle in which letters of different
character were used.   In those cases the accompanying marks afforded
material assistance.   All other letters subsequently found of similar
character to those first ascertained were placed in the cycles and at the

dates to which they appeared to belong, and as a rule they were found to tally with and confirm the first.

A date which is found engraved on antique plate cannot always be relied on as being the date of its manufacture. It has repeatedly happened that pieces of plate which individuals or their families have had in their possession for many years have been subsequently given or bequeathed by them to churches or public bodies, and the date of the presentation or bequest has been engraved on the article. In such cases the period to which the work properly belongs is earlier than the inscribed date. On the other hand, money has been often bequeathed for the purchase of plate, and the purchase has not been made until some years afterwards, but the date of the bequest has been engraved on the plate, which is found to be really of a date later than the inscription records. Again, plate given to public bodies having become much worn has been re-made at subsequent periods, and the date of the original gift has been re-engraved on the new made piece. Mr. Morgan gave one instance in illustration of this: One of the loving cups of the Goldsmiths' Company known as "Hanbury's Cup," is inscribed with the record of its being the gift of Richard Hanbury in 1608. The form and workmanship of the cup are clearly of the period of Charles II., which is confirmed by the Hall marks. This was very perplexing until a memorandum was found in the Company's minutes stating that "Hanbury's Cup, weight 60 oz., was sold with other plate in 1637 and re-made in 1666".

Engraved Dates on Plate often misleading.

Having found that m was the annual letter for 1629-30 Mr. Morgan, in framing his skeleton tables, proceeded to work backwards from that date to an undefined starting point, and knowing that it had been the practice of the Goldsmiths' Company to change the character of the alphabet used every twenty years, he ascribed the examples of the several forms of alphabet which he discovered, to their respective dates. The Lombardic D of 1481-2 on the Anathema Cup of Pembroke College, Cambridge, given in 1497, was a good land-mark, and the inscribed date afforded assistance in setting that date-letter in its proper place. Mr. Morgan, however, assumed a date forty years too early as the time when the use of the alphabetical mark was adopted. A tradition had existed that the "Pudsey" spoon,* long preserved at Bolton Hall and

The tradition attached to the "Pudsey" spoon suggested a table of date-letters forty years too early.

* Now in the Mayer Museum, Liverpool.

Hornby Castle, Westmoreland, had been given by King Henry VI., together with his boots and gloves, to Sir Ralph Pudsey, of Bolton Hall, after the battle of Hexham in 1463, and Mr. Morgan, in order to fit in the marks on the spoon with the tradition, ascribed the Lombardic H, which the spoon bears, as the date-letter for the year 1445-6. This theory involved the assumption of an alphabet for an entire cycle of twenty years (with regard to the use of which no evidence has ever been found) intermediate between the cycle in which he placed this H and that in which the D of 1481 is fixed. This arrangement was copied by Mr. Chaffers, followed by Mr. Cripps, and accepted generally, until it was found that the tradition attached to the "Pudsey spoon,"* like many other traditions, could have had no foundation in fact, as the marks on the spoon could not be of earlier date than 1515; they were therefore assigned to their proper place, viz., 1525. There being no evidence of any earlier use of a date-letter, the adoption by the London Goldsmiths' Company of an alphabetical mark is considered to have been made in the year 1478. The earliest known piece of plate with a date-letter is the Nettlecombe chalice, marked with the Lombardic letter B of 1479-80.† It is believed that the first cycle commenced with the Lombardic A in the preceding year. There is no positive evidence that the use of the date-letter did in fact commence in 1478, as the earliest known recorded reference to it, as such, is in a minute in the Goldsmiths' Company's books of 16th December, 1560, with regard to the letter of the year being "grayved round about for a difference". There is, however, an earlier reference to "the assayer's mark," which appears to be another name for the year mark or date-letter, in an ordinance of the Company, dated 5 Henry VIII. (1513).

We have seen that in the 2 Henry VI. c. 14 (1423),‡ the leopard's head and the maker's mark are the only marks mentioned as being required to be stamped on all wrought silver, and that by the same statute a penalty of double value was imposed on the keeper of the touch "for every harness of silver § which he shall touch that is worse than sterling"; and that in the 17 Edward IV. c. 1 (1477), *the same two marks are mentioned and no other*, and that in addition to the re-enactment of the provision that if the keeper of the touch do mark or touch any

Marginal notes:

Earliest known date-letter is the Lombardic B for 1479-80.†

Assayer's mark mentioned 1513.

Reason for devising "date-letter".

---

* See the Author's monograph on *The Spoon and its History, Archæologia,* Vol. LIII.
† But see page 78, *infra.*
‡ See the Statute in Chapter II.
§ "Harness of silver" appears in this instance to be used to denote any kind of wrought silver.

such harness (wrought silver) with the leopard's head, if it be not as fine The "Craft" made answerable for default of warden in marking bad silver. 1477. as sterling, he shall forfeit double value, it is further provided that *the craft of goldsmiths of London shall be answerable for the default of the Warden.* Here then is a strong reason for devising an additional mark which would fix the date when any particular article was "touched," and thereby enable the "craft" to ascertain "which of their own officers deceived them and from him obtain over a recompence". An additional mark for a similar purpose had already been devised for use at Mont- Date-letter adopted at Montpellier in 1427. pellier, where, in 1427, in consequence of public clamour having been raised against the principal silversmiths for working silver below the standard, process had been issued against them, an inquest was held, they were fined 10 marks each, and, to insure the legal standard being maintained, it was ordained that in addition to the ordinary precaution of the "borihls" (the technical term applied to the metal removed with a buril, burin, or graver for the purpose of assay), a box should be appropriated to each worker, and the borihls, or scrapings, from his work placed in it, to be twice a year assayed, and that the name of the warden of the mystery (inscribed on the register of the city and in the private book of the silversmiths) should be followed by *one of the letters of the alphabet*, which should be reproduced beneath the "ecusson" (escutcheon) of the city, *on each work*, in order that it might be known under what warden it was made. This ordinance was renewed in 1436 with more stringent conditions, and continued in force in the South of France in the time of our Edward IV. It seems, therefore, probable that the London goldsmiths, having acquainted themselves with the practice in force at Montpellier, on their craft being fixed by statute in Whence its probable adoption by the London Goldsmiths in 1478. 1477 with responsibility for the default of their warden, adopted the Montpellier practice of adding a variable letter to the marks already in use, so as to be able to determine at any future time, should the question arise, in whose wardenship any particular article of plate had been "touched".

We have, therefore, the following points :—

1. No mention of any mark other than the leopard's head and maker's mark down to 1477.

2. In 1477 the craft fixed with responsibility for the default of their warden : a strong reason for devising an additional mark to denote the year when the assay was made.

3. Plate found marked with the variable alphabetical mark for the

years 1479-80, 1481-2, 1488-9 and onwards, with an occasional break of a year or two (three at the most), down to the present day, the earliest* (the Nettlecombe Chalice, 1479-80) being marked with the Lombardic B.

4. Three marks, viz., the leopard's head crowned, the maker's mark, and the assayer's mark mentioned in the Goldsmiths' Ordinance of 1513.

On these data it is submitted that the majority of reasonable persons would come to the conclusion that the date-letter or alphabetical mark was first struck on London plate in the year 1478, that the letter first used was A, and that in style or character it probably corresponded with the letters D, H, L, N, O, Q, R, and T, of the first cycle illustrated in the following tables.

Twenty letters used in each alphabet until 1697, when alphabet changed at nineteenth.

The cycles of twenty years, with a change of letter every year, (the letters used being A to U or V, omitting J,) proceeded regularly from 1478 to 1696-7, when, on the new standard being required by the Act of that year, a new alphabet was begun before the twentieth letter of the then current cycle had been reached. The entries in the Minutes of the Goldsmiths with respect to the change of letter are as follows :—

"A.D. 1696, May 29th.—New puncheons received ; the letter for the year being **t** in a scutcheon "

"A.D. 1697, March 27th.—The puncheons for the remaining part of this year were received, being according to an Act of Parliament, a Lyon's head erased, a Britannia, and for the letter, the great court **a** in an escutcheon "

Three letters used in the year 1697.

The court letter **a** was used for only a little more than two months viz : 27 March to 29 May, 1697, and on 29 May the use of the court letter **b** was commenced. A large quantity of plate, however, of the new standard appears to have been assayed in those two months, and in the month of April, 1697, nearly a hundred plate workers took their marks to the Hall to be struck. The date-letters were changed on the day when the wardens were elected, that being St. Dunstan's † day *Letters changed 19 May each year prior to the Restoration, afterwards on 29 May.* (19 May), in each year, prior to the Restoration, and on the 29 May subsequent thereto, except as above mentioned in 1697, when the change was made on 27 March, as well of marks as of standard, and the letter was again changed on the 29 May in the same year.

---

* See marks possibly of 1478-9, page 78.
† St. Dunstan being the Goldsmiths' patron saint.

It will thus be perceived that each letter served from May of one year until May of the following year, except in the one instance when the court letter a was used only from the 27 March to the 29 May, 1697.

With reference to the date-letters represented in the following tables, in facsimile, it will be found that in a number of instances they differ very appreciably from other representations of the same marks which have hitherto been offered in print. To begin with those of Mr. Octavius Morgan : that learned antiquary never pretended that the examples given in his tables were reproductions in facsimile of actual marks on plate. The letters were for the most part copied from the goldsmiths' books, where the style or character of the letter is generally drawn in black without a surrounding field, and does not represent the appearance of an impression struck by a punch. Mr. Morgan continued this system with regard to the date-letters found by him on plate of a date antecedent to the year 1629, the date of the earliest record of the actual letter for the year in the goldsmiths' books. Mr. Chaffers, however, placed the letters (not very accurately drawn) in the fields in which they were supposed to be in the actual impressions represented. Mr. Cripps made a great advance on anything which had been done before by presenting the letters (with some exceptions) from 1479 to the end of the 19th Century with much greater correctness, but still with a great many inaccuracies. In some instances, on these inaccuracies being pointed out to him, he allowed them to remain, on the ground that as they stood they were "traps to forgers". It is submitted that forgers do not resort to representations of marks in black and white for the purpose of forging marks but adopt other means for carrying on their nefarious practice, and it is therefore believed that no harm can arise by the publication of the following tables, which it is hoped will afford some means of assisting in the discrimination of the true from the false rather than be an aid to the latter.

Every letter represented in the following tables has, with one single exception, which will be mentioned further on, been reproduced from an authentic piece of plate.

The characters of the different alphabets used in the several cycles respectively will be found to answer to the following description :—

CYCLE	I.	1478 to 1497.—LOMBARDIC.*
,,	II.	1498 to 1517.—BLACK LETTER, small.
,,	III.	1518 to 1537.—LOMBARDIC and ROMAN, capitals :
		(Lombardic predominating).
,,	IV.	1538 to 1557.—LOMBARDIC and ROMAN, capitals :
		(Roman capitals predominating).
,,	V.	1558 to 1577.—BLACK LETTER, small.
,,	VI.	1578 to 1597.—ROMAN, capitals.
,,	VII.	1598 to 1617.—LOMBARDIC.
,,	VIII.	1618 to 1637.—ROMAN and *Italic* letters, small.
,,	IX.	1638 to 1657.—COURT-HAND.
,,	X.	1658 to 1677.—BLACK LETTER, capitals.
,,	XI.	1678 to 1696.—BLACK LETTER, small.
,,	XII.	1697 to 1715.—COURT-HAND.
,,	XIII.	1716 to 1735.—ROMAN, capitals.
,,	XIV.	1736 to 1755.—ROMAN, small.
,,	XV.	1756 to 1775.—BLACK LETTER, capitals.
,,	XVI.	1776 to 1795.—ROMAN, small.
,,	XVII.	1796 to 1815.—ROMAN, capitals.
,,	XVIII.	1816 to 1835.—ROMAN, small.
,,	XIX.	1836 to 1855.—BLACK LETTER, capitals.
,,	XX.	1856 to 1875.—BLACK LETTER, small.
,,	XXI.	1876 to 1895.—ROMAN, capitals.
,,	XXII.	1896 to 1915.—ROMAN, small.
,,	XXIII.	1916 to 1920.—BLACK LETTER, small.

In the first cycle it will be observed that two letters, viz., the L of 1488-9 and the N of 1490-1, were found and published by the Author in 1905, whereby a gap in that cycle was reduced, and that the T of that cycle (unlike previous representations of that letter) was then for the first time accurately rendered. The small black letters of the second cycle are not the clumsy-looking, ill-formed letters represented in *Old English Plate* and Chaffers' *Hall Marks*; but really beautiful Gothic letters such as one sees in illuminated and other texts of the **Different forms** period. The Author takes no credit to himself for their appearance in **of date-letters.** his tables in a form as nearly accurate as is possible, because the means taken to ensure accuracy has been more mechanical than artistic, as will

---

* It is misleading to describe the first alphabet as " with double cusps," since the only letters that can be described as double cusped are the O of 1491-2, the Q of 1493-4, and the crescent-shaped part of the D of 1481-2, some of which letters are similarly double-cusped in later cycles.

be explained later. It will be observed that some of the letters of the third and fourth cycle in the following tables differ from any representations of those letters published by others. All that is suggested with reference thereto is that an inspection of the marks on the articles from which the following marks have been transcribed will easily settle any question as to which is the more accurate. The letter A for 1538-9, the D for 1541-2, the G for 1544-5, the K for 1547-8 (discovered since the first edition of this work was published), and a second O for 1551-2 have, by the researches of the Author and his friends, all been added to the fourth cycle, so that there is now but one gap in that cycle, which it is hoped may be filled by further research. In the fifth cycle, 1558 to 1577, the letters, generally speaking, as well on large as on small articles, have been found to be smaller than in the preceding cycle, and this difference has been shown in the tables. The letters, too, are not nearly so thick as they are represented in *Old English Plate*, and there is nothing like the extreme breadth of "scutcheon" as shown by Mr. Chaffers. In 1560-1 the letter C is found both without and with an enclosing shield; the shield then used for the first time has, though its form has varied greatly, never since been dispensed with. The introduction of the shield in 1560-1 coincided with, or rather immediately followed, the restoration of the old sterling standard for the silver coinage, and the books of the Goldsmiths' Company contain a minute dated the 16 December, 1560, to the effect that because the standard of the silver moneys had been raised to eleven ounces and upwards, therefore after the feast of the Epiphanie next coming, the assay-master and wardens should " *touch no plate under the fynesse of xi. oz. ij. dwt., and for a certe knowledge to be had between the same plate and other before touched, it is agreed that the letter of the year shall be grayved round about for a difference*".*

The next feature in the date-letters which calls for remark is the pellet under the second k of 1567-8. This is accounted for by the fact that Richard Rogers, who had held the office of assay-master for some time previous, was "discharged of the office of Assayer " on 24 December, 1567, and Thomas Keelynge was appointed as his successor. It therefore became necessary to distinguish between the k used by Rogers, from May, 1567, to December of the same year, and that used by

Reasons why letters of different forms sometimes occur in the same year.

* This is a somewhat strange agreement for the goldsmiths to make, and is suggestive of their having allowed base silver to be "touched" contrary to the terms of every statute and ordinance which had been made concerning wrought silver from the time of Edward I., which provided that none should work silver worse than sterling.

Keelynge thence-forward till May, 1568. Mr. Cripps placed the letter with the pellet beneath it before the one without that distinction, but as it is more probable that the later used letter had the distinguishing spot, it is so placed in the following tables. The author has found two forms of m for 1569-70, but it is suggested that the smaller punch was cut for small articles, or for being struck on ornamental plate which the larger punch might possibly disfigure. The fleur-de-lys and two pellets beneath the second letter s for 1575-6, may be accounted for by the Statute 18 Elizabeth c. 15 (enacted in that year), which raised the standard for gold wares to 22 carats.

It will be observed that in 1583-4, two forms of the Roman letter F are used, one being reversed. The reversed letter is on a fine silver gilt ewer in Lord Swaythling's collection, and may be accounted for by the punch cutter having made the mistake of cutting the F right, instead of reversing it in the punch; the mistake being noticed after the punch was used, a second punch was probably obtained whereby the letter was afterwards struck correctly.

Of the cycle 1618 to 1637 the two forms of the letter b are accounted for by the death of the assayer, Thomas Dymock, in September, 1619, and the appointment of his successor, John Reynolds, in the following month. The two forms of the k of 1627-8 may have happened in the cutting of the second set of punches, without any meaning or intent, for the difference is not very great, and one set of punches can scarcely have lasted for an entire year. Of the letter m for 1629-30, in not a single one of the eight examples seen by the Author are the lower parts of the strokes of the letter barbed and connected, but in each case the three limbs terminate in separate bulbous ends.

In obtaining examples of the letters of the cycle 1638 to 1657 the Author experienced more difficulty than in any other of the completed cycles. For years he was searching and inquiring for plate marked with the court letters for 1643-4, 1644-5, and 1645-6, and it was only after a very protracted search that examples were found. The only instance known of the court letter G (for the year 1644-5) occurs on a piece of Church plate at Snareston-cum-Swepston, Leicestershire, and, as will be observed, it is quite different from the representations of this letter given by Mr. Cripps and Mr. Chaffers. Here, therefore, is another "trap" in *Old English Plate* which the compiler of *Old London Silver* fell into. The examples given by Mr. Cripps and Mr. Chaffers were

Scarcity of Plate bearing marks of 1643 to 1645.

taken from the goldsmiths' books, but it is obvious that the penmanship of their clerk cannot be depended on for absolute exactitude, a reproduction in facsimile being unnecessary in the company's minutes. In *Old English Plate* no reference is given to any article with the date letter for 1644; and for the year 1643 the communion cups made by John Wardlaw, and dated 1644, at the Canongate Church, Edinburgh, are cited, but on examination these cups, though dated 1644, were found to be marked with the Lombardic letter N, the date-letter for 1610.*

It will be observed that there are two forms of the court letter a for 1638-9—one right, the other reversed (due, probably, as in the case of the F of 1583, to the punch-cutter omitting to reverse the letter in the punch). In *Hall Marks on Plate* the error had been committed of making this reversed a do duty for the court letter B of 1639-40, the form of which is quite different.

In the next cycle, 1658 to 1677, the letters for the first two years are all that require comment. As to the first, but for the difficulty of proving a negative, the Author would say what he believes, viz., that one form only of the black letter 𝔄 was used in this cycle, and that one was what Mr. Cripps described as the "blurred" letter; and that the more common form of black letter 𝔄 represented in *Old English Plate* was not used at all. The first representation of the letter for 1658 which appeared in print was copied by Mr. Octavius Morgan from the goldsmiths' books, and was not intended to be a *facsimile* representation. The Author has spoken to dozens of collectors and dealers on the subject, but has never found one who has ever seen on plate the first of the two letters represented in *Old English Plate* as for 1658, hence the Author's belief that it owes its existence entirely to the penmanship of the writer of the Goldsmiths' Minutes. Only one form of letter for 1658-9 For the year 1659-60, however, two distinct forms of the letter 𝔅 have been found, differing from each other very slightly—not more than may be accounted for by the laxity of the die-sinker in cutting the punch— still there is a sufficient difference to warrant the giving of the two forms in the following tables.

As to the next cycle (1678 to 1697) no comment is necessary except with reference to its completion. Mr. Octavius Morgan suggested that there were instances of the letter u having been used in the year

---

* The date-letter for 1643-4 in the following tables has been drawn from parts of three different examples, not one of which was wholly perfect.

1697. It is submitted that the alphabet used in that cycle certainly ended with the letter **t**, and was followed by the court hand **a**, as the Goldsmiths' Minutes record, and that the small Old English letter **u** was not used. In some aspects, and especially when somewhat worn, the letter **n** of that cycle, the limbs of which are connected both at bottom and top, looks very much like the letter **u**, and this appearance probably led to the above suggestion. What, however, did happen, at least in one case which the Author has noted, was that the letter **t** was used on plate of the new standard, marked with the lion's head erased, the figure of Britannia, and the new form of maker's mark enforced by the Act of 1696, as represented in the note on page 151. Of the remainder of the date-letters in the following tables no more need be said than that the greatest possible care has been taken to ensure accuracy.

Since the publication of the first edition of this work, a number of examples of date-letters and other marks (including those of makers) have been found, of somewhat different form from any previously represented, and those new examples will be found illustrated in the following pages.

THE LION PASSANT.

Of this mark Mr. Octavius Morgan wrote as follows :—" Its origin, intention, and the precise date of its adoption are obscure ". The earliest mention of it is in the indictment by the Attorney General in 1597 against Moore and Thomas * for counterfeiting "the marks of Her Majesty's lion, the leopard's head, limited by statute, and the alphabetical mark ". The lion passant had not been found on plate of earlier date than 1543 but is never absent after 1545. It was, therefore, concluded that the lion was first used in 1544 or 1545.

Fortunately the Author has been enabled to clear up what has been a doubtful question as to the precise date of its adoption, as will be gathered by an examination of the following tables, in which the blank for the year 1544-5 is filled. The marks there given (showing the first appearance of the lion passant) are on a seal-top spoon in the Author's collection. There is also in the Author's collection, an apostle spoon of the preceding year, without the lion. The Author has found four examples of the year 1543-4, all without the lion, and four of the year

* See page 44, *ante.*

1545-6, all with the lion.   It is clear, therefore, that 1544-5 is undoubtedly First use of lion passant, 1544. the year when the lion passant guardant was adopted as a mark at Goldsmiths' Hall, London.   It is equally clear that the lion was taken from the Royal Arms of England, but the reason for its adoption, although apparent, is not authenticated by any documentary evidence.   Mr. Morgan suggested the possibility that it was to mark "the inferior silver when Henry VIII. caused the standard to be debased," but it seems more correct to suggest that the lion passant was probably adopted to show Probably devised for showing that the Sterling Standard was maintained for plate, though coinage debased that, notwithstanding the degradation of the standard of the silver coinage, the standard for wrought plate was maintained of the old "sterling" quality.   However this may have been, it is the fact that in 1544 the silver coinage was so debased that it contained only half its weight of pure silver, and there was no enactment authorising the degradation of the standard for wrought plate below that fixed by the Act of Edward I. in 1300, which provided that it should be "as good as sterling".   The first appearance of the lion passant in 1544, in conjunction with the reappearance of the old ducal coronet on the leopard's head,* synchronizes remarkably with the debasement of the silver coinage, and it is highly probable that the lion passant mark was then adopted in order that the purchasers of plate so marked should thereby have a guaranty that it was of the old "sterling" quality.   It is also probable that some Ordinance or Proclamation was made with reference to it in 1544, but the books of the Goldsmiths' Company are silent on the subject, and the registers of the Privy Council for the period in question are missing, but one may venture to re-echo the hope expressed by Mr. Morgan, that "some of those laborious gentlemen who are engaged in calendaring the State papers may fall, in the course of their researches, on some Order in Council or Gracious Proclamation enjoining the addition of this royal lion to the three marks rendered imperative by statute".

     In the early statutes concerning goldsmiths, the leopard's head is The lion passant described as "Her Majesty's Lion," 1597. described as "the King's Mark"; it is remarkable that in the indictment of Moore and Thomas in 1597, it is the lion passant that is given this honourable distinction, being therein described as "*Her Majesty's Lion,*" the "leopard's head" and the "alphabetical mark" being referred to as "limited by statute" and "approved by Ordinance" respectively.   Mr. Cripps asked the question : "Was the lion passant adopted as the King's

* See the observations with reference to the leopard's head, page 53, *ante.*

Mark in place of the leopard's head?" The answer to this question is as yet not forthcoming.

Various forms of the lion passant.

It will be gathered from the following tables that in the first year of its appearance the lion is in a square field; that in the following year and down to 1549-50, the punch is cut to the outline of the animal, and that throughout those six years the head is crowned, at first with a bold upstanding crown, less distinct in the second year, whilst in the last two years it is but barely discernable, and in the following year (1550-1), when the lion is placed in an oblong field, the crown disappears. The form of stamp adopted in 1550 is continued till 1557, when the punch is notched in front, an incipient cutting which in the next year is carried round the entire animal. From 1578 down to 1678 the punch is cut to the outline of the lion. From 1679 to 1697 the punch is gibbous, or oblong with the corners rounded off, and this shape resumed in 1719-20 is continued till 1739. It is then again cut to outline the figure until 1756, when it is placed in a shield with a point at the base and the top corners rounded or clipped, which form is continued until in the cycle commencing in 1896 the shield is invected in chief and base. The shape of the animal at the several periods lends material aid in determining the approximate date of a piece of plate when the other marks are worn. In Cycle IV. the lion appears much more like the conventional heraldic animal than in the later cycles, and from 1821 (when the crown was taken off the leopard's head) the lion passant is no longer guardant, the head being in profile.

Gold and O.S. silver marked alike till 1797.

Lion passant not stamped on gold after 1844.

Until 1797-8, gold and silver of the old standard * had been marked alike, but the 58 Geo. III. provided that gold of the new standard of 18 carats fine should be marked with a crown and 18, in place of the lion, and in 1844 the 7 & 8 Vic. c. 22, s. 15, provided that the crown and 22 should be stamped on gold of 22 carats fine and that thereafter the lion passant should not be stamped on gold.

THE LION'S HEAD ERASED AND "BRITANNIA".

The lion's head erased and figure of Britannia instituted 1696-7. Compulsorily used on plate from 1697 to 1720.

All that need be said with reference to these two marks is that the Statute 8 Wm. III. c. 8 of 1696-7 provided, as we have already seen, that the standard for wrought plate should be raised to 11 oz. 10 dwts. fine (8 dwts. in the lb. finer than the standard theretofore in force, and

---

* The Britannia standard marks of course never appeared on gold.

to the same extent finer than the standard for the silver coinage), and that the marks should be *that of the worker, to be expressed by the two first letters of his surname; the marks of the mystery or craft of the goldsmiths, which instead of the leopard's head and the lion, should be for this plate the figure of a lion's head erased and the figure of a woman commonly called Britannia;* and a distinct variable mark to be used by the warden of the said mystery, to denote the year in which such plate was made; and that the said marks should be affixed, on pain of forfeiture, on all silver vessels, &c., that should be exposed for sale.

These new marks were used exclusively from 27 March, 1697, until 1 June, 1720, when the old standard was restored, since which time both standards have been in use concurrently; but for a long time past the use of the Britannia standard has been very little in comparison with that of the revived old standard, and as it is too soft to withstand much wear there seems no reason for its continuance. At any rate, those goldsmiths who may desire to use it might be allowed to do so, subject to its being marked with the leopard's head, the lion passant, and a set of figures denoting the higher quality; but the use of the lion's head erased and Britannia ought to be abolished, as their continued use may be the means of fraud being practised upon the unskilled. The Author knows of more than one case where young collectors of antique plate have had sold to them by unscrupulous dealers, modern plate bearing the marks of the Britannia standard, but with the date-letter obliterated, the purchasers imagining that they were buying Old English plate of the period 1697-1720. An example of the modern marks of this standard is shown in Cycle XX. of the year 1863-4. By comparing these marks with those of 1716-7 it will be seen how closely they resemble each other, and how easily fraud may be perpetrated upon the unskilled or the unwary.

Objection to present use of " Britannia " marks.

It has been already remarked that on the restoration of the old standard in 1720, the use of the old punches for the leopard's head, lion passant and makers' marks was resumed, or new punches closely resembling them were brought into use. These changes of marks appear to have caused much confusion at the time, and even now, by reason of the close resemblance of some of the marks of the period 1720-29 (excepting the date-letter) to those of 1680-96, unscrupulous dealers have been enabled, by obliterating the date letter from pieces of the later date, to pass off plate of the time of Geo. I. and Geo. II. as that

Resemblance of some marks of 1720-29 to earlier marks of 1680-96.

of the time of Chas. II. To illustrate this, four lines of marks are set out in full on page 86.

THE SOVEREIGN'S HEAD.

This mark, commonly known as the "duty mark," should be found on all gold and silver plate assayed in England and Scotland from 1 December, 1784, to 30 April, 1890, except certain articles enumerated in the following list of exemptions. As mentioned on page 19, a duty had been imposed on plate at an earlier date but no duty mark appears to have been impressed on wrought gold or silver until 1784.

The mark consists of the head of the reigning sovereign in profile, a reproduction in miniature of the heads of the successive Kings and Queen from George III. to Queen Victoria inclusive, as on the coins of the periods, except that from 1 December, 1784, until 29 May, 1786, the head of George III. was not in cameo as it afterwards was, but intaglio, as if the die sinker had engraved the punch as the mark was required to appear in the silver, and on being struck it appeared sunk and reversed. The head, incuse, looking to the left, appears with the date-letter i for 1784-5 and with the k for 1785-6, after which it is always in cameo as on the coins. The heads of George III., George IV. and William IV. all look to the right of the observer, but the head of Queen Victoria looks to the left.

Sovereign's head incuse 1784-5-6 afterwards in low relief.

The intaglio head was in an oblong stamp with the corners clipped off, but from 1786 the stamp was oval. On plate of 1804, 1808, and one or two other years, the head has also been found in a trefoil-shaped stamp. The head of the sovereign was changed at the end of each reign, or shortly after the commencement of the succeeding reign, but in the provincial offices the change was not made until some few years later, and the shape of the stamp varies from that used in London at certain periods, as will be seen further on in the tables of provincial marks.

As the duty mark was not struck before 1 December, 1784, and the date-letters were changed on the 29 May of that year, the letter i was struck during the first half of the goldsmiths' year, without the King's head mark. Plate marked with this letter is therefore found without and with the duty mark.

The duty on gold and silver plate having ceased to become payable on and after 1 May, 1890, thenceforward the Sovereign's head was not stamped on plate of either kind.

List of Gold and Silver Wares exempted from liability to be assayed and from payment of duty (when it was imposed) :—

(The various Statutes imposing the duties are set forth in Chapter II.).

12 Geo. II. c. 26 :—

S. 2. Jeweller's work wherein any jewels or other stones are set (other than mourning rings), jointed night ear-rings of gold, or gold springs of lockets.

S. 6. Rings, collets for rings, or other jewels, chains, necklace beads, lockets, buttons, hollow or raised, sleeve buttons, thimbles, coral sockets and bells, ferrils, pipe lighters, cranes for bottles, very small book clasps, stock or garter clasps jointed, very small nutmeg graters, snuff box rims, whereof tops or bottoms are made of shell, or stone, and sliding pencils, toothpick cases, tweezer cases, pencil cases, needle cases, any filigree work, tippings or swages on stone or ivory cases, mounts, screws or stoppers to stone or glass bottles or phials, ornaments small or slight put to amber or other eggs or urns, wrought, seals, or seals with cornelians or other stones set therein, any gold or silver vessel, plate or manufacture so richly engraved, carved or chased, or set with jewels or other stones as not to admit of an assay to be taken of, or a mark to be struck thereon, without damaging, prejudicing, or defacing the same. Things which, by reason of their smallness or thinness are not capable of receiving the marks, and not weighing 10 dwts. of gold or silver each.

This applied to gold as well as silver originally, but was repealed as to silver by 30 Geo. III. c. 31.

30 Geo. III. c. 31. Exempted the following articles of silver :—

S. 3. Chains, necklace beads, lockets, any filigree work, shirt buckles or brooches, stamped medals, spouts to china, stone, or earthenware teapots of any weight.

S. 4. Tippings, swages or mounts not weighing 10 dwts. of silver each, except necks and collars for casters, cruets, or glasses appertaining to any sort of stands or frames.

S. 5. Any wares of silver not weighing 5 dwts. of silver each, except the following articles—*necks, collars, and tops for casters, cruets, or glasses appertaining to any sort of stands or frames, buttons for wearing apparel, solid sleeve buttons, solid studs,* not having a bisselled edge soldered on, *wrought seals, blank seals, bottle tickets, shoe clasps, patch boxes, salt spoons, salt shovels, salt ladles, tea spoons, tea-strainers, caddy ladles, buckles* (shirt buckles or brooches before mentioned excepted), *pieces to garnish cabinets or knife cases, or tea chests, or bridles, or stands or frames.*

It must be borne in mind that the articles in italics are excepted out of the exemption and are liable to be assayed and were chargeable with duty, and that wedding rings were, by 18 and 19 Vic. c. 60, made liable to duty though of less weight than 10 dwts.

(The tea-strainers mentioned in S. 5 seems to refer to the perforated tea spoons with barbed pointed ends, and apparently settles the question as to what was the purpose of these spoons.)

By the 38 Geo. III. c. 24, watch cases of gold and silver were exempted from duty but not from liability to be assayed, which still attaches to them.

CHAPTER VII.

TABLES OF MARKS ON LONDON PLATE.

The following tables of marks have been prepared with the greatest possible care in the endeavour to insure accuracy. Each set of marks, from first to last, has been taken from an authentic piece of plate.

It will be noticed that in the following tables the raised parts of the marks are white and the depressed parts black—the result of the system adopted in their reproduction—whereby the marks are represented as they appear on the plate from which they have been taken, in actual facsimile. The marks in the tables of other authors have their raised parts black and the sunk parts white in the manner of a rubbing taken from "a brass," by which method it is impossible to portray some of the marks—makers' marks more particularly. Many of the makers' marks in *Old English Plate* and *Hall Marks on Plate* are in some respects misleading for this reason.

Some of the marks in these tables will be found to differ appreciably from other representations of such marks previously published, and in those cases the Author is able to pledge himself to the greater accuracy of the examples herein, by reason of the great care which has been taken in their transcription.

In the first edition of this work, Makers' Marks were included with the Hall Marks in each cycle, but by reason of the large number of makers' marks in many of the lines it has been found somewhat difficult to separately trace in those tables the identity of the makers with their marks. London makers' marks in this edition are all separately illustrated in Chapter VIII., where the names are given in line with the marks, together with a description of the articles on which the marks have been found, and the names of the owners.

There will be found in the following tables a large number of makers' marks never hitherto represented, which, it is hoped, will be of assistance to many collectors in collating marks on their own plate; and although it is extremely difficult to identify the names of makers with marks used before the last quarter of the 17th century, there is no such difficulty from 1697 onwards, and the very voluminous list of makers' names, from the earliest times, which follows the tables of marks will be the means of identifying many makers who worked prior to that year.

The intelligent student will, of course, consult the following tables with the aid of the previous chapters, in which the marks and their history are more fully described, but the following hints (though to the expert quite unnecessary) may to the beginner be of assistance :—*

1. The order of the marks which has been adopted in the tables, for convenience sake, is not that which is most frequently found on plate, where the maker's mark is, for the most part, first in order, sometimes last, but never, or seldom in any other position, except when grouped together, as at the bottom of a tankard or teapot.

2. On early plate, the marks are generally found large and bold in the front or face of the object, and stamped with absolute indifference to the fact that the mark so stamped may interfere with lines of ornamental chasing and occasionally somewhat distort the object stamped on. This seems to have caused some of the goldsmiths of the time of Queen Elizabeth and the Stuart period to have articles intended to be elaborately decorated, assayed and stamped with the Hall marks before being chased. Marks are rarely found hidden in the bottom of an article of earlier date than the latter part of the 17th century. Early tankards are generally marked on the drum to the right of the handle and across the cover. Later ones with domed tops, as well as cups, casters, tea vases, tea and coffee pots, are for the most part marked under the base out of view, and the covers of late tankards are generally marked inside the dome. Early spoons have the leopard's head in the bowl, the other marks on the back of the stem. The date-letter, in the case of spoons "slipped in the stalk," is stamped at the end of the stem well away from the other mark or marks. Spoons dating from about 1670 have all the marks on the back of the stem.

3. One only of the marks illustrated in the space devoted to the maker's mark should be found on one piece of plate, except in the very rare case of the separate parts of which it is composed having been wrought by two distinct workers, or of its having been repaired or added to at a later date.

4. The marks for wrought gold and wrought silver of the old standard were identical until 1798, when the standard of 18 carats fine for gold was first authorised. The marks of a crown and 18 were

* The Assay Marks as to-day stamped on wrought silver are generally in a straight line with which the maker's mark is also in line and not in different places as in earlier times.

ordained for this additional standard in place of the lion passant, which was continued on gold of 22 carats fine until 1844, when the crown and 22 took the place of the lion, which has not since then been struck on gold. The lower standards of 15 carat, 12 carat, and 9 carat, authorised in 1854, are marked with the figures: ᵫ·625, ☒·5 and ⊙·375 respectively;* the crown is, however, not used on those standards but the Sovereign's head is stamped on all wrought gold in respect of which duty has been paid until 1 May, 1890.

TABLE OF MARKS FOUND ON WROUGHT GOLD,

with the dates when the marks were prescribed :—

DATE WHEN PRESCRIBED.	MARKS.	QUALITY OF GOLD.	
1844	👑 22	For gold 22 carats fine.	
1798	„ 18 or 18	„ „ 18 „ „	
1854	15 ·625	„ „ 15 „ „	{ In the London assay marks 15 and ·625 are in one stamp.
„	12 ·5	„ „ 12 „ „	
„	9 ·375	„ „ 9 „ „	

The leopard's head, date-letter, and maker's mark, and until 1890 the Sovereign's head, as illustrated in the following tables, appear in addition to the above marks and the shield is in most cases similar to that enclosing the figure 18 illustrated above. The lion's head erased and figure of Britannia are, of course, never found on gold.

In early days although slight variations of the same mark on different pieces of plate indicate the existence of more than one punch for the same mark in the course of one year, they are yet generally of one (large) size, and it is not until the 18th century that punches of different sizes are found to have been used for different sized articles; some of the punches having been so small as to need a lens to decipher the marks struck with them. In these tables it is the larger sized marks which have been mostly reproduced, but their size has not been exaggerated, the actual size of the largest being considered sufficiently clear, and exaggeration misleading.

* At Sheffield the figures used to denote gold of the lower standards are all placed upright.

The approximate date of plate made between the latter part of the 16th century and the latter part of the 17th, marked only with the maker's mark, may in many cases be ascertained by identifying the marks with those found by the Author on fully marked pieces and represented in the following tables. The Author has seen very many examples of the above period thus deficient in hall marks, and has suggested an explanation in Chapters II. and V. Many small articles, such as very slender tea spoons, caddy and salt spoons, snuff spoons, pierced sugar-tongs, and small toys of the 18th century, will also be found marked only with the lion passant and maker's mark. The approximate date of these objects may be ascertained by identifying the maker's mark with one in the following tables, which will probably fix the date within about 20 years.

The description of the London makers' marks $^{and}_{or}$ names of the makers and of the article (and its owner) from which the marks have been obtained, will be found set forth in the chapter following the tables.

MARKS ON LONDON PLATE.

EXAMPLES OF THE LEOPARD'S HEAD MARK FOUND ON PLATE OF A
DATE ANTERIOR TO 1478.

(THE ASCRIBED DATES ARE APPROXIMATE.)

DATE. (*about*)	MARK.	ARTICLE AND OWNER.
1390		Spoon with hexagonal stem and acorn knop : in the Author's collection.*
1400		,, ,, "dyamond poynt" at end of stem : ,, ,, lion sejant ,, ,, } Mr. J. H. Walter.
1450		,, ,, "dyamond poynt" ,, ,, : Lord Hylton.
,,		,, ,, ,, ,, ,, ,, : Mr. J. H. Walter.

The marks illustrated below are somewhat anomalous. The leopard's head crowned and letter B in a circle appear to be London marks of *c.* 1485, although they differ somewhat from other marks of about that date.

DATE.	MARKS.	ARTICLE AND OWNER.
c. 1470		Spoon topped with seated figure of Our Lady ; leopard's head in bowl, the } Mr. J. H. Walter. other mark on stem :
c. 1485 [probably]		Pre-Reformation Paten : Hartshorne, Derbyshire. (The B is probably the maker's mark.)

Shortly before the printing of this edition was begun the Author was shown by Mr. L. Crichton an Apostle spoon bearing the marks illustrated below. The second of these marks is the letter 𝔄—Lombardic in style—which may perhaps pertain to the year 1478-9.

1478-9 ?   Acquired in 1920 by Mr. L. Crichton.

---

* This spoon, which was sold at Messrs. Christie's on the 3 May, 1905, is of the Mediæval English type, like those described in a Will dated 1392, as six silver spoons "*cum acrinsse de auro*" (*Test. Ebor.* [Surtees Soc. 4] i, 177). The bowl of the spoon is fig-shaped, the stem hexagonal, terminating with a knop formed like an acorn, from which, however, the gilt is worn away. The leopard's head stamped in the bowl—like alt the very early examples of this mark—is without a crown.

MARKS ON LONDON PLATE.

CYCLE I.

THREE STAMPS AS BELOW.

	LEOPARD'S HEAD CROWNED.	DATE LETTER.	MAKER'S MARK.
EDW. IV 1478-9			
1479-80	👑	B	
1480-1			
1481-2	👑	D	
1482-3			
RICH. III. 1483-4			
1484-5			
HEN. VII. 1485-6	👑	h	
1486-7			
1487-8			
1488-9	👑	U	
1489-90			
1490-1	,,	n	V
1491-2	👑	O	
1492-3			
1493-4	,,	Q	
1494-5	,,	R	W
1495-6			
1496-7	👑	T	
1497-8			

CYCLE II.

THREE STAMPS AS BELOW.

	LEOPARD'S HEAD CROWNED.	DATE LETTER.	MAKER'S MARK.
1498-9	👑	a	
1499 1500	,,	b	♡
1500-1	,,	c	
1501-2	,,	d	
1502-3			
1503-4	,,	f	
1504-5	,,	g	
1505-6			
1506-7	👑	i	
1507-8	,,	kk	
1508-9	👑	l	
HEN. VIII 1509-10	👑	m	
1510-1	,,	n	
1511-2	,,	o	
1512-3	,,	p	
1513-4	,,	q	
1514-5	,,	r	
1515-6	👑	s	
1516-7	,,	t	♡
1517-8	,,	u	

* 1492-3    The maker's mark is that of Sir Edmund Shaa, Warden of the Goldsmiths' Company, Master of the Mint, Cup Bearer and Goldsmith to King Richard III., and Lord Mayor in 1482. On Master spoon : Mr. J. H. Walter.

CYCLE III.

THREE STAMPS AS BELOW.

CYCLE IV.

THREE STAMPS TILL 1544, FOUR STAMPS THENCEFORWARD.

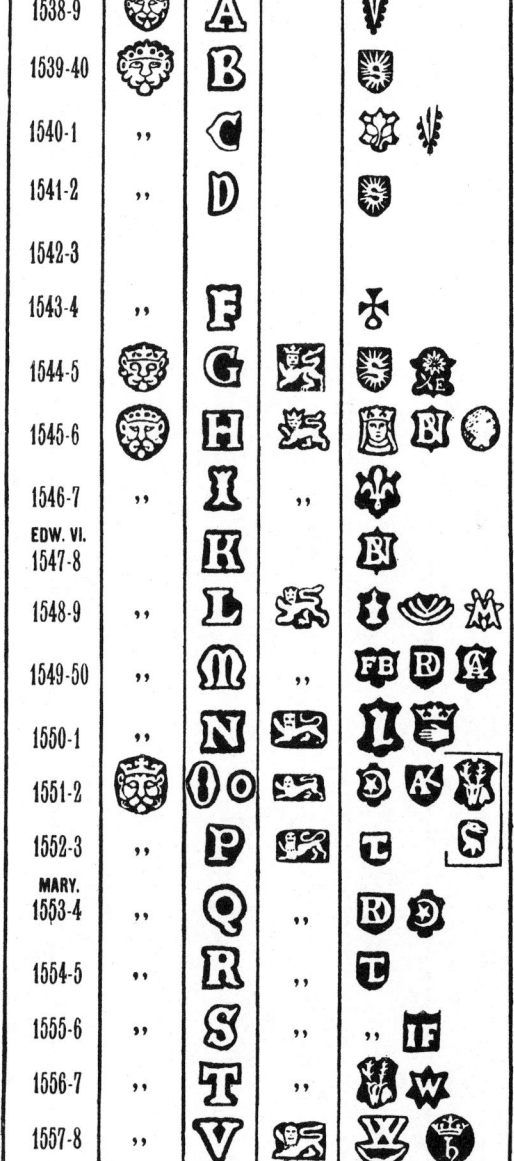

	LEOPARD'S HEAD CROWNED.	DATE LETTER.	MAKER'S MARK.
1518-9		A	
1519-20		B	
1520-1	,,	C	
1521-2		D	
1522-3	,,	E	
1523-4	,,	F	
1524-5	,,	G	
1525-6	,,	h	
1526-7			
1527-8	,,	K	
1528-9	,,	L	,,
1529-30	,,	M	
1530-1	,,	N	
1531-2		O	
1532-3	,,	P	
1533-4	,,	Q	
1534-5	,,	R	
1535-6	,,	S	
1536-7	,,	T	
1537-8	,,	V	

	LEOPARD'S HEAD CROWNED.	DATE LETTER.	LION PASSANT. FROM 1544.	MAKER'S MARK.
1538-9		A		
1539-40		B		
1540-1	,,	C		
1541-2	,,	D		
1542-3				
1543-4	,,	F		
1544-5		G		
1545-6		H		
1546-7	,,	I	,,	
EDW. VI. 1547-8		K		
1548-9	,,	L		
1549-50	,,	M	,,	
1550-1	,,	N		
1551-2		O		
1552-3	,,	P		
MARY. 1553-4	,,	Q	,,	
1554-5	,,	R	,,	
1555-6	,,	S	,,	
1556-7	,,	T	,,	
1557-8	,,	V		

1536·7   Marks on seal-top spoon: Mr. E. A. Bennett.

1544·5   Marks on seal-top spoon: Mr. E. Brand.

CYCLE V.

FOUR STAMPS AS BELOW.

	LEOPARD'S HEAD CROWNED.	DATE LETTER.	LION PASSANT.	MAKER'S MARK.
ELIZ. 1558-9		a		
1559-60	,,	b	,,	
1560-1	,,	cc	,,	
1561-2	,,	d		
1562-3		e	,,	
1563-4	,,	ff	,,	
1564-5	,,	g	,,	
1565-6	,,	h	,,	
1566-7	,,	i	,,	
1567-8	,,	kk	,,	
1568-9	,,	l	,,	
1569-70	,,	mm	,,	
1570-1	,,	n	,,	
1571-2	,,	o	,,	
1572-3	,,	p	,,	EAGLE AS 1562
1573-4	,,	q		
1574-5	,,	r	,,	M AS 1568
1575-6	,,	s	,,	
1576-7	,,	t	,,	
1577-8	,,	u	,,	

London makers' marks from 1479 to 1918 will be found illustrated, accompanied by makers' names, etc , in Chapter VIII.

CYCLE VI.

FOUR STAMPS AS BELOW.

	LEOPARD'S HEAD CROWNED.	DATE LETTER.	LION PASSANT.	MAKER'S MARK.
1578-9		A		
1579-80	,,	B	,,	
1580-1	,,	C	,,	
1581-2	,,	D	,,	
1582-3	,,	E	,,	
1583-4	,,	F	,,	
1584-5	,,	G	,,	
1585-6	,,	H	,,	
1586-7	,,	I	,,	
1587-8	,,	K	,,	
1588-9	,,	L	,,	
1589-90	,,	M	,,	
1590-1	,,	N	,,	
1591-2	,,	O	,,	
1592-3		P		
1593-4	,,	Q	,,	,, D AS 1586
1594-5	,,	R		
1595-6	,,	S	,,	
1596-7	,,	T	,,	
1597-8	,,	V	,,	

1593-4 Another example of the date-letter for this year.

CYCLE VII.

FOUR STAMPS AS BELOW.

	LEOPARD'S HEAD CROWNED	DATE LETTER	LION PASSANT	MAKER'S MARK	
1598-9	●	A	●	TF	✚
1599 1600	,,	B	●	RC	
1600-1	,,	C	,,	HD	
1601-2	,,	D	●	b	✚
1602-3	,,	E	,,	W	IM
JAS. I. 1603-4	,,	F	,,	IG	G
1604-5	,,	G	●	W	AB
1605-6	,,	h	,,	HM	,,
1606-7	,,	I	●	F	RW
1607-8	,,	K	,,	O	C
1608-9	,,	L	,,	O	FV
1609-10	,,	M	,,		C
1610-1	,,	n	●	TP	TI
1611-2	,,	O	,,	V	B
1612-3	,,	P	,,	AB	RB
1613-4	,,	Q	,,	TC	MH
1614-5	,,	R	,,	RB	RC
1615-6	,,	S	,,	CR	IR
1616-7	,,	T	,,	IA	RN
1617-8	,,	V	,,	IV	RS

* Another example of the lion passant for Cycle VIII.

CYCLE VIII.

FOUR STAMPS AS BELOW.

	LEOPARD'S HEAD CROWNED.	DATE LETTER.	LION PASSANT.	MAKER'S MARK.	
*1618-9	●	a	●	IP	WR
1619-20	,,	b	,,	E	,,
1620-1	,,	c	,,	IC	LI
1621-2	,,	d	,,	EL	a
1622-3	,,	e	,,	RD	ER
1623-4	,,	f	,,		WC
1624-5	,,	g	,,		
CHAS. I. 1625-6	,,	h	,,	I·E	IV
1626-7	,,	i	,,	PI	
1627-8	,,	kk	,,	SW	RI
1628-9	,,	l	,,	RM	
1629-30	,,	m	,,	DG	RB
1630-1	,,	n	,,	WM	RS
1631-2	,,	o	,,	RS	
1632-3	,,	p	,,	PB	DC
1633-4	,,	q	,,	IBe	WM
1634-5	,,	r	,,	RS	W
1635-6	,,	s	,,	F	LI
1636-7	,,	t	,,	RB	RW
1637-8	,,	v	,,	RM	RC

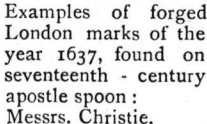

Examples of forged London marks of the year 1637, found on seventeenth - century apostle spoon: Messrs. Christie.

CYCLE IX.

FOUR STAMPS AS BELOW.

	LEOPARD'S HEAD CROWNED.	DATE LETTER.	LION PASSANT.	MAKER'S MARK.	
1638-9	(head)	a b	(lion)	RA	IH
*1639-40	,,	B	,,	IH	WS
1640-1	,,	C	,,	IM	I·B
1641-2	,,	g	,,	WM	TH
1642-3	,,	C	,,	IW	F
1643-4	,,	ff	,,	,,	TT
1644-5	,,	O	,,	BB	
1645-6	,,	R	,,	DW	TG
1646-7	,,	B	,,	NW	IL
1647-8	(head)	B	(lion)	IA	RV
1648-9	,,	P	,,	II	H
COMWTH. 1649-50	,,	y	,,	(mark)	M
1650-1	,,	R	,,	M	IW
1651-2	,,	d	,,	(mark)	SV
1652-3	,,	P	,,	R·S	IB
1653-4	,,	d	,,	WH	HC
1654-5	,,	B	,,	,,	,,
1655-6	,,	O	,,	DR	I·L
1656-7	,,	d	,,	C|S	E·I
1657-8	,,	B	,,	TG	KF

Variations of date-letters of this cycle :

1639-40 (mark)   1643-4 ff   1652-3 (mark)   1657-8 (mark)

* The lion passant is sometimes found thus : (lion)

CYCLE X.

FOUR STAMPS AS BELOW.

	LEOPARD'S HEAD CROWNED.	DATE LETTER.	LION PASSANT.	MAKER'S MARK.	
1658-9	(head)	A	(lion)	WC	P·B
1659-60	,,	B	,,	TG	GS
CHAS. II. 1660-1	,,	C	,,	IG	GS
1661-2	,,	D	,,	SV	TD
1662-3	,,	E	(lion)	HN	ET
1663-4	,,	F	,,	I·F	TK
1664-5	,,	G	,,	IW	WH
1665-6	,,	H	,,	AD	TR
1666-7	,,	I	,,	RD	WM
1667-8	,,	K	,,	M	SS
1668-9	(head)	L	(lion)	(mark)	I·B
1669-70	,,	M	,,	WG	WW
1670-1	,,	N	,,	TM	TK
1671-2	,,	O	,,	DC	IK
1672-3	,,	P	,,	RP	AH
1673-4	,,	Q	,,	EB	SC
1674-5	,,	R	,,	T·G	GG
1675-6	,,	S	,,	GG	(mark)
1676-7	,,	T	,,	M	FS
1677-8	,,	U	,,	XC	WS

Variations of date-letters of this cycle :

1664-5 (mark)   1667-8 (mark)

1671-2 (mark)   1677-8 (mark)

CYCLE XI.

FOUR STAMPS AS BELOW.

	LEOPARD'S HEAD CROWNED.	DATE LETTER.	LION PASSANT.	MAKER'S MARK.
1678-9		a		SR · RN
*1679-80	,,	b		TH · IT
1680-1		c		· IH
1681-2	,,	d	,,	· IC
1682-3	,,	e	,,	IS · AD
1683-4	,,	f	,,	IH · WF
1684-5	,,	g	,,	ILY · IS
JAS. II. 1685-6	,,	h	,,	D · WH
1686-7	,,	i	,,	RS · WM
1687-8	,,	k	,,	RH · CO
1688-9	,,	l	,,	·
WM.&MY. 1689-90		m		HG · D
1690-1	,,	n	,,	FE · WB
1691-2	,,	o	,,	MH · IC
1692-3	,,	p	,,	· IW
1693-4	,,	q	,,	IN · DA
1694-5	,,	r	,,	ST · AN
WM. III. 1695-6	,,	s	,,	P·H · IH
MAY 29, 1696, TO MCH. 27, 1897.	,,	t	,,	W · LH

1695-6 ,, [S] [lion] [H] Tankard: Mr. G. E. Farr.

* [lion] Variation of lion passant occasionally found on plate of 1679 to 1686.

CYCLE XII.

FOUR STAMPS AS BELOW.

	BRITANNIA.	DATE LETTER.	LION'S HEAD ERASED.	MAKER'S MARK.
*1697 MCH. 27 TO MAY 29.		A		TH·RO CA·PA SM·WI
1697-8	,,	B	,,	BI · DU
1698-9	,,	C	,,	GA · MA
1699/1700		D		Lu · Cr
1700-1	,,	E	,,	FA · WA
1701-2	,,	F	,,	SI · Cf
ANNE. 1702-3	,,	G	,,	Sy · EC
1703-4	,,	H	,,	Ra · Ic
1704-5	,,	I	,,	DE · LE
1705-6	,,	K	,,	Ti · FA
1706-7	,,	L	,,	BA · MA
1707-8	,,	M	,,	SL · FL
1708-9	,,	N	,,	MA · Bi
1709-10	,,	O	,,	StPe · CL
1710-11	,,	P	,,	Fo · SM
1711-2	,,	Q	,,	PE · PE
1712-3	,,	R	,,	SU · Ra
1713-4	,,	S	,,	MA · St
GEO. I. 1714-5	,,	T	,,	TB · TA
1715-6	,,	U	,,	AL · Kil

* Solid gold articles are marked with the leopard's head and lion passant as 1696 and not with the figure of Britannia and lion's head erased.

CYCLE XIII.

FOUR STAMPS AS BELOW.

	BRIT- ANNIA.	DATE LETTER.	LION'S HEAD ERASED.	MAKER'S MARK.
1716-7		A		HO / RO
1717-8	,,	B	,,	Tt / KE
1718-9	,,	C	,,	HA / Fa
*1719-20	LEOPARD'S HEAD CROWNED	D	LION PASSANT.	TE / LA / WP / BR
†1720-1	,,	E	,,	CM / FA / TS / GB / Fe / IS IS
1721-2		F		EV / IL
‡1722-3	,,	G	,,	BN / IS / NG / CO
1723-4	,,	H	,,	IE / TF
§1724-5		I		RB / SC / HU / SH
1725-6	,,	K	,,	WT / IB
1726-7		L L		AV / WD
GEO. II. ‖1727-8	,,	M M	,,	IR / IS / RH / WE / GW
1728-9	,,	N	,,	WD / IG
1729-30		O		IJ / TT
1730-1	,,	P	,,	AC / LA
1731-2	,,	Q	,,	IG / EY
1732-3	,,	R	,,	IS / EP
1733-4	,,	S	,,	IE / AC
1734-5	,,	T	,,	R·M / CH
1735-6	,,	V	,,	G·I / TRG C

NOTES ON CYCLE XIII.

* It should be noted that the use of the Britannia standard marks (*i.e.* the figure of Britannia and lion's head erased) was continued after 1720 concurrently with the old standard marks.

† The leopard's head crowned, as 1721-2, is also found with the date-letter for 1720-1.

‡ The date-letter G of 1722-3 is also found in a shield rounded at the base.

§ The date-letter I of 1724-5 is frequently found in a shield rounded at the base.

‖ The leopard's head and lion passant of 1727-8 are also found like those illustrated for 1729-30.

Other variations of marks in this cycle:

1724-5 — Marks on three casters (maker, Thomas Tearle): Mr. Leo. Reid.

1727-8 — Marks on taper stick (maker, Simon Jouett): Mr. Harry Alston.

1728-9 — Marks (with date-letter N of 1728-9) on small cream-jug: Mr Anthony White.

The leopard's head is somewhat like that of 1724, but without the beard. The lion passant resembles that of 1729-30, but the head is more in profile, and the corners of the shield are only slightly rounded.

With respect to the observations on page 71 *ante*, concerning the resemblance of some of the London Hall-marks of the period 1720-9 to others of the period 1680-97, complete sets of marks of 1692-3, 1722-3 and 1726-7, are, for comparison, here interposed ; and to show the resemblance of the date-letter of 1738-9 to that of 1718-9 (illustrated on the preceding page) a set of marks of 1738-9 is added :—

(SUPPLEMENTARY TABLE XIII.A.)

DATE.	MARKS.	MAKER'S NAME.	ARTICLES AND OWNERS.
1692-3		(*Not identified*)	Caster : Presented by Mr. W. W. Simpson to the Victoria and Albert Museum.
1722-3		John Penfold (probably)	Porringer : Mr. Crichton.
1726-7		Benjamin Pyne	Great Mace : Westminster.
1738-9		James Gould	Pair of Candlesticks : Mr. F. W. Kell.

The leopard's head and lion passant of 1722-3 are remarkably like those of 1692-3, and the corresponding marks of 1726-7 resemble others of 1680-9, whilst the makers' marks of 1722-3 and 1726-7 are identical with those used by the respective makers before the Britannia standard for plate was instituted in 1697. In the marks of 1738-9 the old form of lion passant is continued, but the leopard's head differs from every example of that mark of earlier date than 1720. The date-letter, however, is a Roman C, indistinguishable (except by the very slight truncation of the corners of its shield) from that of 1718-9. The possibility of mistaking the letter of 1738-9 for that of 1718-9 and *vice versâ* may be prevented by remembering that the operation of the Act of 1719 (6 Geo. I., c. 11), which restored the old standard for plate, was prescribed to take effect as from the 1st June, 1720,* and that as the new standard was in force exclusively in 1718-9 the letter for that year is accompanied by the lion's head erased and figure of Britannia. From 1720 goldsmiths have had the option of manufacturing plate of either the old or new standard.

---

* The exact date when the letter D of 1719-20 was last used does not appear to be recorded, nor is the day stated when the use of the leopard's head and lion passant was in fact resumed, but as these three marks are found together on plate, and as makers' marks for the restored old standard were entered in every month of the year 1720, from January to May, it seems that the use of the leopard's head and lion passant must have been resumed in 1720 before the 1st June, otherwise the use of the date-letter D of 1719-20 must have been continued in 1720, after the 29th May, the customary date for changing the letter. In view of the number of entries of old standard marks in the month of January, 1720, the former alternative appears the more probable.

CYCLE XIV.
FOUR STAMPS AS BELOW.

	LEOPARD'S HEAD CROWNED.	DATE LETTER	LION PASSANT.	MAKER'S MARK.
1736-7		a		HV
1737-8	,,	b	,,	IA MF
*1738-9	,,	c	,,	R·Z
1739-40	,,	d	,,	WK
				R.B
		d		IW
				Sh
1740-1	,,	e	,,	IR
1741-2	,,	f	,,	D·H
1742-3	,,	g	,,	IG
1743-4	,,	h	,,	WH
1744-5	,,	i	,,	LP
1745-6	,,	k	,,	B·W
1746-7	,,	l	,,	IW
1747-8	,,	m	,,	WG
1748-9	,,	n	,,	EM
1749-50	,,	o	,,	WG
1750-1	,,	p	,,	IP
†1751-2		q		IP
1752-3	,,	r	,,	RC
1753-4	,,	r	,,	GH
‡1754-5	,,	t	,,	P A M
1755-6	,,	u	,,	IS

* 1738-9   Variations of leopard's head and lion passant.   C   G·H

† Although a punch for the leopard's head mark different in form from that of 1739-40 was used between 1751 and 1756, its use was not entirely general, because articles of the latter period are frequently found stamped with the leopard's head mark as here illustrated.

‡ This and other date-letters in this cycle are occasionally found with somewhat broader backgrounds.

CYCLE XV.
FOUR STAMPS AS BELOW.

	LEOPARD'S HEAD CROWNED.	DATE LETTER.	LION PASSANT.	MAKER'S MARK.
1756-7		A		S·W
1757-8	,,	B	,,	D·H
*1758-9	,,	C	,,	IS
*1759-60	,,	D	,,	IK
GEO. III. 1760-1	,,	E	,,	R·R
1761-2	,,	F	,,	R·R
1762-3	,,	G	,,	JI
†1763-4	,,	H	,,	RT
1764-5	,,	I	,,	R D·H
1765-6	,,	K	,,	I W V L
1766-7	,,	L	,,	LH
1767-8	,,	M	,,	DM
†1768-9	,,	N	,,	I·P E·W
1769-70	,,	O	,,	IN
1770-1	,,	P	,,	B·G
†1771-2	,,	Q	,,	I·C T·H
1772-3	,,	R	,,	I·C WP AS 1761
1773-4	,,	S	,,	R D·S
1774-5	,,	T	,,	IS
1775-6	,,	U	,,	W·T

* 1758-60   On articles bearing the hallmarks of 1758-9-60, the leopard's head crowned is occasionally found in a shield with pointed base.

† Date-letters for 1763-4, 1768-9, and 1771-2, are sometimes found to differ from those in general use thus:

1763-4 H   1768-9 O   1771-2 Q

CYCLE XVI.

FOUR STAMPS TILL 1784, FIVE STAMPS THENCEFORWARD.

	LEOPARD'S HEAD CROWNED.	DATE LETTER.	LION PASSANT.	KING'S HEAD.	MAKER'S MARK.
1776-7	(leopard's head)	a	(lion)		CH
1777-8	,,	b	,,		HG
1778-9	,,	c	,,		ID
1779-80	,,	d	,,		I·S
1780-1	,,	e	,,		RJDM
*1781-2	,,	f	,,		C·W
1782-3	,,	g	,,		GS
1783-4	,,	h	,,		IL
†1784-5	,,	i	,,	(king's head)	LI
1785-6	,,	k	,,	,,	WA
1786-7	,,	l	,,	(king's head)	SG EW
1787-8	,,	m	,,	,,	SM
1788-9	,,	n	,,	,,	EI
1789-90	,,	o	,,	,,	ℋℬ 1778
1790-1	,,	p	,,	,,	TP ER
1791-2	,,	q	,,	,,	WP JP
1792-3	,,	r	,,	,,	HC
1793-4	,,	s	,,	,,	I·W R·G
1794-5	,,	t	,,	,,	WF
1795-6	,,	u	,,	,,	TE

CYCLE XVII.

FIVE STAMPS AS BELOW.

	LEOPARD'S HEAD CROWNED.	DATE LETTER.	LION PASSANT.	KING'S HEAD.	MAKER'S MARK.
1796-7	(leopard's head)	A	(lion)	(king's head)	SP
1797-8	,,	B	,,	,,	RC
*1798-9	,,	C	,,	,,	EM
1799 1800	,,	D	,,	,,	WP
1800-1	,,	E	,,	,,	P·S
1801-2	,,	F	,,	,,	RG
1802-3	,,	G	,,	,,	IH
1803-4	,,	H	,,	,,	B·L
†1804-5	,,	I	,,	,,	GW
1805-6	,,	K	,,	,,	DP
1806-7	,,	L	,,	,,	RH SH
1807-8	,,	M	,,	,,	TG IG IC
†1808-9	,,	N	,,	,,	WE WF WC
1809-10	,,	O	,,	,,	CH
1810-1	,,	P	,,	,,	TP ER
1811-2	,,	Q	,,	,,	JB
1812-3	,,	R	,,	,,	TI
1813-4	,,	S	,,	,,	IC WR
1814-5	,,	T	,,	,,	SH
1815-6	,,	U	,,	,,	I·P G·P

* The author has also noted the date-letters f of 1781-2, and the k of 1785-6 in shields with rounded bases, similar to those of the g, h and i of 1782-3 to 1784-5, as well as in shields with pointed bases as illustrated above. On the other hand, the g and h of 1782-3 and 1783-4, are sometimes found in a shield with a pointed base as in the shield for e of 1780-1.

† On some articles dating from 1784 to 1830, the shield enclosing the date-letter has a rounded base, and the lion passant is sometimes found in an oval stamp.

* In 1798 the Stat. 38 Geo. III. c. 69, authorised a new gold standard of 18 carats fine, and provided that it should be marked with a crown and 18 in place of the lion passant. Up to this time gold and silver of the old standard had been marked alike. Gold of the old standard (22 carats) continued to be marked with the same marks as silver of the old standard until 1844, when a crown and 22 were substituted for the lion passant, for the purpose of distinguishing it from silver-gilt.

1798 (R·B G·M) (crown) (leopard's head) (18) (P) An example of the marks on 18 carat gold, as prescribed in the year 1798; on gold snuff box: Mr. Harry Alston.

† For 1804-5, 1808-9, and one or two other years, the duty mark has been found in a trefoil shaped stamp. It has also been found in the oval stamp in the same years. From 1808 to 1815 the king's head is occasionally found like that shown for 1816-17.

CYCLE XVIII.

FIVE STAMPS AS BELOW.

	LEOPARD'S HEAD	DATE LETTER.	LION PASSANT.	KING'S HEAD.	MAKER'S MARK.
1816-7	👑	a	🦁	👤	WB
1817-8	,,	b	,,	,,	TR
1818-9	,,	c	,,	,,	GW
1819-20	,,	d	,,	,,	WS
GEO. IV. 1820-1	,,	e	,,	👤	W·B
1821-2	🦁	f	🦁	,,	TαTα
1822-3	,,	g	,,	,,	PS
1823-4	,,	h	,,	,,	IS
1824-5	,,	i	,,	,,	TH GH
1825-6	,,	k	,,	,,	IC
1826-7	,,	l	,,	,,	IL HL CL
1827-8	,,	m	,,	,,	BP
1828-9	,,	n	,,	,,	WS
1829-30	,,	o	,,	,,	RG
WM. IV. 1830-1	,,	p	,,	,,	C·P
1831-2	,,	q	,,	👤	R·H
1832-3	,,	r	,,	,,	C·P
1833-4	,,	s	,,	,,	PS
1834-5	,,	t	,,	,,	N·M
1835-6	,,	u	,,	,,	CF

CYCLE XIX.

FIVE STAMPS AS BELOW.

	LEOPARD'S HEAD	DATE LETTER	LION PASSANT.	KING'S HEAD.	MAKER'S MARK.
1836-7	🦁	A	🦁	👤	CF / JB / EW
VICT. 1837-8	,,	B	,,	👤	WE / JS / GW / JR
1838-9	,,	C	,,	,,	WT / RA / CR / GS
1839-40	,,	D	,,	,,	WB / DB / FD / WC
1840-1	,,	E	,,	,,	JA / JA / MC / GA
1841-2	,,	F	,,	,,	JS / AS / GA / CF
1842-3	,,	G	,,	,,	JCE / R·H / WB / WS
1843-4	,,	H	,,	,,	WKR / WB / J·A / J·A
*1844-5	,,	I	,,	,,	RGH / BS
1845-6	,,	K	,,	,,	ISH / CTH / GF
1846-7	,,	L	,,	,,	GFP / H·H / EB / &W
1847-8	,,	M	,,	,,	IL / HL / RP / GB
1848-9	,,	N	,,	,,	EJ / BW / RH / JW
1849-50	,,	O	,,	,,	CTF / GF / FD / WRS
1850-1	,,	P	,,	,,	IK / GI
1851-2	,,	Q	,,	,,	EB / JB
1852-3	,,	R	,,	,,	JF / IF
1853-4	,,	S	,,	,,	EB / &JB
+1854-5	,,	T	,,	,,	WR / S
1855-6	,,	U	,,	,,	GA

The shield enclosing the date-letters of Cycle XVIII. and preceding cycles is occasionally found with ts base straight, or slightly rounded.

1825-35 🦁 On plate of the second quarter of the 19th century, the leopard's head is frequently found without whiskers, as here illustrated from an example on a pierced salt cellar: Messrs. Alstons & Hallam.

The date-letter 𝔅 of 1837-8 is accompanied by the head of Wm. IV. from 29 May to 20 June, 1837.
* In 1844 it was enacted that 22 carat gold should be stamped with a crown and 22 instead of the lion passant, and that the lion passant should not thereafter be stamped on any gold.
† In 1854 the lower standards of 15, 12, and 9 carats for gold were authorised; they are marked with the figures 15·625, 12·5 and 9·375. but not with the crown or sovereign's head.

CYCLE XX.

FIVE STAMPS AS BELOW.

	LEOPARD'S HEAD	DATE LETTER	LION PASSANT	QUEEN'S HEAD	MAKER'S MARK
1856-7	(leopard's head)	a	(lion)	(queen's head)	CTF GF
1857-8	,,	b	,,	,,	HW
1858-9	,,	c	,,	,,	JA W·M GR EB
1859-60	,	d	,	,,	GA EE JE
1860-1	,,	e	,,	,,	CR WS
1861-2	,,	f	,,	,,	RH
1862-3	,,	g	,,	,,	R·H
*1863-4	(figure)	h	(lion)	,,	GF
1864-5	Leopard's head as above	i	Lion passant as above	,,	GA
1865-6	,,	k	,,	,,	IJK R·H
1866-7	,,	l	,,	,,	GE GF
1867-8	,,	m	,,	,,	GM HD
1868-9	,,	n	,,	,,	CS H
1869-70	,,	o	,,	,,	J EL·W J
1870-1	,,	p	,,	,,	WS
1871-2	,	q	,,	,,	HF W
1872-3	,	r	,,		Rf
1873-4	,,	s	,,	,,	RM EH
1874-5	,,	t	,,	,,	JEM GW
1875-6	,,	u	,,	,,	W R·R

CYCLE XXI.

FIVE STAMPS TILL 1890, THENCEFORWARD FOUR ONLY.

	LEOPARD'S HEAD	DATE LETTER	LION PASSANT	QUEEN'S HEAD	MAKER'S MARK
1876-7	(leopard's head)	A	(lion)	(queen's head)	C.F.H
1877-8	,,	B	,,	,,	,,
1878-9	,,	C	,,	,,	SS
1879-80	,,	D	,,	,,	DH CH
1880-1	,,	E	,,	,,	JWD
1881-2	,,	F	,,	,,	FH
1882-3	,,	G	,,	,,	CS H
1883-4	,,	H	,,	,,	PW
1884-5	,,	I	,,	,,	JRH
1885-6	,,	K	,,	,,	C.F.H
1886-7	,,	L	,,	,,	,,
1887-8	,,	M	,,	,,	,,
1888-9	,,	N	,,	,,	D&C WD
1889-90	,,	O	,,	,,	CFH
1890-1	,,	P	,,		,,
1891-2	,,	Q	,,		,,
1892-3	,,	R	,,		W.C
1893-4	,,	S	,,		SWS
1894-5	,,	T	,,		JB ER
1895-6	,,	U	,,		J.S

* This is an example of the marks of the Britannia standard very rarely used after 1720 (see page 71 *ante*). Nearly all the plate of the year 1863-4 is marked with the leopard's head crowned and lion passant, as illustrated in the first line of this cycle.

CYCLE XXII.

FOUR STAMPS AS BELOW.

	LEOPARD'S HEAD	DATE LETTER	LION PASSANT	MAKER'S MARK
1896-7	☶	a	⦿	S⁺H C⁰ &
1897-8	,,	b	,,	JBC
1898-9	,,	c	,,	GG
1899 1900	,,	d	,,	C C P
1900-1	,,	e	,,	CCP
EDW. VII. 1901-2	,,	f	,,	C.K
1902-3	,,	g	,,	W.C
1903-4	,,	h	,,	W B J M R D S
1904-5	,,	i	,,	WJ
1905-6	,,	k	,,	TB
1906-7	,,	l	,,	C&C⁰
1907-8	,,	m	,,	W B J M B S
1908-9	,,	n	,,	I B & S
1909-10	,,	o	,,	IMS
1910-1	,,	p	,,	STP
1911-2	,,	q	,,	G H J W
1912-3	,,	r	,,	H&C⁰ LTD
1913-4	,,	s	,,	A P F P
1914-5	,,	t	,,	D&J W
1915-6	,,	u	,,	C&R C

CYCLE XXIII.

FOUR STAMPS AS BELOW.

	LION PASSANT	LEOPARD'S HEAD	DATE LETTER	MAKER'S MARK
1916-7	⦿	☶	A	G&SC⁰ L⁰
1917-8	,,	,,	b	,,
1918-9	,,	,,	c	C&R C
1919-20	,,	,,	d	,,

1909-10	S B H (diamond)	Maker's mark of S. B. Harman: on silver-gilt snuff-box.
1916-17	DF	Mark on Church plate: St. Kerverne, Cornwall.
,,	LAC	Mark of L. A. Crichton.

CHAPTER VIII.

LONDON GOLDSMITHS' MARKS.

CHRONOLOGICAL LIST OF GOLDSMITHS' MARKS FOUND ON PLATE ASSAYED AT GOLDSMITHS' HALL, LONDON.

[FROM A.D. 1479 TO A.D. 1918.]

THE MARKS ON SUCH PLATE HAVING BEEN USED IN CONSTRUCTING THE PRECEDING TABLES.

DATE.	GOLDSMITHS' MARKS.		ARTICLES AND OWNERS.
1479-80		A jug.*	Chalice and paten : Nettlecombe, Somerset.
1481-2		A fetter lock.	The " Anathema " cup: Pembroke College, Camb.
1488-9		A key.	† Spoon with "wrythen" knop: Stanyforth Collection.
1490-1		L.	Apostle spoon (St. Andrew) : the Author's collection.
1491-2		A fish.	Paten : Stow Longa, Kimbolton, Hunts.
1493-4		A horse shoe.	Large rose-water dish : C.C. College, Oxford.
1494-5		A bird's head.	Chalice and paten : Clifford Chambers, Gloucestershire.
,,		W.	Spoon with hexagonal finial : Messrs. Crichton Bros.
,,		?	Spoon with flat knop, having B on the front and W on the reverse: Mr. Harvey Clark.
1496-7		A leaf slipped.‡	Paten : Childrey, Wantage, Berks.
,,		A jug, as in 1479.	Chalice : Dean Darby of Chester.
,,		?	Beaker with farrier's nails : The Holms Collection.
1498-9		MW in monogram.	Pair of chalices : Brasenose College, Oxford.
1499-1500		SW ,, ,,	The Leigh cup : Mercers' Company, London.
,,		Heart as 1516.	Apostle spoon : Messrs. Crichton Bros.

* This mark is certainly not a dimidiated fleur-de-lys as represented in several editions of *Old English Plate*.

† Mr. Cripps (*Old English Plate*) placed this spoon at 1528 ; it is clearly 1488-9.

‡ The maker's mark on the Paten of 1496-7 at Costessy, Norf., is not distinguishable. It is more probably a fish as 1491-2 than a pod with peas in it.

DATE.	GOLDSMITHS' MARKS.		ARTICLES AND OWNERS.
1500-1		A covered jar ?	Font-shaped cup : Lord Swaythling.
1501-2		A hand ?	Two slipped-stalk spoons : Messrs. Crichton Bros.
1503-4		Bow and arrow ?	The Cressener Cup : The Goldsmiths' Company.
1504-5		A horse ?	Paten : Happisborough, near Norwich.
,,		A plant ?	Apostle spoon (St. John) : Messrs. Crichton Bros.
1506-7		A cock's head erased.	Slipped-stalk spoon : ,, ,,
,,		A cross pattée.	Bishop Oldham's spoons with owls at the ends : C.C. Coll., Oxford.
1507-8		A trellis.	Foot of chalice : St. Martin's, Ludgate Hill, London.
,,		A fleur-de-lys.	Bishop Fox's gold chalice and paten : C.C. Coll., Oxford.
,,		A maidenhead.	Chalice and paten : West Drayton, Middlesex.
,,		A fish, as 1491.	Hour glass salt, and the Foundress' beaker : Christ's Coll., Camb.
1508-9		An incuse cross.	Mazer : Whitgift Foundation, Croydon.
,,		A rising sun.	Covered salt : Messrs. Crichton Bros.
1509-10		Two links	Paten : Great Hockham, Thetford, Norfolk.*
1510-1		A flower.	Mazer : Lord Swaythling.
,,		A lamb's head.	Rim of mazer : Franks collection, British Museum.
1511-2		A foot print.	Communion cup : Chewton Mendip, near Bath.
1512-3		A barrel or tun.	Font shaped communion cup : Wymeswold, Leicestershire.
1513-4		Head of pastoral staff	Communion cup : Hethel, Norfolk.
1514-5		Orb and cross.	Large rose-water dish (with spout) : C.C. Coll., Oxford.
,,		Gemini.	Paten : Heworth, Durham.
,,		A leaf.	Paten : Orcheston, St. Mary, Devizes.
,,		A gate ?	Apostle spoon (St. John) : Mr. H. D. Ellis.
,,		,,	Master spoon : Stanyforth Collection.
1515-6		Jack in the green ?	Queen Katherine's (of Aragon) covered cup : C.C. Coll., Oxford.
,,		A fringed S.	Slipped-stalk spoon : Stanyforth collection.

* Lord Hylton has a spoon (with angular knop) of 1509-10, the maker's mark being a heart as figured at 1516. Archbishop Parker's apostle spoon of 1515 at C.C. College, Cambridge, also has this maker's mark.

DATE.	GOLDSMITHS' MARKS.		ARTICLES AND OWNERS.
1516-7		A heart.	Bishop Fox's spoons with balls at the ends: C.C. Coll., Oxford.
1517-8		A sheep.	Paten, with vernicle within sixfoil: Stanyforth Collection.
1518-9		Two links.	Chalice: St. Mary's R.C. Church, Leyland, Lancashire.
,,		HK in monogram?	Mounts of coco-nut cup: The Vintners' Company.
,,		D?	Small alms-dish: St. Mary's, Woolnoth, Lombard Street, E.C.
1519-20		A scorpion?	The "Hamsterley" paten: Durham Cathedral Library.
,,		A fringed S.	Eleven Apostle spoons from the Bernal Collection: Stanyforth Collection.
,,		A bunch of grapes.	Slipped-stalk spoon: Stanyforth Collection.
1520-1		A crescent enclosing a mullet.	Covered cup with scale ornamentation: Christ's College, Cambridge.
1521-2		An escallop.	Font-shaped cup, from Dunn-Gardner Collection: The Holms Collection.
,,		Hand grasping ragged staff.	Mazer, with enamelled rose: C.C. College, Cambridge.
,,		Two links.	Chalice and paten: Jurby, Isle of Man.
,,		A sun.	Maidenhead spoon: The Author's Collection.
1522-3		A short sword.	Hour-glass salt: Ironmongers' Company, London.
,,		A serpent.	Apostle spoon, noted by the Author.
1523-4		A sceptre?	Paten: Beachamwell, Swaffham, Norfolk.
,,		A sun, as 1521.	Spoon slipped in the stalk: Mr. H. D. Ellis.
1524-5		An orb and cross.	Alms-dish (from St. Michael's, Crooked Lane): St. Magnus, London Bridge.
,,		A heart, as 1516.	Six Apostle spoons: Lord Swaythling.
1525-6		Implements crossed.	Mount of ivory cup: The Duke of Norfolk.
,,		A sceptre? see 1523.	Chalice: Wylye, Wilts.
,,		Sc?	Shallow Tudor bowl: Dunn-Gardner Collection.
,,		{ A heart, see 1516. ,, ,,	The " Pudsey " spoon: Mayer Museum, Liverpool. The " Bodkin " cup: Portsmouth Corporation.
1527-8		A maid's head.	Chalice and paten: Trinity College, Oxford.
,,		A fringed S, as 1519.	Eight Apostles spoons: The Marquess of Breadalbane, K.G.
,,		An eagle displayed.	Maidenhead spoon: Mr. Crichton.

Date.	Goldsmiths' Marks.		Articles and Owners.
1527-8		Double-headed arrow.	Mazer : Mr. Crichton.
,,		T, incuse, charged with 3 pellets.	Chalice and paten : South Kensington Museum.
1528-9		Crescent enclosing mullet.	Tazza : Rochester Cathedral.
,,		Orb and cross between I C.—John Carswell.	The " St. Nicholas " spoon from the Dunn-Gardner Collection.
,,		A fringed S, as 1527.	Apostle spoon (St. Thomas) : British Museum.
1529-30		Orb and cross between I C, as 1528.	Standing mazer : All Souls' College, Oxford.
1530-1		A fringed S, as 1519.	Apostle spoon : Stanyforth Collection.
1531-2		A coronet.	Cover of a cup : C.C. College, Cambridge.
,,		Orb and cross between I C, as 1528.	Apostle spoon (St. James the Greater) : Mr. Dobson.
1532-3		A hanap.	Cover of tazza : Rochester Cathedral.
,,		A hand erect.	The " Narford " mazer : Franks Collection, British Museum.
,,		?	" Finial " topped spoon : Messrs. Crichton Bros.
1533-4		An arbalist ?	Two-handled vase with cover : C.C. College, Oxford.
,,		Rose and crown.	Apostle spoon * : Stanyforth Collection.
,,		Thomas Wastell.	Paten : St. Edmund's, Salisbury ; also chalice (1536-7) : Sturminster Marshall, Dorset.
1534-5		Double-headed arrow.	The " Tokerys " mazer : Rev T. W. Braikenridge.
,,		A basket.	Fine Apostle spoon (St. Bartholomew) : The Author's Collection.
,,		A fringed S, as 1519.	Apostle spoon (St. Thomas) : Holburne Museum.
,,		A pair of compasses.	Spoon with "dyamond point " : Mr. J. H. Walter, Drayton, Norwich.
1535-6		A negro's head.	Communion Cup : St. Finn Barre's Cathedral, Cork.
,,		?	Apostle spoon : Mr. R. Meldrum.
,,		?	The " Boleyn " communion cup : Cirencester Church.
,,		An eagle displayed.	Maidenhead spoon : Mr. H. D. Ellis.
,,		A hand grasping a hammer between H C. (Henry Colville ?)	Communion cup (from All Hallows the Great) : St. Michael's, E.C.

* Mr. Cripps (*Old English Plate*) placed this mark at 1493 ; the crown on leopard's head proves it to be later than 1515.

DATE.	GOLDSMITHS' MARKS.		ARTICLES AND OWNERS.
1536-7		A sheaf of arrows.	Set of twelve Apostle spoons and Master : Messrs. Christie, 16-7-03.
1537-8		A fringed S, as 1519.	Apostle spoons : Stanyforth Collection and Holburne Museum.
1538-9		A pheon ?	Spoon with crocketed finial : Mr. Brand.
1539-40		A fringed S, as 1519.	Apostle spoon (St. Julian) : Innholders' Company, London.
1540-1		A spray of leaves.	Communion cup : St. Olave's, Gatcombe, Isle of Wight.
,,		A pheon ? as 1538.	Maidenhead spoon: The late Mr. W. Old, Hereford. Apostle spoon (St. James the less): Mr. A. T. Carter.
1541-2		A fringed S, as 1519.	Seal-top spoon with wrythen knop : Mr. J. H. Walter.
1543-4		Orb and cross incuse.	Standing cup, with statuette on cover : St. Peter Mancroft, Norwich.
,,		A fringed S, as 1519.	Apostle spoon (St. James the Greater) : The Author's Collection.
,,		Marigold and letter E.	Chalice : Messrs. Crichton Bros.
1514-5		A crab.	Seal-top spoon : from collection of Mr. E. Brand.
,,		A fringed S, as 1541.	Seal-top spoon (first appearance of lion passant) : The Author.
1545-6		A queen's head.	Archbishop Parker's ewer and salver : C.C. College, Cambridge.
,,		N B in monogram (Nicholas Bartlemew).	Apostle spoon : Mr. H. D. Ell s.
,,		A head erased.	Communion cup : St. Margaret Pattens, London.
1546-7		A fleur-de-lys.	Mount of crystal jug, with arms of Queen Katherine Parr, from the Strawberry Hill Col. : Mrs. Dent.
1547-8		N B in monogram as 1545.	Apostle spoon : Mr. Lambert.
1548-9		A covered cup.	Large Communion cup : St. Lawrence Jewry, London.
,,		Crescent lines.	Mount of glass jug : Franks Col., British Museum.
,,		M, or W inverted.	Small cup : Messrs. Christie.
1549-50		F B.	⎰ Com. cup and cover : St. James, Garlickhithe, E.C. ⎱ Do. do. : St. Mildred, Bread Street, E.C.
,,		R D in monogram (Robert Danbe).	Communion cup : St. Peter on-Cornhill, London.
,,		C A in monogram.	Mount of stoneware jug : Franks Collection, British Museum.
,,		Crowned cross moline.	Mounts of enamelled stoneware jug : Victoria and Albert Museum.
1550-1		A high boot.	Communion cup : Bridekirk, Cumberland.
,,		A hand under a coronet.	Do. do. : Hunstanton, Norfolk.

DATE.	GOLDSMITHS' MARKS.		ARTICLES AND OWNERS.
1551-2		Crescent enclosing mullet.	Spoon with ornamental finial: The Author's Collection.
,,		A K conjoined.	Communion cup: Totnes, Devon.
,,		Stag's head caboshed.	⎰Do. do.: St. Margaret's, Westminster. ⎱Do. do. (of 1576): Woodford, Wilts.
,,		Swan's head erased.	Do. do.: St. Michael's, Southampton.
1552-3		T L in monogram.	Do. do.: St. James, Garlickhithe, London.
1553-4		Robert Danbe, as 1549.	The "Wm. Bisby" cup: Armourers' Company, London.
,,		As 1551.	Maidenhead spoon: The Author's Collection.
1554-5		As 1552.	Cylindrical salt, with statuette on cover: C.C. College, Oxford.
,,		Queen's head as 1545.	Sir Martin Bowe's cup of the Goldsmiths' Company.
1555-6 ,,		I F (John Freeman). T L., as 1554.	Apostle spoon: Mr. H. D. Ellis. Two-handled cup: C.C. Coll., Cambridge.
1556-7		Stag's head, as 1551.	Archdeacon Wright's jug: Lord Swaythling.
,,		W.	⎰Alms-dish: St. George's Chapel, Windsor. ⎱Also on plate of 1548-9.
1557-8		H crowned.	Mounts of stoneware jug: Messrs. Crichton Bros.
,,		W over a crescent.	Communion cup and cover: Waterbeach, Cambridgeshire.
1558-9		A rose (Henry Gillard).	Communion cup: St. Michael-le-Belfry, York.
,,		C A in monogram.	Mount of stoneware jug from Dunn-Gardner Collection: Lord Swaythling.
1559-60		H W.	Communion cup and paten cover: St. Vedast, London.
,,		A lamp.	Communion cup and paten cover: St. Mary-le-Bow, Cheapside, E.C.
,,		A bird's claw, see 1565.	Apostle spoon: Messrs. Christie; also (156c) lion sejant spoon: Mr. H. D. Ellis.
,,		A mullet.	Communion cup: St. Dunstan, Stepney.
,,		A fleur-de-lys.	Do. do.: St. Stephen, Walbrook.
,,		C C linked.	Do. do.: St. Peter ad Vincula, Tower of London.
,,		S K.	Mount of stoneware jug from Temple-Frere Collection.
1560 1 ,, ,,		? - - - * Mullet in crescent, as 1551. A bird.	Com. cup: St. Magnus the Martyr, London Bridge. Seal-top spoon: The Author's Collection. Communion cup: Christchurch, London, E.C.

* Date-letter without shield. The second and third examples for the year 1560-1 have the date-letter within an angular shield.

DATE.	GOLDSMITHS' MARKS.		ARTICLES AND OWNERS.
1561-2		A spur.	Mark noted by the Author.
,,		P. C.	Communion cup : Beeford, Yorks.
,,		A star radiant.	Do. do. : St. Lawrence, Jewry, London.
,,		Crossed compasses with-in a radiant circle.	Apostle spoon : Innholders' Company, London.
,,		A fleur-de-lys (Wm. Dyxson).	Mount of horn jug : Lord Swaythling.
,,		R B.	Communion cup : St. Mary Magdalen, North Oaken-den, Essex.
,,		{Three mullets over a crescent (R. Durrant)}	Tazza-shaped cup : Messrs. Christie.
1562-3		S R.	Communion cup : Ashby de la Zouch, Leicestershire.
,,		Sun in splendour.	Communion cup : Buckhorn Weston, Dorset.
,,		R M.	Cup with hemispherical bowl on short stem : Messrs. Christie.
,,		W C over a pig (Wm. Cater).*	Communion cup : Headcorn, Kent.
,,		A wallet hook palewise on a cross bendwise.	Mounts of stoneware jug : The Author's Collection.
,,		N S in monogram (Nicholas Sutton).	Standing cup and cover : Armourers' Company, London.
,,		H K conjoined.	Cover of stoneware jug : Messrs. Crichton Bros.
,,		R D in monogram, see 1549 (Robert Danbe).	Standing salt : C.C. Coll., Cambridge.
,,		An eagle displayed (Fras. Jackson).	Seal-top spoon : Messrs. Christie.
,,		Crescent enclosing mullet.	Seal-top and maidenhead spoons : The Author's Collection.
,,		Eagle's (?) head between I C.	Communion cup : St. Mary, Hadley Monken, Middle-sex.
,,		A fleur-de-lys incuse.	Communion cup : St. Olave, Old Jewry, London.
,,		A hand grasping a cross, see 1564.	Communion cup and paten cover : Christchurch, London.
,,		A holly leaf incuse.	Communion paten : St. Stephen, Walbrook, London.
1563-4		3 mullets over a crescent, as 1561.	Small standing salt : South Kensington Museum.
,,		I P (John Pikenynge).	Communion paten : St. Helen and St. Giles, Rain-ham, Essex.
,,		H W, as 1559.	Standing cup (gourd shaped) : Hon. Soc. of Inner Temple.
,,		A bird.	Standing cup : Franks Collection, British Museum. Spoon (1567-8) with cloven-hoof stem : The Author's Collection.
,,		W in radiant circle.	Communion cup : St. Mary Magdalen, East Ham, Essex.

* See p. 43.

DATE.	GOLDSMITHS' MARKS.	ARTICLES AND OWNERS.
1563-4		A spur.	Communion cup: St. Mary, Dunton, Essex.
,,		R D (Robt. Danbe), as 1549.	Do. do. : St. Andrew, Hornchurch, Essex.
1564-5		A mullet.	Do. do. : The Holms Collection.
,,		A hand grasping a branch, see 1562.	Do. do. : Sherburn Hospital, Durham.
,,		A fleur-de-lys, as 1561.	{ Do. do. : Alresford, Hants. Do. do. : Lynn Regis and East Horndon, Essex.
,,		I C (John Cross or John Clark)	Communion cup: St. Peter, Little Warley, Essex.
,,		A horse's head couped (Robert Medley?)	Do. do. : S.S. Peter and Paul, South Weald, Essex.
,,		I S in monogram.	Plain cup: Messrs. Dobson.
,,		A campanula, as 1566.	Apostle spoon: Stanyforth Collection.
,,		A.	Tazza: now at Victoria and Albert Museum.
1565-6		A bird's claw, see 1559.	Seal-top spoon: Messrs. Christie.
,,		I P (John Pikenynge), see 1563.	Seal-top spoon: The Armourers' Company. On many spoons 1560-70: Noted by Author.
,,		As 1562.	Communion cup: Hawkinge, near Folkestone.
,,		A bird's claw (damaged)? see 1559.	Seal-top spoon: South Kensington Museum.
,,		H W, as 1559.	Communion cup and paten: Little Ness, near Baschurch, Salop.
,,		R K.	Seven spoons, with "dyamond poynts": Mercers' Company, London.
1566-7		Stars and crescent.	Small standing salt and cover: Victoria and Albert Museum.
,,		A.	Communion cup: St. Alban, Wood St., London, E.C.
,,		A star radiant, as 1561.	Communion cup: St. Lawrence, Jewry, London, E.C.
,,		A bird's claw, as 1559.	Set of Apostle spoons: C.C. College, Cambridge.
,,		A campanula, as 1564.	Large seal top spoon: Mr. Crichton.
,,		Acorns.	Seal-top spoon: Messrs. Christie.
,,		Tau?	Small standing salt: Mr. Lambert.
,,		W H, pellet below.	Cup on baluster stem: Messrs. Christie.

DATE.	GOLDSMITHS' MARKS.		ARTICLES AND OWNERS.
1567-8		A bull's head erased (Affabel Partridge ?)	Communion cups: Goadby and Marwood, Leicestershire.
,,		A wallet hook.	Standing cup, with Arms of Hull: The Author's Collection.
,,		A bird.	Set of 12 plates, engraved by Peter Maas with the Labours of Hercules, after Aldegraef: Messrs. Garrard—formerly the property of the Cotton family.
,,		F G in monogram.	Apostle Spoon (St. Julian): Innholders' Company, London.
,,		A horse's head couped, as 1564.	Communion paten: St. Alban, Wood St., London, E.C.
,,		R D (Robert Danbe), as 1549.	The "Thos. Tyndale" flagon: The Armourers' Company, London.
,,		A hand grasping a hammer, see 1535.	* Parcel gilt ewer: Corporation of Guildford.
,,		E R in monogram (Edward Ranklyn).	Cup, with agate bowl: S. Kensington Museum.
,,		T B in monogram (Thos. Brown or Benson).	Communion cup and paten-cover: Christ's College, Cambridge.
,,		A talbot ? sejant (Thos. Conell).	Communion paten: St Stephen, Walbrook, London.
,,		A cock's comb ?	Communion cups: Foxton, Kincote and Goadby, Leicestershire.
1568-9		I F, see 1555 (Jasper Fysher ?).	Mount of stoneware jug: Messrs. Spink.
,,		M.	Small cup with engraved hand: Messrs. Christie.
,,		A wallet hook.	Standing cup: Exhibited at Burlington House.
,,		A bunch of grapes.	The "Florence Caldwell" cup: Armourers' Company, London.
,,		F R in monogram.	Communion cup and paten cover: St. Mary-le-Bow, London.
,,		I H, see 1570.	Tazza-shaped cup: Messrs. Christie.
,,		?	Communion cup: Wield, Hants.
,,		A globe.	Communion cup and paten cover: West Tested, Hants.
,,		Two birds.	Communion cup and paten cover: St. John's, Reedham, Norfolk.
,,		R A.	Communion cup and paten: Burcombe.
1569-70		A bunch of grapes, see 1568.	Standing cup, with statuette on cover: C.C. Coll., Cambridge.
,,		F, enclosing T, in monogram.	Master spoon: now in the Author's Collection.
,,		A hand grasping hammer, see 1567.	Apostle spoon ("St. Gilian"): Innholders' Company, London.
,,		Animal's head couped.	Communion cup: Mr. J. Dixon.

* The date-letter on this example has the pellet under the **k**.

Date.	Goldsmiths' Marks.		Articles and Owners.
1569-70		A hooded falcon (Thomas Bampton).	Standing salt (see frontispiece): Vintners' Company, London.
,,		R V, a heart beneath.	Low cup on baluster stem: Mr. W. Boore.
,,		A bunch of grapes, see 1568.	Tall standing cup: C.C. Coll., Cambridge.
1570-1		A millrind.	Communion cup: Stow Longa, Hunts.
,,		An orb and cross.	Do. do.: Charminster, Dorset.
,,		A beaked bassinet.	The " Berry " standing cup and cover: The Author's Collection.
,,		A K conjoined, see 1551.	Communion cup: Lord Swaythling.
,,		T E o, in monogram (Thomas Heard).	Communion cup and paten cover: Walditch, Dorset.
,,		T H in monogram (Thos. Harrison or Hampton).	Communion cup: St. Bees, Cumberland.
,,		A pair of bellows.	Do. do.: Evershot, Dorset.
,,		H B conjoined (Hy. Boswell).	Do. do.: Mr. W. Boore.
,,		M in plain shield.	Paten cover of a cup: St. Augustine, E.C.
,,		Covered cup (John Mabbe).	Communion cup: Shapwick, Dorset.
,,		I H (John Harryson).	Do. do.: Bulford, Wilts. Also pair of silver-gilt tankards: Messrs. Crichton Bros.
,,		A campanula, see 1564.	Seal-top spoon: Messrs. Alstons & Hallam.
,,		R H conjoined.	Do. do.: Messrs. Crichton Bros.
1571-2		F ?	Do. do.: do. do.
,,		A heart.	Mounts of stoneware jug: Mr. Lambert.
,,		Porcupine over T A.	Cover of standing salt: Victoria and Albert Museum.
,,		L reversed.	Communion cup: Caundle Purse, Dorset.
,,		A bird (John Bird ?)	Gilt tankard, given by Archbishop Parker, in 1571: C.C. Coll., Cambridge.
,,		A hand grasping a crosslet, see 1562.	Plain shallow cup on baluster stem: Messrs. Spink.
,,		I piercing G.	Communion cup and paten: St. Mildred's, Bread St., E.C.
,,		A beaked bassinet, see 1570.	Communion cup and paten: Thorncomb, Dorset; Isel, Cumb., &c.
,,		T G in monogram.	Seal-top spoon: Mr. W. Boore.

Date.	Goldsmiths' Marks.		Articles and Owners.
1571-2		T L.	Small plain cup : Mr. Theodore Rossi.
,,		Lombardic A.	Communion cup : Nethercompton, Dorset.
,,		A B conjoined.	Do. do. : Yetminster, Dorset.
,,		N R conjoined.	Beaker : St. Giles, Cripplegate, London, E.C.
1572-3		A trefoil.	Gilt tazza : Christ's College, Cambridge.
,,		A trefoil slipped.	Baluster-top spoon : Mr. H. D. Ellis.
,,		H B conjoined, see 1570.	Communion paten : Northleach, Gloucestershire.
,,		H R.	Mount of stone-ware jug : South Kensington Museum.
,,		A cross couped.	Seal-top spoon : The Author's Collection.
,,		Grotesque object and bunch of grapes.	Tankard : Teffont Ewyas.
1573-4		B.	Communion plate : Tring, Herts.
,,		I F.	Apostle spoon : Stanyforth Collection.
,,		N O in monogram.	Mount of horn cup : St. Giles, Cripplegate, London.
,,		I P in shaped shield.	Communion cup and cover : Risca, Mon.
,,		A beaked helmet, see 1571.	Do. do. do. : Yarlington, Somerset.
,,		A millrind, as 1570.	Seal-top spoon : Armourers' Company, London.
,,		A pelican displayed.	Standing salt : Messrs. Christie.
,,		H S in monogram (Henry Sutton).	Communion cup : Fifehead Magdalen, Dorset.
,,		H R conjoined.	Small tankard : Burlington House Exhibition.
,,		A bird, see 1571.	The Bacon cup : The Holms Collection.
,,		Escallop.	Apostle spoon : Stanyforth Collection.
1574-5		Sun in splendour, see 1562.	Two Apostle spoons (St. Matthew and St. Andrew) : Messrs. Christie.
,,		C P, an axe between.	Tankard : Ashmolean Museum, Oxford.
,,		V S, fleur-de-lys below.	Communion cup : Messrs. Crichton.
1575-6		Hand grasping hammer between H C, see 1535.	Gilt tankard : Mrs. Morgan Williams, St. Donat's Castle.

DATE.	GOLDSMITHS' MARKS.		ARTICLES AND OWNERS.
1575-6		R E in indented border.	Communion paten : Trinity College, Dublin.
,,		A K conjoined, see 1570.	Do. cup : Messrs. Crichton Bros.
,,		W T.	Do. do. : noted by the Author.
,,		T B.	Communion paten : Hedgerley, Bucks.
,,		M.	Do. do. : noted by the Author.
,,		?	Communion cup : Do. do.
,,		A millrind, as 1570.	Seal-top spoon : Armourers' Company.
,,		A pair of bellows, as 1570.	Communion cup : Malmesbury, Wilts.
1576-7		t b.	Do. do. : Sutton-Mandeville, Wilts.
,,		Three trefoils in a trefoil.	The Simon Gibbon standing salt : The Goldsmiths' Company.
,,		I H, bear below.	Communion cup : Damesham, Wilts.
,,		An arrow piercing H.	Communion cups : South Newton, West Grinstead, and Kilook, Wilts.
,,		A fox sejant (John Foxe).	Communion cup : Magor, Mon.
,,		R H in monogram.	A pair of communion flagons : Cirencester.
,,		A caltrap.	Communion cup : Wishford, Wilts.
,,		A bouget.	Do. do. : Ashmore, Dorset.
,,		An arrow piercing H, see above.	Standing cup ; noted by the Author.
,,		W C over a grasshopper (Wm. Cocknidge ?)	Mounts of stoneware jug : S. Kensington Museum.
,,		A snail.	Communion cup : Chilmark, Wilts.
,,		t b, see above.	Do. do. : Teffont Ewyas, Wilts.
,,		A mullet between a pair of compasses.	Do. do. with statuette on cover : St. Mabyn, Cornwall.
1577-8		L R.	Mounts of crystal salt from Stoneyhurst College : Mr. J. Noble.
,,		Do.	Mounts of crystal salt from Stoneyhurst College : Mr. J. Noble.
,,		M.	Tazza : The Holms Collection.

DATE.	GOLDSMITHS' MARKS.		ARTICLES AND OWNERS.
1577-8		A branch.	Small standing salt : South Kensington Museum.
,,		S E in monogram.	Communion plate : Baschurch, Salop.
,,		A H.	Communion cup and cover : Limpley Stoke, near Bath.
.,		W H (Wm. Holborne).	Cup on baluster stem : Messrs. Crichton.
,,		A bird in shaped shield, see 1571 (John Bird ?)	Standing salt with crystal cylinder : The Holms Collection.
,,		R P, crescent below (Robert Planckney).	Seal-top spoon : Mr. W. Boore.
,,		t b, see 1576.	Communion cup : Messrs. Christie.
1578-9		S on a cross (Isaac Sutton ?)	Tazza-shaped cup : South Kensington Museum.
,,		A windmill (Robert Wright).	Communion cup : St. Mary, New Romney, Kent.
,,		P G in monogram.	Bowl of mazer : Armourers' Company, London.
,,		C B in monogram.	Mounts of stoneware jug : Mr. S. Phillips.
,,		A rose slipped.	Paten : noted by the Author.
1579-80		An escallop, see 1573.	Seal-top spoon : The Author's Collection.
,,		Hand grasping hammer between H C, as 1535 (Hugh Crook ?)	Tazza : H.R.H. The Duke of Cambridge.
,,		Three trefoils slipped within a trefoil.	Ewer : The Duke of Rutland.
c. 1580		I H in monogram.	Mounts of lid of stoneware tankard : the Author's Collection.
1580-1		S B (Simon Brooke).	The "Chapman" cup : Armourers' Company, London.
,,		Sun in splendour.	Mount of stoneware jug : Mr. J. Dixon.
,,		A four petalled rose seeded.	Communion cup : Messrs. Christie.
1581 2		Tudor rose.	Do. do. : Exton, Rutland.
,,		Fleur-de-lys incuse.	Mount of stoneware jug : West Malling.
,,		t b, as 1576.	Communion cup : Fugglestone, Wilts.
,,		H W, rose below.	Do. do. : West Dean, Wilts.
,,		R W.	Do. do. : Watermillock, Cumberland, and Grimston, Leic.
,,		R B in monogram (Richard Brooke).	Stoneware jug : B.F.A. Club Exhibition, 1901.

Date.	Goldsmiths' Marks.	Articles and Owners.
1581-2		H W over a star.	Communion cup: West Dean, Wilts.
1582-3		An escallop.	Seal-top spoon: Stanyforth Collection.
,,		A fleur-de-lys.	Apostle spoon: Messrs. Crichton Bros.
,,		A bull's head.	Standing salt: Mr. A. S. M. Smedley.
,,		I F, see 1555, 1568 and 1583.	Tazza: Portsmouth Corporation.
,,		Small letter b ?	Communion cup: Messrs. Phillips and Neale.
1583-4		R S, fleur-de-lys below (Robert Signell).	* Silver-gilt ewer: Lord Swaythling.
,,		A banner bendwise.	Pair of communion flagons: St. Margaret's, Westminster.
,,		I F, see 1555, 1568 and 1582.	Seal-top spoon: Holburne Museum.
,,		I H.	Silver-gilt communion cup: Gray's Inn Chapel.
1584-5		I C.	Covered tazza: Col. Moore Stevens.
,,		W C conjoined.	Standing cup: Plymouth Corporation.
,,		A crown.	Mount of stoneware jug: Franks Collection, British Museum.
,,		Mullet and pellet.	Seal-top spoons: Armourers' Company, London.
,,		Mullet and annulet.	Apostle spoons: The Marquess of Breadalbane, K.G.
,,		R W, as 1581.	Tazza: Mr. W. Boore.
1585-6		A caltrap, as 1576.	Mazer: The Rev. H. F. St. John, Leominster.
,,		An escallop.	The "Joan Doxie" Standing Cup: Armourers' Company, London.
,,		Three trefoils voided.	Mounts of Chinese pot, with spout and handle: South Kensington Museum.
,,		M (line across).	Beaker: Mr. Alfred Trapnell. The acorn-shaped Westbury cup.
1586-7		A newt on a tun (for Newton).	Communion cup and cover: Stanford, nr. Hythe, Kent.
,,		A crescent enclosing W. (Christopher Waiste ?)	Seal-top spoon: Armourers' Company, London.
,,		T, over a crescent.	Do. do. : do. do. do.
,,		T, within a bordure.	Large standing salt: South Kensington Museum.
,,		A mullet and annulet.	Seal-top spoon: Stanyforth Collection.
,,		Orb and cross.	Beaker: Messrs. Crichton Bros.

* This ewer has the date-letter " F " reversed.

Date.	Goldsmiths' Marks.		Articles and Owners.
1587-8		D or I D in monogram. Or E D.	Communion cup and paten: St. Mary-at-Hill, London, E.C.
,,		A chanticleer.	Seal-top spoon: Messrs. Christie.
,,		An escallop.	Apostle spoon: The Author's Collection.
,,		I N in monogram.	Tazza on baluster stem: Lord Swaythling.
,,		T S over a double-headed eagle.	Pair of silver gilt flagons: St. Mary, Woolnoth, London.
1588-9		C B in monogram, see 1578.	Mounts of stoneware jug: Dunn-Gardner Collection.
,,		I S in monogram, see 1578 (John Speilman).	Cylindrical standing salt: Armourers' Company.
.,		W over a rose.	Seal-top spoon: Armourers' Company.
,,		R F (Robert Frye).	Seal-top spoon: The Author's Collection.
,,		W S over a rosette.	Do. do. : Do. do.
1589-90		D, as in 1587 (Edward Delves?).	Tazza-shaped paten: St. Botolph, Aldgate, E.C.
,,		I M (John Morris).	Communion tankard: Fugglestone, St. Peter's, Wilts.
,,		H L conjoined.	Standing cup on baluster stem: Stanyforth Coll. Mounts of stoneware jug, no date-letter: The Author's Collection.
1590-1		P W over I N.	The "Lee" cup: Portsmouth Corporation.
,,		A crescent enclosing a mullet.	Seal-top spoons: Armourers' Company.
,,		A heart over two clubs in saltire.	Gourd-shaped standing cup: St. Magnus, London Bridge.
,,		R M (Richard Matthew?).	The "Offley" rose-water dish: Merchant Taylors' Company, London.
1591-2		T F (Thos. Francknall?).	Communion cup: St. Mary's, Monmouth.
,,		T S over a double-headed eagle, as 1587.	Tankard with raised bands and engraved ornamentation: Lord Swaythling.
.,		N R conjoined.	Parcel gilt beaker: St. Giles, Cripplegate, London, E.C.
,,		T F (Thos. Francknall?).	Cup on baluster stem: Messrs. Christie.
1592-3		I G in monogram.	The "Essex" cup: The V.C. of Cambridge University.
,,		A crescent inclosing W.	Spoon, with lion sejant top: The Author's Collection.
,,		R W.	Mounts of ostrich egg cup: C.C. Coll., Cambridge.
,,		P W.	Communion cup and cover: Ropley, Hants.

DATE.	GOLDSMITHS' MARKS.		ARTICLES AND OWNERS.
1593-4		I G, as 1592-3.	Communion cup and paten: Christ Church, London, E.C.
,,		D, as 1587.	Communion paten: St. Olave, Old Jewry, London, E.C.
1594-5		I M over a billet (John Morley ?).	Communion flagon: Westwell, Kent. Also on mounts of three-handled stoneware vase without hall-marks, dated 1594, in the Author's Collection.
,,		An anchor.	Massive baluster-top spoon: The Author's Collection.
,,		T H, a rose above and below.	Communion cup: St. Botolph, Aldgate, London, E.C.
,,		W H, a rose in base (Wm. Holborne ?).	Low cup, on baluster stem: Messrs. Christie.
,,		A crescent enclosing a mullet, see 1590.	Seal-top spoon: Armourers' Company, London.
1595-6		I H.	Mount of mazer: South Kensington Museum. Seal-top spoon: The Stanyforth Collection.
,,		T N in monogram.	Seal-top spoon: Mr. H. D. Ellis. Also the Hammersley salt: the Haberdashers' Company.
,,		G S, mullet below (Giles Sympson ?).	Communion cup and paten cover: St. Martin, Ruislip, Middlesex.
,,		I B, rose in base (John Brode ?).	Ewer and salver: Bristol Corporation.
,,		T N, rose in base (T. Newton ?).	Rose-water salver: Windsor Castle.
,,		C B in monogram.	Communion cup: S.S. Peter and Paul, Chingford, Essex.
,,		G A, pheon in base.	Small cup: Messrs. Christie.
1596-7		D.	Mounts of coco-nut cup: The Holms Collection.
,,		Crescent enclosing W.	Apostle spoon: Messrs. Spink & Sons.
,,		Sun in splendour.	Small plain wine cup, on baluster stem: The Author's Collection.
,,		Mullet over annulet, see 1584.	Maidenhead spoon: Messrs. Christie.
,,		T, see 1599.	Parcel gilt communion cup: Leigh, Wilts.
1597-8		H B conjoined.	Com. paten: All Hallows, Lombard Street, E.C. Mount of Rhodian-ware jug: Franks Collection.
,,		I H over a bear passant, see 1576.	Small communion flagon: Christ's Coll., Cambridge.
,,		I D over a doe lodged (I. Doe).	Beaker with handle and added cover: St. Giles, Cripplegate, E.C.
,,		I B, badge above.	Bell salt: The Holms Collection.
,,		R B, mullet below (Richard Brooke ?).	Rose-water dish: Merchant Taylors' Company.

Date.	Goldsmiths' Marks.		Articles and Owners.
1597-8		I B, bow in chief.	Small cup, baluster stem : Bateman Collection.
1598-9		T F, see 1591 (Thos. Francknall ?).	Standing cup, on baluster stem : Armourers' Company, London.
,,		Crescent enclosing W, see 1592.	Spoon, slipped in the stalk : the Drane Collection.
,,		Branch between R.P.	{ Communion paten : St. Dunstan-in-the-West, London, E.C. Communion cup : Llanfyllin, N. Wales.
,,		E R.	Mount of coker-nut cup : Burlington House Exhibition.
1599-1600		B W.	Spice box : Mr. B. J. Warwick.
,,		I A.	Tankard : Messrs. Robinson & Fisher.
,,		R C.	The " Grace Gwalter " cup : Innholders' Company, London.
,,		A squirrel.	Large gilt communion cups : St. Mary Abbot, Kensington.
,,		I B, rosette below.	Large communion cup : Whitgift Foundation, Croydon.
,,		T, see 1596.	Bell-shaped salt : Lord Swaythling.
,,		An anchor, see 1594.	Seal-top spoon : Armourer's Company.
,,		A branch.	Communion plate : St. Dunstan-in-the-West, London.
1600-1		S O, a roundlet below.	Fine ewer and salver : The Earl of Ancaster.
,,		Dove, holding olive branch.	Apostle spoon (St. Peter) : Mr. W. Boore.
.,		H D, rosette below.	Cup on baluster stem : Whitgift Foundation, Croydon.
,,		A cock, see 1587.	Cover of Communion cup : St. Margaret Pattens, London.
,,		C B in monogram, see 1595.	Standing cup : Messrs. M. & S. Lyon.
,,		M in plain shield.	Small cup on foot : Messrs. Christie.
,,		Three trefoils slipped, see 1585.	Small beaker : do. do. and (1601-2) standing salt : Goldsmiths' Co.
1601-2		Tau with bar across.	Slipped-stalk spoon : The Drane Collection.
,,		b, see 1582.	Engraved beaker : Lord Swaythling.
,,		Cross couped.	Baluster-top spoon : The Author's Collection.
,,		Two crescents.	Small cup : Messrs. Spink. Also apostle spoon of 1603-4 : The Stanyforth Collection.
,,		A merchant's mark.	Cup : Soc. Antiq. Exhibit. ; also $\left(\begin{smallmatrix}1599\\1600\end{smallmatrix}\right)$ small cup : Armourers' Company.

DATE.	GOLDSMITHS' MARKS.		ARTICLES AND OWNERS.
1601-2		A wine skin tied at the neck.	Communion cup : Holy Trinity, York.
,,		T S in monogram.	Beaker : Mr. Burnet ; also (1600-1) standing salt : Dunn-Gardner Collection.
1602-3		An animal's head erased between W I.	Communion cup : Ellel, Lancashire.
,,		A harp, between L M.	Silver-gilt tankard : Guildford Corporation.
,,		D enclosing C.	Seal-top spoon : Armourers' Company.
,,		M W in monogram.	Standing cup : Messrs. Christie.
,,		T S, over an Imperial eagle, see 1587.	Parcel gilt beaker : St. Giles, Cripplegate.
,,		T W in monogram.	Communion cup : Penmark, Glamorgan.
,,		Anchor.	Seal-top spoon : Messrs. Christie.
,,		A B conjoined, see 1571.	Standing-cup, "ex dono Champerdown" : C.C. College, Cambridge.
,,		b, see 1582.	Bell salt : Trinity House, Hull.
1603-4		I G, annulet below.	Cup dated 1640 : Hedon Corporation.
,,		C I in monogram.	Small tazza-shaped cup, reticulated bowl : Lord Swaythling.
,,		A T, tun below.	Small shallow bowl : Lacock, Wilts.
,,		Three gouttées.	Cup : Franks Collection, British Museum.
,,		I B, fleur-de-lys below.	Standing cup : Hedon Corporation.
,,		A bird over H I.	Cup embossed with escallops : St. Albans Corpn.
,,		A triangle intersected.	Embossed cup : Messrs. Christie.
1604-5		W I, as 1602.	Standing cup made from the Great Seal of Ireland : Dunn-Gardner Collection.
,,		A B conjoined, as 1602.	Pair of beakers : Mercers' Company, London.
,,		W I.	Plain cup on baluster stem : Messrs. Christie.
,,		I A.	Standing cup : Westminster Corporation.
,,		I E.	Tazza : Mr. W. Boore ; also (1599) Communion cup : Charing, Kent.
,,		M B conjoined, a billet below.	Small bowl : Messrs. Christie ; also (1607-8) Paten : Chelmorton.
1605-6		H M conjoined.	Communion paten : St. James', Garlickhithe.

DATE.	GOLDSMITHS' MARKS.		ARTICLES AND OWNERS.
1605-6		{ A B, as 1602. { I A, as 1604.	Beaker : Mercers' Company. Tall flagon : All Hallows, Lombard Street, E.C.
,,		Crescent circling W, see 1598.	Seal-top spoon : British Museum.
.,		G.	The " Cockayne " cups : Skinners' Company, London.
,,		R W, rosette below.	Rose-water dish : Clothworkers' Company, London.
1605-7		F T in monogram (F. Terry).	The " Watt Briant " cup : Portsmouth Corporation.
,,		R W.*	{ Ewer and salver : Sidney Sussex Coll., Cambridge. { Communion cup : St. Alban, Wood Street, E.C.
,,		T R in monogram over W.	Communion cup (cover dated 1607) : Crowmarsh, Oxfordshire.
,,		Orb and cross.	Communion cup : St. Mary, Willesden.
,,		L B, rosette above and below.	Small tazza, baluster stem : Franks Collection, British Museum.
,,		R S.	{ Small tazza : Hull Corporation. { Com. paten : St. Alban, Wood Street, E.C.
,,		F S, star below.	Beaker : Messrs. Christie ; also (1608-9) Communion cup : Stickney, Lincs.
,,		H B.	Tazza : Holburne Museum.
,,		T H, bugle below.	Communion flagon : Holy Trinity, Hull.
,,		W T, animal's head, erased between, see 1602.	Do. do. : Salisbury Cathedral.
,,		G. C.	Pair of bottles : Treasury of the Kremlin.
1607-8		A collar and jewel ?	Communion cup and paten cover : Hendon, Middlesex.
,,		C enclosing W.	Seal-top spoon : Messrs. Christie.
,,		C enclosing M.	Apostle spoon : Stanyforth Collection.
,,		Crescent enclosing I.	Seal-top spoon : Armourers' Company, London.
.,		C enclosing W.	Apostle spoon (St. Simon Zelotes) : The Author's Collection.
,,		T W in monogram.	Standing cup, repoussé with marine monsters : C.C. College, Cambridge.
,,		R S.	Small cup : Messrs. Christie.
,,		I S, crescent under line in base.	Alms-dish : St. Peter-le-Poor, London, E.C.
,,		Crescent enclosing saltire.	Seal-top spoons : Armourers' Company, London.
1608-9		T C.	Standing cup and cover : Trinity Hall, Cambridge.

* Probably the mark of Sir Ralph Warren, Knight and Alderman.

Date.	Goldsmiths' Marks.		Articles and Owners.
1608-9		A fruit slipped.	Cup, indented lozenge ornamentation, baluster stem : St. Albans Corporation.
,,		F W in monogram.	Seal-top spoon : British Museum.
,,		A B, as 1602.	Silver-gilt wine cup : The Author's Collection.
,,		T A, mullet below.	Communion paten : All Hallows the Great, London.
,,		W R.	The "John Maxfield" cup : Armourers' Company.
,,		S O.	{ Pair of tall flagons : All Hallows the Great, London. { Do. do. : B.N. College Chapel, Oxford.
,,		I K.	The "Sampson Leycroft" cup : Armourers' Company.
,,		A helm, see 1573.	Seal-top spoons : Armourers' Company.
,,		N R over a head couped.	Beaker : St. Giles, Cripplegate, London.
,,		A ship.	Bell salt : The Author's Collection.
,,		?	Very small seal-top spoon : Mr. J. H. Walter.
1609-10		A bird over R P.	Communion cup : Wooton, St. Lawrence, Hants.
,,		A cross within a bordure.	The "Bonnor" cup : Portsmouth Corporation.
,,		C enclosing I, see 1607.	Apostle spoon : Holburne Museum.
,,		E W.	Slender wine cup, baluster stem : Lord Swaythling.
,,		Crescent enclosing saltire, see 1607.	Apostle spoon : Innholders' Company.
,,		Staves in saltire, between B T.	Mounts of ostrich egg cup : Franks Collection, British Museum.
,,		A growing plant.	Bell-shaped salt : Mr. J. Dixon.
,,		F S in monogram.	Communion cup : St. Botolph, Aldgate.
,,		W.	Do. do. : St. Mary, Aldermanbury.
1610-11		I W in monogram (John Wardlaw ?).	Communion cups, dated 1644 : Canongate Church, Edinburgh.
,,		T P.	Communion cup and cover : The Author's Collection.
,,		T I, star below.	Toilet box : Messrs. Garrard.
,,		T, over crescent.	Seal-top Christening spoon, inscribed "Margaret Austen, borne ye 11th day of September 1610" : The Author's Collection.
,,		E M in monogram.	Seal-top spoons : Armourers' Company.
,,.		H B.	Beaker : Mr. Alfred Trapnell.

Date.	Goldsmiths' Marks.		Articles and Owners.
1610-11		T C.	Standing cup and cover: St. Mary, Hadley Monken, Middlesex.
,,		T A, star above.	Communion cup: Priors Marston, Warwickshire.
,,		H S, gerbe in base.	Flain cup, baluster stem: St. Albans Corporation.
,,		L M in monogram.	Seal-top spoon: Messrs. Christie.
,,		A pair of compasses.	Seal-top spoon: The Stanyforth Collection.
,.		Trefoil slipped.	Mounts of alabaster casket: Victoria and Albert Museum.
1611-12		T Y Z.	Tall standing cup: Victoria and Albert Museum.
,,		Key between W C.	Communion cup: Hartshorne.
,,		T B in monogram.	Set of three standing cups with steeple-top covers: Lord Swaythling.
,,		F W in monogram.	Communion cup with steeple-top cover: Burford, St. Martin, Wilts.
,,		Two clubs in saltire.	Apostle spoon: Messrs. Crichton.
,,		I T.	The "John Foster" standing cup: Armourers' Company.
,,		Crescent enclosing W, see 1598 and 1605.	Seal-top spoon: The Drane Collection.
1612-13		St. Catherine's wheel.	Cup with steeple cover: Messrs. Crichton Bros.
,,		A crested helmet.	Beaker: The Holms Collection.
,,		Unicorn's head.	Mounts of coco-nut cup: The Holms Collection.
,,		A B conjoined, as 1602.	Tall standing cup with short steeple over arches on cover: The Author's Collection.
,,		R B.	Communion cup: All Hallows, Lombard Street.
,.		N R.	Communion cups: St. Giles', Cripplegate, London.
,,		Key between W C, see 1611.	Do. do.: Nethercerne, Dorset.
,,		F S in monogram, see 1609.	Do. do.: St. Peter, Southgate, Norwich.
,,		W R.	Wine taster: Messrs. Christie.
,,		T H in monogram.	Small wine cup: Messrs. Spink.
,,		A pair of compasses, see 1610.	Maidenhead spoon: Messrs. Crichton.

DATE.	GOLDSMITHS' MARKS.		ARTICLES AND OWNERS.
1613-14		T C between pellets.	Tall communion cup, with pyramidal steeple on cover : Holm Cultram, Cumb.
,,		M H conjoined.	Seal-top spoon : Armourers' Company.
,,		W L conjoined.	Do. do. : Do. do.
,,		N.	Two tankard-shaped flagons : St. Mary Woolnoth, Lombard Street.
,,		H B conjoined, star below (H. Babington).	Tall flagon : All Hallows, Lombard Street.
,,		R S.	The " Edmonds " cup : Carpenters' Company, London.
,,		I M, a bow between.	Bell salt : Holburne Museum.
1614-15		R B.	Cylindrical standing salt : Innholders' Company.
,,		R C.	Seal-top spoon : Armourers' Company.
,,		B F, a trefoil in base (Benjamin Francis).	Small cup : Messrs. Christie; also (1635) patens : Christ's Coll., Camb.
,,		I M and F B.	Tall communion cup, steeple cover : Odcombe, Somerset.
,,		S O, mullet below.	Covered cup : Messrs. Christie.
,,		I D, rose below.	Small cups : Mr. S. J. Phillips.
,,		R M, bird over.	Seal-top spoon : Messrs. Crichton Bros.
,,		H M conjoined.	Bell-shaped salt : Mrs. Davis Gilberts.
1615-16		C R, key between.	Communion cup : Cumrew, Cumberland.
,,		I R, bow beneath.	Do. do. : St. Sampson, Cricklade, Wilts.
,,		M H conjoined, as 1613.	Seal-top spoon : Holburne Museum.
,,		H S, star below.	Wine cup, octagonal bowl : Armourers' Company.
,,		I S in monogram.	Seal-top spoon : Armourers' Company.
,,		Anchor in shaped shield, see 1594.	Apostle spoon : Messrs. Christie.
,,		T F, a dragon between.	Pair of communion flagons : St. Stephen, Walbrook, E.C.
,,		An escallop.	Slender wine cup : Hull Corporation.
,,		R D.	Communion paten : Elsenham Church, Newport and Stanstead Deanery.
,,		A bear.	Covered cup : The Earl of Ancaster.

Date.	Goldsmiths' Marks.	Articles and Owners.
1615-16	A double-headed eagle.	Silver-gilt standish : Noted by the Author.
,,	W. F.	Apostle spoon : The Stanyforth Collection.
1616-17	I A.	Communion flagon : St. Giles, York.
,,	R N.	Standing cup, repoussé and chased with dolphins and marine monsters : The Author's Collection.
,,	I P over a bell.	Two communion patens : Christchurch, London, E.C.
,,	I A, pellet below.	Two communion flagons : St. Giles Ch., Edinburgh.
,,	A phœnix incuse.	Small bell salt : South Kensington Museum.
,,	R over W.	Standing cup, "ex dono Johnson" : C.C. College, Cambridge.
,,	R C, pheon below.	Communion flagon : St. John the Evangelist, Stanmore, Middlesex.
,,	E enclosing C.	Apostle spoon : The Drane Collection.
,,	A trefoil within a bordure.	{ Rose-water dish : Holburne Museum. { Standing cup : St. John's Coll., Cambridge.
,,	F G in monogram.	Tall standing cup : Trinity House, Hull.
,,	I C.	Pierced tazza-shaped fruit-stand : Mr. J. A. Holms.
1617-18	R W.	Wine cup : The Armourers' Company.
,,	H B conjoined.	Beaker : Messrs. Crichton Bros.
,,	I V, star below.	Ewer and salver : Norwich Corporation.
,,	R S, heart below.	Pair of communion flagons : Christchurch, London, E.C.
,,	I C, rose below.	Thistle-shaped cup on baluster stem : Lord Swaythling.
,,	R P, mullet below.	Communion paten : Christchurch, London, E.C.
,,	An arrow between W C.	Rose-water ewer : Windsor Castle.
,,	I F.	Three spoons with lion sejant tops : British Museum.
,,	T H in monogram.	Communion cup : St. Giles, London, E.C.
,,	A tree between C C.	Pair of communion flagons : St. Mildred's, Bread Street, E.C.
1618-19	I P, as 1616.	Tankard with raised bands : Lord Swaythling.
,,	W R, as 1608.	Tankard with raised bands : Norwich Corporation.

DATE.		GOLDSMITHS' MARKS.	ARTICLES AND OWNERS.
1618-19		A V.	Beaker : Mr. D. Davis.
,,		I C.	Communion cup : Overchurch.
,,		Crescent enclosing mullet, see 1594.	Apostle spoon : Holburne Museum.
,,		C enclosing I, see 1609.	Seal-top spoon : The Author's Collection.
,,		R C, mullet below.	Pair of communion flagons : St. Andrew by-the-Wardrobe, London, E.C.
,,		R W, rose below.	The " Northampton " salt : Mercers' Company.
,,		An arrow between W C, as 1617.	Pair of communion flagons : St. Dunstan-in-the-West.
,,		R C.	Seal-top spoon : Holburne Museum.
,,		I S.	Communion cup steeple top : Ambleside, Westmor.
1619-20		T E in monogram.	The " Ridge " cup : Portsmouth Corporation.
·,		F M.	Grace cup : Messrs. Crichton Bros.
,,		A B, roundlet below.	Silver-gilt communion flagon, chased with marine monsters : St. Mary Abbots, Kensington.
,,		R K, rose below.	Spoon with " dyamond poynt " : Mercers' Company.
,,		R G.	Apostle spoon : Messrs. Christie.
1620-1		I C, mullet below.	Communion cup and paten : St. Michael Avery, Essex.
,,		I I, mullet below.	Small cup : Messrs. Christie.
,,		I S, rose below.	Apostle spoon : The Author's Collection.
,,		A I over W T.	Communion cup and paten : St. Peter-le-Poor, London, E.C.
1621-2		E L, fleur-de-lys below.	Tankard : Messrs. Christie.
,,		Small italic *a*.	Apostle spoon : The Drane Collection.
,,		H T in monogram.	Seal-top spoon : The Author's Collection.
,,		T B in monogram within a bordure.	Pair of small maces : Mr. S. Phillips.
,,		R over W.	Small tazza : Hull Corporation.
·,		C.	Master spoon : Messrs. Crichton Bros.
1622-3		R D, over crescent.	Small cup : Messrs. Christie.

DATE.	GOLDSMITHS' MARKS.		ARTICLES AND OWNERS.
1622-3		E R.	Seal-top spoon : The Author's Collection.
,,		Crescent and mullet.	Apostle spoon (St. John) : The Author's Collection.
,,		A H over W W, as 1626.	Communion cup : Chillingham, Northumb.
,,		H T in monogram, as 1621.	Small cup : Hull Corporation.
,,		I F crowned.	Sweetmeat dish : Messrs. Christie.
1623-4		A trefoil slipped.	Mounts of ostrich egg cup : Lord Swaythling.
,,		W C, mullet below.	Communion cup and paten cover : St. Mary-le-Bow, London.
,,		I M, mullet below.	Communion cup and paten cover : St. Mary, Hayes, Middlesex.
,,		R C, pheon below, as 1616.	Communion cup and paten cover : St. Margaret's, Westminster.
,,		E H, pellet above and below.	Seal-top spoon : Messrs. Christie.
,,		R S, a heart below.	Silver-gilt tankard : St. Swithin's, London.
,,		T B, head below.	Goblet : Mr. A. T. Carter.
,,		R S and anchor.	Cup on baluster stem : Victoria and Albert Museum.
,,		I F.	Seal-top spoon : The Stanyforth Collection.
1624-5		T H.	Communion cup : Wooton St. Lawrence, Hants.
,,		A mullet over an escallop.	Communion flagons : St. Mary, Hornsey.
,,		A flower slipped.	Apostle spoon (St. Philip) : The Author's Collection.
,,		A in a lozenge.	Communion cup and paten : All Hallows, Lombard Street.
,,		J in a wreath.	Cup on baluster stem : Mr. W. Boore.
,,		B Y, a gate below (Benj. Yate).	Seal-top spoon : Exhibited Soc. Antiq.
1625-6		I E, a billet below.	The " Moray " cup : Portsmouth Corporation.
,,		I V, a star below.	Tall covered cup in Dutch style : Lord Swaythling.
,,		H S, mullet below.	Slender wine cup : Messrs. Christie.
,,		S over W.	Communion paten : St. Magnus, London Bridge.
,,		H S, star below.	Communion flagon : St. Alban's, Wood Street, E.C.
,,		W S.	Do. do. : St. Peter-upon-Cornhill, E.C.
,,		T B.	Communion cup and cover : St. Alban's, Wood Street, E.C.

DATE.		GOLDSMITHS' MARKS.	ARTICLES AND OWNERS.
1625-6		C B.	Small tazza : Messrs. Christie.
1626-7		P H in monogram, annulet below.	Large Communion flagons : Christ's Coll., Cambridge.
,,		A tree.	Cylindrical salt, steeple cover : Lord Swaythling.
,,		H S, star below.	Pair of standing salts : Innholders' Company.
,,		H B conjoined, as 1613.	Communion cup " given 1626 " : St. Mary, Woolnoth.
,,		R B, mullet below.	Two communion cups and patens : St. Katherine, Creechurch, London.
,,		A H over W W.	Small dish, punched ornament : Messrs. Christie.
,,		B Y, see 1624 (Benj. Yate).	Seal-top spoon : Messrs. Christie.
,,		W S.	Apostle spoon : The Stanyforth Collection.
,,		W S.	Two communion cups and paten covers : Holy Rood, Southampton.
1627-8		S over W, see 1625.	Alms-dish and pair of flagons : St. Dunstan's-in-the-East, London.
,,		R I, mullet below.	Three Apostle spoons : Innholders' Company.
,,		W S linked (Walter Shute).	Communion flagon : All Hallows, Barking.
,,		T B.	Seal-top spoon : Armourers' Company.
,,		T E, fleur-de-lys in base.	Spoon slipped in the stalk : S. Kensington Museum.
,,		J in wreath, as 1624.	Communion cup : Berners Rooding, Essex.
,,		T V, star below.	Cup on baluster stem : Messrs. Christie.
1628-9		R M, heart below.	Communion cup and paten " given 1628 " : Spaldwick, Huntingdon.
,,		An escallop, see 1615.	Tall communion flagon : St. Margaret, Lothbury.
,,		D crossed by a bow sinister wise ?	Apostle spoon (St. James the less) : The Author's Collection.
,,		A pegasus ?	Beaker : Mr. Alfred Trapnell.
,,		B Y, gate in base, as 1626, for B. Yate.	Apostle spoon : Messrs. Christie.
,,		Bow & arrow between W S (Walter Shute ?)	Com. paten : St. Mary, Abchurch, London.
,,		D enclosing C.	Apostle spoon : The Stanyforth Collection.
1629-30		Anchor between D G.	Com. paten : St. Lawrence, Jewry, London. Do. do. : St. Michael, Bassetshaw, London.
,,		R B, mullet below.	Tall covered cup, pyramidal spire : St. John, Hampstead.

DATE.	GOLDSMITHS' MARKS.		ARTICLES AND OWNERS.
1629-30		B P, mullet below.	Cup on stem : Messrs. Christie.
,,		R C, pheon below, in dotted border.	Communion flagons : Exeter Cathedral.
,,		{ C C, as 1617. { W S, as 1628-9.	Paten : St. Peter ad Vincula, Tower of London. Communion cup : St. Mary, Harefield.
,,		I T.	Plain cup on baluster stem : Messrs. Christie.
,,		G G, rose above, round-let below.	Tall cup on baluster stem : Mr. J. Dixon.
,,		P G.	Tankard : Messrs. Crichton Bros.
1630-1		T D in monogram (T. Dove).	Fruit dish : Do. do.
,,		W over M (W. Maunday).	Sweetmeat dish, punched ornament : Messrs. Christie.
,,		R S, heart below.	Communion cup and paten : Exton, near Oakham.
,,		A bolt.	Do. do. : St. Alban's, Wood Street, London.
,,		I M, a bear below.	Communion flagon : St. Augustine's, London.
,,		I A, mullet below.	Two communion flagons : St. Stephen's, Coleman Street, E.C.
,,		W C, mullet below.	Communion cup : St. Vedast, London, E.C.
,,		R S, star below.	Do. do. : Packington, Leicestershire.
1631-2		R S, heart below.	Communion flagon : Exton Church, near Oakham.
,,		T B in monogram.	{ Communion cup : St. Dunstan, Stepney. { Communion paten : Wootton Bassett, Wilts.
,,		H M, rose below.	Communion cup : St. Mary, Aldermanbury, London.
,,		W C, heart below.	Small cup on tall stem : Hull Corporation.
,,		D W.	Tankard : Messrs. Christie.
,,		W R, arch above, pellet below (W. Rainbow).	Sweetmeat dish : Messrs. Christie. Com. paten, dated 1631 : St. Augustine's, E.C.
,,		An orb and star.	Small cup : Messrs. Christie.
,,		C B.	Tazze : The Armourers' Company.
,,		V S over fleur-de-lis.	Communion flagon : St. Briock's, Cornwall.
1632-3		E H.	Seal-top spoon : The Stanyforth Collection.
,,		P B between crescents, see 1658.	Communion paten : St. Pancras Old Church, London.
,,		T E, mullet below.	Apostle spoon (St. James the less) : Messrs. Christie.

DATE.	GOLDSMITHS' MARKS.		ARTICLES AND OWNERS.
1632-3		D enclosing C, see 1602.	Apostle spoon (St. Julian) : Innholders' Company.
,,		I M, bird below.	Communion cups : Shorncote, Wilts ; and St. James', Dover.
,,		Owl holding mouse.	Small cup on tall stem : Messrs. Garrard.
,,		C B in monogram.	Two wine cups : Armourers' Company.
,,		I G over a covered cup.	Two communion cups : St. Mary and St. Lawrence, Great Waltham.
,,		I H between pellets.	Cup on baluster stem : Messrs. Spink.
1633-4		I B, a buckle below (J. Buckle ?)	Pair of communion flagons : St. Lawrence, Jewry, E.C.
,,		W over M (W. Maundy).	Small circular dish : Messrs. Spink.
,,		Walter Shute, as 1628.	Alms dish : All Hallows, Barking.
,,		An escallop, as 1628.	Standing cup : The Author's Collection.
,,		E S in dotted circle.	Communion flagon : St. Mary, Harrow.
,,		H B conjoined, a sun above, see 1626.	Communion cup : St. Stephen, Walbrook.
,,		R C.	Seal-top spoon : The Stanyforth Collection.
1634-5		R S, mullet above and below.	Communion flagon : St. Martin-in-the-Fields.
,,		W over M, see 1633.	Sweetmeat dish : Lord Swaythling.
,,		P G, rose below.	{ Communion cup : St. Dunstan-in-the-West, E.C. { Pierced basket of 1641 : Mr. J. Mallett.
,,		R W between mullet and pellets.	Communion cup : Bradford-on-Avon, Wilts.
,,		D W, a mullet below.	Plain cup on baluster stem : The Author's Collection.
,,		R C, a rosette below.	Apostle spoons : Captain Preston.
,,		P B between two crescents.	Plain cup on baluster stem : Messrs. Christie.
1635-6		F.	Alms-dish, "ex dono Bainbrigge" : Christ's College, Cambridge.
,,		L I, flower below.	Wine cup, with baluster stem : Barber Surgeons' Company.
,,		R S under sun in splendour.	Salver on foot : Mr. W. Lane, Mount Vernon.
,,		An escallop, as 1633.	Communion flagons : St. Olave, Old Jewry, E.C.
,,		R H.	Seal-top spoon : Messrs. Dobson.
,,		R O.	Apostle spoon : Mrs. E. H. Goddard.
,,		R S between a mullet and a heart.	Small salver on foot : Messrs. Garrard.

DATE.	GOLDSMITHS' MARKS.		ARTICLES AND OWNERS.
1635-6		E C in dotted circle.	Communion flagon : St. Mathew, Bethnal Green.
,,		I B, buckle below, as 1633.	Communion paten : St. Mary, Bromley-by-Bow.
,,		E R in rayed shield.	Spoon slipped in the stalk : Messrs. Crichton Bros.
,,		H M conjoined.	Plain cup, baluster stem : Messrs. Christie.
,		B B crowned, six pellets below.	Communion cup : Snareston, Leicestershire.
,,		Owl holding mouse, see 1632.	Do. do. : Llangadwalader, N. Wales.
1636-7		R W, mullet below.	Do. do. : St. John, Hillingdon, Middlesex.
,,		G M, bird below, in dotted border.	Do. do. : Fetcham, near Leatherhead. Do. do. : (1638) St. Mary, Lambeth.
,,		R W between mullets in lozenge.	Communion paten : St. Mary, Islington.
,,		I over W between three mullets.	Cup, granulated bowl : Queen's College, Cambridge.
,,		R over W.	The "Compton" standing cup : Do. do. do.
,,		R H between pellets.	Seal-top spoon : Mr. H. Davison.
,,		B F (Benj. Francis ?)	Small salver on foot : Messrs. Christie.
,,		C R in monogram.	Communion cup : Down Parish Church.
,,		E S, pellet above.	Communion flagon : Bulford, Wilts.
1637-8		R G, heart below.	Cup with baluster stem : Victoria and Albert Museum.
,,		R S, heart below.	Saucer : Mr. J. A. Holms.
,,		I intersecting C.	Seal-top spoon : noted by the Author.
,,		A star over an orb with annulets.	Flagon : Messrs. Crichton Bros.
,		A star over an orb, see 1631.	Communion flagon, "given 1638" : Walpole St. Peter.
,,		R B over an escallop.	Wine taster or sweetmeat dish : Messrs. Christie.
,,		R M, rose below.	Ewer and salver : Portsmouth Corporation.
,,		R C, as 1634.	Master spoon : The Author's Collection.
,,		A pillar between G S.	Paten : Exton Church, near Oakham.
,,		G D, mullet and pellets below (Geo. Day ?)	Communion cup : Holy Trinity, Minories, London.
,,		W C, heart below.	Cup, baluster stem : South Kensington Museum.

Date.	Goldsmiths' Marks.		Articles and Owners.
1637-8		W M, pellets above and below.	Communion flagons : St. Augustine's and St. Mary, Aldermary.
,,		R G, heart below.	Small cup, baluster stem : S. Kensington Museum.
1638-9		R A, quatrefoil below.	Do. do. do. : Barber Surgeons' Company.
,,		I H in circle.	Spoon slipped in the stalk : The Author's Collection.
,,		W T.	Communion plate : St. Newnden.
,,		T I over star and pellets.	Cup : Messrs. Crichton Bros.
,,		T H conjoined.	Apostle spoon : The Stanyforth Collection.
,,		H L conjoined.	Spoon slipped in the stalk : Mr. J. H. Walter.
,,		S V (Stephen Venables), see 1645, 1651-3.	{Do. do. do. : Mr. A. D. George. {Do. do. (1645) : Sir E. Marshall Hall.
,,		R C.	Large seal-top spoon : St. Lawrence, Jewry.
.,		F C in monogram.	Large circular salt : Mercers' Company.
,,		W M, mullet and two pellets below.	Communion cup : Great Greenford, Middlesex.
,,		I G, mullet below.	Communion cup and 2 patens : St. Mary, Harrow.
,,		F C between mullets.	Bleeding basin : South Kensington Museum.
,,		F, as 1635.	Communion paten : Steepleton Iwerne, Dorset.
,,		R R.	Small circular sweetmeat dish : Messrs. Dobson.
,,		B E crowned.	Massive seal-top spoon : Messrs. Christie.
,,		I H.	(With reversed **a** for date-letter) Wine cup : Barber Surgeons' Company.
,,		W S linked, as 1627.	(With reversed **a** for date-letter) Wine cup : Barber Surgeons' Company.
1639-40		C P, rose below.	The " Richard Reeve " salt : Innholders' Company.
,,		T P in shaped shield.	Apostle spoon (St. Mathias) : The Author's Collection.
,,		H B conjoined, see 1613.	{Small trencher salt : South Kensington Museum. {Do. do. do. : Christ's Hospital.
,,		T b in monogram, bird below.	Communion cup, flagon and paten : St. Mary, Acton.
,,		B F, pellet below.	Apostle spoon : Messrs. Christie.
,,		A crowned escallop.	Seal-top spoon : Mr. J. A. Holms.
1640-1		D I.	Feeding bowl : Mr. C. Leo Reid, of Reid & Sons, Newcastle.

DATE.	GOLDSMITHS' MARKS.		ARTICLES AND OWNERS.
1640-1		T I.	Covered cup : Messrs. Crichton Bros.
,,		I M, bear below, as 1630.	Pair of Communion flagons : St. Ives, Cornwall.
,,		I B.	Six wine cups (shallow bowls, baluster stems) : Armourers' Company.
,,		R P, mullet below.	Communion cup : Winterborne, Came, Dorset.
,,		R W, mullet above.	Communion flagon : St. Augustine, City of London.
,,		H B conjoined, see 1639.	Two communion flagons : Great Greenford, Middlesex.
,,		W W in monogram.	Small cup, baluster stem : Mr. H. Davison.
,,		W C.	Communion paten : St. John's, Hampstead.
1641-2		W M.	Communion flagon : St. Magnus, London Bridge.
,,		T H conjoined.	Spoon slipped in the stalk : Submitted to the Author.
,,		R W.	Communion cup, Bramshott, Hants.
,,		I F.	Apostle spoon (St. Andrew) : Messrs. Christie.
,,		E I.	Do. do. (St. Jude) : British Museum.
,,		O M, pheon below.	Plain cup : Messrs. Spink.
,,		T H, fleur-de-lys above and below.	Seal-top spoon : Messrs. M. & S. Lyon.
,,		I I, mullet below.	Do. do. : St. John's, Hackney.
,,		W C, heart below.	Plain cup, baluster stem : Armourers' Company.
,,		I T, pellet below.	Cup with added spout and handle : Holburne Museum.
,,		T over M (Thomas Maundy *).	Sweetmeat dish : Mr. Shaw Smith.
1642-3		I W, tun below.	Cup, "The gift of Coll. Matth. Alured to the Corporation of Hedon, 1658 " : Hedon, Yorks.
,,		F.	Seal-top spoon : Messrs. Crichton.
,,		R S between mullets.	Small dish or taster : Messrs. Christie.
,,		R C, 3 pellets above, star below.	Seal-top spoon : Mr. Simmonds.
,,		W S, mullet below.	Shallow lobed bowl : Messrs. Spink.
,,		R K, mullet below.	Toilet box : Mr. Dobree.
1643-4		I W, as 1642-3.	Paten on foot : Gillingham, Dorset.

* This mark appears on the Leicester mace made by Thos. Maundy in 1649-50, and the accounts, together with Maundy's letters respecting the making of it, are preserved in the Leicester archives.

DATE.	GOLDSMITHS' MARKS.		ARTICLES AND OWNERS.
1643-4		TT (indistinct marks).	Apostle spoon : Messrs. Christie.
,,		T M, see 1641.	Small circular dish : Messrs. Christie.
1644-5		B B.	Paten cover of com. cup : Snareston-cum-Swepston.
1645-6		D W, mullet below.	Communion flagon : St. Mary, Aldermanbury. Do. paten : St. Vedast, E.C.
,,		T G.	Com. cup inscribed " The gift of Captayne John Poyer, Governor of the Towne of Pembroke to the Parish Church of St. Marye in Pembrokeshire, A.D. 1645."
,,		S V (Stephen Venables).	Seal-top spoon : Mr. H. Alex. Trotter.
1646-7		W T.	Communion service : Wickham, Hants.
,,		N W, cinquefoil below (Nicholas Wollaston ?)	Communion cup : Rendcombe, Gloucester.
,,		I L, pellet below.	Seal-top spoon : The Drane Collection.
,,		C O (Cardinal Orme ?)	Do do. : The Author's Collection.
,,		A F (an ancestor of Ant. Ficketts ?).	Standing cup, steeple cover : Vintners' Company.
1647-8		I A.	Mace : Evesham Corporation.
,,		R V. (Richard Vaughan ?)	Small sweetmeat dish : punched ornament : Messrs. Christie.
,,		W M, see 1641.	Large-alms dish : St. Helen's, Bishopsgate, E.C.
,,		S A in monogram.	Small wine cup : Messrs. Debenham.
,,		A bird with branch in beak.	Wine-taster : Mr. J. A. Holms.
1648-9		A hound sejant.	Silver-gilt cup : Plymouth Corporation, " The guift of Sir John Gayer, Alderman of London, 1648 ".
,,		I I, pellet below.	Seal-top spoon : Messrs. Christie.
,,		I H in monogram.	Communion cup : " The gift of Robert Jenner, 1648 " : Marston-Meysey, Glos.
,,		I G, escallop below.	Plain cup : Mansion House, York.
,,		B E, see 1638.	Small punched saucer : Messrs. Christie.
1649-50		Hound sejant.	Twelve-sided silver-gilt cup : Lord Swaythling. Mounts of coco-nut cup of 1657 : Messrs. Crichton Bros.
,,		M, star below.	Communion cup : St. Margaret Pattens, E.C.
,,		C T, two pellets above.	Communion tankard : St. Dunstan's Crawford, Middlesex.
,,		A bird.	Small cup : Col. Harvey, Norwich.

DATE.	GOLDSMITHS' MARKS.		ARTICLES AND OWNERS.
1649-50		S A in monogram.	Wine taster : Messrs. Crichton Bros.
1650-1		I C crowned.	Porringer : Do. do.
,,		A M in monogram (probably A. Moore).	Two alms dishes : St. Vedast, London ; also standing cup : Coach Makers' Company.
,,		I W.	Communion cup : St. Tudy, Cornwall.
,,		H G, between mullets and pellets.	Cup, granulated bowl, baluster stem : Mercers' Company.
,,		I G, crescent below.	Squat cup, baluster stem, spreading foot : Messrs. Spink.
1651-2		Cock on reversed C.	Communion cup : Brokenborough, Malmesbury, Wilts.
,,		S V, see 1638 (Stephen Venables ?)	Puritan spoon : South Kensington Museum.
,,		I T between 3 pellets.	Tankard, spreading base : Messrs. Christie.
,,		I R, cinquefoil below.	Do. : Messrs. Crichton.
,,		I I.	Puritan spoon : The Stanyforth Collection.
1652-3		I B.	Seal-top spoon : Messrs. Attenborough.
,,		A F.	Hoof-shaped spoon : Mr. J. H. Walter.
,,		S V (Stephen Venables).	Seal-top spoon : The Stanyforth Collection.
,,		R S between mullets.	Communion cup and paten : St. Clement Danes.
,,		I B, buckle below, as 1635.	Double salt : Portsmouth Corporation.
,,		S A in monogram, see 1647.	Communion cup : Messrs. Welby.
,,		R F, mullet below.	Large salt : Trinity House, Hull. Saucer-paten : Llanedarne, Cardiff.
,,		A F, see 1646.	Spoon, with horse's hoof at end of stem : Mr. J. H. Walter.
1653-4		W H, star above, pellet in annulet below.	Four plain patens : St. Magnus, London Bridge.
,,		H G between mullets and pellets (Henry Greenway ?)	Tall standing cup and cover: Barber Surgeons' Company.
,,		C T in monogram.	Cup on baluster stem : Messrs. Spink. Do. do. do. (1641) : Messrs. Crichton Bros.
,,		I V, pellet below.	Do. do. do. : Messrs. Christie.
,,		S V, as 1651.	Large basting spoon : Holburne Museum.
,,		E D, roundlet below.	Low tankard : Messrs. Christie.

DATE.	GOLDSMITHS' MARKS.		ARTICLES AND OWNERS.
1653-4		R R.	Puritan spoon : Mr. Dudley Westropp.
1654-5		W H, as 1653-4	Porringer-shaped cup : Lord Swaythling.
,,		H G, as 1653-4.	Pair of tall standing cups : Barber Surgeons' Company. Tall flagon : St. Magnus, London Bridge. Large cup on baluster stem : Innholders' Company.
,,		H N, bird between.	Spoon : Messrs. Crichton Bros.
,,		W C, pellets above, rose and pellets below.	Puritan spoon : The Author's Collection.
,,		I R, crescent above.	Communion cup : Aberavon, Glamorgan.
1655-6		D R, pellet above and below (Daniel Rutty ?)	Do. do. : Navenby, Lincoln.
,,		I L in plain shield.	Seal-top spoon : Messrs. Crichton.
,,		R N between mullets (Richard Neale ?)	Low-lobed bowl : Mr. S. Dean. Beakers (1654) : From Old Independent Meeting House, Great Yarmouth.
,,		T B in monogram, see 1631.	Communion flagon : St. James, Friern Barnet. Flat-top tankard : Mrs. Morgan S. Williams.
,,		R F between pellets.	Plain tankard : Dunn-Gardner Collection.
,,		R over W.	Seal-top spoon : Messrs. Christie.
,,		F W in a circle (Field Whorwood ?)	Two communion cups : St. Paul's, Covent Garden.
,,		I W, tun below.	The " Blacksmiths' " cup : Mr. J. Dixon.
,,		W G between pellets.	Small cup : Mr. A. S. Marsden Smedley.
,,		M G.	Mark noted by the Author.
,,		W G.	Small cup : Mr. A. S. Marsden Smedley.
,,		W G.	Goblet : Do. do.
1656-7		A D conjoined.	Salt : Messrs. Crichton Bros.
,,		C S, a sword in pale (Christopher Shaw ?)	Communion cup : St. Vedast, London, E.C.
,,		E L, escallop below.	Flat-top tankard : Innholders' Company.
,,		G D, mullet and two pellets below.	Two communion cups : St. Paul's, Hammersmith.
,,		W M, as 1647.	Communion cup : St. Nicholas, Lamdon, Essex.
,,		B or J B in monogram.	Plain tankard : Messrs. Christie.
,,		E T, crescent below.	Do. do. : Do. do. also (of 1655-6) small cup : The Earl of Rosebery.
1657-8		N W, as 1646-7.	Beaker : Mr. Alfred Trapnell.
,,		T G in dotted oval.	Large beer tankard : Barber Surgeons' Company.

DATE.	GOLDSMITHS' MARKS.		ARTICLES AND OWNERS.
1657-8		K F, mullet below.	Punched saucer : Messrs. Spink.
,,		I G, pellet between.	Puritan spoon : Mr. R. Meldrum.
,,		I H in monogram between three mullets.	Caudle cups with ring handles : Clothworkers' Company.
,,		A F, see 1652.	Two-handled cup : Peterhouse, Cambridge.
,,		R W.	Plain tankard : Messrs. Christie. / Same mark (with rounded base) on Communion cup and cover : Sherfield-on-Loddon, Hants.
,,		H W, mullet below.	Plain cup on baluster stem : Messrs. Christie.
1658-9		H B conjoined, mullet below, see 1640.	Porringer : Mr. H. D. Ellis.
,,		W C, rose below.	Large seal-top spoon : The Author's Collection.
,,		P B, see 1632-3.	The " Edward Osborn " cup : Innholders' Company.
,,		I or T.	Apostle spoon : Innholders' Company.
,,		?	Flat-topped pint tankard : Sir E. Marshall Hall, K.C.
,,		G B, flower below.	Two communion flagons : St. Peter-le-Poor, E.C.
,,		S A in monogram, mullet below, see 1652.	Porringer : Mr. H. D. Ellis. Also caudle cup and cover : Victoria and Albert Museum.
,,		F L, bird below.	Caudle cup and cover : Mr. F. H. Woodroffe.
,,		Crozier between G S.	Porringer or caudle cup : Trinity House, Hull.
,,		F L over a bird.	Porringer : Mr. J. A. Holms. / Plate at Petrograd : per Mr. E. Alfred Jones.
1659-60		S.	Small salver for porringer : Mr. J. H. M. Kirkwood.
,,		T G in dotted circle.	Loving cup and salver : Evesham Corporation.
,,		G S, a bolt in pale, see 1658.	(Second date-letter B) Two handled cup : South Kensington Museum.
,,		A F, a rose below (Ant. Ficketts ?), see 1657.	Communion cup : All Saints, Springfield, Essex. / Do do. : Euston.
,,		T A, mullet and pellets below.	Caudle cup : Messrs. Christie.
,,		I G, crescent below.	Paten on foot : Do.
,,		M, star below.	Large caudle cup and cover : Mr. S. Phillips.
,,		I C, mullet below.	Do do. : Mr. Hutton, B.F.A. Club Exhibition.
,,		S V, see 1651.	Puritan spoon : The Author's Collection.
,,		R D, fleur-de-lys below.	Two-handled cup and cover : Messrs. Dobson.

DATE.	GOLDSMITHS' MARKS.		ARTICLES AND OWNERS.
1660-1		I G, mullet below.	Communion paten : All Hallows, Lombard Street, E.C.
,,		G S, as 1658.	{ Caudle cup and cover : Victoria and Albert Museum. { Plain pear-shaped caudle-cup : Messrs. Crichton.
,,		T over M for Thomas Maundy, see 1641.	The City Maces : Gloucester Corporation.
,,		An orb and cross.	Tankard : Mr. H. Jefferies.
,,		R F between pellets.	The Royal Font : The Tower of London.
,,		R F and pellets.	Caudle cup and cover : Messrs. Crichton Bros.
,,		G D, mullet below.	Communion flagon : St. Vedast, London, E.C.
,,		E T, crescent below.	Plain tankard : Messrs. Spink.
,,		R A, mullet and two pellets below.	Communion cup and cover : Christchurch, London, E.C.
,,		S V, see 1659.	{ Apostle spoon : Innholders' Company. { Seal-top spoons : The Author's Collection.
,,		T B in monogram, as 1631.	Communion flagons : St. George's Chapel, Windsor.
,,		W M, mullet below.	Do. do. : St. Mary's, Monmouth.
1661-2		S V, see 1659.	Seal-top spoons : Mrs. M. S. Williams, St. Donat's Castle, and the Author.
,,		T D between pellets and a rose.	Two communion cups and paten covers : St. Margaret's, Westminster.
,,		R D over I B.	Two handled cup and cover : Messrs. Crichton.
,,		I I, mullet below.	{ Puritan spoon : The Author's Collection. { Seal-top spoon : The Stanyforth Collection.
,,		R N between 2 mullets.	Communion flagon : St. Paul, Covent Garden.
,,		T G, 3 pellets above and below.	Tankard : Messrs. Christie ; and (1660-1) candlesticks : Christchurch, Oxford.
,,		T D between mullets and pellets.	Puritan spoon : The Author ; and (1662-3) paten : Chester Cathedral.
,,		T A C in monogram.	Small saucer : Messrs. Spink.
,,		T T, mullet below.	Small saucepan with ivory handle : Messrs. Garrard.
,,		R N, mullet and two pellets below.	Altar candlesticks : York Minster.
,,		R L over fleur-de-lys.	Beaker : The Earl of Yarborough.
,,		S R.	Porringer : Messrs. Tessier.
1662-3		D R, stars and pellets above and below.	{ Communion cup : Stratfield Turgis, Hants. { Beaker : Messrs. Spink & Son.

DATE.	GOLDSMITHS' MARKS.	ARTICLES AND OWNERS.
1662-3	D R.	Alms-dish: St. Martin's, Salisbury.
,,	C A in monogram.	Mug: Noted by the Author.
,,	H N, bird with olive branch below.	Small cup on trumpet foot, punched ornaments: Messrs. Christie.
,,	E T, crescent below. Do. without crescent.	Small two-handled wine-taster: The Author's Coll'n. Do. do. do: Do. do.
,,	R F.	Plain tankard: Barber Surgeons' Company.
,,	F P, quatrefoil below.	Puritan spoon: The Author's Collection.
,,	W C.	Tankard (cut card ornament): Barber Surgeons' Company.
,,	G V.	Caudle cup and cover: Messrs. Christie.
,,	D R, as 1655.	Large alms dish: St. Martin's, Salisbury.
,,	I N, mullet below.	Communion flagon: Chester Cathedral.
,,	K S between 2 mullets.	Porringer and cover: Mr. F. H. Woodroffe, B.F.A. Club Exhibition.
,,	T P between 2 pellets.	Caudle cup and cover: Queen's Coll., Oxford.
,,	M, as 1659.	Communion paten on foot: St. John's, Cardiff.
,,	W M, pellet above, mullet below.	Porringer: Mr. H. D. Ellis.
1663-4	I F, fleur-de-lys below.	Tall standing cup, "The gift of Thomas Bell 1663": Barber Surgeons' Company.
,,	T K, fleur-de-lys below.	Two-handled sweet-meat dish, punched ornament: The Author's Collection.
,,	I N, bird below.	Plain tankard: Barber Surgeons' Company.
,,	E T between mullets and pellets.	Small two-handled cup: Lord Swaythling.
,,	A F, mullet and 2 pellets below.	Standing cup "ex dono Henry Barker": Hon. Soc., Middle Temple.
,,	W N, 4 pellets below.	Standing cup, "the gift of Robt. Henley": Hon. Soc., Middle Temple.
,,	I G, mullet below.	Communion cup: All Hallows, Lombard Street, E.C.
,,	T K, cinquefoil below, see 1663.	Wine taster: The Author's Collection. Rose-water dish: Lord Grantley.
,,	I S in heart.	Seal-top spoon: Submitted to the Author.
,,	C H, billet below.	Plain dish, gadrooned edge: Messrs. Garrard.
,,	H N, as 1662.	Communion paten: St. John's, Hackney.
,,	N B, mullet and 2 pellets below.	Small porringer: Mr. J. Ellet Lake.
1664-5	I W, woolsack below.	Beaker, repoussé and chased with tulips: South Kensington Museum.

DATE.	GOLDSMITHS' MARKS.	ARTICLES AND OWNERS.
1664-5	W H, cherub's head below.	Large paten, cabled edge : St. Vedast, London, E.C.
,,	I G, pellet below.	Communion cup : St. Augustine's, London, E.C.
,,	H G between pellets and a mullet.	Porringer and cover : Mrs. Morgan S. Williams, St. Donat's Castle.
,,	F W, a mullet and 2 pellets above and below.	Toilet box, gadrooned edge : Mr. Lowe.
,,	An escallop, a mullet above, see 1624.	Plain tankard : Messrs. Debenham & Storr.
,,	B, 2 mullets over and 1 below.	Tankard-shaped flagon : Batcombe, Somerset.
,,	H I, mullet below, see 1657.	Beaker with moulded base : Messrs. Christie.
,,	R M, between mullets and pellets.	Small repoussé cup : Messrs. Christie.
,,	H in engrailed shield.	Cover of cup : Mr. J. Dixon.
,,	T P, pellets and rosette below.	Stand for caudle cup : Mr. C. Leo. Reid, of Reid & Sons, Newcastle.
,,	D R between mullets.	Large salver on foot : Victoria and Albert Museum.
,,	T P, a rosette above and below.	Cup and cover : Messrs. Reid & Sons.
,,	H B conjoined, a mullet below.	Porringer : Rev. J. A. Brook.
,,	I K, two pellets above, a mullet below.	Church plate : Hunsden.
,,	T L, a pellet above and below.	Communion flagon : St. Mawnan, Cornwall.
1665-6	A D conjoined.	Large salt, with projecting arms for napkin : Portsmouth Corporation.
,,	T R, crescent above.	Covered porringer, caryatid handles : The Author's Collection.
,,	P D, 3 pellets above, cinquefoil below.	Sweetmeat dish : Bateman Collection.
,,	I I, as 1661.	Large seal-top spoon : The Author's Collection.
,,	H R, 3 pellets above and 3 below.	Communion paten : St. Margaret's, Westminster.
,,	P P, star below.	Communion flagon : St. Botolph, Aldgate.
,,	I G, crescent below.	Flat-top tankard : Mrs. Morgan S. Williams, St. Donat's Castle. Standing cup (1668) : Chester Corporation.
,,	A M in monogram, see 1650.	The " Hanbury " cup of the Goldsmiths' Company. Embossed and pierced basket : Mr. A. Baggalay.
,,	C Y in monogram.	Communion cup : Otford, Kent.
,,	T A, mullet between.	Small cup on foot : Messrs. Christie.

DATE.	GOLDSMITHS' MARKS.		ARTICLES AND OWNERS.
1665-6		P M in monogram, a coronet over.	Small waiter, gadrooned edge: Messrs. Vander & Hedges.
,,		F L, bird below.	Skillet with cover: Messrs. Harman; from the Holms Collection.
,,		W G crowned, in a dotted circle.	Candlestick: Mr. A. S. Marsden Smedley.
1666-7		E M in a dotted circle, see 1673 (Edmund Michell).	Plain tankard: Messrs. Spink & Sons.
,,		R D crowned.	Pear-shaped porringer: The Author's Collection.
,,		W M crowned.	Communion flagon: St. Anne and St. Agnes, London.
,,		M, mullet below.	Plain tankard: Fishmongers' Company.
,,		A key between two pellets.	Saucepan: Submitted to the Author.
1667-8		T M in monogram.	Dinner plates: Messrs. Garrard.
,,		S S crowned.	Beaker: Lord Swaythling.
,,		S V, pellet below.	Large spoon, flat stem: Octavius Morgan Collection.
,,		R S, a fleur-de-lys below.	Small tray, gadrooned edge: Mr. Heming.
,,		T S, a bird below.	Small porringer: Edkins Collection.
,,		J W in monogram.	Lion and unicorn porringer: Mr. J. A. Holms.
,,		B P, escallop below.	Large spoon: Mr. A. Bateman.
1668-9		T I, two escallops between.	Peg tankard: Mr. J. A. Holms.
,,		T L in plain stamp.	Tankard: The Earl of Wilton.
,,		B E C G in monogram, star above.	Two-handled covered cup, foliage wrought into the semblance of grotesque masks, in the style of Van Vianen: The Author's Collection. Two-handled cup with open work: The Victoria and Albert Museum.
,,		I B, crescent below.	Cylindrical parcel-gilt cup and cover, on ball feet: Lord Swaythling.
,,		A M in monogram, crowned, see 1665.	Two patens, on feet: St. Paul's, Covent Garden.
,,		R S, mullet above, six pellets below.	Two large communion flagons: St. Sepulchre's, London.
,,		P P, six pellets below, see 1665.	Covered porringer and salver: Mr. J. A. Holms.
,,		I C, mullet below.	Christening basin: St. Paul's, Covent Garden.
,,		G V in engrailed shield.	Large spoon, flat stem: Mr. A. Bateman.
,,		I C, pellet below.	Puritan spoon: Mr. S. Deane.

Date.	Goldsmiths' Marks.		Articles and Owners.
1668-9		R D, mullet below.	Beaker : Messrs. Christie.
,,		R D, mullet above, crescent below.	Alms-dish : Cartmel, Lancashire.
,,		I A in dotted circle.	Caudle cup and cover : Mr. S. Phillips.
,,		A L between three mullets.	Plain tankard : Messrs. Christie.
1669-70		W G, trefoil below.	Beaker : Mr. A. Trapnell ; salver : Mr. J. Dixon.
,,		W W, fleur-de-lys below.	Large mace : Corporation of Hedon, Yorkshire.
,,		T A, star below.	Two small beakers on spreading base : Armourers' Company.
,,		S N, star below.	Small dished salver : The Day Collection.
,,		I W, three pellets above, billet below.	Salver on foot : Burlington Fine Arts Club Exhibition.
,,		R S.	Half-pint mug : Messrs. Debenham & Storr.
,,		F W between mullets and pellets.	Large communion cup : St. Clement Danes, W.C.
,,		T C in monogram, pellet below.	Alms-dish : St. Mary, Monmouth.
,,		R P, pellet below.	Two-handled bowl : Mr. J. Dixon.
,,		I L, flower below.	Plain cup on short stem : Messrs. Christie.
,,		T H crowned.	Large spoon, flat stem, trifid end : Mr. Connel.
,,		T E H (T E conjoined).	Small beaker : Messrs. Robinson & Fisher.
,,		F C.	Child's toy spoon : Mr. H. Davison.
,,		T B E in monogram.	Spoon, flat stem, cut end : O. Morgan Collection.
,,		C over W.	Do. do. do. : Mr. G. Lambert.
,,		O G, fleur-de-lys below.	Small salver on foot : Messrs. Christie.
,,		I S, rosette below.	Porringer-shaped cup : Holburne Museum.
,,		T P, 3 mullets below.	Communion cup and cover : Buriton, Hants.
,,		E G.	Cup : Chester Corporation.
,,		D R, coronet over.	Knightly dish : Mr. L. C. G. Clark.
,,		L C crowned. (Lawrence Coles).	Trifid spoons : Messrs. Crichton Bros.
,,		I I, anchor between.	Porringer : Mr. J. A. Holms.

DATE.	GOLDSMITHS' MARKS.		ARTICLES AND OWNERS.
1670-1		T M over a crown.	Ewer and salver : Hon. Soc. of the Inner Temple.
,,		T K, rosette below.	Plain tankard : Armourers' Company.
,,		I R between rosettes. (John Ruslen ?)	Communion paten and flagon : St. Mary's, Sunbury.
,,		R H, a cinquefoil and 2 pellets below.	Tankard : South Kensington Museum.
,,		T H, anchor between.	Communion cup : St. Paul's, Shadwell, Middlesex.
,,		R N, mullet below.	Do do. : St. Sepulchre's, London.
,,		R P between pellets.	Small tankard : Messrs. Christie.
,,		R D, cinquefoil below.	Sweatmeat dish : Messrs. Dobson.
,,		G crowned, 3 mullets below.	Toy cup : Submitted to the Author.
,,		W H conjoined, mullet below.	Caudle cup and cover : Mr. S. Samuel (B.F.A. Club Exhibition).
,,		E R, mullet below.	Small handbell : Mr. Neale.
,,		I D between pellets and a gerbe.	Spoon, flat stem, trifid end : Mr. B. Jefferis.
,,		E G in oblong punch.	Plain tankard, flat top : The Earl of Wilton.
,,		I L over a crescent and pellet.	Drinking cup : Liskeard.
1671-2		G W over a crescent and pellets.	Beaker : Mr. Allan Cassels, Toronto.
,,		I L, a mullet below.	Trifid spoon : Messrs. Taylor and Laws.
,,		W G conjoined.	Alms-dish : St. Mary, Southampton.
,,		I H over a fleur-de-lys and pellets.	The Dodding tankard : Messrs. Crichton Bros.
,,		M G over a trefoil and pellets.	Tankard : Messrs. Crichton Bros.
,,		D C, rossette below.	Lid of tankard mentioned above : South Kensington Museum.
,,		I K, rose and 2 pellets below.	Spoon, flat stem, trifid end : St. Dionis, Parson's Green.
,,		I D, pellet below.	Communion cup and paten : Do do.
,,		W W linked.	Two-handled cup, porringer shape : Holburne Museum.
,,		R S between mullets.	Spoon, flat stem, trifid end : Mr. A. Bateman.
,,		O S, a trefoil slipped below.	Communion paten : St. Mary, Twickenham.

Date.	Goldsmiths' Marks.		Articles and Owners.
1671-2		A flower slipped.	Spoon, flat stem, trifid end : Mr. A. Bateman.
,,		P D, five pellets below.	Paten on foot : Mr. Dudley Westropp.
,,		C M, three pellets below.	Communion cup : St. Dionis, Parson's Green.
,,		C M, mullet and two pellets below.	Two-handled cup and cover : Holburne Museum.
,,		E G, crescent below.	Small paten on foot : Messrs. West & Son.
,,		I S, two mullets and fleur-de-lys above.	A child's spoon : from the Octavius Morgan Coll'n.
,,		I P, rosette below.	Small wafer box : Messrs. Spink. Similar mark with rosette above and below on handbell : Mr. Anthony White.
,,		R P, star below.	Saucer-shaped paten : St. Nicholas, Lamdon, Essex.
1672-3		D L, a trefoil over and mullet below.	Long toasting fork : Messrs. Crichton Bros.
,,		R K, a star and pellets below.	Trifid spoon : Mr. A. S. Marsden Smedley.
,,		I P, a pellet above and below.	Handbell : Mr. Anthony White.
,,		A H, star above, crescent below.	Porringer and cover : Mr. P. F. Walker.
,,		W G, pellet below.	Alms-dish : St. Margaret's, Barking.
,,		S V, mullet below.	Spoon, flat stem, trifid end : Submitted to the Author.
,,		I C, a pellet below.	Surgeon's bleeding bowl : Mr. G. Lambert.
,,		H L, a pellet below.	A child's spoon, trifid end : Mr. Glading.
,,		S R, cinquefoil below.	Porringer, chased with tulips and foliage : The Author's Collection.
,,		H.	Small wine taster : Messrs. Carrington.
,,		H E, a pellet below.	Small plain saucepan : Messrs. Christie.
,,		R G, star above.	Communion cup : Noted by the Author.
,,		I F, crescent above.	Spoon, flat stem, trifid end : Messrs. Jones & Son.
,,		T R in monogram.	Small salver : Messrs. Christie.
,,		D L.	Small spoon, trifid end : Submitted to the Author.
1673-4		E B crowned.	Spoon, flat stem, trifid end : Mr. B. Jeffries.
,,		S C, fleur-de-lys above and below.	Large tankard : Messrs. Christie.

Date.	Goldsmiths' Marks.	Articles and Owners.
1673-4	I K, rosette below.	Spoon, flat stem, trifid end : Mr. A. Bateman.
,,	E H crowned, crescent below.	Toilet box, gadrooned border : Messrs. Welby.
,,	S S, fleur-de-lys below.	Small three-pronged fork : from the Octavius Morgan Collection.
,,	L C, crown and crescent (Lawrence Coles).	Spoon, flat stem, trifid end : Mr. W. Boore.
,,	H E conjoined.	Small porringer : Messrs. Crichton.
,,	R L, rosette and pellets below.	Plain tankard, flat top : Mr. J. Wintle.
,,	Another mark of Lawrence Coles.	Half-pint mug : Messrs. Jones & Son.
,,	E M, see 1666 (Edmund Michell ?)	Flat stem spoon : The Author's Collection.
,,	Ed. Jones ?	Wafer box : Messrs. Debenham & Storr.
,,	M W (Mathew West ?)	Two-handled cup : from the Temple-Frere Collection.
,,	G W, crescent below.	Small wine-taster, scroll handles : Messrs. Dobson.
1674-5	E M crowned.	Spoon, flat stem, trifid end : Mr. E. W. Colt.
,,	T G, 3 pellets above and 3 below.	Two-handled cup : Lord Swaythling.
,,	G G, George Garthorne (probably).	Communion cup : St. Mary, Ealing.
,,	I S, John Sutton (probably), see 1683.	Two-handled cup : Lord Swaythling.
,,	T L, pellet below.	Alms-dish : St. Dionis, Parson's Green.
,,	R D, comet below.	Do. : St. Pancras Old Church.
,,	G T over a mullet voided.	Two-handled cup, chased with Chinese figures : Messrs. Sotheby.
,,	H K, pellet above and below.	Spoon, flat stem, trifid end : Mr. H. Davison.
,,	W W between mullets and pellets.	Alms-dish, dated 1673 : Crediton, Devon.
,,	E H, pellet above, crescent below.	Rat-tail spoon, flat stem, trifid end : Mr. W. Boore.
,,	W R conjoined, coronet above.	A half-pint mug : Messrs. Debenham and Storr.
,,	J M in monogram.	Hand-bell with ivory handle : Do. do.
,,	W S.	Three-pronged fork : Messrs. Spink.
,,	D W crowned (David Willaume or Williams ?)	Back of round brush : Messrs. Debenham & Storr. / Pair of candlesticks : Messrs. Crichton Bros.

DATE.	GOLDSMITHS' MARKS.		ARTICLES AND OWNERS.
1674-5		A M in monogram, see 1665.	Marks noted by the Author.
,,		G S, a crown and fleur-de-lys above.	Trifid spoon : noted by the Author.
1675-6		G C, mullet below.	Covered cup with lion and unicorn repoussé and chased : Lord Swaythling.
,,		F C, a rosette below.	Repoussé box : Mr. E. W. Colt.
,,		R A, winged figure between.	Caster : Messrs. Christie.
,,		N.	Porringer with acanthus decoration : Messrs. Crichton Bros.
,,		B.	Communion service : Titchfield, Hants.
,,		T D, star below.	Tankard : Carlisle Corporation.
,,		M, fleur-de-lys below.	Communion flagon : St. Bride's, London, E.C.
,,		T I between 2 mullets.	Do. do. : St. Andrew's, Hornchurch, Essex.
,,		I S crowned (Sir Jeremiah Snow).	Spoon, flat stem, trifid end : Mr. W. Boore. Forks of 1673 : Messrs. Crichton Bros.
,,		A R.	Spoon, flat stem, trifid end : Messrs. Christie.
,,		I B, see 1684 (J. Buck ?)	Lemon strainer : Mr. G. Lambert.
,,		I H.	Plain tumbler from the Temple-Frere Collection.
,,		I F, mullet below.	Rat-tail spoon : Messrs. Dobson.
,,		T L, a pellet below.	Sugar caster : Mr. H. Mallett.
,,		I E, a pellet between and below.	Wine taster : Mr. Bennett.
,,		S crowned.	Seal-top spoon : St. Dunstan-in-the-West, London.
,,		C W, a fleur-de-lys above and below.	Paten on foot : Messrs. Christie.
1676-7		R M in monogram (Richard Morrell ?)	Cup, salt, r.-w. ewer and salver : Clothworkers' Co. The " Royal Oak " cup of the Barber Surgeons' Co.
,,		F S.	Paten on foot : St. Luke's, Chelsea.
,,		Y I between escallops.	Cylindrical tankard, loose ornament : British Museum.
,,		F A, fleur-de-lys below	Rat-tail spoon, trifid end : Mr. Howes.
,,		K S between mullets.	Covered cup of porringer shape : South Kensington Museum.
,,		T F, mullet below (Sir Thomas Fowles or ffowles).	Communion cup : Keighley, Yorks.

DATE.	GOLDSMITHS' MARKS.		ARTICLES AND OWNERS.
1676-7		I O or O I.	Small plain ring : Messrs. Robinson & Fisher.
,,		W A in monogram.	Small spoon, trefoil end : Mr. Osborne.
,,		T C, a cat above.	Pair of tripod altar candlesticks : B.N. Coll., Oxford.
,,		A S H in monogram (Thomas Ash ?)	Octagonal salt : The Saddlers' Company.
,,		W W, see 1674.	Small plain porringer, submitted to the Author.
,,		C E, a pellet above and below.	Small octagonal box : Mr. Connell.
,,		S H in dotted circle.	Tankard : The Earl of Wilton.
,,		S R, a cinquefoil and pellets below.	Tankard : Mr. J. A. Holms.
,,		O S, a pellet above.	Trifid spoon : The Author's Collection.
,,		I R, a trefoil above, a pellet below.	Paten cover : Stansted Mountfitchet, Essex.
,,		B R in monogram.	Alms-dish : Willey Church, Broseley.
1677-8		A castle between I C.	Pair of snuffers : South Kensington Museum.
,,		W S, a mullet and two pellets above & below.	Snuffers tray : Do. do. do.
,,		S G crowned.	Child's spoon, flat stem, trifid end : The Author's Collection.
,,		W G, a trefoil below.	Small box : Messrs. Crichton Bros.
,,		W S, a rosette below.	Bleeding bowl with trefoil handle : Victoria and Albert Museum.
,,		H H conjoined, a fleur-de-lys and pellets below.	Pair of vases : The Duke of Portland.
,,		M P conjoined under a crown.	Set of four candlesticks : Messrs. Crichton Bros.
,,		I S crowned.	Spoon, flat stem, trifid end : The Author's Collection.
,,		W C, fleur-de-lys below.	Do. do. : Mrs. Barnett.
,,		F G, mullet below, for Fras. Garthorne ?	Tankard, flat top : Lord Grantley.
,,		A K, pellets above and below.	Hilt of dagger : Mr. F. Weekes.
,,		F S, a pellet above and below.	Small three-pronged fork, flat stem : Messrs. Crichton.
,,		D R, a coronet above.	Tankard, with acanthus leaves at base : Messrs. Christie.
,,		W S linked.	Rat-tail spoon, trifid end : Messrs. Dobson.

DATE.	GOLDSMITHS' MARKS.		ARTICLES AND OWNERS.
1677-8		J G in monogram.	The "Pepys" Cup (no Hall-mark): The Cloth-workers' Company.
,,		I B between pellets.	Toilet box: Mr. W. Townsend.
,,		E M in monogram.	Toy porringer: Messrs. Crichton.
1678-9		I B, pellet below.	Communion cup: Barrow-on-Soar, Leicestershire.
,,		S R, cinquefoil voided below.	Two communion patens: St. Bartholomew-the-less, London.
,,		R N crowned.	Small tankard, acanthus leaves around base: Messrs. Christie.
,,		N C, four pellets below.	Spoon, trefoil end, embossed ornament: Mr. Rowlands.
,,		W N.	Small plain tumbler: Messrs. Spink.
,,		T R crowned.	Trifid spoon, filleted rat-tail: South Kensington Museum.
,,		I A, crescent below.	Trifid spoon, filleted rat-tail: Mr. Heming.
,,		A R, mullet and two pellets below.	Tall flagon, dated 1679: Skinners' Company, London.
,,		W over S (Wm. Sanberry or W. Scarlett?)	Tankard: Messrs. Christie; and (1677-8) plain flagons: Welbeck.
,,		I B, fleur-de-lys below.	Porringer: Messrs. Christie.
,,		C K, pellet below.	Small three-pronged fork: Lord Truro.
,,		I P crowned.	Needle case: Mr. B. Jefferis.
,,		T B in monogram.	Small circular salver or tankard stand: Mr. Lowe.
,,		Double-seed rose.	Plain tankard, flat top: Messrs. Christie.
,,		R S.	Small box: Messrs. Crichton Bros.
,,		A H, pellet above, mullet below.	Alms plate: Do. do.
,,		S crowned.	The Dolben cup: Messrs. Tessier.
,,		N W.	Small plain mug: Mr. Leaman.
,,		I R, crescent below.	Surgeon's lancet case: Mr. G. Roberts.
,,		T A, three pellets above, a device below.	Embossed spoons, trifid ends: Messrs. Crichton.
,,		K S between mullets.	Beaker, threaded base: Messrs. Crichton.
,,		T E in monogram, a coronet above.	Beaker, moulded base: Messrs. Welby.
,,		E C crowned.	Rat-tail spoon, trifid end: Soc. Antiq. Exhibit.

DATE.	GOLDSMITHS' MARKS.	ARTICLES AND OWNERS.
1678-9	I L, a coronet above.	Pair of candlesticks : Messrs. Christie.
1679-80	T H in monogram.	Circular trencher salt : Messrs. Christie.
,,	I T.	Embossed spoon, foliated end : South Kensington Museum.
,,	I M conjoined.	Pair of snuffers : Rev. G. C. Fenwicke.
,,	R H crowned.	Loving cup : Chester Corporation.
,,	C K, mullet below.	Two communion flagons : St. Mary Abchurch, London.
,,	T C, a fish above.	Two patens : St. Edmund-the-King-and-Martyr, London.
,,	T A between pellets (Thos. Allen ?)	Two altar candlesticks : St. Anne's, Soho.
,,	B P, escallop below (Benj. Pyne ?)	Rose-water dish : Hon. Soc. of the Middle Temple.
,,	T M in monogram.	Cover of porringer-shaped cup : South Kensington Museum.
,,	H C crowned.	Embossed spoon, foliated end : Mr. Hawes.
,,	T S in monogram, crowned.	Sweatmeat dish : Messrs. Dobson & Son.
,,	R H, mullet below.	Rat-tail spoon, trifid end : Mr. Bennett.
,,	I S, as 1674.	Fine grace cup : York Corporation.
,,	O S, between trefoils.	Set of dinner plates : Messrs. Garrard.
,,	I S, billet below.	Caudle-cup : Viscount Dillon.
,,	I N, as 1662.	Set of communion plate : Carlisle Cathedral.
,,	D C, a pellet above and below.	Small octagonal box : Mr. Peters.
,,	B, see 1675 and 1687.	Octagonal jar, Chinese decorations : Messrs. Jones & Son.
c. 1680	Mark indistinct.	Forked-stem spoon : Mr. A. S. Marsden Smedley.
,,	F S.	Communion paten : Wilton, Wilts.
1680-1	A goose in dotted circle.	Communion paten : St. James, Garlickhithe, London.
,,	I H, fleur-de-lys below.	Communion cup and paten : St. Mary, Aldermanbury, London.
,,	L C crowned (Lawrence Coles).	Child's spoon, flat stem, trifid end : Mr. H. D. Ellis.
,,	R S, fleur-de-lys below.	Rat-tail spoon, trifid end : Soc. Antiq. Exhibit.
,,	D G and 2 fleur-de-lys in lozenge.	Plain tankard, flat lid : South Kensington Museum.
,,	F G, star below, see 1677 (Fras. Garthorne).	Communion cup : St. Mary, Walthamstow, Essex.
,,	I B, see 1677.	Pair of communion flagons : St. Luke's, Chelsea.

DATE.	GOLDSMITHS' MARKS.		ARTICLES AND OWNERS.
1680-1		W I, star below.	Tankard : Messrs. Christie ; also (1685-6) two-handled cup : Major Marsham, Norwich.
,,		R K, mullet below.	Large rat-tail spoon : Mr. W. Boore.
,,		I S, cinquefoil below.	Tankard with acanthus leaves round base : Messrs. Crichton.
,,		I H, pellets above and one below.	Communion flagon : St. Margaret's, Barking.
,,		T A in lozenge, mullet below.	Communion paten : Guisborough, Yorks.
,,		T I, two escallops be-tween, see 1668 & 1684.	Covered cup : Sir Bourchier Wray.
,,		T L, an escallop and pellets below.	The " Knole " table : Lord Sackville.
,,		F N, a crescent above and pellets below.	Pair of candlesticks : Messrs. Crichton Bros.
,,		R L, a trefoil below.	Offertory Ewer and salver : Hon. Soc. Middle Temple.
,,		B over W, with trefoils.	Ring-handled snuffers : Victoria and Albert Museum.
,,		R H, crowned, crescent below.	Communion cups : Gt. Leighs, Essex ; also cup : Merchant Taylors' Company.
,,		W F conjoined.	Spoon, flat stem, trefoil end : Mr. Leaman.
,,		S E.	Do. do. do. : Mr. Bennett.
1681-2		P B in monogram.	Large punch bowl : Clitheroe Corporation.
,,		I C, mullet below.	Tankard, with acanthus leaves at base : Fishmongers' Company.
,,		R C in dotted circle.	Com. flagons : St. Michael, Paternoster Royal. Large covered porringer (1680-1) : Lord Carysfort.
,,		P L in monogram.	Spoon, flat stem, trifid end : The Author's Collection.
,,		S H linked.	Alms-dish : St. Mary-le-Strand, London.
,,		F B, pellets between.	Porringer, acanthus ornamentation : Messrs. Spink.
,,		I M in dotted circle.	Paten cover of cup : St. Mathew, Bethnal Green. Porringer : Lord Swaythling.
,,		P H.	Circular wafer box : Mr. Howes.
,,		M K in lozenge.	Porringer : Messrs. Christie ; also (1682-3) Communion cup : Rayleigh, Essex.
,,		T E, a coronet above.	Communion flagon (ex bequest of 1678) : Gillingham, Dorset.
,,		L S crowned.	Plain communion paten : Leeds, Kent.
,,		I I between pellets.	Large tankard, acanthus leaves round base : Christ's College, Cambridge.

DATE.	GOLDSMITHS' MARKS.		ARTICLES AND OWNERS.
1681-2		T S, an escallop above and below.	Beaker: The Duke of Rutland.
,,		N W, a star below.	Treasury inkstand.
,,		E N conjoined, under a crown.	Tankard: Messrs. Crichton Bros.
,,		T A, three pellets above, one below.	Trifid spoon: Do. do.
,,		B crowned.	Toilet box, gadrooned border: Messrs. Debenham and Storr.
,,		I H.	Plain tankard: Mr. G. Lambert.
1682-3		I S, cinquefoil below, see 1680.	Communion cup and paten cover: St. Brides, London, E.C.
,,		A D.	Small porringer: Mr. S. Phillips.
,,		T A in monogram.	The " Stockton " cup: Innholders' Company.
,,		H E conjoined, crowned, see 1673.	Hilt of plug-bayonet: Mr. F. Weekes.
,,		A R.	Porringer: Messrs. Welby.
,,		F W, cinquefoil below.	Large paten on foot: St. Peter, Tower of London.
,,		E G crowned.	Plain tankard, flat top: Messrs. Christie.
,,		P M, star above, fleur-de-lys below.	Tankard, Chinese ornamentation: Queen's College, Cambridge.
c. 1682		I A in monogram.	Wager cup: Messrs. Crichton Bros.
1682-3		T E B in monogram.	Porringer: Do. do.
1683-4		I H crowned.	Toilet set, engraved figures, &c., in Chinese style: Lord Swaythling.
,,		W F, knot above, rosette below.	{ Toilet box: Lord Swaythling. { Toilet set: South Kensington Museum.
,,		R L (Richd. Lassels or Ralph Leeke).	{ Large rose-water dish: Barber Surgeons' Company. { Com. cup and flagon: St. James', Piccadilly.
,,		M H, rosette below.	Pair of flagons given by the Duchess of Portsmouth: Portsmouth Corporation.
,,		P R in cypher, pellet below.	Flagons: St. Clement, Eastcheap. Porringer: S. Kensington Museum.
,,		L C crowned (Lawrence Coles).	Spoon, with trifid end: The Drane Collection.
,,		S H.	Spoon, with embossed pattern: The Author's Collection.
,,		I P, star above, crescent below.	Spoon, with trifid end to stem: Messrs. Garrard.
,,		C enclosing K.	Tankard, with flat top: Messrs. Crichton.

DATE.	GOLDSMITHS' MARKS.	ARTICLES AND OWNERS.
1683-4		G C, duplicated in reverse.	Large oval dish : Messrs. Crichton Bros.
,,		T Z, a crown above, a crescent below.	Trifid spoon : Do. do.
,,		I intersecting S, see 1674 and 1684.	Box with hinged cover : Victoria and Albert Museum.
,,		T H conjoined.	{ Spirally-fluted porringer : Mr. R. Meldrum. { Porringer (same date) : Mr. A. L. Henty.
,,		T M (T. Mammal ?)	Early tea-pot : Rev. H. W. Wayne, Willey Rectory, Salop.
,,		W F, knot above.	Toilet set : South Kensington Museum.
,,		I H, 3 pellets above.	Alms-dish : St. Lawrence, Jewry.
,,		R P, pellet below.	Communion flagon : St. Mary-le-port, Bristol.
,,		S H, fleur-de-lys below.	Plain tankard, flat top : Messrs. Christie.
,,		M P conjoined.	Small saucepan : Messrs. Christie.
,,		I S crowned.	Child's rat-tail spoon : Mr. Skinner.
,,		F H E in monogram.	Small mug, scroll handle : Messrs. Jones & Son.
,,		R I.	Small oblong box, hinged lid : Mr. Falk.
,,		I W crowned.	Porringer, acanthus leaf ornament : Messrs. Dobson.
,,		W S, a bird below.	Small circular box : Messrs. Osborne & Gall.
,,		E B, a rosette below.	Rat-tail spoon, trifid end : Mr. Simmonds.
,,		C K, fleur-de-lys below.	Plain tankard : Messrs. Debenham & Storr.
,,		T E, fleur-de-lys above, pellet below.	Small bowl : Messrs. Garrard.
,,		M K, between cinque-foils.	Rat-tail spoon, embossed ornament : Soc. Antiq. Exhibit.
1684-5		I Y, a horse between.	Alms-dish : St. Mary, Abchurch, London.
,,		I S crowned.	Spoon, trifid stem : St. Michael, Wood Street, London.
,,		I I, fleur-de-lys below (John Jackson).	Communion paten : St. Mary-at-Hill, London.
,,		C T.	Communion cup : Mr. Comyns.
,,		I B, see 1675 (J. Buck ?)	{ Paten : Binstead, Hants. { Spoon : Mr. S. J. Phillips.

DATE.	GOLDSMITHS' MARKS.		ARTICLES AND OWNERS.
1684-5		W B, a mullet below.	Cylindrical caster : Mr. Anthony White.
,,		T W conjoined.	Matted beaker : Messrs. Crichton Bros.
,,		D B, a star above, an annulet below.	Two plates : Do. do.
,,		N G, a pellet between.	Salver : Mr. R. Meldrum.
,,		R A, pellets above and below.	Communion flagon : Mr. Alfred Simson.
,,		I intersecting S, see 1674 and 1683 (John Sutton, probably).	Cup : Chester Corporation.
,,		I I, a pellet between, a fleur-de-lys below.	Porringer : Mr. Harman.
,,		T I, escallop above and below in quatrefoil.	Two communion patens on foot and an alms-dish : St. Lawrence, Jewry.
,,		C D.	Rat-tail spoon : Submitted to the Author.
,,		T C in monogram.	Spoon with embossed ornament : Lord Swaythling.
,,		A H between pellets.	Large alms-dish, dated 1685 : St. Lawrence, Jewry.
,,		J S in monogram within a wreath.	Rat-tail spoon, flat stem, trifid end : Mr. J. L. Propert.
,,		P crowned. (Benjn. Pyne).	Communion flagon, dated 1685 : St. Mary, Ealing.
,,		T A between pellets.	Square salts with projecting brackets : Clothworkers' Company.
,,		O S, trefoil below.	Large porringer and cover : Lord Sackville.
,,		E H, crescent below.	Wine taster : Messrs. Crichton.
,,		I G crowned.	Rat-tail spoon, trifid end : Mr. J. B. Stansby.
,,		R K, annulet below.	Do. do. : Mr. W. Boore.
,,		E O, pellet below.	Cylindrical tankard, flat top : The Day Collection.
,,		I S, cinquefoil below, see 1680.	Two-handled cup : Dunn-Gardner Collection.
,,		G G, pellet below, see 1674.	Sugar caster : Lord Swaythling.
1685-6		D.	Large tankard : Messrs. M. & S. Lyon.
,,		W H, fleur-de-lys below.	Two-handled cup : Lord Swaythling.
,,		P R, coronet over.	Plain tankard, flat top : Clothworkers' Company. Com. plate : St. Katherine, Coleman St., E C.
,,		Y Z crowned, crescent below.	Apostle spoon (matching earlier spoons) : Innholders' Company.

Date.	Goldsmiths' Marks.		Articles and Owners.
1685-6		P K, rosette below.	Rose-water ewer and salver: Merchant Taylors' Company.
,,		W K conjoined.	Hilt of plug-bayonet: The Author's Collection.
,,		B B, crescent below.	Sconce: Wallace Collection, Hertford House.
,,		B M, between pellets.	Porringer with acanthus ornamentation: Mr. W. Boore.
,,		I S, coronet over (John Shepherd ?)	Spoon, trifid stem: St. Andrew, Undershaft, London.
,,		T B between pellets.	Small wine taster: Mr. W. Boore.
,,		T D in monogram.	{ Pair of candlesticks: Merchant Taylors' Company. { Octagonal salt: Mercers' Company.
,,		G M, 2 crescents above, 1 below (Geo. Middleton ?)	Porringer (with leopard's head, as 1678): Mr. G. Dunn's Collection.
,,		A F conjoined, a trefoil below.	Porringer: Mr. A. J. Grimes.
,,		I S under a coronet.	Trifid spoon: Messrs. Reid & Sons.
,,		R B.	Small box: Messrs. Crichton Bros.
,,		Benj. Bathurst (ent. 1677).	Tankard: noted by the Author.
,,		H R between pellets.	Mug, with reeded scroll handle: Sir C. Fraser, Bart.
,,		S E between a crescent and annulet.	Small octagonal box: Messrs. Crichton.
,,		L c.	Slender fork for green ginger: Messrs. Christie.
,,		W R, mullet below.	Small bulb-shaped porringer, repoussé and chased: Mr. W. Boore.
,,		T M in monogram.	Lemon strainer: Sir G. Puleston, Bart.
,,		W L, annulet below.	Small salver on foot: Mr. J. S. Hodgson.
,,		M W between pellets.	Plain pap boat: Messrs. Christie.
,,		I L, escallop above and below.	Large communion flagon: St. Clement Danes.
,,		W F conjoined.	Small octagonal candlestick: Viscount Clifden.
,,		P M between two stars.	Alms-dish: Christ Church, London, E.C.
1686-7		R S, mullet below.	{ Wine taster: The Author's Collection. { Do. do.: Messrs. Crichton Bros.
,,		W M, plume and pellets above, and pellet below.	{ Porringer: The Author's Collection. { Do. : Messrs. Crichton Bros.
,,		C K, mullet below.	Communion cup: St. Margaret's, Uxbridge.

DATE.	GOLDSMITHS' MARKS.		ARTICLES AND OWNERS.
1686-7		T R B in monogram.	Small tankard : Messrs. Heming.
,,		T P, a trefoil above, a pellet between.	Porringer : Messrs. Christie.
,,		I C crowned.	Mace : Saltash Corporation.
,,		C K under a mitre ?	Toy paten : Messrs. Heigham.
,,		I C, rosette and 2 pellets below.	Spoon, flat stem, trifid end : The Author's Collection.
,,		W C, cherub's head above.	Small octagonal tray : Mr. W. Boore.
,,		Y T, 2 pellets above, fleur-de-lys below.	Two communion cups and patens : St. Mary, Abchurch, London, E.C.
,,		D B, mullet above, crescent inverted below.	Large paten on foot : St. Dunstan, Stepney ; also (1685-6) punch bowl : The Earl of Wilton.
,,		R I in dotted circle.	Communion flagon : St. John the Baptist, Hillingdon.
,,		F O in monogram.	Communion paten : Kirkland, Cumberland.
,,		C R, mullet below (Christopher Riley ?)	Communion cup : Lowther, Westmorland.
1687-8		R H.	Plain tumbler : Messrs. Christie.
,,		C O, mullet below.	Rat-tail spoon : Messrs. Dobson.
,,		E G between mullets.	Tankard : Mrs. Morgan S. Williams, St. Donat's Castle.
,,		R L, fleur-de-lys below (Ralph Leeke).	Set of dinner plates : Messrs. Garrard.
,,		I B.	Rat-tail spoons, trifid ends : Mr. Hawes.
,,		N G (Nathaniel Greene ?)	Alms dish : Avening, Gloucestershire.
,,		M H.	Small three-pronged fork : Edkins Collection.
,,		T G in dotted circle.	Tankard : Messrs. Christie ; also (1686-7) communion cup : Thryberg, Yorks.
,,		F F, escallop below.	Small oval wafer box : submitted to the Author.
,,		I C in monogram.	Mug with scroll handle : Messrs. Christie.
,,		H T crowned.	Porringer, caryatid handles : Messrs. Sotheby.
,,		B, see 1679.	Rat-tail spoon, trifid end : Mr. Leaman.
,,		E C.	Child's spoon with flat stem : Mr. Davison.
,,		G S crowned.	Mounts of crystal goblet : Mr. W. Boore.

DATE.	GOLDSMITHS' MARKS.		ARTICLES AND OWNERS.
1688-9		I I S and three pellets.	Small caster : Mr. E. W. Colt.
,,		E L, fleur-de-lys below.	Plain tankard, flat top : Messrs. Christie.
,,		A dagger between I D.	Hilt of hunting knife : Mr. J. C. Stevens.
,,		W M crowned.	Spoon, trifid end : Mr. Gould ; another (1684-5) : St. Peter-le-Poor.
,,		W N crowned.	Spoon, trifid end : The Author's Collection.
,,		S D, pellet below (Samuel Dell ?)	Communion flagon : St. Mary, Aldermanbury.
,,		O S, trefoil below.	Communion tankard : St. Mary, Stanwell, Middlesex.
,,		I I, a crown and cinque-foil between.	Small rat-tail spoon : Mr. Denholm.
,,		M S.	Mounts of horn cup : Messrs. Christie.
,,		A pillar between I S.	Communion cup : Fulletby, Lincolnshire.
,,		T V between plumes.	Small salver on foot : Mr. W. Boore.
,,		I F, crescent below.	Plain cup on short stem : Messrs. Debenham & Storr.
,,		I R, annulet below.	Small octagonal candlestick from the Ashford Coll'n.
,,		G S, mullet below.	Cylindrical caster : Messrs. Robinson & Fisher.
,,		T A.	Mug with ribbon handle : Col. Esdail.
1689-90		H G between mullets.	Rat-tail spoon : Soc. Antiq. Exhibit.
,,		F D in monogram.	Small plain salver : Messrs. Christie.
,,		E B.	Circular toilet box : Mr. G. Lambert.
,,		T C and fish, as 1679.	Small beaker : The Author's Collection.
,,		W B.	Small three-pronged fork : Mr. H. Mallett.
,,		I I, see 1684.	Rat-tail spoon, trifid end : Mr. H. D. Ellis.
,,		M E conjoined, bird above.	Tankard : Mr. J. Heming.
,,		H H between rosettes.	Rat-tail spoon : Messrs. Christie.
,,		N B under a coronet.	Wafer-box : Submitted to the Author.
,,		D A.	Small spirit lamp on three ball feet : Do.
,,		I E.	Rat-tail spoon, trifid end : Mr. Davison.

DATE.	GOLDSMITHS' MARKS.		ARTICLES AND OWNERS.
1689-90		R L (Richard Lassels?)	Communion flagon: Farley, Wilts.
,,		C S in dotted oval (Clement Stonor).	{ Alms-dish: Durnford, Wilts. { Porringer and cover (1688): Messrs. Crichton.
,,		T S in monogram in dotted octagon.	Communion cup, dated 1689, but no date-letter: Thornford, Dorset.
,,		A N in monogram (Anthony Nelme).	Dredger: Holburne Museum. (This maker's mark was re-entered as the mark of Francis Nelme in March, 1722.)
,,		R E.	Rat-tail spoon: Messrs. Hancock.
,,		W P, mullet below.	Toy porringer: Messrs. Crichton.
,,		S over W.	Embossed spoon: The Drane Collection.
c. 1690		N G (Nathaniel Green).	Struck thrice on stem of small trifid spoon: Mr. S. Walter, Newbury.
1690-1		T S H E in monogram.	Snuffers and upright stand: Hon. Soc. of Middle Temple.
,,		W B under a coronet.	Toilet box: Messrs. Robinson & Fisher.
,,		S H linked as 1681.*	Plain tankard, flat top: The Author's Collection.
,,		K crowned. (Jonah Kirke?)	Communion flagon: Preston, near Cirencester.
,,		I D crowned.	Cylindrical muffineer: The Day Collection.
,,		E K.	Rat-tail spoon, trifid end: Soc. Antiq. Exhibit.
,,		R L in dotted circle.	Spirally-fluted porringer: Messrs. Christie.
,,		R C in monogram (Robt. Cooper?)	Beaker: Messrs. Crichton; two alms-dishes (1684): St. Mary-le-Bow.
,,		T S O I.	Three-pronged fork: Mr. Tessier.
,,		R Timbrell.	Plain tankard, flat top: Clothworkers' Company.
,,		J S.	Communion flagon: Pangbourne.
,,		T L (Timothy Ley).	Communion flagon: St. Nicholas, Whitehaven, Cumberland.
,,		T A, fleur-de-lys above.	Candlestick: Pem. Coll., Camb.
,,		T S between scroll and star.	Spirally-fluted porringer: Messrs. Spink.
,,		W M.	Small spoon with sucket fork: Mr. J. A. Holms.
,,		G M.	Wine-taster: Noted by the Author.
,,		G N.	Small wine-taster: Victoria and Albert Museum.
,,		T T crowned.	Trifid tea-spoon: Messrs. Crichton Bros.
,,		G S under a crown and fleur-de-lys.	Trifid spoon: Mr. S. Lazarus.

* This mark has a ring of pellets in place of the plain ring shown on the mark of 1681.

DATE.	GOLDSMITHS' MARKS.		ARTICLES AND OWNERS.
1690-1		W B (William Bainbridge ?)	Candlesticks : Noted by the Author.
,,		I I in dotted oval, see 1684 and 1689.	Porringer : Mr. J. A. Holms.
,,		I D, a sexfoil above and crescent below.	Combined spoon and sucket fork : Mr. Lambert.
,,		T H, a crescent below.	Extinguisher : The Author's Collection.
,,		D G under crown and fleur-de-lys (Daniel Garnier).	Toilet set : The Earl of Ilchester.
,,		A H, a crown above and cinquefoil below.	Trifid tea-spoon : Messrs. Crichton Bros.
1691-2		M H crowned.	Communion cup and paten : St James, Friern Barnet.
,,		I C crowned (Jas. Chadwicki ?)	Communion flagon : St. Mary Arches, Exeter.
,,		D.	Communion cup and paten : St. Martin-in-the-fields.
,,		W S.	Small salver on foot : Messrs. Garrard.
,,		S D crowned, fleur-de-lys below.	Trifid spoon : Mr. Colt.
,,		H P in monogram (Henry Penstone ?)	Tankard : Messrs. Christie.
,,		B S.	Small three-pronged fork : Submitted to the Author.
,,		S I.	Communion paten : Wootton Bassett, Wilts.
,,		I E crowned.	Rat-tail spoon : Messrs. Dobson.
,,		I G.	Half-pint mug, ribbon handle : Mr. Peters.
,,		G M between mullets.	Cylindrical flat-top tankard : Mr. Attenborough.
,,		R G.	Rat-tail spoon, trefoil end : Mr. Willett.
,,		Bird over monogram, and 3 annulets.	Oval dish, gadrooned edge : Messrs. Garrard.
,,		N G (Natl. Greene ?), see 1687.	Rat-tail spoon (dessert size) : Mr. Connell.
,,		M H.	Small oblong wafer-box : Mr. Bennett.
,,		A N in monogram (Anthony Nelme).	Snuffers tray : Rev. G. C. Fenwick.
,,		I C over star.	Toy porringer : Messrs. Crichton Bros.
1692-3		Three storks.	Set of communion plates : Swanage, Dorset.

DATE.	GOLDSMITHS' MARKS.	ARTICLES AND OWNERS.
1692-3		I W.	Octagonal taper-holder : Messrs. Christie.
,,	S C, crown and star (Stephen Coleman).	Large rat-tail spoon : Messrs. Crichton.
,,	R T (Robert Timbrell ?)	Communion flagon : St. Olave, Hart Street, E.C.
,,	G G, as 1684 (Geo. Garthorne ?)	{ Coffee-pot : Mr. H. D. Ellis. { Wine cooler : Mr. J. A. Holms.
,,	N L.	Plain tumbler : Edkins Collection.
,,	W E, mullet above and below.	Six candlesticks, fluted shafts : Hon. Soc. Middle Temple.
,	I C in monogram, crowned.	Paten on foot : The Day Collection.
,,	G F, fleur-de-lys below.	Spirally fluted porringer : Ashford Collection.
,,	I H crowned.	Engraved tea-spoon : Mr. A. Le Blond.
,,	L B do.	Cylindrical caster : Victoria and Albert Museum.
,,	B.	Decanter stand : Mr. E. W. Colt.
,,	W G crowned (Wm. Gamble ?)	Communion paten : Tadcaster, Yorks.
,,	W H crowned.	Rat-tail spoon : Soc. Antiq. Exhibit.
,,	T A, 3 pellets, and a trefoil.	Spoon, flat stem, trifid end : Messrs. Crichton.
,,	D G crowned.	Toilet box : Milbank Collection.
,,	C A between cinquefoils.	Punch ladle : Mr. Parkes.
,,	I G crowned.	Small rat-tail spoon : Mr. Ince.
,,	I S (John Spackman ?)	Spirally-fluted porringer : Temple-Frere Collection.
1693-4	I N, star below.	Rat-tail spoon : Ashford Collection.
,,	D A crowned.	Beadle's arm-badge : St. Giles, Cripplegate.
,,	I L, mullet above, fleur-de-lys below.	Punch bowl : Hon. Soc. Middle Temple.
,,	B B, addorsed, in monogram (Benj. Bathurst ?)	Porringer, spiral flutings : Messrs. Crichton.
,,	H C, 3 pellets, mullet and 2 annulets.	Alms-dish : St. Mary, Hayes, Middlesex.
,,	C C in monogram (Christopher Canner ?)	Large caster : Temple-Frere Collection.
,,	D W (Dd. Willaume ?)	Child's mug : Mr. Glading.
,,	M E, mullet below.	Rat-tail spoon : from the Octavius Morgan Coll'n.

DATE.	GOLDSMITHS' MARKS.	ARTICLES AND OWNERS.
1693-4		H P between 2 mullets.	Plain cylindrical tankard: Messrs. Christie.
,,		O, enclosing R.	Toilet box: Mr. J. S. Hodgson.
,,		T K, fish above, trefoil below.	Communion cup and paten cover: Old Romney, Kent.
,,		E T between 2 pellets.	Porringer: Mr. W. Boore.
,,		W S (William Scarlett).	Rat-tail spoon: Soc. Antiq. Exhibit.
,,		R M.	Small hand bell: Messrs. Debenham & Storr.
,,		I G crowned.	Mayor's cup: Totnes.
1694-5		E M.	Toy porringer: Mr. E. W. Colt.
,,		S L in monogram, see 1695.	Per Messrs. Alstons & Hallam.
,,		S T.	Small salver on foot: Mr. Ball.
,,		A N in monogram (Anthony Nelme).	Spirally-fluted porringer: Messrs. Carrington.
,,		R D linked, with 4 annulets.	Communion cup and paten: Didlington, Norfolk.
,,		P crowned (Benj. Pyne).	{Two-handled cup: Messrs. Christie; also (1692), Toilet service: The Marquess of Breadalbane, K.G.
,,		R F conjoined.	Small salver on foot: Sir G. Puleston, Bart.
,,		H B between 2 mullets.	Alms-dish: St. Mary, Aldermanbury, London.
,,		H V.	Small shallow bowl: Mr. J. S. Hodgson.
,,		S H in monogram (Sam Hood).	Two-handled bowl: Mr. J. Dixon.
,,		I in dotted ellipse.	Small octagonal tray: Lyne-Stephens Collection.
,,		I R crowned (John Ruslen?)	{Cups on baluster stems: Mercers' Company. Barber Surgeon's bowl (1682): Messrs. Crichton Bros.
,,		T A, see 1690 (Thomas Allen?)	Pair of octagonal candlesticks: Messrs. Christie.
,,		M G, bird above, crescent below.	Spirally-fluted porringer: Viscount Clifden.
,,		W H bird below.	Rat-tail spoon, trifid-end: Messrs. Spink.
,,		I F.	Small salver: Messrs. West & Son, Dublin.
1695-6		R G, two sexfoils above and one below.	Mug: Messrs. Crichton Bros.
,,		T H conjoined.	Flat-topped tankard: Mr. G. E. Farr.

DATE.	GOLDSMITHS' MARKS.		ARTICLES AND OWNERS.
1695-6		I intersecting S, see 1684.	Porringer : Mr. Ernest A. Sandeman. Mug : Mr. J. A. Holms.
,,		Peter Harache.	Finely-engraved dish : Lord Swaythling.
,,		John Hodson.	Two communion cups : St. John's, Wapping.
,,		M B conjoined (Moses Brown ?)	Plain tumbler, from the Edkins Collection.
,,		William Keatt.	Large two-handled cup : Messrs. Garrard.
,,		S.	Two-handled cup : Mr. W. Boore.
,,		A G, crescent below.	Rat-tail spoon, flat stem, embossed ornament : South Kensington Museum.
,,		M M (Mat. Madden ?)	Plain tumbler : Mr. G. Lowe.
,,		Jonah Kirk.	Pair of octagonal candlesticks : Lord Sudeley.
,,		Isaac Davenport.	Chocolate pot : Burlington House Exhibition.
,,		Anchor between E S crowned.	Rat-tail spoon, trifid end : Mr. Bright.
,,		S L in monogram.	Plain tankard, flat top : Messrs. Christie.
,,		S over W.	Rat-tail spoon, flat stem, trifid end : Mr. A. D. George.
,,		M E conjoined.	Do. do. do. : Mr. G. Lowe.
,,		I S, see 1692.	Small plain saucepan (ebony handle) : Submitted to the Author.
1696-7		W V in monogram.	Fluted porringer : Mr. H. D. Ellis.
,,		G M.	Toy tankard : Messrs. Crichton Bros.
,,		T Z, crown above, mullet below, see 1683.	Embossed spoon : S. Kensington Museum.
,,		John Penfold (probably).	Cup : Messrs. Welby.
,,		T B, crescent below.	Snuffers stand : Col. Croft Lyons.
,,		H C in monogram.	Mark noted by the Author.
,,		T Z crowned, with mullet below.	Do. do. do.
,,		T B, mullet above, crescent below.	Do. do. do.
,,		Lawrence Jones	Spoon, flat stem, trifid end : Mr. H. D. Ellis.

DATE.	GOLDSMITHS' MARKS.		ARTICLES AND OWNERS.
1696-7		Thomas Brydon.	Communion flagon : St. Mary's, Beverley.
,,		Jonathan Bradley.	Small spirally-fluted porringer : Mr. Chilcott.
·,		R W.	Communion paten on foot : Byfield, Northants.
,,		Fras. Garthorne.	Beer jug : Messrs. Christie ; jug (no Hall-marks) · Windsor Castle.
,,		F.	Child's mug : Mr. G. Lowe.
,,		Christopher Canner.	Muffineer : Mr. Frazer ; (1690-1) caster : Dunn-Gardner Collection.
,,		R G.	Small three-pronged fork : Mr. Barnett.
,,		I S in monogram.	Rat-tail spoon, trifid end : Mr. Leaman.
,,		T B, crescent below.	Small porringer : Edkins Collection.
c. 1696-8		G a (possibly Fras. Garthorne).	(With lion's head erased and Britannia—but date letter not clear) : Per Mr. J. H. Walter.

NOTE.—From 27 March, 1697, until 1 June, 1720, while the new standard for plate was compulsory, the use of any of the old marks was prohibited, and makers' marks composed of the first two letters of the surname were required. On the old standard being restored in June, 1719, the old form of maker's mark was resumed for the old standard, the new form being retained for the new standard until 1739. The form, therefore, of the makers' marks from 1697 to 1739 hereafter illustrated will indicate the standard of the plate on which they have been found. The names being printed beside the marks, it can easily be ascertained whether any mark is composed of the initials of the Christian and surname, or of the first two letters of the surname.

The anomalous marks reproduced below, in which the small black-letter t of the old standard is found accompanied by the marks of the new standard, occur on a rat-tail spoon of 1697 made by Lawrence Coles, whose mark in the new form it also bears. The spoon is the property of Mr. E. W. Colt, M.A.

These marks and the spoon on which they occur appear to be perfectly genuine. It is suggested that the date-letter t which pertained to the old standard was stamped by mistake instead of the court-letter a.

Many of the marks appearing in this list from 1697 onwards have been found on plate at Messrs. Christie's and other well-known auction rooms, and on plate in the hands of goldsmiths and dealers, much of which has been family plate sent for appraisement in connection with death duties. The names of the owners in a number of instances are therefore not published.

Some of the marks in the following columns are not to be found in the Goldsmiths' records by reason of the disappearance of one or more of their books and the loss of leaves from others. In several instances also the records appear to have been kept somewhat negligently, inasmuch as marks were sometimes not registered until months after the assay of plate on which they had been struck, and some makers' marks on perfectly genuine plate of the 18th century do not appear to have been entered in the books at all.

Date.	Goldsmiths' Marks and Names.			Articles and Owners.
1697		Lawrence Coles	ent. 1697	Trifid spoon * (with date-letter t) : Mr. E. W. Colt.
,,		——— Thriscross	,, ,,	Do. do. : Bond Street Spoon Exhibition, 1902.
,,		Alexr. Roode	,, ,,	Circular trencher salt : Mr. Peters.
,,		Mathew West	,, ,,	Trifid spoon from the Octavius Morgan Coll. (1706-7); porringer-shaped cup : Temple-Frere Collection.
,,		Jas. Edgar	,, ,,	Small porringer : Mr. J. E. Lake.
,,		Andrew Moore	,, ,,	Mark registered for New Standard, April, 1697.
,,		Edmd. Townsend	,, ,,	Do. do. do. do.
,,		C. Williams	,, ,,	Do. do. do. do.
,,		Mathew Madden	,, ,,	Rat-tail spoon, flat stem, trifid end.
,,		Lawrence Jones	,, ,,	Small paten on foot : Mr. W. Smith.
,,		Wm. Francis	,, ,,	Mark registered for New Standard, April, 1697.
,,		John Hodson	,, ,,	Do. do. do. do.
,,		Edward Ironside	,, ,,	Paten cover : Stansted Mountfitchet, Essex.
,,		? Thos. Ash	,, ,,	Transitional spoon : Mr. S. J. Phillips.
,,		Geo. Garthorne (probably)	,, ,,	Gilt handle of knife and fork in case : The Author's Collection.
,,		Daniel Garnier (see p. 153)	,, ,,	Porringer : Messrs. Lambert.
,,		Isaac Dighton (see p. 155)	,, ,,	Paten : Saffron Walden.
,,		Wm. Gimber	,, ,,	Rat-tail spoon, flat stem, trifid end : The Author's Collection.
,,		Edwd. Courthope	,, ,,	Rat-tail spoon, flat stem, trifid end : Mr. Lowe.
,,		Sam. Hood	,, ,,	A porringer; also (1713-4) com. cup; St. Peter's, Hereford.
,,		Christr. Canner	,, ,,	A trifid spoon; also (1701) a dredger : Hon. Soc. of Gray's Inn.
,,		Fras. Garthorne	,, ,,	Two communion cups : Christchurch, Stepney.
,,		Thos. Parr	,, ,,	Communion paten : Rylstone, nr. Skipton, Yorks.
,,		Wm. Denny & John Backe	,, ,,	Large com. cup : St. Mary Abbots, Kensington. Two candlesticks (Doric columns) : Mr. H. D. Ellis.

* All the marks on this spoon are illustrated on the preceding page.

DATE.	GOLDSMITHS' MARKS AND NAMES.			ARTICLES AND OWNERS.
1697		Jas.	Chadwick ent. 1697	Com. paten : St. Mary Abbots, Kensington.
,,		Wm.	Gibson ,, ,,	Pair of com. flagons : St. Mary's, Chelmsford.
,,		Name not traced.		Oval tobacco-box : The Gurney Collection.
,,		Thos.	Allen ,, ,,	Trifid spoon : Bond Street Spoon Exhibition, 1902.
,,		Moses	Brown ,, ,,	Do. do. : Mr. B. Jefferis.
,,		Danl.	Garnier ,, ,,	Do. do. : The Octavius Morgan Collection.
,,		Thos.	Ash ,, ,,	Do. do. : Do. do. do.
,,		,,	,, ,, ,,	Second mark of Thos. Ash, registered April, 1697.
,,		,,	,, ,, ,,	Third do. : Pair of candlesticks (1709) : Mr. A. Bateman.
,,		Fras.	Archbold ,, ,,	Paten on foot : Mr. H. Hussey.
,,		Benj.	Bradford ,, ,,	Large rat-tail gravy spoon : Mrs. Dawson.
,,		Wm.	Bainbridge ,, ,,	A plain tankard, with flat top.
,,		Jno.	Smithsend ,, ,,	A rat-tail spoon, flat stem, trifid end.
,,		————	Wimans ,, ,,	Do. do. do.
,,		Benj.	Pyne ,, ,,	A plain cylindrical tankard, with flat top.
,,		Jno.	Shepherd ,, ,,	Mark registered for New Standard, April, 1697.
,,		Frances Hoyte	,, ,,	Do. do. do. do. do.
,,		Hugh	Roberts ,, ,,	Large communion flagon : St. Bridget's, Chester.
,,		Ed.	Jones ,, ,,	A toy porringer, spiral flutings, ribbon handles.
,,		Wm.	Brett ,, ,,	Mark registered for New Standard, April, 1697.
,,		Dorothy Grant	,, ,,	Do. do. do. do.
,,		Stephen Coleman	,, ,,	Do. do. do. do.
,		Jno.	Brassey ,, ,,	Do. do. do. do.
,,		Rich.	Nightingale ,, ,,	A rat-tail spoon, flat stem, trifid end.
,,		Geo.	Titterton ,, ,,	A small cup with spreading lip, no handle.
,,		Jn'th'n Lambe	,, ,,	Taper holder : Messrs. Crichton.

Date.	Goldsmiths' Marks and Names.				Articles and Owners.
1697-8		Jos.	Bird	ent. 1697.	A candlestick formed of six columns on rectangular base.
,		Chas.	Overing	,, ,,	Two-handled covered cup with spiral flutings : The Author's Collection.
,,		Thos.	Brydon	,, ,,	A plain tankard with threaded foot, flat top.
,,		Thos.	Issod	,, ,,	Trifid spoon with filleted rat-tail : The Author's Collection.
,,		Robt.	Peake	,, ,,	Communion paten : St. Botolph, Aldgate.
,,		Wm.	Scarlett	,, ,,	Six trifid spoons, with beaded rat-tails : Mr. E. Heron-Allen.
,,		Jos.	Stokes	., ,,	Trifid spoon ; and (1698-9) mark in oblong punch on com. paten : Byford, Herefordshire.
,,		Philip	Rolles	,, ,,	Mark registered for New Standard, April, 1697.
,,		John	Fawdery	,, ,,	Snuffers stand : The Author's Collection.
,,		Thos.	Ash	,, ,,	Struck over a mark MP of 1683 ; Pair of candlesticks : Messrs. Crichton Bros.
,,		James	Edgar	,, ,,	Snuffers : The Author's Collection.
,,		Richard	Syngin	,, ,,	Candlestick : Dr. Wilfred Harris.
,,		Joseph	Bird	,, ,,	Trencher salts : Messrs. Crichton Bros.
,,		Andrew	Moore	,, ,,	Tea spoons : Do. do.
,,		Joyce	Issod	,, ,,	Trifid spoon : Messrs. Spink.
,,		Isaac	Dighton	,, ,,	Paten : Mr. G. Lambert ; also (1699) two-handled cup : South Kensington Museum.
,,		———	Wimans	,, ,,	Porringer-shaped communion cup : Barrow-on-Soar, Leicestershire.
,,		Anthy.	Nelme	,, ,,	Monteith : Pembroke College, Cambridge.
,,		Geo.	Cox	,, 1698.	A beaded rat-tail spoon, flat stem, trifid end.
,,		John	Cove	,, ,,	Mark of a Bristol Goldsmith, registered 4th Jan., 1698.
,,		Wm.	Bull	,, ,,	A bayonet-top sugar caster with modern chasing.
1698-9		Geo.	Garthorne	,, 1697.	Large alms-dish : St. Michael, Cornhill.
,,		Wm.	Mathew	,, ,,	Trifid spoon: Bond Street Spoon Exhibition, 1902.
,,		Jonath'n	Bradley	,, ,,	Rat-tail marrow scoop : Mr. Crichton.
,,		Edwd.	Yorke	,, 1705.	Two communion cups : St. Mary-le-Bow.

DATE.	GOLDSMITHS' MARKS AND NAMES.				ARTICLES AND OWNERS.
1698-9		Henry	Collins?	ent. 1698.	Tankard: Messrs. Carrington.
,,		Richard	Nightingale?	,, 1697.	Mug: Messrs. Crichton Bros.
,,		Isaac	Dighton (see pp. 152 and 154)	,, ,,	Porringer: Messrs. Christie.
,,		Name not traced.			Pair of candlesticks: Messrs. Crichton Bros.
,,		,,	,, ,,		Snuffers tray: Do. do.
,,		Jos.	Sheene.		Plate: Do. do.
,,		Benj.	Bentley	,, 1698.	Table spoon: Reid & Sons.
,,		Wm.	Matthew	,, 1697.	Small bleeding bowl: Victoria and Albert Museum.
,,		Wm.	Fawdery	,, 1698.	Porringer-shaped covered cup: Lord Swaythling.
,,		John	Ruslen	,, 1697.	Monteith, ladle, and salver: Fishmongers' Coy.
,,		Wm.	Scarlett	,, ,,	Six trifid spoons: Mrs. Morgan S. Williams, St. Donat's Castle.
,,		Jno.	Ladyman	,, ,,	Two trifid spoons: Mr. Geo. Lambert.
,,		Robt.	Cooper	,, ,,	Communion paten: St. Dunstan, Cranford, Mids.
,,		Lawrence Coles		,, ,,	Rat-tail spoon, trifid end: Mr. Samuel Deane.
,,		John	Sutton	,, ,,	Do.: Mr. Lowe; also (1697) communion cup: Sollers Hope, Herefordshire.
,,		John	Hely	,, 1699.	Punch ladle from the Octavius Morgan Coll'n.
,,		Job	Hanks	,, ,,	Mark entered for New Standard, 20th May, 1699.
,,		Jno.	Porter	,, 1698.	Cylindrical flat-top tankard: Mr. Geo. Lambert.
,,		White	Walsh	,, ,,	A rat-tail spoon, flat stem, trifid end.
,,		Benj.	Bentley	,, ,,	A large rat-tail hash spoon, with ebony handle.
1699 1700		Wm.	Lukin	,, 1699.	Punch-bowl of "Monteith" fashion: City of London Corporation.
,,		Benj.	Traherne	,, 1687.	Four patens on feet "Synaxi Sacrum A.D. 1700": St. Margaret's, Westminster.
,,		John	Cory	,, 1697.	Two-pronged fork: Lord Swaythling; also (1698) candlestick: Mr. J. Dixon.
,,		John	Diggle	,, ,,	Communion cup, with paten cover: St. Thomas', Neath, Glam.

Date.	Goldsmiths' Marks and Names.			Articles and Owners.
1699 1700		Fras.	Singleton ent. 1697.	The " Somers " salver : Gloucester Corporation.
,,		Sam. Thorne	,, ,,	A fluted and chased Monteith, with coat of arms on a repoussé shield, the rim chased with masks and scrolls.
,,		Isaac Davenport	,. ,,	Transitional rat-tail spoon, flat stem, wavy end : The Author's Collection.
,,		Jno. Chartier	,, 1698.	Set of communion plate : Christchurch, Oxford.
,,		Sam Dell	,, 1697.	Alms-dish : Holy Trinity Church, Coventry.
,,		Pierre Platel	,, 1699.	Rat-tail table spoon : Mr. Ince ; also (1705-6) 12 dessert spoons : Lord Swaythling.
,,		John Downes ?	,, 1697.	Taper stick : Messrs. Crichton Bros.
,,		Isaac Davenport	,, ,,	Transitional spoon : The Author's Collection.
,,		? Gould.		Muffineer : Messrs. Crichton Bros.
,,		John Leach	ent. 1697.	Toilet-boxes : Windsor Castle (per Messrs. Garrard & Co.).
,,		Joseph Ward	,, ,,	Bleeding bowl : Messrs. Crichton Bros.
,,		John Cory	,, ,,	Waiter, chased with conventional foliage : Mr. Waldron.
,,		Richd. Syngin	,, ,,	Communion cup : Puddle Trenthide, Dorset.
,,		Andrew Raven	,, ,,	Two-handled cup, of porringer form, spirally fluted.
,,		John Laughton	,, ,,	Large rat-tail hash-spoon, with hollow stem.
,,		Alex. Roode	,, ,,	Rat-tail table spoon, flat stem, trifid end.
,,		Philip Oyle	,, 1699.	Mark registered 9th October, 1699.
,,		John Broake	,, ,,	Paten, or small salver, on foot.
1700-1		Wm. Fawdery	,, 1700.	Communion cup : Eden Hall, Cumberland.
,.		Jos. Stokes	as 1697.	Fluted oval box : The Author's Collection.
,,		Sam. Wastell	ent. 1701.	Two alms-plates : Christchurch, Southgate.
,,		Jno. Jackson	,, 1697.	Tall communion flagon : St. Martin's-in-the-Fields.
,,		Name not traced		Salver on three feet, used as a paten : St. Mary's, Shenfield, Essex.
,,		Thos. Jenkins	,, ,,	Communion service : St. Mary's, Great Warley, Essex.
,,		David Willaume	,, ,,	Helmet-shaped ewer, cut card ornaments, term. figure handle ; also (1713) a doz. dessert forks : Lord Swaythling.
,,		Ralph Leeke	,, ,,	Communion paten on foot : St. Mary's, Hornsey.

DATE.	GOLDSMITHS' MARKS AND NAMES.			ARTICLES AND OWNERS.
1700-1		Phillip	Roker ent. 1697.	Paten : Stockbridge, Hants.
,,		Mat.	Madden ,, ,,	Tea spoons : Messrs. Lambert.
,,		George	Lewis ,, 1699.	Sucket fork : Messrs. Heming.
,,		Henry	Aubin ,, 1700.	Mark registered 10 June, 1700.
,,		Rich.	Biggs ,, ,,	Rat-tail spoon : Mr. J. Brasher.
,,		Steph.	Edmonds ,, ,,	Plain cylindrical tankard, threaded base, flat top.
,,		Wm.	Gossen ,, ,,	Mark registered 13 July, 1700.
,,		Edm.	Proctor ,, ,,	Rat-tail spoon, flat stem, wavy end.
,,		John	Tiffin ,, 1701.	Small salver, with gadrooned border on foot.
,,		Alex.	Roode ? ,, 1697.	Candlestick : Mr. M. T. Kennard.
1701-2		Frans.	Singleton (see p. 156).	Alms-dish : St. Mary, Stratford-le-Bow.
,,		Ed.	Gibson ent. 1697.	Rat-tail spoon, flat stem, transitional wavy end : Mr. A. Bateman.
,,		Pierre	Harache ,, ,,	Do. do. ; also (1704-5) large soup-tureen : Barber Surgeons' Company.
,,		Benj.	Watts ,, 1698.	Rat-tail spoon, flat stem, transitional wavy end : Captain Garnham.
,,		Sam	Hood ,, 1697.	Communion paten : Cole Orton, Leicestershire. Communion flagon (1699) : Mere, Wilts.
,,		Sam	Jefferys ,, ,,	Large hash-spoon : Chester Corporation.
,,		Henry	Green ,, 1700.	Transitional spoon : Messrs. Crichton Bros.
,,		Wm.	Andrews ,, 1697.	Barber surgeon's bowl : Do. do.
,,		Thos.	Brydon ,, ,,	Snuffers and stand : Do. do.
,,		Wm.	Keatt ,, ,,	Porringer : Mr. Connell ; also (1702-3) com. cup : Wellington, Herefordshire.
,,		Willo'by	Masham ,, 1701.	Salver : Chester Corporation.
,,		Name not traced.		Rat-tail spoon, trifid end to stem : Mr. C. Dobson.
,,		Wm.	Keatt ,, 1697.	Porringer, usual spiral flutings and punched ornamentation.
,,		Sam	Hawkes ,, ,,	Circular punch ladle, with ebony handle.
,,		Fras.	Archbold ,, ,,	Communion paten on drum foot : Ashby-de-la-Zouch.
,,		Josh.	Field ,, 1701.	Rat-tail spoon, rounded stem, wavy end.

Date.	Goldsmiths' Marks and Names			Articles and Owners.
1701-2		John	Goode ent. 1700.	Rat-tail spoon, rounded stem, wavy end.
,,		Ralph	Leeke ,, 1697.	Two-handled covered cup of porringer form : Mr. W. Boore.
,,		John Danl.	Read & Sleamaker ,, 1701.	Paten on foot, plain threaded border.
,,		Alexr.	Hudson ,, ,,	Oval tobacco box, with gadrooned border to lid.
,,		Stepn.	Coleman ,, 1697.	Rat-tail spoon, wavy end to stem.
1702-3		Henry	Greene ,, 1700.	Small cylindrical mug, with scroll handle.
,,		Richd.	Syngin ,, 1697.	Pair of circular toilet boxes : Sir Chas. Welby, Bt.
,,		John	Eckfourd ,, 1698.	Two communion cups and paten covers : St. Mary-le-Strand.
,,		Wm.	Gamble ,, 1697.	Small salver on foot : Messrs. M. & S. Lyon ; also (1710-1) c. paten : Clifford, Hereford.
,,		Jonath'n Crutchfield ,, ,,		Both marks on paten cover of 1702-3 used with a communion cup of 1638-9 before-mentioned : St. James', Garlickhithe, L'don.
,,		Humph. Payne ,, 1701.		
,,		Name not traced.		Alms-dish : St. Margaret Pattens, London.
,,		Thos.	Sadler ,, ,,	Rat-tail spoons, trifid ends : S. Kensington Mus. and Mr. H. D. Ellis.
,,		Jos.	Ward ,, 1697.	Com. cup : Sapperton ; also (1701-2) tankard : The Marquess of Breadalbane, K.G.
,,		Jno.	Downes ,, ,,	Rat-tail spoon, rounded stem, wavy end : Mr. W. Boore.
,,		Jno.	Cope ,, 1701.	Do. do. do. : The Author.
,,		Thos.	Waterhouse ,, 1702.	Mark registered 22 July, 1702.
,,		Wm.	Barnes ,, ,,	Surgeon's lancet case. Also tobacco box of 1698.
,,		Abm.	Russell ,, ,,	Small toilet box, with monogram engraved on lid.
,,		Jas.	Chadwick as 1697.	Fluted tankard : The Author's Collection.
,,		Matt.	Cooper ent. 1702.	Salver : Noted by the Author.
,,		Hy.	Greene ,, 1700.	Porringer : Messrs. Crichton Bros.
,,		Name not traced.		Porringer and cover : Do. do.
,,		Henry Aubin, see 1700. (earliest ment. 1700).		Dessert spoon : Do. do.
,,		?	Fraillon.	Taper stick : Do. do.
,,		Name not traced.		Marrow scoop : Do. do.

DATE.	GOLDSMITHS' MARKS AND NAMES.		ARTICLES AND OWNERS.
1702-3		Jonathan Madden ent. 1702.	Chocolate pot : Messrs. Crichton Bros.
,,		Robt. Lovell ,, ,,	A trifid spoon : Mr. Jefferis ; also (1707-8) com. paten : Ewyas Harold, Herefordshire.
,,		Matt. Cooper ,, ,,	A small tripod stand for a spirit lamp.
1703-4		Jno. Rand ,, 1704.	A repoussé sconce : South Kensington Museum.
,,		Thos. Jenkins ,, 1697.	A salver on foot : Mr. H. D. Ellis.
,,		Ed. Gibson ,, ,,	A rat-tail transitional spoon, wavy end to stem : Mr. H. D. Ellis.
,,		Wm. Andrews ,, ,,	A toy porringer ; and (1698) a covered feeding-cup : Mr. Bateman.
,,		Name not traced.	Coffee-pot : Noted by the Author.
,,		J. Broake.	Dessert forks (shield top) : Messrs. Crichton Bros.
,,		Soane or Soame.	Tobacco box : Messrs. Crichton Bros.
,,		Jonah Kirke ,, ,,	A circular toilet box, with gadrooned border.
,,		Gabl. Player ,, 1700.	A cylindrical tankard, spoiled by bad modern chasing.
,,		Saml. Smith ,, ,,	A small oval tray, with raised gadrooned border.
,,		Chas. Williams ,, 1697.	A bodkin case engraved, with monogram A.M.
,,		Jno. Snelling ,, ,,	A cylindrical tankard, with hollow flutings and punched ornamentation.
,,		Nat. Greene ,, 1698.	A toy tankard without a cover.
,,		Name not traced.	A surgeon's bleeding bowl, with flat handles.
,,		Wm. Warham ,, 1703.	Mark registered 12th November, 1703.
,,		Wm. Charnelhouse ,, ,,	A rat-tail spoon, rounded stem, wavy end.
,,		Andr. Archer ,, ,,	A three-pronged fork, do. do.
,,		Thos. Peele ,, 1704.	A fluted wine-taster, with delicate scroll handles.
,,		Wm. Petley ,, 1699.	A small engraved box, with hinged lid.
1704-5		Robert Stokes ?	Cruet frame : Messrs. Crichton Bros.
,,		Wm. Denny ,, 1697.	Communion cup and paten cover : Holy Innocents' Church, Kingsbury, Mids.
,,		Geo. Lewis ,, 1699.	{ Large com. cup : St. Mary's, Hampton, Mids. { Coffee pot of 1720 : Noted by the Author.

Date.	Goldsmiths' Marks and Names.			Articles and Owners.
1704-5		Thos. Saddler	ent. 1701.	Rat-tail spoon : The Author's Collection.
,,		Henry Penstone	,, 1697.	Rat-tail spoon with wavy end to stem : Do.
,,		Jno. Cole	,, ,,	A toy porringer, usual spiral flutings : Mr. A. Bateman.
,,		Jno. East	,, ,,	A fluted porringer ; also (1720-1) two communion plates : St. Peter's, Hereford.
,,		Jno. Gibbon	,, 1700.	A plain cylindrical jar and cover : Mr. W. H. Fowle.
,,		Chas. Adam	,, 1702.	An octagonal caster, with moulded foot, the top chased with foliage over pierced trellis.
,,		Geo. Havers	,, 1697.	A plain circular trencher salt : Mr. Chisholm.
,,		Wm. Middleton	,, ,,	A salver on foot, with raised gadrooned border.
,,		Alex. Hudson	,, 1704.	A small bowl with one flat pierced handle.
,,		Wm. Spring	,, 1701.	A pair of dessert spoons, with wavy ends to stems.
,,		Jno. Cooke	,, 1699.	A plain helmet-shaped ewer : Mr. W. Boore.
,,		Ishml. Bone	,, ,,	A small octagonal box with hinged lid.
,,		Jno. Fletcher	,, 1700.	A plain cylindrical coffee-pot, with domed lid.
1705-6		Robt. Timbrell	,, 1697.	Fine " Monteith " bowl : late Capt. Reginald Peel.
,,		Wm. Fawdery	,, ,,	Service of communion plate : Holy Trinity Church, Hounslow.
,,		Samuel Pantin	,, 1701.	Standish : The Earl of Ilchester.
,,		Jon. Madden (see 1702)	,, 1702.	Tankard : The Author's Collection.
,,		Isaac Liger (see below)	,, 1704.	{ Bowl : Victoria and Albert Museum. { Porringer : Noted by the Author.
,,		Matthew Pickering	,, 1703.	{ Small mug : Mr. R. Meldrum. { Toy porringer : Messrs. Crichton Bros.
,,		Wm. Fleming	,, ,,	Tobacco box : Mr. G. Lambert ; also (n.d.l.) com. patens, King's Caple, Herefordshire.
,,		Thos. Spackman	,, 1700.	Large spoon, 10½ inches long ; St. George the Martyr, Holborn.
,,		Mathw. Lofthouse	,, 1705.	{ Com. flagon : S.S. Peter and Paul, Chingford. { Candlestick : Glovers' Guild, Carlisle.
,,		Saml. Wastell	,, 1701.	A double set of communion plate : St. George the Martyr, Holborn.
,,		Josh. Readshaw	,, 1697.	An originally plain tankard, spoiled by coarse modern chasing.
,, *		Isaac Liger	,, 1704.	Small salver, with raised moulded edge and drum foot.

* This mark, in a plain oblong punch, is on a communion paten at Lugwardine, Herefordshire.

DATE.	GOLDSMITHS' MARKS AND NAMES.				ARTICLES AND OWNERS.
1705-6		Jonah	Clifton	ent. 1703.	Rat-tail spoon, transitional wavy end.
,,		Jno.	Corosey	,, 1701.	Porringer, with usual spiral flutings: Mr. S. Phillips.
,,		Wm.	Warham	,, 1705.	Octagonal dredger, with trellis-like pierced top.
,,		Thos.	Corbet	,, 1699.	A short octagonal candlestick, with spreading base and gadrooned edge.
,,		Natl.	Lock	,, 1698.	Porringer: Mr. W. Old; also (1709) communion cup: Llansoy, Mon.
,,		John	Barnard	,, 1702.	Pair of tall candlesticks: Mr. Percy Macquoid.
1706-7		Jos.	Barbitt	,, 1703.	Two dozen rat-tail spoons: Hon. Soc. of the Inner Temple.
,,		Wm.	Matthew	,, 1700.	Transitional rat-tail spoon: The Author's Collection.
,,		Wm.	Juson	,, 1704.	Do. do.; one also at St. Mary's, Willesden.
,,		Timothy Ley		,, 1697.	Alms-dishes: All Hallows, Lombard Street, E.C.
,,		John	Backe	,, 1700.	Kettle and stand, with spirit lamp; Lord Swaythling.
,,		Launcelot Keatt		,, 1701.	Nutmeg grater: Messrs. Crichton Bros.
,,		Benj.	Pyne	,, 1697.	Bread dish: St. Edward the Confessor, Romford, Essex.
,,		Jacob	Margas	,, 1706.	Fine ewer: Trinity College, Cambridge; also four candlesticks (1708): Lord Carbery.
,,		Jno.	Ladyman	,, 1697.	Rat-tail table spoon, with ridged stem and rounded end.
,,		Louys	Cuny	,, 1703.	Do. do. do. do.
,,		Jno.	Abbot	,, 1706.	Plain octagonal bottle-shaped tea-caddy, with sliding bottom.
,,		Wm.	Spring	,, 1701.	Tankard: Sidney Sussex College, Cambridge.
,,		Jno.	Crutcher	,, 1706.	Octagonal snuffers tray, with raised gadrooned border.
,,		Wm.	Fordham	,, ,,	An etui, with ivory tablets, scissors and other implements.
,,		Name not traced.			Rat-tailed spoon, with marrow scoop stem.
1707-8		Danl.	Sleath	,, 1704.	Spirit lamp, with pierced stand: The Author's Collection.
,,		Wm.	Fleming	,, 1697.	Porringer, with usual spiral flutings: The Author's Collection.
,,		Thos.	Burridge	,, 1706.	Rat-tail spoons: St. Margaret's, Westminster.
,,		John	Leach	,, 1697.	A pair of toilet boxes: Sir Charles Welby, Bart.
,,		Anthy.	Nelme	,, ,,	Large alms-dish: St. Mary, Hampton, Mids.

Date.	Goldsmiths' Marks and Names.			Articles and Owners.
1707-8		Pierre	Le Cheaube ent. 1707.	Rat-tail spoon, ridge front, round end.
,,		Richard	Hutchinson ,, 1699.	Com. cups and patens: St. Mary's, Chelmsford.
,,		Philip	Roker ,, 1697.	Three-pronged forks, with wavy end to stems.
,,		Benj.	Harris ,, ,,	A plain tumbler cup.
,,		Chr.	Atkinson ,, 1707.	A wine taster, with one pierced handle.
,,		Phil.	Rainaud ,, ,,	An octagonal taper holder.
,,		Thos.	Fawler ,, ,,	An oblong inkstand, with sockets for two bottles.
,,		Jos.	Smith ,, ,,	A plain toy porringer, with roped band under lip.
,,		Samuel	Lee ,, 1701.	Monteith: Messrs. Crichton Bros.
,,		Benj.	Pyne ,, 1697.	Corporation maces: Liskeard.
,,		Saml.	Wastell ,, 1701.	Wine cups: Messrs. Crichton Bros.
,,		John	Backe ,, 1700.	Paten: Selborne, Hants.
1708-9		Mary	Matthew ,, ,,	A small octagonal wafer box.
,,		Jos.	Bird ,, 1697.	Pair of octagonal candlesticks: Mr. H. D. Ellis.
,,		Thos.	Farren ,, 1707.	Rat-tail spoon: Mr. Ince; also (1716-7) set of com. plate: Lucton, Herefordshire.
,,		Philip	Rolles, Jr. ,, 1705.	Communion flagon: Burford, St. Martin, Wilts.
,,		Wm.	Warham ,, 1703.	Scent canister: Windsor Castle.
,,		Lawrence Jones	,, 1697.	Rat-tail spoon with wavy end to stem: Mr. Ll. Davies.
,,		Chris.	Riley ,, ,,	Rat-tail spoon, with wavy end to stem.
,,		Alice	Sheene ,, 1700.	Porringer: Messrs. Spink; and (1707-8) alms-plate: Chedworth, Gloucestershire.
,,		Jno.	Read ,, 1704.	Alms-dish: All Hallows the Great.
,,		Jno.	Bodington ,, 1697.	Pair of communion flagons: St. Mary's, Bromley. One communion flagon: Boscomb, Wilts.
,,		Wm.	Fawdery ,, 1698.	Large ladle: Hon. Soc. of the Middle Temple.
,,		Henry	Greene ,, 1700.	Rat-tail spoon: Mr. Munsey.
,,		Anty.	Blackford ,, 1702.	Porringer, usual spiral flutings.

DATE.	GOLDSMITHS' MARKS AND NAMES.			ARTICLES AND OWNERS.
1708-9		Thos.	Wall	ent. 1708.	Mark registered 25th Sept., 1708.
,,		Jno.	Clifton	,, ,,	Do. do. 21st Oct., do.
,,		Richard	Clarke	,, ,,	Small fluted cup, without a handle.
,,		John	Chartier	,, 1698.	Rat-tail spoon : Mr. W. Boore. / Paten : Dean West, Wilts.
1709-10		Jno. W. Edw.	Stocker & Peacock }	,, 1705.	Communion paten : St. John the Evangelist, Stanmore, Mids.
,,		Jno.	Clifton (?)		A toy tankard : Messrs. Crichton.
,,		Thos.	Allen	,, 1697.	Two dozen rat-tail spoons : Hon. Soc. of the Middle Temple.
,,		Fras.	Turner	,, 1709.	A tiny transitional spoon—a toy, or perhaps a snuff spoon.
,,		Isr'l.	Pincking	,, 1697.	Rat-tail table spoon, ridge front rounded end to stem.
,,		Hy.	Greene	,, 1700.	Dessert spoons : Messrs. Crichton Bros.
,,		Laun.	Keatt	,, 1701.	Caster : Do. do.
,,		Jno.	Rand	,, 1704.	Communion flagon : St. Lawrence, Cowley, Mids.
,,		Simon	Pantin	,, 1701.	Small two-handled cup : Mr. G. Lambert ; also (1699) taper holder : Earl Bathurst.
,,		Phil.	Rolles	,, 1705.	Rat-tail spoon, dessert size.
,,		See 1702.			Oval tobacco box, with loose lid.
,,		Wm.	Francis	,, 1697.	A pair of candlesticks : Sir Charles Welby, Bart.
,,		Andrw.	Dalton	,, 1708.	An octagonal taper holder.
,,		Ebenezr. Roe		,, 1709.	A rat-tail table spoon.
,,		Thos.	Prichard	,, ,,	A child's feeding cup, with two handles.
,,		Hen.	Clarke	,, ,,	A pair of short octagonal candlesticks, with gadrooned bases.
,,		Jas.	Wethered	,, ,,	A pair of circular toilet boxes : The Gurney Collection.
,,		Richd.	Watts	,, 1710.	A rat-tail table spoon : The Octavius Morgan Collection.
1710-1		Thos.	Folkingham	,, 1706.	Octagonal tea caddy : The Author's Collection.
,,		Jno.	Smith	,, 1710.	Tumbler : Mr. Boore ; also (1704-5) com. cup : Driffield, Gloucester.
,,		Wm.	Hinton	,, 1704.	A pair of rat-tail spoons : Mr. W. H. Fowle.
,,		Geo.	Gillingham	,, 1703.	A small ink stand : Sir Frederick Currie, Bart.

DATE.	GOLDSMITHS' MARKS AND NAMES.		ARTICLES AND OWNERS.
1710-1	(ME)	Lewis Mettayer ent. 1700.	Plain rat-tail spoon, rounded stem : The Author's Collection.
,,	(CO)	Ed. Cornock ,, 1707.	Oval tobacco-box : Messrs. Crichton Bros.
,,	(WI)	Jno. Wisdom ,, 1704.	Communion paten on foot : Christ Church, Stepney.
,,	(PE)	Wm. Pearson ,, 1710.	A small circular salver on foot.
,,	(TW)	Wm. Twell ,, 1709.	A marrow scoop.
,,	(B.E)	Jas. Beschefer ,, 1704.	{ Trencher salt : The Author's Collection. Six three-pronged forks, with wavy ends.
,,	(MA)	Jacob Margas ,, 1706.	Candlesticks : Mr. Boore ; and (1719) : Col. Warde.
,,	(RO)	Jas. Rood ,, 1710.	A small mug : Mr. F. L. Fitzgerald.
,,	(KE)	Jno. Keigwin ,, ,,	A pair of rat-tail dessert spoons.
,,	(SL)	Gabriel Sleath ,, 1706.	Small spirit stand : Dr. Wilfred Harris.
,,	(JW)	Name not traced.	Toy porringer : Messrs. Crichton Bros.
,,	(MA)	Jacob Margas ,, ,,	Spoons : Do. do.
,,	(GO)	Jas. Goodwin ,, ,,	A small circular salver on foot.
,,	(RV)	Abm. Russell (?) ,, 1702.	An upright snuffers' stand on fixed tray.
,,	(Ke)	Robt. Keble ,, ,,	A large rat-tail hash spoon.
,,	(SH)	Jos. Sheene ,, ,,	A pair of rat-tail table spoons.
,,	(St)	Jno. Stockar ,, ,,	A small plain mug : Lord Dormer.
,,	(TR)	Wm. Truss ,, ,,	A rat-tail table spoon : Mr. W. H. Fowle.
,,	(Mo)	Hezk. Mountfort ,, 1711.	A small octagonal engraved box.
,,	(MA)	Isaac Malyn ,, 1710.	A pair of small rat-tail spoons, with wavy ends.
,,	(FL)	Jno. Flight ,, ,,	A small octagonal tray, with gadrooned edge.
1711-2	(PE)	Edmd. Pearce ,, 1704.	Communion cup, given 1616 to St. Michael's, Ashford.
,,	(GR)	Dorothy Grant ,, 1697.	Communion paten : Ulverston, Lancashire.
,,	(EA)	John East ,, ,,	Do. do. : Monkton Deverill, Wilts.
,,	(BA)	Joseph Barbitt ,, 1703.	Spirit lamp : Mr. Anthony White.

DATE.	GOLDSMITHS' MARKS AND NAMES.			ARTICLES AND OWNERS.
1711-2		John Porter	ent. 1698.	Communion cup : St. Julien, Southampton.
,,		Richard Williams	,, 1712.	Marks noted by the Author.
,,		Wm. Penstone	,, ,,	Bottle-shaped tea-caddy : The Author's Coll'n.
,,		Ed. Jennings	,, 1709.	Rat-tail spoon : Mr. Webster.
,,		Jno. Read	,, 1704.	Communion cup and paten : St. Mary-le-Strand.
,,		Lewis Mettayer (probably).		Taper holder : Holburne Museum.
,,		Nich. Clausen	ent. 1709.	Spoon : The Author's Collection ; also (1716) standish : Welbeck.
,,		Ed. Holaday	,, ,,	Salver : Mr. Reid ; flagons (1718-9) : Mercers' Company ; com. paten : Kingston.
,,		Aug. Courtauld	,, 1708.	Spoon : Mr. Parkes ; also (1727-8) two sets of com. plate : Madley, Herefordshire.
,,		Hen. Greene	,, 1700.	Com. paten on foot : St. Mary's, Ulverston, Lanc.
,,		Jno. Chamberlen	,, 1704.	Helmet-shaped ewer : General Meyrick.
,,		Isaac Dalton	,, 1711.	Rat-tail table-spoon : Dr. Propert.
,,		Wm. Matthew	,, ,,	Small circular bowl : Lord Dormer.
,,		Jonthn. Newton	,, ,,	Rat-tail table-spoon : Mr. W. H. Fowle.
1712-3		Thos. Sutton	,, ,,	Chamber candlestick : Mr. W. Boore.
,,		Jno. Rand	,, 1704.	Double set of communion plate : St. Michael's, Paternoster Royal.
,,		Seth Lofthouse	,, 1697.	Salver : Mr. Hawes ; also (1702) com. paten : Kington, Herefordshire.
,,		Isaac Dalton	,, 1711.	Three-pronged forks : Mr. J. A. Holms.
,,		Ed. Gibson	,, 1697.	Rat-tail spoon, transitional end : The Author's Collection.
,,		Wm. Lukin	, 1699.	Spirally-fluted porringer : The Author's Coll'n.
,,		Richd. Bayley	,, 1708.	Do. : Mr. Wills ; also (1716-7) paten cover : Dindor, Herefordshire.
,,		Richd. Raine	,, 1712.	Paten, dated 1716 : Ockley, Surrey.
,,		John Hobson	,, 1697.	Rat-tail spoon : Edkins Collection.
,,		Glover Johnson	,, 1712.	Oval, bottle-shaped tea-caddy : Viscount Clifden.
,,		Wm. Turbitt	,, 1710.	Hexagonal taper-holder : Captain Garnham.
,,		Richd. Williams	,, 1712.	Mark registered 11 April, 1712.

DATE.	GOLDSMITHS' MARKS AND NAMES.				ARTICLES AND OWNERS.
1712-3	Be	Thos.	Bevault	ent. 1712.	Mark registered 24 December, 1712.
,,	St	Jno. M.	Stockar	,, 1710.	Small salver on foot : Earl Amherst.
1713-4	MA	Samuel	Margas	,, 1706.	Lion tankard : The Ironmongers' Company.
,,	St	Ambrose Stevenson		,, ,,	Plain tankard, slightly domed top : Mr. H. D. Ellis.
,,	LO	Natl.	Locke	1698.	Pair of tankards : Gloucester Corporation.
,,	RO	Hugh	Roberts	,, 1697.	Tea-caddy : Mr. A. Trapnell.
,,	SL	Gabriel	Sleath	,, 1706.	Paten : St. Dunstan's, Stepney.
,,	PA	Mark	Paillet	,, 1698.	Rat-tail table-spoon : The Author's Collection.
,,	C	Henry	Collins	, ,,	Oval tobacco box, with cabled edge to cover.
,,	V·I	Edw.	Vincent	(?)	Helmet-shaped ewer : Trin. Coll., Oxford.
,,	LV	Jno.	Ludlow	,, 1713.	Plain tumbler : Sir Charles Fraser, Bart.
,,	RO	Gundry	Roode	,, 1709.	Porringer, usual spiral flutings.
,,	MA	Thos.	Mann	,, 1713.	Oval tray, with fluted border : Mr. A. Bateman.
,,	EW	Thos.	Ewesdin	,, ,,	A tumbler : Messrs. Christie.
,,	LO	Wm.	Looker	,, ,,	Plain tankard, reeded foot and domed top.
,,	BA	John	Bathe	,, 1700.	Plate : Mr. Boore ; also (1711-2) com. paten : Brampton Abbots, Hereford.
,,	IV	Wm.	Juson	,, 1704.	Marrow scoop : Messrs. Crichton Bros.
,,	Lo	Seth	Lofthouse	,, 1697.	Communion paten : Brantingham, Yorks.
1714-5	TB	Robt. Timbrell & Benj. Bentley }		,, ,,	Saucepan : Hon. Soc. of the Inner Temple.
,,	TA	David	Tanqueray	,, 1713.	Three pronged fork : The Victoria and Albert Museum.
,,	Fa	Joseph	Fainell	,, 1710.	Tea-caddy : Messrs. Crichton Bros.
,,	BE	Thomas Bevault		,, 1712.	Communion flagon : Ropley, Hants.
,,	Io	Glover	Johnson	,, ,,	Chased octagonal tea-caddy.
,,	BO	Mich'l	Boult	,, ,,	Pair of octagonal baluster-shaped candlesticks.
,,	CO	Name not traced.			Sugar-caster : Messrs. Crichton Bros.

DATE.	GOLDSMITHS' MARKS AND NAMES.			ARTICLES AND OWNERS.
1714-5		Wm. John	England & Vane } ent. 1714.	Communion flagon: Nettleton, nr. Chippenham.
,,		Sam	Welder ,, ,,	An etui, containing a small spoon, tablets, etc.
,,		Rich'd	Green ,, 1703.	Tankard: Mr. Samuel Deane.
,,		Jno.	Holland ,, 1711.	Rat-tail spoon: Mr. H. D. Ellis.
,,		Saml.	Hitchcock ,, 1712.	Rat-tail dessert spoon: Mr. J. Hemingway.
,,		Saml.	Welder ,, 1714.	Plain octagonal muffineer, with small vase surmounting pierced top.
,,		Philip	Brush ,, 1707.	Fluted porringer: From the Temple-Frere Coll'n.
,,		Josiah	Daniel ,, 1714.	Mark registered 21 Feb., 1714.
,,		Nathl.	Bland ,, ,,	Do. do. 10 June, do.
,,		Richd.	Gines ,, ,,	Rat-tail spoon: Mr. B. Jefferis.
,,		Henry	Beesley ,, ,,	Do. do. : Mr. M. Falk.
,,		Henry	Miller ,, ,,	Plain oval snuff-box or wafer-box.
1715-6		Thos.	Allen ,, 1697.	Pepper-caster: Lord Swaythling.
,,		David	Killmaine ,, 1715.	Communion paten: St. Michael's, Ashford.
,,		Fras.	Plymley ,, ,,	Two communion cups and two alms-dishes: St. Clement's, East Cheap.
,,		John	Corporon ,, 1716.	A pair of rat-tail dessert-spoons.
,,		Danl.	Sleamaker ,, 1704.	Octagonal caster: From the Temple-Frere Coll'n.
,,		Humph.	Payne ,, 1701.	Rat-tail spoons: Mr. Peters; also (1721) com. cup: Middleton.
,,		Petley	Ley ,, 1715.	A pap-boat: The Day Collection.
,,		Thos.	Port ,, 1713.	Fluted porringer, usual spiral flutings.
,,		Richard	Greene ,, 1703.	{ Candlesticks: Mr. J. A. Holms. { Do. : Messrs. Crichton Bros.
,,		Edward	Jones ,, 1697.	Salver: Noted by the Author.
,,		Josiah Daniel (see 1714)	,, 1714.	Tea-pot: Messrs. Crichton Bros.
,,		Jas.	Goodwin ,, 1710.	Toy porringer: Mr. S. Phillips.
,,		Danl.	Yerbury ,, 1715.	Oblong snuffers' tray, with rounded corners.
,,		Geo.	Lambe ,, 1713.	Rat-tail dessert spoon.

DATE.	GOLDSMITHS' MARKS AND NAMES.			ARTICLES AND OWNERS.
1715-6		Robt. Hill	ent. 1716.	Mark registered 13 January, 1716.
,,		Thos. Holland	,, 1707.	Small bowl : Messrs. M. & S. Lyon.
1716-7		John Holland	,, 1711.	Rat-tail table-spoon : The Day Collection.
,,		Nat. Roe	,, 1710.	Do. do. : Mr. E. Heron-Allen.
,,		Jos. Clare	,, 1713.	Com. cup and alms-dish : St. Paul's, Shadwell.
,,		Thos. Mason	,, 1716.	Pair of candlesticks : Mr. H. D. Ellis.
,,		Paul Lamerie	,, 1712.	Sauce-boat : Mr. Boore ; also (1712) pair of octagonal salt-cellars : Mr. A. Bateman ; (1717-8) covered cup : The Duke of Devonshire ; and two-handled gold cup and cover : Berkeley Castle.
,,		Thos. Ewesdin	,, 1713.	Com. patens : St. Nicholas, Gloucester.
,,		Jas. Seabrook	,, 1714.	A pair of rat-tail table-spoons.
,,		Petley Ley	,, 1715.	Mug with scroll handle : Mr. A. S. Marsden Smedley.
,,		Phillip Robinson	,, 1713.	Pair of soup tureens : Mr. S. J. Phillips.
,,		Joseph Clare (see above and 1719)	,, ,,	Trencher salt : Messrs. Garrard & Co.
,,		Anty. Nelme	,, 1697.	Sauce-boat : Viscount Clifden.
,,		Geo. Lambe	,, 1713.	Octagonal pepper caster : Captain Garnham.
,,		Wm. Bellassyse	,, 1716.	Taper-holder : Viscount Clifden : also (1720) com. cup : Cross Canonby, Cumb.
,,		David Green	,, 1701.	Candlestick : Cambridge Plate Exhibition.
,,		Jno. Guerrie	,, 1717.	Rat-tail table-spoon.
,,		Danl. Cunningham	,, 1716.	Mark registered 11 Feb., 1716.
,,		Jos. Bell	,, ,,	A cylindrical tankard, with domed top.
,,		Richd. Edwards	,, ,,	An octagonal bottle-shaped tea-caddy : Lady Page Turner.
,,		Jas. Morson	,, ,,	Pair of rat-tail table-spoons.
,,		Wm. Pearson	,, 1717.	Mark registered 21 May, 1717.
1717-8		Jas. (?) Fraillon	,, 1710.	Tazza-shaped covered paten or ciborium on foot : St. Mary's, Ealing.
,,		Robt. Kempton	,, ,,	Lemon strainer : S. Kensington Museum.
,,		Wm. Penstone	,, 1717.	Porringer, spiral flutings, repoussé shield in front.

Date.	Goldsmiths' Marks and Names.			Articles and Owners.
1717-8	**Wa**	Joseph Ward	ent. 1717.	Tea-caddy : Messrs. Crichton Bros.
,,	**BA**	Edward Barnet	,, 1715.	Sugar caster : Do. do.
,,	**IA**	Chas. Jackson (see 1718 below)	,, 1714.	Rat-tail dessert-spoons : Do.
,,	**PE**	William Pearson (see 1716)	,, 1710.	Do. do. do. : noted by the Author.
,,	**RI**	Isaac Riboulau	,, 1714.	{ Rat-tail table-spoon : Sir J. T. Firbank. { Octagonal tea-pot (1718) : Mr. J. A. Holms.
,,	**BA**	Edw. Barnet	,, 1715.	Rat-tail dessert-spoon.
,,	**RO**	Phil. Robinson	,, 1713.	An oblong snuff box, rounded corners cabled band.
,,	**HO**	Thos. Holland	,, 1707.	Rat-tail spoon; also (1713-4) paten : St. Peter's, Hereford.
,,	**Ha**	Jno. Harris	,, 1716.	Pair of octagonal baluster-shaped candlesticks.
,,	**ST**	Wm. Street	,, 1717.	Snuffers and stand on octagonal tray.
,,	**SM**	Jas. Smith	,, 1718.	Repoussé and chased hook for chatelaine.
,,	**SH**	Thos. Shermer	,, 1717.	A plain tumbler.
,,	**WI**	Starling Wilford	,, ,,	A large watch-case : Mr. W. Boore.
,,	**HA**	Paul Hanet	,, ,,	Mounts of shagreen etui.
,,	**BU**	Thos. Burridge	,, ,,	A shaving pot.
,,	**BE**	Wm. Bellamy	,, ,,	Circular salver, with plain raised edge.
,,	**We**	Sam. Welder	,, ,,	Salt spoon : The Day Collection.
1718-9	**St**	Ambrose Stevenson	,, 1706.	Small circular salver on foot : Mr. Hamilton.
,,	**PE**	Wm. Petley	,, 1717.	Do. do. do : Mr. R. G. Hussey.
,,	**HA**	Paul Hanet	,, 1715.	Rat-tail spoon.
,,	**Fa**	John Farnell	,, 1714.	Spoon-tray : Lord Swaythling.
,,	**IA**	Chas. Jackson	,, ,,	Rat-tail spoon; also (1714) paten : Betchworth, Surrey.
,,	**PA**	Thos. Parr	,, 1697.	Snuffers and upright hexagonal snuffers' stand : The Author's Collection.
,,	**BE**	Geo. Beale	,, 1713.	Lemon strainer : Messrs. Carrington.
,,	**Ho**	Ed. Holaday	,, 1709.	Large flagons, presented 1718 : Mercers' Company.

DATE.	GOLDSMITHS' MARKS AND NAMES.			ARTICLES AND OWNERS.
1718-9		David Tanqueray ent. 1713. (see 1714)		Small tea-pot : Mr. W. M. Acworth.
,,		Henry Clarke ,, 1709. (see 1709)		Marrow scoop : Mr. Llewellyn Davies.
,,		Thomas Mason ,, 1716.		Mug : Messrs. Crichton Bros.
,,		Thomas Tearle ,, 1719. (see 1719 below)		Tea-pot : Do. do.
,,		John Keigwin ,, 1710.		Mug : Do. do.
,,		John Sanders ,, 1717.		Octagonal trencher salts : The Author's Coll'n.
,,		Wm. Fawdery ,, 1697. (as 1705)		Flagon : St. Mary Bow.
,,		Wm. Darkeratt ,, 1718.		Plain octagonal sugar casters : Merton College, Oxford.
,,		Hugh Saunders ,, ,,		Octagonal candlestick of baluster form.
,,		John Bignell ,, ,,		A needle-case, engraved with monogram C L.
,,		Geo. Gillingham ,, ,,		Mark registered 25 September, 1718.
,,		Jno. Millington ,, ,,		A rat-tail dessert-spoon.
,,		Jno. Lingard ,, ,,		Mark registered 28 June, 1718.
,,		Do. do. (for O.S.) ,, 1719.		Do. do. 10 June, 1719,
1719-20		Thos. Tearle ,, ,, (see 1718-9)		Alms-plate : Corsham, Wilts.
,,		Thos. Langford ,, 1715.		Com. cup : St. Mary, Bedfont, Mids.
,,		Réné Hudell ,, 1718.		Helmet-shaped milk-jug : Mr. F. D. Wingfield.
,,		Wm. Spackman ,, 1714.		Salver : Messrs. Carrington ; also (1717-8) com. cup : Llanwarne, Herefordshire.
,,		Geo. Boothby ,, 1720.		A plain sauce-boat : Mr. R. N. Crossley.
,,		John White ,, 1719.		Pair of fluted dishes : Mr. Chester-Master.
,,		John le Sage ,, 1718.		Half-a-dozen three-pronged forks.
,,		Benj. Blakeley ,, 1715.		A plain snuff or wafer-box.
,,		Wm. Paradise ,, 1718.		Communion cup : Lazonby, Cumb.
,,		Lawrence (?) Jones ,, 1697.		{ Porringer : Mr. Geo. Dunn. { Mug : Messrs. Crichton Bros.

DATE.	GOLDSMITHS' MARKS AND NAMES.		ARTICLES AND OWNERS.
1719-20		John Gibbons ent. 1700.	Tea-caddy : Messrs. Crichton Bros.
,,		Thomas Shermer ,, 1717.	Marks noted by the Author.
,,		Wm. Darkeratt ,, 1718. (see 1718)	Salvers on foot : Messrs. Crichton Bros.
,,		Edw. Barrett ,, 1715.	Salver of the Mesham family, Pontrhyffydd, Denbigh.
,,		James Smith ,, 1718.	Rat-tail gravy spoon : Messrs. Crichton Bros.
,,		Gabriel Sleath ,, 1706.	Communion paten : Damerham, Wilts.
,,		Thos. Allen ,, 1697. (2nd Mark)	Straining spoon : St. Margaret's, Westminster.
,,		Thos. Morse ,, 1718.	Circular salver on foot : Mr. B. McKay.
,,		Edw. Gibbon ,, 1719.	Rat-tail table spoon : Mr. Davison.
,,		Saml. Smith ,, ,,	Sugar caster from the Londesborough Collection.
,,		Jos. Steward ,, ,,	Cylindrical tankard, moulded foot and band, domed top.
,,		Jos. Clare, as 1716-7.	Alms-dish : St. Magnus the Martyr, London Bridge.
,,		Chris. Gerrard ent. 1719.	Plain octagonal caster.
,,		Edmd. Hickman ,, ,,	Rat-tail table-spoons.
,,		Wm. Pearson ,, ,,	Mark for restored Old Standard, registered 24 Jan., 1720.
,,		Geo. Brydon ,, 1720.	Chased sugar bowl : The Day Collection.
,,		Thos. Gladwin ,, 1719.	Rat-tail dessert-spoons.
,,		Starling Wilford ,, 1720.	Mark for restored Old Standard, registered 30 Jan., 1720.
,,		John Lingard ,, 1719.	Three-pronged forks : Messrs. Crichton Bros.
,,		John Jones ,, ,,	Rat-tail table-spoon.
,,		Paul Hanet ,, 1717.	Oval snuff box : Mr. Hawes.
,,		Edwd. Hall ,, 1720.	Mark for restored Old Standard, registered 14 Jan., 1720.
,,		Bowles Nash ,, ,,	Long rat-tail gravy spoon.
,,		——— Hodgkis ,, 1719.	A pint mug or tankard without lid.
,,		Phyllis Phillip ,, 1720.	Mounts of circular horn box.

DATE.	GOLDSMITHS' MARKS AND NAMES.			ARTICLES AND OWNERS.
1719-20	FA	Joseph Fainell	ent. 1710.	Inkstand: Sir Michael Hicks Beach.
,,	PP	Phyllis Fhillip	,, 1720.	Small cylindrical bodkin or needle case.
,,	RG	Richard Gines	,, ,,	Porringer, with shaped shield in front.
,,	WS	Wm. Scarlett (O.S. as before 1697)	,, ,,	Small oval tray, with fluted border: Mrs. Budd.
,,	RO	Mary Rood	,, ,,	Engraved cover of tablets for memoranda.
,,	CG	Christr. Gerrard	,, ,,	Mark for restored Old Standard, registered 2 July, 1720.
1720-1	EW	John Edwards	,, 1697.	Com. flagon: St. Margaret, Uxbridge.
,,	EV	Thos. Evesdon (see 1721-2)	,, 1713.	This mark is accompanied by the crowned leopard's head as 1721-2. Mug: Mrs. E. H. Goddard.
,,	WL	William Looker	,, ,,	Candlesticks: Messrs. Crichton Bros.
,,	LA	Paul Lamerie	,, 1712.	Tazza: Mr. A. Marsden Smedley.
,,	CR	Paul Crespin	,, 1720.	Shallow saucepan, ebony handle.
,,	LA	Geo. Lambe (widow of)	,, 1713.	Three-pronged forks: Messrs. Crichton Bros.
,,	WF	William Fawdery	,, 1720.	Small saucepan: Mr. Anthony White.
,,	M·I	Henry Millar	,, ,,	Spoon: Do. do.
,,	FO	Thomas Folkingham	,, ,,	Plate: Messrs. Crichton Bros.
,,	LE	Petley Ley (see 1716)	,, 1715.	Coffee-pot: Do. do.
,,	FA	John Fawdery	,, 1697.	Com. flagon and paten: St. Mary's, Harefield.
,,	MC	Matt. Cooper	,, ,,	Two-handled cup and cover: The Marquess Townshend.
,,	TA	Ann Tanqueray	,, 1720.	Sugar caster: The Day Collection.
,,	CI	Chas. Jackson	,, 1714.	Small plain salver: Mr. L. T. Crossley.
,,	HO	Sarah Holaday	,, 1719.	Plain hexagonal taper-holder.
,,	AP	Hugh Arnett & Ed. Pocock	,, ,,	Octagonal coffee-pot, with octagonal spout and lid.
,,	DK	Name not traced.		Alms-dish: St. Magnus, London Bridge.
,,	Ba	Thos. Bamford	,, ,,	Oval tobacco box: Mr. L. Hutchinson.

DATE.	GOLDSMITHS' MARKS AND NAMES.				ARTICLES AND OWNERS.
1720-1		Jno.	Bromley	ent. 1720.	Snuff or powder box, with hinged lid.
,,		Benj.	Watts	,, ,,	Table spoon, ridge in front of stem, round end and double drop at back of bowl, known as the "Hanoverian pattern".
,,		John	Bignell	,. ,,	Mounts of shagreen etui : Mr. Caldwell.
,,		John	Betts	,, ,,	Watch-case : Mr. W. Boore.
,,		Michl.	Boult.	,, ,,	Mark for restored Old Standard, registered 20 June, 1720.
,,		Saml.	Hitchcock	,, ,,	Do. do. do. 19 October, 1720.
,,		Thos.	Sadler	,, ,,	A circular salver on foot : The Day Collection.
,,		Geo.	Boothby	,, ,,	Bottle-shaped tea-caddy : do.
,,		Phil.	Rolles	,, ,,	Octagonal taper-holder.
,,		Jno.	Hopkins	,, ,,	New standard mark, registered January, 1720.
,,		Do.	do.	,, ,,	Old do. do. do.
,,		Saml.	Welder	,, ,,	Do. do. do. 28 July, 1720.
,,		*John	Penfold (probably)	,, ,,	Alms-dish : Witney, Oxfordshire.
,,		Fras.	Turner	,, ,,	Lady's tablet case.
,,		Jas.	Morson	,, ,,	Toy porringer : Mr. Crichton.
,,		Jno.	Millington	,, ,,	Mark for restored Old Standard, registered 23 June, 1720.
,,		Thos.	Folkingham	,, ,,	Snuff-box : Mr. G. Widdowson.
,,		John	Ludlow	,, ,,	Taper-holder : Mr. Hardcastle.
,,		Thos.	Mann	,, ,,	O.S. mark registered 1 July, 1720.
,,		Ed.	Jennings	,, ,,	Lady's thimble-case : Mrs. Wintle.
,,		Do.	do. (O.S.)	,, ,,	Thimble to do. : do. Spoons (1725) : Mrs. E. H. Goddard.
,,		Richd.	Watts	,. ,,	Cylindrical tankard, domed top.
,,		Name not traced.			From impressions supplied to the Author.
,,		J.	Burridge	,, ,,	Do. do. do.
,,		Jno.	Barnard	,, ,,	Do. do. do.
,,		A'brose Stevenson		,, ,,	Salver on foot : Mr. Deacon.

* Old Standard Mark from before 1697 re-used. See also Supplementary Table XIIIA. (p. 86, *supra*).

DATE.	GOLDSMITHS' MARKS AND NAMES.			ARTICLES AND OWNERS.
1720-1	🔲	Edw. Feline	ent. 1720.	Snuff-box: Mr. Carr (see also 1722 on following page).
,,	🔲	Jas. Seabrook	,, ,,	From impressions supplied to the Author.
,,	🔲	Jos. Steward	,, ,,	Do. do. do.
,,	🔲	Henry Miller	,, ,,	Do. do. do.
,,	🔲	Geo. Squire	,, ,,	Do. do. do.
,,	🔲	Gabl. Sleath	,, ,,	Caster: Mr. W. Smith; coffee-pot (1723): Dr. Davies.
,	🔲	Phil. Roker (N.S.)	,, .,	Mark registered 7 April, 1720.
,,	🔲	Do. do. (O.S.)	,, ,,	Do. do. 17 Aug., do.
,,	🔲	Geo. Brydon	,, ,,	Hanoverian pattern spoon.
,,	🔲	Hen. Greene	,, ,,	Meat skewer, with ring at end.
,,	🔲	Edwd. Pearce	,, ,,	Cover of small toilet-box.
,,	🔲	Jno. Brumhall	,, 1721.	From impressions supplied to the Author.
,,	🔲	Jno. Newton	,, 1720.	Do. do. do.
,,	🔲	Wm. Matthew	,, ,,	A pair of moulded octagonal salt-cellars.
,,	🔲	Saml. Lee	,, ,,	A "skittle-ball" tea-pot, with chased band.
,,	🔲	Henry Clarke	,, ,,	Marrow scoop: Edkins Collection.
,,	🔲	Jno. Corosey	,, ,,	From rubbings supplied to the Author.
,,	🔲	Jno. Farnell	,, ,,	Do. do. do.
,,	🔲	Glover Johnson	,, ,,	Small circular cachou or patch-box.
,,	🔲	Wm. Looker	,, ,,	O.S. mark registered 6 July, 1720.
,,	🔲	Phil. Rainaud	,, ,,	Do. do. 26 Oct., do.
1721-2	🔲	Ed. Vincent (probably)	,, ,,	Communion cups: Orton, Westmor.
,,	🔲	Isaac Liger	,, ,,	Oval hot-water jug: Woods' Hotel.
,,	🔲	Henry Jay	,, ,,	Salver: Mr. G. Lambert; also alms-plate of 1716, dated 1718: Hunton, Kent.
,,	🔲	Jos. Clare	,, ,,	Table-spoons, Hanoverian pattern.
,,	🔲	M. Arnett & Ed. Pocock	,, ,,	Salver: Mr. W. Dale; also (1724) com. cup: Barmston, Yorks.

DATE.	GOLDSMITHS' MARKS AND NAMES.			ARTICLES AND OWNERS.
1721-2		Simon Pantin	ent. 1717.	Two-handled cup : Paper-stainers' Company.
,,		John Wisdome (probably)	,, 1720.	Paten on foot, dated 1721 : Pulham, Dorset.
,,		Jane Lambe	,, 1719.	From impressions supplied to the Author.
,,		Ed. Turner	,, 1720.	Small caster : Mr. I. Cathcart White.
,,		Abm. Buteux	,, 1721.	Candlesticks : The Duke of Portland.
,,		Saml. Lee	,, ,,	A circular bowl, matching the tea-pot of 1720.
,,		Geo. Wickes	,, ,,	Plain bottle-shaped tea-caddy : The Day Collection.
,,		Hugh Spring	,, ,,	N.S. mark, registered 22 December, 1721.
,,		Mary Rood	,, ,,	Table-spoon : Hanoverian pattern.
,,		Gundry Roode	,, ,,	Cream-jug chased with figures and foliage : The Marquess Townshend.
,,		Wm. Truss	,, ,,	(of Reading) N.S. mark, registered 22 Sept., 1721.
,,		Do. do.	,, ,,	Do. do. O.S. do. do. do.
,,		Name not traced.		Plate : Messrs. Crichton Bros.
,,		Sarah Holaday (see 1720-1)	,, 1719.	Noted by the Author.
,,		Joseph Bell ?	,, 1716.	Cup : Messrs. Crichton Bros.
,,		Thos. Evesdon (see 1720-1)	,, 1713.	Mug : Mr. Harvey Hadden.
,,		Edmund Pearce	,, 1720.	Pair of bowls : Messrs. Crichton Bros.
,,		Simon Pantin (see above)	,, 1717.	Jug with scroll handle : Victoria and Albert Museum.
1722-3		Bowles Nash	,. 1721.	Alms-dish, dated 1723 : St. Margaret's, Westminster.
,,		Edward Feline (see 1720)	,, 1720.	Salver : Messrs. Crichton Bros.
,,		Jno. le Sage	,, 1718.	Table-spoons, Hanoverian pattern : Mr. D. Gray.
,,		Ed. Wood	,, ,,	Salver, with plain raised moulded border.
,,		Benj. Pyne	as 1706.	Communion cup : Firbank, Westmorland.
,,		Name not traced.		Noted by the Author.
,,		Anth. Nelme	as 1716.	Monteith : Clare Coll., Cambridge.
,,		Edw. Jennings	ent. 1720.	Rat-tail spoons : Mr. H. D. Ellis.

Date.	Goldsmiths' Marks and Names.			Articles and Owners.
1722-3	Jno.	Bignell	ent. 1720.	Com. cup. : Holy Trinity, Minories.
,,	Natl.	Gulliver	,, 1722.	Bread platter : Howden, Yorks.
,,	David	Willaume	,, 1720.	Tankard, moulded band and base, domed top.
,,	Jno.	Eckford	,, ,,	Circular toilet-box.
,,	Isaac	Riboulau	,, ,,	Plain bulbous milk-jug.
,,	Pere	Pilleau	,, ,,	Engraved snuff-box : Mr. Lascelles Carr.
,,	Edw.	Wood	,, ,,	Small taper-holder : Messrs. Spink.
,,	Jas.	Gould	,, 1722.	From a rubbing supplied to the Author.
,,	Nich.	Clausen	,, 1720.	Do. do. do. do.
,,	Phil.	Robinson	,, 1723.	A child's christening mug.
,,	Phil.	Goddard	,, ,,	N.S. mark, registered 23 January, 1723.
,,	Do.	do.	,, ,,	O.S. do. do. do.
,,	Natl.	Gulliver	,, ,,	Milk-jug : Mr. Winstone ; also (1723-4) com. flagon : Weston-under-Penyard, Herefords.
,,	Isaac	Cornasseau	,, 1722.	N.S. mark, registered 20 July, 1722.
,,	Do.	do.	,, ,,	O.S. do. do. do. do.
,,	Michl.	Nicholl	,, 1723.	N.S. do. do. 4 April, 1723.
,,	John	Clarke	,, 1722.	An etui : Mrs. Bromage.
,,	Geo.	Young	,, ,,	Vinaigrette : Mr. A. Thomas.
,,	Jno.	Clarke	,, ,,	Patch-box : Mr. R. Nicholl.
,,	Jas.	Fraillon	,, 1723.	Watch case : Mr. F. R. Hill.
,,	Ed.	Dymond	,, 1722.	Snuff-box : Mr. L. Bennett.
,,	Joseph	Adams ?	,, ,,	Marrow scoop : Mr. A. J. Grimes.
,,	John le Sage		,, 1718.	(Britannia standard marks) : Small tray : Mr. A. S. Marsden Smedley.
,,	Philip	Brush ?	,, 1707.	Alms dish : Alton, Hants.
,,	Isaac	Cornasseau	,, 1722.	Octagonal coffee-pot : Messrs. Crichton Bros.

DATE.	GOLDSMITHS' MARKS AND NAMES.			ARTICLES AND OWNERS.
1722-3		Richard Watts	ent. 1720.	Tea-pot : Messrs. Crichton Bros.
,,		Ed. Dymond	,, 1722.	Small hand-bell, ivory handle : Mrs. Shaw.
,,		Jeremiah King	,, 1723.	N.S. mark, registered 11 Sept., 1723.
,,		Do. do.	,, ,,	O.S. do. do. do.
,,		Wm. Soame	,, ,,	N.S. do. 19 June, do.
,,		Do. do.	,, ,,	O.S. do. do. do.
,,		John Jones	,, ,,	N.S. do. 27 March, do.
,,		Do. do.	,, ,,	O.S. do. do. do.
,,		Henry Dell	,, 1722.	A baby's coral : Mrs. Hammond.
,,		Wm. Owen	,, 1723.	Neck mount and cover of crystal bottle.
,,		John Gibbons	,, ,,	A waist buckle : Mrs. Budd.
,,		Meshach Godwin	,, 1722.	Paten on foot : St. Helens, York.
1723-4		John East	,, 1721.	Large tankard : Armourers' Co.
,,		Thos. Farrer	,, 1720.	Alms-dish : S.S. Peter & Paul, S. Weald, Essex.
,,		Thos. Morse	,, ,,	Cylindrical half-pint mug, with moulded band and base.
,,		Aug. Courtauld	,, 1708.	Two-handled cup : Hon. Soc. Inner Temple.
,,		Jnthn. Madden	,, 1702.	Paten on four feet : St. Lawrence, Cowley.
,,		Edw. Peacock	,, 1710.	Alms-dish : St. Mary, Hadley Monken.
,,		Richd. Scarlett	,, 1723.	A helmet-shaped ewer : Sir Charles Welby, Bart.
,,		John Chartier	,, ,,	Cylindrical tankard, domed top : Col. Fitzgerald.
,,		Arte Dicken	,, 1720.	A plain toddy ladle : General Meyrick.
,,		Paul Lamerie	,, 1712.	Small waiter : Lord Swaythling.
,,		John Jones	,, 1719.	Small milk-jug : Mrs. J. Bird.
,,		Edw. Gibbons	,, 1723.	A small square tray with incurved corners : The Day Collection.
,,		Wm. Spackman	,, 1720.	A small globular tea-pot : Madame de Falbe.
,,		Jnthn. Robinson	,, 1723.	A pair of table-spoons, Hanoverian pattern.

DATE.	GOLDSMITHS' MARKS AND NAMES.			ARTICLES AND OWNERS.
1723-4	I·B	John Bignell ent. 1718. (see 1720 and 1722)		Mark noted by the Author.
,,	G·S	Geo. Squire ,, 1720.		Pair of bowls : St. Albans Corporation.
,,	T·W	Thos. Wall (?) ,, 1708.		Pair of waiters : Messrs. Crichton Bros.
,,	Di	Arte Dicken ? or ,, 1720. John Diggle ,, 1697.		Plate : Do. do.
,,	I·M	John Motherby (?) ,, 1718.		Box : Do. do.
,,	SH	Sam Hitchcock ,, 1712.		Rat-tail gravy spoon : Do. do.
,,	FA	Wm. Fawdery ? ,, 1720.		Communion plate : Stourton, Wilts.
,,	I·R	Jnthn. Robinson ,, 1723.		A helmet-shaped milk ewer ; Mr. H. Mitford.
,,	RE	Richd. Edwards ,, ,,		An octagonal trencher salt, with spreading base.
,,	O	John Owing ,, 1724.		A pair of plain shoe buckles : Mr. F. Martin.
,,	ED PI	John Edwards & Geo. Pitches ,, 1723.		Three rat-tail spoons : Mr. W. Boore.
1724-5	R·B	Richd. Bigge ,, 1700. (probably)		Small porringer : S. Kensington Museum.
,,	S·C	Richd. Scarlett ,, 1719.		(N.S.) Rat-tail spoon : Mr. E. Heron-Allen.
,,	DT	David Tanqueray ,, 1720.		Half a dozen plain dinner plates.
,,	AB	Abm. Buteux ,, 1721.		A porringer, spiral flutings and repoussé shield.
,,	MG	Meshach Godwin , 1722.		Communion cup, dated 1724 : St. Thomas, Cliffe, Lewes.
,,	HP	Humphy. Payne ,, 1720.		Communion flagons: St. Martins-cum-Gregory, York; and (1729) Brockhampton, Hereford.
,,	PC	Paul Crespin ,, ,,		A pair of rat-tail dessert spoons.
,,	I·M	Jacob Margas ,, ,,		A coffee pot (truncated cone) with domed top.
,,	DA	Fleurant David ,, 1724.		Two-handled cup and cover, chased with masks and foliage in relief (1725), given by King Geo. I. to his god-son, George Townshend, son of Charles Lord Viscount Townshend, born 29 February, 1724.
,,	FD	Do. do. ,, ,,		
,,	M	Mathw. Lofthouse ,, 1721.		A pair of shoe buckles : Mrs. Owen.
,,	ED	John Edwards ,, 1724.		A sugar caster : The Day Collection.
,,	EC	Edw. Conen ,, ,,		A toy porringer and saucer.
,,	Io	John Jones ,, 1723.		A watch case converted into a tobacco box.
,,	WD	W'sc'mbe Drake ,, 1724.		A small oval box, with threaded lid.
,,	WH	John White ,, ,,		On Britannia-standard bowl : Mr. C. Ince

DATE.	GOLDSMITHS' MARKS AND NAMES.	ARTICLES AND OWNERS.
1724-5	Jas. Burne ent. 1724.	N.S. mark, registered 4 March, 1724.
,,	Do. do. ,, ,,	O.S. do. do. do.
,,	Saml. Hutton ,, ,,	N.S. do. do. 7 Oct., do.
,,	Do. do. ,, ,,	O.S. do. do. 7 Jan., 1725.
,,	Ed. Peacock ,, ,,	Plain salver on foot.
,,	John Owing ,, ,,	A pair of small three-pronged forks.
,,	Peter Simon ,, 1725.	N.S. mark, registered 14 May, 1725.
,,	John Gibbons ,, 1723.	Large-dish: The Day Collection.
,,	Aug. Courtauld ,, 1708.	Toy tea-set: Sir Redvers Buller.
,,	Josiah Daniel ,, 1714.	Tea-spoons noted by the Author.
,,	Peter Simon ,, 1725.	O.S. mark, registered 14 May, 1725.
,,	John Motherby ,, 1718.	Small toilet box: Mrs. S. Widdowson.
,,	John Pero ,, 1717.	Punch ladle: Mr. H. Middleton.
,,	Jnthn. Newton ,, 1718.	Oval snuff-box: Capt. F. Powell.
1725-6	Abm. de Oliveyra ,, 1725.	Neck-mount and lid of scent bottle.
,,	John Eckfourd ,, ,,	Table-spoons, Hanoverian pattern.
,,	Josh. Healy ,, ,,	N.S. mark, registered 19 August, 1725.
,,	Do. do. ,, ,,	O.S. do. do. do. do.
,,	Robt. Lucas ,, 1726.	A small globular tea-pot: The Marquess Townshend.
,,	Harvey Price ,, ,,	Marrow scoop, with engraved ornament in centre.
,,	John Gorsuch ,, ,,	Plain coffee-pot, domed top: Mr. Chisholm.
,,	Wm. Toone ,, 1725.	Table-spoons: Mr. H. D. Ellis.
,,	Jos. Bird ,, 1724.	Punch ladle: The Drane Collection.
,,	Hugh Saunders ,, 1718.	Pair of flagons: St. Martin, Ruislip, Middlesex.
,,	Paul Hanet ,, 1721.	Spoon, presented by Paul Hanet, St. John, Westminster.
,,	Fras. Garthorne ,, ,,	(As before 1697). Two com. flagons: St. John's, Wapping.

DATE.	GOLDSMITHS' MARKS AND NAMES.			ARTICLES AND OWNERS.
1725-6		Jacob Margas ent. 1720. (see 1724)		Salver: Messrs. Crichton Bros.
,,		Starling Wilford (?) ,, ,, (see 1728 and 1737).		Sugar caster: Do. do.
,,		Edward Feline ,, ,, (see also 1722-1729)		Oval bread basket: Do. do.
,,		John Gibbons ,, 1723.		Dredger: Do. do.
,,		Edw. Vincent ,, ,, (see 1729)		Com. cup: Long Preston, Yorks.
,,		Thos. Mason ,, 1720.		Soup ladle: Mr. Lake; also (1723-4) com. paten: Yarpole, Herefordshire.
,,		Jas. Gould ,, 1722.		Taper stick: The Day Collection.
,,		John Edwards ,, 1724.		Salver: Mr. Boore; also (1728-9) com. cup: King's Caple, Herefordshire.
,,		Geo. Wickes ,, 1721.		Milk-jug: Edkins Collection.
,,		Thos. Clark ,, 1725.		Plain salver on foot: Mr. T. Hutchinson.
,,		Thos. England ,, ,,		A shaving pot: Mr. E. Johnson.
,,		Wm. Scarlett ,, ,,		Table-spoons: Hanoverian pattern.
,,		Peter Tabart ,, ,,		N.S. mark, registered 7 July, 1725.
,,		Do. do. ,, ,,		O.S. do. do. do.
,,		Mathew Cooper ,, ,,		N.S. mark, registered 30 June, 1725.
,,		Do. do. ,, ,,		O.S. do. do. do.
,,		Louis Laroche ,, ,,		Small saucepan: Mr. J. B. Murdoch. Table-spoon: Mr. Geo. Lowe.
,,		John Flavill ,, 1726.		Do. do.: Mr. Edw. Jones.
1726-7		Name not traced.		Com. flagon: St. Mary Mag., Littleton, Mids'x.
,,		Wm. Darkeratt ,, 1724.		Two Com. flagons: St. Martin-in-the Fields.
,,		Richd. Green ,, 1726.		Com. paten: St. Margaret, Uxbridge.
,,		Benj. Pyne (as before 1697).		Great Mace: Borough of Westminster.
,,		Peter Archambo ent. 1722.		Sugar caster, with applied strap ornamentation.
,,		Wm. Fawdery ,, 1720.		Pair of sauce boats, with scroll handles.
,,		Wm. Atkinson ,, 1725.		Pair of octagonal candlesticks of baluster form.

Date.	Goldsmiths' Marks and Names.	Articles and Owners.
1726-7	Robt. Lucas ent. 1726. (variant of mark ot)	Mark noted by the Author.
,,	Thos. Evesdon ,, 1713. (see 1720 and 1721)	Mug: The Hadden Collection.
,,	Fras. Nelme ,, 1722.	Plain two-handled tankard, domed lid.
,,	Bern'd. Fletcher ,, 1725.	Oblong salver on feet, plain moulded edge.
,,	Thos. Bamford ,. 1720.	Muffineer: Jesus Coll., Cambridge.
,,	Robt. Williams ,, 1726.	N.S. mark, registered 2 Oct., 1726.
,,	Do. do. ,, ,,	O.S. do. do. do. do.
,,	Gawen Nash ,, ,,	Large rat-tail hash spoon, with tubular handle.
,,	Chas. Perier ,, 1727.	N.S. mark, registered 6 Jan., 1727.
,,	Do. do. ,, ,,	O.S. do. do. do. do.
,,	Geo. Brome ,, 1726.	Snuff-box: Glasgow Exhibition.
,,	Peter le Chaube ,, ,,	A gold locket: Mr. W. Boore.
1727-8	Isaac Ribouleau ,, 1720.	Rat-tail table-spoons: The Author's Coll'n.
,,	*Jas. Smith ,, ,,	Milk jug: Mr. J. Whaley.
,,	Edw. Wood ,, 1722.	Pair of octagonal salts: The Author's Coll'n.
,,	Ed. Cornock ,, 1707.	Alms-dish: St. Mary Mag., N. Ockenden, Essex.
,,	Saml. Bates ,, 1727.	Trencher salt: The Drane Collection.
,,	Thomas England ,, 1725.	Waiter: Messrs. Crichton Bros.
,,	Richard Pargeter ., 1730.	Pair of octagonal trencher salts: Mr. Anthony White.
,,	Matt. Cooper ,, 1725. (see 1725)	Salver: Messrs. Crichton Bros.
,,	?Andrew Raven ,, 1706.	Teapot: The Day Collection.
,,	Jno. le Sage ,, 1722.	Tankard: Dunn-Gardner Collection.
,,	Name not traced.	Com. paten: Portslade, Sussex.
,,	Sarah Holaday ., 1725.	Table spoons: Hanoverian pattern.
,,	John East ,, 1721.	Large tankard: Armourers' Company.
,,	Jonah Clifton ,, 1720.	Three-pronged forks, dessert size.

* The mark of this maker in a plain oblong punch is on a paten of 1722-3, at Sollers Hope, Herefordshire.

DATE.	GOLDSMITHS' MARKS AND NAMES.			ARTICLES AND OWNERS.
1727-8		Saml. Laundry	ent. 1727.	Double spouted toddy ladle.
,,		Edmd. Bodington	,, ,,	Jug, with short spout and scroll handle : The Day Collection.
,,		Chas. Kandler & Jas. Murray	,, ,,	N.S. mark, registered 29 Aug., 1727.
,,		Do. do.	,, ,,	O.S. do. do. do. do.
,,		Edw. Bennett	,, ,,	Globular teapot, with chased Arabesque band.
,,		Hester Fawdery	,, ,,	A pair of shoe buckles.
,,		Thos. Cooke	,, ,,	Marrow scoop : Mr. Bruford.
,,		Richd. Hutchinson	,, ,,	Helmet-shaped cream jug on three legs.
,,		Chas. Kandler	,, ,,	Soup tureen : Mr. Parkes.
,,		Geo. Weir	,, ,,	This mark is found on a small spoon; also (on a larger scale) on a com. paten and flagon of 1712-3 in Burrington Church, Herefordshire.
,,		Do. do.	,, ,,	O.S. mark, registered 27 July, 1727.
,,		Name not traced.		Snuff-box : Mr. Edward Bass.
,,		Abel Brokesby	,, ,,	Plain octagonal muffineer.
,,		Dike Impey (probably)	,, ,,	An engraved purse ring.
,,		Benj. Bentley	,, 1728.	O.S. mark, registered 31 Jan., 1728.
,,		Mary Johnson	,, 1727.	Mount of crystal bottle.
,,		I. Wichaller	,, 1728.	O.S. mark, registered 2 April, 1728.
,,		Chas. Hatfield	,, 1727.	A pair of plain sauce ladles.
,,		Sam. Laundry	,, ,,	Small straining spoon : Hanoverian pattern.
,,		Matw. Cooper	,, 1725.	A chatelaine hook and thimble case.
,,		David Willaume	,, 1728.	N.S. mark, registered 2 April, 1728.
,,		Danl. Cunningham	,, 1720.	Dessert spoon, Hanoverian pattern : Mrs. A. Wilks.
,,		Richd. Gines	,, ,,	Plain cream-jug : Mrs. Cobb.
,,		Geo. Gillingham	,, 1721.	Lid of glass pomade pot : Mrs. F. Harrison.
,,		Chas. Hatfield	,, 1727.	A tiny three-pronged fork : Mr. Falk.
,,		Jacob Foster	,, 1726.	A plain tankard, domed top.

DATE.	GOLDSMITHS' MARKS AND NAMES.			ARTICLES AND OWNERS.
1727-8		Saml. Green	ent. 1721.	Cream-jug : Dunn-Gardner Collection.
,,		Wm. Shaw	,, 1728.	A small tea-spoon, " H.C.B. 1727 " engraved, but without date-letter.
1728-9		Wm. Darkeratt	,, 1720.	Alms-dish : St. Helen's, Bishopsgate, E.C.
,,		James Goodwin	,, 1721.	Sugar caster : Mr. S. Deane.
,,		Tim. Ley (as before 1697)		Waterman's badge : Barber Surgeons' Co.
,,		Blanche Fraillon	ent. 1727.	Taper holder : Mr. Jas. Gurney.
,,		Isaac Callard	,, 1726.	A plain cream-jug on three legs.
,,		Name not traced.		Hanoverian pattern dessert-spoon : Mr. B. Jefferis.
,,		James Wilkes	,, 1722.	Spoon : Mr. Ince ; also (1737-8) communion flagon, Lugwardine.
,,		Peter Archambo	,, 1720.	A sauce ladle : Lord Dormer.
,,		Josh. Holland	,, ,,	A small trussing skewer : Mr. G. Lowe.
,,		Simon Pantin (see 1729)	,, ,,	A plain cylindrical tankard, moulded band and foot, domed cover.
,,		John Millington	,, 1728.	A small circular salver on drum foot.
,,		Edward Bennett	,, 1727.	A Hanoverian pattern table-spoon.
,,		Ralph Frith	,, 1728.	N.S. mark, registered 24 June, 1728.
,,		Do. do.	,, ,,	O.S. do. do. do. do.
,,		Geo. Hodges	,, ,,	N.S. do. do. 12 Sept. do.
,,		Do. do.	,, ,,	O.S. do. do. do. do.
,,		John Fawdery	,, ,,	A plain hemispherical toddy ladle.
,,		John Montgomery	,, ,,	A table-spoon, with marrow scoop at end of stem.
,,		? John Richardson	,, 1723.	Paten : Rowner, Hants.
,,		? Wm. Fordham	,, 1706.	Cream-jug : Mr. Anthony White.
,,		Starling Wilford (see 1725 and 1737)	,, 1729.	A large gold signet ring : Mr. W. Boore.
1729-30		John Tuite*	,, 1721.	Large salver, shaped and moulded border : Sir Chas. Welby, Bart.
,,		Thos. Tearle	,, 1720.	Ewer with mask spout, handle formed of a female figure : The Author's Collection.
,,		Ed. Vincent (see 1725)	,, ,,	Large oblong tray on four feet : Hon. Soc. of the Middle Temple.

* John Tuite, son of Jas. Tuite, of Drogheda, merchant, apprenticed in 1703 to John Matthews of Dublin, goldsmith, used the above mark in Dublin, where he worked 1710-20. An entry recording his having " gone away " appears in the minute-book of the Dublin Goldsmiths' Company.

DATE.	GOLDSMITHS' MARKS AND NAMES.		ARTICLES AND OWNERS.
1729-30		Anthony Nelme　　ent. 1722.	Mark noted by the Author.
,,		Chas.　　Martin　　,,　1729.	Tankard: Messrs. Spink; also (1731) com. flagon: All Saints, Hereford.
,,		Edwd.　Feline　　,,　　1720. (see 1722 and 1725)	Pair of two-handled sauce-boats: Mr. W. W. Simpson.
,,		Abel　　Brokesby　,,　1727. (see 1727)	Large salver: Chester Corporation.
,,		Simon　Pantin　　,,　1717. (see 1728)	Sauce-boat: Mr. R. Meldrum.
,,		George　Jones　　,,　1724. (see 1735-6)	Dredger: Messrs. Crichton Bros.
,,		Name not traced.	Rat-tail spoon: Mr. Geo. Harrison.
,,		Paul　　Lamerie　　,,　　,,	(O.S.) Escallop shell: Lord Swaythling.
,,		Ralph　　Maidman　,,　1730.	Small salver: Dunn-Gardner Collection.
,,		Richd.　Scarlett　　,,　1720. (see 1723)	Pair of plain octagonal baluster-shaped candlesticks.
,,		Name not traced.	Child's mug: Messrs. Crichton Bros.
,,		John　　Jones　　,,　1729.	A meat skewer, with ring at end.
,,		Saml.　Margas　　,,　1720.	A lion tankard: Mr. Alfred Cock.
,,		Chas.　Alchorne　　,,　1729.	Hanoverian pattern table-spoons.
,,		Sam.　Welder　　,,　　,,	Plain two-handled mug.
,,		Benj.　Goodwin　　,,　　,,	Plain Hanoverian pattern tea-spoon.
,,		Name not traced.	Mark noted by the Author.
,,		Edith　Fletcher　　,,　　,,	A small scissors case for a chatelaine.
,,		Eliz.　　Goodwin　　,,　　,,	O.S. mark, registered 2nd Dec., 1729.
,,		Jas.　　Maitland　,,　1728. of the "Grasshopper," Suffolk Street.	Do.　　do.　　do. June, 1728.
1730-1		Aug.　　Courtauld ent. 1729.	The state salt of the City of London Corporation.
,,		Paul　　Lamerie　　,,　1712.	(N.S.) Coffee pot: Lord Swaythling.
,,		Saml.　Jefferys　　,,　1697.	Do. The "Ludlow cups": Hon. Soc. of the Middle Temple.
,,		Gabl.　Sleath　　,,　1720.	Pair of com. cups and flagons: St. George's, Bloomsbury.

DATE.	GOLDSMITHS' MARKS AND NAMES.			ARTICLES AND OWNERS.
1730-1		Richd. Bayley	ent. 1720.	Com. flagon: St. Mary, Hendon.
,,		Wm. Belassyse	,, 1723.	Plain milk-jug, with short loop handle.
,,		Isaac Callard	,, 1726.	Three-pronged forks: Mr. Boore; and (1737) Lord Amherst.
,,		Wm. Petley	,, 1720.	Perforated Hanoverian pattern wine-straining spoon: St. Magnus, London Bridge.
,,		Perè Pilleau	,, ,,	Plain marrow scoop.
,,		Chas. Kandler	,, 1727.	Mark noted by Author.
,,		John White	,, 1719.	Inkstand: Messrs. Crichton Bros.
,,		Anne Tanqueray	,, 1720.	Cruet-frame: Do.
,,		? Saml. Laundry (see also 1727)	,, 1727.	{ Set of casters: Do. { Toddy-ladle (1733): Mr. Anthony White.
,,		John Chapman (see 1737)	,, 1730.	Plain coffee-pot: Mr. Chisholm.
,·		Samuel Hitchcock	,, ,,	O.S mark, registered 5 Oct., 1730.
,,		Jas. Jenkins	,, 1731.	Do. do. 26 April, 1731.
,,		Wm. Justus	,, ,,	A purse ring: Mr. Connell.
,,		Wm. Reeve	,, ,,	O.S. mark, registered 14 May, 1731.
,,		Aaron Bates	,, 1730.	A plain watch-case: Mr. S. Barnett.
,,		Aug. Courtauld	,, 1708.	Coffee-pot: Mr. W. Comyns.
1731-2		John Gamon	,, 1728.	Table-spoon: Mr. I. Whaley; also (1732-3) com. paten: King's Pyon, Herefordshire.
,,		Edwd. Yorke	,, 1730.	Pair of com. flagons: St. John the Evangelist, Westminster.
,,		Geo. Hindmarsh	,, 1731.	O.S. mark, registered December, 1731.
,,		David Willaume	,, 1728.	Communion cup: Osgathorpe.
,,		Wm. Darker	,, 1731.	Communion flagon: Kington, Herefordshire.
,,		Thos. England	,, 1725.	O.S. mark, registered 26 Aug., 1725.
,,		Jane Lambe	,, 1729.	Tea-spoons: Hanoverian pattern.
,,		Mary Lofthouse	,, 1731.	O.S. mark, registered 30 March, 1731.
,,		Thos. Merry	,, ,,	Tooth-pick and case: Mr. Widdowfield.
,,		Jeffrey Griffith	,, ,,	Handle of pen-knife: Mr. Gwillim.

Date.	Goldsmiths' Marks and Names.			Articles and Owners.
1731-2	SP	Sarah	Parr ent. 1720.	Small circular box for patches or wafers.
,,	G R·A H	Robt. Geo.	Abercromby & } ,, 1731. Hindmarsh }	Salver with escalloped border : Mrs. Du Pasquier.
,,	W·W	Wm.	Woodward ,, ,,	Egg-shaped coffee pot on moulded foot.
,,	C	Thos.	Causton ,, 1730.	Cover of glass toilet pot.
,,	E·R	Etienne Rongent ,, 1731.		A small mug : Mr. F. L. Fitzgerald.
,,	W·D	Wm.	Darker ,, ,, (see 1731)	Punch ladle : Victoria and Albert Museum.
1732-3	R·B	Richd.	Beale ,, ,,	{ Bowl and cover : Mr. Anthony White. { Com. flagon (1737) : Tadcaster.
,,	L S★I G	Sam Jeffy	Laundry & } ,, ,, Griffith }	O.S. mark, registered 2 June, 1731.
,,	I·S	Joseph	Smith ,, 1728.	Coffee pot : Drane Collection ; also (1737) double service of com. plate : St. Giles', Cripplegate.
,,	E·P	Edw.	Pocock ,, ,,	Gravy spoons : Mr. S. Deane ; salver : Mr. Barclay Murdoch ; also (1733-4) com. cup : Bridstow, Hereford.
,,	I·S	John	Sanders ,, 1720.	Silver-gilt spoon : St. Mary-le-Strand.
,,	I·F	John	Fawdery ,, 1728. (see 1728)	Paten : St. John's, Warminster, Wilts.
,,	F·P	Fras.	Pages ,, 1729.	{ Coffee pot : Messrs. Crichton Bros. { Salver (of 1737) : Mr. Anthony White.
,,	L·O	? Matt.	Lofthouse ,, 1705.	Mark noted by the Author.
,,	D·L	Name not traced.		Small waiter : Messrs. Garrard.
,,	W·L	Wm.	Lukin ,, 1725.	Plain sugar caster : Grant Morris Collection.
,,	F·S	Fras.	Spilsbury ,, 1729. (same mark found in square stamp).	Sauce ladle : Messrs. Christie ; also (1733) large salt : Trin. Coll., Camb.
,,	T·P	Thos.	Parr ent. 1732.	A waist buckle, with corner shell-shaped ornaments.
,,	W·M	Wm.	Matthews ,, 1728.	Small octagonal candlestick : Viscount Clifden.
,,	I·S	Jas.	Savage ,, ,,	Gallery of a small ebony tray.
,,	I·P	John	Pero ,, 1732.	Drum-shaped trencher salt.
,,	I·G	Jas.	Gould ,, ,,	Taper holder : The Day Collection.
,,	G·S	Geo.	Smith ,, ,,	Handle of pointed knife.
,,		R.	W. (as 1696).	Trencher salt : Emmanuel Coll., Cambridge.
,,	W·S	Wm.	Soame ,, ,,	Jar-shaped tea-caddy, with Chinese decoration.
,,	C·G	Chas.	Gibbons ,, ,,	Small cylindrical pepper caster, with loop handle.
,,	S·H	Wm.	Shaw ,, 1728.	N.S. squat milk jug, with S-shaped handle.
1733-4	I·E	John	Eckfourd, jr. ,, 1725.	Tankard : Mr. J. Whaley ; com. flagon (1735) : Minchinhampton.

DATE.	GOLDSMITHS' MARKS AND NAMES.			ARTICLES AND OWNERS.
1733 4		Aug.	Courtauld ent. 1729.	A covered bowl on circular foot.
,,		Jas.	Slater ,, 1732.	Pair of com. flagons : St. Luke's, Old St., L'don.
,,		Richd.	Bayley ,, 1720.	Punch ladle : The Drane Collection.
,,		* Henry Herbert ,, 1734. (of the " Three Crowns ")		Large square waiter : S. Kensington Museum.
,,		Wm.	Soame ,, 1732.	Table-spoon : Mr. B. Jefferis.
,,		Eliz.	Buteux ,, 1731.	Small deep oval dish, with fluted side.
,,		Danl.	Chapman ,, 1729.	Short octagonal baluster-shaped candlestick.
,,		Lewis	Pantin ,, 1733.	Octagonal trencher salt.
,,		Chas.	Sprage ,, 1734.	A lemon strainer, with scroll handles.
,,		Robt.	Abercromby ,, 1731. (see 1734)	Waiter : Messrs. Crichton Bros.
,,		Geo.	Braithwaite ? earliest ment. 1728.	Taper-stick : do.
1734-5		Ralph	Maidman ent. 1731.	Small two-handled cup : The Author's Coll'n.
,,		Caleb	Hill ,, 1728.	Table-spoons, with double drop at back of bowl.
,,		Lewis	Mettayer ,, 1720.	Table candlesticks of baluster form, square on plan, with indented quadrant corners.
,,		Wm.	Gould ,, 1732.	A plain coffee-pot : Mr. W. Boore.
,,		Robt.	Abercromby ,, 1731. (see 1733)	Two-handled cup : Gurney Collection.
,,		John	Newton ,, 1726.	Hanoverian pattern table-spoons.
,,		Mary	Pantin ,, 1733.	Oval snuffers' tray.
,,		Richd.	Pargeter ,, 1730.	Table-spoon, double drop : Mr. H. D. Ellis.
,,		Hugh	Arnell ,, 1734.	Mounts of small agate box.
,,		Alex. Edw.	Coates & French } ,, ,,	O.S. mark, registered 29 Aug., 1734.
,,		John	Taylor ,, ,,	Small tea-spoons
,,		Wm.	Gould ,, ,,	Do. do.
,,		John	Jacob ,, ,,	Do. do.
,,		John	Pollock ,, ,,	Do. do.
,,		Jas.	Manners ,, ,,	Table candlestick : Mrs. Dawson.

The lion-passant and maker's mark are the only marks stamped on these spoons.

* See similar mark with three small crowns above the letters at 1735-6, page 188, *infra*.

DATE.	GOLDSMITHS' MARKS AND NAMES.				ARTICLES AND OWNERS.
1734-5	**EF**	Edw.	French	ent. 1734.	A rococo waist-buckle.
,,	**IB**	Jas.	Brooker	,, ,,	Salt spoon (lion-passant and maker's mark only).
,,	**SH**	Sam.	Hutton	,, ,,	A short baluster-shaped candlestick.
,,	**WK**	Wm.	Kidney	,, ,,	An escallop shell.
1735-6	**GI**	Geo.	Jones	,, 1724.	Punch ladle with double spout.
,,	**T·G R·C**	Richd. Thos.	Gurney & Cook }	,, 1734.	Muffineer: Mr. Middleton; cup cover (1738): All Saints, West Ham.
,,	**EB**	Edw.	Bennett	,, 1731.	Table-spoons, double drop: Mr. R. Beauchamp.
,,	**KA**	Fred	Kandler	,, 1735.	Plain vase-shaped caster: Mrs. Du Pasquier.
,,	**B·G**	Benj.	Godfrey (see 1739)	,, 1732.	Globular fluted tea-pot: Dunn-Gardner Collection.
,,	**GE**	Grif.	Edwards	,, ,,	Two small three-pronged forks.
,,	**WS**	Wm.	Shaw	,, 1727.	Oval bread basket: The Earl of Hardwicke's Collection.
,,	**PB**	Peter	Bennett	,, 1731.	A plain coffee-pot: Mrs. Dawson.
,,	**IW**	John	White	,, 1724.	A "double-drop" spoon; also (1733) Set of three tea-caddies: Sir E. Marshall Hall.
,,	**AT**	Wm.	Atkinson	,, 1725.	Salver, with moulded escalloped border, on four feet.
,,	**WY**	Wm.	Young	,, 1735.	Miniature two-handled cup: Mrs. Iggulden.
,,	**EI**	Name not traced, (see 1729-30)			Communion paten: St. Eval, Cornwall.
,,	**FN**	Francis Nelme		,, ,,	Second mark: Noted by the Author.
,,	**I·B**	John	Barbe	,, ,,	Tea-caddy: Sir G. Webbe Dasent.
,,	**GH**	Geo.	Hindmarsh	,, ,,	Table-spoons, double drop pattern.
,,	**CH**	Christn. Hilland		,, 1736.	Marrow scoop, engraved border to centre part.
,,	**D·L**	Name not traced.			Salver: Grant-Morris Collection.
,,	**H·H**	Henry Herbert (of the "Three Crowns")		,, 1734.	Jar-shaped tea-caddy, repoussé and chased.
,,	**LH**	Lewis	Hamon	,, 1735.	Three-quarter-pint mug, with applied band and base moulding.
1736-7	**KV**	Name not traced.			Table-spoons, double drop: The Author's Coll'n.
,,	**WG**	Wm.	Garrard	,, 1735.	Plain globular milk jug, with short neck and loop handle.
,,	**SW**	Sam.	Wood	,, 1733-7.	Sugar caster: Lord Dormer; also cruet stand (1731-2): Major Burton Forster.

DATE.	GOLDSMITHS' MARKS AND NAMES.				ARTICLES AND OWNERS.
1736-7	**BW**	Benj.	West	ent. 1737.	Spoon, double drop: St. Giles', Cripplegate.
,,	**RB**	Robt.	Brown	,, 1736.	Com. paten: St. Cuthbert's, Hawkshead; tankard: Vintners' Company.
,,	**AH**	Ann	Hill	,, 1734.	Three dessert spoons, double drop pattern.
,,	**TM**	Thos.	Mason	,, 1733.	Bulb-shaped tankard, domed top.
,,	**JJ**	John	Jones	,, ,,	Lid of glass toilet-pot.
,,	**IF**	John	Fossey	,, ,,	Pair of snuffers.
,,	**B R T**	Bennet R.	Bradshaw & Tyrill }	,, 1737.	Mark registered 21 March, 1737.
,,	**IK**	Jerem.	King	,, 1736.	Small two-handled cup: Milbank Collection.
,,	**TM**	Thos.	Mann	,, ,,	Pair of rococo candlesticks, Louis XV. style.
,,	**DH**	David	Hennell	,, ,,	Pair of salt spoons, fully marked.
,,	**BW**	Benj.	West	,, 1737.	Small tea-spoon (lion and maker's mark only).
,,	**H·H**	Henry	Herbert	,, 1734.	⎰ The "Sidney" two-handled cup: The Author's Collection. ⎱ Bread platter: Kensington Palace Chapel.
,,	**HP**	? Harvey	Price	,, 1726.	Sauce-pan: Mr. A. G. C. Day.
1737-8	**IA MF**	Joseph	Allen & Co.	,, 1729.	Sauce-boat: Lord Clifden.
,,	**GW**	Geo.	Weekes	,, 1735.	Helmet-shaped cream-jug, on three lion's mask feet.
,,	**JS**	Jos.	Sanders	,, 1730.	Small salver, with shell and scroll border.
,,	**SB**	Saml.	Blackborrow	,, 1720.	Com. cup: Kirkby Iredale, Lancs.
,,	**TW**	Thos.	Whipham	,, 1737.	Pair of table-spoons, embossed with shell.
,,	**G·H**	Geo.	Hindmarsh (see 1735-6)	,, 1735.	Mark noted by the Author.
,,	**S·W**	Starling	Wilford	,, 1729.	⎰ Marrow spoon: Mrs. E. H. Goddard. ⎱ "Double-drop" spoon: Mr. Clement Gadsby.
,,	**IC**	John	Chapman (see 1730)	,, 1730.	Kettle: Messrs. Crichton Bros.
,,	**R·W**	Robt.	Williams	,, 1726.	Snuff-box: The Author's Collection.
,,	**RB**	Richd.	Beale	,, 1731.	Tea-caddy: Sir Charles Crawford Fraser.
,,	**S·I**	Simon	Jouet	,, 1723.	Pair of octagonal salts: The Author's Collection.
,,	**T·I**	Thos.	Jackson	,, 1736.	Plain circular punch ladle, with ebony handle.
,,	**TG**	Thos.	Gladwin	,, 1737.	Pair of dwarf table candlesticks.

DATE.	GOLDSMITHS' MARKS AND NAMES.				ARTICLES AND OWNERS.
1737-8	**IB**	John	Barrett	ent. 1737.	A toasting fork, with tubular sliding handle.
,,	**GB**	Geo.	Baskerville	,, 1738.	Back and corners of a small book cover.
,,	**PP**	Philip	Platel	,, 1737.	A globular tea-pot, with band of fine Arabasque chasing.
,,	**I·I**	Jas.	Jenkins	,, 1738.	Sugar tongs, rococo chasing.
,,	**GR**	Gundry	Roode	,, 1737.	A bulb-shaped tankard, domed top, scroll handle.
,,	**I·R**	John	Robinson	,, 1738.	Six table-spoons, double drop pattern.
,,	**I·S**	Jas.	Schruder	,, 1737.	Pair of octagonal trencher salts.
,,	**WS**	Wm.	Soame	,, 1738.	Plain hemispherical toddy ladle.
,,	**SW**	Sam.	Wood	,, 1737.	A hexagonal baluster-shaped taper-holder.
,,	**DW**	Denis	Wilks	,, ,,	A plain pint mug, with scroll handle.
1738-9	**R·Z**	Richd.	Zouch	,, 1735.	Milk jug: Drane Collection; muffineer: Mr. Edginton.
,,	**TW**	Thos.	Whipham	,, 1739	Com. flagon: St. Andrew's, Boreham, Essex.
,,	**FK**	Fred	Kandler	,, 1735.	Two-handled loving cup: Hon. Soc. of the Middle Temple.
,,	**I·R**	Jno.	Robinson	,, 1738.	Com. paten: Little Baddow, Essex.
,,	**L·D**	Louis	Dupont	,, 1736.	An oblong snuffers tray, with inset quadrant corners.
,,	**T·R**	Thos.	Rush	,, 1724.	Soup ladle, with shell-shaped bowl.
,,	**BB**	Benj.	Blakeley	,, 1738.	Snuff box: Dr. R. F. Woollett.
,,	**HB**	Henry	Bates	,, ,,	Nutmeg box and grater: Mr. Falk.
,,	**PB**	Philip	Brugier	., ,,	Small plain circular salver on foot, with moulded border.
,,	**WW**	Wm.	West	,, ,,	Plain tankard, moulded rib and base, scroll handle and domed cover.
,,	**FP**	Fras.	Pages	,, 1739.	{Oval bread basket: The Hardwicke Collection; also (1750-1) com. cup: Pembridge.
,,	**RH**	Robt.	Hill	,, ,,	A globular tea-kettle, on tripod stand.
,,	**IL**	James	Langlois	,, 1738.	Pair of candlesticks: The Author's Collection.
1739-40	**FK**	Fred	Kandler	,, 1735.	Large salver: Messrs. Crichton Bros.
,,	**RB**	? Richd.	Bayler	,, 1739.	Sauce-boat: do.
,,	**JP**	John	Pero (see 1732)	,, ,,	Covered cup: do.

Date.	Goldsmiths' Marks and Names.*			Articles and Owners.
1739-40	[mark]	Humphrey Payne	ent. 1739.	Covered bowl: Mr. J. B. Carrington.
,,	[mark]	Sarah Holaday	,, 1719.	Coffee-pot: Noted by the Author.
,,	[mark]	Benj. Godfrey (see 1735)	,, 1732.	Sauce-boats: Messrs. Crichton Bros.
,,	[mark]	Thos. Whipham	,, 1737.	Mark noted by the Author.
,,	[mark]	Chas. Hillan	,, 1741.	Sauce-boats: Messrs. Crichton Bros.
,,	[mark]	Wm. Kidney	,, 1739.	Small bowl: Holburne Museum.
,,	[mark]	Paul Lamerie	,, ,,	Pierced and chased cake basket: Sir Charles Welby, Bart.
,,	[mark]	Ben. Blakeley	,, ,,	Haft of hunting knife: Mr. H. D. Ellis; also on table-spoon: The Author's Collection.
,,	[mark]	Isaac Callerd	,, ,,	Table-spoon: S. Kensington Museum.
,,	[mark]	Jeff. Griffith	,, ,,	† Plain globular cream-jug, with loop handle.
,,	[mark]	Thos. Tearle	,, ,,	Tankard with domed cover: The Marquess Townshend.
,,	[mark]	Jnthn. Fossy	,, ,,	Hexagonal baluster-shaped taper-holder.
,,	[mark]	Paul Crespin	,, ,,	Small tea-spoons: Dunn-Gardner Collection.
,,	[mark]	John Harwood	,, ,,	† Small plain globular teapot, with ebony handle.
,,	[mark]	Richd. Bayley	,, ,,	Communion flagon: Cartmel, Lancs.
,,	[mark]	Robt. Abercromby	,, ,,	‡ (Brit. standard) short octagonal muffineer, with tall pierced top.
,,	[mark]	Lewis Dupont	,, ,,	Wine-taster, saucer-shaped, with repoussé knobs in bottom.
,,	[mark]	Wm. Hunter	,, ,,	Oblong moulded salt-cellar, with incurved corners.
,,	[mark]	Wm. Gwillim	,, ,,	Scissors-shaped sugar nippers (maker's mark and lion passant only).
,,	[mark]	Geo. Boothby	,, ,,	Snuff-box, with engraved shell and scroll ornamentation.
,,	[mark]	Edw. Aldridge	,, ,	Baluster-shaped taper-holder, square on plan, with inset quadrant corners.
,,	[mark]	Wm. Soame	,, ,,	Plain bulb-shaped cream-jug on moulded foot.
,,	[mark]	Peter Bennett	,, ,,	Table-spoon: The Author's Collection.
,,	[mark]	Henry Bates	,, ,,	Barrel-shaped beer jug: Lieut.-Col. Milne.
,,	[mark]	John Tuite	,, ,,	Helmet-shaped cream-jug on three legs.

*†‡ On the restoration of the old standard in 1720, most of the London goldsmiths adopted new marks for plate of the restored standard; some, however, resumed the use of marks which had been in use prior to 1697, and thus it became difficult in many cases to identify the makers with their marks during the period 1720-39. To remedy this confusion, the Act of 1739 provided that all makers should destroy their existing marks of every kind, and adopt new marks composed of the initials of their Christian name and surname, of forms different from those previously in use. The marks represented on this and the following pages (of goldsmiths who were working prior to May, 1739) were devised in compliance with that Act. Marks of Robt. Abercromby, Paul Crespin, and Fras. Spilsbury, indicated by ‡ (entered in June, 1739) are composed of the first two letters of their surnames, and do not comply with the Act.

DATE.	GOLDSMITHS' MARKS AND NAMES.				DATE.	GOLDSMITHS' MARKS AND NAMES.			
1739-40		Thos.	England	ent. 1739.	1739-40		Jessie McFarlane	ent. 1739.	
,,		Robt.	Lucas	,, ,,	,,		Wm.	Justus	,, ,,
,,		Ben.	Godfrey	,, ,,	,,		Wm.	Young	,, ,,
,,		Do.	do.	,, ,,	,,		Jas.	Manners	,, ,,
,,		Gawen	Nash	,, ,,	,,		John Harvey		,, ,,
,,		John	Bryan	,, ,,	,,		Chas.	Jackson	,, ,,
,,		Richard	Beale	,, ,,	,,		Thos.	Rush	,, ,,
,,		John	Cam	,, 1740.	,,		Thos.	Gilpin	,, ,,
,,		J.	Barbitt	,, 1739.	,,		Danl.	Chartier	,, 1740.
,,		Richd.	Pargeter	,, ,,	,,		Wm.	Shaw	,, 1739.
,,		Marmdk.	Daintry	,, ,,	,,		Richd. Gosling		,, ,,
,,		Ed.	Bennett	,, ,,	,,		Fras.	Spilsbury ‡	,, ,,
,,		Do.	do.	,, ,,	,,		Louis Hamon		,, ,,
,,		Bennett	Bradshaw & Co.	,, ,,	,,		Sam.	Hutton	,, 1740.
,,		Thos.	Bamford	,, ,,	,,		John	Gamon	,, 1739.
,,		John	Eckfourd	,, ,,	,,		Fras.	Nelme	,, ,,
,,		Wm.	Shaw	,, ,,	,,		Henry Morris		,, ,,
,,		John	Jacobs (see 1750)	,, ,,	,,		Thos.	Pye	,, ,,
,,		John	Pero (see p. 190)	,, ,,	,,		Jas.	West	,, ,,
,,		John	White	,, ,,	,,		Jas.	Paltro	,, ,,
,,		Henry	Herbert	,, ,,	,,		John	Harwood	,, ,,
,,		Richd.	Zouch	,, ,,	,,		Denis	Wilks	,, ,,
,,		Susan'h	Hatfield	,, ,,	,,		Philip	Roker	,, ,,
,,		J.	McFarlane	,, ,,	,,		Simon	Jouet	,, ,,
,,		Henry	Morris	,, ,,	,,		Chas.	Clark	,, ,,
,,		John	Luff	,, ,,	,,		John le Sage		,, ,,

‡ See note at foot of preceding page.

DATE.	GOLDSMITHS' MARKS AND NAMES.			ARTICLES AND OWNERS.
1739-40	𝖡𝖲	Benj.	Sanders ent. 1739.	Tumbler : Edkins Collection.
,,	𝖠𝖮	Abm. de Oliveyra	,, ,,	Snuff-box : Mr. Creighton.
,,	𝖳𝖬	Thos.	Mason ,, ,,	Tea-spoon (no date-letter or leopard's head).
,,	𝖢𝖬	Chas.	Martin ,, 1740.	A pair of garter buckles.
,,	𝖩𝖲	Jos.	Steward ,, 1739.	A billet-shaped needle-case.
,,	𝖦𝖲	Geo.	Smith ,, ,,	Punch ladle : Mr. G. Lowe.
,,	𝖫𝖫	Louis	Laroche ,, ,,	Snuff-box : Mr. Watherston.
1740-1	𝖩𝖱	John	Robinson ,, ,,	Small circular waiter : Rev. C. C. Murray.
,,	𝖦𝖤	Griff.	Edwards ,, ,,	Cream-jug : Mr. Hows.
,,	𝖩𝖯	John	Pollock ,, ,,	Do. do. : The Author's Collection.
,,	𝖨𝖲	Jos.	Sanders ,, ,,	Com. paten : St. Lawrence, Cowley, Mids.
,,	𝖡𝖲	Benj.	Sanders ,, 1737.	† Candlesticks : formerly at Woods' Hotel, Furnivalls Inn.
,,	𝖶𝖦	Wm.	Garrard ., 1735.	Plain tankard : Mr. G. Lambert.
,,	𝖦𝖲	Gabl.	Sleath ,, ,,	Two-handled cup and cover : City of London Corporation.
,,	𝖱𝖦	Richd.	Gurney & Co. ,, 1739.	Ewer : Mr. Bell ; also (1742-3) two sets of com. plate : Stoke Edith, Hereford.
,,	𝖤𝖶	Ed.	Wood ,, 1740.	Sauce-boat on three legs.
,,	𝖢𝖡	Chas.	Bellassyse ,, ,,	Salver, shell and scroll border : Capt. Garnham.
,,	𝖲𝖧	Sarah	Hutton ,, ,,	A plain tumbler : Viscount Clifden.
,,	𝖤𝖫	Ed.	Lambe ,, ,,	A plain cream-jug on three legs.
,,	𝖳𝖬	Thos.	Mercer ,, ,,	Snuff-box : Mr. Jas. Gurney.
,,	𝖩𝖡	John	Barbe ,, 1739.	Plain pint tankard, without lid, scroll handle.
,,	𝖦𝖱	Paul	Crespin ,, 1740.	‡(With Brit. and lion's head erased) cream-jug : Mrs. Earp.
,,	𝖩𝖯	Isabel	Pero ,, ,,	A circular toilet box.
,,	𝖫𝖮	Lewis	Ouvry ,, ,,	A plain mug, with scroll handle.
,,	𝖨𝖦	Jas.	Gould ,, 1741.	Pair of plain Hanoverian pattern table-spoons.
,,	𝖤𝖠	Edwd.	Aldridge ,, 1739. (see 1744)	Vase-shaped pepper caster : Mr. Anthony White.

† ‡ See foot of page 191.

DATE.	GOLDSMITHS' MARKS AND NAMES.			ARTICLES AND OWNERS.
1740-1		? John Owing	ent. 1724.	Three-pronged forks : Messrs. Crichton.
,,		Name not traced.		Table-spoons : The Rev. Harry G. Topham.
,,		Do. do.		Communion cup : Crowan, Cornwall.
,,		John Roker	,, 1740.	Small mug : Miss Sewell, Norfolk.
,,		Abm. le Francis	,, ,,	A long gravy spoon, Hanoverian pattern.
,,		Benj. Gurdon	,, ,,	A small tea-spoon (lion and maker's mark only).
1741-2		David Hennell	,, 1739.	{ Punch ladle : Oswestry Corporation (1740). Do. do. : Holburne Museum (1741).
,,		James Shruder	,, ,,	Com. cup : St. Leonard's, Heston, Mids.
,,		Eliza Godfrey	,, 1741.	Set of three tea-caddies : Sir Charles Welby, Bart.
,,		Saml. Roby	,, 1740.	Table-spoon, with shell ornament : The Author.
,,		Geo. Wickes	,, 1739.	Pair of octagonal candlesticks : Lord Dormer ; also (1756) set of tea-caddies : Lord Carbery.
,,		Thos. Farren	,, ,,	Plain table-spoons, double drop.
,,		Dinah Gamon	,, 1740.	Plain marrow spoon.
,,		John Newton	,, 1739.	Bulb-shaped tankard, domed top.
,,		Thos. Gilpin	,, ,,	Six three-pronged forks : Mr. G. Lambert.
,,		Chas. Hillan	,, 1741.	Helmet-shaped cream-jug on foot.
,,		John Stewart (?)		Communion paten : The Abbey, Romsey, Hants.
,,		Peter Archambo	,, 1739.	Sweet-meat dish : Messrs. Crichton.
,,		Jas. Willmott	,, 1741.	Three-quarter-pint bulb-shaped mug.
,,		John Spackman	,, ,,	Sugar tongs (lion and maker's mark only).
,,		Chas. Laughton	,, 1739.	Pocket nutmeg grater and box.
,,		Thos. Lawrence	,, 1742.	Small three-pronged olive fork.
,,		Jer'mi'h King	,, 1739.	Small oval hair locket.
,,		Benj. Gurdon	,, 1740.	Small tea-spoon, fully marked.
,,		Robt. Tyrrill	,, 1742.	Hemispherical toddy ladle, with slender stem.
1742-3		Jno. Gould	,, 1739.	Four candlesticks : Hon. Soc. of the Inner Temple.

DATE.	GOLDSMITHS' MARKS AND NAMES.			ARTICLES AND OWNERS.
1742-3	P·C	Paul	Crespin ent. 1739.	Circular salt-cellars : Mr. Lowe.
,,	JA MF	Jos. Allen & M'decai Fox	,, ,,	Communion paten : Shenfield, Essex.
,,	RB	Robt.	Brown ,, ,,	Beaker, with moulded band and foot.
,,	FS	Fras.	Spilsbury ,, ,,	Flat circular wafer or patch box.
,,	ET	Eliz.	Tuite ,, 1741.	A pair of plain circular trencher salts.
,,	AC IN	Anne Craig & John Neville (see 1745)	,, 1740.	Covered cup : Messrs. Crichton.
,,	SW	Saml.	Wells ,, ,,	Alms-plate : St. Margaret's, Westminster.
,,	RA	Robt.	Abercromby ,, 1739.	Plain bulb-shaped muffineer.
,,	JM	Jas.	Montgomery ,, 1742.	Handbell, applied moulded band and ivory handle.
,,	IT	Jos.	Timberlake ,, 1743.	Dessert-spoon, with shell at back of bowl.
,,	PG	Phillips	Garden ,, 1739.	Candlesticks : Trinity College, Cambridge.
,,	CR	Paul	Crespin ,, ,,	* (Brit. and lion's head erased) baluster-shaped taper-holder.
,,	IC	John	Cam ,, 1740.	Table-spoons, Hanoverian pattern.
1743-4	DW	Dd.	Williams ,, 1739.	Pair of cups and covers : Messrs. Crichton.
,,	BS	Benj.	Sanders ,, ,,	Flagon : Noted by the Author.
,,	RA	? Robt.	Abercromby ,, ,,	Shell-bordered salver : Mr. Fredk. Bradbury.
,,	WH	Wm.	Hunter ,, ,,	Pair of tea vases : The Author's Collection.
,,	WG	Wm.	Gould ,, ,,	Kettle and stand : Mr. J. Dixon.
,,	JW	Jas.	Wilks ,, ,,	Snuffers tray, plain moulded border.
,,	EF	Ed.	Feline ,, ,,	Com. cup and flagon : Chilmark, Wilts.
,,	AC	Aug.	Courtauld ,, ,,	Milk-jug : Mr. B. Jefferis.
,,	GJ	Geo.	Jones ,, ,,	Table-spoons, Hanoverian pattern.
,,	JA	Jer'mi'h Ashley	,, 1740.	A pocket spirit flask.
,,	HB	Henry	Brind ,, 1742.	Pear-shaped teapot, with ebony handle.
,,	RA	Robt.	Abercromby ,, 1739.	Alms-plate on three feet : Todbere, Dorset.
,,	PP	Pere	Pilleau ,, ,,	A trussing skewer.

* See note at foot of page 191.

DATE.	GOLDSMITHS' MARKS AND NAMES.			ARTICLES AND OWNERS.
1743-4		Thos. Whipham	ent. 1737.	Beaker : Magdalen College, Cambridge.
,,		Name not traced.		Cake-basket : Messrs. Crichton.
,,		Isaac Duke	,, 1743.	Pair of circular salt cellars on lion's mask and claw feet.
,,		Ed. Malluson	,, ,,	Three sauce ladles.
,,		Geo. Methuen	,, ,,	A table-spoon; also (1760-1) com. plate : St. Andrew's, Plymouth.
,,		Chas. Johnson	,, ,,	Chased sugar tongs (lion-passant and maker's mark only).
,,		Ann Farren	,, ,,	Two small tea-spoons do. do.
,,		Geo. Ridout	,, ,,	Double-handled and double-spouted sauce ladle.
,,		Robt. Swanson	,, ,,	Plain dessert-spoon, Hanoverian pattern.
1744-5		Wm. Soame or Wm. Shaw	,, 1723. ,, 1727.	Table-spoon : Rev. E. H. Goddard.
,,		Edwd. Aldridge (see 1740)	,, 1739.	Shell-shaped dishes : Mr. Harry Alston.
,,		Ed. Feline	,, ,,	Coffee-pot : Messrs. Crichton.
,,		Lewis Pantin	,, ,,	Helmet-shaped ewer on foot, with scroll handle.
,,		Robt. Pilkington	,, ,,	A plain vase-shaped sugar-caster.
,,		Chas. Hatfield	,, ,,	Four table-spoons, Hanoverian pattern.
,,		Peter Archambo	,, ,,	A plain soup ladle, do. do.
,,		John Quantock	,, ,,	Two skewers : Mr. Sorby.
,,		Aymé Videau	,, ,,	(1745) Com. cup : Bodenham, Hereford.
,,		John Barbe	,, ,,	A chamber candlestick.
,,		John Edwards	,, ,,	A plain teapot.
,,		Wm. Bagnall	,, 1744.	A pair of rococo table candlesticks, with shell ornamentation in the style of Louis XV.
,,		Wm. Gwillim & Peter Castle	,, ,,	Oval bread-basket, wicker-like pierced sides.
,,		Jas. Smith	,, ,,	A plain sauce ladle.
,,		John Neville	, 1745.	Pair of circular salt-cellars on three feet.
,,		Thos. Jackson	,, 1739.	A large plain gravy spoon.
,,		Nich's Sprimont	,, 1742.	Pair of sauce-boats : Windsor Castle.

DATE.	GOLDSMITHS' MARKS AND NAMES.				ARTICLES AND OWNERS.
1744-5	ℳ	Jas.	Morrison	ent. 1740.	A small waiter, with shell and scroll border.
1745-6	ℬ𝒲	Benj.	West	,, 1739.	Tankards : Mr. Drane and Mr. Whaley.
,,	W·W T·W	Thos. Wm.	Whipham & } Williams }	,, 1740.	Milk-jug : Mr. Parkes ; also (1741-2) com. flagon : St. Martin's, Hereford.
,,	A·C I·N	Ann John	Craig & } Neville } (see 1742) }	,, ,,	Salver : Mr. Boore. Pair of candlesticks (1742-3) : Major T. H. Burton Forster.
,,	𝒥ℋ	John	Holland	,, 1739.	An oval bread-basket with pierced border.
,,	BC	Ben.	Cartwright	,, ,,	Two-handled covered cup : Mr. W. Cosier.
,,	𝒻𝒦	Fred.	Kandler	,, ,,	Bulb-shaped tankard, domed top, scroll handle.
,,	WC	Wm.	Cripps	,, 1743.	Ink-stand : Lord Dormer.
,,	𝒻𝒞	Fras.	Crump	,, 1741.	An escallop shell : Edkins Collection.
,,	IH	John	Higginbotham	,, 1745.	Pair of sugar tongs (lion passant and maker's mark only).
,,	GB	Geo.	Baskerville	,, ,,	Do. do. do. do. do.
,,	IM	Jas.	Manners, Jr.	,, ,,	Small tea-spoon do. do. do.
,,	𝒥𝒦	? Jer'mi'h King		,, ,,	Sauce-boat : Messrs. Crichton.
,,	𝒥𝒮	John	Swift (probably, see 1754-5)	,, 1739.	Teapot and covered bowl.
,,	𝒮𝒦	Sam	Key	,, 1745.	Milk-jug on three feet : Mr. Charles Budd.
,,	RA	Robt.	Andrews	,, ,,	Plain tankard : Mr. C. D. Clarke.
,,	𝒥ℋ	John	Harvey	,, ,,	Cream-jug : Miss Chivers.
1746-7	𝒮·𝒲	Sam	Wood	,, 1739.	Large plain tumbler : The Author's Collection.
,,	𝒥𝒢	Jas.	Gould	,, 1743.	Candlesticks : Mr. Drane and Mr. W. Smith.
,,	𝒲ℋ	Wm.	Hunter	,, 1739.	Eight small waiters : Hon. Soc. Middle Temple.
,,	WP	Wm.	Peaston	,, 1746.	Salver : Mr. W. R. M. Wynne.
,,	𝒥ℳ	Jas.	Morrison	,, 1744.	Sauce-tureen : Mr. W. Holloway.
,,	ℋℳ	Henry	Morris	,, 1739.	Salver : Hon. Soc. of the Middle Temple.
,,	I·B	Jos.	Barker	,, 1746.	Three small tea-spoons (lion passant and maker's mark only).
,,	ℰ𝒱	Ed.	Vincent	,, 1739.	Small salver, with shell and scroll border : The Marquess Townshend.
,,	A·K	Ann	Kersill	,, 1747.	Cruet frame, with casters and bottles : Miss Fox.

DATE.	GOLDSMITHS' MARKS AND NAMES.				ARTICLES AND OWNERS.
1746-7	ES	Ernest	Sieber	ent. 1746.	Table-spoons : Mr. H. Kelston.
,,	GY	Geo.	Young	,, ,,	Globular teapot : Miss Drew.
,,	SM	Saml.	Meriton	,, ,,	Dessert-spoons : Mr. H. Hopkins.
,,	HH	Henry	Herbert	,, 1747.	Pair of vase-shaped tea-caddies.
,,	HH	Do.	do.	,, ,,	Candlestick : The Ilay Collection.
,,	SJ	Simon	Jouet	,, ,,	Pepper caster : Mr. H. Arnold.
,,	BC	Benj.	Cartwright	,, 1739.	Table-spoons : The Author's Collection.
1747-8	IS	Jno.	Sanders	,, ,,	Waiter on three feet : Mr. Hamilton.
,,	WG	Wm.	Gould	,, ,,	Four candlesticks : Noted by the Author.
,,	RK	Richd.	Kersill	,, 1744.	Tumbler : The Author's Collection.
,,	WW	Wm.	Williams	,, 1742.	Pair of com. flagons : St. John's, Hampstead.
,,	S·C	Saml.	Courtauld (see 1750).	,, 1746.	Small waiter on three feet.
,,	I·M	Jacob	Marsh	,, 1744.	Half-a-dozen three-pronged forks.
,,	TC	Thos.	Carlton	,, ,,	Tumbler : The Author's Collection.
,,	J·E	? John	Eckfourd	,, 1739.	Soup-tureen : Messrs. Crichton.
,,	BG	? Benj. / Benj.	Griffin or / Gignac	,, 1742. / ,, 1744.	Table-spoons : The Author's Collection.
,,	JR	John	Richardson	,, 1743.	Pair of tea-caddies, repoussé and chased.
,,	JP	Thos.	Parr	,, 1739.	A child's mug; same maker's mark in circular stamp, on com. plate of 1749; Holmer, Herefordshire.
,,	MD	M'duke	Daintry	,, ,,	Salver, with shell and scroll border : Mrs. Du Pasquier.
,,	W·S	Wm.	Solomon	,, 1747.	Small tea-spoons (lion passant and maker's mark only).
,,	SH	Saml.	Herbert	,, ,,	Plain punch bowl, with lion's head and ring handles.
,,	I·F	John	Fray	,, 1748.	Mark registered 4 Jan., 1748.
,,	B·C	Ben.	Cooper	,, ,,	Do. do. 27 Feb., 1748.
1748-9	E·M	Edwd.	Medlycott	,, ,,	A plain coffee-pot, with domed lid and ebony handle.
,,	JW	John	Wirgman	,, 1745.	Plain milk-jug : Dunn-Gardner Collection.
,,	HP	Hmphy.	Payne (see 1739)	,, 1739.	A "Warwick" cruet frame, with three casters and two bottles.
,,	EC	Elias	Cachart	,, 1742.	Salver on three feet : Mr. G. Hamshaw.

DATE.	GOLDSMITHS' MARKS AND NAMES.			ARTICLES AND OWNERS.
1748-9		M'decai Fox	ent. 1746.	An egg-shaped coffee-pot : Mr. G. Fisher.
,,		Wm. Grundy	,, 1748.	Four candlesticks : Lord Dormer.
,,		John Carman	,, ,,	A wide-mouth porringer : Miss Howard Francis.
,,		Geo. Young	,, 1746.	A cream ewer on three legs.
,,		John Barbe	,, 1739.	Cream-jug : Mrs. M. Arnold.
,,		Geo. Hunter	,, 1748.	Set of four circular salt-cellars, each on three legs.
,,		Phillips Garden	,, ,,	Marrow scoop : The Day Collection.
,,		Wm. Shaw	,, 1749.	Mark registered 3 Jan., 1749.
,,		Eliz. Hartley	,, 1748.	Table-spoons : Mrs. G. Walker.
,,		Eliz. Jackson	,, ,,	Gravy spoon : Messrs. Crichton.
,,		Eliz. Oldfield	,, ,,	Small tea-spoons (lion and maker's mark only).
,,		Ed. Dowdall	,, ,,	Do. do. do. do. do.
,,		Danl. Shaw	,, ,,	Chased and pierced sugar tongs (lion and maker's mark only).
,,		Walter Brind	,, 1749.	Mark registered 7 Feb., 1749.
1749-50		Wm. Grundy	,, 1743.	Com. cup : St. Mary, Gt. Warley, Essex.
,,		Dan. Piers	,, 1746.	Communion cup : Winkfield, Wilts.
,,		Benj. Cartwright	,, 1739.	Snuff-box : The Author's Collection.
,,		Paul Crespin	,, ,,	Inkstand : Messrs. Crichton.
,,		Name not traced.		Pap-boat : Mr. Jas. Owen.
,,		Jerem'h King	,, ,,	Marrow scoop ; also spoon (1740) : Mr. E. H. Goddard.
,,		Abm. Portal	,, 1749.	Mark registered 26 October, 1749.
,,		Abm. le Francis	,, 1746.	Pint mug : Mr. G. Lowe.
,,		Jabez Daniel	,, 1749.	Small " Warwick " frame, with three casters.
,,		Wm. MacKenzie	,, 1748.	Pair of sauce-boats : Mr. Charles Budd.
,,		Wm. Kersill	,, 1749.	Plain gravy spoon : Mr. Geo. Williams.
,,		Andrew Killick	,, ,,	Mark registered 7 September, 1749.
,,		Henry Haynes	,, ,,	Small tea-spoons (lion and maker's mark only).

DATE.	GOLDSMITHS' MARKS AND NAMES.			ARTICLES AND OWNERS.
1749-50	GB	Geo. Bindon	ent. 1749.	Mark registered 13 December, 1749.
,,		Thos. Mann	,, 1739.	Plain tankard, domed cover : Mr. G. Ford.
,,	I·A	John Alderhead	,, 1750.	Mark registered 23 April, 1750.
,,	I T	Jas. Tookey	,, ,,	Chased and pierced sugar tongs (lion and maker's mark only).
,,	WW	Wm. Wooler	,, ,,	Do. do. do. do.
,,	GM	Geo. Morris	,, ,,	Plain tea-spoons fully marked.
,,		Thos. Jeannes	,, ,,	Embossed and chased cream-jug on three legs : Mr. F. Moore.
1750-1	IP	John Priest	,, 1748.	Pair of 3-light candelabra : The Author's Coll'n.
,,	C·C	Chas. Chesterman	,, 1741.	Pap-boat : The Drane Collection ; spoon : Mr. Widdowfield.
,,	EC	Eben. Coker	,, 1739.	Pair of rococo candlesticks on shaped bases.
,,	I·R	John Rowe	,, 1749.	{Mark registered 3 June, 1749. {The Davison cup : The Clothworkers' Company.
,,		Richd. Gurney & Co.	,, 1750.	Com. flagon : Ewenny, Glam.
,,		S. Herbert & Co.	,, ,,	Com. paten. : Urswick, Lancs.
,,		Louis Guichard	,, 1748.	Sugar caster, embossed and chased with festoons of conventional foliage and flowers.
,,	GC	Geo. Campar	,, 1749.	A bulb-shaped tankard with modern chasing : Mr. W. H. Fowle.
,,		Fuller White & / John Fray	,, 1750.	Kettle, with tripod stand and spirit lamp.
,,	HB	Henry Bayley	,, ,,	Mark registered 14 June, 1750.
,,		John Jacobs (see 1739)	,, 1739.	Waiter and tea-caddies : Messrs. Crichton.
,,	S·C	Saml. Courtauld (see 1747 and 1755)	,, 1746.	Caster : Mr. Chas. Davis.
,,	PL	Paul Lamerie (see 1729 and 1730)	,, 1732.	Bowl : Messrs. Crichton.
,,	A·M	A. Montgomery	,, 1750.	Pair of circular salt-cellars, with chased festoons, lion's mask and claw feet.
,,	MW	Michl. Ward	,, ,,	Mark registered 23 July, 1750.
,,	GB	Geo. Bindon	,, 1749.	A rectangular tea-caddy, chased with festoons of flowers and foliage.
,,	IH	John Harvey	,, 1750.	A plain cream-jug on three legs : Mr. Chas. Budd.
,,	TS	Thos. Smith	,, ,,	A pocket nutmeg grater.

DATE.	GOLDSMITHS' MARKS AND NAMES.	ARTICLES AND OWNERS.
1750-1	🔲 John Berthelot ent. 1750.	Combination spoon and marrow scoop.
,,	🔲 L'r'nce Johnson ,, 1751.	Mark registered 3 April, 1751.
,,	🔲 Phillips Garden ,, ,,	Do. do. 18 do.
,,	🔲 Math. Brodier ,, ,,	An oval spice-box with four compartments.
,,	🔲 Fras. Crump ,, 1750.	Mark registered 9 Nov.. 1750.
,,	🔲 Do. do. ,, ,,	Do. do. do. do.
c. 1750-60	🔲 W·F 🔲 Name not traced.	Small tea-spoon : Mr. Harry Alston.
1751-2	🔲 IW ? John Wetherell ,, 1743.	Alms plate : Bishops Sutton, Hants.
,,	🔲 John Payne ,, 1750.	Large alms-dish : St. Lawrence, Jewry.
,,	🔲 Denis Wilks ,, 1747.	Corinthian column candlestick : Lord Dormer.
,,	🔲 FK Fred Knopfell ,, 1752.	Rose-water dish : Synagogue, Duke St., Aldgate.
,,	🔲 Saml. Taylor ,, 1744.	Set of three tea vases : Holburne Museum.
,,	🔲 PW P. Werritzer ,, 1750.	A half-pint mug, with scroll handle.
,,	🔲 Thos. Moore ,, ,,	A vase-shaped caster, chased with flowers and scrolls.
,,	🔲 Wm. Woodward ,, 1743.	A plain tumbler : Mr. W. Vivian.
,,	🔲 G. & S. Smith ,, 1751.	A rectangular tea-caddy, chased with figures in a Chinese garden.
,,	🔲 Geo. Morris ,, ,,	Oval bread-basket, the border pierced, and chased with conventional foliage and scrolls.
,,	🔲 NW Nicks Winkins ,, ,,	A plain tankard : Mr. H. G. Hussey.
,,	🔲 P·P Paul Pinard ,, ,,	A plain three-pronged fork.
,,	🔲 ED Ed. Doweal ,, ,,	Mark registered 8 Nov., 1751.
,,	🔲 T·B Thos. Beere ,, ,,	A small oblong snuff-box, with chased border.
,,	🔲 Phil. Bruguier ,, 1752.	A helmet-shaped milk-jug : Mrs. G. Hill.
1752-3	🔲 RC Robt. Cox ,, ,,	A pear-shaped teapot.
,,	🔲 Lewis Haman ,, 1739.	Tea-caddies : Messrs. Crichton.
,,	🔲 RC Robt. Cox ,, 1752. (see above)	Snuff-box : Mr. S. Lazarus.
,,	🔲 WA Wm. Alexander ,, 1742.	Salver, with shell and scroll border : Lord Dormer.
,,	🔲 John Payne ,, 1751.	Pair of table candlesticks, fluted baluster stem.

Date.	Goldsmiths' Marks and Names.			Articles and Owners.
1752-3	WH	Wm.	Homer　ent. 1750.	A pair of sauce-boats, on lion's mask and claw feet.
,,	W·S P	Wm. Wm.	Shaw & Priest } ,, 1749.	Com. flagon: Wythop, Cumberland.
,,	JB	John	Berthelot　,, 1741.	A "Warwick" cruet frame on shell feet.
,,	IR	John	Richardson　,, 1752.	An octagonal mustard pot: Lord Reay.
,,	DP	Danl.	Piers　,, 1746.	A coffee-pot, chased with flowers and scrolls.
,,	CC	Chas.	Chesterman ,, 1752.	Mark registered 2 Oct., 1752.
,,	I·C	John	Carman　,, ,,	A fluted punch ladle: Mr. W. H. Fowle.
,,	RG	Richd.	Goldwire　,, 1753.	Mark registered 28 March, 1753.
,,	PG	Phillips	Garden　,, 1751.	A large plain gravy spoon.
1753-4	GH	Geo.	Hunter　,, 1748.	Tankard: South Kensington Museum.
,,	DP	Danl.	Piers　,, ,,	Tea vase:　Do.　do.
,,	T&W	Turner & Williams ,, 1753.		Marrow spoon: Mr. S. Deane.
,,	R·G	Richd.	Gosling　,, 1739.	Tea-spoon: The Drane Collection.
,,	RH	Robt.	Hennell　,, 1753.	Do.　do.　do.　do.
,,	J·C	John	Cafe　,, 1742.	Table candlestick, baluster stem: Lord Dormer.
,,	AJ	Alex.	Johnston　,, 1747.	Pair of tea-caddies in case.
,,	FW	Fuller	White　,, 1744.	Beer jug: Holburne Museum.
,,	DW IF	Denis John	Wilks & Fray } ,, 1753.	A plain saucepan, with open spout and cover.
,,	WB	Wm.	Bond　,, ,,	Mark registered 31 July, 1753.
,,	TT	Thos.	Towman　,, ,,	Silver-gilt snuff-box: Mr. W. Boore.
,,	IE	John	Edwards　,, ,,	Mark registered 1 Nov., 1753.
,,	GS FC	Gabl. Fras.	Sleath & Crump } ,, ,,	A "Warwick" cruet frame: Sir Frederick Currie, Bart.
,,	DCF	D. C.	Fueter　,, ,,	Mark registered 8 Dec., 1753.
,,	DS	Dorothy Sarbit　,, ,,		Sugar tongs (lion and maker's mark only).
,,	EA	Edward Aldridge ,, 1743. (see 1740 and 1744)		Cake-basket: Messrs. Crichton.
,,	E·A S	Edwd. John	Aldridge & Stamper } ,, 1753.	Epergne:　Do.　do.

DATE.	GOLDSMITHS' MARKS AND NAMES.			ARTICLES AND OWNERS.
1753-4	**TR**	Thos.	Rowe	ent. 1753.	A pair of table candlesticks : Lady Alice Peel.
,,	**SS**	Saml.	Smith	,, 1754.	A plain waiter, with escalloped border.
,,	**LL**	Simon	Le Sage	,, ,,	An oblong engraved snuff-box.
,,	**HC**	Henry	Corry	,, ,,	Mark registered 6 April, 1754.
,,	**BC**	* Benj.	Cartwright	,, ,,	Third mark registered 22 April, 1754.
,,	**SB**	Sarah	Buttall	,, ,,	A pair of shoe-buckles : Mrs. Holloway.
1754-5	**P·A/P·M**	Peter Peter	Archambo & Meure	} ,, 1749.	Two soup-tureens : Hon. Soc. Middle Temple.
,,	**RP**	? Robt.	Perth.		Table-spoons : The Day Collection.
,,	**WC**	Wm.	Cripps	,, 1743.	A plain coffee-pot.
,,	**I·Q**	John	Quantock	,, 1754.	Pair of plain table-spoons : Miss Chivers.
,,	**E·A/J·S**	Ed. John	Aldridge & Stamper	} ,, 1753.	A pierced and engraved fish trowel.
,,	**P·G**	Phillips	Garden	,, ,,	Beer jug : Lord Dormer.
,,	**IM**	John	Munns	,, ,,	A helmet-shaped milk-jug on three legs.
,,	**DM**	Do'thy	Mills	,, 1752.	A vinaigrette, gilt interior.
,,	**JH**	John	Holland	,, 1739.	A plain soup ladle.
,,	**IS**	John	Steward	,, 1755.	Mark registered 29 January, 1755.
,,	**T·C**	Thos.	Collier	,, 1754.	A lemon strainer.
,,	**HD**	Henry	Dutton	,, ,,	A pair of tea-caddies : Mr. R. Wingfield.
,,	**W·B**	Walter	Brind	,, 1749.	An oval engraved snuff-box.
·,	**GB/WS**	Geo. Wm.	Baskerville& Sampel	} ,, 1755.	A sauce-boat, with double spout and scroll handles.
,,	**DPW**	Dobson Prior & Williams	} ,, ,,		Mark registered 10 February, 1755.
,,	**D**	John	Delmester	,, ,,	Pierced and engraved fish slice.
,,	**W·I**	? Wm.	Justus	,, 1739.	Pair of sauce-boats : Mr. Anthony White.
,,	**JS**	John	Swift	,, ,, (see 1745 and below)	Tankard : Noted by the Author.
,,	**H·M**	Henry	Miller	ent. 1740.	Plain bowl : Dr. Wilfred Harris.
1755-6	**JS**	John	Swift	,, 1739.	Bulbous flagon S.S. Peter and Paul : Dagenham, Essex ; also (1762) the Westfield cup : Clothworkers' Company.

* A maker's mark ℬℭ in script letters (probably the mark of Benj. Cartwright), the lion passant and London date-letter t of 1754-5, occur on a wine taster of Portuguese type with engraved inscription : *Padre Fernando Teixeira Perreira da Veiga, Londres Ao Do* 1754. This taster was no doubt copied from a Portuguese taster and sent from London as a present to the recipient.

DATE.	GOLDSMITHS' MARKS AND NAMES.				ARTICLES AND OWNERS.
1755-6	W·S	Wm.	Sanden	ent. 1755.	Mark registered 30 June, 1755.
,,		Simon	Le Sage	,, 1754.	Sauce tureen and cover with lion's mask and ring handles.
,,		Magd'n	Feline	,, 1753.	A taper-holder : Lyne-Stephens Collection.
,,	JW	? Thos.	Wright	,, 1754.	Communion flagon : Damicham, Wilts.
,,	S·C	Saml.	Courtauld (see 1750)	,, 1746.	Beadle's staff head : Clothworkers' Company.
,,	PC	Paul	Crespin (see 1749)	,, 1739.	Table-spoons : Noted by the Author.
,,	W·B·P	Wm. John	Bond & Phipps }	,, 1754.	Small salver, with shell and gadrooned border : The Marquess Townshend.
,,	WT	Wm.	Turner	,, ,,	A plain half-pint mug.
,,	WB	Wm.	Bond	,, 1753.	Pair of table candlesticks : Mr. J. S. Hodgson.
,,	JJ	Jas.	Jones	,, 1755.	A lemon strainer, with open scroll handles.
,,	P·T	Peter	Taylor	,, 1740.	Salver : Mr. Wickes ; also (1756) tea kettle : Dunn-Gardner Collection.
,,	FV	Fred	Vonham	,, 1752.	Soup ladle, with shell-shaped bowl : Mr. H. G. Hussey.
,,	SS	Saml.	Siervent	,, 1755.	Pair of pierced and engraved coasters.
,,	J.W	John	Wirgman	,, 1745.	Three escallop shells.
,,	RM	Richd.	Mills	,, 1755.	Mark registered 14 July, 1755.
,,	B·B	Benj.	Brewood	,, ,,	Six small tea-spoons (lion and maker's mark only).
,,	ED	Ed.	Doweal	,, 1751.	A small waiter : Mr. J. B. Stansby.
,,	RCox	Robt.	Cox	,, 1755.	A pair of Corinthian column candlesticks : Mr. W. Boore.
,,	R·C	Do.	do.	,, ,,	Another mark of R. Cox, registered 17 Dec., 1755.
,,	T·B	Thos.	Beezley	,, ,,	Sugar nippers (lion and maker's mark only).
,,	A·S	Albert	Schurman	,, 1756.	A pair of sugar nippers (lion and maker's mark only).
,,	JR	John	Robinson	,, 1739.	A plain salver : Lady Alice Peel.
1756-7	S·W	Saml.	Wheat	,, 1756.	Set of sugar casters : Hon. Soc. of the Middle Temple.
,,	P·G	Pierre	Gillois	,, 1754.	Beer jug : Dunn-Gardner Collection.
,,	WR	Wm.	Robertson	,, 1753.	A plain tankard : Mr. W. G. Hussey.
,,	WC	Wm.	Caldecott	,, 1756.	Salver : Mr. Crichton.

DATE.	GOLDSMITHS' MARKS AND NAMES.	ARTICLES AND OWNERS.
1756-7	? Thos. Gilpin ent. 1739.	Pierced epergne : Sir Redvers Buller.
,,	Thos. Heming ,, 1745.	Plate : Messrs. Heming & Co.
,,	Name not traced.	Salver : Mr. E. H. Goddard.
,,	Mathew Roker ,, 1755.	A plain muffineer.
,,	Paul Callard ,, 1751.	A plain coffee-pot, with gadrooned foot.
,,	John Edwards ,, 1753.	A pierced mustard pot, with glass liner.
,,	Wm. Gould ,, ,,	A " clobbered " flagon : Dunn-Gardner Collection.
,,	T. Devonshire ⎫ ,, 1756. & W. Watkins ⎭	A plain coffee-pot. The same letters, etc., within a circle, on skewer : Mr. Dudley Westropp.
,,	Ben. Cartwright ,, ,,	A plain soup ladle : Lord Dormer.
,,	Edw. Jay ,, 1757.	Salver, with scroll border : Rev. W. B. Hawkins.
1757-8	David Hennell ,, 1736.	Plain tumbler : The Author's Collection.
,,	Joseph Clare ,, 1713. (see 1716)	Shield of arms : Messrs. Crichton.
,,	Eliza Godfrey ,, 1741.	A pair of tea vases : Holburne Museum.
,,	John Jacobs ,, 1739.	A small globular teapot : Mr. W. Boore.
,,	W. & R. Peaston ,, 1756.	A lemon strainer, with scroll handles : Mr. W. Boore.
,,	Ed. Darvill ,, 1757.	A pair of rectangular tea-caddies, repoussé and chased.
,,	Robert Innes ,, 1742.	Alms-dish : Swithland, Leicestershire.
,,	Stephen Ardesoif ,, 1756.	A small waiter, with gadrooned border.
,,	Ed. Bennett ,, 1739.	A tea kettle, repoussé and chased, on tripod stand.
,,	John Kentenber & ⎫ 1757. Thos. Groves ⎭	A plain cream-jug on circular foot, scroll handle.
,,	John Frost ,, ,,	A pair of sauce ladles : Mr. J. B. Stansby.
,,	Do. do. ,, ,,	Two table-spoons : do. do.
,,	John Hyatt & ⎫ ,, ,, Chas. Semore ⎭	A plain circular waiter, with moulded border.
,,	Arthur Annesley ,, 1758. (see 1761)	A small plain mug, with scroll handle.
,,	Robt. Burton ,, ,,	A plain milk-jug on three legs : Mr. W. Boore.

Date.	Goldsmiths' Marks and Names.			Articles and Owners.
1757-8	JS	John	Schuppe ent. 1753.	Cow milk-jugs: The Author's Collection; and (1755): Holburne Museum.
,,	WC	Wm.	Cafe ,, 1757.	Candlesticks: Lady Riddell.
1758-9	FN	Fras.	Nelme ,, 1722.	{ Milk-jug: The Drane Collection. Tea-spoons: Mr. Anthony White.
,,	ST	Saml.	Taylor ,, 1744.	Sugar box: The Drane Collection.
,,	WC	Wm.	Cripps ,, 1743.	Heads of four beadles' staves: St. Margaret's, Westminster.
,,	S·C	Name not traced.		Pair of Corinthian-column candlesticks: Mr. H. D. Ellis.
,,	W·S P	Wm. Wm.	Shaw & } Priest } ,, 1749.	Salver: The Day Collection.
,,	C·B	Name not traced.		Pair of waiters on three feet: Holburne Museum; also com. flagon: Landford, Wilts.
,,	I·H	John	Hague ,, 1758.	A chamber candlestick: Lord Dormer.
,,	WB	Wm.	Bell ,, 1759.	A large meat skewer, with shell and ring.
,,	F L★H B	Lewis Francis	Herne & } Butty } ,, 1757.	Standing cup: Mr. R. Meldrum. (See also 1761.)
,,	I·BELL	Jos.	Bell ,, 1756.	{ Table-spoon: Messrs. Crichton. Set of tea-spoons: Mr. Anthony White.
,,	I B S A	Name not traced.		Pierced bread-basket: Lord Hastings, Melton Constable.
1759-60	H· S·H B·	S.	Herbert & Co. ,, 1750.	Bread-basket, with trellis and scroll ornaments between beaded bands, on shell and scroll feet: Mr. H. G. Hussey.
,,	FK	Fred.	Kandler ,, 1739.	Oval pierced cake-basket, engraved with figures, flowers, and appliqué masks: Messrs. Christie.
,,	I★D	John	Delmester ,, 1755.	Mustard pot: The Author's Collection; and (1772) flagon: Wyke-Regis, Dorset.
,,	I·P	John	Perry ,, 1757.	A plain soup ladle: Mrs. Dawson.
,,	S·W	Saml.	Wood, 2nd mk. ,, 1739.	{ Rose-water ewer: The Author's Collection. Cruet-frame: Mr. E. H. Griffiths.
,,	IBBOT	Geo.	Ibbott ,, 1753.	Sugar vase: Messrs. Crichton.
,,	I·P	John	Perry ,, 1757.	Set of candlesticks: Mr. R. Meldrum.
,,	I S·L	Simon	Le Sage ,, 1754.	Ink-stand: Messrs. Crichton.
,,	WB	? Walter Brind ,, 1749.		Sugar vase: Do. do.
,,	WC	Wm.	Cripps ,, 1743.	Pair of fruit dishes: Hon. Soc. of the Inner Temple.
,,	IH	John	Hyatt ,, 1748.	Punch ladle: Mr. W. Boore.
,,	HB	Henry	Bayley (probably).	A chamber candlestick with extinguisher: The Day Collection.

DATE.	GOLDSMITHS' MARKS AND NAMES.			ARTICLES AND OWNERS.
1759-60	𝕊𝕎	? Saml.	Wheat	ent. 1756.	Altar candlesticks : Trin. Coll., Oxford.
,,	SWA	Stephen Abdy & Wm. Jury }		,, 1759.	Two-handled cup and cover : Gregory Coll'n.
,,	AB	Alex.	Barnett	,, ,,	A plain waiter, with scroll and shell border.
,,	TC	Thos.	Congreve	,, 1756.	A cream-jug, chased with pastoral subject.
,,	TD	Thos.	Doxsey	,, ,,	Table-spoons, with embossed scrolls on back of bowl.
,,	WM	Wm.	Moody	,, ,,	A small plain mug, with scroll handle.
,,	WD	Wm.	Day	,, 1759.	A hand candlestick : The Marquess Townshend.
,,	S·E	Saml.	Eaton	,, ,,	A plain tankard, with domed cover and scroll handle.
,,	JK	? Jno.	Kentenber		Table-spoons : The Author's Collection.
1760-1	R·R	Robt.	Rew	,, 1754.	Circular salver : Messrs. Christie.
,,	EW	Edwd.	Wakelin	,, 1747.	Sauce-boats : Hol. Mus. ; and (1756) tea-caddies : Lord Carbery.
,,	C·D	Name not traced.			Tall sugar caster, with gadrooned base.
,,	FW	Fuller	White	,, 1758.	A plain tankard with scroll handle : Mr. H. G. Hussey.
,,	AS	Alex.	Saunders	,, 1757.	A muffineer, the lower part conventionally chased.
,,	JM	John	Moore	,, 1758.	Plain tankard, domed top, scroll handle : The Author's Collection.
,,	CT	C'nst'ne Teulings		,, 1755.	Oblong silver-gilt snuff-box, chased with scrolls and flowers.
,,	WH	Wm.	Howard	,, 1760.	A pear-shaped coffee-pot, with modern chasing.
,,	GM	Geo.	Methuen	,, 1743.	Communion plate : St. Andrew's, Plymouth.
,,	I·E	John	Eaton	,, 1760.	Plain cylindrical tankard, domed top, scroll handle.
c. 1760-1	W·L	Name not traced.			Pair of sugar-nippers : Messrs. Crichton.
,,	Lee	Jeremy Lee		,, 1739.	Do. do. do. do.
1761-2	R·R	Richd.	Rugg	,, 1754.	Circular salver, shell and scroll border, chased centre.
,,	W·P	Wm.	Plummer	,, 1755.	Small pierced basket : The Drane Collection.
,,	LHB	Louis Herne & Fras. Butty }		,, 1757.	Oval meat dishes, with gadrooned borders. (See also 1758.)
,,	FB ND	Fras. Butty & Nicks. Dumee }		,, ,,	Soup tureen : Messrs. Hamilton & Inches.
,,	W·S	Wm.	Shaw	,, 1749.	Communion cup : Llanwern, Mon.

DATE.	GOLDSMITHS' MARKS AND NAMES.			ARTICLES AND OWNERS.
1761-2	I·H	John	Horsley.	Candlestick: Cambridge Plate Exhibition, 1895.
,,	J·G	John	Gorham ent. 1757.	Table-spoons: Mr. W. Boore.
,,	A·A	Arthur	Annesley ,, 1758. (see 1757)	Cake-basket: Messrs. Crichton.
,,	G H	Geo.	Hunter ,, 1748.	Pair of sauce-boats: Do. do.
,,	M·F	Magdalen Feline	,, 1753.	Maces: Okehampton, Devon.
,,	T·H	Thomas	Heming ,, 1745. (see 1756)	Soup-tureen and cover engraved, *Thomas Heming Fecit* 1761: Windsor Castle.
,,	MP	Mary	Piers ,, 1758.	Plain sauce-boat, on three lion's-mask and claw feet.
,,	T·P	Thos.	Powell ,, ,,	Pair of Corinthian column candlesticks.
1762-3	J·J	Jas.	Jones ,, 1755.	Table-spoon: The Author's Collection.
,,	W·T	Wm.	Tant ,, 1773. (probably)	Do. do.: Do. do.
,,	WS	Wm.	Sampel ,, 1755.	Plain cream-jug on three feet: Lady Molesworth.
,,	L·B	Louis	Black ,, 1761.	Pair of circular salt-cellars, each on three feet.
,,	C/T·W	Thos. Chas.	Whipham & Wright } ,, 1757.	Three plain sugar casters: Mr. W. Boore: also (1763-4) com. paten: Dilwyn, Herefordshire.
,,	G·J	Geo.	Ibbott ,, 1753.	Circular salver, with gadrooned border.
,,	SD	Saml.	Delamy ,, 1762.	A plain coffee-pot, with domed lid.
,,	D/W·I	W. & J.	Deane ,, ,,	A lemon strainer, with open scroll handles.
,,	IB	Jos.	Bell ,, 1756.	A large plain gravy spoon: Mr. Lowe.
,,	E/EA/A	Edwd.	Aldridge & Co.	Cream-jug, repoussé and chased with conventional foliage.
,,	WD	Wm.	Day ,, 1759.	A plain bulb-shaped tankard: Mr. Chisholm.
,,	W Wa	Wm.	Watkins ,, 1756.	Marrow scoop: Messrs. Crichton.
,,	E✱A	Edward	Aldridge ,, 1739.	Frame: Mr. Anthony White.
,,	R‡P	R.	Peaston ., 1756.	Pepper caster: Mr. Harry Alston.
1763-4	RT	Richd.	Thomas ,, 1755.	An engraved fish slice, partly pierced.
,,	T·D	Tmpsn.	Davis ,, 1757.	An oval snuff-box: Mr. Peters.
,,	E·A	Edward	Aldridge ,, 1739.	Pierced cake-basket: Trin. Coll., Oxford.
,,	C/T·W	Thos. Chas.	Whipham & Wright } ,, 1758.	Standing cup and cover: Messrs. Harman & Co. (See also 1762.)

DATE.	GOLDSMITHS' MARKS AND NAMES.		ARTICLES AND OWNERS.
1763-4		Danl. Smith & Robt. Sharp	Salver : Holburne Museum.
,,		T. & W. Chawner (probably).	Gravy spoon : Hon. Soc. Grays Inn.
,,		Ebenezer Coker ,,	Com. paten, on three feet : Wythop, Cumb.
,,		Phil. Vincent ent. 1757.	A plain punch ladle, with whale-bone handle.
,,		Wm. King ,, 1761.	A small mug : Edkins Collection.
,,		John Buckett.	A pair of Corinthian column candlesticks.
,,		John Aspinshaw ,, 1763.	A "Warwick" cruet frame, with vase-shaped casters.
,,		John Lamfert ,, 1748.	"Onslow" pattern table-spoons : Mr. Davison.
c. 1763-4		Name not traced.	Tea-spoons : Messrs. Crichton.
,,		Do. do.	Do. do. do.
1764-5		D. & R. Hennell ,, 1768.	Salts, each on four feet : Mrs. Budd.
,,		? Thos. Hannam Rich. Mills	Small waiter : Lord Swaythling.
,,		Name not traced.	Sugar-basket, with glass liner : Mr. Winstone.
,,		W. & R. Peaston (probably).	Candlesticks on vase-shaped stems, gadrooned feet.
,,		Names not traced.	Four sauce tureens : Holburne Museum.
,,		John Hyatt & C. Semore ent. 1757.	Pair of candlesticks : Lady Alice Peel.
,,		Aug. Le Sage ,, 1767.	Plain soup bowl and dish : Lord Dormer.
,,		Thos. Freeman & J. Marshall ,, 1764.	Plain tankard : Mr. Chas. Clarke.
,,		Anthy. Calame ,, ,,	Pair of candlesticks : Lyne-Stephens Collection.
,,		J. A. Calame ,, ,,	Pierced fish-trowel, with ivory handle.
,,		John Innocent (probably).	Table-spoons : The Author's Collection.
,,		W. & R. Peaston ,, (see above)	Tankard : Messrs. Crichton.
,,		Wm. Cafe ent. 1757.	Communion flagon : St. Michael's, Derby.
,,		Name not traced.	Mark noted by the Author.
,,		Do. do.	Plain water-jug : Mr. W. A. Willson.
,,		Thos. Whipham & Chas. Wright ,, 1758.	Fluted soup ladle : Mr. Harry Alston.

DATE.	GOLDSMITHS' MARKS AND NAMES.		ARTICLES AND OWNERS.
1765-6		Names not traced.	Sugar-basket : Mr. H. D. Ellis.
,,	GS	Do.　　do.	Four table candlesticks, with vase-shaped stems.
,,	WC	Wm.　Caldecott ent. 1756.	Milk-jug : The Drane Collection.
,,	EC	Eben.　Coker　(probably).	Candlestick : Do.　　do.
,,		Name not traced.	Alms-dish : St. Mabyn, Cornwall.
,,	ER	Emick　Romer　　,,	Candlesticks : Dunn-Gardner Collection.
,,	BM	Name not traced.	Pyriform coffee-pot : Mr. Hugh Cobb.
,,	R✦P	? R.　　Peaston.	Warwick cruet frame : Windsor Castle.
,,	IA	John　Allen　ent. 1761.	A set of coasters : Sir Charles Welby, Bart.
,,	SH	Sam.　Howland　,, 1760.	Four circular salt-cellars on feet.
,,	GH	Geo.　Hunter　,, 1765.	A gourd-shaped teapot, with Arabesque chasing.
,,	T·C / W·C	T. & W. Chawner (probably).	Table-spoons : The Author's Collection.
1766-7	LH	Name not traced.	Loving cup : Gloucester Corporation.
,,	LC	Louisa　Courtauld.	{ Tea urn : Messrs. Garrard. { Table bell (1766) : Mr. A. S. Marsden Smedley.
,,	JL	John　Lampfert ent. 1748.	"Onslow" pattern sauce ladle : Barber Surgeons' Company.
,,	I / I·L / S	John　Langford & John　Sebille	Cruet frame : The Day Collection.
,,	M·F	Matthew Ferris　　,, 1759.	Tripod salt : Holburne Museum.
,,	T·H / I·C	Thos.　Hannam & John　Crouch	Paten : New Church, Romney Marsh.
,,	FC	Fras.　Crump　　,, 1756.	Epergne, with pierced centre basket : Lord Dormer.
,,	GA	Geo.　Andrews　,, 1763.	A small salver, with shell and scroll border.
,,	TD	Thos.　Dealtry　,, 1765.	Table-spoons : Mrs. Budd.
,,	CM	Chas.　Miegg　　,, 1767.	A plain soup ladle and two sauce ladles.
,,	DM	Dorothy Mills (probably).	Table-spoons : Mr. Lowe.
,,	T·W	Thos.　Wynne　ent. 1754.	Table-spoons : The Author's Collection.
1767-8	JR	Jno.　Richardson ,, 1752.	Sauce-pan : Messrs. Crichton.
,,	I / W·F / K	Names not traced.	Coffee-pot :　　Do.　　do.

Date.	Goldsmiths' Marks and Names.			Articles and Owners.
1767-8		Thos. Bumfries & Orlando Jackson } ent. 1766.		Tea caddy : Edkins Collection.
,,		S. Herbert & Co.	,, 1750.	Pierced basket : Holburne Museum.
,,		Name not traced.		Pair of candlesticks : do. do.
,,		Wm. Abdy	,, 1767.	Oval toilet-box : Rev. W. B. Hawkins.
,,		Geo. Fayle	,, ,,	Two circular salt-cellars : Mr. B. Jefferis.
,,		Wm. Tuite (probably).		Sauce-boat on four legs : Mr. W. Boore.
,,		Name not traced.		A lemon strainer, with two handles : Mr. W. Boore.
1768-9		John Parker & Edwd. Wakelin }		Badge : The Duke of Devonshire ; also (1769) inkstand : Soane Museum.
,,		James Hunt	ent. 1760.	Gold chatelaine : Messrs. Crichton.
,,		T. & W. Chawner (probably).		Large skewer : Hon. Soc. of the Inner Temple.
,,		Dan. Smith & Robt. Sharp }		(See also 1773) ; Standing cup : Messrs. Harman & Co.
,,		Name not traced.		Tobacco-box : Messrs. Crichton.
,,		Fras. Spilsbury, Jr.		Pierced salts : Mr. Cecil B. Morgan.
,,		? Eliz. Tuite (see 1742)	ent. 1741.	Table-spoon : Mrs. E. H. Goddard.
,,		Name not traced.		Pair of soup ladles : Hon. Soc. Inner Temple.
,,		Edward Capper (probably).		Large waiter : Holburne Museum.
,,		Fras. Crump	ent. 1756.	Communion cup and paten : Maryport, Cumb.
,,		W. & J. Priest.		Tankard : Mr. W. H. Fowle, Andover.
,,		John Lamfert	,, 1748.	Table-spoon : The Drane Collection.
,,		Benj. Blakeley	,, 1739.	Table-spoons : Westgate Hotel, Newport, Mon.
,,		John Darwall	,, 1768.	Domed-top tankard, with scroll handle and open thumb piece.
1769-70		John Neville (probably).		Large cruet frame : The Author's Collection.
,,		Chas. Aldridge & Henry Green }		Two-handled cup and cover : Mr. W. Boore.
,,		Fras. Crump	ent. 1756.	Com. cups and flagon : St. Anne's, Limehouse.
,,		Geo. Seatoun.		Milk jug : The Drane Collection.
,,		Chas. Woodward.		Two com. cups : St. Dionis, Parsons Green.

DATE.	GOLDSMITHS' MARKS AND NAMES.			ARTICLES AND OWNERS.
1769-70	I·K	John	Kentenber ent. 1757.	Tall coffee-pot : Mr. Harry Alston.
,,	AL	Aug.	Le Sage ,, 1767.	Tea-caddy : Messrs. Tiffany.
,,	E L	Edwd.	Lowe ,, 1777.	Coasters : Noted by the Author ; (see also 1778).
,,	W·B	Walter	Brind ,, 1757.	A plain pear-shaped coffee-pot, with fluted spout.
,,	WG	Wm.	Grundy ,, 1748.	Pair of pierced oval salt-cellars, with glass liners.
,,	SC I·C	Septimus & James	Crespell }	Set of dishes, with gadrooned edges.
,,	T I	Thos.	Jackson ,, 1769.	A gourd-shaped teapot, with ebony handles.
,,	LC GC	Louisa & Geo.	Courtauld Cowles. }	Candlesticks : Queens' Coll., Cambridge.
,,	RR	Robt.	Rogers ,, 1773.	Gold signet-ring : Mr. B. Jefferis.
,,	JB	John	Baker ,, 1770.	A plain wine funnel with strainer.
1770-1	B·G	Benj.	Gignac ,, 1744.	Two com. cups : St. John's, Hampstead.
,,	TH	Thos.	Heming ,, ,,	{ Sucrier with Adam festoons : S. Kensington { Mus. ; also (1767) Corporation maces : Rye.
,,	JA	Jas.	Allen ,, 1766.	A small pierced muffineer with glass liner.
,,	SC I·C	Septimus & James	Crespell } see 1769.	Hot-water jug : Holburne Museum.
,,	T·P	? Thos.	Powell ent. 1756.	Epergne : Mr. W. Boore.
,,	TA	Thos.	Arnold ,, 1770.	A fluted and engraved coffee-pot.
,,	IB	John	Baxter ,, 1773.	A pierced and engraved cruet frame.
,,	C W	Chas.	Wright.	(See also 1772) tea-urn : Clothworkers' Company.
,,	I·B	? John	Buckett ,, 1770.	Sugar tongs : Messrs. Crichton.
,,	I·L I·S	John John	Langford & Sebille }	Inkstand : Mr. E. H. Goddard.
,,	G·S	Name not traced.		Sauce-boat : Messrs. Alstons & Hallam.
,,	ER	E.	Romer (probably).	Table-spoons : Sir Frederick L. Currie, Bart.
,,	O·J	Orlando	Jackson ent. 1759.	An " Argyle " gravy pot, with hot-water jacket.
,,	SW.	Sam.	Wheat ,, 1756.	Pierced mustard-pot, with glass liner.
,,	I·G V	John Wm.	Gimblett & Vale } ,, 1770.	Muffineer embossed and chased with flowers and foliage.
,,	I·B	J.	Bassingwhite ,, ,,	Table candlesticks (loaded), with fluted stems, circular plinths.
1771-2	I·C T·H	John Thos.	Crouch & Hannam }	Fine tea vase : Barber Surgeons' Company.

Date.	Goldsmiths' Marks and Names.			Articles and Owners.
1771-2	**TF**	Thos.	Foster ent. 1769.	Sauce-boat : Messrs. Alstons & Hallam.
,,	**DB**	David	Bell ,, 1756.	Glass-lined sugar basket : Mr. Arthur J. Finch.
,,	**R I·S**	? Robt. & Jno.	Schofield } ,, 1776.	Standing cup ; Messrs. Harman & Co.
,,	**T I·D D**	Thos. & Jabez	Daniel }	Mark noted by the Author.
,,	**S·B**	? Sarah	Buttall ,, 1754.	Pierced mustard-pot : Mr. Cecil B. Morgan.
,,	**J·A**	Jonathan	Alleine.	Soup ladle, engraved stem, shell pattern bowl.
,,	**WP**	Wm.	Penstone.	Table-spoon : The Drane Collection.
,,	**W·S**	Wm.	Sheen ,, 1755.	Sugar tongs : The Author's Collection.
,,	**T·C**	Thos.	Chawner.	Table-spoons : Mr. G. Hibbert.
,,	**S·H**	Saml.	Howland ,, 1760.	Dish cross, with spirit lamp : Holburne Museum.
,,	**A·U**	A.	Underwood.	Inkstand : Do do.
,,	**C C**	Chas.	Chesterman ,, 1771.	Pierced fish slice : Mr. W. Boore.
,,	**E I**	Edwd.	Jay ,, 1757.	Salver, Mr. W. Boore ; also (1776-7) com. paten : St. Weonard's, Herefordshire.
,,	**T·T**	Thos.	Towman (probably).	Two-handled engraved cup, with moulded band in centre.
,,	**WT**	Wm.	Tuite ent. 1756.	Oblong inkstand, with pierced gallery.
,,	**IR**	John	Romer ent. before 1773.	Soup tureen in the Adam style : The Author's Collection.
1772-3	**I·C**	John	Carter ,, ,,	{ Com. paten : Temple Sowerby, Westmorland. { Tea vase, repoussé and chased with festoons, acanthus leaves at base : S. Kensington Museum.
,,	**TC**	Tho .	Chawner ,, ,,	Three-pronged forks : Mr. W. Boore.
,,	**ET**	Eliz.	Tookey ,, ,,	" Onslow " pattern table-spoons : The Author's Collection.
,,	**WF**	Wm.	Fearn ,, ,,	Large perforated spoon.
,,	**BD**	Burrage	Davenport ,, ,,	Sugar tongs : Dr. Propert.
,,	**I·A**	John	Arnell ,, ,,	Salt-cellars on feet : General Meyrick.
,,	**J·S**	John	Swift ,, ,,	{ Tankard : Mr. Saml. Deane. { Candlesticks (1776-7) : Mrs. E. H. Goddard.
,,	**P·N**	Philip	Norman ,, ,,	A pair of snuffers and octagonal tray.
,,	**CW**	Chas.	Wright ,, ,,	A small cream-jug on three shell feet.
,,	**P·D**	Peter Peter	Desergnes or Devese. }	Pair of sauce-boats : Messrs. Crichton.
,,	**Wa**	? Wm.	Watkins ,, 1756.	Pair of candlesticks : Do do.

DATE.	GOLDSMITHS' MARKS AND NAMES.		ARTICLES AND OWNERS.
1772-3	[mark]	Henry Hallsworth.	Set of candlesticks : Messrs. Heming & Co.
,,	[mark A·F]	Name not traced.	Teapot : Windsor Castle.
,,	[mark I·F]	John Fayle ent. 1772.	Pierced and engraved waist buckle : Lady Page Turner.
,,	[mark WE]	Wm. Eley (probably).	Table-spoons : The Author's Collection.
1773-4	[mark R·S D·S]	Dan. Smith & } ent. before Robt. Sharp } 1773.	Two-handled cup, with festoons of drapery : Messrs. Dobson & Son.
,,	[mark OI]	Orlando Jackson ,, 1759.	O.E. pat. table-spoons, with feathered edges : The Author's Collection.
,,	[mark JH]	John Harvey ,, 1739.	Alms-dish : St. Mary, Ealing.
,,	[mark TS]	Thos. Smith ,, 1750.	Milk-jug : Sir Frederick Currie, Bart.
,,	[mark LV]	Name not traced.	Com. paten : St. Anne's, Limehouse.
,,	[mark AB LD]	Abr'm Barrier & } Lewis Ducornieu }	Silver-gilt spoon : St. Michael's, Highgate.
,,	[mark WS]	Wm. Sheen ,, 1775.	Sauce-boat : Holburne Museum.
,,	[mark T I·D D]	Jabez & Daniel} Thos. see 1771.	Tea-caddy : Mr. W. Boore.
,,	[mark BD]	Burrage Davenport.	Muffineer : Mr. J. L. Propert.
,,	[mark SW]	Saml. Wood (probably).	Set of three tea and sugar vases : Col. Longfield.
,,	[mark P·F]	P. Freeman ent. 1773.	Pair of shoe buckles : Lady Emsley Carr.
,,	[mark MM]	Mary Makemeid ,, . ,,	Nutmeg box : The Author's Collection.
,,	[mark TT]	Thos. Tookey ,, ,,	Watch case : Mr. W. Iggulden.
,,	[mark LD]	Louis de Lisle ,, ,,	Wine labels : Sir Frederick L. Currie, Bart
,,	[mark WLB]	Wm. Le Bas ,, ,,	Vinaigrette, with delicately pierced and engraved inner lid.
1774-5	[mark IS]	Jas. Stamp ,, 1774.	Pair of candlesticks, with fluted vase-shaped stems.
,,	[mark WP]	Wm. Penstone ,, ,,	A fluted and engraved coffee-pot.
,,	[mark E·T]	Eliz. Tookey ,, 1773.	Table-spoons : Mrs. Budd.
,,	[mark T·E]	Thos. Evans ,, 1774.	Milk-jugs : Lady Page Turner ; and (1775-6) : Mrs. E. H. Goddard.
,,	[mark IY OI]	Jas. Young & } Orlando Jackson } ,, ,,	Wine funnel, with gadrooned edge.
,,	[mark I·D]	John Deacon ,, 1773.	Teapot : Holburne Museum.
,,	[mark TD]	Thomas Daniel (probably).	Cruet frame : Holburne Museum.

Date.	Goldsmiths' Marks and Names.				Articles and Owners.
1774-5	**PF**	P.	Freeman	ent. 1774.	An oval cruet frame with reeded borders.
,,	**WF**	Wm.	Fennell.		A small cream jug, chased with wreaths of foliage, a shield in front.
,,	**IY**	Jas.	Young	,, 1775.	"Warwick" cruet frame : Lady Page Turner.
,,	**IS**	Jas.	Stamp	,, 1774.	Engraved punch ladle : Gen. A. W. H. Meyrick.
1775-6	**W·T**	Walter	Tweedie	ent. before 1773.	Small paten : S.S. Peter and Paul, Harlington, Middlesex.
,,	**EC**	? Ed.	Capper	(see 1776).	Argyle : Mr. W. B. Gair.
,,	**WC**	? Wm.	Cox.		Basin : St. Clement, Cornwall.
,,	**IK**	? John Jas. Jas.	Kentish King cr Kingman	ent. 1773.	Straining funnel : Sir Charles E. Welby, Bart.
,,	**WS RC**	Wm. Richd.	Sumner & Crossley	,, 1775.	Wine funnel, with gadrooned rim.
,,	**IY**	Jas.	Young	,, ,,	Vase-shaped tea-caddy, engraved with festoons.
,,	**TL**	Thos.	Langford	(probably).	Plain goblet, on short stem and foot.
,,	**I·E W·F**	? John Wm. Wm.	Easton & Fearn or Fennell, etc.		Engraved tea-kettle : Lord Dormer.
,,	**RR**	Robt.	Ross	ent. 1774.	Circular salver, with chased centre.
,,	**MC**	Mark	Cripps	,, 1767.	Plain tankard, with moulded band and foot.
,,	**CW**	Chris.	Woods	,, 1775.	Hand candlestick and extinguisher : Colonel Fitzgerald.
,,	**RR**	Richd.	Rugg	,, ,,	Fish slice, with stained ivory handle.
,,	**RI**	Robt.	Jones	,, 1776.	Pair of circular salt-cellars on shell feet.
,,	**T G·B M**	Geo. & T.	Baskerville Morley	,, 1775.	A set of four escallop shells.
,,	**RP**	Robt.	Piercy	,, ,,	A circular engraved mustard-pot, with beaded rim.
,,	**{LD}**	Louis	Ducomieu	,, ,,	A pair of plain sauce-boats on feet.
,,	**BS**	Ben	Stephenson	,, ,,	A pair of snuffers and tray : Col. Fitzgerald.
1776-7	**CH**	Name not traced.			Punch ladle : General Meyrick.
,,	**HS**	Henry	Sardet.		Com. flagon and paten : St. Mary-le-bone.
,,	**RP**	Robt.	Piercy	,, ,,	A pair of sugar tongs, with shell ends.
,,	**AB**	Alexr.	Barnet	,, 1759.	A plain oval tea-caddy, with beaded edges.
,,	**N·D**	Nich.	Dumee	,, 1776.	A pair of circular salt-cellars, with gadrooned edges.
,,	**W G·H C**	Geo. & Wm.	Heming Chawner	,, 1774.	Small coffee-pot : Col. Fitzgerald.

Date.	Goldsmiths' Marks and Names.			Articles and Owners.
1776-7	I·L	John	Lautier ent. 1773.	Pierced sugar basket: Holburne Museum.
,,	I·W W·T	John Wm.	Wakelin & } Taylor } ,, 1776.	Standing cup, with serpent handles: St. John's College, Cambridge.
,,	H·A C·G	Chas. Henry	Aldridge & } Green } ,, 1775.	The "Younge" salvers, and two wine-jugs: Clothworkers' Company.
,,	A·C	A.	Calame ,, 1764.	{ Small two-handled cup: Mr. C. M. Morgan. { Cream-jug (1777-8): Messrs. Crichton.
,,	E·C	Edwd. Edwd.	Capper or } Cooke } ,, 1773.	Octagonal teapot: Mr. Rossi, Norwich.
,,	A·L	Aug.	Le Sage ,, 1767.	Two small pierced sugar-baskets: Dr. Wilfred Harris.
,,	P·R	Phil.	Roker ,, 1776.	Table-spoons: Mr. J. M. de Gumacio.
,,	E·R	Eliz.	Roker ,, ,,	Do. do. : do. do.
1777-8	H·G	Henry	Greenway ,, 1775.	Chocolate pot: S. Kensington Museum.
,,	J·A	Jon'th'n Alleine.		Com. patens: St. Andrews, Boreham, Essex.
,,	R·M R·C	Robt. & Richd.	Makepeace } Carter } ,, 1777.	{ Com. flagon and a paten: St. Mary-le-bone. { Pair of candlesticks (1772): Messrs. Spink.
,,	I·H	Joseph	Heriot ,, 1750.	Toilet-box: Holburne Museum.
,,	W·H	Wm.	Holmes ,, 1776.	Urn, with serpent handles: St. John's College, Cambridge.
,,	W·P	Wm.	Potter ,, 1777.	Tea vase in the Adam style: The Author's Collection.
,,	W·H·C	Wm. Wm.	Howe & } Clark } ,, ,,	A circular tripod stand and spirit lamp for a coffee-pot.
,,	W·G	Wm.	Grundy ,, ,,	A plain saucepan and cover with beaded edges.
,,	G·N	Geo.	Natter ,, 1773.	A small circular bulb-shaped and engraved coffee-pot.
,,	R·I I·S	Robt. John	Jones & } Schofield } ,, 1776.	An engraved cream-jug, with beaded base.
,,	G·N	Name not traced.		Sugar nippers: Messrs. Crichton.
,,	T·D	T.	Daniel ,, 1774.	Warwick cruet frame: The Author's Collection.
1778-9	H·C·A·G	Name not traced.		Escallop shells: Windsor Castle.
,,	A·F	Andrew Fogelberg.		Argyle: Messrs. Crichton.
,,	J·D	J.	Denzilow.	Tea vase, with oval shields and festoons of drapery: The Author's Collection.
,,	W·E	Wm.	Eley.	Com. flagon: St. John the Baptist, Leyton-stone, Essex.
,,	H·B	Hester	Bateman. ,, 1774.	Table-spoons, "Onslow" pattern, and pierced salts: The Author's Collection.
,,	W·H N·D	Wm. Nichs.	Holmes & } Dumee } ,, 1773.	A pair of three-legged butter boats, with gadrooned edges.

Date.	Goldsmiths' Marks and Names.				Articles and Owners.
1778-9	**NH**	Nichs.	Hearnden	ent. 1773.	A circular teapot, repoussé and chased with foliage and flowers.
,,	**ED**	Ed.	Dobson	,, 1778.	A pair of oval salt-cellars on four legs.
,,	**RC DS RS**	Rich. Danl. Robt.	Carter, Smith & Sharp	,, ,,	A large plain caster on square base.
,,	**WE GP**	Wm. Geo.	Eley & Pierpoint	,, 1778.	A trowel-shaped pierced fish slice, with ivory handle.
,,	**ID**	John	Deacon	,, 1776.	A snuffers tray, with beaded edge, and the snuffers pertaining to it.
,,	**CK**	Chas.	Kandler	,, 1778.	A meat skewer, with shell and ring at end.
,,	**EL**	Ed.	Lowe	,, 1777.	Four circular salt-cellars, each on three feet.
,,	**GR**	Geo.	Rodenbostel	,, 1778.	A small plain mug, with threaded hoops.
,,	**TW**	Thos.	Wallis	,, 1773.	An engraved caddy spoon.
1779-80	**IS**	John	Schofield	,, 1778.	Stand for supporting a "Queen Anne" monteith: Lord Swaythling.
,,	**EF d**	Edith	Fennell	,, 1780.	(With Britannia standard marks). Rose-water dish: Windsor Castle.
,,	**WG·HC**	Geo. Wm.	Heming & Chawner (see also 1781)	,, 1774.	Soup-tureen: Messrs. Crichton.
,,	**HB**	Hester	Bateman	,, 1774.	Sugar caster: Mr. J. Whaley.
,,	**T·S**	Thos.	Satchwell	,, 1773.	Sugar bowl and milk-jug: Mr. Ince.
,,	**TP RP**	Thos. & Richd.	Payne	,, 1777.	Cream-jug on three legs.
,,	**WF**	W. L.	Foster	,, 1775.	Table-spoons, gravy-spoon, and sauce-ladles.
,,	**E WG F**	Wm. Ed.	Grundy & Fennell	,, 1779.	Chased beaker: Edkins Collection.
,,	**LC SC**	Louisa & Samuel	Courtauld	,, 1777.	A tankard, spoiled by coarse modern chasing.
1780-1	**FS**	Fras.	Stamp	,, 1780.	Pair of Corinthian candlesticks.
,,	**WG**	Wm.	Garrard (probably).		A waiter on three feet.
,,	**R JD M**	Jane Rich.	Dorrell & May	ent. 1771.	An ewer-shaped cream-jug.
,,	**I·S**	Jas.	Sutton	,, 1780.	A soup ladle, with feathered edge.
,,	**WV**	Wm.	Vincent	,, 1773.	Upright oval tea-pot, engraved with festoons.
,,	**IM WH**	Jas. Wm.	Mince & Hodgkins	,, 1780.	A coarsely pierced fruit dish, with glass liner.
,,	**TB AH**	T. P. Arthur	Boulton & Humphreys	,, ,,	Soup ladle, shell-shaped bowl.
,,	**IL IR**	John John of Newcastle	Langlands & Robertson	,, ,,	Bulb-shaped tankard, domed top: Mr. Lowe.

DATE.	GOLDSMITHS' MARKS AND NAMES.		ARTICLES AND OWNERS.
1780-1	H·P	Name not traced.	Sugar-nippers : Windsor Castle.
,,	IP	Joseph Preedy.	Tea-caddy : Messrs. Crichton.
,,	I·K	John Kidder ent. 1780.	A pair of small sauce ladles.
1781-2	TP AH	T. B. Pratt & Arthur Humphreys } ,, 1773.	Engraved tea-caddy : The Author's Collection.
,,	C·W	Chas. Wright ,, 1775.	Two communion cups and a flagon : St. Magnus, London Bridge.
,,	RC	Robt. Cruickshank ,, 1773.	Oval hot-water jug : The Author's Collection.
,,	IC TH	John Crouch & Thos. Hannam } ,, ,,	Two com. patens : St. Mary's, Hanwell, Mids
,,	I·L	Josh. Lejeune ,, ,,	Teapot, with figure of seated Chinaman on lid.
,,	LK	Luke Kendall ,, 1772.	A taper holder of baluster form.
,,	GH WC	Geo. Heming & Wm. Chawner } ,, 1781.	An engraved salver : Edkins Collection.
,,	WP WW	Wm. Playfair & Wm. Wilson } ,, 1782.	A large meat skewer.
,,	TD IW	Thos. Daniel & John Wall } ,, 1781.	A plain circular waiter, with beaded edge.
1782-3	GS	Geo. Smith ,, 1782.	Tea vases with four handles : The Author's Colln.
,,	JW	John Wren ,, 1777.	Do. with rams' heads : Do. do.
,,	GG	George Giles (probably).	Pair of O.E. pattern engraved table-spoons : The Author's Collection.
,,	AF SG	Andr. Fogelberg & Steph. Gilbert } ent. 1780.	Coffee-pot : Mr. Chisholm.
,,	RH	Robt. Hennell ,, 1773.	Engraved snuffers tray : The Author's Colln.
,,	WB	Wm. Bayley.	Communion cup : St. Giles, Ickenham, Mids.
,,	N A·A	This mark is A N S A. Name not traced.	Milk-jug : The Drane Collection.
,,	AP PP	Abm. Peterson & Peter Podie } ,, 1783.	Small two-handled cup on low foot.
1783-4	I·L	John Lamb ,, ,,	O.E. pattern engraved dessert-spoons : The Author's Collection.
,,	IS IB	Jas. Sutton & Jos. Bult } ,, 1782.	Sugar tongs : Mrs. Budd.
,,	WT	Wm. Tant ,, 1773.	Tumbler : The Drane Collection.
,,	W·B	Wm. Brown (probably).	Toy mug and small spirit measure.
,,	SB	? Saml. Bradley.	Hand bell : Messrs. Crichton.
,,	A·F S·G	Name not traced.	Soup-tureen : Mr. S. J. Phillips.

Date.	Goldsmiths' Marks and Names.				Articles and Owners.
1783-4	**E·F**	Ed.	Fennell	ent. 1780.	Two alms-dishes: St. Mary's, Islington.
,,	**SW**	Saml.	Wintle	,, 1783.	Sugar-tongs: Mrs. Briscoe.
,,	**WS**	Wm.	Sumner	,, 1782.	Tea-vase of classic form: Mr. Lowe.
,,	**JH**	Name not traced.			Epergne, with pierced baskets: Lord Dormer.
,,	**I·T**	John	Townshend	,, 1783.	Tumbler: Judge Wynne-Ffoulkes.
,,	**TC**	Thos.	Chawner	,, 1773.	Small oval tray, probably for snuffers.
,,	**I·T**	John	Tayleur	,, 1775.	Bulb-shaped mug, with scroll handle.
,,	**I·S**	John	Schofield	,, 1778.	Two-handled cup: Tailors' Guild, Carlisle.
1784-5	**LI**	Name not traced.			Rose-water salver: The Author's Collection.
,,	**B M**	Do.	do.		Ribbed tankard: Messrs. Crichton.
,,	**C H**	Chas.	Hougham	,, 1785.	Caddy spoon: Mr. A. J. L. Grimes.
,,	**HG**	Hen.	Greenway	,, 1775.	Table-spoon: Mr. E. Heron-Allen.
,,	**SA**	Stephen Adams		,, 1760.	Table-spoon: Do. do.
,,	**SG**	Saml.	Godbehere	,, 1784.	Tea-spoons: Mrs. Budd.
,,	**WS**	Wm.	Simmons	,, 1776.	Teapot stand, oval, with beaded edge.
,,	**PG**	Peter	Gillois	,, 1782.	Engraved mounts of walking stick.
,,	**RI**	Robt.	Jones	,, 1778.	Small engraved waiter, on three feet.
1785-6	**WA**	Wm.	Abdy	,, 1784.	Wine strainer: The Author's Collection.
,,	**I·MF**	Name not traced.			Caddy spoon: Messrs. Crichton.
,,	**HV**	Do.	do.		Pair of folding spoons: Mr. A. J. L. Grimes.
,,	**B·L**	Ben.	Laver	,, 1781.	Three alms-dishes: St. Nicholas, Chiswick.
,,	**W·T**	Walter	Tweedie	,, 1775.	Teapot stand: Mr. Trapnell.
,,	**TW**	Thos.	Wallis	,, 1778.	Gravy spoon: Mr. E. Heron-Allen.
,,	**TD**	Thos.	Daniel	,, 1774.	Oval teapot: Holburne Museum.
,,	**I·K**	John	Kidder	,, 1780.	Plain muffin dish and cover.
,,	**T S**	Thos.	Shepherd	,, 1785.	A shoe-lifter.
,,	**A·B**	Abm.	Barrier	,, 1775.	A mathematical instrument case.

DATE.	GOLDSMITHS' MARKS AND NAMES.			ARTICLES AND OWNERS.
1786-7	**SG EW**	Saml. & Edwd.	Godbehere Wigan } ent. 1786.	Pair of sauce-boats, scroll handles.
,,	**TP·AH**	T. Arth.	Pratt & Humphreys } ,, 1780.	Salt-spoons : Messrs. Crichton.
,,	**W·S**	Wm.	Sutton ,, 1784.	Sugar-tongs : The Author's Collection.
,,	**WR**	Wm.	Reynolds ,, 1773.	Table-spoons : Mr. F. Gothard.
,,		Robt.	Hennell as 1782.	Trencher salt : Pemb. Coll., Cambridge.
,,	**HC**	Henry	Chawner ent. 1786.	Communion cup : Kirk Deighton, Yorks.
,,	**GG**	Name not traced.		Pepper caster : Mr. S. Deane.
,,	**CA**	Chas.	Aldridge ,, 1786.	Pair of shoe buckles : Lady Emsley Carr.
,,	**TD**	Thos.	Daniel ,, 1774.	Sugar basket with glass liner.
,,	**DD**	Danl.	Denny ,, 1782.	Small ring, repoussé and chased.
,,	**WP**	Wm.	Pitts ,, 1786.	Pair of oval entrée dishes.
1787-8	**SM**	Saml.	Massey (probably).	Two com. cups : St. Dunstan, Feltham.
,,	**JH**	Name not traced.		Wine label, pierced and chased.
,,	**WE**	Wm.	Eley.	Fish server and mazarine.
,,	**T·M**	Thos.	Mallison ent. 1773.	Punch ladle : Mr. S. Deane.
,,	**DS RS**	Danl. Robt.	Smith & Sharp } ,, 1780.	Octagonal sugar-bowl with handles.
1788-9	**EI**	Edwd.	Jay ,, 1773.	Two-handled oval tray on four feet : Hon. Soc. of the Inner Temple.
,,	**IC**	John	Carter before ,,	Sauce-boats, with medallions and festoons : S. Kensington Museum.
,,	**TP**	Thos.	Powell, probably 1770.	Epergne, with large centre dish and small dishes on branches : Noted by the Author.
,,	**GB**	Geo.	Baskerville (probably).	Sauce-ladle : Mr. S. Deane.
,,	**HC**	Henry	Cowper ent 1782.	Two-handled vase : Pembroke Coll., Cambridge.
,,	**CB**	Cornls.	Bland ,, 1788.	Sauce-ladle : Westgate Hotel, Newport, Mon.
,,	**TO**	Thos.	Ollivant ,, 1789.	Plain bulb-shaped tankard, domed top.
1789-90	**HB**	Hester	Bateman ,, 1774.	Com cup : St. Paul's, Covent Garden.
,,	**HG**	Henry	Greenway ,, 1775.	Vases, as heads of beadles' staves : St. Clement Danes.
,,	**IT**	John	Thompson ,, 1785.	Tankard, bulb-shaped, domed top : Mr. Chisholm.
,,	**I·E**	John	Edwards ,, 1788.	Engraved snuff-box : Lady Emsley Carr.

DATE.	GOLDSMITHS' MARKS AND NAMES.		ARTICLES AND OWNERS.
1789-90	**TW**	Thos. Willmore ent. 1790.	Vinaigrette : Mr. M. Falk.
,,	**PC**	Name not traced.	Patch box : Messrs. Crichton.
1790-1	**P·P**	Peter Podie ,, 1783.	Sugar basket : Do. do.
,,	**TP ER**	T. Phipps & } E. Robinson }	Com. flagon : St. Mary's, Wanstead, Essex.
,,	**GS WF**	Geo. Smith & } Wm. Fearn } ,, 1786.	{ Large pierced spoon: Do. do. do. { Skewer (1791-2) : Mrs. E. H. Goddard.
,,	**RH**	Robt. Hennell ,, 1773.	Spoon tray : St. Mary's, Wanstead, Essex.
,,	**PB IB**	Peter & Bateman } Jonath'n } ,, 1790.	Pair of gravy spoons : Mrs. Budd.
,,	**SD**	Saml. Davenport ,, 1786.	{ Table spoons : Do. { Paten (1827-8) : St. John's Church, Truro.
,,	**WA**	Wm. Abdy ,, 1784.	Octagonal sugar bowl, with two handles.
,,	**AP**	Abm. Peterson ,, 1790.	Spirit lamp, on cross supports for a dish.
1791-2	**WP JP**	Wm. Pitts & } Jos. Preedy } ,, 1791.	Oval tray : St. Dunstan's, Feltham.
,,	**GB**	Geo. Baskerville (probably).	Table-spoons : Various owners.
,,	**GS**	Geo. Smith ent. 1773.	Do. do. : Do. do.
,,	**RS**	Robt. Salmon ,, ,,	Sugar bowl, on low spreading foot.
,,	**WF DP**	Wm. Fountain & } Danl. Pontifex } ,, 1791.	Oval hot-water jug, engraved ornamentation.
,,	**IB EB**	Jas. & Bland } Eliz. } ,, ,,	Snuffers tray, boat-shaped, with pointed ends.
,,	**JL**	John Lamb ,, 1783.	Plain oval salt-cellars, on moulded feet.
,,	**TS**	Thos. Streetin ,, 1791.	Set of four pierced coasters.
,,	**EB**	Name not traced.	Candlesticks : The Earl of Yarborough.
,,	**S·G R·W**	Do. do.	Cup : Mr. Samuel S. Mossop.
1792-3	**W·L**	Do. do.	Oil and vinegar cruet : Windsor Castle.
,,	**W·P I·P**	Wm. Pitts & (see) Jos. Preedy (above)	Communion cup and cover : Saffron Walden.
,,	**HC**	Henry Chawner ent. 1786.	Fluted baptismal basin : St. Margaret's, Westminster.
,,	**TH**	Thos. Howell ,, 1791.	Table-spoons : The Author's Collection.
,,	**TN**	Thos. Northcote.	Do. do. : do. do.
,,	**GS TH**	Geo. Smith & } Thos. Hayter } ent. 1792.	Alms-dish : Ravenstonedale, Cumberland.

Date.	Goldsmiths Marks and Names				Articles and Owners.
1792-3	**WF PS**	Wm. Pau¹.	Frisbee & Storr	ent. 1792.	Two-handled vase, of Greek form.
,,	**IF**	John	Fountain	,, ,,	Small oval tray for snuffers or tea-spoons.
,,	**TG**	Thos.	Graham	,, ,,	Small muffineer, shaped as an egg-cup and egg.
,,	**EI**	Edwd.	Jay	,, ,,	Two-handled tray: Messrs. Crichton.
1793-4	**I·W R·G**	J. Robt.	Wakelin & Garrard	,, ,,	Half-a-dozen salt-cellars, with lobed bodies.
,,	**IM**	John	Moore	,, 1778.	Plain paten: Marston-Meysey, Fairford.
,,	**I·S**	John	Schofield	,, ,,	Candlestick: Queen's Coll., Cambridge.
,,	**PB AB**	Peter & Ann	Bateman	,, 1791.	{ Cream-jug: The Author's Collection. { Com. cup and paten: Sutton Viney, Wilts.
,,	**RM TM**	Robt. & Thos.	Makepeace	,, 1794.	Sauce tureen, with oval salver pertaining to it.
,,	**DU NH**	Duncan Naphtäli	Urquhart & Hart	,, 1791.	Knob and ferrule of walking-stick.
,,	**I·F I·B**	John John	Fountain & Beadnall	,, 1793.	Pair of gravy spoons converted into salad servers.
,,	**W·F I·F**	Wm. & John	Fisher	,, ,,	Small oval tray, with beaded edge.
1794-5	**WF**	Wm.	Frisbee	,, 1792.	Marrow spoon: Mr. B. Jefferis.
,,	**I·K**	John	King	,, 1785.	Cream-jug: Mr. Trapnell.
,,	**M B**	? Mark	Bock (see 1798).		Wine funnel: Windsor Castle.
,,	**F·T**	? Francis Thurkle.			Sword hilt: Mr. Dudley Westropp.
,,	**JR**	John	Robins	ent. 1774.	Wine labels: Windsor Castle.
,,	**JW**	John	Wren	,, 1777.	Table-spoons: Mrs. Budd.
,,	**MP**	Michl.	Plummer	,, 1791.	Fish slice: Queens' College, Cambridge.
,,	**WF**	W.	Fountain	,, 1794.	Bright-cut O.E. pattern table-spoons.
,,	**TN GB**	Thos. Geo.	Northcote & Bourne	,, ,,	Child's christening mug, with ribbon handle.
1795-6	**RG**	Richd. Robt.	Gardner or Gaze	,, 1773. ,, 1795.	} Plain oval meat dish.
,,	**TE**	Thos.	Ellis	,, 1780.	Argyle: The Hon. Society of the Middle Temple.
,,	**RM**	Robt.	Makepeace	,, 1795.	Communion cup: St. Lawrence, Brentford, Mids.
,,	**PB AB**	Peter & Ann	Bateman	,, 1791.	{ Tea set, of fluted pattern, on ball feet. { Cream jug (1794-5): Mr. Ll. Davies.
,,	**TP AH**	T. B. Arthur	Pratt & Humphreys	,, 1780.	A small muffineer and a nutmeg grater.
,,	**WE**	Wm.	Eley.		Dessert-spoons, noted by the Author.

DATE.	GOLDSMITHS' MARKS AND NAMES.		ARTICLES AND OWNERS.
1795-6	**SH**	Name not traced.	Com. cup.: Grinsdale, Cumberland.
,,	**IP IP**	J. & J. Perkins ent. 1795.	Oblong salt-cellars, rounded corners, lobed bodies.
,,	**HN**	Henry Nutting ,, 1796.	Plain sauce-boats, scroll handles.
1796-7	**SP**	Name not traced.	Table-spoons, dessert-spoons and punch ladle.
,,	**RH DH**	Robt. & David Hennell } ,, 1795.	Two-handled engraved tea-vase.
,,	**IM**	John Mewburn ,, 1793.	Plain oval tobacco box.
,,	**IBO**	Jos. B. Orme ,, 1796.	A small salver, with beaded edge.
,,	**WEH**	Wm. Hall ,, 1795.	Inkstand: Mr. Cecil B. Morgan.
,,	**HC IE**	Hy. Chawner & Jno. Eames } ,, 1796.	Teapot: Dr. Woodhouse.
1797-8	**RC**	Richd. Crossley ,, 1782.	Com. paten and a spoon: St. Mary's, White-chapel.
,,	**HC IE**	Henry Chawner & John Emes } ,, 1796.	Tea and coffee service, and a cake basket.
,,	**GC**	Geo. Cowles ,, 1797.	Small sugar basin, engraved ornament.
1798-9	**EM**	E. Morley.	Two punch ladles: Hon. Soc. of the Inner Temple.
,,	**IP**	Jos. Preedy ,, 1777.	Oval spoon tray: St. Mary's, Hanwell, Mids.
,,	**IB**	John Beldon ,, 1784.	Table-spoons: The Author's Collection.
,,	**WE WF**	Wm. Eley & Wm. Fearn } ,, 1797.	A soup ladle, and a pair of sauce ladles.
,,	**GS**	Geo. Smith.	Gravy spoon: Mr. Saml. Deane.
,,	**IH TL**	Jos. Hardy & Thos. Lowndes } ,, 1798.	Wine straining funnel.
,,	**M·B**	? Mark Bock.	Dessert knives: Windsor Castle.
,,	**JE**	John Emes.	Tea tray: Mr. Lambert.
,,	**T·D**	Thos. Dealtry ,, 1765.	Table forks: Mr. Dudley Westropp.
1799 1800	**WP**	Wm. Pitts ,, 1781.	Pair of classic vases with handles: City of London Corporation.
,,	**WB**	Wm. Bennett ,, 1796.	Snuffers: Holburne Museum.
,,	**WP**	Wm. Pitts ,, 1799.	Small tea-vase with two handles.
,,	**RC**	Richd. Cooke ,, ,,	Large spoon, pierced, for sifting sugar.
,,	**AF**	Andrew Fogelberg ,, 1776.	Oval engraved teapot and stand.
,,	**IH**	John Hutson ,, 1784.	Oval engraved milk-jug, no foot.
,,	**WS**	Name not traced.	Taper stand: The Author's Collection.

DATE.	GOLDSMITHS' MARKS AND NAMES.			ARTICLES AND OWNERS.
1799 1800	**IP**	Jos.	Preedy ent. 1800.	Snuffers and tray : Noted by the Author.
1800-1	**P·S**	Paul	Storr ,, 1793.	Two-handled standing cup, presented to the Hon. Soc. of the Middle Temple by His Majesty King Edward VII. when Prince of Wales and Treasurer of the Inn.
,,	**I·W R·G**	J. Robt.	Wakelin & Garrard } ,, 1792.	Alms-dish : St. Mary's, Stanwell, Mids.
,,	**WH**	Wm.	Hall ,, 1795.	Milk-jug : Noted by the Author.
,,	**SG EW IB**	Saml. Ed. J.	Godbehere Wigan & Bult } ,, 1800.	Soup-ladle : Do. do. do.
,,	**TH IC**	Thos. John	Hannam & Crouch } ,, 1799.	Set of dinner plates, with beaded edges.
1801-2	**RG**	Robt.	Garrard ,, 1801.	Com. flagon : St. Dunstan's, Feltham, Mids.
,,	**I·P**	John	Parker.	{ Table-forks : Mr. Dudley Westropp. { Cream-jug : The Author's Collection.
,,	**JE**	John	Emes ,, 1796.	"Argyle" : Hon. Society of the Middle Temple.
,,	**PB AB WB**	Peter, Ann & Wm.	Bateman } ,, 1800.	Oval mustard-pot : The Author's Collection.
,,	**GS TH**	Geo. Thos.	Smith & Hayter } ,, 1792.	Table-spoons : Westgate Hotel, Newport, Mon.
,,	**RH DH SH**	Robert, David & Saml.	Hennell }	Coffee-jug : The Author's Collection.
1802-3	**IH**	John	Harris ,, 1786.	Waiter : Do. do. do.
,,	**D·S B·S**	Digby Benj.	Scott & Smith } ,, 1802.	Meat dishes, etc. : Windsor Castle.
,,	**WB**	Wm.	Burwash ,, ,,	Small tray : Messrs. Christie.
,,	**PB AB WB**	Peter, Ann & Wm.	Bateman } ,, 1800.	Cruet frame and mounts of cruets : The Author's Collection.
,,	**AB GB**	Alice & George	Burrows ,, 1802.	Two-handled cup : Messrs. Hancock.
,,	**CB TB**	Christr. & T. W.	Barker ,, 1800.	Two-handled tea vase : Mr. Chisholm.
1803-4	**B·L**	Benj.	Laver ,, 1781.	Two sets of com. plate : St. George's, Hanover Square.
,,	**TH**	Thos.	Holland ,, 1798.	Tea service, squat-shaped bulging body.
,,	**GB TB**	G. & T.	Burrows.	Tea-spoons : Mrs. Budd.
,,	**SG W**	Saml. & George	Whitford ,, 1802.	Salt-cellar : The Drane Collection.
,,	**AJ**	Name not traced.		Milk-jug : Do. do. do.
,,	**IR**	John	Robins (probably).	Double set of com. plate : Bromley-by-Bow.
,,	**TR**	? Timothy Renou.		Oval salver : Mr. E. H. Goddard.
,,	**JA**	John	Austin.	Wine labels : noted by the Author.
1804-5	**W·P**	Wm	Purse.	Beaker : Messrs. Crichton.

DATE.	GOLDSMITHS' MARKS AND NAMES.			ARTICLES AND OWNERS.
1804-5	S·B	Name not traced.		Various small articles: Windsor Castle.
,,	RB&R	Rundell, Bridge & Rundell.		Tea service: Messrs. Elkington.
,,	GW	Geo. Wintle	ent. 1804.	Table-spoons: Mrs. Budd.
,,	RG	Robt. Garrard	,, 1802.	Large oval tray, with two handles: The Author's Collection; com. cup: Ulverston, Lancs.
,,	I·H	Jos. Hardy	,, 1799.	Plain Old-English pattern table-spoons.
,,	HN	Hannah Northcote	,, 1798.	Sugar tongs: Mrs. Hammond.
1805-6	DP	Danl. Pontifex	,, 1794.	Muffineer: The Author's Collection.
,,	J·E	John Emes.		Inkstand: Windsor Castle.
,,	TA	? T. Ash.		Salt-cellars: Messrs. Crichton.
,,	W·B R·S	Wm. Burwash & Richd. Sibley	,, 1805.	A hand-bell, with ivory handle.
,,	TS	Name not traced.		Table forks, plain Old-English pattern.
1806-7	RH SH	R. & S. Hennell	,, 1802.	Com. paten.: St. Mary's, Hanwell, Mids.
,,	PB WB	Peter & Wm. Bateman	,, 1805.	Tea-spoons: The Author's Collection.
,,	JS	John Sanders (probably).		A plain soup ladle, and a punch ladle.
,,	CF	Crespin Fuller	,,	Communion cup: St. Mary's, Hornsey. Sugar bowl (1810-11): Mr. Clement Gadsby.
,,	IS	John Salkeld	,,	Cheese scoop, with engraved Vitruvian scroll ornament, as border.
,,	T·R	Thos. Robins	,,	Silver grid: Dunn-Gardner Collection.
,,	WF	Wm. Fountain	ent. 1794.	Com. flagon: Brasenose Coll., Oxford.
1807-8	TG IG IC	T. & J. Guest & Josh. Cradock	,, 1806	Milk-jug (oval shape, without foot).
,,	PB WB	P. & W. Bateman	,, 1805.	Tea-spoons: Mrs. Budd and the Author.
,,	SW	Saml. Whitford	,, 1807.	Vase-shaped cup, with festoons of drapery; also cream-jug: Mr. J. H. Thomas.
,,	T·H	Thos. Halford	,, ,,	Child's mug, with two ribbon bands.
,,	BS	Name not traced.		Meat dish: Windsor Castle.
,,	SR	T. Robins	,, ,,	Soup-tureen: Lady Riddell.
,,	IWS	? J. W. Storey.		Communion cups: Aylsham, Norfolk.
1808-9	I·C	John Crouch	,, 1808.	Cake basket: Messrs. Crichton.
,,	R·E W·E	Name not traced.		Decanter stand: Mr. Anthony White.

DATE.	GOLDSMITHS' MARKS AND NAMES.			ARTICLES AND OWNERS.
1808-9	**TM**	? T. W. Matthews.		Wine-strainer : Mrs. E. H. Goddard.
,,	**I·C**	John Crouch	ent. 1808.	Communion flagon : Illogan (Treverson Chapel), Cornwall.
,,	**E·M**	E. Morley.		Soup-ladle : Mr. Dudley Westropp.
,,	**WE WF WC**	Wm. Eley, Wm. Fearn & Wm. Chawner }	,, ,,	Beaded-pattern table-spoons and forks.
,,	**HN RH**	Henry Nutting & Robt. Hennell }	,, ,,	Mustard-pot, oblong shape, bulging body.
,,	**RC GS**	Richard Crossley & Geo. Smith }	,, 1807.	Perforated spoon : All Hallows, Bromley-by-Bow.
,,	**W·S**	Wm. Sumner	,, 1802.	{ Table-spoons : The Drane Collection. { Large engraved spoon : Mr. J. H. Thomas.
,,	**JC**	John Crouch	,, 1808.	Goblet, on plain stem and foot.
1809-10	**CH**	Chas. Hougham	,, 1785.	Oval engraved milk-jug.
,,	**TW**	Thos. Wallis	,, 1792.	Table-spoons, beaded edge : The Author.
,,	**DW**	David Windsor (probably).		Large spoon : Christchurch, Stepney.
,,	**TJ**	Thomas Jenkinson	,,	{ Com. cup and paten : Kirkby, Ireleth, Lancs. { Small fluted mug : Mr. Clement Gadsby.
,,	**SJ**	Name not traced.		Dish : Windsor Castle.
1810-1	**TH SH**	Do. do.		Wine labels : Do.
,,	**RC**	? Richd. Cooke.	ent. 1799.	Pair of Jardinieres : Messrs. Crichton.
,,	**BS IS**	Benj. Smith & Jas. Smith. }		{ Pierced bread-basket : M. & S. Lyon. { Much plate : Windsor Castle.
,,	**TP ER**	T. Phipps & E. Robinson }		A nutmeg grater. Also tipstaff of 1790 : St. Matthew's, Bethnal Green.
,,	**SB IB**	Name not traced.		Tea-spoons : Mrs. Budd.
,,	**TW JH**	Thos. Wallis & Jonath'n Hayne }	,, 1810.	Snuffers tray (corners clipped), and snuffers.
,,	**IC TH**	John Cotton & Thos. Head. }	,, 1809.	Table-spoons, forks, and dessert-spoons.
1811-2	**JB**	James Beebe	,, 1811.	Do. do. and milk-jug.
,,	**BS IS**	Benj. & Jas. Smith.		Pair of ice pails : Messrs. Dobson & Son.
,,	**WK**	Wm. Kingdon (probably).		A bulb-shaped christening mug.
,,	**RR**	Robt. Rutland	ent. 1811.	Table-spoons and forks. Tea-spoons (1807-8) : Mr. Llewellyn Davies.
,,	**SH**	Saml. Hennell	,, ,,	Wine funnel : Mr. Harry Alston.
,,	**DS BS IS**	Digby Scott, Benj. Smith, Jas. Smith } (probably).		Plate : Windsor Castle.

Date.	Goldsmiths' Marks and Names.			Articles and Owners.
1812-3	**T·B**	? T.	Barker.	Mustard spoons : Windsor Castle.
,,	**J S**	? John	Sanders.	Wine labels : Do. do.
,,	**T I**	Thos.	Jenkinson (probably).	Paten on foot : St. Mary Magdalen, East Ham.
,,	**RE EB**	Rebecca Emes & Edwd. Barnard } ent. 1808.		Com. cup and paten : St. Michael's, Ashford, Mids.
,,	**G S**	Geo.	Smith ,, 1812.	Table-spoons and forks : Woods' Hotel.
,,	**MS ES**	Mary & Eliz.	Sumner ,, 1809.	Plain butter-boat, with salver attached.
1813-4	**IC WR**	Jos. & Wm.	Craddock } ,, 1812. Reid	Small vase-shaped tea-urn with high reeded handles.
,,	**P·S** BRITANNIA	Paul	Storr ,, 1793.	Large caster or dredger (Britannia Standard marks).
,,	**IWS WE**	J. W. W.	Story & } ,, 1809. Elliott	Pair of coasters with vine foliage : Mr. H. D. Ellis.
1814-5	**S H**	Saml.	Hennell ,, 1811.	O.E. pattern gravy spoon : Mrs. Budd.
,,	**RE EB**	Emes & Barnard ,, 1808.		A milk-jug and oblong sugar basin, with rounded corners.
,,	**S A**	Stephen Adams, junr.		Tea-spoons : Mrs. Budd.
,,	**W·B**	Wm.	Bell (probably).	An engraved snuffers tray and snuffers.
,,	**W·E**	Wm.	Elliott ent. 1810.	Pickle fork : Mrs. E. H. Goddard.
,,	**I L WA**	Name not traced.		Snuff-box : H. E. Fernandez.
,,	**SH IT**	S. J.	Hennell & } (probably). Taylor	Tea-set : Messrs. Crichton.
1815-6	**TP ER JP**	Name not traced.		Cucumber slicer : Windsor Castle.
,,	**JE EF**	Do. do.		Mounts of sugar stand : Windsor Castle.
,,	**I·P G·P**	Do. do.		A pair of sauce ladles, and a punch ladle.
,,		Emes & Barnard as above.		Communion cup : St. Mary's, Chelmsford.
,,	**R G**	Robt.	Garrard ent. 1801.	Three com. patens : St. Martin's-in-the-Fields.
,,	**CR DR**	Christ'n Reid & ano'r of Newcastle ,, 1815.		Plain bulb-shaped coffee-pot : Mr. W. Boore.
1816-7	**WB**	Wm.	Burwash ,, 1813.	Asparagus tongs : The Author's Collection.
,,	**I L**	Jas.	Lloyd.	Gold pap bowl : Messrs. Crichton.
1817-8	**S SR IED**	Name not traced.		Teapot : Do. do.

Date.	Goldsmiths' Marks and Names.		Articles and Owners.
1817-8	**WB**	Wm. Bateman ent. 1815.	Basin: Messrs. Crichton.
,,	**M·S**	Name not traced.	Tea-set: noted by Mr. Dudley Westropp.
,,	**WC**	Wm. Chawner ,, ,,	Spoon: Mrs. E. H. Goddard.
,,	**TR**	T. Robins (probably).	Tea-set: Mr. Tessier.
,,	**WC**	Wm. Chawner ent. 1815.	Table-spoons and dessert-spoons.
,,	**GP**	Geo. Purse.	A nutmeg-grater: The Drane Collection.
1818-9	**GW**	Geo. Wintle ,, 1813.	Spoon with perforated bowl: St. Mary's, Stratford-le Bow.
,,	**IW**	Joseph Wilson.	Bowl: Mr. Fredk. Bradbury.
,,	**RG**	Robt. Garrard ,, 1801.	Pair of covered basins and stands: Messrs. Comyns.
1819-20	**SR ID**	Name not traced.	Meat skewers: Windsor Castle.
,,	**A·H**	Do. do.	Dessert-knife: do. do.
,,	**HN**	Henry Nutting ,, 1809.	Teapot, ornamented with foliage in relief.
,,	**WS**	Wm. Stevenson (probably).	Salver on eight claw feet: The gift of Earl Powis to the Corporation of Shrewsbury.
,,	**TI**	See 1812-3 above.	Pap spoon: Mr. Saml. Deane.
,,	**PR**	Philip Rundell ent. 1819.	Oval tray, with concave flutings on border.
1820-1	**W·B**	Wm. Bateman ,, 1815.	Two large silver-gilt maces: Shrewsbury Corporation; also a large ewer presented by Sir Jas. St phen to the Hon. Soc. of the Middle Temple.
,,	**I·L H·L**	John & Henry Lias ,, 1819.	Oval cruet frames for two bottles.
1821-2	**TB**	Thos. Baker ,, 1815. or Thos. Balliston ,, 1819.	} Dessert-knife: Messrs. Crichton.
,,	**IET**	? J. E. Terry & Co. ,, 1818.	Two communion cups: Falmouth.
,,	**ICF**	? John Foligno.	Mark noted by the Author.
,,	**CaCa**	An Exeter maker (probably).	Sugar tongs: The Author's Collection.
,,	**JA IA**	J. & J. Aldous ,,	Top of beadle's staff: St. Mary's, Hampton, Mids.
1822-3	**PS**	Paul Storr ,,	Communion plate: St. Pancras New Church.
,,	**WA**	William Abdy ,,	Cream-jug: Hon. Soc. of the Middle Temple.
,,	**WT**	Wm. Trayes ent. 1822.	King's pattern table-spoons and forks.
1823-4	**IS**	Name not traced.	Helmet-shaped flagon: St. Mary's, Ealing.
,,	**JA**	John Angell (probably).	Teapot: Holburne Museum.

Date.	Goldsmiths' Marks and Names.			Articles and Owners.
1823-4	**I·B**	John	Bridge	ent. 1823.	Ink stand, with pin tray and wafer holder.
,,	**BS**	Benj.	Smith.		Large centre piece, with female figures holding fruit dishes.
1824-5	**TH GH**	Thos. & Geo.	Hayter	,, 1816.	Tea-spoons: The Author's Collection.
,,	**SC**	Name not traced.			Pair of sugar bowls: Hon. Soc. Middle Temple.
,,	**R·H**	Robt.	Hennell.		Two com. patens: St. John's, Wapping.
,,	**F·F**	Name not traced.			Clothes brush: Windsor Castle.
,,	**WE CE IE**	Do.	do.		Egg spoon: Windsor Castle.
,,	**GK**	Geo.	Knight	(probably).	Muffineer: Mr. John B. Wood.
,,	**WE**	Wm.	Edwards	(,,).	Dessert knives: Windsor Castle.
1825-6	**IC**	James	Collins	(,,).	Hash-dish: Hon. Soc. of the Inner Temple.
,,	**I·B**	John	Bridge	ent. 1823.	Half-pint mug, shaped like a swan.
,,	**RP**	R.	Peppin	(probably).	Communion cup: Whitbeck, Cumberland.
,,	**C.E**	C.	Eley	(,,).	Asparagus tongs: Windsor Castle.
,,	**FH**	Fras.	Higgins	(,,).	Tea-spoons: Windsor Castle.
1826-7	**IL HL CL**	John, Henry & Chas. } Lias		ent. 1823.	Shaped venison dish, with gadrooned edge.
,,	**A·B·S**	A. B.	Savory	,, 1826.	Dessert knives and forks: Lady Emsley Carr.
,,	**RC**	Randall Chatterton		,, 1825.	{ Table and dessert spoons: Do. do. { Forks (1831-2): Mrs. E. H. Goddard.
1827-8	**BP**	Name not traced.			Set of communion plate: St. Giles-in-the-Fields.
,,	**T·C·S**	T. Cox Savory		,, 1827.	A cheese scoop, with ivory handle.
,,	**JW**	Jacob	Wintle	,, 1826.	Table and dessert spoons: Woods' Hotel.
,,	**ME**	Moses	Emmanuel (probably).		Marrow spoon: Windsor Castle.
1828-9	**WS**	Wm.	Schofield	(,,).	Tea-spoons: The Author.
,,	**ES**	E. S.	Sampson	(,,).	{ Communion set: St. Day. { Rose-water dish: Truro Cathedral.
1829-30	**IH**	Jas.	Hobbs	(,,).	Communion cup and paten: Mithian, Cornwall.
,,	**EE**	Edward Edwards.			Snuff-box: Trinity College, Dublin.
,,	**RG**	Robt.	Garrard	ent. 1801.	Set of communion plate: St. Paul's, Clerkenwell.
1830-1	**CP**	Chas.	Plumley (probably).		Communion cup: St. Michael's, Highgate.

DATE.	GOLDSMITHS' MARKS AND NAMES.		ARTICLES AND OWNERS.
1830-1	T·D	Thos. Dexter (probably).	Shaving pot: Holburne Museum.
,,	R A W S	Name not traced.	Communion cup and paten: Towednack, Cornwall.
1831-2	W·H	,, ,,	Pair of communion cups: Stansted Mount-fitchet, Essex.
,,	R·H	R. Hennell.	Small oblong tray, with rounded corners.
1833-4	PS	Paul Storr ent. 1793.	Toast rack: The Author.
,,	AS JS AS	Adey, Joseph } Savory ,, 1833. & Albert	Fiddle-pattern asparagus tongs.
1834-5	N·M	N. Morrison (probably).	Nutmeg box: Fitz-Henry Colln., S.K. Museum.
,,	IF	Jas. Franklin ,,	Hand candlestick: Mr. R. Flower.
,,	WB	W. Bellchambers ,,	{ Spoons and forks: Mr. S. J. Phillips. { Meat dishes (1838-9): Windsor Castle.
,,	RP CP	Name not traced.	Alms-dish: Bodmin.
,,	T·E	T. Eley.	Snuff-box: Mr. Harry Alston.
1835-6	CF	Chas. Fox ent. 1822.	Tea-vase: Holburne Museum.
,,	J.C.E	J. Chas. Edington ,, 1828.	Four alms-plates: St. Mary's, Leyton.
,,	CR GS	Reily & Storer (probably).	Mounts of decanters and wine labels.
1836-7	CF	See 1835-6.	Com. flagon and paten: St. Mary's, Little Baddow, Essex.
,,	EB E JB W	Edwd. Barnard, Edwd. Barnard, jr., } ent. 1829. John Barnard, & Wm. Barnard	Hot-water jug: Holburne Museum.
1837-8	WE	Wm. Eaton.	Hand candlestick, with Queen Adelaide's cypher: Mr. H. D. Ellis.
,,	RS	Richard Sibley (probably).	Set of four coasters, with vine leaf ornament.
,,	GW	George Webb ,,	Butter bowl, with salver and knife.
,,	RG	Robert Garrard ent. 1821.	Entrée dishes, stamped "Garrards, Panton Street".
,,	MC	Mary Chawner.	Table-spoons and forks: Messrs. Lambert.
1838-9	WT RA	Wm. Theobalds } & Robt. Atkinson } ,, 1838.	Fiddle-pattern table-spoons and forks: Mrs. Budd.
,,	CR GS	Rawlins & Sumner.	Set of four sauce-boats.
1839-40	WB DB	Wm. Bateman & } ,, 1839. Danl. Ball }	Large teapot, coffee-jug and spirit lamp.
,,	FD	Francis Dexter ,, ,,	Set of four salt cellars, oblong shape, with rounded corners.
,,	WC	Wm. Cooper (probably).	Set of four coasters: Holburne Museum.
,,	I·T	Jos. Taylor ,,	Jug and mustard-pot: Windsor Castle.

DATE.	GOLDSMITHS' MARKS AND NAMES.		ARTICLES AND OWNERS.
1839-40	**EE**	Ed. Edwards (probably).	Church plate, Zennor, Cornwall.
1840-1	**GL**	Name not traced.	Table-fork : Mrs. E. H. Goddard.
,,	**TC**	Thos. Cording ,,	Handles of carving knives : Windsor Castle.
,,	**GA**	Geo. W. Adams ent. 1840.	Table spoons and forks.
,.	**JA JA**	J. & J. Aldous.*	Alms-dish : St. Martin's, Little Waltham, Essex.
,,	**MC GA**	Mary Chawner & Geo. W. Adams ,, ,,	Fish servers, with ivory handles.
1841-2	**JS AS**	Jos. & Albert Savory ,, ,,	Victorian copy of a George III. cake-basket.
,,	**J·L**	John Lacy or John Law (probably).	Box with ink-bottle : Windsor Castle.
1842-3	**JCE**	J. Chas. Edington ent. 1828.	Alms-dish : S.S. Peter & Paul, South Weald, Essex.
,,	**R·H**	R. Hennell.	Vase-shaped hot-water jug, on raised foot.
,,	**WB WS**	Brown & Somersall (probably).	Mustard-pot : Mr. W. Boore.
1843-4	**W·KR**	Wm. K. Reid.	Circular entrée dish and cover.
,,	**WB**	Wm. Brown (possibly).	Alms-dish : St. Mary's, Walthamstow.
,,	**JA J·A**	Joseph & John Angel see 1844.	(1842-3) Com. cup and paten : St. Michael's Highgate.
,,	**R·S**	Richd. Sibley ent. 1837.	Communion flagon : Stansted Mountfitchet, Essex.
1844-5	**R·G**	R. Garrard ,, 1801.	Plate : Messrs. Garrard.
,,	**J·A J·A**	Joseph & John Angel.	Wine strainer : Truro Cathedral.
,,	**RGH**	R. G. Hennell.	Two communion cups : St. George's, Bloomsbury.
,,	**BS**	Benj. Smith (probably).	Tall presentation cup on stand.
1845 6	**ISH**	John S. Hunt ent. 1844.	Milk-jug : Messrs. Hunt & Roskell.
,,	**CTF GF**	Chas. T. Fox & Geo. Fox.	Figure of punchinello : Messrs. Hancock.
1846-7	**GFP**	G. F. Pinnell.	Com. paten : St. James', Friern Barnet.
,,	**H·H**	Hyam Hyams.	Set of circular salt-cellars on three feet.
,,	**EB J &W**	E. J. & W. Barnard.	Communion flagon : Grasmere, Westmor. Do. do. : Wilton, Dorset.
1847-8	**IL HL**	John & Henry Lias.	Table forks : Mrs. H. Morris. Do. do. : Mrs. E. H. Goddard.
,,	**RP GB**	R. Pearce & G. Burrows.	Two com. cups : St. Andrew's, Enfield, Mids.

* Possibly John Angell & Co.

Date.	Goldsmiths' Marks and Names.		Articles and Owners.
1847-8	**EE**	Eliz. Eaton.	Table-forks: Mrs. E. H. Goddard.
1848-9	**EJ BW**	E. J. & W. Barnard. }	Two com. cups: St. Nicholas Shipperton, Mids.
,,	**RH**	R. Hennell.	Com. flagon: St. Peter's, Little Warley, Essex.
,,	**JW**	Jacob Wintle (probably).	Child's fork, spoon, and handle of knife.
1849-50	**C.T.F G.F.**	Chas. T. Fox & } Geo. Fox	Com. flagon: Harleston, Norfolk.
,,	**FD**	Frans. Douglas.	Toilet set: The Author.
,,	**WRS**	W. R. Smily.	Tea-spoons: noted by the Author.
1850-1	**IK**	John Keith.	Four com. cups: All Saints, West Ham.
,,	**GI**	George Ivory.	Com. paten: St. Edward the Confessor, Romford, Essex.
1851-2	**EB JB**	E. & J. Barnard.	Com. cup: St. Lawrence, Brentford, Mids.
1852-3	**JE**	James Edwards (probably).	Do. do.: St. Lawrence, Whitchurch, Mids.
,,	**IF**	I. Foligno.	Set of engine-turned toilet-case fittings.
1853-4	**EB & JB**	E. & J. Barnard.	{ Ink-stand with taper-holder. { Communion cup (1861-2): Wilton, Dorset.
1854-5	**WR S**	W. R. Smily.	Com. cup.: All Saints, Edmonton, Mids.
1855-6	**GA**	George Angell.	Dessert knives and forks, and grape scissors.
1856-7	**CTF GF**	Chas. T. Fox & } Geo. Fox	Ink-stand: Messrs. Hunt & Roskell.
1857-8	**HW**	Henry Wilkinson of Sheffield.	Salver: Mr. W. Comyns.
1858-9	**JA**	Joseph Angell.	Soufflé dish and cover.
,,	**W·M**	W. Mann.	Bulb-shaped coffee-pot.
,,	**GR EB**	Roberts & Briggs.	Pair of sauce-boats and ladle .
1859-60	**GA**	George Angell.	Small sauce-tureen and salver.
1860-1	**EE JE**	Messrs. Eady.	Set of spoons and forks.
,,	**CR WS**	Rawlins & Sumner.	Spirit flask: Mr. W. Boore.
1861-2	**RH**	Robt. Harper.	Milk-jug, with engraved ornamentation.
1862-3	**R·H**	Richard Hennell.	Large hot-water jug, with ivo y handle.
1863 4	**GF**	Geo. Fox.	Brit. Standard candlestick, matching one by A. Nelme of 1700-1.
186 -5	**GA**	Geo. Angell.	Tall milk-jug, in form of ewer on foot.

DATE.	GOLDSMITHS' MARKS AND NAMES.			ARTICLES AND OWNERS.
1864-5	**EKR**			Communion cup : Treslothan, Cornwall.
1865-6	**I.J.K**	I. J.	Keith.	Communion paten : Scole, Norfolk.
,,	**R·H**	Richd.	Hennell.	Sugar bowl, repoussé, with festoons.
1866-7	**GE GF**			Preserve dishes and servers.
1867-8	**GM HD**	Macaire &	Dewar.	Gold watch-case : Mrs. Budd.
,,	**ML HL**			Set of communion plate : St. Thomas, Salisbury.
1868-9	**AS**			Communion set : Davidstow, Cornwall.
,,	**CS H**	Chas. Stuart	Harris.	Brit. St. candlesticks, Wm. III. pattern.
1869-70	**J EB·W J**	J., E., W., & J. Barnard.		Large ink-stand, and a child's mug.
1870-1	**WS**	Wm.	Smiley.	Hot-water jug, with engraved ornamentation.
1871-2	**HE W**	H. E.	Willis.	Communion paten : Harleston, Norfolk.
1872-3	**RS**	Richd.	Sibley.	Small bowl, on moulded foot.
1873-4	**RM EH**	Martin	Hall & Co. of Sheffield.	Frame of hand glass.
1874-5	**JEM GW**	Mappin &	Webb.*	A goblet, on stem, and spreading foot.
1875-6	**IR BR**			A large tea tray and tea set.
1876-7	**GFH**	Messrs.	Hancock.	Large race cup : The Makers.
1877-8	,,	,,	,,	A jewel basket : Do.
,,	**RJL**			Communion set : St. Teath, Cornwall.
,,	**TJ**			Gold snuff-box : Mr. Harry Alston.
1878-9	**SS**	Stephen	Smith.	Large circular salver on feet.
1879-80	**D.H C·B**	Hands &	Son.	Candlesticks, octagonal pattern, George II. style.
1880-1	**JWD**	J. W.	Dobson.	A tea service, of fluted pattern, George III. style.
,,	**EYI**			Church plate : Zennor, Cornwall.
,,	**WIS**			Communion cup : Margenny, Cornwall.
1881-2	**FH**	Francis	Higgins.	Tea-spoons : Lady Emsley Carr.
1882-3	**CS H**	Chas. Stuart	Harris.	Candlesticks, with fluted columns, William III. pattern.

* This may be $\frac{J \, N \, M}{G \, W}$, the middle letter of the upper line not being clear.

DATE.	GOLDSMITHS' MARKS AND NAMES.			ARTICLES AND OWNERS.
1882-3	JA JS			Communion paten : St. John, Truro.
1883 4	JNM			On Cornish Church plate supplied by Messrs. Mappin & Webb.
"	J ASM F			Church plate : Porthleven, Cornwall.
"	PW			Small waiter on three feet.
1884-5	JRH	J. R.	Hennell.	Large punch bowl, plain flutes around base.
1885-6	J W J			Noted by the Author.
"	C.F.H	Messrs.	Hancock.	Large two-handled cup : The Makers.
"	J.W F.C.W	J. F. C.	Wakley & Wheeler.	On plate from 1885 to 1907.
1888-9	D&C			Umbrella mounts : The Author.
"	WD			Two-bottle ink-stand, with rail.
1889-90	CFH	Messrs.	Hancock.	Toilet-box : The Makers.
1891-2	EH			Communion plate : Penzance.
1892-3	E·H			Do. do. : Do.
"	W.C	W.	Comyns.	Toilet set : Mrs. Budd.
1893-4	SWS	S. W.	Smith & Co. (of Birmingham).	Set of three dredgers, George I. pattern.
"	ST			Paten : St. Stythians, Cornwall.
1894-5	IG CL			Communion flagon : Pillaton, Cornwall.
"	JB FR	Brownell & Rose.		Ink-stand : The Author.
"	WBJ	Messrs.	Barnard.	Standing cup : Mr. L. A. West.
1895-6	J.S			Toy windmill.
"	JNN			Communion paten : St. Neot, Cornwall.
1896-7	W&H	W.	Hutton & Sons, Ltd.	Ink-stand : Lord Riddell.
1897-8	JBC	Messrs.	Carrington.	Afternoon tea set : The Makers.
1898-9	GG			Small stew-pan : Mr. Davidson.
1899 1900	ECP	E. C.	Purdee.	Hot-water jug : Do.
"	RP			Church plate : Illogan, Cornwall.

DATE.	GOLDSMITHS' MARKS AND NAMES.			ARTICLES AND OWNERS.
1900-1	CCP	C. C.	Pilling.	Presentation cup : Mr. Ignatius Williams.
1901-2	C.K	C.	Krall.	Communion cup : St. Olave, York.
1902-3	WC	W.	Comyns & Sons.	Butter-dish : The Makers.
1903-4	WBJMBS RD	Edward	Barnard & Sons, Ltd.	Noted by the Author.
,,	HL	H.	Lambert.	Two handled octagonal bowl.
,,	JW			Church plate : St. Elwyn, Cornwall. Also of 1915 by same maker.
,,	JW ECW			Church plate : St. John's, Penzance.
1904-5	WJ			Bust of Duke of Wellington.
1905-6	TB	Thos.	Bradbury of Sheffield.	Inkstand : Messrs. Spink & Sons.
,,	A & H	Alstons &	Hallam.	Sugar caster, etc.
1906-7	C&Cº	Carrington & Co.		Noted by the Author.
1907-8	J&S			Communion plate : Newquay, Cornwall.
,,	LG			Church plate : Mullion, Cornwall.
1908-9	TH &S	Thos. Sheffield.	Bradbury & Son of	Noted by the Author.
,,	HSP LD			Alms dish : Truro Cathedral.
,,	& WW	Wakeley & Wheeler.		Plate from 1908 to 1920.
1909-10	IMS	John	Marshall.	Mark from Messrs. Spink.
1910-1	SJP	S J.	Phillips.	Noted by the Author.
1911-2	TJW H	Thomas & Co., Bond Street.		Tea service and other plate.
1912-3	H&C LD	Heming & Co., Ltd.		Noted by the Author.
1913-4	AP FP	A. &. F.	Parsons, (of Edward Tessier).	Standing-cup.
,,	SG			Gold chalice : Truro Cathedral.
1914-5	D&J W	D. & J.	Welby.	Noted by the Author.
1915-6	PDH CW	Dobson &	Sons.	Cup and bowls.
,,	SJP	S. J.	Phillips.	Coffee-pot and other plate.
1916-7	LAC	Crichton	Bros.	Noted by the Author.
1917-8	HSP			Communion paten : Kenwin, Cornwall.
1918-9	C&R C	Chas. &. Richard	Comyns.	Fruit dish, milk-jug, and other plate.

CHAPTER IX

CHRONOLOGICAL LIST OF NAMES OF LONDON GOLDSMITHS

[FROM A.D. 1090 TO A.D. 1850]

For a large number of the names in the following list, thanks are due to Mr. R. C. Hope, F.S.A., who generously placed the results of his labours in the compilation of lists of the names of the goldsmiths of London and most of the English provincial towns where plate has been assayed, at the disposal of the Author for the purpose of this work. In Mr. Hope's lists the surnames are arranged alphabetically; but having regard to the fact that such arrangement results in names of the eighteenth and nineteenth centuries coming, in many instances, before those of the thirteenth, and so forth, it has been deemed preferable to adopt a chronological order. Moreover, by reason of the rule as to the letters used in makers' marks from 1697 to 1720 being different from that in force before and after that period, no regular alphabetical arrangement could be adopted whereby the identification of marks with names would be rendered easy. The alphabetical order has therefore been disregarded, and the following list has been arranged, chronologically, with the prenomen and surname in their proper order, so that the initials appear as they are generally found on plate.* Mr. Hope's lists have been extended by the addition of several hundred names, which have been collected by the Author from early records, directories and similar sources.

To facilitate the finding of initials, these have all—as well in the case of surnames as Christian or personal names—been printed in vertical lines with a clear space between. Occasionally, names which appear at one date, re-appear at a later date. In these cases, for the

---

* In the case of "firm-names," such as Horne & Temple, in which no Christian name or prenomen occurs, the first surname which appears in the "style" of the firm, is for the sake of convenience printed in the prenomen column. The first two letters of the surname, which appear in makers' marks on plate of the Britannia Standard from 1697 to 1720 and occasionally to 1739, may be easily identified in the following list by reason of the surnames being set clear of the Christian names.

most part, the addresses are different, and although the person may be the same, the reverse is possible. Many names are repeated in the Goldsmiths' books by reason of the re-registration of marks; but wherever it has been ascertained that the same person—not being associated with another—has re-entered his name, the repetition has been avoided, except in a few cases, where a change in the spelling of the name appears to be noteworthy.

Some names have been found recorded in one year only; others in two years, one immediately following the other, or at very short intervals. It should not be concluded in such cases that the goldsmith worked for a period no longer than is thereby indicated, because marks have been found to have been in use for a much longer period than is denoted by records. In many instances marks have been used a year or two before their registration, and in others they have been used by successors after the death of the goldsmiths in whose names they had been entered :—

("Earliest Mention" and "Latest Mention" refer to the earliest and latest mention which has been noted; d. means died; c. means *circa*.)

Name of Goldsmith.	Earliest Mention.	Remarks.	Latest Mention.	Name of Goldsmith.	Earliest Mention.	Remarks.	Latest Mention.
Otto the Elder	1090	Graver to Mint 1090.	1100	Henry de Frowyk	1279		
Leofstane ———	c 1100		1135	William (Sir) Faryngdon	,,	Mayor.	1290
Otto the Younger	c 1120			Thos. (Sir) de Frowick	,,	,,	
William Fitz Otto	c 1130			Hugh Fitz Otho	1280	Master of Mint.	,,
Ralph Flael	1180	First Mayor of London		Laurence Ducket			1284
Henry Fitz Alwyn	1189		1213	William Fitz Otho	1290		1294
Henry de Cornhill	1191	Warden of Mint.	1193	William Torel			
William Fitz William	1212			John le Mazerer	1303		
Ilger the Goldsmith	1221	Master of Mint.	1223	——— Honilane			d 1303
Everard the Goldsmith	1223	Warden.	1225	John le Whympler	1307		
Ralph Essory	1242	Mayor.		John de Louthe	,,	Queen's G'smith.	
William Fitz Otto		King's G'smith.	1243	William de Berkinge	,,	,,	
Richard Abel	1243	Graver to Mint. Sheriff.		Nicholas (Sir) Faren(g)don	1308		d 1361
Hugh Bland	,,			Richard de Wyhall	1323		
William of Gloucester	1255	Master of Mint.	1258	Robert Box	,,		
Thomas Fitz Otho	1265		1275	Thomas de Lincoln	,,		
Ralph le Blount	1267		,,	Walter de Lincoln	,,		
Conrad the Goldsmith			1269	Roger of Ely	,,		
John Fitz Patrick			,,	Richard (Sir) Britane	1326	Mayor.	
Hubert the Goldsmith			,,	Henry of Gloucester			1332
Gregory de Rokesley	1271	Assay Master & Mayor.	1285	Thomas de Berkele	1334	Warden.	
Michael Thovy			1275	Richard Loverye	,,	,,	1337
Josee the Goldsmith	1276	Mint Master.		John de Makenhead	,,	,,	
				Simon de Berking	,,	,,	1349
				William Speron	1336		
				Thomas de Rokesley	1337	,,	
				John de Kingeston	,,	,,	
				William d' Espagne	1339	,,	
				Robert le Shoreditch	,,	,,	1350
				Nicholas de Walyn'wick	,,	,,	
				William Wyndesore	1340		
				William de Walton	1347		

Name of Goldsmith.		Earliest Mention.	Remarks.	Latest Mention.
Nicholas	Walsh	1348		
Adam de	Walpole	,,	Warden.	1350
John de	Walpole			d 1349
John de	Lincoln	1350	,,	
Rafe	Comins	,,	,,	
John (Sir) de	Chichester	1359		1369
Thomas	Raynham	1360		
Thomas	Hessey	1366		
William	Hersey	,,		
Simon le	Maserer	1369		
John /	Standulph	,,	Master.	
John	Hyltoft	,,		,,
John	Walsh	1370		
Thomas	{ Raynham or Reynold	1371		1390
Thomas	Lauleye	1372		
Peter	Randolfe	1376		
Nicholas (Sir)	Twyford	1379	Mayor 1388.	d 1390
John	Edmund	1380	Graver to Mint.	1390
Robert	Lucas	,,	Warden.	
John	Cramb	,,	,,	
Harre	Bame	,,	,,	
Harre	Malvayne	,,	,,	
——	Godfrey	,,		
Adam (Sir)	Bamme	1382	Mayor 1391.	1397
John	Frensshe	,,		
John	Mayhew	1390		1399
John (Sir)	Frances	,,	Mayor 1400.	d 1405
Drugo (Sir)	Barentyne	1394	M.P. for City	d 1415
Thomas	Pole			d 1395
Adam	Browne	1397	Ld. Mayor	
Thomas atte	Hay	,,		d 1405
William	Grantham	1403	Warden.	
Salamon	Oxeneye	,,	,,	1419
Thomas	Senycle	,,	,,	
Robert	Hall	,,	,,	
William	Chicheley	1409	Sheriff.	
John	Bernes	1422		
Gilbert van	Brandenberg	,,	Engraver to Mint.	
Bart'l'mew	Seman	,,		d 1430
William	Russe	1429	Master of Mint.	1432
William	Russ	1430		
John	Hill	,,		
Richard	Whichdale	,,		
John	Orwell	1432	,,	d 1472
John (Sir)	Pattisley	,,	Mayor 1440.	1450
——	Redmonde	1437		
John	Sutton	1440	Sheriff.	d 1450
John	Buching	1441		
John	Thompson	1442		
——	Tomkins	,,		
Robert	Hall	,,		
William	Walton	1443	Warden.	1455
William	Porter	,,	,,	,,
William	Rockley	,,	,,	,,
William	Bismere	,,	,,	,,
Oliver	Davy	,,		1474
Baynham	Dickens		1447	

Name of Goldsmith.		Earliest Mention.	Remarks.	Latest Mention.
Carlos	Spaen		1447	
——	Skinner	1449		
John	Streete	,,		
William	Scales	,,		
William	Rymore	,,		
William	Welstonby	,,		
German	Lyas	1450		1452
William	Breakspeare	,,		d 1461
John	Adys	,,		d ,,
John	Crebit	1451		
John	Waryn	,,		
William	Boston	,,		
Mathew (Sir)	Phillips	,,		1464
Hu'ph'y (Sir)	Hayford	,,	Mayor 1477.	1478
Thomas	Leget	,,		
Robert	Boteler	,,		1488
Matthew	Hall	,,		
John	Crowe	,,		
Roger (Sir)	Brown	,,		
William	Hitches	,,		
John	Walsh	,,		
John	Adys	,,		1512
Thomas	Harrison	1452		
Robert	Harding	,,		1503
John	French	1453		
John	Wicks	,,		
Edward	Clough			1454
William	Wodeward	1455	Engraver to Mint.	
William	Hede	1456		
Hans	Christian	1457		
Edward	Rawdon	1458		
German	Lynche	1460		1483
William	{ Bowdon or Bowden	,,		
William	Flower	1462		
Edm'nd (Sir)	Shaa (or Shaw)	,,		1488
Thomas	Muschamp	1463	Sheriff.	
Mathew (Sir)	Philip	,,	Mayor 1463-4.	1474
Whyte	Johnson	1464		
John	Byrlyney (the elder)	1465		
Diryke	Ryswke	,,		
John	{ Alyn or Alleyne	,,		
Thomas	Cartelage	,,		
Umfrey the	Goldsmythe	,,		
Richard	Mesyngre	,,		
Garrod	Hawerbeke	,,		
Bart'l'mew	Semern	1468		
John	Barker	1469		
Henry	Massey	,,		
Hugh (Sir)	Bryce	,	Alderman 1478.	1497
Robert	Hill	,,		
Richard	Preston	,		
Hu'ph'y (Sir)	Heyford	1477		
Robert	Harding	1478		d 1485
Henry	Coote	,,	Free 1478.	d 1514
Miles	Adys	,,	,,	1492
William	Palmer	,,	,,	
John	Wolk	1480		
Mathew	Shore	,,		
——	Selys	,,		

Name of Goldsmith.		Earliest Mention.	Remarks.	Latest Mention.	Name of Goldsmith.		Earliest Mention.	Remarks.	Latest Mention
Bart'w (Sir)	Reade	1481	Mayor 1502-3.	1503	John	Garrard	1520		
Alen	Newman	1483	Free 1488.		Morgan	Wolff	,,		1553
Stephen	Kelke	,,	,,	d 1511	Henry	Averell	1523		,,
John	Ernest	,,	,,		Robert	Caer	,,		
Henry	Cole	,,			Manasses	Stockton	1528		1569
John (Sir)	Shaa or Shaw	,,	Mayor 1501.	1502	John	Carswell	1529		
Thomas	Wood	1491			Joseph	Allen & ano'r	,,		
John	Vandelf	1497			Robert	Cowper	,,		
Christopher	Eliot	1500		d 1505	Richard	Asplin	,,		
Michael	Dersk	,,			William	Sympson	,,		1531
William	Tallsworth	,,			Robert	Reyns	1530		1533
Louis	Boreman	,,			Thomas	Trappis	,,		1553
John	Frende			d 1505	Cornelius	Hughes or Hayes	,,		,,
Thomas (Sir)	Exmewe	1508	Mayor 1517-8.	d 1528	William	Southwood	,,		d 1557
Richd. (Sir)	Martin	1509		1588	Thomas	Calton	,,		1553
——	Ashley	,,			Richard	Alleyn	1531		,,
John (Sir)	Mundy	,,		1537	Robert	Trappis	,,		,,
Nicholas	Warley	,,		1520	John	Patterson	,,		
Richard	Apulton	,,		1516	Henery	Colville	,,		
John	Banyard	,,			John	Mabbe	1532		1569
Ralph	Latham	,,		1519	John	Harrison	1534		
——	Brokat	,,			John	Frende	1535		1553
——	Lupset	,,			Simon or Symond	Palmer	1538		,,
Henry	Warley	,,			Robert	Spych	,,		
Henry	Coste	,,		d 1509	Edmund	Henrick	,,		
Ralph	Apulston		Free 1510.		Regin.	Horton	,,		1540
John	Barrett	1511			Thomas	Boughton	,,		
John de	Loren	,,	1511		Thomas	Hays	,,		1553
Robert	Fenrother	1512		d 1525	Edmund	Lee	,,		,,
John	Kewe	,,			Henry	Bonsall	,,		
Robert	Mayne	,,			Walter	Lambert	,,		,,
Agas (Mrs)	Harding	1513			Nicholas	Johnson	,,		,,
Christopher	Terry	1515			John	Lewes	,,		,,
E.	Bussey	1516			Vincent	Mundye	,,		,,
——	Melton	,,			George	Webbe	1539		,,
——	Reed	,,			William	Humble	,,		
——	Nele	,,			John	Keale	,,		d 1574
——	Ashley	,,			Robert	Aleyn	,,		1553
T.	Green	,,			Fabyan	Wydder	,,		,,
William	Preston	,,			Robert	Spendley	1540		,,
——	Lowth	,,			Nicholas	Aldewyn	,,		,,
——	Pyke	,,			John	Chaundeler	,,		,,
——	Allen	,,			Robert	Draper	,,		,,
William	Beck	,,			——	Hatwoode	,,		
R.	Vedale or Udall	,,		1519	Martin (Sir)	Bowes	,,	Mayor 1545-6.	1566
R.	Warley	,,			John (Sir)	Williams	,,		
——	Seyley	,,			William	Symonds	,,		d 1543
John	Twisselton	,,		d 1525	Rogier	Mundye	,,		1553
Thomas	Bokys	,,			Silvester	Todd	,,		,,
Thomas	Wastell	,,		1553	Nicholas	Bull	,,		,,
Richard	Bray	,,			John	Freeman	,,		,,
Christopher	Tyrril	,,			William	Chambers	,,		,,
——	Verton	,,			Margery	Herkins	,,		
Edward	Lee	1517			Rowland	Staunton	,,		
Roger	Winburgen		1517		John	Waberley	,,		
John	Nicholl	1518		1521	Thomas	Marshall	,,		
Roger (Sir)	Mundye	,,		d 1537	John	Bolter	,,		,,
Robert	Oxendly	,,			Thomas	Glenton	,,		
Robert	Amades	,,		1520	Robert	Lawerd	,,		,,
Henry	Calton	,,			John	Hart	,,		
Thomas	Reede	,,		1553	John	Harvey	,,		
John (Sir)	Thurston	1519		d 1521	John	Reynolds	,,		1552
Walter	Lamb	,,			John	Barons	,,		1553
Thomas	Banister	,,			Robert	Frew	,,		
					John	Gardener	,,		

Name of Goldsmith.		Earliest Mention.	Remarks.	Latest Mention.	Name of Goldsmith.		Earliest Mention.	Remarks.	Latest Mention.
Thomas	Weltherell	1540			Hugh	Crooke	1558		
Robert	Danbie or Danbe	1541			Henry	Gillard	,,		
					Christopher	Ffulke	,,		1569
Laurence	Warren	1545			———	Franklin	,,		
R.	Maynard	,,			Richard	Martin *	,,		,,
John	Andewerpe	,,			Laurence	Rycle	1559		
Thomas	Hartoppe	,,		1569	John	Ealeston	,,		,,
Thomas	Keeling	1546		1583	Nicholas	Courtnall	,,		
Richard	Lounde	1548			John	Wheeler	,,		
Robert	Brandon *	1549		1569	Hugh	Keale * or Kayle	1560		1571
William	Kelwaye	,,		1553					
Robert	Tayleboys	,,			Richard	Hanberrie	,,		1569
Nicholas	Bartholomew	,,		1569	James	Storke	,,		,,
John	Kettlewood	,,		,,	John	Alsop	,,		
William	Lymson	,		1553	Stephen	Durrant	,,		,,
Thomas	Stephens (Stevyns)	,,		d 1578	Thomas	Maye	,,		,,
					William	Jones	,,		
John	Waterstone			1549	Gabriel	Newman	,,		,,
Henry	Newhall	1550			Robert	Tailbrushe	,,		
Ralph	Lathom	,,		d 1556	George	Gatchet	,,		,,
John	Wickes	,,			William	Carter	,,		1570
John	Cross	,,			William	Cater	,,		,,
Robert	Reyns	,,			Thomas	Green	,		,,
Thomas	Metcalfe	,,		1566	Roger	Hyat	,,		,,
John	Danyell	,,			Edward	Ranklyn	,,		1579
Derrick	Antony	,,		1569	Simon	Brooke	,,		1575
Robert	Harrison	,,			Robert	Taylebois	,,		1566
William	Beereblocke	,,		,,	Thomas	Muschampe	,,		1573
Affabel	Partridge *	,,		1568	Thomas	Gardiner	,,		
Thos. (Sir)	Gresham	,,		d 1579	Peter	Bolton	1561		
Robert	Ffrice	,,			Francis	Heton	,,		1568
John	Palterton	,,			———	Godderyke			d 1561
———	Wark	1551			Thomas	Heard	,,		
John	Clarke	,,	Warden 1566.		Robert	Medley	,,		1569
					Robert	Aske	,,		,,
Richard	Robyns	1552		1569	———	Gylbart			
George	Warrenson	,,		,,	William	Dyckeson (Dyxson)	1562		d 1562
Humphrey	Stephens	,,		,,					,,
Nicholas	Molde	1553			John	Matthew	,,		
———	Lynne	,,		d 1559	Nicholas	Sutton	,,		,,
Ralph	Latham	,,			Antony	Bate	,,		
John	Bardolph	,,			George	Martin	,,		,,
Thomas	Browne	,,			Thomas	Yemans	,,		,,
Raßel	Cornyshe	,,			John	Hallywell	,,		d 1563
John	Dale	,,			Ambrose	Yonge	,,		d ,,
Henry	Goldeville	,,			James	Nutshawe	1564		
Rogier	Horton	,,			———	Stocke	1565		
Edmond	Hatcombe	,,			Edward	Gilberd	,,		
William	Tylsworth	,,			Jasper	Fysher		Warden 1566.	
Thomas	Spooner			1553					
Rogier	Taylour			,,	George	Dalton	1566		
Anthony	Neale			,,	Henry	Gaynsford	,,		,,
Robert	Hortopp			,,	Richard	Rogers	1567		1586
Rafe	Rowlett			,,	Robert	Sharpe	,,		1569
Thomas	Baven			,,	Thomas	Pope	,		,,
Andrew	Pomer	1554			Peter	Maas †	,,		,,
Thomas	Dewey	,,			Thomas	Bampton	,,		
John	Hulson			1555	John (Sir)	Langley (Ald'n)	,,		1586
Robert	Wygge	1557	Warden 1566.	1586	Richard	Robins	,,		
John	Bull	,,		1569	Thomas	Hampton	,,		1569
Henry	Boswell	,,			William	Notte	,,		d 1568
William	Foxe	,,		,,	W.	Calton	1568		1569
John	Pekenynge	,,			John	Bird	,,		,,
R.	Durrant	,,			William	Ffynstwayte	,,		,
Richard	Sharpe	,,		,,	———	Hatcombe	,,		
William	Walker	,,			Thomas	Conell	,,		,,
George	Longedale	,,		,,	Christopher	Wace	,,		,,

* Mentioned in *Queen Elizabeth's Progresses and Processions* as a goldsmith and purveyor to Her Majesty.

† See page 100, year 1567.

Name of Goldsmith.		Earliest Mention.	Remarks.	Latest Mention.
George	Warren	1568		1586
Edmund	Cornwall	,,		
Francis	Jackson	,,		
Robert	Harryson			d 1568
Henry	Gilberd	1569		1569
Robert	Wright	,,		1578
John	Lannyson	,,		
John	Foxe	,,		
Thomas	Turpin	,,		1570
Henry	Sutton	,,		1586
Richard	Howe	,,		
J.	Alleyne	,,		1570
John	Keale	,,		
Thomas	Sympson	,,		,,
Thomas	Benson	,,		
Robert	Frye	,,		
Robert	Signell	,,		
William	Jones, sr.	,,		
William	Jones, jr.	,,		
Robert	Hawkins	,,		
William	Holborne	,,		
William	Burneye	,,		
John	Wetheryll	,,		
Edward	Creake	,,		
John	Harryson			1569
Thomas	Harrison			,,
W.	Alsoppe			,,
Thomas	Clerke			,,
John	Goodrich			,,
William	Marten			,,
Robert	Durrant			,,
Thomas	Denham			,,
John	Pinfold			
John	{ Loveyson, Lavyson or Lannyson *	1570	Master of Mint.	d 1583
Edward	Delves	,,		1599
John	Castell	,,		1572
Nicholas	Hillyard	,,		d 1619
X'pofer	Brickbeck			d 1570
George	Haynes	1572		
Peter	Hibbins	1573		
William	Leighton	,,		
Cuthbert	Crackford	,,		
Isaac	Sutton	1574		d 1589
Francis	Jackson			d 1574
Edward	Lyngard			d ,,
Richard	Phillipps			d ,,
Hance	Payne			d 1575
Thomas	Gough			d ,,
John	Mabbe, jr.	1575		
Samuel	Cole	1576		
John	Wilkins	,,		1599
William	Cocknidge	,,		
Thomas	Jenkinson	,,		
Thomas	Gardner			d 1576
John	Clarke			d ,,
William	Bowyer			d ,,
John	Wetherell	1577		1586
Richard	Robinson	,,		
James	Stocke			d 1578
William	Frank	1579		
John	Cranks	,,		
Cornelius	Vandort	,,		
——	Heydon	,,		
Robert	Hutchinson	,,		1597
Rowland	Johnson	1580		
Edmund	Grete	,,		
George	Newbole	1580		
William	Noke	,,		
Reinard	Trip	,,		
John	Collins	,,		
Robert	Planckney	,,		
Richard	Lory	,,		
Roger	Easton	,,		
Aaudrian	Queeney	,,		
Henry	Gilbert	,,		
Robert	Andrews	,,		
John	Fox	,.		d 1597
James	Poole	.,		d 1581
Nicholas	Johnson			d ,,
Thomas	Nedom			d ,,
George	Osburne			d ,,
Robert	Shewte			d ,,
Thomas	Hartoppe			d 1582
William	Rawlinson	1582		
Richard	Brooke	,,		
Richard	Matthew	1583		
Humphrey	Dutton	,,		1586
Henry	Colley	,,		
Thomas	Kelynge	,,		,,
Thomas	Francknall	,,		
John	{ Speilman or Spilman *	,,	Queen's G'smith.	1597
Edward	Harding	,,		
John	Morris			d 1583
Francis	Heton			d 1584
Francis	Shute	1584		
John	Brode	,,		
Stephen	Mabbe	1585		
John	Morris	,,		
James	Feake	,,		
William	Johnson			1585
Thomas	Taylor	1586		
Harry	Cornford	,,		
John	Fox	,,		,,
Peter	King	,,		
John	Wilson	,,		
Justyne	Spencer	,,		
John	Moothe	,,		
T.	Newton	,,		1596
Henry	Keele	,,		
Thomas	Robinson	,,		
Christopher	Waiste †	,,		1605
Edward	Greene	,,		
William	Ffreeke			1586
Richard	Ballett			d ,,
George	Aley			d 1587
Andrew	Bawdyn			d ,,
John	Morley	1588		
Simon	Sedgwick	,,		1630
William	Franch	1589		
Robert	Tripps	,,		
John	Bull			d 1589
Manasses	Stockton			d ,,
Richard	Williams			d 1590
Francis	Longworth	1590		d 1598
Henry	Hargrave	,,		
Nicholas	Heyrick	,,		d 1601
Giles	Sympson	,,		d 1608
Thomas	Laurence	,,		
John	Robinson	,,		
Thomas	Bowes	,,		
Robert	Durrant			d 1591
Robert	Brandon			d ,,
Thomas	Clarke			d ,,

* See footnote on preceding page.   † See page 105, year 1586-7.

Name of Goldsmith.		Earliest Mention.	Remarks.	Latest Mention	Name of Goldsmith.		Earliest Mention.	Remarks.	Latest Mention
Richard	Cheney	1592		d 1625	F.	Terry	1606		
Albert	Hadock			d 1592	Fabyan	Sympson	,,		
Thomas	Glasse			d ,,	Richard	Phillips	1607		
Nicholas	Herricke			d ,,	William	Rawlins	,,		
Henry	Sutton			d ,,	William	Francis	,,		
Thomas	Jemson			d 1593	Anthony	Bates			d 1607
Robert	Medley			d ,,	Henry	Cheshire	1608		
John	Lovejoy	1594			John	Wheeler	,,		
Richard	Croshaw	,,		d 1621	Richard	Wheeler	,,		
Hugh	Wall *	,,			Arthur	Bassett	1609		
Hugh	Kayle, jr.	,,		1599	John	Broad	,,	of the Irish Society.	
Noye	Farmer	,,		d 1600					
Edward	Brooke	,,			John	Reynolds	,,		1619
Thomas	Bancks			d 1594	Wm. (Sir)	Ward	,,		1630
William	Huntington			d ,,	Robert	Orpwood			d 1609
John	Ballett			d 1595	Humphrey	Lambert			,,
Thomas	Thurseby			d 1596	John	Williams	1610		
Francis	Glanfield	1597			John	Wardlaw	,,		
I.	Doe	,,			Thomas	Savage			d 1611
Edward	Hyde	,,			William	Shordeer	1611		
John	Moore	,,			Oliver	Mantle	,,		
Robert	Thomas	,,			Thomas	Boyce	,,		
Daniel	Binnell	1598			William	King	,,		
William	Carco	,,			Simon	Sedgwick	1612		d 1619
John	Glover			d 1598	Derrick	Beley	,,		
Peter	Blundell	1599			Robert	Shirley (the Elder)	,,		
Balthazar	Lawt	,,							
Hugh (Sir)	Myddleton	1600		d 1631	John	Boultby	1613		
William	Keale	,,		1611	Graves	Heman	,,		
John	Hoare	,,		1607	John	Bowman	,,		
Roger	Bootby	,,			Nicholas	Hooker	,,		1630
Peter	Marmur	,,			Gaius	Newman	,,		d 1613
Anthony	Bull	,,			H.	Babington	,,		1664
John	Acton	,,		1630	Francis	Chapman	1614		1635
Thomas	Ffranklyn	,,			Henry	Blackmore	,,		1651
Richard	Keane	,,			Benjamin	Tate or Yate	1615		1635
Nicholas	Hooper	16—			William	Keble	,,		
John	Lovejoy	1600		1609	Thomas	Simpson	,,		
William	Heyricke	,,			George	Smithies			d 1615
George	Carol or Caro	,,			Robert	Brocklesby	,,		,,
Randall	Rawlinson	,,		1612	Richard	Adams	1616		1648
Timothy	Eman	,,			Richard	Phelce	,,		
Anthony	Herring	,,			William	Ireland	,,		
William	Terry	,,		d 1629	William	Peacock	,,		
Dame Mary	Ramsey	,,			George	Wakefield	,,		1647
Valentine	Judd	,,			Richard	Weld	,,		
Simon	Edmonds	,,			Timothy	Reade			d 1616
William	Rolph	,,		d 1647	Joshua	Walter	1617		
John	Rundall	16—			Michael	Bold			d 1617
John	Colte	1601			Thomas (Sir)	Exmewe	1618		
John	Cooke			d 1601	John	Middleston	,,		
James (Sir)	Pemberton	1602	Mayor 1611-2.	d 1613	Henry	Feake	,,		
					George	Binge	,,		
Barnabe	Gregory	,,			Thomas	Garrett	,,		
Richard	Rogers	,,		1632	Robert	Davies	1619		
Phillip	Strelley	1603			Anthony	Risby	,,		
James	Birkhead	,,	of Knightsbridge.	1620	John	Pemberton	,,		
					Thomas	Dymock			d 1619
George	Heriot	,,		d 1624	————	Tirie	1620		
Philip	Shelley			1603	Michael	Barkstead	,,		
Henry	Duckett			d ,,	George	Willie	,,		
Bennett	Prynne			d ,,	Anthony	Peniston	,,		
John	Elkinton			d 1604	William	Fairfax	,,		
Francis	Haddon	1604			John	Hanfan	,,		
Richard	Man	,,			John	Peacock	1621		
William	Wood	,,			Francis	Malbery	,,		d 1638
Christopher	Wase			d 1605	William	Webbe	,,		
Gabriel	Barber	1606			Henry	Banister	1622		d 1622

Name of Goldsmith.		Earliest Mention.	Remarks.	Latest Mention.	Name of Goldsmith.		Earliest Mention.	Remarks.	Latest Mention.
John	Wilde	1622			John	Perrin	1637		d 1656
Robert	Treat	,,			Richard	Vance	,,		d 1641
Humphrey	Hargrave	,,			William	Eversley	,,		
Thomas	Nevett	,,		d 1655	William	Mainwaring	,,		d 1659
Thomas	Bowen	1623			Charles	Punge	,,		d 1665
John	Leigh	,,			Geo.	Day	,,		
John	Weld	,,			J.	Buckle	1638		
John	Jennings	1624			John (Sir)	Wollaston	,,		d 1658
Edward	Hole	,,			Andrew	Edwards	1639		
———	Patrickson	,,			John	Goodwin	,,		
Thomas	Death	,,			William	Johnson	,,		1652
Arthur	Panter	,,			Robert	Paine	1640		
Walter	Shute	,,			John	Flake	,,		1653
Richard	Snow	1625			Ralph	Robinson	,,		
Arthur	Wright	,,	•		George	Snell	,,		1677
William	Beale	,,			John	Crounton	,,		
Richard	Treat or Trett	1626			Edward	Michell	,,		1652
William	Sandy	,,			Thomas	Smith	,,		
Frances	Bishop	1627		1633	Robert	Jenner	,,		d 1648
Thomas	Treat	,,			John	Westman	,,		
Thomas	Violet	,,		1660	George	Courthope			1649
William	Sanckney	,,			Jacob	Isaac	1641		
Matthew	Paris	1629			Thomas	Maundy	,,		1665
Thomas	Nene	,,			John	Smith	,,		
Matthew	Culleford	1630			Hennifrie	Bates	1642		
Maurice	Walron	,,			Tobias	Coleman	,,		1653
Richard	Gosson	,,			Abraham	Smith	,,		
Thomas	Leadham	,,			Thomas	Hogges	,,		
William	Roger	,,			John	Mackarnes			1643
Humphrey	Banckes	,,			Richard	Marsh			,,
Thomas	Palmer	,,			Edward	Edmunds	1643		
T.	Dove	,,			John	Portman	1644		d 1683
Walter	Furzer	1631			William	Jackson			d 1644
Richard	Crowthaw	,,			Thomas (Sir)	Viner or Vyner	1645		d 1665
W.	Rainbow	,,			Francis	Harris	,,		
William	Mantle	1632		d 1665	William	Comyns	,,		
William	Clent	,,			Gabriel	Marriott	,,		1655
Samuel	Moore	,,		d 1677	Richard	Waring	1646		
Simon	Gibbon	,,			Ant.	Fickets	,,		
William	Feake			1632	William	Hough	,,		,,
Anthony	Bradshaw	1633			Michael	Herring	,,		
Clement	Stonor	,,		1689	Nicholas	Wollaston	,,		
Henry	Futter	,,		1650	Cardinal	Orme	,,		
William	Brown	,,			Robert	Lumpany	1647		
W.	Maunday	,,			Thomas	Hodges	,,		
Richard	Ocall	1634			Richard	Vaughan	,,		
Humphrey	Bedenfield	,,			Thomas	Smithie			1649
William	Harrenden	,,			Thomas	Noel	1649		
Francis	Hall	,,		1649	William	Wayne	,,		1658
Giles	Alleyne	,,			Richard	Morrell	,,		d 1703
John	Gerrard	,,			Richard	Gibbs			,,
William	Daniel	,,			Matthew	Mason			,,
Richard	Clay	,,			Alexander	Jackson			,,
Simons	Gibson	,,			Humphrey	Bath	1650		
Walter	Merrell	,,			A.	Moore	,,		
William	Gibbs	,,			Henry	Pinckney	,,		1660
Edward	Elton	,,			John	Terry			1650
Francis	Ash	,,		1652	Robert	South			,,
Thomas	Collyer	1635			Leonard	Collard	1652		
Stephen	Venables	,,		1688	William	Symonds			1652
James	Beamont	,,			Alexander	Hoult	,,		
Peter	White	,,			Henry	Greenway	1653		
William	Wheeler	,,		1699	George	Pemberton	1654		
James	White	,,			Edward	Backwell	,,		d 1683
John	Pargiter	1636		d 1668	John	Colville	1655		1665*
John	Rayne	,,			Richard	Neale	,,		
Henry	Starkey	,,			Field	Whorwood	,,		
Benj.	Francis	,,			Edward	South			165

* *Pepys' Diary*, 19 June, 1665.

Name of Goldsmith.		Earliest Mention.	Remarks.	Latest Mention.	Name of Goldsmith.		Earliest Mention.	Remarks.	Latest Mention.
Henry	Whittingham			1655	Robert	Fintham	1668		
William	Rawson	1656		1666	Edward	Cossen	,,		
John	Sketcher	,,			Michael	Kirby	,,		
Chris.	Shaw	,,			Edward	Barwell	,,		
William	Smithier	1657			Thomas	Sturgis	,,		
Ralph	Leet	,,		1680	——	Hinton & Co.	,,		
Edward	Abel	,,			John	Maidson	,,		
George	Best	,,			William	Peirson	,,		
Hugh	Lewis			1657	Simon	Middleton	,,		
George	Bullen			,,	Richard	Lucas	,,		
Charles	Everard	1658		d 1665	Augustus	Dudley	,,		
George (Sir)	Viner	,,		d 1673	Jeremy	Gregory	,,		
Henry	Baggs			1658	Henry	Rouse	,,		
Roger	Lee	1659			John	Lindsay	,,		
Simon	Player	,,			——	Waterhouse	,,		1670
John	Garrett	,,			J.	Burt	,,		
William	Sankey			1659	Bartholo'ew	Soane	,,		
Thomas	Bonny			,,	Robert	Tempest	,,		
John	Feake	1660			William	Sanberry	,,		
Edmund	Michell	,,		1665	Edmund	Hinton	,,		
Henry	Fuller	,,			William	Preston (?)	,,		
William	Johnson	,,			John	East	,,		1677
John	Wasson	,,			Edward	East	,,		
——	Cuthbert	,,		1677	Thomas	Rowe	,,		,,
John	Billingsby	1661			Thomas	Potter	,,		
——	Wimbush	1662			Henry	Blomer	,,		
Robert (Sir)	Viner	,,		1689	Bernard	Turner	,,		1670
Francis	Meynell	,,			John	Snell	,,		1680
James (Sir)	Drax	1663			John (Sir)	Shorter	,,		1687
William	Pinchley	,,			William	Gosling	1670		1674
Edward	Greene	,,			John	Temple	,,		1677
Robert	Wealstead	,,		1702	Thos (Sir)	Cook	,,		1686
John	Hinde	,,		1677	Thomas	Kirkwood	,,		
John	Adtherton	1664			John (Sir)	Brattle	,,		1690
Thomas	Panton	,,			Michael	Whaley	,,		
Anthony	Walter	,,			John	Tassel	,,		1692
Nicholas	Clobury	1665	The Dogger Ordinary.		Gilbert	Whitehall	1672		
					George	Portman	,,		
					Richd. (Sir)	Hoare	,,	Mayor 1713.	1718
Nicholas	Sulle	,,							
Will	Wode	,,			Robert	Welstead	,,		
John	Sealey *	,,		1682	Thomas	Williams	1673		d 1697
John	Hind	,,	Foster Lane. The Intelligencer.		John	Innes	,,		
					Edward	Gladin	,,		
John	Harling	,,			James	Whitehead	1674		
					John	Saunders	,,		
John	Marryott	1666			John	Thursby	1675		1677
William	Hall	,,			W.	Pinkney	,,		
John	Smithies	,,			Phillip	Rolles	,,		1720
——	Colfe	,,			Thomas	Ash	1676		1697
William	Hulin	,,			John	Burrow	1677		
Chas. (Sir)	Doe	,,			Thomas	Pardo	,,		
Bartholo'ew	Leyton	,,		1668	John	Blake	,,		
Edward	Backwell	,,		d 1679	——	Brabant	,,		
Joseph	Hornby	,,		1677	John	Bolitho & Wilson	,,	Golden Lion.	
——	Mason	,,							
William	Boteler	1668			Benjamin	Rigforth	,,		
John	Austin	,,			John	Ballard	,,		
John	Gaston	,,			John	Morris	,,		
Isaac	Meynall	,,			Peter	Wade	,,		1681
Nathaniel	Hornby	,,		,,	Charles & Richard	Duncombe Kent	,,	The Grasshopper.	
Nicholas	Dawes	,,			Job	Bolton	,,	The Bolt and Tun.	
Francis	Kenton	,,							
John	Mawson & Co.	,,		,,					
John	Coggs	,,		,,	Henry	Nelthorpe	,,		
John	Gilbert	,,			Samuel	Brabourne	,,		
Jerem'h (Sir)	Snow	,,		d 1702	Peter	Percival &	,,		
Robert	Blanchard	,,		1680	Stephen	Evans			

* *Pepys' Diary*, 11 December, 1665.

(The dates under the heading " Entered " are those of entry or registration at Goldsmiths' Hall.)

Name of Goldsmith.	Earliest Mention.	Remarks.	Latest Mention.
William Depster	1677		
Thomas Cook & } Nicholas Carew	,,	The Griffin.	
Hugh & Jno. Lent	,,		
John Addis & Co.	,,	At the Sun.	
Thomas Price	,,		
John Grimes	,,		
Augustus Allard	,,		
Stat Ahearn	,,		
Humphrey Stocks	,,		
George Copp	,,		
Henry Lamb	,,		1703
Robert Ward & } John Townley	,,		
John Hind & } Thomas Carwood	,,		
Benjamin Hinton	,,	The Flower de-Luce.	
Thomas Kilburne & } James Capill	,,		
James Lapley	,,		
John Mawson & Co.	,,		
Bart. Turner & } Saml. Tookie	,,		
Richard Staley	,,		
John Temple & } John Seale or Sealey	,,		
Thomas Flowerdew	,,		
Edward Blake	,,		
Audrean van Schipcroft	,,		
Thomas White	,,		
Nicholas Lock	,,		
Simon Clark	,,		
Edward Wards	,,		
John Hill & } Thomas Carwood	,,		
William Fasset	,,		
——— Churchill	,,		
Warw Yard	,,		
Major John Wallis	,,		
Paul Alestre	,,		
John Edmonds	,,		
John Ewing & } Benjamin Norrington	,,	The Angel and Crown.	
John Bruse	,,		
James Heriot	,,	The Naked Boy.	1690
Richard Stayley	,,		
Ralph Far	,,		
Benjamin Bathurst	,,		
Michael Schrimshaw	,,		
Peter Vergrew	,,		
Joseph Chapman	,,		
James Caepell	,,		
Thomas Rowe & } Thomas Green	,,		

Name of Goldsmith.	Earliest Mention.	Entered.	Latest Mention.
Robert Blanchard & } Richard Child	1677	The Mary-gold.	
John Nunesan	,,		
John Aldis & Co.	,,		
Samuel Burlingham & Co.	,,		
Thos. (Sir) Fowles	,,	The Black Lion.	1691
James Johnson	,,		
James Hore	,,	The Golden Bottle.	
Joseph Hornby & } Nathaniel Hornby	,,	The Star.	
John Sweetapple	,,		1692
Peter White & } ——— Churchill	,,		
——— Ketch	,,		
Robert Wilstead	1678		
John Hareling	,,		
Barnard Eales	,,		d 1694
Mr. Fells	1679		
Benjamin Pyne	,,	1697	1723
Thomas Jameson	,,		
Ralph Leeke	,,		
Peter White	,,		
Richard Lassels	1680		,,
Francis Garthorne	,,	,,	
Richard Sheldon	,,		
John Butler	,,		
Lawrence Coles	,,	,,	1687
Heneage Price	1681		1687
Nicholas Smith	,,		
Thomas Wilcox	,,		
Charles Wheeler	,,		1681
George Garthorne	1682	,,	
Thomas Seymour	,,		1698
William Walker	1683		1687
Mr. White	,,		
Nicholas Smith & } W. Potter	,,		
John Maurice	,,		
John Batch	1684		
John Phelps	,,		1697
Anthony Fickets	1685		
George Middleton	,,		
D. Buteux	,,		
John Marlow	1686		
Henry Jennings	,,		1688
Edward Pinfold	1687		
John Jas. Saint	,,		
Nathaniel Greene	,,	1698	
Robert Vyner	1688		
Sir Francis Child	,,		
William Pierson	1689		
William Gamble	,,		
Peter Harrache	,,	1697	
Charles Brattle (Assay Master)	1690		1716
Joseph Brandon	,,		
H. Hankey	,,		1708
Nathaniel Poole	,,		
Robert Timbrell	,,	,,	1715

Name of Goldsmith.	Earliest Mention.	Entered.	Latest Mention.
William Scarlett	1691		1725
Philip Booker	,,		
——— Sweetapple	,,		
Richard Snagg	,,		
Middleton & Campbell	1692		
Arthur Maynwaring	,,		
——— Lowders	1693		1694
William Keatt	,,	1697	1698
Robert Mory	,,		
——— Lane	1694		
John Diggle	,,		1700
Edward Jones	,,	,,	
Jeremiah Marlowe	,,		
John Freame	,,		
John Ruslen	,,	,,	
John Freame	,,		
Thomas Allen	,,	,,	1709
John Laughton	,,	,,	
Peter Monga	1695		
Peter Lupart	1696		
William Gladwin	,,		
Land Doyle	,,		
Thomas Brydon	,,	,,	
Robert Cooper		,,	
Joseph Bird		,,	
William Brett		,,	
Andrew Raven		,,	
Matthew Madden		,,	
Stephen Coleman		,,	
Thomas Jenkins		,,	
Jonah Kirk		,,	
Henry Penstone		,,	
Ralph Leeke		,,	
——— Wimans		,,	
Lawrence Jones		,,	
John Hodson		,,	
Timothy Ley		,,	1729
William Matthew		,	
Samuel Dell		,,	1703
Joshua Frenshaw		,,	
Edward Freeman	1697		
John Spackman		,,	
Charles Williams		,,	
Edmund Townsend		,,	
William Gibson		,,	
Francis Hoyte		,,	
Jonathan Bassy		,,	
Joseph Stokes		,,	
Edward Gibson		,,	
John Ladyman	,,	,,	1704
James Chadwick		,,	
John Cory		,,	1702
Thomas Issod		,,	
Israel Pincking		,,	
Samuel Hawkes		,,	
John Jackson		,,	
Dorothy Grant		,,	
Edward Brockes		,,	
John Shepherd		,,	
Andrew Moore		,,	
Mathew West		,,	
William Denny		,,	
Samuel Jeffreys		,,	
James Edgar		,,	
Alexander Roode		,,	
John Brassey		,,	
William Middleton		1697	
Richard Syngin		,,	1701
George Titterton		,,	
William Penstone		,,	
William Gimber		,,	
John Downes		,,	
Seth Lofthouse	1697	,,	1716
Benjamin Braford		,,	
John Penfold		,,	
Jonathan Crutchfield		,,	
Francis Archbold		,,	
Jonathan Lambe		,,	
——— Thriscoss		,,	
Joyce Issod		,,	
Richard Nightingale		,,	
John Edwards		,,	
Samuel Thorne		,,	
Benjamin Harris		,,	
Anne Roman		,,	
Robert Timbrell		,,	
George Havers		,,	
Joshua Readshaw		,,	
Edward Ironside		,,	
Robert Peake		,,'	
Phillip Roker		,,	
Edward Jones		,,	
Samuel Hood		,,	
Isaac Dighton		,,	
William Flemming		,,	
A. Montgomery		,,	
John Snelling		,,	
John East		,,	
Thomas Parr		,,	
Charles Overing		,,	
John Diggle		,,	
William Bambridge		,,	
Francis Billingsley		,,	
John Sutton		,,	
Daniel Garnier		,,	
John Cole		,,	
Jonathan Bradley		,,	
Edward Courthope		,,	
John Smithsend		,,	
Isaac Davenport		,,	
James Blaygrave	,,		
William Denney & John Backe	,,	,,	1716
William Denney		,,	1733
Christopher Riley		,,	
Francis Singleton			1699
Hugh Roberts		,,	1701
William Andrews		,,	1707
John Leach		,,	1710
John Bodington		,,	1715
Joseph Ward		,,	1720
Anthony Nelme		,,	1728
David Willaume		,,	1741
William Gamble		,,	1736
Christopher Canner		,,	1720
Moses Brown		,,	1701
John Fawdery		,,	
Benjamin Traherne		,,	
William Francis	,,		1723
Richard Hutchinson	,,	1699	
Michael Wilson	1698		

Name of Goldsmith.		Earliest Mention.	Entered.	Latest Mention.	Name of Goldsmith.		Earliest Mention.	Entered.	Latest Mention.
John	Pearson &	1698			Ralph	Crowder	1700		
Launcelot	Keate				Thomas	Falkenham	,,		
Henry	Collins	,,	1698		Benjamin	Prynne	,,		1722
Mark	Paillet		,,		Benjamen	Tudiman	,,		1712
Freame &	Gould	,,		1728	Timothy	Lee			1700
Peter	Harrache		,,		Samuel	Lee		1701	1720
Peter	Harrache, jun.		,,	1705	Samuel	Wastell		,,	
John	Cove		,,		Thomas	Sadler		,,	
John	Chartier		,,		John	Cope		,,	
George	Cox		,,		David	Greene		,,	,,
Nathaniel	Lock		,,	1711	William	Spring		,,	
James	Pearce		,,		Jean	Petrig		,,	
John	Porter		,,		Willoughby	Masham		,,	
Benjamin	Bentley		,,		Joshua	Field		,,	
Mark	Paillet		,,		John	Tiffin		,,	
John	Eckfourd	,,	,,	1739	John	Reade &		,,	
———	Coxgrove		,,		Daniel	Sleamaker			
Benjamin	Watts		,,		Gerrard &	Newell		,,	1706
White	Walsh		,,		Samuel	Pantin		,,	1720
William	Bull		,,		John	Corosey		,,	,,
William	Fawdery	,,	1700		Humphrey	Payne		,,	1750
Edward	Lambert	1699			George	Boothby	1701		
Ralph	Gerrard	,,			Launcelot	Keatt	,,	,,	1716
Andrew	Stone	,,			Thomas	Waterhouse		1702	
John	Cooke	,,	1699		Anthony	Blackford		,,	
Pierre	Platel		,,		Jonathan	Madden		,,	
William	Petley		,,		Charles	Adams		,,	
John	Fawdery		,,		Matthew	Cooper		,,	
Job	Hanks		,,		William	Barnes		,,	
Ishmael	Bone		,,		Abraham	Russell		,,	
John	Heley		,,		Robert	Lovell		,,	
Thomas	Corbet		,,		Richard	Morrell	1703		
John	Broake		,,		Joseph	Wilson	,,		1710
Phillip	Oyle		,,		William	Charnelhouse		1703	
Lewis	George		,,		George	Gillingham		,,	
Matthew	Cooper		,,		Richard	Greene		,,	
William	Lukin		,,	1730	Matthew	Pickering		,,	
George	Lewis		,,		Andrew	Archer		,,	
John	Fletcher	1700			Jonah	Clifton		,,	
Gabriel	Player		,,		Joseph	Barbitt		,,	
William	Gosson		,,		Louis	Cuny		,,	1719
Stephen	Edmonds		,,		William	Warham		,,	
Samuel	Smith		,,		William	Juson		1704	
John	Gibbons		,,		Daniel	Sleamaker		,,	
Edmund	Proctor or Procter		,,		Edmund	Pearce		,,	
William	Matthew		,,		James	Beschefer		,,	
Mary	Matthew		,,		Alexander	Hudson		,,	
Richard	Bigge		,,		John	Chamberlen		,,	
John	Goode		,,		Thomas	Peele		,,	
John	Backe		,,		John	Read		,,	
Lewis	Mettayer		,,	1720	John	Wisdome		,,	
Thomas	Spackman		,,		William	Hinton		,,	
Henry	Green		,,		John	Rand		,,	
William	Green		,,		Isaac	Liger		,,	1724
Alice	Sheene		,,		John	Smith	1704	1710	
John	Bathe		,,		Jonathan	Kirk	1705		
Joseph	Moore	1700			John	Hudson	,,		
Charles (Sir)	Duncombe	,,			David	Venables	,,		
Bassy &	Caswall	,,			John Martin	Stocker &		1705	
Benjamen	Tudiman &	,,			Edward	Peacock			
Stephen	Shield				Phillip	Rolles, jun.		,,	
Nathaniel	Woolfrey	,,			William	Warham, jun.		,,	
Henry	Aubin	,,			Matthew E.	Lofthouse		,,	1721
Richard	Morson	,,			Edward	York		,,	1773
Robert	Stokes	,,			James	Thomason	1706		
					Thomas	Burridge		1706	

Name of Goldsmith.		Earliest Mention.	Entered.	Latest Mention.	Name of Goldsmith.		Earliest Mention.	Entered.	Latest Mention.
Thomas	Folkingham		1706		John	Stockar		1710	
Andrew	Raven		,,		William	Pearson		,,	1720
John	Abbott		,,		Thomas	Payne	1711		
William	Denny		,,		Isaac	Dalton		1711	
William	Fordham		,,		Thomas	Sutton		,,	
Jacob	Margas		,,		Jonathan	Newton		,,	
David	Williams		,,		John	Holland		,,	
John	Crutcher		,,		Joshua	Holland		,,	
Gabriel	Sleath		,,	1750	William	Matthew		,,	
James	Hallett	1707			Samuel	Lea		,,	1718
Christopher	Atkinson	1707		d 1753	Hezekiah	Mountford		,,	
Mary	Matthew		,,		Ellis	Gamble	1712		
Pierre le	Cheaube		,,		Thomas	Bevault		1712	
Thomas	Holland		,,		Richard	Raine		,,	
Thomas	Farrar		,,		Samuel	Hitchcock		,,	
Phillip	Rainaude		,,		Richard	Williams		,,	
Phillip	Brush		,,		Paul	Lamerie		,,	1749
Thomas	Fawler		,,		Edward	Vincent	1713		1739
Thomas	Farren		,,		George	Lambe		1713	
Jean	Petrij		,,		Michael	Boult		,,	1720
Edward	Cornac or Cornock		,,	1731	Thomas	Mann		,,	
Mary	Bainbridge		,,		William	Looker		,,	,,
Thos. (Sir)	Rawlinson			1754	Thomas	Evesdon, or Ewesdin		,,	
Robert	Yate	1708			George	Beale		,,	
Henry	Hankey	,,			Thomas	Port		,,	
Augustin	Courtauld		1708	1739	Phillip	Robinson		,,	
Thomas	Wall		,,	,,	John	Ludlow		,,	,,
John	Reade		,,		David	Tanqueray		,,	
John	Clifton		,,		Joseph	Ward		,,	1717
John	Ruslen		,,		Joseph	Clare		,,	
Richard	Bayley		,,		Nathaniel	Bland		1714	
Andrew	Dalton		,,		John	Farnell		,,	1720
Joseph	Smith		,,	1737	Henry	Beesley		,,	
Richard	Clarke		,,		Josiah	Daniel		,,	
Henry	Clarke	1709		1720	Samuel	Welder		,,	
Francis	Turner		,,		William	Spackman		,,	1723
Thomas	Pritchard		,,		Charles	Jackson		,,	
Edward	Holaday		,,		William	England &			
Edward	York		,,		John	Vaen		,,	
Gundry	Roode		,,	1721	Isaac	Riboulau		,,	
Ebenezer	Roe		,,		Samuel	Margas		,,	
William	Twell		,,		Richard	Gines		,,	
Nicholas	Clausen		,,	1718	James	Seabroke		,,	
Edward	Jennings		,,		Thomas	Langford		1715	
James	Wethered		,,		Daniel	Yerbury		,,	
Charles	Shales	1710			Paul	Hanet		,,	
————	Payne & Co.		,,		Edward	Barnet		,,	
James	Fraillon		1710		Benjamin	Blakely		,,	
Richard	Watts		,,		Francis	Plymley		,,	
Edward	Peacock		,,		Petley	Ley		,,	
Nathaniel	Roe		,,		David	Kilmaine		,,	
James	Rood		,,		Benjamin	Howell			d 1715
Robert	Keble		,,		Henry	Jay	1716		1770
Joseph	Fainell		,,		George	Horn	,,		
Andrew	Archer		,,		Richard	Greene	,,	1716	1726
John	Humphrey		,,		James	Morson	,,	,,	
William	Turbit		,,		Robert	Hill	,,	,,	1720
Isaac	Malyn		,,		Daniel	Cunningham		,,	,,
Robert	Kempton		,,		Lewis	Hamon		,,	1738
John	Keigwin		,,		William	Bellassyse		,,	1720
John	Flight		,,		Thomas	Mason		,,	
William	Truss		,,		Richard	Edwards		,,	
James	Goodwin		,,	1721	Joseph	Bell		,,	
John	Matthew		,,		John	Harris		,,	1786
Joseph	Sheene		,,		John	Corporon		,,	

Name of Goldsmith.		Earliest Mention.	Entered.	Latest Mention.	Name of Goldsmith.		Earliest Mention.	Entered.	Latest Mention.
J.	Barbitt		1717		Mary	Roode		1720	1721
Thomas	Shermer		,,		George	Squire		,,	
Paul	Hanet		,,		Isaac	Ribouleau		,,	
William	Bellamy		,,		James	Smith		,,	
William	Street		,,	1720	Benj.	Watts		,,	
William	Penstone		,,		J.	Burridge		,,	
John	Phillips		,,		Ambrose	Stephenson		,,	
Thomas	Parr		,,	1733	Glover	Johnson		,,	
Joseph	Ward		,,		Henry	Miller		,,	
William	Petley		,,		Thomas	Tuite		,,	
John	Sanders		,,	1720	John	Betts		,,	
Samuel	Welder		,,	,,	Jacob	Margas		,,	
Starling	Wilford		,,	1737	Humphrey	Payne		,,	
Simon	Pantin		,,	1720	Francis	Turner		,,	
Thomas	Burridge		,,	,,	Henry	Greene		,,	
John	Guerre		,,		Thomas	Ffarrer		,,	
John	Wisdome		,,		George	Brydon		,,	
John	Pero		,,	1739	Richard	Bayley		,,	
Richard	Gines		,,		Joshua	Holland		,,	
Gabriel	Barber	1717			Thomas	Bamford		,,	
John	Hill	,,			Michael	Ward		,,	
Henry	Hoare	1718		1722	Sarah	Parr		,,	
John	Brumhall	,,			John	Barnard		,,	
René	Hudell		1718		Edmund	Pearce		,,	
John	Millington		,,	1720	John	Wisdome		,,	
George	Gillingham		,,		Phyllis	Phillip		,,	
John	Lingard		,,	1719	John	Newton		,,	
Jonathan	Newton		,,		Samuel	Blackborrow		,,	
William	Paradise		,,		Michael	Boult		,,	
Thomas	Morse		,,		Nicholas	Clausen		,,	
John	Bignel		,,		David	Willaume		,,	
John	Le Sage		,,	1736	John	Farnell		,,	
Hugh	Sanders		,,		Thomas	Folkingham		,,	
James	Smith		,,	1737	Richard	Gines		,,	
William	Darkeratt		,,	1731	William	Scarlett		,,	
John	Motherby		,,		Josiah	Clifton		,,	
Sarah	Holaday	1719		1725	Pere	Pilleau		,,	
John	White		,,	1724	Gabriel	Barber		,,	
Hugh	Arnett & }		,,		Richard	Watts		,,	
Edward	Pocock }				David	Tanqueray		,,	
———	Hodgkis		,,		Matthew	Cooper		,,	
Edmund	Hickman		,,		Benjamin	Watts		,,	
Richard	Scarlett		,,		Hugh	Arnett & }		,,	1724
Jane	Lambe		,,	1729	Edward	Pocock }			,,
Hugh	Arnett		,,		Bowles	Nash		,,	
Joseph	Steward		,,		Edward	Feline		,,	1744
Christopher	Gerrard		,,		John	Lingard		,,	
Samuel	Smith		,,		John	East	1721		1725
Edward	Gibbons		,,		Paul	Hanet		,,	
Thomas	Tearle		,,		Anthony	Jolland		,,	
John	Jones		,,	1733	Gundry	Roode		,,	
Thomas	Gladwin		,,		John	Tuite		,,	1740
Peter	Archambo	1720	1768		John	Emes		,	
John	Bromley		,,		Francis	Garthorne		,,	
Anne	Tanqueray		,,		Hugh	Spring		,,	
Edward	Hall		,,		Samuel	Green		,,	
Edward	Turner		,,		George	Gillingham		,,	
William	Truss		,,		George	Wickes		,,	
William	Fawdery		,,		Abraham	Buteux		,,	1731
Arte	Dicken		,,		Thomas	Cooke & }		,,	
Paul	Crespin		,,		Richard	Gurney }			
Henry	Clarke		,,	1722	David	Willaume		,,	
Phil.	Rolles		,,		George	Boothby		,,	
John	Hopkins		,,		Humphrey	Heyford	1722		
John	Smith		,,		Humphrey	Hetherington	,,		
William	Spackman		,,	1723	Emick	Romer	,,		

Name of Goldsmith.		Earliest Mention.	Entered.	Latest Mention.	Name of Goldsmith.		Earliest Mention	Entered.	Latest Mention.
Augustus	Lesage		1722		Jacob	Foster		1726	
Henry	Dell		,,		George	Weir		1727	
Edward	Dymond		,,		Christian	Claris		,,	
James	Wilkes		,,		Charles	Perier		,,	
George	Young		,,		Charles	Kandler & }		,,	
Nathaniel	Gulliver		,,		James	Murray }			
Francis	Nelme		,,		Edward	Bennett		,,	
Edward	Wood		,,		Richard	Hutchinson		,,	
Meshach	Godwin		,,		William	Shaw		,,	
John	Gould		,,		Charles	Hatfield		,,	
James	Gould		,,		Edmund	Bodington		,,	
Joseph	Adams		,,		Hester	Fawdery		,,	
John	Clarke		,,		Abel	Brokesby		,,	
Isaac	Cornasseau		,,		Mary	Johnson		,,	
William	Soame		1723		Richard	Gurney		,,	
Bernard	Fletcher		,,		Blanche	Fraillon		,,	
Michael	Nicholl		,,		Dike	Impey		,,	
Simon	Jouett		,,		Charles	Kandler		,,	
Phillip	Robinson		,,		Pierre	Bouteiller		,,	
Richard	Scarlett				Thomas	Cooke		,,	
Jeremiah	King		,,		Samuel	Laundry		,,	
John	Edwards & }		,,		William	Shaw		,,	
George	Pitches }				Richard	Pargeter	1727	1730	
William	Owen		,,		George	Braithwaite	1728		
James	Hallett			d 1723	John	Bland	,,		
John	Richardson		,,	1752	James	Savage		1728	
William	Bellasyse		,,		William	Matthews		,,	
James	Fraillon		,,		John	Taylor		,,	
Philip	Goddard		,,		J.	Millington		,,	
John	Gibbons		,,		Samuel	Bates		,,	
Jonathan	Robinson		,,		George	Hodges		,,	
George	Jones		1724		James	Maitland		,,	
John	Owing		,,		John	Swift		,,	
Samuel	Hutton		,,		Ralph	Frith		,,	
James	Burne		,,		John	Fawdery		,,	
Fleurant	David		,,		Joseph	Smith		,,	
Edward	Peacock		,,		Thomas	Potts		,,	
Wescombe	Drake		,,		Deptford	Wichaller		,,	
Thomas	Rush		,,		David	Willaume		,,	
John	Edwards		,,		Edward	Cornac		,,	
Joseph	Bird		,,		I.	Wichaller		,,	
Edward	Conen		,,		James	Wilkes		,,	
William	Toone		1725		Caleb	Hill		,,	
Louis	Laroche		,,		Edward	Pocock		,,	1732
Peter	Tabart		,,		Benjamin	Bentley		,,	
Joshua	Healy		,,		Eraye	Berthet		,,	
Abraham de	Oliveyra		,,		John	Gorham		,,	1730
William	Lukin		,,		Thomas	Glagg	1729		
William	Atkinson		,,		Dennis	Wilks	1729	1729	1753
Thomas	England		,,		Starling	Wilford		,,	
John	Eckfourd, jun.		,,		Daniel	Chapman		,,	
Matthew	Cooper		,,		John	Montgomery		,,	,,
Thomas	Clark		,,		Edith	Fletcher		,,	
Peter	Simon	1725	1726		Elizabeth	Goodwin		,,	
John	Gorsuch	1726	,,		Francis	Spilsbury		,,	
John	Newton		,,		Charles	Martin		,,	
Harvey	Price		,,		Samuel	Welder		,,	
George	Brome		,,		Richard	Mills		,,	
Peter Le	Chuabe		,,		Francis	Pages		,,	
Robert	Lucas		,,		Phillip	Roker		,,	
John	Flavill		,,		Charles	Alchorne		,,	
Robert	Williams		,,		Joseph	Allen & Co.		,,	
John	Gamon		,,		Aug.	Courtauld		,,	
Gawen	Nash		,,		Aaron	Bates		1730	
Isaac	Callard		,,		Benjamin	Godwin		,,	
David	Williams		,,		Joseph	Sanders		,,	

Name of Goldsmith.		Earliest Mention.	Entered.	Latest Mention.
Edward	Yorke		1730	
John	Chapman		,,	
John	Liger		,,	
Jeffrey	Griffith		1731	
Robert	Abercromby		,,	
William	Justus		,,	
Etienne	Rongent		,,	
William	Woodward		,,	
William	Reeve		,,	
William	Darkeratt	1731	,,	
James	Jenkins		,,	
Thomas	Merry		,,	1773
William	Darker		,,	
George	Hindmarsh		,,	
Simon	Pantin, jr.		,,	
Charles	Perier		,,	
Ralph	Maidman		,,	
Richard	Beale		,,	
Peter	Bennett		,,	
Thomas	Causton		,,	
Mary	Lofthouse		,,	
Samuel	Laundry & }		1731	
Jeffrey	Griffith }			
Charles	Gibbons		1732	1734
William	Gould		,,	
George	Smith		,,	
Benjamin	Godwin		,,	
Paul	Lamerie		,,	
James	Slater		,,	
William	Soame		,,	
Benjamin	Godfrey		,,	
Griffith	Edwards		,,	
James	Gould		,,	
John	Pero		,,	
John	Fossy		1733	
Lewis	Pantin		,,	
Mary	Pantin		,,	
Samuel	Wood		,,	1773
Roger	Lee	1734		
Samuel	Hutton		1734	
Hugh	Arnell		,,	
Richard	Gurney & }		,,	
Thomas	Cook }			
John	Quantock		,,	
William	Kidney		,,	
John	Harwood		,,	
Anne	Hill		,,	
John	Tayler		,,	
James	Manners		,,	
John	Gahegan		,,	
Charles	Sprage		,,	
James	Brooker		,,	
Richard	Gurney & Co.		,,	
Henry	Herbert		,,	
Alexander	Coates & }		,,	
E.	French }			
John	Jacob		,,	
John	Pollock		,,	1749
John	Bryan		1735	
George	Weekes		,,	
Bowyer	Walker		,,	
John	Barbe		,,	
William	Garrard		,,	
Gabriel	Sleath		,,	
Richard	Zouch		,,	
Henry	Herbert		,,	
Edward	Wood		1735	1740
William	Young		,,	
Frederick	Kandler		,,	
Freame &	Barclay	1736		
Robert	Ladbrook & Co.	,,		1774
Thomas	Mann		1736	
Louis	Dupont		,,	
David	Hennell		,,	
Robert	Brown		,,	
Dike	Impey		,,	
Thomas	Jackson		,,	1769
Christian	Hilland		,,	
Jeremiah	King		,,	
Benjamin	Sanders		1737	
Dennis	Wilks		,,	1739
John	Barrett		,,	
Samuel	Wood		,,	
Philip	Platel		,,	
Thomas	Whipham		,,	1772
Benjamin	West		,,	
Thomas	Gladwin		,,	
Bennett	Bradshaw & }		,,	
R.	Tyrill }			
James	Shruder		,,	1753
Benjamin	Sanders		,,	
William	Westbrook	1738		
Thomas	Pye		1738	
George	Baskerville		,,	1745
William	West		,,	
Robert	Perth		,,	
Benjamin	Blakeley		,,	
Phillip	Brugier		,,	
David	Mowden		,,	
Thomas	Townsend		,,	
James	Jenkins		,,	
Henry	Bates		,,	
Ebenezer	Coker		,,	
James	Langlois		,,	
John	Robinson		,,	
William	Soame		,,	
John	Pero		,,	
Gabriel	Barber	1739		
William	Garrod	,,		
William	Brown	,,		
Thomas	Turle	,,		
James	Gould		1739	
David	Willaume		,,	
Thomas	Mason		,,	
Edward	Aldridge		,,	1753
John	Robinson		,,	
Edward	Bennett		,,	
John	Pollock		,,	
Richard	Bayley		,,	
George	Boothby		,,	
Griffith	Edwards		,,	
Jonathan	Fossy		,,	
Phillip	Roker		,,	
William	Hopkins		,,	
John	Holland		,,	
John	Eckfourd		,,	
George	Wickes		,,	
John	Barrett		,,	
Thomas	Mann		,,	
William	Hunter		,,	
Jessie	McFarlane		,,	
Marmaduke	Daintry		,,	1747

Name of Goldsmith.		Earliest Mention.	Entered.	Latest Mention.	Name of Goldsmith.		Earliest Mention.	Entered.	Latest Mention.
Richard	Gurney & Co.		1739		Thomas	Farren		1739	
Thomas	Gilpin		,,		John	Gamon		,,	
James	Paltro		,,		J.	Verlander		,,	
William	Justus		,,		James	Wilks		,,	
Daniel	Hayford		,,		John	Swift		,,	
J.	Barbitt		,,		Thomas	Edmonds		,,	
Henry	Bates		,,		Louis	Dupont		,,	
Edward	Feline		,,		Thomas	Parr		,,	
Thomas	Tearle		,,		Griffith	Edmonds		,,	
Joseph	Sanders		,,		Henry	Morris		,,	
Richard	Gosling		,,		William	Young		,,	
Henry	Morris		,,		Robert	Abercromby		,,	
Paul	Crespin		,,		Peter	Bennett		,,	
John	Pont		,,		Gawan	Nash		,,	
Francis	Spilsbury		,,		William	Shaw		,,	
Ayme	Videau		,,		Charles	Jackson		,,	
John	Berthelot		,,		Abraham de	Oliveyra		,,	
William	Kidney		,,		George	Wickes		,,	
James	West		,,		Peter	Archambo		,,	
Roger	Tasker		,,		John	Newton		,,	
Thomas	Rush		,,		Robert	Pilkington		,,	
Charles	Clark		,,		Francis	Nelme		,,	
Lewis	Hamon		,,		Simon	Jouet		,,	
Augustus	Courtauld		,,		George	Jones		,,	
John	Tuite		,,		Joseph	Allen &			
Thomas	Pye		,,		Mordecai	Fox		,,	
John	Gray		,,			Cocker or			
James	Manners		,,		Ebenezer	Coker		,,	1746
Frederick	Kandler		,,		Jeremy	Lee		,,	
Humphrey	Payne		,		Louis	Laroche		,,	
John	Bryan		,,		Benjn.	West		,,	
Richard	Pargeter		,,		J.	Barker	1740		
Pere	Pilleau		,,		Charles	Bellassyse		1740	
Peter	Werritzer		,,	1750	Dinah	Gamon		,,	
James	Shruder		,,		Thomas	Mercer		,,	
Richard	Zouch		,		T.	Whipham &			
William	Gould		,,	1748	W.	Williams		,,	
Benjamin	Godfrey		,,		Samuel	Roby		,,	
Benjamin	Cartwright		,,		John	Roker		,,	
Richard	Bayler		,,		John	Gimblett &			
William	Soame		,,		William	Vale, of		,,	1773
Bennett	Bradshaw & Co.		,,			Birmingham			
Lewis	Pantin		,,		Charles	Martin		,,	
John	Jacobs		,,		Samuel	Hutton		,,	
John	Eckmonds		,,		Benjamin	Gurdon		,,	
Isaac	Callerd		,,		Samuel	Wells		,,	
John	Weatherell		,,		James	Morrison		,,	
Jeremiah	King		,,		Lewis	Ouvry		,,	
Joseph	Steward		,,		William	Gwillim		,,	
Benjamin	Sanders		,,		John	Cam		,,	
John	Barbe		,,		Sussanah	Hatfield		,,	
John	White		,,		Henry	Miller		,,	
Paul	Lamerie		,,		Peter	Taylor		,,	
Daniel	Hayford		,,		Daniel	Chartier		,,	
Thomas	Farrar		,,		S.	Wood		,,	
Francis	Pages		,,		Anne	Craig &			
Thomas	Bamford		,,		John	Neville		,,	
Phillips	Garden		,,	,,	Phillip	Robinson			
David	Williams		,,		Abraham	Le Francis		,,	
Thomas	Jackson		,,	1769	Horne &	Temple			1740
Robert	Lucas		,,		Edward	Lambe		,,	
John	Luff		,,		John	Cafe		,,	
John	Le Sage		,,		Sarah	Hutton		,,	
Richard	Beale		,,		Jerem econ }iah	Ashley		,,	1742
Thomas	England		,,						
John	Edwards		,,		Edward	Wood		,,	

Name of Goldsmith.		Earliest Mention.	Entered.	Latest Mention.
John	Spackman		1741	
Francis	Crump		,,	
John	Hyatt		,,	
James	Willmott		,,	
Elizabeth	Tuite		,,	
Charles	Chesterman		,,	
Charles	Woodward		,,	
Isabel	Pero		,,	
Charles	Hillan		,,	
James	Gould		,,	
Charles	Laughton		,,	
Elizabeth	Godfrey	1742		
Robert	Tyrril		1742	
John	Barbe		,,	
Robert	Innes		,,	
Benjamin	Griffin		,,	
Nicholas	Sprimont		,,	d 1770
Henry	Brind		,,	
William	Alexander		,,	
Jeremiah	King		,,	
Richard	Mills		,,	
George	Smith		,,	
Elias	Cachart		,,	1751
William	Williams		,,	1745
Thomas	Lawrence		,,	
Charles	Johnson		1743	
George	Ridout		,,	
George	Methuen		,,	
Robert	Swanson		,,	
Edward	Aldridge		,,	
John	Stamper		,,	
John	Kineard		,,	
Edward	Malluson		,,	
William	Grundy		,,	
Joseph	Timberlake		,,	
James	Betham		.,	
William	Woodward		.,	
Isaac	Duke		,,	
William	Cripps		,,	
John	Wetherell		,,	
Ann	Farren		,,	
George	Ridout		,,	
Thomas	Carlton		1744	
Samuel	Taylor		,,	
Benjamin	Gignac		,,	
Fuller	White		,,	
John	Fray		,,	
Samuel	Bates		,,	
James	Smith		.,	
William	Bagnall		,,	
William	Gwillim & }		,,	
Peter	Castle			
Jacob	Marsh		,,	
Richard	Kersill		,,	1763
John	Wirgman	1745		
Sir H.	Marshall	,,		1773
John	Harvey	1745		
William	Peaston		,,	1750
John	Neville		,,	1749
Thomas	Heming		,,	
James	Morrison		,,	1780
George	Baskerville		,,	
John	Higginbo tt a		,,	
Hugh	Mills		,,	
James	Manners, jun.		,,	
Robert	Andrews		,,	
Samuel	Key		,,	

Name of Goldsmith.		Earliest Mention.	Entered.	Latest Mention.
George	Young		1746	
Samuel	Courtauld		,,	
Ernest	Sieber		,,	
James	Smith		,,	
Richard	Gurney & }		,,	
Thomas	Cook			
Samuel	Merriton		,,	
Joseph	Barker		,,	
Daniel	Piers		,,	1749
William	Peaston		,,	
Mordecai	Fox		,,	
Abraham	Le Francis		,,	
W.	Benn	1747		
Edward	Wakelin		1747	
Samuel	Herbert		,,	
Alexander	Johnston		,,	
Simon	Jouet		,,	
Anne	Kersill		,,	
Henry	Hebert		,,	
William	Solomon		,,	
Edward	Dowdall		1748	
Elizabeth	Hartley		,,	
Louis	Guichard		,,	
George	Hunter		,,	
Elizabeth	Oldfield		,,	
John	Priest		,,	
William	Grundy		,,	
John	Lamfert		,,	
Benjamin	Cooper		,,	
John	Carman		,,	
William	Mackenzie		,,	
Edmund	Medlycott		,,	
Daniel	Shaw		,,	
Elizabeth	Jackson		,,	
Robert	Cox	1749	1752	1756
Jabez	Daniell		1749	
Peter	Archambo & }		,,	1753
P.	Meure			
Henry	Haynes		,,	
George	Campar		,,	
George	Bindon		,,	
John	Rowe		,,	
Walter	Brind		,,	
Andrew	Killick		,,	
William	Kersill		,,	
William	Shaw		,,	
William	Shaw & }		,,	1758
William	Priest			
Abraham	Portal		,,	1760
Walter	Brind		,,	
William	Garrard		,,	
John	Lavis		,,	
J.	Blackford	1750		
Samuel	Wells		1750	
William	Wooler		,,	
John	Montgomery		,,	
Samuel	Herbert & Co.		,,	
John	Hyatt & }		,,	
Charles	Semore			
Fuller	White & }		,,	
John	Fray			
George	Morris		,,	
Thomas	Moore		,,	
George	Baker		,,	
Thomas	Smith		,,	
James	Tookey		,,	
Thomas	Jeannes		,,	

Name of Goldsmith.	Earliest Mention.	Entered.	Latest Mention.	Name of Goldsmith.	Earliest Mention.	Entered.	Latest Mention.
Joseph Heriot		1750		J. Collins		1754	
John Berthelot		,,		Edmund Ironside			d 1754
Peter Werritzer		,,		Campbell & Coults	1755		
William Homer		,,		William Sanden		1755	
Michael Ward		,,		John Laithwait		,,	
Henry Bayley		,,		William Sheene		,,	
John G. Alderhead		,,		—— Dobson ⎱			
A. Montgomery		,,		—— Prior & ⎰		,,	
John Bayley		1751		—— Williams ⎰			
Phillips Gardener		,,		William Butcher		,,	
Paul Callard		,,		William Sampel		,,	
William Paradise		,,		John Steward		,,	
Matthew Brodier		,,		William Garrard		,,	
John Payne		,,		Edward Dobson		,,	
Thomas Beere		,,		John Delmester		,,	
Paul Pinard		,,		Thomas Beezley		,,	
Lawrence Johnson		,,		William Plummer		,,	
Edward Doweal		,,		Matthew Roker		,,	
G. & S. Smith		,,		George Baskerville ⎱			
Nicholas Winkins		,,		& T. Morley ⎰		,,	
Thomas Watson	1752			Robert Cox		,,	
R. Alsop	,,			Samuel Siervent		,,	
William Brown	,,			Richard Thomas		,,	
John Richardson		1752		Benjamin Brewood		,,	
Dorothy Mills		,,		Constantine Teulings		,,	
John Carman		,,		George Baskerville ⎱			
Charles Chesterman		,,		& William Sampel ⎰		,,	
Frederick Vonham		,,		James Williams		,,	
Frederick Knopfell		,,		Richard Mills		,,	
Philip Bruguier		,,		John Townsend		,,	
William Bond		1753		James Jones		,,	
Thomas Towman		,,		Thomas Powell		1756	
William Robertson		,,		Benj'm. Cartwright		,,	
Gabriel Sleath & ⎱				Francis Crump		,,	
Francis Crump ⎰		,,		David Bell		,,	
Thomas Rowe		,,		William Shaw & ⎱			
Dennis Wilks & ⎱				William Priest ⎰		,,	
John Fray ⎰		,,		Thomas Doxsey		,,	
George Ibbott		,,		Thomas Congreve		,,	
John Munns		,,		William Watkins		,,	
D. C. Fueter		,,		Albert Schurman		,,	
William Gould		,,		William Moody		,,	
Turner & Williams		,,		Samuel Wheat		,,	
John Schuppe		,,		Stephen Ardesoif		,,	
Edmond John		,,		W. & R. Peaston		,,	1763
Magdalen Feline		,,		William Caldecott		,,	
Richard Goldwire		,,		Thomas Powell		,,	
Dorothy Sarbit		,,		Joseph Bell		,,	
Edward Aldridge & ⎱				Edward Bennett		,,	
John Stamper ⎰		,,	1757	William Tuite		,,	1769
Thomas Collier		1754		William Watkins & ⎱			
William Bond & ⎱				T. Devonshire ⎰		,,	
John Phipps ⎰		,,		Francis (Sir) Gosling	1756		d 1768
Samuel Smith		,,		Alexander Saunders		1757	
Benjamin Cartwright		,,		John Kentenber & ⎱			
Peter Gillois		,,		Thomas Groves ⎰		,,	
Richard Rugg		,,		John Frost		,,	
Thomas Wright		,,		William Reynoldson		,,	
Job Trip		,,		John Perry		,,	
Henry Dutton		,,	1773	John Gorham		,,	
John Quantock		,,		Phillip Vincent		,,	
Robert Rew		,,		Paul Crespin		,,	
William Turner		,,		William Cafe		,,	
Henry Corry		,,		Thompson Davis		,,	
Simon Le Sage		,,		Edward Darvill		,,	
Thomas Wynne		,,		Lewis Herne & ⎱			
Sarah Buttall		,,		Francis Butty ⎰		,,	

Name of Goldsmith.		Earliest Mention.	Entered.	Latest Mention.
John	Hyatt &		1757	
Charles	Semore }			
Francis	Waysmith		,,	1773
Edward	Jay		,,	1789
Philip	Vincent		,,	
James	Baker	1758		
Robert	Burton		1758	
My.	Piers		,,	
John	Moore		,,	1793
Thomas	Wallis		,,	1800
Theophilus	Davis		,,	
Fuller	White		,,	
Thomas	Whipham &		,,	1760
Charles	Wright }			
Edward	Bennett, jr.		,,	
John	Barry		,,	
Arthur	Annesley		,,	
John	Hague		,,	
Parker &	Wakelyn	1759		1763
John	Langford &	,,		
John	Sebille }			
Orlando	Jackson	,,	1759	1773
Alexander	Barnet		,,	
Ayme	Videaux		,,	
Wm.	Day		,,	
Matthew	Ferris		,,	
William	Bell		,,	
Samuel	Eaton		,,	
Francis	Butty &		,,	1766
Nicholas	Dumee }			
Stephen	Abdy &		,,	
William	Jury }			
John	Eaton	1760		
Stephen	Adams		,,	1799
James	Hunt		,,	
William	Howard		,,	
Samuel	Howland		,,	
John	Allen	1761		
Louis	Black		,,	
William	King		,,	
W. & J.	Deane	1762		
John	Fountain		,,	
Samuel	Dellamy		,,	
George	Rotherdon	1763		
W.	Dorrell	1763		
John	Aspinshaw	,,		
George	Andrews	,,		
Daniel	Smith &	,,	1780	1782
Robert	Sharp }			
William &	Priest	1764		1773
James }				
Septimus	Crespell	,,		,,
& James }				
Thomas	Freeman &		1764	
J.	Marshall }			
J.A.	Calame		,,	
A.	Calame		,,	
George	Hunter		1765	
Thomas	Dealtry		,,	
William	Abdy		,,	
John	Phipps	1765		
Thomas	Hannam &	1766		1799
John	Crouch }			
Jackson	Bumfries &	,,	1766	
Orlando	Jackson }			
James	Allen		,,	
William	Abdy		1767	
Thomas	Heming		1767	
George	Fayle		,,	
Augustus	Lesage		,,	
William	Cripps, junr.		,,	
Mark	Cripps		,,	
John	Carter	1768		1776
John	Halifax	,,		,,
Fras.	Spilsbury, jr.	,,		
D'd. & Robt.	Hennell		1768	
John	Darwall		,,	
Fuller	White		,,	
Thomas	Hallifax			,,
Joseph	Heriot		1769	
Thomas	Foster		,,	
Jeremiah	King		,,	
Thomas	Jackson		,,	
George	Seatoun	1769		
Charles	Woodward	,,		
W.	Hancock	1770		
John	Baxter	,,		
Tindall	Rushworth	,,		
William	Bayley	,,		1770
John	Buckett	,,		,,
William	Bromage		1770	
Thomas	Arnold		,,	
J.	Bassingwhite		,,	
John	Baker		,,	
Richard	May &		1771	
Jane	Dorrell }			
Charles	Chesterman		,,	
Phillip	Norman	1771		
A.	Underwood	,,		
William	Norman	,,		
John	Nodes	,,		1773
Thomas &	Daniel	,,		
Jabez }				
Peter	Floyer	1772		
John	Wickenden	,,		
Thomas	Wright	,		
Jos.	Adams	,,		1799
Henry	Hoare	,,		
Jonathan	Alleine	,,		
Samuel	Smith	,,		
Luke	Kendal		1772	
J.	Fayle		,,	
Richard	Meade	1773		
William	Meadhurst	,,		
Thomas	Webbe	,,		
Edmond	Vincent	,,		
Thomas	York	,,		
William	Keays	,,		
Thomas	Parr	,,		
Jonas	Osborne	,,		
Lawret	Mertz	,,		
Charles	Miegg	,,		
Anne	Miller	,,		
Richard	Pargetier	,,		
Matthew	Perchard	,,		
My.	Makemeid		1773	
Thomas	Whipham		,,	
James	Young		,,	
William	Weston		,,	
Thomas	Chawner		,,	1783
Louis de	Lisle		,,	
Thomas	Tookey		,,	
Phillip	Freeman		,,	
Herman	Wallis		,,	

Name of Goldsmith.		Earliest Mention.	Entered.	Latest Mention.	Name of Goldsmith.		Earliest Mention.	Entered.	Latest Mention.
Phillip	Goddard		1773		James	Bellis	1773		1780
Arthur	Worboys			1773	Andrew	Fogelberg	,,		
Robert	Hennell		,,		Louis	Benoimont	,,		
Samuel	Wheat		,,		Christopher	Binger	,,		
John	Bennett		,,		Christopher	Biron	,,		
Thomas	Wallis		,,		James	Birkenhead	,,		
John	Weldring		,,	1790	James	Birt	,,		
James	Young		,,	,,	Mark	Bock	,,		
Samuel	Whitford		,,	,,	John	Bourne	,,		
James	Wiburd		,,		Albrecht	Borchers	,,		
John	Kidd		,,	1783	Samuel	Bradley	,,		
William Summer & } Richard Crossley }			,,		Aaron	Bourne	,,		
George	Natter		,,		John	Brockus	,,		
Thomas	Augier		,,		Edward	Capper	,,		
Ralph	Ayscough		,,		John	Chaldecott	,,		
William	Bell		,,		George	Chalmers	,,		
William Holmes & } Nich. Dumee }			,,		B. A.	Chambrier	,,		
John	Burrow		,,		Edward	Cooke	,,		
Orlando	Jackson		,,		James	Cox	,,		
William	Aldridge		,,		William	Cox	,,		
John	Arnell		,,		George	Coyte	,,		
Pointer	Baker		,,		Septimus Crespell & } James Crespell }		,,		
William Le	Bas		,,		Josh.	Creswell	,,		
Richard	Andrews		,,		Jasper	Cunst	,,		
James	Barber		,,		John	Dare	,,		
John	Baxter		,,		John	Deacon	,,		
John	Beadle		,,		John	De Gruchy	,,		
Thomas	Chawner		,,		Peter	Desergnes	,,		
James	Beaty		,,	1773	Fredk.	Deveer	,,		
David	White		,,	,,	Thomas	Devonshire	,,		
William	Winter			,,	Israel	Devonshire	,,		
John	Watkins			,,	Peter	Devese	,,		
Richard L	Wotton			,,	Richard	Dovey	,,		
Samuel	White			,,	Dru.	Drury	,,		
John	Wright			,,	John	Drysdale	,,		
Moses	Willots			,,	Lewis	Dumont	,,		
John	Winter			,,	Stephen	Eastrom	,,		
Paul	Wright			,,	James	Evans	,,		
Samuel	Withers			,,	Thomas	Fair	,,		
Thomas	Wilkinson			,,	John	Farran	,,		
Sacheverel	Wright			,,	Will	Fisher	,,		
James	Wight			,,	William	Flints	,,		
Thomas	Woodhouse			,,	John	French	,,		
Thomas	Wigan			,,	John	Fry	,,		
James	Waters			,,	Rob.	Fryar	,,		
John	Winsmore			,,	Richard	Gardner	,,		
Henry	Walpole			,,	Reynolds	Grignion	,,		
Richard L.	Watton			,,	Benj.	Gurdon	,,		
Edmond	Wells			,,	Thos.	Hall	,,		
William	Whitford			,,	Thos.	Hallows	,,		
John	Williams			,,	Thos.	Harding	,,		
William	Worthington			,,	Thos.	Harrache	,,		
Thomas	Wynne			,,	Henry	Hallsworth	,,		
Herman J.	Walther			,,	L.	Haucher	,,		
John	Westhay			,,	Benj.	Hawkins	,,		
Robert	Wherrit			,,	Maurice	Heeser	,,		
Thomas	Wilson			,,	John	Hoist	,,		
Gabriel	Wirgman			,,	Henry	Hobdell	,,		d 1799
Christ'er Fly Wood & } Thomas Filkin }		1773			Andrew	Hogg	,,		
William	Meers	,,			Edward	Holmes	,,		
Robert	Metham	,,			John	Horsley	,,		
Richard	May	,,			Nat.	Horwood	,,		
Francis	Meynell	,,		1782	George	Houston	,,		
Charles	Wright	,,		1790	William	Howse	,,		
William	Vincent	,,			Jas.	Hughes	,,		
					John	Huntley	,,		

Name of Goldsmith.	Earliest Mention.	Entered.	Latest Mention.
Wm. Hunter	1773		
John Jackson	,,		
Dennes Jacob	,,		
Samuel Jarman	,,		
Nathaniel Jefferys	,,		
John Innocent	,,		
John Johnson	,,		
James Johnston	,,		
Stephen Joyce	,		
John Irvine	,,		
John Kentish	,,		
James King	.,		
James Kingman	,.		
William Kinman	,,		
Fras. Lawley	,,		
John Lautier	,,		
Charles Leadbetter	,		
Josh. Lejeune	,,		
Thos. Liddiard	,,		
Samuel Littlewood	,,		
Lawrence McDuff	.,		
Jos. Malpas	,,		
Wm. Mears	,,		
Lauret Merz	,,		
James Morriset	,,		
Richard Morrison	,,		
Richard Morson & } Benjamin Stephenson {	,,		
Peter Muire	,,		
John Naylor	,,		
Albertus Pars	,,		
James Perry	,,		
John Phillips	,,		
James Phipps	,,		
William Pickett	,,		
Robert Piercy	,		
William Portal	,,		
Edward Price	,,		
John Raeburn	,,		
John Randles	,,		
William Rawle	,,		
John Reynolds	,,		
William Reynolds	,,		
William Robertson	,,		
Robert Rogers	,,		
John Romer	,,		
Peter Romilly	,,		
Fras. Ruffin	,,		
Elias Russell	,,		
John Russell	,,		
Richard Rawlins	,,		
Robert Sallam	,,		
John Saffory	,,		
Robt. Salmon	,,		
John Sarney	,,		
John Scuppe	,,		
Edward Scales	,,		
Samuel Shelley	,		
Richard Simkiss	,,		
William Simons	.,		
James Smith	.,		
William Smith	,,		
John Sterling	,,		
Charles Storey	,,		
Josh. Sutton	,,		
Thos. Swift	1773		
Peter Tabois	,,		
William Tant	,,		
Mark Thomegay	,,		
Fras. Thurkle	,,		
Marmaduke Tokitt	,,		
Eliz. Tookey	,,		
John Hy. Vere	,,		
Wm. Vincent	,,		
John Underwood	,,		
Thomas Webb	,,		
William Weston	,,		
James Wiburd	,,		
Samuel Wood	,,		
William Worthington	,,		
Paul Wright	,,		
Evan Thomas	1774		
John Robins		,,	1800
T. Daniel		,,	1784
J. Denizilow		,,	
Robert Ross		,,	
Wm. Penstone		,,	
James Stamp		,,	1779
John Brown		,,	
George Heming & } William Chawner {		,,	1781
James Young & } Orlando Jackson {		,,	
Hester Bateman		,,	1789
William Fearn		,,	
Louis Ducornieu	1775		
Richard Rugg		,,	
William Fennell		,,	
Benjamin Stephenson		,,	
John Tayleur		,,	
Robert Piercy		,,	
Walter Tweedie		,,	
Thomas Wallis		,,	
Charles Aldridge		,,	
George Baskerville & } T. Morley {		,,	
James Young		,,	
Christopher Woods		,,	
Henry Greenway		,,	
William Sheen		,,	
Abraham Barrier		,,	
W. L. Foster		,,	
Burrage Davenport	1776		
William Holmes		1776	
Robt. & Jno. Schofield		,,	
Thomas Northcote	,,		,,
Robert Jones & } John Schofield {		,,	
Phillip Roker		,,	
William Simmons		,,	
Nicholas Dumee		,,	
Robert Jones		,,	1796
John Deacon		,,	
Elizabeth Roker		,,	
John Wakelin & } William Taylor {		,,	1792
William Potter	1777		
Edwd. Lowe		,,	
William Grundy		,,	
Joseph Preedy		,,	1783

Name of Goldsmith.	Earliest Mention.	Entered.	Latest Mention.
Thos. & Rd. Payne		1777	
Louisa & Samuel } Courtauld		"	
John Wren		"	
Robert Makepeace & Richard Carter }	1772	"	
William How & William Clark }		"	
John Temple & John Searle }	1777		
Bernard Turner & Samuel Tookie }	"		
Abraham Barrier & Louis Ducornieu }	1778		
Richard Carter		1778	
Edward Dobson		"	
John Moore		"	
Thomas Wallis		"	
G. Rodenbostel		"	
William Eley & George Pierpoint }		"	
John Schofield		"	1796
Charles Kandler		"	
Robert Jones		"	"
Richard Carter, Daniel Smith & Robert Sharp }		"	
J. Broughton		1779	
William Grundy & Edward Fernell }		"	
Andrew Fogelberg & Stephen Gilbert }		1780	1791
T. P. Boulton & Arthur Humphreys }		"	
Francis Stamp		"	
John Kidder		"	
James Sutton		"	
Thomas Ellis		"	
James Mince & William Hodgkins }		"	
Edward Fennell		"	"
T. B. Pratt & Arthur Humphreys }		"	
Benjamin Lance		1781	1784
Walter Brind		"	
Thomas Daniel & John Wall }		"	
William Pitts		"	1799
Benjamin Laver		"	1789
William Sumner		1782	1810
Thomas Evans		"	
George Smith		"	
Henry Cowper		"	
Peter Gillois		"	
Richard Crossley		"	
William Playfair & William Wilson }		"	
James Sutton & Joseph Bult }		"	1784
John Lee		"	
John Tweedie		1783	
William Skeene		"	
Thomas Chawner		"	
Samuel Wintle		"	
John Townsend		"	

Name of Goldsmith.	Earliest Mention.	Entered.	Latest Mention.
John Lamb		1783	1791
Abraham Peterson & Peter Podie }		"	
John Beldon		1784	
Samuel Godbehere		"	
William Basnet		"	
William Sutton		"	
John Hutson		"	
William Abdy		"	
Charles Hougham		1785	
John King		"	
William Sanden		"	
John Thompson		"	
Thomas Shepherd		"	
George Smith		"	
John Harris		1786	
Henry Greene		"	
Daniel Denney		"	
William Pitts		"	
——— Godbehere & Edward Wigan }		"	
William Stephenson		"	
Charles Aldridge		"	
Samuel Davenport		"	
George Smith & William Fearn }		"	
Henry Chawner		"	1796
George Wintle		1787	
John Edwards		1788	1791
Cornelius Bland		"	
Thomas Olivant		1789	
Robert Sharp		"	
William Plummer		"	"
Peter & Jonathan } Bateman		1790	
Thomas Willmore		"	
Abraham Peterson		"	
William Pitts & Joseph Preedy }	1790	1791	1800
Thomas Howell		"	
Jas. & Eliz. Bland		"	
Thomas Streetin		"	
Wm. Fountain & Danl. Pontifex }		"	
Michael Plummer		"	
Peter & Anne Bateman		"	
T. Phipps & E. Robinson }	"		
Duncan Urquhart & Naphtali Hart }	1791	"	1805
Thomas Howell	"	"	
Thomas Wallis		1792	1815
George Smith & Thomas Hayter }		"	
John Wakelin & Robert Garrard }		"	1802
Thomas Graham		"	
Thomas Renou		"	
William Frisbee & Paul Storr }		"	
William Frisbee		"	
Paul Storr	1792	1793	1834
Wm. & John Fisher		"	
John Fountain & John Beadnall }		"	

Name of Goldsmith		Earliest Mention	Entered	Latest Mention
Saml.	Godbehere & }		1793	
Edward	Wigan }			
John	Mewburn			1793
William	Fountain		1794	
Daniel	Pontifex		,,	
Jas. & Eliz.	Bland		,,	
Robert & } Thomas }	Makepeace		,,	
Thomas	Northcote & }		,,	
George	Bourne }			
Robert	Gaze		1795	
Robert	Makepeace		,,	
Jonathan	Perkins senr. & junr.		,,	
Robert & } David }	Hennell		,,	
William	Hall		,,	
William	Pitts & }		,,	
Joseph	Preedy }			
Henry	Chawner & }	1796	1796	1808
John	Eames }			
Joseph B.	Orme	,,	,,	
William	Bennett		,,	
Henry	Nutting		,,	1804
William	Eley & }		1797	
William	Fearn }			
George	Cowles		,,	
William	Eley		,,	
Robert	Williams			1797
Jos.	Hardy & }		1798	
Thos.	Lowndes }			
Hannah	Northcote		,,	
Thomas	Holland		,,	
Richard	Cooke		1799	
Jos.	Hardy		,,	
William	Pitts		,,	
George	Smith, Jr.	,,	,,	1815
Thomas	Streetin	1799	,,	1843
John	Lias	,,	,,	1840
Richard	Coote		,,	
Samuel	Godbehere }		1800	
Edward	Wigan & }			
James	Bult }			
Peter, Anne & William	Bateman		,,	
Joseph	Preedy, Jr.		,,	1808
John James	Hill	1800		1803
Timothy	Renou	,,		1804
Robert	Garrard		1801	
Edward	Fernall	1801		1807
Smith	& Son	,,		
Benjamin	Cole	,,		1810
Henry	Lee	,,		,,
D.	Pontifex	,,		,,
Edward	Beauchamp	,,		,,
David	Windsor	,,		1813
G.	Grainger	,,		1815
Tobias	& Co.	,,		,,
George	Dobree	,,		1819
Joseph	Dodds	,,		1811
John	Farmer	,,		1830
Page	& Gordon	,,		1804
John	Shackleton	,,		
Phineas	Barratt	,,		1803
Parker	& Birkett	,,		1804

Name of Goldsmith		Earliest Mention	Entered	Latest Mention
Nathaniel	Jeffreys	1801		1804
John	Parker	,,		,,
Richard	Cooke	,,		1803
Smith	& Sharp	,,		1802
Stephen	Adams	,,		1824
Thomas	Wiltshire	,,		1817
———	Burrows & Son	,,		1819
William	Cordy	,,		1840
W.	Clarke	,,		1807
Thomas	& Evans	,,		,,
W.	Hunter	,,		1803
William	Purse	,,		1806
William	Squire	,,		1813
Horn	& Ash	,,		1814
Edward	Francis	,,		,,
W.	Wattson	,,		1809
Bates	& Doggett	,,		1808
William	Stevenson	,,		1826
William	Holmes	,,		1807
William	Harris	,,		,,
William	Boustred	,,		1809
Thomas	Hoby	,,		1813
T.	Dennett	,,		1806
J. T.	Bartram	,,		1837
Robert	Chandler	,,		1833
Thomas	Hamlet	,,		1840
R.	Needham	,,		1816
James	Tedbury	,,		1817
Joseph	Savory	,,		1818
John	Salkeld	,,		1810
Joseph	Brassbridge	,,		1822
N.	Carter	,,		1824
Thomas	Dean	,,		
M.	Spink & Son	,,		1850
Charles	Chesterman	1802		1814
Robert	Garrard	,,	1802	1822
John	Coles	,,		1808
W.	Cording	,,		1823
John	Steward	,,		1804
George	Purse	,,		1832
William	Burwash	,,	,,	1823
R.	Urquhart	,,		1832
Ellis &	Collins	,,		1803
T.	Carr	,,	,,	1812
Robt. & Sml.	Hennell	,,	,,	
John	Martin	,,		1804
I.	Perry	,,		1836
W.	Bradford	,,		1809
John	Hawkins	,,	,,	1830
John	Denziloe	,,		1808
Peter	Patmore & Co.	,,	,,	1821
Alice & } George }	Burrows	,,	,,	
J.	Dyer	1803		1811
I.	Rogers	,,		1804
James	Godwin	,,		,,
Thomas	Cording	1804		1806
Thomas	Pitts	,,	1804	
Thomas	Dobson	,,		1807
George	Wintle	,,	,,	
Richard	Clark & Son	,,		1823
Benjamin	Gurdon	,,		
Moses	Levy	,,		
Mills &	Whalley	,,		
John J.	Austin	,,		1814

Name of Goldsmith.	Earliest Mention.	Entered.	Latest Mention.
John Blake	1804		
E. and J. Clark	,,		1813
Edward Edlin	,,		1823
Crespin Fuller	,,		1827
T. W. Matthews	,,		
William Plumley			1828
Thos. Paine Dexter	1805	1805	1824
William Burwash & Richard Sibley	,,	,,	
Peter & Wm. Bateman	,,	,,	
Thos. & Jos. Guest & Joseph Cradock	,,	1806	
Thos. Guest, Josh. Guest & Josh. Craddock		,,	
Nicholas Edwards	1806		1807
Urquhart & Whalley	,,		,,
George Like	,,		1814
James Harris	,,		1807
J. L. Simmonds	,,		1839
Joseph Martin	,,		1814
Josiah Parker	,,		1816
William Stephens	,,		1814
Burwash & Sibley	,,		1824
William Davis	,,		1828
Watson & McDowell	,,		
Absalom Marsh	,,		
John Simpson	,,		1823
Peter Purchard	,,		
Richard Cooke	,,		1815
Charles Cording	,.		1827
Samuel Solomon	,,		1813
T. Guest & Son	,,		1809
J. B. Cole	,,		1817
Thomas Layton	,,		1822
Thomas Pace	,,		,,
William Bennet	,,		1823
E. Morley	,,		1818
T. Gosler	1807		1822
Edward Fleming	,,		1819
Thomas Jenkinson	,,		
John Coles	,,		
John Clarke	,,	1807	1811
Thomas Page	,,		1815
John Barber	,,		1817
T. Robins	,,		1820
Edward Fleming	,,		1809
William Bannister	,,		1811
J. Ashman	,,		1819
William Fountain	,,		,,
Thomas Halford		,,	
Grayhurst & Harvey	,,		1816
William Gordon	,,		1810
John Ashley	,,		,,
Will. & Jas. Birkett	,,		
H. Effex	,,		1823
William Parr	,,		1813
William Wakefield	,,		1828
John Butt	,,		1829
Samuel Whitford	,,	,,	
Barber & Lancaster	,,		
Richard Crossley & George Smith	,,	,,	
John Smith	,,		1832
John Dobree	,,		1834
George Morris	1807		1818
B. Massey	,,		1840
Albra & Co.	1808		
Joseph Cording	,,		1809
William Eley, William Fearn & William Chawner	,,		,,
William Parker	,,		1819
Charles Hollingshead	,,		1814
William Allen	,,		1810
Rebecca Eames & Edward Barnard	,,	1808	1828
John Crouch	,,	,,	1813
George Hall	,,		
Henry Nutting & Robert Hennell	,,	,,	
Mary & Eliza Sumner	,,	,.	1814
John Sanders	,,		1813
John Wort	,,		,,
Joseph Taylor	,,		1824
M. Crosswell	,,		1837
James Bruce	,,		1839
G. & B. Blogg	,,		
Eames & Barnard	,.		1828
Salkeld & Acklam	,,		1815
Guest & Gradock	1809		1812
W. Windsor	,,		1810
Joseph Bates	,,		1817
Samuel Durrant	,,		1811
C. W. Auber	,,		
James Turner	,,		
Henry Dobson	,,		1813
Robert Metham	,,		1816
Joseph Folkard	,,		1820
Robert Gaze	,,		1819
S. W. Story & W. Elliott	,,	1809	1810
Robert Hennell	,,	,,	1817
John Cotton & Thos. Head	,,	,,	1811
Joseph Brookes	,,		1811
John Beauchamp	,,		1840
Henry Fleming	,,		
Edward Lees	,,		
Francis Sims	,,		
Read & Son	1810		
Thomas Payne	,,		
Ede & Hewatt	,,		
Thomas Dockwray	,,		1814
Joseph Lewis	,,		1813
Joseph Smith	,,		1816
Thomas Wallis & Jonathan Hayne	,,	1810	
Hugh Brodie	,,		
Nathaniel Pryor	,,		1833
W. H. Fleming	,,		1830
H. Nutting	,,		1815
Thomas Roberts	,,		1813
Joseph Browning	,,		1817
Mary Willis	,,		1835
William Elliott	,,		1844
Storr & Co.	,,		1824
Watson & Chaffers	,,		,,
Wheatley & Evans	1811		

Name of Goldsmith.	Earliest Mention.	Entered.	Latest Mention.	Name of Goldsmith.	Earliest Mention.	Entered.	Latest Mention.
Whitford & Pizey	1811			Daniel Hockle	1814		
David Lamb	,,		1815	Percy & Son	,,		1823
James Fontaine	,,		,,	Joseph Wilson	1815		
H. Wright	,,		1819	Edward Frears	,,		
Samuel Hennell	,,	1811	1818	S. M. Charouneau	,,		1819
H. W. Wilson	,,		1822	Thomas W. Barker	,,		
Thomas Vincent	,,		,,	William Chawner	,,	1815	1837
Jeremiah Hodgkins	,,		1814	Thomas Remett	,,		
John Taylor	,,		1828	William Bateman	,,	,,	1840
Elliott & Storey	,,		1815	Thomas Gardner	,,		
John Wakefield	,,		1819	Joseph Daniel	,,		1822
Moses Emanuel	,,		1815	T. Martin	,,		1817
R. H. Starcke	,,		,,	N. Hart	,,		,,
Samuel Davis	,,			Obadiah Cooper	,,		
S. Phillips & Co.	,,			Richard Brook	,,		1823
Farmer & Son	,,			Eley, Fearn & Eley	,,		,,
Gordon & Foster	,,		1816	John Houle	,,		1843
I. Robinson	,,			J. Fairbrother	,,		
Thomas Holland	,,		1815	John Cowie	,,		1819
Thomas Miller	,,		1819	John Angell	,,		1837
William Frisbee	,,		1815	G. & T. Farmer	,,		
Robert Rutland	,,	,,	1828	E. Souttin	,,		
James Beebe	,,	,,	1847	Matthew Linwood	1816		1817
S. Salmon	1812			Thomas Fisher	,,		1821
T. Pierson	,,		1813	Alston & Lewis	,,		1827
William Flemming	,,		1821	James Collins	,,		1826
George Smith	,,	1812		R. Booth	,,		
Robert Beauchamp	,,		1831	James Cordy	,,		1818
Margaret Gordon	,,		1814	Thomas Sowerby	,,		1830
J. Prior	,,		1817	Brent & Peppin	,,		1823
J. Read	,,			Rowland Hastings	,,		
James Masters	,,			Jane Cotton	,,		1818
Joseph Cradock &				J. Troup	,,		,,
W. Reid }	,,	,,	1826	A. & G. Burrows	,,		,,
William Page	1813		1818	John Murray	,,		1837
George Wintle	,,			George Lane	,,		1821
William Kingdon	,,	1813		George Richards	,,		,,
Rachel Farmer	,,			Samuel Nelme	,,		,,
Samuel Harding	,,		1828	Frederick Seagood	,,	1816	
P. Lindeman	,,			Thos. & Geo Hayter	,,		
James Lloyd	,,		1817	Elizabeth Morritt	,,		1819
J. Wassell	,		1841	Dockwray & Norman	,,		1821
John E. Wilson	,,			Alexander Gordon	,,		1818
William Bell	1814		1817	Lewis Solomon & Co.	,,		1824
Robert Needham	,,		1815	A. Hewat & Co.	,,		1829
A. G. Priestman	,,		,,	Nickolds & Roberts	,,		1817
Jos. & John Wright	,,		,,	Henry Marshall	1817		1818
John Reeve	,,		,,	Edward Gibson	,,		,,
Thomas Sherborn	,,		,,	Thomas James	,,		
Joseph Willmore (of Birmingham)	,,		,,	Page & Ramsey	,,		1821
Samuel Wheatley	,,		,,	David Cameron	,,		1838
John Paul	,,			John Jones	,,		1840
S. Whitaker	,,		1838	William Foster	,,		
John White	,,		1815	Gresham & Barber	,,		1820
Richard Hoby	,,		1822	Needham & Dobson	,,		1818
Edward Clark	,,		1818	William Pulleyn	1818		1819
Richard Sibley	,,		1839	J. Peppin	,,		
Banks Farrand	,		1832	Pemberton, Son & Co.	,,		1826
Charles Norton	,,			J. E. Terry & Co.	,,		1849
William Neate	,,		,,	Hart & Harvey	,,		1825
D. Sutton	,,		1818	R. Hennell & Son	,,		1835
John Tatum	,,		1823	John Banfield	1819		
Ash & Sons	,,		,,	John Bannister	,,		
A. Lee & Co.	,,			John Booth	,,		
				John Brown	,,		

Name of Goldsmith.	Earliest Mention.	Entered.	Latest Mention.	Name of Goldsmith.	Earliest Mention.	Entered.	Latest Mention.
Joshua Bayles	1819			Taylor & Son	1819		1823
John Douglas	,,			Hugh Beavan	,,		
J. C. Grey	,,		1833	H. Cowen	,,		
John Cuff	,,		1828	Lawton & Motley	,,		
John Harvey	,,			H. Lazarus	,,		
J. Harris, junr.	,,		1824	David Farrow	,,		
Philip Rundell	,,	1819		Daniel Folkard	,,		
George Farmer	,,		1823	Daniel Fox	,,		
Thomas Wheeler	,,			George Turner	,,		1840
Griffin & Co.	,,		,,	Henry Walker	,,		1837
William Eaton	,,			George Barker	,,		1827
W. & M. Fillmer	,,			John J. Kembler	,,		1837
Blake & Son	,,			Francis Steele	,,		1838
John & Hy. Lias	,,	,,		Tedbury & Son	,,		1835
Brassbridge & Son	,,			Edward Marshall	,,		1840
Green, Ward & Green	,,			Edward Edwards	,,		1849
Banting & Muncaster	,,			Abel Garnham	,,		
R. W. & T. Hedges	,,			Edward Stammers	,,		1850
William Newby	,,			D. Solome	,,		1822
P. Lawton	,,			Thomas Thomas	,,		1836
William Abdy	,,			David Jennings	,,		
Thomas Clark	,,			Thomas Cotterell	,,		1838
Thomas Cotterell	,,			David Jones	,,		
Thomas Balliston	,,			John Rose	,,		1835
Thomas Carter	,,			A. & M. Stracy	,,		
William Mitchell	,,			William Knight	,,		1850
Wm Geo. Ring	,,			Charles Fox	,,		1842
W. Moon	,,			John Cuffe	,,		1828
S. & N. Latter	,,			Charles Taylor	,,		
Matthew Pryor	,,			William Ingram	,,		
S. Purver	,,			George Jump	,,		1833
Abraham Dry	,,			John Pratt	,,		
Samuel Roberts	,,			Joseph Roberts	,,		
W. M. Smellie	,,			James Ruel	,,		
William Sowerby	,,			Wm. Matthews & Smith	,,		
Barber & Jupp	,,		1837	C. & J. Blake	1820		
W. & S. Mullins	,,			Robert Forrester	,,		1822
Charles Fox	,,	1822	1842	A. Tate	,,		1837
William Sanford	,,			Ashman & Son	,,		1830
Wassell & Marriott	,,			E. S. Sampson	,,		1826
Thomas Thomas	,,		1826	Arrowsmith & Co.	,,		
William Burwash	,,		,,	George Burrows	,,		1849
Cloak & Weatherley	,,		1832	James Wintle	,,		1828
William Baker	,,		1823	J. & J. Aldous	,,		1837
Morritt & Lee	,,		1822	John Robinson	,,		1821
William Edwards	,,			John Robinson & Son	,,		,,
Watson & Co.	,,			Fleming & Hornblow	,,		
Simon Emanuel	,,		1840	Richard Thomas & Son	,,		1830
T. A. Parsons	,,			T. Pilkington	,,		1837
John Thomas	,,			William Dobree	,,		1838
Wise & Page	,,			J. Ely	,,		1839
William Hall	,,			G. H. Cleeve	,,		1828
Thomas Austin	,,		1837	J. Bullard	1821		1827
L. Franklin	,,		1830	Jupp & Barber	,,		,,
J. Stroud	,,		1823	Lawrence Notley	,,		1837
J. Levy	,,			W. H. Sharpe	,,		1828
William Gording	,,			Thomas Richard & Son	,,		
Joseph Marston	,,			S. Barrow	,,		
John Guest	,,			Alexander Purse	,,		1830
James Gatley	,,			Francis Cotton	,,		1838
James Elley	,,			George Knight	,,		1837
J. Elliott	,,			Stonestreet & Poile	,,		1824
John Foligno	,.			John Carter	1822		
John Wells	,,			George Benson	,,		
H. B. Wheatley	,,			John Hayne	,,		

Name of Goldsmith.	Earliest Mention.	Entered.	Latest Mention.
George Fisher	1822		
A. H. Dry	,,		1823
Geo. Hennell	,,		1833
A. T. Parsons	,,		
Charles Needham	,,		1823
Benjn. Moses	,,		
Charles Garraway	,,		,,
John Hobbs	,,		1825
Francis Higgins	,,		1850
Anderson & Post	,,		1823
H. Lambert	,,		,,
Aldred & Tooke	,,		1833
John Garnon	,,		1823
Edward Jenkins	,,		,,
George Sellars	,,		,,
Robert Barker	,,		,,
Stephenson & Farrow	,,		1824
William Mott	,,		1840
Wiltshire & Sons	,,		
J. P. Acklam	,,		1823
James Robinson	,,		,,
R. Marchant	,,		1840
Greenwood & Co.	,,		1823
R. Westwood	,,		,,
Wm. Thos. Barker	,,		
William Fawdington	,,		,,
William Trayes	,,	1822	
William Fleming	,,		,,
Jones & Moxon	,,		,,
Patmore & Routledge	,,		
W. Folkard	,,		1828
Kent. Avery & Vincent	,,		
John Bridge	,,	1823	1829
M. Mariott	1823	1823	1829
Holdsworth & Boyce	,,		
Chaffers & Mills	,,		
Jacob Russell	,,		1837
John Henry & Chas. Lias	,,	,,	
P. R. Higham	,,		
Hopkinson & Brassbridge	,,		
Susan Peppin	,,		1840
Neate & Son	,,		
Thomas Ross	,,		
Hennell & Son	,,		1828
Tobias & Levitt	,,		1824
C. & T. Gray	,,		1825
G. E. Cooke & Co.	,,		1826
E. Thompson	,,		1830
John Westlake	,,		1833
Thos. & J. Stevens	,,		,,
J. Ramsay	,,		1828
William Barrett	,,		1830
J. Robins	,,		,,
W. E. Weatherley	,,		1836
Sophia Bull	,,		1832
W. King	,,		1838
Samuel Norman	,,		1840
A. D. Fleming	,,		1837
Robert Essex	,,		1834
Benjamin Smith	,,		1850
Hyam Hyams	,,		,,
Edwin Alderman	1823		1839
R. Peppin	,,		1832
E. Barton	,,		1846
T. B. Hopgood	,,		1832
Storr & Mortimer	,,		1840
Thos. Paine Dexter		1824	
Edward Barton	1825		1846
Henry Bird	,,		1844
Thomas Burwash	,,		1830
John Lacy	,,		1828
John Law	,,		1835
Kensington Lewis	,,		1839
J. Walker	,,		
R. G. King	,,		1826
Randall Chatterton	,,	1825	
Samuel Cohen	,,		
William J. Prior	,,		1831
William Schofield	,,		,,
W. & Thos. Tyas	,,		
Adey B. Savory	1826	1826	1838
C. Eley	,,		1840
H. Lewis	,,		1827
Joseph Boyd	,,		1834
Joseph Chapman	,,		1828
Jacob Wintle	,,	,,	
James Hobbs	,,		1834
W. Eley	,,		1830
R. J. Baylis	,,		1838
John Smith	,,	,,	1840
Thos. Cox Savory	1827	1827	
Dobson Glover & Co.	,,		1829
J. Cradock	,,		1833
T. Imneys	,,		1832
Pemberton & Scott	,,		1830
William Chaulk	,,		1828
Hart & Co.	,,		1834
Robert Lewis	,,		1840
James Peachey	,,		,,
George Pickett	,,		1839
George Steel	,,		
D. W. Stephenson	,,		
W. Mott	,,		,,
Elizabeth Ramsay	,,		1835
E. Thomas & Co.	,,		
W. Bellchambers	,,		
W. G. Cockerell, jun.	,,		1832
Thomas Cording	,,		1831
Jas. Chas. Edington	,,	1828	
Thomas Goode	,,		1839
Edward Farrell	,,		1850*
C. Mosley	,,		1829
Camper & Rutland	,,		1836
Henry Baron	1829		1832
Furness & Moseley	,,		
James Franklin	,,		1837
E. Baylis	,,	1829	1838
John Bennett	,,		1830
James Collins & Son	,,		1835
Henry Solomon	,,		1837
W. Esterbrook	,,		,,
Clement Cheese	,,		1833

* Many of the names in this list, although appearing as "last mentioned" in 1850 are those of goldsmiths who continued in business long after that date. Some, indeed, of the names which appear here, have been continued in use as "firm-names" down to the present day: it has, however, been deemed expedient to stop at 1850.

Name of Goldsmith.	Earliest Mention.	Entered.	Latest Mention	Name of Goldsmith.	Earliest Mention.	Entered.	Latest Mention.
William Kirkham	1829		1831	Susannah Jupp	1834		1839
Charles Plumley	,,		1832	Judah Hart & Co.	1835		1840
E., E., J. & W. Barnard	,,	1829		Walter Morrisse	,,		1850
E. Barnard & Sons	,,		1850	William Holden	,,		1836
Jabez Woodhill	,,		1838	Matthew Oliver	,,		1840
Thomas C. Savory	,,		1850	M. Phillips	,,		1837
Pearce & Burrows	,,		1840	R. T. Perkins	,		,,
David Jones	1830		1837	I. Behrends	,,		1840
Barnard & Sons	,,		1850	Thomas Stephens	,,		1838
James Cockerell	,,		1831	W. Hewitt	,,		1847
Mann & Muddill	,,		1837	G. F. Pinnell	,,		1850
J. Murray & J. Hall	,,		1832	James Collins	,,		,,
Kirkham & Harrison	,,			Edward Benton	,,		1841
Montague			1839	Griffin & Hyams	,,		1840
Reilly & Storer	,,		1850	Bernoni Stephens	,,		1843
W. & J. Marriott	,,		1840	Glover, Shelley & Carter	,,		1841
Taylor & Perry	,,		1838	C. Randall	1836		
Wm. K. Reid	,,		1850	Chas. Shaw	,,		1850
Waller Smithson	,,		1831	J. T. Neale	,,		1848
William Usherwood	,,		1833	James Catchpole	,,		1839
W. Young	,,		1832	Gass & Sons	,,		,,
J. Gramshaw	,,		1831	M. Hopgood	,,		1850
Henry Glover & Co.	,,		1832	James Bassett	,,		1839
H. G. Ive	,,		1839	R. Hennell	,,		,,
M. Forrestall & J. Bird	1831		1832	G. Newson	,,		1837
B. T. Walter	,,		1838	T. Skrymsher	,		1840
H. W. Fleming	,,		1837	George Beck	,,		1837
John Grant	,,		1834	W. & J. Yates	,,		,,
J. & T. Perry	,,		,,	Henry Dempster	,,		1838
J. Hawkes	,,		1837	William Thomas	,,		,,
T. B. Sowerby	,,		,,	Thomas Johnson	,,		,,
N. W. Morrison	,,		1834	W. Easterbrook	,,		1841
T. J. Bennett	,,		1836	C. J. Willis	,,		1837
Francis Harrison	,,		1840	J. T. Bennett	1837		1839
W. J. Blake	,,		1834	Mary Harding	,,		1838
G. T. Pinnell	,,		,,	Hayne & Co.	,,		1850
John W. Pryor	1832		1840	Thomas L. Vinton	,,		1845
Reynolds & Field	,,		,,	J. Rutland	,,		1840
T. Askey	,,		1834	William Butland	,,		1839
T. & J. Bartram	,,			Edward Dry	,,		
T. Price Jones	,,			William Forrest	,,		,,
W. T. Wilcox	,,		,,	Henry Hall	,,		1840
Purse & Catchpole	1833		1835	Richard Sibley	,,	1837	1850
Forrestall & Bird	,,		,,	W. Hatton	,,		
T. Dexter	,,		1836	Samuel Cave	1838		1840
B. T. Hopgood & Son	,,		1835	Samuel S. Edkins	,,		1841
James Robert	,,		1838	John Jupp	,,		1840
A. B., J. & A. Savory	,,	1833		T. Tate	,,		
John Sarl	,,		1842	Newson Garrett	,,		
Francis Pearce	,,		1850	William Bartram	,,		
Joseph Willmore	,,		1838	Jos. & Jno. Angell	,,		1839
Lowdell & Dempster	,,		1835	William Brown	,,		1844
William Yates	,,		,,	Mary Chawner	,,		,,
Charles Harson	1834		1846	William Crambrook	,,		1839
W. Makepeace & Rob. Henry	,,		1837	T. M. Skyrmsher	,,		,,
W. B. Tomlinson	,,		,,	R. G. Hennell	,,		,,
J. Thompson	,,		1835	J. C. Edington	,,		1850
Edward Lamb	,,		1838	John Gray	,,		
John Simonds	,,		1850	John Hatton	,,		1840
John Hargrave	,,			H. D. Ellis	,,		,,
Edward Pryor	,,		1840	J. A. Muddell	,,		,,
Robert England	,,		1839	James Aldous & Son	,,		,,
				Joseph Ball	,,		
				Henry Fuller	,,		
				H. J. Niblett	,,		,,

Name of Goldsmith.	Earliest Mention.	Entered.	Latest Mention.	Name of Goldsmith.	Earliest Mention.	Entered.	Latest Mention.
Makepeace & Walford	1838		1849	Mahala Jago	1840		1845
Henry Perrin	,,		1843	Mary Chawner & George Adams	,,	1840	
George Mander	,,			M. Moses	,,		1849
G. R. Chatterton	,,		1847	Robert Downes	,,		,,
Charles May	,,		1846	Samuel Foster	,,		
Robinson & Brown	,,		1839	Samuel Jones	,,		
Watson & Cooper	,,		1848	George Adams	,,	,,	
Mark Davis	1839		1840	Thomas Davis	,,		
S. A. Roberts & Co.	,,		1850	T. L. & J. W. Thomas	,,		
Francis Jones & Co.	,,		1842	Thomas Potter	,,		
Leonard Hill & Son	,,		1840	William Best	,		
John Edmonds	,,			Thomas Streetin	,,		1843
Joseph Taylor	,,		1846	T. & W. Vespers	,,		
Francis D. Dexter	,,	1839		Thomas Thresher	,,		
John Nichols	,,		1848	William Bateman, jr.	,,		
John Mortimer & John Saml. Hunt	,,	,,		William Bishop	,,		1850
John Cuisset	,,		1840	William Heath	,,		
William Theobalds & R. Metcalf Atkinson	,,	,,	,,	W. H. Osborn	,,		
Samuel Clark	,,		1842	Emanuel Brothers	,,		
George Knapp	,,		1844	Rawlins & Sumner	,,		
Herman Ball	,,		1843	Roberts & Co	,,		
Charles Bigge	,,			Robinson & Co.	,,		
George Reid	,,		1844	Sharp & Son	,,		
A. B. Savory & Sons	,,		1850	Theobalds & Co.	,,		
Widdowson & Veale	,,		,,	Barker & Co.	,,		
A. L. Newton	,,		1840	James Overan	,,		1845
A. M. Simons	,,		,,	Harvey Denton & Co.	,,		
Charles Vaughan	,,		1843	Joseph Jacobs	,,		1850
Atkins & Somersall	,,			J. & C. Simonds	,,		
William Cochran	,,			J. G. Clark	,,		
Thomas Savage	,,			Benjamin Preston	,,		,,
Thomas Diller	,,		1850	J. Galloway	,	,,	
Thomas Hunt	,,		1840	Charles Boyton	,,		,,
Samuel Skelton	,,		,,	John Cording	,,		
Thomas Wiltshire & Sons	,,		,,	Charles Gibson	,,		
Robert Hufflin	,,			John Burch	,,		
William Bateman & Daniel Ball	,,	1839	,,	Charles Kelk	,,		1848
W. & T. Rowlands	,,		,,	H. Holland	,,		1850
Stephen Noad	,,		1849	Charles Lias	,,		,,
William Neal	,,		1850	Francis Douglass	,,		,,
William Cooper	,,		,,	Charles W. Shipway	,,		1844
William Fitchew	,,			G. Corrie & Co.	,,		,,
Samuel Jackson	,,		1841	David Ellis	,,		
R. Marks	,,			James Beeb	,,		1847
Brown & Somersall	1840		1843	D. & L. Phillips	,,		1842
Chawner & Co.	,,		1850	Gregory Kirby & Co.	,,		
Angell, Son & Angell	,,			David Trail	,,		
W. S. Haynes	,,			George Drury	,,		
William Skeggs	,,			David Calver	,,		
William Potter	,,		,,	George Marshall	,,		
William Day	,,			Edward Dale	,,		
William Else	,,			Godfrey Zimmerman	,,		
William Chinnery	,,		1843	George Wheeler	,,		
William Peirce	,,			H. Abrahams	,,		
J. Perry	,,			I. Foligno	,,		1850
John Pierson	,,			James Andrews	,,		,,
J. T. Grey	,,			James Bult, Son & Co.	,,		
Thomas Perry	,,			Joseph Lomax	,,		
Joseph Wood	,,			J. & N. Johnson	,,		
R. Brook & Co.	,,			T. H. Headland	,,		
J. W. Figg	,,			Alfred Barton	1841		1844
S. Whitford	,,		1848	Wm. J. Fryer	,,		1843
				Alexander Smith	,,		1850
				Edward Foligno	,,		,,

Name of Goldsmith.		Earliest Mention.	Entered.	Latest Mention.
David	Gass & Sons.	1841		
John	Lias & Son.	,,		1850
Edward	Barnard	,,		1843
Jos. & Albert	} Savory	,,	1841	
Angel	& Son.	,,		1842
Pearce	& Co.	,,		1850
Richard	Sullivan	,,		1844
H. L.	Cavalier	,,		1842
James	Hull	,,		,,
John	Angel & Son	,,		1850
Joseph	Angel & Son	,,		,,
James	Edwards	,,		,,
Wm. & John	} Oliver	,,		
John W.	Figg	,,		1862
John M.	Wintle	,,		1850
John	Smee	,,		1848
John	Tearce	,,		1847
Robert	Roberts	,,		1842
Thomas	Burlton	,,		1850
T.	Cook	,,		1846
Thomas	Hastings	,,		1843
William	Marriott	,		1846
William	Mote	,,		
W. Theobalds & Co.		,,		1844
Wrangham	& Moulson	,,		1845
J., C. & G.	Mullins	1842		
John	Evans	,,		
John	Harris	,,		1850
John W.	Denning	,,		1843
Matthew	Weed	,,		
Robert	Death	,,		1850
Thomas	Freeman	,,		1845
W. Butland & Walker		,		
Wm.	Pincher	,,		1843
Wm.	Rickards	,,		
Henry	Glover	,,		1845
Samuel	Hawgood	,,		,,
Joshua	Storrs	,,		,,
C. & G.	Mullins	1843		1850
John R.	Harris	,,		,,
George	Webb	,.		1848
J.	Tapley & Son	,,		1850
Sarah	Clark	,,		
William	Fenner	,,		1844
William	Hunter	,,		1850
W. H.	Jones	,,		,,
William	Ralfs	,,		
Charles	Watson	1844		1848
J. & D. & C.	Houle	,,		1845
John & Jas.	MacRae	,,		1850
John	Perkins	,,		1846
John	Sarl & Sons.	,,		1850

Name of Goldsmith.		Earliest Mention.	Entered.	Latest Mention.
Lewis	Abrahams	1844		1850
Peter M.	Gottheimer	,,		,,
William	Allen	,,		1847
William R.	Smily	,,		1850
George	Bissmire	,,		,,
John Saml.	Hunt	,,	1844	,,
Wolstencroft & Leete		,,		1849
George	Ivory	1845		1850
George	Unite	,,		
George J.	Richards	,,		1849
John	Barber	,,		1850
John	Short	,,		
Thomas B.	Gamson	,,		1851
Thomas	Shepherd	,,		1847
W. & Henry	Papprell	,,		
William	Williams	,,		,,
Wm. Young	Fox	,,		
Frederick	Dear	,,		
Robert	Tallack	,,		,,
D. & C.	Houle	1846		1850
G. & H.	Watson	,,		,,
Henry	Radclyffe	,,		,,
John Jas.	Keith	,,		,,
Michael	Jones	,,		
Samuel	Jacobs	,,		,,
William	Edwards	,,		,,
Hunt	& Roskell	,,		,,
Harris	Brothers	,,		,,
Moulston	& Williams	,,		,,
Andrew	Beaton	1847		1848
Elizabeth	Eaton	,,		1850
William	Grissell	,,		1848
Andrew	Batchelor	1848		1850
David	Phillips	,,		1849
George	Burrows	,,		,,
Henry	Freeth	,,		1850
Joseph	Miller	,,		1849
John	Tease	,,		
John J.	Whiting	,,		1850
Jacob	Wintle	,,		,,
Clothier	& Tarrant	,,		,,
Richard	Britton	,,		
Richard	Ewins	,,		
W.	Cumming	,,		
William	Wheatcroft	,,		1849
William	Wright	,,		
William	Phillips	,,		1850
James	Sayer	1849		
S. Whitford & Son		,,		,,
T. S.	Seagers			,,
William	Stevens			,,
Charles	Bishop	1850		
Robert	Wallis	,,		
S.	Edkins & Son	,,		

CHAPTER X

THE ENGLISH PROVINCIAL GOLDSMITHS

The London Goldsmiths' Company were supposed to have had jurisdiction over all workers of gold and silver within the Kingdom of England, and under their Charters they no doubt had that right. They appear, however, to have exercised their authority only at rare intervals at a distance from the Metropolis, and it seems clear that the Guilds of Goldsmiths at York, Chester, and other provincial towns carried on their affairs independently of the London Company.

There is evidence that goldsmiths worked in the thirteenth century at Chester and Norwich, in the fourteenth century at York and Exeter, and in the fifteenth century at these and other provincial towns. In Chester, one "Nicholas" was known as "the Great Goldsmith" in 1271. In Norwich, in 1285, John Aurifaber and a dozen others carried on the trade of goldsmiths. In Exeter, Johannes Wewlingworth was a goldsmith of note in 1327. A Bishop's crozier is mentioned in 1300 as "Durham-Work,"* and by a will recorded in the York registry, spoons "made in York" were bequeathed as early as 1366.†

Goldsmiths working in Chester, Norwich, York, and Exeter, before A.D. 1400.

In the provincial towns goldsmiths were governed by Guilds composed of the Master Craftsmen of the art or mystery who dwelt and worked there, and by the 28 Ed. I. c. 20 (1300),‡ it was provided that "in all the good towns of England where any goldsmiths be dwelling, they shall be ordered as they of London be, and that one shall come from every good town for all the residue that be dwelling in the same unto London to be ascertained of their touch". The 1 Ed. III. (1327) repeated the above provision as to one goldsmith coming from every good town for all the residue, and required them "there to have a stamp of a puncheon with a leopard's head marked upon their work". It is probable, nevertheless, that the difficulty and danger attendant upon the conveyance of gold and silver wares over considerable distances to the

28 Ed. I. c. 20 (1300). One goldsmith to come to London from every town for the residue, to be ascertained of their "Touch".

* "*De Opere Dunelm.*" Wardrobe Accounts 28 Edw. I.
† "*Coclearia facta in Ebor.*" *Test. Ebor.*
‡ See this Statute set out more fully in Chapter II. (*supra*).

Metropolis prevented the above provisions from being strictly followed, and it seems clear that plate was made and sold in the English provincial towns without being sent to London to be assayed.   That this was

2 Rich. II. (1378).
The Assay of the
Touch belongs to
the Mayors and
Governors of the
Cities and
Boroughs.

so is borne out by the preamble to the Statute 2 Rich. II. (1378-9), which runs : "*Because gold and silver which is wrought by goldsmiths in England is oftentimes less fine than it ought to be because the goldsmiths are their own judges, be it ordained that every goldsmith put his own mark upon his work ; and the assay of the Touch belongs to the Mayors and Governors of the cities and boroughs, with the aid of the Master of the*

Mark of the City
or Borough to be
put on by
Masters of Pro-
vincial Mints.

Mint, if there be such, putting the mark of the city or borough where the assay is".   Here we have it clearly recognised that goldsmiths worked in gold and silver in the cities and boroughs, and were their own judges of the quality or standard of the metal wrought, and in order to insure the gold and silver so wrought being of the legal standard, the Mayors and Governors of the cities and boroughs were charged with control of the assay.   Here too it is laid down that where there was a Mint, the Master of the Mint was to put on the wrought silver and gold the mark of the city or borough where the assay was.   We are thus enabled, even in the absence of other evidence, to distinguish plate stamped with the mark of a particular city or borough as having been assayed and probably made in the city or borough whose mark it bears.

2 Hen. VI. c. 14
(1423).
York, Newcastle,
Lincoln, Nor-
wich, Bristol,
Salisbury, and
Coventry to
have "Touches".

In 1423, the Statute 2 Hen. VI. c. 14, appointed York, Newcastle-upon-Tine, Lincoln, Norwich, Bristow (Bristol), Salisbury, and Coventry* to have divers "touches," and enacted provisions for their guidance "according to the ordinance of Mayors, Bailiffs, or Governors of the said towns".   These provisions were in conformity with the statutes previously enacted relating to the London goldsmiths in particular, and the goldsmiths throughout the realm in general.   With reference to the "touching" or selling of any provincial-made plate in London, it was provided that "No goldsmith nor other workers of silver nor keepers of the said touches within the said (provincial) townes shall set to sell nor touch any silver in other manner than is ordained before, within the City of London" under penalty of forfeiture.†

---

* Chester apparently had a "touch" of its own under the Earl of Chester, and not under the Crown, which accounts for the omission of that city from the Act of 1423, as is more fully explained in Chapter XV.

† Obviously for the preservation of the privileges which had been previously granted to the London goldsmiths.

Notwithstanding that the London goldsmiths claimed the right under their Charter of 1462 to the general control of the working of all gold and silver plate throughout the realm of England and Wales, it seems clear that in the Middle Ages, and later, much plate was made in the provinces without being assayed or marked in any way, " because the goldsmiths were their own judges,"* and that the law requiring them to submit their wares to the " touch," and to set none to sale before being " touched" and " marked" *was "daily broken*, and oftentimes the sign of the worker of the same was not set thereto ".†

Much early provincial-made plate not assayed or marked.

The supervision by the London Goldsmiths' Company when exercised seems only to have been occasional, with intervals extending over many years. Two journeys into the country by the Wardens in a period of six years are recorded in 1512 and 1517. At other times the provincial goldsmiths do not appear to have been interfered with in any way.

In the majority of towns before 1378, when the control of the " touch " was given to the Mayors and Governors,‡ no distinguishing mark appears to have been struck on plate to denote the place of its manufacture. After that date the law as to touching and marking seems to have been largely infringed, if one may judge by recurring references in subsequent statutes to irregularities, and by the amount of antique plate found unmarked, or, at most, marked with the maker's mark only.

The quantity and quality of plate wrought in the provinces varied greatly in the several parts of the realm. In some districts large quantities are found, the work on which will in no way suffer by comparison with London-made plate of the same period, while examples found in other districts (such, for instance, as some of the local-made Church plate in Cumberland) are extremely rude both in design and workmanship, suggestive of having been made by a country blacksmith rather than by a worker in the precious metals.

Excellence of the work of some provincial goldsmiths.

The Statute 2 Hen. VI. c. 14 (of 1423) which appointed touches in the seven towns mentioned in the Act, presumably had some effect at the time, but the most careful research by the Author and others has failed to find any records of action having been taken in any one of these places as an immediate consequence of that statute. Later on—but not until more than a century had elapsed—we find " the mark of the city

---

* 1 Edw. III (1327).
† 17 Edw. IV. c. 1 (1477).
‡ 2 Ric. II. (1378).

or borough" (its badge or armorial bearing) adopted as the mark of the craft of Goldsmiths in several provincial towns.

In York, Norwich, and Exeter, goldsmiths not only worked but flourished from about the middle of the 16th century downwards. They have left behind them records and examples of their work, extending from quite early in the reign of Queen Elizabeth, with slight intervals, down to the time when their assay offices were closed. Of the Chester goldsmiths some records extend back to a time still more remote than those of York, although no examples of Chester plate are known of earlier date than the 17th century. Since that period the Chester goldsmiths have had an active existence, and the assay office there is the only English provincial office remaining of those which existed prior to 1773. Of the Newcastle goldsmiths there are no records earlier than 1536, when, in conjunction with members of other trades, they were incorporated as a Guild of Craftsmen. The goldsmiths of Hull have left ample evidence of their existence from the time of Queen Elizabeth to Wm. III., and an appreciable quantity of Lincoln-made spoons is known to exist, but of the work of the goldsmiths of Bristol, Salisbury, and Coventry (three of the seven towns appointed to have "touches" by the Act of 1423) very little is known. Indeed, if we except a few small articles, which will be referred to hereafter, it may be said that no antique plate is known which may with certainty be ascribed to the craftsmanship of a goldsmith of any one of those three towns.

1677.
References to provincial goldsmiths by the author of *The Touchstone.*

In the latter half of the 17th century the London goldsmiths appear to have had a not very exalted opinion of their provincial brethren, if the expressions of a contemporaneous writer * may be taken as a criterion. He says that he "can give no account of the marks which the respective Governors of York, Newcastle, Lincoln, Norwich, Bristol, Salisbury, and Coventry set on the silver works wrought there "; but he asserts that " by reason of the marks of those places being little known, they bear as little credit ". He refers to the obligation which provincial goldsmiths were under to make their marks known to the Mayors and Governors of their respective cities and boroughs, and to the Wardens of the London goldsmiths, and points out that the privileges then enjoyed by provincial goldsmiths of " having a touch by themselves,"

* *The Touchstone*, London, 1677.

and being excused of the obligation "of bringing their vessels of silver to London to be stamped with the Leopard's Head, were in danger of being lost". Might this be taken as an indication that efforts were being made by the London goldsmiths to get the privileges then enjoyed by provincial goldsmiths revoked? It has the semblance of a sinister foreboding, which certainly, for a time, affected the provincial goldsmiths very prejudicially. The animus of the author of *The Touchstone* against the goldsmiths of the provinces is shown in his reference to the debased quality of their wares (which he attributes to the laxity of the authorities) and in his advice to intending buyers of plate to give their orders to London goldsmiths. It would be interesting, in view of this allegation, to ascertain by assay the actual amount of alloy in the provincial plate of the period. If its quality had been "as good as sterling" it is strange that the Act of 1696-7 * should have provided that all plate stamped with "the mark commonly used at the hall belonging to the Company of Goldsmiths in London besides the worker's mark" should be received at the Mint and paid for without assay at the rate of 5s. 4d. per ounce, and that any not bearing such marks was to be tested by assay, and valued by the Master of the Mint before being paid for.

The Act of 1696-7 * had the effect, foreshadowed by the author of *The Touchstone* twenty years before, of depriving the provincial goldsmiths of the privilege which they had long enjoyed of having their wares assayed at the local assay offices. This resulted from the provision that the standard for wrought plate should be 8 dwts. finer than the standard theretofore in force, and that the marks to be used should be the worker's mark (to be expressed by the first two letters of his surname), the marks of the Mystery of the Goldsmiths, "which *instead of the leopard's head and the lion* should be the figure of a lion's head erased and the figure of Britannia, and the variable mark to denote the year in which such plate was made; and that all plate exposed for sale not so marked should be forfeited. These new marks of the lion's head erased and Britannia having been ordered *in place of the leopard's head and the lion* which theretofore had been used solely by the Mystery of Goldsmiths in London, it followed that only the London Goldsmiths' Company could use the new marks, without which no plate could safely be exposed for sale. Thus all the provincial assay offices were deprived

Effect of the Statute of 1696-7 on Provincial Assay Offices.

Effect of the Statute of 1696-7 on Provincial Assay Offices.

---

* See the Act more fully set forth in Chapter II.

of their business, and all provincial goldsmiths were obliged to send their wares to London to be assayed and marked.

This wrought a great hardship on the provincial goldsmiths, preventing them from exposing any plate for sale which was not London-marked. There seems, however, to have been no penalty attached to the making of plate *to order* without the new marks, and it is suggested that the English provincial plate marked with the stamps of makers of that period and the words "Sterling" ᵃⁿᵈ/ₒᵣ "Britannia," but without any assay office mark, is plate probably "made to order," in the period of three years during which the disability applied to the provincial offices, and that such marks were struck by the makers as their personal warranty of the quality of the plate so made.

With the object of obtaining redress of their grievance, the goldsmiths of Chester, Norwich, and Exeter petitioned Parliament to re-establish their assay offices, and in the year 1700 the Statute 12 Wm. III. c. 4. was passed. This Act recites that the goldsmiths and plateworkers remote from London were under great difficulties and hardships in the exercise of their trades, for want of assayers in convenient places to assay and touch their wrought plate, and for remedy of their grievances and to prevent frauds :—

Statute 12
Wm. III. c. 4
(1700)
re-established
Provincial Assay
Offices.

(Sec. 1.) Appointed the several cities where the Mints had been shortly before erected for re-coining the silver money, viz. :—York, Exeter, Bristol, Chester and Norwich, for the assaying and marking of wrought plate, and for exercising the other powers of the Act :

(Sec. 2.) Incorporated the goldsmiths and plate-workers, freemen of, and living in, any of the said cities and having served an apprenticeship to the said trade, as the Company of Goldsmiths of the said cities respectively, and enabled them annually to choose two wardens to continue for one year and no longer unless re-elected : and

(Sec. 3.) Provided that no goldsmith or plate-worker should work any silver below standard nor sell nor exchange the same until marked with the maker's mark, the lion's head erased, the figure of Britannia, the arms of the city, and a variable yearly letter :

(Secs. 4-6.) That each of the said companies should elect a competent assayer, that he might detain eight grains per lb. Troy of the silver submitted for assay for the purposes of the assay. That the diet box should be in the company's charge, locked with three keys, to be kept by the wardens and assayer and conveyed annually (if required) to the London mint and the diet therein tried as the pyx of the coin is tried, and in case of deceit the company to forfeit £50, recoverable from the company or any member thereof, and if any plate should be "touched" as good by the assayer and any deceit found therein he should forfeit double the value :

(Sec. 7.) That every goldsmith should enter his name, mark and abode, with the wardens, and for striking an unentered mark on plate he should forfeit double its value :

(Sec. 8.) That if any person should counterfeit any of the appointed stamps he should forfeit the sum of £500 : and

(Sec. 9.) Provided for the payment by each goldsmith of a charge not exceeding 6d. per pound Troy for the assayer's trouble in assaying.

Newcastle not having been one of the places wherein a mint had been then recently set up for re-coining the silver moneys of the realm, was not included in the operation of the Act of 1700, and it was not until the year 1702 that the assay office there was re-established, in circumstances detailed in Chapter XIV. This enabled it to again take rank with the other re-established assay offices, of which four only continued in active existence as such until shortly after the middle of the 19th century, when, with the exception of the Chester office, which continues to flourish, each in turn found its work diminishing, and was ultimately closed. *Newcastle Assay Office not included in the Act of 1700, 12 Wm. III. c. 4, but re-established in 1702.*

Meanwhile in 1773 new assay offices had been established at Birmingham and Sheffield. These, however, will be found referred to further on, it being more generally convenient, as well as more consistent with the plan of this work, devised mainly for the purpose of reference, to deal with the personality and work of the goldsmiths of each town separately. Before, however, leaving this general reference to English provincial goldsmiths, mention should be made of a Report on the Assay Offices, which was presented to the House of Commons on the 29th of April, 1773. *Report on the Assay Offices. Presented to Parliament in April, 1773.*

On the 1st of February in that year, a petition was presented to Parliament by plate-workers carrying on business in the town and neighbourhood of Sheffield, setting forth that a considerable trade was being done there, and that the petitioners were put to great and unnecessary expense, inconvenience and delay, in having to send their goods to London to be assayed, and praying that leave might be given to introduce a Bill for establishing an assay office at Sheffield.

On the next day Matthew Boulton and other manufacturers of plate in Birmingham, following the example of the Sheffield plate-workers, prayed that if provision should be made for the establishment of an assay office in Sheffield, a similar privilege should also be granted in the case of Birmingham.

These efforts aroused the opposition of the London Goldsmiths'

Company, who presented counter petitions against the granting of any such privileges to the plate-workers of Birmingham and Sheffield, as were enjoyed by them.

Parliamentary
Inquiry respect-
ing the working
of the Provincial
Offices in 1773.
The matter having been considered in Parliament, a Committee was appointed to inquire into the manner of conducting the assay and marking of wrought plate in the several assay offices in London, York, Exeter, Bristol, Chester, Norwich, and Newcastle-upon-Tyne ; and also to inquire into the frauds and abuses alleged to have been committed and attempted in some of such places.

A further petition by goldsmiths of the City of London and its vicinity, was presented to the House of Commons, alleging that frauds and abuses had been committed in or near Sheffield and Birmingham, or one of them, and that artificers there had plated base metal with silver, and had impressed marks thereon in such manner as to give it the appearance of real plate marked at an assay office, and praying that the petitioners might be heard by the Committee (above-mentioned) in proof of their allegations.   This petition was referred to the Committee with a request that the petitioners be heard.

The Committee thereupon instituted inquiries as directed, and summoned the Assay Masters from the London and provincial assay offices to give evidence touching the matters inquired into.   The evidence given by the Assay Masters of Exeter, Newcastle, and Chester, being of greater interest in connection with the affairs of the goldsmiths of those towns than at this point, will be found set forth in Chapters XIII., XIV. and XV. respectively.   It may, however, be here stated that the evidence with regard to the conduct of the assay offices at Chester and Newcastle was as satisfactory as that respecting the Exeter office was the reverse.   The offices at York and Norwich were at the time of the inquiry both closed, and there was no evidence to show that Bristol had ever availed itself of the Act of 1700.

Inquiry mainly
directed to the
expediency of
establishing
Assay Offices in
Birmingham and
Sheffield.
The main object of the inquiry was with reference to the applications for the establishment of assay offices at Birmingham and Sheffield, and against the granting of these applications the whole strength of the London Goldsmiths' Company—jealous of their own privileges and anxious to prevent the creation of other rival offices—was directed. It was alleged that the plated wares of Sheffield and Birmingham had been made to simulate real silver, and marked so as to deceive the unwary.   These allegations were met by counter allegations as to the

corruption and venality of some of the officers of the London Hall. Mr. W. Hancock, a Sheffield silversmith, said that "his work had been injured by scraping; but that he went to the Hall and gave some drink to the Assay Master and Scraper, after which his plate had been less damaged". Mr. Spilsbury said that "Drawers or Scrapers, if inclined, had opportunities of delivering to the Assayer better silver than that which they scraped from the work; that the Assayer had an opportunity of wrapping in lead whatever scrapings he pleased to put in the cupels delivered by him to the fireman; and as the standard mark was put upon the silver by the report of the Assayer alone, he had opportunities of favouring any silversmith he pleased; that he (Mr. Spilsbury) had several times treated the workmen with drink; and thought it of consequence to be on good terms with the Scrapers, for when plate had been objected to, he had known of difficulties being removed by giving liquor at the Hall ".

These allegations of venality appear to have been established, for although Mr. David Hennell, the Deputy-Warden of the London Goldsmiths' Company; Mr. Fendall Rushworth, the senior Assay Master; Mr. George Fair, the Clerk; and Mr. Richard Collins, Fireman and Drawer, each gave evidence with reference to the assay, the diet, the Charters and other matters pertaining to the Company, the evidence of Messrs. Hancock and Spilsbury was not confuted.

It appeared from the evidence that while the Assay Master of Chester was careful not to pass as good any silver under 11 oz. 2 dwts. fine, without cautioning the sender, it was the practice in London to pass plate which came within two pennyweights of standard.

An ingenious fraud, called a *convoy*, sometimes resorted to by dis- honest workers, was described by Mr. Hennell, who said, "If scrapings or cuttings are taken from different pieces of the same sort of plate, the whole mass so cut or scraped may prove standard, but several of these pieces may not be standard; and that it is common to put good pieces in spoons, &c., to the extent of 10 dwts. to 15 dwts. above standard, amongst the bad ones as a kind of *convoy* for the rest; but if that is suspected, they separate and make different assays of all the parts, and if they find one part worse than standard, they break the whole ".

Several witnesses testified to the practice of inserting iron, brass, &c., in the handles of tankards, sauce-boats, snuffers, &c. (the whole being sold by weight as so much silver), and to its having escaped detection at Goldsmiths' Hall, where articles thus fraudulently increased in weight had been marked as good.

As a result of the inquiry the Committee made a report to the House. The report, after stating the evidence of the witnesses, concluded with the observations that it appeared to the Committee that *the assay offices at Chester and Newcastle had been conducted with fidelity and skill;* that the plating of base metal with silver had been brought to such perfection, that if the practice of putting marks on it similar to those used for silver were not restrained, many frauds might be committed upon the public; that various frauds had been committed with reference to silver plate, contrary to the established legal standards, and that (assuming the new assay offices to be established as prayed for) some further checks and regulations were necessary for the prevention of such frauds, besides those provided by the existing laws.

The recommendations of the Committee were carried out with reference to Birmingham and Sheffield, and assay offices were established in those towns by Acts of Parliament the same year, but nothing was done with reference to the marks on plated wares until eleven years after, when an Act* was passed amending in that respect the Birmingham and Sheffield Acts of 1773.

The old-established provincial assay offices do not appear to have sent their diet to the Mint for verification. In the course of a Parliamentary inquiry on the subject of plate and its assay marks, conducted in 1856, it was shown that no offices other than Birmingham and Sheffield, had ever within living memory sent up their diet boxes to the Mint for the purpose of having the diet tested, being only liable so to do when required by the Lord Chancellor. The Guardians of the Standard of Wrought Plate at Birmingham and Sheffield are obliged by their respective Acts of Parliament to send their diet to the Mint once . in every year to be tested, and the Goldsmiths' Company of Chester, although not legally bound to do so, have taken a similar obligation upon themselves voluntarily.

* The Local Act 24 Geo. III. c. 20 (1784).

CHAPTER XI

THE YORK GOLDSMITHS AND THEIR MARKS

York being the most important provincial city in England in the The Medieval Goldsmiths. Middle Ages, and the first mentioned of the seven provincial towns appointed to have "touches" by the Act of 1423, its goldsmiths are here given precedence over those of all other guilds in the provinces.

York-made spoons are mentioned in a will of the year 1366. That there was a local touch in York as early as 1410-1 is proved by a document* in the archives of the city, concerning a dispute between members of the Craft of Goldsmiths as to whether there should be three or only two "searchers".† The question having been referred to the Mayor, Aldermen, and other good citizens on 5 March, $141\frac{0}{1}$, it was decided that two "searchers" and no more, both to be Englishmen born, should be chosen and duly sworn. The goldsmiths were required to bring their touch and mark, as the statute directs ("*come la statut purport*"), and those who had no mark were to make for themselves punches in compliance with the law, as required by the community ("*en complisiment de justice come le comune lez eut demand*"). It was further decreed that if they sold any article of gold or silver before the common touch of the said city ("*le comune touch de la dite cite*") and the mark of its maker were properly struck on it, they were to forfeit 6s. 8d.

Although the "common touch of the city" is referred to thus early in the city archives, it is not until twelve years later that we find it given statutory recognition as "the touch ordained in the City of York, according to the ordinance of its Mayor," in conformity with the statute,‡ which provided also that no goldsmith anywhere in England should work silver of worse allay than sterling, nor offer any for sale without first setting his mark upon it under the penalty of forfeiture, and empowered the Mayor and Justices of the Peace to hear and determine such matters.

---

* Discovered by Canon Raine.
† Searchers—officers, whose business it is to examine wares as to their quality and mark defects if discovered, otherwise " assayers ".
‡ 2 Henry VI. c. 14 (1423).

Goldsmiths of
the 15th Century.

From 1423 onwards, references are to be found in wills and other documents to goldsmiths who carried on business in York. In 1458, John Luneburgh of York, goldsmith, by his will " bequeaths 6s. 8d. to the working goldsmiths ('*auri fabrorum arti*') towards the cost of a new silver crown, and leaves his tools to his fellow goldsmiths, Robert Spicer and John Pudsay ". In another will, dated 1490, an inventory of the tools, utensils, and other appliances used by the testator, one John Colam, in his trade of goldsmith, is given in complete detail.

A.D. 1560.

In the year 1560, " the ancient ordinances of the mystery or craft of goldsmiths of the citie of Yorke were diligently examined and reformed by the right worshipful Parsyvall Crafourth, Mayour, the Aldermen, and Pryvay Councill," at their assembly in " the Counsell Chamber upon Ousebrig," thenceforth to be firmly observed and kept. The old Ordinance of 1410-1 with reference to the two " searchers " was ratified and confirmed, the two " searchers" (Thomas Sympson and Robert Gylmyn), then in office under the said ordinance, and other good men, Masters of the Craft, being present. It was then also ordained that all

The York Mark
described.

work should be " *towched with the pounce of this citie, called the halfe leopard head and half flowre-de-luyce* " as the statute purporteth ; that wrought gold should be of the " touche of Paryse," that no silver should be worked of " worse alaye than sterlyng," and except that sufficient " sowder" should be allowed, anyone working gold or silver below these standards should forfeit double the value thereof.

The above ordinances were followed by others having reference to apprentices and their admission to the craft, to the punishments to be imposed in respect of fraudulent work, as to what things might be plated with gold and silver, and what exceptions as to gilding might be made in the case of " Ornaments for Holy Church, Knights' spurs, and the apparel that pertaineth to a baron, and above that estate " ; all of which merely repeated the general law of the Kingdom with reference to goldsmith's work as set forth in the Statutes 5 Hen. IV., 8 Hen. V., 2 Hen. VI., and others from 1404 downwards.*

Notwithstanding all these ordinances and declarations of statutory law, the goldsmiths of York do not appear to have been more obedient to them or to have worked together more harmoniously than their brethren in London, where in 1566 no less than twenty-eight were fined for offences. While in London, in 1582-3, the assay master (Kelynge)

* See Chapter II.

himself was not above suspicion, so in York (where the craft elected their Irregularities practised at York in the 16th Century. "searchers" from amongst their own body) in the very same year, malpractices were charged against the two "searchers," Martyn du Biggin and William Pearson. Both were convicted and imprisoned ("committed to ward"), Pearson for a day; du Biggin, however, who seems to have been the greater offender, was deprived of his office and imprisoned during the Lord Mayor's pleasure. Pearson was allowed to continue in office, and Thomas Waddie was elected as his co-searcher in place of Martyn du Biggin, on the 10 May, 1583. Pearson and Waddie do not appear to have been able to perform their duties as assayers without difficulty, for the records show that before they had held office together for a year they had a dispute with George Kitchen, and that the matters in difference were settled by arbitration on the 23 Sept., 1583. Thomas Waddie seems to have tired of his office before he had held it twelve months, for we find that on the 5 Jan., 1584 ($158\frac{3}{4}$), he and his co-searcher had resigned, and that John Stocke and William Ffoster were elected in their place. On the 27th of January in the following year ($158\frac{4}{5}$), the rule formerly observed of electing searchers From 1584 Officers of the Guild elected in July in each year. in the month of January was altered, and it was ordained that thenceforth they were to be elected on the fourth day after the Feast of St. James the Apostle (29 July), and to continue in office till that day year.

This ordinance, however, does not appear to have been regularly observed, for a minute of the 1 Sept., 1684, records that the searchers were fined 40s. a man, for neglecting to call the meeting to choose their successors, and the company was convened to meet that day fortnight to choose them.

In an entry of the year 1606, in connection with some new 1606. Last mention of " halfe leopard head and half flower-de-luce". ordinances concerning "searching," the York mark is referred to, as in former minutes, as the "*towch and mark belonginge to this cittye, called the halfe leopard head and half flower de luce*," and this appears to be the last entry in which the old York mark is thus referred to in express terms.

The York goldsmiths from quite early times appear to have occupied prominent positions amongst the citizens. It will be found mentioned in the list with which this chapter concludes that Thomas Gray was Lord Mayor of the city in 1497, that William Wilson filled that office in 1513, George Gale in 1534, and Rad Pulleyn in 1537. Richard Brerey was Sheriff in 1555; John Thompson Lord Mayor in 1685; Charles Rhoades Sheriff in 1694, and Mark Gill Lord Mayor in 1697.

THE YORK GOLDSMITHS' MARKS

We have seen that from the year 1411 it was incumbent upon all the goldsmiths of York, as well by their own ordinances as by the statute law of the realm, to put their own mark upon their work, which was required to be "brought" to the "searchers" to be touched and marked with the city mark, and that no article of gold or silver was to be sold unless marked with such two marks.

1560.
York mark
described as the
"half leopard
head and half
flowre-de-luyce".

In a minute of 1560, as we have seen, the city mark is described as "the half leopard head and the half flowre de luyce". It is therefore established that from 1411 to 1560 all York-made plate was or ought to have been marked with the leopard's head and fleur-de-lys, both dimidiated and conjoined in one stamp, and the maker's mark, and that these marks were continued in use thenceforward until a change was made in the form of the city mark, or "town-mark" as it is generically termed.

Use of date-letter
appears to have
been adopted
in 1560.

At about the same date as that of the above minute (1560) there was added to the two marks formerly in use, a third, consisting of a date-letter or alphabetical mark, which was from the time of its adoption changed in each successive year. From about 1560, therefore, to 1698, York made plate was, or ought to have been, marked with three marks— viz., the city mark, the maker's mark, and the date-letter. The year 1560 is assumed to have been the date of the commencement of the use of a date-letter, because in April of that year, as we have seen, "the ancient ordynances were diligently perused by the right worshipfull the Mayor, the Aldremen and the Privay Councell" when they were *reformed*, "to be thenceforth firmly observed". There is no express mention of the adoption of a date-letter as an additional mark, but upon the earliest known Elizabethan example of York-made plate (a seal top spoon in the Author's collection) there are three marks—viz., the old York mark (above described), the maker's mark (of Robert Gylmyn) and the date-letter D, which cannot well be ascribed to any other year than 1562-3. It is reasonable to assume that the use of the first alphabet was commenced three years earlier with the letter A. With comparatively few exceptions, the Author has found examples illustrating the successive date-letters which were used from 1562-3 until 1698 when, by reason of the Act of 1696-7, the statutory existence of all the English provincial assay offices was temporarily suspended.

Now with reference to the three marks in use from 1560 to 1698 concerning the maker's mark no question arises, and as to the date-letter, there is only the possible difference (about a year or so) in regard to the position of some of the letters, arising from the doubt as to whether the letter J (as well as I) was used in one or two cycles; but on the question of the "town mark" there has been a most extraordinary conflict of opinion. Mr. Octavius Morgan saw the mark, and described it as "the Leopard's head crowned and fleur-de-lis dimidiated and joined together on one shield". Mr. Cripps, adopting Mr. Morgan's description, used it until the late Mr. Chancellor Ferguson, M.A., F.S.A., found a large number of examples of York plate bearing a mark which he described as "a fleur-de-lis dimidiating a crowned rose in a circular stamp," whereupon Mr. Cripps dropped Mr. Morgan's description and used that of Mr. Ferguson. But later on, Canon Raine and Mr. T. M. Fallow, F.S.A., brought to light the old minutes of 1560 and 1606, in which the mark is described as "the halfe leopard head and half flower de luce," corresponding with the description first given by Mr. Morgan, which was then resumed by Mr. Cripps. Mr. Chaffers, however, persisted (in his *Hall Marks on Plate*) in describing the mark as "half lis and half rose crowned". Now the strange thing about these varying descriptions is that they are each right and each wrong, and the explanation will be seen in the following tables, where every variety of the York mark which has been found, is separately represented in *facsimile*. It will be observed that from 1562 down to 1631 the mark is as described in the minutes of 1560 and 1606, a "halfe leopard head and half flower de luce," but from 1632 till 1698 the place of the half leopard's head is occupied by a half rose crowned. The "town mark" on the example noted by the Author for 1631-2 was much worn, and might possibly have been struck with the earlier stamp, but in all the later examples of the mark, the sinister half can with certainty be distinguished as a dimidiated rose crowned, and not a half leopard's head. How the change came about the Author is unable to say; there appears to be no record of it.

Conflicting opinions in the past regarding the York "town mark".

From 1562 to 1631 the mark is a half leopard's head and half fleur-de-lis, and from 1632 until 1698 a half rose crowned and half fleur-de-lis.

Before leaving the subject of the early York marks it might be suggested that the irregularities of the assayers and their disputes with the craft in the reign of Queen Elizabeth, particularly during the time when Martyn du Biggin, William Pearson, and Thomas Waddie held office, were reflected in the marking of some of the plate of the period.

There is in the Author's collection an apostle spoon with the mark of Thomas Waddie, and the date-letter S (for 1576-7) on the back of the stem ; and in the bowl (where the "town mark" is usually found, and ought to have been struck), instead of the half fleur-de-lis and half leopard's head, the maker's mark is repeated.   The Author has found the same maker's mark with date-letter k (for 1592-3) on another spoon which has the half fleur-de-lis and half leopard's head regularly struck in the bowl. Its absence in 1576-7 may very probably have had some connection with the disputes referred to.

From 1560 to 1584-5 the "searchers" appear to have been elected in the month of January, and thereafter on the 29th of July in each year ; the change of date-letter was probably synchronous with the election of these officers.   The alphabets used were as follows :—

Date-letters, 1560 to 1698.

1560 to 1583—Roman capitals.

1583 „ 1607—Black letter, small, in angular shields, with a few exceptions.

1607 „ 1631—Black-letter capitals in angular shields.

1631 „ 1657—Italics, small (except k, o, t, u, v, and z), in angular shields.

1657 „ 1682—Cursive capitals in angular shields.

1682 „ 1698—Black-letter capitals (except A, B, C, e, and N* which differ from the others), in angular shields.

The difference in the form of the town mark and the makers' marks afford ready means of distinguishing between the alphabets of 1607-1631 and 1682-1698.

On the re-establishment of the York assay office in 1700-1 the distinguishing mark of the office was, in compliance with the Act of Parliament of that year,† changed, and the arms of the city (a cross charged with five lions passant) was thenceforward used as the distinguishing York mark, which in the following tables the Author places under the generic term "town mark".   There were added, also in pursuance of the terms of the Act of 1700-1, the lion's head erased and the figure of Britannia, to mark the higher standard during its compul-

---

* The date-letter N of the year 1694-5 is an italic capital, resembling the date-letter of 1669-70, but the mark of Wm. Busfield (free 1679) which accompanies the letter assigned to 1694-5, is of a form not used by that goldsmith before 1689, and Mr. H. B. McCall, F.S.A., who has examined all the Church plate of Yorkshire, came to the conclusion that the York date-letter used in 1695 was an italic N "somewhat though not exactly like the N of 1670". See *Yorkshire Church Plate*, Vol. I. p. 114.
† 12 Wm. III. c. 4.

sory use; the number of marks struck on York plate having been thereby increased from three to five. The maker's mark was changed also in compliance with the Act, and was from 1700 to 1719 formed of the first two letters of the surname, as in the case of London. The date-letter first used in the 18th century was a cursive capital A; for the next year (1701-2) it was the Roman capital B in a square punch Date-letters, 1701 to 1717. with truncated corners; for 1702-3 the letter was a nondescript C, followed in 1703, 1705, and 1706 by the Roman capitals D, F, and G. No other letters of that cycle have been found except those for 1708-9, 1711-12 and 1713-14, which are Court letters, as illustrated in the following tables.

In 1717 the practice of assaying plate at York was discontinued Assaying of plate at York discontinued, 1717. and not resumed until more than half a century afterwards. John Langwith and Joseph Buckle, who were then the principal goldsmiths in York, entered into an agreement with the Newcastle Goldsmiths' Company for having their plate assayed at the Newcastle assay office and stamped with the Newcastle marks from 1717 onwards by paying an annual fee.

For the years between 1714 and 1779 no York-marked plate has Resumed about 1780. been found, and as the office was closed when the parliamentary inquiry was held in 1773, it seems probable that no assays were made there during that entire period. Articles of a few years later are found marked with the date-letters D, F, G, H and J respectively. On these examples Date-letters, 1780 to 1857. the town mark is in an angular shield, and the leopard's head crowned and lion passant take the places of the lion's head erased and figure of Britannia of the preceding cycle. The communion cup with date letter J, mentioned in Table VIII., has the duty mark, and cannot have been assayed earlier than December, 1784, therefore the flagons marked F, although dated 1780, cannot be earlier than 1781, unless an I was used as well as J. It seems more probable that the money was given for the flagons in 1780, and that they were made and marked the following year. The town mark is in an oval stamp from 1787, when a new alphabet of small Roman letters was commenced. In 1798 the small letters were discontinued and capitals resumed. From 1812 to 1837 small Black letters were used, and from 1837 the letters were Roman capitals, the last letter (for 1856-7) being V and not U as shown in *Old English Plate.*

In 1858 the office was finally closed; and as great irregularities,

York Assay
Office finally
closed, 1858.
such as the marking of plate without assay, are said to have taken place during the later years of its existence, it is not likely ever again to be re-opened.

Many of the marks given in the following tables have not been hitherto represented, and several date-letters, notably the 𝕭 of 1608, the 𝕲 of 1613, the 𝕾 of 1624, the 𝖁 of 1629-30, and a number of makers' marks which will be found here correctly recorded in *facsimile*, have not been accurately represented in any other tables.

Marks on
wrought gold as-
sayed at York.
The marks on wrought gold assayed at York were the same as on plate until 1798. After that date probably no gold was assayed there. If it had been, the remarks would be applicable which occur on page 76 with reference to the substitution of the crown and figures in place of the lion passant on gold of 22 and 18 carats fine respectively, and of figures only in place of the lion passant on gold of the lower standards.

MARKS ON YORK PLATE.

TABLE I.

THREE STAMPS AS BELOW.

	TOWN MARK.	DATE LETTER.	MAKER'S MARK.	MAKER'S NAME.	ARTICLES AND OWNERS.
ELIZ. 1559-60		A		... ...	Date-letter conjectured.
1560-1		B		... ...	Do. do.
1561-2		C		... ...	Do. do.
*1562-3	⊛	D	RG	Robert Gylmyn.	Seal-top spoon : The Author's Collection.
1563-4		E		... ...	Date-letter conjectured.
1564-5	⊛	F	M	... ...	Seal-top spoon : Mr. G. Alderson Smith.
1565-6		G		... ...	Date-letter conjectured.
1566-7	⊛	H	ICI	Christopher Hunton.	Mount of stoneware jug.†
1567-8		I		... ...	Date-letter conjectured.
1568-9	⊛	K	RB / TS / XX / RG	Robert Beckwith. / Thomas Symson. /	Communion cup : St. Mary, Bishop Hill, junr., York.† / Com. cup : Great Salkeld, Cumb. / Com. cup and paten cover : Messrs. Crichton.
1569-70	⊛	L	RG	Robert Gylmyn.	{ Seal-top spoon : Mr. W. Boore. / Communion cup : Handsworth.
1570-1		M	♡	Name not traced.	{ Seal-top spoon : Messrs. Lambert. / Also (with K for 1568) com. cup : Elton.
1571-2		N		... ...	Date-letter conjectured.
1572-3	⊛	O	{ ⊞ / FW	John Lund. / William Foster.	Apostle spoon (pierced bowl) : Dullington Church, Northants. / Seal-top spoon : Messrs. Christie.
1573-4		P		... ...	Date-letter conjectured.
1574-5	,,	Q	GK	George Kitchen.	Communion cup : dated " 1575 ".*
1575-6	⊛	R	,,	,, ,,	Seal-top spoon : Mr. W. Boore.
1576-7		S	fw	Thomas Waddie.	Master spoon : The Author's Coll'n.
1577-8	,,	T		Indistinguishable.	Communion cup : Adwick-on-Dearne, Yorks.
1578-9		V		... ...	Date-letter conjectured.
1579-80		W		... ...	Do. do.
1580-1		X		... ...	Do. do.
1581-2		Y		... ...	Do. do.
1582-3	,,	Z	WR	William Rawnson.	Com. cup : Long Preston, Yorks.

* A York spoon of c. 1490-1500, having a fig-shaped bowl and tapering stem terminating with an ornamental Gothic finial, in the collection of Mr. Harvey Clark, has been noted by the Author. The town mark, stamped in the bowl, resembles that of 1562-3 above, but has a more archaic appearance.

† Noted when in the hands of Bond Street Dealers. Also communion cups at St. Maurice, York, Barnby, Ampleforth and Askham-Bryan, Yorks, and Crosthwaite, Cumberland,

MARKS ON YORK PLATE.

TABLE II.

THREE STAMPS AS BELOW.

	TOWN MARK.	DATE LETTER.	MAKER'S MARK.	MAKER'S NAME.		ARTICLES AND OWNERS.
1583-4		a	WR	Wm.	Rawnson.	Communion cup : Mr. W. Boore.
1584-5		b	,,	,,	,	Do. do. : Troutbeck.
1585-6		c		...	... ...	Date-letter conjectured.
1586-7		d		...	... ...	Do. do.
1587-8	,,	e	GK	Geo.	Kitchen.	Seal-top spoon : Late Mr. W. Old.
1588-9		f		...	... ...	Date-letter conjectured.
1589-90		g		...	... ...	Do. do.
1590-1	,,	h	GK	Geo.	Kitchen.	Seal-top spoon : Messrs. Crichton.
1591-2		i		...	... ...	Date-letter conjectured.
1592-3		k	WR / RG	Wm. / Robt.	Rawnson. / Gylmyn.	Com. cup : Crathorne, near Yarn-on-Tees. / Seal-top spoon : Staniforth Coll'n.
1593-4	,,	l	WH	? Wm.	Hutchinson.	Do. do. : Messrs. Crichton.
1594-5	,,	m	GK	Geo.	Kitchen.	Seal-top spoon : Do. do.
1595-6		n		...	... ...	Date-letter conjectured.
1596-7		o		...	... ...	Do. do.
1597-8	,,	p	CH	Chris.	Harrington.	Small cup, dated 1598 : Mr. Connell.
1598-9		q		...	... ...	Date-letter conjectured.
1599 / 1600	,,	r	FT	Fras.	Tempest.	Seal-top spoon : Messrs. Spink.
1600-1		s		...	... ...	Date-letter conjectured.
1601-2	,,	t	,,	,,	,,	Cup on baluster stem : Messrs. Christie.
1602-3		u		...	... ...	Date-letter conjectured.
JAS. I. 1603-4		w		...	... ...	Do. do.
1604-5	,,	x	CH	Chris.	Harrington.	Seal-top spoon : Messrs. Crichton.
1605-6		y		...	... ...	Date-letter conjectured.
1606-7		z		...	... ...	Do. do.

MARKS ON YORK PLATE.

TABLE III.

THREE STAMPS AS BELOW.

	TOWN MARK.	DATE LETTER.	MAKER'S MARK.	MAKER'S NAME.		ARTICLES AND OWNERS.
1607-8	[mark]	[A]	[IM]	John	Moody ?'	Coco-nut cup : Mr. J. A. Holms.
			[RC]	Robt.	Casson.	Communion cup : Egton.
1608-9	[mark]	[B]	[PP]	Peter	Pearson.	Com. cup : Brantingham, nr. Brough, Yorks.
1609-10	,,	[C]	[FT]	Fras.	Tempest.	Com. cup : Old Cottam, nr. Driffield, Yorks.
1610-1	,,	[D]	[PP]	Peter	Pearson.	Apostle spoon : Mr. B. Jefferis.
			,,	,,	,,	Com. cup : Mr. John Dale, Netherbank.
1611-2	,,	[E]	[CH]	Chris.	Harrington.	Cup on baluster stem : Mr. Colburne.
1612-3	,,	[F]	[FT]	Fras.	Tempest.	Seal-top spoon : Messrs. Dobson & Sons.
1613-4	[mark]	[G]	[PP] [C]	Peter	Pearson.	The "Wrightington" cup : Trinity House, Hull.
1614-5	,,	[H]	,,	,,	,,	Beaker : Messrs. Christie.
1615-6	[mark]	[I]	[CM]	Chris.	Mangy.	Com. cup, dated "1615": St. Cuthbert's, York.
			[FT]	Fras.	Tempest.	Com. cup : Irthington, Cumberland.
1616-7	,,	[K]	,,	,,	,,	Com. cup : Cleator, Cumberland.
1617-8		[L]		...	...	Date-letter conjectured.
1618-9	,,	[M]	[SC]	Sem.	Casson.	Com. cup : Bilbrough, Yorks.
1619-20	,,	[N]	[PP]	Peter	Pearson.	Com. cup: dated "1619": Bempton, Bridlington, Yorkshire.
1620-1	,,	[O]	[SC]	Sem.	Casson.	Small bowl or "taster": Mr. W. Boore.
1621-2	,,	[P]	[PP]	Peter	Pearson.	Foot-rim (dated "1622") of "Scrope Mazer": York Minster.
1622-3	[mark]	[Q]	,,	,,	,,	Com. cup : Holy Trinity Church, Goodramgate, York.
1623-4	[mark]	[R]	[RW] [D]	Robt.	Williamson.	Com. cup and cover, inscribed "Houlden 1638": Howden, Yorks.
				...	...	Seal-top spoon : Mr. E. W. Colt.
1624-5 CHAS. I	[mark]	[S]	[TH]	Thos.	Harrington.	Seal-top spoon : Messrs. Christie. Also S. C. as 1620, com. cup : Naburn.
1625-6	[mark]	[T]	[RH]	Robt.	Harrington.	Seal-top spoon : Mr. Crichton.
1626-7	,,	[U]	[mark]	?		{ Com. cup : Cawthorn, near Barnsley, Yorks. { Apostle spoon : Messrs. Crichton.
1627-8	,,	[W]	[IP]	James	Plummer.	Com. cup : Hayton, near York.*
1628-9		[X]		...	...	Date-letter conjectured.
1629-30	,,	[Y]	[CM]	Chris.	Mangy.	Com. cup and cover inscribed "Bewcastle, 1630": Bewcastle Church, Brampton, Camb.
1630-1	,,	[Z]	[W]	Thomas	Waite.	Com. cup dated 1630: All Saints, North Street, York.

* There was formerly at Thornton-Watlass a communion cup of this year. It was sold for eleven shillings to a dealer ! ! ! The representatives of a deceased incumbent having found the cup somewhat tarnished, in the vicarage, believed it to have been the property of the Vicar, and the marks not having been recognised as silver marks, they were persuaded that the cup was of base metal. This circumstance illustrates the necessity for provincial marks being more widely known.

MARKS ON YORK PLATE.

TABLE IV.

THREE STAMPS AS BELOW.

	TOWN MARK.	DATE LETTER.	MAKER'S MARK.	MAKER'S NAME.		ARTICLES AND OWNERS.
1631-2		a	SC	Sem.	Casson.	Beaker : Messrs. Christie. / Communion cup : Calverley, Yorks.
1632-3		b	,,	,,	,,	Do. do. : St. Helen's, York.
1633-4	,,	c	RH	Robt.	Harrington.	Do. do. : Millom near Carnforth, Yorks.
1634-5	,,	d	TH	Thos.	Harrington.	Communion cup : Threlkeld, Cumb.
1635-6	,,	e	I·T	John	Thomason or Thompson.	Paten cover of cup : Torver, Coniston, Cumb.
1636-7		f	RH	Robt.	Harrington.	Communion cup : Lanercost, near Bampton, Cumb.
1637-8		g	TH	Thos.	Harrington.	Communion cup : Kirk Andrews-upon-Esk, Cumb.
1638-9	,,	h	RW	Robt. or Richd.	Williamson, Senr. Waite.	Communion cup, dated 1638 : Thorner, near Leeds.
1639-40	,,	i	FB	Francis	Bryce.	Seal-top spoon : The Author's Coll'n.
1640-1		j		...	...	Date-letter conjectured.
1641-2	,,	k	I·T	John	Thomason.	Communion cup : Melsonby, near Darlington.
1642-3	,,	l	TH	Thos.	Harrington.	Communion cup : Wheldrake, Yorks.
1643-4	,,	m	I·T	John	Thomason.	Small beaker : Mr. G. Lambert
1644-5		n		...	...	Date-letter conjectured
1645-6	,,	o	CM	Chris.	Mangy.	Communion cup : Speeton
1646-7		p		...	...	Date-letter conjectured
1647-8		q		...	...	Do. do.
1648-9		r		...	...	Do. do.
COMWTH. 1649-50		s	IP	James	Plummer.	Tankard from the Franks family of Beverley.
1650-1		t	,,	,,	,,	Corporation Mace : Richmond, Yorks.
1651-2	,,	u	,,	.,	,,	Six seal-top spoons : Messrs. Crichton.
1652-3	,,	v	,,	,,	,,	Seal-top spoon : Mr. E. W. Colt.
1653-4		w		...	...	Date-letter conjectured.
1654-5	,,	x	TW	Thomas	Waite.	Communion cup : Stockton-on-Forest, Yorks.
1655-6	,,	y	,,	,,	,,	Beaker-shaped cup ; Cumberworth, nr. Huddersfield.
1656-7	,,	z	PM	Philemon Marsh.		Cup : Messrs. Hancock.

Period of Royalist and Parliamentary Wars. Probably very little plate wrought. *(bracket spanning 1643-4 to 1648-9)*

MARKS ON YORK PLATE.

TABLE V.

THREE STAMPS AS BELOW.

	TOWN MARK.	DATE LETTER	MAKER'S MARK	MAKER'S NAME.		ARTICLES AND OWNERS.
1657-8		A	IP	John	Plummer.	Com. paten : Stillingfleet, near York.
1658-9		B	,,	,,	,,	Lion tankard : York Corporation.
1659-60		C	WW / IT	Wm. / John	Waite. / Thomason.	Two-handled cup : Mr. Lowe. / Porringer and cover : Mr. S. J. Phillips.
1660-1	,,	D	IP	John	Plummer.	Com. cup : Thornton, near Pickering, Yorks.
1661-2	,,	E	,,	,,	,,	Large seal-top spoon : Staniforth Coll'n.
1662-3		F	,, / GM	,, / George	,, / Mangy.	Com. cup : Birkin, nr. Ferrybridge, Y'ks. / Small bowl : Judge Wynne Ffoulkes.
1663-4		G	MB	Marmaduke Best.		Com. cup and paten : Bolton Abbey.
1664-5	,,	H	RW	Robt.	Williamson.	Do. do. : Tadcaster, Y'ks.
1665-6	,,	I	IP	John	Plummer.	Peg tankard and "Strickland" death spoon : Mr. R. D. Ryder.
1666-7		K	TM	Thos.	Mangy.	Rose-water dish, "given 1668" : Hull Corporation.
1667-8	,,	L	MB	Marmaduke Best.		Com. cup, dated "1668" : Cartmel, Lancs.
1668-9	,,	M	PM	Philemon	Marsh.	Lining of "Scrope Mazer" ; York Minst.
1669-70	,,	N	TM	Thomas	Mangy.	Peg tankard : The Holms Collection.
1670-1		O	MB	Marmaduke Best.		A chamber utensil : Mansion Ho., York.
1671-2	,,	P	,, / RK	,, / Roland	,, / Kirby.	Gold cup, dated 1672 : Do. do. / Small cruet : Messrs. Christie.
1672-3		Q	IT	John	Thompson.	Com. paten : St. Cuthbert's, York.
1673-4	,,	R	MB	Marmaduke Best.		Tankard : Mansion Ho., York.
1674-5	,,	S	RW / TM	Robt / Thos.	Williamson. / Mangy.	Com. cup : St. Mary, Bishop Hill, sen., York. / Com. plate, dated 1676 : Ripon Minster.
1675-6	,,	T	WM	Wm.	Mascall.	Low covered cup : Mr. Crichton.
1676-7	,,	U	HL	Henry	Lee.	Tankard : Do.
1677-8	,,	V	WB	Wm.	Busfield.	Com. cup and paten, "exchd. 1678" : St. Michael's, Spurrier Gate, York.
1678-9	,,	W	IP	John	Plummer.	Com. cup, "given to Troutbeck Church, 1688".
1679-80		X	IT	John	Thompson.	Spoon, flat stem, trifid end : Mr. Crichton.
1680-1	,,	Y	WB	Wm.	Busfield.	Com. cup : St. Lawrence, York.
1681-2	,,	Z	TM	Thos.	Mangy.	Small com. cup, dated 1684 : Do. do.

MARKS ON YORK PLATE.

TABLE VI.

THREE STAMPS AS BELOW.

	TOWN MARK.	DATE LETTER.	MAKER'S MARK.	MAKER'S NAME.		ARTICLES AND OWNERS.
1682-3		A	GG	George	Gibson.	Mts. of coco-nut cup : Mr. Crichton.
*1683-4	,,	B	WB	Wm.	Busfield.	Large paten: St. Martin-le-Grand, Coney St., York.
1684-5 JAS. II.		C	JC / JP	John John	Camidge. Plummer.	Trifid spoon : The Author. Paten cover of c. cup : St. Maurice, York.
1685-6		D	RC	Richd.	Chew.	Trifid spoon : Mr. Frank Bradbury.
1686-7	,,	E	IS	John	Smith.	Small tankard : Messrs. Lambert.
1687-8	,,	F	IO	John	Oliver.	Alms-dish : St. Michael-le-Belfry, York.
1688-9	,,	G	CW	Chris.	Whitehill.	Com. cup : Oswaldkirk, nr. York.
WM.& MY. 1689-90	,,	H	WB	Wm.	Busfield.	Do. do. : Holtby, Yorks.
1690-1		J	RW	Robt.	Williamson.	Trifid spoon ; also tumbler by Wm. Busfield : Messrs. Crichton.
1691-2		K	CR	Charles	Rhoades.	Spoon, flat stem, trifid end : Mr. Lowe.
1692-3	,,	L	CW	Chris.	Whitehill.	Tankard : Mr. H. Hardcastle.
1693-4	,,	M	MG	Mark	Gill.	Fluted porringer : Messrs. Debenham & Storr.
1694-5		N	WB	Wm.	Busfield.	Noted by the Author.
1695-6 WM. III.		O	CR	Clement	Reed.	Com. cup : Mytton, nr. Whalley, Yorks.
1696-7	,,	P	WB	Wm.	Busfield.	Do. do. : Rylstone, nr. Skipton, Yorks.
1697-8	,,	Q	IS	John	Smith.	Tumbler : Mr. Thos. Boynton.
†1698-9	,,	R		Wm. Busfield as above.		Plain tumbler cup : Messrs. Christie.
1699 / 1700		S		...	...	Date-letter stamped on small brass plate ·from the Assay Office.

* 1683-4		B	TM	Thomas	Mangy.	Communion cup : Todwick.

† Possibly a variant of the date-letter for 1698-9. Stamped on a small brass plate from the Assay Office.

MARKS ON YORK PLATE.

TABLE VII.

FIVE STAMPS AS BELOW.

	TOWN MARK.	BRIT-ANNIA.	LION'S HEAD ERASED.	DATE LETTER.	MAKER'S MARK.	MAKER'S NAME.	ARTICLES AND OWNERS.
1700-1	✠	[mark]	[mark]	A	Gu	Chas. Goldsborough (probably)	Rat-tail spoon: Mr. Alan Garnet.
*1701-2 ANNE.	✠	[mark]	[mark]	B	{ Tu / BE	Danl. Turner. / John Best.	Spoon, flat stem, trifid end, pricked "1702": Mr. Crichton. / Plain tumbler: Mr. Colburne.
1702-3	,,	,,	,,	C	Bu	Wm. Busfield.	Com. cup: St. Michael's, Malton, Yorks.
1703-4	,,	,,	,,	D	LA	John Langwith.	Noted by the Author.
1704-5							
1705-6	,,	,,	,,	F	,,	,, ,,	Communion cup: Addingham.
1706-7	,,	,,	,,	G	RH	Chas. Rhoades.	Tall beaker: Mr. Kenneth Dows.
1707-8					LA	John Langwith.	Com. cup, dated "1715"; Hawkes-well, Yorks.
1708-9	,,	,,	,,	ð	WI	Wm. Williamson.	Com. cup: Kirkby Ravensworth, Yorks.
1709-10					wa	?	Plain tumbler: Birmingham Assay Office.
1710-11							
1711-2	,,	,,	,,	m	LA	John Langwith.	Rat-tail spoon: Mr. Lowe.
1712-3							
1713-4	,,	,,	,,	O	,,	,, ,,	Salver on foot: Mr. Colburne.
GEO. I. 1714-5							
1715-6							
1716-7							

Very little, if any, plate was assayed and marked at York during the sixty years from 1716 to 1776. None has been found bearing a date-letter for any year between 1713 and 1779. In 1717 the Assay Office was closed; it was still closed in 1773 when the Parliamentary inquiry was being held, but was reopened shortly afterwards.

* [mark] Possibly a variant of date-letter for 1701-2. Stamped on small brass plate from the Assay Office.

MARKS ON YORK PLATE.

The date-letter F on communion plate at All Saints', York, and at Burnsall, in Yorkshire, probably stands for the year 1781-2. There is a communion cup without a date-letter, made by Hampston & Prince of York, with the inscribed date 1777, at Selby Abbey, Yorkshire. Assuming the Holme communion cup, with date-letter J and King's head incuse, to have been made in 1784-5, the alphabet of Roman capitals was probably commenced in or about 1776, but no letter of this cycle earlier than the D of 1779 is known to the Author.

TABLE VIII.

FIVE STAMPS UNTIL 1784-5, THENCEFORWARD SIX STAMPS AS BELOW.

	Town Mark.	Lion Passant.	Leopard's Head Crowned.	Date Letter.	King's Head.	Maker's Mark.	MAKER'S NAME.	ARTICLES AND OWNERS.
1776-7				A			... ...	Date-letter conjectured.
1777-8				B			... ...	Do. do.
1778-9				C			... ...	Do. do.
1779-80		🦁	👑	D		HP	J. Hampston & J. Prince	Communion cup: Warthill. Bowls (1783): Messrs. Crichton.
1780-1				E			... ...	Date-letter conjectured.
1781-2	🛡	..	..	F	..	,,	,, ,,	Communion flagons: All Saints', North Street, York.
1782-3	..	..	..	G	..	,,	,, ,,	Paten on foot; All Saints', North Street, York.
1783-4	..	..	..	H	{ HP	,,	,, ,,	Com. cup: Huntington, nr. York. (no town mark.)
1784-5	..	..	..	J	👑 { HP	,,	Hampston & Prince.	Plate: Messrs. Crichton. Com. cup: Holme, nr. York.
1785-6				K			... ...	Date-letter conjectured.
1786-7				L			... ...	Do. do.

The above alphabet was probably not continued beyond L, as a new alphabet of Roman letters was begun in 1787 with a capital A followed by small letters until 1797 when the use of small letters was discontinued, and for the remainder of the cycle capital letters were used.

Some of the marks illustrated in the preceding and succeeding tables have been found on many articles in addition to those mentioned, but it seems unnecessary to multiply instances beyond a sufficient number to establish the tables. The Author has, however, preserved an extensive list of additional examples.

MARKS ON YORK PLATE.

TABLE IX.

SIX STAMPS AS BELOW.

	TOWN MARK.	LION PASSANT.	LEOPARD'S HEAD CROWNED.	KING'S HEAD.	DATE LETTER.	MAKER'S MARK.	MAKER'S NAME.		ARTICLES AND OWNERS.
1787-8	⬡	🦁	▨	👑	**A**	▨	J.	Hampston &	Noted by the Author.
1788-9					**b**		J.	Prince.	Date-letter conjectured.
1789-90	,,	,,	,,	,,	**c**	,,	,,	,,	Table-spoons : Mr. Greenwood.
1790-1	,,	,,	,,	,,	**d**	,,	,,	,,	Com. flagon, dated 1791 : St. John's, Micklegate, York.
1791-2	,,	,,	,,	,,	**e**	,,	,,	,,	Com. flagon, dated 1792 : Kirk Deighton, York.
1792-3					**f**		...	... ...	Date-letter conjectured.
1793-4	,,	,,	,,	,,	**g**	,,	,,	,,	Table-forks : Mr. Greenwood.
1794-5					**h**		...	... ...	Date-letter conjectured.
1795-6	,,	,,	,,	,,	**i**	▨	,,	,,	Com. cup : Askham Bryan, Yorks.
1796-7	,,	,,	,,	🧑	**K**	,,	,,	,,	Goblet : Mr. J. H. Walter, Drayton, Norwich.
1797-8					**l or L**		...	... ...	Date-letter conjectured.
1798-9	,,	,,	,,	,,	**M**	HP &Co	H.	Prince & Co.	Com. flagon, dated 1798 : Warter, Yorks.
1799 1800	,,	,,	,,	,,	**N**	,,	,,	,,	Table-forks : Mr. Greenwood.
1800-1	,,	,,	,,	,,	**O**	H⋆C	,,	,,	Plain cup : Mr. Bradford.
1801-2	,,	,,	,,	,,	**P**	HP &C	,,	,,	Tea-spoons : Mr. Lowe.
1802-3	,,	,,	,,	,,	**Q**	,,	,,	,,	Gravy-spoon : Do.
1803-4	,,	,,	,,	,,	**R**	,,	,,	,,	Beakers and waiter : Messrs. Crichton.
1804-5	,,	,,	,,	,,	**S**	,,	,,	,,	Trowel : Mr. Colburne.
1805-6	,,	,,	,,	,,	**T**	,,	,,	,,	Noted by the Author.
1806-7					**U**		...	... ...	Date-letter conjectured.
1807-8	,,	,,	,,	,,	**V**	RC JB	Robt.	Cattle &	Communion cups : St. John's, Micklegate, York.
1808-9		,,	,,	,,	**W**	,,	J.	Barber.	Skewer : Messrs. Crichton.
1809-10		,,	,,	,,	**X**	,,	,,	,,	Salt-cellars and spoon : Mr. Williams.
1810-1	,,	,,	,,	,,	**Y**	,,	,,	,,	Table-spoon : Messrs. Robinson & Fisher.
1811-2					**Z**		...	... ...	Date-letter conjectured.

1805-6 **T**   1807-8 **V**   1809-10 **X**   Possibly variants of date-letters in above cycle. Stamped on small brass-plate from the Assay Office.

▨ Also example of leopard's head, probably used from 1790 to 1836. Stamped on small brass plate from the Assay Office.

1787 to 1796 🧑   1796 to 1815-6 🧑   1816 to 1820 🧑   1820 to 1830 🧑   🧑 Variants of Sovereigns' heads. Stamped on small brass plate from the Assay Office.

MARKS ON YORK PLATE.

TABLE X.

SIX STAMPS AS BELOW.

	TOWN MARK.	LION PASSANT.	LEOPARD'S HEAD CROWNED.	KING'S HEAD.	DATE LETTER.	MAKER'S MARK.	MAKER'S NAME.		ARTICLES AND OWNERS.
*1812-3	✠	🦁	👑	👤	a	JB WW	James Barber & Wm. Whitwell }		Dessert-forks: Messrs. Crichton.
1813-4					b		...	... ...	Date-letter recorded.
1814-5					c		...	... ...	Do. do.
1815-6	,,	,,	,,	,,	d	,,	,,	,,	Dessert-spoons: Messrs. Crichton.
1816-7					e		...	... ...	Date-letter recorded.
1817-8	,,	,,	,,	,,	f	,,	,,	,,	Salt-cellars and milk-jug: Messrs. Crichton.
1818-9	,,	,,	,,	,,	g	,,	,,	,,	Com. flagon: St. Cuthbert's, York.
1819-20					h		...	... ...	Date-letter recorded.
GEO. IV. 1820-1		,,	,,	,,	i	,,	,,	,,	Table-forks: Messrs. Crichton.
1821-2		,,	,,	,,	k	,,	,,	,,	Table-forks and snuffers tray: Messrs. Crichton.
1822-3					l		...	... ...	Date-letter recorded.
1823-4					m		...	... ...	Do. do.
1824-5	,,	,,	,,	,,	n	JB &Cᵒ	Jas. Barber & Co.		Com. cup: St. John's, Micklegate, York.
1825-6	,,	,,	,,	,,	o	BC&N	Jas. Barber, Geo. Cattle & Wm. North }		Mustard-pot: Messrs. Crichton.
1826-7	,,	,,	,,	,,	p	,,	,,	,,	Noted by the Author.
1827-8					q		...	... ...	Date letter recorded.
1828-9	,,	,,	,,	,,	r	,,	,,	,,	Table-forks: Mr. Maurice Freeman.
1829-30	,,	,,	,,	,,	s	JB GC WN	,,	,,	Fish-slice: Messrs. Crichton.
WM. IV. 1830-1	3	,,	,,	👑	t	JB GC WN	,,	,,	Table-forks: Mr. Arthur J. Brown.
1831-2		,,	,,	,,	u	,,	,,	,,	Communion paten: Slingsby Yorks.
1832-3					v		...	... ...	Date-letter recorded.
1833-4					w		...	... ...	Do. do.
1834-5					x		...	... ...	Do. do.
1835-6					y		...	... ...	Do. do.
1836-7					z		...	... ...	Do. do.

* In examples of marks from 1812 onward, the leopard's head is sometimes found with whiskers and sometimes without.

1812-3	a	1813-4	b	1815-6	d	1819-20 h

1820-1	i	1821-2	k	1823-4	m	1831-2 u	1833-4 w

Possibly variants of date-letters in above cycle. Stamped on small brass plate from the Assay Office.

MARKS ON YORK PLATE.

TABLE XI.

SIX STAMPS TILL 1848, FIVE AFTERWARDS AS BELOW.

	TOWN MARK.	LION PASSANT.	LEOPARD'S HEAD CROWNED. TILL 1848	QUEEN'S HEAD.	DATE LETTER.	MAKER'S MARK.	MAKER'S NAME.	ARTICLES AND OWNERS.
VICT. 1837-3	🛡	🦁	👑	◯	A	J B W N	Jas. Barber & Wm. North }	Waiter: Messrs. Crichton.
1838-9	,,	,,	,,	,,	B	,,	,, ,,	Noted by the Author.
1839-40	,,	,,	,,	,,	C	,,	,, ,,	Communion cup: Otley.
1840-1	,,	,,	,,	👤	D	,,	,, ,,	Communion plate: Bishopthorpe.
1841-2	,,	,,	,,	,,	E	,,	,, ,,	Noted by the Author.
1842-3	,,	,,	,,	,,	F	,,	,, ,,	Com. cup: St. Maurice, York.
1843-4	,,	,,	,,	,,	G	,,	,, ,,	Noted by the Author.
1844-5	,,	,,	,,	,,	H	,,	,, ,,	Paten: Dishforth.
1845-6	,,	,,	,,	,,	I	,,	,, ,,	Alms plate: Bishopthorpe.
1846-7					K		... ...	Date-letter conjectured.
1847-8	,,	,,	,,	,,	L	,,	,, ,,	Com. cup: St. Cuthbert's, York.
1848-9	,,	,,		,,	M	JB	James Barber	Paten: Scrayingham.
1849-50	,,	,,		,,	N	,,	,, ,,	Do. do.
1850-1	,,	,,		,,	O	,,	,, ,,	{ Noted by the Author: also (with maker's mark IG) communion paten: Snainton, Yorks.
1851-2					P		... ...	Date-letter conjectured.
1852-3					Q		... ...	Do. do.
1853-4					R		... ...	Do. do.
1854-5					S		... ...	Do. do.
1855-6					T		... ...	Do. do.
1856-7	,,	,,		,,	V	JB	James Barber	Communion cup: St. Helen's, York.*

*There is at St. Michael-le-Belfry, York, a communion paten stamped with the same marks as those on the communion cup at St. Helens, except that the town-mark is not visible. These examples are understood to have been amongst the last of the plate marked at York, as the office was closed almost immediately afterwards.

1851-2 P 1852-3 Q Possibly date-letters used in the above Cycle. Stamped on small brass plate from the Assay Office.

NAMES OF YORK GOLDSMITHS.

[FROM A.D. 1313 TO 1851.]

ARRANGED CHRONOLOGICALLY FROM THE LIST COMPILED BY
MR. R. C. HOPE, F.S.A.

Name of Goldsmith.	Earliest Date Found.	Free.	Latest Date or Death.
Adœ Munketon	1313		
William Scaiceby		1314	
William de Chester		1333	
John Custance		1339	
John Cayne (Goldbeater)		1340	
John de Scardeburge		1347	
William de Hundmanby		1349	
Thomas de Blackburn		1354	
John Pownell		,,	
William Hovingham		1355	
Henry de Plena		1360	
John de Scarges		1361	
Thomas de Wilberforce		,,	
John de Snaith		,,	
William de Haunby		,,	
William Gaynell		,,	
John de Fforth		1362	
Thomas Winter		,,	
Robert Anghoo		,,	
John de Colonia		1365	
William Hiller		1367	
William Hillensame		1368	
Alan de Alnwyck			d 1374
John Dray (Goldbeater)		1374	
John Rownell		,,	
John de Pinchbeck		,,	
John de Upsale		1376	
John de Parish		,,	
Thomas de Clyff		,,	
Richard de Ede		,,	
John de Grantham		,,	
Wakelenn Wyttecon		,,	
William del Wyke		1384	
Warymebolt de Arlhum		1385	d 1430
John Cateby		,,	
Richard de Aselby		,,	
John Symonet		1386	
Robert de Pickering		,,	d 1403
Henry Wyman		,,	d 1419
William Sampson		1387	
John de Colonia		1388	
Thomas de Menseton		,,	
Richard White		,,	
Peter Porter		1389	
Henry de Stroesburgh		1390	
Henry Selander		,,	
William Fox			d 1393
John de Clyveland (Searcher, 1411)	1393		1411
John de Ipswich (Goldbeater)		,,	
Robert Russell		1394	
William Porter		1395	
John Chamberlayne		,,	
Thomas de Thwayte (Goldbeater)			d 1395
William de Gatesheved		1395	d 1433
Thomas Fforester		1396	
Alan de Bedall		,,	
Gilbert Colonia		,,	
Thomas Foster		,,	
John Duch		1397	1411
John de Colonia		,,	
Roger Grandeson		,,	
William Skyres (Searcher, 1411)	1398	1398	1411
Henry Frese		,,	
John de Berdnay		,,	
Henry Fefe		,,	
Henry Foster		1399	
Jonyn	1400		
Wormod	,,		
Thomas Alberwick		1400	
John Angowe	1401		
Robert Barry			1401
Herman de Tulk (or Gulk)		1402	
William Selar			d 1402
Thomas Holme		1404	
Nicholas Slingsby		1407	
Peter Bruyle		1410	
John Welling		1411	
John Breton		,,	d 1474
John Bewe		,,	
John Paraunt		,,	
Thomas Bright		,,	1452
Thomas Appilton		1412	
William Teesdale		1413	
Bernard Ffemyndyn		,,	
Johannes Seger dictus "Hanse"		1414	
John Watson		,,	
Richard Warter		1415	1421
John Ellis		,,	
Richard Waters		,,	
Walter Spendeluff or Spendlove		,,	1422
William Duke		1416	1440
John Close		,,	d 1442
William Snawsehill		,,	d 1437
John Watson		1417	
John Newland		1419	d 1465
John Wynoll		1420	
Thomas Atkinson	1420		
William de Halton	,,		1433
William Stockton	1422	1440	
William Appilton		1422	
Dirik Johnson		1423	
Nicholas Suldeney		1426	
John Dyke		,,	
John Rode		1429	

Name of Goldsmith.		Earliest Date Found.	Free.	Latest Date or Death.	Name of Goldsmith.		Earliest Date Found.	Free.	Latest Date or Death.
William	Frenland		1429		Thomas	Marshall		1487	
Thomas	Rhoades		"		William	Snawsehill		1488	
Herman	Horn		1430		John	Pulleyn or Polan		"	
William	Heend or Heynde		"	1467	Henry	Smith		"	
Robert	Hedwin		"		John	Colam (Cullam)	1485	1489	
John	Nevergest		1431		Thomas	Austin		1490	
John	Dalburgh		1432		William	Wilson (L'd Mayor 1513)		"	1544
Henry	Halton		1433		John	Hayster		"	
William	Snawsehill		1436		Thomas	Custance		1493	
John	Pudsey		1437	d 1458	Alexander	Jameson		1495	
William	Pudsey		"	1472	William	Newton		"	
John Van	Arstot		1438		Thomas	Bowes		1498	
Thomas	Whixley		1439		Robert	Cure		1500	
John	Buck or Buk		1440		Robert	Wells		"	
Thomas	Widder		"		Rad	Polan or Pulleyn (L'd Mayor 1537)		1501	1537
Nicholas	Colayne		"		Michael	Fennay		1502	
Walter	Gorras		"	1464	Thomas	Francis		"	
John	Field		1442		Thomas	Wilson		1504	
John	Close			d 1442	Richard	Plompton		"	
William	Rotherham		1443	d 1467	Robert	Hutchinson	1506		
John	Eston		1444		George	Gale (L'd Mayor 1534)		1512	1557
John	Nassing		"		William	Goldsmith		1515	
Thomas	Erberry		"		William	Richardson		1517	
Richard	Thwaites		1445		Edward	Burton		"	
Henry	Vancone-honey		"		Christopher	Weatley or Wallis		1518	
John	Colam		1448		Edward	Beckwith		1520	
Thomas	Bispham		1449		Thomas	Hayton		1525	
Thomas	Skelton	1450			John	Bell		"	
Robert	Bagot		1452		Radus	Beckwith		1527	d 1541
John	Gillian		1457		Martin	Soza		1529	
James	Symson		"		Oswald	Chapman		1531	
John	Luneburgh			d 1458	William de	Chester		1533	
Robert	Spicer	1458			Richard	Pigott		1534	
William	Goldsmith		1458	1517	Richard	Bargeman		"	
Thomas	Wells		1459	1499	John de	Ulveston		"	
Thomas	Watson		1460		Richard	Brerey (Sheriff 1555)		"	1562
John	Blackburn		"		Lawrence	Edmonson		"	"
Thomas	Hawkes		"	1462	William	Hopperton		1537	
John	Shingwell		1463		Robert	Wayter		1538	
——	Harmann		1464	1504	Philip	Caverd		1540	
John	Gorras		"	1485	John	Lund		1542	1575
John	Newland			d 1465	James	Howsold		"	
Barthol'm'w	Lampspring		1467		John	Marle		1543	
Thomas	Osbalston		1468		John	Harper		"	
Roland	Kirby		"		Richard	Crawfurth		1545	
Thomas	Gray (L'd Mayor 1497)		"	1497	Robert	Beckwith		1546	d 1585
James	Traves		1469		John	Bargeman		"	1588
Robert	Dickson		"		Thomas	Symson (Searcher 1561)		1547	1586
Christopher	Pudsey		1472		George	Symson		1548	1583
William	Omer		"		Richard	Sympson			1548
Peter	Andrew		1473		Thomas	Hedwin		1550	
Robert	Harrington		1475		Robert	Mower		"	
Harman	Holdsworth		1476		Miles	Gamhell		"	
James	Symson		1477		Robert	England		"	
William	Banes		1478		Milo	Snaweshill		"	
Robert	Hutchinson		"	1506	Robert	Gylmyn (Searcher 1561)		"	1593
John	Tyss or Tyson		"		William	Williamson		1551	
Thomas	Kirk			1479	Christopher	Hunton		"	d 1582
James	Kirk		1481	1490					
James	Simson		"						
John	Dam		1482						
Roger	Marshall		"						
William	Cook		1486						
William	Preston		"						

Name of Goldsmith.		Earliest Date Found.	Free.	Latest Date or Death.	Name of Goldsmith.		Earliest Date Found.	Free.	Latest Date or Death.
Roger	Thompson		1552		John	Hewitson		1606	
Thomas	Banks		1553	d 1572	Robert	Casson		,,	
Richard	Walton		1554	d 1567	Symond	Harrison		,,	
George	Gamhell		1555		Christopher	Mangy		1609	1645
William	Moorhouse		1556		George	Lacy		1612	
Thomas	Blake		1557	1584	Sem	Casson		1613	1635
George	Gylls		1558		Thomas	Waite		,,	d 1663
Rad	Eamonson		1559		Roger	Bargeman		1615	
Richard	Bellerby		,,		John	Waite		1616	
Robert	Denome		,,		Jasper	Foster		,,	
William	Todd		,,	1571	Robert	Harrington		,,	d 1647
John	Skelton		1560		William	Hayton		1617	
George	Kitchen		1561	d 1597	James	Plummer		1619	d 1663
William	Rawnson	1562		1593	John	Frost		1622	
Francis	Hodson or Godson }		1562		Robert	Williamson		1623	d 1667
Mark	Wray		1563	d 1582	Thomas	Harrington		1624	d 1642
Robert	Smith		1564		George	Robinson		1626	
Nicholas	Richard		,,		John	Robinson		,,	
John	Stocke (Searcher 1584)		1565		Henry	Wigglesworth		1629	
John	Bee		1566		William	Sharpe		1631	
Thomas	Hutton		1568	d 1576	John	Hall		1632	
William	Colton		1569		John	Thomason or Thompson (Ld. Mayor, 1685) }		1633	d 1692
William	Foster (Searcher 1584)		,,	d 1610	Francis	Bryne		1634	
William	Lord	1571			John	Lell		,,	
Thomas	Waddie (Searcher 1583)		1571	1609	Francis	Bryce		,,	d 1640
William	Hutchinson		,,		George	Prince	1636		
Martyn du	Biggin (Searcher 1582)		,,		James	Ellis		1636	
Kenrick	Ducheman			d 1571	Edward	Watson		1637	
William	Pearson (Searcher 1582)		1573	1600	Thomas	Cartwright		,,	
Peter	Dangen		1574		George	Mangy		1638	1672
John	Bewe		,,		Thomas	Freeman		,,	
John	Raylton		,,		Richard	Waite		1639	
John	Moody		1575		Robert	Clayton		1640	
Richard	Bonyman			1575	William	Prince		1645	
Joseph	Raylton		1576		Roger	Casson		,,	d 1657
Thomas	Howe		1577		Joshua	Geldart		,,	d 1663
Thomas	Taylor		,,		Francis	Buite		1648	
Thomas	Turner		1580	1586	Christopher	Heward		,,	
B.	Simson		1583		John	Plummer		,,	1688
George	Godson			1583	Henry	Mangy		1650	1672
William	Blake		1584		Thomas	Clarke		1652	
Henry	Sproke		,,		Philemon	Marsh		,,	d 1672
Thomas	Pindar		1587		Robert	Biliffe		1653	
John	Bargeman			1588	Robert	Williamson		,,	1682
John	Dickenson		1589		William	Waite		,,	d 1689
Richard	Gylmyn		,,		Marmaduke	Best		1657	1702
Francis	Johnson			1590	Thomas	Aire or Arie		1659	
John	Share or Shaw		1590		Thomas	Oliver		,,	
Leonard	Beckwith		,,	d 1592	Richard	Plummer		,,	
Edward	Freeman		1591	1638	Michael	Plummer		,,	1689
Christopher	Harrington		1595	d 1614	Leonard	Thompson	1660		d 1698
William	Frost		,,	d 1618	John	Camidge		1660	
Robert	Williamson		1597		Richard	Chewe		1664	
Francis	Tempest		,,	1619	Richard	Shewe		,,	
John	Thompson		1599		William	Mascall		,,	1682
Henry	Frost	1600			Thomas	Mangy		,,	1689
George	Pearson		1600		Richard	Waynes		1666	
Roger	Hornsey		1601		Rowland	Kirby		,,	1684
Thomas	Kitchen		1603		James	Todd		1671	
Charles	Clarke		,,		Isaac	Todd		,,	
Peter	Pearson		,,	1623	John	Geldart		1674	
George	Clarke	1604			William	Elsey		,,	
William	Hutchinson		1604		John	Williamson		,,	
					Timothy	Smith		,,	d 1679
					Henry	Lee		1675	
					George	Mangy		,,	

Name of Goldsmith.	Earliest Date Found.	Free.	Latest Date or Death.
Christopher Whitehill		1676	1693
John Oliver		"	"
Charles Rhoades (Sheriff, 1694)		1677	1707
William Busfield	1677	1679	1705
Edward Ward or Waud }		1678	
George Gibson		"	1684
Edmund Maud		"	1695
John Smith		1679	
Mark Gill (Ld. Mayor, 1697)		1680	1697
Charles Goldsborough		1681	
Roger South		"	
Arthur Mangy		"	d 1696
William Prince		1684	
Timothy Plummer		1688	
Thomas Tomlinson		1689	
Richard Marsh		1692	d 1705
Thomas Reed		1693	
John Best		1694	
William Williamson		"	
Thomas Waite			d 1695
Clement Reed	1695	1698	
John Langwith		1699	1714
Edward Parker	1700		1733
Daniel Turner		1700	d 1704
Christopher Whitehill		1713	
William Bentley		"	
Joseph Buckle		1715	d 1761
Robert Foster			d 1719
John Morrett		1721	
Thomas Barber		"	
Thomas Parker		"	
William Hudson		"	1741
John Bentley		1725	
Michael Bentley			1725
John Busfield		1727	1741
Samuel Todd			1733
Valentine Nicholas		1733	
Jonathan Atkinson		1735	1819
Osward Langwith	1736		
Edward Langwith		1740	
Stephen Buckle		"	1758
William Nicholson (alias Barbour)	1740	"	1741
Ambrose Beckwith	1741		1758
John Ellis	1748		"
Richard Cayley	"	1753	"
William Leake	"		"
John Malton	"		"
Francis Gatcliffe	"		1784
Peter Goullett	"	1756	1758
John Terry		1759	1774
John Agar		1760	1807
William Vincent		1764	1774
Richard Norris		1770	1784
John Prince		1771	1774
Mathew Darbyshire		1772	1807
Richard Clarke		1773	1784
James Brogden		1774	
Joseph Brogden		"	1807
Edward Seagrave		1776	1784
J. Hampston & J. Prince }	1777		1808
Thomas Hornby		1778	1789
John Agar, jr.		1782	1807
Charles Agar		1783	
Richard Morton	1784		
Thomas Hornby	"		1789
William Astley		1784	1830
George Cattle		1785	1807
William Etherington		1788	
John Addison		1789	
H. Prince & Co.	1795		
Thomas Agar		1799	
Jas. Bellamy Carlille		1801	
Etherington & Crossley	1805		
J. James Baker	"		1806
Prince & Cattle	"		1807
William Ashley	"		1819
James J. Barber (Ld. Mayor, 1833)	"		d 1857
Jonathan Astley		1805	1823
J. B. Booth	1806		
W. B. Booth	"		
Richard Cattle			1807
George Bartliff	1807		
Goodman, Gainsford & Co.	"		
William Elliot	"		
G. Booth	"		1810
W. Booth	"		1815
Robert Cattle & J. Barber }	"		1814
Robert Clarke		1807	
Robert Cattle (Ld. Mayor, 1841)		"	d 1842
Francis Agar		1808	
L. Cresser	1809		
R. Cadman & Co.	"		
R. Gainsford & Co.	"		
William Cay		1809	
Henry Watson		"	
Christopher Watson		1810	1830
Joshua Potts		"	1823
Isaiah Cresser		1811	
James Barber & William Whitwell }	1812		1841
Jas. (or Jno.) Burrell (last Assay Master)		1814	1851
Christopher Watson	1815		1830
William Cattle	1816		1823
Wm. Graves North		1816	
G. Addwell	1817		
Edward Jackson	"		1823
James Barber & Co.	1818		1821
David Smith		1818	
John Whip		1820	
William Pulleyn or Polan		"	
Robert Ellison		"	
Joshua Potts	1823		
Matthew Hick	"		
John Whitwell			d 1823
James Barber, George Cattle & William North }	1828		
Thomas Robert		1830	
John Buck		"	
John Bell, jr.		"	1851
James Barber & William North }	1840		1847
(dissolved partnership, 1847)			
Thomas Parker			1851

CHAPTER XII

THE NORWICH GOLDSMITHS

AND THEIR MARKS

Norwich Plate, its antiquity, and excellence of design and workmanship.

As regards the ascertained antiquity of its plate Norwich approaches York very closely. But for the example of York-made plate of the year 1563 recently noted by the Author, it might have been claimed for Norwich that some of its fully marked and authentically dated plate was earlier than that of any other provincial town in England. With reference to quality, the work of the sixteenth century goldsmiths of Norwich is entitled to a place of still higher rank, for in point of design and finish much of the Elizabethan Norwich-made plate is fully equal to the best London-made plate of that period.

Goldsmiths in Norwich from 1285.

The Norwich records show that there were a great many goldsmiths working in Norwich from 1285 to 1305. No goldsmiths' names appear to have been recorded in the next forty-five years, but we find that in 1350 John de Horstede was made free of the city, that Robert de Bumpstead received his freedom in 1366, Robert Rose and William de Denton theirs in 1399, John Hynde and John Goddys were both free in 1409, Robert Boner in 1418, John Nicole in 1419, and John Westwyk in 1422. Norwich was one of the cities appointed to have a " touch " in 1423. Thenceforward, with intervals of a very few years, an unbroken line of goldsmiths is chronicled right down to the end of the seventeenth century.

The earliest existing references to the goldsmiths of Norwich as a company or guild is contained in the lists of " Masters of Crafts " preserved in the records of the Mayor's Court, from which the following entries have been extracted :—

DATE OF ENTRY.			NAMES OF MASTERS OF THE GOLDSMITHS' CRAFT.
Midsummer 6 Eliz.	(1564)	William Cobbolde and William Rogers.
,, 7 ,,	(1565)	Peter Peterson and William Rogers.
,, 8 ,,	(1566)	Peter Peterson and William Cobbolde.
,, 9 ,,	(1567)	William Cobbolde and William Rogers.
,, 12 ,,	(1570)	Peter Peterson and George Fenne.
,, 18 ,,	(1576)	George Fenne and John Tesmond.
,, 29 ,,	(1587)	Peter Peterson and George Fenne.

No further entries are found till Midsummer 20 Ja. I. (1622-3), when the names of Philip Smith and Daniel Aynesworth are recorded. After this date they occur regularly, but as a chronological list of Norwich goldsmiths is printed at the end of this chapter the names are not continued here. Although by the Act of 1423 Norwich was appointed to have a " touch," the guild of goldsmiths there either omitted to put the provisions of that Act into operation or the Act was allowed to fall into abeyance before the year 1565, when goldsmiths wrought wares of all sorts of qualities, as is shown by the following petition, preserved amongst the Norwich Archives and brought to light by Mr. R. C. Hope, F.S.A.

"PRESENTED TO ASSEMBLY HELD DIE MARTIS 2do DIE OCT., 7th ELIZ.* CORAM THO. SOTHERTON Maiore.

" To the Right Worshipfull Mr. Mayor the Shreves Alderman and common councell of the Cittie of Norwich.

" In most humble wyse Sheweth and compleyneth unto yor worshippes your supplyants and daly oratours, the companye or fellowshipp of the Arte or Science of Goldesmethes wthin the Cittie of Norwiche.

" That wheare(as) many and dyverse absurdytes and abuses have heretofore flowed among the said artificers aswell concernyng the unperfecte working of ther works of gold as ther unfaithfull working of ther works of sylver in souche base wyse and manner as the lyke have no wheare be founde. Whiche things have happenyd not only for that no certeyne order, towche or Standerde have been hetherto appoynted or assynged unto the said artificers neyther yet agreid upon among themselves wthin the said cittie towching the manner of working of gold and the directe fyness of silver whereby they shoulde or owght to worke their workes of gold and sylver according to souche fideletie and trewth in that behalf as ben requyred by the Lawes of this Relme, and as hathe ben and yet ys used and practised in other Citties and Townes corporate wthn the same Realme by occasyon whereof some of the said artificers have wrought ther works of golde and sylver after one manner and fynes and som after an other, not according to any perfecte manner and commendable fynes but so unperfectly and in souch base wyse and sorte That the Quenes maiesties subiects have ben thereby greatly deceyved and abused to the greate defasing and slaundour of so famous and worthy an arte or science as the same ys and to the greate reproche and ignomy of souche as do use and frequent the said art wtin the said cittie.† But also for that no good orders and constitucons have ben hetherto made and provided for the dewe investigacon and serche of such abuses and for the condingne ponysshement and correccon of the same. And for that no comon stampp or marke have

Petition of the Goldsmiths of Norwich to the Mayor, Sheriffs, Aldermen, and Common Council of the City, reciting that no " touch " had been appointed as required by the law, whereby great abuses and deceits had been practised, and that no common stamp or mark had been used whereby the fineness of wrought silver might be known and by whom wrought.

* Tuesday, 2 October, 1564.

† This recital shows that notwithstanding the 2 Hen. VI. c. 14 of 1423 appointing Norwich to have a "touch," the provisions of that Act had not been enforced: and that up to 1564 there had been no adoption of any standard mark for gold or silver wrought at Norwich.

thereto ben used and occupied w^thin the saide cittie * whereby the saide works of sylver made and wrought w^thin the said cittie might be stamped and signed * as well for the demonstracon of suche trew and perfecte fynesse as ought to be in the same works of sylver as for a declaracon wheare the same works were made and wrought and by whome. For reformacon whereof it may please yor worshipps the premisses tenderly consideryd wth the concent and assent of Mr. Shreves and the cominaltie of this cittie yt may be ordeyned and decreid by this present assembly in manner and forme hereafter followyng.

" In primis That every artificer of the seide arte of goldsmiths exercising the same w^thin the saide Cittie of Norwich and suburbs of the same shall from and after the feaste of Saynt Michaell tharchangell † next coming after the date of this assembly as well by hymself as by his servants trewly and faithefully worke according to Trewthe and honestie as well all souche works of gold as he from tyme to tyme shall make and work of his owne golde as all souche works of gold as otherwyse shalbe broughte unto hym to be made and wrought by others of what fynes or goodnes so ever they be w^thout any maner of imbasing impayring or otherwyse misusing of the same contrary to trewthe and honestie and contrary to the Truste and confidens in hym reposyd in that behalfe upon payne for every offence in that behalfe founde and taken by the Wardens of the saide arte for the tyme being or presented unto them by any other takyng and fynding the same to be fined by the saide wardens according to the quality and quantitie of every souche offence as it shall seme good to ther decrescions thone halfe of all whiche fynes to be to the Mayo^r of the said cittie for the tyme being and thother to be to the use of the company of the saide arte if the same offence shall be founde by the said wardens or to hym or them other then the saide wardens that so shall fynde present and pursue the same, to be levyed by Mr Mayors officer for the tyme being by waye of distresse of the goods and cattalls of every souche offendo^r and if the same offendo^r do not paye the same fyne w^thin iiij dayes next after the takyng of souche distresse that then it shalbe lawfull to the said Mayo^r or his deputie for the tyme being after thende of the seide fower dayes to cawse the said distresse to be prised by iiij honest men therupon to be sworne before the saide Mayo^r or his Deputie and then to sell the saide distresses and defalking souche sumes of money assessed for fine in that behalffe oute of the price of the same distresse to delyver and render ageyne the overplus and resydew of the price of the same distresse to the owner of the same.

" Itm That from and after the said feaste of St. Michell tharchangell (Sept. 29) the standerde towching the fynes of sylver whereby the said artificers at all tymes hereafter shall worke all ther works of silver within the said Cittie and suberbes of the same shalbe accepted reputed and taken to be of souche and the same fynes and goodnes and better as the Standerde of the lyberds hedde with the crowne ‡ ys and hathe ben alwayes hetherto adiudged and not under the same in enywyse and that a comon stampe or towche of the Armes or Ensigne of the said cittie beyng the castell and the Lyon shall be provided to remayne in the custody and keepyng of the wardens of the saide arte for the time being

* See note (†) on previous page.

† The date of the assembly being 2 Oct., 1564, the next feast of St. Michael (Michaelmas) was 29 Sept., 1565.

‡ The crowned leopard's head, which had been stamped on plate assayed at Goldsmiths' Hall, London, from 1478.

under two severall kyes whereof thone to remayne wth one of the said wardens and the other wth the other warden to thentent to stampe therwithe all souche workes of sylver and every of them as hereafter shall be made and wrought by the saide artificers, beyng founde upon dewe serche thereof made by the said wardens to be of such fynes and goodnes as is before resyted.

"Itm That no artificer of the saide arte nhabityng within the saide cittie and suburbes of the same shall from and after the saide feaste of Sainte Michaell tharchangell work or cause to be wrought for them selves to thentent to put to sale or for any other person or persons any kinde of work of silver beyng of the weight of one oz. but he shall bring the same worke perfectly made and sett together unburnisshed unto the saide wardens to be dewly serched and assigned by them whether the same shalbe of the standerde and fynes before resited or no. Upone payne to forfett for every oz. of suche worke or works so made put to sale or delyvered to the owner or owners and not fyrst brought to the saide wardens to be towched and assaied as is aforesaide xij^d thone half thereof to be to the Mayo^r of this cittie for the tyme beyng. And thother halfe to the wardens of the saide arte or to such other person or persons as so shall finde take and pursue the same. And to be Levied in manner and forme as before ys resited.

After 29 Sept., 1565, no silver above one oz. to be sold before being assayed and marked as "standard," under a penalty of 12d. per oz.

"Itm That the wardens of the saide arte for the tyme being upon the iuste and manifeste profe and assaye by them made as is aforesaide upon every souche worke and workes so brought unto them by the maker and workers thereof shall towche and signe the same worke and workes wth the saide stampe of the armes of the said Cittie taking for ther payment in that behalfe for every pounde weight of any kinde of worke or workes of sylver too pence and so after that rate more or lesse. And if the said wardens shall refuse to towche and signe with the said stampe the saide workes of silver so brought unto them beyng found according to the standerde and fynes aforesaide or shall towche and signe any of the saide works of sylver so brought unto them not being of the standerde and fynes aforesaid the saide wardens to forfett as well for every pece of work so by them refused to be towched and signed as for every pece of worke so by them towched and signed contrary to the forme before resited vj^s viij^d the one moitye thereof to be to the Mayo^r of the Cittie for the tyme being and the other moytie to hym or them that shall fynde the saide defaulte and present and pursue the same to be Levied in manner and forme before declared. And that if the said wardens shall find eny of the seide works of sylver eyther when they shalbe browght unto them to be assayed and signed as is aforesaid or in any of the shoppes or other places wheare the same shall happen to be made or wrought not to be of suche standerde and fynes as is before rememberyd that then it shalbe lawfull to the saide wardens at all tymes to breke suche works and every of them in to peces according to ther discrecons.

The Wardens to mark with the city stamp all works assayed and found according to standard, and to forfeit, for refusing to touch or for stamping work not being standard, 6s. 8d. per piece.

Work below standard to be broken.

"Itm That every artificer of the same arte inhabiting wthin the said Cittie (being an occupier) shall have a severall punche or marke of such devise as he shall thinke good to thentent to sett and stampe the same upon every pece of worke of silver wch he shall hereafter make and after the same pece of worke shalbe serched and stamped by the saide wardens with the saide stampe of the armes of the said Cittie. And that none of the said artificers shall sett ther owne punche or marke upon eny pece of work so by them made and wrought before the same shalbe stamped by the said wardens with the comon towch or stamp of tharmes or ensigne of the Cittie as ys aforesaide. And that every of the saide

Every worker to set his own stamp on his work after being assayed and not before, under a penalty of 6s. 8d. for every offence.

artificers shall sett ther owne stamp upon the saide works so by them made after the same shalbe stamped wth the seid comon stampe of tharmes of the Cittie upon payne to forfett for every tyme they shall offend in eyther of thes thinges contrary to the forme before resited vj^s viij^d whereof the one halfe shalbe to the Mayo^r of this Cittie for the tyme being. And thother halfe to the seide wardens or such other person or persons as shall fynde present and pursue the same to be Levied in manner and forme before rememberyd.

Quarterly search to be made by the Wardens; no artificer to withstand the search under a penalty of 10s.

"Itm That the Wardens of the same arte for the tyme beyng shall every quarter in the yeare at the least make diligent serche and inquisicon for the trew investigacon and finding oute of all and singuler defalts and offenses before rememberid upon payne to forfett for every quarter of the yeare so omytting ther dutie and office in that behalfe x^s thone halfe thereof to be to the Mayo^r of the Cittie for the tyme being and the other halfe to hym or them that shall fynde present and pursue the same to be Levied in forme before resited. And that no artificer or artificers of the said crafte shall lett withstande interrupte or by eny meanes denye or geynsaye the saide wardens to com and enter into his shopp or howse for the dewe serche and inquisicon of the premises upon payne to forfett for every such offence contrary to the trew meanynge hereof x^s thone moytie thereof to the Mayo^r of the said for the tyme being. And thother moytie to the saide wardens or souche other person or persons as shall fynde and diligently pursue the same to be Levied in manner and forme afore declaryd."

This petition establishes the fact that no plate was officially marked at Norwich before 1565, and that the compulsory assaying and marking of plate with the city arms (the lion and castle), and the maker's mark, took effect as from the 29 Sept., 1565. No mention is made of the date-letter, but as the earliest marked examples of Norwich plate have date-letters A, B, C, D., etc., in regular rotation, and as there are in the county of Norfolk a large number of communion cups * and patens marked with the letter C, dated 1567 and 1568, it seems clear that the use of a date-letter was commenced on the 29 Sept., 1565, and that it was regularly changed at Michaelmas in each succeeding year. The letter A, therefore, appears to have been used from Michaelmas, 1565, till the recurrence of that feast in the following year, each succeeding letter having served for three months of one year and nine months of the next.

With reference to the assaying of plate, as established in 1565, the following is extracted from the Mayor's Book, page 136 :—

"SAY MASTERS OATHE OF THE SILVER SMITHS TRADE.

The Assay Master's Oath

"You shall sweare that you will well and truly execute the office of a Say Master to the Company of Silver Smithes within the City of Norwich, & not sett the stampe of the Rose and Crowne † upon any Plate but what is according to the standard. And allsoe doe & execute All other matters & things relating to the said Office according to your best skill & cuninge. So helpe you God."

---

* No less than fifty have been found so marked, of which eighteen are dated 1567 and a dozen dated 1568.

† The mention of the " Rose and Crown " indicates that the date of this entry is later than 1574-5.

The following is from the "Norwich Liber Albus," f. clxxvi. :—

"THE OTHE OF THE STRAWNGERS * GOLDESMYTHES.

"Ye shall swere That ye shall be feithfull and trewe to our liege Lorde the king † and to his heyres Kynges And noo latten ne copper worke nor doo to worke whereby the king and his peopull mighte be deceyved But ye shall worke and doo to werke trewe golde and Sylver that is to saie The goldeworke to be as goode as the Alaye of the iiij^th ‡ and noon worse And the saide Sylver worke to be as goode as the money of our sovereign Lord the kyng. And all suche workes as ye make, and doo to make, of gold and sylver, *ye shall thereuppon set your marke to you assigned by the wardens of the crafte or misterye of the Goldesmythes of the cittie of London.* And noo glasses ne counterfette Stones sette in golde contrary to the goode Rewle and honeste of the crafte or misterye aforeseide. Also if ye knowe any disceiptfull worke of golde or sylver made or put to sale ye shall thereof gyve knowleadge to your wardens as sone as ye goodly maye for amendement of the same. And that ye sette noo man a worke without he bring A Testymoniall from the wardens that he is admitted and sworn as a brother. And all the goode ordynaunces of the same crafte or mistereye of Goldesmythes made and to be made not repealed ye shall kepe And the Secrettes and privyties of the same crafte ye shall not discover ne tell. But as a goode man and obedyent to your wardens ye shall behave you at all tymes soe healpe you God and hollidame by this Booke."

The list of names of Norwich goldsmiths at the end of this chapter will be found to comprise all those who are known to have worked in the city from A.D. 1285 to 1735; as no plate was assayed there by virtue of the 12 & 13 Wm. III. c. 4 (1700-1), it is unnecessary to extend the list further. The goldsmiths residing in the city after 1700 are more likely to have been dealers in plate than manufacturers, there being no evidence of any plate having been made or assayed in Norwich later than the year 1701-2.

Much of the Norwich plate appears to have been designed in the Dutch taste of the best period, and the names of the goldsmiths in many cases suggest a continental origin. There was a colony of Dutch people in Norwich, and the first mentioned Peter Petersen was called the "Dutchman".§ He is found so described in the city records. He became free in 1494 and worked in the city for a number of years before the establishment of the "touch" there in 1565. His son (or grandson) Peter Peterson was apprenticed to John Basyngham, and was admitted

(margin notes:) The Oath of the strangers or immigrant goldsmiths.

Dutch Colony in Norwich.

Peter Peterson, of Dutch descent.

* Strangers working in the city not having been admitted freemen.
† This entry is not dated, but the "King" referred to may have been Henry VII, Peter Peterson (the Dutchman) having been admitted in 1495.
‡ Meaning one-fourth alloy and three-fourths gold, which was the standard for gold wares at that time, c. 1571 and up to 1575, when it was increased to 22 carats fine. See p. 30 *ante*.
§ Zachary Shulte ("*indigena et alienigena*") was another.

a freeman in 1553. He wrought plate for about fifty years, and died in 1602-3 at the age of 84, having made a bequest to "the poorest sort of the Dutch nation settled in Norwich". This Peter Peterson was the most celebrated of the Norwich goldsmiths of the time of Elizabeth, and wrought a large quantity of plate which was highly esteemed for the excellence of its design and workmanship.

In each line of the following tables (except where the date-letter is stated to be "conjectured") the marks are represented in *facsimile*, as found on the plate from which they have been transcribed.

Norwich Town mark "a Castle and Lion".

It will be seen that the town mark* (the castle and lion—the arms of the city) is practically unchanged from 1565 to 1575, from which date, until 1581, no example has been found. The marks for 1581 have been transcribed from the silver mounts of a coco-nut cup in the South Kensington Museum. They are a rose crowned, a date-letter R, and a maker's mark, consisting of a five-petalled flower. If the silver of this cup is Norwich work, it is the earliest known example of Norwich plate marked with the crowned rose. The cup appears to have been acquired by the Museum authorities as an example of Norwich work, and is or was described as such, but grave doubts have been expressed with regard to its provenance. It has been, in fact, repudiated by the best informed of the Norwich collectors, and its marks are included by the Author in his Norwich tables solely on the representations of the South Kensington authorities. The crowned rose bears a strong resemblance to that found in the bowls of a great number of apostle spoons of *circa* 1600-40 of Dutch origin (which have been purchased by some unwary collectors as Norwich spoons, whereas no authentic example of a Norwich apostle spoon is known), and it is quite possible that the Norwich collectors are right in saying that the marks on the mounts of this cup are Dutch and not Norwich.†

First cycle of date-letters commenced 1565.

With reference to the date-letters, it is conjectured that the first cycle was one of twenty letters, as shown in the tables, but this assumption rests on no authority. It is merely put forward as being that which is most probable, the examples found being the A, B, C, D, E, F, G, I, and K, from 1565-6 to 1574-5, and the doubtful R on the South Kensington cup. As to the accuracy of the dates assigned to the letters in

---

* More correctly "city mark," but the use of the generic term "town mark" is continued.

† The nut itself is admittedly "Dutch"; it has, however, been suggested that the silver work was probably executed in Norwich by a Dutch settler, but on that hypothesis the Dutch character of the marks is still unexplained.

facsimile which precede K, there can scarcely be a question. All the subsequent letters of the first cycle are, however, hypothetical, no example of Norwich plate of a date between 1574 and about 1590 (if we exclude the doubtful R of 1581) being known, and there being no records which throw any light on the subject.

With regard to the period intervening between 1585 and 1624, all that the Author, after minute and long extended research, has been able to discover, tends only to indicate the probability that no date-letter was used, and that the marks which were used as town-marks were various.

Probably no date-letters used from 1585 to 1624.

Early examples of marks used in this period are found on four beaker cups which formerly belonged to the Dutch church at Norwich. The marks are three in number, repeated on each of the four cups, and are illustrated in the following tables, in line with the date *c.* 1595. The cups bear the inscription : " The gift of Mr. Rychard Browne of Heigham," the donor being a gentleman who was sheriff of Norwich in 1595 and died in that year, which gives us the approximate date of the making of the cups. The marks are :

Marks on the beakers from the Dutch Church, Norwich.

1. The lion and castle—a conventional heraldic castle, different from that of 1565-74.
2. An orb and cross in a shaped shield.
3. A wyvern's head erased.

The second and third marks appear to be makers' marks and may indicate that the cups were wrought by two goldsmiths working in partnership.* The mark of the orb and cross is attributed to the great Peter Peterson, but three forms of the orb and cross mark have been found on Norwich plate, and it has been suggested that the mark of the "great" Peter Peterson was the sun in splendour represented in the following tables opposite 1566-7 and not the orb and cross.. Mr. William Minet, F.S.A., the present owner of two of these cups, said in 1897 with reference to these marks :

"The first is the Norwich City mark, which, as we have seen, dates the cups as not earlier than 1565.† The second is the maker's mark. Now in the collection of plate which belongs to the Norwich Corporation is a cup stamped with the

---

* Another suggested explanation of the two makers' marks is that the cups were imported from Holland in the "rough" or plain state, and that one of the two makers' marks is that of a Dutch manufacturer, the other being the mark of the Norwich goldsmith who finished them. There is, however, no evidence to support this suggestion.

† Notes on the communion cups of the Dutch church at Norwich. *Proc. Huguenot Soc. London.*

Lion and Castle and the Orb and Cross in a shaped shield, with this inscription, in cusped letters, round its edge :—

THE + MOST + HERE + OF + IS + DVNE + BY + PETER + PETERSON.

" It has generally been assumed that the history of this cup is explained by the following entry in the Assembly Book, under date September 21st, 1574 :—

" ' This daye by the hole concent of this howse, at the humble suit request and desyer of Peter Peterson of the same cittie, goldsmith, the same Peter Peterson is dispensyd with and discharged from beryng the office of Shrevaltie and all other offices within the cittie, only the office of Chamblyne excepted : for the wch dispensacon the same Peter Peterson have agreed to geve one standing cupp gylte of the weight of xv. oz. and xl^li in money, to be payed in forme following, viz., xx^li between this and the purificacon of o^r Lady next ; x^li at Michelmas next after that, and the other x^li that tyme twelvemonths.' *

" It has very generally been assumed that the cup now in the possession of the Corporation, is the cup referred to in this entry ; but, unfortunately for this theory, the existing cup weighs 31 oz. 2 dwts., or just double the weight of what may be called the ransom cup,† and the two can only be connected by crediting Peterson with great generosity (unless some subsequent arrangement was made for the acceptance of the extra weight of silver instead of a part of the money agreed to be paid).‡

" The fact remains, that we have a cup of Norwich make with the orb and cross in a shaped shield, the inscription on which declares the greater part of it to be the work of Peterson : it would seem therefore but reasonable to attribute the beakers from the Dutch church to him also. The discovery and publication of Peterson's will has, however (to some minds) ‡ imported a considerable element of doubt into the matter.§

" This will bequeaths specifically a large amount of plate, and much of what is so bequeathed is identified as having the ' sonne ' on it. This caused the suggestion to be made that the ' sonne,' and not the orb and cross, was Peterson's mark. A good deal, however, turns on the exact way in which the ' sonne ' is spoken of in connection with these pieces. In the will many spoons are mentioned as having ' knoppes of the sonne ' ; others have ' the knoppe of the sonne, and are graven and guylt on the back side wth the sonne '. Again we find a ' tankard of silver graven with the sonne,' a ' cup with a cover, of London tuch wch cover hath the sonne mentioned in the top thereof with the goldsmith's arms graven upon it ' ; a ' silver pot graven upon the covers wth the sonne, the Lion and Castle of Norwich tuch, of my own making.' In addition to the silver so

---

* *History and Description of the Insignia and Plate belonging to the Mayor, Aldermen and Citizens of the City of Norwich :* Norwich, 1890, 17. In the same collection is another example of plate, attributed to Peterson, known as the Reade salt, date about 1568, and stamped with the lion and castle, and the orb and cross ; but the latter is in a lozenge, and not in a shaped shield, as on these cups.

† " *Corporation Plate and Insignia of Office of the Cities and Towns of England and Wales.* Ll. Jewitt & W. H. St. John Hope, London, 1895 ; ii., 189. Nor can the existing cup be the one bequeathed by Peterson to the Corporation (though in this case the weights more nearly correspond), for this latter is specified in the will as of ' London tuch '."

‡ The words in parentheses are the Author's and not Mr. Minet's.

§ *Nor. Arch.,* xi, 259. A paper by C. R. Manning, F.S.A. The will is in the Norwich Archdeaconry ; 1603, fo. 190.

bequeathed, mention is also made of a 'garnish of pewter marked with the sonne,' and a 'half garnish' marked in the same way. In none of these instances, however, is the sun spoken of as being the maker's mark. On the contrary, it may well be argued that it was more in the nature of a badge or crest. It will be noticed for instance :—

"1. That the sun is always spoken of as 'graven,' while a maker's mark would be punched.

"2. The sun was, in the instances quoted above, admittedly used otherwise than as a maker's mark; the spoons, for example, have it for a 'knoppe' or seal end.

"3. In the case of cups having covers, the sun is expressly stated to be 'graven on the cover,' whereas we should expect the maker's mark to be punched both on the cup and cover, being separate pieces.

"4. In one case we are distinctly told of a cover which 'hath the sonne mentioned in the top thereof wth the goldsmith's arms graven on it'; the inference being, that the sun and the arms were both treated in the same way, the arms being evidently graven and not punched.

"5. A cup, of London 'tuch' (and therefore not likely to be Peterson's work), has the sun graven upon it.

"6. The pewter (and we have no evidence that Peterson was a pewterer) also has the sun on it.

"7. Lastly—and this is important as proving what seems clear from the other cases, namely, that the sun was at any rate used otherwise than as maker's mark—a bequest of coals is directed to be distributed by means of leaden tokens stamped with the sun.

"So far as all this goes, it might fairly be argued that the sun was used by Peterson merely as a badge; and that the absence of any mention in his will of the orb and cross does not exclude the possibility of his having used this as his craft mark. Hence, if the question could be left here, it might be assumed, on the evidence of the Corporation cup, and notwithstanding the silence of the will, that the Dutch church beakers were from his workshop. We have, however, one further piece of evidence, which supports the surmise arising from the will, that the sun was Peterson's mark. In the Churchwardens' Accounts for the parish of St. Margaret, Norwich, is an entry under date 1567 : 'p^d to Peter Peterson ye gold-smyth for making ye comunyon cuppe—and for making ye cover '.* This cup still exists, bearing the date 1568, and for maker's mark, a full human face surrounded by rays, known heraldically as a head affrontée, and often used as the conventional representation of the sun. Here, then, we have a piece of plate identified as Peterson's work, bearing the mark which his will has told us he certainly used for some purposes, and, moreover, of about the same date as the Dutch cups.

"In the sixth edition of *Old English Plate* it is suggested, on the authority of a communion cup at Haddiscoe in Norfolk, that the orb and cross mark may have belonged to John and Robert Stone; but the mark on that cup is in a plain angular shield with a pointed base. The orb and cross mark is a common one in the county, some twenty instances of it being given in *Norfolk Archæology*;† most of these are however in a lozenge, while the mark on the beakers is in a shaped shield."

* *Norf. Arch.*, X. 92, 392. The cup has a further mark, viz., a trefoil slipped.
† *Ibid.*, X. 95.

It remains to be suggested that Peterson used both marks, the sun as well as the orb and cross, and that John and Robert Stone may have used the orb and cross within an angular shield to differentiate it from the mark of the same description used by Peterson. That the orb and cross in a shaped shield as found on the " Ransom " cup of the Norwich Corporation was the mark, or at least one of the marks, of Peter Peterson (in view of the contemporary inscription on the cup represented below) cannot be denied, and that the four beakers from the Dutch church at Norwich were also the work of Peterson, or were made in his workshop under his eye, a comparison of the work on the respective pieces forces one to admit. In the character of the lettering the following points of similarity may be observed : the manner of the bifurcation of the limbs and the bulbs across them ; the conjunction of the letters H and E, and N and E respectively, and the dip in the centre of the cross bar of the H. These coincidences are in the circumstances too remarkable for any other explanation than that the inscriptions were in both cases engraved by or under the superintendence of the same goldsmith. In comparing the lettering, allowance must of course be made for the difference in size of the " Ransom " cup and the Dutch church beakers ; the size of the letters in each case being commensurate with the size of the vessel.

The large-size inscription illustrated in the first two lines below is reproduced from the " Ransom " cup, around which it runs in one continuous line ; the smaller letters in the third line are reproduced from the beaker in the possession of Mr. W. Minet. In both cases the letters are reduced to a common scale of $\frac{5\text{ths}}{9}$ linear.

✠ THE ✠ MOST HERE ✠ OF HIS ✠
ƆVNE ✠ BY ✠ PETER ✠ PETERSON

THE · GIFT · OF · MARYCHARD · BROWNE · OF · HEIGHAM

It is submitted that the " Ransom " cup of the Norwich Corporation and the four beakers from the Dutch church all emanated from Peter Peterson's "shop," and that therefore the mark of the orb and cross in a shaped shield was his mark. The Author is also of opinion that the standing salt of the year 1567-8 belonging to the Norwich Corporation, with the orb and cross mark in a lozenge ; the communion cup at Diss of

1565-6 with the same mark, and the standing cup of the year 1566-7 with the "sun in splendour" mark, are also Peterson's. The Author has had the opportunity of consulting several of the best known collectors of Norwich plate with reference to these marks, each of whom agrees with the opinion here expressed.

Returning to the consideration of the remainder of Table II. the fourth line is remarkable. The four marks are stamped on a seal-top spoon in the collection of Mr. J. H. Walter, of Drayton, Norfolk. They are: (1) The newly introduced mark—the double-seeded rose crowned—struck in the bowl and on the back of the stem; (2) an indistinguishable mark—probably a maker's mark—and (3) and (4) two London Hall-marks, viz., the lion passant and date-letter (the Lombardic n) for the year 1610-1.

The crowned rose mark.

London marks on Norwich-made spoons of 1610-1.

The following explanation of these London marks on Norwich-made spoons is suggested by the Author: There is no evidence of the existence of any regular system of assaying and marking plate at Norwich between 1584-5 and 1624-5, and no record of the election of any officers between 1587 and 1622. In all probability there was no official "touch," in the interval, and the excellent system inaugurated in 1565 had fallen into abeyance, so that in the absence of a local "touch," anyone who required his plate to be Hall-marked would be obliged to get it assayed in London. Thus the Norwich marks found on Norwich-made plate of the period under consideration were in no sense "Hall marks," but merely the marks struck by the makers, the lion passant and date-letter having been struck at Goldsmiths' Hall, London, in 1610-1, when the spoon was assayed there. This, however, while being the obvious explanation, has no documentary evidence to support it.

The next four marks in Table II. occur on another of Mr. Walter's seal-top spoons; they are the crowned rose and castle-over-lion marks (resembling those on the communion flagon of 1627-8 at St. Simon and St. Jude's, Norwich), and for maker's mark a lion rampant in shaped shield, as illustrated in Table III. at 1632 and 1634. Because the castle and crowned rose marks resemble those of 1627 rather than the later examples, its date is ascribed to about 1620.

Table III. (1624-44) presents a fairly regular cycle of date-letters, all in elaborately shaped shields, and the crowned rose is seen to have been regularly used during this period, probably as a standard mark. It is in no sense a maker's mark, since it appears on every piece of plate

The crowned rose mark, whence adopted?

mentioned in that table, no matter by whom made. How the rose crowned came to be adopted as a Norwich mark the Author is unable to determine. It has not been found on any plate of the first cycle, with the exception of the mounts of the South Kensington coco-nut, and its use in the reign of a Stuart can scarcely have been because it was a Tudor badge, as is sometimes suggested. Its first appearance on the Dutch work of the South Kensington coco-nut cup suggests the question —was the mark introduced from Holland? In view of the fact that it is very like the Dordrecht mark, and that there was constant communication between Norwich and Holland, the answer is probably in the affirmative.

Probably from Dordrecht.

It would be interesting, if it were possible, to ascertain how the regularity of the cycle 1624-44 was brought about. The municipal records contain a minute to the effect that at a "Court held 29th May, 9 Jas. I. (1611) a proclamacion from the Counsell was delivered concerning goldsmythes," but whether it had reference to plate being sent to London to be "touched," or to the system which had been established in 1565 having fallen into abeyance, is not stated. We are therefore left to conjecture that before 1624, abuses and deceits had again been practised, and in order to stop them, some regularity of procedure was in that year re-established. We have the fact that while there are no records of the election of officers between 1587 and 1622, it is recorded that in 1622-3 Philip Smyth and Daniel Aynesworth were elected as Masters or Wardens of the Norwich goldsmiths; and for a number of years afterwards these officers were regularly chosen, and authentic assays made. No plate had been found by the Author for any one of the first three years of the cycle 1624-44, until after the publication of the first edition of this work in 1905. The Author has since then noted plate marked with the A, B, and C of the years 1624-5, 1625-6, and 1626-7, and all the succeeding letters from 1626-7 to 1642, with only two exceptions, and the pricked or engraved dates on the respective articles agree so well with the date-letters that it may be regarded as an established fact that the cycle was commenced with the letter A in 1624 That it was continued down to and including the T of 1642-3 is also proved, but whether it stopped there, or was continued to and terminated with the V of 1643-4, as is conjectured, or was continued to Z, as it may have been, it is, in the absence of further information, which appears at present unattainable, impossible to say.

Use of date-letter resumed 1624.

After 1643 no cycle of date-letters is found until 1688. In the interval No date-letter found between 1643 and 1688. marks of several kinds were used, and plate of that period is for the most part stamped with marks, consisting of the castle and lion, a crown on a separate stamp, a rose-slip also on a separate stamp, and a maker's mark usually composed of two letters, generally conjoined. The fourth table with its amendments and additions, for which the Author is largely indebted to Mr. J. H. Walter, covers to a great extent the period in question. The marks in the first line of this table (set opposite the date *c.* 1645) occur on a seal-top spoon which belonged to the late Mr. W. Boore and on another spoon belonging to the Author. In this case the marks are three only: a very curious kind of rose with a rosette in the centre and four pellets round it, a castle incuse, and a maker's mark also incuse, the last being a representation of the sun in splendour, something like the mark ascribed to Peter Peterson,* but without the face in the centre. The marks in the next line occur on a seal-top spoon in the collection of Mr. J. H. Walter. The first of these marks is a rose in form, the second a five-petalled rose, the third a crown unlike any other crown which the Author has found stamped on Norwich plate and the fourth the maker's mark (A H conjoined) which is ascribed to Arthur Heaslewood (free 1661). The spoon was in the possession of a Norwich family for several generations before it was acquired by Mr. Walter. In Norwich it has always been believed to be a Norwich spoon, and there appears to be no doubt as to its authenticity. The other marks in this table vary so much that it might be suggested that every individual maker struck all the marks on his own plate with his own puncheons, and that none were stamped by a duly authorised "searcher". In the numerous examples of Variety of contemporaneous Norwich marks 1645 to 1685. roses there are several varieties, one being a single rose, the others rose-slips; and in the whole table, consisting of eleven examples, there are six kinds of castle marks, and ten varieties of crowns. It is worthy of note that the rose crowned is never found in combination with the rose-slip. The control of the craft during this period (1645-85) must, if any control existed, have been indifferently exercised, and the records cannot have been consistently kept, if kept at all. It is possible to identify one goldsmith (Thomas Havers) of this period, by his initials, not from any of the records of the craft, but because of his description on being appointed sheriff in 1701 and mayor in 1708.

* See Table I. at 1566-7.

More regular
system of mark-
ing resumed in
1688 which
lasted till 1697
when it ter-
minated.

The fifth and last table or group of marks presents indications of some spasmodic efforts having been made to resuscitate a regular system of Hall-marking.   In 1688 a new cycle was started with a small black-letter **a** and continued with **b**—probably **c** also, although the Author has found no example of that letter—and **ò**, after which, until 1696, the existence of date-letters is merely conjectural, no letter having been found between the **ò** of 1691 and the Roman capital I of 1696, which was followed lastly, so far as is known, by K in 1697.   Apart from the eccentricity in the choice of date-letters in this cycle, the other marks from 1689 show an amount of consistency not apparent in the preceding thirty-five or forty years.

The Act of 1697 prevented the Norwich goldsmiths from continuing to work under the old regime, and there does not appear to have been sufficient vitality amongst the few who survived in 1701 to take advantage of the Act of that year, whereby they were enabled, had they been so disposed, to re-establish an assay office.   Being unable or unwilling to do so, with the end of the 17th century the existence of the craft of Norwich goldsmiths, as a working body, also ended.   It is recorded that one Robert Hartsonge was sworn in as assayer on July 1st, 1702, but no record appears to have been found as to his having assayed any wrought gold or silver, or that any was wrought in Norwich after his appointment.

The marks on wrought gold assayed at Norwich were the same as on wrought silver.

The Author cannot conclude this chapter without acknowledging his indebtedness to Mr. J. H. Walter, of Drayton, Norfolk, and to Messrs. Walter Rye and Theodore Rossi, of Norwich, for their valuable assistance in the collecting of many of the facts here recorded and in the compilation of the following tables.

MARKS ON NORWICH PLATE.

TABLE I.

THREE STAMPS AS BELOW.

	CASTLE OVER LION.	DATE LETTER	MAKER'S MARK.	DESCRIPTION OF MAKER'S MARK.	ARTICLES AND OWNERS.
1565-6		A		Orb and cross in lozenge.	Communion cup: Diss, Norfolk. Do. do. : Saxlingham, (1566-7).
1566-7	,,	B		Sun in splendour. Mark of Peter Peterson.	Standing cup: South Kensington Museum.
1567-8		C		IV over a heart.	Communion cup: Bintry, Norfolk.
				Maidenhead in shield.	Communion cup: dated 1568: Northwold, Norfolk.
				Flat fish in oval.	Communion cup, dated 1568: St. Martin-at-Oak, Norwich.
				Estoile of six curved rays.	Communion cup, undated: Beighton, Norfolk.
1568-9		D		Trefoil slipped.	Communion cup, dated 1570: St. Stephen, Norwich.
1569-70		E		Orb and cross in plain shield.	Communion cup, inscribed " Made by John Stone and Robert Stone ": Haddiscoe, Norfolk.
1570-1		F		,, ,, {Mark of Christ'r. Tannor.	Com. cup: Little Witchingham. Patens at Arminghall and Burgh, Norfolk.
1571-2	,,	G		Orb and cross in shaped shield.	Mounts of stone-ware jug: Mr. W. Boore.
1572-3		H		... ...	Date-letter conjectured.
1573-4	,,	I		Trefoil slipped.	Wine-taster: Messrs. Crichton.
1574-5	,,	K		A flower with foliated stem and orb and cross as 1571-2	Seal-top spoon: Messrs. Christie.
1575-6		L		... ...	Date-letter conjectured.
1576-7		M		... ...	Do. do.
1577-8		N		... ...	Do. do.
1578-9		O		... ...	Do. do.
1579-80		P		... ...	Do. do.
1580-1	ROSE CROWNED.	Q		... ...	Do. do.
*1581-2		R		Flower of five petals.	Mounts of coco-nut cup: South Kensington Museum.
1582-3		S		... ...	Date-letter conjectured.
1583-4		T		... ...	Do. do.
1584-5		V		... ...	Do. do.

c. 1570   Norwich mark, and mark of Christopher Tannor (free 1562) on seal-top spoon: Mr. J. H. Walter.

* See remarks on page 306 *ante.*

MARKS ON NORWICH PLATE.

TABLE II.

STAMPS VARIOUS AS BELOW.

DATE (ABOUT).	MARKS.	DESCRIPTION OF MAKER'S MARK.	ARTICLES AND OWNERS.
1590		A bird.	Communion cup and paten, Guestwick.
1595		Orb and cross, and wyvern's head erased	Four beakers from the Old Dutch Church, Norwich, now in the possession of Mr. Wm. Minet, F.S.A., Miss Colman, and the Nederlandsch Museum, Amsterdam.
1600-10		Orb and cross.	Goblet on baluster stem: Messrs. Crichton.
1610		* Indistinguishable.	Seal-top spoon: Mr. J. H. Walter.
1620		Lion rampant.	Do.　　　　do.
,,		Mark of Wm. Hayden.	Beakers: Mr. R. Levine.
,,		W. is probably an Assayer's mark.	Spoon: Mr. J. H. Walter.
1620-40		T.S.	Castle struck twice at right angles, one over the other, and castle (in bowl), maker's mark and castle on back of stem; massive seal-top spoon, pricked 1640: Messrs. Crichton.
1624		Arthur Heaslewood (free 1625).	The first mark in bowl, the other three marks on stem; seal-top spoon: Mr. J. H. Walter.

In order to appreciate the marks illustrated in the preceding and succeeding tables, it is necessary to read the few pages of letterpress with reference to the Norwich Goldsmiths and their marks, where observations are made in explanation of the absence of a date-letter and the irregularity of the marks found on Norwich plate of the period covered by this and the fourth table.

* These marks are in part only those of Norwich, the lion passant and date-letter being London Hall-marks.

MARKS ON NORWICH PLATE.

TABLE III.

FOUR STAMPS AS BELOW.

	CASTLE OVER LION.	ROSE CROWNED.	DATE LETTER.	MAKER'S MARK.	DESCRIPTION OF MAKER'S MARK.	ARTICLES AND OWNERS.
1624-5			A		A pelican, as 1628.	Seal-top spoon: Mr. J. H. Walter.
1625-6	,,	,,	B		A pegasus, as 1632.	Do. do.; Messrs. Crichton. Mounts of wood bowl: Mr. Theodore Rossi.
1626-7		,,	C		Timothy Skottowe.	Seal-top spoon: Mr. J. H. Walter.
1627-8	,,	,,	D		Orb and cross.	Chalice: Attleburgh.
					A ship.	Seal-top spoon: Messrs. Lambert. Do. do.: Mr. R. Levine.
1628-9		,,	E		A pelican in her piety.	Seal-top spoon, dated 1629: Mr. A. D. George.
1629-30			F		... ...	Date-letter conjectured.
1630-1	,,		G		W. D. conjoined.	Tall flagon: Norwich Corporation. Seal-top spoon: Mr. J. H. Walter.
1631-2			H		... ...	Date-letter conjectured.
1632-3	,,	,,	I		A pegasus.	Com. cup: Great Melton, Norfolk
					A lion rampant.	Seal-top spoon: Mr. J. H. Walter.
1633-4	,,	,,	K		Arthur Heaslewood.	Com. cup: Aspall, Suffolk.
1634-5	,,	,,	L		A lion rampant.	Com. cup: S.S. Simon & Jude, Norwich.
*1635-6			M		Do. do.	Spoon with virgin and child finial: Mr. R. Levine.
1636-7			N		A crowing cock † (Herald of the Morn.)	Seal-top spoon: Burlington Fine Arts Club Exhibition.
1637-8			O		Timothy Skottowe.	Beaker, dated 1638, from a Congregational Ch., Great Yarmouth: Pierpont Morgan Collection.
					A pelican in her piety.	Seal-top spoon, pricked 1637: Mr. J. H. Walter.
1638-9	,,	,,	P		A crowing cock,† see above.	Com. paten: Skeyton, Swanton-Abbot, Norfolk.
1639-40			Q		A pelican in her piety.	Communion cup at St. Margaret's, Swanington, Norfolk.
1640-1	,,	,,	R		Timothy Skottowe.	Com. paten: Riddlesworth, Norfolk.
1641-2	,,	,,	S		A tower incuse.	Mounts of coco-nut cup: The Marquess of Breadalbane, K.G.
					D.	Com. paten: St. Etheldreda, Norwich.
1642-3	,,	,,	T		Timothy Skottowe. †	Seal-top spoon: Messrs. Christie.
1643-4			V		... ...	Date-letter conjectured.

* 1635-6 **M** Accompanying this date-letter, are the mark of Arthur Heaslewood (maker) as 1633-4 and Norwich town-marks as 1637-8; communion paten: Coston, Leicestershire.

† Crowing cock rising from pot or skillet (old legend).

MARKS ON NORWICH PLATE.

TABLE IV.

FROM ABOUT 1645 TO ABOUT 1685. MARKS VARIOUS AS BELOW.

DATE (ABOUT).	MARKS.	ARTICLES AND OWNERS.
1645		Seal-top spoon : Mr. W. Boore.
,,		* Seal-top spoon (pricked 1650) : Mr. J. H. Walter.
1653		* Seal-top spoon ; (pricked 1653 : Mr. J. H. Walter. EM / SA
1661		* Trifid-spoon : Messrs. Crichton.
,,		Communion cup, inscribed 1661 : Southwold, Suffolk.
1670		* Spoon, flat stem, trifid end : Mr. J. H. Walter.
,,		* Do. do. do. : Do. do.
,,		* Seal-top spoon, pricked WF / PC : Do. do.
,,		* Table-spoon : Mr. Thurlow Chamness.
1675		† Communion paten : St. Peter Hungate, Norwich.
1676		† Flat-top tankard, dated 1676 : Messrs. Christie.
1679		† Communion paten, dated 1679 ; St. Peter's, Mountergate, Norwich.
,,		Seal top spoon : Mr. A. D. George.
1680		Communion cup, dated 1680 : East Dereham, Norfolk.
1685		† Crown, rose, and maker's mark of Thos. Havers ; cream jug : Lord Hastings.
c. 1660		Small jug : Mr. J. H. Walter.

* This maker's mark is probably that of Arthur Heaslewood.
† Maker's name : Thomas Havers.

MARKS ON NORWICH PLATE.

TABLE V.

FROM 1688 TO 1697. FOUR STAMPS AS BELOW.

	ROSE CROWNED.	CASTLE OVER LION.	DATE LETTER.	MAKER'S MARK.	MAKER'S NAME.	ARTICLES AND OWNERS.
1688			a	EH	... ...	Beaker : Messrs. Christie.
1689			b	TH	Thomas Havers.	Tankard : Major H. S. Marsham. Bleeding bowl : Mr. J. H. Walter.
1690			c		... ...	Date-letter conjectured.
1691	,,	,,	d	,,	Thomas Havers.	Communion flagon, dated 1694 : St. Michael's-at-Plea, Norwich.
	,,	,,	,,	ID	James Daniel.	Alms-dish and basin : St. Stephen's, Norwich. Dome-top tankard : Mr. R. J. Colman.
	,,	,,	,,	EH	... ...	Small mug : Messrs. Christie. Salver on foot : Mr. R. J. Colman.
	,,	,,	,,	LG	... ...	Communion cup, dated 1694 : Stockton, Norfolk.
1692			E		... ...	Date-letter conjectured.
1693			F		... ...	Do. do.
1694			G		... ...	Do. do.
1695			H		... ...	Do. do.
1696	,,	,,	I	ID	James Daniel.	Spoon, flat stem, trifid end : Messrs. Spink.
1697	,,	,,	K	PR	... ...	Beaker, pricked 1697 : Messrs. Spink.
			,,	EH	... ...	Beaker and spoon : Mr. J. H. Walter.

c. 1697 ,, Castle as 1688, no date-letter.   ... ... Trifid spoon : Mr. Arthur Irwin Dasent.

1701-2   HA Robt. Hartsonge ? Communion paten on foot : Kirkstead, Norfolk.

NAMES OF NORWICH GOLDSMITHS.

[FROM 1285 TO 1735.]

ARRANGED CHRONOLOGICALLY FROM LISTS COMPILED BY

MR. WALTER RYE OF NORWICH, MR. R. C. HOPE, F.S.A., AND OTHER SOURCES.

Names have not been found to correspond with initials appearing on some of the makers' marks of the 17th century illustrated in the preceding tables ; on the other hand, some of the earlier names which appear in different forms very probably refer to the same persons.

Name of Goldsmith.		Earliest Date Found.	Free.	Latest Date or Death.	Name of Goldsmith.		Earliest Date Found.	Free.	Latest Date or Death.
John	Aurifaber	1285			George	Hamchirche		1457	
John de	Attleburgh	,,		1300	John .	Kebyll		,,	
Nicholas de	Swathing	1286			Thomas	Graye		1461	
Walter de	Swathing	,,			Richard	Herry		1466	
Henry the	Goldsmith	,,			Robert	Saunders		,,	
Geoffrey de	Cons'tinople	,,			William	Bond		1467	
Robert le	Orfevre	1289			John	Rich or		1480	
John le	Orfevre	1295				Sutton			
Nicholas le	Rus	,,			John	Smart		1481	
Robert de	Byrri	,,			John	Belton		1491	1520
Henry le	Orfevre	1299			Thomas	Worcester		1492	
Daniel de	Swathing	,,			Robert	Alman		1493	
Stephen de	Wells	,,		1306	Peter	Petersen		1494	
John de	Derham	,,			Thomas	Maskey		1495	
Walter de	Birlingham	,,			Edward	Belton		1499	
Robt. de St.	Edmund	,,			Walter	Man		1501	
Henry de	Brabant or	1305			John	Hunt		1502	
	Boubon				John	Basyngham		1517	
John de	Horstede		1350		Thomas	Bere		1518	
Robert de	Bumpstead		1366		Felix	Puttok		1524	
Robert	Rose		1399		William	Porter		,,	
William de	Denton		,,		William	Petyer		1530	
John	Hynde		1409		Nicholas	Isborn		1535	
John	Goddys		,,		John	Elger		1537	
Robert	Boner		1418		Nicholas	Heyward		1538	
John	Nicole		1419		John	Basyngham		1539	
John	Westwyk		1422		Zachary	Shulte		1543	
Richard	Brasyer		1425		William	Umfrey		1547	
John	Cok		,,		Thomas	Wharlow		1548	
Thomas	Wrentham		1426			or Wurlow			
Richard	Bere		1428		Henry	Sheef		1549	
John	Elger		1429		Augustine	Stywarde *	1549		
Thomas	Burton		1433		Henry	Shulte			
John	Belton		1437		William	Cobbolde		1552	1581
Thomas	Grene		1442			(Master 1564)			
John	Cok		1443		Peter	Peterson		1553	d 1603
James	Caron		1446			(Master 1565)			
John	Clerk		,,		Valentine	Isborne		1554	
William	Underwode		,,		William	Rogers		1558	
John	Mathieson		,,			(Master 1567)			
William	Toftes		1449		Christopher	Tannor		1562	
	(alias Chapman)				Walter	Man		,,	
Richard	Fraunceys		,,		George	Bladon		1563	
Thomas	Chapman		,,		Thomas	Buttell		1564	
	(alias Toftes)				John	Tesmond		1566	
Reginald	Clerk		,,			(Master 1576)			
John	Dyghton		1454		George	Fenne		1567	1587
Thomas	Sheef		,,			(Master 1570)			
Thomas	Gelyngham		1455		Robert	Stone	1569		
Thomas	Sellers		,,		John	Stone	,,		
Thomas	Willeson		,,						

* Made the Chamberlain's mace 1549-50.

NAME OF GOLDSMITH.		Earliest Date Found.	Free.	Latest Date or Death.	NAME OF GOLDSMITH.		Earliest Date Found.	Free.	Latest Date or Death.
John	Graye		1591		James	Rayner		1631	
Nicholas	Wharlow		1593			(Armourer)			
Matthew	Cobbolde		,,	d 1603	Elias	Brown		1633	d 1660
James	Grundy		1594	1594	William	Weston		1634	
Simon	Borrowe		1596		William	Kettleburgh		,,	
Emmanuel	Garratt		1597		James	Grundy		1636	
Daniel	Eynsworth				Thomas	Proctor		1641	
	or Aynesworth		1600	1626	Daniel	Mathew		,,	
	(Mstr 1622-3)				George	Grundy		1645	
Richard	Baspoole		1603		John	Woolfe		1648	
Edward	Woolfe		1607		Edward	Wright		1649	
	(Armourer)				A.	R.	1650		
Peter	Peterson		,,	d 1609	William	Edwards		1653	
Richard	Shipdam		1610	1629	Robert	Neave		1655	
William	Haydon		1613		E.	D.	c. 1660		
John	Wright		,,		M.	E.	1661		
William	Smyth		,,		Daniel W.	Hutcheson		1661	
Philip	Smyth		,,	1624	Arthur	Heaslewood	,,	,,	1665
	(Warden 1624)				Robert	Osborne		1665	
Edward	Wright		1616	1629	Robert	Hartsonge		1672	1701
(Searcher 1624-5, Master 1626-9)					Thomas	Havers		1674	d 1732
Timothy	Skottowe		1617	1644		(Sheriff 1701. Mayor 1708)			
	(Warden 1624)				M.	H.	1680		
John	Howlett		1620	1627	E.	H.	1688		1697
	(Warden 1626-7)				James	Daniel	1691	1693	1696
Arthur	Heaslewood		1625		L.	G.		,,	
	(Warden 1628-9)				P.	R.	1697		
Daniel	Aynesworth	1625		1626	Thomas	Harwood		1698	d 1755
	(Warden 1625-6)				Robert	Hartsonge		1702	
William	Skerry		1627		Arthur	Heaslewood		,,	
Augustine	Grundy		1628		Nathaniel	Rowe	1735		
W.	D.		1630						

CHAPTER XIII

THE EXETER GOLDSMITHS

AND THEIR MARKS

Antiquity of the
Exeter
Goldsmiths.

Next to Norwich in order of antiquity, judging by the examples of their work which have survived to our own times, come the goldsmiths of Exeter.   The Statute 2 Hen. VI. c. 14 (1423) makes no mention of Exeter amongst the provincial towns appointed to have touches, and its assay office appears to have had no statutory existence until 1701, when it was established in compliance with the Act 12 and 13 Wm. III. which authorised the appointment of wardens and assay masters to control the assaying and marking of wrought plate.   Conse-

No Assay Office
records made
earlier than 1701.

quently no Exeter assay-office records earlier than those of the year 1701 are to be found.   The names of Exeter goldsmiths, who worked in times prior to that date, have been collected from civic and ecclesiastical records not immediately connected with the " craft," but having indirect reference to its members.   At St. Petrock's Church, in the city of Exeter, there is an entry in the churchwardens' accounts of a payment

But other re-
cords are in
existence.

in 1571 "to Iohn Ions, goldsmith,* for changing the chalice into a cup, £1 15s. 5d.".   However much we may regret the conversion of a medieval chalice into a post-Reformation communion cup, we have some little compensation, inasmuch as the entry referring to the payment for the " changing " enables us to identify the work of the Elizabethan goldsmith who made the cup (preserved amongst the St. Petrock's sacramental vessels) which bears the stamp " I IONS," and has the date " 1572 " engraved on the knop of its paten-cover.

A guild or mystery of goldsmiths existed in Exeter long anterior to the time of Queen Elizabeth.   It is recorded that John de Wewlingworth, a goldsmith, flourished there in the 14th century, and in all probability the existence of this guild was continued down to the 7th of August, 1701, when eleven members of the craft met for the purpose of exercising the powers conferred upon them by the Act of that year.

---

* This goldsmith who used the stamp I IONS was really John Jones, the I and J being at that time identical.   He is the best known of the early Exeter goldsmiths, examples of his work being found in most parts of Devon, Somerset, and Cornwall.

Exeter was too far removed from London for the sending of all its wrought plate to the Metropolitan assay office to have been practical in the 16th and 17th centuries, and there is no evidence of the establishment of any adjacent "touch". Salisbury and Bristol were mentioned in the Act of 1423, but no evidence has been found to prove that assay offices were ever established in those cities. It is, therefore, probable that until towards the end of the 17th century the goldsmiths of Exeter worked under the privileges of a Royal Charter, although its existence has not been discovered. A craft, from whose hands emanated the numerous examples of Elizabethan and Stuart plate with which the counties of Devon and Cornwall abound, is not likely to have continued an illegal existence for so long a period as is indicated by such evidence of their activity.

The distinguishing Exeter plate mark, or "town mark," * of the 16th and 17th centuries was the Roman letter X. On some of the earlier Elizabethan examples of Iohn Ions' work the mark is found without a crown within a circle of pellets, as it is also found on some of Easton's work. In other examples the X has a crown over it and a mullet or pellet on each side, generally within a circle of very small pellets or elliptical dots. It is, however, also found in a circular stamp without surrounding dots, and on plate of about the middle of the 17th century it is occasionally found in a stamp shaped to the outline of the crowned X. Towards the end of the century instances are found of the crowned X incuse, instead of being raised within a depressed field as in all other cases. The Exeter "town mark"

In the 16th century the workers' marks consisted of their surnames, generally accompanied by a single letter (which in the cases of I. IONS, I. NORTH, and others appear to be the initials of Christian names, although in other cases this interpretation seems improbable), and the "town mark" (the letter X as above described). Makers' marks.

Several of the early marks which in the first edition of this work were ascribed to Exeter, have since been found by the researches of the Rev. J. F. Chanter, M.A., to pertain to Barnstaple, to which town they have now been allocated.

Other makers' marks found on early examples of Exeter plate are R H conjoined, R O in a heart-shaped punch, H H conjoined, S MORE,

---

* More properly city mark, but the generic term town mark is preferable.

HORWOOD, YEDS, ESTON or EASTON, BENTLY, HERMAN, $\frac{B}{W}$, $\frac{E}{A}$, WB, IR, RADCLIFF, OSBORN, IL, IP, HP, TB in monogram, MW with the crowned X between the letters, S beneath the crowned X, IS, JM in monogram, and an incuse cross pattée charged with pellets. All these marks and several others will be found represented in *facsimile* in the following tables. In the earlier marks of IONS the letter N is reversed, as is often the case in lettering of the 16th century. In OSBORN and BENTLY letters are conjoined so that one limb serves for two letters, a practice frequently resorted to in Elizabethan lettering.

With reference to the initial letters referred to above as having been found accompanying makers' names, it is stated in *Old English Plate* * that where there are two of such letters "on stone-ware jugs and communion cups, one might be for dating them, but nothing at all like a date-letter is found on spoons". That observation must now be accepted only with considerable qualification, inasmuch as several spoons have been discovered of about the year 1600, with single letters in plain angular shields, two of them with the letter "*a*" and one with the letter "*b*," as set out in *facsimile* in Table II. (*infra*). It is submitted that these marks can be nothing other than date-letters. In Table I. will be found the letters A, B, N, and P. It is suggested that each of these is a date-letter for the year opposite which it is set. The A is found on church-plate, dated (in contemporary engraving) "1575". The B occurs on church-plate similarly engraved with the date "1576". The cup at St. Andrew's, Plymouth, bearing the letter N is dated "1590". The lion-sejant spoon in the Victoria and Albert Museum, marked "C ESTON P," has no inscribed date, but it is suggested that the letter "P" is the date-letter for the year 1592. The several inscribed dates on the examples above-mentioned correspond so closely with the dates considered to be indicated by the respective letters, that it is difficult to imagine any other explanation of the coincidence than that each letter was intended to indicate the year in which it was struck on the article which bears it. The letters which it is contended are date-letters, are not ranged in columns as in other tables, but are set forth in the order in which they occur on the examples of plate from which they have been transcribed, so that the Author's contention may not appear to

Early date-letters.

* See 6th Ed., 101.

gain support from any factitious aid. Seeing that the letters in question are different in size and general appearance from the name-letters which accompany them, and that these (date?) letters in the first table are in the second table succeeded by "*a*" and "*b*" of a different character, and that the latter are within shields, it seems clear that an alphabet of a kind of Roman capital type was used from 1575 to somewhere near the end of the 16th century, and that about the year 1600 a cycle of small Italic letters was commenced.

In the absence of records it is impossible to say what plan was followed in testing and marking Exeter plate prior to 1701, but as the " craft " probably elected from time to time some or one of their most respected members to be master $^{and}_{or}$ wardens, one of these was probably entrusted with the punch for striking the "town mark". Each worker would naturally strike his own mark on his work, and where a mark occurs (not being a maker's mark or date-letter), which differs from the common mark of the city, it seems probable that this also was struck by the maker and not by the master or warden. It does not appear that there was a regular assay by cupel at any time before 1701, but probably the "touchstone" was used when a test was deemed necessary, and considered sufficient in view of the fact that all the old Exeter plate appears to have a maker's mark struck on it, and that the maker could have been identified and held liable had his mark been found upon bad plate. It is not known whether, in consequence of the Act of 1696, the Exeter goldsmiths ceased working, or sent their plate to London in compliance with the requirements of that Act until the new powers were conferred upon them by the Statute 12 & 13 Wm. III. c 4 (170^0_1), whereby they were authorised to assay and mark plate as from 29 September, 1701. It is, however, certain that other Devonshire goldsmiths, many of whom entered their names and marks at Exeter in 1701, wrought plate between 1696 and 1701. This is proved by the Eddystone lighthouse salt made by Rowe of Plymouth during the interval.

Probably no regular assay by cupel before 1701.

No time was lost after the passing of the Act of 1700 before the Exeter goldsmiths commenced preparations for carrying out its provisions. They assembled on the 7 August, 1701, to the number of eleven, and met again on the 17 September, and having elected William Ekins and Daniel Slade as first wardens under the Act, they made arrangements for obtaining premises suitable for their assay office. They subsequently passed resolutions with reference to the conduct of the assay, ordered

The Exeter Goldsmiths and their marks subsequent to the 17th century.

punches to be made for marking plate, and appointed Edmond Richards to be their first assay-master.   He was sworn in before the mayor on the 19 November, and continued in office till January 1707-8, when he was succeeded by Robert Palmer.

Work having been commenced by assaying plate for those goldsmiths of the city who had entered their names and marks, notices were sent out early in 1702 to goldsmiths known to be carrying on business in other parts of Devon and the neighbouring counties of Cornwall, Somerset and Dorset, informing them that the office was ready to assay plate in accordance with the provisions of the Act of 170_1^0, and in response a number of goldsmiths from Plymouth, Dartmouth, and other towns entered their names and marks.   The names of all these goldsmiths were entered in the assay office books with sketches of their marks (composed of the first two letters of their names) adjoining ; but the leaf of the book which contained the first series of entries is missing, and the first page extant commences with the name of Peeter Elliott of Dartmouth, who entered his name and mark on the 13 November, 1703.

According to the provisions of the Act of 170_1^0 the Exeter town mark was composed of the arms of the city, viz. : per pale *gules* and *sable* a triple-towered castle, turreted, *or*, and the use of the old town mark (the letter X crowned) was discontinued.   For nineteen years, during which only plate of the new standard was allowed to be worked, the marks of Exeter were five in number, viz., the town mark, the lion's head erased, the figure of Britannia, the annual letter, and the maker's mark, which consisted of the first two letters of the goldsmith's surname. Between 1701 and 1882 the design of the town mark, while still answering the above description, was considerably modified on several occasions as illustrated in the following tables.   At one period—1831 to 1837—the castle consisted of three separate towers.   In 1720, consequent upon the restoration of the old standard by the Act of 1719, the leopard's head crowned and the lion passant took the place of the lion's head erased and figure of Britannia, except on plate of the higher standard, which goldsmiths had the option of continuing to work ; the form of the makers' marks was also changed, and new marks, composed of the initials of the makers' Christian and surnames, were entered at the office and thenceforward used on all plate of the restored standard.   The leopard's head was not used after 1777.   In 1784 the sovereign's head was added.

Throughout the first cycle of twenty-four years after the passing of the Act of 1700, the date-letters used at the Exeter assay office were Roman capitals, and were, with one exception, enclosed in plain angular shields, every letter of the alphabet excepting J and U having been employed. The letter B of 1702-3 is found in an ornamental or " shaped " escutcheon. The letter A which marked the first plate assayed under the new regime in November, 1701, was continued in use till the 7th of August, 1702. Thenceforward the date-letter was changed annually on the anniversary of that day or on such other day as was appointed for the election of wardens for the next ensuing year. The first mention of a date-letter in the existing records is contained in a minute of the year 1710 which refers to the letter K as being the letter for the year 1710-1. In the cycle of twenty-four years, 1725-49, small letters, some Italic and some Roman, were used, as represented in Table V., j

The date-letter from 1701 to 1883.

and v having been omitted. From 1749 to 1773, the letters were Roman capitals in square shields, with similar omissions. In the following cycle Roman capital letters were again employed down to and including the P of 1788-9, after which small Roman letters were used down to and including the y of 1796-7 with which the cycle ended—all the letters being in plain angular shields, the omitted letters of this alphabet being the capital J and the small v and z. As the use of the leopard's head mark was discontinued in 1777-8, the only letters of this cycle which could possibly be mistaken for those of any other are the A, B, C, D, and E, and these may be distinguished from those of the preceding cycle by the shape of their enclosing shields, and from similar letters in later cycles in the same manner. The next cycle (1797-1816) consisted of twenty Roman capital letters A to U, omitting J, in rect-angular shields. The castle and lion passant of this cycle are also in rectangular shields. The cycle 1817-37 consisted of twenty small Roman letters a to u inclusive, omitting j : these are, for the most part, found in square or oblong shields with the upper corners clipped and the bases rounded ; some are, however, left rectangular, but the appearance of all the marks throughout this cycle differs so much from that of any other cycle in which small Roman letters are used that no mistake can easily be made. From 1837 to 1857 twenty Black-letter capitals 𝔄 to 𝔘 were used, and from 1857 to 1877 twenty Roman capitals A to U (J having been omitted). The presence of the Queen's head stamp affords an easy means of distinguishing these from the letters of any other cycle.

Lastly, from 1877 to 1883 (when the office was closed) plain block letters **A** to **F** inclusive were used. It will be observed that from 1797 the date-letters corresponded with those used at Goldsmiths Hall, London, the Exeter letter was, however, a year later than London, but except in this respect and in the shape of the enclosing shields the letters were alike from 1797 to 1856.

The duty-mark of the sovereign's head first appeared in 1784 as on London plate, and was thereafter continued, but the change of stamp denoting the change of reign was considerably delayed, in one instance— that of Wm. IV. in succession to Geo. IV.—as much as four years.

Parliamentary Inquiry in 1773.

In March, 1773, when the Parliamentary Committee appointed to inquire into the working of the Provincial Assay Offices was conducting its inquiry, the Exeter assay-master was called before the committee to give evidence concerning the conduct of the business of that office, and the following account of his testimony is copied from the report of the committee presented to Parliament on the 29 April, 1773 :—

Method of conducting the Assay Office at Exeter.

" Mr. Matthew Skinner (Assay Master of the Goldsmiths' Company of Exeter), produced, pursuant to the Order of your Committee, the several accounts annexed in the Appendix, No. 4 : and informed your Committee, that two of the members of the Goldsmiths' Company of Exeter are not freemen of the City of Exeter, but follow the trade of goldsmiths, and that all the other members are ; that all the members inhabit within the city ; and that two of them served only a part of their apprenticeships.

" That he took an oath before Benjamin Heath, town clerk, which was not the oath directed by Act of Parliament ; but thinks it was as binding as that in the Act ; that he is guided in his duty by an Act passed in the Reign of King William the Third ; that he has heard of the said Act from time to time, but never read it until he received an order to attend your Committee.

" That he never received instructions from any man living how to assay ; but when he had purchased the lanthorn, the scales, and all the other implements necessary for assaying, from the late assay master, he then made various experiments by coppelation and fire ; that he believes his assay pound weighs about 13 or 14 grains ; that he has compared all his assay weights, and found that they all bore a due proportion to each other ; that his smallest weight is a halfpenny weight ; and that he never made an assay of gold in his life.

" That after silver is assayed, if it is half a pennyweight better or worse than Standard, he reports it as such, but has no assay tables ; that he gets his bone ashes from town to make coppels, and makes as many at one time as serve him for half a year ; that his muffles are eight inches long, are arched, and have holes in the sides to give air while the metal is in fusion ; that he does not make them himself ; and that they will hold from six to nine coppels ; that he assays his silver with lead, which he receives from an assay master in London, whom he can confide in.

" Being desired to describe his method of assaying silver ; he said, I take a small quantity of silver from each piece (the quantity allowed by Act of Parliament is eight grains from every pound troy weight) which I weigh by the assay pound weight: I wrap it up in a thin sheet of lead, and when the furnace is properly heated, the assays are put in and fired off; they are taken out when cool, and then weighed; and from the waste we ascertain its goodness.

" That no officer is employed by the company in assaying Plate besides himself; that he has no salary, and takes what silver is allowed by law for assaying; that he was brought up a jeweller, and is in no way concerned in the manufacturing of plate, but buys all his plate from London.

"That the standard for plate is 11 oz. 2 dwt. of fine silver; and 18 dwt. of alloy; but they allow a remedy of 2 dwt. in the pound, because it would be hard upon a working tradesman, if he was not allowed something, as he does his best, and may be mistaken; that many times he had allowed it, and sometimes had found it over standard.

" Being asked if the trade of a working goldsmith, silversmith or plate-worker was necessary for qualifying a person for scraping or cutting wrought plate properly? he said, he thought a person bred to those trades the best qualified to know if all the plate in one parcel be of the same sort of silver, and whether the plate is forward enough in workmanship, but that he had acquired that knowledge without being brought up to the business, so as to be able to judge; and further said, he thought great judgment was necessary to know all the pieces that were affixed together in a piece of plate, such as a sword hilt, or an epergne; and thinks it impossible for an assay master to judge of the solder necessary for joining a piece of work, unless he was brought up to the trade of a silversmith.

" That the makers of wrought plate send a note with their names to the assay office, containing the name of the owner, the weight of the silver, and what articles it consists of; that he receives a halfpenny per ounce for assaying and marking such plate, which is entered in a book particularizing the day of the month when the plate was assayed, the name of the owner, the species of plate, and, if cut, he enters the worseness.

" That he has heard of convoys, which are intended by workmen to deceive the assayer; that he examines the work as near as he can, but never found out any such thing as convoys.

" That the marks he strikes upon wrought plate are the lion, the leopard's head, the Exeter mark (which is a castle), and the letter for the year; that the letter for the present year is Z, in Roman character; that the letter is appointed annually at the first Hall meeting after the 7th of August, and goes through the whole alphabet, and that A will be the letter for the next year.

" That the workman sets his own mark before the plate is sent to the office; that the witness has the custody of the marks, and if plate is doubtful upon the first assay, he detains it for a second trial; that he puts four grains of silver into the diet box for every pound weight of plate he assays and marks; that there are three locks and two keys to the diet box, one lock being spoilt; and the senior warden who has the custody of the diet box, keeps one of the keys and the junior warden the other; that the diet is put into the box once a year, on the 7th of August, being first wrapped up in paper, and marked what year's diet it is, and the witness has the custody of it until it is put into the box; and knows not when it was sent to the Tower; and that there are many years' diet now in the office.

"That he makes the assays of plate at such times as best suit his convenience, and never had any person to assist him in assaying ; and when he is absent or ill the thing stops.

"That he thinks the trust too great to be reposed in one man, and apprehends such a hall as Goldsmiths Hall is safer to the public, where there are so many checks, and no temptation to dishonesty, the officers having good salaries ; and he should prefer plate marked at Goldsmiths Hall, because of the sanction. That some years ago he assayed plate marked at Goldsmiths Hall, out of curiosity, and found it Standard.

"That he has been at Goldsmiths Hall, and seen the progress of business there ; and has used the remedy he has spoken of ever since he has been in the office."

In 1773 the Exeter company of goldsmiths consisted of five members, but there were other goldsmiths then working, and having their plate assayed at the Exeter assay office, who had not been admitted to the freedom of the company. Many of these resided at Plymouth and Dartmouth. The office appears to have done a fairly large amount of business until about the middle of the 19th century, when the number of manufacturing goldsmiths in Exeter, and the West of England generally, became considerably reduced. After 1850 the work dwindled away until at last the charges for assaying were found insufficient to cover the working and establishment expenses of the office, and it was closed in the year 1883.

Marks on wrought gold assayed at Exeter.

The marks on wrought gold assayed at Exeter were the same as on plate until 1798. If any were assayed there after that date, what has been said with reference to the substitution of the crown and figures in place of the lion passant in the case of York, on page 284, would be applicable here.

Following the tables of marks will be found a list of the names of Exeter goldsmiths from the 14th to the 19th century, compiled from various sources, with as. much completeness as it has been possible to attain. For many of the names in the list, and for assistance in compiling the tables of marks, the Author is indebted to Mr. J. Ellett Lake, Mr. F. T. Depree, of Exeter, and the Rev. J. F. Chanter, M.A., and other clergymen of the counties of Devon, Cornwall, Somerset and Dorset, who have, with the greatest possible cordiality, assisted the Author in this portion of his work.

MARKS ON EXETER PLATE.

No Exeter town mark has been found of earlier date than c. 1571; before that date only makers' marks appear to have been used.

TABLE I.

FROM 1544 TO 1592 OR THEREABOUT.

(The dates are approximate except where the articles are described as dated.)

DATE.	MARKS.	MAKER'S NAME.	ARTICLES AND OWNERS.
c. 1544-98	RH	Richard Hilliard.	Communion cups: St. Edmund's and St. Sidwell's, Exeter.
c. 1562 / 1607	RO	Richard Osborne.	Communion cups: Catteleigh.
c. 1568-74	I NORTH	John North.	Do. cup: Curry Mallett.
c. 1570	HH	Henry Hardwicke.	Chalices: Parkham and Holsworthy.
1570-3	X IONS	John Ions (Jones).	Communion cup: St. Petrock's, Exeter.
,,	I IONS	Do. do do.	Cover paten: Whitstone.
c. 1570 / 1600	S MORE ✿	Steven More.	Communion cup: Halwell.
1571	I N	John North.	Do. do., dated 1571: St. Davids, Exeter.
,,	I N	Do. do.	Communion cup: Messrs. Crichton.
,,	X I IONS	John Jons.	Do. do., dated 1571: Trevalga.
1572	IW	John Withycombe.	Trencher used as paten: Berrynarbor.
1575	X I IONS ✿	John Jons.	Mounts of cylindrical salt (ivory drum): Lord Swaythling.
,,	,, ,, ,, ✿	Do. do.	Standing salt: Mr. J. Dixon.
,,	X I ,, A	Do. do.	Com. cup, dated 1575: Lympstone, nr. Exeter.
,,	,, IO ,, ,,	Do. do.	Com. cup: Duloe, Cornwall.
1576	I IONS X B	Do. do.	Do. do., dated 1576: Tamerton, Devon.
,,	VI X	... ...	Do. do.: Eggesford and Broadwood-wiger, dated.
1580	X HORWOOD	Wm. Horwood.	Mounts of stone-ware jug: Messrs. Christie.
c. 1580	X I YEDS	John Eydes.	Mounts of stone-ware jug: Victoria and Albert Museum. Chalice and paten: Harpford.
1582	X C ESTON	C. Eston.	Com. cup, dated 1582: Cadbury, Devon. Do. do. do. 1585: Talaton, do. Lion-sejant spoon: Mr. A. S. Marsden Smedley.
,,	EASTON ✿	C. Easton.	Com. cup, dated 1582: formerly at Fen Ottery, Devon.
1585	X BENLY	— Bently.	Mounts of stone-ware jug: Ashmolean Museum.
,,	X HERMAN	R. Herman.	Seal-top spoon: Messrs. Christie.
1590	X ESTON N	C. Eston.	Com. cup, dated 1590: St. Andrew's, Plymouth.
1592	X C ESTON P	Do. do.	Lion-sejant spoon: Victoria and Albert Museum.

MARKS ON EXETER PLATE.

TABLE II.

FROM 1600 TO 1640 OR THEREABOUT.

(The dates are approximate except where the articles are described as dated.)

DATE.	MARKS.	MAKER'S NAME.	ARTICLES AND OWNERS.
1600		Richd. Osborn.	Maidenhead spoon : Mr. J. H. Walter.
,,		R. Herman.	Seal-top spoon : Do. do.
,,		No maker's mark.	Lion-sejant spoon : Do. do.
c. 1600		Richd. Osborn.	Apostle spoon : Mr. Crichton.
1606		,, ,,	Lion-sejant spoon, pricked 1606 : Noted by the Author.
c. 1610-20		William Bartlett. (1597-1646).	{ Com. cup : Crewkerne. { Seal-top spoons : Mr. W. Boore.
1620		,, ,,	Lion-sejant spoon : Messrs. Christie.
,,		Edward Anthony (1612-67).	Seal-top spoon : The Author's Collection.
,,		,, ,,	Do. do. : Dunn-Gardner Collection.
,,		?	Six maidenhead spoons : Mr. R. E. Brand.
c. 1630		Wm. Bartlett (probably).	Communion cup and paten, dated 1630 : Helston.
,,		Anthony mark, &c.*	Exeter mark in bowl, other marks on stem of seal-top spoon : Mr. H. D. Ellis.
c. 1635		John Lavers.	{ (Crowned X repeated after second IL). { Chalice : Ashwater.
,,		I. P.	Apostle spoon : noted by the Author.
c. 1635-8		John Lavers.	{ Seal-top spoon, pricked 1638 : do. do. { Do. do. : Sir Edward Marshall Hall, K.C.
c. 1640		... ...	Apostle spoon : Messrs. Crichton.
,,		H. P.	Do. do : Messrs. Bruford.
,,		Jasper Radcliffe.	Do. do. : Messrs. Christie.
,,		L. M.	Snuff-box : Mr. G. Henderson.
,,		Jasper Radcliffe.	Com. cup, dated 1640 : St. Petrock's, Exeter.
,,		Richd. Osborn.	Apostle spoon : Messrs. Christie.
,,		John Lavers.	{ Do. do. : Holburne Museum. { Seal-top spoon, with dot at each side of X : Sir { E. Marshall Hall, K.C.
,,		No maker's mark.	Apostle spoon : Holburne Museum.

* See Truro Marks, p. 462 *infra*.

MARKS ON EXETER PLATE.

TABLE III.

FROM 1640 TO 1698 OR THEREABOUT.

(The dates are approximate except where the articles are described as dated.)

DATE.	MARKS.	MAKER'S NAME.	ARTICLES AND OWNERS.
c. 1640-50		{ John Elston { Anthony Tripe	IE stamped twice, TA in monogram once, on chalice: Broadhembury; also on decorated trifid spoon: Messrs. Crichton.
,,		P. R.	Paten: Gerrans, Cornwall.
,,		Thomas Bridgeman.	Apostle spoon (St. Matthew): Mr. A. D. George.
,,		Edward Anthony.	Apostle spoon (St. Peter): Mr. J. H. Walter.
,,		Do. do.	Puritan spoon: Do. do.
c. 1646-98		I. F.	Patens: Bralton and Nymet St. George.
c. 1670		Jasper Radcliffe.	Snuffers tray: Messrs. Crichton.
1676		M. W.	Flat-stem spoon (pricked 1676): The Author's Collection.
,,		— S.	Embossed spoon, flat stem, foliated end: Mr. J. H. Walter.
c. 1680		... ...	Paten: Kingsnympton.
,,		No maker's mark.	Spoon, trifid end (pricked 1690): Mr. J. H. Walter.
,,		I. S.	Spoon, flat stem: Mr. J. H. Walter.
1690		John Mortimer.	Do. do. (pricked 1690): Mr. J. H. Walter.
c. 1690		Daniel Slade.	Flat-stem spoons: Mr. J. H. Walter, Mr. J. Bennett Stanford, and Messrs. Tessier.
,,		Wm. Ekins.	Flat-stem spoons: Mr. C. H. Chichester.
,,		Do. do.	Do. do.: Messrs. Debenham.
,,		John Mortimer.	Paten on three feet: St. Erth, Cornwall.
,,		... ...	The X mark in bowl, lion and castle (incuse) on stem of Apostle spoon: Kenwyn.
,,		I. P. (See Barnstaple, p. 459 *infra*).	Communion cup and paten: Lanteglos-by-Fowey.
,,		I. P.	Spoon, flat-stem: Mr. J. H. Walter.
1694		Nichs. Browne.	{ Rat-tail spoon: The Marquess of Breadalbane, K.G. { Same mark, with WE for Wm. Ekins, as above, { on trifid spoon: Mr. H. D. Ellis.
1698		No maker's mark.	Rat-tail spoon: Mr. J. H. Fitzhenry.

MARKS ON EXETER PLATE.

TABLE IV.

FIVE STAMPS AS BELOW.

	CASTLE.	BRIT-ANNIA.	LION'S HEAD ERASED.	DATE LETTER.	MAKER'S MARK.	MAKER'S NAME.	ARTICLES AND OWNERS.
1701-2	🛡	🛡	🛡	A	🛡	J. Elston.	Small mug : Mr. F. L. Fitzgerald.
ANNE. 1702-3	🛡	,,	,,	B	FO	Thos. Foote.	Trifid spoon : Mr. Lambert.
1703-4	🛡	,,	,,	C	Mu / Au	Hy. Muston. / John Audry.	Alms-dish : St. Stephen's, Exeter. / Trifid spoon : Mr. J. B. Stansby.
1704-5	,,	,,	,,	D	Br	Wm. Briant.	Straining spoon : St. Petrock's, Exeter.
1705-6	,,	,,	,,	E	FR	Richd. Freeman.	{ * Tankard : St. Goran, Cornwall. / { Also paten 1702 : St. Clear.
1706-7	,,	,,	,,	F	RE	Thos. Reynolds.	Rat-tail spoon : Mr. B. Jefferis.
1707-8	,,	,,	,,	G	WI / SA	Richd. Wilcocks. / Thos. Salter.	Do. do. : Messrs. Christie. / Porringer : Mr. J. E. Lake.
1708-9	🛡	,,	,,	H	Pl	Richd. Plint.	Rat-tail spoon : Mr. S. Deane.
1709-10	🛡	,,	,,	I	FV	Name not traced.†	Com. cup : St. Stephen's, Exeter.
1710-1	,,	,,	,,	K	Ri	Ed. Richards.	Rat-tail spoon : Mr. F. T. Depree.
1711-2	,,	,,	,,	L	TR / SW	Geo. Trowbridge. / Ed. Sweet.	Do. do. : Do. do. / Do. do. : Holburne Museum.
1712-3	,,	,,	,,	M	Ri	Ed. Richards.	Com. flagons : St. Sidwell's, Exeter.
1713-4	🛡	,,	,,	N	SL	Danl. Slade.	Rat-tail spoon : Holburne Museum.
GEO. I. 1714-5	,,	,,	,,	O	To / Mo	——— Tolcher. / John Mortimer.	Com. paten : St. David's, Exeter. / Rat-tail spoon : Mr. Glading.
1715-6	,,	,,	,,	P	TR	Geo. Trowbridge.	Com. plate : Redruth, Cornwall.
1716-7	,,	,,	,,	Q	Sy / Lo	Pent. Symonds. / Ab'm. Lovell.	Com. cup & paten : Do. do. / Small salver : Messrs. Christie.
1717-8	,,	,,	,,	R	SP	Pent. Symonds.	Com. paten : Tamerton Foliott.
1718-9	,,	,,	,,	S	AR	Peter Arno.	Rat-tail spoon : S. Ken. Museum.
1719-20	,,	,,	,,	T	WO	Andr. Worth.	Do. do : Mrs. Smithers.
1720-1	,,	,,	,,	V	BL / IE	Saml. Blachford / J. Elston.	Com. flagon : Tamerton Foliott. / Salver : Exeter Museum.
1721-2	🛡	🛡	🛡	W	IS	Thos. Sampson.	Rat-tail spoons : Mr. A. Rowe.
1722-3				X	SB	Saml. Blachford	Do. do. : Mr. Ince.
1723-4	,,	,,	,,	Y	IE	J. Elston.	Tankard : Messrs. Debenham and Storr.
1724-5	,,	,,	,,	Z	IW	Jas. Williams.‡	Rat-tail spoons : Mr. Chisholm.

* " Ex Dono Trevanion, 1706."
† A name such as Fuller, probably entered on missing page of Register.
‡ An IW, but without crown and mullett, was used at this date by John Webber.
See also additional Makers' Marks on p. 342 *infra.*

MARKS ON EXETER PLATE.

TABLE V.

FIVE STAMPS AS BELOW.

	CASTLE.	LEOPARD'S HEAD CROWNED.	LION PASSANT.	DATE LETTER.	MAKER'S MARK.	MAKER'S NAME.		ARTICLES AND OWNERS.
1725-6	⌂	⌂	⌂	a	SB	Saml.	Blachford.	Communion flagon: Uny-Lelant, Cornwall.
1726-7	,,	,,	,,	b	TS	Thos.	Sampson.	Gravy spoon: Victoria and Albert Museum.
GEO. II. 1727-8	,,	,,	,,	c	{ IC / PE	Joseph / Philip	Collier. / Elliott.	Coffee-pot: Mr. Stevens. / Rat-tail spoon: Mr. Davison.
1728-9	,,	,,	,,	d	IE	John	Elston, jr.	Paten: Morwenstow.
1729-30	,,	,,	,,	e	{ ,, / JS	Do. / James	do. / Strang.	Com. paten: Melksham, Wilts. / Small com. cup: S. Martin's, Exeter.
1730-1	,,	,,	,,	f	IB	John	Burdon.	Chocolate-pot: Messrs. Christie.
1731-2	,.	,,	,,	g	PE	Peter	Elliott.	Small mug: Mr. Lowe, Chester.
1732-3	,,	,,	,,	h	IC	Joseph	Collier.	Chocolate-pot: Messrs. Tiffany.
1733-4	,,	,,	,,	i	IE	John	Elston, jr.	Coffee-jug: Mr. Chappell.
1734-5	,,	,,	,,	k	SB	Sampson	Bennett.	Table-spoon: Messrs. Debenham & Storr.
1735-6	,,	,,	,,	l	PE	Philip	Elston.	Paten: Little Hempstead; Flagon: Bow.
1736-7	,,	,,	,,	m	JS	James	Strang.	Com. cup: Bishops Nympton.
1737-8	,,	,,	,,	n	PE	Philip	Elston.	Tankard: Collampton.
1738-9	,,	,,	,,	o	PS	Pent.	Symonds.	Small salver: Mr. W. Boore.
1739-40	,,	,,	,,	p	IB	John	Burdon.	Coffee-pot: Mr. A. J. Grimes.
1740-1	,,	,,	,,	q	IB	Do.	do.	Flagon: Talland Polperro, Cornwall.
1741-2	,,	,,	,,	r	Sy	Pent.	Symonds.	Tankard (Brit. std.): Mr. W. Boore.
1742-3	,,	,,	,,	s	IF	Name not traced. J.	Freeman?	Paten: Down St. Mary.
1743-4	,,	,,	,,	t	IB	John	Babbage?	Pair of alms-basins: St. Ives, Cornwall.
1744-5	,,	,,	,,	u	,,	Do.	do.	Coffee-pot: Messrs. Christie.
1745-6	,,	,,	,,	w				
1746-7	,,	,,	,,	x	PS	Pent.	Symonds.	{ Table-spoon: Mr. Lowe / Tankard (1750): St. Austell.
1747-8	,,	,,	,,	y	TB	Thos.	Blake.	Alms-dishes, dated 1747: Crediton.
1748-9	,,	,,	,,	z	JS	Jas.	Strang.	Small paten: St. Martin's, Exeter.

Variant of date-letter for 1748-9   z   ... ...   Mr. A. J. Grimes.

MARKS ON EXETER PLATE.

TABLE VI.

FIVE STAMPS AS BELOW.

	CASTLE	LEOPARD'S HEAD CROWNED.	LION PASSANT.	DATE LETTER	MAKER'S MARK.	MAKER'S NAME.	ARTICLES AND OWNERS.
1749-50	🏰	🐆	🦁	A	TB	Thomas Blake.	Table-spoon, double drop : Mr. Chisholm.
1750-1	,,	,,	,,	B	,,	,, ,,	Small salver : Mr. S. Phillips.
1751-2	,,	,,	,,	C	,,	,, ,,	Table-spoon : Mrs. Smithers.
1752-3	,,	,,	,,	D	WP	W. Parry.	Commun on cup : Yealmpton.
1753-4	,,	,,	,,	E	DC	Danl. Coleman.	Snuffers tray : Messrs. Spink.
1754-5	,,	,,	,,	F	WP	W. Parry.	Paten, etc. : Dunkeswell.
1755-6	,,	,,	..	G	,,	,, ,,	Tankard : Buckfastleigh.
1756-7	,,	,,	,,	H	TB	Thomas Blake.	Table-spoon : Mr. Crichton.
1757-8	,,	,,	,,	I	,,	,, ,,	Soup-ladle : Mr. J. B. Stansby.
1758-9	,,	,,	,,	K			
1759-60	,,	,,	,,	L	SF	Name not traced.	Tankard : Mr. E. A. Sandeman.
GEO. III. 1760-1	,,	,,	,,	M			
1761-2	,,	,,	,,	N			
1762-3	,,	,,	,,	O	MS	Mat'w Skinner.	Sauce-boat : Col. Fitzgerald.
1763-4	,,	,,	,,	P			
1764-5	,,	,,	,,	Q			
1765-6	,,	,,	,,	R			
1766-7	,,	,,	,,	S	RS	Richard Sams.	Lemon strainer : Messrs. Christie.
1767-8	,,	,,	,,	T	,,	,, ,,	Table-spoons : Mr. W. Boore.
1768-9	,,	,,	,,	U	JH	James Holt.	Tea-pot : Messrs. Crichton.
1769-70	,,	,,	,,	W	TC	Thomas Coffin.	Pap-boat : Mr. H. Mallett.
1770-1	,,	,,	,,	X	IF	J. Freeman.	Tankard : Hon. Mrs. Tremayne.
1771-2	,,	,,	,,	Y	RS	Richard Sams.	Do. : Holcombe Roger.
1772-3	,,	,,	,,	Z		... ...	Date-letter recorded.

MARKS ON EXETER PLATE.

TABLE VII.

FIVE STAMPS AS BELOW. NO LEOPARD'S HEAD AFTER 1777-8. KING'S HEAD FROM 1784.

	CASTLE.	LEOPARD'S HEAD CROWNED	LION PASSANT.	DATE LETTER.	MAKER'S MARK.	MAKER'S NAME.	ARTICLES AND OWNERS.
1773-4	🏰	🦁	🦁	A	RS	Richd. Sams.	Table-spoon : Judge Wynne Ffoulkes.
1774-5	,,	,,	,,	B			
1775-6	,,	,,	,,	C	TE / WW	Thos. Eustace. William West of Plymouth.	Table-spoon : Mrs. Smithers. Sauce pan : Mr. G. E. Farr.
1776-7	,,	,,	,,	D			
1777-8	,,	,,	,,	E			
1778-9	,,		🦁	F	,,	Thos. Eustace.	Table-spoon : Mr. E. Heron-Allen.
1779-80	,,		,,	G	,,	,, ,,	Do. do. : Do. do.
1780-1	,,		,,	H			
1781-2-3	,,		,,	I	,,	,, ,,	Do. do. : Do. do.
1783-4	,,	KING'S HEAD	,,	K	W·P	W. Pearse.	Skewer : Judge Wynne Ffoulkes.
1784-5	,,	👑	,,	L		Thos. Eustace (as 1775-6).	Table-spoon: Mr. E. Heron-Allen.
1785-6	,,	,,	,,	M	TE	Thos. Eustace.	Sauce-ladle : Mr. G. E. Farr.
1786-7	,,	👑	,,	N	JH	Joseph Hicks.	Table-spoons : Mr. B. Jefferis.
1787-8	,,	,,	,,	O	,,	,, ,,	Do. do. : Do. do.
1788-9	,,	,,	,,	P	,,	,, ,,	Do. do. : Do. do.
1789-90	,,	,,	,,	q	JP	J. Pearse.	Communion cup : Twitchen.
1790-1	,,	,,	,,	r			
1791-2	,,	,,	,,	f	JH	Joseph Hicks.	Paten : St. Lawrence, Exeter.
1792-3	,,	,,	,,	t			
1793-4	,,	,,	,,	u			
1794-5	,,	,,	,,	w			
1795-6	,,	,,	,,	X	RF	Richd. Ferris.	Table-spoon : Mr. E. Heron-Allen.
1796-7	,,	,,	,,	y			

MARKS ON EXETER PLATE.

TABLE VIII.

FIVE STAMPS AS BELOW.

	CASTLE.	LION PASSANT.	DATE LETTER.	KING'S HEAD.	MAKER'S MARK.	MAKER'S NAME.		ARTICLES AND OWNERS.
1797-8	🏰	🦁	A	👑	RF	Richd.	Ferris.	Small salver : Mr. Lowe.
1798-9	,,	,,	B	,,	,,	,,	,,	Coffee-pot : Do. do.
1799 / 1800	,,	,,	C	👑	JH / ww	Joseph / W.	Hicks. / Welch.	Table-spoon : Mr. Geo. Henderson. / Do. do. : Messrs. Debenham.
1800-1	,,	,,	D	,,	JH	Joseph	Hicks.	Do. do. : Mr. Lowe.
1801-2	,,	,,	E	,,	,,	,,	,,	Alms dish : Mesham.
1802-3	,,	,,	F	,,	,,	,,	,,	Tea-spoons : Mr. Fuller.
1803-4	,,	,,	G	,,	TE	Thos.	Eustace.	Tankard : East Worlington.
1804-5	,,	,,	H	,,	RF	Richd.	Ferris.	Table-spoon : Mr. Crichton.
1805-6	🏰	🦁	I	,,	,,	,,	,,	Do. do. : Mr. Payne.
1806-7	,,	,,	K	,,	,,	,,	,,	Table plate : Mrs. Budd.
1807-8	,,	,,	L	,,	,,	,,	,,	Do. do. : Do. do.
1808-9	,,	,,	M	,,				
1809-10	,,	,,	N	,,	JL	J.	Langdon	Waiter : Rumonsleigh.
1810-1	,,	,,	O	,,	ww	W.	Welch.	Alms-dish : Holy Trinity, Exeter.
1811-2	,,	,,	P	,,	JH	Joseph	Hicks.	Tea-spoons : Mr. Bruford.
1812-3	,,	,,	Q	,,	,,	,,	,,	Dessert-spoons : Mr. Chisholm.
1813-4	,,	,,	R	,,	GT	G.	Turner.	Table-spoon : Mr. Harris.
1814-5	,,	,,	S	,,	,,	,,	,,	Table plate : Mr. F. T. Depree.
1815-6	,,	,,	T	,,	,,	,,	,,	Do. do. : Do. do.
1816-7	,,	,,	U	,,	GF	Geo.	Ferris.	Skewers : Messrs. Crichton.

MARKS ON EXETER PLATE.

TABLE IX.

FIVE STAMPS AS BELOW.

	CASTLE.	LION PASSANT.	DATE LETTER.	KING'S HEAD.	MAKER'S MARK.	MAKER'S NAME.	ARTICLES AND OWNERS.
1817-8	🏰	🦁	a	◐	GF	Geo. Ferris.	Table plate : Mr. F. T. Depree.
1818-9	,,	,,	b	,,	,,	,, ,,	Do. do. : Do. do.
1819-20	,,	,,	c	,,	JH	Joseph Hicks.	Table-spoons : Mr. G. Lowe.
GEO. IV. 1820-1	,,	,,	d	,,	,,	,, ,,	Do. do. : Do. do.
1821-2	,,	,,	e	,,	,,	,, ,,	Do. do. : Do. do.
1822-3	,,	,,	f	◐	GF	Geo. Ferris.	Table plate : Mr. F. T. Depree.
1823-4	,,	,,	g	,,	,,	,, ,,	Tankard : Uffculme.
1824-5	,,	,,	h	,,	,,	,, ,,	Com. cup : Holcombe Baswell.
1825-6	,,	,,	i	,,	IE	John Eustace.	Table plate : Mr. F. T. Depree.
1826-7	,,	,,	k	,,	GM	Name not traced.	Do. do. : Do. do.
1827-8	,,	,,	l	,,	JO	J. Osmont.	Do. do. : Do. do.
1828-9	,,	,,	m	,,	,,	,, ,,	Table-spoon : Mrs. Budd.
1829-30	,,	,,	n	,,	JH	Joseph Hicks.	Butter-knife : Do.
WM. IV. 1830-1	,,	,,	o	,,	,,	,, ,,	Tea-spoons : Do.
1831-2	🏰	🦁	p	◐	WS	W. Sobey.	Table-spoons : Messrs. M. & S. Lyon.
1832-3	,,	,,	q	,,	JS	John Stone.	Salt-spoons : Do. do.
1833-4	🏰	🦁	r	,,	WP	Wm. Pope.	Table plate : Mr. F. T. Depree.
1834-5	,,	,,	s	◐	JO	J. Osmont.	Do. do. : Do. do.
1835-6	,,	,,	t	,,	WRS	W. R. Sobey.	Do. do. : Do. do.
1836-7	,,	,,	u	,,	WW	William Welch.	Toast-rack : The Day Collection.

MARKS ON EXETER PLATE.

TABLE X.

FIVE STAMPS AS BELOW.

	CASTLE.	LION PASSANT.	DATE LETTER.	QUEEN'S HEAD.	MAKER'S MARK.	MAKER'S NAME.	ARTICLES AND OWNERS.
VICT. 1837-8			A		SOBEY	W. R. Sobey.	Table plate : Mr. F. T. Depree.
1838-9	,,	,,	B		J·O	J. Osmont.	Salt-spoons : Mr. G. Lowe.
1839-40	,,	,,	C		TB	Thos. Byne.	Tea-spoons : Mr. F. T. Depree.
1840-1	,,	,,	D	,,	J·S	J. Stone.	Egg-spoons : Mr. G. Lowe.
1841-2		,,	E	,,	RAM SEY	— Ramsey.	Tea-spoons : Mr. F. T. Depree.
1842-3	,,	,,	F	,,	SOBEY	W. R. Sobey.	Com. paten : St. Stephen's, Exeter.
1843-4		,,	G	,,	,,	,, ,,	Table-spoon : Mr. G. Lowe.
1844-5	,,	,,	H	,,	WRS	,, ,,	Fish-slice : Do. do.
1845-6	,,	,,	I	,,	,, SOBEY	,, ,, ,, ,,	Table-spoon : Mr. F. T. Depree. Com. paten : All Hallows, Exeter.
1846-7	,,	,,	K	,,	,,	,, ,,	Tea-spoons : Mr. Fuller.
1847-8	,,	,,	L	,,	W W W	? Williams.	Do. do. : Judge Wynne-Ffoulkes.
1848-9	,,	,,	M	,,	J·S	J. Stone.	Table plate : Mr. F. T. Depree.
1849-50	,,	,,	N	,,	WRS	W. R. Sobey.	Do. do. : Do. do.
1850-1	,,	,,	O	,,	,,	,, ,,	Do. do. : Do. do.
1851-2	,,	,,	P	,,	J·O	J. Osmont.	From Assay Office marks, supplied by Mr. J. E. Lake.
1852-3	,,	,,	Q	,,	,,	,, ,,	Do. do. do.
1853-4	,,	,,	R	,,	IP	Isaac Parkin.	Do. do. do.
1854-5	,,	,,	S	,,	,,	* ,, ,,	Do. do. do.
1855-6	,,	,,	T	,,	,,	,, ,,	Do. do. do.
1856-7	,,	,,	U	,,	J·S	J. Stone.	Table plate : Mr. F. T. Depree.

* Also mark of W. R. Sobey, on Communion cup : Harberton.

MARKS ON EXETER PLATE.

TABLE XI.

FIVE STAMPS AS BELOW.

	CASTLE.	LION PASSANT.	DATE LETTER.	QUEEN'S HEAD.	MAKER'S MARK.	MAKER'S NAME.	ARTICLES AND OWNERS.
1857-8	🏰	🦁	A	👑	J·S	J. Stone.	Paten cover of communion cup: Alderholt.
1858-9	,,	,,	B	,,	,,	,, ,,	Table plate: Mr. F. T. Depree.
1859-60	,,	,,	C	,,		... ...	From the Assay Office plate.
1860-1	,,	,,	D	,,	PO	Name not traced.	Tea-spoons: Mr. T. Perrett.
1861-2	,,	,,	E	,,	J W	Jas. Williams.	Table plate: Mr. F. T. Depree.
1862-3	,,	,,	F	,,		... ...	From the Assay Office plate.
1863-4	,,	,,	G	,,		... ...	Do. do. do.
1864-5	,,	,,	H	,,		... ...	Do. do. do.
1865-6	,,	,,	I	,,		... ...	Do. do. do.
1866-7	,,	,,	K	,,		... ...	Do. do. do.
1867-8	,,	,,	L	,,		... ...	Do. do. do.
1868-9	,,	,,	M	,,	HL	Henry Lake.	Butter dish: Mr. Barnet.
1869-70	,,	,,	N	,,		... ...	From the Assay Office plate.
1870-1	,,	,,	O	,,		... ...	Do. do. do.
1871-2	,,	,,	P	,,		... ...	Do. do. do.
1872-3	,,	,,	Q	,,		... ...	Do. do. do.
1873-4	,,	,,	R	,,		... ...	Do. do. do.
1874-5	,,	,,	S	,,		... ...	Do. do. do.
1875-6	,,	,,	T	,,		... ...	Do. do. do.
1876-7	,,	,,	U	,,		... ...	Do. do. do.

MARKS ON EXETER PLATE.

TABLE XII.

FIVE STAMPS AS BELOW.

	CASTLE.	LION PASSANT.	DATE LETTER.	QUEEN'S HEAD.	MAKER'S MARK.	MAKER'S NAME.	ARTICLES AND OWNERS.
1877-8			A		J.W & Co	J. Whipple & Co.	Engraved goblet: Mr. Bruford.
1878-9	,,	,,	B	,,		... ...	From the Assay Office plate.
1879-80	,,	,,	C	,,		... ...	Do. do. do.
1880-1	,,	,,	D	,,		... ...	Do. do. do.
1881-2	,,	,,	E	,,		... ...	Do. do. do.
1882-3	,,	,,	F	,,	WE FD JT	Ellis, Depree & Tucker }	Com. plate: St. Matthew's, Exeter.

The communion plate at St. Matthew's above-mentioned appears to have been some of the last work assayed at Exeter, as the office was finally closed in 1883.

SUPPLEMENTARY LIST OF MARKS OF GOLDSMITHS

Impressed at Exeter, but not illustrated in the preceding tables :—

DATE.	MARK.	NAME.	DATE.	MARK.	NAME.
1701	S1	Daniel Slade.	1722	PS	Pentecost Symonds.
c 1706	JO	Peter Jouett.	1728	TC	Thomas Coffin.
1707	Sa	Thos. Sampson.	1730	IR	John Reed
1708	Wi	Richard Wilcocks. ?	1732	TC	Thomas Clarke.
1709	SY	Pentecost Symonds.	,,	IS	John Suger.
1710	JP	John Pike.	1741	MM	Micon Melun.
,,	Be	Joseph Bennick.	1771	RB	Richd. Birdlake (Plymouth).
1713	Su	John Suger.	1825	SL	Simon Lery.
1714	Tr	Anthony Tripe.	1830	IP	Isaac Parkin.
1717	Wi	Zacariah Williams.	1835	GT TT	G. Turner & partner (? Son).
1719	BE	Joseph Bennick.	1845	JG	J. Golding (Plymouth).
1721	ER	Edward Richard.	1847	HE	Henry Ellis.
,,	IM	John March.	1850	IP GS	Isaac Parkin & Geo. Sobey.

NAMES OF EXETER GOLDSMITHS.

[FROM A.D. 1327 TO 1883.]

CHRONOLOGICALLY ARRANGED.

(Many of the Goldsmiths mentioned in this list may have worked at an earlier date than the first mentioned, and may have continued working later than the last-mentioned date.)

Name of Goldsmith.		Earliest Mention.	Entered.	Latest Mention.
John de	Wewlingworth	1327		
John	Busse	1330		
John	Russel	1395		1397
John	Goldsmith	1424		
Thomas	Colyne	1474		
Thomas	White	1477		
William	Colton	1512		1560
William	Kitylton	1513		
Henry the	Goldsmith	1518		
Richard	Bassett	1527		
Thomas	Erryt	1528		1552
Henry	Bestet	,,		1533
William	Smith	,,		1556
Hugh	Page	1533		
Richard	Hilliard	1545		d 1594
James	Walker	,,		1562
William	Pynnefold	1559		
Francis	Lavender	1560		
John	Dayman	,,		
Richard	Osborne	1562		1607
Gawey	Furney	,,		
Roger	Wodes	,,		
William	Ottery	,,		
William	Nicholls	,.		1566
John	Ions, Jons or Jones	1565		1580
T.	Mathew of Tregoney	,,		1585
D.?	Coton	,,		
John	Coton	,,		
John	North	1568		1574
Edward	Spicer	,,		
John	Averie	1569		1621
Steven	More	1570		1600
Philip	Driver	1571		
Henry	Hardwick	,,		
Nicholas	Reeve	,,		
George	Lyddon	,,		
H——	D——	,,		
Edward	Harman	1572		
William	Nicholls	,,		
M——	H——	1574		
John	Yeds or Eydes	1575		
C.	Eston or Easton	1576		1592
Thomas	Bridgeman	1577		1620
William	Horwood	1580		1613
——	Bently	1585		
——	Benetlye	,,		
Ralph	Herman	,,		c. 1620
Jeremy	Hilliard	1586		
John	Lavers	1595		1648
William	Bartlett	1597		1646
William	Horwood	1598		1613
William	Bartlett	1600		1640
Edward	Anthony	1610		1667
B. Y. or	Y. B.	1620		,,
R.	Osborn	c. 1620		
Jasper	Radcliffe	1624		1675
Roger	Mallock	1630		1654
George	Barnes	1640		1648
H——	P——	1646		
Thomas	Bridgeman	1650		
George	Knowling	1658		1676
Nicholas	Tripe	1662		1685
William	Wootton	,,		1690
William	Reed	1664		1680
Samuel	Cowley	1665		1687
John	Ridler	1668		1700
Thomas	Wood	1672		
M——	W——	1676		
John	Palmer	1677		1698
James	Tucker	1678		1708
Thomas	Salter	1679		1723
Samuel	Bidwell	1680		1691
John	Mortimer	1684		1716
William	Bryant	1685		1706
Edward	Spicer	,,		1713
Nicholas	Glanville	1686		
William	Ekins	1687		1712
John	Cleek	,,		
Daniel	Slade	1688		1713
William	Drake	1690		1725
I——	S——	,,		1715
I——	P——	,,		
Nicholas	Browne	1692		1728
Nicholas	Kennicot	1693		
Edmond	Richards	1694		1736
	(Assay Master 1701-8)			
Anthony	Tripe	1695	1712	1728
Peter	Townsend	1698		
	(Disfranchised this year)			
John	Audry	1701		
Thomas	Foote	,,		d 1708
Joseph	Leigh	,,		1728
J.	Elston	,,		,,
Henry	Muston	,,		1721
John	Browne	,,		c 1730
Peter	Elliott	1703	1703	1730
	(Dartmouth)			
Jacob	Tythe	,,	,,	
	(La'n'ston)			
Mary	Ashe		,,	
	(La'n'ston)			
Richard	Vavasour		1704	
	(Totnes)			
Richard	Willcocks		,,	
	(Plymouth)			
Richard	Holin		,,	
	(Truro)			
Edward	Sweet		,,	1710
	(Dunster)			
James	Strang		1705	1726
Robert	Catkill		,,	
Thomas	Reynolds		,,	1709
Thomas	Haynshaw or Haysham	1705		
	(Bridgewater)			

Name of Goldsmith.		Earliest Mention.	Entered.	Latest Mention.	Name of Goldsmith.		Earliest Mention.	Entered.	Latest Mention.
John	Manly (Dartmouth)	1705			John	Torkington (Totnes)		1727	
Richard	Freeman (Plymouth)	,,		1729	Richard	Freeman	1729		1769
Richard	Plint (Truro)		1705	,,	Moses	Pelet	1730		1734
Peter	Jouet (Topsham)	,,	1706		Francis	Trowbridge (Assay Master, 1731-51)	,,		1757
Samuel	Blachford (Plymouth)		,,	1728	Daniel	Coleman	1738		1758
Pentecost	Symonds (Plymouth)	1706	,,	1742	James le	Compt	1739		1743
Thomas	Sampson		,,	1728	Samuel	Glyde	1740		1753
Phillip	Elston	1707	1723	1748	Joseph	Pearse	1748		
Benjamin	Browne	1708		1716	W.	Parry	1750		1768
Robert	Palmer (Assay Master, 1708-31)	,,		1726	William	Browne	1753		1759
————	Fu———	1709			Lewis	Courtail	1756		1757
John	Pike, jr. (Plymouth)		1710		Thomas	Coffin	1757		1773
Joseph	Bennick (Liscard)		,,		Matthew	Skinner (Assay Master, 1757-73)	,,		,,
George	Trowbridge		,,	1741	Richard	Sams (Assay Master, 1787-9)	,,		1815
————	Tolcher (Plymouth)		1711		————	Shatlin	,,		
William	Adams (Falmouth)		,,		Ed.	Broadhurst (Plymouth)		1757	
John	Suger		1712		Roger B.	Symons (Plymouth)		1758	1773
Joseph	Collier (Plymouth)		1713	1728	William	Welch (Plymouth)		,,	,,
Joseph	Coles	1713		1730	Richard	Jenkins (Plymouth)		1760	1806
Adam	Hutchings (Totnes)		1714		Thomas	Thorne (Plymouth)		,,	1773
Andrew	Worth (Modbury)		,,	1721	David	Jones		,,	1781
Edward	Strong or Strang (Fowey)		1715		————	Symons, jr. (Plymouth)		1761	
John	Brinley	1715		1717	Thomas	Strong (Plymouth)	1766		1773
Peter	Arno (Barnstaple)		1716		Thomas	Kaynes or Raynes	1767		1770
Abraham	Lovell (Plymouth)		,,	1722	James	Holt	1768		1773
A.	Brinley		,,		David	Hawkins (Plymouth)	1769		,,
John	Reed	1716	,,	1720	Thomas	Beer (Plymouth)	1770		
James	Williams		1717	1725	William	Coffin (Assay Master, 1773-87)	1773		1787
John	Burdon	1719		1723	Thomas	Gilbert	,,		
Micon	Melun (Falmouth)	1720		1727	William	Harvey (Plymouth)			1773
Francis	Bishop (Bodmin)	,,		1773	Benjamin S.	Nathan (Plymouth)			,,
John	Murch (Tiverton)		1720		John	Tingcombe (Plymouth)			,,
Zachariah	Williams (Plymouth)		,,		William	Evelegh (Dartmouth)			,,
James	Stevens		1721	1750	James	Jenkins (Plymouth)			,,
Sampson	Bennett (Falmouth)		,,	1736	Richard	Birdlake (Plymouth)			,,
Jane	Maryon (Penryn)		1722		Edward	Broadhurst (Plymouth)			,,
Samuel	Wilmott (Plymouth)		1723		John	Brown (Plymouth)			,,
John	Elston, jr.	1723	,,		Jason	Rolt (Plymouth)			,,
Thomas	Blake	1724		1759	John	Eustace (per two)	1776		1826
John	Webber (Plymouth)		1724		Ezchiel	Abraham	1780		
Thomas	Clarke		1725		William	Upjohn	,,		
James	Marshall		,,		Richard	Crutchett	,,		
John	Babbage	1725		1741	W.	Pearse	,,		1790
John	Boutel (Plymouth)		1726		J.	Balle	1782		
					W———	P———	1783		
					Joseph	Hicks	1784		

Name of Goldsmith.	Earliest Mention.	Entered.	Latest Mention.	Name of Goldsmith.	Earliest Mention.	Entered.	Latest Mention.
Moses Mordecai		1788		E. Ramsay		1840	1860
Richard Sams, jr.	1789		1816	I. Fulton		,,	,,
(Assay Master, 1789-1816)				W. W. W.			1848
James Traies		1790		W. H. Row		1849	
(Dartmouth)				Wm. Thos. Maynard	1854		1883
William Dunsford		1792		(Assay Master, 1854-83)			
(Plymouth)				Joseph Head		1855	
Richard Ferris	1794		1810	W. W. Hill		,,	
G. Turner	1812		1834	James Williams		1857	1867
Edward C. Maynard	1816		1849	Philip Osmont		,,	
(Assay Master, 1816-49)				George Ferris, jr.			1859
George Ferris	1817		1838	Thos. H. Stone		1861	
John or Jas. Osmont	1827	1835	1855	Henry Lake		1868	1883
G. M.			1827	Jas. Croad Ross		1869	
J. Langdon	1830			Josiah Williams		,,	
Samuel Lery		1830		Wm. Geo. Caunter		1875	,,
William R. Sobey	1831	1835	1851	John Ellett Lake		,,	1886
W. S.	,,			J. Whipple & Co.			1877
John Stone	1832	1841	1859	W. Ellis			
W. Pope	1833			F. Templer Depree &		1882	
Jacob Nathan		1833		J. Tucker			
Isaac Parkin	1835	1835	1856	Thomas Salter			1883
(Assay Master, 1849-54)				W. T. Maynard			,,
E. Sweet	1836			(Assay Master)			
H. Norris	,,			W. Woodman	1883		
William Welch	1799		1837				
Thomas Byne	1839	1855					

CHAPTER XIV

THE NEWCASTLE GOLDSMITHS
AND THEIR MARKS

For much of this chapter the Author is indebted to a monograph on *The Goldsmiths of Newcastle*, by Mr. J. R. Boyle, F.S.A., by means of whose kind introduction access was obtained to large collections of plate, both ecclesiastical and secular, in Hull and other parts of Yorkshire, which furnished material for a considerable part of the tables of York, Newcastle, and Hull marks appearing in this work.

History of the
Company.

The earliest known reference to Newcastle goldsmiths occurs in an ordinance of the 33 Henry III. (1248), commanding the bailiffs and men of Newcastle-upon-Tyne to choose four of the most trusty persons of their town for the office of moneyers, and other four like persons for the keeping of the king's mints there, *and two fit and prudent goldsmiths to be assayers of the money to be made there*, and one fit and trusty clerk for the keeping of the exchange ; and to send them to the Treasurer and Barons of the Exchequer, to do there what by ancient custom and assize was required to be done. By the 2 Hen. VI. c. 14 (1423), an Act previously mentioned, it was ordained that Newcastle-upon-Tyne should have a touch according to the ordinance of its mayor, bailiffs, or governor,

The Goldsmiths
of Newcastle
Incorporated
with other
Craftsmen,
1536.

After that, no reference to the goldsmiths of Newcastle appears till 1536, when they were incorporated, together with freemen of other trades, as a company of goldsmiths, plumbers, glaziers, pewterers, and painters. The original charter of incorporation, granted by the mayor, sheriff, and aldermen of Newcastle, still exists amongst the archives of the Plumbers' Company.

"The Company," as Mr. Boyle explains, "was to be governed by four wardens, viz., a goldsmith, a plumber, a glazier, and a pewterer or painter. No brother was to follow any trade except that to which he was apprenticed, on pain of a penalty of 3s. 4d. Any brother taking 'a Scots man borne in Scotland' as apprentice or workman was to be fined 40s., half of which went to the company, and the other half to 'the upholdyng of the works of tyne Bridge'. Every apprentice on obtaining his freedom was to pay 6s 8d., 'and a pott of ale w^t thappurtenances'. If any brother defamed another by calling him 'a Scott, a morderer, a thefe,' and 'at sise or sessions was ffounde culpable,' he was to be expelled from the company, and not received again till 'such tyme that he be clerely & duely purged & acquited by dew order of the law'."

Of the original members of the company, five were goldsmiths, viz., Thomas Cramer, James Chawbre, Geoffrey Hall, Humphrey Coyll, and Nicholas Cramer. From the number of goldsmiths' names recorded, it seems that their art flourished in Newcastle in the 16th century, for although no Newcastle plate of earlier date than about the middle of the 17th century is now known, it is more probable that 16th century plate was melted down in the troublous times of Charles I. than that none was wrought. From 1536 to 1650 thirteen goldsmiths appear to have been admitted to the company. They were Valentine Baker, James Austold, Nicholas Brutte, John Harper, John Cramer, Francis Sose, Anthony Sympson, William Seaton, John Sympsoun, Oswald Carr, John Baker, James Wylson, and John Baynes.

Goldsmiths of the 16th and 17th centuries.

The goldsmiths who joined the company from 1656 to 1697 signed the first transcript of the charter of 1536. At the very bottom the almost obliterated signature of William Ramsay appears, certainly enough identifiable by the long tail of his R. The column headed "Gold-Smiths," after a transcript of the names appended to the original, bears the signatures of William Ramsay, John Wilkinson, William Robinson, John Dowthwaite, John Norris, Francis Batty, Albany Dodson, Eli Bilton, Ffrancis Anderson, Cuthbert Ramsay, William Ramsay (junior), Abraham Hamer, Robert Shrive, and Thomas Hewitson. The last-named attained his freedom in 1697.

One of these persons, Ffrancis Anderson, was not a goldsmith but a confectioner.

In 1598 the company consisted apparently of only 14 members, of whom three were goldsmiths, viz., Anthony Sympson, James Wilson and John Baynes. On the 19 June, 1599, Baynes paid 40s. to the company for some "agrementt" which "shold have ben thre pound," but 20s. were generously "remitted for his wyffe". On the 17 August in the same year he took one Thomas Royd, son of Thomas Royd, "mylliner," as apprentice ; and on the 3 February, 1599-1600, he took as apprentice one John Nicholson, son of George Nicholson.

From this time till 1656, in which year William Ramsay joined the company, the society had no goldsmith amongst its members.   There is indeed one person (William Robinson), described as a "Goulsmith, late of Newcastle, deceased," in the enrolment of his son's apprenticeship (20 Aug., 1657) and once elsewhere as an "imbroderer"; doubtless a manufacturer of gold and silver lace, then largely employed in the enrichment of costume.   Ramsay's accession to the company was followed two years later by that of John Wilkinson, from which time till 1697 the goldsmiths of Newcastle appear to have been prosperous.

The Act 8 & 9 Wm. III. c. 8, which raised the standard for plate and inferentially gave to the Goldsmiths' Company of London the sole right of assaying, inflicted a hardship and inconvenience upon the goldsmiths of Newcastle similar to that suffered by all other manufacturers in the provinces, who were put to the risk, expense, and delay of sending their plate to London to be assayed.   To remedy this hardship, the Act 12 & 13 Wm. III. c. 4, was passed in 1700, establishing assays at York, Exeter, Bristol, Chester, and Norwich, but by reason probably that Newcastle was not one of the places where mints had been established for recoining the silver money, it was not mentioned in that Act.   But although plate could not have been legally assayed in Newcastle between 1696 and 1702, there is little doubt about its having been wrought there during the interval, for at All Saints' Church, Newcastle, there are two communion flagons bearing the marks of Thomas Hewitson, dated the 25 Dec., 1697 and 1698 respectively; a mug of 1701 bears the mark of Eli Bilton.   On the 9 February, 170$\frac{1}{2}$, a petition was presented to the House of Commons by the goldsmiths of Newcastle, supported by another from the Mayor, Alderman, Sheriff, and Common Council setting forth the inconvenience they suffered by being compelled to send their plate to York to be assayed, whereby they were in "danger of losing the greatest part of their trade, which chiefly consists of plate bespoke to be wrought up in a short time, and they cannot have it returned from York in less than a fortnight's time".   In consequence of these petitions an Act of Parliament, 1 Anne, Stat. 1, c. 9, was passed, which received the royal assent on 30 March, 1702, re-establishing the assay office at Newcastle.

This Act (reciting that "whereas in the town of Newcastle upon

Tyne there is and time out of mind hath been an ancient company of goldsmiths, which, with their families are like to be ruined" by the operation of the Act of 1696-7, and their trade "utterly lost in the said town; and whereas by the statute of the second of Henry the sixth, the town of Newcastle upon Tyne is one of the places appointed to have touches for wrought silver plate"), enacted that the town of Newcastle should be appointed for the assaying and marking of wrought plate, to execute all "the powers, authorities, and directions" conferred upon other towns and cities by the Act of 1700-1, "as fully and amply to all intents, constructions, and purposes as if the said town had been expressly named in the said act". The same Act provided that the gold-smiths, silversmiths, and plate-workers, who had served apprenticeships to those trades and were freemen of Newcastle, should be incorporated and known as the Company of Goldsmiths of Newcastle-upon-Tyne. The Act further provided for the election of two wardens annually and for the appointment of an assay master, and stated the marks which were to be impressed upon all plate assayed there.

The marks required at this time were, first, the maker's mark (which consisted of the first two letters of his surname); second, the lion's head erased; third, "the figure of a woman commonly called Britannia"; fourth, the arms of the city or town where the plate was assayed; and, lastly, a variable letter or mark to denote the year in which the assay was made. The only difference between the marks then appointed for Newcastle and those of the other re-established provincial offices being in the respective town marks, which in each case consisted of the arms of the city. London differed from the provincial offices in having no distinguishing town mark.

Although the Act of Parliament constituted the goldsmiths of New-castle an independent corporation, they continued in association with the plumbers, pewterers, painters, and glaziers (with the exception of an interval from 1707 to 1711), till 1716, when they finally separated themselves. It must, however, be stated that during considerable portions of this period they held meetings independently of the rest of the association, formulated their own regulations, and kept their own minute books, which are perfectly complete from the establishment of the company in 1702 to the time when the assay office was closed in 1885. Their first assay book, however, begins in 1747 and ends in 1755. The next book which has been preserved begins in 1761, and

The Newcastle goldsmiths continued in association with other trades till 1716, when they became a separate body.

from this date the series is complete down to the closing of the office. Almost their most precious record, however, is the circular copper plate on which from shortly after 1702 the punches of the makers whose plate was assayed at Newcastle were impressed. It contains 287 different marks, most of which can be identified. On this copper plate are also to be found the marks of John Langwith and Joseph Buckle, of York, who by agreement (in consideration of an annual fee) had their plate assayed and stamped at Newcastle from the year 1717 when the York office was temporarily closed.

In the early part of 1773 the goldsmiths of Sheffield and Birmingham having petitioned Parliament for the establishment of assay offices in their respective towns, the Goldsmiths' Company of London, in opposing the establishment of these rival offices, suggested that great irregularities, if not frauds, were practised at the provincial halls and, as already stated, a committee was appointed to enquire into the matter and to report thereon to Parliament. The Newcastle Company appealed to their representatives, Sir W. Blackett and Mr. Ridley, to watch and protect their interests. The replies of both members are preserved amongst the company's archives.

Parliamentary Committee appointed to enquire into the working of the provincial assay offices, 1773.

Mr. Ridley stated that a separate committee had been appointed to enquire into the alleged malpractices of provincial offices, and suggested that "perhaps the London Gent^n. may attempt to take away those assay offices already established". He added that a messenger from the House of Commons would be sent to Newcastle to serve the assay master, " who I understand is Matt. Prior," with a notice to attend the committee on the 22 March. The committee ordered a return from each assay office, giving the number and names of the members of its company, the names and trade of the wardens and assessor, an account when and before whom the assayer had been sworn, the names and places of abode of all persons who sent plate to be assayed, and the weight of all gold and silver plate which had been assayed, marked, broken and defaced during the preceding seven years.

Matthew Prior posted to London, and was examined by the committee on the 22 March. His evidence, copied from the minutes of the committee, reported by Mr. Thos. Gilbert and presented to Parliament on the 29 April, 1773, appears on the two following pages.

METHOD OF CONDUCTING THE ASSAY OFFICE AT
NEWCASTLE UPON TYNE.

" Mr. Matthew Prior (a musical and mathematical instrument maker and tuner, assay master of the Goldsmiths Company of Newcastle upon Tyne) produced, pursuant to the orders of your committee, the several accounts annexed in the appendix, No. 5 ; and informed your committee that upon his being elected to the office of assay master, he took an oath prescribed by the Act of King William the Third, and is guided in his duty by that Act.

The Assay Master's evidence before the Parliamentary Committee in 1773.

" That he attended the assay office for his father, who was assay master many years before he died, and that the Company had often seen him make assays for his father.

" He also produced to your committee his assay weights, and said he bought them in London ; that he had weighed them to see if they bore a due proportion and had tried them with reports of assays of silver made in London, and found they agreed to about a pennyweight ; and that the lowest subdivision in his reports is half a pennyweight.

" That he makes his assays upon coppels made of bone ashes, which he prepares himself several months before he uses them ; that his muffles are of the same size and form as those made in London, and made of the same sort of clay that glasshouse pots are made of, and will hold about 21 coppels ; that he assays two days a week ; that he puts refined lead with the silver into the coppel in order to make the assay, and assays the lead before he uses it, but never found any silver in it.

" Being desired to describe his method of assaying silver, he said, we scrape a quantity of silver from every part of the vessel that comes to the office ; we weigh that in the assay scales very exactly with the twelve ounce weight ; we then add a quantity of fine lead to the assay, put it upon a coppel, and refine it to fine silver ; when it is fine we draw it out of the fire, and weigh it with 11 oz. 2 dwt., and if it weighs that, we call it standard, though we pass it at 11 oz. ; it has been the practice of the office to allow a remedy of two pennyweight ; that the London office does the same, and it is an indulgence which has always been allowed ; and that he never made use of any other flux but lead in assaying silver. And being asked, if he used any other flux than lead in the assaying of gold ? he said, yes, aqua fortis, fine silver, and lead.

" He also informed your committee, that one or both of the wardens always attend on the two assaying days, which are Tuesdays and Fridays, from nine in the morning till the assaying is over, and that they sometimes assist him ; that the scrapings are taken off, the assays made, and the plate marked, in the presence of the wardens ; that he has no fixed salary, but is paid one halfpenny an ounce for all the plate which comes to be assayed, by the owners of it.

" Being asked, if the knowledge of the trade of a working goldsmith, or plate worker, was necessary to qualify a person for scraping or cutting wrought plate properly ? he said, he imagined it was ; but also said, that an assayer not brought up to the trade of a silversmith might judge whether all the plate in one parcel was of one sort of silver, and might know whether plate was forward enough in the workmanship for assaying, and whether loaded with unnecessary solder, as well as if he had been brought up to the trade ; and that by the practice he has had at the assay office he has learnt to examine every visible part of the plate very nicely.

"That the makers of wrought plate send a note with each parcel of plate which is entered in a book kept for that purpose, called 'The Assay Book'.

"That he never heard of convoys; but has known in the same parcel some plate better, and some worse, than standard, but knows not whether it was from fraud or mistake. Being asked, what method he took, when he suspected that some plate in a parcel was better and some worse, to prevent the company marks being obtained? he said, that he made a different assay of all the pieces he suspected, and has done so for many years.

"That when all the pieces in one parcel appear to be of one sort of silver, he takes a small quantity from every piece, as much as will make an assay; that when plate appears under standard, he sometimes re-assays it, and has re-assayed plate three times, in order to satisfy the owner; that he puts four marks upon the plate, viz.: the lion, the leopard's head, the three castles, and the letter for the year; and that the letter for the present year is D; that these marks are kept in a box which has three locks upon it; that the wardens keep each of them a key at their own houses, and the witness keeps the other in his pocket; and the box cannot be unlocked without producing the three keys; that the diet (which is eight grains from every pound of silver that is marked) is kept in the same box; and all the diet, except two or three ounces is taken out of the box every year by the wardens, and appropriated to defray the expence of the office; and that the company thought two or three ounces a sufficient quantity to be kept.

"That the diet in the office remains in its original state, as scrapings and cuttings from the plate, and he never knew any of it to be assayed, nor does he remember the diet box ever to have been sent or required by the Lord Chancellor to be sent, to the Mint; that he knows nothing of the annual weight of the diet, but the wardens do, as they keep an account of it in a book kept for that purpose;—that there are scrapings now in the office taken in several years, but are mixed together.

"The witness further said, that there never was an assay made at Newcastle by any other person than himself, since he was appointed assay master; that the office is kept in a private house; that there are in it two assay furnaces, and a pair of scales, so exact that a hair off the back of his hand will turn them either way."

Later in the day on which Prior was examined by the committee, Mr. Ridley wrote to Messrs. Langlands and Kirkup with reference to Prior's examination as follows :—

"Burlington Street, March 22nd, 1773.

"Sirs,

"I have the pleasure of acquainting you, that this day we got through Mr. Prior's examination, wherein he acquitted himself with great precision and judgement, and the Committee came to a Resolution, 'That the Assay Office at Newcastle upon Tyne had been conducted with Fidelity and Skill'. Mr. Prior was discharged from farther attendance, and will set forward on his return to Newcastle next Wednesday. I am very happy that we have got this matter well over, notwithstanding the most violent opposition of the Goldsmiths of London.

I am S[rs]

Your most obed[t.] servant

M. RIDLEY.

Mr. John Langlands &
Mr. John Kirkup.

Gold does not appear to have been assayed at Newcastle before 1785. The Company, however, then determined to undertake the assaying of gold plate, and the following information with reference to the matter is cited by Mr. Boyle in his monograph : " Mr. Fendall Rushforth, one of the assayers at Goldsmiths' Hall, London, procured and sent to Mr. Robertson, of the firm of Langlands and Robertson, the necessary implements. These cost £13 1s., and were sent to Newcastle by ship. The company manifested its gratitude by sending Mr. Rushforth a salmon which cost 7s. 6d., and the carriage of which to London cost 6s." The first gold plate was assayed for John Mitchison, of the Side, on the 11 March, 1785.

In 1844 the Goldsmiths' Company of London endeavoured to obtain jurisdiction over all provincial offices, and they procured a Bill to be introduced into Parliament, giving the London Company the right to sue the wardens and assayers of provincial halls, on proof that they had passed gold or silver below the standard. " This," says Mr. Boyle, " led to an extensive correspondence between the secretary of the Goldsmiths' Company at Newcastle (Mr. F. Sanderson) and Mr. W. Ord, then one of the representatives of Newcastle. Mr. Ord conducted the goldsmiths' case with energy and tact, and the result of his efforts was that the objectionable clause was so amended as to place all companies upon the same footing, and give provincial offices a right to sue the wardens and assayers of the London Company itself, should they offend against the provisions of the Act."

In 1855 another attempt was made by the London Company to abolish the assay offices at Newcastle and some other provincial towns, and as a consequence, the House of Commons ordered on the 22 June, 1855, that returns should be made by the Inspector-General of Stamps and Taxes on the assaying and marking of plate at Newcastle and other towns, and a report on the same subject by Messrs. Garrard and Johnson, wardens of the London Company. Mr. Boyle having carefully examined a great number of documents relating to this matter, says that he is "convinced that the accusations and insinuations against the practices of the Newcastle Office were entirely without foundation".

In 1853 the weight of the silver assayed at Newcastle was 9644 oz. In 1863 it had fallen to 4394 oz. · In 1873 it had further decreased to 1982 oz., whilst in 1883, the last complete year in which the office was open, it had fallen to 316 oz. At the annual meeting of the company in 1884 it was resolved to discontinue the Newcastle assay.   On 20 May in that year the stamps and dies, 21 in number, were delivered to Mr. Alfred Sheriff, the collector of Inland Revenue, and on 13 June the local dies, 11 in number, were effaced in the presence of Mr. Sheriff, Mr. James W. Walkinshaw, and Mr. Thomas Arthur Reed (the wardens appointed in 1883), and Mr. James Robson, the last assay master. The tenancy of the room in Dean Court, for which the company paid Messrs. Mather and Armstrong a rental of £11 per annum, terminated on the 1 May, 1885, since when the company has held its meetings at the Salutation Hotel, Bridge Street.   The last assay of silver was made of 30 teaspoons on 22 April, 1884, and the last assay of gold of 30 rings on 2 May.   In both cases the property assayed belonged to Mr. R. M. Craig.

There are now no relics of the Newcastle Assay Office except the books and papers, the round copper plate of makers' marks, a square plate on which, from 1864 to 1884, the date-letter was impressed, and two old oaken boxes, in one of which the diet was formerly kept.   These are preserved by the Society of Antiquaries of Newcastle-upon-Tyne.

From the time of the separation of the goldsmiths from the plumbers in 1716, the annual meeting of the former was regularly held on 3 May, except when that day fell on a Saturday or Sunday, and then the meeting was held on the Monday following.

THE NEWCASTLE GOLDSMITHS' MARKS.

It does not appear that the marks set on Newcastle plate before the Act of 1702 came into operation, were stamped by any duly authorised officer, after an assay had been first made.   There appears to be no evidence of the appointment from time to time of "searchers" or assayers as at York.   The town mark on plate of the 17th century made by different goldsmiths differs in appearance very considerably, and this difference is noticeable even in cases where the stamps have apparently been struck at about the same time.   It seems probable that every master goldsmith who had been admitted to the freedom of the company was allowed to have a "town-mark" stamp for his own use, and that there was no regular assay by cupel, the mark of each maker being his warranty that his wares were of standard quality, the touch-stone being probably used when a test was considered necessary.

Prior to 1702 probably each Newcastle goldsmith marked his own plate without any official assay.

The "town mark" of Newcastle was at first a single castle, derived The "town mark." probably from the arms of the borough, which are : *Gules*, three castles *argent*. It is found in a plain heraldic shield on communion cups and other plate of about the middle of the 17th century.

From about 1670 the mark was the entire coat-of-arms of Newcastle —"the three castles"—at first in a plain heraldic shield. About 1685-6, and again ten years later, it is found in an elaborately-shaped shield, but a plain shield is also found to have been occasionally used at about the same time.

The earliest authenticated examples of Newcastle plate (1658-72) The lion passant "to sinister" peculiar to Newcastle. have, in addition to the town mark of the single castle, the mark of a lion passant, "to sinister". A lion "to sinister" is not known to have been used at any other assay office. After the restoration of the old standard the lion is again found "to sinister" in the years 1721 to 1725, although in some examples of 1722-3 it is to dexter, as it invariably is after 1725.*

A small mug belonging to the Glovers' Guild of Carlisle, apparently made between 1697 and 1702 by Eli Bilton, bears not only the Britannia standard marks of the lion's head erased and figure of Britannia, with the first two letters of Bilton's surname, but also a single castle in a plain shield. This curious marking clearly shows that the piece was not stamped according to the Act of Parliament, which required the "town mark" to be the arms of the borough, as struck in all cases from 1702 onwards. It was probably made and stamped after 1697 but before the re-establishment of the Newcastle office in 1702.

From 1702 till 1720 the mark used at Newcastle, in addition to the lion's head and figure of Britannia (which closely resemble those of London of the same period), was the "town mark" of the three castles in a shield, quite plain at the sides and base, but with a central notch in the top, or "chief," and the corners clipped. From 1707 to 1710 the shield found is hollowed between the points of the central notch and the corners, and from 1712 to 1720 the shield is quite plain except for the little notch in centre of "chief". Throughout this cycle the maker's mark, in compliance with the Act, is formed of the first two letters of his surname.

After the restoration of the old standard for plate in 1719-20, the marks of the leopard's head and lion passant are found resembling those of London, except that in 1721-2, 1723-4, and 1724-5 the lion is

---

* See late example of a lion " to sinister," under Table VI., p. 365.

"to sinister". The maker's mark is formed of the initials of his Christian and surname. The town mark is in a heart-shaped shield from 1722 until 1757, when it was changed to a plain elliptical shield, but in 1759 the use of the heart-shaped shield was resumed and continued until 1772; from 1772 onwards the shield is egg-shaped.

The date-letter, made obligatory by the Act of 1701, was regularly changed every year for the first few years, but subsequently the rule was not always followed. The character of the letters used from 1702 till 1720 was a kind of Black-letter capital, and each letter from 𝕬 to 𝕱 was used in proper rotation—𝕬 and 𝕭 having a mullet or star on their dexter side. The first letter is found in an oblong punch, the others in a squat oval. 𝕱 and 𝕰 seem to have been used for at least three, and possibly five years. The next letter found after 𝕲 is the 𝕸 of 1712-3. No example of the letter 𝕹 for this cycle has been found. 𝕺 appears to have been used for about three years, followed by 𝕻 and 𝕼 (each for one year); the letter next in succession was not 𝕽 but a second 𝕯. Many articles have been found of this cycle (1702-20) bearing the letters 𝕬, 𝕭, 𝕮, 𝕯, 𝕰, 𝕱, 𝕲, 𝕸, 𝕺, 𝕻, 𝕼 respectively, but not one has been found with 𝕳, 𝕵, 𝕽, 𝕷, or 𝕹, and it seems highly probable that some of the letters were used for more than a year. It is clear that 𝕬 was the letter for 1702-3, but the next *recorded* date-letter is 𝕸 for 1712, the other letters in that cycle fixed by the records being 𝕻 for 1717, 𝕼 for 1718, 𝕯 for 1719, and 𝕰 for 1720.

In 1721 a new cycle of date-letters in Old English characters was commenced and the alphabet was used consecutively, a distinct letter for each year, from 𝕬 to 𝕾, and terminating with a Roman capital T in a plain angular shield, in 1739-40.

In 1740 was commenced a third cycle consisting of 19 Roman capital letters, A to T inclusive (omitting J), in plain heraldic shields. The letters of this cycle (with the exception of I for 1748) are recorded in the minutes, and as five pieces of plate with the I of this cycle are known, there can be no question about that letter. There is, however, considerable doubt as to whether the T was ever actually struck in 1758-9, inasmuch as while examples of every other letter have been found in plenty, not a single piece has been found with the letter T for that year. It is suggested therefore that the letter S, which by the way has terminations of a Lombardic character, was used for 1758-9 as well as for 1757-8. It will be observed by a reference to the tables that the top of the shield enclosing the C of 1742-3 is waved, as in a less degree is that enclosing the S.

In 1759 the fourth cycle was commenced with the cursive capital letter *A* for 1759-60 followed by the *B* for 1760-1, both being recorded in the Company's minutes, but the next succeeding entry is dated 1769, recording that the letter for the ensuing year is "*C*". No explanation, whatever, of the hiatus is made, and the only suggestion of an explanation seems to be that no letter was used other than the *B* adopted in 1760 until the *C* was resolved upon in 1769. As a quantity of plate bearing the marks of makers who worked at about this time has been found without a date-letter, it is probable that for several years no date-letter was used. After the *C* of 1769-70 each letter of the alphabet, *D* to Z (omitting J and V), follows in proper sequence, cursive capitals being used up to and including *F*, and Roman capitals afterwards. Each letter is in a plain angular shield until 1771-2, thenceforward a shield shaped in the base is used with slight variation until 1780, after which date a square shield is, with two exceptions, found till the end of the cycle in 1790-1. Before leaving this cycle, mention must be made of a point in the evidence of Mr. Matthew Prior, the assay-master, given before the Parliamentary Committee in 1773. The report states that he said, "the letter for the present year is D". The Author has made several attempts to make his tables agree with this statement, but has utterly failed. In *Hall Marks on Plate*, Mr. Chaffers appears to have evaded the difficulty by the simple expedient of discarding the last three letters (X, Y and Z) of the cycle, and in succeeding editions of that work the same course was followed ; but from G downwards every letter of the cycle in question is represented in that book in cursive characters, whereas, in fact, every letter from G to Z actually used was a Roman capital. The three letters, X, Y and Z of this cycle have been found in repeated instances, and it is impossible to disregard them. Prior's reported statement that the letter for 1772-3 was D is not referred to in *Old English Plate*, where *F* is given as the letter for that year. If D really had been the letter for 1772-3, then, as S is fixed as the letter for 1784-5 by the fact of its being found both without and with the incuse king's head, C must have been used for three years in succession ; and as all the letters represented in Table V. have been found on plate, there must have been changes of the letter twice a year for at least two years between 1773 and 1784. This seems extremely improbable, and the suggestion that some mistake was made either by Mr. Prior or the reporter in stating that the letter for 1772-3 was D, seems to be the only feasible explanation.

In the next cycle, 1791 to 1814, the letters (Roman capitals) are recorded, and as examples of all have been found on plate, there can be no question about them.   The presence of the king's head mark through-out this cycle—absent in the preceding cycle except with the last seven letters—distinguishes all but those ; and the truncated corners of the shields of the letters in the later cycle, as well as the slight differences in the form of the other stamps, should prevent confusion, albeit that three-fourths of the letters of both cycles are alike in form.

In the following cycle, 1815 to 1838 inclusive, the date-letters are again Roman capitals, but somewhat narrower in proportion to their height than in any of the preceding cycles.   The lowness of the crown over the leopard's head (as well as its general form) and the slight differences in the other marks, enable one to distinguish with a little careful observation these marks from others.   There were not many goldsmiths or silversmiths working at Newcastle after 1815 and marked examples of their work are not often found.   The Author has not found more than eighteen different examples of the marks of the last three cycles, but as the date-letters are all recorded, actual examples are not necessary for the framing of the tables.   The marks of the cycle 1839 to 1863 in-clusive may easily be distinguished by the head of Wm. IV. in the first two years, and of Queen Victoria thereafter ; the leopard's head being generally crowned.   In the last cycle, 1864 to 1884, in which year the office was closed, small Roman letters were used, unlike any of previous years.   The other four Hall-marks resemble those of 1846-7, and it is un-necessary to repeat them in the table.

The date-letters were as a rule changed immediately after the annual meetings on 3 May, so that, except when the rule was broken, each letter ran from May of one year until May of the succeeding year.

The following tables of marks and the list of names of makers do not appear to require any further explanation than is contained above and in the tables themselves.   It may, however, be as well to mention that for the marks down to 1815 the Author has depended not entirely on the examples mentioned in the tables, but on those and many others too numerous to particularize.

The marks stamped on wrought gold at Newcastle were the same as on plate until 1798. From that date the crown and figures 18 were substituted in place of the lion passant on gold of 18 carats fine, gold of 22 carats being stamped as before until 1844, when the crown and 22 were substituted for the lion. After that date the lion was not stamped on gold. From 1854 the three lower standards of 15, 12 and 9 carats fine then authorised, were stamped with the figures 15 ·625, 12 ·5, and 9 ·375 respectively, and neither the crown nor the sovereign's head was stamped on gold below 18 carats in fineness.

MARKS ON NEWCASTLE PLATE.

TABLE I.

(The dates given in this Table, although in most cases inscribed on the article, must be regarded as approximate, and not actually fixed.)

DATE (ABOUT).	MARKS.	MAKER'S NAME.	ARTICLES AND OWNERS.
1658		John Wilkinson.	Communion cup: Trimdon, Durham.
1664		,, ,,	Do. do.: Ryton-on-Tyne.
1668		,, ,,	Tankard: Mr. Geo. Dunn.
1670		John Dowthwaite.	Com. flagons, dated 1672: St. Mary's, Gateshead.
1672		,, ,,	Marks noted by the Author.
,,		Wm. Ramsay.	Com. flagon, dated 1670: Sawley, Yorks.
1675		,, ,,	Com. cup: Aspatria, Cumberland.
,,		,, ,,	Do. do.: St. John's, Newcastle.
1680		,, ,,	Do. do. dated 1680: Ennerdale, Cumb.
1684		,, ,,	Do. do. dated 1684: Rose Castle, Carlisle.
,,		,, ,,	Com. paten and flagon: Do. do.
,,		,, ,,	Marks noted by the Author.
1685		Wm. Robinson.*	Com. cups and paten, dated 1686: St. Nicholas Cathedral, Newcastle.
,,		,, ,,	{ Com. flagon: St. Nicholas Cathedral, N'cas. { Punch bowl: Mr. Cecil B. Morgan.
1686-7		Eli Bilton.	Com. cup: Chollerton, Northumberland.
1686-8		Wm. Robinson.	Com. paten: St. Nicholas Cathedral, New-Castle.
1690		,, ,,	Tankard: Mr. S. Phillips.
1692		,, ,,	Do. : Blackgate Mus. Exhib., Newcastle.
1694		Robt. Shrive.	Fluted porringer: Major Widdrington.
,,		Eli Bilton.	Chocolate pot: Mr. S. J. Phillips.
,,		,, ,,	Mug: Messrs. Crichton.
1695		Wm. Robinson.	Tankard: Do. do.
1697		Thos. Hewitson.	Large two-handled cup: The Marquess of Breadalbane, K.G.
1698		,, ,,	Com. flagons, dated 1698: All Saints' Church, Newcastle.
1698-9		Eli Bilton.	Tankard: Mr. S. Phillips.
1700		,, ,,	Porringer: Taylors' Guild, Carlisle.
,,		John Ramsay.	Tankard: Tanners' Guild, Carlisle.
1701		Eli Bilton.	Half-pint mug: Glovers' Guild, Carlisle.

* Or Wm. Ramsay. It is suggested that the W R conjoined is the mark of Wm. Robinson (son of William Robinson, imbroderer, apprenticed 1657), who worked in Newcastle from 1665 till 1698. The mark W R conjoined is found on plate which appears to have been made after Wm. Ramsay's death.

MARKS ON NEWCASTLE PLATE.

TABLE II.

FIVE STAMPS AS BELOW.

	THREE CASTLES.	BRIT ANNIA.	LION'S HEAD ERASED.	DATE LETTER.	MAKER'S MARK.	MAKER'S NAME.		ARTICLES AND OWNERS.
ANNE. 1702-3	🏰	🏛	🦁	A	Ra	John	Ramsay.	Tankard: Blackgate Museum Exhibition.
1703-4	,,	,,	,,	B	Ba	Fras.	Batty.	Com. cup: Askham, Westmor.
1704-5	,,	,,	,,	C	Sh	Robt.	Shrive.	Rat-tail spoon (trifid): Mr. Crichton.
1705-6	,,	,,	,,	D	Bi	Eli.	Bilton.	Com. paten: Kirkandrews-upon-Esk.
1706-7	,,	,,	,,	E	,, / Yo	John	Younghusband.	Com. cup: Castle Eden, Durham. / Tumbler: Mr. J. Cotterell.
1707-8	🏰	,,	,,	F	Yo / Fr	,, ,, / J'nath'n French.		Com. cup: Ainstable, Cumb. / Tumbler: Tailors' Guild, Carlisle. / Com. flagon: St. Mary-the-less, Durham.
1708-9	,,	,,	,,	G	Bv	John	Buckle of York.	Tumbler: Messrs. Crichton.
1709-10	,,	,,	,,	,,	Ki	James	Kirkup.	Mug: Mr. Colt.
1710-11								
1711-2					Bi	Eli.	Bilton.	Com. cup: "re-made, 1712": Holy Island.
1712-3	🏰	🏛	🦁	M	H	Richd.	Hobbs.	Monteith: Corporation of Morpeth
1713-4					LA	John	Langwith.	Rat-tail spoon: Mr. Hardcastle. / Com. cup.: Newton Kyme, Yks.
GEO. I. 1714-5	🏰	,,	,,	D	Fr / Ba	J'nath'n French. / Fr. Batty, jr.		Tankard: noted by Author. / Tankard: Messrs. Crichton. / ¾-Pint mug: The Author's Coll'n.
1715-6					Sh	Nathl.	Shaw.	Tumbler: Mr. Geo. Dunn.
1716-7								
1717-8	,,	,,	,,	P	BV	Joseph	Buckle.	Small mug: Mr. Lowe, Chester.
1718-9	,,	,,	,,	Q	Ba	Fras.	Batty, as above.	Tankard: The Author's Coll'n.
1719-20	,,	,,	,,	D	Ki / MaBa / Ca	James Kirkup. / R. & F. Makepeace Batty. / John Carnaby.		Muffineer: Mr. J. R. Carr-Ellison. / Punch-bowl: Mr. Tinley Dale, Westoe. / Rat-tail spoon: Mr. Crichton.
1720-1	,,	,,	,,	E	Wh	Wm.	Whitfield.	Tankard: Mr. R. Meldrum.
,,	🏰	🏛	🦁		IH	John	Hewitt.	Tankard: Mr. G. Dunn.

MARKS ON NEWCASTLE PLATE.

TABLE III.

FIVE STAMPS AS BELOW.

	THREE CASTLES.	LION PASSANT.	LEOPARD'S HEAD CROWNED.	DATE LETTER.	MAKER'S MARK.	MAKER'S NAME.	ARTICLES AND OWNERS.
1721-2	(castles)	(lion)	(leopard's head)	a	FB IR	Fras. Batty, jr. John Ramsay, jr.	Com. plate, dated 1722: St. John's, N'cas. Cup: Tanners' Guild, Carlisle.
1722-3	(castles)	(lion)	,,	B	RM I·K	Robt. Makepeace. Jas. Kirkup.	Coffee-pot: Mr. J. R. Carr-Ellison. Tankard, dated 1730: Carlisle Corporation.
1723-4	,,	(lion)	,,	C	IF	Jthn. French.	Beakers: St. Andrew's, Bishop Auckland.
1724-5	,,	,,	,,	D	IC TP	John Carnaby. Thos. Partis.	Communion cup: St. Mary's, Gateshead. Com. cup: Monk Hesledon.
1725-6	(castles)	(lion)	(leopard's head)	E	IR	Fras. Batty, jr.	Pint mug: Mr. G. Dunn.
1726-7	,,	,,	,,	F	WW IB	Wm. Whitfield. John Busfield of York. ?	Noted by the Author. Plate: Messrs. Reid & Son.
GEO. II. 1727-8	(castles)	,,	(leopard's head)	G	IC	Isaac Cookson.	Small mug: Mr. Geo. Lowe.
1728-9	,,	(lion)	,,	H	GB WW WD	Geo. Bulman. Wm. Whitfield. Wm. Dalton.	Cup: Messrs. Crichton. Gravy spoon: Mr. G. Lowe. Noted by the Author.
1729-30	,,	,,	,,	I	GB	Geo. Bulman.	Salver: Mr. J. R. Carr-Ellison.
1730-1	,,	,,	,,	K	WD	Wm. Dalton.	Small mug: The Author's Collection.
1731-2	,,	,,	,,	L	TG IF	Thos. Gamul? Jon. French.	Noted by the Author. Do. do.
1732-3	,,	,,	,,	M	TM IB	Thos. Makepeace. John Busfield of York. ?	Salver: Cordwainers' Company, N'castle. Sauce-boat: Rev. Jas. Allgood.
1733-4	,,	,,	,,	N	IC	Isaac Cookson.	Tankard: York Corporation. Coffee-pot, kettle and stand: Mr. J. R. Carr-Ellison.
1734-5	,,	,,	,,	O	TP	Thos. Partis.	Com. cup and alms-dishes: Sunderland.
1735-6	,,	,,	,,	P	GB	Geo. Bulman.	Plain salver: Mr. Chisholm.
1736-7	,,	,,	,,	Q	WP	Wm. Partis.*	Small mug: Mr. Widdowfield.
1737-8	,,	,,	,,	R	IC	Isaac Cookson.†	Tankard: Mrs. Hodgson Huntley.
1738-9	,,	,,	,,	S	WB IB	Wm. Beilby&Co.‡	Coffee-pot: Major Widdrington.
1739-40	,,	,,	,,	T	IC R·M	Isaac Cookson. Robt. Makepeace.	Salver: Mr. W. Orde. Small mug: Weavers' Guild, Alnwick.

* Possibly Wm. Prior.

† This mark of Isaac Cookson was found on a coffee-pot (belonging to Mr. W. H. Willson) with the hall-marks and date-letter for 1722-3, although no record of his name as a goldsmith has been found of earlier date than 1724.

‡ Perhaps Wm. and John Busfield of York.

MARKS ON NEWCASTLE PLATE.

TABLE IV.

FIVE STAMPS AS BELOW.

THREE CASTLES.	LION PASSANT.	LEOPARD'S HEAD CROWNED.	DATE LETTER.	MAKER'S MARK.	MAKER'S NAME.	ARTICLES AND OWNERS.
1740-1				A { S·B / I·K	Stephen Buckle. / James Kirkup.	Com. flagon: St. Martin-cum-Gregory, York. / Com. flagon: Kirkandrews-upon-Esk.
1741-2	,,	,,	,,	B { WB / JB	W. Beilby & Anor. Perhaps Jno. Busfield (of York.)	Gravy spoon: Mr. H. Dawson.
1742-3	,,	,,	,,	C { IC	Isaac Cookson.	Two-handled cup: Blacksmiths' Co., Carlisle.
1743-4	,,	,,	,,	D { TS / WP	Thomas Stoddart. / William Partis.	Cream-jug: Mr. W. H. Willson. / Sauce-boat: Submitted to the Author.
1744-5	,,	,,	,,	E { FM	F. Martin (probably).	From Assay Office plate.
1745-6	,,	,,		F { JB	Thomas Blackett (probably).	Do. do.
1746-7				G { IC	Isaac Cookson.	Cream-jug: Mr. Crichton.
1747-8	,,	,,	,,	H { IW	John Wilkinson of Sheffield (probably).	From Assay Office Plate.
1748-9	,,	,,	,,	I { TR	? Thos. Reid of York.	Do. do.
1749-50	,,	,,	,,	K { RG / R·M / TP	R. Gillson (of Sunderland). / Robert Makepeace. / Thos. Partis II. (of Sunderland).	Do. do. / Beaker on moulded feet: Dr. Embleton. / From Assay Office Plate.
1750-1	,,			L { WB	William Beilby.	Small plain tankard: Rev. J. Allgood.
1751-2	,,	,,	,,	M { WP	William Partis.	Com. plate: Bridekirk, Cumb.
1752-3	,,	,,	,,	N { WD / I·B	William Dalton. / Perhaps John Barrett (of Sunderland).	Com. paten: Berwick-on-Tweed. / From Assay Office Plate.
1753-4	,,	,,	,,	O { IC	Isaac Cookson.	Sauce-boats: Mr. J. Caldcleugh and Mr. Hesketh-Hodgson.
1754-5	,,	,,	,,	P { IL / IG	Langlands & Goodriche.	{ Coffee-pot: Mr. J. Kirsopp. / Salver: Mr. W. Orde.
1755-6	,,	,,	,,	Q { JK	John Kirkup.	Table spoons: Mr. B. Jefferis.
1756-7	,,	,,	,,	R { I·L	John Langlands.	Tankard: Mr. Lowe, Chester.
1757-8		,,		S { JL / IL	,, ,, / ,, ,,	Do. : Mr. H. D. Ellis. / Mustard-pot: Submitted to the Author.
1758-9				T { RB	Ralph Beilby.	Noted by the Author.

MARKS ON NEWCASTLE PLATE.

TABLE V.

FIVE STAMPS TILL 1784, THENCEFORWARD SIX, AS BELOW.

	THREE CASTLES.	LION PASSANT.	LEOPARD'S HEAD CROWNED.	DATE LETTER.	KING'S HEAD.	MAKER'S MARK.	MAKER'S NAME.	ARTICLES AND OWNERS.
1759-60	(mark)	(mark)	(mark)	A		SI	Samuel James.	Tankard: Messrs. Spink.
GEO. III. 1760-8	,,	,,	,,	B		{ SJ / IB }	Saml. Thompson. / John Barrett of Sunderland.	(No date-letter) table-spoon: Miss Allgood. / From Assay Office plate.
1769-70	,,	(mark)	,,	C		{ SI / RP }	Saml. James. / Robt. Peat.	Do. do. / Three-quarter-pint mug: Mr. Lowe, Chester.
1770-1	(mark)	,,	(mark)	D		{ IK / IF }	John Kirkup. / John Fearny of Sunderland.	Two-handled cup: Mr. T. Watson. / From Assay Office plate.
1771-2	,,	,,	,,	E		IL	John Langlands.	Do. do.
1772-3	(mark)	,,	,,	F		IC	James Crawford.	Com. flagon, dated 1773: Holy Trinity, Whitehaven.
1773-4	,,	,,	,,	G		{ JJ / IH }	John Jobson. / Jas. Hetherington.	From Assay Office plate. / Small mug: Messrs. M. & S. Lyon.
1774-5	,,	,,	,,	H		{ WS / IM }	Stalker & Mitchison.	Tankard: Mr. J. A. Holms, Paisley.
1775-6	,,	,,	,,	I		{ IH HE / FJ }	Hetherington & Edwards. / Francis Solomon of Whitehaven.	Soup ladle: Mr. Arthur. / From Assay Office plate.
1776-7	,,	,,	,,	K		{ H&E / JH }	Hetherington & Edwards. / James Hetherington.	Gravy-spoon: Mr. Lowe. / From Assay Office plate.
1777-8	,,	,,	,,	L		DC	David Crawford.	Small two-handled cup: Mr. Welby.
1778-9	,,	,,	,,	M		{ IL IR }	Langlands & Robertson.	Com. cup: Newbiggin, Westmor.
1779-80	,,	(mark)	(mark)	N		DC	David Crawford.	Sauce-boat: Mr. H. D. Ellis.
1780-1	,,	,,	,,	O		{ RP RS }	Pinkney & Scott.	Gravy-spoon: Mr. L. W. Adamson.
1781-2	,,	,,	,,	P		{ IL IR }	Langlands & Robertson (as below).	Plain oval tea-pot: Rev. J. Allgood.
1782-3	,,	,,	,,	Q		{ IS / BD }	John Stoddart. / Ben. Dryden.	From Assay Office plate. / Do. do.
1783-4	,,	,,	,,	R		JJ	John Stoddart.	Do. do.
*1784-5	,,	,,	,,	S	(mark)	{ RP RS }	Pinkney & Scott.	Com. flagon: St. Mary's, Gateshead; sauce boats: Col. Adamson.
1785-6	,,	,,	,,	T	,,	IM	John Mitchison.	Two sauce-boats: Capt. Bates.
1786-7	,,	,,	,,	U	(mark)	,,	,, ,,	Oval tea-pot and stand: Mr. Neale.
1787-8	,,	(mark)	(mark)	W	,,	{ TG / L&R }	Name not traced. / Langlands & Robertson.	Tea-set: Mr. Lowe, Ch's'r. / Tankard: Messrs. Debenham & Storr.
1788-9	,,	(mark)	,,	X	,,	CR	Chrstn. Reid.	Com. flagon: Greystoke, Cumberland.
1789-90	,,	,,	,,	Y	,,	P&S	Pinkney & Scott.	Meat skewer: Mr. Lowe, Chester.
1790-1	,,	,,	,,	Z	,,	IM	John Mitchison.	Coffee-pot: The Author's Coll'n.

* The letter S of the year 1784-5 is found both without and with the King's head stamp incuse.
See also Supplementary List of Makers' Marks on page 368 *infra*.

MARKS ON NEWCASTLE PLATE.

TABLE VI.

SIX STAMPS AS BELOW.

	LION PASSANT.	THREE CASTLES.	LEOPARD'S HEAD CROWNED.	KING'S HEAD.	DATE LETTER.	MAKER'S MARK.	MAKER'S NAME.	ARTICLES AND OWNERS.
1791-2	[lion]	[castles]	[leopard]	[king]	A	IL / IR	Langlands & Robertson.	Tankard: Mr. J. W. Pease.
1792-3	,,	,,	,,	,,	B	R·S	Robert Scott.	Engraved cup: Mr. W. Boore.
*1793-4	,,	,,	,,	,,	C	O / AH	Anth. Hedley.	Large tankard: Messrs. M. & S. Lyon
1794-5	,,	,,	,,	,,	D	{ MA / GW	Mary Ashworth of Dur. / G. Weddell.	From Assay Office Plate. Do. do. do.
1795-6	,,	,,	,,	,,	E	I·R / D·D	Robertson & Darling.	Com. cup, dated 1795: Chester-le-Street, Durham.
1796-7	,,	,,	,,	,,	F	{ TW / R&D	Thos. Watson. / Robertson & Darling.	Milk-jug: Mr. Fred. L. Fitzgerald. / Table-spoon: Mr. Davison.
1797-8	,,	,,	,,	[king]	G	GL / JW	Geo. Laws & John Walker. ?	Table-spoons: Mr. L. W. Adamson.
1798-9	,,	,,	,,	,,	H	CR / IR	Chrstn. Reid. / John Robertson.	Tea-spoon: Mr. E. Heron-Allen. / Cake basket: Lord Riddell.
1799/1800	,,	,,	,,	,,	I	{ JR / SC	,, ,, / Sarah Crawford.	From Assay Office Plate. / Do. do. do.
1800-1	[lion]	[castles]	[leopard]	[king]	K	IL	John Langlands, jr.	Tea-pot: Mr. W. Smith, Glasg'w.
1801-2	,,	,,	,,	,,	L	{ TW / A·R	Thos. Watson. / Ann. Robertson.	From Assay Office Plate. Do. do. do.
1802-3	,,	,,	,,	,,	M	{ D·D / CR DR	David Darling. / Chrstn. K. Reid & David Reid.	Do. do. do. / Do. do. do.
1803-4	[lion]	,,	,,	[king]	N	A·K	Alexr. Kelty.	Do. do. do.
1804-5	,,	,,	,,	,,	O	IL	John Langlands, jr.	Table-spoon: Mr. Skinner.
1805-6	,,	,,	,,	,,	P	GM	George Murray.	Oval bread basket: Mr. W. Boore.
1806-7	,,	,,	,,	,,	Q	TW	Thos. Watson.	Com. flagon, "given to the church of Hesket-in-the-Forest, 1807".
1807-8	,,	,,	,,	,,	R	,,	,, ,,	Table-spoons: Mr. Ince.
1808-9	,,	,,	,,	,,	S	DD / TB	Darling & Bell.	From Assay Office Plate.
1809-10	[lion]	[castles]	[leopard]	[king]	T	I·L	John Langlands.†	Pint mug: Mr. Lowe, Chester.
1810-1	,,	,,	,,	,,	U	T·W	Thos. Watson.	From Assay Office Plate.
1811-2	,,	,,	,,	,,	W	{ D·L / IR IW	Drthy. Langlands. / Robertson & Walton.	Hot-water jug: Mr. H. D. Ellis. / From Assay Office Plate.
1812-3	,,	,,	,,	,,	X	{ RP / M&R	Robert Pinkney. / Name not traced.	Table-spoons: Mrs. Budd. / From Assay Office Plate.
1813-4	,,	,,	,,	,,	Y	CR / DR / CR	Chrstn. Ker Reid, David Reid, & Chrstn. Bruce Reid.	Do. do. do.
1814-5	,,	,,	,,	,,	Z	IW	John Walton.	Milk-jug: Mr. Williamson.

* 1793-4 C [mark] [mark] M·MILLER	Maker, M. Miller.	Sugar tongs: Mr. Frank Bradbury. (*Note.* — The lion passant is to sinister.)
1805-6 AC [mark] [mark] [mark] P	Maker, Alexander Cameron, of Dundee.	Tea-spoons: The Marquess of Breadalbane, K.G.

† Mark probably used after J. Langlands' death by his widow, Dorothy Langlands.

MARKS ON NEWCASTLE PLATE.

TABLE VII.

SIX STAMPS AS BELOW.

DATE LETTER.	KING'S HEAD.	LION PASSANT.	THREE CASTLES.	LEOPARD'S HEAD CROWNED.	MAKER'S MARK.	MAKER'S NAME.	ARTICLES AND OWNERS.
1815-6	A	🂠	🦁	🏰	😐	T·W	Thos. Watson.	Punch-ladle : General Meyrick.
1816-7	B	,,	,,	,,	,,	TW	,, ,,	Tea-spoons : Messrs. Crichton.
1817-8	C	,,	,,	,,	,,	C·D	Christ'r. Dinsdale, of Sunderland.	Milk jug : S. & A. Mus., Dublin.
1818-9	D	,,	,,	,,	,,	I R I W	Robertson & Walton.	From Assay Office plate.
1819-20	E	,,	,,	,,	,,			
GEO. IV. 1820-1	F	,,	,,	,,	,,	TW	Thos. Watson.	Do. do. do.
1821-2	G	◗	,,	,,	,,	,,	,, ,,	Marrow scoop : Submitted to the Author.
1822-3	H	,,	,,	,,	,,	,,	,, ,,	Tea-spoon : Mr. E. Heron-Allen.
1823-4	I	,,	,,	,,	,,	,,	,, ,,	Small mug : Messrs. Debenham.
1824-5	K	,,	,,	,,	,,	TW	,, ,,	Large two-handled cup : The Earl of Yarborough.
1825-6	L	,,	,,	,,	,,			
1826-7	M	,,	,,		,,			
1827-8	N	,,	,,	,,	,,			
1828-9	O	,,	,,	,,	,,			
1829-30	P	,,	,,	,,	,,			
WM. IV. 1830-1	Q	,,	,,	,,	,,			
1831-2	R	,,	,,	,,	,,			
1832-3	S	◗	,,	,,	,,	,,	Thos. Watson.	Sauce-ladle : Mr. J. B. Stansby.
1833-4	T	,,	,,	,,	,,			
1834-5	U	,,	,,	,,	,,	WL	Wm. Lister.	From Assay Office plate.
1835-6	W	,,	,,	,,	,,			
1836-7	X	,,	,,	,,	,,			
VICT. 1837-8	Y		,,	,,	,,	TW	Thos. Watson.	Salt-spoons : Messrs. Crichton.
1838-9	Z	,,	,,	,,	,,	WL CL WL	Lister & Sons.	From Assay Office plate.

See also Supplementary List of Makers' Marks on p. 368, *infra.*

MARKS ON NEWCASTLE PLATE.

TABLES VIII. AND IX.

SIX STAMPS AS BELOW.   LEOPARD'S HEAD UNCROWNED FROM 1846.

	KING'S HEAD.	LION PASSANT.	THREE CASTLES.	LEOPARD'S HEAD CROWNED.	DATE LETTER.	MAKER'S MARK.	MAKER'S NAME.	ARTICLES & OWNERS.		DATE LETTER.
1839-40	●	●	●	●	A	IW	John Walton.	Com. cup & paten : Aspatria.	†1864-5	a
1840-1	,,	,,	,,	,,	B	,,	,, ,,	Do. do. do.	1865-6	b
1841-2	●	,,	,,	,,	C	TW	Thos. Watson.	Small mug : Col. Fitzgerald.	1866-7	c
1842-3	,,	,,	,,	,,	D	,,	,, ,,	Goblet : Mr. W. Boore.	1867-8	d
1843-4	,,	,,	,,	,,	E				1868-9	e
1844-5	,,	,,	,,	,,	F		Lister & Sons (as 1838-9).	Sugar ladle : Messrs. Crichton.	1869-70	f
1845-6	,,	,,	,,	,,	G				1870-1	g
*1846-7	,,	●	●	●	H	GG	Name not traced.	Egg-spoon : Mr. Lowe.	1871-2	h
1847-8	,,	,,	,,	,,	I				1872-3	i
1848-9	,,	,,	,,	,,	J				1873-4	k
1849-50	,,	,,	,,	,,	K				1874-5	l
1850-1	,,	,,	,,	,,	L				1875-6	m
1851-2	,,	,,	,,	,,	M				1876-7	n
1852-3	,,	,,	,,	,,	N				1877-8	o
1853-4	,,	,,	,,	,,	O				1878-9	p
1854-5	,,	,,	,,	,,	P				1879-80	q
1855-6	,,	,,	,,	,,	Q				1880-1	r
1856-7	,,	,,	,,	,,	R				1881-2	s
1857-8	,,	,,	,,	,,	S				1882-3	t
1858-9	,,	,,	,,	,,	T				1883-4	u
1859-60	,,	,,	,,	,,	U					
1860-1	,,	,,	,,	,,	W					
1861-2	,,	,,	,,	,,	X					
1862-3	,,	,,	,,	,,	Y					
1863-4	,,	,,	,,	,,	Z					

The office was closed in 1884.

†Mustard spoon of this year with leopard's head *un*crowned : Messrs. Reid & Sons.

	KING'S HEAD.	LION PASSANT.	THREE CASTLES.	LEOPARD'S HEAD CROWNED.	DATE LETTER.	MAKER'S MARK.	MAKER'S NAME.	ARTICLES & OWNERS.
1850-1	●	,,	,,	●	M	DR	David Reid.	Marrow scoop : Mr. A. J. Grimes.
1869-70	●	●	●	●	f	CJR	C. J. Reid.	Pair of salt-spoons : Messrs. Reid & Sons.

* In some cases the leopard's head has been found with a crown.

SUPPLEMENTARY LIST OF MARKS OF GOLDSMITHS.

Impressed at Newcastle from c. 1750 to c. 1880, but not illustrated in the preceding tables :—

MARK.	NAME.	MARK.	NAME.	MARK.	NAME.
GL	Name not traced.	L & SONS	Lister & Sons.	I·M	John Miller.
WJ	,, ,,	L&S	,, ,,	C·D	Cuthbert Dinsdale.
WB	Mr. Bartlett ?	I·B	John Brown.	G·L	Geo. Sam. Lewis.
SI	Samuel Jones.	J·B	,, ,,	M Y & SONS	M. Young & Sons.
PI	Peter James.	JB	,, ,,	SJ	Simeon Joel.
H·I·I	Name not traced.	WS	Wm. Sherwin.	J·C	John Cook.
F·S	F. Somerville or Summerville, Sen., and F. S. Junr.	J·D	James Dinsdale.	RD	R. Duncan of Carlisle.
		JS	Name not traced.	J & IJ	Joseph and Israel Jacobs.
P·B	Peter Beatch.	CJR	Chrstn. J. Reid.	J·F	James Foster.
I·T	Name not traced.	RR	Robert Rippon.	W & JW	Wm. and Jno. Wilson.
RD	,, ,,	JS	John Sutler.	TR	Thos. Ross of Carlisle ?
R·W	Robt. Wilson.	J.W	John White.	TALBOT	A. Y. Talbot of Crook, Darlington.
D&B	Darling & Bell.	DR	David Reid.	TS	Thos. Sewill.
T·H	Thos. Huntingdon.	BUXTON	Wm. Buxton of Bishop Auckland.	IR	Name not traced.
H·B	Hugh Brechinridge.	I·D	John Deas ?	E.J.C	,, ,,
PL	Peter Lambert of Berwick.	OSWALD	Robt. Oswald of Durham.	WR	,, ,,
CR DR	Chrstn. K. Reid & David Reid.	OY	Oliver Young.	E·O	,, ,,
CAM ERON	Alexr. Cameron of Dundee.	IC	John Cook.	RO	,, ,,
J·R	John Robertson.	W W & SONS	W. Wilson & Sons.	IH HB	,, ,,
		LP	L. Pedrine of Carlisle.		
		A & S	Alder & Sons of Blyth.		

NEWCASTLE-ON-TYNE GOLDSMITHS.

[FROM 1536 TO 1884.]

Name of Goldsmith.		Earliest Mention.	Free.	Latest Mention.
Thomas	Cramer	1536		
James	Chawbre	,,		
Geoffrey	Hall	,,		
Humphrey	Coyll	,,		
Nicholas	Cramer	,,		
Nicholas	Brutte	,,		
James	Austold	c 1560		
Nicholas	Brutte	,,		
John	Harper	,,		
John	Cramer	,,		
Francis	Sose	,,		
Anthony	Sympson	1572		1597
William	Seaton	,,		
John	Sympsoun	,,		1589
Oswald	Carr	,,		
John	Baker	,,		
Valentine	Baker	1579		1594
James	Wilson	1594		1597
James	Wilkinson	1597		
John	Baynes	1598		1600
Thomas	Royd (apprenticed)	1599		
Thomas	Bishop	1626		1634
John	Williamson	c 1634		1670
Richard	Barkston	1646		1652
John	Wilkinson	1650	1658	1665
William	Robinson			d 1652
William	Ramsay (Mayor 1690)	1656	1656	d 1698
William	Robinson	,,	1666	1698
John	Dowthwaite		,,	d 1673
John	Norris		1674	
Francis	Batty, senr.	1674	,,	d 1706
Thomas	Armstrong (Warden 1702)	1676		1704
Albany	Dodson	1679		d 1718
Augustine	Float	1681		
Cuthbert	Ramsay	c 1682		1692
Efi	Bilton		1683	d 1708
Ffrancis	Anderson			1687
Abraham	Hamer		1690	1717
William	Ramsay, jr.		1691	d 1716
Robert	Shrive		1694	d 1704
Thomas	Hewitson		1697	1722
John	Ramsay		1698	1708
———	Ramsay (or Ramsgill)	1700		1703
Margaret	Ramsay	1702		
Roger	West	,,		
Alexander	Campbell	,,		
Richard	Hobbs	,,		1744
Thomas	Lightly	,,	1703	1707
Jonathan	French		,,	d 1732
Thomas	Gannil	1703	1717	1717
Eli	Bilton, jr.	1704		
John	Younghusband		1706	d 1718
Francis	Batty, jr.	1706	1708	1728
Thomas	Snowden	1707		1708
James	Shrive		1710	
Mark	Martin	1710		
John	Langwith (York Assay Master)	1712		1718
Mark Grey	Nicholson	,,	1718	1754
James	Kirkup		1713	d 1753
Moses	Touyen	1714		
William	Ramsay	c ,,		1741
John	Hewitt (Durham)	1714		
Joseph	Buckle (York)	1716		d 1761
John	Carnaby		1717	d 1733
Thomas	Gamul		,,	1757
Nathaniel	Shaw	1717		1741
Henry	Martin	,,		
Abraham	Hamer			1717
Robert	Makepeace		1718	1755
Abraham	Anderson	1718	1728	1753
Thomas	Partis	1720		1734
William	Whitefield	c ,,	1720	1742
John	Ramsay, jr.		,,	1728
William	Prior (Assay Master)	1722		1738
Richard	Holes	c ,,		1741
Daniel	Albert (Gateshead)	1724		
George	Bulman		,,	1743
William	Dalton		,, 1725	1767
*Isaac	Cookson		,, 1728	1757
Thomas	Makepeace		,, ,,	d 1739
Edward	Gill	1725		1754
———	Thompson (Durham)		1725	
Alexander	Coats	1729		
William	Partis		1731	d 1759
John	Langlands, sen.	c 1732		
William	Beilby	1733		1765
Edward	French	1734	1737	1780
William	Carr (Mayor 1737)			
William	Wilkinson	1739		1744
Stephen	Buckle (of York)	1740		1749
Edward	Hewitson	1741		
Robert	Peat	,,		
John	French	,,		1780
Richard	Nicholson	,,		,,
John	Kirkup	,,	1753	,,
John	Stoddart	,,		,,
Thomas	Blackett	,,		,,
Nicholas	Armstrong	,,		,,
Richard	Armstrong	,,		,,
Thomas	Stoddart	,,	1752	
Stephen	Buckles	c ,,		
John	Langlands	,,	1754	d 1793
Abraham	Anderson, jr.		1742	
Thomas	Gill	1745		1795
Robert	Makepeace, jr.	,,	1755	d 1790

* See footnote † at bottom of Table III., page 362.

Name of Goldsmith.	Earliest Mention.	Free.	Latest Mention.	Name of Goldsmith.	Earliest Mention.	Free.	Latest Mention.
Samuel Thompson	1750		1785	Pinkney & Scott	1779		1790
John Goodrick	1751	1754	1757	George Hogg			1780
John Langlands & }	1754		1756	Robert Mitchell			,,
John Goodrick }				John Walker	1783		1797
Alexander Bruce	,,		1764	John Mitchison	1784		1792
Wm. Geo. Chalmers	1755		1780	F. R.	1788		1796
Matthew Prior (Assay Master)	1759		1773	Anthony Hedley	1789		1800
John Clarke	1760			Robert Scott	1790		1793
Samuel Thompson (of Durham)	c ,,		1780	Robert Pinkney	,,		1825
James Crawford	1763		d 1795	W. R.	1793		
David Crawford	,,		1784	Thomas Watson	,,		d 1845
Joseph Hutchinson	.,	1765	,,	John Langlands, jr.	,,		1804
Samuel James	,,		d 1774	William Gray	,,		
James (or John) Jobson	1763		1784	John Robertson & }	1795		1801
Robert Mitchel	1764		,,	David Darling }			
Peter James	1765		1767	John Robertson	,,		,,
Robert Scott	1770	1781	d 1793	Christopher Dinsdale	,,	1813	,,
(From 1779 to 1790 Pinkney & Scott)				G. L. & I. W.	1797		
Francis Somerville	1771		1800	W. Crow	1798		
John Fearney	1772		1773	Anne Robertson	1801		
James Hetherington	,,		1782	Joseph Watson	,,	1809	
William Stalker & }	1773	1774	1792	Dorothy Langlands	1804		d 1845
John Mitchison }				Francis Somerville, jr.	1806	1815	1827
Robert Armstrong	1774		1777	John Robertson	1813		
Hetherington & Edwards	.,		,,	James Walkingshaw			1815
Matthew Wilkinson	,,		1780	C. D.	1817		1818
Patrick Redamachen	,,		1787	R. C. }	1819		1820
Robert Makepeace	,,			R. D. }			
John Armstrong	,,		1780	John Walton	1820		
Nicholas Armstrong, jr.	,,	1775	,,	I. W.	1839		1840
Richard Armstrong	,,		,,	G. G.	1846		
Thomas Armstrong	,,	,,	,,	Reid & Son.			1851
John Wilkinson	,,		,,	J. Somerville (Assay Master)			,,
John Hackworth	,,		,,	Thomas Sewill (Warden 1851)			1880
John Halden	1777		,,	James W. Walkinshaw (Warden)			1884
William Wilkinson	,,		,,	Thos. Arthur Reed (Warden)			,,
Timothy Wilkinson	,,		,,	James Robson (Assay Master)			,,
Robert Pinkney	,,		1798	R. M. Craig			,,
John Langlands & }	1778		1795				
John Robertson }							
Christian Ker Reid	,,		d 1834				
Anthony Hedley	,,		1789				

The following names and places of residence are those of goldsmiths who had plate assayed at Newcastle and stamped with the Newcastle assay marks but were not members of the Newcastle Guild of Goldsmiths. The dates given refer to the years in which their plate was assayed.

Joseph	Buckle, York,	c 1717.	John	Fearney, Sunderland,	c 1773.
John	Langwith, do.	c 1722.	Francis	Sollomon, Whitehaven,	c 1775.
Mr.	Thompson, Durham,	1725.	James	Thompson, Darlington,	,,
Mr.	Bainbridge do.	1733.	Samuel	Thompson, Durham,	c 1776-85.
James	Lamb, Whitehaven,	c 1748.	John	Thompson, Sunderland,	c 1778-1801.
James	Brock, do.	1749.	Anthony	Hedley, Durham,	c 1780-99.
William	Williamson, do.	,,	Mary	Ashworth, do.	c 1787-98.
Robert	Gibson, Sunderland,	c 1750.	Christopher	Dinsdale, Sunderland,	c 1798-1800.
John	Barrett, do.	c 1751.	Mary	Ashworth, Durham,	c 1799-1800.
John	Waller, Whitehaven	c 1766.			

CHAPTER XV

THE CHESTER GOLDSMITHS

AND THEIR MARKS

The goldsmiths of Chester have been placed after those of New-castle, not by reason of their inferiority, but because, unlike all the other provincial guilds, they have an assay office which is still alive, and in full exercise of a healthy competition with modern rivals, thus being a connecting link between the provincial goldsmiths of the Middle Ages and of the twentieth century.

The goldsmiths of Chester, a connecting link between the Middle Ages and the 20th century

In regard to antiquity precedence might well be claimed for the goldsmiths and moneyers of Chester over all their provincial brethren. The names found on Chester coins are those of the earliest of its citizens whose names are recorded. The British Museum list of Chester moneyers contains twenty-seven whose names appear on coins of the time of Athelstan (925-40), one of the reign of Edmund (940-46), twelve of the time of Edgar (959-75), twenty-three of the time of Ethelred, thirty of the time of Canute, sixteen of the time of Harold I. (1035-40), six of the time of Hardicanute (1040-42), and the names of twenty-one are recorded as of the time of Edward the Confessor. It is, however, recorded in Domesday Book that in the reign of Edward the Confessor the legal number of moneyers in Chester was seven only. Mr. J. Brownbill, of Chester, suggests that this limitation of the number may have been made in The Confessor's reign, and directs attention to the similarity of the names of seven moneyers to the names of a like number appearing in Domesday Book as holders of land in the county in 1066—many of the names being identical. They are as follows :

The Saxon " Moneyers " of Chester.

ON COINS.	IN DOMESDAY BOOK.
Alxxi	Alsi.
Arngrim or Ærngrim ...	Aregrim or Haregrim (for Arengrim).
Dunninc	Dunning.
Godric	Godric.
Leofwine	Leuuin (for Levwin).
Leofnoth	Leuenot (for Levenoth).
Wolfnoth or Wulnoth ...	Ulnod (for Wulnoth).

In a paper read by Mr. Wm. Fergusson Irvine before the Chester Archæological Society, in 1903, on some documents which had been discovered relating to Chester in the 12th and 13th centuries, it is pointed out that the names of several goldsmiths appear described not as moneyers but as goldsmiths (" aurifab ").

Names of Chester gold-smiths occur in 13th century deeds.

The earliest of these documents (all of which are in the abbreviated law-Latin of the period) is undated, but the date is otherwise proved to be about 1225. It is a deed whereby one " Adam son of Haman son of Herbert the Skinner quit-claims in full Portmoot (the city court) to Nicholas son of Herbert and his heirs all his lands within the walls of Chester and outside for three marks of silver ". One of the many witnesses to the deed is *John the Goldsmith*.

By a later deed (*circa* 1265) Lady Alice de la Haye, Prioress of the nuns at Chester, and the convent there, granted to Margery Erneys, formerly wife of Richard of Rhuddlan, a certain piece of land in the city of Chester (which the said Richard gave to the grantors in pure and perpetual alms) in St. Werburgh's lane in Chester, lying between the land of Henry, nephew of the said Richard, and the land of *Bartholomew the Goldsmith*.

Mr. Henry Taylor, F.S.A., has traced three generations of gold-smiths in Chester in the 13th and 14th centuries. Amongst a number of ancient deeds exhibited by him at a meeting of the Chester Archæologi-cal Society on the 24th March, 1903, there were some of particular interest in this connection. The first of these was undated, but from the fact of the Mayor and the two Sheriffs of the city having been witnesses to the execution of this deed the date is fixed as within the years 1271-2. This was a bond from *Nicholas called the Great* (*goldsmith*) to pay to John de Stanlow, son of Thurstan de Stanlow, 5s. of silver at four terms of the year for certain land of his in Foregate Street of the city of Chester.

In another Chester deed, dated 1282-3, *Matthew the Goldsmith* (" aurifabir ") is a witness ; in another, dated 1292, the names of *Nicholas the Goldsmith* (" aurifabro ") and *Walter the Goldsmith* appear as witnesses, and in another deed, also dated 1292, *Nicholas the Goldsmith* (" aurifabro ") is a witness.

A deed dated " Thursday before the feast of St. Mark," 28 Ed. I. (1309) is an appointment by William de Doncaster [by Richard Candelan, citizen of Chester, as his attorney] to put Adam his (Doncaster's) son in seisin *inter alia* of one other messuage with the appurtenances and the cellar " which I bought of Nicholas son of *Bertram the Goldsmith* in

Eastgate Strete of the city aforesaid and in one messuage with appurtenances in Foregate Strete of the city aforesaid lying between the land of Richard the Clerk of Chester on the one part and the lane called Cow Lane on the other part the which I have of the demise of the aforesaid Nicholas called the Goldsmith ".

Mr. Taylor suggests, apparently with sufficient reason, that the latter Nicholas (called the Goldsmith) was a grandson of Nicholas "called the Great" (goldsmith), thus :—

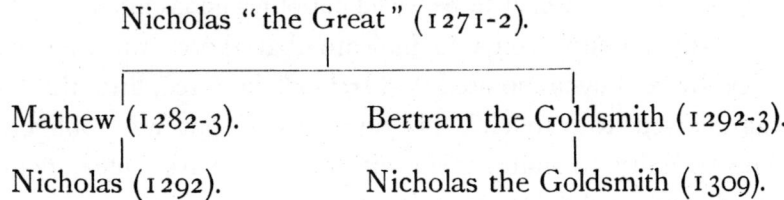

Nicholas "the Great" (1271-2).

Mathew (1282-3).   Bertram the Goldsmith (1292-3).

Nicholas (1292).   Nicholas the Goldsmith (1309).

No other goldsmith is found mentioned after Nicholas (the younger) until 1402, when the name of Richard Pratt is found. There is a long gap after this, no other being found mentioned until 1540, when Lawrence Smith, of Chester, goldsmith, was Mayor of the city. He was Mayor also in 1558 and in 1570. Thenceforward goldsmiths' names are found recorded in a fairly continuous line down to the present day.

Chester is not mentioned in the Statute 2 Henry VI. (1423), by which York and five other towns were appointed to have "touches"; the explanation of the omission being that Chester appears already to have had a "touch". Inasmuch as there were mints in the city certainly as early as the time of Athelstan, 925-40, and goldsmiths (that is to say, workers of gold and silver as distinguished from makers of coin) were established there in the 13th century, as we have seen by the above references, it seems clear that no statutory provision was necessary in the 15th century for establishing a privilege which had been enjoyed for two centuries previously. It should also be borne in mind, as Mr. Henry Taylor pointed out to the Author, that "from early Norman days both the county and the city of Chester were under the Earl of Chester, who held his court at Chester Castle, and not under the crown ; wherefore Chester sent no members to Parliament until the time of Henry VIII.". It is probable therefore that the "touch" of Chester was regulated by its Earl and not by Parliament as York and the other provincial touches appear to have been. A charter granted by Queen

Chester not mentioned in the Act of 1423 as one of the towns appointed to have a "touch," probably because that privilege was already enjoyed.

Elizabeth recognised, inferentially, the existence of more ancient privileges. Whatever may be the date of the origin of those privileges they certainly appear to have been exercised in the 16th century, for the records prove the existence of a guild or company of goldsmiths in 1573, in October of which year a brother was made free of the "mystery". The undated minute preceding that which relates to the admission of a brother in 1573 runs as follows :—

Maker's mark required to be struck on all plate before 1573.

"Itm that noe brother shall delevere noe plate by him wrought unles his touche be marked and set vpon the same beffore deleverie thereof vpon paine of forfeiture of everie deffalt to be levied out of his goods iij^s· iiij^d·"

This minute seems to indicate that there was then no system of assay by a duly appointed "searcher" in force, and that each brother was allowed to "touch" his own wares, but was obliged under the above penalty to stamp them with his own mark before delivery, so that remedy might be obtained by the purchaser in case the plate should prove worse than standard.

An entry of 1585 in the company's books contains a list of the members of the guild then working, and their names will be found in the chronological list of goldsmiths which follows the tables of Chester marks.

The guild appears to have been careful in regulating the charges to be made for work by its members, so that no one should undersell the others, as the following entries, dated 8 March, 1603, with reference to the prices to be charged for the silver arrows and bells given as prizes at the Shrovetide sports, testify :—

No goldsmith to undersell his fellow-craftsmen.

"Y^t is agreed by the whole compeney of gouldsmyths y^t this order shall be houlden and kept amongst us all, that the brood arrows against Shrooftid shall way everie one vj^d 'stalling' and every one of the compeney shall not sell vnder ix^d and for every on that selles vnder ix^d shall fforfyt xij and it is fourther agreyed that the Steward for y^t time shall come and sey them wayd and touchte and have for his paynes ij^d a duzen."

"It is agreed by the Alderman and Steward of the gouldsmiths y^t whosover shall make the bell * that shalbe made against Shrovetide for the Sadlers shall have for his paines iij^s· iiij^d· and yf any of the compeney shall offend in the premisses, he shall pay unto the alderman and steward and the reste of the compeney iij^s· iiij^d·"

"And y^t all the oulde bells shalbe broke and not any of the compeney to by any to be new burnished or sould to the peneltee aforesaid iij^s· iiij^d·"

The books of the company contain entries from the time of Queen Elizabeth downwards, but the minutes and accounts of the 17th cen-

---

* The silver bell appears to have been given as a prize for the fleetest horse in one of the races held in Chester in 1512. This race was the forerunner of the celebrated "Chester cup" race.

tury down to the end of the reign of Charles II. refer for the most part to feasts, processions, charities and fines upon admission to the freedom of the company.* There is no reference to an assay other than by " touch," as mentioned above with reference to the arrows, nor to any marks other than the worker's own mark, and it seems probable that no regular assay was made, and no town mark or date-letter used till after 6 March, $168\frac{5}{6}$—the date of the charter granted by King James II. The most persistent search has been made but no evidence has been found indicating their use prior to $168\frac{6}{7}$.

No evidence of the use of a Chester town mark or date-letter before 1686.

It seems clear that the cycle of date-letters for the period 1664-5 to 1688-9 and the three marks, consisting of (1) the city arms, (2) the crest (a sword erect), and (3) a date-letter, as set forth in *Hall Marks on Plate,*† are entirely inaccurate, just as the reference to a fleur-de-lis having been used as a Chester mark from 1689 to 1696 most certainly is, as will presently be demonstrated. The first establishment of a regular assay and adoption of assay marks seems beyond doubt to have been in $168\frac{6}{7}$, consequent upon the Charter of James II. in $168\frac{5}{6}$.

Much plate disappeared from Chester in the time of Chas. I., as is proved by a minute in the Records of the Chester Corporation of the last day of June, 1645, recording a resolution "*to sell so much of the Corporation plate as would amount to £100 to be forthwith converted into coin for the necessary use and defence of the 'citty'*".

Recorded sale of Chester plate for conversion into coin.

This would not, however, account for the disappearance of all Chester-made plate from private hands, and there is probably much still in existence, but as only a maker's mark appears to have been stamped on Chester plate before $168\frac{6}{7}$, the identification of any of earlier date is extremely difficult. On this point, it is interesting to note that the Chester mace of the year 1668 has only a maker's mark stamped on it.

The operation of the Charter of James II. was very short-lived, for the rights and privileges conferred by it were suspended by the Act of 1696, but by the Act 12 and 13 Wm. III. c. 4 ($170\frac{0}{1}$), Chester, being one of the several cities where mints had been erected, was re-established as an assay town, and under that Act, as modified by the 12 Geo. II. c. 26, it has continued a flourishing existence down to the present day, the

Chester assay office re-established by 12 & 13 Wm. III. c. 4 ($170\frac{0}{1}$).

* The following extract from the minute book—" Memorandum that the 22nd of Aprill, 1631, came into the company of the goldsmiths Sillvaynus Glegg and was sworn and paid his money "—is of interest in connection with the fact that six years later he is found to have been established as a goldsmith at Dublin, and named in the charter of 1637 as one of the original members of the Dublin Goldsmiths' Company. There was from very early times a close connection between Chester and Dublin.

† Chaffers' *Hall Marks on Plate*, 8th edn., pages 141, 143-4.

work done there of recent years being greatly in excess of anything recorded in its past history.

　　The Chester goldsmiths, like those of other cities, appear to have been well represented amongst the civic dignitaries, as is testified by the number of them who from time to time filled the offices of Mayor and Sheriff. Certain families seem to have furnished goldsmiths in succeeding generations. In the earliest records, as we have seen, Nicholas "the Great," goldsmith, was the father and grandfather of two others ; then, there are the Lynglays, followed by the Edwardses in three generations, and, later on, the Pembertons in two generations ; the Richardsons, father, son and grandson, apparently, for as there was a Richard Richardson working in connection with the assay office, either assaying or having his wares assayed for no less than eighty-three years, there could not well have been less than three generations of them. Mr. Lowe, the present Assay Master, says that there were at least two in a direct line, for one of them died in 1768, and the name was continued uninterruptedly in working connection with the office from 1708 to 1791, as shown by the following entries :—

			£	s.	d.
"1708.	Recd. of Mr. Richd. Richardson in lieu of a feast ...		2	10	0*
1721.	May 20.	L'kwiss Mr. Willm. Richardson	2	10	0*
1724.	Sept. 29.	Sums recd. by members from Owen Jones's legacy :			
		To Thomas Maddock, Warden	3	0	0½
		Wm. Richardson, Warden	3	0	0½
		Richard Richardson, Assay Master ...	3	0	0½
1734.	Aug. 19.	Richard Richardson at his admission to the Worshipfull Company of Goldsmiths	2	10	0
1772.	July 14.	To paid the Children of the late Mr. Richardson for arrears due to their late Father.	5	6	4 "

　　The last entry relating to the Richardsons is dated 1791, and is in connection with " Duty ".

　　In more recent times, there have been goldsmiths of the Lowe family in a continuous line from 1796 down to the present day, the family being now represented by the Assay Master, Mr. W. Foulkes Lowe, and the firm of Lowe & Son, goldsmiths.

　　It may not be out of place to mention in connection with the Chester

---

* Formerly, it appears to have been the custom for members of the Company, on admission, to give a feast. This was subsequently commuted to a fine or money payment of £2 10s. 0d.

goldsmiths the name of the late Mr. Joseph Mayer, F.S.A., who, although not a Chester man, had a long continued connection with the city. Born at Newcastle-under-Lyne in 1803 and educated at Chester, after serving an apprenticeship with a relative named Wordsley—a goldsmith in Lord Street, Liverpool—Mayer himself started in the same street a business which he carried on with remarkable success until 1873. For nearly thirty years he sent wrought gold and plate to the Chester assay office, where most of his work, celebrated for its excellence at a time when goldsmiths' work was not generally remarkable for good taste, was assayed. He was a collector of Greek, Roman and Anglo-Saxon antiques, and of British plate, and bequeathed the whole of his collections (amongst which is the celebrated Pudsey spoon) to the town of Liverpool where, in a museum bearing his name, they are preserved. He died in 1886.

In March, 1773, Mr. John Scasebrick,* then the Assay Master at Chester, was summoned to appear before the Parliamentary Committee appointed to enquire into the manner in which the provincial assay offices were then being worked. The following is Mr. Gilbert's report of his evidence :—

METHOD OF CONDUCTING THE ASSAY OFFICE AT CHESTER.

" Mr. John Scasebrick (essay master of Chester and a jeweller) informed your committee, that there is a company of goldsmiths and watchmakers at Chester, which consists of two wardens and about eight other members ; and produced, pursuant to the order of your committee, the several accounts annexed in the appendix No. 3, and said, that he never made any entries of, nor took any diet from, plate that proved worse than standard ; but upon his report of it to the wardens it was defaced and returned to the owners ; that he cannot recollect the quantity of plate broke since he has been in the office, but about a month ago, one dozen of watch cases, that came from Liverpool to be assayed, were broke ; and that he has broke other kinds of plate about a year or two ago, which belonged to a silversmith in Chester ; that he is paid for plate which is broke and defaced, the same prices as if it was standard, according to Act of Parliament, and enters such payments in a book ; but no entry is made of plate broken.

" The witness further informed your committee, that the plate which has been sent by Messrs. Boulton and Fothergill, of Soho, near Birmingham, to be assayed and marked at the Chester office, has generally been 2 or 3 dwt. above standard,

---

* Mr. Henry Taylor suggests that the name is properly " Scarisbrick," that of a well-known Lancashire family. It probably became " Sca'sbrick " by contraction, and eventually as written by the Parliamentary reporter.

and that he never received any plate from the said Boulton and Fothergill which was under standard ; that he calls 11 oz. 2 dwt. standard and 11 oz. 1 dwt. or anything under 11 oz. 2 dwt. under standard ; and never received any plate in his time from Birmingham or Sheffield that was under standard.

"Being asked if he had any Assistant in the Office ?—he answered, when I am not well, I have a person whose name is Farmer, and who assisted Mr. Richardson my predecessor ; that Farmer was not a sworn officer, neither was he appointed by the company.

"That the witness served his apprenticeship with Alderman Richardson, the late assay master, and that the assay office is at Alderman Richardson's house, where all the utensils remain ; that he never knew an instance of several things in one parcel of plate sent to be assayed that were made of different sorts of silver as to fineness ; and that when there are a great number of pieces, he scrapes some off most or all of them, and assays them altogether ; that he never knew an instance of buckles worse than standard, having pieces of silver soldered to them in order to obtain the company's marks ; and believes he could very safely swear they were all as they were cast.

"Being asked his method of drawing, he answered : If pieces come, from which I can cut off bits, I cut them off ; but if there are no pieces fit for cutting, I scrape them with a sharp scraper.   I then take an assay weight, called 12 ounces, but which is about 17 grains, and weigh as much of such cuttings or scrapings as are equal to the 12 ounces, which is then wrapped in lead, and when the furnace and coppels are hot enough, the assay is put in and refined, but no flux is used, because the lead refines it ; if it comes out 11 oz. 2 dwt. fine silver, we mark it with the lion, the leopard's head, the city arms (being three lions and a wheat sheaf) and the letter for the year ; the letter for the present year is U.   Sometimes we pass it at 11 ounces, but when only 11 ounces, I write to the owners and give them a caution to take care another time.

"The witness said he wrote to some silversmiths at Liverpool, whose plate was full 11 ounces, not long since, and had done so to others ; and his intentions were not to pass it again if they sent it only 11 ounces fine, but they took care to mend their silver.

"That if there is a great deal more solder than necessary upon watch cases, and they were melted down into one mass, the standard of such silver would be reduced in proportion to the quantity of solder, because solder has one third of allay in it ; and believes solder may be added to silver wares after they are assayed ; that he knows nothing of the solder necessary for tankards, because he is not acquainted with tankards, having never assayed any ; and never returned any silver wares for having apparently too much solder.

"That he marks the plate after it is assayed, if it proves standard, and keeps the marks locked up.

"That the late Mr. Richardson was a manufacturer of silver at the time he was assayer, and generally kept two or three people at work in that manufacture ; and that Farmer (who sometimes assays for the witness when sick or out of town) worked for Mr. Richardson near thirty years, and assayed and marked his plate ; that the witness never heard of Mr. Richardson's plate being objected to as under standard ; and believes it was not in the power of any man living to object to it, as there never was better silver worked ; that it was oftener above standard than under, and that he had tried it and found it so himself; and never found any of Mr. Richardson's plate under 11 ounces.

"That the witness works a little in the jewelling way; but never worked above ten or twelve ounces since he has been in that trade; that he has no fixed salary as assay master; his profit arises from the prices allowed by Act of Parliament, which never amounted to £10 in any one year.

"That he doth not assay the lead before he puts the silver in it, because he uses litharidge lead, which has had all the silver taken out of it; and although it may happen, that by an overstrong blast upon the test some of the silver may be blown over with the litharidge, yet the quantity is so small that it would make very little difference.

"That he takes ten grains upon every pound of silver which he puts into the diet box, besides which he is paid for the assay; because it is the custom of the town, and allowed by Act of Parliament.

"That the diet was never sent to the tower to be assayed, nor was ever required by the Lord Chancellor, or anybody else, in the witness's time. Being asked what quantity of diet there was now in the office at Chester? he said he could not tell; for when he wanted silver he had taken some out.

"That he has tried all his assay weights, down to the pennyweight, and they all bear a due proportion; and that he has a halfpenny weight.

"That he never met with any silver allayed with tin, and imagines it would not be malleable enough to bear the hammer, but would be too brittle. Upon being asked, how he knew when silver was sufficiently assayed? he answered, we know by the assay, it has first a cap over it, then that works off in various colours and after that it grows quite bright, and then we know all the lead is worked away; we always use a sufficient quantity of lead."

As the result of the inquiry concerning the manner of working at the Chester assay office the following report was made to Parliament :— " Your committee upon closing the evidence relative to the assay office at Chester, in order to testify their approbation thereof, made the following observation, viz., 'that it appears to this committee that the assay office at Chester has been conducted with fidelity and skill'."

The reputation gained in 1773 appears to have been maintained and increased since then. Under the Acts of Parliament governing its conduct there is no obligation on the Chester Goldsmiths' Company to send its diet to the mint; the Chester authorities, however, in 1889 voluntarily undertook to send it up annually as a guaranty of the propriety with which the business of the assay office is conducted.

The management of the affairs of the assay office is conducted by the Chester Goldsmiths' Company, admission to which is by servitude only, and no person is eligible until after he has served an apprenticeship of seven years to a free brother of the Company.

CHESTER GOLDSMITHS' MARKS.

The Chester
"Coat and
Crest" on two
punsons and
annual letter
adopted as
Warden's marks
168⁶⁄₇.

The following entry, extracted from the minute book of the Chester Goldsmiths' Company, is the first reference which has been found to any mark other than the maker's mark :—

" 1686, Feb. 1st.*—And it is further concluded the warden's marks shall be the coat and crest of the citty of Chester on two punsons with the letter for the year, and the wardens according to the statute made in the third year of King Edward the fourth shall go from shop to shoppe once every week or as oft as they see needful to make search for all goldsmiths' wares exposed to sale without such marks as aforesaid.

" And that every Brother of the said Mistery of Goldsmiths shall bring in his mark to be stamped in their office on a table of copper, the impression thereof to remain to the end that every one's perticular mark may be known."

The following entries in the cash accounts and minute book go to show that although the resolution as to marking was carried out, *the letter was not changed every year.*

FROM THE CASH ACCOUNT.

		£	s.	d.
" 1687	Paid for ye tuches engraving	0	12	0
	Paid for ye three punsons	0	00	6 "

FROM THE MINUTE BOOK.

" June 2nd 1690. Memorandum it was this day agreed upon by the Company of Goldsmiths and Watch Makers that the second day of June shall be the election day for Mr· and Wardens and accordingly Peter Edwards senior was chosen Mr· and Peter Edwards junior and Timothy Gardner Wardens *and the same day the letter was changed from A to B for one year.*"

FROM THE CASH ACCOUNT.

" Paid for 5 essayes att the tower	0	02	06
For a box and three locks and hinges ...	0	09	06
For one ounce of fine silver to make essay of...	0	05	00
1692	April 11th Paid for a puncheon and engraving ye letter C	0	01	06
1694	June 11th To Mr. Bullen for a new letter punson	0	01	00
1697	June 2nd Paid for the punson and carriage ...	0	05	08 "

The minute of 2 June, 1690, to the effect that on that day the letter was changed from A to B, and the cash entry of 11 April, 1692, " Paid for a puncheon and engraving ye letter C, 1s. 6d.," show that the letter A was not changed until 2 June, 1690, and that from June, 1690, until

* *I.e.* 168⁶⁄₇.

April, 1692, the letter B was used.   From April, 1692, until June, 1694, the letter used was C.

The letter on the new puncheon procured from Mr. Bullen in 1694 is not described, but it may be conjectured that it was D.   What the " punson " was, which was obtained on 2 June, 1697, does not appear. Possibly it may have been E, but there is no authority for saying that it was that letter, and the ordering by the company of any kind of punch at a time when the right to assay and mark plate was suspended seems to require some explanation.

There appears to have been much misconception as to what the two marks adopted by the Chester Goldsmiths by their resolution of 1 February, 168⁶⁄₇, really were.   Mr. Chaffers * made the mistake of imagining that a Chester spoon belonging to the Marquess of Breadalbane bore the mark of a fleur-de-lis (a mark entirely foreign to Chester) and his editor, Mr. Markham, having continued that error, the Committee of the Burlington Fine Art Club were thereby apparently misled into describing in connection with their excellent loan exhibition of plate in 1901 some plainly marked 17th century Lincoln spoons as of " Chester manufacture ".   In *Hall Marks on Plate* it is stated that " in an old minute book there is a sketch of a fleur-de-lis, from which it may be inferred that the fleur-de-lis was an old Chester mark ".   A search of all the old minute books reveals no such sketch, and no evidence that any such mark was ever used at Chester.   In order to settle this question, Lord Breadalbane lent the (Chester) spoon referred to above (and several other pieces of plate) to the Author for the purpose of transcribing their marks for this work. The way in which the above mistake originated was then revealed. The marks on the spoon are : 1. AP conjoined, in a shaped shield—the mark of Alexander Pulford ; 2. The Chester town mark—three garbes surmounted by a sword in pale ; 3. A plume of three feathers encircled with a coronet in a plain shield—the badge of the Prince of Wales, who is also Earl of Chester ; and 4. A small black letter a in a shield.   The third mark (placed second in Mr. Chaffers' illustration) was so inaccurately drawn in *Hall Marks on Plate* that it is made to appear like a fleur-de-lis, and on the following page two lines of Lincoln marks with the fleur-de-lis in a circular stamp are given as examples of " uncertain Chester marks," apparently because the plume of feathers had been made to present the appearance of a fleur-de-lis.

The Author has found no other example of the plume of feathers on

The fleur-de-lis erroneously ascribed to Chester.

* Chaffers' *Hall Marks on Plate,* 8th edn., pages 143-4.

Chester plate.   In the other six examples of Chester-marked plate of the period 1687-92, the town mark is the same (on a slightly different shield), but a sword erect with a riband attached takes the place of the plume of feathers.   With reference to this mark, Mr. Chaffers also fell into an error in describing the sword as "issuing from an earl's coronet, the five pellets underneath indicating the balls of the coronet".   What Mr. Chaffers imagined to be pellets indicating the balls of a coronet is in reality a crest-wreath from which the sword issues.*   All the date-letters of this period which have been found are A, B and C in a hybrid black-letter and court-hand type.   It will be noticed that the date-letter

The date-letters prior to 1701.

a on Lord Breadalbane's spoon is different in character from the other letters.   The B and C which follow are nondescript.   It seems absurd to suggest on the basis of these four letters that an entire alphabet of black-letter capitals was used from 1664 to 1688, and that eight letters of another alphabet were used from 1689 to 1696, when there is not a tittle of evidence indicating the use of any date-letter before $168\frac{6}{7}$.   Yet one complete cycle of date-letters, and a third of another, covering this period of thirty-four years, were illustrated in *Hall Marks on Plate* upon less foundation than that exhibited in the first of the following tables.   The construction of this imaginary table is supported by placing the date-letter " B " of 1690-92 as far back as 1665, without any other reason than that the name of Peter Pemberton (whose initials compose the maker's mark) has been found in the minute book from 1677 until 1702.   Tables so constructed cannot but be misleading to those who have not had the time or opportunity to ascertain the facts for themselves.

"Sterling" Mark on Chester plate.

It will be observed that in the first of the following tables a "sterling" mark is illustrated.   The first instance of such a mark occurs on an alms-dish, dated " 1683," in the Church of St. John the Baptist, Chester, and the last on a spoon with flat stem and trifid end, which in 1901 belonged to Mr. Heming.   The first bears the mark of Ralph Walley, 1682-92, and the last bears what is suggested to be the mark of either Puleston Partington or Peter Pemberton (1677-1701).   The alms-dish was probably made before the adoption of the town-mark and date-letter in $168\frac{6}{7}$, and the "sterling" stamp was probably the maker's guaranty that the silver was of the "sterling" standard.   The appearance of the "sterling" stamp, with the date-letter C of 1692-94, after the

* In one of the sword-erect marks a coronet appears : it is, however, not an earl's coronet but one resembling an Eastern crown.

adoption of the town mark in 168⁶⁄₇, is much more puzzling, and, in the absence of evidence regarding its use, it is scarcely worth while suggesting an explanation.

It appears clear that the date-letters shown in Table I. were each used for more than a year and, having regard to the smallness of the number of goldsmiths and plate-workers at Chester at this time, and the small amount of plate then assayed and marked, it is not surprising that one date-letter stamp should have served for two or three years.

It seems probable, in view of the entry in the cash account of 5s. 8d. paid for a punch in 2 June, 1697, that work was continued after the Act of 1696 had been passed, but what the marks were does not appear by any record, and the Author has found no Chester-marked plate which can be ascribed to the period between 1695 and 1701.

On the re-establishment of the Chester assay office in 1701 by the *Marks used from 1701 onwards.* 12 & 13 Wm. III., c. 4, the marks used were the lion's head erased and figure of Britannia—as in London and all the other English provincial offices—a new form of the town mark, viz., the three lions or leopards of England dimidiating the three garbes of the Earldom of Chester in a plain shield, and a date-letter. The cycle of date-letters from 1701 to *The date-letters from 1701 to 1726.* 1725-26 inclusive was an alphabet of twenty-five Roman capitals A to Z, excluding J, the top corners of the C, G, and K and the two extremities of the S terminating in a curl. The maker's mark was composed of the first two letters of his surname until 1725.

The following extracts from the assay office cash accounts show all the entries in respect of letter-punches from 1702-24 :—

				£	s.	d.
"9 July,	1702.	Paid Mr. Bullen for puncheon	(B)	0	2	6
„	1703.	„ Mr. Bullen for Letter	(C)	0	2	6
10 July,	1704.	Paid Mr. Bullen for the Letter	D	0	02	06
25 Feb.,	1705.	Paid Mr. Bullen for the Letter	E	0	02	06
9 July,	1706.	„ Mr. Bullen for the Letter	F	0	02	06
19 March,	1707.	for the Letter	G	0	02	06
9 July,	1708.	Paid Mr. Bullen for the Letter	(H)	0	2	06
21 July,	1709.	Paid Mr. Bullen for the Letter	(I)	0	2	06
9 July,	1710.	Paid Mr. Bullen for „ „	(K)	0	2	06
9 July,	1711.	Paid Mr. Bullen for the Letter	(L)	0	2	06
9 July,	1712.	Paid Mr. Bullen for the Letter	(M)	0	02	06
9 „	1713.	Paid Mr. Bullen „ „ „	(N)	0	2	06
9 July,	1714.	For the Letter	O			
9 July,	1715.	For the Letter	P			
9 July,	1716.	For the Letter	Q			
20 Feb.,	1724.	For five Hall Marks		1	0	0"

All the twenty-five letters of the cycle 1701-26 are struck in the copper plate preserved in the Chester assay office, as also are the marks of makers whose plate was assayed there during the period of that cycle.

It should be noticed in the marks of the cycle 1701-26 that, although on the restoration of the old standard in 1720 the leopard's head crowned and lion passant took the places of the lion's head erased and figure of Britannia, the maker's mark—composed of the first two letters of the maker's surname—continued to be used for several years, and the maker's mark, composed of the initials of his Christian and surname, has not been found in conjunction with an earlier date-letter than that of 1725-26.

After the first cycle the accounts for date-letters do not appear to have been kept regularly, as the following extracts show :—

		£	s.	d
"11 July, 1726.	For punch (A) to Mr. Richardson ...	0	2	6
18 June, 1727.	New Mark	0	2	6
9 July, 1728.	For a new Mark	0	2	6
10 July, 1749.	The Mark	0	2	6"

The date-letters from 1726 to 1751.

The entry of 1726 establishes the fact that the letter *A* was procured for use in that year. The alphabet used from 1726 to 1751 inclusive consisted of cursive capital letters *A* to *Z*, excluding *J*.

The date-letters from 1751 to 1776.

The letters of the following cycle, 1751-2 to 1775-6, were given by both Mr. Chaffers and Mr. Cripps as Roman capitals, whereas six—the a, c, e, h, m and n—have been found to be small Roman letters. The G of this cycle is a Roman capital, the O might, of course, be either. The form of the town mark and leopard's head fixes the a at 1751-2, because in the following cycle these marks are differently formed. Moreover the a of 1776-7 has a much more modern appearance. The form and date of the m of 1762-3 is fixed by the communion cup at Tattenhall, Cheshire, inscribed, " *The gift of the Rev. Samuel Peploe, LL.B., Rector 1762,*" the other date-letters by the particulars given in the tables. No question arises here, as sometimes happens in the case of a bequest. The cup was given to the church by the Rector while he filled that office. The next fixture is the R of 1767-8, which is on a communion paten also at Tattenhall, inscribed " *The gift of the Rev. Samuel Peploe, LL.D., Rector, 1767,*" by which time the Rector had taken his degree of Doctor. It seems, therefore, that there can be no question as to the placing of the date-letters down to this point. Following the R of 1767-8 the letters down to and including the Y as illustrated in the table have been found.   See also the footnote as to letter Z, p. 391 *infra*.

From 1776-7 onwards the arrangement of the date-letters is perfectly simple, the cycle 1776-7 to 1796-7 being composed of twenty-one small Roman letters—a to v inclusive, excluding j.   In the cycle 1797-8 to 1817-8 the same number of Roman capitals were used. Before proceeding further it should, however, be remarked that throughout the cycle 1751-2 to 1775-6 the town-mark and leopard's head appear to have been struck with the same two punches, which well might have been the case in view of the comparatively small amount of work done in those years, the only new punch other than date-letter punches being one for the lion-passant mark for which a new punch appears to have been obtained in 1768.   In 1779 an entirely new set of punches were procured and put into use, the town mark being changed and the representation of the city arms (as it appears in the town mark from 1687 to 1692) was again adopted, the enclosing shield, however, being plain instead of shaped.   In the same year (1779) two new stamps were obtained for the leopard's head and lion-passant marks respectively, and these continued in use until December, 1784, when, on the duty-mark— the king's head incuse—being brought into commission, an entire set of new stamps was obtained of smaller size than those which preceded them.   The earlier marks are to be seen on a communion cup at St. Mary's Church, and the later on a pair of gravy spoons belonging to the Goldsmiths' Company, Chester, both being of the year 1784-5.

In 1823 the leopard's head first appears uncrowned, and thenceforward the use of Roman capital letters was continued till 1838-9, in which year the cycle ended with the letter U, and at the same time the use of the leopard's head terminated.   In 1839 a new cycle of black letter capitals was commenced with the letter 𝔄.   In the next year the following entry occurs in the minute book : " 5th Aug., 1840, at this meeting the letter was changed from A to B ".

After this there is no entry referring to the date-letter until " 5th Aug., 1843, that the letter be changed from 𝔇 to 𝔈 ".

Thenceforward the change of letter was made regularly on the 5 August or following day in each year until 1900, since when it has been made on 1 July ; and the letters and other marks used were as they appear in the following tables.

It remains to be said, with reference to the marks stamped on

The date-letters from 1776 to 1818.

Town mark changed in 1779.

Leopard's head (uncrowned 1823) not used after 1839.

Marks on wrought gold.

wrought gold assayed at Chester, that the observations regarding gold wares assayed in London are applicable, *mutatis mutandis*, to wrought gold assayed at Chester, namely, that the marks on gold and silver were identical until 1798, when for 18-carat gold, then first authorised, a crown and 18 took the place of the lion passant, which was continued on 22-carat gold until 1844, when the crown and 22 were substituted for it. Since then the lion passant has not been used on gold. From 1854 the new standards of 15, 12, and 9 carats have been stamped with the figures 15·625, 12·5, and 9·375, respectively, but the crown is not to be found on gold of less fineness than 18 carats.

By the courtesy of the Goldsmiths' Company and the assay master, the marks in the following tables have been compared with those struck on the copper plates so far as they exist at the assay office, whereby their accuracy has, to that extent, been verified.

The names of Chester goldsmiths and of other goldsmiths and plate workers who have had their plate assayed at Chester, which appear in the lists following the tables of marks, were nearly all supplied to the Author by the assay master, the late Mr. Jas. F. Lowe, B.A. ; the names of those still working have, by a rule of the office, been withheld, and where any such appear they have been obtained from other sources.

MARKS ON CHESTER PLATE.

TABLE I.

DATE.	MAKER'S MARK, TOWN MARK AND DATE-LETTER.	MAKER'S NAME.	ARTICLES AND OWNERS.
1668	GO	George Oulton.	Mace: Presented in 1668 by the Earl of Derby to the Chester Corporation.
c. 1683	RW STER LING RW	Ralph Walley.	Alms-dish, dated 1683: St. John the Baptist, Chester.
,,	NB	Nathanl. Bullen.	Large paten: St. Mary's Church, Chester.*
c. 1685	NB Sterlᵗ	,, ,,	Com. cup: Llanfihangel-Bachellaeth, Carnarvonshire.
,,	NB	,, ,,	Rat-tail spoon: Messrs. Christie.
1686-90	AP	Alexand'r Pulford.	Spoon, flat stem, trifid end: The Marquess of Breadalbane, K.G.
,,	PE	Peter Edwards.	{ Punch bowl: Messrs. Carrington. Oval tobacco box: Genl. Wynne.
,,	PE	,, ,,	Punch bowl: Messrs. Carrington.
,,	RW	Ralph Walley.	Spoon, flat stem, trifid end: Mr. Crichton.
1690-2	RW	,, ,,	Com. flagon: Congregational Church, Oswestry.
,,	PP ,, ,, ,,	Peter Pemberton.	Fluted porringer: Messrs. Christie.
,,	P *	,, ,,	Com. flagon: St. Mary's Cathedral, Limerick.
,,	PP STER LING	,, ,,	Com. cup: Shotwick, near Chester.
c. 1692	PP STER LING C	,, ,,	Com. cup: Llangian, Carnarvonshire.
1692-4	P·P STER LING STER LING	,, ,,	Spoon, flat stem, trifid end: Mr. Heming.
1695-1700	BB STER LING BB	Name not traced.	Tankard: The Day Collection. (Tentatively ascribed to Chester.)
1695	D	... ...	Date-letter conjectured.
1696	E	... ...	Do. do.
1697	F	... ...	Do. do.

The observations in the preceding pages should be read in connection with this and the following Tables.

* Inscribed " The Gift of Thomas Barlow, of Upton, to St. Mary's Church, Chester, 1683 ".

MARKS ON CHESTER PLATE.

TABLE II.

FIVE STAMPS AS BELOW.

	BRIT-ANNIA.	LION'S HEAD ERASED.	DATE LETTER.	TOWN MARK.	MAKER'S MARK.	MAKER'S NAME.	ARTICLES AND OWNERS.
1701-2 ANNE.	[Britannia]	[Lion's head]	A	[shield]	Ri	Richd. Richardson.	Rat-tail spoon : Mr. G. Lambert.
1702-3	,,	,,	B	,,	Bi	John Bingley.	Do. do. : Messrs. Christie.
1703-4	,,	,,	C	,,	Bu / Bi	Nath. Bullen. / Chas. Bird.	Table-spoon: Mr. Lowe, Chester. / Assay Office Plate, Chester.
1704-5	,,	,,	D	,,	Ri	Richd. Richardson.	Oval tobacco box, dated 1704 : Chester Corporation.
1705-6	,,	,,	E	,,	Pe / H	Peter Pemberton. / Name not traced.	Large rat-tail table-spoon: Mr. Lowe. / Assay Office Plate, Chester.
1706-7	,,	,,	F	,,	Ha	,, ,,	Do. do. do.
1707-8	,,	,,	G	,,	Ro	Thos. Robinson.	Tumbler cup : Judge Wynne-Ffoulkes.
1708-9	,,	,,	H	,,	Gi	Name not traced.	Assay Office Plate, Chester.
1709-10	,,	,,	I	,,	Co	,, ,,	Do. do. do.
1710-11	,,	,,	K	,,	Ie	,, ,,	Do. do. do.
1711-2	,,	,,	L	,,	Sa	,, ,,	Do. do. do.
1712-3	,,	,,	M	,,	Ta	— Tarleton.	Do. do. do.
1713-4 GEO. I.	,,	,,	N	,,	Ri	Richd. Richardson.	Com. cup and flagon, " given 1716 " : St. Peter's, Chester.
1714-5	,,	,,	O	,,	Ri	,, ,,	Com. paten : Church of St. John Baptist, Northgate, Chester.
1715-6	,,	,,	P	,,	Du	Barth. Duke.	Gravy spoon : Mr. Hignett.
1716-7	,,	,,	Q	,,	Ma / Ma	Thos. Maddock. / ,, ,,	Rat-tail spoon : Mr. Crichton. / Assay Office Plate, Chester.
1717-8	,,	,,	R	,,	Ri	Richd. Richardson.	Alms-plate, inscribed 1719 : St. John's, Chester.
1718-9	,, LION PASSANT.	,, LEOP's HEAD C?	S	,,	,,	,, ,,	Com. cup : St. Bridget's (now at St. Mary's), Chester.
1719-20	[Lion passant]	[Leopard's head]	T	.	Ri	,, ,,	Small oar : Chester Corporation.
1720-1	,,	,,	U	,,	Ma	Thos. Maddock.	Rat-tail spoon : The Day Collection.
1721-2	,,	,,	V	,,	Ri	Richd. Richardson.	Small cup with one handle : Cordwainers' Guild, Carlisle.
1722-3	,,	,,	W	,,	Ri	,, ,,	Rat-tail spoon : Chester Corpn.
1723-4	,,	,,	X	,,	Ri	,, ,,	{ Paten, on foot, dated 1723 : St. Michael's, Chester. / Gravy spoon : late Miss Farmer.
1724-5	,,	,,	Y	,,	Ri	,, ,,	Plate paten : St. Michael's, Ches.
1725-6	,,	,,	Z	,,	{ Ri / JM	,, ,, / John Melling.	Com. cup : St. John's, Chester.* / Table-spoon: Judge Wynne-Ffoulkes.

1716-7 Mark on small cup at Llanerchymedd ; possibly the mark of a Richardson widow.

* Also water-bailiff's oar, dated 1726, badge of jurisdiction over the river : Beaumaris.

MARKS ON CHESTER PLATE.

TABLE III.

FIVE STAMPS AS BELOW.

	LION PASSANT.	LEOPARD'S HEAD CROWNED.	TOWN MARK.	DATE LETTER.	MAKER'S MARK.	MAKER'S NAME.	ARTICLES AND OWNERS.
1726-7	[stamp]	[stamp]	[stamp]	A	BP	Benj'n Pemberton.	Small salver : Messrs. Christie.
GEO. II. 1727-8	„	„	„	B	BP	„ „	Large skewer : Messrs. G.
1728-9	„	„	„	C	RR	Richd. Richardson.	Com. cup, dated 1728 : Kendal.
1729-30	„	„	„	D	RP	Richd. Pike.	Rat-tail spoon : Mr. W. Boore.
1730-1	„	„	„	E	WR	Wm. Richardson.	Do. do. : Do.
1731-2	„	„	„	F		R.R. conjoined as at 1728 above.	Pipkin : Mr. Lowe, Chester.
1732-3	„	„	„	G	RR	Richd. Richardson.	Com. cup and cover, dated 1732 : Whitehaven.
1733-4	„	„	„	H	RR	„ „	Assay Office Plate.
1734-5	„	„	„	I	„	„ „	Com. cup and cover : Workington.
1735-6	„	„	„	K	{ RR	„ „	Do. do. : Kirkby Lonsdale. Do. do., dated 1735 : Poulton-le-Fylde, Lancashire.
1736-7	„	„	„	L	„	„ „	Half-pint mug : Messrs. Comyns.
1737-8	„	„	„	M	RR	„ „	Pair of alms-basins, dated 1737 : Chester Cathedral.
1738-9	„	„	„	N	„	„ „	Large gravy spoon : Mr. W. Boore.
1739-40	„	„	„	O	WR	Wm. Richardson.	Assay Office Plate.
1740-1	„	„	„	P	BP	Benj'n Pemberton.	Table-spoon : Mr. G. Lambert.
1741-2	„	„	„	Q	RR	Richd. Richardson.	Sauce-boat : Judge Wynne-Ffoulkes.
1742-3	„	„	„	R	TM	Thos. Maddock.	Pap bowl : Messrs. Spink.
1743-4	„	„	„	S	RR	Richd. Richardson.	Do. do. : Mr. Lowe, Chester.
1744-5	„	„	„	T	„	„ „	Sauce pan : Messrs. Crichton.
1745-6	„	„	„	U	…	… … …	Date-letter conjectured.
1746-7	„	„	„	V		… … …	Do. do. do.
1747-8	„	„	„	W		Thos. Maddock as above.	Table-spoon : Mr. Payne.
1748-9	„	[stamp]	„	X	RR	Richd. Richardson.	Pair of beakers : Judge Wynne-Ffoulkes.
1749-50	„	„	„	Y	„	„ „	Plate : Messrs. Comyns.
1750-1	[stamp]	„	„	Z	RR	„ „	Tumbler : Mr. W. Keir, Corwen.

[Y] Variant of date-letter for 1749-50 : Assay Office Plate ; and tumbler : Mr. Lowe.

MARKS ON CHESTER PLATE.

TABLE IV.

FIVE STAMPS AS BELOW.

	LION PASSANT.	LEOPARD'S HEAD CROWNED.	TOWN MARK.	DATE LETTER.	MAKER'S MARK.	MAKER'S NAME.	ARTICLES AND OWNERS.
1751-2	🦁	👑	🏛	**a**	RR	Richd. Richardson.	Plate submitted to the late Mr. Jas. F. Lowe.
1752-3	,,	,,	,,	**B or b**			
1753-4	,,	,,	,,	**C**	,,	,, ,,	Do. do. do.
1754-5	,,	,,	,,	**D or d**			
1755-6	,,	,,	,,	**e**	,,	,, ,,	Tumbler cup: Messrs. Crichton.
1756-7	,,	,,	,,	**F or f**			
1757-8	,,	,,	,,	**G**	RR	,, ,,	Cup won at a cock-fight, inscribed, "Drink and be sober": Dr. Jenkins, Ruthin.
1758-9	,,	,,	,,	**h**	RR	,, ,,	Tumbler cup: Messrs. Crichton.
1759-60	,,	,,	,,	**I or i**			
GEO. III. 1760-1	,,	,,	,,	**K or k**			
1761-2	,,	,,	,,	**L or l**			
*1762-3	,,	,,	,,	**m**	RR / RR	,, ,, / ,, ,,	Com. cup, inscribed, "The gift of the Rev. Samuel Peploe, L.L.B., Rector, 1762": Tattenhall, Cheshire. Com. cup: St. Peter's, Chester.
1763-4	,,	,,	,,	**n**	RR	,, ,,	Tumbler cup: Messrs. Crichton.
1764-5	,,	,,	,,	**o**	RR	,, ,,	Table spoon: Mr. B. Jefferis.
1765-6	,,	,,	,,	**P**	,,	,, ,,	Mug: Sir P. Egerton, Bart.
1766-7	,,	,,	,,	**Q or q**			
*1767-8	,,	,,	,,	**R**	RR	,, ,,	Com. paten, inscribed, "The gift of the Rev. Samuel Peploe, LL.D., Rector, 1767": Tattenhall, Cheshire.
1768-9	🦁	,,	,,	**S**	,,	,, ,,	Ring, noted by the late Mr. Jas. F. Lowe, B.A.
1769-70	,,	,,	,,	**T**	B&F	Bolton & Fothergill, Birm.	Mazarin or fish strainer: Birm. Assay Office.
†1771-2	,	,,	,,	**U**	I·W	Joseph Walley.	Table spoon: Mr. W. Boore.
1773	,,	,,	,,	**V**	GW / I·D	Geo. Walker. / James Dixon or Jos. Duke.	Noted by the Author. Ring: Mr. B. Jefferis. Sauce boat: Mr. Stansby.
1774	,,	,,	,,	**W**	ID	,, ,,	Noted by the Author.
1775	,,	,,	,,	**X**	GW	Geo. Walker.	Tumbler: Dr. Jenkins, Ruthin.
1775-6	,,	,,	,,	**Y**	RR	Richd. Richardson, jr.	Mustard pot: Messrs. Comyns.

1755-6   **E**   Another example of date-letter for this year: Assay Office Plate. Also on a sugar basin (with mark of Joseph Walley): The Goldsmiths' Co.

* See the observations on pages 384-5.
† Fixed by Mr. Scasebrick's evidence before Parliamentary Committee, March, 1773.

MARKS ON CHESTER PLATE.

TABLE V.

FIVE STAMPS TILL 1784, SIX AFTERWARDS, AS BELOW.

	LION PASSANT.	LEOPARD'S HEAD CROWNED.	TOWN MARK.	DATE LETTER.		MAKER'S MARK.	MAKER'S NAME.	ARTICLES AND OWNERS.
1776-7	🦁	👑	🛡	a		RR	Richd. Richardson.	Tumbler: Judge Wynne-Ffoulkes.
1777-8	,,	,,	,,	b		GW	George Walker.	Table-spoon: Judge Wynne-Ffoulkes.
1778-9	,,	,,	,,	c		RR	Richd. Richardson.	Soup ladle: Mr. Parkes.
1779-80	🦁	👑	🛡	d		,, TW	Joseph Walley.	Gravy spoon: Judge Wynne-Ffoulkes, Beaker: Mr. Lowe, Chester.
1780-1	,,	,,	,,	e		,,	,, ,,	Lemon strainer: Mr. D. Key.
1781-2	,,	,,	,,	f		GW	George Walker.	Table-spoon: Mr. W. Boore.
1782-3	,,	,,	,,	g		,,	,, ,,	Table-spoon: Mr. Lowe.
1783-4	,,	,,	,,	h		JA	John Adamson.	Tobacco box: Mr. Skinner.
1784-5 {	,, 🦁	,, 👑	,, 🛡	i i	KING'S HEAD. 👑	R̄ RR	Richd. Richardson. ,, ,,	Com. cup: St. Mary's, Chester. Pr. gravy spoons; Goldsmiths' Co., Chester.
1785-6	,,	,,	,,	k	,,	JC	J. Clifton or } James Conway. }	Table-spoon: Mr. W. Smith.
1786-7	,,	,,	,,	l	👑	TP	T. Pierpoint.	Beaker: Judge Wynne-Ffoulkes.
1787-8	,,	,,	,,	m	,,	RB	Robt. Boulger.	Watch-case: Mr. Pattison.
1788-9	,,	,,	,,	n	,,	IG RJ	John Gilbert. Robert Jones.	Purse-ring: Mrs. Bass. Watch case: Mr. T. Priest.
1789-90	,,	,,	,,	o	,,	WH	Wm. Hull.	Do. do.: Mrs. Dickson.
1790-1	,,	,,	,,	p	,,	WT WT	Wm. Tarlton.* ,, ,,	Snap-spring tobacco box: Mr. Scandrett.
1791-2	,,	,,	,,	q	,,	IB	James Barton.	Assay Office Plate, Chester.
1792-3	,,	,,	,,	r	,,	EM	E. Maddock.	Watch-case: Mr. Paris.
1793-4	,,	,,	,,	s	,,	TA	Thos. Appleby.	Do. do.: Mr. Osborne.
1794-5	,,	,,	,,	t	,,	TH	Thos. Hilsby.	Assay Office Plate: Chester.
1795-6	,,	,,	,,	u	,,	TM	Thos. Morrow.	Watch-case: Mr. Williamson.
1796-7	,,	,,	,,	v	,,	IA&S	John Adamson & Son.	Assay Office Plate: Chester.

1790-1   IH   Mark of Joseph Hewitt, mentioned 1786; or Isaac Hadwine, mentioned 1792.

* or Wm. Twemlow.

When the above Table of Marks was being printed, the Author was shown, by Messrs. Jay Richard Attenborough & Co., a silver cake basket stamped with the lion passant, the leopard's head, the Chester town mark and the RR mark of Richard Richardson, as in the first line of this Table; and in addition thereto the date-letter Z as in the last line of Table II. (page 388) *ante*. Whether this date-letter was stamped on any other Plate assayed at Chester between 1775 and 1777 the Author is unable to say.

MARKS ON CHESTER PLATE.

TABLE VI.

SIX STAMPS AS BELOW.

	LION PASSANT.	LEOPARD'S HEAD CROWNED.	TOWN MARK.	DATE LETTER.	KING'S HEAD	MAKER'S MARK.	MAKER'S NAME.	ARTICLES AND OWNERS.
1797-8	🦁	👑	🛡	A	👤	GL	George Lowe.	Large skewer : Judge Wynne-Ffoulkes.
1798-9	,,	,,	,,	B	,,	R·I	Robt. Jones.	Extinguisher : Messrs. Crichton.
1799 1800	,,	,,	,,	C	,,	RG	Robert Green.	Watch-case, noted in Manchester.
1800-1	,,	👑	,,	D	,,	NC	Nicholas Cunliffe.	Do. do. do.
1801-2	,,	,,	,,	E	,,		Maker's mark indistinct.	Goblet : Messrs. Welby.
1802-3	,,	,,	,,	F	,,	GW	George Walker.	Gravy-spoon : Messrs. Debenham.
1803-4	,,	,,	,,	G	,,		,, ,,	Table-spoon : Mr. W. Boore.
1804-5	,,	,,	,,	H	,,	I·E	Name not traced.	Marks noted by the Author.
1805-6	,,	,,	,,	I	,,	NL	Nicholas Lee.	Watch-case, noted in Manchester.
1806-7	,,	,,	,,	K	,,		,, ,,	Do. do. do.
1807-8	,,	,,	,,	L	,,	GL	George Lowe.	Skewer : Mr. Lowe, Chester.
1808-9	,,	,,	,,	M	,,		Mark indistinct.	Table-spoon : Mr. Wills.
1809-10	,,	,,	,,	N	,,	WJ	Name not traced.	Marks noted by Author.
1810-1	,,	,,	,,	O	,,	IW	John Walker.	Watch-case : Mr. Spiridion.
1811-2	,,	,,	,,	P	,,	WP	William Pugh (of Birmingham).	Sugar-tongs : Mr. Harris.
1812-3	,,	,,	,,	Q	,,	A&I	Abbott & Jones.	Watch-case noted by the Author.
1813-4	,,	,,	,,	R	,,		,, ,,	Do. do. do.
1814-5	,,	,,	,,	S	,,	JM	Jas. Morton.	Sauce-boat : Mr. Crichton.
1815-6	,,	,,	,,	T	,,		,, ,,	Fish-slice : Mr. Phillips.
1816-7	,,	,,	,,	U	,,	H·A	Hugh Adamson.	Watch-case noted by the Author.
1817-8	,,	,,	,,	V	,,	JA	John Abbott.	Do. do. do.

MARKS ON CHESTER PLATE.

TABLE VII.

SIX STAMPS AS BELOW.

	LION PASSANT.	LEOPARD'S HEAD.	TOWN MARK.	DATE LETTER.	KING'S HEAD.	MAKER'S MARK.	MAKER'S NAME.	SOURCE OF MARKS.
* 1818-9	[lion]	[leopard]	[town]	A	[king]	J·A·W	J. Walker.	From wax impression : Mr. J. F. Lowe, B.A.
* 1819-20	,,	,,	,,	B	,,	V&R	Vale & Co.	Assay Office Plate and Records.
GEO. IV. * 1820-1	,,	,,	,,	C	,,	J&R	Jones & Reeves.	Do. do. do.
* 1821-2-3	,,	,,	,,	D	,,	H·V·A	Hy. Adamson.	Do. do. do.
* 1823-4	,,	[leopard]	,,	E	[king]	M·H	Mary Huntingdon.	Do. do. do.
1824-5	,,	,,	,,	F	,,	J·T	John Twemlow.	Do. do. do.
1825-6	,,	,,	,,	G	,,	J·M	J. Morton.	Small cream-jug : Mr. Crichton.
1826-7	,,	,,	,,	H	,,	G·L	Geo. Lowe.	Plate : Mr. Lowe, Chester.
1827-8	,,	,,	,,	I	,,	R·B	Robt. Bowers.	Assay Office Plate, Chester.
1828-9	,,	,,	,,	K	,,	T·N	Thos. Newton.	Do. do. do.
1829-30	,,	,,	,,	L	,,	J·H / JH	John Hilsby, L'pool. ,, ,, ,,	} Do. do. do.
WM. IV. 1830-1	,,	,,	,,	M	,,	J·C	John Coakley.	Gravy spoon : Mr. Lowe, Chester.
1831-2	,,	,,	,,	N	,,	J·P	John Parsonage.	Assay Office Plate, Chester.
1832-3	,,	,,	,,	O	,,	T·W	Thos. Walker or } Thos. Woodfield	Do. do. do.
1833-4	,,	,,	,,	P	,,	R·L	Robt. Lowe.	Do. do. do.
1834-5	,,	,,	,,	Q	,,	R·L	Richd. Lucas.	Do. do. do.
1835-6	,,	,,	,,	R	[king]	I·W	John Walker.	Do. do. do.
1836-7	,,	,,	,,	S	,,	I·L·S	Jos. L. Samuel.	Do. do. do.
VICT. 1837-8	,,	,,	,,	T	,,	J·S	John Sutters.	Large quantity of table plate, Liverpool.
1838-9	,,	,,	,,	U	,,	H·C	Henry Close.	Pocket compass case : Captain Williams.

* See the observations on page 385.

MARKS ON CHESTER PLATE.

TABLE VIII.

FIVE STAMPS AS BELOW.

	LION PASSANT.	TOWN MARK.	DATE LETTER.	QUEEN'S HEAD.	MAKER'S MARK.	MAKER'S NAME.	SOURCE OF MARKS.
1839-40			A		LTL	J. & Thos. Lowe.	Sauce-boat; Mr. P. Lannon.
* 1840-1	,,	,,	B	,,	I&TL	,, ,, ,,	Assay Office Plate and Records.
1841-2	,,	,,	C	,,	HYA	Henry Adamson.	Do. do. do.
1842-3	,,	,,	D	,,	PL	P. Leonard.	Do. do. do.
* 1843-4	,,	,,	E	,,	WS	Wm. Smith.	Do. do. do.
1844-5	,,	,,	F	,,	RS	Ralph Samuel.	Do. do. do.
1845-6	,,	,,	G	,,	AB / WC	Adam Burgess. / Wm. Crofton.	Do. do. do. / Do. do. do.
1846-7	,,	,,	H	,,	JB	J. Burbidge.	Do. do. do.
1847-8	,,	,,	J	,,	IFW	John F. Wathew.	Do. do. do.
1848-9	,,	,,	K	,,	CJ	Christr. Jones.	Do. do. do.
1849-50	,,	,,	L	,,	TW	T. Wilson.	Do. do. do.
1850-1	,,	,,	M	,,	EK	E. Kirkman.	Do. do. do.
1851-2	,,	,,	N	,,	GW	Geo. Ward.	Do. do. do.
1852-3	,,	,,	O	,,	TC	T. Cubbin.	Do. do. do.
1853-4	,,	,,	P	,,	RA / GCL	Richard Adamson. / G. C. Lowe. (Manchester).	Do. do. do. / Do. do. do.
1854-5	,,	,,	Q	,,	TW	Thos. Wooley.	Do. do. do.
1855-6	,,	,,	R	,,	AGR	A. G. Rogers.	Do. do. do.
1856-7	,,	,,	S	,,	JL	John Lowe.	Do. do. do.
1857-8	,,	,,	T	,,	JM	Joseph Mayer.	Do. do. do.
1858-9	,,	,,	U	,,	EJ	Edwd. Jones.	Do. do. do.
1859-60	,,	,,	V	,,	E.N	Elias Nathan.	Do. do. do.
1860-1	,,	,,	W	,,	GR	Geo. Roberts.	Do. do. do.
1861-2	,,	,,	X	,,	HF	H. Fishwick.	Do. do. do.
1862-3	,,	,,	Y	,,	HS	H. J. Stuart.	Do. do. do.
1863-4	,,	,,	Z	,,	FB	Francis Butt.	Do. do. do.

* See the observations on page 385.

MARKS ON CHESTER PLATE.

TABLE IX.

FIVE STAMPS AS BELOW.

	LION PASSANT.	TOWN MARK.	DATE LETTER.	QUEEN'S HEAD.	MAKER'S MARK.	MAKER'S NAME.
1864-5	[lion]	[town]	B	[head]	WD	Wm. Dodge.
1865-6	,,	,,	b	,,	IR	John Richards.
1866-7	,,	,,	c	,,	SW	Saml. Ward, Manchester.
1867-8	,,	,,	d	,,	GL	Geo. Lowe, junr.
1868-9	,,	,,	e	,,	HT / HT	Henry Tarlton, Liverpool.
1869-70	,,	,,	f	,,	WR	W. Roskell, Liverpool.
1870-1	,,	,,	g	,,	S.Q	S. Quilliam.
1871-2	,,	,,	h	,,	GR	Geo. Roberts.
1872-3	,,	,,	i	,,	RO	Robt. Over.
1873-4	,,	,,	k	,,	TR	Thos. Russell.
1874-5	,,	,,	l	,,	HG	Hugh Green.
1875-6	,,	,,	m	,,	S&R	Samuel & Rogers.
1876-7	,,	,,	n	,,	AC	A. Cruickshank.
1877-8	,,	,,	o	,,	SQ	S. Quilliam.
1878-9	,,	,,	p	,,	GFW	Geo. F. Wright, Liverpool.
1879-80	,,	,,	q	,,	JK	Joseph Knight, Birmingham.
1880-1	,,	,,	r	,,	TP&S	T. Power & Son, Liverpool.
1881-2	,,	,,	s	,,	B.N	Benge Nathan.
1882-3	,,	,,	t	,,	WS	Wm. Smith, Liverpool.
1883-4	,,	,,	u	,,	AR	A. Rogers, Liverpool.

TABLE X.

FIVE STAMPS TILL 1890,
FOUR AFTERWARDS.

	LION PASSANT.	TOWN MARK.	DATE LETTER.	QUEEN'S HEAD.	MAKER'S MARK.
1884-5	[lion]	[town]	A	[head]	NBS
1885-6	,,	,,	B	,,	A.B
1886-7	,,	,,	C	,,	JT&S
1887-8	,,	,,	D	,,	A&M
1888-9	,,	,,	E	,,	W.T
1889-90	,,	,,	F	,,	EW
1890-1	,,	,,	G		J.W
1891-2	,,	,,	H		T.C
1892-3	,,	,,	I		JH / AH
1893-4	,,	,,	K		H.W
1894-5	,,	,,	L		JD / WD
1895-6	,,	,,	M		A.M
1896-7	,,	,,	N		W.N
1897-8	,,	,,	O		H.K
1898-9	,,	,,	P		W.A
1899 1900	,,	,,	Q		T.P.B
1900-1	,,	,,	R		GN / RH
EDW. VII. 1901-2	,,	,,	A		J.F
1902-3	,,	,,	B		B.B

MARKS ON CHESTER PLATE.

TABLE XI.   FOUR STAMPS, WITH MAKER'S MARK.

DATE.	LION PASSANT.	TOWN MARK.	DATE-LETTER.	SOURCE OF MARKS.		
1903-4	🦁	⛨	C	From Assay Office Records.		
1904-5	,,	,,	D	Do.	do.	do.
1905-6	,,	,,	E	Do.	do.	do.
1906-7	,,	,,	F	Do.	do.	do.
1907-8	,,	,,	G	Do.	do.	do.
1908-9	,,	,,	H	Do.	do.	do.
1909-10	,,	,,	J	Do.	do.	do.
1910-1	,,	,,	K	Do.	do.	do.
1911-2	,,	,,	L	Do.	do.	do.
1912-3	,,	,,	M	Do.	do.	do.
1913-4	,,	,,	N	Do.	do.	do.
1914-5	,,	,,	O	Do.	do.	do.
1915-6	,,	,,	P	Do.	do.	do.
1916-7	,,	,,	Q	Do.	do.	do.
1917-8	,,	,,	R	Do.	do.	do.
1918-9	,,	,,	S	Do.	do.	do.
1919-20	,,	,,	T	Do.	do.	do.
1920-1	,,	,,	U	Do.	do.	do.
1921-2	,,	,,	V	Do.	do.	do.

MARKS ON CHESTER GOLD WARES.

22 carat	🔲🔲🔲🔲
18 ,,	🔲🔲🔲🔲
15 ,,	🔲🔲🔲🔲
12 ,,	🔲🔲🔲🔲
9 ,,	🔲🔲🔲🔲

The $\mathcal{S}$ is the date-letter for 1918-9.
The date-letter for 1920-1 is $\mathcal{U}$, as in the table for silver marks above.

For MARKS ON FOREIGN PLATE assayed at Chester, see page 27, *ante*.

NAMES OF CHESTER GOLDSMITHS.

[From 1225 to 1878.]

Name of Goldsmith.	Earliest Mention.	Remarks.	Latest Mention.
John the Goldsmith	1225		
Bartholomew the Golds'ith	1265		
Nicholas "the Great" Goldsmith	1271		1292
Mathew the Goldsmith	1282		1293
Bertram the Goldsmith	1292		
Walter the Goldsmith	,,		
John the Goldsmith	1297		
Nicholas (son of Bertram) the Goldsmith	1309		1315
Richard Pratt	1402		
Laurence Smith, Knt.	1540	Mayor 1540, '58 & '70.	1585
Richard Bexwick		Free 1546.	
John Trevis	1560		
Thomas Trevis	,,		
Robert Smith	1573		1615
Richard Warmingshaw	1577		1609
Christ'r Conway	,,	Free 1583.	1603
John Lynglay	1585		1612
Griffith Edwards	,,	1607	d 1640
Thomas Price	,,	,,	d 1635
John Lynglay, jur.	1594		1609
Richard Gregorie	,,	1594	1615
Sylvanus Glegg	1631	1631	
Gerard Jones	1632	Mayor 1638	1674
Dutton Bunbury	1636	Free 1636.	d 1652
Peter Eddwardes	1651	Mayor 1682.	1696
George Oulton	1658		1680
Thomas Chapman	1661	Free 1661.	1702
Thomas Wright	1664	Sheriff 1675.	1676
John Buck	,,	Free 1664.	1677
William Warmenshaw	1666	1666	1670
Nathaniel Bullen	1668	1669	1712
Joseph Billington		,,	
Puleston Partington	1673	Sheriff 1686.	Mayor 1706.
Robert Drew	1675	Free 1675.	d 1680
Symon Wynn	1676	1676	
Peter Pemberton	1677	1677	1706
Peter Edwards, jur.	1679	Mayor 1682.	1700
Ralph Walley	1682	Warden 1686.	1692
Charles Ashton		Free 1682.	
Thomas Robinson	1682		1712
Joseph Clarke	1685		1686
Timothy Gardener	1687		1696
Alexander Pulford	,,		1710
John Deane	,,	Free 1695.	
John Wrench	1696	1696	1725
Samuel Edwards	,,	,,	1700
Charles Bird	,,		1704
John Bingley	1697	1697	1706
Bart'mew Duke	,,	1715	1726

Name of Goldsmith.	Earliest Mention.	Remarks.	Latest Mention.
Richard Richardson (I.)	1701	Sheriff 1714.	
Richard Richardson (II.)		Mayor 1751.	d 1768
—— Tarleton	1712		
William Wrench	1717		1753
Benj'n Critchley	,,		1752
Thomas Maddock	,,	Mayor 1744.	d 1761
Robert Downes		Free 1720.	
William Richardson	1721		1751
Thomas Duke	1722	Mayor 1740.	d 1764
John Melling	1723		1725
Benjamin Pemberton	,,		1753
John Sharman	,,		1726
Robert Cawley	1727		d 1772
Robert Pike		Entered 1727.	
Jon. Jones			1730
Charles Brother		Free 1731.	
George Crookes			1731
Samuel Pemberton	1732		1752
John Eccles	1733	1733	1796
Richard Richardson (III.)	1734		1787
John Wrench	,,		1751
John Warrington	1743		,,
William Wrench	1746		1753
Gabriel Smith	1752	Mayor 1779.	1796
James Conway	,,		,,
Joseph Duke	,,		1776
John Scasebrick or Scarisbrick	,,	Assay M'r. 1772-9.	1782
Thomas Brown	1772		1796
George Walker	,,		1809
Thomas Duke	,,		1796
Joseph Walley		Mention'd 1773.	
George Smith		,,	
Ralph Wakefield		,,	
James Dixon		,,	
W. Fisher		,,	
John Gimlet		,,	
John Gunble & William Vale		,,	
Christian Thyne		,,	
John Wyke & Thomas Green		,,	
William Hardwick		,,	
Wm. Pennington		,,	
Ralph Walker		,,	
T. Pritchard		,,	
Robert Bowers	1796		1813
George Walker, junr.	,,	Sheriff 1823.	1823
Robert Barker	,,		1801
George Lowe	,,		1841
William Twemlow	1797		1823

Name of Goldsmith.		Earliest Mention.	Remarks.	Latest Mention.
Robert	Bowers, junr.	1798	Mayor 1811.	1826
Joseph	Duke	1804		1814
John	Walker	1808	Sheriff 1827.	1839
Henry	Spencer	1817		1830
Mary	Huntington	1822		1827
John	Twemlow	1823		1846
George	Hyatt		Entered 1824.	
John	Lowe	1826	Sheriff 1842.	d 1864
Thomas	Lowe	,,	Assay M'r. 1842-64.	1866
H. M. & S.	Huntington	1827		1831
John	Walker, junr.	1829		1840
Thomas	Walker	1832		,,
John	Walker	1834		,,
Arthur D.	Walker	1837		,,
Chas. B.	Walker	1838		,,
Henry	Walker	,,		,,
William	Hyatt	,,		1846
Edward	Jones	1839		1867
James	Evans	,,		1846
John	Lowe &	}1840		1841
Thomas	Lowe			
Richard	Hall	1841		1843
John	Davies		Mention'd 1841.	
———	Comtene		1841	
P.	Leonard	1842		1847
John	Garner	,,		1861
John	Lowe	,,		1864
John F.	Wathew	1843		1852
Geo. Lowe	Whitehouse	1845		1893
William	Crofton		1845.	
Thomas	Wooley	1852	Warden 1861-1903	
Francis	Butt	,,	Sheriff 1865	d 1869
Daniel	Davies	1853		1862
Joseph	Jones		Entered 1857.	
John	Foulkes Lowe	1858	Sheriff 1897.	
Edward	Tatler	1861	Assay Master	
Jas.	Foulkes Lowe, B.A.	1862	Assay M'r. 1864-1903	
John	Wooley	,,		
John	Foulkes Lowe ⎫	}1864	Entered 1864⎫	
Geo.	Bennett Lowe ⎬		1885⎭	
Lowe &	Sons ⎭	1871		
W.	Foulkes Lowe, F.I.C.	,,	Assay M'r. Ent. 1871.	
Andr.	Nixon Godwin		City Councr. 1878	
Alfred	W. Butt	1872		
Geo. Hy.	Williams		Warden	

Names of Liverpool Manufacturing Goldsmiths, Silversmiths and Watch-case Makers registered at Chester, whose goods have been assayed there. The Watch-case Makers are denoted by (w.m.).

Name of Goldsmith.		Earliest Mention.	Remarks.	Latest Mention.
John	Adamson (w.m.)	1784		1796
John	Clifton	,,		1785
John	Fisher	,,		1795
Thos.	Green (w.m.)	,,		1799
Thos.	Pierpoint ,,	,,		1786
Henry	Rigby ,,	,,		1787
Wm.	Tarlton ,,	,,		
James	Barton&Co. ,,	1785		1798
D.	Beyendroff ,,	,,		1792
William	Hull ,,	,,		1801
Thos.	Harrison ,,	,,		
Walley &	Jones	,,		1788
J.	Gilbert	1786		1797
Joseph	Hewitt	,,		1793
Richard	Morrow	,,		1792
Richard	Boulger	1787		
R.	Preston	,,		1793
Robt.	Jones	1788		
Edward	Maddock	,,		1815
Robert	Green	1791		1803
Isaac	Hadwine	1792		
Thomas	Helsby (w.m.)	1793		1816
John	Ellison ,,	1794		1808
James	Richards ,,	,,		1863 (?)
John	Adamson & Son ,,	1796		
Nicholas	Lee (w.m.)	1796		1817
Thomas	Morrow	,,		
Nicholas	Cunliffe	1798		1815
Richard	Kilshaw	1802		
Hugh	Adamson	1807		1820
Burrell & Co.		1809		
William	Jones	,,		1821
Abbot &	Jones	1812		1816
Robert	Jones & Son	1813		1832
J.	Clarke	1814		1833
Compton	& Parry	1815		1816
M.	Solomon	,,		
J.	Abbot	1817		1826
Henry	Adamson (w.m.)	1818		1849
Jones	& Reeves	1820		1822
Wm.	Cumpsty	1822		1824
W.	Ball	1823		1826
J.	Taylor	1825		
J.	Miller	,,		,,
Edward	Christian	,,		1829
John	Coakley	1828		1834
D.	Lloyd	,,		1831
William	Helsby	1830		
John	Helsby (w.m.)	,,		1857
H.	Close	1831		1842
John	Parsonage	,,		1831

Name of Goldsmith.		Earliest Mention.	Remarks.	Latest Mention.	Name of Goldsmith.		Earliest Mention.	Remarks.	Latest Mention.
William	Hemming .	1831		1851	T.	Wilson	1846		1850
T. M.	Bowen	1832		1832	H.	Stuart	1849		1866
Thomas	Armit	,,		1835	T. W.	Willim	,,		1851
Thos.	Woolfield	,,		1845	Thos.	Over	1850		
E.	Kirkman (w.m.)	,,		1857	W.	Roskell	,,		1875
Richard	Lucas ,,	,,		1853	Thos.	Russell	,,	still working.	
Richard	Adamson	1833		1858	J. F.	Quick	1852		1868
John	Sutters	1835		1856	Henry	Tarlton	,,		1869
Joseph L.	Samuel (w.m.)	,,			G.	Roberts (w.m.)	1855		1875
Thos.	Cumming ,,	1837			R.	Over	1858		1879
Jas.	Hemming	,,			S.	Quilliam (w.m.)	1861		1882
T.	Cubbin	,,		1855	Samuels & Rogers		,,		1881
Samuel	Close	1838			John	Richards (w.m.)	1863		1866
Ralph	Samuel (w.m.)	,,		1858	A.	Cruickshank	1864		1880
Richard	Adamson	1840			Hugh	Green (w.m.)	1865		1882
J. R.	Goepell	1842		1847	A. G.	Rogers	{ 1855		1861
H.	Fishwick	1843		1865			1867		1894
R.	Burgess	,,		1851	William	Smith	1870		1887
Christr.	Jones	,,		1859	T. J.	Paris	1875		1878
W.	Lucas	,,		1846	Geo. F.	Wright	1878		
W.	Smith	,,			Benjn.	Nathan	1879		
Adam	Burgess	1845		1846	T.	Power & Son	,,		
J.	Burbidge	1846		1849					
Joseph	Mayer, F.S.A.	,,		1873					

Names of Manchester Goldsmiths and Plate Workers registered at Chester whose Goods
have been assayed there.

Name of Goldsmith.		Earliest Mention.	Remarks.	Latest Mention.	Name of Goldsmith.		Earliest Mention.	Remarks.	Latest Mention.
James	France	1785		1819	Thos.	Newton	1828		1845
Thos.	Appleby	1791			Robert	Lowe (Preston)	1830		1842
Hemming & Glover		1808		1810	George	Ward	1840		1858
Joseph	Morton	1811			G. C.	Lowe	1853		
James	Glover	1812			William	Dodge	1854		1868
John	Hemmingway	1813		1814	Samuel	Ward	1858		1870
Elizabeth	France	1819		1822	Elias	Nathan	1859		1866
Newton & Hyde		1822		1829	Isaac	Vickers	1869		1878

Other Goldsmiths who have had goods assayed at Chester.

Name of Goldsmith.					Name of Goldsmith.					
Matthew	Boulton & } Birmingham		...	1769-73	Joseph	Tetter	...	...	...	1861
James	Fothergill }				Isaac	Vicars	...	...	...	1869-78
———	Jackson ...	...	...	1841	E.	W., Coventry	...	...	...	...
———	Hayne & Co. ...	...	...	1842	H.	Y., ,,	...	...	...	...
George	Lowe, junr., Glo'ster ...		...	1847-74	A.	M., ,,	...	...	...	...
Fredk. W.	Ward ...	...	...	1851	Joseph	Knight ...	...	...	...	1878

CHAPTER XVI

THE BIRMINGHAM GOLDSMITHS

AND THEIR MARKS

Birmingham
Assay Office
Established 1773. The establishment of the assay office at Birmingham in the year 1773 was due mainly to the exertions of one man—perhaps the greatest Birmingham man of his time—Matthew Boulton, who, whether as an inventor, designer, or manufacturer of great and small things, useful and ornamental, left his mark, and that an estimable one, on everything he touched.

From the fact that petitions were presented to Parliament on the 1st of February, 1773, by manufacturers of plate in Sheffield, and on the following day by others of Birmingham, praying for the establishment of assay offices in their respective towns, it would appear that concerted action had been arranged. The petition from Birmingham was prepared by Matthew Boulton on behalf of himself and the rest of the manufacturers of wrought silver in Birmingham. After referring to the Sheffield petition, it stated that the petitioners were engaged in the manufacture of plate, which might be considerably improved if an assay office were established in their own town, that the inconvenience of sending their goods to Chester, the nearest assay office, greatly interfered with their success, and it prayed that if provision should be made for establishing an assay office at Sheffield, a similar privilege might be extended to Birmingham.

The opposition of the London Goldsmiths Company to the applications from Birmingham and Sheffield, the evidence with respect to the matter, and the Committee's report thereon, have already been referred to.* The result was that an Act (13 Geo. III. c. 52) was passed, whereby new assay offices were established at Birmingham and Sheffield. This Act, so far as it related to Birmingham, recited the difficulties and hardships suffered by the plate workers of that town in the exercise of

---

* See Chapter X., pp. 273-6.

their trades for want of assayers in convenient places (as set forth in their petition), appointed Birmingham as a place for assaying and marking wrought plate, and incorporated a Company (with perpetual succession and the right to use a common seal) entitled " The Guardians of the Standard of Wrought Plate in Birmingham," with exclusive jurisdiction over all silver plate made in the town of Birmingham or within thirty miles thereof. The Act provided that the Company should be composed as follows :—

"The Rt. Hon. the Earl of Dartmouth, The Rt. Hon. Lord Archer, The Rt. Hon. Heneage Finch—commonly called Lord Guernsey, The Rt. Hon. Geo. Greville—commonly called Lord Greville, The Rt. Hon. Francis Conway—commonly called Lord Beauchamp, Sir John Wrottesley, Bart., Sir Hy. Bridgeman, Bart., the Hon. John Ward, Richard Geast, John Wyrley, Isaac Spooner, Henry Gough, Charles Colemore, John Taylor, Samuel Garbett, Henry Carver, Senr., Joseph Wilkinson, Sampson Lloyd, Junr., Thomas Ingram, Edward Palmer, John Kettle, Joshua Glover, Matthew Boulton, John Francis, Thomas Mynd, Samuel Pemberton, John Turner, senr., John Lee, William Sawyer, John Lane of Moseley, James Alston, Matthew Barker, Joseph Adams of Walsall, James Wright, Samuel Galton, and James Jackson."

The Act of 1773 was, so far as it related to Birmingham, repealed, but in substance re-enacted by the 5 Geo. IV. c. 52 (1824-local), whereby the right to assay and mark wrought gold was conferred on the Birmingham Company in addition to the other powers granted by the former Act. By this later Act the Birmingham assay office has since that date been and is now mainly regulated.

Of the thirty-six guardians of which the Company now consists, not more than nine nor less than six are to be goldsmiths or silversmiths. They are required to elect from their number annually not more than six nor less than four wardens, to appoint an assay master, a treasurer and other officers. The guardians are empowered within the terms of their Act of Incorporation to make bye-laws for the management of the assay office. They had, until 1854, exclusive jurisdiction over all gold, as well as silver, wrought in or within thirty miles of Birmingham, and any person in that district offering for sale any gold or silver ware made therein without having it assayed at the Birmingham assay office, was liable to the forfeiture of the ware or its value. Now, however, by the 17 & 18 Vict. c. 96 (1854), goldsmiths may register their marks and have their wares assayed and marked at any assay office in the kingdom. All workers of gold and silver are required to enter their names, places of abode, and marks at the assay office where their wares are assayed, and if they stamp on any wrought gold or silver any mark other than that so entered, they are liable to a penalty of £100 for every offence.

The wardens, Assay Master, and other officers employed at the office are bound by their oaths, in form provided by the Act, faithfully to discharge their duties and not to disclose the design of any plate sent to be assayed.

The marks appointed to be used at Birmingham are described further on. The prices to be charged for assaying are limited by the Act. The "diet" or scrapings to be taken from each article for the purpose of the assay is also defined, and it is provided that the monies received for assaying and marking and from the sale of the diet are to be applied to the payment of the expenses of the office and the prosecution of offenders, and the surplus is to be invested in the Public Funds or Government Securities.

The wardens and Assay Master are obliged as part of their duties :—

To provide a trial plate for each standard which is to be assayed at the Mint.

Duties of the Wardens and Assay Master.

To provide punches for striking the statutory marks and a box for their safe custody, with three different locks and keys, a key to be kept by each of the two wardens and by the Assay Master. The punches are not to be taken out except in the presence of the Assay Master and two wardens, and are to be used only for the purpose of marking wares which have been assayed.

To provide a box for the diet, with three different locks, the two wardens and the Assay Master each to have a key, and this box is to be opened only in presence of all three, and no diet is to be taken out except once a year for the purpose of trial.

To examine all work sent to be assayed in order to ascertain whether each article is of one sort of gold or silver, whether all the parts have been joined together which are intended to be joined, whether it is marked with the maker's mark or has any unnecessary solder, and to return to the worker such as may be objected to. If free from all the foregoing objections, scrapings are taken from each article in their presence, and they are to see that no more is taken than in the proportion of six grains to a pound from gold, and eight grains to a pound from silver.

The scrapings from each article of gold and silver submitted to him are to be divided by the assayer ; and in the presence of the wardens and assayer, one part is to be put into the diet box and the other part into the assayer's box.*

To be present whilst articles reported by the assayer to be as good as standard are marked, and whilst articles reported as worse than standard are broken to pieces.

To cut open all work suspected of having base metal concealed, and if any base metal be found, to have the article broken, which is then forfeited for the benefit of the office. If the suspicions prove groundless, the owner of the article is to be recompensed out of the funds of the guardians.

The diet box is to be opened once in every year in the presence of four wardens and the Assay Master, the diet taken out (each standard to be kept in a separate parcel) the whole is to be made into one parcel without opening the respective parcels of which it is composed, the entire parcel is to be sealed with their respective seals, and delivered to a messenger in each other's presence, to be by him conveyed to the Mint.

The diet returned from the Mint is to be sold by the wardens and Assay Master and the produce accounted for.

The duties of the Assay Master, in addition to the foregoing are :—

To assay wrought gold and silver and report thereon to the wardens.

To receive all moneys paid for assaying and marking.

To keep books containing the names of every owner of wrought gold or silver brought to be assayed, and the particulars of the weight of the same, and an account of monies received for assaying, and for scrapings and cuttings, and an account of the expenses of the office, including salaries and wages, and to allow every guardian to have access to such books.

To see that nothing except the diet is put into the diet box.

He is liable to a penalty of £200 and loss of office if he divulge the design or invention of any plate brought to be assayed, or permit it to be viewed by any person except those who are necessarily employed at the assay office, or if he mark any plate not assayed and found as good as standard, or if the diet should not be of the same fineness as the trial plate.

He is required to provide two sureties of £500 each to the Master

* In assay office practice, the use of the word "Diet" is confined to that portion of the scrapings which is placed in the diet box.

of the Mint for the performance of his duties, and the payment of the fines should any become payable.

Growth of the
Business of the
Assay Office.

For a number of years the office was open only two days a week, but the business grew to such an extent that for half a century it has been open on every working day, and for a number of years past there have been no less than ten thousand ounces of gold and silver wares per day assayed and marked there. The equipments of the office are amongst the most perfect and complete in the whole world, and not even at the Metropolitan Mint is the machinery better suited for its purpose. The wares are assayed with the most minute care, and the marking is performed by means of machinery of the most delicate construction, worked by electrical power. It is, of course, impossible with such an enormous amount of work that the wardens and Assay Master should personally superintend the marking of each separate article, but the system of responsibility cast upon every individual assayer, marker, and other officer, from the highest to the lowest, is such that it would be impossible for any irregularity to take place without immediate detection. The growth of the gold and silver trade of Birmingham in recent years has been so remarkable, and the consequent increase in the work of the assay office has been so great as to be almost incredible to persons unfamiliar with the subject. The following table, compiled from the annual reports of the Guardians, shows the progress made in twenty years :—

WORK DONE AT THE BIRMINGHAM ASSAY OFFICE

IN QUINQUENNIAL YEARS FROM 1883 TO 1918.

	1883.	1888.	1893.	1898.	1903.	1908.	1913.	1918.
Gold Wares Assayed and Marked ... Ounces	91,053	122,743	229,016	333,741	358,437	381,957	389,914	366,456
Gold Wares Assayed and Broken ... Ounces	1,142	1,024	2,226	1,772	2,749	1,918	2,354	2,550
Silver Wares Assayed and Marked ... Ounces	851,957	775,901	1,276,317	2,530,019	3,791,474	3,588,640	4,248,843	2,283,155
Silver Wares Assayed and Broken ... Ounces	4,223	1,438	2,672	616	2,280	2,974	2,781	780
Number of Gold and Silver Wares entered for Assaying	2,649,379	3,347,974	6,467,922	11,889,093	13,248,255	13,355,074	12,715,798	6,923,236
Number of Assays made	101,012	109,760	171,643	286,750	436,238	478,330	508,761	209,455

THE BIRMINGHAM GOLDSMITHS' MARKS.

The Act of 1773 provided that all plate assayed at the Birmingham assay office, being of the standard of 11 oz. 2 dwts. fine, should be marked with :— Marks prescribed by Act of 1773.

1. The mark of the maker, which should be the first letters of his Christian and surname.
2. The lion passant ; and for plate of the standard of 11 oz. 10 dwts. fine the figure of Britannia * in lieu of the lion.
3. The mark of the Company (an anchor), and
4. A distinct variable mark or letter which should be annually changed upon the election of new wardens.

Very small wares incapable of being marked without injury being done to them are excepted from the operation of the Act.

From December, 1784, to June, 1890, in addition to the above marks, the Sovereign's head stamp, indicating the payment of duty, was struck on all plate made during that period. Sovereign's head 1784 to 1890.

The only one of the four marks (named in the Act of Parliament) requiring any particular mention is "the mark of the Company," which is an anchor. The reason why it was appointed to be the mark of the Birmingham assay office does not appear. It is referred to in the Act of 1773 as "the mark of the Company," and the only explanation of its adoption which the Author has been able to obtain, is that it was probably because of the extent of the over-sea commerce of Birmingham.

The date-letter, or—in the words of the Act—the "distinct, variable mark or letter which shall be annually changed," has been changed every year since the office was opened in 1773.

The guardians meet annually in the month of July, when they fill up any vacancies which have occurred in their body.

The first cycle of date-letters commenced in 1773 and terminated in July, 1798, the letters used being the entire alphabet of Roman capitals, excluding J. Strangely enough, both in *Old English Plate* and *Hall Marks on Plate*, the mistake was made of including the J in this cycle (one apparently copied from the other) whereby the cycle was made to comprise twenty-six instead of twenty-five letters. The first appearance of the duty stamp (the Sovereign's head) is thus in those books associated with the letter L, whereas the King's head is first seen with the letter M, The Birmingham date-letters from 1773 to 1798.

---

* The lion's head erased is never used at Birmingham.

some articles marked with that letter being found without and some with the King's head incuse.

The date-letters from 1798 to 1824.

The second cycle, from 1798-9 to 1823-4, comprehends the entire twenty-six letters of the alphabet in small Roman characters. It is by no means easy to distinguish the letters o, s, v, w, x and z of the second cycle from the same letters of the first cycle, as the form, and on small articles, the size, of the letter is identical in both. It is only by carefully noting the few very slight differences between the shields surrounding these letters in the two cycles and by ascertaining the makers' marks which were used in each cycle that the date of an article can with certainty be determined. The makers' names and dates of registration contained in the list which succeeds the tables in the following pages will be found of assistance in a case of difficulty.

The date-letters from 1824 to 1849.

In the third cycle, 1824-5 to 1848-9, twenty-five black-letter or old English capitals were used. No letter I, like that illustrated in *Hall Marks on Plate* for 1833-4 nor 𝔍, like that shown in *Old English Plate* for 1845 was ever used. The letter actually used in 1844-5 was, as illustrated in Table III., really a small black-letter 𝔲 with a fine upright line, two curved lines, and a spur, added to give it the character of a capital letter.

The date-letters from 1849 to 1875.

In the fourth cycle, 1849-50 to 1874-5, the entire alphabet of twenty-six Roman capital letters was used, the first eighteen being in oblong punches with clipped corners, the rest in oval shields. The Queen's head forms a ready means of distinguishing the letters of this cycle from those of any other; there is also a marked difference in the shape of the letter punches.

The date-letters from 1875 onwards.

The fifth cycle, 1875-6 to 1900, comprises twenty-five small old English letters—j not being used. Seventeen of these letters are found in oval punches, the others are in oblong shields with clipped corners.

In July, 1900, the sixth cycle was commenced, the letters used being small Roman letters in shields, the sides and tops of which are straight with clipped corners, and the bases waved, finishing with a point in the centre.

The duty mark.

The Sovereign's head stamp was changed with each succeeding Monarch from 1784 to 1890 as on London plate, except that the changes were not made until some few years after the succession, the head of Wm. IV. not appearing until 1834, and of Queen Victoria not until 1839.

Marks on wrought gold.

Since 1824, when the right to assay gold was conferred by the Act

5 Geo. IV. c. 52, the marks on gold work assayed at Birmingham have been the same as at London, except that the anchor takes the place of the leopard's head. Examples of the marks are given on page 414 *infra*.

By the courtesy of the Birmingham wardens and the Assay Master, Mr. Arthur Westwood, the marks in the following tables—obtained from articles of plate examined by the Author—have been compared with the assay office records. Marks not obtained from articles of plate have been reproduced from impressions struck by the punches on the trial plates at the office.

By the same courtesy the list of names entered at the Birmingham assay office from 1773 to 1850, which follows the tables of date-letters, has been furnished to the Author for the purpose of this work. Names of recent date have not been disclosed because of the objection to their being used for advertising purposes ; any such names printed in the following tables have been supplied by others.

The hall marks on foreign plate assayed at Birmingham are illustrated on page 27 *ante*.

MARKS ON BIRMINGHAM PLATE.

TABLE I.

FOUR STAMPS UNTIL 1784, THENCEFORWARD FIVE, AS BELOW.

	LION PASSANT.	ANCHOR.	DATE LETTER		MAKER'S MARK.	MAKER'S NAME.	ARTICLES AND OWNERS.
1773-4	🦁	⚓	A		MB IF	Matthew Boulton & John Fothergill.	Pair of salts: Birmingham Assay Office.
1774-5	,,	,,	B		,, ,,	{ ,, ,, Do. ,, ,,	Candlesticks: Mr. M. B. Huish. Do. : B'm'ham Assay Office.
1775-6	,,	,,	C		CF	Charles Freeth.	Mounts of horse-pistols: Mr. F. Weekes.
1776-7	,,	,,	D		,,	,, ,,	Light striker: Mr. F. Weekes.
1777-8	,,	,,	E		{ RB CF MB IF	Richard Bickley, Charles Freeth. Boulton & Fothergill.	Mounts of pistol: Mr. Dudley Westropp. Cake-basket: Mr. H. D. Ellis.
1778-9	,,	,,	F		,, ,,	,, ,,	Candlesticks : Mr. W. Boore.
1779-80	,,	,,	G		TW	T. Willmore & Alston.	Pair of shoe buckles: B'm'ham Assay Office.
1780-1	,,	,,	H			... ...	Marks from B'm'ham Assay Office Records.
1781-2	,,	,,	I			... ...	Do. do. do.
1782-3	,,	,,	K		TW	T. Willmore & Alston.	Pair of shoe buckles: B'm'ham Assay Office.
1783-4	,,	,,	L	KING'S HEAD	,,	,, ,,	Pair of shoe buckles: Mr. Dicker.
1784-5	,,	,,	M	👑	SP	Samuel Pemberton.	Snuff-box: Mr. Falk.
1785-6	,,	,,	N	,,	HH	Henry Holland.	Watch-case: B'm'ham Assay Office.
1786-7	,,	,,	O	👤	SP	Samuel Pemberton.	Snuff-box: Messrs. Robinson and Fisher.
1787-8	,,	,,	P	,,	IT	Joseph Taylor.	Caddy spoon: Do. do.
1788-9	,,	,,	Q	,,	,,	,, ,,	Marrow spoon: Mr. Simmonds.
1789-90	,,	,,	R	,,	TW	Thos. Willmore.	Pair of shoe buckles: The Author's Collection.
1790-1	,,	,,	S	,,	MB	Mathw. Boulton.	Tripod fruit stand: B'm'ham Assay Office.
1791-2	,,	,,	T	,,	SP	Samuel Pemberton.	Patch-box: B'm'ham Assay Office.
1792-3	,,	,,	U	,,	,,	,, ,,	Snuff-box: Mr. Lowe, Chester.
1793-4	,,	,,	V	,,	MB	Mathw. Boulton.	Candelabrum: Birmingham Assay Office.
1794-5	,,	,,	W	,,	IT	Joseph Taylor.	Caddy spoon: Birmingham Assay Office.
1795-6	,,	,,	X	,,	IS	John Shaw.	Vinaigrette: The Author's Collection.
1796-7	,,	,,	Y	,,	TW	Thos. Willmore.	Scent bottle case: B'm'ham Assay Office.
* 1797-8	,,	,,	Z	👤	,,	,, ,,	Vinaigrette: B'm'ham Assay Office.

* The King's head is found in stamps both of oval and indented outline for the year 1797-8, and in some instances the King's head mark is stamped twice.

See also additional makers' marks on page 414 *infra*.

MARKS ON BIRMINGHAM PLATE.

TABLE II.

FIVE STAMPS, AS BELOW.

	LION PASSANT.	ANCHOR.	DATE LETTER.	KING'S HEAD.	MAKER'S MARK.	MAKER'S NAME.	ARTICLES AND OWNERS.
1798-9	🦁	⚓	a	👑	TW	Willmore & Alston.	Nutmeg box : Mr. Fitzhenry.
1799 / 1800	,,	,,	b	,,	SP	Samuel Pemberton.	Snuff-box : Messrs. Spink.
1800-1	,,	,,	c	,,	F&W	Forrest & Wasdell.	Nutmeg grater : Messrs. Spink.
1801-2	,,	,,	d	,,	IT / T.W	John Turner ? / Thos. Willmore ?	Vinaigrette : B'ham Assay Off. / Patch-box : The Author's Collection.
1802-3	,,	,,	e	,,	MB	Matthew Boulton.	Toast rack : B'ham Assay Off.
1803-4	,,	,,	f	,,	IS	John Shaw.	Vinaigrette : The Author's Collection.
1804-5	,,	,,	g	,,	IT	Joseph Taylor.	Mustard spoon : Mr. Fitzhenry.
1805-6	,,	,,	h	,,	ML / WP / JW	Matthew Linwood. / William Pugh. / Joseph Willmore.	Snuff-box : The Author's Coll. / Caddy spoon : B'm Assay Off. / Snuff-box : Do. do.
1806-7	,,	,,	i	,,	C&B	Cocks & Bettridge.	Nutmeg grater : Mr. Ballard.
1807-8	,,	,,	j	,,	WP	William Pugh.	Snuff-box : The Author's Coll.
1808-9	,,	,,	k	,,	MB	Matthew Boulton.	Chees. scoop : Messrs. Christie.
1809-10	,,	,,	l	👑	IS	John Shaw.	Snuff-box : Mr. Bruford.
1810-1	,,	,,	m	,,	T&T	Thropp & Taylor.	Do. : B'ham Assay Office.
1811-2	,,	,,	n	,,	S&S	T. Simpson & Son.	Snuff-box : Messrs. Spink.
1812-3	,,	,,	o	👑	,, / IT	,, ,, / Joseph Taylor.	Do. : B'ham Assay Office. / Salt-spoons : Messrs. M. & S. Lyon.
1813-4	,,	,,	p	,,	C&B	Cocks & Bettridge.	Mustard-spoon : The Author.
1814-5	,,	,,	q	,,	L&C	W. Lea & Co.	Vinaigrette : Do.
1815-6	,,	,,	r	,,	,,	,, ,,	Snuff-box : Messrs. Spink.
1816-7	,,	,,	s	,,	SP / W&K	Samuel Pemberton. / Wardell & Kempson.	Vinaigrette : Mr. G. Lowe. / Child's coral : Miss Jackson.
1817-8	,,	,,	t	,,	E.T	Edward Thomason.	Tea-spoon : B'ham Assay Off.
1818-9	,,	,,	u	,,	J.W	Joseph Willmore.	Snuff-box : Do. do.
1819-20 GEO. IV.	,,	,,	v	,,	,,	,, ,,	Vinaigrette : The Author's Collection.
1820-1	,,	,,	w	,,	ML	Matthew Linwood & Son.	Sandwich box : Messrs. Robinson & Fisher.
1821-2	,,	,,	x	,,	L&C	Lea & Clark.	Seal : Birmingham Assay Office.
1822-3	,,	,,	y	,,	L&Cº	John Lawrence & Co.	Snuff-box : Do. do.
1823-4	,,	,,	z	,,	J.W	Joseph Willmore.	Vinaigrette : Do. do.

On plate of 1801 to 1811 the King's head mark is frequently found in a stamp of oval shape, and on plate of 1812 to 1825 it is sometimes found in a foliated stamp as shown at 1797-8 and 1809-10.

MARKS ON BIRMINGHAM PLATE.

TABLE III.

FIVE STAMPS AS BELOW.

	LION PASSANT.	ANCHOR.	DATE LETTER.	KING'S HEAD.	MAKER'S MARK.	MAKER'S NAME.	ARTICLES AND OWNERS.
1824-5	(lion)	(anchor)	A	(head)	TP / C.J	T. Pemberton & Son. / Charles Jones.	Salt-spoons: B'm. Assay Office. / Sugar-tongs: Do. do.
1825-6	,,	,,	B	,,	LV&W / T.S	Ledsam, Vale & Wheeler. / Thomas Shaw.	Snuff-box: Messrs. Spink. / Do. : Mr. John Fullerton.
1826-7	,,	,,	C	(head)	L&Co / NM	John Lawrence & Co. / Nathaniel Mills.	Do. : The Author's Coll'n. / Do. : B'm'ham Assay Office.
1827-8	,,	,,	D	,,	U&H / MB / J.W	Unite and Hilliard / M. Boulton & Plate Co. / Joseph Willmore.	Caddy spoon: Do. do. / Taper-stand : Do. do. / Snuff-box: The Author's Coll'n.
1828-9	,,	,,	E	,,	ET / WF	Edward Thomason. / William Fowke.	Cake-basket: M's'rs. Smith & Rait. / Table-spoon: B'm'ham Assay Off.
1829-30	,,	,,	F	(head)	IB / LV&W	John Bettridge. / Ledsam, Vale & Wheeler.	Snuff-box : Do. do. / Wine-labels : Do. do.
WM. IV. 1830-1	,,	,,	G	,,	TR&S / MB	Thos. Ryland & Sons. / M. Boulton & Plate Co.	Pair of spurs: Do. do. / Cake-basket : Do. do.
1831-2	,,	,,	H	(head)	JW	Joseph Willmore.	Handles of knife and fork : Birmingham Assay Office.
1832-3	,,	,,	I	,,	,,	,, ,,	Silver-gilt knife, fork, and spoon : Birmingham Assay Office.
1833-4	,,	,,	K	,,	ES / VR	Edward Smith. / Vale & Ratheram.	Snuff-box: Messrs. Spink. / Watch-case: B'm'ham Assay Off.
1834-5	,,	,,	L	(head)	T&P / WP	Taylor & Perry. / William Phillips.	Caddy-spoon: Do. do. / Snuff-box: Mr. Bruford.
1835-6	,,	,,	M	,,	GW	Gervase Wheeler.	Vinaigrette: Mr. G. Lowe.
1836-7	,,	,,	N	,,	FC / J&Co	Francis Clark. / Joseph Jennens & Co.	Snuff-box: The Author's Coll'n. / Baron's coronet: Messrs. Crichton.
VICT. 1837-8	,,	,,	O	,,	T.S / R.E.A	Thomas Spicer. / Robinson, Edkins & Aston.	Watch-case: B'm'ham Assay Off. / Standish : Do. do.
*1838-9	,,	,,	P	(head)	GU / N.M	George Unite. / Nathaniel Mills.	Wine labels: Do. do. / Snuff-box : Do. do.
1839-40	,,	,,	Q	,,	N&R	Neville & Ryland ?	Do. : Do. do.
1840-1	,,	,,	R	,,	,,	,, ,,	Do. : B'm'ham Assay Office.
1841-2	,,	,,	S	,,	... ...		From Birmingham Assay Office Records.
1842-3	,,	,,	T	,,	R.E.A	Robinson, Edkins & Aston.	Hand candlestick: Messrs. M. & S. Lyon.
1843-4	,,	,,	U	,,	ES	Edward Smith.	Snuff-box: Messrs. Spink.
1844-5	,,	,,	V	,,	N.M	Nathaniel Mills.	Do. : B'm'ham Assay Office.
1845-6	,,	,,	W	,,	W&ET	Wm. & Ed. Turnpenny.	Oval strainer: Mr. Peters.
1846-7	,,	,,	X	,,	Y&W / N.M	Yapp & Woodward. / Nathaniel Mills.	Apple scoop: B'm'ham Assay Off. / Snuff-box : Do. do.
1847-8	,,	,,	Y	,,	,,	,, ,,	Vinaigrette : Messrs. Spink.
1848-9	,,	,,	Z	,,		... ...	From Birmingham Assay Office Records.

* On plate of the early part of 1838-9 the head of King William is sometimes found stamped, although Queen Victoria succeeded to the throne in 1837.

MARKS ON BIRMINGHAM PLATE.

TABLE IV.

FIVE STAMPS AS BELOW.

	LION PASSANT.	ANCHOR.	DATE LETTER	QUEEN'S HEAD.	MAKER'S MARK.	MAKER'S NAME.	ARTICLES AND OWNERS.
1849-50	🦁	⚓	A	👑	NM	Nathaniel Mills.	Snuff-box: Messrs. Christie.
1850-1	,,	,,	B	,,	{ ES	Edward Smith.	Match-box: B'ham Assay Office. Vinaigrette: Messrs. Spink.
1851-2	,,	,,	C	,,	,,	,, ,,	Snuff-box: Mr. A. W. Cox.
1852-3	,,	,,	D	,,		Nathl. Mills, as 1849.	Wine label: B'ham Assay Office.
1853-4	,,	,,	E	,,		... ...	From B'ham Assay Office Plate.
1854-5	,,	,,	F	,,		... ...	Do. do. do.
1855-6	,,	,,	G	,,	GU	George Unite.	Caddy spoon: B'ham Assay Office.
1856-7	,,	,,	H	,,		... ...	From B'ham Assay Office Plate.
1857-8	,,	,,	I	,,		... ...	Do. do. do.
1858-9	,,	,,	J	,,		... ...	Do. do. do.
1859-60	,,	,,	K	,,	GU	George Unite.	Small box: Mr. Bruford.
1860-1	,,	,,	L	,,		... ...	From B'ham Assay Office Plate.
1861-2	,,	,,	M	,,		... ...	Do. do. do.
1862-3	,,	,,	N	,,		J. H. & Co., as on page 414.	Church plate: Lanlivery.
1863-4	,,	,,	O	,,		... ...	From B'ham Assay Office Plate.
1864-5	,,	,,	P	,,	JM&Cº	Names registered after 1850 not disclosed.	Communion paten: All Saints, York.
1865-6	,,	,,	Q	,,		... ...	From B'ham Assay Office Plate.
1866-7	,,	,,	R	,,		... ...	Do. do. do.
1867-8	,,	,,	S	,,	JG	... ...	Dessert knife: Messrs. M. & S. Lyon.
1868-9	,,	,,	T	,,		... ...	From B'ham Assay Office Plate.
1869-70	,,	,,	U	,,		... ...	Do. do. do.
1870-1	,,	,,	V	,,		... ...	Do. do. do.
1871-2		,,	W	,,	JT	Crown and 18 instead of lion passant.	Gold mounts of studs: The Author.
1872-3	,,	,,	X	,,		... ...	From B'ham Assay Office Plate.
1873-4	,,	,,	Y	,,		... ...	Do. do. do.
1874-5	,,	,,	Z	,,		... ...	Do. do. do.

MARKS ON BIRMINGHAM PLATE.

TABLE V.

FIVE STAMPS TILL 1890, THENCEFORWARD FOUR ONLY.

	LION PASSANT.	ANCHOR.	DATE LETTER.	QUEEN'S HEAD.	MAKER'S MARK.	MAKER'S NAME.			ARTICLES AND OWNERS.
1875-6	🦁	⚓	a	👤	TP&S	Names registered after Jan. 1, 1850, not disclosed.			Fish slice : The Author.
1876-7	,,	,,	b	,,	,,	...	...	...	Memorial trowel : Birmingham Assay Office.
1877-8	,,	,,	c	,,	H&T	...	...	...	Caddy spoon : Birmingham Assay Office.
1878-9	,,	,,	d	,,		...	...	...	From B'm'ham Assay Office Plate.
1879-80	,,	,,	e	,,		...	...	...	Do. do. do.
1880-1	,,	,,	f	,,		...	...	...	Do. do. do.
1881-2	,,	,,	g	,,		...	...	...	Do. do. do.
1882-3	,,	,,	h	,,	H&T	...	...	...	Napkin rings : Mrs. Budd.
1883-4	,,	,,	i	,,	,,	...	...	...	Breakfast cruet : Do.
1884-5	,,	,,	k	,,		...	...	...	From B'm'ham Assay Office Plate.
1885-6	,,	,,	l	,,		...	...	...	Do. do. do.
1886-7	,,	,,	m	,,		...	...	...	Do. do. do.
1887-8	,,	,,	n	,,		...	...	...	Do. do. do.
1888-9	,,	,,	o	,,		...	...	...	Do. do. do.
1889-90	,,	,,	p	,,	N&H	...	...	...	Match-box : The Author.
1890-1	,,	,,	q		T.W.D	...	...	...	Umbrella mount : Mr. Day.
1891-2	,,	,,	r		N&H	...	...	...	Milk-jug : Mr. S. Deane.
1892-3	,,	,,	s		J.M.B	...	...	...	Cigarette-case : The Author.
1893-4	,,	,,	t		SWS	...	...	...	Toilet fittings : Do.
1894-5	,,	,,	u		L.G	...	...	...	Stick mounts : Do.
1895-6	,,	,,	v		T·H	...	...	...	Candlestick : Mrs. Budd.
1896-7	,,	,,	w		HM	...	...	...	Paperknife : The Author.
1897-8	,,	,,	x		HH&Co JHW	... ...	... ...	... ...	Pin trays : Do. Toilet fittings : Do.
1898-9	,,	,,	y		A& JZ	...	...	...	Do. do. : Do.
1899 1900	,,	,,	z		J.S SS	...	...	...	Cigar-holder : Do.

MARKS ON BIRMINGHAM PLATE.

TABLE VI.

FOUR STAMPS AS BELOW.

DATE.	An-chor.	Lion Passant.	Date Letter.	Maker's Mark.	MAKER'S NAME.			ARTICLES AND OWNERS.
1900-1	⚓	🦁	a	E&CₒLᵈ	Names registered after 1850 not disclosed.			Set of communion plate: Illogan, Cornwall.
1901-2	,,	,,	b	HWE	...	...	...	Sweet meat dishes: The Author.
1902-3	,,	,,	c	IS G	...	...	...	Candlesticks: Mr. J. S. Greenberg.
1903-4	,,	,,	d	L&Cº	...	...	...	Set of communion plate: Lelant, Cornwall.
1904-5	,,	,,	e	H&F	...	...	...	Com. cup and paten: St. Mawgan-in-Pystar.
1905-6	,,	,,	f		...	...	...	
1906-7	,,	,,	g		...	...	...	
1907-8	,,	,,	h		...	...	...	
1908-9	,,	,,	i		...	...	...	
1909-10	,,	,,	k		...	...	...	
1910-1	,,	,,	l		...	...	...	
1911-2	,,	,,	m		...	...	...	
1912-3	,,	,,	n		...	...	...	
1913-4	,,	,,	o		...	...	...	
1914-5	,,	,,	p		...	...	...	
1915-6	,,	,,	q		...	...	...	
1916-7	,,	,,	r	R&TW	...	...	...	Ciborium: Lanarth, Cornwall.
1917-8	,,	,,	s		...	...	...	
1918-9	,,	,,	t		...	...	...	
1919-20	,,	,,	u		...	...	...	
1920-1	,,	,,	v		...	...	...	
1921-2	,,	,,	w		...	...	...	
1922-3	,,	,,	x		...	...	...	
1923-4	,,	,,	y		...	...	...	
1924-5	,,	,,	z		...	...	...	

SUPPLEMENTARY LIST OF ADDITIONAL MARKS OF GOLDSMITHS,

Impressed at Birmingham, not illustrated in the preceding tables.

DATE.	MARK.	MAKER'S NAME.	ARTICLES AND OWNERS.
1776-7	JA&S	Jos. Adams & Son.	Pierced sugar-tongs : Messrs. Crichton.
1778-9	E·S	Edward Sawyer.	Do. do. : Do. do.
1783-4	S𝒫	Samuel Pemberton.	Do. do. : Do. do.
1804-5	W	... ...	Caddy spoon : Mr. P. Phillips.
1806-7	H&Co.	... ...	Do. do. : Do. do.
1807-8	M	... ...	Do. do. : Do. do.
1811-2	W	... ...	Do. do. : Do. do.
1814-5	J L	... ...	Do. do. : Do. do.
1820-1	T N	Thos. Newbold.	Musical snuff-box : Mr. A. J. Grimes.
1822-3	S P	... ...	Caddy spoon : Mr. P. Phillips.
1826	T & K	Geo. Tye & Jas. Kilner.	Fox-mask box : Messrs. Crichton.
1832-3	G T	Geo. Tye.	Do. do. : Do. do.
1876-7	T T & Co	... ...	Church plate in several Cornish parishes.
1862-3	J H & Co	... ...	Church plate : Lanlivery.
1892-3	H W	... ...	Church plate in several Cornish parishes.

HALL MARKS ON BIRMINGHAM GOLD WARES.

THE MARKS HERE GIVEN ARE FOR THE SEVERAL CLASSES OF GOLD WARES ASSAYED AT BIRMINGHAM.

22 Carat	👑	22	⚓	V
18 „	„	18	„	„
15 „	15	·625	„	„
12 „	12	·5	„	„
9 „	9	·375	„	„

The date-letter for 1920-1
is a small Roman V,
as here illustrated.

For the MARKS ON FOREIGN PLATE assayed at Birmingham see p. 27 *ante.*

NAMES OF GOLDSMITHS ENTERED AT THE

BIRMINGHAM ASSAY OFFICE.

FROM 1773 TO 1850.

Entered from 1773 to 1800.

Matthew Boulton &
John Fothergill
Benjamin May
James Benton
Joseph Adams, Walsall
John Gimblett, Junr., &
William Vale
Charles Freeth
Thomas Phipson
James Wright
Thomas Clowes
William Phillips
Joseph Bunney
Edwd. Parker
Benjn. Dewson &
William Taylor, W'hampt'n
John Turner
William Grice
Thos. Mynd
Richd. Bickley
William Tutin
Thos. Richards
Joseph Roper
Willmore & Alston
Samuel Baker
James Horton
Geo. Crowther
Edwd. Sawyer
John Gimblett, Junr.
James Burbidge
Jos. Adams & Son, Walsall
James Greaves
Samuel Pemberton
Henry Clay
Henry Holland
Joseph Taylor
Richd. Porter
Thomas R. Porter
Henry Wood &
Thos. Withnoll
Joseph Sharp
Saml. Baker
Isaac Bissell, Cradley
John Jesson, W'hampton
James Greaves
John Whitehouse, Wednesbury
John Goodall
Edward Winfield
Thos. Heath, Coventry
John Moore
James Alston
Levy Perry
Geo. Skipp
Jno. Tayleur, London
John Guest

James Benton
Thos. Warner
Wm. & Ben Lewin
Thos. Clocker
John Bentley
Thos. Eggerton
Samuel Baker
Thomas Hales, Coventry
Henry Harding, Coventry
John Shaw
Jos. Fendall
William Stringer, West Bromwich
David Blair
Matthew Linwood
Charles Westley
John Smith
Samuel Harvey
Edward Taylor
William Smith
Henry Meadows
Thos. Willmore
Joseph Warren
Thos. Parsons
Joseph Fletcher, Walsall
Richard Turner
Joseph Inshaw
Robert Wheeler
John Phillips & Co.
John Piercy
Robt. Turner
William Bennett
Richd. Evans
Joseph Jukes
Charles Wyatt &
Thomas Dixon
Richd. Morrow, Liverpool
John Adamson, do.
James Barton, do.
Willm. Hull, do.
Joseph Taylor
George Smith
James Woolley
Thomas Beilby
Thomas Green, Liverpool
Saml. Flower
Josh. Hart
William Ryley, Coventry
John Thornton
William Wright
Thomas Challener
Robt. B. Cooper
Robt. Simpson, Derby
John Barnett
Cocks & Bettridge
Charles Willmore
Bishop & Waterhouse
Edward Betts
Jones & Barker

Thos. Gill
Ford & Slater
John Phillips & Co.
Kendrick & Astbury
Wm. & R. Smith
Elizth. Cook
Horton & Bewley
Porter & Mills
Saml. Buggins & Co.
Saml. Malkins
Henry Osborn
Robert Emuss
Thos. Cheston
Daniel Hunt
William Bingley
Matthew Linwood
Thos. Ryland
Robt. Skinner, Coventry
Jos. Ford
William Ryland
John White
Forrest & Wasdell
Thos. Turner
Rudder, Ledsam & Co.
Sheldon & Skinner, Coventry
William Pugh
Thos. Turner
Wm. & Sam. Dawes

1801.

John Sheldon, Coventry
Wm. Platt
Wm. Selkirk
William Howard, Coventry
John Hipkiss
Laurence & Allen
Benjamin Beardsmore, Kettinsall
W. Cartwright &
S. Horton
Emerson & Buggins

1803-7.

D. Hill & Co.
Mills & Langston
John Shaw
Thomas Pemberton
Underhill & Dutton
Wm. Boot
Woolley Deakin
Dutton & Johnson
Joseph Willmore
John Freeth
Wm. Stych
Joseph Pearson

John	Parrock
J. B.	Rolls
Willm.	Woolley
Harding	& Son, Coventry
John	Moore, Coventry
Waterhouse	& Co.
John	Hart & Co.
John	Rock, Walsall
Thos.	Tompson
Mary	Tart & Co.
Edwd.	Thomason
John	Corfield & ⎱
John	Munslow ⎰
Waterhouse & Lightfoot, ⎱	
(now Waterhouse & Ryland) ⎰	
James	Elkington
Joseph	Pearson
E.	Medlycott, Coventry
John	Munslow
John	Corfield
Geo.	Barnett
Edwd.	Betts & Son

1808.

Geo.	Thickbroom, Coventry
Jas.	Rock, Walsall
William	Simpson
Joseph	Timmins
Henry	Adcock
John	Hadley
Thomas	Lacey
Charles	Hancock
Rudder,	Ledsam & Vale
John	Thropp
James	Humphreys
Mosely	Solomon & ⎱
Saul M.	Solomon ⎰
(Solomon	Brothers)
Worton	& Ratheram
I.	Lilly & Co.

1809.

Geo.	Hanson
Josiah	Emes & ⎱
Samuel	Carpenter ⎰
Ann	Fuller
Thomas	Simpson & Son
Moses	Westwood
Wm.	Nicholls & Co.
Amos	Moor
(Matthew	Boulton, died 1809)

1810.

Thomas	Hughes
Saul M.	Solomon
Thomas	Davis
Packwood & Harris	
John	Thropp & ⎱
Thos.	Taylor ⎰
Saml.	Horton
John	Ashton, Coventry
Benj.	Barlow
Daniel	Hill & Renshaw

1811.

Mary	Hanson
Geo.	Bower

Jos.	Walker
Geo.	Bragg & ⎱
Thos.	Crockett ⎰
Jesse	Parkes
John	Andrews
William	Lea & Co.

1812.

Josiah	& G. Richards
Robt.	Mitchell & Co.
Thomas	Bartlett
John	Bewlay
Richard	Brittain
David	Jenkins
Saml.	Pemberton, ⎱
Son	& Mitchell ⎰

1813.

John	Parkes
Joseph.	Harrison
I.	Thrasher, Coventry
Jabez	Vale, Coventry
Thomas	Timmins
John	Lawrence & Co.
William	Wardell & ⎱
Peter	Kempson ⎰
Joseph	Taylor
Cocks	& Bettridge
Matthew	Linwood & Son
Joseph	Rock, Walsall
James	Bourne, Coventry

1814.

I. & B.	Cook
Thomas	Taylor
John	Thropp
Geo.	Sanders, Coventry
Saml.	Horton
John	Cottrill
Reubin Wm.	Buggins

1815.

John	Thropp & ⎱
Ann	Thropp ⎰
William	Lander
William	Spooner
Geo.	Barnett
John	Oswin, Coventry
Jeremiah	Ross, Walsall
John	Moore, Coventry
Matthew	Dixon
Saml.	Allport

1816.

Saml.	Vale ⎱
John	Carr ⎰
John	Ratheram ⎱ Coventry
Richard	Ratheram ⎰
Thomas	Bartleet, Junr.
Thomas	Spicer, Coventry
Hannah	Howard, Coventry
James	Cox & ⎱
William	Lander ⎰
John	Barber
James	Collins
Pemberton	& Mitchell

1817.

John	Sherwood
Wm.	Linsley
Wm.	Brown, Coventry
John	Bettridge
John	Thrasher & ⎱ Coventry
Robt.	Mathers ⎰
Bragg	& Baldwin

1818.

William	Gregory
Stephen G.	Onion & ⎱
Mark	Perkins ⎰
Jane	Timmins
Ann & Eliz.	Freeth & ⎱
William	Jones ⎰
John & Ann	Thropp
Saml.	Oughton & ⎱
Thomas	Smith ⎰
Robt. A.	Mathers, Coventry
Ledsam	& Vale

1819.

William	Brown & ⎱ Coventry
John	Hands ⎰
Isaac	Parkes
John	Barlow
James	Bourne
James	Hewlett
David	Jee, Coventry
William	Johnson
William	Edwards
Thomas	Smith
John	Godfrey
John	Cook
Wm.	Postans & ⎱
Geo.	Tye ⎰
Thomas	Kettle
William	Spooner & ⎱
Thomas	Clowes ⎰

1820.

Thos.	Newbold
M.	Boulton & Plate Co.
John	Shaw
Peter	Kempson, junr.
Chas. & Ed.	Ratherham

1821.

Thos.	Parkes & ⎱
Thos.	Latham ⎰
William	Brown, Coventry
Ths. & Wm.	Simpson
S.	Pemberton & Son
John	Wood, Coventry
Robert	Mitchell
Ann	Freeth, ⎱
Elizabeth	Freeth & ⎰
William	Jennings
Charles	Shaw
Thomas	Millington
Edwd.	Thomason
John	Hebbert
John	Wells, Coventry
Saml.	Horton

1822.

Vale	& Ratheram, Coventry
Lea	& Clark
Peter	Kempson
Joseph	Farrar, Coventry
Thos.	Freeman
James	Heales, Coventry
Richard	Corfield & ⎫
Josh.	Patrick ⎭
Thos.	Shaw
John	Parkes
John	Bettridge
Samuel	Haines
John	Fox
Edwd.	Walker
Fredk.	Moore
Richd.	Corfield
Matthew	Davis, Coventry

1823.

Thomas	Priest
Jeremiah	Scudamore
George	Waterhouse
William	Platt
William	Russell, Coventry
Joseph	Hardy & Co.
Slack	& Wilkinson
Joseph	Bower

1824.

Spooner	Clowes & Co.
Thos.	Walker
Lea	& Clark
Geo.	Bower & Son
James	Heales, Coventry
George	Horton
William	Ryley, Coventry
John	Horton
James	Heales, Coventry
James	Spratt
John	Clark
William	Smith
Charles	Jones
Samuel	Ashton
Charles	Read, Coventry
John	Woolley

1825.

Edward	Day
William	Simpson & Son
Thomas	Simpson, junr.
John Edwd.	Clark & ⎫
Edward	Smith ⎭
Joseph	Taylor
Nathaniel	Mills
Charles	Ratheram
William	Steen, junr.
Kempson	& Kindon
Thos.	Parkes
Elizth.	Brown, Coventry
William	Simpson
George	Ravenscroft
Geo.	Unite & ⎫
Jas.	Hilliard ⎭
George	Perton
Ledsam	Vale & Wheeler
John	Cook

1826.

John	White
Willm.	Mitchell
John	Turton
Manoah	Bower
Thomas	Shaw
Benjamin	Kirby, Coventry
Joseph	Hayes
James	Collins
John Edwd.	Clarke
Edward	Smith
George	Walton & Son
John	Hopkins
Carnall	& Turner
Francis	Clark
Spooner	Clowes & Co.
John F.	Parker
George	Collins
Thomas	Brooks, Coventry
John	Wilkinson
Richard	Slack
George	Tye & ⎫
James	Kilner ⎭

1827.

Joseph	Joyce
Geo.	Richards & ⎫
Geo. Richds.	Elkington ⎭
John	Woodhill
Spooner	Clowes & Co.
Richard	Neale, Coventry
Thos.	Freeman
Edwd.	Day
Thos.	Wakelam
William	Turner
John Ll'n.	Clark, L'pool
John	Parkes
John	Wood, Coventry
Josh.	Jennens & Co.
Thomas	Brooks, Coventry

1828.

John & Wm.	Lilly
Joseph	Carnall
William	Anchor
Joseph	Jee, Coventry
William	Kendrick
Thos. & Jno.	Twiss
Edward	Kirkman, Liverpool
Theophilus	Kirkham
Saml.	Hargrove
Charles	Jones
Elizth.	Brown & ⎫ Coventry
Fredk.	Brown ⎭
William	Such
William	Fowke
William	Sabin & ⎫
John	Willis ⎭

1829.

Charles	Read, Coventry
Wm. W.	Richards ⎫
Henry	Edwards ⎭

Willm.	Simpson
Willm.	Fouke & ⎫
James	Thomas ⎭
Thomas	Smith & ⎫
Edward	Vernon ⎭
Wm.	Chambers & ⎫
Wm.	Cotterell ⎭
Thomas	Freeman
John	Oswin, Coventry
Samuel	Edwards
Willm.	Mordan
Willm.	Pinches & ⎫
James	Laughton ⎭
William	Steen, junr.
Elizabeth	Brown, Coventry
Edward	Walker, Coventry
Samuel	Evans
Joseph	Bettridge
John	Taylor & ⎫
John	Perry ⎭
John	Coley
John A.	Moss
Urban & F.	Luckcock
William	Robinson & ⎫
James	Allport ⎭

1830.

George	Tye
Thomas	Waterhouse & ⎫
George	Waterhouse ⎭
Job	Winchurch & ⎫
John	Pritchard ⎭
Joseph	Bower
Thomas	Platt
William	Guest
Thos.	Ryland & ⎫
Wm.	Ryland ⎭
George M.	Horton
Thomas	Woodward
Thomas	Graves
Vale	& Ratheram, Coventry
George	Richards
George	Perton
William	Pearsall & ⎫
John	Ensor ⎭
John	Gilbert
Elizabeth	Brown, Coventry
Chas.	Hancock & ⎫
Saml.	Keeley ⎭
Thomas	Spicer, Coventry
William	Nock, Coventry

1831.

Jacob L.	Samuel, Liverpool
William	Pipe
Horatio	Powell
Thomas	Millington
Thomas	Freeman
William	Simpson
John	Thrasher, Coventry
J. Anthony	Moss
John	Tongue
Gervase	Wheeler
Thomas	Hastelow & ⎫
Jonathan	Harlow ⎭

27

1832.

Joseph	Wickes, Coventry
John	Wood, Coventry
William	Phillips, Handsworth
John	Newton, do.
Henry	Manton
William	Witcomb
David	Lloyd, Leominster
John	Taylor & ⎱
John	Perry ⎰
Francis	Swinden
Jonathan	Liggins, Coventry
Joseph	Willmore
George	Unite
Joseph	Bent & ⎱
James	Tagg ⎰
Thomas	Spicer, Coventry
John	Horton
Saml.	Horton
J. Anthony	Moss

1833.

Frederick	Brown, Coventry
George	Ravenscroft, Dudley
William	Steen
Joseph	Perkins
James	Timmins, ⎱
Joseph	Stock & ⎬
Wm.	Sharp ⎰
James	Collins
Henry	Edwards
James	Adams
Michael	Burgess & ⎱
John	Wyon ⎰
Jonathan	Liggins & ⎱ Coventry
Edward	Salisbury ⎰
John	Lilly
Charles	Read, Coventry
Thomas	Freeman
Thomas	Bickley, Coventry

1834.

John	Robinson ⎱
Saml. S.	Edkins & ⎬
Thos.	Aston ⎰
John	Willis
Job	Winchurst
John	Pritchard
Mary	Platt
J.	Robinson, S.S.
Jesse	Sargeant
William	Edwards
Charles	Mainstone
Edward	Walker, Coventry
James	Heales, Coventry
James	Gregory
William	Spooner & ⎱
Charles	Painter ⎰
Edwin	Jones
Chas.	Read, Coventry
John	Oswin, Coventry
Thomas	Lawrence
James	Gargory

Spooner	Painter & Co.
Christopher	Jones, Coventry
Joseph	Willmore, ⎱
John	Yapp & ⎬
John	Woodward ⎰
George	Barnet
Richard	Thelwell
John	Ensor
Henry	Osborn
James A.	Hardy
George	Unite
Thomas B.	Bragg

1835.

Robert	Nevill
James	Widowson, Coventry
John	Wilmot & ⎱
Wm.	Roberts ⎰
Edward	Brown, Coventry
John	Britain
Thomas	Wilkinson & ⎱
James	Shaw ⎰
William	Jennings
Samuel	Keeley
Samuel	Clark
Joseph	Redfern
George R.	Collis & ⎱
George	Whitgrave ⎰
Christopher	Jones, Liverpool

1836.

W.	Maddock, Liverpool
Nathaniel	Mills
Edward	Barnett & ⎱
George	Wright ⎰
Thomas M.	Livett & ⎱
Henry C.	Parker ⎰
Jas. & Josiah	Cox
Thomas	Richards
Thomas	Waterhouse & ⎱
Thomas	Parker ⎬
Thomas	Mole ⎰
John	Parkes & ⎱
William	Parkes ⎰
John	Parker
James	Loveridge

1837.

G. R.	Collis & Co.
Richard	Whitehead, Coventry
John	Shaw
Thomas	Hastelow
John	Timms
Edward	Kerby, Coventry
James	Roadknight
John P.	Hodgkins & ⎱
James	Booth ⎬
Joseph	Jennens ⎰

1838.

William	Ryland
John	Hilliard

George	Perton
Edward	Parsons
John	Willis
James	Collins
Charles	Read, Coventry
William	Thompson
John	Woolley
Benjamin	Humphries
Henry	Manton
Richard	Baker, Coventry
Geo. C.	Stringer, Dudley

1839.

Edward	Parsons
Thomas	Freeman
Isaac	Simmons, Manchester
William	Waterhouse, Coventry
Henry	Edwards & ⎱
Edwd. Jno.	Ball ⎰
James	Griffin, Aston
Thos.	Wilkinson & ⎱
James	Shaw ⎰
Francis	Marrian
Wm. & Jno.	Page, Derby
John	Yardley, Coventry
Harry	Gill

1840.

William	Parkes
James	Perry & ⎱
John	Keys ⎰
Saml. Isaac	Neustadt & ⎱
David	Barnett ⎰
George	Carrington
John	Oswin, Coventry
Thomas	Colson, Coventry
Edward	Nock, Coventry
William	Sanders, Coventry
George	Perton & ⎱
Wm.	Sabin ⎰
Edward	Smith
William	Gough
Francis	Clark

1841.

Jno. & Wm.	Guest
John	Sheldon
Thomas	Aston
Richd. K.	Ratheram & ⎱
John	Ratheram ⎰ Coventry
George	Richards
William	Spooner
John	Moore & ⎱
Hannah	Sabin ⎰
William	Pendrell

1842.

Abraham	Kemp
Joseph	Redfern

Benjamin	Cole
Gloster	& Docker
John	Ashton, Coventry
Joseph	Bent
Joseph	Harris, Coventry
William	Williams
Sarah	Clark
Thomas	Spicer, Coventry
Wheeler	& Cronin
Brittain	& Waddams
Mary	Wheeler & ⎫
Jas. Barth.	Cronin ⎭
John	Dolman,
	Nottingham

1843.

Wm. & Geo.	Field
Willm.	Naul, Coventry
John	Holloway
G. Richards	Elkington, ⎫
Henry	Elkington & ⎬
Josiah	Mason ⎭
Edward	Waithman,
	Coventry
John	Jones, Coventry
John	Gee, Coventry
William	Clarke, Coventry
John	Hardman, sen. & jr. ⎫
Jer. & Chas.	Iliffe ⎭

1844.

Wm. & Ed.	Turnpenny
John	Reddall
John	Balleny
Samuel	Perry

1845.

Frederick	Marson
Francis	Skidmore, Coventry
Timothy	Parker & ⎫
Thomas	Acott ⎭
Wm. Hy.	Hill, Coventry
Thomas	Harwood
John	Yapp & ⎫
John	Woodward ⎭
Harry	Gill
John	Bannister & ⎫
Dalton	Stephenson ⎭
John	Hardman & ⎫
Wm.	Powell, junr. ⎭
James	Deakin & ⎫
Wm. Hy.	Deakin ⎭

1846.

Edward	Adams
John	Jones, Coventry
Mary	Clarke, Coventry
Jas. Bart.	Cronin ⎫
Sarah	Wheeler & ⎬
Geo.	Wheeler ⎭
Chas. & Rd.	Nevill
Thomas	Prime
Richard	Whitehouse
Sarah	Loveridge

1847.

John	Hilliard & ⎫
John	Thomason ⎭
Charles	Birch & ⎫
Thomas	Morrall ⎭

Edward	Wilmot
Wm.	Roberts & ⎫
Charles	Daniel ⎭
Henry	Wells, Coventry
Phillip	Vaughton
David	Pettifer
Edward	Ratheram
Edward	Turnpenny
William	Hall
Wm. Henry	Dukes & ⎫
John	Clemmens ⎭
James	Capell

1848.

Edward	Barnett
Henry	Gloster
Chas. E.	Ballam
Benjn.	Kerby, Coventry
William	Dudley
Edward	Wilmot & ⎫
Charles	Roberts ⎭

1849.

Francis	Marrian & ⎫
John Baker	Gausby ⎭
James	Pagett
William	Wood, ⎫
George	Wood & ⎬
Samuel	Wood ⎭
William	Swingler
Henry	Manton
Henry	Elkington
James	Walker, Coventry

CHAPTER XVII

THE SHEFFIELD SILVERSMITHS

AND THEIR MARKS

Only silver
assayed at
Sheffield until
1 March, 1904.

This chapter is headed "silversmiths" and not goldsmiths, because, although the term "goldsmith" is understood to include silversmith, it might possibly be misleading to speak of Sheffield goldsmiths, when, as a fact, gold had never been officially assayed at Sheffield until 1 March, 1904.

Sheffield assay
office established
1773.

As mentioned in the preceding chapter, the establishment of an assay office at Sheffield by the Act 13 Geo. III. c. 52, in 1773, was consequent upon a petition to Parliament on 1 February in that year. The Act, reciting that the silversmiths and plate-workers in Sheffield were under great difficulties and hardships in the exercise of their trades for want of assayers in convenient places to assay and touch their plate, appointed Sheffield to have an assay office for assaying and marking wrought plate, and incorporated a company, entitled "Guardians of the standard of wrought plate within the town of Sheffield," with perpetual succession and power to use a common seal. The following noblemen and others—several being plate manufacturers—are named in the Act as the first members of the company thereby incorporated :—

The Marquess of Rockingham, the Earl of Strafford, the Earl of Effingham, Godfrey Bagnall Clark, Anthony St. Leger, Samuel Shore, jun., Saml. Tooker, Henry Howard, Walter Oborne, the Rev. James Wilkinson (clerk), Benjamin Roebuck, Thos. Broadbent, John Shore, Geo. Greaves, John Turner, Thos. Bland, George Brittain, Samuel Staniforth, Simon Andrews Young, Joseph Matthewman, John Hoyland, Henry Tudor, John Winter, Albion Cox, John Rowbotham, Joseph Hancock, Matthew Fenton, William Marsden, Thomas Law, and Joseph Wilson.

No time was lost after the Act was passed before the company proceeded to business. They met on the 5 July, 1773, under the presidency of the Earl of Effingham and elected Joseph Hancock, John Rowbotham, Simon Andrews Young, and Samuel Staniforth as the first four wardens; they appointed Daniel Bradbury, of Carey Lane, London, to be assayer, and ordered that the letter to be stamped on the silver wares for the ensuing year should be the old text capital letter **E**.

The Act of 1773, modified by the 24 Geo. III. c. 20, which authorised a somewhat increased scale of charges for assaying, still regulates the proceedings of the corporation. A district consisting of the town of Sheffield and twenty miles around was assigned to it, and no silver wares made within that district could be assayed and marked except at the Sheffield office, and all plate made for sale must have been assayed there until 1854, when by the 17 & 18 Vic. c. 96 workers and dealers were allowed to have their plate assayed and marked at any legally established assay office in the kingdom.

The principal officers are four wardens,* the Assay Master, and a law clerk, and the regulations of the office are similar to those in force at Birmingham.

At first this office, like that of Birmingham, was open on two days only in each week, but now by reason of the extent of the business it is open every day except Sundays and holidays.

THE SHEFFIELD SILVERSMITHS' MARKS.

The marks required to be stamped on wrought silver assayed at Sheffield are :—

1. The maker's mark, which must be the first letters of his Christian and surname ;
2. The standard mark, which for plate 11 oz. 2 dwts. fine is the lion passant, and for plate 11 oz. 10 dwts. fine (which, however, is very rarely manufactured in Sheffield), the figure of Britannia, in a square stamp ;†
3. The peculiar mark of the company, as prescribed by the 13 Geo. III. c. 52, sec. 5, namely a crown ;
4. A distinct variable mark or letter, which must be annually changed on the election of new wardens ; and
5. From December, 1784, to June, 1890, a further mark representing the head of the Sovereign : indicating that duty had been paid in respect of the plate on which the mark was stamped.

The variable mark or date-letter is changed on the first Monday in

(margin note: Proceedings regulated by the Act 13 Geo. III. c. 52, as modified by the 24 Geo. III. c. 20.)

(margin note: The marks on silver wrought at Sheffield.)

* Any two of whom are empowered to act.
† The lion's head erased is not one of the Sheffield marks.

July in every year, when any vacancies in their body are filled by the guardians, and the wardens for the next ensuing year are elected.

Capricious use of letters for date-marks.

Though letters of various alphabets have been used, as at other offices, for date-marks, the letters used at Sheffield prior to 1824 followed each other in no regular order. During the twenty-six years from the establishment of the office, to 1799, letters were selected from at least three distinct alphabets, none of which were arranged consecutively. This must have made their meaning very obscure, in fact indeterminable except by a table such as follows.

As the term "cycle" has been applied to an alphabet taken in regular order (though frequently curtailed) to represent the successive years of a series, it is somewhat inappropriate to the early Sheffield tables, but for the sake of convenience its use is continued.

The date-letters from 1773 to 1799.

The first cycle commenced in 1773 and continued to July, 1799. The date-letters of this series are twenty-six in number, the first twelve being old English capitals, the thirteenth and fourteenth being 𝔭 and 𝔨 respectively in small old English letters. The next five letters are old English capitals, the following four, 𝔲, 𝔬, 𝔪, and 𝔮 being small old English letters. The last three letters are Roman capitals, Z, X, and V respectively. The description of the letters of this cycle in the minute book of the company is merely that they are "Text Capital Letters," the letters having been written in the book in the handwriting of the clerk. It will be observed that they differ very materially from most illustrations of these letters which have been represented by other authors. The letters of this cycle and the next, unlike any others, commence with E, and proceed without order, having been selected arbitrarily by the guardians at their annual meeting. The letter E, being the initial of the title of the Earl of Effingham, the first chairman of the guardians, was, it is presumed, selected by way of compliment to his lordship. Other letters, the initials of the names of other members of that body, may have been selected for a similar reason.

The date-letters from 1799 to 1868.

The twenty-five letters of the second cycle (July, 1799, to July, 1824) are all Roman capitals in square or oblong punches.* In the third cycle, from 1824 to 1844, twenty small Roman letters—a to z—were used, selected in regular order, except that i, j, n, o, w and y were omitted.

* Except when the crown and letter are in one stamp, when the shape is as illustrated in the table.

In the fourth cycle (1844 to 1868) twenty-four Roman capital letters were used, in square or oblong punches with the corners clipped,* the letters having been chosen in regular order right through the alphabet from A to Z, except that J and Q were omitted. The Queen's head stamp of this cycle affords an easy means of distinguishing between the marks of this and those of earlier cycles.

In the fifth cycle (1868 to 1893) the date-marks are twenty-five plain block letters, **A** to **Z**, omitting **I**, in oblong punches with truncated corners.† The sixth cycle was commenced in 1893, the letters being small Old English characters in oblong punches with clipped corners, proceeding in regular order from 𝖆 onwards, the letter 𝖏 being omitted.

The date-letters from 1868 to 1918.

A new cycle (see Table VII.) was commenced in 1918 with a small Roman letter 𝖆.

In 1890, on the repeal of the duty on plate, the use of the Sovereign's head stamp was discontinued. With reference to this mark it will be noticed that, as in the case of other provincial offices, the change in the form of the head with each reign was not made until a few years had passed after the accession of the new monarch.

Disappearance of Sovereign's head stamp on repeal of plate-duty.

The Author is indebted to the courtesy of the Assay Master (Mr. B. W. Watson) and Mr. F. Bradbury for their kind assistance with reference to the revision of the following tables. With the aid of their notes and casts of the marks found on existing articles of plate the tables have been carefully reconstructed. The marks, where so described in the tables, have been reproduced from articles there mentioned and compared with similar marks found on many other examples which it is unnecessary to mention in detail.

From 1780 to 1853 in the case of small articles, the crown is found above or at the side of the date-letter, combined in the same stamp, as illustrated in the following tables at 1780, 1785, 1791, 1810, 1814, 1819, 1825, and other years. This occurs simultaneously with the more common method of striking each mark separately, but the practice of

The crown and date-letter struck by one punch, simultaneously with the more common method of striking each mark with separate punches.

---

* The date-mark for the year 1854-5, the letter L, is in a circular stamp, quite an exceptional form for a Sheffield letter-punch.

† In Chaffers' *Hall-Marks on Plate* **I** is given in error as the date-letter for 1876-7, and it is there stated that "the variable letter for each year was furnished by Mr. J. Watson, the Assay Master". The mistake arose, it appears, through the late Mr. J. Watson, a former Assay Master, having informed the late Mr. Chaffers, some time prior to the year 1876, that the variable letters appointed to be used in the cycle of twenty-four years, from July, 1868, to July, 1893, were plain block letters. It was then anticipated that **J** would not be used, and the table for that cycle was framed accordingly. In July, 1876, however, the letter selected for the then ensuing year was **J**, (**I** having been discarded), but in subsequent editions of *Hall-Marks on Plate* the mistake has been passed without correction by the editors of that work.

grouping the crown and date-letter together in one stamp was discontinued many years ago and has not been resumed. In some cases the enclosing shield is oval, and in others oblong.

From 1815 to 1819 the crown is found stamped upside down. The most probable explanation of this singular proceeding is that the intention was to differentiate more clearly between letters used at this period and those struck in earlier years. For example, **X** is the date-letter for both the years 1797 and 1817, but confusion is avoided by the crown being placed upside down in the latter year. Originally it was the custom for the Assay Master to strike each mark separately, but of late years the method adopted has been to include the lion, town mark, and date-letter in one punch, though in distinct shields.

Order of marks. The order of the marks generally observed, is as described on page 421. Proceeding from left to right, as you look at them, the maker's mark is the first of the series. It is placed last in the tables, for convenience of reference to the names in type.

The heading "Marks on Sheffield Silver Wares" has been adopted to prevent mistake, because the term "Sheffield plate" has been misappropriated to the old *plated* wares of Sheffield, which were made of copper sheets, coated with a plate of sterling silver.

MARKS ON SHEFFIELD SILVER WARES.

TABLE I.

FOUR STAMPS TILL 1784, FIVE STAMPS AFTERWARDS, AS BELOW.

	LION PASSANT.	CROWN.	DATE LETTER.	KING'S HEAD (from 1784)	MAKER'S MARK.	MAKER'S NAME.	ARTICLES AND OWNERS.
1773-4						Rich'd. Morton & Co.	Coasters: B'ham Assay Office.
						S. Roberts & Co.	Candlesticks: V. and A. Museum.
						Mat'w. Fenton & Co.	Salt-cellars: Mr. Dudley Westropp.
1774-5	,,	,,				Geo. Ashforth & Co.	Candlesticks: S. Kensington Museum.
1775-6	,,	,,				John Winter & Co.	Pair of Candlesticks: Messrs. G.
1776-7	,,	,,				Wm. Damant.	Do. do.: Mr. Lowe, Chester.
1777-8	,,	,,				Tudor and Leader.	Sauce tureen: Col. Longfield.
						Fenton Creswick & Co.	Candlesticks: Messrs. M. and S. Lyon.
1778-9	,,	,,				John Smith ?	Candlesticks: S. Ken. Museum.
1779-80	,,	,,			,,	,, ,,	Do. : St. John's College, Cambridge.
* 1780-1	,,	,,				Nath'l. Smith & Co.	Pair of salt-cellars: Mr. H. D. Ellis.
1781-2	,,	,,				Fenton Creswick & Co.	Salver: Mr. Cecil Woods.
1782-3	,,	,,				John Winter & Co.	Candlesticks: S. Ken. Museum.
1783-4	,,	,,				Danl. Holy & Co.	Tea-urn: Mr. W. Boore.
						John Parsons & Co.	Pair of candlesticks: Do.
† 1784-5	,,	,,			,,	,, ,,	Do. do.: Messrs. Christie.
‡ 1785-6	,,	,,		,,		Richd. Morton & Co.	Inkstand: Messrs. Spink.
1786-7	,,					John Parsons & Co.	Candlesticks: Queen's College, Cambridge, & Mr. J. H. Walter.
1787-8	,,	,,		,,	,,	,, ,,	Candlesticks: Messrs. G.
1788-9	,,	,,		,,		John Younge & Sons.	Do. : Mr. H. D. Ellis.
1789-90	,,	,,		,,		R. Sutcliffe & Co. (?)	Do.: Sir F. L. Currie, Bart.
1790-1	,,	,,		,,		John Parsons & Co.	Do.: South Kens. Museum.
* 1791-2	,,	,,		,,		John Younge & Sons.	Large skewer: Mr. H. Davison.
1792-3				,,		John Parsons & Co.	Table candlestick: Mr. Arthur.
1793-4	,,	,,		,,		Thos. Law.	Small stopper: Col. Longfield.
1794-5	,,	,,		,,		John Green & Co.	Candlesticks: Oswestry Corpn.
1795-6	,,	,,		,,		John Younge & Sons, as above.	Sugar basket: Mr. F. Bradbury.
1796-7	,,	,,		,,		Geo. Eadon & Co.	{ Candlesticks: Messrs. Comyns. { Cake-basket: Mr. D. Davis.
‖ 1797-8	,,					T. Law.	Candlestick: Messrs. Comyns.
1798-9	,,	,,				Saml. Roberts, jr. } Geo. Cadman & Co. }	Candlestick: Mr. F. Bradbury.

1779-80    John Younge & Co.   Pierced cruet: Mr. H. D. Ellis.

1796-7    Maker's mark of Henry Tudor & Thos. Leader.

* See sixth paragraph, page 423 *ante.*

† The J of 1784-5 is found without and with the King's head.

‡ With the R of 1786-7 the King's head is found both incuse and cameo.

‖ From July, 1797, to April, 1798, the duty mark was struck twice to denote the higher duty.

MARKS ON SHEFFIELD SILVER WARES.

TABLE II.

FIVE STAMPS AS BELOW.

	LION PASSANT.	CROWN.	DATE LETTER.	KING'S HEAD	MAKER'S MARK	MAKER'S NAME.	ARTICLES AND OWNERS.
1799 1800	🦁	👑	E	👤	IL&Cº JG&Cº	John Love & Co. John Green & Co.	Candlesticks: Mr D. Westropp. Do. : Messrs. Foster.
1800-1	,,	,,	N	,,	GA &Cº IG&Cº	Geo. Ashforth &Co. John Green & Co.	Bread-basket: Mr. W. Boore. Candlesticks: The Author.
1801-2	,,	,,	H	,,	,, TW&Cº	Thos." Watson & Co.	Candelabrum: Trinity Ho., Hull. Candlesticks: Messrs. Christie.
* 1802-3	,,		M	,,	TL DL R·M	Thos. & Danl. Leader. Richd. Morton & Co.	Teapot stand: Mr. S. Deane. Candlestick: Messrs. Spink.
1803-4	,,	,,	F	,,	N·S&Cº	Nathan Smith & Co.	Candlesticks: The Author.
1804-5	,,	,,	G	,,	IE &Cº	Jas. Ellis & Co.	Do. : Messrs. Christie.
† 1805-6	,,	,,	B	,,	AG&Cº	Alexr. Goodman & Co.	Coasters: Mr. Dudley Westropp.
1806-7	,,	,,	A	,,	ITY &Cº	J. T. Younge & Co.	Candlestick: Mr. Bright.
1807-8	,,	,,	S	,,	WT&Cº	W. Tucker & Co.	Noted by the Author.
1808-9	,,	,,	P	,,	T·B &Co	Thos. Blagden &Co.	Do. do.
1809-10	,,	,,	K	,,	I·R&Cº	John Roberts & Co.	Coasters: Mr. Dudley Westropp.
* 1810-1	,,		L	,,	,, GE &Cº	Geo. " " &Co.	Do. : Holburne Museum. Candlesticks: Mr. Day.
‡ 1811-2	,,	,,	C	👤		John Roberts & Co., as 1809-10 above.	Candlestick: Mr. F. Bradbury. See also marks of J. Staniforth & Co. and R. Gainsford on p. 432 *infra*.
1812-3	,,	,,	D	,,	ST N&H	Smith, Tate & Co. (Nicholson & Holt).	Noted by the Author.
1813-4	,,	,,	R	,,	I·K·I·W&Cº	Kirkby, Waterhouse & Co.	Candlesticks: Mr. Goldman.
* 1814-5	,,	,,	W	,,	I·L	John Law	Snuff-box: Messrs. Spink.
1815-6	,,	,,	O	,,	JE&CO	J. Ellis & Co. (?)	Small salver: Mr. Lowe.
1816-7	,,	,,	T	,,	I·W	John Watson.	Candlesticks: Messrs. Christie.
1817-8	,,	,,	X	,,	,, I&T·S·	John and Thos. Settle.	Do. : Do. do. Cake-basket: Mr. Arthur.
1818-9	,,	,,	I	,,	SCY &Cº	S. C. Younge & Co.	Pair of salvers: Messrs. Christie.
* 1819-20	🦁	,,	V	,,	T·I·C IKIW &CO	Thos. and Jas. Creswick Kirkby, Waterhouse & Co.	Candlesticks: Messrs. Crichton. Do. : Mr. B. W. Watson.
GEO. IV.			V	,,	GC·&Cº	G. Cooper & Co.	Noted by the Author.
1820-1	,,	,,	Q	,,	ST H&T	Smith, Tate, Hoult & Tate.	Candlesticks: Mr. W. Boore.
1821-2	,,	,,	Y	,,	JL	Joseph Law	Do. : Messrs. Christie.
1822-3	,,	,,	Z	,,	IG&Cº	John Green & Co.	Do. : Do. do.
1823-4	,,	,,	U	,,	W·B	Wm. Briggs.	Do. : Do. do.

* See sixth paragraph, page 423 *ante*.
+ The King's head for this year is in an oval stamp.

‡1811-2. 👤👤👤👤👤 The outline of the King's head stamp has varied in the same year, being oval in some cases and indented in others. The marks here illustrated are very small, and occur on dessert knives and forks: Messrs. Crichton.

On small articles assayed in 1815 the crown is upside down below the date-letter in one stamp; from 1815 to 1820 inclusive the crown is upside down above the date-letter, as illustrated at 1810-20 above. See page 424 *ante*.

MARKS ON SHEFFIELD SILVER WARES.

TABLE III.

FIVE STAMPS AS BELOW.

	LION PASSANT	CROWN	DATE LETTER	KING'S HEAD	MAKER'S MARK	MAKER'S NAME.	ARTICLES AND OWNERS.
1824-5	(lion)	(crown)	a	(head)	SCY&Co	S. C. Younge & Co.	Candlesticks : Messrs. Christie.
					WB&Co	Wm. Blackwell & Co.	Coasters : per Mr. Dudley Westropp.
1825-6	,,		b	,,	I&IW&Co	Waterhouse, Hodson & Co.	Candlesticks : Mr. Lowe, Chester.
*1826-7	,,	,,	c	,,	BH&H	Battie, Howard & Hawksworth. }	Do. : Messrs. Christie.
1827-8	,,		d	,,	TJNC	T. J. & N. Creswick.	Do. : Mr. H. D. Ellis.
1828-9	,,	,,	e	,,	BH&H	Battie, Howard & Hawksworth. }	Do. : Messrs. Christie.
1829-30	,,		f	,,	JS HW	John Settle & Henry Williamson. }	Bread-basket : Mr. W. Boore.
WM. IV. 1830-1	,,		g	,,	TJNC	T. J. & N. Creswick.	Bedroom candlestick : Mr. R. Day, F.S.A.
1831-2	,,	,,	h	(head)	JB	Jas. Burbury.	Dessert knife : Mr. Crichton.
1832-3	,,	,,	k	,,	S&N A&O	Stafford & Newton. Atkin & Oxley.	Caster : Do. Dessert knives and forks : Do.
1833-4	,,		l	,,	TJNC WA&Co	T. J. & N. Creswick. Wm. Allanson & Co.	Candlestick : Mr. Bruford. Do. : Messrs. Spink.
1834-5	,,		P	,,	I&IW&Co	Waterhouse, Hodson & Co.	Do. : per Mr. Dudley Westropp.
1835-6	,,		P	(head)	H&H	Howard & Hawksworth.	Coasters : Holburne Museum.
1886-7	,,	,,	q	,,	... ...	Assay Office Record.
VICT. 1837-8	,,		r	,,	HW&Co	Hy. Wilkinson & Co.	Candlestick : Mr. Stansby.
1838-9	,,		s	,,	HW&Co	,, ,, ,,	Inkstand : Mr. Arthur.
1839-40	,,	,,	t	,,	SH	Samuel Harwood.	Decanter labels : The Author.
1840-1	,,	,,	u	(head)	,,	,, ,,	Plate : per Mr. B. W. Watson.
1841-2	,,	,,	v	,,		... ...	Assay Office Record.
1842-3	,,		x	,,	HE&Co	Hawksworth, Eyre & Co.	Plate : per Mr. B. W. Watson.
1843-4	,,	,,	z	,,		... ...	Assay Office Record.

In the two preceding cycles (1773 to 1799 and 1799 to 1824) the date-letters were selected without any regular order. In the cycle illustrated above (1824 to 1844) the date-letters were, for the first time, selected in regular alphabetical order; the letters i, j, n, o, w and y were, however, omitted without any apparent reason.

See sixth paragraph, page 423 *ante*.

* Additional examples for the year 1826-7 :—

(lion) (crown) c (head)   JN   Maker's mark of J. Nowill)
,, ,, ,, ,,   WN   ,,   ,,   ,, W. Nowill. } Dessert knives and forks : Messrs. Crichton.
,, ,, ,, ,,   T•R   ,,   ,,   ,, T. Rodgers.)

MARKS ON SHEFFIELD SILVER WARES.

TABLE IV.

FIVE STAMPS AS BELOW.

	CROWN.	DATE LETTER.	LION PASSANT.	QUEEN'S HEAD.	MAKER'S MARK.	MAKER'S NAME.	ARTICLES AND OWNERS.
*1844-5	👑	A	🦁	👤	HE&Co	Hawksworth, Eyre & Co.	Milk-jug : Mr. Lowe.
1845-6	,,	B	,,	,,		... ...	Assay Office Record.
1846-7	,,	C	,,	,,		... ...	Do. do.
1847-8	,,	D	,,	,,		... ...	Do. do.
1848-9	,,	E	,,	,,		... ...	Do. do.
1849-50	,,	F	,,	,,	,,	Hawksworth, Eyre & Co.	Tea-set : per Mr. D. Westropp.
1850-1	,,	G	,,	,,		... ...	Assay Office Record.
1851-2	,,	H	,,	,,		... ...	Do. do.
1852-3	,,	I	,,	,,		... ...	Do. do.
1853-4	,,	K	,,	,,		... ...	Do. do.
1854-5	,,	L	,,	,,		... ...	Do. do.
1855-6	,,	M	,,	,,		... ...	Do. do.
1856-7	,,	N	,,	,,		... ...	Do. do.
1857-8	,,	O	,,	,,		... ...	Do. do.
1858-9	,,	P	,,	,,		... ...	Do. do.
1859-60	,,	R	,,	,,	MH&Co	Martin Hall & Co.	Salad server : The Author.
1860-1	,,	S	,,	,,		... ...	Assay Office Record.
1861-2	,,	T	,,	,,		... ...	Do. do.
1862-3	,,	U	,,	,,	H·H	Harrison Bros. & Howson.	Fish knives : Mr. Bruford.
1863-4	,,	V	,,	,,		... ...	Assay Office Record.
1864-5	,,	W	,,	,,	FBs	Fenton Bros.	Hot-water jug : Mr. R. Day.
1865-6	,,	X	,,	,,	HA	Hy. Archer & Co.	Dessert knife : Mr. Crichton.
1866-7	,,	Y	,,	,,	RMEH	Martin Hall & Co., Ltd.	Communion plate : Ulverston.
1867-8	,,	Z	,,	,,		... ...	Assay Office Record.

* WA&Co 🦁 👤 A   A further example of the marks for 1844-5.   Makers' mark of W. Allanson & Co.
Candlesticks : Windsor Castle.

MARKS ON SHEFFIELD SILVER WARES.

TABLE V.

FIVE STAMPS TILL 1890, FOUR STAMPS AFTERWARDS, AS BELOW.

	CROWN.	LION PASSANT.	DATE LETTER.	QUEEN'S HEAD.	MAKER'S MARK.	MAKER'S NAME.	ARTICLES AND OWNERS.
1868-9	👑	🦁	A		RM EH	Martin Hall & Co., Ltd.	Dessert knife: Messrs. M. & S. Lyon.
1869-70	,,	,,	B	,,	,,	,, ,,	Fruit dish: Messrs. Christie.
1870-1	,,	,,	C	,,		... ...	Assay Office Record.
1871-2	,,	,,	D	,,		... ...	Do. do.
1872-3	,,	,,	E	,,		... ...	Do. do.
1873-4	,,	,,	F	,,	IH	John Harrison & Co., Ld.	Goblet: Messrs. M. & S. Lyon.
1874-5	,,	,,	G	,,		... ...	Assay Office Record.
1875-6	,,	,,	H	,,		... ...	Do. do.
1876-7	,,	,,	J	,,		... ...	Do. do.
1877-8	,,	,,	K	,,		... ...	Do. do.
1878-9	,,	,,	L	,,		... ...	Do. do.
1879-80	,,	,,	M	,,		... ...	Do. do.
1880-1	,,	,,	N	,,		... ...	Do. do.
1881-2	,,	,,	O	,,		... ...	Do. do.
1882-3	,,	,,	P	,,		... ...	Do. do.
1883-4	,,	,,	Q	,,		... ...	Do. do.
1884-5	,,	,,	R	,,		... ...	Do. do.
1885-6	,,	,,	S	,,		... ...	Do. do.
1886-7	,,	,,	T	,,		... ...	Do. do.
1887-8	,,	,,	U	,,		... ...	Do. do.
1888-9	,,	,,	V	,,	J·K·B	Hawksworth, Eyre & Co., Ltd.	Candlesticks: Mr. W. Boore.
1889-90	,,	,,	W	,,	WB JA	W. Briggs & Co.	Butter cooler: Mrs. Budd.
1890-1	,,	,,	X		RM EH	Martin Hall & Co., Ltd.	Toilet fittings: The Author.
1891-2	,,	,,	Y		J·D&S	Jas. Dixon & Sons.	Spirit flask: Do.
1892-3	,,	,,	Z		H·S	Henry Stratford.	Candlesticks: Messrs. Debenham.

Excepting the letter I every letter of the alphabet was used in regular succession in the above cycle.

MARKS ON SHEFFIELD SILVER WARES.

TABLE VI.

FOUR STAMPS AS BELOW.

	CROWN.	LION PASSANT.	DATE LETTER.	MAKER'S MARK.	MAKER'S NAME.	ARTICLES AND OWNERS.
1893-4	👑	🦁	𝖆	J.D & S	James Deakin & Sons.	Grape scissors : Mrs. F. Budd.
1894-5	,,	,,	𝖇	JR	John Round & Son, Ltd.	Fruit dish : Do.
1895-6	,,	,,	𝖈	JD WD	Jas. Deakin & Sons.	Cake-basket : Do.
1896-7	,,	,,	𝖉	M&W	Mappin & Webb.	Candlesticks : Mappin & Webb.
1897-8	,,	,,	𝖊	WF AF	Fordham & Faulkner.	Hot-water jug : Mr . F. Budd.
1898-9	,,	,,	𝖋	H.W	Lee & Wigfull.	Large dredger : Do.
1899 / 1900	,,	,,	𝖌	HA	Atkin Brothers.	Lemon-strainer : Do.
1900-1	,,	,,	𝖍	W&H	Walker & Hall.	Biscuit-barrel : Walker & Hall.
EDW. VII. 1901-2	,,	,,	𝖎	R&B	Roberts & Belk.	Tea-set : Mrs. Ince.
1902-3	,,	,,	𝖐	GH	Harrison Bros. & Howson.	Table plate : noted by Author.
1903-4	,,	,,	𝖑	...	... ...	Assay Office Record.
1904-5	,,	,,	𝖒		... ...	Do. do.
1905-6	,,	,,	𝖓		... ...	Do. do.
1906-7	,,	,,	𝖔		... ...	Do. do.
1907-8	,,	,,	𝖕		... ...	Do. do.
1908-9	,,	,,	𝖖		... ...	Do. do.
1909-10	,,	,,	𝖗		... ...	Do. do.
1910-1	,,	,,	𝖘		... ...	Do. do.
1911-2	,,	,,	𝖙		... ...	Do. do.
1912-3	,,	,,	𝖚		... ...	Do. do.
1913-4	,,	,,	𝖛		... ...	Do. do.
1914-5	,,	,,	𝖜		... ...	Do. do.
1915-6	,,	,,	𝖝		... ...	Do. do.
1916-7	,,	,,	𝖞		... ...	Do. do.
1917-8	,,	,,	𝖟		... ...	Do. do.

MARKS ON SHEFFIELD SILVER WARES.

TABLE VII.

FOUR STAMPS AS BELOW.

DATE.	CROWN.	LION PASSANT.	DATE LETTER.	MAKER'S MARK.	MAKER'S NAME.	ARTICLES AND OWNERS.
1918-9	👑	🦁	**a**	TB &S	Thos. Bradbury & Sons.	Various articles of plate.
1919-20	,,	,,	**b**	W & H	Walker & Hall.	Do. do. do.
1920-1	,,	,,	**c**	,,	,, ,,	Do. do. do.

HALL MARKS ON SHEFFIELD GOLD WARES.

The Sheffield assay office is now authorised* to assay and mark gold wares. It commenced doing so on 1 March, 1904.

The York Rose is the local mark which distinguishes gold assayed at Sheffield. It corresponds with the crown on silver wares. The date-letter has been changed yearly, the same as for silver, and for 1920-1 the letter is C. The other marks which denote the five gold standards are similar to those of London, Chester, and Birmingham, the crown used with the figures 22 and 18 respectively on gold of the two higher standards having no connection with the crown stamped on silver.

The examples of marks illustrated below have been reproduced on an enlarged scale from the assay office stamps.

MARKS ON THE SEVERAL CLASSES OF GOLD WARES ASSAYED AT SHEFFIELD FROM 1 MARCH TO 4 JULY, 1920-1.

22 Carat	🌹	👑	**22**	**C**
18 Carat	,,	,,	**18**	,,
15 Carat			**15** **·625**	,,
12 Carat			**12** **·5**	,,
9 Carat			**9** **375**	,,

For MARKS ON FOREIGN PLATE assayed at Sheffield see p. 27 *ante*.
* By the Act 3 Edw. VII., c. 255.

SUPPLEMENTARY LIST OF MARKS OF GOLDSMITHS

Impressed at Sheffield, not illustrated in the preceding tables, from 1773 to 1905 :—

DATE.	MARKS.	MAKER'S NAME.	DATE.	MARKS.	MAKER'S NAME.	DATE.	MARKS.	MAKER'S NAME.
1773	W·H / I·R	W. Hancock & J. Rowbotham.	1784	T·F&Co	T. Fox & Co.	1822	A·H	A. Hadfield.
"	WB &Co	W. Birks & Co.	1788	P·S	P. Spurr.	1824	CHS	C. Hammond & Co
"	IL STERLING / LAW STERLING	T. Law. / " "	1789	W·J	W. Jervis.	1825	RG	R. Gainsford.
"	WB &Co STERLING	W. Birks & Co.	1790	RS	R. Sporle.	1828	GH	G. Hardesty.
"	IR ,,	J. Rowbotham ?	1791	I·B	J. Bailey.	1829	D&S	J. Dixon & Son.
"	IL ,,	J. Littlewood.	"	MF &Co	M. Fenton & Co.	1833	JM	J. Mappin & Son.
"	SO ,,	Name not traced.	1792	LP &Co	? Luke, Proctor & Co.	1836	K&W	Kitchen & Walker.
"	IK&Co	John Kay & Co.	1796	G·A &Co	G. Ashforth & Co.	1840	L&M	Lee & Middleton.
"	JN / WN	J. Nowill. W. Nowill.	1797	CP	C. Proctor.	"	WK &Co	Walker, Knowles & Co.
1774	I·M	J. Mappin.	"	EG	E. Goodwin.	1843	W&S	Waterhouse & Co
"	WM &Co	W. Marsden & Co.	"	IC	J. Creswick.	1844	BW&A	Badger Worrall & Co.
"	SR	S. Roberts.	"	HT&Co	Mark of Henry Tudor & Co.	1846	R&S	Roberts & Slater.
1775	IR·Co	J. Rowbotham & Co.	1798	GG&Co	Goodman, Gainsford & Co.	1847	P·P &Co	Padley, Parkins & Co.
"	R·K	R. Kippax.	"	SK&Co	S. Kirkby & Co.	1853	JC / NC	J. & N. Creswick.
"	I·M&Co	J. Mappin & Co.	1799	RJ	R. Jewesson.	1856	WS / HS	W. & H. Stratford.
1776	T·H	T. Hoyland.	1801	TP	T. Poynton.	1857	F&A	Fenton & Anderton.
"	IT	J. Tibbitts.	1804	IJ	Name not traced.	1858	WH	W. Hutton.
1777	IH Co	J. Hoyland & Co.	"	IS	J. Staniforth.	"	WS / GS	W. & G. Sissons.
"	IH&Co	" "	1807	WT&Co	W. Tucker & Co.	1859	MB	Mappin Bros.
1778	S·W	S. Warburton.	1808	JW	J. Watson.	"	EM&Co	Elkington Mason & Co.
"	DH	D. Holy.	1810	G·W	G. Wostenholme	1861	WWH	W. W. Harrison.
1779	M&T	Madin & Trickett	1811	IS / TS	J. Staniforth & Co.	1862	W&H	Walker & Hall.
1780	Y·G&H	Young, Greaves & Hoyland.	"	RG	R. Gainsford.	1863	LB	Levesley Bros.
"	N·S	N. Smith & Co.	1813	I·R	J. Rogers.	1864	M&W&Co	Mappin & Webb.
1781	I·D	J. Dewsnap.	1817	RG	R. Gainsford.	1866	W& MD	W. & M. Dodge.
1783	S·K	S. Kirkby.	1818	B·R	B. Rooke & Son.	1867	J·H·S	J. Slater & Son.
			"	W·W	W. Wrangham	1868	CL TL	Levesley Bros.
			1820	TJ&NC	T. J. & N. Creswick.	1869	AB	A. Beardshaw.
			1822	T&IS	T. & J. Settle.	1905	IE &S	Name not traced.

NAMES OF SILVERSMITHS ENTERED AT THE

SHEFFIELD ASSAY OFFICE,

FROM 1773 TO 1890.

Entered 1773.

Geo.	Ashforth & Co.
Wm.	Birks & Co.
Matthew	Fenton & Co.
John	Hoyland & Co.
W. Hancock & J. Rowbotham	
Thos.	Law
Jonathan	Littlewood
John	Littlewood
Richard	Morton
Richard	Morton & Co.
W.	Marsden & Co.
James	Margrave & Co.
Chas. & L.	Proctor
Samuel	Roberts
Samuel	Roberts & Co.
John	Rowbotham & Co.
Robert	Trickett
H.	Tudor & T. Leader
John	Winter & Co.
Jos.	Wilson

1774.

Isaac	Cosins
Thos.	Greaves
Sam.	Greaves & Co.
Thos.	Holy & }
W.	Newbold }
John	Ibberson
Paris	Justice
Robert	Kippax & Co.
Wm.	Marsden
J.	Rowbotham & Co.
Samuel	Warburton & Co.

1775.

Wm.	Damant
W.	Fox
John	Henfrey & Son
John	Jervis
Chas.	Kelk
J.	Mappin & Co.
Jonathan	Mappin
W. & W.	Smith
John	Smith

1776.

Thos.	Hoyland
Thos.	Lamborn
Maurice	Rogers
John	Rowbotham
Jos.	Shemeld & Co.
J.	Watkinson

1777.

Thos.	Allen
Joseph	Creswick
Daniel	Holy & Co.
W.	Hoyland & Co.

1778.

John	Green
John	Harrison
Naylor & Settle	
Thos.	Prior
Thos.	Ratcliffe
James	Tibbitts
John	Winter
John	Younge & Co.

1779.

Benjamin	Blonk
David	Cadman
Joseph	Dickenson
Josia	Kemp
Mary	Kirkby
Madin & Trickett	
Wm.	Patten

1780.

Richard	Foster
R.	Morton
Nathaniel	Smith & Co.
Thos.	Shaw
T.	Settle & Co.

1781.

W.	Birks & Son
Benjn.	Broddrick
Geo.	Briddock
John	Dewsnap
Sam.	Deakin & Co.
Michael	Hunter & }
Josiah	Twig }
P.	Madin & }
R.	Trickett }
R.	Morton & Co.
S.	Roberts & Co.
Thos.	Settle
Shemeld,	Parkin & Co.
R.	Sutcliffe & Co.
J. D.	Sykes & Co.
Benjn.	Withers

1782.

Josiah	Cawton

1783.

Thos.	Colley
John	Green
J.	Jones & }
H.	Greenway & Co. }
John	Love & Co.
J.	Nowill
John	Parsons & Co.
J.	Staniforth & Co.

1784.

Geo.	Brittan & Co.
John	Cooper
Thos.	Fox & Co.
W.	Green & Co.
Geo.	Hawley
Saml.	Kirkby & Co.
J.	Swift & Co.
Wm.	Wild & Co.

1785.

Jos.	Bailey
W.	Darby
James	Green
Luke,	Proctor & Co.
John	Seynor

1786.

W.	Denning
W.	Dewsnap
Hague & Nowill	
Jas.	Makin
J.	Micklethwaite & }
J.	Hounsfield }
Thos.	Nowill
Chas.	Roebuck
Saml.	Roberts, jun., }
Geo.	Cadman & Co. }
John	Roberts
Jos.	Spooner
Robt.	Tricket & Co.

1787.

Jos.	Barraclough & Co.
Luke	Marriott
I.	Davidson
Stafford & Newton	

1788.

John	Borwick
Robert	Barnard

Geo. Cooper
John Lindley & Co.
Robert Owen & Son
Thos. Settle & Co.
Peter Spur & Son
W. Urton
John Younge & Sons

1789.

W. Greaves
W. Jervis
Nathaniel Travis
John Wright

1790.

Luke Brownell
John Law
T. Nowill
Thos. Rodgers
Dollif Rollinson
John Wilkinson

1791.

Benjn. Brocklesby
Thos. Parkin
Eben. Rhodes

1792.

R. Barnard & }
W. Hadfield }
Saml. & Ann Fox & Co.
John Green & }
George Hague }
John Green & Co.
Richard Loy
John Parkin & }
Ab. Wigham }
 Proctor & Beilby
James Rotherham
John Sykes & Co.
Dennis Sykes
J. & S. Saynor
Robert Sporle & Co.
Henry Whitelock & Co.
Hannah Watkinson

1793.

James Marsh
James Ellis & Co.
Edmund Sporle & Co.
Smith, Knowles, }
 Creswick & Co. }
James Sharrow & Co.
H. Watkinson & Co.
Jos. Wilson & Co.
J. Rowbotham
 Kirkby, Waterhouse & Co.

1794.

Geo. Dalton

1795.

Geo. Eadon & Co.
Jas. Gregory & Co.
John Kay & Co.

James Moore
Isaac Sampson
 Watson, Bradbury & Co.
John Watson

1796.

E. Goodwin
Richard Gregory & Co.
W. Jessop
S. Kirkby & Co.
W. Tucker, Fenton & Co.
Thos. Warris & Sons

1797.

 Goodman, Gainsford & Co.
Dan Leader
 Tudor & Nicholson
W. Linley

1798.

Thos. Blagden
Hamond Blake
Geo. Hague
Thos. & Dan Leader
J. Makin & Co.
 Middleton, Jewesson & Co.
 Peacock & Austin
Henry Rock

1799.

Daniel Barnard & }
John Settle }
John Fenton & Co.
Henry Hewett & }
Henry Rock }
J. Hinchcliffe
Jos. Hardy
Jn. Shore & Co.
Ebenezer Smelle

1800.

Alexr. Brailsforth & Co.
G. Cooper
Alexr. Goodman & Co.
Robert Jewesson
Jos. Kirkby

1801.

Sam. Bennett & }
Peter Spurr }
Geo. Battie & Bros.
Thos. Watson & Co.
John Ellis
Peter Spurr & }
Peter Cadman }
W. Harwood & Co.
Thomas Poynton & Flower

1802.

Thomas Cooper
Thomas Rodgers
John Settle & }
W. Hatfield }

1803.

Henry Coar
Jos. Quixall & Co.

1804.

J. Kay
John Poynton & Co.
John Staniforth

1805.

 Roberts, Moseley & Settle
John Rodgers, & Co.
R. F. Wilkinson
Jas. Drabble & Co.

1806.

Wm. Coldwell

1807.

 Clark, Hall & Clark
Benj. Polack
Thos. Sansom

1808.

Thos. Blagden }
Thos. Hodgson & Co. }
Robert Gainsford
J. Kirkby
J. Waterhouse & }
J. Hodgson }
Thomas Nixon & Co.
J. Sykes & Co.

1809.

Gregory Wostenholme & Co.
James Kirkby
 Thompson & Barber
George Wostenholme
 Wright & Fairbairn

1810.

Jos. Brammar &}
Sam. Horrabin }
Thos. & Jas. Creswick
 Furness, Poles and Turner
Thomas Kitchen
Chas. Needham
 Smith, Tate, Nicholson & Hoult
W. Tucker }
J. Fenton & }
E. G. Machon }
Robt. Wass

1811.

Saml. Mearbeck
 Wardell & Kempson
S. & C. Younge & Co.

1812.

Jos. Rodgers & Son

1813.

Jos.	Nowill
Roberts,	Clayton & Co.
Young & Deakin	

1815.

Battie,	Howard & ⎫
	Hawksworth ⎭
Jno. & Thos. Settle	
Thos. & Jno. Settle	

1816.

Blackwell & Parkin	
W.	Blackwell & Co.
Jas.	Crawshaw
Fenton,	Allanson & Co.

1817.

Thos.	Best
Wm.	Parkin
W.	Proctor
Wm.	Wrangham

1818.

Aaron	Hadfield
John	Eyre
B.	Rooke & Son
T.	Vaughan

1819.

Geo.	Dodd
T. J. & N.	Creswick
Peter	Dewsnap

1820.

Wm.	Bagshaw
Benjn.	Martin
Francis	Morton
Thos.	Clayton
John	Etches

1821.

Jonathan	Briggs & Co.
Castleton,	Milner & Co.
S. & W.	Kirkby

1822.

Alex.	Hunt
Kirkby,	Gregory & Co.
John	Taylor
Webster,	Danby & Co.
John	Watson & Son.
Waterhouse, Hodgson & Co.	
John	Whip & ⎫
John	Rose ⎭

1823.

William	Briggs
William	Blackwell & Co.
J. & G.	Fearn

Fenton,	Danby & Webster
A.	Hatfield & Sons
Benjn.	Rowlings

1824.

Chas.	Hammond
Joseph	Law
Law,	Oxley & Atkin
Samuel	Tinker

1825.

Geo.	Addy & Son
John	Ashforth
Jasper	Cutts & ⎫
T.	Anderton ⎭
John	Houlden
Settle,	Gunn & Co.
Wm. & John Nowill	

1826.

Ashforth, Hartshorn & Co.	
Ashforth, Creswick & Co.	
Thomas	Champion & Son
Ashforth	Crawshaw
Roberts,	Smith & Co.
Underdown, Wilkinson & Co.	
W. Watson & T. Bradbury.	

1828.

Atkin &	Oxley
Green,	Bradbury & Firth
Geo.	Hardesty
Sam	Hennell
J.	Newton & Son
Chas.	Picksley & Co.

1829.

Jas.	Burbury
Jas.	Dixon & Sons
Jas.	Smith & Son

1831.

Bartol	Hounsfield
Hardy,	Bell & Co.
Henry	Wilkinson & Co.
Wilkinson & Roberts	

1832.

W.	Allanson & Co.
Thos.	Bradbury & Sons
Kitchen,	Walker & Cerr
Wm.	Watson & Co.

1833.

Hawksworth, Eyre & Co.	
John	Harrison & Co.
Geo.	Stokes
Joseph	Mappin & Son
Sansom & Harwood	
H. Dawson, Wilkinson & Co.	

1834.

Geo.	Hibbert
Thorpe,	Glossop & Middleton

1835.

Abraham	Dyson
Howard & Hawksworth	
Saml.	Harwood
Patrick	Leonard
William	Sansom
Kitchen & Walker	

1836.

Thos.	Hardy
John	Waterhouse & ⎫
Edward	Hatfield ⎭
W.	Hutton
Samuel	Walker & Co.
Chas. Fred.	Younge

1837.

Henry	Duke
Wm. & Hy.	Hutchinson

1839.

W.	Carter
Isaac	Simmons

1840.

Lee &	Middleton
T. P.	Lowe
Henry	Walker & ⎫
John	Wilkinson ⎭
Glossop & Nutt	
Walker,	Knowles, & Co.

1841.

Henry	Atkin
Edwin	Bradley
John	Gilbert
John	Oxley

1842.

Jno. Priston	Cutts
Geo.	Waterhouse & Co.

1843.

John & Jonathan Bell	
Osborn & Elliott	

1844.

Badger,	Worrall & Armitage
Charles	Boardman
Roberts & Slater	
T. W.	Eaton
J.	Harrison
J.	Roberts
Thompson & Brown	

1845.

Thomas   Freeman

1846.

James   Green
George   Ward
  Martin Bros. & Naylor
  Padley,   Parkin & Co.
Josephus   Smith

1847.

Thomas   Badger
  Roberts & Hall

1848.

Joseph & Ed. Mappin
J.   Needham

1849.

George   Deakin & Co.
  Harrison Bros. & Howson

1850.

James   Wolstenholme
W. F.   Wolstenholme

1851.

Thomas   Royle

1852.

W.   Watson & Co.
H.   Wilkinson & Co.

1853.

H. W.   Atkin Bros. & Co.
Thomas   Turner

1854.

  Archer,   Machin & Marsh
Jonathan   Bell
John   Bell
J. Y.   Cowleshaw
James   Fenton (B'ham)
  Martin,   Hall & Co.
Joseph   Machin }
Henry   Archer & Co. }
  Martin,   Hall & Co., Ltd.
  Sansom & Davenport

1855.

John   Biggin
  Lockwood Bros.
Thomas   Marples
  Rhodes   Bros.
W, & H.   Stratford

1856.

Hukin &   Fenton
J. F.   Fenton
George   Hawksley & Co.
W. W.   Harrison & Co.
J.   Mappin & Bros.
Henry   Stacey & Orton
  Sansom & Creswick

1857.

  Creswick & Co.
  Fenton & Anderton
John Fred.   Fenton
W. W.   Harrison & Co.
W.   Hutton & Son
  Padley,   Stanforth & Co.
Fred Ellis   Timm
F. E.   Timm & Co.

1858.

Thomas   Aston & Son (B'ham)
G.   Hawksley
John   North
S. H.   Ward (M'chester)
Jos. & Jas.   Rodgers, Ltd.
W. & G.   Sissons
W. & S.   Ward

1859.

  Elkington, Mason & Co. (B'ham)
  Brown & Clark (B'ham)
  Mappin Bros.
  Roberts & Briggs
  Slater,   Son & Horton
George   Teasdell
  White & Johnstone

1860.

  Fenton   Bros.
John   Knowles & Son
  Mappin & Webb

1861.

Geo.   Edwards (Glasgow)
  McKay & Chisholm
                (Edinburgh)
  Pryor,   Tyzack & Co.
Wm.   Skidmore
Geo.   Unite (B'ham)

1862.

Jas.   Chesterman & Co.
  Slack   Bros.
  Walker & Hall

1863.

  Briddon   Bros.
Chas.   Favell (Creswick & Co.)
  Levesley   Bros.

1864.

A. J.   Beardshaw & Co.
S.   Bright & Co.
  Brookes & Crookes
G.   Hawksley & Co.

1865.

  Harrison Bros. & Howson
  Mammatt, Buxton & Co.
  Robinson & Co.
  Towndrow Bros.
T.   Turner & Co.

1866.

W. & M.   Dodge (Manch.)
J.   Harrison & Co.
W.   Hutton & Sons
  Parkin &   Marshall
  White,   Henderson & Co.

1867.

Michael   Beal
Thos.   Bradbury & Sons
J.   Dixon & Sons
T.   Ellis
W.   Gallimore & Co.
J. E.   Makin
  Roberts & Belk
John   Round & Son, Ltd.
Jos.   Slater & Son

1868.

Wm.   Brearley
James   Thompson, Son & }
                Jenkins }

1869.

Albert John   Beardshaw
W.   Morton

1870.

Thos.   Prime & Son
                (Birmingham)
James A.   Rhodes
John   Sherwood & Son
                (Birmngham)
Jos.   Wilkinson

1871.

  Boardman & Glossop
  Manton & Cook (Birmingham)
W.   Webster & Son
  Wilson & Davis

1872.

Wm.   Adams
P.   Ashbury & Sons
Geo.   Butler & Co,
Geo.   Cutts

Henry	Cook	R. M.	Johnson & Co.		**1885.**	
John	Hunter & Son	Lee &	Wigful			
Thos.	Hall & Co.	Hy.	Stratford	W.	Fairbourne & Sons	
Francis	Knowles & Co.	George	Wish	John	Gallimore	
Lucas &	Johnson			Wm.	Mammatt & Sons	
			1880.	Wm.	Morton	
	1873.			Parkin &	Marshall	
		John	Batt.	J. & H.	Potter	
W.	Biggs & Co.	John	Fee.	Albert H.	Thompson	
Fee &	Swift	Joseph	Haywood & Co.	George	Warris	
J.	Kilpatrick & Co.	Meyers &	Davis.			
	(London)	Chas Edw.	Nixon.		**1886.**	
Sampson,	Wish & Co.	John	Sanderson			
Sheffield	Nickel Plating Co.			Ed.	Brailsford & Co.	
			1881.	Howell &	James	
	1874.			John Wm.	Kilpatrick	
		Allison &	Lonsdale.	W.	Spiridion	
John	Pinder & Co.	Sandy	Beatson			
		Gibson &	Langman		**1887.**	
	1875.	W.	Batt & Sons			
		E.	Draper & Co.	Adams &	England	
James	Dewsnap	John	Nowill & Sons.	Allen &	Darwin	
Lewis D.	Gibaud	John	Needham	Wm. Allen	Beevers	
John	Hunter	Henry	Price & Co.	Chas.	Favell & Co.	
W.	Padley & Son	Joseph	Ridge & Co.	Geo. & Hy.	Hulley	
B. W.	Ramsden			John	Jenkins	
Edwin	Round & Son, Ltd.		**1882.**			
Jos.	Swift & Co.				**1888.**	
Mark	Willis & Son	W.	Beatson.			
		John B.	Carrington.	Ballas &	Co.	
	1876.	Thos. de la	Rue & Co.	Saml.	Biggin & Son	
		Holland Son & Slater		Z.	Barraclough & Sons	
Hayllar &	Lonsdale	W. Clark	Manton.	Bracker &	Sydenham	
		Chas.	Stokes & Son	Carrington & Co.		
	1877.			W.	Dawson	
			1883.	Fenton	Bros.	
Edmund	Bell			Frank	Fidler	
Muirhead &	Arthur	Geo.	Ashmore	James	Neill	
Peter	Skidmore	Bethel	Barnett	S. D.	Neill	
		Bradley &	Blake	Pinder	Bros	
	1878.	Francis	Cholerton	Arthur W.	Staniforth	
		W. Chas.	Eaton.			
John Cook	Clarke	T. W.	Eaton		**1889.**	
Cooper	Bros.	Robt.	Mosley, Fead & Co.			
William	Davis	Geo.	Harvey Whitaker.	Joseph	Adams	
James	Deakin & Sons	Fred.	Witson & Co.	Thos.	Bradbury & Sons.	
John	Fullerton			Walter	Bullas	
Francis	Howard		**1884.**	Francis	Corthorn	
Morton &	Green			G. & I. W.	Hawkesley	
J. & H.	Rhodes & Backer	Barnett &	Scott	Heeley	Bros.	
Sibray	Hall & Co.	Jas. W.	Benson	Jenkins &	Timm	
F. E.	Timm & Co.	Maurice	Baum	W. & J.	Sears	
White,	Sons & Co.	F.	Hall	Priestley &	Shaw	
William	Yates		(Shaw & Fisher).	E. L.	Thompson & Co.	
		Joseph	Price			
	1879.	Richd.	Richardson		**1890.**	
		Shaw &	Fisher			
W.	Beatson & Sons	Geo. H.	Whitaker & Co.	Sandy	Beaston	
Thos.	Otsley & Sons			Fordham &	Faulkner	

CHAPTER XVIII

ENGLISH PROVINCIAL GOLDSMITHS
OF THE MINOR GUILDS

HULL

Judged by what remains of their work, the goldsmiths of Kingston-upon-Hull are entitled to first place amongst the guilds of English Provincial Goldsmiths remaining to be noticed.

Hull Goldsmiths mentioned in the Fifteenth Century. Hull had a mint in the reign of Edward I., and in all probability goldsmiths were working there then, but it is not mentioned in the Statute 2 Hen. VI. c. 14 (1423) as one of the towns "appointed to have touches of their own". Names of Hull goldsmiths are, however, found recorded from the 15th century onwards. One "Swethero, Goldsmyth" is mentioned in the Hull chamberlain's roll of 1427 in connection with the greater corporation mace, and "Willelmus and John Goldsmyths" are mentioned in the same connection in 1440. The names of a number of other Hull goldsmiths will be found in the following list.

No evidence of Incorporation. No evidence that the goldsmiths of Hull were ever incorporated either by Statute or Charter has been found. It may have been that their guild existed by sufferance and not by direct authority from the Crown. Their remoteness from London and comparative inaccessibility, except by sea, would account for their immunity from interference. In the 17th century the goldsmiths of Hull, as in many other towns, are found to have been combined with workers in brass as "The Company of Goldsmiths and Braziers".

Marks on Hull Plate. A number of examples of plate have been found in and around Hull bearing marks which have been traced to Hull goldsmiths. The earliest of such examples has the letter H, the initial of Hull, as the town mark; in the 17th century, however, the arms of the town—*three ducal coronets in pale*—was adopted as the town mark. It is generally found in a plain shield on plate stamped also with makers' marks, formed of initials of the names of goldsmiths known to have been working in Hull at that period.

There is no evidence of the existence of any regular assay office, and there probably never was one at Hull. An attempt seems to have been made towards the end of the 17th century to establish a system of marking with date-letters, but the examples which have been found are too few to compile an entire table from, those discovered being no more than a Lombardic E and the letters *A*, *D*, *E* and *F*, in cursive capitals, and the Roman capital K.

The Hull goldsmiths do not appear to have troubled themselves much about the Act of 1696, for they seem to have worked on for a few years regardless of its provisions ; their existence, however, as workers of plate terminated early in the 18th century. Goldsmiths' names are recorded in the archives of the borough down to 1774, but the majority of those mentioned after 1706 were probably dealers in gold-smiths' work and not manufacturers. No more than one example of Hull plate of the period of Queen Anne is known, and not any of later date.

The examples of Hull plate known to the Author number about thirty-four in all, and the different combinations of marks amount to seventeen varieties, the others being repetitions of some of the seventeen which are represented in the table on the following page.

NAMES OF HULL GOLDSMITHS,

FROM 1427 TO 1774.

NAME OF GOLDSMITH.		Earliest Date Found.	Free.	Latest Date or Death.	NAME OF GOLDSMITH.		Earliest Date Found.	Free.	Latest Date or Death.
Swethero	"Goldsmyth"	1427			H[enry(?)]	R[ussell (?)]	1621		
John	do.	1440			Christopher	Watson	1638		1660
Willelmus	do.	,,			James	Birkby		1651	
Robert	Alnwick	1499			A[braham (?)]	B[irkby (?)]	1651		
John	Norton	1500			Edward	Mang$^{ie}_{y}$	1660	1660	1724
Robert	Norton	1540			John	Watson		,,	
George	Harwood	1572	1572	1616	T——	G——	1666		
P[eter (?)]	C[arlille (?) / asson (?)]	1580			Katherine	Mangy	1680		1697
James	Watson	1582	1582	1609	Thomas	Hebden	1681	1681	1690
James	C[arlille (?) / asson (?)]	1585		1610	Abraham	Barachin		1706	
James	Carlille	1592	1592	1599	Hawse	Brampton	1724		
Martin	Moore	,,	,,	,,	Christopher	Thompson	17—		1750
Edward	Russell			,,	Richard	Moxon		1750	
Jeconiah	Watson	1600		1620	Stephen	Bramston	1760		1772
Robert	Robinson	1617	1617	1649	John	Dove		1772	
James	Watson		1620		Edward	Hardy		,,	
					James	Dewitt		1774	

MARKS ON HULL PLATE.

THE DATES IN COLUMN I ARE APPROXIMATE EXCEPT TO THE EXTENT THAT THE INSCRIBED DATES
MAY BE RELIED ON.

DATE.	TOWN MARK.	MAKER'S MARK.	TOWN MARK.	MAKER'S MARK.	MAKER'S NAME.	ARTICLES AND OWNERS.
1580	[H]	[PC]			Peter Carlille.	Com. cups: Beverley Minster, and Gatwick Church.
1587		[I.C]	[H]		James Carlille.	Com. cup, dated 1587: Holy Trin. Ch., Hull. Seal-top spoon: Trinity House, Hull.
1621	[crown/W]	[IC]	[crown/RR]	[IB]	„ „ *	Beaker, dated 1621: Trinity House, Hull.
1629	[H]	[RR]	[H]		Robt. Robinson.	Mount of coco-nut cup, dated 1629: Trinity House, Hull. Com. cup and paten: N. Frodingham, Yorks.
1635	[crown/W]	[*RR]	[„]		„ „	Two com. cups: Holy Trinity Ch., Hull. Seal-top spoon: Trinity House, Hull.
1638	[H]	[CW]	[H]		Chr. Watson.	Com. cup, dated 1638: St. Mary's Church, Hull.
1651	[crown/W]	[IB]	[crown/W]		James Birkby.	Small caudle cup: Mr. B. Barnett.
1666	[crown/W]	[EM]	[crown/W]	DATE LETTER.	Edwd. Mangie or Mangy. }	Posset cup and small beaker: Trin. Ho., Hull. Com. cup, dated 1666: Beverley Minster.
1666-70	[crown/W]	[TG]		[E]	Name not traced.	Beaker: Victoria and Albert Museum.
1670-80	„	„		[K]	„ „	Noted by the Author.
†„	[crown/W]	[EM]		[A]	Edwd. Mangie or Mangy. }	Porringer: Messrs. Gilder & Son.
1680	„	[M]			„ „	Small mace: Hull Corporation.
„	„	[EM]	„	[D]	„ „	Trifid spoon: Mr. J. H. Walter. Com. cup: Copgrove, Yorks.
1680-97		[KM]	„	[E]	Kath. Mangy.	Com. cup: Trinity House, Hull.
„		[KM]			„ „	Cover of do.: Do. do.
„	..	[EM]	„	[I]	Edwd. Mangy.	Tankard: Do. do.
1689	„	[TH]	„		Thos. Hebden.	Peg tankard, dated 1689: Hedon Corporation; tumbler, dated 1689, and a porringer: Trinity House, Hull; and two trifid rat-tail spoons: Mr. Robson.
1690-7	[crown/W]	[KM]	[crown/W]		Kath. Mangy.	Tobacco box, dated 1697: Trinity House, Hull.
1697	[ornate]	[KM]			„ „	Trifid spoon: Messrs. Crichton.
1706	[crown/W]	[AB/crown]	„		Abm. Barachin.	Com. cup: Preston-in-Holderness, Nr. Hull.

* Probably repaired by R. Robinson in 1621 and by Hawse Brampton, c. 1724, as it bears their marks as well as the mark of Jas. Carlille.

† 1670  Date-letter on porringer: Messrs. Gilder & Son.

LINCOLN.

Lincoln was one of the seven towns appointed by the Act of 1423 "to have divers touches," but no records concerning the proceedings of its goldsmiths have been brought to light. That there were goldsmiths working in Lincoln from the 12th century onwards, is, however, proved by deeds, in which one or more of the parties, or an attesting witness, is described as "Aurifaber". In a deed undated, but the date of which is otherwise ascertained to be A.D. 1155 to 1163, one "William," grantee of land from Walter, Abbot of St. Oswald, of Bardney, is described as "Aurifaber," and in two others of *c*. A.D. 1200 and 1216 the attesting witnesses are similarly described. Names of goldsmiths have been found in other documents and in the registers of the city, extending, with intervals, down to the year 1708. Goldsmiths from Lincoln appear also to have gone to London and pursued their calling there in the Middle Ages, for in a deed dated 19 May, 1323, conveying·certain lands to the Goldsmiths' Company of London, the name of "Thomas de Lincoln, aurifaber," occurs as one of the witnesses, and in the same year, in another document, "Walter de Lincoln, goldsmith," is mentioned as holding land in the way called St. Vedast, in the parish of St. John Zacary, London, bordering upon land then purchased by the Goldsmiths' Company. In 1350 John de Lincoln was one of the wardens of the London Goldsmiths' Company. Extracts from *Lincoln Wills* go to show that a considerable amount of gold and silver plate was possessed by Lincoln residents in the 14th, 15th and 16th centuries.*

The arms of Lincoln are :—*Argent, on a cross gules, a fleur-de-lys or*,† and the device of a fleur-de-lys is borne on all the old seals of the borough, the earliest now in existence having been made in accordance with a resolution of the 2nd February, 165$\frac{5}{6}$.‡ Impressions are, however, known of a seal of 1449, in which year it was resolved "that a new common seal should be made, stamped with the representation of a castle with five towers and one gate, and to have a shield of the arms of the city of Lincoln, and on each side of the castle *one Flourdelyssh*, with a writing about the 'girum,' viz., *Sygillum Coe Civitatis Lincoln*".‡

The adoption by the goldsmiths of Lincoln of the principal charge in the coat-of-arms of their city as their distinguishing "town mark," was in accordance with the ancient custom which obtained in the provinces.

Marginal notes:

Lincoln appointed to be an Assay-town in 1423.

Lincoln goldsmiths found mentioned in the 12th century.

The Lincoln "town mark" a fleur-de-lys.

---

*.Vols. I.-V., *Lincoln Record Society*.

† The fleur-de-lys has reference to the Blessed Virgin Mary, whose emblem it is, and in whose honour the cathedral church of Lincoln is dedicated.

‡ *Civitas Lincolnia*, by John Ross (printed by Cousans), p. 50.

Plate which has been found in recent years bearing the Lincoln mark consists for the most part of spoons of the various types which prevailed in the 16th and 17th centuries. In the earlier examples the fleur-de-lys is stamped in the bowl, in the later—the flat-stemmed varieties —all the marks are struck on the backs of the stems. Four pieces of church plate have been found with the Lincoln mark; they are :—a communion cup and paten at St. Audoen's, Dublin, a communion cup at Wherwell, Hants, and a paten at Holy Trinity Church, Goodramgate, York.

A beaker, a mug, and other articles, have been found, marked with the fleur de-lys of Lincoln and a maker's mark identical with that of Timothy Skottowe who worked at Norwich from 1617 to 1644, and who, it is suggested, also carried on business at Lincoln simultaneously, or shortly after the year 1644. Both the beaker and mug have the mark of a Roman capital-letter G, similar to the Norwich date-letter for 1630, and what is more remarkable, both have an additional mark of a lion's face, which also occurs—together with the mark of Timothy Skottowe, and the Norwich date-letter T—on a beaker belonging to Mr. Wm. Minet, F.S.A.

Communion cups, dated 1569, at Osbournby, North Cockerington, and Marsh Chapel; others dated 1570, at Auborn and Upton-cum-Kexby, and others undated at Lea near Gainsborough, Haxey, Boultham, Heapham, Scotton, and Thimbleby—all in or near the County of Lincoln—bear a mark (illustrated in the fourth line of the following table), believed to be that of a Lincoln goldsmith, but no other mark is distinguishable to connect it with the city; in view, however, of the fact that no less than eleven examples so marked have been found in the neighbourhood of Lincoln, it seems reasonable to suppose that they were wrought there.

The list of names of Lincoln goldsmiths which follows the tables of marks, has been compiled from the documents mentioned, and placed at the Author's disposal by Colonel John G. Williams, of Lincoln. The only name which has been found to correspond with any of the makers' initials in the tables of marks is that of John Woodward of Chesterfield, who was apprenticed to Thomas Turpin of Lincoln, goldsmith, from Christmas, 1577, for eight years ;—which is not surprising, in view of the facts that no records expressly pertaining to the craft have been discovered, and that there are gaps without names at periods contemporaneous with the making of the articles which have been found.

MARKS ON LINCOLN PLATE.

TABLE I.

FROM ABOUT 1560 TO ABOUT 1650.

(THE DATES ARE APPROXIMATE EXCEPT TO THE EXTENT THAT THE INSCRIBED DATES MAY BE RELIED ON.)

DATE (ABOUT).	MARKS.	ARTICLES AND OWNERS.
1560		Apostle spoon (St. Jude): The Author's Collection. The three fleur-de-lys grouped, are in the bowl: the three in line, on back of stem.
,,		Hexagonal seal-top spoon: Messrs. Crichton.
,,		Elizabethan seal-top spoon: Mr. J. W. Usher, Lincoln.
1569		Com. cups, dated 1569 and 1570 (maker's mark only visible): Osbournby, and ten other parish churches in Lincolnshire.
c. 1590		Seal-top spoon: The Author's Collection.
1617		Seal-top spoon, pricked 1617: Mr. J. H. Walter, Drayton, Norfolk.
1624		Com. cup and paten, inscribed "Ex Dono Petri Harison Anno 1624": St. Audoen's, Dublin.
1628		Seal-top spoon, pricked "Ianu. 4, 1628": Mr. J. H. Walter.
1633		Do. do., do. 1633: Messrs. Crichton.
1639		Do. do., do. 1639: Do. do.
1640		Do. do., do. 1640: Mr. W. Boore.
1640-50		Puritan spoon: Mr. J. H. Walter.
,,		Struck thrice on small porringer: Mr. R. G. Westmacott.
,,		Communion plate: Hintlesham.

MARKS ON LINCOLN PLATE.

TABLE II.

FROM ABOUT 1650 TO ABOUT 1706.

(THE DATES ARE APPROXIMATE EXCEPT TO THE EXTENT THAT THE INSCRIBED DATES MAY BE
RELIED ON).

DATE. (ABOUT).	MARKS.	ARTICLES AND OWNERS.
1640-50		Communion cup : St. Margaret's, Ipswich.
,,		Do. do. : Noted by Mr. J. H. Walter.
,,		Seal-top spoon : Mr. J. H. Walter.
,,		Do. do. : Mr. H. D. Ellis.
1642		*(Timothy Skottowe ?) Beaker : Mr. Wm. Minet, F.S.A.
1650	,, ,,	,, ,, (?) { Beaker : Mr. A. D. George. Mug found in Norwich : submitted by Mr. J. H. Walter. Puritan spoon ; S. Ken. Museum. Tankard : The Goldsmiths & Silversmiths & Co. }
,,		Mark stamped thrice on Com. cup : Wherwell, Hants.
1650-6		,, ,, ,, ,, plain flat-stemmed spoon : Messrs. Christie.
1660		* Puritan spoons : Mercers' Company, and S. Kensington Museum.
,,		Do. do. : The Author's Collection.
1686	,, ,,	Trifid spoon, dated 1686 : Mr. A. W. Stone.
1690		Trifid spoon, pricked $169\frac{0}{1}$: South Kensington Museum.
,,		Rat-tail spoon, flat stem : Goldsmiths' Company, London.
,,		Do. do., pricked 1690 : Mr. E. W. Colt.
1706		Communion paten, inscribed " Given to the Holy Trinity Church, Goodramgate, 1706 " : Holy Trinity Church, Goodramgate, York.

* See pages 317 and 321 *ante*.

NAMES OF LINCOLN GOLDSMITHS.

FROM MEDIÆVAL REGISTERS IN THE POSSESSION OF THE DEAN AND CHAPTER OF LINCOLN.

DATE.

1155-63. William "Aurifaber". Grantee of Land from Walter Abbot of St. Oswald of Bardney: Lib. Cant. No. 178.

1200. Jordan "Aurifaber". Attesting Witness: Registrum Antiquissimum. No. 819.

1216. Thomas "Aurifaber". Attesting Witness: Reg. Antiq. No. 790.

1217. Alanus "Aurifaber". Owner of Land in St. Laurence, Lincoln: Sempringham Charter.

1225. Thomas "Aurifaber". Attesting Witness: Lib. Cant. 172.

„ Magister Radulphus "Aurifaber". Lib. Cant. 172.

1250 to 1263. Richard "Aurifaber" and Michael "Aurifaber". Attesting Witnesses, sometimes alone, sometimes coupled: Lib. Cant. 100, 128, 162, 191, 192, 201, 202, 203, 222.

1254. Ynon "Aurifaber". House of: 217 Lib. Cant.

1260. Alan "Aurifaber". Witness: Lib. Cant. 178.

1270. Peter "Aurifaber". Grant to Roger Son of Benedict: Lib. Cant. 191.

„ Galfridus "Aurifaber". Son of Peter son of Benedict: Lib. Cant. 191.

1275. William "Aurifaber". Attesting Witness: Lib. Cant. 214.

1284 Nicholas de Shirbec (? Skirbeck) "Aurifaber": Lib. Cant. 184.

1289. Richard (Son of Richard) "Aurifaber". Grant to Nicholas of Hibaldston: Lib. Cant. 196.

1296. William Findelove de Ballio (of the Bail of Lincoln) "Aurifaber". Grant to Simon le Holm: Lib. Cant. 126.

FROM LINCOLN MUNICIPAL REGISTERS.

1567 (19 June). Nicholas Tooley, Goldsmith, admitted to the Freedom of the City by purchase.

DATE.

1574. Thomas Turpyne, Goldsmith, admitted to the Freedom of the City by purchase.

1577-85. John Woodward, Son of John Woodward, of Chesterfield, apprenticed to Thomas Turpyne, Goldsmith, from the Feast of Nativity 20 Eliz. (1577) for 8 years. Enrolled.

1592 (24 July). Robert Stockeld to Nicholas Towley, Goldsmith. Indre. of Apprenticeship dated 22 March, 29 Eliz. (1586) for 8 years. Enrolled.

FROM REGISTER OF LEASES 1612-33. LINCOLN CORPORATION.

1623 (14 Aug.). William Watson, Goldsmith, obtained a Lease of meadow land from the Corporation for 30 years.

1625 (13 Mar.). John Tooley, Goldsmith, obtained a Lease of 2 Closes of marsh land from the Corporation.

1629 (11 Feb.). William Watson, Goldsmith, obtained a Lease of other land from the Corporation.

FROM BOOK OF FREEMEN, 1706-26. LINCOLN CORPORATION.

1706 (24 Sept.). Thomas Colson, Son of Thomas Colson, of the City of Lincoln, Goldsmith, deceased, admitted to the Freedom of the City by birth (his father having been a Freeman).

1707. William Colson, Son of Thomas Colson, of the City of Lincoln, Goldsmith, deceased, admitted to the Freedom of the City by birth.

1708. Christopher Colson, Son of Thomas Colson, of the City of Lincoln, Goldsmith, deceased, admitted to the Freedom of the City by birth.

SHREWSBURY.

Shrewsbury, though not one of the towns appointed " to have divers touches " by the Act of 1423, was a place where gold and silver wares were wrought in the Middle Ages.   The provisions of the Statute 28 Ed. I., c. 20 (1300), repeated in subsequent Acts, requiring that " no manner of vessel or other work of silver should be set to sale without having the mark of the leopard's head set upon it," were an aid rather than a hindrance to the Shrewsbury goldsmiths.   The arms of Shrewsbury being *azure, three leopard's heads, or,* one of such leopard's heads would be the mark which the Shrewsbury goldsmiths would naturally, in accordance with the custom which obtained in the Middle Ages, select as their own proper town mark.   Many possessors of spoons marked with an uncrowned leopard's head in the bowl wrongly ascribe them to London, on the assumption that because an uncrowned leopard's head had been found on what appeared to be a London-made spoon of a date anterior to 1478, all plate so marked is therefore London-made plate of a date earlier than the year in which the date-letter was first adopted.   The Author, in drawing attention for the first time to this particular mark, in a paper on *The Spoon and its History*, read at a meeting of the Society of Antiquaries in the year 1890, and published in Vol. LIII. of *Archæologia*, never intended to suggest that all marks in any way resembling the one referred to should be assumed to be mediæval London marks.   It is much more likely that the greater number of such marks were struck in Shrewsbury in the 16th century than that they were struck in London before 1478.

The margin note: The Shrewsbury "town mark" a leopard's head.

The Author believes that the marks represented below are Shrewsbury marks of about the dates which are set against them, and he is supported in this belief by other antiquaries who have given consideration to the subject.

EXAMPLES OF SHREWSBURY MARKS.
(THE DATES ARE, OF COURSE, APPROXIMATE.)

DATE.	MARKS.	ARTICLES AND OWNERS.
1530		*Maidenhead spoon : Mr. H. D. Ellis.
1560		Apostle spoon : Mr. J. H. Walter, Drayton, Norfolk.
,,		Communion cups at Tugby and Saxton, Leicestershire.

* It has been suggested that this is a London mark of c. 1470, and that each of the two lower marks represents a bucranium.   See page 77, *ante.*

The following names of goldsmiths found in the Shrewsbury Records of the 15th, 16th and 17th centuries show a goodly succession, and indicate that the craft or "mysterie" of goldsmiths flourished there before the Act of 1696 deprived them, in common with all other English provincial goldsmiths, of the right of marking their wares.

In the "Dublin Roll of Names" of the latter part of the 12th century one "Willielmus 'Aurifaber' de Srobesburi" is mentioned, which appears to indicate that the art of the goldsmith was practised in Shrewsbury at a period more than two centuries earlier than the date with which the following list commences :—

NAMES OF SHREWSBURY GOLDSMITHS.

FROM 1465 TO 1695, COMPILED BY MR. R. C. HOPE, F.S.A., FROM SHREWSBURY RECORDS.

NAME OF GOLDSMITH.	Earliest Date Found.	Free.	Latest Date or Death.	NAME OF GOLDSMITH.	Earliest Date Found.	Free.	Latest Date or Death.
Thomas Stalbrook		1465		Edward Mind	1568		
Thomas Syward		,,		John King	1581	1581	
Thomas Engylfelde	14—	1470		Gregory Fryer	1590		
John Massy		1476		Isaac Fewe	1600	1617	
Richard Phillips		1480	1510	Thomas Fryer		1605	
Robert Hyckoks	1482	1482		John Whitakers	1658		c. 1667
Ellice Decka	,,	1504	,,	Thomas Jenks	1661		1676
Gregory Fewe	1500			James Kinsey	,,		
William Dodilwick		1503		Thomas Whitakers		1662	1674
Llewelyn Ap John	1510	1510		Thomas Gittins	1667	1673	1695
Robert Heyffyle		,,		Henry Jenks		1668	
Nicholas Phillips		,,		Daniel Pugh	1672		
Roger Phillips	1510	1518	c. 1547	Charles Wood	1676	1676	
Matthew Dillory		1544		Henry Vaughan	1677	1678	
William Phillips		1548		Thomas Sandford	1687		d. 1741
George Burton	1568	1568		Thomas Gittins	1695	1695	,,

LEWES.

The Common Seal of Lewes, the county town of Sussex, is of late 14th century date, and bears a shield : *checky (or and azure)* on *a canton sinister gules a lion rampant or*, which was used by the goldsmiths of Lewes as their town mark. This mark has been found, together with the maker's mark, as illustrated below, on spoons of the latter part of the 16th and first half of the 17th century.

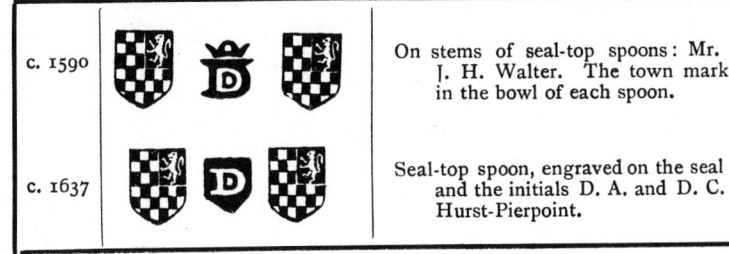

c. 1590	On stems of seal-top spoons: Mr. H. D. Ellis, and Mr. J. H. Walter. The town mark alone is stamped once in the bowl of each spoon.
c. 1637	Seal-top spoon, engraved on the seal end with the date 1637, and the initials D. A. and D. C.: Mr. J. E. Couchman, Hurst-Pierpoint.

ROCHESTER.

The marks illustrated below for 1560 consist of (1) a reversed R, and (2) BR in monogram within a ring of pellets—transcribed from an Elizabethan communion cup at Snave, Kent. A 16th century spoon sold at Messrs. Christie's in March, 1905, had a reversed R within a ring of pellets stamped in the bowl. It sometimes happened in the 16th and 17th centuries that letter-marks instead of being reversed in the punch were (probably by oversight on the part of the die-sinker) so cut that the stamped mark was reversed, as is the case with one of the two London date-letters F for 1583-4, and with one of the two letters **a** for 1638-9. The reversed R in the bowl of the 16th century spoon, suggested the idea of its being a town mark ; and as the principal charge in the arms of the city of Rochester is the letter R borne on the fess point of the shield, it seems safe to conclude that in conformity with the rule which obtained in the 16th century, the goldsmiths of Rochester adopted as their town mark the letter R from their city arms, and that the reversed R stamped on the Snave communion cup is the Rochester town mark. The arms of Rochester here illustrated show the R, borne as above described.

THE ARMS OF ROCHESTER.

In some late representations of the arms, the principal charge is a small black-letter **r**, but in Gwyllim's work on Heraldry a Roman capital letter R is displayed.

EXAMPLES OF ROCHESTER MARKS.

DATE.	MARKS.	ARTICLES AND OWNERS.
1560	℟ ℝ	Elizabethan communion cup : Snave Church, Kent.
c. 1640	ℝ	Mark stamped in bowl, and thrice on stem of seal-top spoon : Mr. H. D. Ellis.

John Cresswell of Rochester is mentioned in records as a goldsmith there *c.* 1710.

SANDWICH.

The town mark of the goldsmiths of Sandwich—one of the Cinque Ports—was a lion passant and a ship's hull, both dimidiated and conjoined. The device was taken from the arms of the Cinque Ports, which are composed of the three lions of England dimidiated with the hulls of three ships, as found in the Mayor's seal, which is here illustrated.

SEAL OF THE MAYOR OF SANDWICH.

On the only known example of Sandwich plate the town mark is found between two other marks—an apple slipped, and a serrated leaf, also slipped, as illustrated below :—

These marks occur on a communion cup shaped like a miniature baptismal font, at St. Mary's, Sandwich. The date of the cup is about the end of the 15th or early part of the 16th century ; Lord Swaythling owns one of similar form with London Hall-marks for 1500-1 ; another is used as a communion cup at Wymeswold in Leicestershire. Each of these cups has an inscription in plain Lombardic lettering round the vertical side of the bowl, that of Sandwich being "THIS IS THE COMMVNION COVP'. Neither the Sandwich nor the Wymeswold cup was originally an ecclesiastical vessel ; both were probably given to the respective churches some time after the Reformation, perhaps in the reign of Edward VI., and the above words then engraved. Before 1547 such a cup would not have been called a communion cup. The name of Christopher or Coper Johnson, of Sandwich, Goldsmyth, appears in *Letters and Papers Foreign and Domestic of the Reign of Henry VIII*. It is possible that he was the maker of the abovementioned communion cup, but no evidence of that has been found.

29

LEICESTER.

There were goldsmiths working in Leicester in the 16th and 17th centuries as proved by the following entries extracted from the Books of the Leicester Corporation :—

"1541.—Item paid to *Thomas Goldsmith* ffor mending of the Town Waytes collars ... ... liij^s· iiij^d·

1576-7.—Item paid to *Dod the Goldsmith* for xv^{ten} ounces of silver for the Waytes collars and for mendinge or making of them new ... ... vli^s· x^d·

1593-4.—Item p^d to *John Woodward goldsmythe* for mendinge and gyldinge of the olde mace ... xiij^s· iiij^d·

Item p^d to hym for makinge and gyldinge of Twoe of the lesser maces ... ... xvj^s·

Item p^d to hym for iij ounces & a halfe of old sylver for making the said two maces stronger ... ... xv^s·

Item p^d to hym for flyers (*scrolls*) for the said ij maces wch were wantinge ... ... iij^s· vj^d·

1601.—Item p^d to the *Goldsmiths* for mending the Wayts collors or Chaynes & the olde Town Mace ... ... xiij^s· iiij^d·"

One *Robert*, a goldsmith, is also found mentioned in 1554.

The name of *John Turvile*, written also Turvill and Turville, a Leicester goldsmith, appears in the accounts of the Leicester Corporation in 1647-8, 1650 and 1659-60, with reference to the making of a new mace, altering others and making seals.

The Leicester goldsmiths, although capable of executing work of an unimportant character, do not appear to have been equal to re-making the large Corporation mace for which the order was given to Mr. John Turvile in 1650. Turvile entrusted the work to Thomas Maundy, of the Grasshopper, in Foster Lane, London, who had made the Parliament mace a short time before that. The Corporation accounts with reference to this matter are as follows :—

"1649-50.—Item paid to John Turvile ffor the newe Mace wayhinge 87·0 ounces and 12dwt., besides screws and pins and staffe att a 11s. p. oz., more than were made of the old mace as apps. by bill ... ... xxxiij. xvij. vj.

Item paid to John Turvile for carriage of the Mace and his charge to London and paines and care taken about the making of the Newe Mace by order of the commissioners ... ... iij. vj. viij."

The sum of £33 17s. 6d. being what Turvile paid Maundy, and the other amount—£3 6s. 8d.—Turvile appears to have received for his own services.

In 1660, Turvile was paid a further sum of £45 for four small new maces, and for "making the great mace new and guilding it all over with gold, with a globe and crosse and ye King's Arms on it," (consequent upon the restoration of Charles II. in that year), "£41 being paid by him to the London goldsmith, and £4 for his own pains; he having been a month away from home on the matter".

The plate actually made by the Leicester goldsmiths appears to have been limited to spoons and cups of the plainer sort, many of which have been found in different parts of the county.

On the subject of "Spoons," the following occurs in the Hall-book of Leicester relating to the "Merchant-Gild," under date 1599-1600:—

"Willm Heyricke, late of London, Goldsmythe, now of Bewmanor, in the Countie of Leic. esquier, and one of the sonnes of Mr. John Heyricke, Ironmonger, decessed, made free, for the wch he dothe give to the Town in Kyndenes one dozen of sylver spoones wth the sinckefyle upon the knobbes thereof."

The following occurs in the accounts of 1650-1 :—" Item paid John Turvile for exchanging the old silver spoones and for six new spoones & for engraving them iiij*li* ix*d*.".

The "sinckefyle" mentioned above, is the *cinquefoil* borne on the coat of arms of the Borough of Leicester, which has appeared in the seal of the borough for several centuries. With reference to one of these seals, the following entry occurs in the borough accounts for 1593-4 :—" Item p^d for a sinckefoyle of sylver to seale capyacs * wth all...... iiijs."

The cinquefoil is as represented below, in which form it appears in a circular brass badge preserved in the Leicester Museum.

SCALE ½ LINEAR.

The cinquefoil is in the centre of the badge, and is surrounded with a ring bearing the inscription :—

" EDMVND SVTTON MAIOR OF LEICESTER ANNO 1676."

* "Capyacs" is probably a corruption of *capias*, a writ.

A cinquefoil of similar form occurs on a waits' badge of 1695-6, with the legend " BVRGVS LEICESTRVE ".

A cinquefoil after the form of the above badge, more or less modified at different times, was used by Leicester goldsmiths as their town mark in the 16th and 17th centuries as appears below ; the dates mentioned are approximate :—

EXAMPLES OF LEICESTER MARKS.

DATE.	MARKS.	ARTICLES AND OWNERS.
1540		Spoon, with " Dyamond " point at end of stem : Mr. E. W. Colt.
1590		Maidenhead spoon : Mr. J. H. Walter.
1600		Seal-top spoon : Mr. H. D. Ellis. The same mark, with the addition of L.R. in monogram, on a seal-top spoon : Mr. Letts.
„		Seal-top spoon : Mr. H. D. Ellis.
1575 to 1600		Communion cups : Thurnby, Welham, and 15 other Churches in Leicestershire.
1630		Seal-top spoon, pricked 1631 : Mr. H. D. Ellis.
„		Do. do. : Messrs. Christie.

The following short list contains the names of all the Leicester goldsmiths of the 16th and 17th centuries which the Author has been able to trace.

NAMES OF LEICESTER GOLDSMITHS.

FROM 1541 TO 1695.

NAME OF GOLDSMITH.	Mentioned.	NAME OF GOLDSMITH.	Mentioned.
Thomas "Goldsmith"	1541	John Woodward	1593
Robert "Goldsmith"	1554	John Turville	1638-60
Robert Dodd	1576	John Lee	1695

CARLISLE.

The late Mr. R. S. Ferguson, F.S.A., who was Chancellor of the Diocese of Carlisle, discovered in or about the year 1880 a number of communion cups in Cumberland and Westmorland churches which, from the similarity of their workmanship, were attributed to the same hand, and, from the rudeness of the work, to some local silversmith. Some of these cups bear the marks illustrated in the first line of the examples of Carlisle marks, and are believed to be of about the date " 1571," which is inscribed on the cover of one of the cups.

The marks on these cups are, as will be observed : (1) the maker's mark, composed of the two letters ED in monogram in a rounded stamp— believed to be the mark of Edward Dalton ; (2) a four-petalled rose—also in a circular stamp ; and (3) the second mark repeated. The arms of Carlisle are : *or, a cross pattée between four roses, gules, charged with a similar rose of the field.* A single rose, doubtless taken from the ancient arms of the city, has long been used by the Corporation of Carlisle as a stamp for weights and measures, and would in all probability have been used for authenticating the standard of wrought silver.

That there were goldsmiths and silversmiths in Carlisle in the 16th century is proved by the fact that the full title of the Smiths' Guild is " The Ancient ffraternite of Blacksmiths, Whitesmiths, Goldsmiths and Silversmiths " whose rules appear in a revise made in the year 1562. This guild of associated hammermen continued in existence in Carlisle for two centuries after the time of Queen Elizabeth, and apprentices who were bound to members of the guild continued, down to the year 1728, to be taught—in pursuance of a covenant in their indentures —the " trade, faculty, mistery, and occupation of a blacksmith, whitesmith and goldsmith ". After 1644, however, very little goldsmiths' work appears to have been executed in Carlisle. In 1660 the city maces had to be sent to Newcastle to be repaired, and it appears clear that before the end of the 17th century the art of manufacturing gold and silver wares at Carlisle had become extinct.

That the rose was a Carlisle mark was strongly believed by Mr. Ferguson. His belief is supported by the fact that a similar rude rose is found struck on the siege pieces which were minted in Carlisle, and since the 27th of June, 1883, when Mr. Ferguson drew attention to these marks in a paper read at a meeting of the Cumberland Archæological Society at Kirkby Lonsdale, they have been accepted by antiquaries as Carlisle marks.

EXAMPLES OF CARLISLE MARKS.

(THE DATES ARE APPROXIMATE.)

DATE.	MARKS.	ARTICLES AND OWNERS.
1571	🔵 🔵 🔵	Communion cups: Bolton, Ireby and Lazonby, Cumb., and Cliburn, and Long Marton, Westmor.
1630	🔵	Seal-top spoon: Mr. H. D. Ellis.
,,	🔵 🔵	Spoon, slipped in the stalk: Mr. W. Boore.
1670	🔵	Do. flat stem, foliated end: The Goldsmiths' Company, London.

GATESHEAD.

The Gateshead mark, a goat's head erased in a circular stamp, and a maker's mark " A F " with an annulet between the letters, both stamps repeated as illustrated below, are found on a tankard and christening mug, of about 1680, belonging to Sir Robert Mowbray, Bart. The tankard has engraved on it the arms of a Northumbrian lady named Reed, who was married to one of Sir Robert's ancestors in 1738, and brought an estate in the county, together with the tankard and mug, into the Mowbray family. A goat was called a "gate" by Spenser, and in the North of England as late as the time when the Mowbray tankard and mug were made, the term "gates head" would be equally applicable to the head of a goat and the name of the town. Hence the representation of a goat's head is found on the 17th century token of a Gateshead tradesman named John Bedford,* and carved on a chair of the year 1666 in the Gateshead Parish Church. A goat's head is also represented on a torse over a castellated gateway on the seal of the borough.

EXAMPLE OF GATESHEAD MARKS.

c. 1680	🔵 🔵 🔵 🔵	On a tankard and a mug inscribed " Ex dono XXX." : Sir Robert Mowbray, Bart.

The Author has not discovered the name of the goldsmith who bore the initials " A F " nor the name of any other early Gateshead goldsmith.

* Boyne—*Tokens of the 17th Century*—" John Bedford, who was a draper, was one of the *Four and Twenty of Gateshead* nominated by the Protector in 1658, in place of others who were ejected for profanity and divers other crimes."

LEEDS.

The mark of the golden fleece found on communion cups at Almondbury and Darrington, and on other plate in Yorkshire, is ascribed to Leeds, not because the plate on which the mark is stamped is found in that neighbourhood, but for the reason that the badge of the golden fleece appears on the seal of the borough, dated 1626, as well as on one of an earlier date. It appears also in the town arms: *azure, the golden fleece, on a chief sable three mullets argent*. As before observed, it was the common practice amongst provincial goldsmiths, long before the Act of 1700, to adopt the arms of their town, or one of its charges, as their town mark. The Author has not been able to obtain the name of any Leeds goldsmith of the 17th century other than that of Arthur Mangey, who, according to Mr. St. John Hope, made the town mace in 1694, and was hanged at York in 1696 for clipping and forging the current coin of the realm. The names of the goldsmiths whose marks appear below are therefore not suggested. The plate on which the marks are stamped, in each case, appears to belong to the 17th century, although one of the patens is dated as late as 1702.

EXAMPLES OF LEEDS MARKS.

DATE.	MARKS.	ARTICLES AND OWNERS.
1650		Communion cup: Almondbury, Yorks, and other Yorkshire plate.
TO		
1702		*Paten, dated 1702: Harewood, Yorks; and other Yorkshire plate.
„	„ „	The TS in monogram mark stamped thrice on communion cup: Darrington, Yorks.
1660		Maker perhaps R. Williamson of York. Maker's mark struck once, the fleece twice, on flat-topped tankard: Judge A. Clearwater, New York.
1680	„	Trifid spoon: Mr. J. H. Walter.
1690		Do. do. made by Arthur Mangey (see above): Mr. J. H. Walter.
„	„	Beaker: Mr. D. T. Davis.

* This mark bears a strong resemblance to the mark of Timothy Skottowe, illustrated on page 444 *ante*, which makes it seem possible that Skottowe may have worked at Leeds as well as at Norwich and Lincoln.

KING'S LYNN.

The arms of King's Lynn are : *azure, three dragons' heads erect, each pierced with a cross crosslet, or ;* in allusion to St. Margaret, whose figure—standing on a dragon and holding in her right hand a long cross with which she is piercing the dragon in the mouth—is borne on the town seal, believed to date from the year 1300. The town mark of the goldsmiths of King's Lynn was a stamp containing the arms as above described in a plain shield. In the marks here represented, the charges appear more like the heads of congers than of dragons, but in so small a mark one would not expect to find the teeth and other features of a dragon's head portrayed with minute exactness. The maker's mark illustrated last below has been struck deeply on the sinister side, but on the dexter side it is quite shallow and worn; the first letter, however, seems to be H, the second is certainly W. The name of the goldsmith, whose mark it is, is not known. The TS in monogram may be compared with a somewhat similar mark illustrated in the table of Lincoln Marks, page 444. See also the footnote at the bottom of the preceding page.

EXAMPLES OF KING'S LYNN MARKS.

DATE.	MARKS.	ARTICLES AND OWNERS.
1632		Communion cup and paten cover (inscribed : " Elizabeth Wilton gave 40s. and Mary Griffin gave 10s. toured this bowle for the parish Church of Middleton in Norfolke Anno Dom. 1632 ") : Middleton near King's Lynn.
1635	,,	Communion cup (inscribed : " The Quest of Thomas Clarke to the Church of Barmar) : Bagthorpe * near King's Lynn.
1640	,,	Communion paten : St. Nicholas Chapel, King's Lynn. ,, cup of slender shape on baluster stem : St. Etheldreda's, Southgate, Norwich.

* The Parish Churches (livings) of Bagthorpe and Barmar are held by the same incumbent.

TAUNTON.

The mark T and a tun (T on tun) too obviously stands for Taunton to require any argument to support it.   Even in the absence of any evidence directly proving that rebus to be the town mark of the Taunton goldsmiths, it may well be accepted as such, in view of the facts that there is a paten dated 1676 so marked at Wooton Courtney Church in Somersetshire (within an easy distance of the county town), that spoons with this mark have been found in other parts of Somersetshire with inscribed dates ranging from 1670 to 1690, and that Somersetshire antiquarians are agreed in ascribing this mark to Taunton.

The Author has found this mark with the initials of three distinct makers, viz., T.D., S.R. and I.S., but has not discovered the names of the goldsmiths to whom they pertain.   The marks illustrated in the first three lines below occur on apostle spoons, bearing every appearance of having been wrought between the years 1640 and 1650.   The other marks have been found on spoons and a paten ranging in date from about 1660 to 1689.   The marks are illustrated in *facsimile* in the table, the dates given being, of course, approximate.

EXAMPLES OF TAUNTON MARKS.

DATE (ABOUT).	MARKS.			ARTICLES AND OWNERS.
1645	🛡	TD	g	Apostle spoons : Mr. E. W. Colt and Dunn-Gardner Collection.
,,	,,	SR		Do. do. : Mr. Crichton.
,,		TD		Do. do. : Mr. S. Phillips.
1660	🛡			Seal-top spoon : Mr. A. Trapnell.
1676-82	B	🛡	B	{ Paten, dated 1676 : Wooton Courtney, Somerset. { Spoon, flat stem, foliated end, pricked " 1682 " : South Kensington Museum.
1689	IS	🛡	IS	Apostle spoon, engraved 1689 : Messrs. Crichton.

BARNSTAPLE.

Judged by existing records, Barnstaple ranks very little later than Exeter in having goldsmiths established within its boundaries, for in A.D. 1370, Hugh Holbrook, goldsmith, and Alice, his wife, are mentioned in the Borough Records * with reference to bequests to the Wardens of the lights of St. Mary and to the Wardens of the lights of SS. Peter and Paul in the Parish Church.   From that time onwards, till the end of the 17th century, mention is found at short intervals of goldsmiths who worked in the town.   John Frend, a goldsmith, was Mayor in A.D. 1426, 1428 and 1430.   The *Receiver's Accounts* of 1477 record a payment to Adrian Goldsmith for repairing the Maces, and in the 16th century there was carried on at Barnstaple a very considerable business in the manufacture of silver plate, Barnstaple being the only town in Devonshire other than Exeter in which goldsmiths were then registered; the number registered there in the year 1571 was six, as compared with twelve in Exeter, six in Bristol and four in Taunton.

The following list contains the names of Barnstaple goldsmiths and the years during which they worked, as chronologically arranged by the Rev. J. F. Chanter after searching the Borough Records.

Hugh Holbrook .	1370.	Richard Lovering .	1630-1632.
John Frend .	1420-1430.	John Seldon .	1642-1680.
Adrian Goldsmith.	c. 1477.	Richard Punchard .	1645-1660.
Symon Hill .	1548-1596.	John Peard ? I. .	c. 1650.
Thomas Mathew .	1563-1611.	Raleigh Clapham .	1650-1676.
John Coton or Cotton	1567-1601.	John Peard, II. .	1662-1680.
Peter Quick, I. .	1571-1610.	John Peard, III..	1680-1699.
Richard Diamond .	1572.	John Smith .	1682-1708.
John Davy .	1575-1581.	Henry Servanté .	1692-1738.
J. Parnell .	c. 1579-1590.	Francis Servanté .	1694-1700.
Peter Quick, II. .	1600-1623.	Peter Arno .	1710-1735.
Robert Mathew .	1622-1632.		

The most celebrated of all the goldsmiths who are known to have worked in Barnstaple is Thomas Mathew.   He worked there for forty-eight years and examples of his work are to be seen in most of the parishes in the neighbourhood of Barnstaple, and also in other parishes in Devon and Cornwall.   Much of the plate wrought by him bears, in addition to being stamped with his name, the mark of a flower or fruit on

---

* *Receiver's Accounts*, No. 2016.   See *The Barnstaple Goldsmiths' Guild*, by the Rev. J. F. Chanter, to whom the author is indebted for nearly all the information with reference to the goldsmiths of Barnstaple herein contained.

a slipped and leaved stalk which, it has been thought, is intended as a representation of a pomegranate, the device portrayed in the Tregoney arms. Because of that mark it has been suggested that Mathew was a native of Tregoney, but no evidence has been found to confirm that suggestion. Having lived and worked at Barnstaple for nearly fifty years and being mentioned as one of the Barnstaple Burgesses in 1587, 1589, 1592, 1594 and 1596 there can be no doubt that he is properly described as a Barnstaple goldsmith.

The next in rank to Mathew is John Coton (or Cotton) of whose work a number of examples of the Elizabethan period are still in existence, and of others of the late Tudor and early Stuart period mentioned in the above list it may be said that their work was largely influenced by that of Mathew and Coton.

There are no less than three goldsmiths of the name of John Peard mentioned in the Borough Records for the latter half of the 17th century. Examples of marks attributed to one or other of them will be found illustrated in the table of Barnstaple marks.

The earliest Barnstaple town mark found on wrought silver is a bird in a circular stamp, adopted from the Borough seal (as here illustrated),

SEALS OF THE BOROUGH OF BARNSTAPLE.

said to have been in use from A.D. 1272 till 1624-5. From 1625 until the end of the 17th century, the mark of a triple-turreted tower (as here illustrated) was granted to Barnstaple as its arms, and, in a modified form, was used as the town mark. In the earlier forms of this mark the castle has a large doorway with a portcullis lowered; in the later ones the letters B A R appear above the castle and V M below it, making BARUM, the shortened form of Barnstaple.

BARNSTAPLE MARKS.

DATE (ABOUT).	MARKS.	MAKER'S NAME.	ARTICLES AND OWNERS.
1568-1601	IC	John Coton.	Chalice: Abbotsham.
c. 1570-75	M	Thos. Mathew.	Noted by the Author.
1576	T MATEV	,, ,,	Communion cup, dated 1576: St. Genny's, Bude. / Lion-sejant spoon: Messrs. Christie.
1578	D COTON	J. Coton.	Com. cup: Stoke-Rivers, near Barnstaple.
1580	M MATEV	T. Mathew.	Seal-top spoons: Mr. W. Boore.
,,	IC	*J. Coton.	Communion cup: Tresmere. / Spoon with cherub's head: Mr. J. H. Walter.
1584	I COTON	,, ,,	Communion cup: Morwenstow, Bude.
c. 1650	I·P	John Peard	Tankard: Noted by the Author.
1670-80	IP I·P IP	,, ,,	Spoon with flat stem: From the Temple-Frere Collection.
1680	IP	,, ,,	Porringer of about 1680 but pricked 1703: Noted by the Author. / Com. paten and flagon: St. Ewe, Cornwall.
1687	IP	,, ,,	Trifid spoon, pricked 1687: Noted by the Author.
1695	I·P	,, ,,	Trifid spoon, pricked 1695: Noted by the Author.

* The mark of John Coton is also found on spoons bearing the Barnstaple town mark.

MARKS OF LOCAL MAKERS FOUND ON PLATE IN DEVON AND CORNWALL.

The Rev. Canon Mills, Rector of St. Stephen-in-Brannel, Cornwall, who has prepared for publication a catalogue of ecclesiastical plate in the Diocese of Truro, has very kindly furnished the Author with impressions of a number of marks not hitherto published which had been noted on plate in that diocese. Included in those impressions are several Local Marks found only in or near the Truro diocese.

In collecting particulars with reference to the Makers of Cornish Plate, Canon Mills was, after a diligent search, unable to find any evidence of the existence of an Assay Office in Cornwall, or that any mark which might fairly be called a "Cornish Town Mark" was ever in general use.

Many of the goldsmiths and silversmiths who worked in Devon and Cornwall appear to have used a private mark as well as their initials and/or their names, and although the crowned X may be properly described as the Exeter Town Mark, it differs slightly in form as found stamped on the works of Exeter makers of the Elizabethan period, and it is therefore not improbable that—even in the case of plate stamped with an Exeter mark—the punch with which the mark was impressed may have belonged to the silversmith who wrought the plate and not to the Assay Office.

In the following groups, a number of goldsmiths' marks found on plate in Devon and Cornwall (other than the marks pertaining to Exeter and Barnstaple), are illustrated, but the names of the goldsmiths whose marks are there represented have not been traced. In the first group are representations of an animal which the Author thought, when writing the first edition of this work, was intended to portray an elephant, but having carefully compared a number of similar marks found on Devon and Cornwall plate, it has become obvious that the mark referred to is the representation of a pig with a bell pendent from its neck. Accompanying this pig-and-bell mark is the letter T, and as the pig, bell and Tau cross are emblems of St. Anthony, the suggestion of Mr. H. D. Ellis that the marks were in some way connected with the name of Anthony was accepted by a number of Antiquaries when it became known that one Edward Anthony worked in Exeter as a goldsmith in the first half of the 17th century; these marks are now ascribed to Edward Anthony, as well as marks on plate assayed at Exeter illustrated in Tables II. and III. of the Exeter marks. Nearly all of these Anthony marks have been found stamped on the stems of spoons, on several of which the mark TR in monogram is stamped in the bowl. This covened TR mark has been ascribed by Mr. Ellis to Truro. Should that ascription be correct, the monogram was probably used by Edward Anthony as an indication of the spoons having been wrought by him in that city, or perhaps for one who resided there. As no evidence has yet been found of that or any other mark having been in general use as a Truro mark, its ascription by the Author to Truro is merely tentative.

EXAMPLES OF TRURO MARKS. (See page 461.)

DATE (ABOUT).	MARKS.	ARTICLES AND OWNERS.
1560 / 1600		In bowl of apostle spoon : The Author's Collection.
,,		{ Massive seal-top spoon : Do. do. { Also on many spoons in other collections.
,,	,, ,,	Seal-top spoons : Mr. H. D. Ellis and others.
1600		Baluster-topped spoon : Messrs. Crichton.
1620		TR in monogram in bowl, the other marks on stem of spoon with lion-sejant terminal : Mr. H. D. Ellis.
,,		An anchor (one of the Saltash bearings or devices) in bowl, the pig mark on stem, of spoon with baluster and seal top : Mr. H. D. Ellis.
,,		Seal-top spoon : The Author's Collection.
1630	,,	Spoon : Mr. Du Cane.

EXAMPLES OF DEVON AND CORNWALL LOCAL MAKERS' MARKS.

DATE. (ABOUT).	MARKS.	ARTICLES AND OWNERS.
1576-80		Communion cups at St. Levan, Sancreed, Morvah, St. Ives, St. Hilary, Wendron, and St. Anthony, West Cornwall.
,,		Mark resembles a bunch of grapes. Communion cup : St. Columb Minor, Cornwall.
1580		Chalice of Exeter pattern : Wembworthy, Devon.
? c. 1600		Patens : St. Anthony-in-Meneage, and several other parishes in West Cornwall.

DEVON AND CORNWALL LOCAL MAKERS' MARKS (*continued*).

DATE. (ABOUT).	MARKS.	ARTICLES AND OWNERS.
c. 1600-30		Stamped twice on communion cup : St. Erth, Cornwall.
,,		Communion cup and paten : St. Eval, Cornwall.
,,		Paten : St. Hilary, Cornwall. The larger mark is on the flat part of paten, and the smaller mark on foot.
,,		Paten : Kenwyn, Cornwall.
,,		Spirally-fluted porringer : Gerrans, Cornwall.
,,		Embossed spoon, flat stem, trifid end : Mr. J. H. Walter.
1610		Com. cup and paten : North Hill Church, Cornwall.
1610-50		Do. do. do. cover : Treaeglos, Cornwall.
1630		{Do. do. : Liskeard, Cornwall. / {Apostle spoon : Mr. J. H. Walter.
1641		Com. cup and paten, dated 1641 : St. Ives, Cornwall.
1650 / 1700		{Do. do. do. do. cover : St. Wenn. / {Do. do. : St. Erwun, Cornwall.
1675		Paten (inscribed : " Mr. Abraham Heiman of this towne gave this plate to the Church in the year '75 ") : Bideford.
1680-5		Spoon, flat stem, trifid end, pricked 1684 : Mr. J. H. Walter.
1690		ID conjoined, stamped thrice on paten : West Putford, Devon.
1695		Communion cup and paten, dated 1695 ; also on flagon, dated 1712 : Paul Church, Cornwall.
,,		Struck thrice on beaker : St. Ervan, Cornwall.
1700		The R H stamped thrice, the B once, on com. plate with engraved date 1701 : Mevagissey, Cornwall. Probably mark of Richard Holin of Truro, who registered his mark at Exeter in 1704. The B may indicate Britannia standard.
1715		Probably mark of Richard Plint of Truro. Com. paten (dated 1719) St. Enoder. Also com. cup and paten (dated 1728) : St. Clement, Truro.

PLYMOUTH.

When the first edition of this work was being compiled, the Author had found no Plymouth-marked plate of earlier date than about the end of the 17th century, but he has recently noted two spoons of the Elizabethan period, each of which is stamped in the bowl with a mark representing the arms of the Borough of Plymouth : *a saltire between four castles*, as illustrated below.   Mr. Dudley Westropp has found the name Barsie or Bardsly mentioned as that of a goldsmith of Plymouth in the Lismore Papers, *c.* 1603-28.   A flat-stemmed spoon, with trifid end, of the late Stuart period, stamped with the Plymouth arms in a shield, maker's mark HM in monogram, and the word *Sterling*, as illustrated below, has been submitted to the Author by Mr. Frederick Bradbury.

The marks of one Rowe of Plymouth occur on the " Eddystone Lighthouse" salt,* and a tankard, of about 1699, and are illustrated below. The standing salt—probably one of the last made of the old form of upright salts—is a miniature reproduction in silver of Winstanley's lighthouse, which was built on the Eddystone rock in 1698, considerably altered in the following year, and completely destroyed in the storm of November, 1703.   The marks on the salt, which have been reproduced with the greatest possible care so as to ensure accuracy, and represented below in *facsimile*, are " Rowe Plm° BritAN," and not Plin°, as stated in *Old English Plate*.   The salt cannot well be earlier than 1698, the date of the building of the lighthouse, nor later than the date of the re-establishment in 1701 of the Exeter assay office, or it would have been assayed and marked there, in common with the work of R. Wilcocks, P. Symonds, and Tolcher, of Plymouth.   These marks may, therefore, be safely ascribed to 1698-1700.   The second group occurs on a tankard with flat cover, which, although by the same maker, bears marks of a different form ; the name " Rowe" has the " e " carried to the top of " Row," " Plm° " is changed to " Ply°," and instead of " Britan" the stamp " N$\overset{\text{St.}}{\text{ew}}$ " appears. Both examples must have been wrought about the same time, and from the fact that in the case of the tankard marks the standard is described as New Standard (New St), while in the lighthouse stamps the standard is described by the technical term " Britan " (for " Britannia "), it may be suggested that the tankard marks are the earlier and were struck in 1697, immediately after the introduction of the new standard, before it became technically known as the Britannia standard.   Both of these marks indicate the higher standard of 11 oz. 10 dwts. fine.

* This salt is illustrated and fully described on page 564 of the author's *History of English Plate*.

A number of Plymouth goldsmiths entered their names at the Exeter assay office from early in the 18th century, as will be seen by reference to the List of Exeter Goldsmiths, pages 343-5 *ante*.

William Pope, a goldsmith whose mark is recorded with reference to table plate assayed at Exeter in 1833-4, and is illustrated in Table IX. of Exeter marks, also worked in Plymouth, where he had a house and workshop in King Street, and wrought plate for other gold and silversmiths who carried on the business of dealers in wrought gold and silver in the West of England.

EXAMPLES OF PLYMOUTH MARKS.

DATE.	MARKS.	ARTICLES AND OWNERS.
c. 1600		In bowls of two spoons with Vishnu knops: Noted by the Author. Apostle spoon: Dr. Wilfred Harris.
1690-5		Spoon, flat stem, trifid end: Messrs. Crichton.
1695-9		Spoon, flat stem, foliated end, embossed ornamentation, dated 1699: Mr. J. H. Walter.
,,		Spirally fluted mug, riband handle: Mr. J. H. Walter.
c. 1694		Flat stem spoon, with trifid end, pricked 1694: Messrs. Page, Keen, and Page, Plymouth.
1698 to 1700		The "Eddystone Lighthouse" salt belonging to Miss Rous, of Cwrt-yr-Ala, Glam. Flat-top tankard: Mr. Crichton.

BRISTOL.

Although Bristol ("Bristow") was mentioned in the Act of 1423 as one of the towns appointed "to have divers touches," the Author has been unable to glean any information concerning either its mediæval goldsmiths or their touch. It seems very extraordinary that a city of such wealth and importance, with a mint established within its walls from very early times, should have been without a guild of goldsmiths, while in other towns of much less importance the mystery or craft of the goldsmiths not only existed but flourished. Further, it appears remarkable that Bristol should again be mentioned nearly three

30

centuries later—in the Act of 170^0_1—as one of the towns appointed to have assay offices, and that no trace of either an assay office or guild of goldsmiths should be found.   It is to be hoped that some local antiquary may be sufficiently interested in the subject and sufficiently industrious to make a thorough search of the city archives for some reference to the subject.

All that is at present known is that the late Mr. R. C. Hope, F.S.A., discovered in 1880 in the Temple Church, Bristol, a perforated silver straining spoon bearing the following marks: (1) R G ; (2) the letter A in a pointed shield ; (3) a lion passant guardant ; (4) a leopard's head crowned ; and (5) an oblong punch-mark bearing the arms of the city of Bristol—*a ship issuing from a castle.*   This discovery Mr. Hope communicated to the late Mr. Cripps, who dismissed the matter with the remark that "it seems almost certain that Bristol never exercised the power of assaying plate.   There are some anomalous marks on a spoon at the Temple Church, Bristol, which might be taken for Bristol hall-marks, but the civic archives do not record the establishment of any goldsmiths' company nor the swearing in of any assay-master before the mayor, as prescribed by the Act."

About twelve years after Mr. R. C. Hope's discovery of the Bristol spoon, a Bond Street dealer submitted to Mr. W. H. St. John Hope, M.A. (Sec. Soc. Antiq.), and to the Author, for their respective opinions, a milk-jug, bearing five marks, the 1st, 3rd, 4th and 5th being exactly like those on the above-mentioned spoon, but having, instead of the letter A—the second mark on the spoon—a capital-letter B, in a pointed shield similar to that enclosing the A on the spoon.

The Author has made numerous inquiries with the object of ascertaining the possibility of some origin other than Bristol for these marks.   It was suggested that Cork may have been the place, but a ship is never seen issuing from behind a castle in any Cork mark, and no variable alphabetical marks were ever used there.   The late Mr. R. Day had in his possession an old buckle, badge and medal, dated 1814, pertaining to the Bristol militia, with a ship and castle almost identical in drawing with the ship and castle mark on the spoon.   Can it be doubted, in view of the fact that the spoon so marked was found with the communion plate of the Temple Church, Bristol, where it was believed to have been for generations, that the marks are Bristol marks, and that the letters A and B respectively are date-letters?   The form of the spoon—Hanoverian pattern, with a ridge along the centre of stem in front and a double drop at back of bowl—indicates its date to be about 1730, and the tall bulbous shape of the plain milk-jug shows that to be of about the same date. In the face of such evidence as that above-mentioned it does not seem likely that "Bristol never exercised the power of assaying plate" when it appears almost unquestionably to have marked it.

EXAMPLES OF BRISTOL MARKS.

DATE.	MARKS.	ARTICLES AND OWNERS.
c. 1730	RG A	Straining spoon : Temple Church, Bristol.
c. 1731	,, B ,, ,, ,,	Milk-jug : Mr. Crichton.
c. 1780-90	FEL XOJ SALMON	Reeded-edged gravy spoon, with oval (not pointed) bowl and pointed oval end to stem: Noted by the Author.

DORSETSHIRE.

Dorsetshire is particularly rich in the work of its local goldsmiths, about fifty examples of Elizabethan and Jacobean work, proved by their marks to have been of local origin, having been found within and closely adjacent to the county. Some of these are referred to in the English unascribed marks, page 475 *infra*.

DORCHESTER.

The three following marks are those of Lawrence Stratford, a Dorchester goldsmith, mentioned in the Dorchester Corporation and other local records from 1579 to 1593. His marks are a monogram formed of the raised letters L.S. within a ring of small pellets, a small rudely-formed incuse mullet of six points on one side, and a small saltire cross, also incuse, on the other. These marks were found by the late Mr. J. E. Nightingale, F.S.A., on communion plate (dated from 1573 to 1578) in more than thirty parish churches in Dorset, Wilts and Somerset.

DORCHESTER MARKS.

Mark of Lawrence Stratford, of Dorchester.		Communion cup and paten cover (dated 1574) : West Purley ; and (dated 1575) : Bothenhampton ; and communion plate in many other Dorset churches.

Other Dorchester goldsmiths whose names have been found are John Stratforde, mentioned in the time of Henry VIII., and one Radcliffe, who was fined by the London Goldsmiths' Company in 1617.

SHERBORNE.

The first of the three following marks has been found on about a score of examples of church plate in the county of Dorset and bordering parishes in Somersetshire. Many of such examples are dated, the dates being 1572, 1573, 1574, 1582 and 1607. The marks are all believed to be those of Richard Orenge, a Sherborne goldsmith of the Elizabethan period.

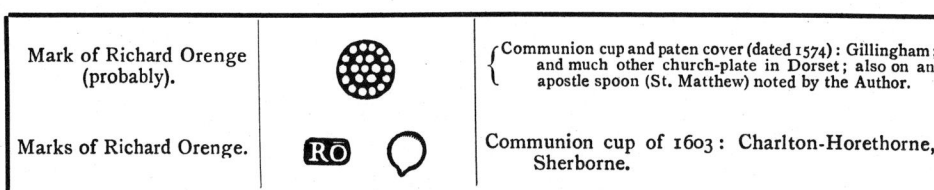

| Mark of Richard Orenge (probably). | | Communion cup and paten cover (dated 1574): Gillingham; and much other church-plate in Dorset; also on an apostle spoon (St. Matthew) noted by the Author. |
| Marks of Richard Orenge. | | Communion cup of 1603: Charlton-Horethorne, Sherborne. |

In connection with these marks, the late Mr. Cripps observed in *Old English Plate* that "it was the example of 1603 at Charlton-Horethorne, Som., which led to the identification of the mark" (referring to that composed of a central pellet surrounded by six other pellets which are again surrounded by a ring of similar pellets, as illustrated above, and which had been found on communion cups at Gillingham, and other churches in Dorset, by Mr. Nightingale) "as that of Richard Orenge". The marks on the Charlton-Horethorne cup were not illustrated in *Old English Plate*, and were in the first edition of this work shown for the first time in *facsimile*. The Author is, therefore, unable to understand how the mark composed of pellets could have been identified by means of the marks on the Charlton-Horethorne cup, which are—there can be very little doubt—the marks of Richard Orenge, of Sherborne, goldsmith, who was churchwarden at Charlton in 1585 and 1596, and whose Will was proved in 1606. The letters R.O. are obviously his initials, and the mark at the side of the initials may be intended for an orange, but in the mark composed of pellets no connection with the identified mark appears. Still, the pelleted mark may be, and probably is, a mark of Richard Orenge, but there is scarcely sufficient evidence to establish it as a fact.

POOLE.

Three escallops in chief occur in the arms of the Borough of Poole. The marks illustrated below, which are found struck in the bowls, and sometimes on the backs of the stems of rather rudely-made apostle and seal-top spoons of the 16th and the early part of the 17th centuries, are probably the marks of Poole goldsmiths.

DATE.	MARKS.	ARTICLES AND OWNERS.
c. 1540		In bowls of maidenhead spoon : Messrs. Crichton.
,,		Seal-top spoon : Messrs. Crichton.
c. 1560		Apostle spoon (St. Paul) : The Author's Collection.
c. 1580		Apostle spoon (St. Mathias) : Mr. F. W. Kell.
,,		Seal-top spoon : Sir E. Marshall Hall, K.C.
c. 1620		Apostle spoon : Mr. J. H. Walter. Do. do. : Holburne Museum, Bath. Do. do., and seal-top spoon : Sir E. Marshall Hall, K.C.

SALISBURY.

Although Salisbury was mentioned in the Act of 1423 as one of the towns appointed to have a "touch" of its own, no plate-marks have been found which can with certainty be ascribed to it. A number of marks, reproduced from plate in various parts of Wilts, are included in the following list of "unascribed marks," some of which may possibly be the marks of Salisbury goldsmiths, but no evidence has as yet been found to prove it. No goldsmiths' names have been discovered in connection with any plate wrought in the city, and no evidence that a guild of goldsmiths was ever established there is obtainable. Sir R. C. Hoare—*Hist. of New Sarum*—says that, in 1665, the great mace of the city was repaired by Mr. Thornborough, goldsmith, of Salisbury, at a cost of £3 10s. ; this is all the information concerning Salisbury goldsmiths which the Author has been able to glean.

The discovery of a number of spoons recently dug up in the course of excavations near Salisbury has led to the marks here illustrated being ascribed to that city.

EXAMPLES OF SALISBURY MARKS.

DATE.	MARKS.	ARTICLES AND OWNERS.
c. 1596		Seal-top spoon (one of seven found near Salisbury), date 1596 pricked on seal end.
,,		Two seal-top spoons (part of above seven) ; one pricked 1596 and EH, the other 1621 and IE.
c. 1620		Seal-top spoon (one of above seven) ; has 1621 and $\frac{MA}{WE}$ pricked on seal end.
,,		Do. do. do. do. ; has 1621 and $\frac{BE}{IE}$ pricked thereon.
c. 1627		Silver-gilt Vishnu-topped spoon ; pricked "S.W.L.P. 1627" : Messrs. Christie.
c. 1629		Seal-top spoon (one of above seven) : has 1629 and $\frac{I.\,I}{B.\,E}$ pricked on seal end.
,,		Do. do. do. do. ; has "$\frac{IS}{EE}$ 1629" pricked on seal end.

COVENTRY.

Coventry appointed to be an Assay-town, in 1423

Although Coventry was one of the seven towns appointed "to have divers touches" by the Act of 1423, very little remains that can be connected with the guild of goldsmiths which flourished there in the Middle Ages. The Corporation at one time possessed a goodly array of plate, consisting of "bason and ewer, high-standing cup with cover double guilt, beer boles, wine boles, dishes, salts, tankards and spoons," but all that now remains of its former display are four pewter plates bearing the Coventry arms. The history of its plate-workers seems to have disappeared almost as completely as its plate ; we, however, find that one John Talance, who was Mayor of the borough in 1544 and again in 1562, was a goldsmith, and there is evidence which proves that goldsmiths' work was executed in the city at various dates in the 16th and 17th centuries. In 1597 the name of Wm. Tonks appears in the city accounts as having been paid 33s. 4d. for gilding the hilt of the new sword ; in 1607 it is recorded that one Bulling was paid 20s. for making and engraving the common seal, which is of silver ; and the name of

Richard Blackwell appears in an account of 1651 for the "great mase" and "the little mase," amounting to £61 14s. 6d., and as the maces have no hall-marks they were probably made by the same Richard Blackwell in Coventry.

When writing the first edition of this work, it was thought by the Author that the marks TR conjoined and the representation of an animal (having the appearance of an elephant in outline) were Coventry marks, but since the publication of the first edition, evidence has been found that the above-mentioned marks had been used by a goldsmith who worked in Devon and Cornwall, who appears to have had no connection with Coventry. The marks referred to have, therefore, in this edition, been placed with others of somewhat similar form in the part of this chapter where marks on silver wrought in Barnstaple and other places in Devon and Cornwall are illustrated and described (see pp. 461-2).

The Coventry "town mark".

COLCHESTER.

The marks R. HUTCHINSON and COLCHESTER, illustrated below, are stamped on a punch ladle of the early Georgian period. It is suggested by these marks that a silversmith of that name worked or carried on business at Colchester in the early part of the 18th century, although no other evidence that the ladle was wrought at Colchester has come to the Author's knowledge. In the absence of any other suggestion as to their origin, the marks are ascribed to Colchester.

EXAMPLE OF COLCHESTER MARKS.

DATE.	MARKS.	ARTICLE AND OWNER.
c. 1723		Marks of R. Hutchinson, on punch ladle engraved T M HA IM: Mr. Fredk. Bradbury. 1723 17 23

THE CHANNEL ISLANDS.

The first three marks illustrated below were, in the first edition of this work, grouped with "Unascribed Irish Provincial Marks," because it was thought that the middle mark may have been intended as a representation of the Harp of Ireland, although it does not resemble the harp-mark stamped on plate assayed at Dublin. Examples of plate, dating, apparently, from about 1690 to 1730, stamped with three similar marks, were about twenty years ago exhibited at the Burlington Fine Arts Club, London, and other places, where they were described as " Dublin-wrought plate," and it is only within the last ten years that through information imparted by Mr. E. R. du Parcq, a goldsmith born at Jersey and now associated with Messrs. Crichton, it has become known to collectors of antique plate and dealers that those marks pertain to the Channel Islands.

The other marks illustrated below are stamped on spoons belonging to Mr. du Parcq and on other plate brought to the Author's notice by him, and the names of the makers here mentioned have been obtained from the same source.

EXAMPLES OF CHANNEL ISLANDS MARKS.

DATE (ABOUT).	MARKS.	ARTICLES AND OWNERS.
GUERNSEY, c. 1690-1730	(three marks)	Small two-handled cups : Dublin Museum and Mr. M. T. Kennard. Chalice : Dominican Convent, Cabra, Channel Islands. Salver, with shell pattern border : Goldsmiths and Silversmiths Co., Ltd. Set of three two-handled cups : Fitzhenry Collection.
c. 1740	(two marks)	Chalice : Messrs. Crichton.
c. 1750	(mark)	Beaker : Do. do.
,,	(mark)	Struck thrice on Cup, with engraved date 1776 : Messrs. Crichton.
,,	I H	Cup : Messrs. Crichton.
,,	I A	Do. do. do.
JERSEY, c. 1760	G B	" Double-drop " table-spoon : Mr. E. R. du Parcq.
c. 1780	G M	Do. do. : Do. do.
,,	(marks)	Jersey marks of J. Le Gallais ; tea-spoons : Do.
c. 1790	P N	Mark stamped thrice on table-spoon : Mr. E. R. du Parcq.
c. 1800	C W Q	Mark of C. W. Quesnel, on table-spoon : Do. do.
,,	I Q	Do. I. Quesnel, on tea-spoons : Do. do.
,,	J . Q	Do. do. do. do. : Do. do.
c. 1830	T.DG J.LG	Do. T. de Gruchy and S. Le Gallais, on tea-spoons : Do.

CALCUTTA.

Although gold and silver wares have doubtless been wrought in India for centuries past, the articles manufactured there have, until about the end of the 18th century, probably been the work of natives of India, or adjoining countries, and do not come within the scope of this work.

The earliest date when silver articles were wrought in India by workers of British origin as to which the Author has been able to obtain information is the year 1808 when the firm of Hamilton & Co. was established in Calcutta by Robert Hamilton under licence from the East India Company. This information was given to the Author by Mr. A. G. Sandeman, J.P. of London and Bexhill-on-Sea, who has in his collection several fine examples of plate stamped with the marks of Hamilton & Co. as illustrated below.

Mr. Frederick Bradbury of Sheffield, who has a spoon similarly marked, received from Messrs. Hamilton & Co., in reply to an inquiry by him, a letter dated 5 March, 1919, stating that the mark on his spoon was theirs and that their mark for over a hundred years had been H. & Co. with an elephant, and that their firm, which was established in 1808, had been carried on continuously ever since by a succession of partners, and has branches in Delhi and Simla.

DATE.	MARKS.	ARTICLES AND OWNERS.
c. 1810	H&Cº [elephant] [urn] A	Mark of Messrs. Hamilton & Co. of Calcutta : Various articles of plate : Mr. A. G. Sandeman ; spoon : Mr. Fredk. Bradbury.
"	A [lion] P&Cº	Mark of Pillar & Co. of Calcutta : per Messrs. Bruford.

EXAMPLES OF JAMAICA MARKS.

DATE.	MARKS.	ARTICLE AND OWNER.
c. 1800	[head] J.EWAN [lion]	Marks on fiddle pattern sugar tongs : Noted by the Author.

UNASCRIBED ENGLISH MARKS.

The following marks have been found on old English plate un-accompanied by any known town mark. It is therefore impossible, except in a few instances, to assign them respectively to particular places. The examples, however, on which the marks have been found appear unmistakably English in character, and the period of their manufacture is indicated by the style, confirmed in some instances by engraved dates. It must, however, be understood that the dates assigned are approximate, and a possible variation of a quarter of a century either way should in some cases be allowed. Many of these marks are, possibly, the marks of pewterers who have made silver spoons for their own use.

DATE (ABOUT).	MARKS.	ARTICLES AND OWNERS.
1500		Spoon with "wrythen knop": The Author's Collection.
,,		The only mark on the "Richmond Cup": The Armourers' Company.
1510		Pre-Reformation chalice and paten: The Author's Collection; S. Kensington Mus. Loan Exhibit.
1520		Spoon (lion sejant top): Mr. H. D. Ellis.
1530		Pre-Reformation paten; Buckhorn Weston Church, Dorset.
,,		Spoon with "dyamond poynt": Messrs. Christie.
1550		Lion sejant spoon: Sir E. Marshall Hall, K.C.
,,		Small scent flask: Victoria and Albert Museum.
1560		{Maidenhead spoon: The Author's Collection. (The mark may be HN, it reads equally well with either side up.)
,,		Apostle spoon (acorn in bowl, RH twice on stem): Major Chichester.
1570		Apostle spoon: Major Chichester.
,,		In bowl of seal-top spoon: Mr. John Vincent.
,,		Mounts of stoneware jug: Messrs. Christie.
1570		Do. do. do.: S. Kensington Museum.

UNASCRIBED ENGLISH MARKS—*Continued.*

DATE (ABOUT).	MARKS.	ARTICLES AND OWNERS.
1570-7		Elizabethan communion cups, dated 1570-6-7: Cricklade, and Somerford-Keynes, Wilts. Also on seven other communion cups of the Elizabethan period, in Gloucestershire and Worcestershire.
"		Elizabethan communion cups, dated 1571; Nethercompton and Upcerne, Dorset.
"		Elizabethan communion cups: Goadby, Leicestershire.
"		Do. do. do. : Walton-le-Wolds, do.
"		Do. do. do. : Dadlington 1573, Sutton Chaney 1575, and Swepston 1577.
1570-80		First mark in bowl, second mark twice on stem of Apostle spoon: Major Chichester.
"		Two finial-topped spoons : Messrs. Crichton.
"		Maidenhead spoon : Messrs. Crichton.
"		Seal-top spoon : Do. do.
"		Baluster-top spoon : Mr. R. Levine, Norwich.
1576	IW	Paten (dated 1576): Bodmin. Also on plate at other Churches in Cornwall.
1580		Seal-top spoon : Holburne Museum, Bath.
"		Maidenhead spoon : per Mr. H. D. Ellis.
"		Silver gilt tazza : The Author's Collection.
"		Spoon with figure of Virgin : Messrs. Spink.
"		Probably a mark of Christopher Hunton of York. Apostle spoon: The Author's Collection.
1590		Spoon (lion-sejant top): Mr. J. H. Walter, Drayton, Norfolk.
"		Elizabethan communion cup: Long Sutton.
"		Spoon (lion-sejant top) : The Author's Collection.
"		Do. do. : Mr. W. Boore.
"		Mount of stoneware jug: The Author's Collection. This mark is found on London-made cups of 1589 and 1590.
"	PARR	* {Spoon (lion-sejant top): Mr. E. W. Colt. Apostle spoon (St. Peter): The Author's Collection.

* Seal-topped spoons and other Elizabethan spoons are found similarly marked, but with PARK or PARN instead of PARR.

UNASCRIBED ENGLISH MARKS—*Continued.*

DATE (ABOUT).	MARKS.	ARTICLES AND OWNERS.
1590		Maidenhead spoon : Mr. Edmund James.
,,		A spray of hawthorn, on communion cup and paten : North Carlton, Lincs.
,,		Apostle spoon : Noted by the Author.
1600		Seal-top spoon : Holburne Museum, Bath.
,,		Do. do. : Messrs. Christie. This mark within a ring of pellets occurs on a seal-top spoon in the collection of Mr. J. H. Walter.
,,		Maidenhead spoon : Mr. H. D. Ellis.
,,		Apostle spoon : The Marquess of Breadalbane, K.G.
,,		Seal-top spoon : Messrs. Christie.
,,		Apostle spoon : Mr. E. W. Colt.
,,		Seal-top spoon : Holburne Museum.
,,		Maidenhead spoon : Mr. J. H. Walter.
,,		Mount of stoneware mug : The Author's Collection.
,,		Maidenhead spoon : Mr. E. Brand.
,,		Apostle spoon : Do.
,,		Communion cup : Bursledon, Hants.
,,		Do. do. : St. Nicholas, Boarhunt, Hants.
,,		Do. do. : Mr. R. Meldrum.
,,		Lion-sejant spoon : Mr. J. H. Walter.
,,		Apostle spoon : Messrs. Spink.
,,		Beaker : Noted by the Author.
,,		Maidenhead spoon : Mr. J. E. Page.
,,		Stamped once in bowl and twice on stem of Apostle spoon : Mr. J. H. Walter.

UNASCRIBED ENGLISH MARKS—*Continued.*

DATE (ABOUT).	MARKS.	ARTICLES AND OWNERS.
1600		Seal-top spoon: Mr. J. H. Walter.
,,		First mark in bowl, second on stem, of seal-top spoon: Mr. S. J. Phillips.
,,		Small wine-cup: Mr. S. Lazarus.
1600-50		Struck thrice on chalice with Norwich-stamped bowl, but stem as London communion cups of c. 1640: Noted by the Author.
1609		Master spoon, pricked 1609: Sir E. Marshall Hall, K.C.
1610		Rose-sprig in bowl, and also lion as London, 1604, on small seal-top spoon: Mr. H. D. Ellis.
,,		Mounts of alabaster scent box: Victoria and Albert Museum.
,,		Seal-top spoon: Noted by the Author.
,,		Do. do. : Mr. H. N. Veitch.
,,		Do. do. (pricked 1611): Messrs. Crichton.
,,		Do. do. : Mr. J. H. Walter.
,,		Do. do. : The Author's Collection.
,,		Do. do. : Mr. E. W. Colt.
1620		Do. do. : Mr. S. Phillips.
,,		Do. do. : Dunn-Gardner Collection.
,,		Do. do. : Mr. W. Boore.
,,		Spoon with baluster and seal end to stem: Mr. Assheton Bennett.
,,		Communion cup: South Stoneham, Hants.
,,		The first mark in bowl, the second and third on stem, of seal-top spoon: Mr. J. H. Walter.
,,		Provincial Buddha-topped spoon, pricked 1624. Mark in bowl, and once on stem: Mr. John Vincent.
,,		Seal-top spoon: Noted by the Author.

UNASCRIBED ENGLISH MARKS—*Continued.*

DATE (ABOUT).	MARKS.	ARTICLES AND OWNERS.
1620		The first mark in bowl, the others on stem : Seal-top spoon lent to Mr. Fredk. Bradbury—suggested as Bristol spoon by owner.
1623		Seal-top spoon, pricked 1623 : Major C. H. Chichester.
1625		Apostle spoon : Messrs. Spink.
1630		Do. do. : British Museum.
,,		Do. do. : Mr. F. W. Kell, and Mr. A. Trapnell.
,,		Large apostle spoon : Messrs. Christie.
,,		Seal-top spoon : Mr. H. D. Ellis.
,,		Spoon, slipped in the stalk : Mr. W. Boore.
,,		Communion cup : St. Martin-cum-Gregory, York.
,,		Seal-top spoon : Dunn-Gardner Collection.
,,		Spoon with Buddha top to stem : Mr. Alan Garnett.
,,		Seal-top spoon : Messrs. Crichton.
,,		Communion flagon and patens : Kingston Deverill and Corsley.
,,		Spoon with Buddha top to stem : Victoria and Albert Museum.
1630-5		Master spoon : Messrs. Crichton.
,,		Seal-top spoon, pricked 1633 : Mr. Arthur W. Stone.
,,		Do. do. : Dunn-Gardner Collection.
,,		Do. do. : British Museum.
,,		Do. do. : Messrs. Christie.
,,		Apostle spoon : Holburne Museum, Bath.
,,		Seal-top spoon : Mr. Crichton. (I.P. in bowl, R over W on stem.)
,,		Apostle spoon : South Kensington Museum.

UNASCRIBED ENGLISH MARKS—*Continued.*

DATE (ABOUT).	MARKS.	ARTICLES AND OWNERS.
1630-5		Seal-top spoon : Mr. Samuel Deane.
,,		Do. do. : Mr. W. Boore.
,,		Apostle spoon : Mr. G. Lambert.
,,		Circular stand for china bowl : Mr. Ball.
,,		Seal-top spoon : Messrs. Crichton.
,,		Communion cup : Oulton, and other Church plate in the County of Suffolk.
1637		Paten, dated 1637 : East Knoyle, near Salisbury.
,,		Chalice, pricked " CPH 1637 " : Mr. Frederick Bradbury.
1638		Alms-box : All Saints, Milford, Hants.
1640		On stem of St. John Apostle spoon : Mr. Vincent. Also on Apostle spoon of 1640 at Holborn Museum, and two belonging to Mr. H. D. Ellis.
,,		Seal-top spoon : Sir E. Marshall Hall, K.C.
,,		Buddha-topped spoon : Do. do.
,,		Spoon, with hoof at end of stem : Dunn-Gardner Collection.
,,		Apostle spoon : Holburne Museum, Bath.
,,		Do. do. : Do. do. do.
,,		*Do. do. : Do. do. do.
,,		Do. do. : Do. do. do.
,,		Do. do. : Do. do. do.
,,		Seal-top spoon : Messrs. Crichton.
,,		(Possibly R. Williamson, of York.) Apostle spoon : Mr. H. D. Ellis.
,,		In bowl and twice on stem of seal-top spoon : Mr. E. Brand.
,,		Seal-top spoon : Mr. Edmund James.
,,		Apostle spoon, pricked " 1647 " : Messrs. Spink.
,,		Do. do. " 1663 " : Do. do.

* Mark of George Reve of Bath, who made Bath tokens of the year 1638.

UNASCRIBED ENGLISH MARKS—*Continued.*

DATE (ABOUT).	MARKS.	ARTICLES AND OWNERS.
1640		Seal-top spoon : Messrs. Crichton.
,,		Do. do. : Holburne Museum, Bath.
,,		Do. do. : Mr. Crichton.
,,		Apostle spoon : Holburne Museum, Bath.
,,		Seal-top spoon : Messrs. Christie.
1640-8		Do. do., dated 1648 : Mr. E. W. Colt.
1640-50		Apostle spoon : Messrs. Spink.
,,		Porringer : Messrs. Christie.
,,		Apostle spoon (1670 pricked on nimbus) : Messrs. Crichton.
,,		Seal-top spoon : Messrs. Christie.
1650		Communion cups : Grateley and Whitsbury, Hants.
,,		Seal-top spoon : Messrs. Crichton.
,,		St. Peter apostle spoon : Mr. J. Bennett Stanford.
,,		Puritan spoon : Noted by the Author.
,,		Late apostle spoon : Major J. Herbert How.
,,		Communion cup : St. Peters, Wherwell, Hants.
,,		Gold communion cup : Chapel Royal, St. James's Palace.
,,		Seal-top spoons : S. Kensington Museum, Mr. J. H. Walter, Mr. H. D. Ellis, and the Author's Collection.
,,		Seal-top spoons, pricked 1652 : Dunn-Gardner Collection.
,,		Do. do. : Dunn-Gardner Collection.
,,		Do. do. : Mr. W. Boore.
,,		Communion cup : Mugginton, Derbyshire.

UNASCRIBED ENGLISH MARKS—*Continued.*

DATE (ABOUT).	MARKS.	ARTICLES AND OWNERS.
1650		Communion flagon : Mugginton, Derbyshire.
,,		Communion cup : West Walton, Norfolk.
,,		Seal-top spoons : Holburne Museum ; and communion paten : Bishop's Knoyle, Wilts.
1658		Seal-top spoon (pricked 1658) : Mr. S. Phillips. (First mark in bowl, second stamped twice on back of stem).
1660		Tankard : Mr. Lambert. Also on Tangier communion flagon : St. Thomas of Canterbury, Portsmouth.
,,		Puritan spoon : Noted by the Author.
··		Mounts of blue and white porcelain jug of the Ming period : Victoria and Albert Museum.
,,		Cylindrical tankard, flat top : Mr. Munsey.
,,		Communion cup : St. Sidwell's, Exeter.
,,		Communion paten : Crathorne, Yorks.
,,		*Seal-top spoon : Messrs. Spink.
1660-70		{ Small box : The Author's Collection. { Flat stemmed trifid spoon : Mr. W. H. Willson.
,,		Flat-stem spoon with engraved decoration : Messrs. Crichton.
1667		Communion cup : St. Andrews, Mottisfont, Hants.
1670		Flat-stem spoon : Messrs. Bruford.
,,		Flat-stem trifid spoon : Mr. J. H. Walter.
1670-4		*Spoon, flat stem : Mr. J. H. Walter.
,,		Porringer, dated 1674 : Mr. W. H. Fowler, Andover.
1674		Marks noted by the Author.
,,		Flat-stem spoon : Mr. Theodore Rossi.
,,		Vertical-sided porringer, with " Prudena Hobson, April, 1674," pricked thereon.

* Probably the mark of Wm. Ramsay or Wm. Robinson, of Newcastle.

UNASCRIBED ENGLISH MARKS—*Continued.*

DATE (ABOUT).	MARKS.	ARTICLES AND OWNERS.
1674		Flat-stem spoon: Mr. A. S. Marsden Smedley.
1675		Do. do. : Mr. J. H. Walter.
,,		Flat-stem spoon: Messrs. Franklin & Hare.
1677		Seal-top spoon: Major C. H. Chichester.
,,		Two com. cups and patens, dated 1677: East Knoyle, Dorset.
1680		Two communion patens, on feet: Tisbury, Wilts.
·,,		Communion paten, inscribed "Ex dono M B 1681": Kingston Deverill, Wilts.
,,		Flat-top tankard: Mr. D. H. Lane.
,,		Pair of candlesticks: Mr. L. Crichton.
,,		Flat-stem spoon: Mr. Fredk. Bradbury.
,,		Paten: Farleigh Wallop, Hants.
·,,		Cup stand: Marquess of Breadalbane, K.G.
,,		Nell Gwyn snuff-box: Col. Croft Lyons.
,,		Snuffers: Messrs. Crichton.
,,		Trifid rat-tail spoon: Mr. J. W. Colbran.
,,		{Trifid spoon: Messrs. Tessier. {Communion paten: Farleigh Wallop, Hants.
,,		Spoon with flat stem: Mr. J. H. Walter. (Possibly a Bridgwater mark.)
,,		Paten: Churchstanton, Somerset.
,,		Trifid spoon, chased, pricked 1699: Sir E. Marshall Hall, K.C.
,,		Snuffers: Victoria and Albert Museum.
,,		Trifid spoon: Messrs. Carrington.

UNASCRIBED ENGLISH MARKS—*Continued.*

DATE (ABOUT).	MARKS.	ARTICLES AND OWNERS.
1680		" Clobbered " tankard : Holburne Museum.
,,		Decorated trifid spoon : Messrs. Crichton.
,,		Spoon, flat stem, trifid end : Mr. H. D. Ellis.
,,		Spoon, flat stem : Goldsmiths' Company, London.
1680-5		{ Do. do. trifid end (pricked 1698) : Noted by the Author. { Do. do. do. : Mr. F. W. Kell. (First mark only.)
,,		(Two coronets, counter-ranged, conjoined in base)—Spoon, flat stem, trifid end : Mr. H. D. Ellis.
,,		Rat-tail spoon, flat stem, trifid end : Messrs. Christie.
,,		Do. do. do. do. : Mr. F. W. Kell.
,,		Surgeon's lancet case : Messrs. Crichton.
,,		Spoon, flat stem, trifid end : Mr. A. D. George.
,,		Do. do. do. : Do. do.
,,		Do. do. do. : Mr. Dudley Westropp.
,,		Do. do. do. : Mr. A. D. George.
,,		Do. do. do., pricked 1683 : Mr. J. H. Walter.
,,		Trifid spoon : Mr. S. Lazarus.
,,		Do. : Mr. Aubrey Le Blond.
,,		Do. : Mr. H. C. Pulley.
,,		Flat-stem spoon : Mr. Dudley Westropp.
1682		Oval tobacco-box : Messrs. Reid & Son, Newcastle.
1684-5		Tumbler : Noted by the Author.
,,		Do. (engraved : " *James Harrington of New Malton* 1684 ").
,,		Nutmeg grater : Messrs. Crichton.

UNASCRIBED ENGLISH MARKS.—*Continued.*

DATE (ABOUT).	MARKS.	ARTICLES AND OWNERS.
1685		On mace, given 1685 to Wilton Corporation.
1687		Mark noted by the Author.
1690		Trifid spoon: Mr. Arthur Irwin Dasent.
,,		Do. do. : Do do.
,,		Rat-tail gravy spoon, pricked "1719": Mr. E. W. Colt.
,,		Spoon, flat stem, trifid end: Mr. Franklin.
,,		Plain tankard: Victoria and Albert Museum.
,,		Large toilet-box: Windsor Castle.
1690-1		Com. cup and flagon, dated 1691: Todwick, near Sheffield.
1690-5		Infant's pap bowl: Mr. J. L. Propert.
,,		Spoon, flat stem, trifid end, embossed bowl: Mr. Crichton.
,,		Do. do. do. : Mr. W. Boore.
,,		Communion paten: St. Mary-le-Bow.
,,		Chocolate pot: Dunn-Gardner Collection.
,,		Rat-tail spoon, flat stem, trifid end: Dunn-Gardner Collection.
,,		Do. do. do. : Do. do.
,,		Do. do. do. : Mr. Crichton.
,,		Oval box with arms of Brooke: South Kensington Museum.
,,		Cover of communion cup inscribed, " This chalice bought att yᵉ charge of ye parish of Warter 1695 ": Warter, Yorks.
1690-9		Spoon with wavy end to stem: Mr. Lowe, Chester.
,,		Do. do. do. : Messrs. Crichton.
1693		Spoon, pricked 1693: Messrs. Crichton.

UNASCRIBED ENGLISH MARKS—*Continued.*

DATE (ABOUT).	MARKS.	ARTICLES AND OWNERS.
1695		Toy teapot : Mr. Claud Malcolmson.
,,		Plain tankard : Mr. S. Phillips.
,,		
,,		Toy cups and porringers : Messrs. Crichton.
,,		
1700		Half-a-dozen tiny forks : Lieut. A. W. Stone, R.N.V.R.
,,		Nutmeg box and grater : The Drane Collection.
1700-5		Rat-tail spoon, flat stem, wavy end : Mr. Crichton.
,,		Com. flagon, "given 1700" : Corsby, Wilts; and paten, inscribed "Mary Curtis, widow, 1704" : Kingston Deverill, Wilts.
1700-40		Fluted saucer on foot : Major Thorold, Sidmouth.
1702		Flat-stemmed rat-tail spoon : Mr. Fredk. Bradbury.
1706-9		Wine funnel : Messrs. Crichton.
,,		Set of com. plate, dated 1706 : Bruton, Somerset; paten, dated 1707 : Poulshot, Wilts; and other church plate in Wilts and Somerset.
,,		Three-pronged table forks, flat stems, wavy ends : Mr. Crichton.
1710		Large rat-tail basting spoon : Mr. W. H. Wilson.
,,		Gravy spoon : Messrs. Crichton.
1720-5		Small teapot : Rev. R. McCheane.
1720-30		* Punch ladle : Mr. Lowe, Chester.
1725-30		Toy tea-set : Mr. Claud Malcolmson.
,,		Table-spoon : The Marquess of Breadalbane, K.G.
,,		Globular teapot : Mr. W. Boore. Mr. Dudley Westropp has noticed this mark stamped thrice (with an additional mark representing a bishop's mitre) on a kettle-stand on three feet.
1730		Small wine-cup, cylindrical bowl on plain moulded circular foot : Mr. Fredk. Bradbury.

* This mark resembles that of Louis Laroche ent. London, 1725.

UNASCRIBED ENGLISH MARKS—*Continued.*

DATE (ABOUT).	MARKS.	ARTICLES AND OWNERS.
1730		Toilet set : Mr. W. A. Baird, Lennoxlove.
,,		Newmarket cup : Mrs. Aldsworth.
,,	G·BC	Candlestick : Mr. C. Ince.
,,	TW	Plain coffee pot : brought to the Author's notice by Mr. E. Alfred Jones.
1730-4	C·I	Marrow scoop : Windsor Castle.
1730-40	MC MC	Table-spoon : Goldsmiths' Company, Chester.
,,	TM STER LING TM	* Marrow scoop : Mr. Arthur Irwin Dasent.
,,	GS Y	Tiny three-pronged fork : Mr. Crichton.
,,	I·H	From a wax impression, taken by Mr. Jas. Lowe, B.A., Chester.
,,	GT GT	Table-spoon, double drop : Goldsmiths' Company, Chester.
,,	S IT IT S	Globular teapot : Mr. W. Ball.
,,	L DF	Rat-tail spoon : Messrs. Crichton.
1740	I·D F	} Pint mug : Messrs. Comyns.
1750	RS MG	} Sugar bowl on three legs : Mrs. Middleton, Merrion.
1750-60	AD	Probably London maker's mark. Pair of nut-crackers : Mr. A. S. Marsden Smedley.
c. 1760	A·L	Toaster : Mr. A. J. Davis.

* Possibly a mark of Thomas Maddock of Chester (1717-61).

CHAPTER XIX

THE SCOTTISH GOLDSMITHS
AND THEIR MARKS.

Whatever uncertainty may exist with reference to the exercise of jurisdiction over English provincial goldsmiths in early times by the London Goldsmiths' Company, there is no such uncertainty with regard to the goldsmiths of Scotland. They have never been subject to any interference in the exercise of their craft by any authority outside their own borders. Nor has there been any influence, either affecting their manner of working or the design of what they wrought, which can be traced as having passed from the English centre to the Scottish goldsmiths. We have seen, in the history of the Newcastle goldsmiths, evidence of the sort of feeling that existed between the craftsmen of the respective countries in the 16th century, from which it may be gathered, that so far from the goldsmiths of either country being inclined to adopt anything "from over the border," the exact opposite was more probably the case. It is therefore not surprising that early Scottish examples of the goldsmith's art bear a much greater resemblance to continental than to English work.

The Scottish goldsmiths were never subject to interference from outside their borders.

The earliest records concerning Scottish goldsmiths, pertain, as may be expected, to the goldsmiths of Edinburgh, whose minutes, containing the names of the deacons of the craft and the dates of their election from 1525 downwards, are preserved. The art of the goldsmith was, however, practised in Scotland much earlier than the 16th century. The Scottish statutes reflect some light on the mediæval goldsmiths in the absence of other evidence. Following the practice which obtained on the continent of Europe, whence, as we have seen, English legislation on the subject derived its inspiration, the laws affecting Scottish goldsmiths were enacted not for the purpose of conferring privileges upon the members of the craft, but for the protection of the public against being defrauded by having inferior metal passed off as good gold or good silver.

Earliest records of Scottish goldsmiths pertain to Edinburgh.

Enactment of 1457. To this end it was enacted in the year 1457 * that :—"As anent the reformacione of golde and siluer wroᵗ be goldsmythis ande to eschewe the desaving done to the Kingis liegis thair salbe ordanyt in ilk burghe quhair goldsmythis wirkis ane vnderstandande † and cunnande ‡ man of gude conscience quhilk sall be dene § of the craft. And quhen the werk is broᵗ to the gold-smyᵗ and it be golde quhat golde that ever it beis broᵗ till him he sall give it furᵗ agane in werk na weᶠ ‖ than xx. granys. And of siluer quhat ever be broᵗ him he sall gif it furᵗ agane na weᶠ ‖ na xj. granys. And the said gold-smyᵗ sall tak his werk or ** he gif it furthe and pass to the dene of the craft and ger examyn that it be sa fyne as is befor wrettyn. And the said dene of the craft sall set his merk and takyn †† thairto togidder wᵗ the saide goldsmytis. And gif faute be fundyne thairin afterwartis the dene forsaide and goldesmytis gudis salbe in eschet to the King and their liffis at the Kingis will. And the saide dene sall haif to his fee of ilk vnce wroᵗ jd. And quhair ther is na gold-smyᵗ bot ane in a town he sall schawe that werk takinit wᵗ his awne merk to the hede officiaris of the town quhilkis sall haif a merk in like manner ordanyt thairfor and salbe set to the saide werk. And quhat goldsmyt that giffis furth his werk vthrwayis thane is befor wrettyne his gudis salbe confyskyt to the Kyng and his life at the Kingis will."

Scottish goldsmiths wrought the gold and silver of their customers.

From this Statute we gather that in the 15th century it was the custom in Scotland, for those who required goldsmith's work, to take their own gold and their own silver to the goldsmith to be wrought according to their order, and it appears that dishonest craftsmen had resorted to the practice of obtaining illicit profit by adulterating gold and silver so brought to them, with undue quantities of alloy.   With a view to stopping this dishonest practice, the amount of alloy which might legally be added to gold and silver by goldsmiths was restricted, so that in every 24 grains (or carats) of wrought gold there should not be less than 20 of fine gold, and in every 12 grains (or ounces) of wrought silver there should not be less than 11 of fine silver. We find here also the first reference to the marking of wrought gold and silver, which was to be marked with the mark of the dean or deacon of the craft, and with the maker's own mark, so that if deceit should be afterwards discovered to have been practised, the lives of both the deacon and the worker were held forfeit.   In towns where there was but one goldsmith he was to take his work, with his own mark on it, to the chief officer of the town to be marked with the town-mark, on pain of having his goods con-fiscated, and his life held at the King's will.

Amount of alloy restricted.

Gold and Silver required to be marked with the deacon's mark and the maker's mark.

* Reign of James II. (of Scotland), March 6th, 1457.
† " vnderstandande "=understanding, *i.e.*, discerning.
‡ " cunnande "=cunning, skilful.
§ " dene "=dean, deacon, warden (of the craft).
‖ " na wer na "=no worse than.
** " or "=ere, before.
†† " merk and takyn "=mark and token.

In 1483 * it was further enacted that whereas :—"throw the negligence and avirice of the wirkaris and goldesmithis the said siluer gevin to thaim is mynging † with laye and uthir stuife that is put in the said werk that fra the siluer cum agane fra the werkmen it is sa fer scaithit of the avale fra the fyne siluer that the pupill is ouer gretly scaithit and dissauit therthrow.‡   And thairfor the lordis avis and think speidfull that in ilk a tovne quhair that golde smithis ar and thair craftis exersit and vsit that thair be deput and ordanit a wardane and a decane of the craft that salbe suorne thairto and examyn al the werkmanschip that cummys fra thair handis, and quhair thai fynd it sufficient set thair merkis thairto, and quhair thai fynd it vnsafficient thai sal refusit and punice the wyrkar efter his demeritis and quhair ony werkman walde culour or stele away his werk w^tout examinacioun it salbe eschetit quhaireuer it may be fundin, and the dampnage thairof fall in the werk manis hand."

Enactment of 1483.

A skilful warden to be appointed to mark work proved sufficient, and to refuse insufficient work and punish offenders.

THE GOLDSMITHS OF EDINBURGH.

In the same year (1483) the Edinburgh goldsmiths (who were then associated with other hammer-wielding trades under the general description of "Hammermen") presented a petition to the Town Council complaining of certain things whereby they were prejudiced, contrary to the "auld gude rule and statutes of their craft".   In response to their petition the Council granted them certain privileges and prescribed certain rules for their observance.   In less than fifty years after the date of that grant they must have dissociated themselves from the other trades, because in the year 1525—the date of their oldest minute-book—they were an independent corporation.

Edinburgh goldsmiths originally associated with other hammermen.

By a Statute of the year 1485 "a dekin and a sercho^r of the craft" were appointed, and it was ordained that "al goldsmytis werk be markit w^t his avn mark, the dekynis mark, and the mark of the tovne, of the finace of xjd. fyne".§

A deacon and searcher appointed by the Edinburgh goldsmiths in 1485.

On the 20th June, 1555, an Act of the sixth Parliament of Queen Mary was passed, whereby it was ordained that :—"Forasmuch as there is great fraud and hurt done unto the lieges of the realme by goldsmiths that make silver and gold of no certaine finesse but at their pleasure by which there is some silver warke set furth of such baseness of alloy of six and seven penny fine against the public weal of the realme . . . na goldsmith should make in warke nor set foorth either of his awn or uther mennis silver under the just

Statute of 1555.

---

* Reign of James III., February 24th, 1483.
† "Mynging with laye and uthir stuife"=mixed with alloy and other stuff.
‡ So far depreciated in value below fine silver that the people are greatly wronged and deceived thereby.
§ Of the fineness of xjd. fyne: xjd.=11 deniers: "denier" (from the French brass coin so-called, worth three-tenths of a farthing English), an arbitrary weight, which was divided into 24 grains. Silver without alloy was xijd. fine, therefore plate xjd. fine contained eleven parts of pure silver and one part of alloy.

finance of elleven pennie under the paine of death and confiscation of all their gudes moveable And that everie goldsmith marke the silver warke that he makis with his awin marke and with the townis mark And als that na goldsmith make in warke or set furth of his awin or other mennis gold under the just finesse of twentie twa carat fine under the pains aforesaid."

The "Craft" authorised to search for and test the quality of all gold and silver work.

In January, 1586, James VI. (afterwards Jas. I. of England) granted to the "deacon and masters of the goldsmiths craft in Edinburgh" a letter under his privy seal (confirmed by statute in the following year) whereby they were empowered amongst other things to search for "all gold and silver wark wrocht and made in ony pairt within this realme," and to try if it were of the fineness required by statute and to seize all such as should be deficient.

Rules of the craft approved 1591.

In August, 1591, the deacon and brethren of the craft presented to the Town Council of Edinburgh certain rules for the government of their body, whereupon the Council having declared them to be agreeable to all good laws, equity and reason, confirmed them.

Charter granted by James VII. (Jas. II. of Eng.) 1687.

On the 10th of November, 1687, King James VII. (Jas. II. of England) granted a charter to the Edinburgh goldsmiths, whereby all their previously enjoyed privileges were confirmed unto them and in addition they were granted more extensive powers with reference to searching for gold and silver work and punishing offenders. Pursuant to this charter they issued notices to the goldsmiths of other Scottish towns directing their attention to the necessity of maintaining their gold and silver work up to the required standard. In examining the records of the Edinburgh goldsmiths, Mr. A. J. S. Brook found a draft of one of these notices (undated, but assigned to about the year $168\frac{7}{8}$) on the back of which is written the names of the persons to whom copies were sent, from which it appears that the number of goldsmiths in various towns of Scotland at that time was as follows :—In Glasgow, 5 ; Aberdeen, 3 ; Perth, 1 ; Inverness, 1 ; Ayr, 1 ; Banff, 1 ; and Montrose, 1. From the minute-books of the Edinburgh Goldsmiths' Incorporation, it appears that the number of goldsmiths in Edinburgh at that date was about twenty-five.

Thirteen provincial goldsmiths found mentioned about 1687.

The Britannia standard of 11oz. 10dwt. fine never enforced in Scotland.

The Act 8 and 9 Wm. III. c. 8, which was passed by the English Parliament in 1696 (before the union of the parliaments of England and Scotland), whereby the standard for wrought plate in England was raised to 11oz. 10dwt. fine, was not operative in Scotland. The Act 6 George I. c. 11, however, which restored the old English standard, provided that "from and after June 1st, 1720, no goldsmith or silversmith or other person whatsoever should work or cause to be wrought any plate less in fineness than 11 oz. 2 dwt. of fine silver in every pound *Troy*, nor put to sale, exchange, or sell any plate until it should be touched, assayed and marked in manner provided by the laws then in force". That Act having been passed after the union of the English and Scottish parliaments, became operative over the whole of Great Britain, and as a result the Scottish standard for plate was raised on 1 June, 1720, from 11 oz. fine, at which it had previously stood, to 11 oz. 2 dwt. fine (agreeably with the English standard), which, ever since that date, has remained unchanged. By the same Act a duty of sixpence per ounce was imposed on plate manufactured in or imported into Great Britain. The option of manufacturing plate of the higher or Britannia standard of 11 oz. 10 dwts. fine was also conferred by this Act, but it does not appear to have been exercised by the Scottish goldsmiths.

In 1757-58 the duty on plate was repealed by the Act 31 Geo. II. c. 32, and a licence tax, payable by every person dealing in gold and silver wares, was imposed in substitution, but in 1784 the above duty of 6d. per ounce was (by the Act 24 Geo. III. c. 53) reimposed, and extended to gold, on which 8s. per ounce became payable. In 1797 the duty on plate was increased to 1s. per ounce. In 1804 the duty on gold was increased to 16s. per ounce and on silver to 1s. 3d. per ounce. By the Act 55 Geo. III. c. 185 (1815) the duty on gold was raised to 17s. per ounce and on silver to 1s. 6d. per ounce, at which rate it remained until the abolition of the duty on the 28 May, 1890.*

The manufacture of gold and silver wares in Scotland is now regulated by the Statutes 59 Geo. III. c. 28 (1818-19) and the 6 & 7 Wm. IV. c. 69 (1836). The former relates only to Glasgow, and will be referred to in connection with the Glasgow goldsmiths ; the later Act extends to the whole of Scotland, except the Glasgow district.

The supervision of the standards appointed for Scotland is entrusted to *the Wardens of the Incorporation of Goldsmiths of the City of Edinburgh*. They have, under the Act of Wm. IV., jurisdiction over the whole of Scotland, excepting Glasgow and forty miles round it, which excepted district is subject to the control of the Glasgow Goldsmiths' Company. The provisions for the election of wardens, the appointment and duties of assayers, the custody and trial of the diet and the entries to be made are similar to those in the Birmingham Act (*supra*). The duties of the

* A list of gold and silver wares exempted from liability to duty will be found on page 73 *ante*.

wardens are merely to be present when requested by the assayer at the breaking of any plate in respect of which fraud is suspected, and four times a year to superintend and keep an account of the weighing of the scrapings deposited in the assayer's box; to be present at the opening of the diet-boxes once a year, and to sell the diet after it has been sent to and returned from the mint. The assayer's box and the diet-boxes are each required to have two different locks : the key of one to be kept by the assayer and that of the other by the deacon of the incorporation.

The dies or punches for marking gold and silver wares are entrusted to the assayer alone, under very heavy penalties in case of improper use.

Penalties for offences.

The penalties for offences against the standards and marks are heavier than in England. "Every person who shall make, sell, or export out of Scotland, any wrought gold or silver, less in fineness than the Act provides is (Sec. 1) liable to a penalty of £100 for each piece of plate; and every person who shall knowingly sell, exchange, keep for sale, export, or attempt to export any gold or silver wares not marked with the proper marks, as required by the Act, is also liable to a penalty of £100 for each article."

THE EDINBURGH GOLDSMITHS' MARKS.

First enactment as to marks 1457.

There were probably no marks struck on gold and silver wares wrought in Scotland before 1457 when, as we have seen, the statute of that year provided for the appointment of deacons or other officers to regulate the quality of wrought gold and silver. Before this it seems to have been a common practice amongst some working goldsmiths to increase their profits by substituting an undue amount of alloy in place of the precious metals entrusted to them by their customers. Therefore, if any plate whatever had been marked prior to this date, it would in all probability have been only such goldsmiths as were conscious of their own rectitude, and were prepared to warrant the honesty of their work, who would have stamped their marks on it. We see, however, that from 1457 the marks of the deacon and of the worker were required by statute to be set on all wrought gold and silver.

The obligatory marking of plate devised for the prevention of fraud enables the date of its manufacture to be determined.

These requirements with respect to the marking of plate, although intended as a means of preventing fraud or detecting its perpetrator, and in no way meant to serve the purpose of enabling the antiquary and the plate collector in after years to fix the date of the manufacture of any particular article of plate, do, as a matter of fact, incidentally afford the means of doing so. Firstly, the maker's mark enables one to ascertain the maker when, as is mostly the case from 1525 onwards, the name is to be found in the records; whence we have an approximate date, limited by the working-lifetime of the maker; and, secondly, by reason of the names of the Edinburgh deacons being recorded from the year 1525 onwards, we are enabled to reduce the range of possible dates to the very narrow limit of time during which the deacon, whose mark any particular article bears, held office.

By a statute of the year 1485 it was, as we have seen, ordained that the mark of the town, in addition to the goldsmith's own mark and the deacon's mark, should be struck on all goldsmiths' work, and these three marks continued to be the marks by law required to be struck on all wrought gold and silver down to 1681. *" Town mark " added 1485.*

The " town mark " of the Edinburgh goldsmiths, according to the rule generally followed, was taken from the arms of the burgh, which are :—*Argent, on a rock proper, a castle, triple towered and embattled, sable.* This triple towered castle, slightly modified in design from time to time, has been used as the Edinburgh " town mark " from the year 1485 down to the present day. *Edinburgh town mark taken from the arms of the burgh.*

In 1681 the Edinburgh Goldsmiths' Incorporation, following the practice which originated at Montpellier, adopted a variable annual letter for stamping on gold and silver wares, whereby any fraudulent practice in the manufacture of plate might be more easily detected. From that time a date-letter, changed annually in the month of September (when the officers for the next ensuing year are elected), has been regularly used. Therefore, from 1681 downwards it is possible to determine the exact year when any fully marked piece of Edinburgh plate was made and assayed. *Date-letter adopted 1681.*

At the time when they adopted the use of the date-letter, the Edinburgh goldsmiths abolished the deacon's mark and substituted the mark of the assay master, whereby the official assayer was fixed with responsibility for his assay by the striking of his mark. At first this mark consisted of the initials of the assayer in monogram in script letters; afterwards it was composed of separate Roman capital letters. *Assayer's mark substituted for deacon's mark.*

In 1759 the use of the assay master's initials was discontinued and the mark of a thistle was substituted, in accordance with the following minute :— *1759. Mark of a thistle substituted for assayer's initials.*

" 15th September, 1759: Thereafter Hugh Gordon the Assay Master being called in and having delivered the last year's puncheon to the Deacon, the

Incorporation did unanimously nominate and re-elect the said Hugh Gordon to be Assay Master to the Incorporation for the ensuing year and appointed him the Saxon letter 𝕮 to be put on the plate said year with the stamp or impression of a Scots thistle in place of the initial letters of the Assay master's name, which initial letters they discharge in time coming."

Mr. Brook, who copied this minute in 1892, pointed out * the mistake which had been made by Mr. Chaffers and Mr. Cripps in assigning the date of the substitution of the thistle for the assayer's initials to the year 1757, and Mr. Cripps consequently corrected his error in the succeeding edition of *Old English Plate*.

1784. Sovereign's head (duty mark) added.

Consequent upon the re-imposition of duties (at the rate of 8s. per oz. on gold and 6d. per oz. on silver in lieu of licences) over the whole of Great Britain, a fifth mark, consisting of the sovereign's head, indicative of the payment of duty, was ordered to be struck on all gold and silver plate assayed from and after the 1 December, 1784, in Scotland, as in England. This duty-mark continued thenceforward to be used in Edinburgh† as in London, except that the change in the form of the head, consequent upon the accession of a new monarch, was longer delayed in Edinburgh. After the accession of Queen Victoria, as much as four years elapsed before the change was made. This mark continued in use until 1890, when the duty on plate was repealed, and it ceased to be used.

Marks prescribed by the Statute 6 & 7 W. IV. c. 69, 1836.

The Statute 6 and 7 Wm. IV. c. 69 (1836) prescribed the marks to be struck on silver plate in the following terms :—

On silver of 11 oz. 2 dwts. fine (the Old English standard) the maker's initials, the thistle, variable letter, and the peculiar mark of the company (a castle) ; and on silver of 11 oz. 10 dwts. fine (the new English or "Britannia" standard) the same marks with the addition of the figure of Britannia.

In addition to the above marks the duty mark was required to be struck, until 1890, as before mentioned. The Britannia standard has been very rarely, if ever, used in Scotland ; the Author has not in all his researches met with a single piece of Edinburgh-made "Britannia" plate, and that standard was most certainly not enforced from 1700 to 1720, as implied by Mr. Chaffers in *Hall Marks on Plate*.

---

* *Old Scottish Communion Plate*, page 537.

† The duty-mark was, of course, not stamped on articles exempted from the payment of duty, a list of which appears on page 73 *ante*.

For gold of 22 carats the prescribed marks were until 1844 identical with those prescribed for silver of the old standard; now, however, the figure 22 is added to denote the number of carats fine.

For gold of 18 carats the marks are similar, with the addition of the figure 18 instead of 22; and for the three lower standards the figures 15, 12 and 9 respectively are used to denote the fineness of each quality.

In the following tables the marks are represented in *facsimile* exactly as they appear (in a row, side by side) on the plate from which they have been taken, and have been reproduced from the originals in the same manner as the English marks, the sunk parts being black and the raised parts white. For impressions of several of the marks the Author is indebted to the late Mr. A. J. S. Brook, whose assistance was most generously accorded in the compilation of these tables, which will be found to agree (as far as a comparison can be made) with Mr. Brook's tables in *Old Scottish Communion Plate*. On the other hand, they will be found to differ very considerably from the marks illustrated in Chaffers' *Hall Marks on Plate*, which cannot have been obtained from authentic sources; and to differ also from the Edinburgh marks illustrated by Mr. Cripps in *Old English Plate*, which, having been prepared by Mr. Sanderson from drawings of marks made by different hands, cannot possibly have the same accuracy as is attained by reproducing the actual marks by means of castings from impressions taken from the plate itself.

In Mr. Chaffers' *Hall Marks on Plate* it was stated that most of the date-letters—1681 to 1705—were taken from the minutes of the Goldsmiths Corporation, in many cases from an impression of the actual punch given on the paper, and a somewhat similar statement appeared in *Old English Plate*. On Mr. Brook directing attention to the fact that there were no such impressions struck in the books, but merely some sketches of the marks roughly drawn with the pen, having a very remote resemblance to the actual marks, the statement was withdrawn from the subsequent edition of *Old English Plate*, but the erroneous statement was re-repeated by the editors of Chaffers' *Hall Marks*. In the year 1901, by the courtesy of the deacon and officers of the Goldsmiths' Incorporation, the Author was allowed to inspect their books, and he is able to verify the statement of Mr. Brook as to there being no impressions of the actual punches in the paper of the minute book from 1681 to 1705. There are, however, impressions of 19th century punch marks struck on copper-plates, and of these, the Author, by the same courtesy, was allowed to

[margin: The marks in the following tables are in facsimile; reproduced from marks on authentic examples of plate.]

[margin: No impressions of early marks stamped in the goldsmiths' books.]

[margin: 19th century marks are struck on copper-plates.]

take castings which have been compared with the marks reproduced from articles of plate. In the following tables all the marks found on each article are printed in line, so that any one desiring to compare the marks on a given piece of plate with the marks here recorded will be able to do so without referring to several pages for each of the several marks.

It is unnecessary to further describe the marks which appear in the tables, as by reason of the way in which they are arranged they "speak for themselves". It may, however, be as well to observe that the Roman capital letters O, S, V, W, X and Z, date-marks of the cycle 1780-1806, are not readily distinguishable from the corresponding small letters of the following cycle, but by bearing in mind that the shields of the letters of the former (after H) all have angular bases, while the shields of the date-letters (from e onwards) in the cycle which follows all have bases which curve downwards to a point in the centre, the difference between the marks may be easily detected. It may also be added that concurrently with a castle such as those illustrated in line with 1799-1800 and 1824-25, the more common form of town mark as represented opposite 1780-81, 1806-07 and 1826-27 is found to have been used on other examples of plate not mentioned in the tables. In some instances the castle, thistle, and date-letter are rather close to each other and are so regularly placed as to appear as if the three marks had been grouped in one punch and stamped with a single stroke, while the maker's mark— which was always separately stamped by the maker—and the duty-mark, appear much more irregularly spaced. A few other noteworthy observations regarding certain marks will be found above and below several of the tables.

It will be observed that the marks in the Edinburgh tables have been placed in a different order from that observed with regard to the English marks, where for the sake of convenience the mark of the maker has been placed in the last column. On old Edinburgh plate the maker's mark occupies the first place (to the left as you look at the marks) : the deacon's mark being third, with the castle between the two. The relative position of the marks being, therefore, of importance in distinguishing which is the maker's mark and which the deacon's, these relative positions have been maintained in the tables. The same relative positions of the maker's mark and town mark were continued after the deacon's mark ceased to be applied ; the place of the deacon's mark being

Similarity of certain date-marks in two cycles.

The relative position of marks of importance prior to 1681.

taken by that of the assay-master, for which in 1759 the thistle was substituted, as before explained.

While the deacon held office he was not precluded from making plate, and therefore examples are found with the same mark on either side of the castle, the first being his mark as maker and the last as deacon. *Deacons marked their own plate as deacon and maker.*

In 1740 a dispute occurred between the Incorporation and Archibald Ure as to his tenure of office as assayer. The dispute was terminated by the appointment of Hugh Gordon to the office of assay-master in 1744. Meanwhile, in lieu of the assay-master's mark, plate was stamped with the mark of the oldest and youngest master, who in turn temporarily undertook the assayer's duty. Hence we find plate stamped with the marks of Dougal Ged, Edward Lothian and other goldsmiths in the place of that of the assay-master.

Following the tables of marks there will be found a list of the names of the deacons who held office from 1525 to 1681 ; after 1681 the deacon's mark was not used. A large number of goldsmiths' names appear opposite their marks in the tables from 1552 to 1903. These are supplemented by the names of goldsmiths which have been found recorded, but of whose work the Author has not met with any example. *List of deacons and names of goldsmiths follow the tables of marks.*

The recording of goldsmiths' names does not appear to have been made with the same care in the nineteenth century as seems to have been exercised previously ; it is consequently difficult to identify some of the makers' marks represented in the later tables.

Marks on Edinburgh-wrought gold are described on page 509 *infra*.

The marks on Foreign Plate assayed at Edinburgh are illustrated on page 27 *ante*.

MARKS ON EDINBURGH PLATE.

TABLE I.

FROM ABOUT 1552 TO ABOUT 1633.

THREE STAMPS AS BELOW.

The date within parentheses which follows the maker's name is the date of his *admission* to the Incorporation : his first work having been previously assayed and found satisfactory.

The period during which each deacon held office is stated on page 510.

DATE.	MAKER'S NAME.	MAKER'S MARK	TOWN MARK CASTLE	DEACON'S MARK	DEACON'S NAME.	ARTICLES AND OWNERS.
1552-62	Alex. Auchinleck				Thos. Ewing.	Foot of Mazer, dated 1567: St. Mary's Coll., St. Andrews.
1563-4	Henry Thompsone (1561)		,,		James Cok.	Bowl of com. cup : Forgue.
c. 1570	(*Mark indistinct.*)		,,		George Heriot, senr.*	Mount of rock-crystal jug† : Lord Swaythling.
1576	Adam Craige				James Mosman.	Mazer on foot, dated 1576 : Sir Charles Ferguson, Bart.
1585-6	John Mosman (1575)		,,		John Mosman.	Two com. cups : Roseneath.
1590-1	Adam Allane, jr. (1589)				Geo. Heriot, senr.*	Tazza-shaped cup : Messrs. Christie.
1591-2	James Craufuird		,,		Do. do.	Mazer on tall foot : Lord Semphill.
1591-4	David Gilbert (1590)		,,		Wm. Cok (Cokie).	Baptismal basin : East Church, Perth.
,,	James Craufuird (1591)				Do. do.	Spoon, thistle-sh'd top : The Author's Coll'n.
1596 / 1600	Hugh Lindsay (1587)		,,		David Heriot.	Two com. cups : Currie.
1609-10	Gilbert Kirkwood (1609)		,,		Robert Denneistoun.	Do. do. Arbirlot.
1611-3	Robert Denneistoun (1597)				David Palmer.	Mts. of nautilus shell cup : Heriot's Trust.
,,	George Craufuird, jr. (1606)		,,	,,	Do. do.	Com. cups : Fala & Soutra.
1617-9	Do. do.	,,			John Lindsay.	Pair of cups : Earl Cawdor.
,,	John Lindsay (1605)		,,	,,	Do do.	Com. cups : Closeburn.
,,	George Robertsone (1616)		,,	,,	Do. do.	Com. cups : Holywood, Dumfries.
,,	Thos. Thompson (1617)		,,	,,	Do. do.	Com. cups : Middlebie, Ecclefechan.
c. 1617	Hew. Anderson		,,		George Craufuird.	Plate : Messrs. Crichton.
1613-21	Gilbert Kirkwood (1609)				James Denneistoun.	Com. cup : Straiton and Blantyre.
1616-35	George Robertsone (1616)		,,		George Craufuird.	Corporation Mace : Edinburgh.
1633	Adame Lamb (1619)		,,	,,	Do. do.	Com. cup, dated 1633 : Old Greyfriars, Edinburgh.
,,	Thos. Kirkwood (1631)		,,	,,	Do. do.	Com. cup‡ : Aberchirder.
1633 (?)	(*Mark indistinct.*)				Alexr. Reid (probably).	Com. cup, dated 1633 : Fintray.

* Father of the famous George Heriot.

† Presented by Queen Elizabeth to the Regent Mar.

‡ Also bread-plates, dated 1633, Trinity College Church, Edinburgh.

MARKS ON EDINBURGH PLATE.

TABLE II.

FROM ABOUT 1637 TO ABOUT 1677.

THREE STAMPS AS BELOW.

(See notes above Table I. on preceding page.)

DATE.	MAKER'S NAME.	MAKER'S MARK.	TOWN MARK. CASTLE.	DEACON'S MARK.	DEACON'S NAME.	ARTICLES AND OWNERS.
1637-9	Jon Scott (1621) Adm.				Jon Scott.	Two com. cups, given 1645: South Leith.
1640-2	Thos. Clyghorne (1606)				Thos. Clyghorne.	Spoon: Glasgow Exhibition of 1901.
1642	Patrick Borthwick (1642)		,,		John Fraser.	Com. cups *: Tolbooth Church, Edinburgh.
1643	Jon Scott (1621)			,,	Do. do.	{ Com. cups, dated 1643: Canongate. Also com. cups at St. Giles', Edinburgh, and South Leith.
,,	Nicoll Trotter (1635)		,,	,,	Do. do.	Com. cups: Tolbooth, Church, Edinburgh.
1644-6	George Cleghorne (1641)		,,		Adam Lamb.	Com. cup: Newbattle.
,,	Andro Denneistoun (1636)		,,	,,	Do. do.	Do. do.
,,	Thos. Clyghorne (1606)		,,	,,	Do. do.	Do. do.
1644	{ John Myln or Jas. McAulay		,,	,,	Do. do.	Wine taster: Messrs. Crichton.
1649	Andro Burrell (1642)		,,		George Cleghorne.	Baptismal basin dated 1649: Old Greyfriars, Edinburgh.
1648-57	Peter Neilsone (1647)		,,	,,	Do. do.	Two spoons: Mrs. Maxwell.
1650	Thos. Scott (1649)		,,	,,	Do. do.	Com. cup: Dalmellington.
1651-9	Robert Gibsoune (1627)		,,		James Fairbairne.	Com. cups: Dalkeith.
1657	John Wardlaw (1642)		,,	,,	Do. do.	Com. cups, dated 1657: Dunbar.
1660	Edwd. Cleghorne (1649)		,,		Andro Burrell.	Com. cups, dated 1660: Abercorn.
1665-7	Wm. Law (1662)		,,		James Symontoun.	Baptismal basin: North Leith Church
,,	Andrew Law (c. 1665)		,,	,,	Do. do.	{ Cup: Glasgow Exhibition. Communion cup: Wemyss.
1665	Alexr. Reid		,,		Do. do.	Quaich: Messrs. Crichton.
1669-75	Alexr. Scott (1649)		,,		Alexr. Reid (2nd).	Com. cup: Arbroath.
1674	James Cockburne (1669)		,,	,,	Do. do.	Do. given 1674: Longformacus.
1663-81	Alexr. Scott (1649)		,,		Edwd. Cleghorne.	Com. cup: Linlithgow.
1675-7	George Rolland (1675)		,,		Wm. Law.	Large spoon: Glasgow Exhibition of 1901.
1677	Alexr. Reid (3rd) (1677)		,.	,,	Do. do.	Do do.: Do.
1650	Patrick Borthwick.				John Fraser.	Wine cup: The Author's Collection.

* Dated 1642. John Fraser's mark as deacon has been found on the communion plate of no less than four parishes in and near Edinburgh, and two near Paisley, but no record of his election to the office of Deacon has been discovered. He may have been elected between terms to fill the place of some deacon deceased or incapacitated.

MARKS ON EDINBURGH PLATE.

TABLE III.

FROM 1681 TO 1705—TWENTY-FOUR YEARS, FOUR STAMPS AS BELOW.

The order of marks, for convenience of reference, has been arranged differently in this and the nine following tables from that previously observed.

ARTICLES AND OWNERS.	MAKER'S NAME.	MAKER'S MARK.	TOWN MARK. CASTLE.	ASSAY MASTER'S MARK.	DATE LETTER.	DATE.	ASSAY MASTER'S NAME.
Spoon : Mr. S. Phillips.	Alexr. Reid (1660) Adm.						John Borthwick.
Communion cups, dated 1682 : Duddington.	Edwd. Cleghorne (1649)					1681-2	
Two cups : Heriot's Trust.	Andrew Law (c. 1665)		,,			1682-3	,,
Two communion cups : Culross.	Wm. Law (1662)						
Do. do. do. : Peebles.	Thos. Yorstoun (1673)		,,	,,		1683-4	,,
Flagon : Glasgow Exhibition.	John Lawe (1661)		,,	,,		1684-5	,,
Communion cup : Pittenweem.	James Penman (1673)		,,	,,		1685-6	,,
Do. do. : Dunblane.	Do. do.	,,	,,	,,		1686-7	,,
Do. do. : Sprouston.	James Cockburne (1669)		,,	,,		1687-8	,,
Sauce-pan : Messrs. Christie.	George Scott (1677)		,,	,,		1688-9	,,
Two com. cups, given 1689 : Temple Church, Edinburgh.	Wm. Scott (1686)		,,	,,		WM. & MY. 1689-90	,,
Spoon : Mr. Chisholm ; com. cups : Bothkennar.	James Cockburne (1669)		,,	,,		1690-1	,,
Spoon : Messrs. Smith & Rait.	Robert Bruce (1687)		,,	,,		1691-2	,,
Do. : Mr. Wilson : com. cups : Hawick.	Robert Inglis (1686)		,,	,,		1692-3	,,
Communion cups, dated 1694 : Kirriemuir.	James Sympsone (1687)		,,	,,		1693-4	,,
Mug : The Author's Collection.	Geo. Yorstoune (1684)		,,	,,		1694-5	,,
Communion cups, dated 1695 : Borthwick.	Alexr. Forbes (1692)		,,	,,		WM. III. 1695-6	,,
Quaich : Lord Breadalbane.	James Sympsone ? (1687)		,,			1696-7	James Penman.
Spoon : Glasgow Exhibition.	(Not identified).		,,	,,		1697-8	,,
Communion cup, dated 1698 : Trinity College, Edinburgh.	Thos. Ker (1694)			,,		1698-9	,,
Rat-tail spoons : Mr. Chisholm.	Alexr. Kincaid (1692)		,,	,,		1699 1700	,,
Punch-bowl : Sir Jas. Menzies ; Com. cups : Dalserf.	Colin McKenzie (1695)		,,	,,		1700-1	,,
Tankard : Glasgow Exhibition.	Geo. Scott, jr. (1697)		,,	,,		1701-2	,,
Spoon : Do. do.	Mungo Yorstoun (1702)		,,	,,		ANNE. 1702-3	,,
Do. : Messrs. Christie.	Thos. Cleghorne (1689)		,,	,,		1703-4	,,
Rat-tail spoon : Mus. of Antiq., Edinburgh.	James Sympson (1687)		,,	,,		1704-5	,,
Mug : Glasgow Exhibition.	Patrick Murray (1701)						

Six trifid table-spoons : Mr. Crichton.	James Cockburne					1682-3	John Borthwick.
Variant of date-letter for 1687-8.	James Penman, as 1685					1687-8	,,
Do. do. do. 1697-8.	Colin McKenzie, as 1700-1					1697-8	James Penman.

MARKS ON EDINBURGH PLATE.

TABLE IV.   FROM 1705 TO 1730—TWENTY-FIVE YEARS. FOUR STAMPS AS BELOW.

ARTICLES AND OWNERS.	MAKER'S NAME.	MAKER'S MARK.	TOWN MARK. CASTLE.	ASSAY MASTER'S MARK.	DATE LETTER.	DATE.	ASSAY MASTER'S NAME.
Rat-tail spoon: Soc. Antiq. (1889)	Patrick Murray (1701) Adm.	PM	[castle]	[TP]	A	1705-6	James Penman.
Communion cups: Rattray.	James Tait (1704)	IT					
Bapt. laver: Old Greyfriars, Ed.	Walter Scott (1701)	WS	,,	,,	B	1706-7	,,
Com. cups, "gifted 1708": Crieff	Wm. Ged (1706)	WG		EP	C	1707-8	Edward Penman.
Do. "gifted 1709": Broughton.	John Penman, jr. (1703)	IP	,,				
Tankard: Mr. Chisholm.	Harry Beathune (1704)	HB	,,	,,	D	1708-9	,,
Plaid-brooch: Glasgow Exhib.	John Seatoune (1688)	IS	,,	,,	E	1709-10	,,
Com. cup: Borthwick.	James Mitchellsone (1706)	IM	,,	,,	F	1710-1	,,
Do. dated 1711: Penninghame.	Patrick Turnbull (1689)	PT	,,	,,	G	1711-2	,,
Large spoon: Glasgow Exhib.	Robert Ker (1705)	RK	,,	,,	H	1712-3	,,
Quaich: Lord Breadalbane.	Robert Inglis (1686)	RI	,,	,,	I	1713-4 GEO. I.	,,
Com. cups: Maryton, Montrose. Milk-jug: Mr. W. Boore.	Mungo Yorstoun (1702) ,, ,,	MY M·Y	[castle]	,,	K	1714-5	,,
Rat-tail spoon: Mr. Chisholm.	Thos. Ker (1694)	T·K	,,	,,	L	1715-6	,,
Do. do.: Glasgow Exhib. Do. do.: Mr. Crichton.	Harry Beathune (1704) John Seatoun (1685)	HB IS	,,	,,	MM	1716-7	,,
Bread plates: North Leith. Small mug: Glasgow Exhib.	Chas. Dickson (as 1721) Chas. Blair (1707)	CB	,,	,,	NN	1717-8	,,
Rat-tail table-spoon: The Author's Collection.	Wm. Ure (1715)	WU	[castle]	EP	N	,,	,,
Hash-spoon: Mr. J. Guthrie.	James Mitchellsone (1706)	IM	,,	,,	O	1718-9	,,
Rat-tail spoons: Messrs. G. Do. do.: Mr. W. Smith.	Mungo Yorstoun (1702) Alexr. Sympsone (1710)	M·Y AS	,,	,,	PP	1719-20	,,
Rat-tail table-spoon: The Author's Coll.	Jas. Inglis (1720)	II	,,	EP	P	,,	,,
Com. cups: Pencaitland. Spoon: Mr. Chisholm.	,, ,, David Mitchell (1700)	DM	,,	,,	q	1720-1	,,
Communion cups: Ayr.	Chas. Dickson (1719)	CD	,,	,,	R	1721-2	,,
Small spoon: Lord Breadalbane.	James Clarke (1710)	IC	,,	,,	S	1722-3	,,
Com. cups: Kinnaird, Dundee.	Colin Campbell (1714)	CC	,,	,,			
Small cup: Messrs. Christie.	Ken'th McKenzie (1714)	KM	,,	,,	T	1723-4	,,
Table-spoon: Mr. W. Smith.	Chas. Blair (1707)	CB					
Do.: Mr. Davison.	Alexr. Edmonstoune (1721)	AE	,,	,,	U	1724-5	,,
Do.: Mr. Chisholm.	Archd. Ure (1715)	AU	,,	,,	V	1725-6	,,
Do.: Messrs. Hamilton & Inches.	James Taitt (1704)	IT	,,	,,	W	1726-7 GEO. II.	,,
The "Bruce" cup: St. Salvador's, St. Andrews.	Harry Beathune (1704)	HB	,,	,,	X	1727-8	,,
Table-spoon: Glasgow Exhib.	Patrick Graeme (1725)	PG	,,	,,	Y	1728-9	,,
Do.: S. Kensington Mus. Salver †: Mr. Crawfurd.	Wm. Aytoun (1718) Wm. Jameson (1729)	WA WI	,,	AU	Z Z	} 1729-30	Archibald Ure.
Variant of date-letter for 1711-2. Mug: Mr. J. A. Holms.	Colin Campbell	CC	G			1711-2	Edward Penman.
Variant of assay master's mark, castle, and date-letter. Salver, etc.: Mr. North.	... ...	EP	N	[castle]		1717-8	,,
Teapot: Messrs. Crichton.	James Ker	IK				1723-4	,,
Octagonal basin: Messrs. Crichton.	Thos. Mitchell	TM				1724-5	,,

MARKS ON EDINBURGH PLATE.

TABLE V.

FROM 1730 TO 1755—TWENTY-FIVE YEARS.

FOUR STAMPS.

ARTICLES AND OWNERS.	MAKER'S NAME.	MAKER'S MARK.	TOWN MARK. CASTLE.	ASSAY MASTER'S MARK.	DATE LETTER	DATE.	ASSAY MASTER'S NAME.
Milk-jug : Lady Molesworth.	James Anderson (Adm. 1729)	IA	🏰	AU	A	1730-1	Archibald Ure.
Communion cups : Kilsyth.	Hugh Gordon (1727)	HG	,,	,,	B	1731-2	,,
Table-spoon : Glasgow Exhib.	George Forbes (1731)	GF	,,	,,	C	1732-3	,,
Com. cups : Birsay & Harray.	John Main (1729)	IM	,,	,,	D	1733-4	,,
Salver : Mr. Wm. Beattie.	Edw'rd Lothian (1731)	EL	,,	,,	E	1734-5	,,
Spoon : Col. Esdaile; com. cups : Stow.	John Rollo (1731) (afterwards Lord Rollo).	IR	,,	,,	F	1735-6	,,
Spoon : Mr. W. Smith; com. cups : Kinross.	Hugh Penman (1734)	HP	,,	,,	G	1736-7	,,
Small mug : Mr. Crichton.	Alexander Farquharson (1734)	AF	🏰	,,	H	1737-8	,,
Waiter : Messrs. G.	James Ker (1723)	I·K	,,	,,	I	1738-9	,,
Teapot : Messrs. Hamilton & Inches.	Dougal Ged (1734)	GED					
Mug : Edinburgh Museum.	James Ker (1723)	I·K	,,	,,	K	1739-40	,,
Spoon : Glasgow Exhibition.	,, ,, (1737)	,,	,,	,,			,,
Spoon : The Marquess of Breadalbane.	Ebenr. Oliphant (1737)	EO	,,	GED	L	1740-1	†
Hash-spoon : Mr. Chisholm.	Law'ce Oliphant (1737)	LO	,,	,,	M	1741-2	†
Spoon : Mr. H. D. Ellis.	William Aytoun (1718)	WA					
Communion cups : Auldearn.	Robert Gordon (1741)	RG	,,	EL	N	1742-3	†
Spoon : Mr. W. Smith; com. cups : Kirkcudbright.	Edwd. Lothian (1731)	EL	,,	,,	O	1743-4	†
Teapot : Messrs. Hamilton & Inches.	Chas. Dickson (1738)	CD	🏰	HG	P	1744-5	Hugh Gordon.
Mug : Mr. Chisholm; Bapt. basin : Kirkcaldy.	Ebenr. Oliphant (1737)	EO	,,	,,	Q	1745-6	,,
Coffee-urn : Mr. Crichton.	John Kincard (1726)	IK	,,	,,	R	1746-7	,,
Spoon : Glasgow Exhib. Sauce-boat : Mr. J. F. Lowe.	(Not identified.)	CL	,,	,,	S	1747-8	,,
Spoon : Mr. Davison.	William Gilchrist (1736)	WG	,,	,,	T	1748-9	,,
Teapot : Mr. Iggulden.	Edward Lothian (1731)	EL	,,	,,	U	1749-50	,,
Quaich : Glasgow Exhibit'n.	Robert Lowe (1742)	LOW	,,	,,	U	1750-1	,,
Salver : Mr. Bull. Jas. Sterling's kettle & stand : Glasgow Exhibition.	Ebenr. ,, Oliphant (1737)	EO	,,	,,	W	1751-2	,,
Table-spoon : Mr. Chisholm.	James McKenzie (1747)	IM	,,	,,	X	1752-3	,,
Hash-spoon : Glasgow Exn.	James Weems (1738)	IW					
Small tray : Mr. W. Smith.	John Edmonston (1753)	IE	,,	,,	Y	1753-4	,,
Sugar caster : Mr. W. Beattie.	Wm. Davie (1740)	WD	,,	,,	Z	1754-5	,,

Tea-pot : Mr. O. J. Charlton.	George Forbes	GF		1737-8	...
With date-letter O for 1743-4, Edinburgh Castle, and mark of assay master as 1742-3. Coffee-pot : Mr. Hugh Cobb.	Robt. Hope	HOPE		1743-4	...
Mug : Mr. Colt.	Wm. Aytoun	WA	HG	1744-5	Hugh Gordon.

† Dougal Ged and Edward Lothian each stamped plate with his own mark while temporarily performing the assayer's duties.

MARKS ON EDINBURGH PLATE.

TABLE VI.

FROM 1755 TO 1780—TWENTY-FIVE YEARS.

FOUR STAMPS.

ARTICLES AND OWNERS.	MAKER'S NAME.		MAKER'S MARK.	TOWN MARK. CASTLE.	ASSAY MASTER'S MARK.	DATE LETTER	DATE.
Spoon: Messrs. McKay & Chisholm.	Ker & Dempster.		K&D	🏰	HG	𝔄	1755-6
Do. : The Author's Collection.	Rbt. Gordon	Adm. (1741)	RG	,,	,,	𝔅	1756-7
Small salver : Miss Forbes.	Wm. Taylor	(1753)	WT				
Spoon : Glasgow Exhibition.	John Clark	(1751)	CLARK	,,	,,	ℭ	1757-8
Teapot : Earl of Harrington.	Lothian & Robertson.		L&R				
Coffee-pot : Messrs. Crichton.	James Welsh	(1746)	IW	,,	,, THISTLE	𝔇	1758-9
Spoon : Mr. Chisholm.	James Gilsland	(1748)	IG	,,	🏰	ℭ	1759-60
Sugar-tongs : Glasgow Exhibition.	Alexr. Aitchison	(1746)	AIT			𝔉	GEO. III.
Table-spoons : Mr. Murdoch.	Jas. Somervail	(1754)	I.S	,,	,,		1760-1
Salver : Messrs. Hamilton & Inches.	John Robertson	(1758)	J.R				
Table-spoon : Mr. G. Lambert.	Wm. Dempster	(1742)	W.D	,,	,,	𝔊	1761-2
Do. : Mrs. Kerr.	,, ,,						
Com. cups : Liberton, Edinburgh.	John Welsh	(1742)	IW	,,	,,	𝔥	1762-3
Hash-spoon : Messrs. Wilson & Sharp.	John Taylor	(1760)	IT				
Snuffers tray : Miss Forbes.	James Hill	(1746)	JH	,,	,,	𝔍	1763-4
Hash-spoon : Mr. John Denholm.	Milne & Campbell ?		M&C	,,	,,	𝔎	1764-5
Small mug : Mr. Sorley.	Rbt. Clark	(1763)	RC				
Table-spoons : Colonel Milne.	Wm. Drummond	(1760)	WD	,,	,,	𝔏	1765-6
Table-spoons : Mr. Smith ; and communion cup : Dundee.	John Stirling ?	(1757)	IS	,,	,,	𝔐	1766-7
Table-spoons : Mr. Hough.	Benjn. Tait	(1763)	TAIT				
Do. : Mr. H. D. Ellis.	Gillsland & Ker.		G&K	,,	,,	𝔑	1767-8
Do. : Messrs. McKay & Chisholm.	Patk. Robertson	(1751)	PR	,,	,,	𝔒	1768-9
Coffee-pot : Edinburgh Museum.		,,					
Salt-spoon : Messrs. Smith & Rait.	Daniel Ker."	(1764)	DK	,,	,,	𝔓	1769-70
Sugar-spoon : Lord Breadalbane.	(not identified.)		JB				
Small quaich : Do. do.	James Gilsland	(1748)	IG	,,	,,	𝔔	1770-1
Teapot : Mr. W. Boore.	Wm. & Jno. Taylor.		WT IT	,,	,,	𝔕	1771-2
Soup-ladle : B'ham Assay Office.	Wm. Davie	(1740)	WD	,,	,,	𝔖	1772-3
Communion cups : Lanark.	,, ,,						
Quaich : Mr. Chisholm.	Alexr. Gairdner	(1754)	AG	,,	,,	𝔗	1773-4
Teapot : Messrs. Crichton.	James Welsh	(1746)	IW	,,	,,	𝔘	1774-5
Plate noted by Mr. A. J. S. Brook.	... ...			,,	,,	𝔙	1775-6
Sugar spoon : Mrs. Walker.	Wm. Davie	(1740)	WD	,,	,,	𝔛	1776-7
Table-spoons : Mr. Davison.	James Dempster	(1775)	ID	,,	,,	𝔜	1777-8
Tea-urn : Edinburgh Museum.	Patk. Robertson	(1751)	PR	,,	,,	𝔝	1778-9
Sauce-ladle : Mr. Chisholm.	James Hewitt	(1750)	JH	,,	,,	𝔘	1779-80

Small salver : Mr. McKay.	... ...		MW	ℭ	1759-60
Pepper caster : Messrs. Crichton.	{ Wm. Ker. { Wm. Taylor ?		KER WT	𝔊	1761-2
Sweet basket : Do. do.	... ...		YR	𝔑	1767-8
Teapot : Mr. Jefferis.	... ...		DE	𝔯	1771-2

MARKS ON EDINBURGH PLATE.

TABLE VII.

FROM 1780 TO 1806—TWENTY-SIX YEARS.

FOUR STAMPS TILL 1784, THEREAFTER FIVE STAMPS AS BELOW.

(See the observations on page 496 with reference to certain marks of this and the following cycles.)

ARTICLES AND OWNERS.	MAKER'S NAME.		MAKER'S MARK.	TOWN MARK CASTLE	THISTLE	DATE LETTER	DATE.
Table-spoon: Glasgow Exhibition of 1901.	W. & P. Cunningham.		W & PC	⛫	✿	A	1780-1
Toasting fork: Lord Newlands.	David Downie	Adm. (1770)	DD	,,	,,	B	1781-2
Tea-spoons: Messrs. Smith & Rait.	Fras. Howden	(1781)	FH	,,	,,	C	1782-3
Do. : Do. do.	Robt. Bowman	(1780)	RB	,,	,,	D	1783-4
Teapot: Messrs. Hamilton & Inches.	Alex. Edmonston	(1779)	AE	KING'S HEAD. ⬤	,,	,,	E	*1784-5
Table-spoons: Messrs. McKay & Chisholm.	David Marshall	(1782)	DM	,,	,,	F	1785-6
Salt cellar: Mr. Propert.	James Dempster	(1775)	ID	⬤	,,	,,	G	†1786-7-8
Mustard-pot: Mr. G. Lowe.	Thos. Duffus	(1780)	TD	,,	,,	,,	H	1788-9
Hash-spoon: Mr. J. Barclay Murdoch. Toddy-ladle: Glasgow Exhibition.	Alex. Gairdner James Douglas	(1754) (1785)	AG JD	,,	,,	IJ	‡1789-90
Ewer and basin: Tolbooth Ch.	W. & P. Cunningham.		WC PC	,,	,,	,,	K	1790-1
Waiter on 3 feet: Mr. Lowe.	Geo. Christie	(1791)	GC	,,	,,	,,	L	1791-2
Teapot: Mr. W. Boore.	Alex. Zeigler	(1782)	AZ	,,	,,	,,	M	1792-3
Sauce-boat: Mr. Nesbit.	Peter Mathie	(1774)	PM	,,	,,	,,	N	§1793-4
Table-spoon: Mr. E. Heron Allen.	Wm. Robertson	(1789)	WR	,,	,,	,,	O	1794-5
Mustard-pot: Messrs. Christie.	Alex. Henderson	(1792)	AH	,,	,,	,,	P	1795-6
Com. cup: Fortingall. Table-spoon: Mr. Chisholm.	Geo. Christie Alex. Spence	(1791) (1783)	GC AS	,,	,,	,,	Q	1796-7
Com. cup: Tulliallan.	W. & P. Cunningham.		WPC	⬤	,,	,,	R	¶1797-8
Spoon: Lord Breadalbane.	Thos. Duffus	(1780)	TD	,,	,,	,,	S	1798-9
Spoon: Messrs. McKay & Chisholm. Com. cups: Symington and Dunlop.	Alex. Graham & Co. ? W. & P. Cunningham.		AG&C⁰ WPC	,,	⛫	✿	T	1799 1800
Hash spoons: Mr. Chisholm.	John Zeigler	(1798)	IZ	,,	,,	,,	U	1800-1
Table-spoons: Do.	Fras. Howden	(1781)	FH	,,	,,	,,	V	1801-2
Do. : Do.	Matt. Craw.		MC	,,	⛫	,,	W	1802-3
Cup: Glasgow Exhibition.	Wm. Auld	(1788)	WA	,,	,,	,,	X	1803-4
Marrow spoon: Messrs. Crichton.	Simon Cunningham	(1800)	SC	,,	,,	,,	Y	1804-5
Tea-spoons: Mr. E. Eggleton.	(*Not identified*).		M&R	,,	,,	,,	Z	1805-6

* The King's head mark (incuse) which first came into use on the 1 December, 1784, is not to be found on plate which was stamped with the date-letter E before that day.

† The date-letter G was used in the latter part of 1786, the whole of 1787, and the first part of 1788, and with that letter the King's head mark is found both incuse and cameo.

‡ The letter I was used in the latter part of 1789, followed by J, which continued to be used until September, 1790.

§ In some instances the letter N of 1793-4 is found in a shield, the top of which extends on each side slightly beyond the vertical line, and the base of which is not angular but finishes in a point with a waved line on each side, like the last twenty in the following table.

¶ The King's head outlined as illustrated at 1797-8, is also found with the date-letter Q used in the early part of 1797.

MARKS ON EDINBURGH PLATE.

TABLE VIII.

FROM 1806 TO 1832—TWENTY-SIX YEARS.

FIVE STAMPS AS BELOW.

(See the observations on page 496 with reference to certain marks of this and the preceding cycle.)

ARTICLES AND OWNERS.	MAKER'S NAME.	MAKER'S MARK	KING'S HEAD	TOWN MARK CASTLE	THISTLE	DATE LETTER	DATE.
Tea-spoons : Miss Forbes.	R. Green or R. Grierson.	RG	(king's head)	(castle)	(thistle)	a	1806-7
Salt-spoons : Messrs. M. & S. Lyon.	Cunningham & Simpson.	PC&S	,,	,,	,,	b	1807-8
Communion cup : Kelso.	(*Not identified*).	D&M					
Cup : Messrs. R. & W. Sorley.	Do. do. *	IH	,,	,,	,,	c	1808-9
Punch-bowl : Mr. Geo. B. Murdoch.	George Fenwick.	GF					
Teapot : Messrs. Hamilton & Inches.	John McDonald.	IMD	,,	(castle)	,,	d	1809-10
Snuff-box : The Earl of Ancaster.	Robt. Gray & Son (of Glasgow).	RG&S	,,	,,	,,	e	1810-1
Plaid brooch : Glasgow Exhibition.	Math. Craw.	MC	,,	,,	,,	f	1811-2
Cup : Messrs. R. & W. Sorley.	Alexr. Henderson.	AH	,,	,,	,,	g	1812-3
Quaich : Do. do.	J. McKay. †	JMc	,,	,,	,,	h	1813-4
Table-spoons : Glasgow Exhibition.	Frs. Howden.	FH					
Tea-spoon : Lord Breadalbane.	R. K. (a Perth maker).						
Beer-jug : Messrs. Crichton.	Wm. Zeigler.	WZ	,,	,,	,,	i	1814-5
Toddy-ladle : Mr. Skinner.	Js. & Wm. Marshall.	J&WM					1815-6
Salt-spoons : Mr. Arthur.	Chas. Dalgleish.	CD	,,	,,	,,	k	1816-7
Punch-ladle : Messrs. Mackay & Chisholm.	J. McKay.	JMc	,,	,,	,,	l	1817-8
Table-forks : Mr. J. R. Garstin, F.S.A	Do. do.						
Nutmeg box : Mr. FitzHenry.	Redpath & Arnot.	R&A	,,	,,	,,	m	1818-9
Quaich : Messrs. Mackay & Chisholm.	J'n'th'n Millidge ?	JM	,,	,,	,,	n	1819-20
Waiter : Messrs. Hamilton & Inches.	Frs. Howden.	FH	,,	(castle)	(thistle)	o	GEO. IV. 1820-1
Meat-skewer : Mr. Davison.	Do. do.	,,	,,	,,	,,	p	1821-2
Toddy-ladle : Messrs. Mackay & Chisholm.	Redpath & Arnot.	R&A	,,	,,	,,	q	1822-3
Table-spoon : Do. do Quaich : Lord Breadalbane. }	Alexr. Zeigler.	AZ	(king's head)	,,	,,	r	1823-4
Punch-ladle : Mr. George Young.	Marshall & Sons.	M&S	,,	(castle)	,,	s	1824-5
Tea-set : Messrs. Hamilton & Inches.	J. McKenzie ? †	Mc	,,	,,	,,	t	1825-6
Punch-ladle : Messrs. Smith & Rait.	J. McKay.	JMc	,,	(castle)	,,	u	1826-7
Tea-spoons : Messrs. Mackay & Chisholm.	Leon'd Urquhart.	LU	,,	,,	,,	v	1827-8
Dessert-spoon : B'm'ham Assay Office.	(*Not identified*).	WC	,,	,,	,,	w	1828-9
Punch-bowl : Messrs. R. & W. Sorley.	J. McKay.	JMc	,,	,,	,,	x	1829-30
Toddy-ladle : Messrs. Mackay & Chisholm.	Do. do.	,,	,,	,,	,,	y	WM. IV. 1830-1
Small mug : Mr. W. Boore.	Peter Sutherland.	PS	,,	,,	,,	z	1831-2

Milk-jug : Mr. Adams.	Cunningham & Simpson	PC&S					1808-9
Mustard-pot : Messrs. Crichton.	(*Not identified*).	GMH	P				1821-2

* The names of John Hay, J. Haldane, Jas. Haxton, John Henderson and John Horn occur about this time ; the initials I H might pertain to any one of these.

† The names of James Mackie, John ? McKay, and James McKenzie occur between 1773 and 1845. The mark JMc. which is most probably that of John McKay (adm. 1793), has been found from 1803 to 1845 ; the mark Mc. is probably that of Jas. McKenzie.

MARKS ON EDINBURGH PLATE.

TABLE IX.

FROM 1832 TO 1857—TWENTY-FIVE YEARS.

FIVE STAMPS AS BELOW.

ARTICLES AND OWNERS.	MAKER'S NAME.	MAKER'S MARK.	KING'S HEAD.	TOWN MARK CASTLE.	THISTLE.	DATE LETTER	DATE.
Sauce-boat : Messrs. G.	Marshall & Sons.	M&S	☉	▦	◈	A	1832-3
Snuff-box : Birm. Assay Office.	Jas. Nasmyth.	JN	,,	,,	,,	B	1833-4
Tea-spoon : Do. do.	(*Not identified*).	GB	,,	,,	,,	C	1834-5
Table-spoon : Do. do.	Elder & Co.	E&Cᵒ	,,	,,	,,	D	1835-6
Tea-spoons & ladle : Marquess of Breadalbane.	R. & R. Keay, of Perth.	R&RK	,,	,,	,,	E	1836-7
Small quaich : Do. do.	J. McKay.	JMᶜ	,,	,,	,,	F	VICTORIA. 1837-8
Table-spoon : Mr. Drummond, of Stirling.	A.D. (see the Arbroath Marks).		,,	,,	,,	G	1838-9
Large salver : Mr. Chisholm.	Jas. Howden & Co.	JH&Cᵒ	,,	,,	,,	H	1839-40
Snuff-box : Messrs. Spink.	Jas. Nasmyth & Co.	JN&Cᵒ	,, QUEEN'S HEAD	,,	,,	I	1840-1
Sauce-ladle : The Marquess of Breadalbane.	Geo. Jameson, of Aberdeen.	GJ	☉	,,	,,	K	1841-2
Small waiter : Mr. Falk.	Marshall & Sons.	M&S	,,	,,	,,	L	1842-3
Goldsmiths' Hall Plate, Edinbr.	... ...		,,	,,	,,	M	1843-4
Table-spoons : Mr. Chisholm.	J. McKay.	JMᶜ	,,	,,	,,	N	1844-5
Goldsmiths' Hall Plate, Edinbr.	... ...		,,	,,	,,	O	1845-6
Tea-spoon : The Marquess of Breadalbane.	* D G as Canongate c. 1836 (page 514).		,,	,,	,,	P	1846-7
Cream-jug : Messrs. Christie.	Marshall & Sons.	M&S	,,	,,	,,	Q	1847-8
Table-spoon : Glasgow Exhibn.	J. Hay.	JH	,,	,,	,,	R	1848-9
Hash-spoon : The Makers.	Mackay & Chisholm.	M&C	,,	,,	,,	S	1849-50
Table-spoon : Do.	Do. do.	,,	,,	,,	,,	T	1850-1
Goldsmiths' Hall Plate, Edinbr.	... ...		,,	,,	,,	U	1851-2
Do. do. do.	... ...		,,	,,	,,	V	1852-3
Do. do. do.	... ...		,,	,,	,,	W	1853-4
Do. do. do.	Chas. Robb.	CR	,,	,,	,,	X	1854-5
Do. do. do.	J. Hay.	JH	,,	,,	,,	Y	1855-6
Do. do. do.	(*Not identified*).	RN	,,	,,	,,	Z	1856-7

* The maker's mark " D G " on Lord Breadalbane's tea-spoon (above) is identical with the mark on a Canongate toddy-ladle of about 1836, and a Perth tea-spoon with Edinburgh marks for 1855-6. It is probably the mark of David Greig, junr., of Perth (and possibly of Canongate about 1836).

MARKS ON EDINBURGH PLATE.

TABLE X.

FROM 1857 TO 1882—TWENTY-FIVE YEARS.

FIVE STAMPS AS BELOW.

ARTICLES AND OWNERS.	MAKER'S NAME.	MAKER'S MARK.	QUEEN'S HEAD	TOWN MARK CASTLE.	THISTLE.	DATE LETTER	DATE.
Goldsmiths' Hall Plate, Edinbr.	J. & W. Marshall.	J&WM	⬤	🏰	🌿	A	1857-8
Do. do. do.	Jonthn. Millidge?	JM	,,	,,	,,	B	1858-9
Do. do. do.	(*Not identified*).	JU	,,	,,	,,	C	1859-60
Fruit knife : Museum of Antiq., Edinburgh.	Alex. Hay.	AH	,,	,,	,,	D	1860-1
Goldsmiths' Hall Plate, Edinbr.	J. Asherheim.	JA	,,	,,	,,	E	1861-2
Do. do. do. Do. do. do.	R. L. Christie. J. E. Vernon.	RLC JEV	,,	,,	,,	F	1862-3
Do. do. do.	Wm. Crouch.	WC	,,	,,	,,	G	1863-4
Do. do. do. Do. do. do.	D. Blackley. W. J. McDonald.	DB WJM'D RMC	,,	,,	,,	H	1864-5
Do. do. do.	Wm. Marshall.	WM D.M&C	,,	,,	,,	I	1865-6
Do. do. do.	Elder & Co.	E&C° JM	,,	,,	,,	K	1866-7
Do. do. do. Do. do. do. Do. do. do.	J. Smith or Scott. D. & J. Sanderson. Cockburn & McDonald.	JS D.&J.S COCKBURN	,,	,,	,,	L	1867-8
Teapot : Lord Newlands.	Geo. Edwards & Son.	GE &S	,,	,,	,,	M	1868-9
Goldsmiths' Hall Plate, Edinbr.	J. Hamilton & Son.	J HASON GEO. ST	,,	,,	,,	N	1869-70
Do. do. do. Do. do. do.	George Laing. Walter Neil.	GL WN	,,	,,	,,	O	1870-1
Do. do. do. Do. do. do. Do. do. do.	Wm. Carstairs. Carlisle & Watt. W. Fraser.	WC C&W WF	,,	,,	,,	P	1871-2
Do. do. do.	Jas. Aitchison.	AITCHISON	,,	,,	,,	Q	1872-3
Do. do. do. Do. do. do.	J. Johnston. Jas. Hamilton.	JJ HAMILTON JHAC°	,,	,,	,,	R	1873-4
		M&GS	,,	,,	,,	S	1874-5
Do. do. do.	John Crichton.	J°CRICHTC°					
Do. do. do.	M. Crichton.	JH&C MC JG&C	,,	,,	,,	T	1875-6
Do. do. do.	Robb & Whittet.	R&W J&WM	,,	,,	,,	U	1876-7
Do. do. do.	C. or J. Gray.	GRAY	,,	,,	,,	V	1877-8
Do. do. do.	Mackay & Chisholm.	M&C	,,	,,	,,	W	1878-9
Do. do. do.	J. Crichton.	JC	,,	,,	,,	X	1879-80
Do. do. do.	Hamilton & Inches.	H&I	,,	,,	,,	Y	1880-1
Do. do. do.	... ...		,,	,,	,,	Z	1881-2

Church Plate : Egloskerry. ... ... WM 1871-2

MARKS ON EDINBURGH PLATE.

TABLE XI.

FROM 1882 TO 1906.   FIVE STAMPS TILL 1890, THENCEFORWARD FOUR ONLY, AS BELOW.

ARTICLES AND OWNERS.	MAKER'S NAME.	MAKER'S MARK.	QUEEN'S HEAD.	TOWN MARK. CASTLE.	THISTLE.	DATE LETTER.	DATE.
Goldsmiths' Hall Plate, Edinbr.		CS	●	🏰	●	𝖆	1882-3
Do. do. do.	Wm. Knaggs.	WK	,,	,,	,,	𝖇	1883-4
Do. do. do.	Hamilton & Inches.	H&I	,,	,,	,,	𝖈	1884-5
... ...	... ...	,,	,,	,,	,,	𝖉	1885-6
Do. do. do.	Mackay & Chisholm.	M&C	,,	,,	,,	𝖊	1886-7
Do. do. do.	Jas. Duncan.	JD	,,	,,	,,	𝖋	1887-8
Do. do. do.	Milne of Aberdeen.	MILNE ABDⁿ	,,	,,	,,	𝖌	1888-9
Do. do. do.	W. Crouch & Sons.	WC&S	,,	,,	,,	𝖍	1889-90
Do. do. do.	Hamilton & Inches.	H&I		,,	,,	𝖎	1890-1
" Bute " cup : Cardiff Corp'n.	J. Crichton & Co.	JC&C				𝖐	1891-2
Goldsmiths' Hall Plate, Edinbr.	Jas. Duncan.	JD		,,	,,		
Do. do. do.	Brook & Son.	B&S		,,	,,	𝖑	1892-3
Do. do. do.	J. Crichton & Co.	H&Cⁿ		,,	,,	𝖒	1893-4
Do. do. do.	Lewis Cohen.	L.C					
Do. do. do.	Latimer & Sons.	L&SONS		,,	,,	𝖓	1894-5
Do. do. do.	Jas. Duncan.	JD					
Do. do. do.	D. Crichton.	D.C		,,	,,	𝖔	1895-6
Do. do. do.	J. Crichton & Co.	J&Cⁿ		,,	,,	𝖕	1896-7
Do. do. do.	McDonald & Horne.	M&H					
Do. do. do.	J. Hardy & Co.	H&Cⁿ / C&K		,,	,,	𝖖	1897-8
Do. do. do.	W. Crouch & Sons.	WC&S		,,	,,	𝖗	1898-9
Do. do. do.	W. & J. Milne.	W&JM					1899
Do. do. do.	Hamilton & Inches.	H&J		,,	,,	𝖘	1900
Do. do. do.	Thos. Johnston.	TJ					
Do. do. do.	Young & Tatton.	Y&T		,,	,,	𝖙	1900-1
Do. do. do.	Jas. Robertson.	JR		,,	,,	𝖚	EDW. VII. 1901-2
Plate of the Makers.	Brook & Son.	B&S		,,	,,	𝖛	1902-3
Goldsmiths' Hall Plate, Edinbr.				,,	,,	𝖜	1903-4
Do. do. do.	... ...			,,	,,	𝖝	1904-5
Do. do. do.	... ...			,,	,,	𝖞	1905-6
Do. do. do.	... ...			,,	,,	𝖟	1906-7

MARKS ON EDINBURGH PLATE.

TABLE XII.

SOURCE OF MARKS.	MAKER'S NAME.	TOWN MARK. CASTLE.	TRISTLE.	DATE LETTER.	DATE.
Goldsmiths' Hall Plate, Edinburgh	.. ..	🏰	🌣	**A**	1907-8
Do. do. do.	... ...	,,	,,	**B**	1908-9
Do. do. do.	... ...	,,	,,	**C**	1909-10
Do. do. do.	... ...	,,	,,	**D**	1910-1
Do. do. do.	... ...	,,	,,	**E**	1911-2
Do. do. do.	... ...	,,	,,	**F**	1912-3
Do. do. do.	... ...	,,	,,	**G**	1913-4
Do. do. do.	... ...	,,	,,	**H**	1914-5
Do. do. do.	... ...	,,	,,	**I**	1915-6
Do. do. do.	... ...	,,	,,	**K**	1916-7
Do. do. do.	... ...	,,	,,	**L**	1917-8
Do. do. do.	... ...	,,	,,	**M**	1918-9
Do. do. do.	... ...	,,	,,	**N**	1919-20
Do. do. do.	... ...	,,	,,	**O**	1920-1
Do. do. do.	... ...	,,	,,	**P**	1921-2

MARKS ON EDINBURGH-WROUGHT GOLD.

For gold 22 carats fine, the marks were the same as for plate until **1844**, when the mark 22 was ordered to be added, to denote its fineness. A lower standard for gold—18 carats fine—had been authorised in 1798, since which date the mark 18 (as prescribed) has (in addition to the marks illustrated in the tables), been stamped on such gold to denote its quality. In 1854 three still lower standards of 15 carats, 12 carats and 9 carats fine, respectively, were authorised, for which the marks $\frac{15}{6}$·625, $\frac{12}{5}$·5, and $\frac{9}{6}$·375 respectively were prescribed, in addition to those illustrated in the tables.

For MARKS ON FOREIGN PLATE assayed at Goldsmiths' Hall, Edinburgh, see p. 27 *ante*.

EDINBURGH GOLDSMITHS.

SUCCESSION OF DEACONS OF THE INCORPORATION OF GOLDSMITHS FROM 1525 TO 1681.

(AFTER 1681 THE DEACON'S MARK WAS NOT STAMPED ON PLATE.)

The Deacon was the prime warden, or president of the Incorporation, and was elected to serve for one year, at the end of which he retired from office unless re-elected. The dates which precede the names indicate the terms during which the diaconate was held by the respective deacons.

The Author is indebted to the late Mr. A. J. S. Brook, F.S.A., Scot., for the following list, which was with the greatest possible care transcribed by Mr. Brook from the books of the Incorporation for the pages of *Old Scottish Communion Plate** where the list first appeared.

It will be observed that the spelling of several of the names is varied in the tables and in this and the following list. In some parts of the records from which these lists have been compiled, the names are spelled in one way, and in other parts quite differently. Again, when goldsmiths have signed their names to early documents and to entries in old minute books, the orthography is often found to be quite different from that of the same names in the body of the document or entry in minute book. For example "William Cok" and "William Cokie" refer to the same man. In the same way "George Craufurd" is also "George Craufuird," "Adame Lamb" is "Adam Lamb". In the 16th century, and later, goldsmiths, like other good citizens, were often illiterate and this kind of eccentric spelling was quite common.

DATE.	DEACON'S NAME.		DATE.	DEACON'S NAME.	
1525-6	Adam	Leis	1599-1600-1	David	Heriot † (see 1596)
1526-7	Thomas	Rynd	1601-2-3	George	Foullis
1529-30	Micheall	Gilbert	1603-4	George	Heriot † (see 1589)
1530-1	James	Cokkie	1604-5	Robert	Cokie
1531-2	Allane	Mossman	1605-6-7	George	Foullis (see 1601)
1532 3	John	Kyle	1607-8	George	Heriot (see 1603)
1534-5	George	Heriot	1608-9-10	Robert	Denneistoun †
1535-6	Thomas	Rynde (see 1526)	1610-1	George	Fowlis (see 1605)
1536-7	John	Rynde	1611-2-3	David	Palmer †
1537	Thos.	Rynde (see 1535)	1613-4-5	James	Denneistoun †
1537-8	Richard	Young	1615-6-7	George	Craufuird †
1539-40	William	Rynd	1617-8-9	John	Lindsay †
1542-3	Do.	do.	1619-20-1	James	Denneistoun † (see 1613)
1544-5	Johne	Kyle (see 1532)	1621-2	George	Craufuird † (see 1615)
1547-8	Archibald	Maissone	1623-4-5	Gilbert	Kirkwood †
1548-9	Johne	Gilbert	1625-6-7	Alex.	Reid †
1550-1	Johne	Kyle (see 1544)	1627-8-9	Adame	Lamb †
1551-2	Micheall	Rynd	1629-30-1	Alex.	Reid † (see 1625)
1552-3-4	Thomas	Ewing †	1631-2-3	Jas.	Denneistoun † (see 1619)
1555	No deacon elected.		1633-4-5	George	Craufuird † (see 1621)
1556-7	Thomas	Ewing (see 1552)	1635-6-7	Adame	Lamb † (see 1627)
1558-9	Micheall	Gilbert (see 1529)	1637-8-9	Jon	Scott †
1561-2	Thomas	Ewing (see 1556)	1639-40	Adame	Lamb † (see 1635)
1562-3	George	Rind	1640-1-2	Thos.	Clyghorne †
1563-4-5	James	Cok †	1642	John	Fraser (?) †
1565-6-7	George	Heriot †	1642-3-4	Jas.	Denneistoun (see 1631)
1568-9	James	Mosman	1644-5-6	Adame	Lamb † (see 1635)
1572-3-4	Adam	Craige	1646-7-8	Jon	Scott † (see 1637)
1574-5	David	Denneistoun	1648-9-50	George	Cleghorne †
1575-6	George	Heriot † (see 1565)	1650-1	Nicoll	Trotter †
1576-7	James	Mosman	1651-2-3	Jas.	Fairbairne †
1577-8-9	William	Cokie, otherwise Cok †	1653-4	Andro	Burrell †
1579-80-1	Edward	Hairt	1654-5	The same (probably, but not recorded).	
1581-2	David	Denneistoun (see 1574)	1655-6-7	George	Cleghorne † (see 1648)
1582-3	Edward	Hairt (see 1579)	1657-8-9	Jas.	Fairbairne † (see 1651)
1583-4	Thomas	Annand	1659-60-1	Andrew	Burrell † (see 1653)
1584-5	George	Heriot † (see 1575)	1661-2-3	Patrick	Borthwick †
1585-6	John	Mosman †	1663-4-5	Edward	Cleghorne †
1587-8-9	Adame	Craige (see 1572)	1665-6-7	Jas.	Symontoun †
1589-90-1	George	Heriot † (see 1584)	1667-8-9	Alex	Scott †
1591-2-3-4-5	William	Cok † (see 1577)	1669-70-1	Alex	Reid †
1596-7	David	Heriot †	1671-2-3	Edward	Cleghorne † (see 1663)
1597-8	Daniell	Craufuird (Jr.)	1673-4	Thomas	Cleghorne † (see 1640)
1598-9	George	Heriot † (Jr.)	1674-5	Alex	Reid † (see 1669)
			1675-6-7	William	Law †
			1677-8-9	Alex	Reid † (see 1674)
			1679-80-1	Edward	Cleghorne † (see 1671)

* *Old Scottish Communion Plate* by T. Burns and A. J. S. Brook (Edinburgh: R. R. Clark 1892).
† His mark either as maker or deacon appears in the preceding tables.

SUPPLEMENTARY LIST OF EDINBURGH GOLDSMITHS.

FROM 1525 TO 1798.

The marks of many of the under-mentioned goldsmiths not having been found by the Author, their names do not appear in the preceding tables. Their names are, however, recorded in the minutes of the Incorporation as having been *admitted* to its privileges, each in the year set opposite the name below.

DATE.	NAME OF GOLDSMITH.		DATE.	NAME OF GOLDSMITH.	
1525	William	Curror	1598	James	Denneistoun
,,	Henrie	Young	1599	Adame	Wilsone
1526	Robert	Melvin	1600	William	Stalker (Jr.)
,,	Patrick	Lindsay	1601	John	Galbraith
1529	James	Achieson	1603	John	Brown
,,	John	Achieson	1605	Archibald	Cokie
1530	Thomas	Mosman	,,	James	Stalker
,,	James	Kyle	1606	James	McAulay (Jr.)
1532	Thomas	Wood	1608	Hercules	Weddell
,,	John	Vaitche	1609	David	Thomson
,,	James	Brown	1610	Andro	Boyes
1534	Walter	Cokburne	1616	Thomas	Craufuird
,,	Robert	Craige	1618	James	Stalker
1535	John	Mosman	1619	William	Crichton
1536	Patrick	Gray	1624	David	Haldane
,,	George	Allane	1627	William	Craufuird
,,	Alexander	Mosman	1635	James	Cunynghame
1539	Nichol	Syme	1636	James	Aytoun
,,	Robert	Rynd	,,	Alexander	Heriot
,,	Adam	Denneistoun	1643	George	Robertsone (Jr.)
1547	William	Bassintaine	1644	John	Myln
,,	William	Aitken	,,	James	McAulay (3rd)
,,	John	Ba·sintyne	1653	David	Bag
,,	George	Law	1658	Robert	Lowe
,,	William	Touris	1662	John	Leishman
1551	William	Uric	,,	William	Gray
1557	Hew	Mosman	1663	Robert	Gibsone
1558	Alexander	Gilbert	,,	Samuel	Meickle
,,	Robert	Murray	1664	Thomas	Cleghorne
,,	Edward	Bassintyne	1666	John	Cockburn
,,	Andro	Gray	1668	Andrew	Merstoun
1561	Mungo	Brydie	1672	Zacharias	Mellinus
,,	Gavin	Frechman	1673	William	Rae
,,	Adame	Allane	1674	John	Threipland
1563	Henrie	Stalker	1681	William	Wallace
1564	John	Mosman	,,	John	Aikman
1567	Michael	Heriot	1686	William	Law
,,	Thomas	Frechman	,,	Andro	Gilmour
,,	James	Stalker	1687	Thos.	Hutcheson
1573	John	Barrane	1688	Geo.	Mayne
,,	David	Mylne	1694	Andrew	Law (Jr.)
,,	James	Cok	,,	Edward	Cleghorne (Jr.)
1574	Michael	Syme	1696	Adam	Gordon
1575	George	Heirysone	1697	Robt.	Scott
,,	James	Mosman	,,	John	Yorstoune
1577	James	Lumsdaine	1700	Wm.	Burtoun
1580	William	Duncane	1702	John	Penman
1581	Thomas	Foullis	,,	Robt.	Craig
1586	William	Stalker	1703	Richd.	Rae
1587	John	Lindsay	,,	Hugh	Law
1588	John	Cuninghame	,,	Wm.	Law (Jr.)
1589	Robert	Thompson	1706	Chas.	Duncan
,,	George	Craufuird	,,	Robert	Robertson
1591	John	Duncane	1709	Thos.	Mitchell
,,	James	Craufuird	1710	Jas.	Yorstoune
1594	James	Heriot	,,	Colin	Campbell
1597	Andro	Stalker	1714	Thos.	Leslie
,,	Johne	Lamb	1715	Geo.	Yorstoun (Jr.)
,,	Robert	Fairlie	1719	Thos.	Hay
1598	James	McAulay	1720	John	Cumming

DATE.	NAME OF GOLDSMITH.		DATE.	NAME OF GOLDSMITH.	
1722	Jas.	Scott	1768	Ronald	McDonald
1726	Chas.	McKenzie	1770	Geo.	Beech
1732	Patk.	Murray (Jr.)	,,	Alexr.	Aitchison (Jr.)
1734	Jas.	Campbell	1772	Archibald	Ochiltree
1736	Alexr.	Campbell	1773	Jas.	Mackie
,,	Jas.	Hally	,,	Jos.	Ritchie
1743	Robt.	Hope	1775	Jas.	McKenzie
1753	Peter	Spalding	1778	Wm.	Hewit
1754	Geo.	Auld	1779	Benj.	Buchanan
,,	Benj.	Coots	1782	Neil	Paton
,,	Jas.	Craig	1783	Wm.	McKenzie
1760	Alexr.	Reid	1786	Robt.	Swan
,,	Jas.	Reid	1788	John	Simpson
,,	Wm.	Ker	1789	Saml.	Kerr
,,	Jas.	Oliphant	1791	Thos.	Sempill
1763	John	Anderson	1796	Geo.	Bayne
1764	Thos.	Anderson	1798	John	Cunningham
1765	Adam	Davie	,,	Robt.	Hamilton
1768	John	Irvine			

CANONGATE (EDINBURGH).

Canongate was in early times a distinct burgh with its own Chartered Incorporation of Hammermen.

Canongate, now an integral part of Edinburgh, and never divided by more than the narrowest boundary line from the Scottish metropolis, was in early times a distinct and separate burgh, with its own guilds, and chartered incorporations. As was very commonly the case in provincial towns, the goldsmiths of Canongate were associated with other trades, such as blacksmiths, whitesmiths and coppersmiths, with whom they were incorporated under the comprehensive term of " Hammermen ".

Mr. Mackay * says that " disputes were of frequent occurrence between the trades of the Canongate and those of the city of Edinburgh, on account of members of the craft of one burgh attempting to execute work within the liberties of the other, and whenever ' Ratification ' of a Charter was granted to one, ' Protestatioun ' was taken either to Parliament or to the magistrates and council ' that the granting of the samyn should be no ways prejudicial to the privileges and liberties of the trades and the remanent of the Incorporation ' of the other ".

Canongate mark, a stag's head.

The Canongate mark was a stag's head. In the earliest example of its plate which the Author has found, the mark is a stag lodged, and in some of the later examples an additional mark of an anchor wreathed

* *History of the Burgh of Canongate.*

about with a cable is seen. A stag's head erased, charged between the antlers with a cross crosslet fitchée, was the crest of the burgh, and, as illustrated below, it is to be seen on several buildings within its ancient boundaries, and in the old burgh seal.

In all the known examples of Canongate plate there is no cross between the antlers of the stag's head in the town mark. The head, moreover, although in the majority of instances erased, is sometimes couped.

No cross between the antlers in any known plate stamp.

The Author has not succeeded in tracing the connection of the stag lodged and the anchor, with the stag's head, and, in the absence of evidence, refrains from making a suggestion. The anchor wreathed about with a cable is the Edinburgh crest, and if the ancient records of Canongate were brought to light, both the stag lodged and the anchor might be found to have been " charges " in the ancient coat of arms of the burgh.

The only goldsmith's name in connection with Canongate which can with certainty be stated at present is that of M. Hinchsliffe. His mark appears in the thirteenth line of the following table. An exhaustive examination of the minutes of the Hammermen's Incorporation might result in connecting names with all the marks, but the Author has not been able to get access to any minute books and cannot even say that they are preserved.

Only a very small amount of plate (consisting of spoons and ladles) appears to have emanated from Canongate since the end of the eighteenth century. The Author has been unable to ascertain that any plate at all was wrought by any member of the old Canongate Guild later than 1836. Before the middle of the nineteenth century the guild was extinct.

The examples on which the first two lines of marks are found—spoons in the Edinburgh Museum of Antiquities—would, from their general character, have been ascribed by the Author to a date about half a century later than that which they bear. The inscribed lettering and date on the second spoon appear to be perfectly genuine, and although the stem is suggestive of the middle of the 17th century, the earlier form is preserved in the bowl, and both spoons, therefore, may perhaps be fairly described as early Scottish examples, or varieties of the type of spoon which was adopted in England about the time of Charles II.

CANONGATE GOLDSMITHS' MARKS.

FROM ABOUT 1680 TO ABOUT 1836.

(The dates are approximate, except to the extent that the inscribed dates may be relied on.)

DATE (ABOUT).	MARKS.	MAKER'S NAME.	ARTICLES AND OWNERS.
1680	GC 🐇 XI·D *	... ...	Spoon : Edinburgh Museum of Antiquities.
,,	GC 🐇 KI·D	... ...	Spoon, with flat stem, dated 1689 : Edinburgh Museum of Antiquities.
,,	MZ 🦅 MZ	... ...	Two com. cups, carried off 1689, recovered 1697 : Flisk.
1696	G:Z G:Z	... ...	Two com. cups, dated 1696 : Bolton, Haddington.
1700	P XI ASN	... ...	Wine taster : Messrs. Crichton.
,,	P XX FIS XI·	... ...	Do. do. do.
1760	CM CM	... ...	Table-spoon,† " double drop " back of bowl : Glasgow Exhibition, of 1901.
1763	WC ,, WC	... ...	Two com. cups, dated 1763 : Auchtertool.
1780-90	F GIG GA	... ...	Oil lamp, which may also have been used as a candlestick : Mr. G. Glass. Also stag's head over R, on fork : Mr. Clement Gadsby.
	PC PC	... ...	Table-spoon (fiddle pattern) : Rev. J. Carr.
1790	K	... ...	Tea-spoon (fiddle pattern) : The Marquess of Breadalbane.
TO	K HINCHSLIFFE M	M. Hinchsliffe.	Tea-spoons (fiddle pattern) : The Marquess of Breadalbane and the Author.
1820	e IP	... ...	Tea-spoon : Mr. Geo. Henderson.
	M M	... ...	Table-spoon (fiddle pattern) : Mr. Chisholm.
1836	K DG	‡David Greig (?)	Toddy ladle (fiddle pattern) : Mr. Dudley Westropp.

* The meaning of the stamp XI.D is 11 deniers (i.e. 11 pennyweights) fine, the standard established in Scotland in the 16th century.

† Mr. A. J. S. Brook has a spoon with these marks, and an additional mark of a large Roman letter L in a square punch. *Vide Old Scottish Communion Plate,* 569.

‡ See Edinburgh marks, Table IX. (1846-7), and the Perth table.

CHAPTER XX

THE GLASGOW GOLDSMITHS

AND THEIR MARKS

Glasgow, although not always, as it now is, the largest and most populous town in Scotland, may well claim premier place amongst the Scottish provincial burghs, because of its importance as a centre of the goldsmith's art or craft, both in the past and present.

The Glasgow goldsmiths were incorporated with other metal workers, saddlers and belt-makers under the designation of "Hammermen". They were incorporated by a "Seal of Cause" granted by the Town Council of Glasgow, with the concurrence of the Archbishop (Gavin Dunbar) on 14 October, 1536. *Glasgow gold-smiths were associated with other crafts as an Incorporation of Hammermen.*

The only existing minute-book of the Incorporation runs from 1616 to 1717. The earliest book, and another extending from 1717 to 1775, have been lost. From the existing book of the Incorporation, supplemented by extracts from the Burgess rolls and directories, the list of names which follows the tables has been compiled.* The names of members of all trades who were not likely to have been concerned with goldsmith's work have been excluded from the list, but because in the old days the goldsmith's art, or some branch of it, was frequently exercised by jewellers and watch and clock-makers, the names of such as followed those trades have been retained.

No Glasgow plate of earlier date than 1681 is known to the Author, and the earliest known Glasgow-marked communion plate is of the year 169⅝. The disappearance of plate of earlier date is accounted for by entries of proclamations in the old Burgh Records; the following may be taken as an example of many such :—"15th June, 1639. Proclamatioun anent Silver Plait. The said day it is ordanit that publicatioun be made throw the toun, be sound of drum, that the inhabitantis of this brughe bring their haill † silver plait, to be bestowit in defence of the good comoun cause in hand, conforme to the ordinance of the committee at Ed ⁿ⁻, and ordaines James Stewart lait provest, Walter Stirling, deane of gild, John Barnes and Gawaine Nisbit to attend *Disappearance of much of the early Glasgow plate accounted for.*

* The Author is indebted to Messrs. W. & R. Sorley, of Glasgow, for the list of Hammermen.
† haill = whole, unimpaired.

upon the reassauing * of the said silver plait, and to meitt the days following at nine houris."

The Glasgow "town mark".

The Glasgow town mark is the burgh arms, which are —" *Argent, on a mount in base an oak tree proper, the trunk surmounted by a salmon proper with a signet ring in its mouth, or, on the top of the tree a red breast, and on the sinister fesse-point a hand-bell both proper*". It is commonly called the "fish, tree and bell" mark. The marshalling of these charges is not strictly followed in the mark, which differs very considerably at times. In some examples the bell is on the dexter fesse-point. The bird and salmon are generally "to dexter" but occasionally "to sinister". In most of the early examples the salmon is placed below the trunk of the tree, where the mount should be, and in nearly all cases the size of the bird and fish is Brobdignagian compared with that of the oak-tree. In many cases the letter G (for Glasgow) occupies the sinister fesse-point and the letter is sometimes reversed. As appears to have been the case in some other burghs, each of the Glasgow goldsmiths in the old times had a "town mark" punch of his own. In the case of one maker—William Clerk—his surname, in full, is actually in the field of the burgh mark.

Date-letters used in the latter part of the 17th and early part of the 18th centuries, on Glasgow plate.

In 1681 a date-letter appears to have been adopted, contemporaneously, in all probability, with the first use of the variable letter in Edinburgh, but its use was discontinued about 1710, and it is not again found to have been regularly used until 1819. From that year it has been used without interruption. Between 1763 and 1770 the letters E and F—which may have been date-letters or possibly deacons' marks—are found on plate made by Adam Graham, but there is no evidence to prove that they were either the one or the other.

From about 1730 to about 1800, the letter S in variously shaped punches was generally used in addition to the town and maker's marks. There is no evidence to prove the meaning of this letter or by what authority it was added. It is clear, however, that it cannot be a date-letter, and the probable and generally accepted explanation is that it stood for standard or sterling (S being the initial of both words) whereby plate so marked was guaranteed as of standard or sterling quality, just as the word "STERLING" in full was struck on plate made at Chester, Cork and some other towns.

A mark which at first sight may be mistaken for a date-letter is

---

* reassauing = resaving, receiving, *i.e.* to attend at the receiving of the plate.

found on plate made between 1760 and 1800. It is the Roman letter O in a square punch with the corners clipped, and is found on all or nearly all the plate manufactured by Milne and Campbell. It cannot therefore be a date-letter. The same letter, sloping backwards diagonally, is found in a perfectly square punch on plate made by John Donald (1785-95), while on other plate by the same maker the customary S (for sterling or standard) is found. It would be interesting to know the meaning of this letter O, but the Author is unable to make a suggestion regarding it, except that as it is not found together with the letter S, it may, as an alternative mark, have been an indication of quality; possibly *Old* standard.

There appears to be no evidence of the existence of a regular assay at Glasgow before 1819, and in view of the variety in the form of the "town mark" used by different makers at the same time, the presumption is that there was no such office until the assay office was established in Glasgow by the Statute 59 Geo. III. c. 28 (1819). This statute constituted the Glasgow Goldsmiths' Company a body corporate, and gave to it powers and placed it under regulations similar to those which were subsequently defined by the Act 6 and 7 Wm. IV. c. 69 with reference to Edinburgh. A regular assay office established in Glasgow, in 1819.

The Act established a district comprising Glasgow and forty miles round it, and required that all plate made in that district should be assayed at the office of the company. It provided also for the election of new members to fill up vacancies in the corporation.

The Act contains an extraordinary direction to the assayer : He is required to weigh the plate in water and try the effect of magnetism ! The Glasgow assayer directed to weigh plate in water, and to try the effect of magnetism.

The selling of plate made in the district not having the marks appointed by the Act, subjects the offender to forfeiture of the plate or its value, to which by the later Act is added a further penalty of £100 in respect of every piece of plate sold without being marked as prescribed.

The marks prescribed by the Act are :— Marks prescribed by Act of 1819.

(1) The lion rampant (the standard mark) ;
(2) The city arms—a tree, fish and bell (the town mark) ;
(3) The maker's mark—the initials of his name ;
(4) A variable letter or date mark ; and
(5) The sovereign's head—the duty mark.

The standard for silver is 11 oz. 2 dwt. fine ; the higher quality

(11 oz. 10 dwt. fine) may be used, in which case the figure of " Britannia " is to be *added* to the above marks.

The additional marks indicating the several qualities of gold are the same as at Edinburgh.

The duty mark was abolished on the repeal of the duty on plate 28 May, 1890. All the other marks continue in use.

Pursuant to the above Statute the use of the date-letter was resumed in 1819 with the Roman capital A. The letter is changed in the autumn of each year, and from 1819 each cycle has consisted of twenty-six years. In each cycle an entire alphabet of twenty-six letters has been used.

It will be observed on referring to Table III. of the Glasgow marks which follows hereon, that the lion rampant was used before its statutory appointment in 1819.

By the courtesy of the Glasgow Incorporation and their Assay Master, the Author has been furnished with impressions of the marks used from 1871 to 1921, from which Tables VI. and VII. have been compiled.

The makers' marks which follow the tables have also been reproduced from the impressions struck in the copper plates at the assay office. The date when each of these makers' marks was registered is not recorded.

For MARKS ON FOREIGN PLATE assayed at Glasgow, see page 27 *ante*.

MARKS ON GLASGOW PLATE.

TABLE I.

FROM ABOUT 1681 TO 1706.

FOUR STAMPS, in the order represented below, the town mark being stamped between the duplicated maker's mark, the date-letter last.

The date following a maker's name is that of his *admission* to the Incorporation of Hammermen.

DATE.	MAKER'S MARK.	TREE, FISH & BELL.	MAKER'S MARK.	DATE LETTER	MAKER'S NAME.			ARTICLES AND OWNERS.
1681-2				a	Thos.	Moncrur	(1665)	Quaich (without date-letter) : Mr. B. Warwick.
1682-3				b	...	...	...	Date-letter conjectured.
1683-4				c	Robt.	Brook	(1673)	Large quaich : Mr. J. A. Holms.
1684-5				d	...	...	...	Date-letter conjectured.
1685-6	,,	,,	,,	e	Robert Brook		(1673)	Table-spoon, flat stem, trifid end : Messrs. Crichton.
1686-7				f	...	...	...	Date and date-letter conjectured.
1687-8				g	...	...	...	Do. do. do.
1688-9				h	...	...	...	Do. do. do.
1689-90				i	Jas.	Stirlıng	(1686)	Trifid spoons : Mr. R. Meldrum.
1690-1	,,	,,	,,	k	Do.	Do.		Do. do. do.
1691-2				l	...	...	...	Date-letter conjectured.
1692-3				m	...	...	...	Do. do.
1693-4				n	...	...	...	Do. do.
1694-5				o	Robt.	Brook	(1673)	Quaich : The Day Collection.
1695-6				p	...	...	...	Date-letter conjectured.
1696-7		,,		q	Robert Brook		(1673)	Communion cup dated 1697 : Hamilton.
1697-8				r	...	...	...	Date-letter conjectured.
1698-9				s	Wm.	Clerk	(1693)	Quaich : Glasgow Exhib., 1901.
1699 1700				t	Robert Brook		(1673)	Two com. cups : Strathblane.
1700-1				u	John	Luke*		Rat-tail spoon, trifid end : The Marquess of Breadalbane, K.G.
1701-2		,,		v	James Luke		(1692)	Rat-tail spoon, trifid end : Glasgow Exhibition, 1901 ; also communion cups dated 1703 : Renfrew.
1702-3				w	...	...	...	Date and date-letter conjectured.
1703-4				x	...	...	...	Do. do. do.
1704-5		,,		y	Thos.	Cumming	(1682)	Ladle : Glasgow Exhibition ; also com. cups dated 1704 : Kilpatrick.
		,,			John	Luke, jr.	(1699)	Mug (applied ornamentation) : Mr. J. Barclay Murdoch.
1705-6	,,	,,	,,	z	Do.	do.	do.	Rat-tail hash spoon, with mace handle : The Marquess of Breadalbane, K.G.

* John Luke (or Louk) first mentioned 1659, died 1702.

MARKS ON GLASGOW PLATE.

TABLE II.

FROM ABOUT 1706 TO 1765.

STAMPS VARIOUS, AS BELOW, the town-mark being stamped between the duplicated maker's mark.

DATE (ABOUT.)	MAKER'S MARK.	TREE, FISH & BELL.	MAKER'S MARK.	LETTER	MAKER'S MARK.			ARTICLES AND OWNERS.
1706-7				A	...	...	...	Date and (date ?) letter conjectured.
1707-8	⃝	⃝	⃝	B	John	Luke, jr.	(1699)	Tankard, dated 1707: Mr. Thos. Maxwell; and com. cups, dated 1708: Greenock.
1709-10	,,	,,	,,	D	Do.	do.	,,	Com. cups, inscribed " For the Baronie Kirk 1704": Barony Ch., Glasgow.
1709-10	W.C	⃝	W.C	,,	William	Clerk	(1693)	Large quaich : The Marquess of Breadalbane.
1709-20	IF	⃝	IF		John	Falconer	(1709)	Quaich and rat-tail spoon : Glasgow Exhibition, 1901.
,,	JL	,,	JL		James	Lockhart	(1707)	Soup-ladle : Messrs. Smith & Rait.
1717-49	IB	,,	IB		Johan Got-helf-Bilsings (1717)			{ Table-spoon : Glasgow Exhibition; { Snuff-box : Messrs. Smith & Rait.
1728-31	,,	,,	,,	S	Do.	do.	,,	Com. cups, dated 1728 : Douglas, and (1731) Dumbarton.
1725-35	RL	,,	RL	S	Robert	Luke	(1721)	Two com. cups, dated 1734 : Barony Church, Glasgow.
1743-52	IG	⃝	IG	S	James	Glen	(1743)	{ Small quaich : The Marquess of { Breadalbane. { Hash-spoon : Mr. J. Barclay Murdoch.
,,	GLN	,,	GLN	,,	Do.	do.	,,	Teapot : Messrs. Smith & Rait.
1747-60	ST		ST	S	Saml.	Telfer	(1747)	Table-spoon : Mr. W. Boore.
1756-76	D.W	,,	D.W	S	David	Warnock	(1756)	Four com. cups : The Marquess of Breadalbane.
,,		,,		S	(*No maker's mark*).			Table-spoon : Mr. J. Barclay Murdoch.
1757-80	IC	⃝	IC		John	Campbell	(1757)	Snuff-box : The Marquess of Breadalbane.
,,	JL	⃝	JL		(*Not identified.*)			Table-spoon (double drop) : Messrs. Smith & Rait.
,,	J·S	⃝	J·S	,,	Do.	do.		Do. do. do.
1758-65	WN	,,	WN		Wm.	Napier	(1758)	Do. do. do.
,,	B&N	,,	B&N	S	Bayne & Napier.			Com. cup, dated 1765 : St. Quivox Ch., near Glasgow.

The observations in the text preceding Table I. should be read in connection with the above marks, especially with reference to the letters in the last column of marks in this and the succeeding table.

MARKS ON GLASGOW PLATE.

TABLE III.

FROM ABOUT 1763 TO ABOUT 1813.

STAMPS VARIOUS, AS BELOW: The town-mark is generally found between the duplicated maker's mark, both impressions of the maker's mark having been struck with the same punch.

DATE (ABOUT).	MAKER'S MARK.	TREE, FISH & BELL.	MAKER'S MARK.	LETTER.	MAKER'S NAME.			ARTICLES AND OWNERS.
1763-70	AG	(tree)	AG		Adam	Graham	(1763)	Quaich, salts, spoons and sugar tongs: The Marquess of Breadalbane.
,,	,,	,,	,,	E	Do.	do.		Table-spoon: Mr. J. Barclay Murdoch.
,,	,,	,,	,,	F	Do.	do.		Do. do. do.
1773-80	IT	S	IT	S	James	Taylor	(1773)	Four table-spoons: The Marquess of Breadalbane.
1776-80	M&C	(tree)		O	* Milne & Campbell.			Teapot and sugar-bowl: Mr. John Denholme.
,,	M&C	(tree)	M&C	O	* Do.	do.		Snuff-box and spoons: Mr. J. Barclay Murdoch.
,,	RG	(tree)	RG		Robert	Gray	(1776)	Soup-ladle: Messrs. Smith & Rait.
,,	RG	(tree)	RG	S	Do.	do.	,,	Hash-spoon: Mr. John Denholme.
1783	T&H	(tree)	T&H		Taylor & Hamilton.			Shoulder-brooch: Glasgow Exhibition.
,,	J·Mc	(tree)	J·Mc	,,	James	McEwen	(1783)	Large punch-bowl: The Marquess of Breadalbane.
1777-90	WL	,,	WL	,,	Wm.	Love	(1777)	Table-spoons: Messrs. Smith & Rait.
1782-92	J·W	(tree)	J·W		James	Wright	(1782)	Table-spoons: Glasgow Exhibition.
1785-95	ID	(tree)	ID	S	John	Donald	(1785)	Do. do. do.
,,	,,	,,	,,	O	Do.	do.	,,	Do. do. do.
1781 / 1800	MF	(tree)	MF	S	†Patrick	McFarlane	(1781)	Pair of gravy-spoons: Messrs. Crichton.
1811-3	MF	(lion) LION RAMPANT.			‡Archibald McFadyen	(1811)		Pair of table candlesticks: Mr. W. Boore.

The observations in the text preceding Table I. should be read in connection with the above marks, especially with reference to the letters E, F, O and S, which appear after the maker's marks.

* The marks in the fifth and sixth lines, though apparently resembling each other, are appreciably different in size and otherwise. In the town mark, in the fifth line, the letter G (for Glasgow) appears where the bell should be and *is* in the mark below it. The maker's mark is struck only once on the articles bearing the marks in the fifth line instead of twice, as is generally the case.

† In this case (as in that of firms), no initial of Christian name is included in the maker's mark.

‡ This seems to be the first appearance of the lion rampant (from the Royal Standard of Scotland), as a mark on Glasgow plate—the mark prescribed by the Act 59 Geo. III. c. 28 to be stamped on all plate assayed at Glasgow from 1819 onwards, to indicate that plate so stamped is of standard quality.

MARKS ON GLASGOW PLATE.

TABLE IV.

FROM 1819 TO 1845, FIVE STAMPS AS BELOW.

The date following a maker's name is that of his *admission* to the Incorporation of Hammermen; in the case of firm-names it is that of their first known appearance.

	TREE, FISH & BELL.	LION RAMPANT.	DATE LETTER.	KING'S HEAD.	MAKER'S MARK.	MAKER'S NAME.	ARTICLES AND OWNERS.
1819-20	🦁	🦁	A	👤	B.SCOTT / M&R	B. Scott. *(Not identified.)*	Sugar tongs: The Author. / Salt spoon: B'm'ham Assay Office.
GEO. IV. 1820-1	🦁	,,	B	,,	LFN / JD	Luke F. Newlands (1816) / Jas. Downie (1812)	Teapot: Messrs. Smith & Rait. / Tea-spoon: B'm'ham Assay Office.
1821-2	,,	,,	C	,,	RG&S	Robt. Gray & Son (1819)	Tea-spoons: Glasgow Exhibition.
1822-3	,,	,,	D	,,	RD	Robt. Duncan (1813)	Lemon strainer: Do. do.
1823-4	,,	,,	E	,,	JB	John Bruce (1815)	Snuff-box: Mr. Arthur.
1824-5	,,	,,	F	,,	M&S	*(Not identified.)*	Punch bowl: Mr. George Young.
1825-6	,,	,,	G	,,	AM	Alexr. Mitchell (1822)	Table-spoon: Glasgow Exhibition.
1826-7	,,	,,	H	,,	AMcD	Angus McDonald (1824)	Tea-spoons: Mr. Chisholm.
1827-8	,,	,,	I	,,	PA	Peter Arthur (1808)	Do. : Messrs. Smith & Rait.
1828-9	,,	,,	J	,,	EB	Edwd. Bell (1827)	Toddy ladle: Glasgow Exhibition.
1829-30	,,	,,	K	,,	JB CO	Jas. Burrell & Co. (1825)	Sugar tongs: Mr. Wilkinson.
WM. IV. 1830-1	,,	,,	L	,,	DR	Danl. Robertson (1829)	Small circular box: Messrs. Spink.
1831-2	,,	,,	M	,,		John Mitchell ... (as 1835-6 below).	Plain bowl: Messrs. Crichton.
1832-3	,,	,,	N	👤	RG&S	Robt. Gray & Son (1819)	Lemon strainer: Messrs. Smith & Rait.
1833-4	,,	,,	O	,,	PA	Peter Arthur (1808)	Tea-spoon: Messrs. Smith & Rait.
1834-5	,,	,,	P	,,	DCR	D. C. Rait (1832)	Toddy ladle: Mr. Harrison.
1835-6	,,	,,	Q	,,	JM	John Mitchell (1834)	Salt spoons: Messrs. Smith & Rait.
1836-7	,,	,,	R	,,	DCR / JW	D. C. Rait (1832) *(Not identified.)*	Tea-spoons: Do. do. do. / Snuff-box: Messrs. Crichton.
VICT. 1837-8	,,	,,	S	,,	WP	W. Parkins (1835)	Shoulder-brooch: Mr. Mitchell.
1838-9	,,	,,	T	,,	RG&S	Robt. Gray & Son (1819)	Large beer-jug: Messrs. Crichton.
1839-40	,,	,,	U	,,	,,	Do. do. ,,	Spirit lamp: Messrs. Smith & Rait.
1840-1	,,	,,	V	,,	JM	John Mitchell (1834)	Hilt of small dirk: Mr. Jefferis.
1841-2	,,	,,	W		HM	*Henry Muirhead (1838)	Watch-case: Mr. Lannon.
1842-3	,,	,,	X		HD	*Henry Downs (1831)	Waist buckle: Mr. Falk.
1843-4	,,	,,	Y		DCR	*D. C. Rait (1832)	Book clasp: Glasgow Exhibition.
1844-5	,,	,,	Z		CB	*Chas. Bryson (1834)	Top of scent-bottle: Mrs. Budd.
1823					PG	Philip Grierson.	Punch ladle: Messrs. Crichton.
c. 1826					JK JL JK	John Law.	Wine labels: The Marquess of Breadalbane, K.G.

* The head of Queen Victoria was first used as a duty-mark in Glasgow in 1841-2. These articles were, however, exempt from duty and had no duty-mark.

MARKS ON GLASGOW PLATE.

TABLE V.

FROM 1845 TO 1871; FIVE STAMPS AS BELOW.

	TREE, FISH & BELL.	LION RAMPANT.	DATE LETTER.	QUEEN'S HEAD.	MAKER'S MARK.	MAKER'S NAME.			ARTICLES AND OWNERS.
1845-6	🐟	🦁	𝕬	👑	WB	Walter	Baird	(1845)	Sugar bowl: Messrs. Hamilton & Inches.
1846-7	,,	,,	𝕭	,,	RG &S	Robt.	Gray & Son	(1819)	Small mug: Messrs. R. & W. Sorley.
1847-8	,,	,,	𝕮	,,		...	...	...	Glasgow Assay Office Plate.
1848-9	,,	,,	𝕯	,,	JR	John	Russell	(1845)	Pair of salt shovels: Mrs. Marshall.
1849-50	,,	,,	𝕰	,,	PAJʀ	Peter	Aitken, jr.	,,	Shoulder-brooch: Mr. J. Stevens.
1850-1	,,	,,	𝕱	,,	J&WM	J. & W.	Mitchell	(1834)	Tea-caddy spoon: The Author.
1851-2	,,	,,	𝕲	,,		...	...	...	Glasgow Assay Office Plate.
1852-3	,,	,,	𝕳	,,	RG&S	Robt.	Gray & Son (1819) (second mark)		Sugar tongs: Messrs. Smith & Rait.
1853-4	,,	,,	𝕴	,,		...	...	...	Glasgow Assay Office Plate.
1854-5	,,	,,	𝕵	,,	AM	A.	McMillan	(1837)	Watch-case: Mr. Falk.
1855-6	,,	,,	𝕶	,,	RS	R.	Stewart	(1842)	Tea-spoon: Messrs. R. & W. Sorley.
1856-7	,,	,,	𝕷	,,		...	...	...	Glasgow Assay Office Plate.
1857-8	,,	,,	𝕸	,,	AMcD	A.	McDonald	(1845)	Spectacle-case: Mr. J. Walker.
1858-9	,,	,,	𝕹	,,	WA&S	W.	Alexander & Son.		Tea-spoon: Glasgow Exhibition.
1859-60	,,	,,	𝕺	,,		...	...	...	Glasgow Assay Office Plate.
1860-1	,,	,,	𝕻	,,		...	...	...	Do. do. do.
1861-2	,,	,,	𝕼	,,		...	...	...	Do. do. do.
1862-3	,,	,,	𝕽	,,	JM	J.	Murray	(1862)	Mustard spoon: Birmingham Assay Office.
1863-4	,,	,,	𝕾	,,		...	...	...	Glasgow Assay Office Plate.
1864-5	,,	,,	𝕿	,,		...	...	...	Do. do. do.
1865-6	,,	,,	𝖀	,,		...	...	...	Do. do. do.
1866-7	,,	,,	𝖁	,,		...	...	...	Do. do. do.
1867-8	,·	,,	𝖂	,,		...	...	...	Do. do. do.
1868-9	,,	,,	𝖃	,,		...	...	...	Do. do. do.
1869-70	,,	,,	𝖄	,,		...	...	...	Do. do. do.
1870-1	,,	,,	𝖅	,,		...	...	...	Do do. do.

MARKS ON GLASGOW PLATE.

TABLE VI.

FROM 1871 TO 1897.

FIVE STAMPS TILL 1890, THENCEFORWARD FOUR ONLY.

	TREE, FISH & BELL.	LION RAMPANT.	DATE LETTER.	QUEEN'S HEAD.	MAKER'S MARK.
1871-2	(tree, fish & bell)	(lion rampant)	A	(queen's head)	
1872-3	,,	,,	B	,,	
1873-4	,,	,,	C	,,	
1874-5	,,	,,	D	,,	
1875-6	,,	,,	E	,,	
1876-7	,,	,,	F	,,	
1877-8	,,	,,	G	,,	
1878-9	,,	,,	H	,,	
1879-80	,,	,,	I	,,	
1880-1	,,	,,	J	,,	
1881-2	,,	,,	K	,,	
1882-3	,,	,,	L	,,	
1883-4	,,	,,	M	,,	
1884-5	,,	,,	N	,,	
1885-6	,,	,,	O	,,	
1886-7	,,	,,	P	,,	
1887-8	,,	,,	Q	,,	
1888-9	,,	,,	R	,,	
1889-90	,,	,,	S	,,	
1890-1	,,	,,	T		
1891-2	,,	,,	U		
1892-3	,,	,,	V		
1893-4	,,	,,	W		
1894-5	,,	,,	X		
1895-6	,,	,,	Y		
1896-7	,,	,,	Z		

FOR MAKERS' MARKS SEE LIST ON FOLLOWING PAGES.

TABLE VII.

FROM 1897 TO 1921.

FOUR STAMPS TILL 1913, THENCEFORWARD FIVE.

	TREE, FISH & BELL.	LION RAMPANT.		DATE LETTER.	MAKER'S MARKS.
1897-8	(tree, fish & bell)	(lion rampant)		A	
1898-9	,,	,,		B	
1899 1900	,,	,,		C	
1900-1	,,	,,		D	
EDW. VII. 1901-2	,,	,,		E	
1902-3	,,	,,		F	
1903-4	,,	,,		G	
1904-5	,,	,,		H	
1905-6	,,	,,		I	
1906-7	,,	,,		J	
1907-8	,,	,,		K	
1908-9	,,	,,		L	
1909-10	,,	,,		M	
1910-1	,,	,,		N	
1911-2	,,	,,		O	
1912-3	,,	,,		P	
1913-4	,,	,,		Q	
1914-5	,,	,,	(thistle)	R	
1915-6	,,	,,	,,	S	
1916-7	,,	,,	,,	T	
1917-8	,,	,,	,,	U	
1918-9	,,	,,	,,	V	
1919-20	,,	,,	,,	W	
1920-1	,,	,,	,,	X	
1921-2	,,	,,	,,	Y	

FOR MAKERS' MARKS SEE LIST ON FOLLOWING PAGES.

MARKS ON GLASGOW PLATE.

The marks in Tables VI. and VII. and the makers' marks which follow have been reproduced from the impressions struck in the copper plate preserved at Glasgow Assay Office.

See the text preceding Table I.

MARKS ON GLASGOW-WROUGHT GOLD.

The marks for gold, 22 carats fine, were the same as for plate until 1844, when the mark 22 was ordered to be added to denote its fineness. For the lower standard of 18 carats (authorised in 1798) the mark 18 had been ordered to be added. In 1854 three lower standards of 15 carats, 12 carats and 9 carats fine respectively were authorised, for which the marks ·625, ·5, and ·375 were prescribed in addition to those illustrated in the tables.

For MARKS ON FOREIGN PLATE assayed at Glasgow, see page 27 *ante*.

NAMES OF GLASGOW GOLDSMITHS, PLATEWORKERS, &c.,

WITH THE DATES OF THEIR ADMISSION TO THE GLASGOW INCORPORATION OF HAMMERMEN, FROM 1616 TO 1848.

Copied from the Minute-books of the Incorporation, supplemented by extracts from the Burgess Rolls and Directories. The names of members of trades other than goldsmiths, silversmiths, watch and clockmakers, and jewellers, have been omitted.

G.S. = Goldsmith; S.S. = Silversmith; W.M. = Watchmaker; C.M. = Clockmaker; J. = Jeweller.

Date of Admission.	Name and Designation (see above).			Date of Admission.	Name and Designation (see above).		
1616	John	Kirkwood	G.S.	1777	William	Love ‡	G.S.
1649	John	Neill	C.M.		Walter	Wright	
*1660	William	Cockburn	G.S.		James	Taylor	S.S.
1665	Thomas	Moncrur	,,		Wm.	Hamilton	,,
1673	Robert	Brook ‡	,,	1778	Charles	Clyphon or Clephan	,,
	John	Luke ‡	,,	1779	James	Stewart	W. & C.M.
1680	George	Louck or Luke	,,		Thos.	Brydone	J.
1682	Thomas	Cumming ‡	,,		James	McLenan	W. & C.M.
1686	Jas.	Stirling	,,		Wm.	Dunn	,, ,,
1687	James	Cumming	,,	1781	Patrick	Macfarlane ‡	,, ,,
1689	Wm.	Hodgy or Hodgert	,,		John	Frazer	
1692	James	Luke ‡	,,		Peter	Frazer	G.S.
1693	Wm.	Clerk ‡	,,		John	Inglis	S.S.
1699	John	Luke, jr. ‡	,,		Archd.	Miller	W. & C.M.
1707	James	Boyd		1782	James	Wright ‡	J.
	James	Lockhart ‡	,,		Bery	Parkhill	,,
1709	John	Falconer ‡	,,	1783	James	McEwen ‡	G.S. & J.
1717	Johan	Got-helf-Bilsings ‡	,,		James	Cullen	S.S.
†1721	Robert	Luke ‡	,,	1784	Archibald	Lang	J.
1735	John	Bilctzing			John	Wyllie	,,
1743	James	Glen ‡	,,	1785	John	Donald ‡	S.S.
1747	Saml.	Telfer ‡		1788	James	Wyllie	G.S. & J.
1756	David	Warnock ‡	,,		James	Duncan	J.
1757	John	Campbell ‡	,,		John	Patterson	,,
1758	Wm.	Napier ‡	,,	1790	James	Ross	W. & C.M.
1759	John	Napier		1791	James	Pennecuick	,, ,,
1761	John	Bayne	,,		James	McKendrick	S.S.
	Archibald	Graham	,,		Alexr.	Bell	W. & C.M.
1763	Adam	Graham ‡	,,	1792	John	Thomson	S.S.
1767	Peter	Lang			James	Muir	W. & C.M.
1773	James	Taylor ‡	,,		Archd.	McVicar	,, ,,
	Robt.	Wilson		1793	James	Gray	G.S.
1775	John	Calder	W & C.M.		James	Spittal	W.M.
	James	Muir			James	Adshead	J.
1776	Robert	Gray ‡	G.S.		James	Graham	W.M.
	James	Kirkland	W. & C.M.	1796	Robert	Thomson	,,
	James	Cullen	S.S.		Hay	Lapsley	G.S.
					Wm.	Hannington	W.M.
				1797	Alexr.	Mitchie	S.S.
				1798	Richard	McLean	S. & J.
					Wm.	Mitchell	W.M.
					Robert	Sommerville	W. & C.M.
				1800	Walter	Macadam	,, ,,
					George	Easton	S.S.

* William Cockburn, described as "an Edinburgh goldsmith," was by an Act of Council, of 1660, allowed "to exercise his calling in the burgh".

† The Minute-book for the period 1717 to 1775 has been lost, and the names during the interval have been copied from the Burgess Roll.

‡ His mark represented in preceding tables.

NAMES OF GLASGOW GOLDSMITHS—*Continued.*

Date of Admission.	Name and Designation (See previous page).			Date of Admission.	Name and Designation (See previous page).		
1800	William	Halbert	W. & C.M.	1825	Wm.	Innes	W. & C.M.
	John	Graham	J.		Thomas	Burtie	J.
1801	James	Turnbull	S.S.		John	McKell	S.S.
	Ebenezer	Robertson	W. & C.M.		John	Welsh	W.M.
1802	John	Dobbie	,, ,,	1826	Wm.	Spencer	J.
	Wm.	Russell	W.M.		Thomas	Muir	S.S.
	Robert	Robertson	W. & C.M.		John	Dobbie	W.M.
1803	Alexander	Phillip	,, ,,		John	Law	
1805	David	Reid	C.M.		John	Waddell	W. & C.M.
	Jas. Brown	Adshead	J.	1827	Edward	Bell ‡	G.S.
1806	Wm.	Cowan	W.M.		James L.	Spencer	J.
	Walter	Grey	S.S.		Andrew	Thomson	W.M.
	John	Smith	W.M.		William	Russell	W.M. & J.
	Robert	Reid	,,	1828	David	McDonald	S.S. & J.
	Thomas	Adshead	J.	1829	John	Cree	C. & W.M.
1807	James	Finlayson	G.S.		Daniel	Robertson ‡	G.S. & J.
1808	Peter	Arthur ‡	J.		George	Brown (Airdree)	W.M.
	James	Newlands	,,	1830	George	Brown	,,
1809	James	Gibson	W.M.		John	Wotherspoon	W. & C.M.
	John	Gibson	,,		Arch'd.	Armstrong	S.S.
1810	Philip	Grierson	J.	1831	David	Sutherland	J.
	Saml.	Whelar	W.M.		Wm.	Adshead	,,
	Archd.	Cochrane	J.		Henry	Downs ‡	G.S.
	Thomas	Cochrane	W. & C.M.	1832	George	Railton	G.S. & J.
	John	Neilson	,, ,,		D. Crichton	Rait ‡	,, ,,
1811	James	Coghill	W.M.	1833	George	Thomson	W.M.
	Archd.	McFadyen ‡	J.	1834	Charles	Bryson ‡	J.
	John	Austin	,,		Alex'r.	Wood	W. & C.M.
1812	John	Mann	G.S.		John	Mitchell ‡	J.
	James	Downie ‡	S.S.		Wm.	Mitchell ‡	,,
	Thomas	Finlayson	J.		Wm.	McInnes	W.M.
1813	Walter	Inglis	W.M.		Andrew	Kelly	,,
	Robert	Duncan ‡	G.S. & J.	1835	Joseph	Graham	G.S. & J.
1814	John	Calder, jr.	W.M.		Wm.	Alexander	,,
1815	Donald	McCallum	J.		Robt.	Buchanan, jr.	W. & C.M.
	John	Bruce ‡	,,		Alex. Walker	Alexander	,, ,,
1816	Robert	Smith	W.M.		Wm.	Parkins ‡	S.S.
	Luke Frazer	Newlands ‡	G.S.	1836	Alex.	Aitken	W.M. & J.
	James	Scrymgeour	W.M.	1837	George	McLean	W.M.
1817	James	Muirhead	,,		Alex'r.	Brown	,,
1818	John	Buchanan	J.		Andrew	McMillan ‡	,,
	William	Steel	W. & C.M.	1838	Henry	Muirhead ‡	,,
1819	Robert	Gray & Son ‡	G.S.	1839	John	Donaldson	,,
1820	Andrew	Dobbie	,, ,,	1840	John	Arthur	J.
1821	Thomas	Beggs	W.M.		Wm.	McCracken	W.M.
1822	Alexr.	Mitchell ‡	W.M. & S.S.	1841	John	Gibson	;,
	David	Crichton	W.M.	1842	Robert	Stewart ‡	J.
	John	Aitken	S.S.	1843	Wm. Clarke	Shaw	G.S. & J.
	John	Ferguson	,,	1844	Alexander	Lucas	G.S.
	Robert	Corbet	W. & C.M.		Robert	Arthur	J.
	James	Middleton	J.	1845	Walter	Baird ‡	G.S. & J.
1823	James	Muirhead	W. & C.M.		John	Russell ‡	J.
	Francis	Reid	W.M.		Alexander	McDonald ‡	,,
	John	Campbell	,,		Peter	Aitken, junior ‡	,,
	John	Todd	,,				
1824	Angus	McDonald ‡	S.S.	1848	Francis	Chapman	W.M.
1825	James	Burrell ‡	G.S.				

‡ His mark represented in preceding tables.

The names and marks of Goldsmiths who have had plate assayed at Glasgow between 1848 and 1903 will be found on the two following pages.

MARKS AND NAMES OF GLASGOW GOLDSMITHS.

1848 TO 1903.

THE DATE WHEN EACH MARK WAS FIRST USED IS NOT RECORDED.

MARK.	NAME.	MARK.	NAME.	MARK.	NAME.
(R)	J. Russell.	(IH)	J. Hall.	T.SMITH&SON GLASGOW	T. Smith & Son.
WG	W. Gordon.	J.R.&W.L.	J. R. & W. Laing.	TS&S	Do. do.
VL&Co	V. Levy & Co.	LAING	Do. do.	MF JBM	(Not identified).
SK	D. Sprunt.*	M&M	McIntosh & McCulloch.	A.W.P	A. W. Peden.
JDD	J. D. Davidson.	AB	A. Brown.	R&AA	R. & A. Allen.
M&A	Muirhead & Arthur.	RK	Robt. Kerr.	D.T	D. Todd.
M&A	Do. do.	CCM	C. C. McDonald.	W.S.&Co	W. Scott & Co.
GA	G. Alexander.	H·L	H. Low.	J.W.	J. Wallace.
JB&S	J. Ballantyne & Son.	J.W	Jas. Weir.	T.W.C	T. W. Crawford.
WR	W. Russell.	WEIR	Do. do.	AWA	A. W. Allison.
WC	W. Corbett.	J.E	J. Easton	W.W	W. Warrington.
A&T	Aird & Thompson.	J.P.C	J. P. Campbell.	MVW	M. V. Wilks.
T.S.&S	T. Smith & Son.	S.&McL	S...... & McLellan.	(JM)	J. Moir.
T.S.&S	Do. do.	JHS	J. H. Storer.	K&P	Kerr & Phillips.
R&WS	R. & W. Sorley.	M.G	Mungo Guthrie.	M&A	Muirhead & Arthur.
(R'S/W.S)	Do. do.	H&L	Hamilton & Laidlaw.	A.McD	A. McDonald.
(G.E/C.E)	Geo. Edward & Son.	W.A	W. Allan.	GJEFFREY	G. Jeffrey.
DE·GE	Do. do.	A.L.B	A. L. Boston.	H&M	Hyslop & Marshall.
P&CO.	Parr & Co.	D&M	Duff & Millar.	W.G.T	W. G. Taylor.
GWS	G. W. Stratton.	J.ADAIR DUMFS	John Adair (Dumfries).	T.M	Thos. Mutter.
KELLY DUBLIN	Kelly & Co., Dublin.	L&Co	Lawson & Co.	ALEXR&SN	Alexr. & Son.
HOWELL	A. Howell.	FR	J. Riddoch.	JM	J. Mark.
DS	D. Simpson.	D.T	D. Todd.	F&F	Finlay & Field.
GM	G. Mitchell.	D.F.T	D. F. Turnbull.	WP	W. Paul.
J.E.A.	J. E. Ainsley.	J.D	Jas. Douglas.	JP	Jas. Porter.
J.H&Co	Jos. Haywood & Co.	TF	T. Fyfe.	GMcP	Geo. McPherson.
PG	(Not identified).	M&Co	Mitchell & Co.	T.S.	Thos. Stewart.
WG	W. Gordon.	R.S	Robt. Scott.	JF	J. Fettes.
K.C.B	(Not identified).	SCOTT	Do. do.	D.F.	Duncn. Ferguson.
G.E.R	G. E. Rattray.	D.C.R.&S	D. C. Rait & Son.	WVJ	W. V. Jackson.
T.C.G	T. C. Garstang.	DD	David Dow.	G.J.	Geo. Jackson.
D.M.C	D. M. Cameron.	W.J	W. Jenkins.	T.R&S	Thos. Ross & Sons.
DM	D. Munro.	T&W	Thomson & Williamson.	R.T	R. Tennent.
F.&J.S.	F. & J. Smith.	WR	Wm. Russell.	DMcC	D. McCallum.
(MF)	M. Friedlander.	MACFARLANE PARTICK	—— Macfarlane (of Partick).	J.D	John Donald.
M·F	Do. do.	HG	Hector Gollun.	D.S	Danl. Sutherland.
JR	J. Reid.	MW	Mark Wilks & Co.	J.M	Jas. Myres.
JF	J. Ferrier.	J.C	Jas. Crichton.	JB&S	J. Blond & Son.

* S.K. seem strange initials for D. Sprunt; the mark is, however, registered in that name.

MARKS AND NAMES OF GLASGOW GOLDSMITHS.

1848 TO 1903.—*continued.*

THE DATE WHEN EACH MARK WAS FIRST USED IS NOT RECORDED.

MARK.	NAME.	MARK.	NAME.	MARK.	NAME.
W.S	W. Semple.	B & M	Brown & Miller.	J.N	J. Neville.
J.D.R	J. D. Reid.	JS	Jas. Simpson.	D&S	Davis & Son.
WR&S	Wm. Russell & Sons.	J.R	Jas. Ross.	LM&Cº	Lorimer, Moyes & Co.
R·Mc·I	R. McInnes.	J & Cº	Johnston & Co.	AA	Andrew Allison.
W. & W. LOGAN	W. &. W. Logan.	L & L	Lyle & Lock.	AF	A. Ferrier ?
D & M	Duff & Miller.	J.LYᴸ	J. Lyle.	J.M.JB	J. Muir, jr. ?
J.S	Jas. Smith.	J.M.B.&C	J. M. Ballantyne & Co.	H.T	H. Tennant.
J.F	Jas. Forrest.	G.D & Cº	Geo. Drummond & Co.	GD	Geo. Drummond.
J.H.G.	(*Not identified.*)	M & T	Miller & Thompson.	W&S	Wilson & Sharp, Edinbro.
J. STEVENSON	J. Stevenson.	AT&S	A. Taylor & Son.	M.BROS	Mitchell Bros.
R&F	Ross & Ferrier.	W.M&Cº	W. Miller & Co.	F.N	F. Neville.
R.R	Robt. Ross.	H & I	Hamilton&Inches,Edinbro.	L.K	L. King.
WJ	W. Jaffray.	G.W	George White (or Wilson).	RKM	R. K. Muirhead.
W.J	Do. do.	W.M	W. Mitchell.	AAP	Anton Pfaff.
PM	Peter Martin.	J.McA	J. McArthur.	R.L.R	R. L. Rawson.
R.B.F.	R. B. Forrest.	RA	Robt. Arthur.	J&AH	J. & A. Howell.
J&AK	Jas. & Andrew Kelly.	R&G	Reed & Garrick.	G&S	Guthrie & Shear.
T&D	Taylor & Downes.	G.T	Geo. Thomson.	TLL	T. L. Leck.
JM&S	J. Muirhead & Sons.	GL	(*Not identified.*)	DH	D. Howie.
G.I	Geo. Innes.	R.B	Robt. Buchanan.	S&R	Smith & Rait.
SB GG	Barclay & Goodwin.	J.HERON	J. Heron.	ABA	Alex. B. Arthur.
		J.McD	J. McDonald.	AW	Alex. Wotherspoon.
D.S &Cᴵʸ	Dl. Sutherland & Co.	T.F	T. Finlayson.	HD	Hugh Downs.
JL	J. Laing.	D.T	David Taylor.	J.B	J. Brown.
J & WM	J. & W. Mitchell.	TR	Thos. Ross.	AS	A. Sterling.
WA	W. Allan.	WB	Walter Baird.	CCC	Colin C. Campbell.
YOUNG	—— Young.	ARS	A. & R. Stewart.	A·L	Alex. Lucas.
G&W	Gilmore & Watson.	RH	Robt. Hyslop.	MM	M. Michael.
L&P	Lindsay & Paisley.	LA	Lawrence Aitchison.	W.N	W. Noble
LH	L. Hymens.	WCM	(*Not identified.*)	J.C.S	(*Not identified*)
W.C	Wm. Coghill.	W&P	Watson & Pozzie.	JA F	John A. Fetter.
J.Mᴵ	J. McInnes.	D.McD	D. McDonald.	J.F	Do. do.
W.S	Wm. Sharp.	RD	Robt. Duncan.	R.B.G	(*Not identified.*)
JMᴵG	J. McGregor.	AC	A. Coghill.	RGL	Do. do.
P&Cº	Panton & Co.	T.C	Thos. Chapman.	M&H	Do. do.
R.L	R. Laing.	MᴵK&Cº	McKenzie & Co.	GL	Do. do.
T&Cº	Tennent & Co.	WSR	(*Not identified.*)	W&D	Do. do.
J&WB	J. & W. Boyd.	L&M	Lorimer & Moyes.	McH&S	Do. do.
RRK	Robt. Rankin.	L.G.&Cº	Leckie, Graham & Co.	R.W.F	Do. do.
J.C	Jas. Crichton.	AMC	(*Not identified.*)	S&R	Smith & Rait.
		G.S.B	Do. do.		

CHAPTER XXI

SCOTTISH PROVINCIAL GOLDSMITHS

OF THE MINOR GUILDS

AND THEIR MARKS

ABERDEEN.

Formerly two burghs—Old Aberdeen and New Aberdeen.   There were two Burghs of Aberdeen in juxtaposition, Old Aberdeen and New Aberdeen, each having its own distinct guilds and trading privileges. The distinction which (as in the case of Edinburgh and Canongate) was maintained for centuries, was only abolished in quite recent times by the merging of the old burgh in the new.

In both burghs the goldsmiths were associated with other crafts, such as pewterers, wrights, armourers and saddlers, and incorporated under the common designation "Hammermen".

The town mark in both cases composed of letters.   In neither burgh was the "town mark" of the goldsmiths taken from its arms, but was in both composed of the first two, or the first two and the fifth letters of the town name (AB or ABD). Mr. Brook suggested that this curious departure from the general practice by the goldsmiths of (Old) Aberdeen was because the arms of their burgh were so much like those of Dundee—the charge on the shield of the former is a pot with three lilies, the first closed, the second half open, and the third in full bloom; in the case of the latter it is a pot with three lilies all in full bloom—a variation so slight as to be hardly distinguishable in a punch-mark. Why the goldsmiths of New Aberdeen should have taken a similar course down to the 18th century does not appear, as their arms resemble neither those of Dundee nor of Old Aberdeen.

OLD ABERDEEN.

Old Aberdeen.   Of the goldsmiths of the old burgh the names of two only can be found; the name of the first—Robert Cruickshank—is recorded in the minutes of the Incorporation of Hammermen as having been admitted a member on the 31 October, 1699; the second—Coline Allan—was enrolled as a burgess on 9 January, 1762.

The marks illustrated below are found on a beer-jug (at King's College, Aberdeen), made by Robert Cruickshank about the year 1700.

ↄ RC AB

This being the only known example of plate bearing the Old Aberdeen mark, it seems useless to speculate with regard to the signification of the first mark—the small old English ↄ. It might perhaps have been a deacon's stamp. A somewhat similar letter is represented in Table I., line 11, of the Aberdeen marks (page 533), and in line 3 of the Banff marks (page 540).

ABERDEEN (or NEW ABERDEEN).

Aberdeen, or *New Aberdeen* as it was called until by the extension of its boundaries it embraced the adjoining burgh, has in its Council Register, entries referring to at least two goldsmiths of the 15th century : the earliest being a record of the admission of James Kemp into the service of a goldsmith named Theman, on 23 September, 1464.

Aberdeen or New Aberdeen.

The Council Register, the Burgess Rolls, the Minutes of the Incorporation of Hammermen, Parish Registers, and other records contain references to Aberdeen goldsmiths from the 15th to the 19th century.

Goldsmiths' names recorded from the 15th to the 19th century.

Two " Seals of cause " appear to have been granted to the Hammermen, in 1519 and 1532 respectively.

The appointment by the Town Council in 1649 of William Anderson to be "tryar of all gold and siluer wark" is recorded in the Council Register, under date 7 November, 1649, as follows :—

"The said day, the Counseil, taking to their consideratioun the insufficiencie of siluer wark maid within this brughe have nominat and appojntit, and be the tennour heirof nominatis and appointis William Andersone, Goldsmyth, to be tryar of all gold and siluer wark to be maid within the said brughe for the yeir to cum, and being sufficient and markit with the prob,* to put on the towne's mark, and for that effect nominatis and appointis the said William Andersone keiper of the towne's mark for this present yeir : the said William Andersone being personallie present, acceptit the said office, and gave aith *de fideli administratione*, and obleist him that all wark that sowld pas his mark, and the towne's mark sall be elewin pennie fyne [11dwt fine] : and if thair be ony wark fund of less walew, markit as said is, he sall be lyable for the samen according to the ordinar rait. *Sic sub^r.*,† William Andersone."

Mr. Brook, for whom the above was originally extracted by Mr. Jas. Aitchison, observed that "this appointment does not appear to have been renewed after William Anderson ceased to fill the office. At any rate, if it was continued (as to which there is no evidence) the provision as to silver plate being stamped with the 'tryar's' mark and a municipally appointed 'town-mark' would seem to have fallen into desuetude, for an examination of all the marks undoubtedly shows that each goldsmith used a town-mark of his own."‡

---

* "markit with the *prob*" (probe), *i.e.* marked as having been tested.   † sub^r = subscripsit.
‡ *Old Scottish Com. Plate*, p. 570.   No mark of this Wm. Anderson has been found.

Weakness of
supervision
at Aberdeen
illustrated by
the variety of
" town marks ".
An examination of the Aberdeen marks represented in the following tables, which have been reproduced in *facsimile* from the original marks on the plate described, will show that Mr. Brook's observations with reference to the weakness of the supervision—if any there were—over the Aberdeen goldsmiths, are well founded, for not only the makers' marks but the town marks on different articles of plate vary in character in the most extraordinary manner.   Such a variety of marks as was used at Aberdeen is not found in any other Scottish burgh.

Marks found on
Aberdeen plate.
The earliest known example of the town mark consists of the letters A B in Roman capitals, which was followed shortly after by A B D, sometimes with a contraction mark over.   These three letters in a single stamp (either with or without the contraction mark) appear to be the most common form of town mark, but on 18th century plate the letters A B D are found both in Roman and Script characters.   Occasionally the three letters appear as if each had been struck by a separate stamp. In a few instances the first two letters, A B, are in a single stamp ; in others the letters A B D N are found struck by separate stamps, some- times, however, they are combined in one stamp.   The Roman capital letter A is also found struck thrice, and the same letter, of a peculiar char- acter—as if formed of twisted ribbon—is also to be seen on plate of about the end of the 18th and the early part of the 19th centuries.   The letters B D without the initial A—as represented in *Old English Plate*—are, however, not to be found except where the A has been worn out or otherwise obliterated.

Eccentricity of
Aberdeen marks.
Early in the 18th century a stamp composed of three castles in a shaped shield, somewhat resembling the Newcastle mark, was used by Geo. Robertson as the town mark, and he was followed in this respect by others.   The adoption of this mark is accounted for by the fact that the arms of the burgh are :—*gules, three castles, triple towered, within a double tressure flory counter flory, argent.*   The use, however, of the various eccentric marks such as a gate, a rose, a hand grasping a dagger, and other devices which are found in some combinations, seems quite in- explicable.   The signification of the letters ♂ and ♀, ℭ, ℯ, and B is also difficult to explain.   The letter ♂ has already been referred to in connec- tion with Old Aberdeen and Banff.

The dates set opposite the marks in the tables must be considered as merely approximate, except where the inscribed dates on some of the examples may be depended on.

MARKS ON ABERDEEN PLATE.

TABLE I.   FROM ABOUT 1600 TO ABOUT 1770.

The date within parentheses which follows the maker's name is the date of admission to the Aberdeen Incorporation of Hammermen, entry on the Burgess Roll, or earliest mention.

DATE (ABOUT).	MARKS.	MAKER'S NAME.	ARTICLES AND OWNERS.
1600-25		... ...	AB in bowl, castle thrice on stem of an Apostle and a seal-top spoon: Mr. H. D. Ellis.
,,		... ...	Lion-sejant spoon: Sir Arthur Evans.
,,		... ...	Seal-top spoon: Messrs. Crichton.
1650		Thomas Moncrur (1649)	Noted by the Author.
,,		Do. do. ,,	Small quaich: Messrs. Crichton.
,,		*Walter Melvil (1650)	Mace, dated 1650: King's College, Aberdeen. Strathnairn cup: Mareschal College, Aberdeen.
1660-70		(*Not identified.*)	Small bowl: The Marquess of Breadalbane, K.G.
1670-7	WS VS	Wm. Scott (1666)	*Engraved marks* on medals dated 1670 and 1677: Grammar School, Aberdeen.
1672-8	A·G AG	Alexr. Galloway (1671)	*Engraved marks* on medals dated 1672, 1673, 1674, 1675 and 1678: Grammar School, Aberdeen.
1690		(*Not identified.*)	Sugar bowl: The Author's Collection.
1691-7		Geo. Walker (1685)	Spoon (flat stem): Messrs. Crichton. Com. cups: Monymusk (1691) and Fintray (1697).
1703		Do. do. ,,	Com. cup, dated 1703: Longside.
1708-14		Geo. Robertson (1708)	Rat-tail spoon (pricked 1714): Glasgow Exhibition of 1901.
1710-20		Do. do. ,,	Plain paten: Messrs. Reid & Son.
1718-27		†John Walker (1713)	Rat-tail spoon, dated 1718: Glasgow Exhibition. Communion cups, dated 1727: Dyke and Alford.
1730	J WALKER	Do. do. ,,	Salt spoon: Birmingham Assay Office.
,,		George Cooper (1728)	Salver: The Dunn Collection.
,,		Alexr. Forbes (1728)	Two communion cups, bought 1731: Mary-culter.
,,		George Cooper (1728)	Mug and spoon: Glasgow Exhibition.
,,	,, ,,	Do. do. ,,	Porridge bowl and tray: Mr. W. M. Acworth.
1734-51	JA	Jas. Abercrombie (1734)	Tea-spoon: The Marquess of Breadalbane, K.G.
1748-67	CA ABD	Coline Allan (1748)	Tea-spoon: Glasgow Exhibition. Two spoons: King's College, Aberdeen.
1750	CA ABD	Do. do. ,,	Waiter: Messrs. Crichton.
1763-70	IW	James Wildgoose (1763)	Com. cups: East Church, Aberdeen.
,,	IW ABD	Do. do. ,,	Table-spoon: Glasgow Exhibition.

* The first two marks in line are alike (WM conjoined for Walter Melvil), but the first mark is struck upside down.

† The "three-castles" mark is sometimes struck with the single castle uppermost as represented by Mr. Brook, but it is clear from the shape of the shield that the mark is upside down when so struck, the arrangement of the charges in the arms of the burgh being two castles in chief and one in base.

MARKS ON ABERDEEN PLATE—*Continued.*

TABLE II.

FROM ABOUT 1760 TO ABOUT 1820.

The date within parentheses which follows the maker's name is the date of admission to the Aberdeen Incorporation of Hammermen, entry on the Burgess Roll, or otherwise the date of the earliest mention which has been found of the name.

DATE (ABOUT).	MARKS.	MAKER'S NAME.	ARTICLES AND OWNERS.
1760	BL ✕✕ ABD	(*Not identified.*)	Hash-spoon : Glasgow Exhibition.
,,	BL ✣ BL	Do. do.	Tea-spoon : Do. do.
1766-79	IG ABD ✕✕	Jas. Gordon (1766)	Table-spoon : Marquess of Breadalbane, K.G. Com. cups : New Machar (dated 1779), and West Church, Aberdeen.
	IG ABD	Do. do.	Six table-spoons : Birm. Assay Off.
	,,	Do. do.	Tea-spoons : Glasgow Exhibition.
1772-7	AT ABD·	Alexr. Thompson (1772)	Table-spoon : The Marquess of Breadalbane, K.G.
1777-8	IL ABD ✕✕	Jas. Law (1777)	Small quaich : Glasgow Exhibition.
	,, ,,	Do. do.	Com. cups, dated 1778 : Birnie.
1782-96	I·L ♉ ✕✕	*Do. do.	Toddy ladle : Messrs. Crichton.
	IL ✕✕ ABD	John Leslie (1782)	Table-spoon : Glasgow Exhibition.
	I·L ABD	Do. do.	Mug & dessert-spoon : Lord Breadalbane.
	IL ♉ ✕✕	*Do. do.	Tea-spoon : Mr. Chisholm.
	,, ,,	Do. do.	Toddy-ladle : The Marquess of Breadalbane.
	,, ,, ✿	Do. do.	Tea-spoons : Messrs. Smith & Rait.
1783-90	J·S ABD	Jas. Smith (1783)	Sauce ladle : Birm. Assay Office.
	JS ABD	Do. do.	Table-spoons : Mr. Chisholm.
	✿ JS ✿	Do. do.	Do. : Glasgow Exhibition.
1785-95	PR ABD	(*Not identified.*)	Do. : Mr. R. Meldrum.
1786 to 1818	⟳ NG	Nathl. Gillet (1786)	Tea-spoon : The Marquess of Breadalbane, K.G.
	,,	Do. do.	Sugar-tongs : Glasgow Exhibition.
	NG ☒ ✿ ✿	Do. do.	Toddy-ladle : The Marquess of Breadalbane, K.G.
1790 to 1800	NG⟳ Z	Do. do.	Sugar-bowl : Noted by the Author.
	,, ,, N ⟳	Do. do.	Tea-spoons : Lord Breadalbane.
1796 to 1820	E 🏛 ✕✕	James Erskine (1796)	Do. : Do. do.
	,, ,,	Do. do.	Tea-spoon : Glasgow Exhibition.
	JE ♉	*Do. do.	Do. : Lord Breadalbane.
	JE ✿ ✿ ✿	Do. do.	Pair of salt spoons : Do.
	R&S A B D	(*Not identified.*)	Salt-spoon : Birm. Assay Office.

* Compare the second mark with a similar mark inverted in Table III.

MARKS ON ABERDEEN PLATE—*Continued.*

TABLE III.
FROM ABOUT 1800 TO 1871.

DATE (ABOUT).	MARKS.	MAKER'S NAME.	ARTICLES AND OWNERS.
1800	WB 🦁	(*Not identified.*)	Plain tea-spoons: Mr. Dudley Westropp.
	DOUGLAS ⬭ ⬭ ID	*J. Douglas (?)	Small toddy ladle: The Marquess of Breadalbane, K.G.
	JA AB 🦁	John Allan (1797)	Dessert spoon: Glasgow Exhibition. (The third mark appears to have been stamped bottom upwards.)
	J.A	Do. do.	Tea-spoon: The Marquess of Breadalbane, K.G.
	ID 🛡 🛡	*J. Douglas (?)	Tea-spoons: Messrs. Smith & Rait.
1800	I·D	*Do. do.	Communion cup: Foveran.
TO	GB ABD	(*Not identified.*)	Fiddle-pattern tea-spoon: Marquess of Breadalbane, K.G.
1830	GB AB GB AB	Do. do.	Do. dessert spoon: Do.
	G.B A B D N	Do. do.	Toddy ladle and decanter label: Do.
	WJ ABD WJ	Do. do.	Dessert spoon: Do.
	WJ A B D WJ	Do. do.	Tea-spoons: Do.
	A A A	Do. do.	Do. : Do.
1820	IB ABD	Do. do.	Fiddle-pattern sugar-tongs: Messrs. Crichton.
1830	WJ A B D ⚇	Do. do.	(These marks are stamped irregularly as drawn.) Tea-spoons: Reid & Sons.
1841	GJ ABDN	Geo. Jamieson	Pair of sauce ladles (also Edin. marks for 1841): Marquess of Breadalbane, K.G.
1850	W·W A B D N	(*Not identified.*)	Toddy ladle and sugar spoon: Do.
	WW ⫿⫿⫿ ABD WW	Do. do.	Tea-spoon: Do.
1871	GS ABD	Do. do.	Butter knife (with Edinburgh marks for 1871 added): B'ham Assay Office.

* These are believed to be Aberdeen marks, but there is no proof to that effect.

The following names of Aberdeen Goldsmiths, *in addition to those whose marks appear in the preceding tables*, are recorded in the Aberdeen Council Register, the minutes of the Incorporation of Hammermen, or other records—the date preceding the name is the year in which the name is first mentioned.

1464 James Kemp	1617 Hew Anderson	1679 Patrick Scott
„ —— Theman	1629 James Robertson	1685 Alexr. Galloway
1473 Andrew Robertson	1632 Walter Hay	1691 Wm. Scott
1508 David Theman	1636 William Anderson	1693 Robt. Sharp
„ David Brois	1649 Thomas Moncur	1695 Wm. Lindsay
1590 Alexr. Duff	1651 Wm. Crystie	1755 James Morrison
1592 Patrick Hay, died 1592	1667 Robt. Lindsay	1784 George Rodger

ARBROATH.

Arbroath marks traced to their origin by Lord Breadalbane and Mr. Gregor Drummond.

Until the publication of the first edition of this work nothing had been published concerning the goldsmiths of Arbroath, or—to give the burgh its ancient name—"Aberbrothock," and it is due to the researches of the Marquess of Breadalbane, who very cordially placed his notes at the Author's disposal, that the marks illustrated below have been ascertained to be those of an Arbroath plate-worker. Lord Breadalbane, having in his possession some of the objects mentioned below, made inquiries concerning their marks and received in 1901 from Mr. Gregor Drummond of Stirling (whose acquaintance with Arbroath and its history was intimate) a very interesting letter, from which the following is transcribed :—

"I send impressions of two Hall marks, one with the reputed Arbroath mark [a portcullis], the other with the same AD [maker's mark] but smaller, with Edinburgh Hall-marks in addition, indicating the year 1838 as its date. I got the loan of the tablespoons [from which the impressions were taken] from the Rev. John Chalmers, a native of that part—he was Free Church minister in Arbroath and is now in Stirling. The spoon with the Arbroath mark came to him from a grand-aunt who died about ten years ago aged over 90. The Edinburgh spoons with the AD mark were gifted to Mr. Chalmers by an old Arbroath resident. The initials and make of the spoons being exactly alike seem to point to the same Arbroath maker. A note to the Edinburgh Hall would get his name.

"The spoon with the Arbroath mark seems to be older, but not much. I send a rubbing of the Arbroath seal from a book on the History of Arbroath, which I have looked carefully through, but can find no reference to silversmiths, but as Arbroath formerly had, like Elgin, important ecclesiastical dignitaries, they would probably have had men of that craft there to make their church plate, and they would have had a distinctive mark. The Abbot had large powers as a justiciary, and appointed the Earls of Airlie as his baillies of the Regality. They continued to hold their office until it was abolished in 1748. I mentioned in a former note that the Airlie crest [or charge] was a portcullis with a lady behind it. I do not know whether the lady was introduced after Argyll tried to burn her out in her Lord's absence."

Application was made to the Edinburgh Hall and a search instituted, but as very few names of makers whose plate was assayed at Edinburgh in the second quarter of the 19th century are recorded, the name of the Arbroath worker with initials A D was not to be found. It may, however, still be possible by a more exhaustive inquiry in Arbroath (which, as yet, the Author has been unable to make), to ascertain the name.

Mr. Chalmers always understood that the spoons were made by an Arbroath silversmith ; he had been so informed, and the fact of the mark being a portcullis like that on the burgh seal, is corroborative evidence of the statement. The portcullis marks illustrated in the table below are inverted on the objects mentioned : an accident of striking which is frequently seen, and makes no difference as regards the identity of the mark. The second mark on the first spoon, and on Lord Breadalbane's snuff-box, has the appearance of a crowned head, but, being somewhat worn, the details are not clear.

THE ARBROATH BURGH SEAL.

MARKS ON ARBROATH PLATE.

DATE (ABOUT).	MARKS.	ARTICLES AND OWNERS.
1830	𝗔𝗗 ♡ ♡ ⊞	Table-spoon : The Rev. John Chalmers.
1838	𝗔𝗗 ⊞ ⊛ ⊛ ⊛	Do. (with Edinburgh Hall Marks of 1838-9) : The Rev. John Chalmers.
1830-9	𝗔𝗗 ☺ 𝗔𝗗 ⊞	Lid of snuff-box : The Marquess of Breadalbane, K.G.
,,	⊞ 𝗔𝗗 ⊞ ⊞	Toddy ladle : Do do. do.

AYR.

The mark (MC conjoined), here illustrated, is stamped twice on a

𝗠𝗖   𝗠𝗖

quaich of the 17th century in the possession of Mr. J. Barclay Murdoch of Capelrig. It is probably the name-punch of Matthew Colquhoun of Ayr, one of the thirteen Provincial Goldsmiths whose names are endorsed on the draft of the letter of the year 1687 or thereabouts, previously mentioned in connection with the Edinburgh Goldsmiths' Incorporation.

BANFF.

Banff goldsmiths
incorporated
with other
Hammermen.

The goldsmiths of Banff, like their fellow-craftsmen of Aberdeen, were incorporated with other hammer-wielding trades under the general title of "Hammermen".

In *The Annals of Banff*, by Dr. Cramond, reference is made to the following goldsmiths (silversmiths, &c.) whose connection with the burgh is traced by means of the burgh registers and other records :—

1670 to 1699 William Scott (the elder), goldsmith. This is the same Wm. Scott who was admitted a burgess in Aberdeen in 1666, where he was deacon of the Hammermen in 1673, 1678 and 1685. He appears to have carried on business from 1670 to 1699, both at Aberdeen and at Banff. His wife died in Banff in 1697, and he is believed to have died there about two years afterwards.*

1687 to 1748 William Scott (the younger), goldsmith, son of the above, first mentioned in 1687, as then married. He also carried on his trade both at Aberdeen and Banff. He was made a burgess of Aberdeen in 1691, and paid fines in Banff in 1723 and 1728, in respect of his being allowed to work there. He was appointed assay master in 1733, and died in 1748.*

1710 to 1729 Patrick Scott, goldsmith, first mentioned in 1710. His name occurs in the Council books in 1712. He died 1729.

1720 to 1740 John Reid, watchmaker, worked in Banff from about 1720 to 1740.

1732 to 1741 Patrick Gordon, gold and silver smith. Admitted to the Incorporation of Hammermen 1732, on paying as composition 30s. and 40s. (Scots.) as loft money. His " Sey " was appointed to be a silver watch-case, a spoon, and a gold (stoned) ring. He worked as a goldsmith, silversmith, jeweller and watch-case maker.

1747 to 1750 Thomas Forbes. Free 1747. His "Sey" was a gold mourning ring, a pair of silver buckles and a punch-ladle. He was to give the ordinary treat and pay £6 (Scots.) as composition. His name is not found mentioned after 1750.

1749 to 1760 Ernest Mearns, watchmaker, mentioned 1749 to 1760.

1750 to 1761 Alexr. Shirras, silversmith, died 1761.

1771 to 1795 John Argo, silversmith, admitted 1771 as hammerman (burgess 1785).

1774   Alexr. Mackay, watchmaker, married 1774.

1778 to 1792 William Byres, master of the craft in 1778 and deacon in 1781. He was admitted to the Incorporation without an essay, paying £3 stg. as composition.

1794 to 1797 David Izat, mentioned only 1794 and 1797.

1794 to 1824 John Keith, master of the craft in 1798, and deacon in 1804.*

1819 to 1843 George Elder, gold and silver smith, mentioned at intervals 1819 to 1843.

1829 to 1839 John McQueen, silversmith.

1840 to 1855 William Simpson, silversmith.

Various marks
used by Banff
goldsmiths.

The town mark of Banff varied considerably at different times on the work of successive members of the craft. The earliest known mark—that of Wm. Scott the elder—consisted of his monogram and the letters "ABC". He subsequently used the same monogram with the name BANF, as town mark. The same town mark was used by Patrick Scott, John Argo, Wm. Byres and John Keith. Wm. Scott the younger used a fish, about 1720, as did John Keith and another maker, who stamped plate about the beginning of the 19th century with the initials

---

* The elder and younger Wm. Scott and John Keith worked in Elgin as well as Banff, and John Keith appears to have worked in Perth also.

S.A., but whose name has not been identified. Sometimes BAF was used, or merely the initial letter—a Roman capital B, or an ornamental letter ß formed in a semblance of ribbon-work.

In the second line in the table of Banff marks, the Roman capital letter D appears in connection with the marks of the elder Wm. Scott— transcribed from the Banff communion cup, on which they are stamped. In the third line a small old English ð is represented in connection with the marks of Wm. Scott, jun. Similar marks occur on plate of Aberdeen and Old Aberdeen, and are mentioned in the text concerning the Aberdeen goldsmiths, to which the reader is referred.

With the marks of Patrick Scott, represented in the fourth line of Banff marks, a crowned heart occurs between his duplicated stamp—his initials with a mullet below them, in a heart-shaped shield. This symbol has probably no signification apart from the fancy of the particular maker who adopted it ; similar devices were frequently used by English and Irish goldsmiths in the 17th and 18th centuries, but are not often found to have been used in Scotland.

On one of Lord Breadalbane's table-spoons and a dessert-spoon, made by John Keith, about 1795 to 1820, a stamp resembling a man's head appears, the meaning of which is obscure. It is probably not a duty-mark, being unlike any such mark known to the Author. With regard to this, the absence of a duty-mark in the case of Scottish provin- cial plate manufactured after 1784 (except on that which was assayed and marked at Edinburgh) is remarkable, and seems to indicate a lack of active interference by the authorities who were at that period respon- sible for carrying out the provisions of the Act 24 Geo. III. c. 53, with regard to the collection of plate duty, and to the mark prescribed for indicating its payment.

Another mark, with reference to which no explanation appears to be forthcoming, is the letter H in a square stamp, occasionally found with the marks of John Keith (1794-1824) and Wm. Simpson (1840-55).

The following table illustrates examples of the marks of nearly all the known Banff goldsmiths :—

MARKS ON BANFF PLATE

FROM ABOUT 1680 TO ABOUT 1850.

DATE (ABOUT).	MARKS.	MAKER'S NAME.	ARTICLES AND OWNERS.
1680		Wm. Scott.	Beaker-shaped communion cup : Cullen.
1698		Do. do.	Do. do. do : Banff.
1720		Wm. Scott, junr.	Table-spoon : Mr. H. D. Ellis.
1725		Patk. Scott.	{ Table-spoon : Glasgow Exhibition. { Beaker-shaped com. cup : Auchterless.
1732-41		Patrick Gordon.	Ewer : Messrs. Crichton.
1750		Alexr. Shirras.	Table-spoon : Glasgow Exhibition.
1775		John Argo.	Do. : Do. do.
1780		Do. do.	Toddy-ladle : Do. do.
1785		Wm. Byres.	Table-spoon : Do. do.
1795		John Keith.	Tea-spoon : Lord Breadalbane.
,,		Do. do.	Table-spoon : Do. do.
1800-20		Do. do.	Do. & toddy ladle : Do. do.
,,		Do. do.	Dessert-spoon : Do. do.
,,		Do. do.	Tea-spoon : Do. do.
,,		Do. do.	Gravy-spoons : Do. do.
,,		Do. do.	Toddy ladle : Do. do.
,,		Do. do.	Four-pronged fork : Do. do.
,,		(*Not identified.*)	Tea-spoon : Do. do.
1820		Geo. Elder.*	Table-spoon : Glasgow Exhibition.
1835		John McQueen.	Dessert-spoon : Mr. Chisholm.
1850		Wm. Simpson.	Table-spoon : Messrs. Smith & Rait.
,,	,, ,,	Do. do.	Tea-spoon : Glasgow Exhibition.

* The mark of Geo. Elder, as above (with the figure of mother and child in addition), is stamped on a communion cup at Rhynie.

DUNDEE.

The goldsmiths of Dundee were also incorporated with other trades under the common denomination of "Hammermen". This association of trades was at one period discontinued, but it was subsequently revived.

(margin note: Dundee goldsmiths incorporated with other hammermen.)

The earliest reference to any goldsmith contained in the burgh records is of the year 1550, when one David Stevenson, a goldsmith, is mentioned. Of their charter no trace is to be found, and the oldest record which pertains to the Dundee goldsmiths is known as the "locked-book," the entries in which were commenced in 1587. It contains the names of the master-goldsmiths then working and (with apparently some omissions) the names of others admitted from that date down to the 19th century.

The following list was furnished to the Author by the Marquess of Breadalbane, for whom it was compiled by Mr. James Ramsay, of Dundee, under the supervision of Mr. Thos. Thornton, the Town-clerk, who in his official capacity had the custody of all the Dundee Records.

The names of watch and clock makers, jewellers and engravers are included in the list as they often combined the trade of a gold and silversmith with their principal business.

NAMES OF DUNDEE GOLDSMITHS.

FROM 1550 TO 1834.

G.S. = Goldsmith; S.S. = Silversmith; W.M. = Watchmaker; C.M. = Clockmaker; J. = Jeweller; E. = Engraver.

The date is that of admission as a "Hammerman" or earliest mention of name.

1550	David	Stevenson, G.S.
1587	Thomas	Ramsay, ,,
,,	Charles	Ramsay, ,,
1602	Thomas	Lindsay, ,,
1611	Alexdr.	Duncan.
,,	John	Ramsay.
,,	Thomas	Kyd.
1628	Alexdr.	Lindsay, G.S., son of James Lindsay.
1660-2	Thomas	Lindsay. In the town council in 1660 and following years was a Thos. Lindsay who subscribed the Act of Council, 14 Nov., 1668, ordaining "that no man be admitted master without he give one faithful tryall of his profession".
1664	William	Smith, W.M.
1683	David	Scrymgeour, G.S.
,,	Robert	Gairdyne, or Gairdine, G.S.
1700	George	Smith, Knocksmith (*i.e.* clocksmith, clockmaker).
1722	Charles	Dickson, G.S.
1724	Alexdr.	Smith, C.M. (son of George Smith).
1726	Alexdr.	Smith, G.S.
1736	Charles	Farquharson, W.M. (address in 1782—Cross).
1738	Charles	Dickson, G.S. (son of Charles Dickson, goldsmith).
1763	William	Bisset, W.M. (address in 1782—Overgate).

1764	John	Steven, G.S.
1767	James	Ivory, W.M. (address in 1782—Cross).
1782	Alexdr.	Ferguson, W.M. (address in 1782—back of Guard).
,,	William	Scott, J. (address in 1782—Cross).
1795	Thomas	Ivory, W.M. & E. (son of James Ivory; in 1809 at 18 High Street, S.).
1803	Colin	Salmon, W.M. (in 1809, Overgate, N.S.).
1806	William	Constable, S.S., J. & W.M. (5 High Street, S.).
1809	Alexdr.	Buchan, C.M. (Hill E.).
,,	John	Crichton, W.M. (Castle Street).
,,	Thomas	Dall, W.M. (Murraygate).
,,	Edward	Livingstone, J. & S.S. (top of Castle Street, W.S., and 1809 & 1818-24-5, at 6 High Street).
,,	David	Manson, J. & S.S. (1809-18, Crichton Street).
,,	James	Robertson, W.M. (till 1845, High Street, removed in 1845-7 to 10 Murraygate).
,,	William	Young, C. & W.M. (High St.).
1817	William	Scott, jr., C. & W.M.
1818	Alexdr.	Cameron,* J., S.S., C. & W.M. (till 1847 at 78 High Street).
,,	John	Lundie, W.M. (46 High Street).
,,	William	Millar, J. (Nethergate, S.).
1834	Robert	Donaldson, J. & S.S. (till 1845 at 16 Crichton St., E.).

* The mark of Alexander Cameron is found on Newcastle Plate of 1805-6.

The Dundee town mark—a pot of lilies—taken from the arms of the burgh.

The arms of the burgh of Dundee—adopted by its goldsmiths as their town mark—are *azure a pot of growing lilies argent*. It appears, with four exceptions, upon every example of Dundee plate which the Author has seen. The pot has always two handles, varying slightly in form, as do the flowers, but all are easily recognisable by the general resemblance they bear to each other. There were no such inexplicable varieties of the town mark used at Dundee as have been found to have been used at Aberdeen and some other burghs.

Other marks used by Dundee goldsmiths.

Early in the 19th century Alexander Cameron added the mark of a thistle, after the manner of the Edinburgh mark. The thistle mark was used also by Edward Livingstone, and two other goldsmiths whose initials were " RN " and " RH " respectively, but whose names have not been ascertained. Cameron used an additional stamp bearing the town name DUN DEE in full. A similar stamp was also used by a goldsmith with initials " WK," whose name has not been ascertained. With the marks of RH a crown in an octagonal stamp and a mark resembling a basket appear; and the marks of WK are accompanied by an incuse star of six points charged with a pellet.

From an early date in the 18th century various single letters occur with the other marks, some being Script others Roman, and one a small Black-letter m. These can scarcely have been " date-letters " in the sense generally understood by that expression. They were perhaps used to indicate some kind of test or assay to which the plate had been subjected.

The dates placed before the names in the list of goldsmiths, and (in parenthesis) after the names in the table of marks, are not in all cases the dates of admission, but the dates when the names are found first mentioned. For instance, the date (1683) appended to the name of Robert Gairdine is half a century later than the date of some of his work and 1683 may be the date (or about the date) of his death, as cups made by him are found dated 1631, 1643 and 1648 respectively. There may, of course, have been two goldsmiths whose initials were R.G. and the earlier perhaps was the father of the Robert Gairdine mentioned in 1683. Again, the mark of John Steven, whose name is found mentioned in 1764, is stamped on a rat-tail table-spoon belonging to Lord Breadalbane, which has every appearance of having been made not later than 1730. The observations, therefore, which have been made with reference to Robert Gairdine may be applied, *mutatis mutandis*, to John Steven.

MARKS ON DUNDEE PLATE

FROM ABOUT 1628 TO ABOUT 1840.

The date in the first column is the approximate date of the plate; that in the third column is the date when the name has been found mentioned.

DATE (ABOUT.)	MARKS.	MAKER'S NAME.	ARTICLES AND OWNERS.
1628	AL 🏆 AL	Alexr. Lindsay (1628)	Com. cups: Kettins and Bel-helvie.
1631	RG 🏆	Robt. Gairdine (mentioned 1683)	Com. cup, dated 1631: Brechin.
1643	RG 🏆 RG	Do. do.	Do. do. 1643: Do.
1648	RG 🏆 RG	Do. do.	Do. do. 1648: Do. Tazza-shaped cup: Exeter College, Oxford.
1667	TL 🏆 TL	Thos. Lindsay (1662)	Com. cup, dated 1667: St. Vigeans, Arbroath.
1722	CD 🏆 CD E	Chas. Dickson (1722)	Table-spoons: Glasgow Exhib.
1730	IS 🏆 IS M	John Steven (mentioned 1764)	Rat-tail spoon: The Marquess of Breadalbane, K.G.
1742	AI ,, AI K	Alexr. Johnston (1739)	Baptismal basin, dated 1742: Oathlaw.
1764	JS 🏆	John Steven (1764)	Toddy ladle: The Marquess of Breadalbane, K.G.
1776	WS ,, WS W	Wm. Scott (1776)	Hash-spoon and table-spoons: The Marquess of Breadalbane, K.G.
,,	,, ,, M	Do. do.	Com. cup: Oathlaw.
	AC 🏆 C 🦁	Alexr. Cameron (1818)	Three-pronged forks: The Marquess of Breadalbane.
	EL ,, D ,,	Edwd. Livingstone (1809)	Toddy ladle: Glasgow Exhib.
	CAMERON ,, C ,, DUNDEE	Alexr. Cameron (1818)	Tea-spoon: The Marquess of Breadalbane, K.G. Hash-spoon: Birm. Assay Off.
	RN 🏆 🏆 🏆	Robt. Naughton? (see Inverness, p. 549)	Sugar tongs: The Marquess of Breadalbane, K.G.
1800	T.S ,, ,,	Thos. Stewart? (see Inverness, p. 549)	Toddy ladles: Do.
TO	WC ,, ,,	Wm. Constable (1806)	Tea & caddy spoon: Do.
1840	RH S 👑 ☐ 🏆 DUNDEE	(*Not identified.*)	Table-spoon: Do.
	EL 🏆 EL m	Edwd. Livingstone (1809)	Do. : Do.
	WK DUN DEE ✡	(*Not identified.*)	Do. : Do.
	DM 🌸 DM	David Manson (1809)	Tea-spoon: Birm. Assay Office.
	DM ,, DM	Do. do.	Soup ladle: Messrs. Smith & Rait.
1809	WY 🏆 D 🏆	Wm. Young (1809)	Toddy ladle: Messrs. Crichton.

ELGIN.

Elgin Gold-
smiths probably
never incorpor-
ated.

There does not appear to have been any Incorporation of goldsmiths at Elgin, and the earliest mention of any goldsmith in the burgh records is in 1701, when the elder and younger Scott were admitted freemen. The entries are:—

"1701 William Scott (the elder) * and
  ,,   William Scott (the younger) * being found qualified in their trade of gold and silversmiths are admitted freemen.
1712 James   Guthrie (from Edinburgh), having satisfied the hammermen craft that he was a duly qualified gold and silversmith was admitted a freeman.

1715 Alex. Innes.
1720 James Tait.
1729 Wm. Livingston.
1754 James Humphrey, to whom were bound as apprentices,
  ,,   John M'Beath and
  ,,   John Cruickshank.
1790 Chas. Fowler.
1808 John Keith."

The Elgin
town mark.

The town mark was the name of the burgh, usually contracted either as ELG or ELN, but sometimes in full, as in one of the marks of Chas. Fowler.   With some of the earlier examples the figure of a mother and child in an upright oblong stamp is found.   From about 1790 to about 1830 a stamp representing the west front of Elgin Cathedral Church was added, which was sometimes accompanied by another stamp representing the figure of St. Giles, its patron saint.   In one instance (with the marks of Wm. Livingston of 1728) the letter O is found, as with the Glasgow marks of Milne & Campbell and John Donald.   On a tea-spoon of about 1820 a thistle in an oval stamp occurs, in addition to the Elgin stamp and the initials W.F.

The table below illustrates all the examples of Elgin marks which have been noted by the Author.   In the third line the letter A in a separate stamp will be observed.   Mr. Brook noted an example in which he found the letter B in a separate stamp.   No explanation can be given of these letters other than that suggested in the case of Dundee.

MARKS ON ELGIN PLATE,

FROM ABOUT 1728 TO ABOUT 1830.

DATE (ABOUT.)	MARKS.	MAKER'S NAME.	ARTICLES AND OWNERS.
1728	WL ELG O	Wm. Livingston.	Com. cup dated 1728 : Boharne.
1730	ER 🝆 ER	E. R.........	Table-spoon, embossed back: The Marquess of Breadalbane, K.G.
1754	IH ELN 🝆 A	James Humphrey.	Do. do. do.
1760	🝆 IH	(E on its back and LN for Elgin). James Humphrey.	Half-a-dozen table forks : Mr. E. A. Sandeman.
1770	JP ELN RS	... ...	Half-a-dozen tea-spoons : Messrs. Reid & Sons, Newcastle.
1790 to 1820	CF ELN	Chas. Fowler.	Table forks (three pronged) : Do.
	,, ,, 🝆	Do. do.	Tea-spoons : Glasgow Exhibition.
	CF ELGIN ,, 🝆	Do. do.	Table-spoon: Do. do.
	WF ,, 🝆	W. F.........	Tea-spoon : Lord Breadalbane.
1830	TS ELN 🝆	Thos. Stewart (see Inverness, p. 549).	Toddy ladle : Do. do.

* The names of the elder and younger Wm. Scott appear also in the Aberdeen and Banff lists.

GREENOCK.

The goldsmiths of Greenock do not appear to have ever been incorporated, and the names of those who worked there can only be

No incorporation of goldsmiths at Greenock.

MARKS ON GREENOCK PLATE

FROM ABOUT 1750 TO ABOUT 1830.

DATE (ABOUT).	MARKS.	MAKER'S NAME.	ARTICLES AND OWNERS.
1750		W. L.........	Table-spoons : Messrs. Smith & Rait.
		Jonas Osborne, of Glasgow.	Do. : Glasgow Exhib., 1901.
1765		Do. do.	Do. : Do. do.
		Do. do.	Do. : Do. do.
		Do. do.	Do. : Lord Breadalbane.
		James Taylor, of Glasgow.	Do. : Messrs. Smith & Rait.
1780		G. B.........	Do. : Lord Breadalbane.
		W. C.........	Do. : Do. do.
,,		M. C.	Toddy ladle : Messrs. Crichton.
1790		B. C.	Do. do. : Do.
,,		N. H.	Fiddle-pattern fish slice : Mr. Dudley Westropp.
1800		J. H.	Fiddle-pattern fish forks : Mr. Dudley Westropp.
,,		R. N.	Egg-spoon : Lord Breadalbane.
,,		P. H.	Tea-spoons : Messrs. Crichton.
		John Heron.	Tea- and gravy-spoon : Do.
		Do. do.	Dessert-spoons : Do.
1800		Thos. Davie.	Table-spoon : Glasgow Exhibition.
		Do. do.	Toddy ladle : Lord Breadalbane.
		John Heron.	Table-spoon : Glasgow Exhibition.
		J. & G. Heron ?	Tea-spoon : Do. do.
1800 TO 1830		Do. do.	Toddy ladle : Lord Breadalbane.
		W. H. T.........	Tea-spoon : Do. do.
1820		Do. do.	Sugar basin : Mr. W. Farr.
,,		Peterhead and Greenock mark.	Fiddle-pattern tea-spoons : Lord Breadalbane.

traced in directories and burgh or parish records, where their names and calling are incidentally mentioned. The names of those in the table on page 545 have been so found. The names of John Campbell, Long Vennel, John McFarlane and John Menzies appear in directories of Glasgow and district between 1780 and 1800, as Greenock goldsmiths and jewellers, but no examples of plate made by them have been seen by the Author, and whether they ever made any is uncertain.

Greenock marks.

The marks found on Greenock plate are an anchor, a ship in full sail, a green oak (obviously a rebus representing the name of the town), or some one or two of them, and the maker's initials. In one case a rat (or mouse) sejant is found, and in another a crescent enclosing a mullet.

The letter S was probably meant to indicate sterling or standard. The letters G, C, W and O may have some reference to an assay, as suggested in the case of Dundee. Additional marks found recently comprising a star, a two-handled cup, and a thistle, have been inserted in this edition, but the Author makes no suggestion as to their origin.

INVERNESS.

Earliest known work of any Inverness goldsmith is of about 1640.

The earliest date which can be assigned to any known work by an Inverness goldsmith is about the year 1640. This is the approximate date of a quaich in the collection of the Marquess of Breadalbane made by a goldsmith whose initials (MK conjoined) are also to be found on a communion cup inscribed " GIVEN BY IOHN NICOLSON, WRITER IN EDN^R TO THE KIRK OF FORRESS ANNO 1643 AND REPAIRED 1724 BY Y^E ANNUAL RENTS OF MORTIFICATIONS LEFT BY THE DONATOR TO THIS BURGH ". The name of this goldsmith has not been discovered, nor has the identity been ascertained of three others who used the letters MR, ML, and the single letter M, respectively, as their marks. It is, however, known from the endorsement of the draft of the circular letter sent about 1687 by the Goldsmiths' Incorporation of Edinburgh to provincial goldsmiths, that one, by name " Robert Elphingstoun," carried on the business of a goldsmith at Inverness at that time, but no example of his work has been found.

No official records of Inverness goldsmiths earlier than 1740 are known.

There appear to be no official records known containing the names of Inverness goldsmiths of a period anterior to about 1740. A chronological list has, however, been compiled by Mr. James MacBean, of

Inverness, giving substantially all the names of goldsmiths who worked there from that date to the present day. This list having been courteously placed at the Author's disposal, the names of the makers of most of the known Inverness plate will be found in the following tables annexed to their marks. The Stewarts, whose names appear in the list, were members of a family of goldsmiths who worked in the North of Scotland for about two centuries. They lived to all intents and purposes the lives of gipsies, moving about from town to town, and were called "tinkers," the material which they wrought being found by their customers, as was the custom in the old days. They stayed at each place long enough to execute the work with which they were entrusted, and then tramped to the next town, returning after a time, and repeating their round of travels as before. Hence their marks as makers are found on plate with the town marks of Dundee, Elgin, Inverness, Tain, and Wick, in each of which places they worked in turn, while, strictly speaking, they belonged to none.

The earliest known Inverness town mark is (as in the case of Aberdeen, Banff and Elgin), an abbreviated form of the town name, the letters "INS" in an oblong punch. It is so found on almost all the known examples of Inverness plate. Early in the eighteenth century an additional stamp representing a cornucopia—the crest of the burgh—was used along with the town mark. In two instances it appears to have been used instead of the usual town mark, but its use was by no means continuous; it is found at intervals from about 1715 to about 1815. About the year 1730 an additional mark, possibly a town mark (as illustrated in Table I.) was stamped on forks, together with the marks of John Baillie and another; the reason for the use of the Roman capital A which is found on these forks, as well as on other examples of Inverness plate, has yet to be explained. From about 1740 a further additional stamp representing a dromedary—the dexter supporter of the burgh arms and the central device in the burgh seal, the other being an elephant—was occasionally used with the town mark, and in one instance it is found used with the cornucopia: the usual town mark being absent. In the nineteenth century a stamp representing a thistle is occasionally found; two or three anomalous marks and letters, the meaning of which is not apparent, have also been found. In the latest example, the town mark is "INVS".

Earliest Inverness town mark is "INS". Later additional marks are a cornucopia and a dromedary.

MARKS ON INVERNESS PLATE.

TABLE I.

FROM ABOUT 1640 TO ABOUT 1800.

(THE DATES ARE APPROXIMATE.)

DATE (ABOUT).	MARKS.	MAKER'S NAME.	ARTICLES AND OWNERS.
1640	 MK IᴧS	M. K......	Quaich : The Marquess of Breadalbane, K.G.
1643	 ,, ,, T	Do. do.	Com. cup, given 1643 : Forres.
1680	 MR INS	M. R......	Mug : Messrs. Ferguson & MacBean.
1708	M ,, M	M. L......	Quaich : Glasgow Exhibition, 1901.
1715	 M ,, �️	—— M......	Two-handled cup : Messrs. Ferguson & MacBean.
1720	 RI INS A	R I......	Rat-tailed gravy- and table-spoons : The Marquess of Breadalbane, K.G.
1730	 IB FB ⚜	John Baillie (and another)	{ Spoons : Do. do. do. Beaker-shaped com. cups : Drainie-by-Elgin.
,,	 IB FB 🔳 A	Do. do.	A dozen three-pronged forks : Mr. Burnett Stuart.
1740	 IB INS 🗙	John Baillie	Quaich : Glasgow Exhibition.
,,	 TB 🐫 INS	Thos. Baillie	Plaid-brooch : Museum of Soc. Antiq., Edinburgh.
1770	 AS INS	Alexr. Stewart	Table-spoon : Glasgow Exhibition.
1780	 RA 🐫 C INS	Robert Anderson	Soup-ladle and spoons : The Marquess of Breadalbane, K.G.
1790	 AS INS Ⓞ	Alexr. Stewart, jr.	Toddy-ladle : Glasgow Exhibition.
,,	 🐫 🖐	(*No maker's mark.*)	Small quaich : The Marquess of Breadalbane, K.G.
,,	 H&Cº 🐘 🌿 A ⌃	* Hamilton & Co.	Strainer or movable ewer top : The Marquess of Breadalbane, K.G.
,,	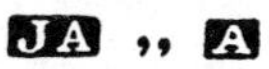 JA ,, A	J. A.	Sugar-basin : Mr. John G. Gray, Corowa, New South Wales.
,,	 T&Cº 🐫 🖐	T. & Co.	Table-forks : Mr. Broadbent.
,,	 AS ✺	Alexr. Stewart, jr.	Mustard-spoon : Lord Breadalbane.
1800	 CJ INS	Chas. Jamieson	Egg-spoons : Do. do.

* Compare with Calcutta marks, p. 473, *supra.*

MARKS ON INVERNESS PLATE.

TABLE II.

FROM ABOUT 1800 TO ABOUT 1880.

(THE DATES ARE APPROXIMATE.)

DATE (ABOUT).	MARKS.	MAKER'S NAME.	ARTICLES AND OWNERS.
1800	J&N INS 🦐	Jameson & Naughton.	Mustard-spoons: The Marquess of Breadalbane. Dessert-spoons: Mr. Fitzhenry, S. Ken. Museum.
,,	MAC MAS ,,	———— Macmas.	Tea-spoon: Lord Breadalbane.
,,	DF INS	Donald Fraser.	Toddy ladle: Do. do.
1810	CJ INS 🐎 CJ	Charles Jamieson.	Soup ladle: Do. do.
,,	,, ,, ,,	Do. do.	Small quaich: Do. do.
,,	J.McR INS 🌿	J. McR.	Egg-spoon: Do. do.
1815	RN INS J RN	Robt. Naughton.	Soup ladle: Do. do.
,,	RN 🌿 🔵	Do. do.	Table-spoon and toddy ladles: Glasgow Exhibition, 1901.
1820	AM INS ○ ○	Alexr. MacLeod.	Tea-spoon: Lord Breadalbane.
,,	AMcL INS ⚫⚫⚫	Do. do.	Dessert-spoon: Do. do.
1830	TS INS 🐾	Thos. Stewart.	Toddy ladle: Glasgow Exhibition.
,,	D·F INS	Donald Fraser.	Table-spoon: Lord Breadalbane.
,,	A·S INS ♠	Alexr. Stewart.	Dessert-spoon: B'ham Assay Office.
1840	🐖	... ...	Mark noted by Mr. James MacBean.
1857	F BROS	Ferguson Brothers.	Do. do. do. do.
1880	F&M 🐾 INVS	Ferguson & MacBean.	Small ornaments: The Makers.

MONTROSE.

The names of the early goldsmiths of Montrose.

Of the Montrose goldsmiths the names of eleven have been found, as printed in the following list.

The name of William Lindsay occurs in the Montrose Kirk Session Records for 1708, and his mark is found on eight communion cups— the oldest dated 1671—of excellent design and workmanship, in different churches. Of David Ouchterlony no more is known than that his name, as a goldsmith then working at Montrose, is endorsed on the draft of the letter previously mentioned, of the year 1687 or thereabouts, at Goldsmiths' Hall, Edinburgh. The name of David Lyon occurs in the Kirk Session Records for the year 1718. The name of Thomas Johnston occurs in the same Records for the year 1752, and his mark is stamped on a pair of communion cups at Marykirk, Montrose.

MARKS ON MONTROSE PLATE.

DATE (ABOUT).	MARKS.	MAKER'S NAME.	ARTICLES AND OWNERS.
1670		Wm. Lindsay (probably).	Table-spoon, pricked 1672, Mr. A. W. Stone.
1671		Wm. Lindsay.	Com. cups, "gifted 1671": Forfar. Spoon with flat stem: Mr. W. Boore.
	" " " 	Do. do.	Com. cup, "given 1688": Laurencekirk, Montrose.
1680-3		Do. do.	Com. cups, "gifted 1680": Bervie, and (1683) Aberlemno.
1710		... ...	Wavy-end spoon: Mr. J. H. Walter.
1752		Thos. Johnston.	Com. cups: Marykirk, Montrose. Table-spoon: Mr. H. Dawson.
1788		Benj. Lumsden (admitted 1788).	Dessert-spoon: The Marquess of Breadalbane, K.G.
1811		Wm. Mill (1811)	Tea-spoon : Do. do.

The Montrose "town mark" was a rose.

The Montrose town mark was a rose. As found on the cups made by William Lindsay it is a double rose (like that associated with the Tudor dynasty), in a circular punch, generally struck twice, with Lindsay's own mark—WL surmounted by a crown, with a hammer between the letters—occupying a central position between the two roses.

In the earlier examples of Lindsay's mark a hand is seen grasping the hammer, but in the later examples the hand is absent. The town mark on the cup made by Thomas Johnston is a single rose in a plain shield. On the plain cup at Laurencekirk the letter E is stamped, and on the Marykirk cups the letter B, the meaning of which is not apparent.

On a spoon recently noted, the letter H is accompanied by other marks ascribed to Montrose. In the last two lines below there are further marks discovered since the first edition of this work was published, to which have been added the names of the goldsmiths to whom the marks are ascribed.

LIST OF MONTROSE GOLDSMITHS.

(MENTIONED IN THE TOWN'S RECORDS, KIRK SESSION OF MONTROSE.)

Date.	Marks.	NAME OF GOLDSMITH.
1649	JM	James Mudie [offered to put up two new horologes: probably a watch and clockmaker].
1674	TB	Thomas Browne, "Knockmaker" [ordered to be paid a sum of £3 by the Town Treasurer, 4 February, 1674].
1687	DO	David Ouchterlony.
1688	WL	Wm. Lindsay [was called upon by the Dean of Gild to admit himself as a Burgess: Gild-brother of Montrose. He refused to do so on the grounds that his father was a Burgess and Gild-brother. He was not allowed to work within the limits of the Burgh. At 4 April, 1688, he was again charged for non-admitting himself, and admitted that he had wrought (worked) and would again; the Dean fined him 10s. Scots (equal to 10d. of present money) and ordered him to be imprisoned if the fine was unpaid, but he was liberated afterwards as the cost of his incarceration was too much for the local Treasury. 28 November, 1688: He was admitted a Burgess and Gild-brother on condition that he would "undertake to cutt ane new seal for the Towne's use," and in his admission he is described as a goldsmith. He was elected a member of the Town Council in 1672, as representative from the Blacksmiths' Incorporation.]
1702	JS	John Seton [of Edinburgh, Goldsmith. £816 6s. was disbursed by the Town for silverwork wrought by John Seton.]
"	JT	John Thomson [watchmaker; mentioned as working in Montrose].
1718	DL	David Lyon [Goldsmith: made a Burgess and Gild-brother].
1743	TI	Thomas Johnston [Goldsmith: admitted a Burgess and Gild-brother, 19 August, 1743].
1788	BL	Benjamin Lumsden [admitted 24 December, 1788].
1811	WM	William Mill [an apprentice: admitted 22 June, 1811].
1817	JG	John Glenn [Goldsmith's apprentice: admitted 31 May, 1817].

PERTH.

The Perth Gold-
smiths were
associated with
other crafts in
a Guild of
Hammermen.
The goldsmiths of Perth had no distinct guild, but were associated with the blacksmiths, whitesmiths, gunsmiths, armourers, brass workers, pewterers, watch and clock makers, carriage makers, bell hangers, potters, and saddlers in the Hammermen's Incorporation. Whether they were incorporated by charter is not known. There is no charter in existence, and if there ever was one it has been lost or destroyed.

The Minutes
date from 1518.
The goldsmith's art is said to have been practised in Perth in the 13th century by one Henry the Bald, but the earliest minutes date from the year 1518. They are contained in a book in which the first entry is dated 1584, when by order of the craft the original minutes of 1518-84 were copied from an older book which is not now to be found.

The names of several goldsmiths entered in the minute-book of the Perth Hammermen's Incorporation from 1567 to 1808, appear below. In most cases the marks which they used are sketched in the book at the side of their names. Of these, four were deacons of the Incorporation. Other goldsmiths worked in Perth at various dates, in addition to those whose names appear below, but as the minute-book frequently omits to state the calling of the members of the Incorporation, their identification is extremely difficult. Perth marks have been found on spoons and punch ladles of the first half of the 19th century with marks of makers whose names the Author has been unable to trace.

The following names were copied from the minute-books of the Hammermen's Incorporation by Mr. David Hepburn for the Marquess of Breadalbane, to whose courtesy the Author is indebted for this list.

NAMES OF PERTH GOLDSMITHS.

Date of Admission.	Name of Goldsmith.	Remarks.	Date of Admission.	Name of Goldsmith.	Mentioned.
	Findlay-goldsmyth (c. 1518-32)	Mentioned in minutes	1808	John Scott	
	Adam Denholme	Deacon 1567	,,	John Sid	
	Robert Ramsay	Deacon 1604, 1610-12		David Greig	1810
				Colin Richardson	1813
	Robert Gardiner	Deacon 1669, 1673-9		John Hogg	,,
				Charles Murray	1816
1772	James Cornfute			Robert Greig	1817
1791	Robert Keay			James Stobie	1821
	R. & R. Keay	Partners, c. 1795		Robert Keay (Jr.)	1825
1796	Wm. Ritchie	Deacon 1806-8		John Pringle	1827
1804	Thomas Sim			Colin Pensford	1829
				David Greig (Jr.)	1850

The ancient name of Perth was St. John's-toun, and its device—a lamb bearing the banner of St. Andrew—was the earliest known town mark of the Perth goldsmiths.   This mark, as illustrated in the following table, has been found in several different forms on domestic spoons (with trifid ends to the stems) of about 1670-80, on communion cups at Coupar Angus and Muthil of a few years' later date, and on cups, as well as other articles of plate ranging in date from about 1675 to 1710. On work of later date the more modern town mark—an eagle displayed —is found, adopted from the arms of the burgh, which are : *an Imperial eagle surmounted on the breast with an escutcheon charged with the holy lamb passant reguardant carrying the banner of St. Andrew.*   This device, with the motto *Pro rege lege et grege*, is on the burgh seal as here illustrated :—

The ancient name of Perth was St. John's-toun.

The earliest "town mark" a lamb and flag.

Afterwards an eagle displayed, both taken from the burgh arms.

The device on the Perth burgh seal.

In the more modern town mark the eagle is sometimes found with one head only, differing from the "charge" in the burgh arms: probably by reason of inattention to precedent on the part of the die-sinker.

The eagle sometimes with one head only.

In only one mark as yet discovered—that of Robert Keay, junior (1821)—is the escutcheon charged with the lamb, bearing the banner of St. Andrew, defined.   Mr. Brook noted this instance, but the lamb as seen in the mark is too small to be represented in print, except on a greatly enlarged scale, which would be out of proportion with the other marks illustrated here in *facsimile.*

In the first two lines of marks in the table of Perth marks to be found on the following page there are letters (𝔅 and 𝔞 respectively), the signification of which is not apparent.   In later examples the letter S appears, probably indicative of the standard or sterling quality of the silver used.   With the marks of John Sid the figures of a cup and an ewer appear, and in two other instances a mark resembling the Glasgow town mark is added to the Perth mark.

MARKS ON PERTH PLATE.

The date in the first column is the approximate date of the plate; that after a maker's name is the date of his admission to the Incorporation of Hammermen.

DATE (ABOUT).	MARKS.	MAKER'S NAME.	ARTICLES AND OWNERS.
1675		W. M......	Table-spoon, trifid end: Mr. J. H. Walter.
1680		Robert Gardiner (1669)	Table-spoon, trifid end: Messrs. Crichton.
1687		Do. do. do.	{ Pair of cups: The Earl of Kinnoul. Com. cup, dated 1687: Coupar Angus.
1710		William Scott, of Banff	Hash-spoon: The Marquess of Breadalbane, K.G.
1750		... ...	Punch ladle and spoons: Mr. Geo. Henderson.
1772		James Cornfute (1772)	Six table-spoons: The Marquess of Breadalbane, K.G.
1780		T. F......	Table-spoon: Glasgow Exhibition.
,,		Robert Keay (1791)	Tea-spoons: Mr. Geo. Henderson.
,,		J. J.	Sugar tongs: Do. do.
1791		Robert Keay (1791)	Salt-spoons and toddy-ladle: The Marquess of Breadalbane, K.G.
1800		William Ritchie (1796)	Tea-spoons: Lord Breadalbane.
1810		John Sid (1808)	Do. : Do. do.
,,		R. & R. Keay	Do. : Do. do.
1815		David Greig (c. 1810)	Do. & toddy ladle: do.
1816		Charles Murray (1816)	Do. & sugar tongs: do.
,,		(*No maker's mark.*)	Tea-spoon: Glasgow Exhibition.
,,		R. McG.	Do. : Lord Breadalbane.
,,		I. H.	Dessert-spoons: Do. do.
1820		Robert Greig (1817)	Do. : Do. do.
1830		Robert Keay, jr. (1825)	Two punch ladles: Birm. Assay Off.
,,		A. M......	Tea-spoon: Lord Breadalbane.
,,		John Pringle (1827)	Do. : Do. do.
,,		Robert Keay, jr. (1825)	Do. : Do. do.
,,		John Pringle (1827)	Mustard-spoon: Do. do.
1830 TO 1850	{	J. K......	Punch-ladle: Do. do.
		R. D......	Tea-spoon: Do. do.
1856		David Greig, jr.	Tea-spoon (also Edinbro' marks of 1846-7): Lord Breadalbane.

ST. ANDREWS.

The above marks, found on a communion cup dated 1671, belonging to the Town Church, St. Andrews, and on a salt-cellar of about the same date belonging to St. Mary's College, illustrate the St. Andrews town mark—*a saltire or St. Andrew's cross*—and the mark of the goldsmith—Patrick Gairden—who made both examples of plate.

STIRLING.

The second of these two marks is believed to be the town mark of Stirling; the first is a maker's mark. Both occur on an oval tobacco box of about the last quarter of the 17th century, in the collection of the Marquess of Breadalbane. The lid of the box is engraved with a coat of arms and an inscription in the style of the period of Charles II. The name of the maker—whose initials GR appear in his mark under a mermaid and star of six points, in an oval stamp—is not known.

What are believed to be other Stirling marks are here illustrated :—

These marks were noted on an 18th century table-spoon in the Glasgow Exhibition of 1901. Similar marks were found by the late Mr. A. J. S. Brook* on two table-spoons belonging to an old Stirling family.

The arms of Stirling are :—*on a mount a castle, triple towered.* The second mark in the first example, and the first in the second, are supposed to be crude representations of a triple-towered castle.

WICK.

The town mark of Wick, the principal burgh in Caithness, was the name of the town as illustrated above. The marks occur on a tea-spoon, of about the end of the 18th or beginning of the 19th century, belonging to Lord Breadalbane. The name of the maker has not been ascertained.

TAIN.

Mr. Brook made several incidental references to goldsmiths who plied their craft in Tain, the county town of Ross-shire.*

The town mark is the town name in Roman or Italic capital letters, accompanied in some instances with the mark of a Scotch thistle.

The EXAMPLES OF TAIN MARKS illustrated below are on articles of plate of about the latter part of the 18th century.

MARKS.	ARTICLES AND OWNERS.
HR SⓄB 𝒜	Table-spoon : The Marquess of Breadalbane, K.G.
H·R TAIN SⓄB ℒ	Tea-pot : Mr. Willoughby Farr.
A·S TAIN ⚓	Toddy ladle : The Marquess of Breadalbane, K.G.
RW ,, 🏰	Dinner fork : Do. do.
W.I. TAIN ,,	Tea-spoon : Do. do.

In some of the Scottish provincial burghs the manufacture of small articles of plate was continued after the passing of the Statute 6 and 7 Wm. IV. c. 69, which from the year 1836 gave to the Edinburgh Goldsmiths' Incorporation, jurisdiction over the whole of Scotland, excepting the Glasgow district. The manufacture of small articles, such as mounts for dirks and their sheaths, plaid brooches and other ornaments, was continued through the 19th century and is carried on at the present day in Aberdeen and Inverness. Such small articles being exempt from liability to be assayed, and from payment of duty (during the time when a duty was levied on plate), are not within the operation of the above statute and are stamped with the local marks only.† When, as has frequently happened, larger articles which come within the operation of the statute are made in any provincial burgh they have to be sent to the assay office at Edinburgh (if within the Glasgow district to Glasgow) to be assayed and marked, and in these cases the articles are impressed with the marks of the assay office as well as those of the provincial maker.

* See *Old Scottish Communion Plate*, p. 597.
† See the list of articles exempt from liability to be assayed on page 73, *ante*.

UNASCRIBED SCOTTISH MARKS.

The following marks have been found on articles of plate also believed to be of Scottish manufacture.   With two or three exceptions the articles have been found in Scotland, and the thistle mark on the greater number of them points to a Scottish origin, but the Author has not been able to locate with certainty the place where any one of them was made.

THE DATES APPENDED—WHICH ARE CONJECTURED APPROXIMATELY—ARE SUCH AS THE CHARACTER OF THE ARTICLE AND STYLE OF THE WORK IN EACH CASE SUGGEST.

DATE (ABOUT).	MARKS.	ARTICLES AND OWNERS.
1500		Possibly an Inverness mark. Spoon with "wrythen" knop: Lord Breadalbane.
1690		Folding rat-tail spoon : Museum of Antiquities, Edinburgh.
1700		Fork, with seal at end : Do. do. do.
"		Small quaich : Lord Breadalbane.
1720		Plaid brooch : Do. do.
1730		Taper stand, etc. : Windsor Castle. (? Chas. Alchorne, ent. 1729.)
1750		Dessert-spoons : Lord Breadalbane.
"		Salt-box : Mr. Dudley Westropp.
"		Small bowl : Messrs. Crichton.
"		Large soup ladle : The Marquess of Breadalbane, K.G.
"		Small quaich : Mr. Nyberg.
"		* {Bonbonnière : The Marquess of Breadalbane, K.G. {Table-spoons : Lord Newlands.
1760		Tea-spoons : The Marquess of Breadalbane, K.G.
"		Tea-spoon : Do. do.
"		Two-handled tray : Mr. A. J. Davis.
1770		Table spoon : The Marquess of Breadalbane, K.G.
"		Dessert-spoon : Messrs. Mackay & Chisholm.

* Lord Breadalbane suggests that these marks emanate from some place near Glasgow.

UNASCRIBED SCOTTISH MARKS—*Continued.*

DATE (ABOUT).	MARKS.	ARTICLES AND OWNERS.
1780		Sugar tongs : The Marquess of Breadalbane, K.G.
,,		Tea-spoon : Do. do.
1790		Sauce ladle : Do. do.
,,		(Perhaps Dundee marks). Each mark struck twice on table-spoons : Messrs. Crichton.
,,		Dessert-spoons : Messrs. Crichton.
,,		Fiddle-pattern forks : Noted by Mr. Dudley Westropp.
1800		*(Perhaps Dundee marks) Marrow scoop : Lord Breadalbane.
,,		†Shell-pattern caddy spoon : Lord Breadalbane.
,,		Small tea-spoon : Do. do.
,,		Salt-spoon : Do. do.
,,		Table-spoon and mounts of shell snuff-box : The Marquess of Breadalbane, K.G.
1816		‡ Pepper caster : Messrs. Crichton.
1800-20		*Perhaps John Glenn of Montrose. Half a dozen tea-spoons : Lord Breadalbane.
,,		*Dozen fiddle-pattern table-spoons : Lord Breadalbane.
,,		* Dozen fiddle-pattern tea-spoons : Do. do.

* These are believed to be the marks of travelling goldsmiths, called " Tinkers ".
† It has been suggested that these are Leith marks.
‡ It is with considerable hesitation that this line of marks is included. The work, however, not appearing to be continental, as suggested by the striking of the full date " 1816," the marks have been placed here as " doubtful " Scotch because of the thistle.

CHAPTER XXII

THE IRISH GOLDSMITHS
AND THEIR MARKS

THE GOLDSMITHS OF DUBLIN.

The existence of highly skilled goldsmiths in Ireland at a period Early Dublin
Goldsmiths. anterior to the Norman Conquest is referred to in Chapter I. Many famous examples of their work, of great antiquity and extraordinary artistic merit, are preserved in the National Museum, Dublin.* In the *Dublin Roll of Names,*† a document which appears to have been written about the latter part of the 12th century, the following goldsmiths are mentioned :—

> *Willielmus aurifaber de Srobesburi (Shrewsbury), Rogerus aurifaber, Willielmus aurifaber, Giles aurifaber, and Godardus aurifaber de London.*

In the list of free citizens of Dublin, 1225-50, the names of *Thomas* and *John*, goldsmiths, and *William de St. Helena*, goldsmith, are included.†

The name of *Oliver de Nichol*, goldsmith, occurs in a Dublin "Gild Merchant" roll of 1226, and in one of 1257 the names of the following goldsmiths occur :—*William Frend, Maurice of Connaught, and Cristinus.*

In the accounts of the Seneschal of the Holy Trinity Priory, Dublin, for the year 1344 ‡ the name of *Walter the goldsmith* appears as having received 9d. for marking one dozen pewter saucers, one dozen dishes, one dozen plates and two chargers, which had been purchased for the use of the Prior.

In the 15th century the following goldsmiths were admitted to the freedom of the city of Dublin :—

1469.	*Patrick Kenne, and Nicholas Browne.*	1474.	*John Savage.*
1473.	*Dermot Lynchy.*	1477.	*Walter Foile (Foley ?).*
		1482.	*Meiler Trevers.*

* For a description of these see Dr. Joyce's *Social History of Ancient Ireland* (2 vols. Longmans, 1903). See also the *Illustrated History of English Plate* by the Author of this work.
† *Historic and Municipal Documents*, vol. i. (Sir J. Gilbert). See also a paper by Mr. H. F. Berry in the Journal of the Royal Society of Antiquaries of Ireland, vol. xxxi, pp. 119-38 (1901).
‡ *Account Roll, Holy Trinity Priory*, 1337-46 (Mills).

Earliest refer-
ence to a Guild
of Goldsmiths
(1498).

The earliest known reference to a Guild of Goldsmiths in Ireland is contained in the archives of the Dublin Corporation, where it is recorded that on the festival of Corpus Christi in the year 1498 the goldsmiths of the city were represented by members of their guild who " rode worshipfully with the ' offerance,' and a star before them ". The inclusion of gold in the offering probably suggested the guild being represented in that manner.

Dublin
Goldsmiths
incorporated
prior to 1555,
but Charter
accidentally
burnt.

The date of the first incorporation of the Dublin goldsmiths is not now known, nor is it known by whom their first charter was granted. They, however, appear to have presented a petition to the City Corporation in the year 1555, stating that the charter which they had possessed had been accidentally burnt, and praying that the enjoyment of the privileges to which they were entitled under it might be continued. In April, 1557 (3 and 4 Philip and Mary), they applied to the City Assembly for leave to bring in a copy of the enrolment of their charter. Their application was granted, as testified by the following minute in the Dublin Corporation Records :—

" April 1557. It is ordained and agreed by authority aforesaid that the Corporation of Goldsmiths of this city for that their Charter by chance was burnt, that bringing the true copy of the enrolment of their charter hither before Mr. Mayor and Sheriffs they shall have the exemplification thereof under the common seal of this city."

Goldsmiths ask
the Dublin City
Council to
concede
privileges like
those conferred
by their burnt
Charter.

In October of the same year the Goldsmiths again appeared before the City Council and stated that they had been incorporated by the progenitors of Queen Mary, and that privileges such as were usual in the case of similar fraternities had been conferred on them by their charter which had been accidentally burnt. They besought the Council to prohibit foreigners from practising the art of the goldsmith in the city, and made certain other requests, which were granted, as appears by the following minute :—

Request granted,
1557.

" The fourth Friday after Michaelmas (29th Septr.), 1557 :—Whereas, as well by the humble supplication of the Goldsmiths of this City made unto us the Mayor and Sheriffs citizens and Commonalty of this city of Dublin in our assembly presently holden the fourth Friday after the feast of St. Michael the Archangel in the fourth and fifth years of our Sovereign Lord and Lady, King Philip and Queen Mary, as by ancient writing exhibited by them it doth appear that they have been from ancient time incorporate by the progenitors of our said sovereign Lady and endowed with privileges as is accustomable used in cases of like fraternities erected, which their charter was by misfortune burnt as they do grievously complain, whereupon they do humbly beseech us to relieve them with grant from us that no foreigner shall exercise the faculty within this franchise but that the same may be used and practised in such decent and comely order as heretofore it hath been in this city, and presently in all places of civil rule and regiment. We, well considering the same their request to stand with reason and to be much beneficial for all their Majesties' subjects, do by these presents by the authority of this present assembly, grant and agree that John Hanne, John Latton, Terence Byrne and Adam Colman, goldsmiths of this city and free citizens of the same, shall use and exercise within the franchise of this city the art or faculty of goldsmiths as brethren of that art or science ; and that they shall yearly choose of themselves and such other as they shall admit and receive into their fellowship or brotherhood a master and two wardens, as in other fraternities of this city is used, and that the said master and wardens with the rest of the fraternity, shall assemble themselves together and make and establish orders and laws for the good and reasonable use of the said faculty and for the peaceable conservation of the brethren thereof, and that none shall within this city or franchise thereof, use or exercise the said art or faculty of goldsmith unless he be thereunto received, admitted and allowed by the master and wardens for the time being, upon pain to be punished as other usurpers upon any franchise or liberty within this city may by the point of the same charters be corrected and punished, and the said master and wardens shall have the correction order and punishment of all such of the said faculty as shall be found within this city or franchise to violate or break these good orders or otherwise to offend in anything touching the said faculty or art in such and like manner as other masters and wardens in this city may : And that they shall have and appoint such officers and ministers as shall be requisite for their fraternity and fellowship. Provided that the Mayor of this city for the time being shall have the oversight and correction of these orders and doings so oft as he shall think expedient. Provided also that none shall be admitted to the said fraternity without he be of English name and blood of honest conversation and also free citizen of this city. And also it is granted by the authority of this said assembly that none of the faculty or art of goldsmith shall be admitted or received into the franchise of this city, unless he be first admitted and received to use the said faculty by the master and wardens for the time being.

> Four goldsmiths appointed by the city council to choose annually a master and two wardens to govern the craft.

" In witness whereof the said Mayor, Sheriffs, citizens and Commonalty have caused the common seal of the said city to be herewith appended. Dated the day and year above written." *

The goldsmiths appear not to have restricted members of other crafts from joining their association, for it is recorded that in 1590 the master and company of the goldsmiths were fined £10 for admitting Thadius Tole, coppersmith, he not being sworn a freeman of the city. The fine was afterwards reduced to £5. It is also recorded that in 1593 the Corporation of Smiths and Goldsmiths took a lease for sixty-one years of premises " on Gormond's, otherwise Ormond's Gate, at a rental of 4s.".* In 1640 the lease was renewed for a further term of sixty-one years at a rental of £8.

No entry occurs in the records down to the end of the 16th century with reference to any "touch" for gold or silver. There appears

---

* *Dublin Corporation Records*, edited by Sir J. Gilbert,

to have been no regular assay and no marks required to be stamped on wrought gold or silver. Fraudulent practices and abuses appear to have been resorted to, respecting which complaints had been made from time to time, and in order to maintain the standard of silver wares it was resolved by the Dublin City Council in the year 1605 * that thenceforward certain marks should be stamped on all wrought plate, which in quality should be equal to the silver standard coin then current, and provision was made for testing the quality, as appears in the following minute :—

"The 4th Friday after Sept. 29th, 1605.

A.D. 1605 : Resolution of Dublin City Council.

"Whereas the Commons complained that whereas in time past there hath been great abuse in this city by the indirect and sinister dealing of the goldsmiths, and that there hath for many years been divers parcels of plate made of every base and corrupt silver, notwithstanding they have by credible report received good silver of those that caused it to be made, greatly hindering the flourishing state of this Commonwealth, for remedy whereof it is therefore ordered and agreed

Every goldsmith to have a special mark, and all plate made for sale to be stamped with the figures of a lion, a harp, and a castle.

by the authority aforesaid, that every goldsmith that shall exercise that trade within this city shall have a special mark to stamp all such plate as he shall work or sell, and withall that the Mayor and constables of the staple yearly shall be assay-masters of all plate wrought or to be sold from the first day of January next within this city, and that a stamp shall be made with the figures of a lion, a harp and a castle, and the same to be locked by the seal of the staple, with which stamp all plate to be sold by any goldsmith in this city shall be marked before the same shall be put to be sold, and if any goldsmith after the first day of January next shall sell or put to be sold any plate not marked with his own mark and the stamp aforesaid, that the same shall be forfeited, and the said goldsmith fined in the sum of five shillings for every ounce of plate sold by him and not stamped and marked as aforesaid. The said fine to be levied off his goods by warrant of the Mayor and recorder of this city upon presentment thereof by twelve men sworn before them at their general quarter session.

"And further we do agree that the mayor and constables of the staple shall call to their assistance for the touch and trial of the said plate when the same shall be stamped, the preferrer of the bill or some other that hath skill in such work, and that trial shall be made before they put the stamp to any parcel of plate, and if by such trial or upon touch thereof it appears to be corrupt, mingled with baser, or not made altogether of as pure silver as the silver standard coin now current in this Kingdom, that then every such parcel of plate to be forfeited, the one moiety thereof to the mayor and constables of the staple and the other moiety to the use of the mayor of the city, of which moiety the mayor and constables of the staple shall yield an account yearly after their year is ended before the city auditors. Further we do agree that for every parcel of plate to be touched and stamped before the mayor and constables of the staple as aforesaid they shall have the allowance of an halfpenny for every ounce, to be paid by the goldsmith that have or goeth about to sell the same, and the moiety of the allowance to be given by them to the presenter of the bill, and whosoever else shall be assisting them in that touch and trial by their appointment. And further that the preferrer

* *Dublin Corporation Records*, edited by Sir J. Gilbert.

of the bill or whosoever else the mayor and constables of the staple shall call to their assistance shall be sworn for the careful honest and true trial of every parcel, and if any parcel whereunto the stamp shall be put shall prove corrupt or mixed with baser metal and not meet to be stamped, that the preferrer of the bill or whosoever shall be assistant to the said mayor and constables, shall forfeit twenty pounds for every parcel so stamped *toties quoties*, and endure imprisonment for six months upon complaint made to the mayor of the city, and that therefore the mayor and constables of the staple shall keep note in writing of all such parcels as they shall stamp and the names of such persons as they shall call to their assistance."

The assayer to forfeit £20 and be imprisoned for six months for every parcel stamped as standard plate which should prove corrupt.

The above extract shows that what was expressed in the Statute 2 Rich. II.* concerning English goldsmiths, viz., that "the assay of the touch belongs to the mayors and governors of the cities and boroughs" was applicable also to Ireland, and was enforced by the above order of October, 1605. It is the earliest known reference to the marking of Dublin-wrought plate. The figures of a lion, a harp, and a castle, in addition to the mark of the goldsmith, were by this resolution clearly required to be stamped on all plate, but not a single example appears to be known bearing those marks. When, however, it is borne in mind that there are no more than about twenty pieces known, bearing the marks of a later period of over forty years (1638-79), and that between 1641 and 1680 there are no less than thirty years without a single known example of Dublin-marked plate, it is not strange that none has been brought to light with the lion, harp and castle mark of 1605-37.

A contributory cause of the disappearance of Irish plate of the period in question is disclosed by the following extract, dated 1642:—

Disappearance of early Irish plate accounted for.

"By order of the Lords Justices, the citizens brought in their plate to be coined, to the amount of £12,000! to supply the exigencies of state."†

Apart from the "exigencies of state," it appears to have been a common practice amongst people of good position in the 17th century, in case of need—which frequently arose—to resort to their plate cupboards, as an easy means of obtaining ready money. It is not surprising that so little early Irish domestic plate remains; indeed, it is wonderful that any of a date anterior to the time of Charles II. has survived.

In 1637 the Dublin goldsmiths appear to have become dissatisfied with their status under the domination of the City Corporation. They probably felt the inferiority of their position as compared with the London

In 1637 the Dublin Goldsmiths petition the King for a Charter.

* See Chapter II., p. 9, *ante*.
† Proclamation by the Lords, Justices and Council, 14 Jan., 164⅔: All persons living in Dublin to bring in half their plate to be paid for at the rate of 5s. per oz. Gilbert Tonques and Peter Vaneijndhoven to assist in viewing it.

goldsmiths, who had the management and control of all matters connected with the assaying and marking of wrought gold and silver in
their city without interference by the civic authorities.   The Dublin
goldsmiths presented a petition to the King representing that great abuses
and deceits had been practised, and were being daily committed in Ireland
by persons who were not duly qualified goldsmiths, that these abuses
were attributable to the absence of an established standard for gold and
silver wares, and to the fact that the craft was not controlled by men
skilled in the art of the goldsmith.   They prayed that they might be
incorporated by Royal charter, and be given the control and management
of the assaying and marking of wrought gold and plate in Ireland.
Charter granted 22 December, 1637. Their petition was favourably received, and a charter, dated 22 December 13 Charles I. (1637), was granted to them.

The original charter, beautifully engrossed on vellum, and with an
impression of the Great Seal of Ireland attached,* is in the custody of the
Master of the Company.   It is a lengthy document in Latin (excepting
the forms of oath, which are in English), and its enrolment in Chancery
occupies six skins of the Patent Roll of the 13th of Charles I. part 9, now
in the Dublin Record Office.   With the original is an English translation
(called a copy) which in some parts is so much worn that the writing is
undecipherable.   In *Assay of Gold and Silver Wares* (Ryland, 1852),
what purports to be a copy of this translation appears, which, however,
on being collated with the original was found to contain a great many
inaccuracies.   A new translation of the charter has therefore been
made, and is here set forth in full, because Mr. Ryland's little book is
now very rare and the printed calendars of the Patent Rolls of Ireland
stop at an earlier year in the reign of Charles I. than the date of the
charter.

Mr. Ryland made the double mistake of stating that this charter was
"*granted by Charles II. in the year* 1638".   Mr. Cripps and Mr. Chaffers
both made the same error as to the year.   The grant having been made
by *Charles the first* in the *thirteenth* year of his reign, its date cannot have
been other than 1637, which is the date engraved on the original seal of
the Dublin Goldsmiths' Company, by whose permission this representation in *facsimile* of an impression of it has been made.

---

* A representation in *facsimile* of the obverse and reverse of this seal is given on page 574, *infra*.

THE SEAL OF THE WARDENS AND COMPANY OF GOLDSMITHS OF DUBLIN.

CHARTER OF THE GOLDSMITHS' COMPANY OF DUBLIN.

"Charles, by the Grace of God, King of England, Scotland, France and Ireland, Defender of the Faith; To all people unto whom these Our present letters shall come Greeting. WHEREAS of late we have received certain intelligence, through the great abuses and deceits which heretofore have been and are daily committed within the said Kingdom of Ireland, by such men and persons who are bold, and do presume in themselves to take upon them and to exercise the art or mystery of goldsmiths, not altogether being expert, but unskilful therein, to the general loss and grievous damage of us and of our good subjects there. And whereas we having consideration to the premises, it is observed and is manifestly known, and appeareth unto us, that all those things do fall out and happen through want of a certain mark—in English a standard—and of good rules and ordinances to and for the government and better ruling of the said mystery within our said Kingdom of Ireland.

The reason for the grant:— Deceits practised through want of a certain stamp or standard, and rules for the government of the mystery in Ireland.

"We, therefore, willing and taking care graciously to provide a convenient redress and fitting reformation in this behalf, and to the intent that from henceforth for ever, a perpetual company and body incorporate of the aforesaid mystery of goldsmiths may be set up and established in our city of Dublin, within our said Kingdom of Ireland, as now it is, and for many years last gone and past hath been, in our city of London, within our said Kingdom of England, it hath been thought good, and doth seem meet unto us, to give, grant, and vouchsafe to the goldsmiths hereafter named, and their successors, which shall hereafter be of our said city of Dublin within our said Kingdom of Ireland, full and free license, power, and authority to discover, punish, and correct all, and all manner of the aforesaid abuses and deceits of the said mystery within our said Kingdom of Ireland, hereafter to be done or committed. And that our said royal intention in the premises, for the good and profit of our commonwealth and of our said subjects of our said Kingdom of Ireland may more speedily, better, and more effectually be brought to pass and perfected, KNOW YE that we, of our especial grace and of our certain knowledge, and mere motion, also with the advice, assent, and consent of our right well-beloved and right trusty cousin and counsellor, Thomas Viscount Wentworth, our Deputy-General of our Kingdom of Ireland aforesaid, and President of our Council established in the north parts of our said Kingdom of England, have willed, ordained, and granted, and by these presents for us, our heirs and successors, do will ordain and grant, that our beloved subjects, William Cooke, of our said city of Dublin, in the county of the said city, gold-smith, John Woodcocke, of the same, William Hampton, of the same, James Vnderbegg,* of the same, William Gallant, of the same, John Banister, of the

A Company of Goldsmiths incorporated in Dublin the same as in London with power to discover, punish and correct all abuses throughout Ireland.

The names of the first members of the Incorporation.

* So in enrolment, but the name was Vanderbegg, sometimes written Vanderbeck.

same, Nathaniel Stoughton, of the same, James Acheson, of the same, Clement Evans, of the same, George Gallant, of the same, Sylvanus Glegg,* of the same, William St. Clere,† of the same, Gilbert Tongues,‡ of the same, Edward Chadsey, of the same, Peter Vaneinthoven,§ of the same, Matthew Thomas, of the same, William Crawley, of the same, Thomas Duffield, of the same, John Cooke, of the same, and John Burke, of the same, goldsmiths, from henceforth shall be one Society and body incorporate of itself, in deed and in name, and shall have perpetual succession, to continue for ever hereafter, and may be and shall be in deed, name and fact, one body incorporate by itself for ever by the name of WARDENS AND COMPANY OF GOLDSMITHS OF OUR SAID CITY OF DUBLIN ; and those Wardens and Company of Goldsmiths of our said City of Dublin and their successors, we have incorporated established and united, and the said body incorporate by the same name, and under the same name of Wardens and Company of the Mystery of Goldsmiths of our City of Dublin, for ever to continue, we really and fully do create, erect, incorporate, establish, ordain, make, and appoint by these presents, and that they may have perpetual succession and a common seal to serve for the affairs of the aforesaid mystery.

To have perpetual succession and be known by the name of WARDENS AND COMPANY OF GOLDSMITHS OF DUBLIN, and to have a common seal.

" And we will, and by these presents do nominate, ordain, create, make, and appoint the aforesaid William Cooke, John Woodcocke, William Hampton, and John Banister the first and present Wardens of the said mystery of Goldsmiths of our city of Dublin aforesaid, from the making of these our Letters Patent, until the Feast of All Saints next following after the date of these presents, to remain and continue, and for a longer or shorter time, as to the Wardens and Company of the said mystery of Goldsmiths of our said city of Dublin aforesaid, or to the greater part of them, shall seem to be fit and necessary.

The Wardens' Oaths.

" And further, we will, and by these presents for us our heirs and successors we do ordain and appoint that the said William Cooke, John Woodcocke, William Hampton and John Banister above in these presents named to be the first and present Wardens of the said Company of the aforesaid mystery, before they be admitted to execute the office of the Wardens of the said Company of the mystery aforesaid, take and receive and every of them take and receive, before our Chancellor of our said Kingdom of Ireland for the time being, the oath or pledge following, in these English words, ' You and every of you shall swear to be true and faithful to the King our Sovereign Lord, his heirs and successors. You shall not be against his profit or advantage, but that you shall be to the advancement of his crown as much as in your power shall lie. Furthermore you and every of you, shall duly and truly execute and perform the office of Wardens of the Company of Goldsmiths, and in that place or office whereunto you and every of you are now appointed, you and every of you shall faithfully and uprightly behave yourselves. Ye shall therein, to every person and persons who shall bring or cause to be brought unto your hands, within your office, any manner of silver plate to be tried or touched, or any weight called Troy weight, to be assized, according to his Majesty's standard, use yourselves in the due execution of the same according to right, equity, and justice, and also that

To truly execute the duty of Wardens according to justice.

---

* Sylvanus Glegg had been admitted as a goldsmith to the freedom of the Company of Goldsmiths in Chester on 22 April, 1631.

† Or Sinclair.

‡ So in enrolment, but the name was Tonques, often written Tonks.

§ So in enrolment, but the name was Van eynde Hoven, often written Vaneijndhoven and more frequently Vandenhoven.

you or any of you do not set, nor by your powers shall not suffer to be set, the King's Majesty's Stamp called the *Harp Crowned*, now appointed by his said Majesty, in no manner of plate of silver to you brought unto your said office by any manner of person or persons, unless the said silver plate be in every part and parcel thereof according to his Majesty's standard, otherwise called eleven ounces two pennyweights. And in case it be under and not of the said fineness, you and every of you shall cause it to be broken ere it pass your hands, whose plate or of what value soever it be. And you and every of you shall also make true and diligent search from time to time as often as need shall require, for all deceivable wares of gold and silver, and do and perform all other things whatsoever touching the said office, according to the law and according to the purport of his Majesty's grant in that behalf made unto the said Company of Goldsmiths, without fear, favour, love, hatred, or affection by you or by any of you to be borne, to any manner of person or persons, so help you God and the contents of this book.'

The harp crowned not to be set on plate below the standard of 11 oz. 2 dwts.: any less fine to be broken.

To search for all deceivable wares of gold and silver.

"Wherefore we will, and by these presents for us our heirs and successors, we do give and grant full power and authority unto our said Chancellor of our said realm of Ireland for the time being, to give and administer unto the aforesaid William Cooke, John Woodcocke, William Hampton, and John Banister, and every of them respectively, the aforesaid oath and pledge of the office of the Wardens of the said Company of Goldsmiths as aforesaid, without any other Commission or Warrant from us, our heirs, or successors to be procured or obtained.

The Lord Chancellor of Ireland empowered to swear in the first Wardens.

"And further for us our heirs and successors, we will, and by these presents do grant, that the said Company of the said mystery of Goldsmiths of our city of Dublin aforesaid, and their successors, of themselves, can and may at our said city of Dublin choose every year, from time to time for ever, four wardens, of the men of the Company aforesaid, to supervise, rule, and duly govern the mystery and Company aforesaid. And all and every man or men of them for ever, in the self-same like manner and form as the Wardens and Company of the said mystery of Goldsmiths of our said city of London within our said Kingdom of England, or the greater part of them may choose or have used to choose, and that the said Wardens of the said mystery within our city of Dublin aforesaid, for the time being, have the selfsame, so much, such, and the like power and authority of Goldsmiths of the Company aforesaid, and of all the men of the same, within our said Kingdom of Ireland, in all things and according to all things, to govern, rule, and order, as the Wardens of the said Company of the said mystery, within our city of London in our said Kingdom of England, now have, do, exercise, or use, or ought, or can lawfully have, enjoy, exercise, or use, by reason or pretence of any grant or grants by us, or any of our progenitors, late Kings or Queens of England, or of any statute law, ordinance, custom, or lawful prescription, or use, or otherwise by any lawful manner whatsoever.

The Company empowered to elect members of the Company every year as Wardens to supervise and govern the Company,

and to have the same rights and powers as the London Company.

"And furthermore, we will, and by these presents for us, our heirs and successors, we do ordain, grant, and appoint, that all and every person and persons, who hereafter may be chosen to be Wardens of the said Company of the said mystery of Goldsmiths, and every of them before they exercise the said office, shall from time to time take their corporal oath, according to the effect of the oath or pledge above, in these presents specified and ordained for the aforesaid First Wardens, before the last precedent Wardens of the said Company of the mystery aforesaid, yearly at the feast of All Saints, to which the last precedent Wardens of the Company of the mystery aforesaid, for us, our heirs and successors, we do

Wardens empowered to administer the oath to their successors.

give and grant full power and authority, from time to time by these presents, to give and administer the oath and pledge aforesaid, without any other commission or warrant from us, our heirs and successors, in that behalf to be procured or obtained. And that after such an oath so taken, the aforesaid office, unto which they shall be chosen and named for one whole year (to wit) until the feast of All Saints then next following, they may and can respectively execute, and further, until four others unto the office of Wardenship of the said Company of the mystery aforesaid, be appointed and sworn respectively, according to the provisoes and ordinances above in these presents expressed and declared.

> Wardens to remain in office for one year from All Saints Day and until successors elected.

"And furthermore we will, and do by these presents, for us, our heirs and successors, ordain, grant, and appoint, that all and every the freemen, and every of them, who hereafter shall be admitted or received from time to time into the Company of the mystery aforesaid, shall undertake the oath or pledge of their liberties and immunities before the Wardens of the same Company of the mystery aforesaid, for the time being, and full power and authority to the Wardens of the said Company of the said mystery for the time being to give and administer the corporal oath to all and every the freemen, and every of them, who hereafter shall be admitted and received into the said Company of the mystery aforesaid from time to time the oath or pledge of their several liberties or immunities respectively, for us our heirs and successors, we do give and grant, by these presents, without any other commission or warrant from us, our heirs or successors, in that behalf to be procured or obtained.

> Everyone received into the Company to undertake the oath upon being admitted.

> Wardens empowered to administer the oath to new members.

"And furthermore, for us, our heirs and successors, we grant to the said Wardens and Company of the mystery aforesaid, within our said city of Dublin, and to their successors, that they and their successors for ever, by the name of Wardens and Company of the mystery of Goldsmiths of our city of Dublin aforesaid, henceforth may and shall be one body incorporate in the law, sufficient, capable, able, and fit to plead and be impleaded and to implead, prosecute, answer, and defend, before what Judges and Justices whatsoever of us, our heirs and successors, as well spiritual as temporal, and other persons whatsoever in all the Courts of us, our heirs and successors, and other Courts and places whatsoever, within the said realm of Ireland, in all and all manner of actions, real, personal, and mixed, *assise of novel disseisin* and in all other pleas, suits, plaints, actions and demands whatsoever, of what kind or nature soever they be, touching, concerning, or appertaining to the said Wardens and Company of the aforesaid mystery of Goldsmiths within our said city of Dublin, or the lands, tenements, affairs, wares, merchandizes, bargains, agreements, debts, or any other thing of theirs. And that the said Wardens and Company of that mystery, and their successors from time to time for ever, may make honest and reasonable ordinances and constitutions for the better government of the said mystery, as often as to them shall seem expedient. Provided always, that none of their ordinances or constitutions be of force or put in execution, until the same be seen and approved of by our two Chief Justices and our chief Baron of the Exchequer, of us our heirs and successors, within our said realm of Ireland for the time being, and be allowed before the Deputy or other Chief Governor, and our Council of our aforesaid Kingdom of Ireland.

> The Company empowered to plead and be impleaded in any action.

> Empowered to make reasonable ordinances for the government of the craft, to be approved by the two Chief Justices, the Chief Baron of the Exchequer, the Lord Lieutenant and Privy Council of Ireland before becoming operative.

"And furthermore we will, and by these presents, for us, our heirs and successors, do grant and give special license unto the said Wardens and Company of the said mystery of Goldsmiths of our city of Dublin aforesaid, and to their successors to have, possess, receive, and acquire, them and their successors for ever, such manors, messuages, lands, tenements, meadows, feedings, pastures, woods, underwoods, rectories, tithes, rents, services, reversions, and other hereditaments whatsoever, within our said realm of Ireland, as well from us, our heirs and successors, as from any other person or persons whatsoever, which are not held of us, nor shall be held of our heirs or successors *in capite* or by knight's service, provided that the said manors, messuages, lands, tenements and other hereditaments, so by them to be had, received, and acquired, do not exceed in the whole the clear yearly value of twenty pounds sterling by the year, beyond all burdens and reprises, the statute ' of lands and tenements not to be placed in mortmain ' or any other statute, act, ordinance, or proviso, heretofore had, done, ordained, or provided, or any other thing, cause, or matter whatsoever to the contrary thereof in anywise notwithstanding. We have also given, and by these presents for us our heirs and successors, grant unto every subject and subjects of us, our heirs and successors, special license and free power and authority that they and any of them may and can give, grant, sell, bequeath, and alien such manors, messuages, tenements, meadows, feedings, pastures, woods, underwoods, rectories, tithes, rents, services, reversions, and other hereditaments whatsoever within our said realm of Ireland, as are not now held of us, neither shall be held of our heirs or successors *in capite*, nor by knight's service, to the aforesaid Wardens and Company of the said mystery of Goldsmiths of our said city of Dublin, and to their successors. So nevertheless that the aforesaid manors, messuages, lands, tenements, and other hereditaments, so as is aforesaid, to the aforesaid Wardens and Company of the mystery aforesaid and their successors (by force and virtue of these presents) to be given, granted, bequeathed, or aliened, may not exceed in the whole the clear yearly value of twenty pounds sterling yearly beyond all burdens and reprises—the said statute ' of lands and tenements not to be placed in mortmain ' or any other statute, act, ordinance, or proviso, or any other thing, cause, or matter whatsoever, done, had, proclaimed, ordained, or heretofore provided to the contrary thereof, in anywise notwithstanding.

Empowered to buy and hold land and other hereditaments of every kind,

not exceeding in value £20 a year and to grant, sell or bequeath the same.

"And furthermore, of our like especial grace, with the advice, assent, and consent aforesaid, we do grant, and by these presents for us, our heirs and successors, firmly enjoining, we give, charge, ordain, and command that no master goldsmith whatsoever within our said realm of Ireland, shall hand over, deliver, or cause to be delivered unto his workmen, or any of them, any gold or silver to be wrought in handiwork, of less value than that of the Standard in our said realm of England upon assay thereof to be made, or such moneys as are well and commonly known and recognised to be of the selfsame value and goodness ; to the intent that if the said workmen, or any of them, [after] the delivery thereof into their hands, or the hands of any of them, shall make the said gold or silver worse (as often times they are accustomed to do), whereas they shall be punished for their offences, on that behalf he nor they shall not allege that such inferior and base gold and silver was delivered to them.

No master goldsmith to deliver to any workman any gold or silver (to be wrought) below the English standard.

"And furthermore, for the honesty of the men of the aforesaid mystery in our said city of Dublin, for the time being and dwelling, and for the avoiding and eschewing of the damages and losses which daily do happen and arise, or may happen and arise, as well to us and our heirs and successors, as to other our liege people and subjects, out of the unjust and indiscreet government of certain of our subjects, and others using the aforesaid mystery, little weighing the honesty of the said mystery, and also for the cutting off and removing the subtleties and deceits in

The Company entrusted with the search, supervision, assay and government of all manner of gold and silver work throughout Ireland.

that mystery often used, we have given and granted, and do by these presents for us, our heirs and successors, give and grant, unto the aforesaid present Wardens and Company of the aforesaid mystery and their successors for ever, that they the aforesaid present Wardens, and the Wardens of the aforesaid mystery for the time being for ever, may have the search, supervision, assay, and government of all and all manner of gold and silver, wrought and to be wrought, or exposed for sale, within our city of Dublin, and in all fairs, markets, and marts, and also in cities, towns, and boroughs, and other places whatsoever, in and through our said whole Kingdom of Ireland, as well within liberties as without, and to punish and correct the defects and deceits in the same works found, or to be found, if occasion shall be, by the help of the Mayor and Sheriffs of our said city of Dublin, and of the Mayors, bailiffs, or others of our officers whatsoever, in whatsoever fairs, markets, marts, cities, boroughs, and towns, and other places without the afore-said cities, where such search and searches shall happen to be made; and that the present Wardens, and the Wardens of the aforesaid mystery for the time being, may have full power for ever to make and exercise due search of and in all and singular the premises, as also of all and singular works touching and concerning the said mystery, as well on men of the aforesaid mystery of goldsmiths, as also on others whatsoever, selling, making, or working their affairs, merchandizes, or works, to the said mystery belonging or the said mystery concerning, as well in our aforesaid city of Dublin and suburbs thereof, as elsewhere without the said city of Dublin, in whatsoever fairs, markets, marts, cities, boroughs, and towns, and other places whatsoever in and through our said whole realm of Ireland, by themselves, or any of them; and all such deceitful works and merchandizes of

All deceitful works found, made, wrought, or set to sale to be broken, and the makers, sellers and work-ers thereof to be punished accord-ing to their deserts.

gold and silver, of what kind or nature soever they be (if any be), by them or any of them in any such of their searches found, and for the deceiving of the people of us, our heirs and successors, made or wrought and exposed for sale, to be broken, and the makers, sellers, and workers of the same works, according to their deserts, to punish and correct (if need be) by the help of the Mayor, sheriffs, bailiffs, seneschals, and other such like officers, according to the laws, statutes, and ordinances in such cases made and provided, and this as often as it shall seem best to be done, by the aforesaid present Wardens and those for the time being. We will also, and by these presents for us, our heirs and successors, we do grant, and, firmly commanding, charge, that all and singular Mayors, sheriffs, bailiffs, seneschals, and other our officers whatsoever, and every of them, in fairs, markets, marts, cities, boroughs, and towns, and other places where such search shall happen to be made, shall be from time to time for ever advising, favouring, and assisting in all things, as is seemly to the aforesaid Wardens and every of them, making such search, in the exercise and execution of the premises.

"And moreover we having received certain intelligence that divers men both native and foreign, exercising and using the aforesaid mystery in divers parts of our said Kingdom of Ireland, and fraudulently coveting their dishonest gains, and studying and propounding unto themselves the deceits and losses of the rest of our subjects, divers ways do work and expose for sale gold and silver deceitfully and cunningly wrought, of less value than duly it ought to be, and wrought contrary to the ordinances thereof made, within our said Kingdoms of England and Ireland, and counterfeit stones which are of no value, in such like gold and silver, as if precious stones subtlely and splendidly to glitter, according to the nature of such gems wrought and set, do daily sell for a great price to divers of our subjects, not experienced therein, as well in privileged places, as in fairs, markets, and other places, cities and boroughs of our said realm of Ireland, and herein they fear not nor are afraid to be punished or brought to justice; wherefore because due search or some due punishment for such a defect in that mystery, was not executed anywhere heretofore, by which means so much fraud, deceit and unjust workmanship of gold and silver, and of counterfeit gems and works of gold and silver and otherwise, in divers ways, in the mystery aforesaid, by the workmen of that mystery, in every part of our said Kingdom of Ireland, doth daily increase, to the great damage and loss of us, and all our liege people and subjects; and we, willing (as becometh us), the deceitful, insufficient, and unjust works and wares of gold and silver, precious stones, and stones of pearl, coral, and such like in the mystery aforesaid, insufficiently and not duly wrought, and counterfeit, used to be set forth to sale, to be forfeited, abolished and punished, of our certain knowledge and mere motion, as also with the advice, assent, and consent aforesaid, have given and granted, and by these presents, for us, our heirs and successors, do give and grant, unto the aforesaid Wardens and Company of the aforesaid mystery, and their successors, that they the aforesaid Wardens and their successors, and every one of them for the time being, have and may have for ever, by virtue of these presents, full power, force, and authority, in every defect, offence, crime, and deceit, made, or attempted, or committed against the ordinances of the aforesaid mystery, done within our said Kingdom of England or Ireland, in all their searches and assays of gold and silver, and wares, and precious stones, and stones of pearl, coral, or precious stones whatsoever, counterfeit stones, in gold and silver, as in necklaces, signets, rings, or girdles, or otherwise in any manner wrought or put in within our said Kingdom of Ireland, wheresoever it is justly proved against the workmen or users of any of the same premises to be exposed for sale, by the same Wardens for the time being, all and every person or persons whatsoever of the said mystery working so deceitfully, or exposing for sale, to be punished according to their offences, and according to the laws, statutes, and ordinances, in that behalf published and provided. We have also granted, and by these presents, for us and our heirs, we do grant, to the same Wardens and Company and their successors, that whensoever, how-often soever, or wheresoever, as well within liberties as without, any wares of gold or silver, or pearl, or any other whatsoever counterfeit stones, and deceitfully wrought and fixed, in the nature of gems or pearl, in gold or silver, and by assay thereof they be of less value, and insufficient in the work of gold or silver than of right they ought to be wrought—to wit—of the value sterling, according to the ordinances and statutes of us and our progenitors or predecessors, Kings and Queens of England, within our said realm of England or Ireland, in such cases published, or any such deceitful wares of gold and silver, wrought within our said Kingdom of Ireland, or by any native or foreign workman, and users of the aforesaid mystery, wheresoever sold or exposed for sale, or not assayed, approved and marked as they ought, in deceit of our people, and offending contrary to the form of the ordinances and statutes aforesaid; that then they the Wardens for the time being, or any two of them, may have power and authority to arrest, and seize on, and break, and damnify, all and all manner of such wares of gold and silver, counterfeit stones, and pearls, or other stones whatsoever, and deceitfully wrought and exposed for sale, wheresoever they can find them, so that our people be no more thereby deceived. And that in all the searches of those Wardens and their successors for the time being, of and in the

[marginal note:] Gold and silver of less value than it ought to be, and counterfeit jewels, to be sought for, seized, broken, and the workers or others exposing the same for sale to be punished according to their offences.

In and within three miles of Dublin the Wardens may cause all works of gold or silver and jewels to be brought to the Goldsmiths' Hall, Dublin, to be assayed, and if sufficient to be marked with the stamp as good, and if not sufficient to be dealt with as before provided.

premises from time to time, in whatsoever places within the space of three miles, on this side and near the said city of Dublin, near or adjoining, where any workman, or users of the aforesaid mystery shall remain, work and abide, the same Wardens, or some of them for the time being, all manner of works and wares of gold and silver, aforesaid, or in gold or silver whatsoever, and set in necklaces, gems and precious stones, there wrought, and to be wrought, may cause to be brought into the Common Hall of those Wardens and Company of the mystery aforesaid, being within our aforesaid city of Dublin (within which the common assay of gold and silver is had and tried according to the ordinances thereof), there to be tried and assayed, and if there shall be any defect therein in any manner, to be duly amended, and being so amended there then to be affirmed for good ; and to be marked with their mark for that purpose to be used and put to ; and all defective works whatsoever, as well of or in gold or silver deceitfully wrought, with counterfeit stones set in the same for gems, and falsely wrought, or tried, known, and found in alloys not sufficient, be dealt with according to the laws, statutes, and ordinances, in that behalf published and provided.

The Dublin Goldsmiths' Company to have all such rights, privileges, authorities and jurisdictions as the Goldsmiths Company of London have.

"And moreover, of our special grace, certain knowledge and mere motion, we will, and by these presents, for us, our heirs and successors, do grant to the said Wardens and Company of the aforesaid mystery, and to their successors for ever, and to every one of the goldsmiths of the said Company, that they the said Wardens and Company of the mystery aforesaid, and every goldsmith of the said Company of the mystery aforesaid, as well present, as to come, for the time being, may and can have, hold, use, enjoy, exercise and execute, within our said realm of Ireland, such like liberties, customs, franchises, privileges, powers, authorities, pre-eminences, jurisdictions, immunities, commodities, and all other rights whatsoever, of what sort, kind, nature, quality or condition, whatsoever

Not being contrary or repugnant to this Charter or to the laws of England and Ireland.

they be, have been, or shall be, not being repugnant, or contrary to these presents, or to any article in the same contained, or specified, or to the laws and statutes of this our Kingdom of Ireland, as many such, and as much, and what the Wardens and Company of the aforesaid mystery of Goldsmiths of London aforesaid, or any Wardens and Company of goldsmiths within our said realm of England or Ireland, now have, enjoy, exercise, and use, by reason or pretence of any statutes or Acts of Parliament, or any letters patent, by any of our progenitors, Kings and Queens of England, had or made, or of any prescription or custom, or by any other lawful manner, right, or title, whatsoever.

In every city and town in Ireland where there are goldsmiths they are to observe the like ordinances as those of Dublin are bound to observe, and to acquaint themselves of the "touch" of gold and silver and obtain their punch to mark their works.

"And furthermore of our like special grace, and of our certain knowledge, and mere motion, and also of the advice, assent and consent aforesaid, we do, for us, our heirs and successors, grant, and by these presents, ordain, that in all and every city and town within our said realm of Ireland, in which there are goldsmiths, and to which merchants frequent, they hold and from time to time shall observe the same and the like ordinances, which men of the same mystery within our said city of Dublin are bound to observe, and that one or two men of the same mystery, of every of the said cities and towns, may come and draw near to our said city of Dublin, to know the science of the said mystery, and there to ask and seek for the same, their touch of gold and silver and also their punch—namely, a harp crowned—to mark, denote and impress their works and wares and every of them within the same, as of old it was accustomed and ordained within our city of London.

"We also give charge, and firmly enjoining, do command that the aforesaid Wardens and Company of the said mystery of Goldsmiths in the said city of Dublin, for themselves and their successors, do covenant and agree to and with our heirs and successors, by these presents, that the aforesaid Wardens and Company, and their successors, of the said mystery, or any of them, exercising the said mystery hereafter, shall not nor will, work, sell, or exchange, or procure to be sold, wrought or exchanged, any vessels or any other goldsmiths' works, of gold of less value than that of two and twenty carats; and that they shall not use certain things called solder, anneal, or stuffings, in any of their works, more than necessary to perfect the same, and that they shall not take beyond the rate of twelve pence for every ounce of gold (over and above the fashioning) more than the buyer thereof can obtain, or is allowed for the same, at the Exchange and money office of us our heirs and successors, upon pain of forfeiture of the value of the thing so sold and exchanged, and that henceforth no goldsmith of the mystery aforesaid in the city aforesaid, shall make, or sell, or exchange in any place within our said realm of Ireland, any vessels or goldsmiths' works of silver of less value than that of eleven ounces two penny weights, nor shall take beyond the rate of twelve pence for every pound weight of silver vessels and merchandizes (over and above the fashioning) more than the buyer thereof is or can be allowed for the same at the Exchange and money office of us, our heirs and successors, neither shall he expose for sale, exchange, or sell any vessels or goldsmiths' silver works, before his workman shall have put his proper mark to so much thereof as the same conveniently can carry,* under pain of forfeiture of the value of the thing so sold or exchanged; And if any of the aforesaid goldsmiths of the said mystery shall hereafter make any vessels or goldsmiths' works, and they be touched, marked, and allowed for good by the Wardens or Masters of the aforesaid mystery, and if in the same afterwards any falsehood or deceit be found, that then the Wardens and Company of the said mystery for the time being shall forfeit and pay the value of the things so exchanged or sold, and that the one half of whatever forfeit thereof may remain to the use of us, our heirs and successors, and the other half to the use of the party who sustained loss by the same, and who will in any court of record, by action, bill, plea, or information, or otherwise, in which no essoin, protection, or surety of the law shall be allowed, be defendant.

"And furthermore we will, and by these presents, do declare, our princely good pleasure to be, that no man shall be admitted to be privileged, or made free of such company of the mystery aforesaid, until he be approved by men of the said mystery to have served seven years an apprentice in said mystery, and from thenceforth to be a sufficient workman or craftsman; also to have made and framed with his hands a certain work or vessel of gold, in English called his masterpiece,† tried and approved by the Wardens aforesaid, for the time being; and also, that the aforesaid Wardens and Company of the said mystery of Goldsmiths in our said city of Dublin, may be, and be from time to time, subject, bound, conformable and obedient to all and singular the Acts, ordinances, instructions, and provisoes whatsoever of the aforesaid Wardens and Company of the said mystery and their successors, or touching or concerning in anywise

Marginal notes:

No gold to be wrought or sold less fine than 22 carats, nor silver less than 11 oz. 2 dwts. No more solder or stuffing to be used than necessary.

No more than 12d. for every oz. of gold and 12d. for every lb. of silver (besides the making) to be taken by any goldsmith beyond the Exchange value. No work to be sold, exchanged or set to sale without being marked with the goldsmith's proper mark. If plate marked as good be afterwards found deceitful, the Company to forfeit the value.

None to be admitted to the Company but after seven years apprenticeship and proof of ability, and being bound to conform to the rules and ordinances in force.

* Objects so small as to be incapable of conveniently carrying a goldsmiths' mark being impliedly exempt from liability to be marked.

† A similar practice was followed in Scotland, where a time-expired apprentice had to submit an example of his work to be approved by the masters of the guild before he was admitted to its privileges, see page 538, *ante*.

the premises or any part thereof, had, done, published, ordained, or provided by us, our heirs or successors, or by our Deputy, or other Chief Governor or Governors, and our Council, of us, our heirs and successors, of our said realm of England or Ireland for the time being or hereafter to be had, made, ordained or provided, anything in these presents to the contrary thereof notwithstanding.   And finally of our more abundant special grace, and of our certain knowledge and mere motion, with the advice, assent, and consent aforesaid, we will, and by these presents, for us, our heirs and successors, grant, and, strictly enjoining, do command and give charge that the aforesaid Wardens and Company of the aforesaid mystery and their successors be from henceforth for ever freed, acquitted and discharged, and exonerated of and from all other companies, societies, fraternities, guilds, incorporations, and bodies incorporate whatsoever, and of and from all observances, service and appearances, and all manner of actions, fines, and other burdens and demands whatsoever, by reason or occasion of being incorporated with the same or any of them, by any name or names or ways whatsoever, any act, ordinance, restriction, proviso, or any other thing, cause or matter whatsoever to the contrary thereof in anywise notwithstanding.   We will also, etc.; and without a fine in the Hanaper etc.; although express mention, etc.   In witness whereof, we have caused these our letters to be made patents.

"Witness our aforesaid Deputy-General of our said Kingdom of Ireland at Dublin, on the twenty-second day of December in the thirteenth year of our reign."   [A.D. 1637.]

Margin note: The Company freed from all other Companies, Guilds, &c., and from all obligations by reason of having been incorporated with them.

THE GREAT SEAL, ATTACHED TO THE CHARTER OF THE DUBLIN GOLDSMITHS' COMPANY.
(Scale ½ Linear.)

The above illustration is a photographic reproduction of the obverse and reverse of the great seal, which is suspended from the charter by a ribbon (passed through the skin where it is doubled at the end of the engrossment) embedded in the composition of the seal, below which the two ends of the ribbon appear.

RECORDS OF THE DUBLIN GOLDSMITHS' COMPANY.

The wardens mentioned in the Charter having elected William Cooke as their president, under the style or title of "Master," continued in office until 1639, when Peter Vaneijndhoven was elected as a warden and William Hampton was re-elected—two wardens only being mentioned in that year. In 1640 John Woodcocke was appointed master, and James Vanderbeck warden. Gilbert Tonques and Peter Vaneijndhoven were wardens 1644-5-6.* Gilbert Tonques was master, and Daniel Burfeldt warden in 1646-7. Nathaniel Stoughton was master, and Daniel Burfeldt and Daniel Bellingham were wardens 1648-9. The names of masters and wardens between 1649 and 1654 are not recorded. Possibly no new wardens were elected during the interval, in which case the wardens of 1649 continued, by virtue of the Charter, to hold office until their successors were appointed. In 1654-5 Joseph Stoaker was master and John Woodcocke and Thomas Hooker were wardens. In 1656-7 Joseph Stoaker continued to be master, with William Huggard and Daniel Bellingham as wardens. Thenceforward, except during the most troublous year of the war period (1689-90), the names of the officers for each successive year are recorded. It is, however, noticeable that for twenty years from 1654 there appear to have been only two wardens and the master in office each year.

A minute of the year 1686 records that it was "ordered that Michaelmas day be the day for choosing new Wardens, and on St. Andrew's day (30th November) the old Wardens are to give up their accounts". The new master and wardens, although elected on the 29 September, do not appear to have taken office until the 1st of November (All Saints' Day) in each year. (The Dublin Goldsmiths' Company was formerly styled "The Guild of All Saints".) *[margin: Officers to be chosen on Michaelmas day and to take over the accounts from their predecessors on 30 November.]*

From about three months after the date of their incorporation by the charter of 1637 to the present day, the proceedings of the Dublin Goldsmiths' Company appear to have been recorded with tolerable regularity. A volume or two of the early records are, however, missing, and one of the existing volumes seems to have been substituted for an earlier one, for in the book of proceedings commenced in 1686, an ordinance of the year 1667 is transcribed. The archives at present comprise:—assay books, minute books, lists (compiled for the most part annually) of the wardens and freemen of the Company (the latter being called "Free *[margin: The existing records of the Company date from April, 1638.]*

* In a proclamation of 8 July, 1643, three Goldsmiths (Sir John Veale, Peter Vaneijndhoven and Gilbert Tonques) were authorised to coin silver brought to them by private owners.

Brothers "); lists of " Quarter Brothers " (goldsmiths admitted to certain privileges by the payment of quarterly contributions); and lists of apprentices, with the names of their parents and the masters to whom they were bound.   There are also an index book and a volume containing entries of gifts and benefactions conferred on the Company.

The earliest recorded assays.

About three or four months appear to have been absorbed after the Charter was obtained, in making preparations for the performance of the duties newly conferred upon the Wardens and Company, and in the establishment of an assay office, for the earliest entries in the Company's books are dated 6 April, 1638.   They refer to plate of various descriptions brought in to be assayed, the names of the makers of each parcel being also recorded.   The articles include beer bowls, sugar boxes, Spanish cups, caudle cups, ewers and basins, trencher-salts, cans, porringers, saucers, spoons and candlesticks, which were assayed for the following brethren :—William Hampton, John Woodcocke, William Cooke, Mathew Thomas, George Gallant, Peter Vaneijndhoven, Daniel Underwood, James Vanderbeck, Edward Chadsey, George Greene, and John More.   Entries of plate assayed are continued to 1649, when a break occurs, owing, apparently, to the loss of records, and no further entry appears until 1694, whence they proceed with some regularity until 1700.   Thenceforward the entries appear to have been made fairly regularly, but only a few of the assay books of the 18th and 19th centuries are preserved.

The amount of plate assayed annually, at different periods from 1638 to 1904.

The amount of plate assayed at Dublin varied considerably at different periods.   From 1638 to 1644 the yearly average was about 1300 oz. From 1644 to 1649—the time of the struggle between Royalist and Parliamentary forces, when very little plate was manufactured in any part of the three Kingdoms—it was no more than 230 oz.   From 1657 to 1666 the business had increased to about 8500 oz. a year.   From 1694 to 1700, it had still further increased to about 26,000 oz. a year, and between 1725 and 1730 the yearly average was about 60,000 oz.   In the three years following the imposition of plate duty, it fell to about 50,000 oz. a year, but it soon more than recovered its lost ground, for in the year 1787-8 the aggregate weight of plate assayed was over 80,000 ounces.   In the 19th century the business fell off very appreciably.   In 1810 the amount of plate assayed was about 70,000 oz., but in 1835 it had diminished to 6000 oz.   After that year, however, the trade revived, and in 1848 plate to the amount of about 13,000 oz. was assayed.   In 1870 it had increased to 15,000 oz., but it afterwards fell off considerably, for in 1885 no more than about 5000 oz. were assayed.   In the succeeding years another revival of business set in, which has continued, and it appears as if the flourishing condition of trade which was enjoyed in the last quarter of the 18th century will be regained.   In the two years 1903-4 no less than 60,600 oz. of plate were assayed.

There are a number of interesting entries in the volume containing records of gifts and benefactions.   The apartments of the Company were, in the three years 1638-40, equipped largely by the generosity of those " Brethren " who were named in the Charter of 1637, as, for instance :— *Gifts to the Company.*

"William Hampton, the third first-warden gave one pewter standishe and a picture of S^r· George Ratcliffe, Knt.*   Gilbert Tonques, a brother, gave the New Testament and David's Psalms.†   William Cooke the first M^r· gave the Kinge's arms to adorne ye Hall.   John Woodcocke, the first second-warden gave one carpett of good stuffe.   Israel Aprill (a frenchman and moste lovinge brother) gave a picture of Henrietta Maria, Queen of England, the daughter of Henry 4th french Kinge.   James Vanderbeck, warden, gave *the picture of our most dread soveraigne Lord Kinge Charles, Kinge of Greate Britayne, france and Ireland, Defendr. &c. (of whose gratious Bountye and good will we houlde and received our Charter, whom God graunt long to raigne over us and his seede, so long as the sonne and moone indureth).*   Nathaniel Stoughton, a brother, gave the armes of the Companie to adorne the hall."   On "Feb 2nd, 164$\frac{0}{1}$, John Woodcocke, now M^r· of this Corporacon, gave unto the use of this Companie one crimson silke Damask Cushion wth Silke Tassels, lyned wth greene say, to lye before the M^r· and Wardens att every generall meetinge of the said companye ".

On " May 1st, 1646, Daniel Burfelt, third-warden of this companye, in his extraordinary love to the same, did give thereunto an iron boxe to keep our moneys ".

In 1698, it was resolved that the Hall Chest should have a padlock added, a key of which was to be in the master's keeping.   The three wardens also were each to hold a key of the chest, and a strong oak box in which the money and diet were to be kept, was to be placed within it.

The records of the Company (Liber A, pp. 81-2) contain an amusing account of the Riding of the Franchises just before the breaking out of the Rebellion in 1649.   The Mayor's warrant required the master and wardens to attend "at four of the clock in the morning (!) decently furnished with horse and arms ".   They held a meeting and made a collection to defray expenses ; the names of ten subscribers are given. N. Stoughton (the master warden) perhaps not being an equestrian, deputed Gilbert Tonques to represent him, and they rode, in all *The Riding of the Franchises in 1649 and 1656.*

---

* *A good and honble. furtherer of our Charter.*
† Printed at Edinburgh in 1633 by Robert Young, King's Printer for Scotland.   The cover is inscribed in gold letters, *The Goldsmiths' Booke, Dublin,* and inside is written, " Ex dono Gilberti Tonques 1 Nov., 1638 ".   It was perhaps used for administering oaths.

seventeen, whose names are recorded, as are the several items of the dinner which followed. In 1656 this ceremony was repeated, but as the company had no tent they dined at the "George," in St. Thomas Street, where thirty persons enjoyed "a carcase of lamb, colly flowers, rabbots, and vinegar, sack, claret, and beer". In 1776 a motion was made declaring the Corporation "incapable of riding the Franchises this year".*

On 12 February, 165⅞, Alderman Daniel Bellingham,† goldsmith, a past warden of the Company, was appointed by the guild to try the *diet* which had accrued from 10 June, 1654. On being all melted together and tested in the presence of the master and wardens it was found to be 11 oz. 2 dwts. fine. By general consent 12 oz. 14 dwts. were taken out of the mass to make a head for the leading staff.

The following curious record of a gift occurs under date 9 February, 1693 :—"This day John Phillips master warden of this Corporacon, bestowed upon them a melting Ingott,‡ and the same is to be kept by the Assay Master thereof for the time being, and not to be lent to anybody but one of the free brothers of this Company, leaving a pledge for the same ".

Every apprentice to execute an approved master-piece before admission to the Company.

The earliest existing volume of the orders and proceedings of the Company commences in 1686. Into it is transcribed an ordinance of the year 1667 prohibiting the admission of an apprentice to the freedom of the Company until he had wrought his "master-piece" and it had been approved of, before which he had to pay five shillings quarterly as a foreigner or quarter-brother. No money was to be taken in respect of an admission to the franchise. The fine was to take the form of a piece of plate.

On 10 November, 1687, it was ordered that all brothers bring their punches to be struck in the house of Capt. Richard Lord,§ and that thenceforth no one should make plate without striking his mark on it, under a penalty of ten shillings.

In March, 1688, a new Charter was obtained from James II., and two silver flagons belonging to the Company were sold to defray the expenses. The same year James fled from England and, with French aid, commenced the war with his successor which was carried on

---

* Mr. Garstin, F.S.A., had a full transcript, besides many similar notes supplied by Messrs. Water-house; see also Mr. Berry's paper, *Journal of the R.S.A.I.*, vol. xxxi., pp. 119-38.

† Daniel Bellingham was the first *Lord* Mayor of Dublin, the title having been conferred in 1665. His portrait with a label describing him as "Knight and Baron" (*sic*) now hangs in the City Hall. He was Under Secretary of State, and obtained a Baronetcy which became extinct on the death of his son and successor.

‡ The term "melting Ingott" in this instance obviously means a melting-pot and not an ingot or ingot-mould as the expression would now be understood.

§ Master of the Company in 1673-4 and for many years Assay Master.

for nearly four years on Irish soil, to the interruption both of manufactures and trade. Its effect on the Dublin goldsmiths was, that little or no work was done during the interval, and no minutes were recorded for nearly two years—16 February, $168\frac{8}{9}$, till 1 November, 1690. In November, 1691, however—the army of King James having been vanquished in the meantime—the Company voted £6 "for the carrying on a treate for General Ginckle, General-in-chief of the forces in Ireland of their Majesties King William and Queen Mary". On the 30th of the same month it is recorded that John Cuthbert handed over to Adam Soret, the newly-elected master, "several pieces of plate which had been placed in his custody by the Corporation some time before the late troubles".

Shortly after this the ordinary business of the Company was re- sumed, and the privileges of its members were strenuously maintained. In 1693 one Timothy Hevin was required to answer for keeping "open shop" as a goldsmith, he not being a free brother. He was ordered to "shut down" same within seven days, but was given permission to work privately in his room, paying the fee of a quarter brother. In 1694 (29 Sept.) it was ordered that no one should be allowed to strike his mark to any plate or bring plate to be "touched" who was not a free brother; all others were required to bring to Goldsmiths' Hall on 1 November their several stamps to be disposed of as the master and wardens saw fit. In the same year John Cuthbert, a free brother and past warden, was ordered to "show cause" for having employed a Frenchman to work for him for some time before he had acquainted the master and wardens with the fact. The above restriction was soon afterwards modified, and goldsmiths who were not freemen were allowed to make and put their marks on plate, on payment of quarterly fees. In 1698 "Thomas Eliot, an English watchmaker who had worked some time in the city, prayed admission as a free brother, which was granted, in consideration of his good service in the late wars in reducing this kingdom".

Offences against the laws of the Guild.

The records show that the Company was both vigilant and per- sistent in the detection and punishment of offences against the standard. In 1687 John Humphries, Robert Smith, John Clifton, John Phillips, George Thornton, Francis Sherwin, John Wall, and Timothy Heyvin, were fined various sums from 2s. 6d. to 30s. for working silver worse than standard. In the same year it was resolved that £4 should be allowed towards the costs of prosecuting William Keogh, a "pretended" goldsmith in Kilkenny, for selling plate as sterling which was not worth

Vigilance of the Company in the detection of frauds.

Offenders
rigorously dealt
with.

2s. per ounce. In 1691 Abraham Voisin, Vincent Kidder, John Phillips, James Cotton, and John Cuthbert were all fined for working bad silver. In July, 1693, twelve pairs of shoe-buckles below standard were seized from David Swan. He was fined for the offence but undeterred from repeating it, as a search of his shop three months afterwards resulted in four dram-cups and other articles being found, made of bad silver. He opposed the master and wardens in a contemptuous and unworthy manner, when they were making the search, by " forcing back said cups and putting them down into his breeches pockets ; he ran into a room behind his shop and hid same in an obscure place ". When taken into custody and required to produce the cups he cursed, and swore that same were melted down. Immediately afterwards, in fear of punishment, he delivered up the cups, which were beaten down. On the 25 October he attended at the Hall and acknowledged his crime.

In the same year (1693) Michael Haines and William Billinghurst were fined for working base silver and gold, and several sets of breast buttons made of bad silver were seized from Mr. Nelthorp, some with Mr. Wall's mark 8 dwts. worse, others with Mr. Sherwin's mark 2 dwts. worse. They were broken up and delivered back. In 1717 a complaint was made by Mr. Hore that George Farrington, a goldsmith, had sold him a teapot not "touched" at the Hall, but which had soldered on to it a piece of silver "touched" with the harp crowned, and the mark of Richard Archbold struck twice on it. Archbold having been summoned, and owning his marks and soldering, was fined £5. In 1723 Will. Matthews was fined for having wrought base silver, and in 1729 Andrew Patterson, of Drogheda, was " indicted for silver worse than standard ". In the same year (1729) a silver cup very much worse than sterling was brought in by Thomas Walker to be assayed. It weighed 19 oz. and was said to have been made by one Buck, of Limerick. It bore the mark of the harp crowned on a piece of silver which had formerly been part of some other article, soldered into the side of the cup—" a most notorious fraud and cheat " the record adds.

In 1708 the Company built a new Hall in Werburgh Street, where the meetings were held and the assays conducted until the early part of the 19th century. The assay office is now in the basement of the Dublin Custom House—a government building.

CHAPTER XXIII.

THE DUBLIN GOLDSMITHS' MARKS.

We have seen that in 1605 it was ordered by the city council that all Dublin goldsmiths should have every article of plate assayed, and stamped with the figures of a lion, a harp, and a castle, as well as the goldsmith's special mark, before being sold, exchanged or offered for sale. In the absence of examples of plate bearing these marks it is impossible to illustrate them. This, however, is not of much importance in view of the fact that their use was short-lived, the order of 1605 having been annulled by the Charter of December, 1637, which not only prescribed the standards for gold and silver wares—the former to be 22 carats and the latter 11 oz. 2 dwts. fine—but also prescribed the marks with which they should be stamped. Marks used prior to 1605 not known, and no example known of the " lion, harp and castle " mark in force 1605-37.

The marks prescribed by the Charter of 1637 were (1) the harp crowned (which was the King's Majesty's stamp, and the standard mark) indicating that gold and silver wares so marked had been proved to be of the standard quality ; and (2) the goldsmith's proper mark. The first assay in pursuance of the Charter was made on the 6 April, 1638, and every article then assayed was stamped with the two marks above described ; and from that date to the present day no Dublin-made article of silver or gold can have legally been sold or exchanged without being so marked. Marks prescribed by the Charter of 1637: the harp crowned, and the maker's mark.

A third mark, namely, a date-letter, has been used from 1638, in addition to the two above-mentioned. This mark is not prescribed ; in fact, it is not mentioned in the Charter, but it is provided that " if any goldsmiths' work be touched, marked, and allowed for good, and if in the same any deceit be afterwards found, the wardens and Company shall forfeit and pay the value of the thing ". It was obviously, therefore, to the interest of the Company that they should have the means of ascertaining in whose year of office any particular work had been stamped, and it was probably with that object that they followed the practice instituted by the London goldsmiths more than a century and a half earlier, and adopted a date-letter. A date-letter, used from 1638.

The date-letter, one of the marks prescribed by Statute in 1729, but afterwards frequently omitted.

These three marks were made statutory by an Act of the Irish Parliament in 1729, which provided that all articles of gold and silver should be assayed by the assay master appointed by the company of goldsmiths, and that they should be marked with the three marks which had been used from 1638, viz., the harp crowned, date-letter, and maker's mark. The date-letter, however, appears to have been very frequently omitted in the case of plate made in the latter half of the 18th century.

A fourth mark—the figure of Hibernia—was adopted in 1730 or 1731, and a fifth mark, consisting of a representation of the head of the Sovereign, was used from 1807 to 1890. The reasons for the use of these marks will be found explained further on.

A great deal of misconception has existed with respect to the Dublin Hall-marks, more particularly the date-letter. In no work dealing with the subject have the marks been represented with even a reasonable approximation to accuracy, and in a recently published *Magazine for Collectors*, an article appeared, with accompanying tables of marks, purporting to be correct representations; but in each of the tables previously published errors were copied, with the difference merely that the size of the representations was increased (the errors being thereby exaggerated) and that the marks, which in the previously published tables had been arranged vertically, were, in the tables as copied, arranged horizontally.

The following tables of marks, are the result of the collaboration of the Author with several members of learned societies in Ireland.

The correction of the errors which have so long existed with regard to the marks on Dublin plate, and the presentation of tables of marks of Irish goldsmiths with the nearest obtainable approach to accuracy, has been the aim of the Author, and the collection of material for this purpose has been the work of years. The succeeding tables of marks and names are the result of the collaboration of the Author with the following Irish gentlemen :—the late Mr. John Ribton Garstin, F.S.A., formerly President of the Royal Society of Antiquaries of Ireland, and Vice-President R.I.A.; the late Mr. Robert Day, F.S.A., of Cork; Mr. Henry F. Berry, Assistant Keeper of the Records in Ireland, a Member of the Royal Irish Academy; Mr. Langley Archer West, Master of the Dublin Goldsmiths' Company; and last but by no means least, Mr. Dudley Westropp, M.R.I.A., who has left nothing unexamined in the archives of the Goldsmiths' Company, or the Dublin civic records, which could in any way elucidate this subject.

Of all the tables of Dublin date-marks which have hitherto been published, one compiled by Dr. Waterhouse in 1881—reproduced here —is most nearly accurate :—

[TENTATIVE.]

TABLE OF DUBLIN DATE-MARKS.

COMPILED BY DR. W. D. WATERHOUSE.

3 Stamps	3 Stamps	3 Stamps	3 Stamps	5 Stamps to 1732 / 4 after 1732 GEORGE I	4 Stamps GEORGE II	4 Stamps AFTER 1784 GEORGE III	4 Stamps to 1807 / 5 after 1807 GEORGE III	5 Stamps Shields various GEORGE IV	5 Stamps VICTORIA	5 Stamps VICTORIA
				1721	1746	1771	1796	1821	1846	1871
1638	1658	1678	1698	1722	1747	1772	1797	1822	1847	1872
1639	1659	1679	1699	1723	1748	1773	1798	1823	1848	1873
1640	1660	1680	1700	1724	1749	1774	1799	1824	1849	1874
1641	1661	1681	1701	1725	1750	1775	1800	1825	1850	1875
1642	1662	1682	1702	1726	1751	1776	1801	1826	1851	1876
1643	1663	1683	1703	1727	1752	1777	1802	1827	1852	1877
1644	1664	1684	1704	1728	1753	1778	1803	1828	1853	1878
1645	1665	1685	1705	1729	1754	1779	1804	1829	1854	1879
1646	1666	1686	1706	1730	1755	1780	1805	1830	1855	1880
1647	1667	1687	1707	1731	1756	1781	1806	1831	1856	1881
1648	1668	1688	1708	1732	1757	1782	1807	1832	1857	
1649	1669	1689	1709	1733	1758	1783	1808	1833	1858	
1650	1670	1690	1710	1734	1759	1784	1809	1834	1859	
1651	1671	1691	1711	1735	1760	1785	1810	1835	1860	
1652	1672	1692	1712	1736	1761	1786	1811	1836	1861	
1653	1673	1693	1713	1737	1762	1787	1812	1837	1862	
1654	1674	1694	1714	1738	1763	1788	1813	1838	1863	
1655	1675	1695	1715	1739	1764	1789	1814	1839	1864	
1656	1676	1696	1716	1740	1765	1790	1815	1840	1865	
1657	1677	1697	1717	1741	1766	1791	1816	1841	1866	
			1718	1742	1767	1792	1817	1842	1867	
			1719	1743	1768	1793	1818	1843	1868	
			1720	1744	1769	1794	1819	1844	1869	
				1745	1770	1795	1820	1845	1870	

(First column note: cycle letters S, H, I, K, L, T. "These Letters taken from Goldsmiths Corporation Books.")

In this table by Dr. Waterhouse it will be observed that at 1766, 1791, and 1816 respectively, shields are left unoccupied by date-letters. In explanation of these blanks, when placing his table at the Author's disposal in 1899, Dr. Waterhouse said : " I examined tons of plate for the construction of that table, and although I found every other letter used in those cycles, I never met with a letter V earlier than 1841. I left the shields blank in case they should subsequently turn up. If they were not used, the result is that the letters in those cycles are a year or two, may be three, out of their place." Mr. Cripps, who had been given permission to use Dr. Waterhouse's table, adapted it to the columns of *Old English Plate*, but in so doing (without mentioning any authority) *materially altered it, by interpolating an entirely factitious letter 𝔙 at 1741 and filling each subsequent blank with a Roman capital* V, *in not one of which cases was the addition authentic, for there is no instance of the use of the letter* V *before 1841.* * What Mr. Cripps printed in *Old English Plate*, Mr. Chaffers, or his editors, copied (with acknowledgment) in *Hall Marks on Plate*, and a contributor to *The Connoisseur* of March, 1904, again copied, without naming the source of his marks, which is, however, disclosed by the errors reproduced.

We will now consider the marks in detail in chronological order :—

THE HARP CROWNED.

The harp crowned : the various shapes of the enclosing stamp used from 1638 downwards.

Firstly, the *Harp-crowned*, or Sovereign's mark : The appearance of this mark has varied so much from time to time since 1638 that its successive changes cannot well be described in words, and for that reason the reader is referred to the following tables, where its various forms are represented as they have been found on authentic articles of plate. It may, however, be stated that the broad distinctions are as follows : From 1638 until 1787 the shape of the stamp followed the outline of the device which it enclosed ; from 1787 until 1794 the outline was oval, and from 1794 until 1809 it was octagonal, or, to be more precise, an upright parallelogram with the corners clipped off. In the earlier examples of 1809 the stamp with the octagonal outline is still found. In 1794 and 1795 both the oval and octagonal-shaped crowned-harp stamps appear to have been used, marks of both forms having been found in conjunction with the letters X and Y, and the marks of the three years 1794-5-6 present a poor appearance, as if the punches with which they were struck had been cut by a somewhat incompetent die-sinker. The harp-crowned punch used in 1808 and 1809 appears to have been much worn, since in many examples of the mark for those years, the outline presents the appearance of a square with rounded corners rather than an octagon. In the latter part of the year 1809 and thenceforward for eleven years, the harp was in a regular heraldic shield with straight sides, engrailed top, and curved base, terminating in a point. In 1821 and the five following years the oval-shaped stamp was resumed.

---

* With reference to the absence of V before 1841, Mr. Garstin observed : " It need cause no astonishment, if it be borne in mind that neither it nor the ' double U ' was originally in the Roman alphabet, and when employed they were regarded as only different forms of the same letter, and were so treated in Dictionaries. Similarly, I and J were not deemed separate letters. Apart from Black-letter, in which they are usually indistinguishable, j is only found, as an Irish date-letter, in small Roman letter for 1854 (not 1879 as shown in Dr. Waterhouse's Table)."

From 1827 until 1846 the crowned harp was enclosed in a shield, the shape of which was changed no less than eleven times in nineteen years. From 1846 until 1871 the mark was again enclosed in a regular shield, the top of shield being invected. From 1871 to the present time the outline of the stamp has been similar in form to that of 1794-1809, namely, an upright parallelogram with clipped (or slightly rounded) corners. In recent years the size of the stamp has been smaller than it was in the 17th and 18th centuries, and while on early plate the same (large size) mark is found stamped on small articles as on large, on plate of the 19th and 20th centuries several sets of stamps varying in size from large (but not so large as the early stamps) to very small, have been used.

THE MAKER'S MARK.

(2) The maker's mark, or, as it is designated in the Charter, "the goldsmith's proper mark": This mark, from the date of the first operation of the Charter of 1637 till about the middle of the 19th century, is almost invariably found composed of letters, either separate or in monogram, indicating the Christian name and surname of the maker. In the 18th century two or three instances have been found of a single letter having been used for a maker's mark; on the other hand, in some cases where the maker's surname was composed of no more than three or four letters such as LAW, SLY, and WEST, the entire surname was used. The practice of using the entire surname in the maker's mark became much more common in the 19th century, when names as long as WATER-HOUSE are found to have been so used, indicating the seller rather than the maker. John Letablere used the first three letters of his surname for his mark about 1740-50. Two or three instances are to be found between 1715 and 1740 of marks such as Sa and Su, composed apparently of the first two letters of the maker's surname as used in England on plate of the Britannia Standard, but marks such as these are very rare.

The letters in the makers' marks of the 17th and the first half of the 18th century are often found accompanied by a device, such as a rosette, an anchor, an arrow, a fleur-de-lys, a mullet, a lion, a bird, a plume, a thistle, and the like, or with a crown or coronet over the letters enclosed in a single stamp. The use of a crown or coronet in a maker's mark appears to have caused some jealousy and misconception with regard to its meaning. It was suggested that the use of such a device tended to delude the public into believing that Royal authority

(marginal note beside "THE MAKER'S MARK" paragraph:) The maker's mark.

(marginal note beside final paragraph:) Use of devices in conjunction with letters in early makers' marks.

or warrant was thereby indicated. The Goldsmiths' Company having resolved to prohibit the use of such devices, the following order was entered in the minutes :—

Crowns and other ornaments in makers' marks forbidden in 1731 but used occasionally afterwards until about 1780.

"1731 Nov. 1st. Ordered that all [persons] working in gold and silver having crowns, coronets, or other ornaments with their punches are forthwith to bring such punches to [the] Master and Wardens to have the same defaced, and that no one hereafter use crowns, coronets or any ornaments. In case of such use [offenders] to be proceeded against with the utmost severity of the law."

What was meant by "the utmost severity of the law" does not appear, nor does it appear that the order was immediately attended to, for we find that coronets and other ornaments were used in makers' marks with nearly as much frequency for a few years after the promulgation of the order as before. From 1745, however, the use of these "ornaments" became much less common, but a coronet is found in a maker's mark as late as 1780. Possibly the resolution : "1744 *Samuel Walker ordered to change his mark,*" may have had some effect on the goldsmith named and others.

In 1783, by the 23 and 24 Geo. III. c. 23 (Ireland) it was enacted that "from and after 9 Septr. 1784 no person being a merchant manufacturer or dealer in gold or silver wares should sell or expose for sale, buy or exchange or export any wares of gold or silver or of both or any jewels either set or unset without first registering his name and place of abode with the Company of Goldsmiths in Dublin in a book to be kept by the said Company for that purpose under a penalty of £100 for every offence.

"No hawker pedler or other trading person going from town to town should buy sell or export to sell exchange or barter any wares of gold or silver under a penalty of £50 for every offence.

"That it should be lawful on or after the 1st June 1784 for any person making or causing to be made any goldsmith's work to enter an impression of his mark or punch together with his or her respective name and place of abode at the Assay Office at Dublin (or New Geneva) upon paying 5s. to the Assayer or Wardens of such office who were required to make in a plate or sheet of pewter or copper an impression of such mark and also make an entry of such mark and the name and place of abode of the owner in a book to be kept for the purpose and that no person should be entitled to have any goldsmith's work made by him or her assayed or stamped at such assay office until after it should have been stamped by the maker with his mark (entered as aforesaid) and that no goldsmith's work should be assayed or marked at such assay office if marked with any other mark but such as should have been duly entered as aforesaid."

Registration of Marks in 1784.

Consequent upon this Act, a large number of Dublin and provincial goldsmiths complied with its provisions in the year 1784, and the marks of many of them are to be found struck in the plates of copper preserved in the assay office. But the marks of all are not so recorded, and after a while the requirements of the Act appear to have fallen into abeyance. The register—commenced in 1784—of the names and marks of manufacturing goldsmiths does not contain all the makers' marks found to have been used during the first half of the century which succeeded the passing of the Act of 1783. The books of the Company, however, contain the names of many for whom plate was assayed, and the names and places of abode of goldsmiths carrying on their trade in provincial towns which were registered at Goldsmiths' Hall, Dublin, in compliance with the above Act.

In the 19th century the makers' marks consisted for the most part of the bare initials of the goldsmiths' names. These marks were then and are now much smaller and simpler than those of earlier times. The lists of goldsmiths' names which follow the tables of marks, will be found of great assistance in the identification of makers, and will to a great extent enable the date of the manufacture of a piece of plate to be approximately fixed in cases where no date-letter has been stamped, and the maker's mark and the harp crowned only are distinguishable. It must, however, be observed that in many cases the names of goldsmiths appearing in the tables have not been verified by contemporary records as those of the owners of the marks, but have been conjectured because the initials correspond with the marks.

[margin note: The following lists of goldsmiths' names will be of assistance in fixing, approximately, the date of plate without a date-letter.]

THE DATE-LETTER.

(3) The Date-letter : The earliest record of a date-letter in the Chronicles of the Goldsmiths' Company is that of the letter G for 1644-5. This entry is followed by others, which record that the letters appointed for the four succeeding years were H, I, K and L respectively. We are left in no doubt as to the letter with which the cycle was commenced in April, 1638, for there is at Trinity College, Dublin, a communion flagon inscribed in contemporaneous lettering " *Par fratrum pariles fecerunt esse lagenas. Moses et Eduardus Hill generosi, Anno Domini* 1638."* This

[margin note: The date-letter.]

---

* The late Mr. J. R. Garstin, wrote :—" A representation of this flagon is given in *The Book of Trinity College* (1891), at page 44, and a description in the Chapter on the College plate, page 267. It is of paramount interest as the oldest known piece of Irish plate with a date-letter. But its inscription is also curious, and has not hitherto been explained. In order to make it intelligible, it is necessary to mention that the Chapel of Trinity College previously possessed a flagon which was presented by one of the Fellows, John Richardson (who became Bishop of Ardagh), but it was of London make. Two undergraduates of T.C.D., desiring to emulate him, had the flagon in question made to match the other, and so the inscription (the first part of which is in verse) may be thus rendered in doggrel English :—' Edward and Moses [Hill], a *pair* of brothers, made these a pair by giving this other '. "

flagon is marked with the harp crowned of the early form, the date-letter A in a curiously shaped shield, and IVB in monogram, the "proper mark" of James Vanderbeck. At Fethard in co. Wexford, there is a communion cup inscribed "*Ex dono Nicolai Loftus Anno Salutis,* 1639," marked with the harp crowned, the date-letter B in a plain shield for 1639-40, and IT the "proper mark" of John Thornton.* In the same church there is a communion paten with a similar crowned harp, the "proper mark" of the same goldsmith, and date-letter C for the following year. In Derry cathedral there is a communion cup also marked with the same kind of harp crowned, the date-letter D (in a plain shield), and the "proper mark" of William Cooke. The Dublin Museum possesses a spoon "slipped in the stalk" marked with the crowned harp of the early form, the date-letter S (in a plain shield), and the "proper mark" of Daniel Bellingham (warden 1656-7); and one of 1639—the earliest hall-marked spoon known. At this point an entry in the Goldsmiths' minute book is of importance. It runs as follows :—

"Nov. 9th, 1660. *Trial was this day made at G.S. Hall, Dublin, of all the diet of all the plate that had been touched there from the 12th day of Feb.* 1657 *to the day of the date aforesaid* at the rate of 2grs. to the lb. being plate touched 21,977oz. 5dwts. and upon trial made it fell out to be by the assay better 1dwt. being present wt. of the diet 7oz. 11dwts. *letter ꟑ and lett. b.*" (The remainder of the page is torn off.)

In other words, the period during which the diet tested on 9 Nov., 1660, had accumulated, extended from 12 Feb., 165⅞, to the day of trial. At the commencement of such period the letter T was the date-letter in use, and during the last year of such period the letter in use was *b* as is proved by the following entry, "*November 12th,* 1659:—*Order that the letter b, a small Roman letter, be struck by the assay-master upon all the silver plate which shall be brought to his office and approved of by him from after the day of the date hereof until the first day of November next*".

The letter T having been the date-letter for 1656-7, and *b* the letter for 1659-60, it seems safe to assume that U was the letter for 1657-8, and that *a* was the letter for 1658-9 with which the second alphabet or cycle was commenced. It is, moreover, extremely probable that the

---

* During the first three years after the incorporation of the Company the records appear to have been regularly entered. Thornton's name, however, does not appear in the list of freemen until 1653, but as John Thornton is the only goldsmith known to have been working about 1639 whose initials fit the above mark, it is suggested that he was probably working then as a goldsmith, and allowed certain privileges before being admitted as a free brother to the enjoyment of all the amenities pertaining to the full freedom of the Company. This frequently happened.

Dublin Goldsmiths were acquainted with the fact that their London brethren had been using alphabetical marks arranged in cycles (of twenty years) in each of which the first twenty letters of the alphabet —A to U (or V)—were employed, and that during the first forty years of the existence of the Dublin Company, under the Charter of 1637, a similar practice was followed.

The next certain mark in the tables of Dublin date-letters is the Old English 𝕮 for 1680. This letter occurs on the great tankards of the Merchant Taylors' Company, London, which bear a contemporary inscription stating that they were "*made* in the year one thousand six hundred and eightie, being the plate of the Guild of St. John Baptist, Dublin". The guild was a company of Merchant Tailors like the Company in London, into whose possession the tankards passed directly upon the dissolution of the Dublin Guild.

𝕮 fixed as the date-letter for 1680 by contemporary inscriptions on the Merchant Taylors' tankards.

It is therefore obvious that from 1659-60 to 1680 the rotation of the date-letters must have been as shown in the second and third of the following tables. In view of the dates when new Wardens were elected and the old Wardens retired from office, it also seems clear that the first date-letter, the Roman capital A, was used from the date of the first assay—6 April, 1638—to November, 1639, and that each succeeding letter was used from November of one year until the same month in the succeeding year. It should be borne in mind that at this period it was a common practice to retain the date of the old year until Lady Day in the new year. The next point of time, after 1680, at which a date-letter is fixed, is the year 1693-4. It is recorded in the goldsmiths' books that the letter appointed for that year is 𝕳. The letter itself is written in the book in a kind of hybrid cursive hand, but as there are known to the Author at least nine authentic examples of the letter itself (which is an old English capital), it is unnecessary to reproduce the written character. Several of the objects on which this letter occurs are dated in contemporary engraving. One with maker's mark J W (probably for Joseph Walker) is inscribed "*Chalice given to St. Michael's, Dublin*, 1693"; another with maker's mark W D (William Drayton) at St. Michan's and a paten at St. Werburgh's (made by John Clifton) are similarly dated. In Abbeyleix church there is a communion cup inscribed "*Jan.* 169$\frac{4}{5}$, *Abbey Leix*". Now the goldsmiths' books contain no record of any plate having been assayed in the year 1693, nor until February in the following year, that is to say 169$\frac{3}{4}$. It

The letter 𝕳, recorded as adopted in 1693, used for more than one year.

is obvious that at this period each date-letter was used for more than one year, and as the examples of plate referred to above are inscribed with dates in such a manner as to indicate exactitude, it appears clear that the old English capital 𝕶 found on those examples may be safely ascribed to 1693-4-5. The fixing of the letters between the year 1680-1

War troubles of 1688-92 caused a break of continuity.

and 1693 is, however, not so simple a matter, principally owing to the break caused by the war troubles of 1688-92, during which period very little plate (if any) appears to have been either made or assayed.

There is an entry in the goldsmiths' books of a regulation in 1686 that "the assay master for the time being shall yearly and every year hereafter enter with the clerk of the company the letter of the year with which he marks each brother's plate".

This regulation, however, appears to have been very much neglected and for a whole century the entries of the letter of the year are only occasional.* The date-letters which have been found between 𝕮 and 𝕶 are 𝕯, 𝕰, 𝕲, and 𝕳, and as there is no reason for supposing that any break occurred either in the business of the company or the order of the date-letters during the reign of Charles II., it has been assumed that the letter 𝕱 was used in its proper place, although no example of that letter pertaining to the cycle in question has been found. The date-letter 𝕲 occurs on a communion cup bearing a contemporary inscription recording its gift by Alderman John Rogerson A.D. 1685, and on the "Dogget" paten "given 1693" to St. Werburgh's, Dublin. Since the first edition of this work was printed, the letter 𝕳 has been traced as having been used from 1688 to 1693. Whether the letter 𝕴 was used or not is a matter for conjecture. The 𝕷 for 1697-9 is stamped on the mace of New Ross, dated 2 October, 1699, as well as on other articles of plate mentioned in Table III.

The letter 𝕸 recorded with entries of 1699-1700.

The next "land-mark" is the Old English capital letter 𝕸, which has been stamped in the thick paper of the assay book with the same punch as that with which the date-letter was struck on a communion cup, at Abbeyleix (from Ballyroan), dated 1700. The mark is stamped on the last page containing entries referring to articles assayed 9 February, 1700. This record gives us the date-letter for 1699-1700, and in further confirmation of the ascription of the letters of this period, there is the Lifford mace, with the date-letter 𝕺 (in the possession of Lord

---

* Mr. Dudley Westropp suggests that the entries may have been regularly made in accordance with the resolution of 1686, and that the book containing them has probably been lost.

Erne), dated 1701. The letter 𝔓, of 1702-3, is also stamped in one The letter 𝔓 recorded with the names of officers appointed for 1702-3. of the Goldsmiths' books on the page containing the list of wardens and members of the company for that year; and confirmation of the fact of its being the letter for the year 1702-3 is its occurrence on Dromore Cathedral Church plate, dated 1703. It seems clear, therefore, that the letter 𝔜 must have been used during three years (1696-7-8), as was almost certainly the case with the letter 𝔎 (1693-4-5).

The following entries with reference to punches occur in the cash accounts of the Dublin Goldsmiths' Company :—

" March 21st, 1702.	Paid for punches	...	...	£0	6s.	0d."
" Feb. 1st, 1705.	Paid for cutting letters	...	4	6s.	0d."
" Oct. 9th, 1708.	2 letter punches	...	...	0	10s.	0d."
" Sept., 1712.	Paid Brown for 4 punches	...	0	10s.	0d."
" Feb. 2nd, 1715.	Cutting 6 punches	...	...	0	15s.	0d."
" July, 1716.	Paid for punches	...	...	0	12s.	0d."
" Sept., 1721.	Paid for punches	...	...	0	16s.	3d."

These entries, however, afford very little assistance, as it is not Other records having reference to date-letters. stated what letters were cut in any of the punches. After the 𝔓 of 1702-3 there is really no entry in any of the Company's books which affords any information concerning date-letters, until 2 February, 1747, when it is recorded that the sum of "*7s. 7d. was paid for two punches, letter* A". We are, therefore, restricted in a measure to dated examples of plate (of which there are, fortunately, a considerable number in the hands of corporate bodies in Ireland), for information enabling us to arrange the date-letters which were used from 1703 until 1747, in chronological order. The Old English letter 𝕆 has been found only on undated plate, but the 𝔅 is found on a communion paten inscribed "*New St. Mary's Church Dublin* 1705," and on a communion cup and paten, dated 1706, at St. Nicholas (without), Dublin. The 𝔖 is found on a communion cup and paten inscribed "*Bartholomew Vigors Bp. of Ferns and Leighlin Anno Dom.* 1707," at Staplestown, co. Carlow. The 𝔗 is found on communion plate dated 1709, presented in that year to Dromiskin Church, co. Louth, by Sir Thomas Fortescue. The 𝔘 is found on two communion patens at St. Mary's, Dublin, "given by Dr. Pooley, 1712," and on two flagons, similarly dated, in Cloyne Cathedral. The 𝔚 is on a communion cup, dated 1714, at Rathclaren, co. Cork. The 𝔛 occurs on six pieces of church plate, dated 1714 (from the demolished church of the once flourishing but now merged parish of St. Brides), in the possession of the Irish Church Representative Body, and on communion cups, dated

1715, in St. John's Cathedral, Cashel; and the 𝕭 is found on a communion flagon, dated 1716, at Killeshandra. A number of other examples have been found marked with the above date-letters, both with and without inscribed dates, but as they bear marks similar to those which are represented in the tables, it is unnecessary to increase the number mentioned by

Several letters used for more than one year.

referring to them in detail. Each of the letters between 𝕺 and 𝑿, judging by the dated examples of plate which have been found, served for more than a single year, and there appears sufficient reason for assigning each letter to the years set opposite to it in the tables. The quantity of plate assayed between 1703 and 1714, in the aggregate, was not large, and during this period some one or more of the wardens held office for two or more years; there was therefore no necessity for changing the letter every year. No example of plate marked with the letter Z for 1716-7 has been found, but the letter in all probability was used, and an authentic example may some day be brought to light. With the single exception of the letter A of 1638-9, all the enclosing shields of the date-letters have straight tops, until that of the

Shape of the tops of shields.

𝕾 of 1706-8, the top of which is engrailed, as are the tops of the two following letters (𝕿 and 𝖀). The 𝖂 of 1712-3-4 has been found only in shields with straight tops; the next two letters (𝑿 and 𝕭) are known to the Author in shields with engrailed tops only.

With respect to the date-letters used from 1717 to 1746, although we are not assisted in assigning them to their proper places by any entries in the goldsmiths' records, we have otherwise the means of fixing the letters for 1727-8 and 1746. The letter 𝕭 in a shield with engrailed top, an 18th century crowned harp—larger than that used in the time of James II.—and the "proper mark" of Robert Calderwood, occur on a communion paten dated 1727 at St. Werburgh's, Dublin; the same date-letter and harp crowned, with the "proper mark" of Thomas Walker are on the mace of the Borough of Portarlington, which was sold in the 19th century and acquired by Mr. T. A. H. Poynder, who presented it to the London Goldsmiths' Company in 1864. This mace is inscribed in contemporary engraving with the date 1728. Now, a mace is not an article which any goldsmith would make "for stock," and it is not likely to have been made for a private person, and, after a year or more had elapsed, dated and presented—as often happened in the case of cups and other vessels. This mace was no doubt made to order for the Borough of Portarlington at the date which it bears, and in view of the fact that the St. Werburgh's paten with the same date-letter is dated 1727, this letter 𝔅 is confidently assigned to the year 1727-8.   The ascription of the respective date-letters from 1717-8 to 1727-8 is a simple matter, because a distinct letter is found for every intervening year.

The letter 𝔅 of 1727-8.

In 1717 a Court-hand alphabet was commenced with the letter 𝖆, followed by the letters 𝔅 and ℭ respectively in the two succeeding years. This alphabet must have been soon abandoned, for in 1720, without any apparent reason, an alphabet of old English capitals was again resorted to, the letters being changed and taken in consecutive order yearly, down to the 𝔏 of 1730-1.   These letters are easily distinguishable from those of the preceding cycle by the fact that the enclosing shields of all the earlier letters of the same character are straight topped, while the tops of the later shields are each engrailed.   Apart from these distinguishing features there is a marked difference in the design of the crowned harps of the two cycles, as will be at once observed on referring to the tables.

Three Court-hand letters interposed between old English alphabets.

The distinction between the old English capitals 1720-46 and those of earlier years.

In 1730 or 1731 a new stamp, namely, the figure of Hibernia, was adopted for a reason which will be presently explained.   The addition of this stamp affords of itself a feature of distinction in the Dublin marks.   The date-letter 𝔏 appears to have been used for two years. When without the Hibernia mark, it is, in the following tables, assigned to 1730-1, and when accompanied by the figure of Hibernia, it is assigned to 1731-2.   From 𝔐 to 𝔄 the alphabet proceeded regularly, each year having a distinct letter.   The latter, however, instead of being followed by 𝔙, was followed by 𝔚.   The letter V was not used until 1841, and every table in which it appears before that date is inaccurate.   Two sorts of 𝔚 were used, one with a straight top to its enclosing shield, that of the other being engrailed, as illustrated in Table VI.*   In the absence of a record it is impossible to say which form of 𝔚 is the earlier, they are therefore bracketed in the table for the years—1741 to 1743.†   The accuracy of the dates ascribed to the letters in this table is confirmed by the contemporary inscription on the Athy mace marked with the date-letter Z.   It runs as follows : " *The gift of the Rt. Honble. James Earl of Kildare to the Borough of Athy Sept 29th, 1746*".

At some time between 1743 and 1747 the date for changing the annual letters appears to have been altered.   There is reason to believe

---

* In a table of supplementary marks on page 619 *infra*, the date-letter ℭ is also represented in a straight-topped shield.   It was so found after the tables had been arranged.

† The repetition of 𝔚 may possibly be explained by recalling the origin of its name—double of U (V was also a " double " of U in the sense of being interchangeable with it), just as, in the Greek alphabet, Omega (or great o) was constructed by repeating or doubling Omicron (or little o).

From about 1747 to 1826, letters changed on 1st (or 2nd) of January.

that the letter $\mathcal{X}$ was used from 1 November, 1743, to 31 December, 1744, a period of fourteen months. Thenceforward, until the year 1826, the change of letter was made each year on the 1st (or 2nd) of January, or 25 March, as mentioned below.

In January, 1747, a new cycle (the first of four in succession, each consisting of Roman capitals and consequently causing much confusion) was commenced with the letter A. This is confirmed by a record in the accounts (current from 1 Nov., 1746), of the approval on 2 February, 1747, of the payment of " 7s. 7d. for two punches letter A," which, as already mentioned, appears in the goldsmiths' books. All the letters of this alphabet except J and V were used in regular succession, a different letter for each year with two exceptions, namely : (1) There were two kinds of the date-mark E used in the year 1751-2, of which one has the top of its enclosing shield formed of two waved lines invected in the middle, the shield of the other being engrailed ; (2) the date letter H seems to have been used from 8 January, 1754, for a period of at least two years. On the first page of the Assay Book commencing 27 March, 1752, a capital letter F is written, and in an entry dated 26 March, 1753, the letter G is written ; while in an entry dated 8 January, 1754, the letter H appears.

Twenty-four letters served for 26 years—1747 to 1772 inclusive.

From those entries it has been assumed that the dates on which the letters F, G and H were first used are thereby indicated. As no date-letter V has been found to have been in use earlier than 1841, and no J earlier than 1854, it seems clear that in two years of this cycle a letter must have been used which had been used before, and as several examples of plate have been found with date-letters and also engraved dates, ranging from 1765 to 1769, in accordance with the arrangement now adopted in Table VII, it has been assumed that the date-marks were used as there indicated.

The shields of the date-letters in this cycle are all straight sided, except that of the S which has slightly hollowed sides, and the tops are all engrailed, except that of one of the two examples of the letter E which is as above described ; the bases are all pointed, and all angular at the sides of the base, except four, which are slightly rounded as shown in the table.

The four letters, B, C, N and O of this cycle are not easily distinguishable from the same letters of the following cycle, but in the later alphabet they are less broad in proportion to their height and the main lines less thick than is the case with those of the earlier. The upper central point of the shield of the letter C in the later cycle is raised above the outer points, unlike the shield of that letter in the earlier cycle.

The allocation of the date-letters to their respective years in Table VIII. (1773 to 1796) has been an easy task, by reason of the discovery in the Goldsmiths' cash accounts of the following entries of payments for letter-punches :—" Letter P for 1787," "Q for 1788," and " R for 1789 ". These three letters being fixed, all the others, before as well as after, fall into their proper places without question. The letter A of this cycle is differentiated from that of the preceding cycle by the shape of its shield, which is markedly different from that of the earlier letter A as will be readily observed by glancing at the tables. The letters B, C, N and O have already been discussed. There is a pellet under each of the letters D, E, F, H, I, K, L, and M of this cycle, and a pellet within the G, whereby they are easily distinguished from similar letters in the preceding cycle. The base of the shield of the letter G of 1779 is rounded, while that of the G of 1754 is angular. The alteration which was made in the outline of the crowned-harp stamp in 1787 prevents the possibility of the marks from that year onwards being mistaken for any of an earlier date and *vice versa;* but as this alteration was not made until after some plate had been stamped in that year, the letter P of 1787 is found with the crowned-harp stamp of both the old and new form.

The letters for 1773-96 distinguished from those of 1747-72.

The following lines, which refer to payments for letter-punches, have been copied from accounts in the archives of the Dublin Goldsmiths' Company :—

							£	s.	d.			
" Jan.	4th	1791	3 letter punches	T				10	10	Henry Standish."		
"	„	3rd 1792	„ „ „	U				„		„	„	„ "
"	„	3rd 1793	„ „ „	W				„		James Standish."		
"	„	4th 1794	„ „ „	X				„		„	„	„ "
"			„ „ „	Z	for 1796			„		„	„	„ "
" Jan.		1797	„ „ „	A	for 1797			„		„	„	„ "
"		1798	„ „ „	B				„		„	„	„ "
"		„	2 harp „				I	12	6	„	„	„ "
" Jan.	2nd	1799	3 letter „	C				10	10	„	„	„ "
"	„	2nd 1800	„ „ „	D				„		„	„	„ "
"	„	3rd 1801	„ „ „	E				„		„	„	„ "
"	„	2nd 1802	„ „ „	F				„		„	„	„ "
" Aug.	26th	„	2 letter punches	F				5	5	„	„	„ "
" Dec.	30th	„	3 „ „	G				10	10	„	„	„ "
" Feb.	10th	1803	I „ „	G				2	8½	„	„	„ "

						£	s.	d.		
"Jan.	1st	1804	2 steel	punches	H		5	5	Will. Mossop. "
"	„	„	2 Hibernia	„		1	2	9	„	„ "
"	„	2nd 1805	4 steel	„	I		10	10	„	„ "
"Dec.	17th	„	4 punches		K		„		„	„ "
"July	28th	1806	„	„	L		„		„	„ "
"Dec.	31st	1807	2 letter punches		M		5	5	„	„ "
"Jan.	3rd	1811	3	„	„	P	8	1½	„	„ "
"Oct.	24th	„	2	„	„	„	5	5	„	„ "
"Jan.	5th	1814	cutting 2 letters		S		„		„	„ "
"Feb.	2nd	„	1 letter S dessert size No. 3			2	8½	„	„ "
"Jan.	6th	1825	2 punches letters		E		5	5	„	„ "

These accounts prove that the date-letters in the following tables from 1791 to 1807 (except possibly 1795), and for the years 1814 and 1825, have been put in their proper places, and that no such letter as V was, or could have been, used in the year 1791, as represented in *Old English Plate* and *Hall Marks on Plate.* The two letter punches paid for on Aug. 26, 1802, were probably required to replace two of the three which had been procured on Jan. 2nd, 1802, and which had very likely become damaged or worn by use, as the business done at that period was considerable. The payment of 10s. 10d., on July 28th, 1806, for four punches letter L (not required before Jan. 1, 1807), is the only recorded occasion (shown in these extracts) where punches appear to have been obtained (five months) in advance. There seems, however, to be no other feasible explanation than that they were obtained in advance from Wm. Mossop of Dublin, the die-sinker who cut them.

Date-letters for 1797 to 1820 distinguished from those of other years. The date-letters in Table IX. (1797 to 1820) may, although they also are Roman capitals, be readily distinguished from others of the same character by the fact that from 1797 to 1808 they are in oblong stamps with clipped corners. The letters M (of 1808) and N (of 1809) are for the most part in square stamps with the corners rounded. The N is, however, also found in a shield with engrailed top, and waved base terminating in a point, a form of shield in which all the later letters of this cycle are respectively enclosed. The letter O is also found in two forms of shield, one with engrailed top, the other having a straight top with corners slightly hollowed. None of these letters, N to Z (1809-20), can be mistaken for similar characters of any other cycle, by reason of the shapes of the crowned-harp and Hibernia stamps, and the sovereign's head which accompany them. The date (1813) to which the letter R of this cycle is assigned, is proved to be correct by the fact that the Masonic cup at Limerick, which bears that date-mark, was ordered in February and made by the month of May in that year.

The cycle of date-letters 1821 to 1845-6, represented in Table X., is again, with one exception, composed of Roman capitals. The shape of the enclosing shields of these letters varies so much that their forms will be better understood by a reference to the illustrations in the table than by reading a mass of descriptive matter, which therefore is not given. The marks of this cycle cannot be mistaken for those of any other, as will be seen immediately on consulting the tables.

[margin: 1821 to 1845-6.]

An order is recorded in the goldsmiths' books dated 2 February, 1822, "that an entire new set of punches be made annually and put into use on Jany. 1st each year," and it is also recorded that "On Novr. 30th, 1822, on the New Master taking office there were handed to him thirteen hand punches and twelve press punches all defaced; four gold punches, three press punches and fourteen hand punches to be used until Jan. 1st, 1823, also twelve new hand punches not to be used until Jan. 1st, 1823".

The above order merely confirmed the practice which had been followed for a number of years previously, and which in the third year from the date of that order was altered in the following manner: The date-letter brought into use in January, 1825 (the Roman capital E), was discontinued on 20 September, 1825, when it was "*ordered that new punches be made with letter e for remainder of year*". This change of letter was effected by the direction of the Commissioners of Stamps (to whom the collection of the duty on plate had been transferred from the Commissioners of Excise by the Statute 6 Geo. IV. c. 118), in order to mark the reduction of the allowance of variation from standard to $1\frac{1}{2}$ dwt. per 12 oz., so as to assimilate the practice with that of the London Assay Office.* The allowed variation at the Dublin Office had up to this time been $2\frac{1}{2}$ dwts. per lb.

[margin: 20 Sept., 1825; letter changed from E to e to mark reduction of allowance of variation from Standard.]

On 5 December, 1825, it was resolved that the change of marks should be made annually on 28 May, when all old punches should be defaced in the presence of the Master and Wardens. Accordingly, the small Roman letter e continued in use for a period of eight months. It was defaced in pursuance of the above resolution on 28 May, 1826, when new date-letter punches, composed of the Roman capital F, were put into commission. The practice of changing the marks at about the end of the month of May was continued until 1840, when the change was

[margin: 5 Dec., 1825; resolved to change marks annually on 28 May.]

[margin: 1840, change of marks made in September.]

---

* It will be observed that the change of letter from E to e was in reality the exact reverse of that stated in *Old English Plate.*

not made till 23 September.   In the following years of the cycle illustrated by Table XI., the change was made in the months of August and July respectively, and after 1845, in June.

From the year 1822, all marks have been struck on plates of copper, and date of change recorded.

From the year 1822 until the present time, every hall-mark used by the Dublin Incorporation has been struck on copper plates preserved at the Assay Office, and the dates recorded.   The remaining tables numbered XI., XII. and XIII. have each been compared with those records and their accuracy verified.   Down to 1824, every date-letter represented in the following tables—the proper date of which has been ascertained to be as shown—has an asterisk placed against the date in the table to which it pertains; but as the proper date of every letter subsequently employed has been recorded, there is no necessity to continue those marks further.

Many of the marks here represented differ materially from all representations of the like marks which have hitherto been published. In particular, the twenty-five letters of the cycle extending from 1871 to 1896, which have been represented in edition after edition of several well-known books on this subject, as Roman capitals, are nothing of the kind.   They are plain block letters as illustrated in Table XII. hereafter. How such a mistake could have been perpetuated when the means of correcting it was at hand, is incomprehensible.

The date-mark requires no further comment than is necessary to explain its absence from much Dublin plate of the 18th century.

Much plate marked in the reign of Geo. III. without a date-letter.

For several years during the reigns of George II. and George III. the assaying and marking of plate at Dublin appears to have been carried on with some laxity, and plate was often sold without being assayed or marked,* the date-letter having been omitted to be stamped in numerous instances.†   The only marks which appear on many examples of this period are the crowned harp, the figure of Hibernia, and the maker's mark.   In such cases it is impossible to determine the exact year in which an article so marked was made.   The various forms of the harp and Hibernia marks illustrated in the following tables will afford the means of fixing the date approximately, and the lists of goldsmiths' names which follow the tables will (except where there are two or more with the

---

* With reference to this subject the following note has been copied by Mr. Dudley Westropp from the Act of Parliament, 25 Geo. II. c. 10, s. 21. " Silver plate often sold without being assayed and marked, Buyers relying on the credit of silversmiths that it is standard.   Enacted that from May 21st, 1752, no one to buy from Goldsmiths any plate unmarked except silver wire and objects not exceeding 4 dwt.   If bought, plate to be forfeited, and penalty as in Geo. II. c. 3.   Penalty and forfeiture laid on Buyer and Seller to be for sole use of informer."

† See *Transactions of Royal Irish Academy*, Vol. XXXIV., Sec. C., No. 5, by Mr. D. Westropp, M.R.I.A.

same initials at about the same time) enable anyone to identify the maker.   This neglect to impress the date-letter on plate appears to have been contemporaneous with the forgery of marks, which was perpetrated by Michael Keating and others for the purpose of avoiding payment of the duty.*†   It is astonishing that this omission of the date-letter should have been allowed, in view of the fact that its adoption was for the very object of preventing and detecting fraud.   The only alternative, however, to the conclusion that this neglect was suffered by the authorities, is the highly improbable one, that on all the plate (and that is a large quantity) which is found without a date-letter, the harp-crowned and Hibernia stamps have been forged.

THE DUTY MARKS:—(1) HIBERNIA.

"An Act for the encouragement of tillage" appears to be a strangely incongruous statute to cite in connection with goldsmiths' marks, yet such is the title of the Act 3 Geo. II. c. 3 (1729), an enactment of the Irish Parliament which imposed a duty upon a number of things, amongst others manufactured gold and silver, the proceeds of which were to be applied to the purpose indicated by the title of the Act. *(Duty imposed on Irish plate by the Irish Act 3 Geo. II. c. 3 (1729).)*

Section 30 of the Act provided "that from and after the 25th day of March 1730 for a term of twenty-one years a duty at the rate of sixpence per ounce Troy should be charged on all gold and silver plate wrought in Ireland at any time or times after the 25th day of March 1730". This duty was re-imposed for a further 21 years by 23 Geo II. c. 5.

Section 32 provided "that no wrought gold or silver plate should be sold before being assayed touched and marked," and

Section 33 provided "that the assay master should stamp without fee or reward all gold and silver wares with such stamp as the commissioners of His Majesty's Revenue or any three or more of them should from time to time appoint".

With reference to this Act it is stated, in *Old English Plate* that to the marks previously used at the Dublin Assay Office, "another was added in the year 1730, by order of the Commissioners of Excise, who introduced the figure of Hibernia to denote the payment of the duty first charged upon plate in that year". This statement, however, appears to be somewhat inaccurate, there being no evidence that the mark was added by order of the Commissioners of Excise in 1730, as will presently be demonstrated. The stamp of the figure of Hibernia was adopted by the Dublin Goldsmiths' Company (probably of their own initiative) to indicate the payment of duty, for the collection of which they were held

* See the paragraph with reference to the prosecution of Michael Keating (*infra*).
† 18th century spoons nearly always have the date-letter, while larger articles have not.

responsible, but it was not until August, 1752 (after the mark had been in use for more than twenty years), that an Act was passed making it penal to sell or exchange plate without this evidence of the payment of sixpence per ounce for duty.

It will be noticed that the duty was chargeable only on gold and silver plate "*wrought in Ireland after* 25*th March*, 1730". The Dublin gold-smiths appear to have known beforehand that the duty would be imposed. In the first three months, 1 January to 31 March, of the year 1730, the "touch money" received by the assay master in respect of assays amounted to no less than £121 11s. 1d., whilst in the remaining nine months of the year it amounted to no more than £106 15s. 8d. It is not stated how much of the plate assayed after March, 1730, had been wrought before the duty was imposed, nor is it now known on what date the first duty was actually paid, nor is there any record of the date

The figure of Hibernia adopted as a duty-mark in 1730 or 1731.

when the duty mark—the figure of Hibernia—was first stamped on plate. It was at some time after the 25 March, 1730, and probably not later than 1 January, 1731. There is an entry in the goldsmiths' books :— "21 *April*, 1730, *Duty came on this day*". That may mean that the first duty was paid on that day, and the Hibernia stamp may have been then struck to mark its payment. There is as much (or more) plate marked with the date-letter 𝔚 without the Hibernia mark as with it, and as the letter 𝔚 appears to have been used for two years, the new mark may not have been adopted until 1 January, 1731.

The Act of 1729, whereby the duty of 6d. per oz. was imposed upon all plate wrought in or brought into Ireland from and after 25 March, 1730, was occasionally evaded, and to remedy such evasion another Act of Parliament (25 Geo. II. c. 10) was passed in 1752, which provided that from and after 1 May, 1752, no person should buy, take, or receive in the way of purchase, barter, or exchange any wrought or manufactured gold or silver plate from any goldsmith or silversmith or any person working or trading in gold or silver (excepting silver wire and articles not exceed-ing 4 dwt.) not assayed, touched and marked before delivery to the buyer upon pain of forfeiting the value thereof.

The figure of Hibernia was in an oval stamp from the time of its adoption until 1794 (except in one or two instances, where it appears

Its shape varied

in a stamp outlined to the figure). In 1794 the shape of the stamp was changed to an upright parallelogram with clipped or slightly rounded corners, and it so continued until 1810, when it is found in a shield with engrailed top, in which it was continued until 1821. In that and the following years, until 1827, it is again found in an oval stamp. Thenceforward it appeared in stamps of various shapes until 1846, when the stamp was made with parallel sides, invected top, and straight base, with the lower corners hollowed. This form of stamp was continued until 1864 when the octagonal shape was resumed, and has been continued to the present day.

The imposition of the tax on wrought gold and plate was followed Attempts to evade the duty. by a new form of offence, perpetrated with the object of avoiding its payment. In earlier times, the frauds which called for the attention of the wardens of the craft were the adulteration of gold and silver with an undue quantity of alloy. In the reigns of Geo. II. and Geo. III. their attention was directed to the forgery of marks. In the year 1739, " Baldwin Potter, of Mullingar, was indicted for counterfeiting Hall-marks on spoons". In May, 1750, " Kirk Reeves was fined for counterfeiting marks by casting buckles with marks from Dies ". The offence of counterfeiting marks was not, however, stopped by those measures. It appears to have been practised with great persistency, and the omission of the date-letter in numerous instances tended to make detection more difficult.

In view of this persistent forgery of marks in the 18th century, it may possibly be the case that some plate of that period now exists which is fully up to the legal standard, but which may have been made by dishonest goldsmiths, who, by counterfeit marks, defrauded their country of the duty which they ought to have paid.

In August, 1776, Michael Keating, a Dublin goldsmith, was tried for counterfeiting the duty mark. In the course of the trial it was found that *the Commissioners of Revenue had not appointed a mark to be used by* Michael Keating escapes punishment for forging the duty mark—on a technicality—in 1776, *the assay master of the Corporation of Goldsmiths to denote the payment of duty as required by the Act*, and in the result Keating was acquitted. It was not until after the failure of this prosecution that the omission of the Commissioners to appoint a duty mark was made good, as recorded in the goldsmiths' books as follows : " Having received a full certificate that Mr. Thomas Nuttall had been appointed assay master of the Dublin Goldsmiths' Corporation, the commissioners made the proper order and appointed a particular mark (the figure of Hibernia) to be used by him in the future and to be struck on all sterling plate pursuant to the said Act of Parliament ".

Keating did not escape punishment altogether, for in the following

but was
afterwards
punished for
forging the
standard mark.

year—1777—he was tried for counterfeiting the harp crowned (the standard mark), found guilty, sentenced to six months' imprisonment, and fined £50.

The conviction of Michael Keating, however, did not stop the counterfeiting of marks, for we find in the goldsmiths' books the following entries :—

In 1794, "William Gethin, Back Lane, Dublin, Goldsmith, reported for counterfeit marks".

"John Daly, Hoey's Court, Dublin, Goldsmith, for ditto."

What (if any) steps were taken with reference to these two cases does not appear, but it does appear that at this date the shape of the Hibernia and crowned-harp stamps was altered as already described— possibly with the object of more effectually preventing or more readily detecting further forgeries.

Efforts had been made by the Dublin goldsmiths to get the duty repealed. In a petition dated 13 November, 1773, addressed "to the Right Honourable and Honourable the Knights Citizens and Burgesses in Parliament assembled," by "the Master, Wardens, Brethren and Commonality of the Corporation of Goldsmiths, Dublin," and signed by their clerk (J. Robinson), it was alleged that the trade of the city was impeded by it, and in proof, it was stated that whilst for three years before the duty was imposed, plate to the amount of 187,637 oz. was manufactured, during the following three years only 114,783 oz. were made and that a large quantity of plated ware was imported. The duty was, however, not then repealed, and the re-imposition of the duty on plate in England in 1784 probably was the obstacle which prevented its repeal in Ireland until 1890, when it was abolished throughout the United Kingdom.

DUTY MARKS :—(2) THE SOVEREIGN'S HEAD.

Sovereign s
head duty mark
prescribed 1807.

In pursuance of the statute 47 Geo. III. c. 15 (1807)—an Act of Parliament subsequent to the union—it was provided that thenceforward the mark of the Sovereign's head should be stamped on all gold and silver plate wrought in Ireland to denote the payment of duty, assimilating the practice to that of every other assay office then open in the United Kingdom.* The fact that the "Hibernia" stamp had been duly appointed

---

* The precise provisions of the Act so far as they affected the marks, were that "gold and silver wrought in Ireland should be touched and marked with the marks as by law required, as (then) in use, or with such stamp or mark as the Commissioners of Inland Excise should from time to time devise and appoint," and the Commissioners forthwith appointed the Sovereign's head mark to be used to denote the payment of duty.

By the same statute a penalty of £100 was imposed for selling goods not assayed, and it was

as a duty mark in 1776 was ignored, and as by the appointment of the King's-head mark (pursuant to the Act of 1807) it was superseded, it can be regarded now only as a mark pertaining solely to the Dublin Goldsmiths' Company, and of the nature of a "town mark" for Dublin.

The new duty mark having been appointed to be used on and after 10 August, 1807, the date-letter L of that year is consequently found both without and with the head of George III. On the death of the Sovereign, the form of the head was not immediately changed, but after a year or two the head of the succeeding monarch appeared in the duty stamp, facing in the opposite direction to that which preceded it. The shape of the stamp containing the head varied considerably from time to time. For ascertaining the different forms it will be better to consult the following tables, where all are represented, from that of 1807, when the mark was first appointed, down to 1890, when the duty was repealed and the mark denoting its payment disappeared.

(marginal note: Form of the head.)

THE BRITANNIA STANDARD.

The Britannia standard was never in force in Ireland, and no marks peculiar to such standard were ever used there.

(marginal note: Britannia standard never in force in Ireland.)

Makers' marks have been found—(as Sa of 1717-8 in Table V., and Su, of about 1740, represented in the table of supplementary marks on page 619) which appear as if they were composed of the first two letters of the goldsmiths' surnames, as prescribed in England in 1696-7, rather than initials of the Christian and surnames as usual.

THE MARKS ON WROUGHT GOLD.

The marks for wrought gold and silver assayed at Dublin were alike until 1784, when by the Statute 23 and 24 Geo. III. c. 23 (Ireland), two new standards of 20 and 18 carats respectively were added to the old standard for gold, namely 22 carats. From that date the marks for gold 22 carats fine have been continued as before ; the figures 22, however, were added as from 1 June, 1784, to denote its fineness. The marks for gold 20 carats fine are, in addition to the marks which are struck on plate, a plume of feathers (as represented in the last line of Table X) and the figures 20. Gold 20 carats fine is peculiar to Ireland, and not often manufactured there. The marks for gold 18 carats fine are, in

(marginal note: Marks on gold wares assayed in Dublin.)

provided that any person buying plate not marked should forfeit its value, and for forging or transposing marks a penalty of £200 was imposed.

addition to the marks which are struck on plate, a unicorn's head "erased" (as represented in Table XI. at 1867-8) and the figures 18. The harp crowned is omitted in the case of jewelry. In the case of gold work of the lower standards of 15, 12 and 9 carats fine, allowed since 1854, the harp crowned is always omitted, and the several qualities of the gold are distinguished by the figures $\overset{\llcorner}{\cap}$·625, $\overset{\sqcap}{\sqcup}$·5 and $\cap$·375 respectively,* stamped by the assay master. The figures on wrought gold of 22, 20 and 18 carats fine were, by the above statute, required to be in one stamp with the makers' initials, and to be struck by the makers so that the image should be indented below the surface of the work. As a rule the duty mark was not stamped on articles exempt from duty,† but it appears on a watch-case of 18 carat gold in company with three incuse marks (Hibernia, the unicorn's head, and date-letter S for 1814), the crowned harp being absent.‡ The marks are here illustrated :—

Dublin 1814.   Watch-case by Arthur O'Neill :
Mr. Dudley Westropp.

The MARKS ON FOREIGN PLATE assayed at Dublin will be found illustrated on page 27 *ante*.

Tables of marks.

The marks used on Dublin plate from 1638 to 1921 will be found illustrated in the tables on pages 606-18. With reference to the marks generally, it may be mentioned that the relative position of each varied considerably at different times and on different articles. Though the words of the Charter may appear to indicate the use of two marks in one stamp, plus the maker's own mark, they are not so arranged on early examples of plate, where the marks are found to have been struck by separate punches, quite irregularly, and it must not be supposed that the marks occur in a straight row as in the following tables. Not only were

Collocation of marks.

---

* The figures set on their sides represent the number of carats of fine gold in every 24 carats of the alloyed gold in the article marked. The figures set upright represent the proportion (in decimal fractions) of fine gold contained in the amalgam of gold and copper or other alloy of which the several qualities of " gold " are composed. These figures are usually raised in a depressed stamp as illustrated on page 76 *ante*.

† See List of Exemptions on page 73. They are the same in Ireland as in England.

‡ The duty mark also occurs on a silver watch-case of about the same date belonging to Mr. Westropp, from which it seems probable that at that period the duty on such articles was remitted *after* they had been assayed and stamped.

the marks scattered, but there was no apparent rule as to their order, and some of them frequently pointed in different directions. In more recent examples, however, the tendency was to bring all the marks into line, except perhaps that of the maker, which was struck separately; they often appear as neatly arranged as if they had all been struck by one blow on a single punch. The present practice is to impress the *Present practice.* marks on large articles with separate punches; but for small objects one punch containing all the marks, except the maker's, is used.

The marks on a very large number of articles, in addition to those mentioned in the tables, have been examined and impressions taken for the purpose of comparison with the marks illustrated, but the tables being limited in size, repetitions have been largely excluded. Where repetitions appear, they have been included mainly for the purpose of illustrating different examples of makers' marks.

The tables of marks are followed by names of goldsmiths, transcribed *Lists of goldsmiths' names, &c.* from Dublin records dating from about 1200 to 1630. These are followed by lists of the Masters, Wardens, and Freemen of the Dublin Goldsmiths' Company; lists of apprentices with the names of the masters to whom they were bound; lists of Quarter-brothers and journeymen (who were admitted to some of the privileges of the Company without being free brothers); and lists of names of other Irish goldsmiths registered in the books of the Company, with some account of the articles of plate assayed for them—all transcribed from the records of the Goldsmiths' Company. These are supplemented by names of goldsmiths found in other records pertaining to the city of Dublin, and in old directories.

There is not a book or document in the possession of the Dublin *Documents examined.* Goldsmiths' Company which has not been thoroughly examined. Everything of importance in the elucidation of this subject, has been extracted and is set forth either in full or in a tabulated or condensed form, in this and the following chapters.

MARKS ON DUBLIN PLATE.

The dates to which asterisks are affixed, have been *ascertained* to be those of the marks in line with them (see pages 587-9). The date-marks of intervening years cannot be fixed with absolute certainty, but the arrangement set forth in these tables is consistent with ascertained facts.

The names which appear in the maker's-name columns are such as appear to pertain to the marks, but as the earliest existing register of Dublin goldsmiths' marks commences in the year 1765, the evidence connecting the marks with the names is, for the most part, merely circumstantial. See also additional makers' marks, &c., on pages 619-24 *infra*.

TABLE I.

FROM 1638 TO 1658—TWENTY YEARS.

THREE STAMPS AS BELOW: The date-marks being twenty Roman capital letters—A to U.

	HARP CROWNED.	DATE LETTER.	MAKER'S MARK.	MAKER'S NAME.	ARTICLES AND OWNERS.
CHAS. I. 1638-9		A		James Vanderbeck,	Com. flagon, dated 1638: Trinity College, Dublin.
1639-40		B		John Thornton.	Com. cup, dated 1639: Fethard, co. Wexford.
				Edwd. Chadsey.	Com. cup, "ex dono T.B. 1638": St. Finn Barre, Cork.
1640-1	,,	C		John Thornton.	Com. paten: Fethard, co. Wexford.
1641-2	,,	D		Wm. Cooke.	Com. cup: Derry Cathedral.
1642-3		E		... ...	(Date-letter conjectured.)
1643-4		F		... ...	Do. do.
* 1644-5		G		... ...	(Records of the Dublin Goldsmiths' Co.)
* 1645-6		H		... ...	Do. do. do.
* 1646-7		I		John Burke (or John Banister).	Com. paten: Sutton Mandeville, Wilts.
* 1647-8		K		... ...	(Records of the Dublin Goldsmiths' Co.)
* 1648-9		L		... ...	Do. do. do.
COMWTH. 1649-50		M		... .	(Date-letter conjectured.)
1650-1		N		... ...	Do. do.
1651-2		O		... ...	Do. do.
1652-3		P		... ...	Do. do.
1653-4		Q		... ...	Do. do.
1654-5		R		... ...	Do. do.
1655-6		S			Daniel Bellingham.	Spoon slipped in the stalk, fig-shaped bowl: Dublin Museum.†
* 1656-7	,,	T		Joseph Stoaker (or John Slicer).	{ Mace, from Carlow: Dublin Museum. Plain porringer: Noted by Mr. Dudley Westropp.
1657-8		U		... ...	See page 588.

| 1639-40 | | B | | George Gallant. | Slip-topped spoon: National Museum, Dublin. |

† Also spoon slipped in the stalk, oval bowl, by J. Stoker or J. Slicer: National Museum, Dublin.

MARKS ON DUBLIN PLATE.

TABLE II.

FROM 1658 TO 1678—TWENTY YEARS.

THREE STAMPS AS BELOW: The date-marks being twenty small Italic (or Roman) letters—*a* to *u*.

(See also pages 588-9, and notes at head of Table I.)

	HARP CROWNED.	DATE LETTER.	MAKER'S MARK.	MAKER'S NAME.	ARTICLES AND OWNERS.
1658-9		*a*		... ...	(*Date-letter conjectured*).
*1659-60	[harp crowned / crowned V]	*b*	[I S mark] [I S mark]	Joseph Stoaker.† Do. do.	Com. cup and paten : Dromore Cathedral. Do. do. (dated 1659) : St. John's-in-the-Vale, Crosthwaite, Cumb.
CHAS. II. 1660-1		*c*		... ...	(*Date-letter conjectured*.)
1661-2		*d*		... ...	Do. do.
1662-3		*e*		... ...	Do. do.
1663-4	[harp crowned]	*f*	[I S mark]	Joseph Stoaker.†	Alms dish : Kilkenny Cathedral. Double set of communion plate : St. Peter's Drogheda. (See also page 619.)
1664-5	,,	*g*	[A R mark]	Abel Ram.‡	Alms plate : St. Columb's, Kells, co. Meath.
1665-6		*h*		... ...	(*Date-letter conjectured*.)
1666-7		*i*		... .	Do. do.
1667-8		*k*		... ...	Do. do.
1668-9		*l*		... ...	Do. do.
1669-70		*m*		... ...	Do. do.
1670-1		*n*		... ...	Do. do.
1671-2	[harp crowned]	*o*	[I S mark]	Joseph Stoaker.†	Shallow bowl : Messrs. G. Plain tankard, flat top : Messrs. Christie.
1672-3		*p*		... ...	(*Date-letter conjectured*.)
1673-4		*q*		... ...	Do. do.
1674-5		*r*		... ...	Do. do.
1675-6		*s*		... ...	Do. do.
1676-7		*t*		... ...	Do. do.
1677-8		*u*		... ...	Do. do.

* Date-letter recorded.
† Or John Slicer.
‡ Another mark of Abel Ram (of 1663-4) with a ram's head below his monogram, is illustrated in the supplementary table on page 619 *infra*.

MARKS ON DUBLIN PLATE.

TABLE III.

THREE STAMPS AS BELOW: The date-marks being Old English capital letters.

(This and Table IV. comprise one cycle, covering a period of thirty-nine years—1678 to 1717.)

	HARP CROWNED.	DATE LETTER	MAKER'S MARK	MAKER'S NAME.			ARTICLES AND OWNERS.
1678-9		𝕬		...	...	...	(*Date-letter conjectured.*)
1679-80		𝕭	T̆B	Timothy	Blackwood.‡		Large com. flagon: Christ Church Cath'l., Dublin.
			S·M	Samuel	Marsden.		Com. cup and cover: St. Michan's, Dublin.
			I·K	James	Kelly.		Com. cup: St. Audoen's, Dublin.
			AG	Andrew	Gregory.		Pair of com. cups and a flagon: St. Werburgh's, Dublin.
*1680-1		𝕮	"	Do.	do.		Pair of tankards, "*made* 1680": Merchant Taylors' Company, London. (See page 589.)
			IP	John	Phillips.		Com. flagon: St. John's, Limerick.
			WL	Wm. Walter	Lucas or Lewis. }		Alms-dish: St. Werburgh's; and mace: Royal Irish Academy, Dublin.
1681-2	"	𝕯	E·S	Edwd.	Swan.		Two-handled cup: Messrs. G.
1682-3	"	𝕰	I·K	James	Kelly.		Tankard: Messrs. Christie.
1683-4		𝕱		...	...	...	(*Date-letter conjectured.*)
JAS. II. 1685-6-7	"	𝕲	IF	John	Farmer.		Com. cup, dated 1685: St. Werburgh's, Dublin.
			IC	John	Cuthbert.		Com. paten, inscribed " Deo in usum 1693": St. Werburgh's, Dublin.
			RN	Robert	Nevill.		Plain tankard, flat top: Messrs. Christie.
			IH	John	Humphrys.		Com. cup and paten cover: St. Werburgh's, Dublin.
†{ 1688 to 1692		𝕳	DK	David	King.		Chamber candlestick: The Marquess of Sligo.
			RS	Robt.	Smith (warden 1701).		Salver: Mr. Day.
		𝕴		...	...	...	(*Date-letter conjectured.*)
WM. III. 1693-4-5		𝕶	IW	Joseph	Walker.		{ Com. cup, dated 1693: St. Michael's, Dublin. { Altar candlesticks: Trin. Coll., Dublin.
			WD	Wm.	Drayton.		Two com. patens, dated 1693: St. Michan's, Dublin.
			WM	Wm.	Myers.		Com. cup: St. Michael's (now at Christ Church Cathedral), Dublin.
			AS	Ant'ny	Stanley.		Com. cup, dated Jan., 1694-5: Abbeyleix.
			B	Thos.	Bolton.		{ Two-handled cup: Lord Carbery. { Com. cup: Trinity College, Dublin.
1696-9	"	𝕷	IP	John	Phillips.		Two com. flagons, inscribed: "Belongs to New St. Michan's, Dublin, 1698".
			DK	David	King.		Lemon strainer: Messrs. G.
			IW	Joseph	Walker.		Salver, on foot, gadrooned edge: Mr. Dudley Westropp.
			IH	John	Humphrys.		Toilet set: Lord Swaythling.
			A·S	Anth'y	Stanley.		Plain tankard, and chalice dated 1698: Noted by Mr. Dudley Westropp.

* Date-letter ascertained. (See pages 589-91, and note at head of Table I.)

† 1688 to 1692—period of the war troubles. See pages 578-9 and 590.

‡ Timothy Blackwood died 1675, but the W (over the initials) probably indicates " widow," and that the flagon was made while the business was carried on, in Blackwood's name, by his widow.

MARKS ON DUBLIN PLATE. TABLE IV.

THREE STAMPS AS BELOW : The date-marks being Old English capital letters.
(This and Table III. comprise one cycle, covering a period of thirty-nine years, 1678 to 1717.)
In the letterpress of pages 581 to 605 the DATA will be found on which the arrangement of the
marks of this as well as the preceding and succeeding cycles is based.

HARP CROWNED.	DATE LETTER.	MAKER'S MARK.	MAKER'S NAME.	ARTICLES AND OWNERS.
* 1699/1700			Ant'ny Stanley (as 1693-4-5.)	Com. cup, dated 1700 : Abbeyleix.
			Edward Workman.	Rat-tail spoon, flat stem : Holburne Museum, Bath.
1700-1	,,		Alexr. Sinclair.	Cylindrical tankard, flat top : Messrs. G.
* 1701-2			Joseph Walker.	Com. cup, paten and flagon : Christ Ch. Cath'l., Dublin. (D K as 1696-9), The Lifford mace, dated 1701 : Lord Erne.
			Thomas Boulton.	Com. paten, dated 1703 ; St. Mary's, Dublin.
ANNE. * 1702-3			Do. do.	Com. plate dated 1703 : Dromore Cathedral. Com. cup : Trinity College, Dublin.
1703-4	,,	,,	Do. do.	Two-handled cup : Messrs. G. Small bowl : The Day Collection.
1704-5-6			Henry Matthews.	Com. paten, inscribed " New St. Mary's Ch., Dublin 1705 " : St. Mary's, Dublin.
			Joseph Walker.	Alms-dish, dated 1705 : Finglas, co. Dublin. Com. cup, dated 1706 : St. Nicholas (without) Dublin.
1706-7-8			David King.	Communion flagon : Killeshandra.
			Edward Barrett.	Plain two-handled cup : Mr. Arthur Irwin Dasent.
			Thomas Bolton.	Com. cup and paten, dated 1707 : Staplestown, co. Carlow.
1708-9-0	,,	,,	Do. do. (Maker's mark indistinct)	University mace : Trinity Coll., Dublin. Com. plate, dated 1709 : Dromiskin.
1710-1-2			David King. (Maker's mark indistinct)	Com. cup, " given 1713 " : Killeshandra. Com. patens, " given by Dr. Pooley, Bishop of Raphoe, 1712 " : St. Mary's, Dublin.
1712-3-4			Edward Workman.	Two com. flagons and a paten, dated " Dec. 1713 " : St. Mary's, Shandon, Cork.
			Walter Archdall.	Communion cup, dated 1714 ; Rathclaren, co. Cork.
			John Clifton.	Two-handled cup : Mr. John R. Lloyd, Dublin.
GEO I. 1714-5	,,		Wm. Archdall.	Com. cup and paten, two flagons and two alms dishes, dated 1714, from St. Bride's : Irish Church Rep. Body.
1715-6			John Tuite.†	Small tray : Dublin Museum.
			John Cuthbert, jun.	Com. cup, dated 1718 : Clonmeen, Castlemagner, co. Cork.
			Joseph Walker. David King (as 1706 above).	Circular dish, fluted sides : Dublin Museum. Com. flagon, dated 1716 : Killeshandra.
1716-7			... ...	(Date-letter conjectured.)

* Date-letter ascertained, see pages 590-2.
† John Tuite removed to London in 1723, where he afterwards used the same mark : (see page 183 *ante* and footnote on same page). A similar mark is illustrated on page 191. Tuite died in 1740 and the business was continued in London by his widow who used a similar mark, the initial I merely being altered to E (for Eliz.). Her mark is illustrated on page 195.

1703-4   ... ...   Paten : Mr. M. Falk, Dublin.

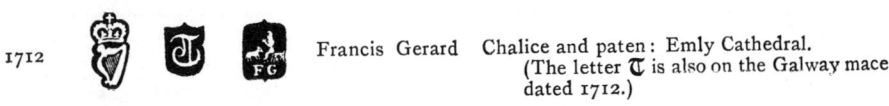

1712   Francis Gerard   Chalice and paten : Emly Cathedral.
(The letter T is also on the Galway mace, dated 1712.)

MARKS ON DUBLIN PLATE.

TABLE V.

THREE STAMPS AS BELOW: The date-marks 1717-20 being Court-hand letters, and from 1720, old English capitals in shields with engrailed tops, the completion of this cycle being illustrated in Table VI.

	HARP CROWNED.	DATE LETTER.	MAKER'S MARK.	MAKER'S NAME.	ARTICLES AND OWNERS.
1717-8				Joseph Walker.	Salver, on foot: Messrs. Christie.
				Christr. Thompson.	Soup ladle: the late Mr. J. R. Garstin, F.S.A.
				Wm. Clarke (of Cork).	Pair of salvers: Messrs. West & Son.
				John Hamilton.	Three-pronged fork: Dublin Museum.
				John Savage ?	Marrow scoop: Messrs. G.
,,		,,		Thos. Parker.	Two-handled cup: Sir J. T. Firbank.
1718-9				Erasm's Cope.	Paten cover of small communion cup: St. Werburgh's, Dublin.
1719-20				Henry Daniell.	Small two-handled cup: Colonel Longfield. / Salver: Messrs. West & Son. / Small salver, on foot: Messrs. G.
				John Clifton, jr.	
,,				John Clifton, sr.	Two-handled cup: Mr. Arthur Irwin Dasent.
1720-1				John Hamilton.	Sauce-boat: Messrs. G.
1721-2				Do. do.	Bishop Crowe's plate: Donoughmore, Cork.
				Thos. Sutton.	Lemon strainer: Mr. John R. Lloyd.
1722-3				John Clifton, sr.	Two-handled cup: Messrs. Sotheby.
				Edwd. Barrett.	Table-spoon: Messrs. G.
1723-4				Robert Harrison.	Gravy-spoon: Mr. H. Davison.
				Thos. Walker.	Two-handled cup: Messrs. West & Son.
				Wm. Duggan.	Paten, at Belfast, noted by Mr. D. Westropp.
1724-5				Thos. Slade.	Small circular tray, scolloped edge: Dublin Museum.
				John Taylor.	Candlesticks: Mr. Frayne and Mr. Ellis.
				Thos. Bolton.	Circular salver: The Day Collection.
1725-6		,,		Mathw. Walker.	Two com. cups: St. Nicholas (now at St. Audoen's), Dublin.
				Michl. Hewitson.	Soup-ladle, noted by Mr. Dudley Westropp.
				Mathw. Walker.	Cup, with two harp-shaped handles: Messrs. G.
1726-7		,,		Noah Vialas.	Lemon strainer: Messrs. G.
				Philip Kinnersly.	Two-handled cup: Messrs. Christie.
GEO. II. *1727-8				Robert Calderwood.	Com. paten, dated 1727: St. Werburgh's, Dublin.
				John King.	Dessert-spoon: The Author's Collection.*
				Wm. Clarke (of Cork).	Small tray : Do. do.
1728-9		,,		John Robinson.	Small two-handled cup: Messrs. G.
				Bolton Cormick.	Small freedom box: Mr. Dudley Westropp.
1729-30				Robert Calderwood.	Small bowl: The Author's Collection.
				John Moore.	Pair of cups: Mr. P. M. Lindsay, Cork.
				Wm. Archdall.	Coffee-pot: Mr. Ball.
1730-1		,,		David King.	Communion paten: St. Ann's, Belfast.

* Also (but with maker's mark T.W., as 1723-4), the Portarlington mace, dated 1728: Goldsmiths' Company, London. See the observations concerning date-letters on pages 592-3.

MARKS ON DUBLIN PLATE.

TABLE VI.

FOUR STAMPS AS BELOW: the date-marks being Old English capital letters in shields with engrailed tops (except one 𝔚 with straight top) in continuation of the cycle commenced 1720. The letter 𝔏 of Table V. is repeated and a new mark (Hibernia) added. See pages 593-4.

	HARP CROWNED.	DATE LETTER.	HIBERNIA.	MAKER'S MARK.	MAKER'S NAME.	ARTICLES AND OWNERS.
1731-2	(harp crowned)	𝔏	(Hibernia)	EF	Esther Forbes.	Rat-tail spoon: Mr. Geo. Lambert.
				EC	Erasmus Cope?	Do. do. : Do. do.
1732-3	,,	𝔐	(Hibernia)	AL	Anthony Lefebure.	Pair of sauce-boats: Messrs. Christie.
				JD	James Douglas.	Waiter on three feet: Mr. J. Dixon.
1733-4	,,	𝔑	,,	WW	Wm. Williamson.	Plain two-handled cup: Colonel Longfield.
				CL	Charles Lemaitre.	Two-handled cup: Mr. Dudley Westropp.
				IT	John Taylor.	Gravy-spoon: Mr. H. Davison.
1734-5	(harp crowned)	𝔒	(Hibernia)	WT	Wm. Townsend.	Salver: Messrs. Christie.
				CL	Chas. Leslie.†	Cake-basket: Messrs. G.
				TW	Thos. Williamson.	Plain cup, harp handles: Do.
1735-6	,,	𝔓	,,	BM	Barth Mosse.	Table-spoon: The Day Collection.
				AB	Alexr. Brown.	Do. : do. do.
1736-7	,,	𝔔	,,	IW	John Williamson.	Large salver and bread-basket: Mr. Frederick L. Fitzgerald.
				IW	John Wilme.	Oval hot-water jug: Lord Swaythling.
				AG	Andrew Goodwin.	Rat-tail spoon: Mr. Dudley Westropp.
				IT	James Taylor.	Perforated spoon: St. Werburgh's, Dublin.
1737-8	,,	𝔕	,,	DK	David King?	Two-handled cup: Messrs. G.; com. paten: Camerton, Cumb.
1738-9	,,	𝔖	,,	SW	Samuel Walker.	Rat-tail spoon: Noted by the Author.
				MW	Matthew Walker.	Table-spoon: Mr. S. Phillips.
1739-40	,,	𝔗	,,	AG	Andrew Goodwin.	Salver: Mr. Harry Alston. / Two-handled cup: Messrs. Hancock.
				FW	Francis Williamson.	Com. cup, dated 1741: Kildare Cath'l.
				JW	John Walker.	Two com. flagons: St. Mary's, Dublin.
1740-1	,,	𝔘	,,	JM	John Moore.	Waiter on three feet: Messrs. G.
				AR	Alexr. Richards.‡	Table-spoon: Mr. H. Davison.
1741-2-3	(harp crowned)	𝔙 𝔚	,,	ID	Isaac D'Olier.	Do. : Mr. E. W. Colt.
			,,	I·L	John Laughlin.	Perforated cover for bowl: Holburne Museum, Bath.
1743-4	,,	𝔛	,,	CL	Christr. Locker.	Two com. flagons, dated 1743: St. Anne's, Belfast.
				RH	Robt. Holmes.	Gravy-spoon: Dublin Museum.
				Let	John Letablere.	Large alms dish: Trin. Coll., Dublin.
1745	,,	𝔜	,,	IW	James Whitthorne.§	Sauce-boat: Messrs. G.; salt on three legs: Mr. D. Westropp.
				M	John Moore.	Table-spoon: Messrs. Crichton.
*1746	,,	𝔷	,,	W	Jas. Whitthorne. (see 1745).§	Mace inscribed "The Gift of the Rt. Honble. James Earl of Kildare to the Borough of Athy Sept. 26th, 1746": The Duke of Leinster.

* See the observations concerning date-letters on pages 593-4.
† Leslie was of Scotch origin. His work was not inferior to that of Paul Lamerie.
‡ The mark of this maker is also found with a pellet between A and R.
§ Probably Jas. Whitthorne (master 1744-5), but possibly John Williamson or John Wilme.

MARKS ON DUBLIN PLATE.

TABLE VII.

FROM 1747 TO 1772 (INCLUSIVE)—TWENTY-SIX YEARS.

FOUR STAMPS AS BELOW: The date-marks being Roman capital letters. See pages 594-5.

	HIBERNIA.	DATE LETTER.	HARP CROWNED.	MAKER'S MARK.	MAKER'S NAME.	ARTICLES AND OWNERS.
*1747		A		[WW]	Wm. Williamson.	Fine com. flagon: St. Nicholas (without) Dublin.
				[CF]	C. Fox.	Soup-ladle: Noted by Mr. Dudley Westropp.
				[WW]	Will. Walsh.	Table-spoon: Dublin Museum.
1748	,,	B	,,	[W·B]	Will. Beates.	Plain table-spoon: Mr. G. Lambert.
				[IC]	John Christie.	Small bowl: Messrs. West & Son.
1749	,,	C		[IL]	John Laughlin.	Table-spoon: Mr. C. D. Oliver (Cork Exhibition).
				[M·B]	Mathias Brown.	Do. : The Day Collection.
1750	,,	D	,,	[ID]	Isaac D'Olier.	Table-spoons: Messrs. West & Son.
1751-2	,,	E		[IP]	John Pittar.	Soup-ladle: Dublin Museum.
				[WR]	William Ring.	Com. cup: Christ Ch. Cath'l., Dublin.
1752-3	,,	F	,,	[MH]	Mich'el Homer.	Table-spoons: Messrs. Debenham & Storr.
1753-4	,,	G	,,	[W·T]	Wm. Townsend.	Small bowl on three feet: Messrs. Christie.
				[AR]	Alexr. Richards.	Gravy-spoon: Messrs. G.
1754-5	,,	H	,,	[CS]	Christr. Skinner.	Table-spoon: Sir E. Marshall-Hall.
1757	,,	I	,,	[A]	Matt'w Alanson.	Sauce-boat: Messrs. G. / Also (1733-4) salver: Mr. Dudley Westropp.
1758	,,	K		[D·P]	Daniel Popkins.	Table-spoons: Mr. R. H. Woods, Dublin.
				[M·S]	(*Not identified.*)	Table-spoon: Cork Exhibition.
1759	,,	L	,,	[SW]	Saml. Walker.	Table-spoon: Col. Longfield.
				[IP]	J'nth'n. Pasley.	Pair of Corinthian candlesticks: Mr. H. D. Ellis.
GEO. III. 1760	,,	M	,,	[R·C]	Robt. Calderwood.	Cup: Messrs. West & Son; dish ring: Messrs. Christie.
1761	,,	N	,,	[GH]	Geo. Hill.	Small tray: Messrs. Vander & Hedges.
				[TJ]	Thos. Johnston.	Pierced cake-basket: Mr. J. R. Garstin, F.S.A.
1762	,,	O		[..]	Do. do.	Small mace: Dublin Corporation.
				[X/A]	Matt'w Alanson.	Table-spoon: Mr. G. Lambert.
1763	,,	P	,,	[DP]	David Peter.	Plain table-spoon: Mr. Dudley Westropp.
1764	,,	Q	,,	[W·C]	Wm. Currie.	Dish ring: Cork Exhibition.
				[WH]	Wm. Homer.	Salver on three feet: Mr. W. Boore.
1765	,,	R	,,	[FI]	Francis Jones.	Pierced ladle, dated 1765: St. Werburgh's, Dublin.
				[IC]	Joseph Cullen.	Table-spoons: Messrs. West & Son.
1766	,,	S	,,	[MC·IL]	M. Cormick & J. Locker.	Gravy-spoon: Mr. J. Talbot Power, Dublin.
				[F&K]	French & Keating.	Table-spoon: Col. Longfield.
1767	,,	T		[JW]	John West.	Goblet: Cork Exhibition.
				[RW]	Richd. Williams.	Fish server: Mr. Michael Frayne.
†1768	,,	U	,,	[R·T]	Richd. Tudor.	Hot-water jug: Messrs. G.
				[ID]	Jer'm'h D'Olier.	Sauce-boat : Do.
1769		W		[J·S]	John Shields.	Table-spoon: Cork Club.
				[IG]	James Graham.	Dish ring: Holburne Museum, Bath.
1770	,,	X	,,	[IL]	John Locker.	Small waiter: Barber Surgeons' Coy.
				[CH]	Christr. Haines.	Sauce-boat: Mr. Webster.
1771	,,	Y		[TK]	Thos. Kinsela.	Dish ring: Col. Claude Cane.
				[IL]	John Lloyd.	Coffee-pot: Mr. Jas. F. Darcy.
1772	,,	Z	,,	[CT]	Chas. Townsend.	Two-handled cups: Messrs. West & Son
				[CM]	Chas. Mullin.	Teapot: The Day Collection.

 The Hibernia stamp of this form was used between 1752 and 1754, as well as the one of oval outline.

* Date-letter A for 1747 recorded in the goldsmiths' books. See page 594.

† The letter U of this cycle is found with the Hibernia stamp in an oval and also in a stamp the outline of which follows the figure, as represented above.

MARKS ON DUBLIN PLATE.

TABLE VIII.

FROM 1773 TO 1796 (INCLUSIVE)—TWENTY-FOUR YEARS.

FOUR STAMPS AS BELOW: The date-marks being Roman capital letters. See pages 594-6.

	HIBER-NIA.	DATE LETTER.	HARP CROWNED.	MAKER'S MARK.	MAKER'S NAME.	ARTICLES AND OWNERS.
1773	(Hibernia)	A	(harp)	JW	John Walker.	Sauce-boat: Messrs. G. / IL as 1771, butter dish: Mr. J. H. Fitzhenry.
				WH	Wm. Hughes.	Dish ring: Colonel Claude Cane.
1774	,,	B	,,	I·C	John Craig.	Table-spoon: Mr. E. Heron-Allen.
				A·B	Ambrose Boxwell.	Two-handled cup: Mr. T. W. Rolleston.
1775	,,	C	,,	R·W	Richd. Williams.	Do. do.: Dublin Museum.
				C·T	Chas. Townsend.	Urn-shaped communion cup: Donoughmore, co. Cork.
1776	,,	D	(harp)	MW	Matthew West.	Salver on three feet: Dublin Museum.
				HA	Hay Andrews.	Candlestick: Mr. Arthur.
1777	,,	E	,,	DK	Darby Kehoe.	Table-spoons: Mr. W. Boore.
				SW	Stephen Walsh.	Bulb-shaped tankard: Messrs. Christie.
1778	,,	F	,,	MH	Michael Homer.	Marrow spoon: The late Mr. J. R. Garstin, F.S.A.
				J·P	John Pittar.	Table-spoon: Mr. E. Heron-Allen.
1779	,,	G	,,	I·I	Jos. Jackson.	Fine pierced dish ring: Mr. Jas. F. Darcy, Dublin.
				M·K	Michael Keating.	Shell-pattern soup-ladle: Lord Wm. Fitzgerald.
1780	,,	H	,,	MW	Michael Walsh.	Pair of candlesticks: Messrs. G.
				J·B	John Bolland.	Salad servers: Colonel Longfield.†
1781	,,	I	,,	I·K	John Kelly.	Table-spoons: Messrs. Crichton.
				I·I	Jos. Jackson.	Dish ring: Col. Claude Cane.
1782	,,	K	,,	T·J	Thomas Jones.	Plate presented 1781: St. Mark's, Dublin.
				W·W	Wm. Ward.	Gravy- and table-spoons: Mr. E. Heron-Allen.
1783	,,	L	,,	HL	John Laughlin, jr.	Dinner plates, gadrooned edges: Messrs. G.
				R·W	Robert Wyke.	Dish ring: Dublin Museum.
1784	,,	M	,,	W·T	Wm. Thompson.	Two-handled cup: Mr. Jas. F. Darcy.
				MW	Matthew Walsh.	Small bowl on three legs: Messrs. G.
1785	,,	N	,,	C·H	Christr. Haines.	Set of four coasters: The late Mr. J. R. Garstin, F.S.A.
				W·S	Wm. Supple.	Two-handled cup: Glasgow Exhibition.
1786	,,	O	,,	W·J	Wm. Johnson.	Cream-jug: Mr. T. L. O'Shaughnessy, K.C.
				L&B	(Not identified.)	Shoe buckles: The Author's Collection.
* 1787	(Hibernia)	P	(harp)	J·P	John Pittar.‡	Table-spoon: The late Mr. J. R. Garstin, F.S.A.
				MW	Matthew West.	Two-handled cup: Do. do.
* 1788	,,	Q	,,	MK	Michael Keating.	Bright cut fork: Sir Robt. H. Woods.
				I·S	John Stoyte.	Wine labels: The Author's Collection.
* 1789	,,	R	,,	WL	Wm. Law.	Bright cut spoons: Messrs. West & Son.
				R·W	Robt. Williams.	Pierced fish slice: The Author's Collection.
1790	,,	S	,,	A·C	Arthur Clark.	Dish ring: Messrs. West & Son.
				O·N	Arthur O'Neill.	Dessert-spoon: The Day Collection.
* 1791	,,	T	,,	B·T	Benjn. Tait.	Gravy-spoon: Mr. Nicholson.
				T·J	Thos. Jones?	Wire cake-basket: Mr. Jas. Talbot Power.
* 1792	,,	U	,,	R·S	Robt. Smith.	Table-spoons: Messrs. Christie.
				WB	Wm. Bond.	Salver on three feet: Messrs. Smith & Rait.
				I·K	James Keating.§	Snuff-box: Mr. T. L. O'Shaughnessy, K.C.
				MK	Michael Keating.	Sauce-ladle: Colonel Longfield.
* 1793	,,	W	,,	J·P	John Power.	Table forks: Lord Carbery.
				GW	George West.	Helmet-shaped cream-jug: The Day Collection.
* 1794	(Hibernia)	X	(harp)	L&B	(Not identified.)	Large table-spoon: Victorian and Albert Museum.
1795	,,	Y	,,	I·L	John Laughlin, jr.	Dish ring: The Earl of Wilton.
				I·E	James England.	Dish ring: The Author's Collection.
* 1796	,,	Z	,,	GW	Geo. Wheatley.	Small teapot: South Kensington Museum.
				FB	Fredk. Buck.	Milk-jug: Dublin Museum.

The date-letters D and G have been found both with and without a pellet in base of shield, which is sometimes rounded.

    * Date-letters recorded, see pages 595-6.

    † The mark of John Bolland also occurs on spoons of 1756.

    ‡ The P of 1787 is also found with the harp crowned as represented at 1776 (above).

    § Also on a pretty little snuff-box of 1795: Sir E. Marshall-Hall.

MARKS ON DUBLIN PLATE.

TABLE IX.

FROM 1797 TO 1820 (INCLUSIVE)—TWENTY-FOUR YEARS.

FOUR STAMPS UNTIL 1807, THENCEFORWARD FIVE, AS BELOW: The date-letters being Roman capitals.

	HIBERNIA.	DATE LETTER.	HARP CROWNED.	MAKER'S MARK.	MAKER'S NAME.	ARTICLES AND OWNERS.
1797		A		J·R	John Rigby.	Salt-spoon : Mr. Cecil C. Woods.
					Geo. West (as 1794.)	Engraved goblet : Mr. W. Boore.
* 1798	,,	B	,,	J·K / JD	John Keene. / John Daly.	Dessert-spoon : The Author's Collection. / Salad servers : Colonel Longfield.
* 1799	,,	C	,,	I·K WEST / IS	James Keating.† / James Scott.	Waiter, on three feet : Mr. Lowe, Chester. / Snuffers tray : The Day Collection.
* 1800	,,	D	,,	J·K / WP	John Kearns. / Walter Peter.	Bright cut tea-spoons : Do. / Gold watch-case : Mr. Reed.
* 1801	,,	E	,,	IC / JP	Jas. Connor. / John Power.	Milk-jug : Mr. Goldman. / Plain table-spoon : Mr. Cecil C. Woods.
* 1802	,,	F	,,	RS / WH	Richd. Sawyer. / Wm. Hamey.	Teapot : Messrs. R. & W. Sorley. / Sugar tongs : Messrs. Mackay & Chisholm.
* 1803	,,	G	,,	O AN / IB	Arthur O'Neil. / J. Brady.	Coffee-pot, noted by the late Mr. R. Day, F.S.A. / Bright-cut spoons : Mr. D. Westropp.
* 1804	,,	H	,,	RB / DE	Robt. Breading. / Danl. Egan.	Teapot : West & Son ; sugar bowl : Dub. Mus. / Helmet-shaped sugar-bowl : Cork Exhibition.
* 1805	,,	I	,,	W·D / DM	Wm. Doyle. / (Not identified.)	Snuffers tray : Mr. M. Falk. / Milk-jug : Do.
* 1806	,,	K	,,	S·N / T&W / W·W	Samuel Neville. / Tudor & Whitford. / Wm. Ward.	Dessert-spoon : The late Mr. J. R. Garstin, F.S.A. / Table-spoon : Do. do. do. / Table-forks : Colonel Longfield.
* 1807	,,	L	,, KING'S HEAD.	GB	Gust'v's Byrne.	Teapot stand : Mr. J. Talbot Power.
‡ 1808	,,	M	,, ,,	C·T I·W / SN	Terry & Williams (of Cork). / Saml. Neville.	Snuffers tray : Mrs. Annie Lindsay. / Soup ladle : Mr. Cecil C. Woods.
‡ 1809	,,	N N	,,	JJ / RB	Joseph Johnson. / Robt. Breading.	Cream ewer : Do. do. / Pierced fish slice : Dublin Museum.
1810		O O		,, I·L·B / T·R	Jas. Le Bass. / (Not identified.)	Com. cups : St. Mark's, Dub.; goblet : Mr. Boore. / Table-spoons : Messrs. G.
1811	,,	P	,,	,, C·S / W·N	Chas. Stewart. / W. Nowlan.	Watch-case : Mr. M. Halkett. / Snuff-box : Do.
1812	,,	Q	,,	,, HAMY R·S / PM	W. Hamy & R. Smith. / P. Moore.	Table-forks : Mr. Lowe, Chester. / Mustard-pot : Messrs. Crichton.
§ 1813	,,	R	,,	,, WR / J·P	Wm. Rose. / John Pittar.	Teapot : Lord Carbery. / Table-spoon : The Day Collection.
* 1814	,,	S	,,	,, I·S / LAW / I·N	Jas. Scott. / Wm. Law. / John Nicklin.	Set of skewers : Messrs. G. / Butter cooler : The Day Collection. / Bread fork : Messrs. G.
1815	,,	T	,,	,, PG / SB	Phineas Garde (Cork). / S. Bergin.	Table-spoon : Cork Club. / Egg-spoons : Mr. Cecil Woods.
1816	,,	U	,,	,, DE / RC	Danl. Egan. / Randall Cashell.	Three patens, on feet : St. Werburgh's, Dublin. / Two-handled cup : Messrs. R. & W. Sorley.
1817	,,	W	,,	,, J·M / WC / NWB	James Moore. / W. Cummins. / Sir N. W. Brady.	Snuffers tray : Mr. Winstone. / Table-spoons : Mr. Cecil Woods. / Candlesticks : Messrs. M. & S. Lyon.
1818	,,	X	,,	,, T·R / I·B	T. Read. / J. Buckton.	Mustard-spoon : Messrs. Crichton. / Snuff-box : Mr. M. Falk.
1819	,,	Y	,,	,, I·L·B / I·F WEST	Jas. Le Bass. / Jas. Fry.†	Tripod dish stand : Dublin Museum. / Alms dish : Trinity College, Dublin.
GEO. IV. 1820	,,	Z	,,	,, JS / EM	J. Salter (Cork). / Edwd. Murray.	Table-spoon : Mr. Lannon. / Milk-jug : Mr. Bruford.

* Date-letters recorded, see pages 595-7.
† Made for Alderman West by J. Keating and J. Fry respectively.
‡ All the marks for 1808 and 1809 are frequently found in square stamps with rounded corners.
§ The R is fixed as the date-letter for 1813 by the "Masonic Cup" at Limerick, which was ordered in February, 1813, and *made* within the following three months.

MARKS ON DUBLIN PLATE.

TABLE X.

FROM JANUARY, 1821, TO JUNE, 1846—TWENTY-FIVE AND A HALF YEARS.

FIVE STAMPS AS BELOW: The date-marks being Roman capital letters (with an additional letter є, as to which see page 597); every mark and its date being recorded from 1821 onwards.

Year	Date Letter	Maker's Mark	Maker's Name		Articles and Owners
*1821	A	MW&S	M.	West & Sons.	Table forks: Messrs. Waterhouse.*
		WM	Wm.	Morgan.	Cream-jug: Messrs. Wilson & Sharp.
		EC	E.	Crofton.	Teapot: Mr. M. Falk.
1822	B	I·B	J.	Buckton.	Four salts: Messrs. Mackay & Chisholm.
		LAW	Wm.	Law.	Tea-spoons: Do. do.
1823	C	EP	Edwd.	Power.	Do. : Mr. Cecil Woods.
		IF	Jas.	Fray.	Paten on foot: St. Mark's, Dublin.
1824	D	SN	Saml.	Neville.	Straining spoon: Do. do.
		SB	Saml.	Beere.	Fruit knife: Mr. Cecil C. Woods.
1825-6	E є	WT	Wm.	Teare.?	Table-spoon: Do.
		R·G	Richd.	Garde (Cork).	Fish slice: Cork Club.
1826-7	F	W&Cº	Ald'm'n	West (& Co.).	Table forks: Mr. Cecil C. Woods.
		J·S	J.	Smith.	Salt-spoon: Do.
1827-8	G	CM	Chas.	Marsh.	Fish slice: The late Mr. J. R. Garstin, F.S.A.
		I·R	J.	Read.	Snuff-box: Messrs. Spink.
1828-9	H	TWY†	Edwd.	Twycross.	Com. flagon, dated 1829: St. Mark's, Dublin.
		HF	Hy.	Flavelle.	Memorial trowel: Messrs. Debenham & Storr.
		LN	L.	Nowlan.	Tea-spoons: Cork Club.
1829-30	I I	C·M	Chas.	Marsh.	Do. : Do.
WM. IV.		& M·G	D. W.	Moulang & Gibson.	Wine labels: Mr. Jones, Long Acre.
1830-1	K	S&G	Smith & Gamble.		Jewel-box: Messrs. G.
		E·J	Edmd.	Johnson.	Large ewer: Mr. W. Boore.
1831-2	L	R·S	Richd.	Sawyer, jr.	Oval teapot: Messrs. West & Son.
		TF	T.	Farnett.	Oval salt-cellar: Do.
1832-3	M	PM	P.	Moore.	Candlestick: Messrs. Christie.
		HF	Hy.	Flavelle.	Small strainer: Mr. Chappell.
1833-4	N N	TM	Thos.	Meade.	Dessert-spoon: Mr. Michael Falk.
		EJ	Edmd.	Johnson.	Salver: Messrs. Christie.
1834-5	O O	LN	L.	Nowlan?	Tea-spoons: Cork Club.
		WS	Wm.	Sherwin.	Cream-jug: Mr. W. Boore.
1835-6	P P	PW	P.	Weeks?	Fish slice: Mr. M. Falk.
		I·M	J.	Moore.	Table-spoon: Messrs. Debenham & Storr.
1836-7	Q Q	WS	Wm.	Sherwin.	Tea-spoons: Mr. Cecil C. Woods.
		R·G	Richd.	Garde (Cork).	Punch ladle: Cork Club.
VICT. 1837-8	R R	IL	Josiah	Low.	Table-spoons: Mr. Chisholm.
		S&G	Smith & Gamble.		Small inkstand: Messrs. Spink.
1838-9	S	H&F	Hughes & Francis.		Sauce tureen: Messrs. Dobson.
1839-40	T	PW	Peter	Walsh.	Salt-spoon: Messrs. M. & S. Lyon.
1840-1	U U	E&JJ	E. & J.	Johnson.	Sauce-boat: Messrs. Christie.
		LN	L.	Nowlan.	Toilet fittings: Mr. M. Falk.
1841-2	V	GA	G.	Alcock.	Large teapot: Messrs. M. & S. Lyon.
1842-3	W	IW	John	Warren.	Small cruet: Mr. M. Falk.
		I·L·B	Jas.	Le Bass.	Plate, dated 1483: St. Werburgh's, Dublin.
1843-4	X	IF	J.	Francis.	Mount of ivory paper-knife: Messrs. Sotheby.
		GW	Geo.	West?	Salt-spoon: Mr. Goldman.
1844-5	Y	MN	Michl.	Nowlan.	Whisky label: Mr. B. Jefferis.
1845-6	Z	JG	J.	Gamble.	Small waiter: Mr. Ince.
		JJ20	‡ Joseph Johnson.		Gold rim of agate snuff-box: Messrs. Debenham.

* The duty stamp with the head of Geo. IV. was made in Feb., 1821. The letter A of that year is found with head as 1821 and as 1822. Mr. Garstin had an egg-spoon, of 1821 (maker's mark WC as 1817), with the King's head as 1822.

† Letter changed from E to є Sept., 1825 (the reverse of what is stated in *Old English Plate*).

‡ The plume of feathers and 20 indicate gold 20 carats fine, a standard peculiar to Ireland. The date-marks on gold and silver are alike (see page 603).

The shields for Hibernia, and the harp crowned, have, in examples of the year 1823, been found like those illustrated at 1810 in Table IX. The Hibernia for 1834-5 has also been found in a plain rectangular shield, while the harp for the same year has been found in an oval shield.

MARKS ON DUBLIN PLATE.

TABLE XI.

FROM JUNE, 1846, TO JUNE, 1871—TWENTY-FIVE YEARS.

FIVE STAMPS AS BELOW : The date-marks being small Roman letters (except Q and Y—large).

	HIBER-NIA.	DATE LETTER.	HARP CROWNED.	QUEEN'S HEAD.	MAKER'S MARK.	MAKER'S NAME.	ARTICLES AND OWNERS.
1846-7	(mark)	a	(mark)	(mark)	JJ	Joseph Johnson.	Salt cellars : General Meyrick.
1847-8	,,	b	,,	,,	J·M / TM	J. Mahoney. / Thos. Mason.	Small spirit flask : Mr. W. Boore. / Sugar tongs : Messrs. Robinson & Fisher.
1848-9	,,	c	,,	,,	CC / WL / RS	C. Cummins, jr. / Wm. Lawson. / R. Samuel.	Child's coral : Mr. Skinner. / Cheese scoop : Messrs. Debenham & Storr. / Watch-case : Mr. T. H. Priest.
1849-50	,,	d	,,	,,	D&W	Donegan & Co.	Ink-stand : Mr. J. L. Propert.
1850-1	,,	e	,,	,,	JG / HF	J. Gamble. / Henry Flavelle.	Asparagus tongs : Mr. D. Keys. / Mounts of scent bottle : Mrs. Murray.
1851-2	,,	f f	,,	,,	IN / AC	Joseph Needham. / Ann Cummins.	Sauce-ladle : Lord Dormer. / Sugar scoop : Mr. G. Lowe.
1852-3	,,	g g	,,	,,	GARDNER / JS	— Gardner. / J. Smyth.	Lady's card-case : Mrs. O'Gorman. / Dessert-spoon : Cork Club.
1853-4	,,	h h	,,	,,	RS / T&W	R. Sherwin. / *Topham & White.	Mace : College of Surgeons, Dublin. / 22 carat gold locket : Mr. J. Barry.
1854-5	,,	j	,,	,,	M·K	Michael Keating.	Toast rack : Mrs. Du Pasquier.
1855-6	,,	k	,,	,,	CC	C. Cummins.	Small trowel-shaped fish slice : Mr. J. M. de Gumacio.
1856-7	,,	l	,,	,,	W·A	W. Atcheson.	Pair of salad servers : Messrs. Christie.
1857-8	,,	m	,,	,,	D&W / AJ	*Donegan & Co. / Arthur Johnson.	22 carat gold matchbox : Do. / Engraved bowl : Messrs. M. & S. Lyon.
1858-9	,,	n	,,	,,	J.R.N / NEILL	†J. R. Neill. / Do. do.	15 carat gold locket : Mrs. Corrigan. / Engraved cups : Mr. J. Darcy.
1859-60	,,	o	,,	,,	S·LB	Samuel Le Bass.	(Maker's mark registered 15 Dec., 1859.)
1860-1	,,	p	,,	,,	WP / W&IP	Wm. Percival. / W. & I. Percival.	(Do. do. do. 17 Jan., 1860.) / (Do. do. do. do.)
1861-2	,,	Q	,,	,,	EP	E. Powell.	(Do. do. do. 2 May, 1861.)
1862-3	,,	r	,,	,,	JK / EJ·JJ	J. Keating. / E. & J. Johnson.	(Do. do. do. 1 Aug., 1861.) / Plate : Edmond Johnson & Joseph Johnson.
1863-4	,,	s	,,	,,	JS	John Smyth.	Grape scissors : Mr. Lane.
1864-5	(mark)	t	,,	,,	IS / RYAN&CO	J. Scriber. / Ryan & Co.	Sugar sifter : Mr. John Wells. / 22 carat gold locket : Mr. Coltman.
1865-6	,,	u	,,	,,	I·W / WATERHOUSE / FM	Jas. West. / Waterhouse & Co. / Francis Martin.	Engraved chatelaine hook : Miss Doherty. / Table plate : Messrs. Waterhouse & Co. / (Maker's mark registered 12 Jan., 1862.)
1866-7	,,	v	,,	,,	AH / BRUNKER DUBLIN	A. Hutton. / Thos. Brunker.	(Do. do. do. 4 Oct., 1864.) / (Do. do. do. 18 March, 1865.)
1867-8	,,	w	,,	(mark)	PD / WL	§Patk. Donegan. / §Wm. Lawson.	On gold work 18 carats fine. / Do. do. do.
1868-9	,,	x	,,	,,	EJ / MT	§Edmd. Johnson, jr. / §Mars. Trench.	Do. do. do. / Do. do. do.
1869-70	,,	Y	,,	,,	WL	§Wm. Lawson.	Do. do. do.
1870-1	,,	Z	,,	,,	TDB	§T. D. Bryce.	Do. do. do.

* The figures 22 are stamped in addition, indicating the fineness of the gold.   See page 603.

† Crowned harp omitted, and the figures 15 added.

§ On gold wares liable to duty the Sovereign's head also appeared until the repeal of the duty in 1890.   These marks were, however, transcribed from articles exempt from duty and therefore bore no duty-mark.   The number of carats fine is also indicated in figures.   On jewelry, neither the crowned harp nor the Sovereign's head appears.   The date-marks on gold and silver are alike.   See pages 603-4.

MARKS ON DUBLIN PLATE.

TABLE XII.

FROM JUNE, 1871, TO JUNE, 1896—TWENTY-FIVE YEARS.

FIVE STAMPS TILL 1890, THENCEFORWARD FOUR, AS BELOW : The date-marks being plain block letters in plain shields.

	HIBERNIA.	DATE LETTER	HARP CROWNED.	QUEEN'S HEAD.	MAKER'S MARK.	MAKER'S NAME AND DATE OF REGISTRATION OF MARK.	
1871-2	●	A	●	●	J·W W&R	J. Weir	Wickham. & Rogers.	(1871). ,,
1872-3	,,	B	,,	,,	J·D	John	Donegan.	(1872).
1873-4	,,	C	,,	,,	EGAN CORK	Wm.	Egan & Son (of Cork).	,,
1874-5	,,	D	,,	,,	IC	Ignatius	Cummins.	(1874).
1875-6	,,	E	,,	,,	McD.BS	McDowell	Bros.	(1875).
1876-7	,,	F	,,	,,	M'DB	Do.	do.	,,
1877-8	,,	G	,,	,,	W&S	West	& Son.	(1877).
1878-9	,,	H	,,	,,	JR	J.	Redmond.	(1876).
1879-80	,,	I	,,	,,	W&S	West	& Son.	(1879).
1880-1	,,	K	,,	,,	OC &D	O'Connor	& Dillon.	(1880).
1881-2	,,	L	,,	,,	E.JOHNSON E.J	Edmond Do.	Johnson. do.	(1881). (1882).
1882-3	,,	M	,,	,,	W.C H.H	Wm. Henry	Carty. Hopkins.	(1881). (1883).
1883-4	,,	N	,,	,,	DM	Danl.	Moulang.	,,
1884-5	,,	O	,,	,,	W&L	Winder	& Lamb.	,,
1885-6	,,	P	,,	,,	F.B.S	Frengley	Bros.	(1885).
1886-7	,,	Q	,,	,,	A&Cº	Austin	& Co.	(1886).
1887-8	,,	R	,,	,,	MA J.E.P	M. Jas. E.	Anderson. Pim.	(1887). ,,
1888-9	,,	S		,,	TB F·H	Thomas Fredk.	Barton. Hill.	(1871). (1889).
1889-90	,,	T	,,	,,	WQ J·F	Wm. Joseph	Quinlan. Fray.	(1888). (1889).
1890-1	,,	U	,,		HLS	Henry L.	Stewart (of Limerick).	,,
1891-2	,,	V	,,		S·D·NEILL	Sharman D.	Neill (of Belfast).	(1890).
1892-3	,,	W	,,		H&H MOSLEY	Hopkins Jas.	& Hopkins. Mosley (Waterford).	(1883). (1892).
1893-4	,,	X	,,		CH E.J	C. Edmond	Harris (Coventry). Johnson.	(1893). ,,
1894-5	,,	Y	,,		C.H.L K&G	Chas. Howard Lawson. Kane	& Gunning	(1894). ,,
1895-6	,,	Z	,,		R·D C.L C&S	Richard Charles Chancellor	Dillon (Waterford). Lamb. & Son.	(1893). (1895).

MARKS ON DUBLIN PLATE.

TABLE XIII.

FOUR STAMPS AS BELOW.

	HIBER-NIA.	DATE LETTER.	HARP CROWNED.	MAKER'S MARK.	MAKER'S NAME AND DATE OF REGISTRATION OF MARK.		
1896-7		A		R&W / J·M	Richards & Walsh. / John Morton.		(1895). / (1896).
1897-8	,,	B	,,	G LTD	Gibson, Ltd. (Belfast).		(1897).
1898-9	,,	C	,,	R K / M&C / R V	Robert Knaggs. / Moore & Co. / Robert Valentine.		(1898). / ,, / ,,
1899 / 1900	,,	D	,,	W J G / LAWSON DUBLIN	W. J. Gethings. / Chas. Howard Lawson.		,, / (1900).
1900-1	,,	E	,,	L AW	Langley Archer West.		,,
EDW. VII. / 1901-2	,,	F	,,	H&T / M^cC&D	Henderson & Thompson (Belfast). / McCutcheon & Donaldson (Belfast).		,, / (1901).
1902-3	,,	G	,,	& W S	West & Son.		(1902).
1903-4		H		JEB	J. E. Byrne (Belfast).		(1909).
1904-5	,,	I	,,	JAMESON	——— Jameson.		,,
1905-6	,,	K	,,	R LTD	Russell Ltd. (Manchester).		,,
1906-7	,,	L	,,	A. DUFFNER TIPPERARY	A. Duffner (Tipperary).		(1907).
1907-8	,,	M	,,	F S LD	Finnegans Ltd. (Manchester).		(1912).
1908-9	,,	N	,,	E&C	Elkington & Co. (Birmingham).		,,
1909-10	,,	O	,,	W.E&SNS LTD	W. Egan & Sons (Cork).		(1910).
1910-1	,,	P	,,	N	——— Neill (Belfast).		(1906).
1911-2	,,	Q	,,	Y. A.M W	Youghal Art Metal Works Co.		,,
1912-3	,,	R	,,	FALLER.GALWAY	——— Faller (Galway).		,,
1913-4	,,	S	,,	J McD	J. McDowell.		,,
1914-5	,,	T	,,	C.CROMER LIMERICK	C. Cromer (Limerick).		(1907).
1915-6	,,	U	,,	& W W	Wakeley & Wheeler (London).		(1909).

TABLE XIV.—FOUR STAMPS AS BELOW.

	HIBER-NIA.	DATE LETTER.	HARP CROWNED.	MAKER'S MARK.	MAKER'S NAME AND DATE OF REGISTRATION OF MARK.		
1916-7		A		W·S	Will Stokes.		(1910).
1917-8	,,	b	,,	WALDRON SKIBBEREEN	M. Waldron (Skibbereen).		,,
1918-9	,,	C	,,	JR	Jas. Ramsay (Dundee).		(1912).
1919-20	,,	D	,,	R S	R. Sharman.		(1908).
1920-1	,,	e	,,	LAC	Crichton Bros. (London).		(1912).

MARKS ON DUBLIN PLATE.

SUPPLEMENTARY MARKS.

DATE.	MARKS.	MAKER'S NAME.	ARTICLES AND OWNERS.
1663-4		Abel Ram.	Spoon, with flat stem, trefoil end: National Museum, Dublin.
1708-10		Philip Tough.	Cylindrical tankard, domed top: Mr. Nyburg.
1715-6		Wm. Archdall.	Small salver: Mr. Arthur Irwin Dasent.
1731		——— Sutton?	Tankard: Noted by Mr. Dudley Westropp.
1739		Robert Holmes.*	Table-spoon, Hanoverian pattern: Mr. Dudley Westropp.
1740		Will. Walsh.	Do. do.: Do. do.
		Jane Daniell.†	Salver: Mr. Arthur Irwin Dasent.
,,	,, ,, ,,	——— Sutton?	{ Sauce boat, with date-letter as in Table VI.: Mr. Dudley Westropp.
c. 1750			{ No date letter (but date about 1750), Paten: Donabate. The communion cup pertaining to it is dated 1751. Also on soup ladle with D for 1750: Noted by Mr. Dudley Westropp.

* Or Robert Hunter.   † Widow of Henry Daniell.

The five goldsmiths' marks illustrated below are copied from the Dublin Assay Office book, in which they appear at the date set opposite each respectively.

1660	Æ	Andrew Edwards.	1704	IG	John Garrett.
1704	AⱯ	Abraham Voisin.	,,	IW	James Walker.
,,	RS	Robert Smith.			

For MARKS ON WROUGHT GOLD, see page 603 *ante*.

For MARKS ON FOREIGN PLATE assayed at Dublin, see page 27 *ante*.

SUPPLEMENTARY LIST OF MARKS OF GOLDSMITHS,

impressed at Dublin but not illustrated in the preceding tables.

DATE.	MARK.	MAKER'S NAME.	ARTICLES AND OWNERS.	DATE.	MARK.	MAKER'S NAME.	ARTICLES AND OWNERS.
1636		John Woodcocke.	Com. cup: Parsonstown.	1706		Thos. Bolton.	Hexagonal teapot: Lord Oranmore.
1663-4		Francis Coffee or Clifton.	Noted by Mr. Dudley Westropp.	1710		Henry Sherwin.	Mounts of coco-nut bowl: Noted by Author.
1679		Edward Swan.	Chalice: Miltown Collection.	1710-2		Thos. Bolton?	Chalice: Noted by Mr. Dudley Westropp.
1680		„ „	Large ladle and cup: Noted by Mr. Dudley Westropp.	„		J. Pennyfather or J. Palet?	Harp-handled cup: Noted by Mr. Dudley Westropp.
„		Lawrence Salmon.	Hilt of sword: The Marquess of Sligo.	1712-4		... ...	Chalice: Noted by Mr. Dudley Westropp.
„		John Seager.	Octagonal box: Messrs. Crichton.				
1685		John Phillips.	Noted by Mr. Dudley Westropp.	1715		Geo. Smart.	Toy porringer: Noted by Mr. D. Westropp.
1685-7		John Cuthbert.	Tankard: Noted by Mr. Dudley Westropp.	„		Ed. Dowdall.	Chalice: Pro. Cath'l., Dublin.
1696-7		(*Not identified*.)	Cruet stand: Noted by Mr. Dudley Westropp.	1715-6		Mark Twelves.	Cup: Messrs. Crichton.
1698		A. Stanley?	Chalice, dated 1698: Noted by Mr. Dudley Westropp.	1716-7		... ...	Porringer: Messrs. Crichton.
1699		Cyriac Mallory.	Six transitional spoons: Mr. H. S. Guiness.	1717-8		W. Bell.	Teapot: Messrs. Crichton.
„		George Lyng.	Sugar caster: Noted by Mr. Dudley Westropp.	1718-9		Thos. Walker.	Oval dish: Mr. Day.
1700		Alexr. Mackay.	Salver: Noted by Mr. Dudley Westropp.	1719-20		Arthur Weldon.	Two-handled cup: Noted by Mr. Dud. Westropp.
1701-2		Thos. Sumpner.	Candlestick: Noted by Mr. Dudley Westropp.	1720		Thos. Racine.	Rat-tail ladle: Noted by Author.
„		... ...	Paten: Noted by Mr. Dudley Westropp.	1722-3		Ed. Fitzgerald.	Forks: Messrs. Crichton.
1702-3		Edward Barrett.	Beaker: Noted by Mr. Dudley Westropp.	1723-4		... ...	Rat-tail spoon: Noted by the Author.
„		Thos. Hartwell.	Cup: Messrs. Tessier.	1724-5		Phillip Kinnersly.	Saucer: Mr. Dudley Westropp.
1703-4		... ...	Sugar caster: Messrs. Crichton.	1725-6		John Sale.	Waiter: Messrs. Crichton.
„		David King.	Do. do.	„		Robt. Pilkington.	Chalice: noted by Mr. Dudley Westropp.
1706		Robt. Forbes.	Spoon: Noted by Mr. Dudley Westropp.	„		Matt. Copeland.	Cup: Messrs. Crichton.

SUPPLEMENTARY LIST OF MARKS OF GOLDSMITHS—*Continued.*

DATE.	MARK.	NAME OF MAKER.	ARTICLES AND OWNERS.	DATE.	MARK.	NAME OF MAKER.	ARTICLES AND OWNERS.
1725-6		Mary Barrett.	Fork: Mr. Dudley Westropp.	1737-8		Thos. de Limarest.	Punch ladle: Mr. S. Phillips.
,,		Thos. Wheeler.	Gold watch-case: Mr. Dudley Westropp.	1740-1		Peter Desenard.	Mug: Noted by Mr. Dudley Westropp.
1726-7		Peter Racine.	Harp-handled cup: Messrs. Crichton.	,,		... ...	Table-spoon: Mr. Dudley Westropp.
				,,		Jas. Champion ?	Soup ladle: Mr. Dudley Westropp.
1728-9		... ...	Mug: Noted by Mr. Dudley Westropp.	,,		... ...	Mug: do. do.
1729		Esther Forbes.	Small tazza: Messrs. Spink.	,,		John Letablere.	Waiter: Mr. Lambert.
,,		Thos. Sutton.	Two-handled cup: Messrs. Crichton.	,,		Thos. Burton.	Salt-cellars: Messrs. Crichton.
				,,		Thos. Sutton.	Bowl: Noted by the Author.
1730-1		George Cross.	Mug: Mr. Dudley Westropp.	c. 1740		? Henry Jago.	With harp and Hibernia, but no date-letter.
,,		Geo. Cartwright.	Rat-tail spoons: Mr. Dudley Westropp.	1743-4		Wm. Bonynge.	Waiter: Messrs. Garrard.
,,		Dorothy Monjoy.	Bowl: Sir J. Nutting.	,,		Robt. Calderwood.	Cup: Messrs. Comyns.
1731		Matthew Alanson.	Ribbed table-spoon: Sir E. Marshall-Hall, K.C.	1745		George Beere.	Bowl: Messrs. Crichton.
				,,		Robt. Glanville.	Do. : Mr. Veitch.
1732-3		Erasmus Cope.	Two-handled cup: The Marquess of Sligo.	1746		John Hamilton ?	Plain cup: Mr. E. W. Colt.
1734		John Gumly.	Waiter: Messrs. West.	,,		Wm. Faucett ?	Gravy-spoon: Mr. Dudley Westropp.
1735		Isaac D'Olier.	Marrow scoop: Mr. A. J. L. Grimes.	,,		Bart'mew Stokes.	Candlesticks: Messrs. Crichton.
1736-7		Thos. Maculla ?	Two-handled cup: Mr. Dudley Westropp.	,,		Wm. Walsh.	Six table-spoons: Sir E. Marshall-Hall.
,,		Anthony Lefebure.	Sauce-boat: Messrs. Welby.	c. 1750		Joseph Taafe.	Marrow scoop: Mr. Dudley Westropp.
,,		Ralph Woodhouse.	Soup ladle: Messrs. Crichton.	1751		Nathan Murray.	Spoon: Mr. Dudley Westropp.
,,		... ...	Noted by the Author.	,,		J. Pittar.	Soup ladle: Dublin Museum.
1737-8		John Freebough.	Trencher salt: Messrs. Carrington.	,,		Wm. Betagh.	Soup ladle: Noted by the Author.

SUPPLEMENTARY LIST OF MARKS OF GOLDSMITHS—*Continued.*

DATE.	MARK.	MAKER'S NAME.	ARTICLES AND OWNERS.	DATE.	MARK	MAKER'S NAME.	ARTICLES AND OWNERS.
1752	E R	Edward Raper.	Noted by the Author.	1780	HO	Hugh O'Hanlon or Owen Hart?	Cream-jug: The Day Collection.
1754	R+C	Robt. Calderwood or Cope.	Dish ring: Do.	c. 1780	O·C	Owen Cassidy.	Sugar tongs: Mr. D. Lane.
"	H★W	Hy. Waldron.	Spoon-tray: Mr. Dudley Westropp.	"	A B	Alex. Barry?	Noted by Mr. Dudley Westropp.
1757	M·F	Michael Fowler.	Large jug: Mr. Dudley Westropp.	1780-5	B D	Barnaby Dela-hoyde?	Spoons: Mr. Dudley Westropp.
1758	WW	Wm. Williamson.	Salver: Mr. Hurman.	1785	D·E	Dan. Egan?	Processional cross: Mr· Dudley Westropp.
"	CS	Christr. Skinner.	Table-spoons: Mr. W. H. Willson.	1792	MH	Michael Homer?	Teapot stand: Mr. Bond.
c. 1760	H★W	See 1754 above.	Sugar-bowl: Mr. Dudley Westropp.	1795	JASK	J. R. Ash.	O.E. pattern spoons: Noted by the Author.
1762	I·M	John Moore, Jr.	Cream-jug: Messrs. Crichton.	c. 1795	I·W	... ...	Tea-spoons: Mr. Dudley Westropp.
1764	I D	John Dawson.	Sauce-boat: Messrs. Garrard.	c. 1797	TT	Thos. Tudor.	Caddy spoon: Noted by Mr. Dudley Westropp.
"	FI	... ...	Spoon: Mr. Dudley Westropp.	1798	IB	John Brooks?	Dessert-spoons: Messrs. Crichton.
1766	RV	Ralph Vizard?	Sauce - boat: Mr. Dudley Westropp.	1800	S·T	Saml. Teare.	Sleeve links: Noted by Mr. Dudley Westropp.
1767	W★F	Wm. French.	Spoon: Mr. Dudley Westropp.	1800-1	JB	John Bolland.	Dinner forks: Noted by Mr. D. Westropp.
c. 1767	WT	Wm. Townsend.	Sweet dishes: Messrs. Crichton.	"	G&PW	... ...	Bowl: Do. do.
1768	JW	Jno. Williamson.	Salver: Noted by Mr. Dudley Westropp.	1802	JD	John Daly?	Spoons: Do. do.
"	B·W	Benj. Wilson.	Table-spoon: Messrs. Welby.	1807	C&W	Clarke & West.	Spoons: Do. do.
"	A·T	Abraham Tuppy.	Table-spoon: Messrs. Welby.	"	ÆR	Æneas Ryan.	Snuff-box: Heming & Co.
1769	W·T MC	... ...	Chalice dated 1769: Noted by Mr. Dudley Westropp.	1810	RS	Richard Sawyer.	Fish knives: Mr. Dudley Westropp.
"	GH	George Hall.	Cream-jug: Messrs. Crichton.	"	IT	John Teare.	Wine labels: Noted by Mr. Dudley Westropp.
1770	KAR	John Karr.	Skewer: Noted by Mr. D. Westropp.	1811	JK RF	... ...	Spoons: Mr. Dudley Westropp.
1776	I◦B	... ...	Spoons: Noted by Mr. D. Westropp.	1812	JH	J. Henzell?	Two-handled cup: V. & A. Museum.
1779	IL	John Locker?	Epergne: Noted by Mr. D. Westropp.	"	JK	... ...	Cup: V. & A. Museum.
"	M S	... ...	Ladles: Noted by Mr. D. Westropp.	1815	R·W	Richard Whitford.	Spoons: Noted by Mr. Dudley Westropp.

DUBLIN GOLDSMITHS' MARKS.

The marks illustrated below are reproduced from a plate of pewter preserved at the Dublin Assay Office, in which marks in use at various dates, from about 1765 to 1812, have been stamped. The plate contains a number of other marks which it is unnecessary to illustrate here, as they appear in the preceding tables.

MARK.	NAME.	MARK.	NAME.	MARK.	NAME.
RA	Robt. Atkinson?	JSB		WG	
ET		EB		LT	
RID	Richard & Jeremiah } D'Olier.	CF		W·S	Will. Stafford?
GM		JN	Joseph Nixon.	I·E	John Ebbs.
JA	John Austin.	RB	Robert Breading.	TA	
JC	John Clarke.	RH		EC BC	
T·F	Thos. Farley.	JE	Joshua Emerson.	GN	George Nangle.
II	Joseph Jackson.	SR	Saml. Reily (Cork).	IH	James Hadmill.
TS		RL		G·ALLEY	Geo. Alley.
W·D	Will. Digby?			IK	James Kenzie.
JK	John Keene.	G·T	Geo. Thompson.	IA	Jerome Alley?
G&B		JJ	James Jones.	ID	John Dalrymple.
TW	Thos. Williamson.	PM		WS	
WB	Will Beere.	M·CL	Mark M'Cloughlin.	PS	
TP		WFG	Wm. Fitzgerald (Limerick).	TM	Thos. Martin.
JC	John Coleman.	HL		WJ	Will. Johnson.
MB	Michael Byrne.	TN		AT	Alex. Ticknell.
WP	Walter Peter.	AN	Ambr'se Nicklin.	JO	John Osborne.
CD	Chas. Dowdall.	O M·N		HN	Henry Nicholson.
T·C	Thos. Cooksey.	HM		RT	
J·J	James Jones.	NICOLSON	J. Nicolson (Cork).	WS	
IP		JA		S·R	Saml. Reily (Cork).
GW		WK	Wm. Keene.	H&H	Hopper & Hannay.
CC	Christr. Clarke?	JJ	James Jones?	JG	
I·W	Jacob West.	IN		TH	Thos. Hunt?
I·M		LM	La'rence Martin (Kilkenny).	GN	George Nangle.
L·A		C·G		PF	

DUBLIN GOLDSMITHS' MARKS, 1765 TO 1812—*Continued.*

MARK.	NAME.	MARK.	NAME.	MARK.	NAME.
LH		W·W		FB	Fredk. Buck.
W·H	Will. Hughes ?	BT	Benjn. Tait.	ST	Samuel Taylor.
CK		PW	Peter Wingfield.	RC	Randall Cashell ?
WG	Will. Gethin ?	TA	Thos. Adams.	W·H	Wm. Hannay ?
I·T	John Tweedie ?	HM		I·C	
R°S	Robt. O'Shaughnessy (Limerick).	TR	Thos. Rourke.	JL	John Lloyd.
I·H	James Hewitt ?	DP		E&B	
IW	John West ?	RC	Randall Cashell ?	WF	Will French.
JR	J'n'th'n Robinson ?	GIBSON	Joseph Gibson (Cork).	W·W	Will Ward.
SLY	Thos. Sly.	GR		AM	Arthur Murphy.
G&PW		JJ	Joseph Johnson.	W·L	
MS		JC	James Campbell ?	R·D	
TE		D·P		BP	
IM	James Mills ?	ID	Isaac Davis ?	J·T	
WL	Wm. Law ?	MW&S	Matt. West & Son.	I·G	
WH	Will. Hamey ?	I·C	Jas. Connor ?	WH	
T·B	Thos. Baker ?	B·B		IB	John Bolland ?
W·F		SINGLETON	—— Singleton.	TSW	
FR		T·T	Thomas Townsend.		

THE FOLLOWING MARKS, WHICH ARE STAMPED ON A COPPER-PLATE OF LATER DATE, RANGE FROM ABOUT 1813 TO ABOUT 1850.

MARK.	NAME.	MARK.	NAME.	MARK.	NAME.
WG		GF		LK	
TK JF		TT		GW WM	
TK		CM		GA	
HL	Henry Lazarus.	IH		JT	John Townsend.
DM		WHT	Wm. H. Townsend.	W·N	Wm. Nelson.
S&W		SB	S. Bergin.	K&F	
J·M &E·M		J·MOORE	James Moore.	RE	
IM	J. Moore.	WC		TO	
BOYLE	—— Boyle.	FM &S		GRAYS	—— Grays.
EM	Edwd. Murphy.	LEE		PG	
		RWS	R. W. Smith.	IS	

CHAPTER XXIV

CHRONOLOGICAL LISTS OF NAMES OF DUBLIN GOLDSMITHS,

FROM A.D. 1200 TO A.D. 1904

INCLUDING THE MASTERS AND WARDENS, FREEMEN, AND QUARTER BROTHERS OF THE DUBLIN GOLDSMITHS' COMPANY FROM ITS INCORPORATION IN 1637.

The names of earlier date than 1637 have for the most part been extracted from *Historic and Municipal Documents*, and *Dublin Corporation Records*—edited by Sir J. Gilbert. From 1637 onwards the names have been copied from the Records of the Dublin Goldsmiths' Company, supplemented by some which have been found in enrolments of Wills in Dublin and District, and in Dublin Directories.

The records of the Dublin Goldsmiths' Company are more perfect and complete than those of any other company of goldsmiths in the Kingdom, and, but for the fact that one or two books are missing, an unbroken record of its members and their work, from 1637 to the present day, would be contained in the archives of the company. Even as it is, very little is wanting; in fact, much less is missing than, having regard to the state of similar archives in other parts of the Kingdom, might reasonably have been expected. The Dublin Goldsmiths' Records are of the highest value to the antiquary and the plate collector, and of no little importance to the present day goldsmiths and other citizens of Dublin who take an interest in the history of a "craft," which has shown by work which emanated from its members, that the skill of Dublin goldsmiths in former times was quite equal to that of their contemporary London brethren.

A perusal of the following names brings to one's notice the extent to which the craft in Dublin was enriched by French Huguenots and other continental goldsmiths, of whom a large number were driven by persecution from their native countries, which thereby lost many highly talented workmen, whom Ireland gained.

The observations which occur on page 510 with reference to the different ways in which certain Scottish goldsmiths' names are spelled at different times, are also applicable, but in a less degree, to some of the names which appear spelled in different ways in the following lists.

NAMES OF GOLDSMITHS FOUND IN DUBLIN RECORDS

FROM ABOUT A.D. 1200 TO A.D. 1630.

NAME OF GOLDSMITH.				Date.	NAME OF GOLDSMITH.					Date.
Willielmus de	Srobesburi	...	...	c. 1200	Dionyse	Carie	...	...	...	1558
Rogerus	aurifaber	...	...	,,	William	Calfe	...	...	...	1562
Willielmus	,,	...	...	,,	Thomas	Pinnock	...	...	...	1565
Giles	,,	...	...	,,	William	Jackson	...	...	...	1577
Godardus	,,	de London.		,,	Robert	Bee	...	...	...	1578-95
Thomas	goldsmith	...	...	1225-50	Philip	Kenreaght	...		...	1580
John	,,	...	...	,,	Nicholas	Ford	...	...	...	1584
William de	St. Helena	...	...	,,	John	Hand	...	...	...	,,
Oliver de	Nichol	...	...	1226	Francis	Trassy	...	...	...	,,
William	Frend	...	...	1257	John	Fyan	...	...	...	1591
Maurice of	Connaught	...	...	,,	Edward	Wylkes	...	...	...	,,
Cristinus	...	...	...	,,	Lawrence	Doyne	...	...	...	1595
Will	Rudestan	...	...	1263	George	Miller	...	...	...	1603
Walter the	goldsmith	...	...	1344	James	Gerland	...	...	...	1605
Thomas	O'Carty	...	...	1418	James	Bee	...	...	...	,,
Nicholas	Priour	...	...	1432-42	Brian	Ratlyffe	...	...	...	1612
Patrick	Kenne or Keyne		...	1469	Thomas	Bee	...	...	...	1613
Nicholas	Browne	...	...	,,	William	Calfe	...	...	...	1618
Dermot	Lynchy	...	...	1473	Henry	Cheshire (Alderman)		...		1611-21
John	Savage	...	...	1474	Barnaby	Ratlyffe	...	...	...	1621
Walter	Foile	...	...	1477	Edmond	Needly	...	...	...	1622
Meiler	Trevers	...	...	1482	Edmond	Murray	...	...	...	,,
David	Locke	...	...	1542	Edmond	Medley	...	...	...	,,
John	Ellys	...	...	1547	William	Bee	...	...	...	,,
John	Anwarp	...	...	1552	Will	Ward	...	...	...	1625
John	Hanne	...	...	1557	John	Coulson	...	...	...	1627
John	Latton	...	..	,,	Robert	Coffee	...	...	...	,,
Terence	Byrne	...	...	,,	Thomas	Mennan	...	...	...	1630
Adam	Colman	...	...	,,						

THE GOLDSMITHS COMPANY OF DUBLIN.
(GUILD OF ALL SAINTS.)

LIST OF MASTERS AND WARDENS OF THE COMPANY FROM ITS
INCORPORATION IN 1637.

COMPILED FROM THE COMPANY'S JOURNALS.

1637-9	William	Cooke	master	1668-9	Abel	Ram	master
	John	Woodcocke	warden		Edmond	Coghlan	warden
	William	Hampton	,,		Abraham	Voyseen (Voisin)	,,
	John	Banister	,,	1669-70	Abel	Ram	master
1639-40	William	Hampton	,,		Abraham	Voisin (Voyseen)	warden
	Peter	Vaneijndhoven	,,		John	Dickson	,,
1640-1	John	Woodcocke	master	1670-1	Thomas	Pennant	master
	James	Vanderbeck	warden		John	Dickson	warden
1641-4					Timothy	Blackwood	,,
1645-6	Daniel	Burfeldt	master	1671-2	Thomas	Rutter	master
1644-5-6	Gilbert	Tonques	warden		Timothy	Blackwood	warden
	Peter	Vaneijndhoven	,,		Paul	Lovelace	,,
1646-7	Gilbert	Tonques	master	1672-3	John	Dickson	master
	Daniel	Burfeldt	warden		Paul	Lovelace	warden
1647-8					John	Cope	,,
1648-9	Nathaniel	Stoughton	master	1673-4	Richard	Lord	master
	Daniel	Burfeldt	warden		John	Cope	warden
	Daniel	Bellingham	,,		James	Cottingham	,,
1649-54				1674-5	Paul	Lovelace	master
1654-5	Joseph	Stoaker	master		James	Cottingham	warden
	John	Woodcocke	warden		Thomas	Sterne	,,
	(decd., and Giles Goodwin				Richard	Webb	,,
	elected in his place).			1675-6	Paul	Lovelace	master
	Thomas	Hooker	,,		James	Cottingham	warden
1655-6					Thomas	Sterne	,,
1656-7	Joseph	Stoaker	master		Richard	Webb	,,
	William	Huggard	warden	1676-7	Abraham	Voisin	master
	Daniel	Bellingham	,,		Richard	Webb	warden
1657-8	David	Jean (or John)	master		James	Kelly	,,
	John	Slicer	warden		Gerard	Grace	,,
	Isaac	Jean (or John)	,,	1677-8	James	Cottingham	master
1658-9	John	Slicer	master		James	Kelly	warden
	Isaac	John	warden		Gerard	Grace	,,
	Nicholas	Seward	,,		Samuel	Marsden	,,
1659-60	Isaac	John	master	1678-9	James	Kelly	master
	Nicholas	Seward	warden		Gerard	Grace	warden
	Edward	Harris	,,		Samuel	Marsden	,,
1660-1	John	Thornton	master		John	Hyatt (Hyett)	,,
	Edward	Harris	warden	1679-80	John	Cope	master
	Edward	Swann	,,		Samuel	Marsden	warden
1661-2	Thomas	Parnell	master		John	Hyett (Hyatt)	,,
	John	Parnell	warden		Andrew	Gregory	,,
	George	Southaick	,,	1680-1	Gerard	Grace	master
1662-3	David	Harris	master		John	Hyett	warden
	George	Southaick	warden		Andrew	Gregory	,,
	John	Partington	,,		Adam	Soret	,,
1663-4	Edward	Harris	master			(watchmaker)	
	John	Partington	warden	1681-2	Samuel	Marsden	master
	George	Lambert	,,		Andrew	Gregory	warden
1664-5	George	Southaick	master		Adam	Soret	,,
	George	Lambert	warden			(watchmaker)	
	Thomas	Rutter	,,		John	Cuthbert	,,
1665-6	George	Lambert	master	1682-3	Abel	Ram	master
	Thomas	Rutter	warden		Adam	Soret	warden
	George	Taylor	,,		John	Cuthbert	,,
1666-7	John	Partington	master		Walter	Lewis	,,
	George	Taylor	warden	1683-4	Edward	Harris	master
	Abel	Ram	,,		John	Cuthbert	warden
1667-8	John	Parnell	master		Walter	Lewis	,,
	Abel	Ram	warden		John	Shelley	,,
	Edmond	Coghlan	,,				

LIST OF MASTERS AND WARDENS—*Continued.*

1684-5	James	Cottingham	master	1701-2	Joseph	Walker	master
	Walter	Lewis	warden		Alexander	Sinclare	warden
	John	Shelly	,,		Robert	Smith	,,
	Burleigh	Cuffe	,,		Thomas	Billing	,,
1685-6	James	Cottingham	master	1702-3	Robert	Rigmaiden	master
	John	Shelly	warden		Robert	Smith	warden
	Burleigh	Cuffe	,,		Thomas	Billing	,,
	John	Moseley	,,		Abraham	Soret (watchmaker)	,,
1686-7	Adam	Soret (see 1680-1)	master	1703-4	John	Harris	master
	Burleigh	Cuffe	warden		Thomas	Billing	warden
	John	Deane	,,		Abraham	Soret	,,
	William	Drayton	,,		Richard	Grosvenor	,,
1687-8	John	Shelley	master	1704-5	James	Welding	master
	John	Deane	warden			(decd., and 21 June, 1705, Robert Smith elected for remainder of the year).	
	William	Drayton	,,				
	John	Phillips	,,		Abraham	Soret	warden
1688-9	John	Cuthbert	master		Richard	Grosvenor	,,
	William	Drayton	warden		John	Gregory	,,
	John	Phillips	,,	1705-6	Robert	Smith	master
	John	Clifton	,,		Richard	Grosvenor	warden
1689-90					John	Gregory	,,
1690 1	William	Drayton	master		Benjamin	Racine	,,
	Thomas	Bolton	warden			(jeweller)	
	James	Weldon	,,	1706-7	Edward	Slicer	master
	John	Bryerley (or Brearly)	,,		John	Gregory	warden
1691-2	Adam	Soret	master		Benjamin	Racine	,,
	Thomas	Bolton	warden		Mortagh	Dowling	,,
	Capn. Benj.	Burton	,,	1707-8	Edward	Slicer	master
	John	Billing	,,		Benjamin	Racine	warden
1692-3	Thomas	Bolton	master		Mortagh	Dowling	,,
	Benjamin	Burton	warden		John	Mathews	,,
	John	Billing	,,	1708-9	Thomas	Browne (graver)	master
	Joseph	Wesencraft	,,		Mortagh	Dowling	warden
		(decd., 24 Jan., 1692, Robt. Rigmaiden elected in his stead).			John	Mathews	,,
					Edward	Workman	,,
1693-4	John	Phillips	master	1709-10	Mortagh	Dowling	master
	Benjamin	Burton	warden		John	Mathews	warden
	Robert	Rigmaiden	,,		Edward	Workman	,,
		(watchmaker)			William	Archdall	,,
	Vincent	Kidder	,,	1710-11	Benjamin	Racine	master
1694-5	Capn. Benj.	Burton	master		Edward	Workman	warden
	Robert	Rigmaiden	warden		William	Archdall	,,
	Vincent	Kidder	,,		Francis	Girard	,,
	Walter	Bingham (clockmaker)	,,			(decd., and 2 Feb., 1710, John Hamilton elected in his stead).	
1695-6	Benjamin	Burton	master				
	Vincent	Kidder	warden	1711-12	Thomas	Billing	master
	Walter	Bingham	,,		William	Archdall	warden
	John	Humphrys	,,		John	Hamilton	,,
1696-7	Vincent	Kidder	master		Henry	Mathews	,,
	Walter	Bingham	warden			(decd., and 11 Sept., 1712, Philip Tough elected in his stead).	
	John	Humphrys	,,				
	David	King	,,				
1697-8	John	Clifton	master	1712-13	Edward	Workman	master
	John	Humphrys	warden		John	Hamilton	warden
	David	King	,,		Philip	Tough	,,
	Joseph	Walker	,,		John	Pallet	,,
1698-9	John	Humphrys	master	1713-14	William	Archdall	master
	David	King	warden		Philip	Tough	warden
	Joseph	Walker	,,			(decd., and 18 June, 1714, Henry Daniell elected in his stead).	
	John	Harris	,,				
1699 1700	David	King	master				
	Joseph	Walker	warden		John	Pallett	,,
	John	Harris	,,		Erasmus	Cope	,,
	Alexander	Sinclare (Sinclair)	,,	1714-15	John	Hamilton	master
1700-1	Walter	Bingham	master		Erasmus	Cope	warden
	John	Harris	warden		Henry	Daniell	,,
	Alexander	Sinclare	,,		John	Burton	,,
	Robert	Smith	,,				

LIST OF MASTERS AND WARDENS—*Continued.*

1715-16	Erasmus	Cope	master	1731-2	Roger	Finch	master
	Henry	Daniell	warden		William	Sinclare	warden
	John	Burton	,,		Noah	Vialas	,,
	William	Barry	,,		Charles	Leslie	,,
1716-17	John	Pallet	master	1732-3	Roger	Finch	master
	John	Burton	warden		Noah	Vialas	warden
	William	Barry	,,		Charles	Leslie	,,
	John	Crampton (clockmaker)	,,		William	Williamson	,,
1717-18	John	Sterne (jeweller)	master	1733-4	William	Barry	master
	William	Barry	warden		Charles	Leslie	warden
	John	Crampton	,,		William	Williamson	,,
	Martin	Billing	,,		Robert	Calderwood	,,
1718-19	William	Barry	master	1734-5	William	Sinclare	master
	John	Crampton	warden		William	Williamson	warden
	Martin	Billing	,,		Robert	Calderwood	,,
	Charles	Norton	,,		Thomas	Williamson	,,
1719-20	William	Barry	master	1735-6	Charles	Leslie	master
	Martin	Billing	warden		Robert	Calderwood	warden
	Charles	Norton	,,		Thomas	Williamson	,,
	Thomas	Cope	,,		George	Cartwright	,,
1720-1	Martin	Billing	master	1736-7	Robert	Calderwood	master
	Charles	Norton	warden		Thomas	Williamson	warden
	Thomas	Cope	,,		George	Cartwright	,,
	Edmond	Sturgys	,,		John	Wilme	,,
1721-2	Charles	Norton	master	1737-8	William	Williamson	master
	Thomas	Cope	warden		George	Cartwright	warden
	Edmond	Sturgys	,,		John	Wilme	,,
	Mathew	Walker	,,		Martin	Kirkpatrick (watchmaker)	,,
1722-3	Erasmus	Cope	master	1738-9	George	Cartwright	master
	Edmond	Sturgys	warden		John	Wilme	warden
	Mathew	Walker	,,		Martin	Kirkpatrick	,,
	Edward	Barrett	,,		Andrew	Goodwin	,,
	(decd., and 28 June, 1723, John Clifton elected in his stead).			1739-40	John	Wilme	master
					Martin	Kirkpatrick	warden
1723-4	Erasmus	Cope	master		Andrew	Goodwin	,,
	Mathew	Walker	warden		Isaac	D'Olier	,,
	John	Clifton	,,	1740-1	Martin	Kirkpatrick	master
	Philip	Kinnersly	,,		Andrew	Goodwin	warden
1724-5	Mathew	Walker	master		Isaac	D'Olier	,,
	John	Clifton	warden		David	Bomes	,,
	Philip	Kinnersly	,,	1741-2	Noah	Vialas	master
	Thomas	Crampton (watchmkr)	,,		Isaac	D'Olier	warden
1725-6	John	Clifton	master		David	Bomes	,,
	Philip	Kinnersly	warden		James	Whitthorne (watchmaker)	,,
	Thomas	Crampton	,,	1742-3	Robert	Billing (jeweller)	master
	Simon	Young	,,		David	Bomes	warden
1726-7	Arthur	Weldon	master		James	Whitthorne	,,
	Thomas	Crampton	warden		Thomas	Isaac	,,
	Simon	Young	,,	1743-4	David	Bomes	master
	John	Taylor	,,		James	Whitthorne	warden
1727-8	Philip	Kinnersly	master		Thomas	Isaac	,,
	Simon	Young	warden		Thomas	De Limarest (jeweller)	,,
	John	Taylor	,,	1744-5	James	Whitthorne	master
	Joseph	Blundell	,,		Thomas	Isaac	warden
1728-9	Edmond	Sturgys	master		Thomas	De Limarest	,,
	John	Taylor	warden		Thomas	Blundell (clockmaker)	,,
	Joseph	Blundell	,,	1745-6	John	Freeze	master
	Roger	Finch	,,		Thomas	De Limarest	warden
1729-30	Thomas	Cope	master		Thomas	Blundell	,,
	Joseph	Blundell	warden		Deacon	Standish (jeweller)	,,
	Roger	Finch	,,	1746-7	Andrew	Goodwin	master
	William	Sinclare	,,		Thomas	Blundell	warden
1730-1	Henry	Daniell	master		Deacon	Standish	,,
	Roger	Finch	warden		William	Townsend	,,
	William	Sinclare	,,				
	Noah	Vialas	,,				

LIST OF MASTERS AND WARDENS—*Continued.*

1747-8	Thomas	Blundell	master	1761-2	Nathan	Murray, sen.	master
	Deacon	Standish	warden			Fishamble Street	
	William	Townsend	,,		Thomas	Burton	warden
	James	Champion	,,		Henry	Billing	,,
		(jeweller)			Jonathan	Ruston	,,
1748-9	Deacon	Standish	master			Cole Alley (jeweller)	
	William	Townsend	warden	1762-3	Edward	Mockler	master
	James	Champion	,,		Henry	Billing	warden
	Daniel	Onge	,,		Jonathan	Ruston	,,
1749-50	William	Townsend	master		William	Wilme	,,
	James	Champion	warden			Hoey's Court	
	Daniel	Onge	,,	1763-4	Thomas	Burton	master
	Barth'mew	Mosse	,,		Jonathan	Ruston	warden
1750-1	John	Moore	master		William	Wilme	,,
	Daniel	Onge	warden		Benjamin	Stokes	,,
	Barth'mew	Mosse	,,			Skinners' Row	
	(decd., and 21 May, 1751,			1764-5	Andrew	Goodwin	master
	Christopher Skinner elected					Skinners' Row	
	in his stead).				William	Wilme	warden
	John	Letablere	,,		Benjamin	Stokes	,,
		(a lapidary)			Richard	Williams	,,
1751-2	Daniel	Onge	master			Castle Street	
	(decd., and 3 July, 1752, John			1765-6	Thomas	Blundell	master
	Moore elected in his stead).					Ormond Quay	
	John	Letablere	warden		Benjamin	Stokes	warden
	Christ'r	Skinner (jeweller)	,,		Richard	Williams	,,
	Richard	Eaton	,,		John F.	Sherwin	,,
1752-3	Isaac	D'Olier	master			Skinners' Row	
	Christ'r	Skinner	warden	1766-7	William	Wilme	master
	Richard	Eaton	,,		Richard	Williams	warden
	Thomas	Parsons	,,		John F.	Sherwin	,,
1753-4	James	Champion	master		Benjamin	Willson	,,
	Richard	Eaton	warden			Skinners' Row	
	Thomas	Parsons	,,	1767-8	Benjamin	Stokes	master
	Mathias	Browne	,,		John F.	Sherwin	warden
		(silversmith)			Benjamin	Willson	,,
1754-5	Christ'r	Skinner	master		Henry	Waldron	,,
	Thomas	Parsons	warden			Christchurch Yard	
	Mathias	Browne	,,	1768-9	Richard	Williams	master
	George	Beere	,,		Benjamin	Willson	warden
1755-6	Thomas	Parsons	master		Henry	Waldron	,,
	Mathias	Browne	warden		Richard	Tudor	,,
	George	Beere	,,			Skinners' Row	
	William	Wilson	,,	1769-70	John	Sherwin	master
1756-7	William	Currie	master		Henry	Waldron	warden
	George	Beere	warden		Richard	Tudor	,,
	William	Wilson	,,		Nathan	Murray, junior	,,
	Nathan	Murray	,,			Fishamble Street	
1757-8	George	Beere	master	1770-1	Benjamin	Willson	master
	William	Wilson	warden		Richard	Tudor	warden
	Nathan	Murray	,,		Nathan	Murray, junior	,,
	Robert	Hopkins	,,		William	Nugent	,,
1758-9	William	Wilson	master			Skinners' Row	
	Nathan	Murray	warden	1771-2	Richard	Tudor	master
	Robert	Hopkins	,,		Nathan	Murray, junior	warden
	Edward	Mockler	,,		William	Nugent	,,
1759-60	James	Vidouze	master		George	Clarke	,,
		Fownes' Street (jeweller)				Dame Street (toy seller*	
	Robert	Hopkins	warden			and seal graver)	
		Ormond Quay		1772-3	Henry	Archdall	master
	Edward	Mockler	,,			Coleraine Street	
		Ormond Quay			William	Nugent	warden
	Thomas	Burton	,,		George	Clarke	,,
		Skinners' Row			John	West, Skinners' Row	,,
1760-1	Robert	Hopkins	master	1773-4	James	Vidouze	master
	Edward	Mockler	warden		George	Clarke	warden
	Thomas	Burton	,,		John	West	,,
	Henry	Billing	,,		Thomas	Nuttall	,,
		Werburgh St. (jeweller)				Skinners' Row	

* " Toy seller " = one who sold *trinkets*, not playthings.

LIST OF MASTERS AND WARDENS—*Continued.*

1774-5	Nathan	Murray	master
	John	West	warden
	Thomas	Nuttall	,,
	John	Wilme	,,
		Hoey's Court (resigned)	
	Ambrose	Boxwell	warden
		Skinners' Row (in his stead)	
1775-6	George	Clarke	master
	Thomas	Nuttall *	warden
		resigned, and	
	John	Locker	,,
		(in his stead)	
	Ambrose	Boxwell	,,
	William	Raymond	,,
		Abbey St. (watchmaker)	
1776-7	John	West	master
	John	Locker	warden
		Parliament Street	
	William	Raymond	,,
	Richard	Shaw	,,
		Essex Bridge (sword cutler)	
1777-8	James	Warren, Cork Hill,	master
	John	Locker	warden
	Richard	Shaw	,,
	John	Lloyd, Dame St.	,,
1778-9	Ambrose	Boxwell	master
	Richard	Shaw	warden
	John	Lloyd	,,
	Charles	Townsend	,,
		Skinners' Row	
1779-80	John	Locker	master
	John	Lloyd	warden
	Charles	Townsend	,,
	Robert	Murray	,,
		Skinners' Row	
1780-1	John	Lloyd	master
	Charles	Townsend	warden
	Robert	Murray	,,
	Matthew	West	,,
		Skinners' Row	
1781-2	Jeremiah	D'Olier	master
		Dame Street	
	Robert	Murray	warden
	Matthew	West	,,
	Thomas	Jones	,,
		Cole Alley	
1782-3	Charles	Townsend	master
	Matthew	West	warden
	Thomas	Jones	,,
	Poole	Taylor	,,
		Cole Alley (jeweller)	
1783-4	Matthew	West	master
	Thomas	Jones	warden
	Poole	Taylor	,,
	Arthur	Clarke	,,
		Dame Street	
1784-5	Benjamin	Willson	master
		Skinners' Row	
	Poole	Taylor	warden
	Arthur	Clarke	,,
	William	Sherwin	,,
		Skinners' Row	
1785-6	Richard	Williams	master
	Arthur	Clarke	warden
	William	Sherwin	,,
	Barthw.	Delandre	,,
		Skinners' Row	
1786-7	Ambrose	Boxwell	master
	William	Sherwin	warden
	Barthw.	Delandre	,,
	Samuel	Close, Capel St.	,,
1787-8	Poole	Taylor	master
	Barthw.	Delandre	warden
	Samuel	Close	,,
	William	Law	,,
		Parliament Street	
1788-9	Barthw.	Delandre	master
	Samuel	Close	warden
	William	Law	,,
	George	Harkness	,,
		Stephen St. (jeweller)	
1789-90	Arthur	Clarke	master
	William	Law	warden
	George	Harkness	,,
	John	Pittar, Ross Lane	,,
1790-1	William	Sherwin	master
	George	Harkness	warden
	John	Pittar	,,
	John	Wade, Essex Quay	,,
1791-2	Thomas	Jones	master
	John	Pittar	warden
	Joseph	Jackson	,,
		Hoey's Court	
	Richard	Fitzsimons	,,
		Crow Street (jeweller)	
1792-3	George	Harkness	master
	Joseph	Jackson	warden
	Richard	Fitzsimons	,,
	Henry	Wilme	,,
		Dame Street	
1793-4	William	Law	master
	Richard	Fitzsimons	warden
	Henry	Wilme	,,
	William	Osborne	,,
		South Gt. George's St. (jeweller)	
1794-5	Richard	Fitzsimons	master
	Henry	Wilme	warden
	William	Osborne	,,
	Edward	Rice, Capel Street	,,
1795-6	Joseph	Jackson	master
	William	Osborne	warden
	Edward	Rice	,,
	William	Keene, Dame Street	,,
1796-7	John	Pittar	master
	Edward	Rice	warden
	William	Keene	,,
	John	Stoyte	,,
		Kennedy's Lane	
1797-8	Henry	Wilme	master
	William	Keene	warden
	John	Stoyte	,,
	John	Keene	,,
1798-9	William	Osborne	master
	John	Stoyte	warden
	John	Keene	,,
	Thomas	Taylor	,,
1799 / 1800	John	Stoyte	master
	John	Keene	warden
	Thomas	Taylor	,,
	Robert	Williams	,,
1800-1	{ William	Keene (died)	master
	{ Ambrose	Boxwell	,,
	Walter	Peter	warden
	Thomas	Taylor	,,
	Robert	Williams	,,

* Thomas Nuttall, having resigned the office of warden, was elected assay master in 1776.

LIST OF MASTERS AND WARDENS—*Continued.*

Year	First	Last	Office		Year	First	Last	Office
1801-2	John	Keene	master		1818-19	Rich. Wm.	Osborne	master
	Robert	Williams	warden			Edward	Murray	warden
	Walter	Peter	,,			John	Browne	,,
	George	Connor	,,			William	Mossop	,,
1802-3	Edward	Rice	master		1819-20	John	Twycross	master
	Walter	Peter	warden			John	Browne	warden
	George	Connor	,,			William	Mossop	,,
	William	Clarke	,,			Henry	Rooke	,,
1803-4	Robert	Williams	master		1820-1	Edward	Murray	master
	George	Connor	warden			William	Mossop	warden
	William	Clarke	,,			Henry	Rooke	,,
	Jacob	West, jun.	,,			James	Moore	,,
1804-5	George	Connor	master		1821-2	William	Mossop	master
	William	Clarke	warden			Henry	Rooke	warden
	Jacob	West, jun.	,,			James	Moore	,,
	Samuel	Neville	,,			William	Morgan	,,
1805-6	William	Clarke	master		1822-3	Henry	Rooke	master
	Jacob	West, jun.	warden			James	Moore	warden
	Samuel	Neville	,,			William	Morgan	,,
	John	Dalrymple	,,			Isaac	Hinds	,,
1806-7	Walter	Peter	master		1823-4	James	Moore	master
	Samuel	Neville	warden			William	Morgan	warden
	John	Dalrymple	,,			Isaac	Hinds	,,
	John	Tudor	,,			Hy. Thos.	Gonne	,,
1807-8	Samuel	Neville	master		1824-5	William	Morgan	master
	John	Dalrymple	warden			Issac	Hinds	warden
	John	Tudor	,,			Hy. Thos.	Gonne	,,
	Robert	Breading	,,			John	Gaskin	,,
1808-9	Jacob	West	master		1825-6	Isaac	Hinds	master
	John	Tudor	warden			Hy. Thos.	Gonne	warden
	Robert	Breading	,,			John	Gaskin	,,
	Matthew	West	,,			Joseph	Johnson	,,
1809-10	John	Tudor	master		1826-7	John	Brown	master
	Robert	Breading	warden			Joseph	Johnson	warden
	Matthew	West	,,			Forward	Rumley	,,
	George	Warner	,,			George	Harkness	,,
1810-11	William	Sherwin	master		1827-8	Samuel	Neville	master
	Matthew	West	warden			Joseph	Johnson	warden
	George	Warner	,,			Forward	Rumley	,,
	John	Lloyd, jun.	,,			Benj. S.	Brunton	,,
1811-12	John	Dalrymple	master		1828-9	Joseph	Johnson	master
	George	Warner	warden			Forward	Rumley	warden
	John	Lloyd, jun.	,,			Benj. S.	Brunton	,,
	Thomas	Gonne	,,			Edward	Thompson	,,
1812-13	Matthew	West	master		1829-30	Forward	Rumley	master
	John	Lloyd, jun.	warden			Benj. S.	Brunton	warden
	Thomas	Gonne	,,			Edward	Thompson	,,
	Arthur	O'Neill	,,			William	McQuestion	,,
1813-14	John	Lloyd, jun.	master		1830-1	Bj. Shafton	Brunton	master
	Thomas	Gonne	warden			Edward	Thompson	warden
	Arthur	O'Neill	,,			William	McQuestion	,,
	Matthew	Law	,,			Edmond	Johnson	,,
1814-15	George	Warner (Alderman)	master		1831-2	Edward	Thompson	master
	Arthur	O'Neill	warden			William	McQuestion	warden
	Matthew	Law	,,			Edmond	Johnson	,,
	Richard W.	Osborne	,,			Stephen	Cox	,,
1815-16	Thomas	Gonne	master		1832-3	William	McQuestion	master
	Matthew	Law	warden			Edmond	Johnson	warden
	Richard W.	Osborne	,,			Stephen	Cox	,,
	John	Twycross	,,			Edward	Power	,,
1816-17	Arthur	O'Neill	master		1833-4	Edmond	Johnson	master
	Richard W.	Osborne	warden			Stephen	Cox	warden
	John	Twycross	,,			Edward	Power	,,
	Edward	Murray	,,			Josiah	Lowe	,,
1817-18	Matthew	Law	master		1834-5	Hy. Thos.	Gonne	master
	John	Twycross	warden			Edward	Power	warden
	Edward	Murray	,,			Josiah	Lowe	,,
	John	Browne	,,			Richard	Sawyer	,,

LIST OF MASTERS AND WARDENS—*Continued.*

Year	First	Last	Role	Year	First	Last	Role
1835-6	Edward	Power (resigned)	master	1852-3	William H.	Nelson	master
	Joseph	Johnson	,,		Theophilus	Barton	warden
	Josiah	Lowe	warden		Joseph	Johnson, jun.	,,
	Richard	Sawyer	,,		John	Teare	,,
	James	Le Bass	,,	1853-4	Arthur	Johnson	master
1836-7	Edward	Thompson	master		Joseph	Johnson, jun.	warden
	Richard	Sawyer	warden		John	Teare	,,
	James	Le Bass	,,		Henry E.	Flavelle	,,
	George	Twycross	,,	1854-5	Edward	Thompson	master
1837-8	Richard	Sawyer	master		John	Teare	warden
	James	Le Bass	warden		Henry E.	Flavelle	,,
	George	Twycross	,,		Edward	Quigley	,,
	Wm. Hy.	Sherwin	,,	1855-6	John	Teare	master
1838-9	Stephen	Cox	master		Edward	Thompson	,,
	George	Twycross	warden		Henry E.	Flavelle	warden
	Wm. Hy.	Sherwin	,,		Edward	Quigley	,,
	Rd. West	Smith	,,		Robert	Nelson	,,
1839-40	George	Twycross	master	1856-7	John	Teare	master
	Wm. Hy.	Sherwin	warden		Robert	Nelson	warden
	Rd. West	Smith	,,		(the only warden in 1856)		
	Anthony	Willis	,,	1857-8	John	Teare	master
1840-1	Richard	Sawyer	master		Edward	Quigley	warden
	Rd. West	Smith	warden		Arthur	Johnson	,,
	Anthony	Willis	,,	1858-9	John	Teare	master
	Edward	Murray, jun.	,,		Edward	Quigley	warden
1841-2	Edward	Thompson	master		Arthur	Johnson	,,
	Anthony	Willis	warden	1859-60	John	Teare	master
	Edward	Murray, jun.	,,		Edward	Quigley	warden
	James	Willis	,,		Richard	Sawyer	,,
1842-3	Edward	Thompson	master	1860-1	John	Teare	master
	Edward	Murray, jun.	warden		Edward	Quigley	warden
	James	Willis	,,		Robert	Nelson	,,
	James	Fray	,,		Richard	Sawyer	,,
1843-4	Edward	Thompson	master	1861-2	Edmond	Johnson	master
	James	Willis	warden		Edward	Quigley	warden
	Henry E.	Flavelle	,,		Robert	Nelson	,,
	James	Wickham	,,		Richard	Sawyer	,,
1844-5	Edmond	Johnson	master	1862-3	Edmond	Johnson	master
	Henry	Flavelle	warden		Edward	Quigley	warden
	James	Wickham	,,		Robert	Nelson	,,
	Henry	Flavelle, jun.	,,		Richard	Sawyer	,,
1845-6	Edmond	Johnson	master	1863-4	Edmond	Johnson	master
	James	Wickham	warden		Joseph	Johnson	warden
	Henry	Flavelle, jun.	,,		George	Twycross	,,
	Joseph	Johnson, jun.	,,	1864-5	Joseph	Johnson	master
1846-7	Edmond	Johnson	master		George	Twycross	warden
	Henry	Flavelle, jun.	warden		Edmond	Johnson, jun.	,,
	Joseph	Johnson, jun.	,,	1865-6	Joseph	Johnson	master
	Henry E.	Flavelle	,,		George	Twycross	warden
1847-8	Henry	Flavelle, jun.	master		Edmond	Johnson, jun.	,,
	Joseph	Johnson, jun.	warden	1866-7	Joseph	Johnson	master
	Henry E.	Flavelle	,,		George	Twycross	warden
	Arthur	Johnson	,,		Edmond	Johnson, jun.	,,
1848-9	Joseph	Johnson, jun.	master	1867-8	Joseph	Johnson	master
	Henry E.	Flavelle	warden		Richard	Sawyer	warden
	Arthur	Johnson	,,		Edward	Thompson	,,
	Thomas	Brunker	,,		Edmond	Johnson, jun.	,,
1849-50	Henry E.	Flavelle	master	1868-9	Joseph	Johnson	master
	Arthur	Johnson	warden		Richard	Sawyer	warden
	Thomas	Brunker	,,		Edward	Thompson	,,
	William H.	Nelson	,,		Edmond	Johnson, jun.	,,
1850-1	Arthur	Johnson	master	1869-70	Joseph	Johnson	master
	Thomas	Brunker	warden		Richard	Sawyer	warden
	William H.	Nelson	,,		Edward	Thompson	,,
	Theophilus	Barton	,,		Edmond	Johnson, jun.	,,
1851-2	Thomas	Brunker	master	1870-1	Joseph	Johnson	master
	William H.	Nelson	warden		Richard	Sawyer	warden
	Theophilus	Barton	,,		Edward	Thompson	,,
	Joseph	Johnson, jun.	,,		Edmond	Johnson, jun.	,,

LIST OF MASTERS AND WARDENS—*Continued.*

1871-2	Joseph	Johnson	master
	Richard	Sawyer	warden
	Edward	Thompson	,,
	Edmond	Johnson, jun.	,,
1872-3	Joseph	Johnson	master
	Edmond	Johnson	warden
	Robert G.	Norman	,,
	Edward	Thompson	,,

After 1872 only two wardens, a senior and a junior, were appointed.

1873-4	Joseph	Johnson	master
	Edmond	Johnson	sen. warden
	Robert	Norman	jun. warden
1874-5	Joseph	Johnson	master
	Samuel	Le Bass	sen. warden
	Robert	Norman	jun. warden
1875-6	Joseph	Johnson	master
	Robert	Norman	sen. warden
	William	Lawson	jun. warden
1876-7	Joseph	Johnson	master
	Robert	Norman	sen. warden
	William	Lawson	jun. warden
1877-8	Joseph	Johnson	master
	Robert	Norman	sen. warden
	William	Lawson	jun. warden
1878-9	Joseph	Johnson	master
	William	Lawson	sen. warden
	John	Smyth	jun. warden
1879-80	Joseph	Johnson	master
	William	Lawson	sen. warden
	John	Smyth	jun. warden
1880-1	Joseph	Johnson	master
	William	Lawson	sen. warden
	Edmond	Johnson	jun. warden
1881-2	Joseph	Johnson	master
	William	Lawson	sen. warden
	Edmond	Johnston	jun. warden
1882-3	Joseph	Johnston	master
	William	Lawson	sen. warden
	Edmond	Johnson	jun. warden
1883-4	Edmond	Johnson	master
	William	Lawson	sen. warden
	W. P.	Lewis	jun. warden
1884-5	Edmond	Johnson	master
	William	Lawson	sen. warden
	W. P.	Lewis	jun. warden
1885-6	Edmond	Johnson	master
	William	Lawson	sen. warden
1886-7	Edmond	Johnson	master
	William	Lawson	sen. warden
1887-8	Edmond	Johnson	master
	William	Lawson	sen. warden
1888-9	Edmond	Johnson	master
	William	Lawson	sen. warden
1889-90	Edmond	Johnson	master
	William	Lawson	sen. warden
1890-1	William	Lawson	master
	Samuel	Le Bass	sen. warden
	Jacob	Frengley	jun. warden
1891-2	William	Lawson	master
	Samuel	Le Bass	sen. warden
	Jacob	Frengley	jun. warden
1892-3	Langley A.	West	master
	Jacob	Frengley	sen. warden
	William	Sharland	jun. warden
1893-4	Langley A.	West	master
	William	Sharland	sen. warden
	James E.	Pim	jun. warden
1894-5	Langley A.	West	master
	James E.	Pim	sen. warden
	Thomas	Smyth	jun. warden
1895-6	Langley A.	West	master
	James E.	Pim	sen. warden
	Thomas	Smyth	jun. warden
1896-7	Langley A.	West	master
	James E.	Pim	sen. warden
	Thomas	Smyth	jun. warden
1897-8	Langley A.	West	master
	James E.	Pim	sen. warden
	Thomas	Smyth	jun. warden
1898-9	Langley A	West	master
	James E.	Pim	sen. warden
	Thomas	Smyth	jun. warden
1899	Langley A.	West	master
1900	Thomas	Smyth	sen. warden
	Charles	Lamb	jun. warden
1900-1	Langley A.	West	master
	Thomas	Smyth	sen. warden
	Charles	Lamb	jun. warden
1901-2	Langley A.	West	master
	Charles	Lamb	sen. warden
	Richard	Hopkins	jun. warden
1902-3	Langley A.	West	master
	Richard	Hopkins	sen. warden
	James	Wallace	jun. warden
1903-4	Langley A.	West	master
	James	Wallace	sen. warden
	Daniel	Moulang	jun. warden
1904-5	Langley A.	West	master
	Daniel	Moulang	sen. warden
	W. Forbes-	Howie	jun. warden

ASSAY MASTERS.

1638-44	Will.	Cooke.
1644-9	{ Gilbert	Tonques &
	Peter	Vaneijndhoven.
	Richard	Lord.
1692-7	Thomas	Bolton.
1697-'36	Vincent	Kidder.
1736-51	William	Archdall.
1751-4	John	Wilme.
1754-70	William	Williamson.
1770-5	William	Townsend.
1775-6	Richard	Forster.
1776-'25	Thomas	Nuttall.
1795-'04	{ Nathan	Murray.
	*Deputy Assay Master.**	
1825-33	William	Clarke.
1833-5	R. W.	Osborne.
1835-54	Edward	Murray.
1854-80	George	Twycross.
1880-90	Samuel	Le Bass.
1890-'05	Sam'l. Wm.	Le Bass.
1905	Albert A.	Le Bass.

   * In 1783-4 a Statute was passed for the appointment of a Deputy Assay Master, to be "payed" out of duty money seventy pounds a year and forty pounds to be "payed" by the Corporation as a free gift. It was by this Act that a gold standard of 20 carats fine was established, mainly for the accommodation of the New Geneva workmen.

CLERKS OF THE COMPANY, WITH THE DATES OF THEIR APPOINTMENT.

Each of those whose names appear in the third column (from 1856 downwards) had been respectively appointed as " Secretary of the Company ".

1693.	Nicholas Peters.	1739.	Yeomans Sinclare.	1856.	Thos. Ryves	Metcalf.
1697.	Edmund Butler.	1755.	Noah Vialas.	1872.	Robt. E.	Norman.
1701.	John Seward.	1767.	Luke Kelly.	1885.	J. E.	Pim.
1709.	Francis Andrews.	1772.	John Robinson.	1892.	C. H.	Lawson.

LIST OF FREEMEN OF THE COMPANY FROM ITS INCORPORATION IN 1637.

G.S. = goldsmith ; S.S. = silversmith ; Sp.M. = spoonmaker ; J. = jeweller ; E. = engraver ; L. = lapidary ; W.M. = watchmaker ; W.C.M. = watch-case maker ; C.M. = clockmaker ; S.G. = seal-graver ; d = died ; g = marked in list as gone away ; off = disappearance of name from annual lists. When no letters follow the name it is presumed from the fact of his membership of the Goldsmiths' Company that the bearer of the name was a goldsmith.

In the great majority of instances freemen were goldsmiths or silversmiths, although not so described in the entries, and often the business of a goldsmith or silversmith was combined with that of jeweller, watch and clockmaker, lapidary, &c. Many goldsmiths worked as such for several years before being made freemen of the Company, while others were elected shortly after having completed their apprenticeship.

Name of Goldsmith.		Free.	Last Notice or Death.	Name of Goldsmith.		Free-	Last Notice or Death.
James	Acheson *	G.S.	1637		Daniel	Burfeldt	G.S.	1646	d 1654
John	Bannister *	,,	,,	Daniel	{ Gould } §	,,	,,	
John	Burke *	,,	,,		{ Bould }			
William	Cooke *	,,	,,	Joseph	Stoker (Stoaker)	,,	1647	1671
John	Cooke *	,,	,,	Nathaniel	Stoughton	J.	,,	off 1662
William	Crawley *	,,	,,	Ambrose	Futtrell §	G.S.	1648	
Thomas	Duffield *	,,	,,	Christr.	Wright §	,,	,,	
Clement	Evans *	,,	,,	d 1654	George	Carmick §	,,	1649	
William	Gallant *	,,	,,	Thomas	Taylor §	,,	1651	
George	Gallant *	,,	,,	John	Powell §	,,	,,	
Sylvanus	Glegg *	,,	,,	Stephen	Bostock		1652	d 1672
William	Hampton *	,,	,,	John	Bevan	G.S.	,,	d 1669
Nathaniel	Stoughton *	,,	,,	1653	Giles	Goodwin	,,	,,	
Will.	St. Cleere † *	,,	,,	,,	Edward	Harris	,,	,,	1688
Edward	Shadesy ‡ *	,,	,,	,,	Thomas	Heiden	,,	,,	d 1666
Gilbert	Tonques *	,,	,,	,,	Arthur	Padmore §	,,	,,	
Matthew	Thomas *	,,	,,	,,	John	Carr §	,,	,,	
James	Vanderbegg *	,,	,,	1642	William	Harrison §	,,	,,	
	or Vanderbeck				Francis	Harris	,,	1653	1664
Peter	Vaneijndhoven *	,,	d 1650	Robert	Thornton	,,	,,	1675
		G.S.		John	Thornton	,,	,,	1666
John	Woodcocke *	,,	,,	,,	Edward	Burgess §	,,	,,	
George	Greene	S.S.	(mentd.	1638)	Ralph	Allen	,,	1654	1663
Daniel	Underwood	,,	,,	,,	Henry	Bellingham	,,	,,	d 1669
Ambrose	Browne §	G.S.	,,	,,	Thomas	Barker		,,	g 1659
Edward	Bentley §	,,	,,	,,	James	East		,,	g 1669
John	More		,,	,,	George	Hewet	G.S.	,,	off 1670
Israel	Aprill		1639	d 1654	Isaac	John	,,	,,	1675
William	Huggard	G.S.	1640	d 1673	Bryan	Hughes	,,	,,	off 1670
David	Carny §	,,	,,		Robert	Lawe	,,	,,	
Daniel	Bellingham	,,	1644	d 1671	John	Slicer	,,	,,	1672

* Named in the charter of 22 December, 1637.
† Sometimes written " Sinclare," more commonly " Sinclair ".
‡ More commonly " Chadsey," sometimes " Shadsey ".
§ Not in Company's list, but described as a goldsmith in list of Dublin Freemen.

LIST OF FREEMEN OF THE DUBLIN GOLDSMITHS' COMPANY—*Continued.*

NAME OF GOLDSMITH.			Free.	Last Notice or Death.	NAME OF GOLDSMITH.			Free.	Last Notice or Death.
Edward	South	G.S.	1654	off 1660	Will	Lucas		1672	1700
Richard	Street	,,	,,	d 1654	Thomas	Sterne	G.S.	,,	1678
Edward	Swan	,,	,,	off 1683	Elizabeth	Slicer		,,	1675
Thomas	Wale	,,	,,	1665	John	Popkins	W.M.	,,	1679
David	John	,,	1655	1666	John	Powell		,,	1685
Robt.	Hughes		1656	off 1662	Andrew	Gregory		1673	d 1709
Thomas	Heydon		,,	1666	Richard	Lord, jun.		,,	off 1674
Amos	Ogden §	G.S.	,,		Samuel	Marsden		,,	off 1695
James	Heydon	,,	,,	1662	Paul	Lovelace		1674	1679
Thomas	Parnell, sen.	,,	,,	1663	Thomas	Linnington		,,	1692
John	Parnell	,,	,,	1679	Walter	Lewis		,,	off 1682
Nicholas	Seward	,,	,,	1667	George	Southwick	G.S.	,,	
Edward	Mason §	,,	,,		George	Taylor †	,,		1674
James	Lee §	,,	,,		Denis	Byrne		1675	d 1689
Theoph.	Sandford §	,,	,,		Gerrard	Grace	G.S.	,,	d 1694
Stephen	Burton		1657	g 1663	Adam	Soret		,,	d 1723
Miles	Graham	G.S.	,,	d 1665	Christr.	Palles		,,	off 1706
George	Lambert	,,	,,	1666	Willm.	Hewetson		1676	l'ft 1676
Richard	Lord	,,	,,	1692	Willm.	Elphinston		1677	g 1682
George	Southaick		,,	1683	John	Martin		,,	l'ft 1683
Charles	Butler	G.S.	1658	g 1670	John	Moseley		,,	l'ft 1684
John	Partington		,,	1669	Will	Norton		,,	l'ft 1679
David	Williams	G.S.	,,	off 1663	James	Ross		1679	g 1679
Phillip	Jones		1659	1680	John	Segar	G.S.	,,	1686
Edmund	Hoyle		,,	1667	Francis	Sherwin		,,	g 1694
Patrick	Russell		,,	off 1669	John	Phillips	G.S.	,,	1703
Edward	Short	G.S.	,,	off 1667	Walter	Bingham	W.M.	1680	d 1727
James	Wheatley		,,	1674	John	Barnard		,,	d 1681
Andrew	Edwards	G.S.	1661	d 1663	Willm.	Keating		,,	,,
Francis	Coffey		1662	off 1682	Matthew	La Roche	G.S.	,,	1697
George	Taylor		,,	d 1667	Eliz'b'th	Lovelace		,,	off 1683
Richard	Woodcock		,,	off 1670	James	Moseley		,,	
Thomas	Rutter		1663	g 1679	Willm.	Myers		,,	d 1700
Timothy	Blackwood	G.S.	1664	d 1675	Francis	Nevill		,,	1681
Abraham	Voizin (Voyseen)		,,	1704	George	Taylor		,,	g 1694
Robt.	Walsh	W.M.	,,	off 1677	Willm.	Archbold		1681	d 1699
Francis	Clifton	G.S.	1665	d 1667	John	Clifton	G.S.	,,	d 1726
Edmond	Coghlan		,,	g 1681	Nathl.	Higgins		,,	off 1695
Robt.	Dillon		,,	g 1676	John	{O'Heime or} {O'Hem}	J.	,,	1683
Nathaniel	Drake		,,	g 1670					
Abel [Sir]	Ram, Aldn. 1670 G.S.		,,	d 1698	Thomas	Somervill	C.M.	,,	1707
					Richard	Archbold †	G.S.	,,	1681
John	Dickson	,,	1666	d 1695	Henry	Bond		1682	1691
Will	Hanway		1667	off 1672	John	Baskett		,,	,,
Will	Walshman		,,	d 1671	John	Deane		,,	d 1704
Thomas	Tenant		,,	1700	Will.	Dermott	G.S.	,,	d 1685
John	Cope	G.S.	1668	d 1704	John	Shelley		,,	off 1688
James	Cottingham	,,	,,	d 1702	Thomas	Goodwin †	G.S.	,,	d 1689
George	Kirkman		,,	1674	Joshua	Cobham	,,	1683	d 1707
Andrew	Ram		,,	off 1683	Ebenezer	Cawdron		,,	g 1694
Thomas	Godfrey		1669	d 1682	George	Cartwright		,,	1695
John	Hyett (Hyatt)		,,	off 1678	Burleigh	Cuffe		,,	off ,,
John	Cuthbert	G.S.	1670	1705	Will.	Drayton		,,	d 1694
John	Farmer		,,	l'ft 1680	David	Swan	G.S.	,,	off 1712
Ferdinand	Matthews		,,	1681	Nathl.	Unit		,,	off 1695
Richard	Web		,,	off 1694	John	Brearly		1684	d 1689
Edward	Ashton		1671	d 1674	Will.	Billinghurst	G.S.	,,	d 1692
Hugh	Madden		,,	off 1683	Joseph	Bayley		,,	d 1694
Joseph	Stoker	G.S.	,,	1672	Alex.	Forbes		,,	g ,,
Will	Davison		1672	l'ft 1682	Benjamin	West		,,	off 1695
John	Destaches	G.S.	,,	d 1699	Henry	Chaloner		1685	g 1700
James	Kelly		,,	1697	John	Humphrys		,,	g 1704

§ Not in Company's list, but described as a goldsmith in list of Dublin Freemen.
† ,, ,, ,, ,, ,, ,, ,, ,, ,, ,, ,, ,, District Wills.

LIST OF FREEMEN OF THE DUBLIN GOLDSMITHS' COMPANY—*Continued.*

NAME OF GOLDSMITH.			Free.	Last Notice or Death.	NAME OF GOLDSMITH.			Free.	Last Notice or Death.
Alex.	Mackey		1685	1707	Edward	Workman	G.S.	1702	1719
Robt.	Smith		,,	1720	Willm.	Archdall	,,	1704	d 1751
Joseph	Teate		,,	d 1704	Joseph	Blundell	C.M.	,,	d 1732
John	Turner	W.M.	,,	,,	John	Crampton	,,	,,	
Joseph	Wesencroft	,,	,,	1688	Mortagh	Dowling	W.M.	,,	
Benjamin	Burton		1686	d 1727	Francis	Girard	G.S.	,,	d 1710
Thomas	Bolton		,,	d 1736	John	Paturle	J.	,,	d 1721
Arthur	Bryan		,,	g 1694		("Served" in France.)			
Peter	Devine		,,		George	Parker	W.M.	,,	
Robt.	Hopkins		,,	off 1695	John	Pennyfather	G.S.	,,	g 1721
Robt.	Rigmaiden	W.M.	,,	off 1734	Thomas	Racine		,,	
James	Welding	G.S.	,,	1705	John	Sterne	J.	,,	
Peter	Tobin	,,	(men	t'd 1693)	Robt.	Cuffe	G.S.	1705	g 1727
Thomas	Elliott	,,	(,,	1698)	Phillip	Tough	,,	,,	1714
Adam	Buck	,,	1690	g 1695	George	Lyng		1706	
John	Billing	,,	,,	d 1694	Edward	Sweetenham		,,	off 1728
Samuel	Clarke	,,	,,	off 1695	Henry	Matthews	G.S.	,,	1712
Vincent	Kidder	G.S.	,,	d 1735	Solomon	Condart		1707	
David	King	,,	,,	d 1737	Erasmus	Cope	J.	,,	d 1748
George	Montgomery		,,	off 1696	Christr.	Kindt		,,	1720
Henry	Nelthorp	G.S.	,,	1695	Benjn.	Mountjoy	G.S.	,,	d 1714
Abraham	Soret	W.M.	,,	1715	John	Pallet	,,	,,	⎰ran away.
Joseph	Walker	G.S.	,,	1722					⎱ 1718
Michael	Haines		1693	1700	Daniel	Pineau	J.	,,	1752
Conway	Mace		,,	off 1695	John	Whitefield	G.S.	,,	1712
Edward	Slicer	J.	,,	off 1752	Francis	Humphrey		1708	off 1735
Benjamin	Pemberton	G.S.	,,	1710	Peter	Lemaistre	W.M.	,,	off 1719
Nicholas	Pontaine		,,		Willm.	Barry		1709	
Thomas	Brown	E.	1694	d 1733	Stephen	Golding		,,	d 1716
Willm.	Berry		,,		John	Hamilton	G.S.	,,	d 1751
John	Harris	J.	,,	1708	Arthur	Weldon		,,	d 1760
Robt.	Ince		,,	g 1712	John	Burton	W.M.	1710	
Alex.	Sinclair	G.S.	,,	1718	Abraham	Barboult	,,	,,	d 1751
James	Thompson		,,	1694	Edward	Hall		,,	off 1728
Samuel	Wilder		,,	1700	James	Somervill		,,	g 1727
Thomas	Parker	W.M.	,,	d 1751	Henry	Daniell	G.S.	1711	d 1738
Thomas	Billing		1695	d 1722	Charles	Norton	,,	,,	1724
John	⎰ Gerrard or		,,	d 1714	Richard	Baker ‡	,,	(men	t'd 1725)
	⎱ Garrett				Martin	Billing	J.	1712	
Henry	Sherwin	G.S.	,,	1719	Will	Patten		,,	d 1717
Thomas	Desbrough		1696		Richard	Eycott ‡	S.S.	(men	t'd 1712)
Floris	Six		,,	1709	Andrew	Ross ‡	G.S.	,,	1719)
Samuel	Berry		,,	1706	George	Lennan ‡	,,	,,	,,)
	(descr'bed as G.S.)				Thomas	Bellingham		1713	
Richard	Grosvenor		1697	d 1714	Matthew	Darousseau	G.S.	,,	
Robert	Whitfield*	G.S.	,,		Daniel	Washburn	W.M.	,,	
Henry	Ireland †	,,		d 1717	Bolton	Cormick		1714	
Christian	Waggoner	,,	1698	g 1704	James	Mackey		,,	g 1727
James	Byrne	,,	1699	g 1724	Michael	Read	,,	,,	1732
Thomas	Meakins	C.M.	,,	1709	Thomas	Walker	G.S.	,,	1776
Cyriac	Mallory		,,	1705	George	Farrington ‡	,,	(men	t'd 1717)
Benjamin	Racine		,,	1723	Richard	Archbold ‡	,,	(,,	,,)
Anthony	Donoe		1700	d 1707	James	Champion	J.	1715	d 1719
John	Matthews	G.S.	,,	1733	Thomas	Cope		,,	d 1739
Peter	Baullier §	J.	1701	d 1725	Robert	Forbes	G.S.	,,	d 1718
Ahasuerus	Hartwick	G.S.	,,	g 1705	Peter	Gervais	,,	,,	d 1730
Will.	Skinner	,,	,,	1710	Edmond	Sturgys	W.M.	,,	off 1751
Edward	Barrett	,,	1702	d 1722	Mark	Twelves	G.S.	,,	off 1744
John	Cuthbert, jun.	,,	,,	off 1729	William	Walsh ‡	,,	(men	t'd 1733)
John	Gregory	J.	,,		George	Berford ‡	,,	(,,	1734)
Christr.	Hartwick	G.S.	,,	g 1705	John	Giles ‡	,,	(,,	1735)
Will.	Palmer		,,	d 1704	John	Barry	L.	1716	d 1719

* Not in Company's list of Freemen, but described as a goldsmith in St. Werburgh Records.
† ,, ,, ,, ,, :, ,, ,, ,, ,, ,, ,, ,, list of Dublin District Wills.
‡ ,, ,, ,, *Bolio* ,, ,, ,, mentioned as such in Company's journals.
§ Also written *Bolio* and *Beaulieu.*

LIST OF FREEMEN OF THE DUBLIN GOLDSMITHS' COMPANY—*Continued.*

Name of Goldsmith			Free.	Last Notice or Death.	Name of Goldsmith			Free.	Last Notice or Death.
Thomas	Deane		1716	d 1716	Francis	Williamson		1730	
John	Hodgkinson		,,	d 1720	Isaac	D'Olier	G.S.	1731	d 1779
Philip	Kinnersly		,,	off 1742	John	Gumley	,,	,,	1739
Will.	Proctor		,,	g 1729	Anthony	Lefebure		,,	1737
Matthew	Walker	G.S.	,,	d 1760	Barth.	Popkins	,,	,,	off 1741
John	Williamson	,,	,,	1734	Kirk	Ryves		,,	g 1731
Benjamin	Beauvais	,,	1717		Michael	Smith		1732	1754
Edward	Loftus		,,	off 1718	Peter	Usher		,,	{ g abroad 1750
Noah	Vialas	,,	,,	1774	Peter	Verdon		,,	
Willm.	Aicken	,,	1718	g 1722	John	Wilme	G.S.	,,	1754
John	Barrett		,,	c 1755	Thomas	Blundell	C.M.	1733	d 1774
James	Bollegne		,,	g 1720	Thomas	Parsons	G.S.	,,	d 1759
Thomas	Crampton	W.M.	,,	d 1751	Charles	Smith	C.M.	,,	d 1743
John	Drew		,,	g 1720	Francis	Gore	G.S.	(men t'd 1745)	
John	Freeze		,,	g 1749	Barth.	Mosse	,,	1734	d 1771
Will.	Streeter		,,	1732	Will.	Reily		,,	off 1739
John	Clifton, jun.	G.S.	1719	off 1751	Edward	Tench		,,	
John	Taylor	,,	,,	off 1740	Burton	Wright	G.S.	(men t'd 1751)	
John	Bradley	J.	1720	d 1728	Willm.	Aldridge (Aldn.)		1735	
Thomas	Sutton		,,	d 1744	John	Broadhurst		,,	d 1755
Matthew	Wilson	G.S.	,,	1731	James	Douglas	G.S.	,,	off 1768
Simon	Young		,,	off 1739	Richard	Forster	J.	,,	
Martin	Kirkpat'k	W.M.	1721	1769	Charles	Hunter	G.S.	,,	1739
John	Mitchell		,,	g 1727	Charles	Lemaitre		,,	1741
John	Freebough		1722	g 1748	Daniel	Onge	J.	,,	1752
John	King	J.	,,	d 1727	Henry	Sadire		,,	
Willm.	Duggan		1723	g 1727	John	Walker		,,	
John	Fenny	C.M.	,,		John	Banks	G.S. & W.M.	,,	off 1743
Robt.	Harrison		,,	g 1723	David	Bomes	G.S. & J.	,,	d 1787
Charles	Leslie	G.S.	,,	1757	Spranger	Barry		1736	off 1745
Mark	Martin		,,	off 1735	John	Brooks	E.	,,	off 1746
Will.	Smith	,,	,,	1728	Vere	Forster	G.S.	,,	off 1772
Henry	Wilme	,,	,,	1740	Robt.	Glanville		,,	off 1762
Robt.	Aicken	,,	1724	g 1728	Thomas	Isaac	G.S.	,,	1750
Will.	Challenor		,,		Christr.	McCarthy		,,	off 1743
Will.	Sutton		,,	1733	Nathaniel	Pearson		,,	
Thomas	Wheeler	W.M.	,,	g 1729	Alexr.	Richards		,,	d 1768
Morris	Nash		1725	g 1732	Solomon	Savage	G.S.	,,	d 1763
Charles	Prendergast	G.S.	,,	g 1732	Philip	Simms		,,	off 1749
Peter	Racine	J.	,,	g 1729	Christr.	Skinner	G.S.	,,	1780
Will.	Sinclaire	,,	,,	1779	Will.	Townsend	,,	,,	d 1775
Will.	Stopleare		,,	1740	Adam	Teate		,,	off 1737
Richard	Workman	G.S.	,,	off 1736	John	Letablere	L.	1737	d 1754
James	Whitthorne	,,	,,	1779	Thomas	De Limarest	J.	1738	
Dd. Alex.	Brown		1726	off 1740	Philip	Portal		,,	g 1739
Robt.	Billing	J.	,,	d 1754	Deacon	Standish		,,	1790
Will.	Swift		,,	g 1727	Yeomans	Sinclaire		,,	
Thomas	Williamson	G.S.	,,	1740	Christr.	Locker		1739	1751
Will.	Williamson	,,	,,	1782	James	Vidouze	J.	,,	1781
Edward	Adams		1727		John	Whitshed	J.	,,	1768
Robt.	Calderwood	,,	,,	d 1765	Will.	Wilson	G.S.	,,	1768
Roger	Finch		,,	off 1753	Thomas	Borr		1741	off 1745
Jasper	Graddell		,,	1733	Michael	Connor		,,	d 1763
Michael	Hewetson		,,	1728	Peter	Painter	G.S.	(men t'd 1758)	
Robt.	King		,,		Willm.	Bonynge	J.	1742	d 1746
John	Slicer		,,		James	Champion		,,	d 1761
Richard	Eaton	G.S.	1728		Clotw'thy	O'Neal		,,	
John	Moore	,,	,,	1767	Jonathan	Ruston		,,	off 1769
Will.	Fawcett		1729	d 1763	Matthias	Brown	S.S.	1743	d 1759
John	Taylor		,,	g 1732	Daniel	Walker		,,	
Daniel	Walker	,,	,,		Mervyn	Archdall		1744	
Will.	Currie	,,	1730	d 1772	Eneas	M'Phearson	G.S.	,,	
Fleetw'd	Daniel	,,	,,		George	Beere	,,	1745	d 1797
Andrew	Goodwin	,,	,,	1787	Jonathan	Thomas		,,	off 1748
Francis	McManus		,,						

LIST OF FREEMEN OF THE DUBLIN GOLDSMITHS' COMPANY—*Continued.*

Name of Goldsmith.	Free.	Last Notice or Death.	Name of Goldsmith.	Free.	Last Notice or Death.
William Walsh* G.S.	1745	d 1755	John Douglas	1761	d 1779
Isaac Parker* ,,	,,	d 1756	Adam Fraigneau L.	,,	d 1766
Robt. Pearson	1746	1798	John Harrison	,,	
Henry Archdall	1747	d 1790	Francis Jones G.S.	,,	d 1765
Charles Darragh G.S.	,,		Robt. Murray	,,	d 1786
Nathan Murray, sen. ,,	,,	1772	Will. Minemey	,,	off 1789
Edward Raper ,,	,,	d 1755	John Pringle	,,	
Benjamin Stokes ,,	,,	1771	Will. Richards G.S.	,,	
James Bloxham ,,	1748	d 1751	George Wilme J.	,,	1780
Thomas Croker	,,		Thomas Cooksey	1762	d 1775
Daniel O'Neill	,,		George Clarke S.G.	,,	1792
Will. Savile W.M.	,,	d 1761	Abraham Davis	,,	off 1764
Giles Roberts* G.S.		d 1761	Alexr. Gordon W.M.	,,	1787
Peter Wingfield ,,	,,	1777	Thomas Hagarty L.	,,	,,
Mar'duke Webb W.M.			John Karr G.S. & J.	,,	1778
Thomas Green	1749	1757	Will. Nugent G.S.	,,	1807
Edward Lord J.	,,	1790	Will. Raymond W.M.	,,	
Fleetwo'd Powell	,,	d 1763	John Shields G.S.	,,	1784
James Templeton	,,		John West	,,	d 1806
James Wyer G.S.	,,	1767	Isaac D'Olier, jun. J.	1763	
Thomas Burton ,,	1750	d 1784	Willm. Cordner	1764	
William Betagh	1751	d 1770	John Dawson	,,	
Michael Fowler G.S.	,,		Thomas Hammersley G.S.	1765	d 1784
John Loughlin Sp.M.	,,	1773	Richard Shaw ,,	,,	1781
Nicholas Le Maistre	,,		George Campbell ,,	1766	d 1789
Edward Mockler G.S.	,,	1786	John Ebbs W.M.	,,	
Thomas Shepherd ,,	,,	d 1765	John Houston ,,	,,	
Arthur Annesley ,,	1752	d 1795	David Karr J.	,,	
Robt. Fisher J.	,,		Richard Laughlin G.S.	,,	
George Murphy G.S.	,,	1759	Thomas Nuttall ,,	,,	d 1825‡
Daniel Mc.Neil ,,	,,	1789	John Sherwin ,,	,,	1783
Gray Townsend W.C.M.	,,	1757	Will. Smith ,,	,,	1776
James Warren G.S.	,,	1789	Benjamin Slack ,,	,,	1771
Richard Williams ,,	,,	1798	Ezekl. G. Townsend ,,	,,	1782
Will. Wilme ,,	,,	1774	James Fulton J.	1767	d 1791
Samuel Walker* ,,	,,	d 1773	Willm. Hughes G.S.	,,	1781
Michael Cormick* ,,	,,	d 1780	Will. Moore J.	,,	d 1821
Henry Billing J.	1753	d 1770	Oliver Moore ,,	,,	1784
Henry Cullen	,,		Ebenezer Orr J.	,,	,,
Joseph Cullen G.S.	,,	off 1767	David Peter G.S.	,,	1806
Owen Cassidy ,,	,,	d 1816	Robt. Billing	1768	d 1812
Richard Keightley ,,	,,	1776	Ambrose Boxwell G.S.	,,	d 1823
Richard Sonley W.M.	,,		Wm. Beere ,,	,,	d 1784
Will. Steele G.S.	,,	1776	J. Moses Dufour J.	,,	d 1803
John Wilme ,,	,,	d 1774	Francis N. Gervais	,,	d 1786
Robert Mirfield† ,,		d 1771	Richard Graham	,,	
Thomas Green† ,,		d 1783	Richard Harrison G.S.	,,	
Joseph Thompson ,,	1754	1782	John Lloyd ,,	,,	1790
Benjamin Wilson ,,	,,	1797	John Laughlin ,,	,,	d 1821
Daniel Savile	1755	1805	Henry Nicholson ,,	,,	d 1813
Richard Tudor ,,		1801	Thomas Proctor J.	,,	1770
Henry Waldron	,,	d 1814	Poole Taylor ,,	,,	d 1801
John Pittar G.S.	1756	1757	George Wilkinson G.S.	,,	1779
John St. John	,,	1795	Patrick Walsh J.	,,	d 1814
Thomas Williamson G.S.	,,		William Bate ,,	1769	d 1783
Joseph Bridgman ,,	1758	d 1761	John Craig G.S.	,,	d ,,
Nathan Murray, jun. ,,	,,	1803	George Furnace W.M.	,,	
John Sherwin	,,	1773	Charles Stokes J.	,,	1789
John Locker G.S.	1759	d 1825	Will. Supple G.S.	,,	1794
Joseph Nixon J.	,,	1803	Matthew West, sen. ,,	,,	1806
Daniel Popkins G.S.	,,	1775	Jeremiah D'Olier ,,	1770	d 1816
Willm. Barry J.	1761		Barthw. Delandre ,,	,,	off 1825

* Not in Company's lists, but described as a goldsmith in list of Dublin Prerog. Wills.
† ,, ,, ,, ,, ,, ,, ,, ,, ,, ,, ,, Dublin District Wills.
‡ T. Nuttall made no plate during the period in which he was assay master, 1776-1825.

LIST OF FREEMEN OF THE DUBLIN GOLDSMITHS' COMPANY—*Continued.*

Name of Goldsmith.			Free.	Last Notice or Death.	Name of Goldsmith.			Free.	Last Notice or Death.
Robt.	Field	E.	1770	d 1809	John	Dalrymple	S.S. & W.M.	1789	d 1823
James	Holmes	J.	,,		John	Keene	G.S.	,,	1807
Charles	Townsend	G.S.	,,	1784	John	Moore		,,	d 1798
Alexr.	Christie	W.M.	1771	d 1801	John	Nuttall		,,	d 1790
Isaac	Fraigneau		,,	d 1786	David	Peter		,,	d 1821
Darby	Kehoe	G.S.	,,		John	Rice	J.	,,	
Thos. E.	Strahan	J.	,,		John	Stoyte	G.S.	,,	1805
Charles	Wright	G.S.	,,		Thomas	Taylor	J.	,,	d 1825
John	Clarke	G.S.	1772	d 1798	Robert	Williams	G.S.	,,	d 1846
Hugh	Cunningham	W.M.	,,	d 1776	Will.	Keene	,,	,,	d 1800
Will.	Osborne		,,	d 1813	Thomas	Bridgman		1790	off 1808
Jonathan	Robinson	J.	,,	1790	Thos.	Walsh	,,	,,	
Samuel	Teare	G.S.	,,	d 1812	Walter B.	Nugent		,,	{ abroad 1832
Gordon	Whitthorne	W.M.	,,	d 1819					
William	Whitthorne	,,	,,	d 1826	John	Powell		1791	d 1837
John	Wade	J.	,,	1790	John	Moore, jun.		1792	d 1802
George	Beere, jun.		1773	1835	Denis	M'Owen		,,	d 1807
Samuel	Bermingham	,,	,,	d 1802	George	West		,,	d 1828
Arthur	Clarke	G.S.	,,	d 1821	Humph'y	Byrne	G.S.	1793	d 1817
Will.	Piers		,,	1779	Matt.	West, jun.		1794	d 1820
G. Davis	Sherry		,,	1794	Walter	Peter		,,	d 1845
Thomas	Jones	G.S.	1774	1803	Edward	Supple		,,	d 1838
Arthur	Keen		,,	d 1817	Thomas	Higginson		,,	{ struck off 1803
William	Law		,,	d 1820					
John	Martin		,,		George	Connor		1795	d 1837
William	Ward		,,	d 1822	Edward	Egerton	G.S.	,,	
Robt.	Dent		1775		Samuel	Nevill	,,	,,	d 1851
Lawrence	Fowler		,,	d 1826	Anthony	Willis	,,	,,	d 1848
Richard	Fowler		,,	d 1798	Joseph	Johnston	J.	1796	
Joseph	Jackson		,,	1807	John	Teare	G.S.	,,	
John	Wilson	W.M.	,,	1809	Willm.	Clarke	G.S.	1798	d 1828
Richard	Beere		1776	d 1807	Will.	Delandre		,,	off ,,
George	Forster		,,	d 1809	Robt.	Turner	G.S.	1799	d 1818
John	Kelly	J.	,,	d 1794	Oliver	Moore		1801	d 1845
Will.	Morrison		,,		Jacob	West, jun.		,,	to 1859
John	O'Neill	W.M.	,,		John Jos.	Peter		1802	off 1815
William	Power		,,	1806	Thos. A.	Harrison		,,	d 1846
Will.	Bridgman	G.S.	1777	d 1804	Richard	Whitford		,,	d 1824
George	Harkness		,,	1798	Alfred	Delessart		,,	off 1832
Samuel	Close	J.	1778	d 1821	James	Thorpe	C.M.	,,	off ,,
Daniel	Beere	,,	,,	d 1828	John	Lloyd, jun.		,,	d 1853
Peter	Warren		,,	off 1837	John	Tudor	G.S.	,,	d 1838
Will.	Sherwin		1779	d 1823	John	Townsend		,,	to 1855
Joshua	Adamson	G.S.	1780		John	Boxwell		,,	to ,,
John	Pittar		,,	d 1825	Francis	Boxwell		1803	to 1810
Solomon	Williams		,,	d 1823	Wm. Hy.	Townsend		,,	d 1853
Will.	Beere		1781	d 1853	John	West, jun.		1804	off 1836
Edward	Boyce	G.S.	1782	d 1791	Matthew	West		,,	d 1820
James	{ McKay or M'Coy		,,	off 1807	John	Ward		,,	d 1823
					Nicholas	Fell		,,	d 1809
Robert	Breading	G.S.	,,	d 1822	Joseph	Johnson		,,	to 1855
Richard	Fitzsimmons		1783	d 1798	John	Pittar, jun.		1805	to ,,
Richard	Gibbings		,,	d 1821	Will.	Morgan		1806	to ,,
Will.	Skinner		,,	d 1793	George	Warner		,,	d 1820
John	Franks		1784	d ,,	Pask	Pittar		1807	to 1855
Gore	Sherwin	J.	,,	1803	Thos.	Gonne		,,	d 1844
Jacob	West		,,	d 1824	Will.	Peter		,,	d 1825
Benjamin	Wilson, jun.		,,	d 1853	Richard	Sawyer		,,	d 1812
Edward	Rice	G.S.	1785	d 1815	Henry	Nixon		,,	off 1815
Henry	Wilme		,,	d 1818	George	Fivey		,,	d 1812
Thomas	Wilson		1786	d 1843	Hy. Dd.	Peter		,,	
Garrett	English	G.S.	1788	d 1791	Peter	Turpin		,,	
Joseph	Ridley	,,	,,	d 1810	John	Twycross		1808	
John	Austin		1789		Edward	Kevill		,,	

LIST OF FREEMEN OF THE DUBLIN GOLDSMITHS' COMPANY—*Continued.*

Name of Goldsmith.		Free.	Last Notice or Death.	Name of Goldsmith.		Free.	Last Notice or Death
Arthur	O'Neal	1808	d 1820	Stephen	Cox	1827	
Saml. J.	Pittar	,,		Jonathan	Osborne	1828	
Will.	Mossop	1809	d 1826	James	Fray	1829	d 1842
Richard	Gaskin	1810	d 1821	John	Laing	,,	d 1847
Matthew	Law	,,	to 1855	Richard	Sawyer	1830	
Henry	Rook	,,		Henry	West	,,	d 1881
W. Deane	Stubbs	,,		James	Willis	,,	
Thos.	Manning	,,	d 1853	John	Sawyer	,,	
Henry	Manning	,,		John H.	Hogan	1831	d 1853
George	Beere, jun.	1812		Edward	Twycross	,,	d 1851
John	Keene	,,	d 1828	James	Bourne	1833	
John	Browne	,,	d 1847	George	Twycross	1835	
John	Sherwin	,,	d 1820	Chas.	Kevill	,,	
Edward	Murray	,,	d 1853	Richard	Williams	,,	d 1835
R. W.	Osborne	,,	d 1834	Oliver	Moore	,,	
Thos.	Turpin	1813	d 1818	W. H.	Sherwin	,,	
Isaac	Hinds	,,	d 1849	Will.	West	,,	d 1837
John	Corry	1814	d 1853	Richard	Sherwin	1836	
Edward	Murphy	,,		F. E.	Gibbon	1837	
Poole	Taylor	,,		A. B.	Keene	,,	
John	Teare, jun.	,,	mr 1885	John	Moore	,,	
David T.	Peter	1816		Joseph	Pointz	,,	
Edward	Power	,,	d 1846	Henry	Flavelle	,,	
J. W. C.	Peter	,,		Rich'd Edw'd	Keene	1838	
John	Gaskin	,,	d 1834	Thos. Ryves	Metcalf	,,	
H. Thos.	Gonne	,,		Will.	Logan	,,	
Will.	Gainsford	1817		Will. Henry	Stanford	,,	
James	Moore	1818	d 1849	John	Ward	1839	
R. W.	Smith	,,		Richard	Richardson	,,	
George	Connor, jun.	,,		Edward	Murray, jun.	,,	
Samuel	Beere	,,	d 1818	Chas. Mat'w	West	1840	d 1883
Josiah	Low	1819	d 1846	James	McCord	,,	
John	Wade	1820		Thos.	Clarke	,,	
Forward	Rumley	,,		Alfred	De Lessart	,,	
J. F.	Sherwin	1822		Chas. G.	De Lessart	,,	
Edward	Thompson	,,		Arthur	Johnson	1843	
John	Warren	,,	d 1845	Joseph	Johnson, jun.	,,	
James	Le Bass	1824	d ,,	Edward	Quigley	,	
Starkey	Doyle	,,	d ,,	Henry	Flavelle, jun.	,,	
B. S.	Brunton	,,		Thos.	Smyth	1844	
Henry	Beere	,,		Thos.	Smith	,,	
Will.	McQuestion	,,		Thos.	Ayre	,,	
H. W.	Teare	,,		Will. Henry	Finlay	1845	
James	Wickham	1825		Thos.	Brunker	,,	
James	Johnson	,,		Matthew	Powell	,,	
Edmond	Johnson	,,		Theophilus	Barton	,,	
W. J.	Whitehorne	,,		Henry E.	Flavelle	,,	
Gordon	Whitehorne	,,		Wm. Horatio	Nelson	,,	
Henry	Whitehorne	,,		Walter	Askins	1847	
Walter	Askin	1826					

The books of the Company contain lists of its Freemen compiled as late as the year 1855, but the lists of later date than 1847 consist of repetitions of the names of goldsmiths on whom the freedom of the Company had been conferred in 1847 and earlier years, and no record has been found of any goldsmith having been admitted as a freeman between 1847 and 1855; about forty years ago the term "*member*" was adopted instead of "*freeman.*" The company now consists of twenty-five "members," including the master and two wardens.

In the above list, and in the list of goldsmiths compiled from directories and other sources, there are a few names which appear more than once—a number of years generally intervening between the dates of the respective entries. In those cases, as it is not known whether the repeated name was that of the same or a different person, the repetitions have been allowed to stand, because in many instances a father, son, and other relative—sometimes also strangers in blood—have borne a name identical with that of the person to whom the earliest record pertained.

ENROLMENTS OF APPRENTICES TO DUBLIN GOLDSMITHS FROM THE YEAR 1632.

The following list of apprentices extends over a period of nearly two hundred years and will be found of considerable service in ascertaining the names of the makers of Dublin plate of the 17th, 18th and early part of the 19th centuries. It will also—to a limited extent—afford assistance in fixing the approximate date of much of the plate wrought in Dublin in the 18th century on which no date-mark appears.

Each apprentice was bound for a term—seven years as a rule—to a master who engaged to teach him the art or mystery of the goldsmith. The dates which appear in the following list are the dates of the commencement of the apprenticeship, and no apprentice could have worked as a master-goldsmith before the expiration of the term for which he had been bound. As a rule, a date seven years subsequent to that appearing before his name in the list would be the earliest year in which he could legally have stamped his mark on plate, the latest being, of course, the last of his working life. It must, however, be borne in mind that in a few instances the business of a goldsmith has been continued by his widow who perhaps for a few years used her deceased husband's mark.

It is interesting to note that the names of many appearing in the following list as apprentices, recur periodically in later years as master-goldsmiths to whom in turn other apprentices were bound. The names of many may also be traced in this and the accompanying lists through the various stages of "apprentice," "goldsmith," "freeman of the Goldsmiths' Company" and "warden," to "master of the Company".

NOTE.—The entries in this list are not all in strict chronological order, but are printed as they occur in the volume from which they are taken. It seems that in some cases the indenture of apprenticeship was not brought to the Company's Hall for enrolment immediately after the apprentice was bound, but that as many as six years were sometimes allowed to elapse between the signing of the indenture and enrolment, which, however, except in the case of immigrants, appears to have been a necessary preliminary to ultimate recognition as a "goldsmith". When the indenture had been produced, it was the date of its execution, and not of its production, which was recorded, and that is the reason why some of the entries are out of chronological order.

G.S. = goldsmith ; W.M. = watchmaker ; J. = jeweller ; L. = lapidary.

NAME OF APPRENTICE.	NAME OF PARENT.	MASTER TO WHOM BOUND.
1632 Thomas Penn.	Humphrey Penn.	Clement Evans.
1637 Daniel Bellingham.	Robt. Bellingham.	Peter Vaneijndhoven.
Daniel Bould.	Peter Bould, of Chester.	John Woodcock.
Peter Hacket.	Will. Hacket, of Preston.	George Gallant.
1639 Will Culme.	Will. Culme, of Barnstaple.	Edward Bentley.
1640 Joseph Stoker.	Thos. Stoker, of Drogheda.	Gilbert Tonques.
1641 Roger Pointon.	Edward Pointon, of Chester.	James Vanderbeck.
1643 John Kinge.	John Kinge, of Edenderry.	Daniell Bellingham.
1640 Thomas Taylor.	Thomas Taylor, of Bellturbet, co. Cavan.	⎰ Daniel Burfelt. transferred to ⎱ John Williams.
1644 John Parnell.	Orphan of the Sittye of Dublin.	Thos. Parnell.
1646 Thos. Hall.	Orphan of the Sittye of Dublin.	Daniel Burfelt.
Benjamin Baysatt.	Benjamin Baysatt, decd.	Peter Vaneijndhoven.
1647 Francis Coffee.	Patrick Coffee, decd.	Robert Coffee.
1656 John East.	John East, watchmaker, London.	Daniel Bellingham.
1653 Edwd. Meredith.	Eliz. Meredith, Dublin, widow.	John Thornton.
1654 James Keally.	Philip Keally, Limerick, merchant.	John Slicer.
1662 George Benson.	Geo. Benson, co. Kerry, gent.	John Thornton.
1654 Nathaniel Withers.	... ...	Robert Lawe.
1655 Thomas Castle (signed Cashell).	... ...	Robert Lawe.
1654 Edmond Coghlan.	Daniel Coghlan, of Barony of Garrycastle, King's County, gent.	Isaac John.
1666 Richard Lord.	Richard Lord.	Isaac John.
1655 Edmond Palmer. (ran away June, 1657).	Emanuel Palmer, Ballyturlagh, co. Roscommon, gent.	Edwd. Swan.
1656 Wm. Williams.	Robert Williams, late of Dublin, ironworker.	Nich. Seward.
1660 Wm. Trevis.	Wm. Trevis, late of Dublin, gent.	Geo. Lambert.
1662 Wm. Harborne.	Wm. Harborne, Dublin, gent.	John Parnell.
1663 David Aickin.	(br. of Robert Aickin, merchant.)	Geo. Lambert.

ENROLMENTS OF APPRENTICES—*Continued.*

	NAME OF APPRENTICE.		NAME OF PARENT.	MASTER TO WHOM BOUND.	
1658	Chas.	Brackenberry.	John Brackenberry, Dublin, gent.	Thos.	Barker.
	Hugh	Hughes.	Elizabeth Hughes, Holyhead, widow.	Rt.	Thornton.
	Valentine	Hammond.	Henry Hammond, of Preston, decd.	Geo.	Southicke.
1659	Thos.	Doran.	Chas. Doran, maltster, decd.	Miles	Graham.
1660	Andrew	Presland.	Richard Presland, of Issaroyd, co. Denbigh, gent., decd.	Tho.	Parnell.
1658	Lancelott	Brauthwaite.	Anthony Brauthwaite, Lamplouth, Cumberland, yeoman.	Ed.	Swan.
1664	Joseph	Stoker.	Jos. Stoker.	Jos.	Stoker.
	Thos.	Rutter.	Thos. Rutter.	Thos.	Rutter.
1665	Samuel	Marsden.	Samuel Marsden, Dublin, tallow chandler.	Timy.	Blackwood.
1666	John	Phillips.	Griffantius Phillips, Gloucester, gent.	Abm.	Voysin.
	Walter	Lewis.	Thos. Lewis, Dublin, joiner.	Edmd.	Coghlan.
1667	John	Moore.	Thomas Moore.	Abel	Ram.
	Thos.	Linnington.	Geo. Linnington, late of Wexford, decd.	Abel	Ram.
	Walter	Lloyd.	Jenkin Lloyd, D.D., Treaprise, Pembrokeshire.	John	Dickson.
1669	Richd.	St. Lawrence.	Richard St. Lawrence, Rathenie, co. Dublin, gent.	Tho.	Godfrey.
	Abm.	Blanchard.	Isaac Blanchard, Rowslouch, co. Worcester, gent.	Isaac	John.
1670	John	Clifton.	Francis Clifton, goldsmith, decd.	John	Cope.
1673	Walter	Bingham.	Walter Bingham, Dublin, gent.	Ed.	Ashton.
	Samuel	Peirson. (ran away)	John Peirson, late of Cominstown, co. Westmeath, gent. decd.	Tim.	Blackwood.
	Edmond	Coffey.	Edmond Coffey, Ballykeran, co. Westmeath, decd.	Fras.	Coffee.
	John	Baskett.	... ...	Abm.	Voysin.
1672	John	Deane.	... ...	Paul	Lovelace.
1674	Wm.	Dermott.	... ...	John	Cope.
	John	Mosely.	... ...	Isaac	John.
1673	Fras.	Nevill.	... ...	Jas.	Cottingham.
	Thos.	Tennant.	Thos. Tennant.	Thos.	Tennant.
1674	Stephen	Marmion.	... ...	Abel	Ram.
1672	John	Segar.	Richard Segar, clk.	Tho.	Sterne.
1674	Thos.	Bradshaw.	E. Bradshaw, Woodstock, co. Kildare, gent.	John	Hiett.
1675	Wm.	Close.	Wm. Close, Lisburn, Esq., decd.	Tho.	Sterne.
1676	Benj.	West.	Thos. West, Belgeight, co. Meath, gent.	John	Farmer.
	Ebenezer	Cawdron.	Geo. Cawdron, Dublin, gent.	Jas.	Kelly.
1674	John	Shelley.	Jno. Shelley, Ratoath, gent.	Tim.	Blackwood.
1675	John	Bennett.	Jno. Bennett, Kidwelly, Carmarthenshire.	John	Popkins.
	David	Sibbald.	Henry Sibbald, Carrickmcroe, co. Wicklow, gent., decd.	Samuel	Marsden.
	David	Swan.	John Swan, Baldwinstown, co. Wexford, Esq., decd.	Abm.	Voysin.
	John	Bulkeley.	Wm. Bulkeley, Anglesey, N.W., gent.	Walter	Lewis.
	Thos.	Yeates.	Thos. Yeates, Dublin, vintner, decd.	Christr.	Palles.
1676	Joseph	Bayly.	Jos. Bayly, Casterton, Cumberland, apothecary, decd.	Paul	Lovelace.
	James	Walsh.	Edmd. Walsh, Shanganoth, co. Dublin, gent., decd.	Dennis	Bryne
	Ben.	Breviter.	Richard Breviter, Norwich, clk., decd.	Abm.	Voisin.
1675	Geo.	Cartwright.	—— Cartwright, decd.	Jas.	Cottingham.
1676	Wm.	Drayton.	... ...	Andrew	Gregory.
1675	Chas.	Wilton.	Roger Wilton, Curglass, co. Cavan, gent.	Jas.	Cottingham.
	Joseph	Wesencroft.	Ralph Wesencroft, Dublin, hammerman.	Adam	Sorett.
1676	Thos.	Bolton.	Henry Bolton, Ratoath, clk.	Gerard	Grace.
1677	John	Turner.	John Turner, Dublin, periwig maker.	John	Martin.
	Ezekiel	Bourne.	John Bourne, physician.	John	Martin.
1678	Henry	Chabenor.	Tho. Chabenor, Dublin, decd.	Geo.	Sowthaick.
1677	John	Ebzery.	... ...	Samuel	Marsden.
	Thos	Osborn.	... ...	John	Cope.
1675	Burley	Cuffe.	... ...	Abel	Ram.
1678	Benj.	Burton.	... ...	Abel	Ram.
1679	Michael	Haynes.	... ...	John	Powell.

ENROLMENTS OF APPRENTICES—*Continued.*

	NAME OF APPRENTICE.		NAME OF PARENT.	MASTER TO WHOM BOUND.	
1673	Wm.	Keatinge.	(br. to Oliver Keatinge, Dublin, gent.)	Rd.	Webb.
1679	Thos.	Bayly.	... ...	Thos.	Godfrey.
	Geo.	Thornton.	... ...	Jas.	Kelly.
	Geo.	Newbold.	Francis Newbold, Ballyfinnen, Queen's co., gent.	Walter	Lewis.
1675	John	Brearley.	John Brearley, Dublin, gent.	Tho.	Linnington.
1678	Wm.	Mainwaring.	Wm. Mainwaring, Athy, gent.	Adam	Sorett.
1679	John	Billing.	John Billing, Kingstowne, gent.	John	Mosely.
	Timothy	Charnock.	Geo. Charnock, Gallygallerie, Queen's co., farmer.	John	Segar.
1677	John	Nowlan.	Patrick Nowlan, Dublin, tailor.	Edmd.	Coghlan.
1679	Arthur	Bryne.	Barn. Bryne, Colebuck, co. Westmeath, Esq., decd.	Denis.	Bryne.
1680	Chas.	Danter.	Son-in-law to John Durey, Limerick, gent.	John	Phillips.
1679	James	Willoe.	... ...	Elizab'th	Lovelace.
1680	Steph.	Shatling.	Daniel Shatling, Dublin, merchant.	Matw.	La Roch.
1678	Joseph	Whitechurch.	Jos. Whitechurch, Dublin, decd.	Andrew	Gregorie.
1680	Oliver	Nugent.	Nich. Nugent, Castledelvin, co. Westmeath, gent., decd.	Christr.	Palles.
1681	Henry	Moore.	Nich. Moore, Ardestown, co. Louth, Esq., decd.	Walter	Lewis.
1680	John	Webb.	Richd. Webb, Kilkenny, gent., decd.	John	Farmer.
1681	Geo.	Stewart.	Jas. Stewart, Newry, gent., decd.	Andrew	Gregory.
	John	Peryman.	Geo. Peryman, gent., decd.	Samuel	Marsden.
	Thos.	Meekins.	John Meekins, Dublin, blacksmith, decd.	Walter	Bingham.
	Christr.	Fitzgerald.	Richard Fitzgerald, Rathrone, co. Meath, Esq., decd.	Christr.	Palles.
	Walter	Dougherty.	Daniel Dougherty.	Wm.	Myas.
1682	Walter	Fitzgerald.	Thos. Fitzgerald, gent.	Denis	Bryne.
1681	James	Moussoult.	... ...	Abm.	Voisin.
1683	Samuel	Clarke.	Henry Clarke, Belfast, innkeeper.	Abm.	Voisin.
1682	Wm.	Ormsby.	Wm. Ormsby, Grange, co. Roscommon, gent.	John	Deane.
1683	Alex.	Dickson.	Archibald Dickson, Tourland, Scotland, gent.	John	Dickson.
1678	Joseph	Teate.	Joseph Teate, Dean of Kilkenny, decd.	John	Cuthbert.
1680	Geo.	Montgomerie.	—— Montgomery, decd.	John	Cuthbert.
1681	David	King.	James King, gent.	John	Cuthbert.
1683	Wm.	Pridham.	Wm. Pridham.	John	Phillips.
1681	Joseph	Chiven.	James Chiven, Drogheda, merchant.	Wm.	Archbold.
	John	McLaughlin.	Phelim McLaughlin, Dublin, butcher.	Wm.	Archbold.
	Wm.	Stockley.	Tho. Stockley, Liverpool, innholder.	Geo.	Taylor.
1683	Samuel	John.	Isaac John, Dublin, jeweller, decd.	Abm.	Voisin.
	Samuel	Wilder.	Mathew Wilder, Carlingford, gent.	John	Hyett.
	Joseph	Walker.	John Walker, Dublin, weaver, decd.	John	Cuthbert.
	John	Powell.	Robert Powell, gent.	Walter	Lewis.
	Robert	Sheilds.	Robert Sheilds, gent.	John	Shelly.
1685	Joseph	Malbon.	Samuel Malbon, London, clk., decd.	Wm.	Billinghurst.
1684	Robert	Mollineux.	Richard Mollineux, Newhall, in Darby, Lanc., gent.	Geo.	Taylor.
1685	John	Harlin.	Edmd. Harlin, Dublin, innholder.	Jos.	Bayly.
1684	Alex.	Tweedy.	Patrick Tweedy, Dublin, gent.	Wm.	Myas.
1685	Wm.	Price.	Lewis Price, Dublin, shoemaker.	John	Deane.
1686	John	Martin.	Thos. Martin, Rabuck, co. Dublin, gent.	Ebenezer	Caudron.
	Isaac	Dawson.	John Dawson, Heaton Rhodes, Lanc., weaver, decd.	Wm.	Drayton.
1685	Isaiah	Grosvenor.	Francis Grosvenor, Dublin, brewer.	John	Deane.
1686	Robert	Ince.	Robert Ince, Dublin, haberdasher.	John	Brearly.
	Conway	Mace.	Elizabeth Berry, Dublin.	John	Cuthbert.
	Patrick	Cadell.	Richard Cadell, Dublin, baker.	John	Morphy.
1681	Francis	Bovet.	Elias Bovet, Rochelle, France, merchant.	Adam	Sorett.
1687	Alex.	Sinclare.	Wm. Sinclare, Belfast, merchant.	John	Cuthbert.
1685	John	Ward.	Wm. Ward, Dublin, butcher.	John	Shelly.
1686	John	Bennett.	John Bennett, Dublin, victualler.	Thos.	Boulton.
1690	Jas.	Kinnier.	(br. of William Kinnier, clk.).	John	Humphreys.
1685	Anthony	Stanley.	Chr. Stanley, Drogheda, merchant.	Chr.	Palles.

ENROLMENTS OF APPRENTICES—*Continued.*

NAME OF APPRENTICE.		NAME OF PARENT.	MASTER TO WHOM BOUND.	
1686	Thos. Melaghlin.	Thos. Melaghlin, Ardrum, co. Meath.	Chr.	Palles.
	Henry Sharp.	Henry Sharp, late of Lazyhill, Dublin.	John	Phillips.
	John Bennett.	John Bennett, Dublin, victualler.	Robert	Smith.
	Benjamin Haslehurst.	John Haslehurst, Dublin, joiner.	John	Brearly.
1688	Samuel Berry.	John Berry, late of Clonehan, King's co., gent.	John	Humphry.
	*John Gerrard.	Wm. Gerrard, woodmonger.	John	Dixon.
1692	*Ciriac Mallory.	Thos. Mallory, late minister of Maynooth.	John	Phillips.
	John Cuthbert, jun.	John Cuthbert.	John	Cuthbert.
1693	Samuel Ruchant.	... ...	Mat.	La Roch.
1692	James Brenan.	(br. of Daniel Brenan.)	David	Swan.
	James Standish.	... ...	Tho.	Bolton.
1693	Robert Evers.	... ...	Wm.	Lucas.
1690	Henry Miller.	John Miller, Dublin, gent.	Henry	Chabenor.
1694	Chas. White.	John White, Ballymore Eustace, decd.	John	Phillips.
1693	Edwd. Workman.	Richd. Workman, Portadown, tanner.	Jas.	Welding.
1694	Chas. Crompton.	Thos. Crompton, co. Wexford, gent.	John	Cuthbert.
1695	John Sterne.	Thos. Sterne, Dublin, goldsmith, decd.	Edwd.	Slicer.
(no date)	Geo. Pilkington.	Thos. Pilkington, Dublin, gent., decd.	Robert	Rigmaiden.
1694	Edwd. Fitzgerald.	Oliver Fitzgerald, Tara, co. Meath, gent.	Walt.	Bingham.
1695	Jas. Drysdale.	Jas. Drysdale, co. Kilkenny, clk., decd.	Thos.	Bolton.
	Wm. Archdall.	John Archdall, Lusk, clk., decd.	David	King.
	Philip Tough.	Thos. Tough, Dundalk.	Jas.	Welding.
1697	Thos. Paris.	Lt.-Col. Henry Paris, Dublin.	Fras.	Cuthbert.
1698	Edwd. Hall.	Thos. Hall, Dublin, gent.	John	Harris.
	Chas. Brigham.	Sebastian Brigham, Dublin, gent.	John	Harris.
1699	Jas. Blanchard.	Samuel Blanchard, Dublin, farrier.	Jos.	Walker.
	Gilbert Lane.	Wm. Lane, late co. Tipperary, gent.	Jos.	Walker.
	Anthony Walsh.	Pierse Walsh, Dublin, milliner, decd.	Ed.	Slicer.
1700	Jacques Foucault.	Peter Foucault, Dublin, Surgeon.	John	Harris.
	Wm. Ross.	Henry Ross, Drogheda, gent.	Jas.	Welding.
	Mark Mottershead.	John Mottershead, Dublin, farmer.	Saml.	Wilder.
1699	Richard Brown.	Richard Brown, Dublin, yeoman.	R.	Grosvenor.
1701	John Whiting.	John Whiting, Dublin, wheelwright.	Ed.	Slicer.
	Thos. Deane.	Zachary Deane, Dublin, gent.	And.	Gregory.
1697	Thos. Rasin.	Edward Rasin, Dublin, victualler.	John	Turner.
1702	Ambrose Bruffe.	Amb. Bruffe (or Brough).	Thos.	Meekins.
1700	Wm. Sheilds.	Roger Sheilds, Wainestown, co. Meath, gent.	A.	Sinclare.
1702	Stevens Golding.	John Golding, Dublin, gent.	A.	Sinclare.
1701	Benj. Hawley.	Wm. Hawley, James St., Dublin, saddler.	A.	Sinclare.
	Henry King.	Peter King (late of France).	Ben.	Racine.
	Vincent Trott.	Martin Trott, late of Dublin, gent.	Ed.	Workman.
1702	Chas. Gordon.	Alex. Gordon, Dublin, gent.	Chr.	Waggoner.
1703	†John Tute.	James Tute, Drogheda, merchant.	John	Matthews.
1699	John Whitfield.	Robert Whitfield, Dublin, girdler.	Thos.	Bolton.
1700	Nehemiah Donnellan.	Dorothy Jones.	Thos.	Bolton.
1703	Henry Daniell.	Richard Daniell, Coombe, Dublin, clothier.	Thos.	Bolton.
1704	Wm. Smith.	Wm. Smith, Ballyshannon, gent.	Chr.	Hartwick.
1701	Geo. Harris.	Wm. Harris, Bandon, gent.	Walter	Bingham.
1704	Wm. Brady.	John Brady, Dublin, gent.	Cyriac	Mallory.
1703	Lawrence Burke.	Mary Burke, Ross, co. Wexford.	Ed.	Barrett.
1705	John Fourreau.	Aymé Fourreau, Dublin, gent.	Ed.	Barrett.
1706	James Cole.	James Cole, late of England, gent.	Jno.	Matthews.
	Robert Willmore.	Wm. Willmore, Dublin, tailor, decd.	Mortagh	Dowling.
1704	Abm. Crosle.	John Crosle, Armagh.	John	Crampton.
1702	Robert Coleman.	James Coleman, Dublin, gent.	Joseph	Walker.
1706	Wm. Caddow.	John Caddow, Dublin, shoemaker.	Ben.	Pemberton.
	Wm. Patten.	Wm. Patten, Drogheda, gent.	John	Matthews.
1704	Cornelius Malone.	Mary Malone, Dublin, widow.	Robert	Ince.
1706	Bolton Cormock.	John Cormock, Dublin, gent.	And.	Gregory.
1705	Rd. Chinn.	Rd. Chinn, Newnham, Gloucester, gent.	Ed.	Slicer.
1707	John Coudert.	Bernard Coudert, Dublin, gent.	Mortagh	Dowling.

* There are no entries between 1688 and 1692, which may be explained by the state of Ireland during this period while the respective armies of Jas. II. and Wm. III. were contending there.

† John Tute, or Tuite, moved to London in 1723, where he afterwards worked for many years. He advertised in the Dublin Weekly Journal of 3 May, 1729.

ENROLMENTS OF APPRENTICES—*Continued.*

NAME OF APPRENTICE.		NAME OF PARENT.	MASTER TO WHOM BOUND.	
1706	James Young.	Simon Young, co. Wexford, decd.	Ed.	Slicer.
1707	Thos. Walker.	Thos. Walker, Dublin, smith.	John	Whitefield.
	Jas. Balaquier.	Barthw. Balaquier, Dublin, clk.	Daniel	Pineau.
	John Frees.	Jas. Frees, Dublin, brasier.	Christian	Kindt.
	Mathew Copeland.	Geo. Copeland, Dublin, shoemaker.	Ben.	Mountjoy.
	John Steele.	Fabian Steele, Dublin, gent., decd.	Ben.	Mountjoy.
	Wm. B. St Lawrance.	Chr. St. Lawrance, Dublin.	John	Crampton.
	Benj. Boové.	John Boové, Dublin, gent.	Fran.	Giraud.
1704	*Walter Bingham.	... ...	John	Harris.
1707	Wm. Bennett.	Wm. Bennett, Dublin, merchant.	Erasmus	Cope.
	Henry Cope.	John Cope, Dublin, goldsmith, decd.	David	King.
1708	John Nicholas.	John Nicholas, Maguiresbridge, gent., decd.	John	Cuthbert.
	Wm. McMurray.	... ...	Ed.	Slicer.
	John Downes.	Richard Downes.	Wm.	Skinner.
1707	Wm. Williamson.	Richd. Williamson.	Jos.	Blundell.
1709	Chas. Moneypeny.	Rev. Henry Moneypeny.	Fran.	Humphry.
	Jas. Rickisson.	Robert Rickisson, Dublin, shoemaker, decd.	Fran.	Humphry.
	Robert Aickin.	Geo. Aickin, Paulstown, co. Dublin, gent.	Henry	Sherwin.
	Henry Sherwin.	John Sherwin, Dublin, shoemaker, decd.	Henry	Sherwin.
1707	Wm. Sherwin.	Henry Sherwin, Dublin, goldsmith.	John	Palet.
1709	John Wilme.	Wm. Wilme, Dublin, brewer.	John	Harris.
1708	Isaac Neau.	Martin Neau, Dublin, merchant, decd.	Christn.	Kindt.
1709	Simon Young.	Simon Young, Ballytange, co. Wexford, gent., decd.		
1708	Jas. Trubshaw.	Thos. Trubshaw, Dublin, merchant, decd.	Fran.	{ Gerrard (or { Giraud).
1711	John Taylor.	Robert Taylor, Dublin, skinner.	David	King.
1709	Hugh Hamilton.	(br. of John Hamilton, goldsmith).	John	Hamilton.
1710	Wm. Parker.	John Parker, Limerick, gunsmith.	Christn.	Kindt.
	John Mitchell.	John Mitchell, Knockdruman, co. Dublin.	Wm.	Archdall.
	Adam Tate.	Moses Tate, Augher, co. Tyrone, gent.	John	Hamilton.
	Geo. Peregrine	Mary Peregrine, Dublin, widow.	Ed.	Workman.
1712	Robert Billing.	... .	Thos.	Billing.
	John Clifton.	... ...	John	Clifton.
	Wm. Eycott.	Richard Eycott, Dublin, silversmith.	Ed.	Barrett.
1713	Matthew Roper.	Mary Roper, Dublin, widow.	Ed.	Barrett.
1710	Wm. Aickin.	Geo Aickin, The Murrow, co. Dublin.	Philip	Tough.
1715	Asahell Mason.	Rebecca Mason, widow.	Erasmus	Cope.
1712	Martin Kirkpatrick.	... ...	John	Burton.
	Jas. Correges.	... ...	Daniel	Pineau.
1715	Wm. Scott.	John Scott, Santry.	John	Pallett.
1714	Francis Gerard.	... ...	Mary	Gerard.
	Robinson Augier.	... ...	Daniel	Pineau.
1712	Wm. Fawcett.	... ...	Thos.	Parker.
1715	Wm. White.	Wm. White, Sconagh, co. Wexford.	John	Clifton.
1716	Richd. Hall.	Mable Hall, Dublin, widow.	Ed.	Workman.
	Richard Cody.	John Cody, co. Westmeath, gent., decd.	Mark	Twelves.
	Joseph Semirot.	Anthony Semirot, Cork.	Thos.	Deane.
	Thos. Butler.	Thos. Butler, Waterford, periwig maker.	John	Cuthbert.
	Richard Workman.	Ed. Workman, goldsmith.	Ed.	Workman.
	Chas. Prendergrass.	(stepson of Rd. Burnham, Dublin, gardener.)	Ed.	Workman.
1712	Chas. Maynou.	... ...	John	Paterell.
1714	John Price.	... ...	John	Burton.
1715	Thos. Chapel.	... ...	John	Paturel.
1716	Jas. Truelove.	James Truelove, Dublin, gent.	Mary	Gerard.
1715	John Taylor.	John Taylor, Dublin, skinner.	Ben.	Mountjoy.
1714	Benj. Correges.	Eliz. Correges, Dublin, widow.	Peter	Gervais.
1717	Wm. Smith.	Robert Smith, goldsmith.	Tho.	Walker.
	Geo. Dougherty.	John Dougherty, Rossmagh, co. Dublin, gent.	John	Crampton.
	John Robinson.	... ...	Mat.	Walker.
	Jas. Whitehorne.	... ...	Geo.	Parker.
	Alex. Richards.	Alex. Richards, Dublin, grocer.	Robt.	Forbes.
1715	Wm. Sumner.	Thos. Sumner, Dublin, cabinet maker.	Jos.	Blundell.

* Not in the regular list, but mentioned in the Company's Journal as having been "enrolled an apprentice" in 1704.

ENROLMENTS OF APPRENTICES—*Continued.*

	NAME OF APPRENTICE.		NAME OF PARENT.	MASTER TO WHOM BOUND.	
1714	Robt.	Williamson.	Mary Williamson, Wicklow, widow.	Tho.	Parker.
	John	Brown.	Jas. Brown, Dublin, coachmaker.	Jas.	Champion.
1715	Daniel	Nixon.	Rev. Adam Nixon, Drumcrow, co. Fermanagh, clk.	David	King.
	Francis	Thornhill.	Francis Thornhill, Ballybough Lane, co. Dublin, farmer.	Ed.	Sturgys.
1716	Stephen	Delile.	... ...	Daniel	Pinsane.
1712	William	Fawcett.	... ...	Tho.	Parker.
1717	Roger	Finch.	Sarah Finch, Wigan, Lanc.	John	Williamson.
	Richard	Foster.	... ...	John	Sterne.
	Jas.	Templeton.	... ...	Wm.	Archdall.
	John	Broadhorst.	John Broadhorst, Dublin, gent.	John	Hamilton.
	John	Moore.	Alice Moore, Boley, co. Wexford, widow.	Jos.	Walker.
1716	John	King.	Jas. King, Dublin, merchant.	John	Patturell.
1717	John	Rogers.	Thos. Rogers, Dublin, founder.	John	Barry.
1718	Wm.	Townsend.	John Townsend.	Chr.	Keindt.
	Wm.	Reily.	Chas. Reily.	Edmd.	Sturgys.
1717	Jas.	Lasalle.	Mark Lasalle, Dublin, gent.	Daniel	Pineau.
1718	Wm.	Currie.	Mary Currie, Dublin, widow.	Peter	Gervais.
	John Jas.	Turner.	... ...	Noah	Vialas.
	Daniel	Brogan.	... ...	Tho.	Cope.
	Henry	Cole.	... ...	Eras.	Cope.
	Thos.	Rone.	... ...	Jos.	Walker.
	John	Jones.	... ...	Tho.	Bolton.
	Benjamin	Hocks.	... ...	Dorothy	Monjoy.
	Timothy	Pontt.	... ...	John	Pallett.
	Wm.	Ryan.	... ...	Geo.	Parker.
	James	Lintoun.	... ...	Philip	Kinersly.
	Peter	Racine.	Benj. Racine.	Benj.	Racine.
	Chas.	Ball.	... ...	Ph.	Kinnersly.
	Chr.	Jackson.	... ...	Tho.	Cope.
1717	Nich.	Workman.	Ed. Workman.	Ed.	Workman.
1719	Esaias	De Lorthe.	Esaias De Lorthe.	Jas.	Balaquier.
	Peter	Audouin.	... ...	Daniel	Pineau.
1718	Wm.	Stoppelaer.	Chas. Stoppelaer, Dublin, painter.	Arthur	Weldon.
1719	John	Nangle.	Geo. Nangle.	Eras.	Cope.
	Elias	Maquay.	(bro. to Rev. Thos. Maquay.)	Mat.	Walker.
	Thos.	Grey.	Deborah Grey.	Jas.	Champion.
	Ansloey	Lavally.	(stepson of John Price, Stoneybatter, gent.)	Ed.	Barrett.
	John	Chauvin.	John Chauvin, Dublin wigmaker.	Peter	Gervais.
	Richd.	Eaton.	Burleigh Eaton, Dublin, clothier.	John	Williamson.
1720	Geo.	Cross.	Thos. Cross, Dublin.	Thos.	Crampton.
	Henry	Cope.	Rev. Anthony Cope, clk., decd.	John	Williamson.
1719	David	Homan.	M'y Homan, Dromcooly, King's co., widow.	John	Williamson.
	David	Baumes.	Ann Baumes, widow.	Martin	Billing.
1718	James	Robison.	Geo. Robison, Limerick, gent.	John	Paturle.
1717	John	Moore.	Alice Moore, Buoly, co. Wicklow, widow.	Jos.	Walker.
1718	Wm.	Cearey.	Wm. Cearey, Dublin, gent.	Jos.	Blundell.
1720	Wm.	Savill.	Kath. Savill, Dublin, widow.	Walter	Bingham.
	John	Tench.	John Tench, Navan.	Tho.	Sutton.
	Francis	Moseley.	John Moseley, Wicklow.	Henry	Daniel.
1721	James	Weir.	James Weir, Sligo, farmer.	John	Clifton.
1722	And.	Goodwin.	And. Goodwin, decd.	Henry	Daniel.
1721	Fras.	Williamson.	Fras. Williamson, Dublin, shoemaker.	Ed.	Barrett.
1720	Barth.	Popkins.	Nicholas Popkins, Dolphin's Barn, surgeon.	Simon	Young.
1721	Isaac	D'Olier.	Isaac D'Olier, Dublin.	John	Williamson.
	John	Pagett.	Rich'd. Pagett, Dublin, merchant.	Thos.	Sutton.
	Stephen	Royall.	Stephen Royall, Dublin, gent.	Noah	Vialas.
	Deacon	Standish.	James Standish, Dublin, gent.	Martin	Billing.
	Michael	Connor.	Ann Connor, widow.	Wm.	Streeter.
	Thos.	Hall.	Edward Hall, goldsmith.	Ed.	Hall.
	Samuel	Taylor.	Samuel Taylor, Dublin, silk dyer.	Eras.	Cope.
	Chas.	Gouy.	Wm. Gouy, Dublin, mariner.	Noah	Vialas.
1722	Thos.	Connor.	Wm Connor, Dublin, gent.	Ph.	Kinnersly.
	John	Young.	John Young, late of London, distiller.	John	Freboul.

ENROLMENTS OF APPRENTICES—*Continued.*

NAME OF APPRENTICE.		NAME OF PARENT.	MASTER TO WHOM BOUND.	
1722	Abm. Mondet.	Lodowick Mondet, Dublin, merchant.	Arth.	Weldon.
	Daniel Walker.	Thomas Walker, Dublin, distiller.	Dorothy	Monjoy.
	Wm. Babington.	Thos. Babington, co. Donegal, gent.	Geo.	Parker.
1723	Henry Crosle.	John Crosle, Armagh.		
	Wm. Minchin.	Wm. Minchin, Busherstown, King's co., Esq.	Tho.	Walker.
	Hugh Martin.	Simon Martin, Dublin, merchant.	Ed.	Sturgys.
	Philip Barrett.	Mary Barrett.	Mary	Barrett.
	Thos. Jolly.	Thos. Jolly, Dublin, gent.	Dorothy	Manjoy.
	Peter Desinards.	Lamotte Desinards, Dublin, merchant.	John	Sterne.
	Joshua Mirfield.	Joseph Mirfield, Dublin, carpenter.	John	Bradley.
	Peter Lacoste.	Hercules Lacoste, Portarlington, gent.	Mark	Martin.
	Richd. White.	Robert White, Ballymore, Eustace, gent.	Wm.	Doogan.
	Jas. Champion.	Jas. Champion, Dublin, jeweller.	Henry	Wilme.
	Jas. Douglas.	Thos. Douglas, Dublin, tailor.	John	Hamilton.
	Peter Dennard.	Mark Dennard, Dublin, merchant.	John	Sterne.
	Geo. Lapier.	Stephen Lapier, Dublin, merchant.	Tho.	Sutton.
	Joseph McMun.	... ...	Mat.	Walker.
1724	Cleare Bate.	Wm. Bate, Dublin, engraver.	Thos.	Cope.
	Tho. Parsons.	Tho. Parsons, Dublin, sword cutler.	Matthew	Walker.
	Robert Glanvile.	Francis Glanvile, late of Longford, gent.	John	Hamilton.
1723	Elias Tankerfeild.	... ...	Martin	Kirkpatrick.
1724	Philip Walsh.	Richard Walsh, Dublin, Tailor.	Ph.	Kinnersley.
	Robert Burfield.	Jane Burfield, Dublin, widow.	Eras.	Cope.
1723	Peter Vicars.	Wm. Vicars, Grantston, Queen's county.	Wm.	Barry.
1725	John Gaskin.	Mary Gaskin, Dublin, widow.	Tho.	Crampton.
	Anthony Lefebure.	Jacob Lefebure, Dublin, Merchant.	Mary	Barrett.
	Richard Baker.	Rd. Baker, Dublin, goldsmith.	Roger	Finch.
	John Alexander.	John Alexander, Dublin, gent.	Chas.	Leslie.
	John Fortin.	Thos. Fortin, Waterford, merchant.	Tho.	Walker.
	Peirce Bass.	John Bass, Dublin, slater.	Esther	Forbes.
	Peter Usher.	Peter Usher, Dublin, founder.	Roger	Finch.
	Benj. Mosley.	John Mosley, Dublin, weaver.	Jas.	Whitthorne.
1722	John Jesson.	Elizabeth Jesson, Dublin, widow.	John	Freeze.
1724	Silvester Ince.	Randolph Ince, Dublin, apothecary.	Peter	Gervy.
1725	Wm. Sheilds.	Martha Sheilds, als. Walsh, Dublin, widow.	Ph.	Kinnersly.
	Albert Hamon.	Albert Hamon, Dublin, gent., decd.	Arth.	Weldon.
	Forbes Lovett.	Thos Lovett, Dublin, sword cutler.	Wm.	Sinclare.
1726	Peter Faure.	Elizabeth Faure, Dublin, widow.	Wm.	Barry.
	Wm. West.	Robert West, Waterford.	John	Hamilton.
	John Ball.	Elizabeth Ball, Dublin, widow.	Peter	Racine.
	George Williams.	Edward Williams, Dublin, apothecary, decd.	Wm.	Sutton.
	Daniel Beringuier.	Stephen Beringuier, Dublin, merchant.	John	Bradley.
	Samuel Walker.	Elizabeth Walker, Dublin, widow.	John	Taylor.
	Geo. Berford.	Richard Berford, Dublin, gent.	Tho.	Williamson.
	Reasin Foley.	Wm. Foley, late of Dublin, victualler.	Robert	Billing.
	Daniel Hamond.	Albert Hamond, late of Dublin, gent., decd.	John	Williamson.
	James Vidouze.	James Vidouze, gent.	Daniel	Pineau.
	Jno. La D. Letablere.	Rene La Douespe Letablere, Dublin, Esq.	Wm.	Streeter.
	Philip Thompson.	John Thompson, Dublin, gent.	Geo.	Parker.
	Richard Forster.	Richard Forster, late co., Tipperary, gent.	Noah	Vialas.
	Matthias Brown.	Edwd. Brown, late of Mosson, G.B., mariner.	Simon	Young.
	John Strahan.	Jane Strahan, Dublin, widow.	Tho.	Sutton.
	Wm. Gaughagan.	Chas. Gaughagan, late of Dublin, founder.	Ch.	Prendergast.
	Daniel Calderwood.	Andrew Calderwood, Dublin, gent.	Arth.	Weldon.
	Barthw. Mosse.	Michael Mosse, Ballywish, co. Wexford, clk., decd.	William	Williamson.
1727	Daniel Onge.	(nephew of Abel Onge, Dublin, merchant.)	Wm.	Sinclare.
1726	Thos. De Limarest.	Mary de Limarest, Dublin, widow.	Martin	Billing.
1727	Thos. Burton.	John Burton, London, chandler.	Dorothy	Manjoy.
	Wm. Gratton.	Richd. Gratton, Edenderry, gent.	Peter	Jervis.
	Matthew Alanson.	John Alanson, Dublin, merchant.	Mark	Martin.
	Solomon Savage.	Robert Savage, Dublin, merchant.	John	Sterne.
	Wm. Hadlock.	Samuel Hadlock, Dublin, gent.	Walter	Bingham.
	Chas. Boucher.	Peter Boucher, late of Rochelle, merchant.	Alex.	Brown.
	Robert Baker.	(br. of Geo. Baker, Dungannon, gent.)	John	Williamson.

ENROLMENTS OF APPRENTICES—*Continued.*

	NAME OF APPRENTICE.		NAME OF PARENT.	MASTER TO WHOM BOUND.	
1727	Wm.	Teatte.	... ...	M.	Billing.
	Æneas	McPherson.	Daniel McPherson, Dublin, merchant.	Ch.	Leslie.
	Henry	Lyndon.	Chas. Lyndon, Dublin, merchant.	Eras.	Cope.
	Vere	Forster.	Richd. Forster, Dublin, gent.	Robt.	Calderwood.
1728	Joshua	Crampton.	John Crampton, goldsmith.	John	Crampton.
1727	Philip	Portal.	John Portal, Dublin, gent.	Simon	Young.
1728	Robert	Mirfield.	Joseph Mirfield, Dublin, carpenter.	John	Bradley.
	Archd.	Scott.	Mary Scott, Dublin, widow.	John	Crampton.
	John	Hawtrey.	(br. of Ralph Hawtrey, Armagh, gent.)	Wm.	Streeter.
	Joseph	Donnellan.	Chas. Donnellan, Lisonhacody, co. Galway, gent.	John	Sterne.
	Henry	Pepyat.	Rev. John Pepyat, decd.	Eras.	Cope.
	Chris.	McCarthy.	(br. of Theo. McCarthy, Dublin, chandler.)	Jos.	Blundell.
	Thos.	Graham.	Wm. Graham, Dolphin's Barn Lane, weaver.	Tho.	Crampton.
	Peter	Paintard.	... ...	Mat.	Wilson.
	Thos.	Bolton.	John Bolton, Park, co. Galway, gent.	Robt.	Calderwood.
	Mark	St. Maurice.	Mark St. Maurice, Dublin, Esq.	Gaspard	Gradell.
	Thos.	Bigham.	Thos. Bigham, Belfast, merchant, decd.	Edm.	Sturgys.
	Samuel	Goodeau.	John Goodeau, merchant.	Peter	Gervis.
	Henry	Jago.	Henry Jago, Dublin, merchant.	Noah	Vialas.
1726	Mark	Mott.	James Mott, Dublin, yeoman.	Henry	Daniell.
1728	Thos.	Isack.	Wm. Isack, Redcross, co. Donegal, gent.	Wm.	Williamson.
	Wm.	Carroll.	Robert Carroll, Dublin, grocer.	Henry	Wilme.
	Philip	De Glatigny.	Adam De Glatigny, Dublin, gent.	Geo.	Parker.
1729	René	Letablere.	René Letablere, Dublin, gent.	Daniel	Fineau.
	Henry	Watts.	James Watts, late of Moygounagh, co. Mayo.	Wm.	Sinclare.
	Geo.	Hodskisson.	Henry Hodskisson, late of Dublin, glover, decd.	Roger	Finch.
	Edwd.	Barrett.	Wm. Barrett, Dublin, smith.	Mark	Martin.
	Fras.	Thompson.	Elinor Thompson, Dublin, widow.	John	Williamson.
	James	McGwire.	Patrick McGwire, Clarendon Street.	Mau.	Nash.
1730	John	Forbes.	Robert Forbes, decd.	Robert	Billing.
	Stanley	White.	Patrick White, Dublin, victualler.	Thos.	Cope.
1729	Peter	Walker.	Peter Walker, Dublin, merchant.	Thos.	Walker.
1730	Chris.	Barry.	Humphry Barry, Trim., gent., decd.	Arth.	Weldon.
	Berecah	Low.	John Low, Kilbeggan, gent.	John	Barrett.
1728	Archibald	McNeall.	Loughlin McNeall, Bellicon, co. Antrim, gent.	Arth.	Weldon.
1730	Jno. A.	Bere.	Peter Bere, Dublin, merchant.	Noah	Vialas.
	Thos.	Mitchell.	Caleb Mitchell, Dublin, carpenter, decd.	John	Sterne.
1731	Robert	Browne.	Robt. Browne, Dunleary, co. Dublin.	Dorothy	Manjoy.
	Wm.	Smith.	Samuel Smith, Dublin, weaver.	John	Hamilton.
	Wm.	West.	Dorothy West, Dublin, widow.	Roger	Finch.
	Robert	Hopkins.	Patience Hopkins, Dublin, widow.	John	Gumley.
	Wm.	Wilson.	Fras. Wilson, Dublin, widow.	Barth.	Popkins.
	Jonathan	Ruston.	John Ruston, Dublin, goldsmith.	Robt.	Billing.
	Laurence	Darquier.	(br. of Wm. Darquier, Dublin, gent.)	Mark	Martin.
1732	Geo.	Lehunt.	Geo. Lehunt, Cashel.	Isaac	D'Olier.
1731	John	Cooksey.	Wm. Cooksey, Kilkenny, Alderman.	John	Hamilton.
1732	Thos.	Collins.	Robt. Collins, Rathfarnham, gent.	Jas.	Whitehorne.
	Maurice	Deane.	Matthew Deane, co. Limerick, gent.	Anty.	Lefebure.
	Henry	Gifford.	Wm. Gifford, Powlemaloe, co. Wexford, gent.	A. D.	Browne.
	Chas.	Gifford.	Wm. Gifford, do. do. do.	Noah	Vialas.
	Isaiah	Dezouche.	Isaac Dezouche, Dublin, silk weaver.	Dan.	Pineau.
	Anthony	Sargent.	Humphry Sargent, late of Trim, farmer.	M.	Billing.
	St. Leger	Brafett.	Thos. Brafett, Dublin, weaver.	Wm.	Sinclare.
	John	Stern, jun.	John Stern, goldsmith.	John	Stern.
	Wm.	Taylor.	John Taylor, Dublin, skinner, decd.	Arth.	Weldon.
1733	Wm.	De Laune.	Gideon De Laune, Dublin, gent., decd.	Arth.	Weldon.
1732	Benj.	Smith.	Roger Smith, Dromcoo, co. Fermanagh, gent., decd.	Noah	Vialas.
1733	John	Fearns.	John Fearns, late of Kilkenny West.	Wm.	Stopleare.
	Edmond	Cogan.	Thos. Cogan, late of Dublin, tailor.	Jas.	Whithorn.

ENROLMENTS OF APPRENTICES—*Continued*.

NAME OF APPRENTICE.		NAME OF PARENT.	MASTER TO WHOM BOUND.	
1733	Robert Savage.	John Savage, Dublin, gent.	N.	Vialas.
	Geo. Murphy.	Elizabeth Murphy, widow.	Roger.	Finch.
1734	James St. Maurice.	James St. Maurice, Dublin, Esq., decd.	B.	Popkins.
	Wm. Steel.	Alex. Steel, Derryvullin, co. Fermanagh, clk.	N.	Vialas.
	Wm. Eeds.	Wm. Eeds, Clanroosk, King's co., farmer.	Th.	Blundell.
	John Davisson.	John Davisson, Athy, gunsmith.	Philip	Simms.
	Geo. Charleton.	... ...	Wm.	Currie.
	David Riausset.	Peter Riausset, Dublin, merchant, decd.	Mark	Martin.
	Daniel O'Neill.	Arthur O'Neill, Dublin, gent.	M.	Billing.
	Robert Fisher.	... ...	John	Sterne.
	John McCormick.	Wm. McCormick, Dublin, grocer.	John	Gumley.
	Thomas Bor.	Humphry Bor, Cloonard, co. Meath, gent.	Wm.	Williamson.
	Edwd. Cavenagh.	Denis Cavenagh, Dublin, feltmaker.	Peter	Usher.
1735	Henry Rash.	Henry Rash, London, gent.	Wm.	Currie.
	John R. Whitmore.	Lieut. Edwd. Whitmore.	Tho.	Walker.
	Robert Hunter.	Richard Hunter, co. Meath, gent.	Tho.	Parsons.
	John Horner.	John Horner, Dublin, smith.	Wm.	Stopleare.
	Wm. Ball.	Jonathan Ball, Dublin, weaver.	Daniel	Onge.
1736	Wm. Teat.	co. Wicklow.	Isaac	D'Olier.
	Chas. Darragh.	John Darragh, Dublin, dyer, decd.	Wm.	Sinclare.
1739	David Roche.	Thos. Roche, Dublin, merchant.	Roger	Finch.
1736	Samuel South.	Mary South, Stoneybatter, widow.	Mort.	Dowling.
	Richd Johnson.	John Johnson, Dublin, innholder.	John	Wilme.
	Philip Deane.	Thos. Deane, Dublin, gent.	Fras.	Williamson.
	Benj. Willson.	Frances Willson, Dublin, widow.	Mat.	Walker.
	John Christie.	Alex. Christie, Dublin, merchant.	Peter	Usher.
	Edwd. Jn. Raper.	Wm. Raper, Dublin, gent.	A. D.	Brown.
	Thos. Crampton.	Thos. Crampton, goldsmith.	Tho.	Crampton.
	Mar'duke Webb.	Ann Webb, widow.	Tho.	Crampton.
	James Wyer.	Corns. Wyer, Hallohoyse, co. Kildare, gent.	John	Moore.
	Oliver Dillon.	Barthw. Dillon, Ballymackallen, co. Westmeath, gent.	John	Gumley.
1737	John Rumble.	Isaac Rumble, Whitehaven, jeweller.	Rob.	Glanvile.
	Richd. Graham.	John Graham, Dublin, gent.	Peter	Usher.
	John Rawleigh.	Walter Rawleigh, Mitchelstown, decd.	N.	Vialas.
	Richd. Keightly.	John Keightly, Kendalstown, co. Wicklow.	R.	Finch.
	Henry Chadwick.	Treacey Chadwick, late of Dublin, coachmaker.	W.	Williamson.
	Leonard Blackham.	John Blackham, co. Dublin, decd.	John	Hamilton.
	James Gillespie.	Hugh Gillespie, Peace, co. Meath, farmer.	Jane	Daniell.
1736	Robt. Finlay.	Robert Finlay, London, gent.	Rob.	Calderwood.
1738	Thos. Green.	Susana Green, Dublin, widow.	Chr.	Skinner.
	Richd. Bristo.	Anthony Bristo.	Tho.	Sutton.
	Wm. Wilme.	Henry Wilme, goldsmith.	Henry	Wilme.
	Patk. Thornton.	Thos. Thornton, Dublin, stocking-weaver.	Chr.	McCarthy.
	Ebenezer Orr.	John Orr, Dublin, tailor.	Daniel	Onge.
	Jonathan Thomas.	Joseph Thomas, Dublin, gent, decd.	John	Gumley.
	Peter Rieusset.	Peter Rieusset, Dublin, merchant, decd.	B.	Popkins.
1737	Wm. Rd. Beck.	Edwd. Beck, Dublin, farmer.	R.	Billing.
1738	Richd. Sloper.	John Sloper, Mountdesey, co. Mayo, gent.	J.	Wilme.
	Const'tine Sloper.	John Sloper, Mountdesey, co. Mayo, gent.	M.	Kirkpatrick.
	Thos. Jones.	Wm. Jones, Dublin, gent.	Tho.	Blundell.
	Daniel McNeal.	Neal McNeal, Dundalk, gent., decd.	R.	Calderwood.
	Wm. Irwin.	John Irwin, Drumsilla, co. Leitrim, gent.	John	Hamilton.
1739	Robt. Andrews.	Elizabeth Andrews, Dublin, widow.	Tho.	De Limarest.
	John Kidd.	Thos. Kidd, Ballinstraw, co. Wexford.	B.	Popkins.
	Wm. Sewell.	Eliz. Sewell, Dublin, widow.	Wm.	Currie.
	James Clanchy.	Eliz. Elsey, Dublin, widow.	David	Bomes.
	Mich. McDaniel.	Dominick McDaniel, Dublin, merchant.	Wm.	Stoplear.
	Paul Palmer.	Mary Palmer, Birr, widow.	Roger	Finch.
	John Haggarty.	Edward Haggarty, Dublin, smith.	Tho.	Isack.
	Mich. Lemaistre.	Eliz. Lemaistre, Carlow, widow.	Cha.	Lemaistre.
1740	John Ronan.	Garrett Ronan, Dublin, victualler.	N.	Vialas.
1739	John Craig.	Ann Craig.	Wm.	Townsend.

ENROLMENTS OF APPRENTICES—*Continued.*

NAME OF APPRENTICE.		NAME OF PARENT.	MASTER TO WHOM BOUND.	
1740	Fleetw'd Powell.	John Powell, Dublin, merchant.	Rt.	Billing.
1738	Robt. Pearson.	Roger Pearson, Dublin, baker.	Th.	Delimarest.
1740	Mich. Shuckmell.	Jane Bradstreet (wife of Dudley Bradstreet), Dublin.	Vere	Forster.
	Laurence Doran.	Mary Bell, Dublin, widow.	Ph.	Simms.
	Wm. Soubiran.	Capt. John Soubiran, Dublin.	David	Bomes.
	Wm. Popkins.	Wm. Popkins, Dublin, smith.	Chr.	Locker.
1741	John Wilme.	Henry Wilme, Dublin, goldsmith.	Roger	Finch.
	John Freboul.	Peter Freboul, Kilkenny, merchant.	Jas.	Vidouze.
	Robert King.	John King, co. Wicklow, gent.	Rob.	Calderwood.
	John Irish.	John Irish, Cork, gent.	Wm.	Williamson.
	John Douglass.	Nathaniel Douglass, Dublin, victualler.	Jas.	Douglass.
	Matthew Sleater.	Mat. Sleater, Dublin, bricklayer.	Isaac	D'Olier.
	Thos. Williamson.	Mary Williamson, Dublin, widow.	Wm.	Currie.
	Samuel Walmsley.	Jas Walmesley, Dublin, merchant.	John	Whitshed.
	James Bloxham.	Wm. Bloxham, Dublin, decd.	N.	Vialas.
	Geo. Campbell.	James Campbell, Dublin, merchant, decd.	Wm.	Sinclare.
1742	James Warren.	Robert Warren, Dublin, merchant, decd.	And.	Goodwin.
	Thos. Hagarty.	Thos. Hagarty, Dublin, smith.	Ml.	Connor.
	Jonathan Pasley.	Elizabeth Mills by her former husband, Jonathan Pasley.	John	Wilme.
1741	Whitney Swarbrick.	Geo. Swarbrick, co. Antrim, draper, decd.	John	Letablere.
1742	James Lee.	Wm. Lee, Dublin, lace weaver, decd.	Jno.	Bancks.
	Richd. Ussher.	John Ussher, Dublin, merchant.	John	Moore.
	John Archbold.	Patrick Archbold, Dublin, M.D.	Wm.	Wilson.
	Fredk. Wilson.	James Wilson, Dublin, gunsmith.	John	Sterne.
	Edward West.	Hamilton West, co. Dublin, gent.	Daniel	Onge.
1743	Henry King.	John King, co. Wicklow, gent.	Rt.	Calderwood.
	Joseph Walker.	Ann Walker, Dublin, widow.	Tho.	Walker.
	Thomas Lee.	Wm. Lee, Dublin, merchant, decd.	John	Hamilton.
	Joseph Cullen.	Ann Cullen, (now wife of John Saul).	Tho.	Sutton.
	Joshua Payne.	Geo. Payne, co. Wicklow, farmer.	Mathias	Brown.
	Richard Williams.	Solomon Williams, Wicklow, slater.	John	Wilme.
	Joseph Nixon.	Rev. Eccles Nixon, co. Tyrone.	Rd.	Foster.
	Wm. Betagh.	Robert Betagh, Dublin, gold lace weaver.	And.	Goodwin.
	Arthur Annesley.	Wm. Annesley, co. Wexford, gent.	John	Moore.
1744	John Willoughby.	Frances Willoughby, Drogheda, widow.	Th.	De Limarest.
1745	John Horne.	John Horne, Dublin, merchant.	Robt.	Billing.
1744	John Ranson.	Wm. Ranson, Dublin, gent.	David	Bomes.
	Samuel Tyrer.	Elizabeth Tyrer, Dublin, widow.	Tho.	Blundell.
	Josias Vivian.	Henry Vivian, tallow chandler, decd.	Ph.	Simms.
	Edmond Milne.	Thos. Milne, co. Meath, yeoman, decd.	Isaac	O'Olier.
	Henry Waldron.	Luke Waldron, Dublin, sword cutler, decd.	Wm.	Williamson.
	Wm. Wiseman.	Henry Wiseman, ship-carpenter, decd.	Ch.	Skinner.
1745	Geo. Horne.	John Horne, Dublin, merchant.	Rt.	Calderwood.
	Simon Williams.	Thos. Williams, decd.	David	Bomes.
	John Houston.	Henry Houston, co. Roscommon, gent.	Jas.	Whitthorne.
	Wm. Morrison.	Samuel Morrison, Borris Kane, gent.	Geo.	Beere.
	Joseph Cullin.	Ann Cullin (now wife of John Saul).	Jno.	Hamilton.
1746	James Clenahan.	And. Clenahan, Dublin, merchant, decd.	Peter	Usher.
	James Holmes.	Robert Holmes, Dublin, watchmaker.	Jas.	Champion.
	John Shiels.	James Shiels, Drogheda, chandler.	Rt.	Calderwood.
	John Clark.	Wm. Clark, co. Meath, farmer.	Wm.	Townsend.
	Gordon Whitthorne.	James Whitthorne, goldsmith.	Jas.	Whitthorne.
1747	John Deane.	Robert Deane, Dublin, shoemaker.	M.	Kirkpatrick.
	John Semple.	Rev. And. Semple, decd.	Wm.	Williamson.
	Geo. Gratton.	Mary Gratton, widow.	John	Letablere.
	Heck'field Stanford.	Ann Stanford, co. Louth, widow.	And.	Goodwin.
	John Henderson.	John Henderson, mariner.	Daniel.	Onge.
	Richard Harrison.	Ann Harrison, co. Dublin, widow.	Wm.	Currie.
	Isaac D'Olier.	Isaac D'Olier, goldsmith.	Rt.	Billing.
1748	John West.	Jacob West, Q'nsboro', co. Kildare, farmer.	B.	Mosse.
	Jno. Moses Dufour.	Isaac Dufour, Dublin, weaver.	Jas.	Vidouze.
	John Catherwood.	Wm. Catherwood, Belfast, mariner, decd.	Edw.	Raper.
	Samuel Bury.	John Bury, co. Wicklow, gent.	John	Moore.
	Isaac Parker.	Paul Parker, Dublin, merchant.	Isaac.	D'Olier.

ENROLMENTS OF APPRENTICES—*Continued.*

NAME OF APPRENTICE.	NAME OF PARENT.	MASTER TO WHOM BOUND.
1748 Roger Pearson.	Wm. Pearson, Golden Lane, innkeeper.	Mathias Brown.
John Teare.	John Teare, Athlone, gent.	Ben. Stokes.
Wallis Hewetson.	Wallis Hewetson, co. Kilkenny, decd.	David Bomes.
John Carmick.	Robert Carmick, Longford, apothecary, decd.	John Wilme.
Daniel Savill.	... ...	Wm. Savill.
Thomas Jones.	Isaac Jones, co. Wexford, farmer, decd.	M. Brown.
1749 Robert Cassidy.	Frances Cassidy, Dublin, widow.	Rd. Eaton.
John Standish.	Henry Standish, Dublin, seal cutter.	Deacon Standish.
James Fulton.	James Fulton, Dublin, gent.	Jas. Champion.
Mark Meares.	Rachel Meares, widow.	Wm. Currie.
Wm. Raymond.	Mary Raymond, co. Dublin, widow.	Tho. Blundell.
Walter Wilson.	John Wilson, Carrick-on-Shannon, merchant.	Ch. Darragh.
John St. John.	... ...	John Wilme.
Wm. Smith.	Robert Smith, Finglas, decd.	Jas. Douglass.
1750 Henry Jones.	Amos Jones, decd.	Robt . Calderwood.
Simon Isaac.	Robert Isaac, Clough, co. Down, gent.	Wm. Williamson.
John Garstin.	Barthw. Garstin, Dublin, gent., decd.	Wm. Townsend.
John Clouney.	Dominick Clouney, Dublin, draper, decd.	B. Mosse.
William Rainsford.	Henry Rainsford, Dublin, weaver.	D. Standish.
J.Langton May.	Wm. May, Roscrea, merchant.	Vere Forster.
Wm. Whitthorne.	James Whitthorne, goldsmith.	Wm. Whitthorne.
1751 Simon Surman.	Wm. Surman.	Peter Wingfield.
John Karr.	Hugh Karr, co. Cavan, decd.	Edw. Raper.
Thomas Karr.	Thomas Karr, gent.	Edw. Raper.
Wm. Hodgson.	Wm. Hodgson, Scotland, tanner.	Chr. Skinner.
Robert Moore.	Brent, Moore, co. Meath, gent.	Ml. Fowler.
John Moore.	John Moore, goldsmith.	John Moore.
Thomas Harris.	James Harris, co. Kildare, gent.	Edw. Mockler.
Samuel Taylor.	Jonathan Taylor, Dublin, brewer, decd.	Wm. Currie.
John Wogan.	Robert Wogan, Naas, yeoman.	John Moore.
1752 Wm. Kathrens.	Esther Kathrens. Dublin, widow.	Rr. Forster.
Geo. Gates.	Jacob Gates, decd.	David Bomes.
Francis Dunn.	... ...	Wm. Savill.
John Deane.	John Deane, Cork, decd.	Wm. Savill.
John Locker.	Mary Locker, widow.	Wm. Williamson.
Richd. Mockler.	Mary Mockler, widow.	Edw. Mockler.
1746 Wm. Harrison.	Ann Harrison, Donnycarny, widow.	Jas. Robertson.
1747 Jas. Charnock.	John Charnock, Dublin, mariner, decd.	Jos. Bridgman.
1748 Richard Fenimore.	John Fenimore, Balliward, co. Wicklow, farmer.	Tho. Shephard.
1749 Wm. Currie.	Wm. Currie, Dublin, goldsmith.	Henry Billing.
Robert McCrea.	Robert McCrea, Dublin, Tailor.	Alex. Lilly.
1750 Levallen Oldfield.	John Oldfield, Howth, farmer.	Ch. Gillespy.
Joseph Rankin.	Geo. Rankin, Chamber St., clothier.	David Gordon.
1751 Geo. Roycraft.	Gilbert Roycraft.	Geo. Chalmers.
1752 Samuel Ormsby.	Samuel Ormsby, co. Mayo, Esq.	John Ringland.
Thomas Nuttall.	James Nuttall.	Will Townsend.
Will Richards.	Alex. Richards.	James Douglas.
Maurice Fitzgerald.	James Fitzgerald.	Vere Forster.
Richard Grace.	Deborah Grace.	Will. Wilme.
Thomas Graydon.	Philis Graydon, widow.	James Champion.
James Lamie.	Oliver Lamie.	David Bomes.
George Eaton.	Thomas Eaton.	James Wyer.
Francis Jones.	Edward Jones.	John Laughlin.
Lodowick Cathcart.	Archibald Cathcart.	Nicholas Lemaistre.
Fred. Elliott.	Robert Elliott.	Matthias Browne.
1753 Compton Roe.	... ...	Robt. Smith.
Thomas Atkinson.	... ...	Thos. Johnston.
Alex. Bate.	... ...	John Ringland (watchmaker).
John McCrea.	... ...	Robt. Potter.
Valentine Cannon.	... ...	Robt. Rose.
George Graydon.	... ...	Chas. Gillespy.
Joseph Murphy.	... ...	Philip Glasco.

ENROLMENTS OF APPRENTICES—*Continued.*

NAME OF APPRENTICE.		NAME OF PARENT.	MASTER TO WHOM BOUND.	
1753	John Clinton.	James Clinton.	James	Vidouze.
	John Pringle.	Anne Pringle, widow.	James	Warren.
	Henry Cassidy.	Deborah Cassidy.	Benj.	Stokes.
	Robert Murray.	to serve 7 years from June, '49. }	Nathan	Murray
	Nathan Murray.	both sons of Nathan Murray, goldsmith. }		
	Robert Wogan.	Thomas Wogan.	John	Letablere.
	Joshua S. Green.	... ...	Robert	Calderwood.
	Whaley Hughes.	Patrick Hughes.	Willm.	Wilme.
	Richard D'Olier.	Isaac D'Olier, goldsmith.	Isaac	D'Olier.
	William Keen.	Edward Keen.	Isaac	D'Olier.
	Willm. Nugent.	Walter Nugent.	Will.	Townsend.
	Richard Raymond.	... ...	Thomas	Blundell.
1754	Caple Harrison.	Theophilus Harrison.	Thomas	Blundell.
	Will. Hy. Morton.	Anne Morton.	Edward	Raper.
	George Hamilton.	... ...	Sam	Walker.
	James Hamilton.	Will. Hamilton.	Andrew	Goodwin.
	James Rothe.	Oliver Rothe.	Richard	Forster.
	John Lloyd.	Will. Lloyd.	Matthias	Brown (d. 1759)
	John M'Crea.	Robert M'Crea.	James	Wyer.
	James M'Grath.	Luke M'Grath.	David	Bomes.
	Henry Rogers.	Rev. George Rogers.	R.	Calderwood.
	George Wilme.	Eleanor Wilme.	Will.	Wilme.
	Richard Shaw.	Richard Shaw.	Thomas	Shepherd.
	Phillip How.	Thomas How.	Nichol.	Lemaistre.
	Will Beere.	Samuel Beere.	Benj.	Wilson.
	Will. Smith.	(remainder of term from James Douglas.)	John	Moore.
1755	Robert Chester.	Anne Chester.	Nichol.	Lemaistre.
	Will. Cordner.	Robert Cordner.	Richard	Williams.
	Will. Mills.	Mary Mills.	James	Champion.
	Will. Ball.	Mildred Ball, widow.	Henry	Billing.
	Edward Coles.	... ...	James	Vidouze.
	Richard Vincent.	Winifred Vincent.	Robert	Hopkins.
	Abdy Man.	Rev. Robert Man.	W.	Curry.
	J.Langton May.	Will. May (remainder of term from Vere Forster).	Will.	Steele.
	John Watters.	... ...	Jonath'n	Ruston.
	Nicholas Skinner.	Christr. Skinner.	Christr.	Skinner.
1756	Patrick Walsh.	Edward Walsh.	Henry	Billing.
	Darby Kehoe.	Isabella Kehoe.	Benj.	Stokes.
	Ambrose Boxwell.	John Boxwell.	John	Moore.
	Poole Taylor.	Thomas Taylor.	John	Wilme.
	John Dawson.	Rev. John Dawson.	Will.	Wilme.
	John Pearson.	... ...	James	Black
	John Lawler.	... ...	Alex.	Lilly.
	Richard Babington.	... ...	Chas.	Gillespy.
	Gerrard Fitzsimons.	Rosana Fitzsimons.	Benj.	Wilson.
	Charles Wright.	John Wright.	Charles	Darragh.
	Thomas Williams.	... ...	Peter	Wingfield.
	John Nelson.	John Nelson.	Willm.	Savile.
1757	Richard Harper.	... ...	John	Dalrymple.
	Shaw Williamson.	... ...	Hugh	Cunningham.
	Joseph Cunningham.	...	Philip	Glasco.
	Ebenezer Straughan.	Rev. E. Kilburn.	Will.	Wilme.
	Thomas Dawson.	Rev. John Dawson.	Richard	Williams.
	(left R. Williams in 1761).			
	William Martindall.	Roger Martindall.	Will.	Savile.
	Gregory McCannon.	Will. McCannon.	Thomas	Shepperd.
	Joseph Currie.	Will. Currie.	Will.	Currie.
	Thomas Hammersley.	John Hammersley.	Will.	Wilme.
1758	Miles Cunningham.	... .	Robt.	Pitts.
	Gregory Langholt.	... ...	Henry	Billing.
	Arthur Hamilton.	Arthur Hamilton.	Nathan	Murray.
	Richard Laughlin.	John Laughlin.	John	Laughlin.
	Daniel Harrison.	Will. Harrison.	David	Bomes.
	Will. Hughes.	Philip Hughes.	John	Moore.
	Hall Fitzsimons.	James Fitzsimons.	Benj.	Willson.

ENROLMENTS OF APPRENTICES—*Continued.*

NAME OF APPRENTICE.		NAME OF PARENT.			MASTER TO WHOM BOUND.	
1758	John Hicks.	James Hicks.			James	Wyer.
	Edward Welsh.	Michael Welsh.			James	Champion.
	Henry Vincent.	Winifred Vincent.			James	Champion.
	Joyce Fonvielle.	...	...	...	John	Sherwin.
1759	Christn. Haines.	Christn. Haines.			Richard	Williams.
	R. Grah'm Bridgman.	Joseph Bridgman, goldsmith.			Joseph	Bridgman.
	Samuel Gordon.	...	...	...	Robert	Glanville.
	Laurence Fowler.	John Fowler.			Will.	Steele.
	Thomas Proctor.	Margaret Proctor.			Will.	Steele.
	Richard Graham.	Richard Graham.			John	Sherwin.
	James Nixon.	Rev. Eccles Nixon.			Joseph	Nixon.
	Bart'mew Delandre.	Will. Delandre.			Thomas	Burton.
	Charles Wright.	...	...	...	Thomas	Burton.
	John McGowan.	Edward McGowan.			Thomas	Shepherd.
	Joshua Emerson.	Joshua Emerson.			Benj.	Willson.
	Joseph Bennett.	...	...	...	Chas.	Gillespy.
	Will. Moore.	...	...	...	Alex.	Kelly.
	Chas. Wright.	...	...	...	Sam	Teare.
1760	Chas. Barrington.	...	...	...	John	Moore.
	Valentine Meyler.	...	...	...	Philip	Glasco.
	Joseph Bonynge.	...	...	...	Thos.	Green.
	John Pearson.	...	...	...	Thos.	Johnston.
	Edmund Low.	...	...	...	Chas.	Gillespy.
	Will. M'Gee.	...	...	...	Thos.	Johnston.
	James Dunn.	...	...	...	John	Graham.
	Jonathan Robinson.	George Robinson.			James	Vidouze.
	David Peter.	David Peter.			Owen	Cassidy.
	Lambert Dupuy. ("Eloped".)	...	...	...	Alex.	Richards.
	George Johnson.	Elizabeth Johnson.			Robert	Calderwood.
	John Clarke.	Frances Clarke.			John	Locker.
	Fredk. McCannon.	Will McCannon.			David	Bomes.
	Edward Haines.	...	...	...	Joseph	Thompson.
	Henry Hatchell.	Henry Hatchell.			David	Hopkins.
	Garrett Fitzgerald.	Richard Fitzgerald of Limerick.			Will.	Townsend.
1761	John Laughlin.	John Laughlin, goldsmith.			Joseph	Nixon.
	James Kennedy.	James Kennedy.			Benj.	Slack.
	Joseph Jackson.	Henry Jackson.			Robt.	Glanville (dead in 1762).
	Edward Bury.	John Bury.			John	Douglas.
	Willm. Pyers.	Elizabeth Pyers.			John	Moore.
	Willm. French.	Paulgry French.			Francis	Jones.
	James Jonquier.	James Jonquier.			Jonathan	Ruston.
	Robert Field.	John Field.			Nathan	Murray.
	Will Ward.	John Ward.			Christr.	Skinner.
	Charles Stokes.	Benj. Stokes, goldsmith.			James	Vidouze.
	Edward Actison.	...	...	...	Will.	Bate.
	George Hetherington.	...	...	...	Isaac	Crab.
	Thos. Hicks.	...	...	...	Thos.	Green.
1762	Isaac Boothman.	...	...	...	George	Thompson.
	Charles Barrington.	James Barrington.			James	Douglas.
	John Martin.	Benj. Martin.			Benj.	Wilson.
	John Case.	Benj. Case.			Thos.	Shepperd.
	Josiah Adamson.	Benj. Adamson.			John	Locker.
	James Franck.	Chas. Franck.			Will	Wilme.
	Barnaby Nangle.	Morton Nangle.			Joseph	Thompson.
	Matthew West.	Jacob West (of Kildare).			John	West.
	Robert Cullen.	...	...	...	T.	Billing.
	Lang, W. Palmer.	Jeffrey Palmer.			Will	Currie.
	Willm. Main.	John Main.			James	Champion.
	Thomas Sullivan.	Eugene Sullivan.			Vere	Forster.
	John Murray.	...	...	...	James	Wyer.
	John Carter.	Theophilus Carter.			Joseph	Nixon.
	Robert Dent.	...	...	...	John	West.
	Henry Nicholson.	Henry Nicholson.			Owen	Cassidy.
1763	James Nelson.	James Nelson.			Benj.	Wilson.
	Isaac Fraigneau.	Isaac Fraigneau.			Adam	Fraigneau, L.
	Richard Snow.	...	...	...	Will	Williamson.

ENROLMENTS OF APPRENTICES—*Continued.*

	NAME OF APPRENTICE.		NAME OF PARENT.	MASTER TO WHOM BOUND.	
1763	John	Adams.	Richard Adams.	Alex.	Gordon.
	George	Harkness.	George Harkness.	Jonath'n.	Ruston.
	Anthony	Van Trieght.	George Van Trieght.	Vere	Forster.
	Thomas	Rylans.	Edward Rylans.	Francis	Jones.
	Robert	Cowell.	George Cowell.	Henry	Billing.
1764	Willm.	Gordon.	Alex. Gordon, clockmaker.	Alex.	Gordon.
	Christr.	Nangle.	Martin Nangle.	John	Sherwin.
	Willm.	Osborn.	Richard Osborn.	Wm.	Wilme.
	Denis	M'Owen.	Edward M'Owen.	T.	Billing.
	John	M'Cannon.	Hector M'Cannon.	C.	Skinner.
	John	Wade.	Thomas Wade.	Joseph	Nixon.
	Robert	Clarke.	Robert Clarke.	John St.	John.
	Will.	Finlay.	John Finlay.	Francis	Jones.
	James	Corcoran.	Silvester Corcoran.	Will.	Raymond.
	Geo.Davis	Sherry.	Andrew Sherry.	W.	Wilme.
	Anthony	Lee.	Anthony Lee.	R.	Calderwood.
	George	Brush.	James Brush.	R.	Calderwood.
	John	Mestayer.	Chas. Mestayer.	David	Bomes.
	Mark	Walsh.	Matthew Walsh.	James	Dyer.
	Robt. Jno.	Smith.	... ...	Robt.	Smith.
	Daniel	Crosby.	...:	Thos.	Nuttall.
1765	Henry	Kelly.	... ...	Will.	Dolittle.
	Joshua	Wolfe.	... ...	Will.	Bate.
	John	Earls.	... ...	Chas.	Dowdall.
	Will.	Law.	Will. Law.	Will.	Townsend.
	Samuel	Bermingham.	Joanna Bermingham.	W.	Wilme.
	Sam.	Laughlin.	Philip Laughlin.	Alex.	Richards.
	Joseph	Fish.	Rev. John Fish.	John	Locker.
	John	Anderson.	James Anderson.	Dan.	Popkins
	Matthew	Goggin.	Will. Goggin.	W.	Townsend.
	George	Beere.	Geo. Beere, goldsmith.	Geo.	Beere.
1766	Will.	Smythe.	Will. Smythe.	David	Bomes.
	Joseph	Kingsmill.	P. Kingsmill.	John	Moore.
	Anthony	Bourne.	Anthony Bourne.	John	Locker.
	Francis	Bower.	Jonathan Bower.	Richard	Williams.
	James	Jacob.	James Jacob.	Jonath'n	Ruston.
	Robt.	French.	Calfrey French.	John	Ebbs.
1767	James	Spring.	George Spring.	James	Vidouze.
	John	Leake.	John Leake.	Will.	Steele.
	James	St. Clare.	Charles St. Clare.	Henry	Billing.
	George	Hamersley.	John Hamersley.	W.	Wilme.
1768	Lewis	Johnson.	Francis Johnson.	Benj.	Wilson.
	David	Henderson.	John Henderson.	David	Peters.
	Thomas	Blundell.	Joseph Blundell.	Thomas	Blundell.
	Will.	Power.	Richard Power.	Joseph	Nixon.
	Robt.	Breading.	John Breading.	Will.	Hughes.
	John	Dalrymple.	John Dalrymple, goldsmith.	John.	Dalrymple.
	Alex.	Barry.	John Barry.	Will.	Beere.
	Alex.	Laughlin.	... ...	John	Laughlin, jun.
	John	Grant.	St. Neil Grant.	Poole.	Taylor.
1769	John	Beauchamp.	Joseph Beauchamp.	Will.	Townsend.
	Robert	Moore.	John Moore.	John	West.
	John	Franks.	Thos. Franks.	Patrick	Walsh.
	John	Kelly.	Will. Kelly.	James	Vidouze.
	Henry	Nalty.	Henry Nalty.	Will.	Hughes.
	James	Wilson.	Benj. Wilson, Dublin, goldsmith.	Benj.	Slack.
	James B.	Esdall.	... ...	John	Laughlin.
	Michael	Graham.	... ...	Will.	Steele.
	Will.	Bridgman.	Joseph Bridgman, Dublin, goldsmith (decd.)	John	Sherwin.
1770	Daniel	Beere.	George Beere, goldsmith.	George	Beere.
1771	James	Fletcher.	... ...	Joseph	Nixon.
	Sam.	Allen.	... ...	John	Laughlin, J.
	Gustavus	Burne.	Thos. Burne, Dublin, goldsmith.	Chas.	Townsend.
	Michael	Connor.	... ...	David	Peter, G.S.
	Will.	Sherwin.	John Sherwin, goldsmith.	John	Sherwin, G.S.
	Garrett	English.	... ...	Matthew	West, G.S.
	Robert	Cubbin.	(From Isle of Man).	Darby	Kehoe, G.S.
1772	Alex.	Gordon.	Alex. Gordon, watch and clock maker.	Alex.	Gordon.

ENROLMENTS OF APPRENTICES—*Continued.*

NAME OF APPRENTICE.	NAME OF PARENT.	MASTER TO WHOM BOUND.
1772 Arthur Farrell.	... ...	W. Wilme, J.
Francis Barnett.	... ...	John Clarke, G.S.
James Thorp.	... ...	A. Gordon, W.M.
1773 Gore Sherwin.	John Sherwin, Dublin, goldsmith.	Poole Taylor, G.S.
Walter Young.	... ...	Thos. Blundell, W.M.
Robert Turner.	... ...	Richard William, G.S.
Robert French.	... ...	John Ebbe, W.M.
Michael Graham.	from W. Steele to	Abrah'm Bate, J.
1774 Henry Wilme.	Will. Wilme, jeweller.	Will. Wilme, J.
John Austin.	... ...	Nathan Murray, Eng'vr.
Chas. Blundell.	... ...	Will. Osborne, J.
Robert Thornhill.	... ...	Will. Hughes, G.S.
1775 James McCoy.	... ...	Matt. West, G.S.
Prussia Powell.	... ...	Matt. West, G.S.
1776 John Forster.	Vere Forster, Dublin, jeweller, decd.	John Laughlin, J.
George Fitzpatrick.	... ...	Will. Hughes, G.S.
Humphy. Byrne.	Thos. Byrne, Dublin, goldsmith.	W. Law, G.S.
James Jones.	... ...	Thos. Jones, G.S.
John Brooks.	... ...	Chas. Townsend, G.S.
1777 Will. McMurray.	... ...	Ebenezer Orr, J.
James Jones.	... ...	Will. Hughes, G.S.
Robert Holmes.	Robert Holmes, Dublin, jeweller.	W. Bates, J.
1778 John M'Clenihan.	... ...	C. Townsend, G.S.
Matt. Bellew.	... ...	Pat. Walsh, J.
Thos. Anderson.	... ...	Thos. Jones, G.S.
Joseph Brownly.	... ...	David Peter, G.S.
Joseph Ridley.	... ...	John Lloyd, G.S.
1779 Edward Jollie.	... ...	R. Williams, G.S.
1780 Christr. Donovan.	... ...	John Lloyd, G.S.
Sam Hawthorn.	... ...	Joseph Jackson, G.S.
J. Orson Walsh.	Stephen Walsh, Dublin, goldsmith.	Poole Taylor, J.
(ran away 1784).		
John Tudor.	Richard Tudor, Dublin, goldsmith.	Richard Tudor, G.S.
1781 George Mason.	... ...	John Wade, J.
1782 Joseph Johnson.	... ...	John M. Dufour, J.
Isaac Jones.	... ...	Thos. Jones, G.S.
1784 John Charles.	... ...	Joseph Jackson, G.S.
Edward Breading.	... ...	Robert Breading, G.S.
John Power.	... ...	Will. Power, G.S.
Thomas Shannon.	... ...	John Wade, J.
1785 Will. Wheeler.	... ...	John Wade, J.
Henry Nalty.	... ...	Joseph Jackson, G.S.
1786 Thos. Egerton.	... ...	Robt. Breading, G.S.
1787 Edward Fisher.	... ...	Will. Ward, G.S.
Thos. Townsend.	... ...	R. Breading, G.S.
1788 Tobias Shannon.	... ...	John Wade, J.
Arthur O'Neill.	Arthur O'Neill, Dublin, goldsmith.	George Campbell, G.S.
1789 James Hartley.	... ...	Joseph Jackson, G.S.
1790 Barth. Austin.	... ...	John Austin, G.S.
1791 Daniel Nelson.	... ...	Will. Power, G.S.
1792 Will. Teare.	... ...	Sam. Teare, G.S.
1794 Jonathan Close.	Sam. Close, Dublin, goldsmith.	Robt. Williams, G.S.
1795 Edward Egerton.	Nephew of Edward Egerton, goldsmith.	Edward Egerton, G.S.
1796 James Richardson.	... ...	James M'Coy, G.S.
1800 Will. D. Stubbs.	... ...	Joseph Jackson, G.S.
1801 Geo. Hy. Burke.	... ...	Sam. Close, Engr'ver.
1802 Matt. Law.	Will Law, Dublin, goldsmith.	Will. Law, G.S.
John. Keene.	John Keene, Dublin, goldsmith.	John Keene, G.S.
1804 Philip Weekes.	... ...	Sam. Nevill, G.S.
1806 Will. Gaisford.	... ...	John West, G.S.
1804 John Cockburn.	... ...	R. Breading, G.S.
1806 John Brown.	... ...	M. West, G.S.
1808 Thos. Gonne.	Thos. Gonne, Dublin, jeweller.	Thos. Gonne, J.
1809 Will. Robinson.	... ...	Thos. Gonne, J.
1810 Rich. Chichester.	... ...	S. Nevill, G.S.
1823 Joseph Scrutten.	... ...	Matt. Law, G.S.

[END OF ENTRIES].

LIST OF QUARTER BROTHERS AND JOURNEYMEN

WHO WORKED IN DUBLIN FROM 1661 (THE EARLIEST ENTRY) TO 1775.

Quarter Brothers (sometimes called " Foreigners," a comprehensive term which included all goldsmiths who were not "freemen" of the Company), were time-expired apprentices and immigrant goldsmiths who were allowed to work and enjoy certain privileges by paying *quarterly* contributions to the funds of the Company. The date over each group of names is that of first appearance in the Company's books. Many of the names reappear at later dates, but are not repeated in the following list except when they seem to pertain to a different person.

	1661-3.		1674.		1682.
John	East	John	Wyse	Nicholas	Pantain
Thomas	Rutter	George	Webster, gone	Thomas	Dalston
John	Haynes	Andrew	Mainwaring, gone	Ebenezer	Cawdron
Paul	Lovelace	Thos.	Cleghorne, d. 1675	Edmund	Waller
Francis	Clifton	John	Boillot	John	Melcarkern
Thomas	Godfrey	Francis	Souder	Alex.	Forbes
Richard	Hiol (Hill ?)	James	Kirkwood, gone 1674	John	Humphreys
Will.	Claw	John	Atkins, gone 1675		
John	Dixon	Will.	Norton		1683-4.
Abraham	Voyseen (Voisin)			John	Bulkley
Nathaniel	Drake		1675-6.	Thomas	Marker
Robt.	Walsh	Will.	Elphinstone	Timothy	Heyvin (or Hevin),
Robt.	Dillon	Matthew	La Roche		d. 1708
John	Vallance, gone 1664	Thos.	Rutter, jun.	Nicholas	Delamain
		John	Philips	———	Doble (gone 1686)
	1664-5.	John	Martin		
Ralph	Johnson	Henry	Jones		1685-6.
Edmond	Cohland (Coghlan ?)	Andrew	Rewsoe (Rousseau)	Mark	Cooke, d. 1692
Andrew	Gregory	Peter	Mysser	John	Murphy
		John	Heath	George	Lyon
	1666-7.			Henry	Sherwin
John	Cope		1677-8.	Henry	Nevill
James	Kelly			Edward	Farr
Fred.	Mansell	Edmund	Godfrey	Arthur	Maungee
John	Hyett (Hyatt)	Will.	Fitzgerald	Abraham	Sorett
John	Cox	Glover	Johnson	Oliver	Platt, d. 1691
Francis	Bennett, gone 1672	Richard	St. Lawrence	Peter	Devin
Will.	Davison	Will.	Bedford	Alexander	Gordon
		Robt.	Elphinstone	Michael	Snelling
	1668-9.	Abraham	Blanchard	Samuel	{ Williamson
John	Shaw	Humphrey	Nevill		{ Wilson
John	Dickson	George	Pomfrett	Thomas	Fisher
Nicholas	Arras	Will.	Billinghurst	James	Fawcett
		Lawrence	Salmon	John	Wall, d. 1692
	1669-70.			Edward	Starkey
John	Farmer		1679.	Walter	Goughagan
Thomas	Walsh, d. 1671	Thomas	Oven	Thomas	Jenkins
Denis	Bryne	Robt.	Chappell	Gregory	Street, d. 1688
Peter	Mercer	John	Lewis, d. 1680	Michael	Gavan
Daniel	Boltee, gone 1673	John	Ohem	Robt.	Nevill, d. 1691
		John	Cressy		
	1670-1.	David	Weston, d. 1680		1690-1.
Will.	Barnard, gone	John	Barnard	Joseph	Jones
Peter	Racyne (Racine)	Richard	Hill	Nicholas	Pountain
Thomas	Sterne	Edmund	Lambe, gone 1680	John	Elkins
John	Destaches	Alexander	Forbes	Edwd.	Wall
Ferdinand	Corry	Nicholas	Shaller	Joseph	Jones
Will.	Rowse	Humphrey	Hanwell, gone 1680	Will.	Cooper
Thos.	Brooks, gone 1673			Peter	Paris (or Parry)
John	Henman		1680-1.	Will.	Berry
		David	Weston	Michael	Haynes
	1671-2.	Nathaniel	Hutchinson, d. 1682	John	Melkerkern
Thomas	Clement, gone 1673	Job	Hopkins	Timothy	Hevin
Nathaniel	Hutchinson	Richard	Archbold		
Robt.	Balme	William	Archbold		1692-3.
Thos.	Hartstone, gone 1672	John	Elkins (or Ecklin)	Conway	Mace
Richard	Archbold	Chas. De la	Main, gone 1681	Floris	Sykes (or Six)
John	Powell	James	Weldon	Anthony	Stanley
Lewis	Farran, gone 1673	Stephen	Nollably	Richard	Hill
Francis	Cobham	James	Barrett, gone 1681	James	Thompson

LIST OF QUARTER BROTHERS AND JOURNEYMEN—*Continued.*

1692-3.		1698-9.		1702-3.	
Joseph	Whitchurch	Peter	Lemesier	Will.	Sinclair
Jasper	Lavell	Will.	Sinckler	Edward	Dowdall
Nathaniel	Higgins (mentioned)	Thos.	Hall	John	Slater
Robt.	Ince	Ahasuerus	Hartwick	Will.	Wheatley
Jarvis	Thurlby	Christopher	Hartwick	Thos.	Wheeler
Anthony	Dono	Isaac	Cousin	Thos.	Matthews
John Dan.	Dalhusius	Thomas	Elliott	John	Sterne
John	Matthews	Will.	Palmer	Thos.	Hartwell, & to 1739
Samuel	Wilder	Thos.	Burton	Thos.	Slade
Jabin	Hawkins	Anthony	Teare	Philip	Kinnersly
Thomas	Desborough	Peter	Venables	Robt.	Cuffe
John	Tims	Jonathan	Kingham	John	Crampton
		Francis	Boyd	Paul	Romey
	1694-5.	George	Joyce	John	Carter
Francis	Rivers, d. 1715	Walter	Sherlock	John	Smart
John	Doutoung	Gideon	Donoe	Will.	Bates
Thomas	Parker	Robt.	Pilkington	Benj.	Goodwin
John	Parker			Christopher	Kind
John	Bennett		1700.	Gamaliel	Mauritius, gone 1706
Joseph	Bennett	———	Gamuell	Will.	Lyons
Joseph	Graves	John	Ruston		
Will.	Croft	Nichs.	Smart		1704-5.
Jabes	Morris	James	Colton	Henry	Matthews
Will.	Price, d. 1702	———	Chosey	Paul	Townsend
Solomon	Goodaire	David	Rummy (or Romey)	Edw.	Sweetenham
Thos.	Cooper	James	Champion	Thos.	Rasin (Racine ?)
Christopher	Waggoner	John	Paturle	George	Gillingham
Richard	Smart	Richard	Bouchett	Will.	Shields, d. 1707
		James	Cotton	Thos.	Coakeley
	1696.	Will.	Keys, d. 1702	James	Blanchard
John	Matthews	Nicholas	Leiness	Francis	Humphreys
Thomas	Cooke	John	Sale	Robt.	Evers
Timothy	Mullineux	Thos.	Court	Will.	Marshall
Will.	Pridham	Robt.	Anderton	James	Young
Peter	Bolio (or Beaulieu)	Nathaniel	Bulling	George	Farrington
George	Lyng	John	Pattison	George	Smart
Thos.	Mekins	Hugh	Law	Jas.	Scott
John	Rouston	Robt.	Nevill	Paul	Romey, Jr.
		Dan	Norris		
	1697-8.	Henry	Tyre		1706-7.
Isaac	Swan	Samuel	Lemesier	John	Williams
Will.	Norris	Fergus	Reily	John	Whitfield
Charles	Rossiter	Robt.	Noble	David	Price
Robt.	Gursuch	Edward	Workman	Richard	Cahill
David	Rummy (or Romey),	Mortagh	Dowling	Erasmus	Cope
	d. 1729			Edward	Hall
Will.	Skinner		1701.	John	Walker
James	Walker	Will.	Palmer	Will.	Ross
Thos.	Daniel	Anthony	Girard	James	Foucault
		Dan	Norris	Will.	Betagh
	1698-9.	Henry	Vyse	John	Wise
Richard	Eycott	Robt.	Forbes	Will.	Hester
Peter	Leroy	Jonathan	Gerrard	Abraham	Barboult
Thos.	Bradshaw	John	Cooper	Gilbert	Lane
Isaac	Finch	George	Parker	Richard	Archbold
Alexr.	Masterson	Edward	Nelthorp	Richard	Coban, and in 1715
Edward	Barret	Prosser	Brown	Benjamin	Hawley
John	Bollard	John	Williams	Lawrence	Burke, gone 1712
James	Burne			Robt.	Gilchrist
Robt.	Shepperd		1702-3.		
Peter	Pennet	Benj.	Manjoy		1709.
Patrick	Smith		(or Mountjoy)	John	Norton
Richard	Preston	Mangham	James	John	Whiting
Thos.	Sumpner	John	Norton	Charles	Moore
Thos.	Burton	Joshua	Travers	John	Lewis

LIST OF QUARTER BROTHERS AND JOURNEYMEN—*Continued.*

1709.

Richard	Holden (or Holding)
George	Lyons, d. 1722
John	Williamson
Nehemiah	Donallan
Joseph	Jones

1710.

Matthew	Hoes, and in 1721
Henry	Tyrer
Robert	Forbes
Nicholas	Leiness
Mahon	James
Will.	Bates
Joseph	Walker
Francis	Betagh
Chas.	Norton
John	Lennies
George	Gillingham
Jabez	Tench
Henry	Daniel
Matt.	Wilson
John	Carrick
Samuel	Fitteley
Daniel	Washbourne, d. 1713
Martin	Billing
Thomas	Deane
Thomas	Carrick
Jacob	Pountson
Jas. Matt.	Daniel
Henry	Gardner
Thomas	Williamson
John	Walker
Phillip	Kinnersley, jun.
John	Tuite { went to London 1723
Hosea	Lumley
Richard	Clarke
Henry	Ireland

1711.

Joshua	Travers
Jabes or Jacob	} Touch, d. 1723

1712.

Philip	Brush
Mark	Twelves
George	Carr
Peter	Franaux
Thomas	Dean
John	Sully
Richard	Matthews
Thomas	Duell, and in 1715
Peter	Gervais
David	Parry
Jeremiah	Morgan

1713-14.

Francis	Florio
Isaac	Bedford
Will.	Stone
Richard	Scott
Christopher	Thompson
Will.	Streeter
John	Hodgkinson

1713-14.

Benjamin	Boové
Will.	Jones
Jonas	Headon
Michael	Read
Will.	Waples
Edward	Sturgess
James	Mackey
Jacob	Ferrar
Stephen	Ferrar
Charles	Harris
Thomas	Daniel
John	Barry
Matthew	Copeland
Walter	Bendall
John	Hood (also Whood)
Stephen	Ferrne
Joseph	Wright
Alexr.	Moore
Matthew	Dawson
Will.	Whithorne
Will	Hunt
John	Ferrne
George	Pilkington.
Noah	Vialas
John	Ball
Will	Hester

1715-16

Robt.	Wilmore
Daniel	Heyford
Thos.	Craven
Thos.	Huddy
John	Ball
Samuel	Desserett
Joseph	Booth
John	Sully
Robert	Nevill
Anthony	Stanley
Richard	Scott
Will	Smith
Will	Proctor
James	Quinn
Thomas	Whood
Will.	Caddow
Jas.	Farlow

1717-18.

John	Whiting
Francis	Begg
Robert	Aiken, G.S.
Thos.	Jolly
Thos.	Sutton
Charles	Mayo
John	Downs
John	Mitchell
Edward	Tute
Nicholas	Bird
Richard	Cahill
John	Labase
John	Willme
John	Hall
J.	Rigby
Will	Hester, dead 1722
Henry	Willin
Will	Caddock

1717-18

Will	Bennett
John	Bradley
Richard	Baker
Charles	Duplasey
Will	Freeze
Will	Stones
Thos.	Jones

1719.

Will	Bennett
Samuel	Marchant
Nathan	Murray
Charles	Good (d. 1721)
Joel	Hulbert
John	Bingham
Isaac	Rumble
Jasper	Gradelle
Joseph	Herrick
Rutland	Gill
Robt.	Punch
John	Gale
Eleazer	Jones, dead 1723
Richd.	Jones
James	Bollegne (ment'd.)
Matthew	Duruson „

1720-1.

Charles	Wall
John	Turner
Martin	Kirkpatrick
Will.	Hildreth
Robt.	Holmes
Alexr.	Lorimer
Chas.	Leslie
Joseph	Tate
John	Sale, d. 1739
Richd.	Bakers
Joseph	Nevill
Chas.	Lemaitre
Will.	Boales
James	Taylor
Will.	Williamson
John	Wilmott
Edward	Somerwell
Will.	Fawcett
Edward	Morris
Benj.	Wood
John	Gumley
Solomon	Gibbs, d. 1728
Robt.	Willmore
Samuel	Glades
John	Brown
John	King, d. 1727
John	Hall (mentioned)

1722.

Will.	Rhodes
Thos.	Tompion
Richard	Spencer
Will.	Madders or Mathers
Will.	Sutton
James	Carter
Joseph	Holland
Edward	Jones (ment'd. 1723)

LIST OF QUARTER BROTHERS AND JOURNEYMEN—*Continued.*

1724-5.

Robt.	Pilkington
Michael	Hewitson
Robt.	Williamson
James	Thiboe
Richard	Barry
James	Correges
Samuel	Truelove, d. 1726
Michael	Smyth
James	Turner
Richard	Forester
George	Cartwright
Robt.	Billing
David	Gordon
John	Ravenscroft
John	Wilme
John	Moore
Robt.	Smith
John	Williams
Will	Sinclaire
Wingfield	Broderick
Thomas	Smarley (Cork)
Richd.	Matherson
Alexr.	Larimore
Alex. D.	Browne
Rich.	M'Donell
John	Taylor
Will	Murray
Robt.	Catherwood
Thos.	Prue
Michael	Dowdall
Charles	Duplessy
Robt.	Nevill
Will	Swift
Benj.	Fenner
Will	Oven
Sam	Brown
Peter	Tonnery
Edward	Smallwood
Stephen	Gerry
Matt.	Roper
Warham	Tearfield
Barth.	Potts
Ben.	Correges, d. 1728
George	Saunderson
Thos.	Barron
John	Johnson
Charles	Ball
George	Croft (or Cross)
Henry	Cole
John	Nangle
Will.	Walsh
George	Lyon
John	Smallpage
Robt.	Lyon

1727-8.

John	Fenny
Ralph	Vizard
Thos.	Hayford
Nicholas	Dowdall
Jacob	Mills
Will.	Walsh
John	Turner
James	Glascoe
Isaac	Doloares (D'Olier) ?

1727-8.

Henry	Gardiner
Richard	Pollard
Will.	Savile
Will.	Bates, jun.
Nathaniel	Fawden
Joseph	Holland (ment'd.)

1729.

Will.	Curry
Robt.	Cope
Daniel	Walker
John	Rogers
Barth.	Popkins
John	Gyles
Philip	Glascoe

1731.

John	Davis
Richard	Farren
Henry	Sadears
Andrew	Peterson
John Jas.	Turner
James	Templeton
Thos.	McCullagh
John	Jesson
Thos.	Quin, d. 1735
Richard	Wyat, d. 1755
James	Douglas
Samuel	Walker
James	Taylor
John	Bingham
Will.	Minchin
Robt.	Rogers
Ralph	Woodhouse
David	Bomes
Will.	Madden
Michael	Conner
James	O'Neale
Thos.	Rogers, d. 1732
Ambrose	Colcott, d. 1735
Francis	Quinn
Kirk	Ryves
Stephen	Royall
Silvester	Ince
John	Rigmaiden
Robt.	Savage
Will.	Berney
George	Smart
James	Champion
Richd.	Masterton
Thos.	Hayford
Thos.	Guire, d. 1735
John	Smith
Joshua	Hagne
Andrew	Patterson

1732-3.

James	O'Neal, d. 1733
Peter	Lacost
Rowland	Savage
Richard	Foster
Thos.	Maculla
Samuel	Shelly, d. 1739
Richard	Rice
Barth	Stokes

1732-3

Dan	Walker
Josias	Mears
John	Gaskin
Paul	Custos
Thos.	Coote
Archibald	Smith
Garrett	Farrell
Benjamin	Stokes
Robt.	Burfield, d. 1737

1733-4.

Patrick	Smith
Thos.	Bell
John	Hawtrey
George	Burford
Benj.	Stokes
Richd.	Baker
Matt.	Browne
Jos.	Carter
D.	Hamon
Dan.	Benjamin
Philip	Portall

1734-5.

Peter	Desenard
Will.	Williamson, jun.
John	Fortnum
Matthew	Brown
Alexr.	Richards
Clear	Bates
Will.	Burie
Robt.	Glanville
Albert	Hamon
Joseph	Foxall
Vere	Foster
John	Banks
Daniel	Beringues
Matt.	Alanson or Allison
Edward	Walsh
Edw.	Broadhurst
Will.	Hadcock
Will.	Townsend
Will.	Skinner
Christr.	Skinner
Daniel	Hainon
Thomas	Foxcroft
Abraham	Mandett
Will.	Percival
Will.	Teate, d. 1736

1736.

Septimus	Ciscell
Christopher	Clarke
Will.	English
Philip	Portall
Adyhaduck	Andrews
Archibald	Smith
Christopher	Lockard
Henry	Standish
Henry	Pepitt
Richard	Wyatt
George	Dent
Thos.	Wadman
Arthur	Leech
Will.	Wilkinson

LIST OF QUARTER BROTHERS AND JOURNEYMEN.—*Continued.*

1736.

Alexander	Power
Will.	Carroll
Will.	Guppy
David	Radford
John	Burdett
John	Whitchott
Angus	Dowding
John	Daniel
John	Loe
Thomas de	Lemerest
Benj.	Martin

1737.

Benj.	Shelly
George	Wilkinson
Alexr.	Power
James	Vidouze
James	Pickering

1738.

Benj.	Smith
Francis	Smith
Joshua	Crampton
James	Delasale
Nathaniel	Lowe
Thomas	Mitchell
George	Townsend
Adam	Tate, jun.

1739-43

Thomas	Huddy
Nathaniel	Murray
Joseph	Taafe, d. 1753
Richard	Masterson
Robert	Holmes
David	Gordon
Will.	Walsh
James	Glasco
Philip	Glasco
Richard	Pollard
Thomas	Hayford
Richard	Farren
John	Rogers
Robert	Rogers
Will.	Beates
Barth.	Potts
Samuel	Walker
George	Hodgkisson
Thomas	Johnson
Thomas	Lilly
Joseph	Bridgman
Thomas	Burton
James	Walker
Grey	Townsend
Nathaniel	Lowe
Francis	Quinn
Will	Burn
Jas.	Bingham
Jas.	Carter
Jas.	Delasalle

1744.

James	McCreary
Thomas	Verney
Francis	Gore

1744.

Daniel	Bringy
Levy	Wolf
Daniel	Pineau
Samuel	Epwell
John	Fearns
Will.	Digby
Jas.	Robinson
Edward	Lord
David	Radford
John	Nearny (or Warney)
Anthony	Sergeant
John	McDowal
George	Murphy
Marmaduke	Webb
Daniel	Pomerede
Robert	Hopkins
——	Finlay
Will.	Meager

1745-6.

John	Ringland
Thomas	Cornwall
Sam.	Wilson
Thomas	Hart
Thomas	Saunderson

1747-8.

Thomas	Shepperd
Thomas	McConnell
Peter	Dumain
Anthony	Cavanagh
Charles	Gillespie
Edward	Moore
John	Laughlin
Peter	Wingfield
Robert	Rose
George	Clarke
Edward	Cogan
Edward	Wright
Henry	Sankey
Francis	Daniel
John	Pittar
George	Chalmers

1749-50.

Will.	Byrne
Thomas	Bull, d. 1760
Benj.	Slack
George	Wilkinson
Henry	Chadwick
——?	Carmichael
Henry	Billing
Alexr.	Lilly
Nicholas	Lemaitre
Thos.	Williamson
Thos.	Appleby
George	Williamson
Robt.	Smith
John	Field
George	Trulock
John	Gaskin
Richd.	Sonly
John	Reilly
Will.	Steele
Dan.	McNeal

1749-50.

Edward	Mockler
Chas.	McLaughlin
Jonathan	Hutton
Richard	Keatley
Jas.	Pickering
John	Seawell

1751

John	Correge
Anthony	Bate
Wallace & Warman	
John	Kelly
Thos.	Lee
Michael	Fowler
Will.	Parry
George	Furnace

1752-3.

Henry	Molier
Robt.	Fisher
Burton	Wright
James	Wyer
Robt.	Cope
Lawrence	Doran
John	Nangle
Edward	Eccleston
Michael	Byrne
John	Slater
Robt.	Graham
John	Walker
——	Freeth

1753-4.

Daniel	Gordon
Will	Walsh
Christr.	Clarke
Owen	Cassidy
John	Douglas
Richd.	Coggan
——	Mason
George	Thompson
Joseph	Taafe
Francis	Crookshank
Peter	Gillois
Will.	Knox
Benj.	Smalley
Will.	Stafford

1754-5

John	Dalrymple
Richard	Sonley
John	Stedman
Adam	Fragneau
Matthias	Chambers
Richard	Gardiner, d. 1762.
Hugh & John Cunningham	
Alexr.	Stewart
Will.	West

1756.

Moses	Verney
Hugh	Caddell
Alexr.	Gordon
John	Sherwin
Matthew	Read

LIST OF QUARTER BROTHERS AND JOURNEYMEN.—*Continued.*

1756.

Samuel	Wilson

1758.

Peter	Rousset
Richard	Kelly
Will.	Homer, d. 1773
Alexr.	Christie
Edward	Walsh

1759.

George	Hill
Sam.	Teare
Thos.	Hart
Matt.	Lemaistre
John	Harrison

1760.

Jas.	Holmes
Will.	Moore
Michael	Cormick, d. 1780

1761.

Robt.	Holmes, d. 1787
Chas.	Craig
Will.	Williamson
Francis	Smith
Haydock	Andrews
Daniel	Pomarede
Jas.	Black
Edmund	Coggan
John	Gaskin
Moses	Verney
Michael	Walsh
Edward	Grumly
Richard	Harrison
——	McDonell
——	Bruce
Charles	Hull, d. 1766
John	Davison
Robt.	Atkinson
John	Moore, jun.
Jacob	Wills
Israel	Wolfe
Will.	Bond
Thos.	Green
Philip	Brew
——	Sturdy
Isaac	Bull, d. 1762
John	Ruxton
Thos.	Martin
Thos.	Meakins
George	Bambridge
Richard	Graham
Chas.	Caffrey
——	Campbell
David	Jonquer
Abraham	Tuppy
Eleazer	Warren
Thos.	Nuttle

1761.

Matt.	Copeland, d. 1764.
Joseph	Donallan
Will.	English
Thos.	Barron.

1762.

George	Horn
John	Ebbs
Chas.	Jones
Joshua	Hutton

1763.

Sam.	Busby
Will.	Digby
Edward	Eccleston
Ambrose	Nicholan (Nicklin)

1764.

Michael	Archdeacon
Paul	Barnwell
Isaac	Crab
Joshua	Emerson
Chas.	Gillespie
George	Graydon
Thos.	Hunt
George	Horn
Matt.	Lemaitre
George	Layng
Ebenezer	Orr
Robt.	Owens
Francis	Smith
Robt.	Smith
Jonathan	Taylor

1765-6.

Darby	Kehoe
Barnaby	Vizier
Will.	Bond
——	Bruce
Chas.	Carthy
	French & Keating
Sam.	Holmes
Owen	Hart
Michael	Keating
Sam.	Wilson
George	Wilkinson

1767.

John	Davison
Will.	French
Will.	Howard, W.M.
Richard	Bristow, G.S. ment'd
Richard	Ward

1768.

Willm.	Wiseman, ment'd as dead
Edward	Moore, W.M., ment'd

1769.

Will.	Moore
John	Moore

1770.

Hay	Andrews
George	Crossthwaite
Samuel	Close
Joy	Fumbaily
Garrett	Fitzgerald
John	Nicholan (Nicklin)
Jas.	Black
Anthony	Bate
Isaac	Bull
George	Bainbridge
Alexr.	Brown
Chas.	Craig
Christr.	Clarke
Richd.	Fitzsimons
Thomas	Johnston
John	Kelly
Arthur	O'Neile
Jacob	Stedman
Henry	Standish
Chas.	Wright

1771-2.

Chas.	Cathry
Bernard	Dolahoyde, W.M.
——	Howan
John	Reilly
Robt.	Smyth
Nugent	Booker.
James	Brush
John	Bolland
John	Digby
Thos.	Howes
Will.	Keen
Thos.	Williamson
John	Walker
Jas.	Carter, J'yman, G.S.

1773.

Robt.	Woggan
Francis	Walsh

1775.

Thos.	Martin
John	Pittar.

1784.

(Last entry of Quarter Brothers.)

Henry	Andrews
Samuel	Basley
George	Chalmers
Will	French
Will	Stafford
John	Steadman
John	Taafe
Jacob	Wills

NAMES OF DUBLIN GOLDSMITHS REGISTERED IN THE BOOKS OF THE COMPANY IN 1784 AND FOLLOWING YEARS.*

* The Statute 23 and 24 George III. c. 23 (Ireland 1783) enacted that from and after 9 September, 1784, no merchant, manufacturer, or dealer in gold or silver wares should buy, sell, exchange, or export any gold or silver wares or pearls without first registering his name and place of abode with the Company of Goldsmiths in Dublin, under a penalty of £100. (See page 586).

1784.		1784.		1784.	
Alexr. D.	Brown	Mary	Dunne	Jeremiah	Bridgman
James	Kinzie	Joseph	Daffron		
Samuel	Guinness	Ignatius	Christian	**1785.**	
Thomas	Hill	Joseph	Bayley	Robt.	Thompson
C. A.	Kelly	James	Norton	Young	Martin
Joshua	Whitehouse	James	Jones	John	Begg
Thomas	Whitehouse	Samuel	Baird	John	Laughlin
Benjamin	Henfrey	Samuel	Wilkinson	Richard	Singleton
N. W.	Brady	John	Leake	John	Shekleton
Job	Montgomery	John	Russell	Griffin	Jones
Shean	Houston	Will.	Power	Alex.	Barry
John	Young	Samuel	Busby	Archibald	Buchanan
John	Jellett	Thos.	Turpin	John	Fawcett
Eneas	Ryan	Will. Izod	Dogherty	Barnaby	Delahoyde
Frederick	May	Robt.	Roth	Samuel	Scott
Israel	Wolf	John	Keen	Thomas	Farrell
Peter	Magennis	Michael	Homer	Christopher	Clarke
John	Clarke & }	Elinor	Champion	Samuel	Taylor
James	Rice }	Robt.	Smith	Will.	Howard
Thomas	Kennan	Samuel	Taylor	John	Huddy
Arthur	Farrell	Christopher	Haines	John	Tweedie
Robert	Hunter	James	Mills	Richd.	Williams
Ann	Stafford	Eleazer	Warren	Alex.	Robertson
Will. D.	Moore	James	Hewett	Patrick	Somers
James B.	Mahon	Will.	Johnson	John	Gibson
Samuel	Holmes	John	Shiels		
Ann	Cormick	Robt.	Deane		
Charles	White	Charles	Johnson	**1786.**	
Will. Thos.	Archer	Joseph	Thrist (or Tuist)	John	Paine
Thomas	Baker	Alexander	Ticknell	Thos. Pat.	Reilly, & }
Henry	Clements & }	Rich.	Williams	A.	Reilly }
John	Smith }	George	Fivey	Thomas	Marley
Ambrose	Nicklin	Weston	Warrely	Gaspard	Truitte
Robert	Wyke	John	Freth	Will.	Gethin
Samuel	Jacobs	Lion	Davis	Leonard J.	Long
Nicholas	Butler	Jacob	Jetz	Edward	Percy
Thomas	Kelly	Robt.	Botts	John	Daley
Will.	Ward	John	Gibson		
Charles	Stokes	George	Robertson	**1787.**	
Benjamin	Taitt	Nathaniel	White	D. Peter	Bayley, & }
Owen	Cassidy	Matthew	O'Brien	T.	Bayley }
John	Kelly	Philip	McDermot	John	Rice
James	Spring	Wright,	Pike, & Co.	Isaac	Davis
Francis	Vidouze	Thomas	Martin		
John	Nicklin	Will.	Greer	**1788.**	
Thomas	Connor	Peter	Covey	John	Broome
John	Wilkinson	Thomas	Barber	James	Hamill
Jonathan	Robinson	Michael	Archdeacon	George	Nangle
Samuel	Close	Thomas	Kinsela	Thomas	Hart
James	Campbell	Alexis	Livernet	Robt.	Eccleston
Dennis	Frey	Will.	Rose	Henry	Nicholson
James	Vigne	James	Robertson		
Thos. Eben.	Strahan	John	McLean	**1789.**	
Patrick	Walsh	Robt.	Moore	Martha	Gregory
Moses	Moses	James	Kennedy	Joseph	Mandals
Andrew	Pitman	Michael	Rogers	Robert	Roth
Thomas	Atkinson	John	McCraith	Peter	Lemaistre
Andrew	Savage	Richard	Wilde	Surdeville	Kiernan
James	Brush	Rice	Jones	Thomas	Nixon
John	Wade	Will.	Lemaistre	John	Payne
John	Cox	Jerome	Alley		
John	Gordon	Henry	Martin	**1790.**	
Arthur	O'Neill	Charles	Craig	Isaac	Jones
Will.	Moore	John	Smith		

GOLDSMITHS REGISTERED IN THE BOOKS OF THE COMPANY—*Continued.*

1791.

Thomas	Adams
James	England
John	McEllray
Patrick	McEllray
Gustavus	Byrne
William	Bond

1792.

Michael	Smith
Will.	Packer
Eneas	Ryan
Henry	Morgan
Christopher	Donovan
John	Rigby
John	Hart

1793.

Thomas	Sly
John	Wharton
George	West
Thomas	Fowler
George	Matthews

1794.

Christopher	Haines, jun.
Patrick	Kainan
James	Anderson
John	Coleman

1795.

James	McCoy
James	Keating
Edward	Egerton
Will.	Doyle
Henry	Nowlan
Will.	Thompson
Samuel	Neville

1796.

Jeremiah	D'Olier
John	West

1797.

Thomas	Townsend
Richard	Sawyers
Thomas	Le Fevre
John	Kearns
George	Connor
Archibald	Bell
John Ash	Rainey
John	Jackson
George	Wheatley
Thomas	Tudor
Joseph	Johnston
Robt.	Tomlinson

1798.

Roger	Carson
Thos.	Tracy
James	Poole & ⎫
Thomas	Adams ⎭
Randall	Cashell
Walter	Peter
Thos.	Hopper & Co.

1799.

Joseph	Ravill
Fred.	Buck

1799.

Daniel	Vennant
John	Willington
James	Henderson
Thomas	Wilson

1800.

Daniel	Egan
James	Connor
Michael	Murphy
Thomas	Bayley
George	Warner
Francis	Dunn
James	Scott
Thomas	Rourke
Houston &	Farley
Hopper &	Hannay
Roger	Kennedy
Mark	McLoughlin
Will.	Bradbury
Perkins	Flood

1801.

Will.	Hannay

1802.

Henry	Nowland
Will.	Hamey
Will.	Binns
Henry	Rooke
Alex.	Wheatley
Lewis	Williamson
Barnaby	Vizer
Will.	Gurty

1803.

Christr.	Robinett
John	Twycross
Charles	Stewart
Will.	Frederick
J. B.	Jamillion
John	Clarke & ⎫
Jacob	West ⎭
Richard	Archbold

1804.

Matt.	West, junr.
Thos.	Eley
Will	Law
Will	Sherwin & Co.
John	Egan
John	Macpherson
Hugh	McConnell
Samuel	Smith
Will.	Morgan
Edward	Kelly
John	West
Isaac	Parrington

1805.

Thomas	Farley
Francis	Johnston
Christopher	Holmes
Isaac	Barrington
Arthur	Murphy
James	McGliddon
George	Rooke
Edward	Heyland
Joseph	Francis

1806.

James	Brush
Hugh	Buckley

1807.

Arthur	Calloway

1809.

Richard	Speer
Joshua	Franklin
Henry	Nowlan
Charles	Harris
Will	Hanlon

1811.

Bernard	Mcguire
James	Keating & ⎫
Richd.	Flood ⎭
James	Flanagan

1812.

John	Brown

1813.

Mich.	Flanagan
Jas. A.	Henzell
John	Teare, junr.
John	Hendrick
Jas.	Green
Rich.	Fell
Crabb &	Cummins
Jas.	Fray
Will.	Cumyng
Edw.	Martin

1814.

Edwd.	Murray
Lawrence	Nowlan

1815.

Thos.	Farnell

1816.

Peter	Godfrey
Chas.	Marsh
Philip	Weekes

1817.

Hugh	Patrick
Francis	Holmes

1818.

Joseph	Eades
John	Shekleton

1819.

Chas.	Campbell
George	Bayley
Jas.	Bourke
	Jenkins
John	Tate
Will.	Farquhar

1821.

Hy.	Flavelle
Thos.	Groves
Jas.	Johnson
Baker	Smith
Dan.	Mason
Baker	Smith

GOLDSMITHS REGISTERED IN THE BOOKS OF THE COMPANY—*Continued.*

1821.

Warren	McDermott
Turvey	Flower
Will	Bullock
Mic.	Doyle
Josiah	Lowe
Alex.	Ross
Will	Boyle
Jas.	Brady
Christ'r.	Eades
Willett &	Doyle
Chas.	Browne
Jas.	Johnston
Thos.	Grove

1822.

Rich. Wm.	Osborne
Smith &	Gamble
Adam	Martin
Arthur	O'Neill
John	George
Lawrence	Isaacs

1823.

Joshua	Weathered
Arthur	Sergison
Richd.	O'Donnell

1824.

Mich.	Myers
Edw.	Topham
H. J.	Deveaux

1825.

Robt.	Whitstone
Will.	Broderick
Christr.	Byrne

1826.

Am.	O'Neill
Jas.	Brady
Pat.	Morin

1827.

D.	Moulang
Will.	Nowlan
Lawrence	Kearny
Will	Brady
Dan	Moulany
Henry	Rooke
Henry	Flavelle
David	Foster
John	Gaskin
Will	Mossley
Rich.	Craig
John	Smith
Will	Hanlon
Robt.	Hampson
Edw.	O'Reilly
Mary A.	Johnson
Henry	Booth
Nicholas	Walsh
Lamb &	Duffy
Thos.	Lindley
Thos.	Morgan
Pierce	Brett
Joseph	Pinkney
Edw.	Adams
J. & W.	Cohen
Jas.	Lynch
John	Lawlor
Evan	Fairclough

1827.

Thos.	Read & Co.
John	Read & Son
John	Bassegge
Matt.	Law
Thos.	Kennedy
John	Russell
Will.	Broderick
Thos.	Ayre
Baxter	Star
Rich.	Smith
Jas.	Jesson
John	McDermott
Will.	Gibton
J. & C.	Butler
J. T.	Lebel
Thos.	Fannin
Sam.	Smith
J.	Barnier
West &	Son
Joseph	Hodson
Arthur	Wise
Jas.	Fagan
Philips &	Cohen
Henry	Gregory
Will.	Boyle
Mich.	McCulloch
Edw.	Crofton
E.	Jackson
Fred.	Hodges
Robt.	Cortigan
W. J.	Cainen
John	Tate
Thos.	Kelly
Will.	Mooney
——	West
George	Gillington,
McWilliams & Gibton	
John	Littledale
Sam	Smith
Joseph	Johnston
George	Walker

1828.

John Joseph Deveaux	
Sam.	Garre
Joseph	Sherlock

1829.

Ralph	Walsh
Anthony	Lestrange
Thos.	Morpie
Chas.	Byrne
Jas.	Nowlan
George	Mills
John	Holbrook
John	Wilson
A.	Jones
G.	Mitchell
Roderick	Burk
Sam.	Spencer
Edw.	Farrell
Thos.	Murphy
J. W.	Milliken
W. or I.	Parkes
John	Cullinan
Rich.	Sawyer
Will.	Broderick

1830.

Thos.	Morpe

1831.

Edmd.	Johnson

1832.

Thos.	Low
George	Butler

1834.

Jas.	Brady
John	Mooney

1835.

Thos.	Meade
John	Warren

1836.

John	Clark
Hughes & Francis	
Ed. & Jos.	Johnson
Jas.	Richardson
Edw.	Smith
Sam.	Page
J. J.	Nolan
Jas.	Harris

1837.

Geo.	Twycross

1838.

Nowlan & Stewart	
Mich.	Bennett

1840.

J.	Francis

1841.

Michael	Nowlan

1842.

N.	Burdge

1845.

T.	Barton
J.	Gamble
J.	Mahony
J.	Smyth
Jos.	Johnson

1847.

C.	Cummins, jun.
Thos.	Mason

1848.

Ann	Cummins
J.	Donegan
W.	Lynn

1849.

—.	Gardner

1850.

Joseph	Needham

1851.

Arthur	Johnson
Michael	Keating

1853.

Edwd.	Topham

1855.

Kapp Bros	

1856.

Hy.	Flavelle, jun.
W.	Atcheson

GOLDSMITHS REGISTERED IN THE BOOKS OF THE COMPANY—*Continued.*

1859.
D. Goyer
Samuel Le Bass

1860.
W. Percival
Thos. Smyth

1861.
J. Keating
Ed. Powell
J. Scriber

1862.
Mars. Trench
Francis Martin

1864.
◉ Hutton
J. R. Ryan
James West & Son

1865.
Thos. Brunker
Ed. Johnson, jun.
—. Waterhouse

1866.
C. Stewart
Patrick Donegan

1867.
J. D. Bryce
Wm. Lawson
Thos. Mason
John Pelin

1869.
I. Panton

1870.
Jas. Walsh

1871.
J. Wickham
Wur & Rogers
Parder & Werner

1872.
Thos. Weir
A. Rogers

1874.
Ignatius Cummins

1875.
McDowell Bros.
Jos. Walsh

1876.
J. Redmond

1877.
Wm. Hendricken
West & Son

1880.
O'Connor & Dillon.

1881.
Saml. H. Wright

1883.
D. Moulang
Walker & Pim
Winder & Lamb
Henry Hopkins

And others whose names appear in the maker's-name columns of the last three tables of Marks on Dublin Plate, on pages 616-8, *ante.*

NAMES OF DUBLIN GOLDSMITHS FOUND IN DIRECTORIES FROM 1760 TO 1808,

BUT NOT IN OFFICIAL LISTS OF FREEMEN OF THE GOLDSMITHS' COMPANY.

G.S. = goldsmith; S.S. = silversmith; W.M. = watchmaker; W.C.M. = watch-case maker; J. = jeweller.

Date.	Name and Designation.			Date.	Name and Designation.		
1800-8	Rainey	Asshe	W.M.	1798	Patrick	Cainen	J. & W.M.
1762	Elizabeth	Brown		1800-8	Michael	Cainen	G.S. & W.M.
1764	Isaac	Bull	W.M.	1786	Ambrose	Clarke	W.M.
	Robert	Burton	G.S.	1798-08	William	Clarke	G.S. & J.
1786-98	George	Bainbridge	W.M.	1786-8	Christopher	Clarke	W.M.
1795	William	Bailie	S.S.	1808	Clarke & West		G.S. & J. (wholesale)
1786-91	Thomas	Baker	J.				
1800	John	Bayly	G.S.	1786-8	George & A. Clarke		G.S. & J.
1786	George	Bambrick	W.M.	1786-90	Clements & Smyth		G.S. & J. to His Majesty.
1798	James	Baker	J.				
1798-08	Charles	Barker	J. & W.M.	1808	Thomas	Connor	Mfg. G.S. & J.
1788-98	Isaac	Bedford	W.M.	1788	Close & Jones		G.S & J.
1786-8	Anthony	Bate	,,	1786-8	John	Crosthwaite	W.M.
1798	Robert	Beeth	,,	1798	Alexr.	Christie	,,
1785-98	John	Bolland	S.S.	1764-88	John	Dalrymple	,,
1786-98	Archibald	Buchanan	W.M.	1770	Richard	D'Olier	G.S.
,,	Isaac	Bull		1764	Isaac	D'Olier & Son	,,
1798-00	Gusty	Byrne	G.S. & S.S.	1798-08	Joseph	Daffron	J. & W.
1786	Samuel	Busby	W. & Cl.M.	1786	John	Daniel	J.
1800-8	Jeremiah	Bridgman	G.S.	1786-08	James	Dalrymple	W.M.
1764	Robert	Calderwood	,,	1795-08	John	Daly	S.S.
,,	James	Champion	J.	1800	Michael	Devereux	G.S.
,,	Richard	Cogan	W.	1798	William	Donovan	J.
1786-91	Eleanor	Champion	J.	1770	Samuel	Epwell	G.S.

NAMES OF DUBLIN GOLDSMITHS FOUND IN DIRECTORIES—*Continued.*

Date.	Name and Designation.		Date.	Name and Designation.	
1798	Egerton & Pittar	G.S. & J.	1808	J. Manley	Mfg. J. & S.S.
1800	Egerton & Brown	G.S.	1786-8	Thomas Martin	W.M.
1786-8	James Esdall	J.	1798	William Mills	J.
1795-8	James England	S.S.	1786-8	Frederick May	W.M.
1808	Barthw. Farley	J.	1808	Thomas Morgan	S.S.
1786	Francis Fitzpatrick	W.M.	1786-8	John Mestayer	J.
1808	Joshua Franklin	G.S.	1786-95	Ambrose Moore	G.S. & J.
1786-8	Hugh Fleming	W.M.	1798	Michael C. Mullen	J.
1788	Henry Gardiner	,,	1786-8	Robert Murray	G.S.
1786	Thomas Glascoe	,,	,,	John Nelson	W.M.
1808	Thomas Gonne	J.	1808	Osborne & Kevell	J.
1786-8	Alexander Gordon & Son	W.M.	1788	John Peel	W.M.
,,	George Graydon	,,	1808	William Poole	J.
1760-4	Robert Hopkins	G.S.	,,	John Power	S.S.
1790-1	Walter Harley	J. & G.S.	1764-86	John Reily	W.M.
1786-98	James Hewett	G.S.	1798	Robert Richardson	J.
1788-90	Thomas Hill		1764	William Sinclair	
1808	John Hawkesley & Co.	G.S. & J.	1786	Jno. & Wm. Sherwin	G.S.
,,	Jane Hewett	J.	1795-08	Robert Smith	S.S. & J.
,,	James Henderson	G.S. & J.	1786-08	Mary Anne Stafford	G.S. & W.M.
1786-8	Willm. Howard	W.M.	,,	William Sterling	W.M.
1808	J. A. Henzel	S.S. & J.	1798	Matthew Stewart	J.
,,	F. Hull	W.C.M.	1786-98	Poole Taylor	W.M.
1786-8	Isaac Hutchinson	J.	1762	Thomas Thorp	G.S.
1764	David Johnson	W.M.	1786	Joshua Tomey	W.M.
1788	Josiah Jackson	G.S. & J.	1808	James Twycross	G.S.
1808	Erasmus W. Jenkins	J.	1788	Francis Townsend	,,
1786	Thomas Johnson	W.M.	1798-08	John Tudor (warden 1808)	,,
1788	Willm. Johnson	J.	1808	George Turvey	J.
1786-8	Griffith Jones	G.S.	1786-08	James Vigné	,,
1788	David Jonquiere	J.	1788	Barnaby Vizer	W.M.
1785-08	John Kavanagh	S.S. & J.	1761	Arthur Weldon	G.S.
1788	Charles Kavanagh	W.M.	1764	James Warren	,,
1786	John Kavanagh	G.S.	,,	Thomas Walker	,,
1800	Michael Keating	S.S.	1775	Francis Walsh	J.
1808	Jane Keen	G.S.	1786-8	George Walker	W.M.
,,	Edward Kelly	J.	,,	Francis Walsh	J. & S.S.
1764-86	Alexander Lilly	,,	1808	Peter Walsh	J.
1788-98	George Laing	,,	1786-8	Richard Ward	W. & Clk.M.
1788	Henry Le Maitre	W.M.	1808	William Ward	G.S.
1761-4	John Moore, sen. & jun.	G.S.	1786-8	James Warren	W.M.
1764	Nathan Murray, sen. & jun.		,,	John Weldon	
1775	Charles Mullin	G.S. & J.	1808	Robert Williams	G.S. & J.
1798-08	Owen Macram	J.	,,	Henry Wilme	
1786-8	John M'Donough	W.M.	,,	T. Wright	J.
1798-08	Thos. & Hy. Manning	G.S. & J.	1788	Martin Young	W.M.
1786-8	John M'Lean	W.M.			

LIST OF GOLDSMITHS FOR WHOM PLATE WAS ASSAYED IN DUBLIN.

[FROM 1638 TO 1811.]

Compiled by Mr. Dudley Westropp from the following Assay Books of the Goldsmiths' Company (all that are preserved):—Book 1, 1638-49, 1694-1700; Book 2, 1705-13; Book 3, 1725-8; Book 4, 1729-33; Book 5, 1744-8; Book 6, 1752-5; Book 7, 1758 (only a few leaves left); Book 8, 1787-9, giving details of plate; Book 9, 1788-99; Book 9a, 1796-1802; Book 10, 1809-11, giving details of plate; Book 11, 1811-17, giving details of plate; Book 12, 1818-20, giving details of plate.

The books obviously do not contain accounts of *all* the plate assayed from the incorporation of the Company, nor the name of every Dublin goldsmith, but the entries here transcribed cover considerable ground.

PLATE ASSAYED FOR—

1638-44.

Will.	Cooke
Will.	Hampton
John	Woodcock
Matthew	Thomas
George	Gallant
Peter	Vaneijndhoven
Daniel	Underwood
James	Vanderbeck
Edward	Chadsey
Will.	Gallant
John	Moore
George	Greene

1644-5.

Thomas	Parnell
Dan.	Bellingham
Gilbert	Tonques
Robt.	Coffee
Nathaniel	Stoughton
Peter	Vaneijndhoven

1645-6.

Daniel	Bellingham
Nathaniel	Stoughton
Peter	Vaneijndhoven
Edward	Shadsey
Gilbert	Tonques
Ambrose	Futrell
Christopher	Wright
Robt.	Coffee

1646-7.

Nathaniel	Stoughton
Peter	Vaneijndhoven
Robert	Coffee
Christopher	Wright
Daniel	Bellingham

1647-8.

Peter	Vaneijndhoven
Gilbert	Tonques
Daniel	Bellingham
Nathaniel	Stoughton

1648-9.

Daniel	Burfeldt
Peter	Vaneijndhoven
Gilbert	Tonques
Nathaniel	Stoughton
Daniel	Bellingham

1676.

John	Cope
John	Hyett
Timothy	Blackwood
Elizabeth	Slicer

1694.

John	Billing
Thos.	Bolton
George	Cartwright
John	Philips
David	King
Robt.	Smith
John	Cuthbert
Matthew	Laroche
Benj.	Pemberton
John	Humphreys
Joseph	Walker

1694-5.

Samuel	Wildar
Edward	Nelthorp
Alexr.	Mackey
John	Clifton
James	Thompson
Andrew	Gregory
Vincent	Kidder
Christopher	Wright
Anthony	Stanley
James	Weldon
Will. or Richard	} Archbold
David	Swan
Adam	Buck
James	Thompson
John	Dickson
Will	Mayars
Timothy	Hevin
Abraham	Voyseen
Alexr.	Sinkler (Sinclair)

1696.

Erasmus	Cope
Robt.	Ince
Robt.	Smyth
Stephen	Kennedy
———	Aspole
Thos.	Disbrough

1697.

John or Joseph	} Bennett

1697.

John	Garrett
Christian	Waggoner
John	Matthews
David	Swan
Francis	Jones
Joseph	Whitchurch
David	Rumie
John	Eakin
Floris	Six

1698-9.

Samuel	Wildar
Alexr.	Sinclair
David	King
James	Wilding
Joseph	Walker
Thomas	Boulton
John	Clifton
Stephen	Kennedy
Anthony	Stanley
Christian	Waggoner
John	Cuthbert
John	Phillips
John	Humphreys
Andrew	Gregory
Benjamin	Pemberton
Christr. ?	Wright
Robert	Smyth
——— ?	Heather
——— ?	Garrold
Abraham	Voyseen
David	Rummieu
Erasmus	Cope
Isaac or Dd.	Swan
——— ?	Hanon
——— ?	Griffe, or Griffith
Will.	Mias
Timothy	Heaven
John	Garret
Alexr.	Mackey
Cyriac	Mallory
John	Eakin
Will.	Skinner

To Feb. 9th, 1700.

1701.

Thomas	Lovet
James	Cotton
Anthony	Stanley
John	Matthews
Abraham	Voisin

GOLDSMITHS FOR WHOM PLATE WAS ASSAYED IN DUBLIN.—*Continued.*

1702.

David	Swan
John	Cuthbert, sen.
John	Phillips
John	Matthews
Jonathan	Gerrard

1704.

Abraham	Voisin
Robert	Smith
John	Garret
James	Walker

1705-13.

Thos.	Billing
John	Philips
Will.	Skinner
John	Pennyfather
John	Cuthbert, sen.
Burleigh or Robert	} Cuffe
David	King
Edward	Barrett
Jno. or Thos.	Matthews
Robert	Forbush (Forbes)
Thomas	Slade
Alexr.	Sinclair
Robert	Smith
Will.	Archdall
Joseph	Walker
John	Carter
John	Cuthbert, jun.
A. or C.	Hartwyck
Francis ?	Jones
John	Clifton
Philip	Tough
Edward	Workman
Jonathan	Gerard
Alexr.	Mackey

1706.

T.	Bolton
John	Ruston
Peter ?	Beaulieu
John	Wyes
George	Ling
David	Rummieu
Adam	Buck
Christian	Kindt
David	Swan

1707.

John	Palet
Francis	Girard
Henry	Sherwin
Thomas	Slade
Richard	Scott
George	Parker
Will.	Skinner
John	Pattison
John	Matthews, jun.
John	Eakin
Benj.	Pemberton
John	Wyes
John or Hy.	Matthews, sen.
James	Welding
—— ?	Killreigh
Richd.	Archbold
Robert	Pilkington

1709.

John	Hamilton
George	Farrington
John	Williamson
Jas. Matt.	Daniell

1710.

Mortagh	Dowling
John	Whitefield
Stevens	Golding
Henry	Sherwin
Will.	Clarke

1711.

Mark	Twelf, or Twelves
Rich.	Lord
Christian	Waggoner
—— ?	Wilks
John	Tuite
Henry	Ireland
George	Ling
Thomas	Paris
——	Lhomine ?

1712.

Thomas	Ovin
Nehemiah	Donelan
Thomas	Lovet
Thomas	{ English, or Inglish
Jabes	Tench
Richard	Houlding
Will.	Paton
John	Garrett

1713.

—— ?	Lloyde
Benj.	Manjoy
George	Gillingham

1715.

Edward	Barrett
Thos.	Walker
John	Cuthbert
Thomas	Jolly

1716.

Will.	Smith
John	Williamson
Benj.	Mountjoy
Edward	Barrett

1718-24.

Joseph	Francis
Mark	Twelves
Chas.	Leslie
Thos.	Williamson

1725-28.

Joseph	Teafe,* or Taafe (spoons)
Mary	Barrett (Mrs.)
Will.	Archdall
Will.	Duggan

1725-8

Thos.	Walker
Esther	Forbes (Mrs.)
Erasmus	Cope
Philip	Kinnersly
Will.	Sutton
Thos.	Bolton
Matt.	Walker
David	King
Chas.	{ Pendergras Prendergast
George	Cartwright
John	Hamilton
John	Taylor
John	Williamson
—— ?	Baker (Mrs.)
Roger	Finch
Thos.	Williamson
Matthew	Wilson
Will.	Jones
Daniel	{ Hofford or Heyford
John	Freebough
Henry	Daniel
Simon	Young
Chas.	Leslie
John	Robinson
Will.	Swift
Thos.	Slade
Will.	Sherwin
John	Clifton
Samuel	Truelove
John	Freeze
Michael	Hewitson
Edward	Dowdall
Richard	Barry
—— ?	Beatly
Noah	Vialas
Michael	Smith
Robert	Harrison
Peter	Gervais
Elias	Maquay
Henry	Williams
Edward	Workman
Thos.	Brown
Will.	Sinclair
Dorothy	Manjoy (Mrs.)
Richard	Spencer
Thos.	Walker

1726.

Matt.	Walker
Anthony	Stanley
Daniel	Hayford
Will.	Williamson
Thos.	Sutton
Peter	Tonnery
Michael	Hewitson
John	Taylor
—— ?	Clinton
Will.	Welsh
Benj.	Woods

1727.

—— ?	Williams (Mrs.)
—— ?	{ Tirre or Terry

* Joseph Teafe (or Taafe) made a large quantity of spoons 1725-28 and onwards to 1748.

GOLDSMITHS FOR WHOM PLATE WAS ASSAYED IN DUBLIN—*Continued.*

1727.

Robt.	Calderwood
John	Hamilton
John	Frebough
John	Ravenscroft
———?	Renchors

1728.

Thos.	Slade
Richard	Pollard
Caleb	Colbeck (Limerick)
Will.	Barry
Richard	Eaton
Thomas	Lovet
———?	Hill (Limerick)

1729-33.

Matt.	Walker
Philip	Kinnersly
Will.	Archdall
Chas.	Leslie
John	Jones
Alexr.	Brown
Joseph	Teafe
Esther	Forbes
Will.	Williamson
Thos.	Williamson
Francis	Williamson
Mary	Barrett (Mrs.)
Robt.	Calderwood
John	Hamilton
Richard	Pollard
John	Giles
John	Jesson
Thomas	Hayford
Roger	Finch
Dorothy	Manjoy (Mrs.)
Richard	Baker
Henry	Daniell
Thos.	Sutton
E.	Cope
Edward	Dowdall
Thos.	Walker
Will.	Sutton
Will.	Walsh
John	Taylor
Peter	Gervais
Richard	Farren
Thos.	Slade
Spranger or Will.	} Barry
George	Cartwright
John	Hamilton
Thomas	Hefford (Heyford)
Simon	Young
Anthony	Lefebure
Noah	Vialas
Henry	Sherwin
Will.	Sinclair
John	Freebough

1730.

Peter	Tonnery
John	Williamson

1730.

———?	Randsford
Richard	Eaton
Henry	Wilme
Capt. Matt.	Wilson
Caleb	Colbeck (Limerick)
———?	Mulligan
Chas	Ball
Thos.	Hartwell
———?	Patterson
Richard	White
———?	Reynolds
John	Robinson (Limerick) also in 1738
Jonathan	Buck (Limerick)
Thos.	Parsons

1731.

Barth.	Popkins
James	Douglas
Abraham	Barboult
Will.	Curry
Kirk	Ryves
Isaac	D'Olier
Samuel	Walker

1732.

Samuel	Shelly
———?	Stoyte
John	Wilme
John	Gumley
James	Whithorn
Fleetwood	Daniel
———?	Fegan
Rattle	White
John	Moore
———?	Duffy
Richard	Rice
Michael	Smith
George	Smart
Christ.	{ Locker or Lockart
Hercules	Morgan (Clonmel)

1733.

Peter	Usher
———?	Herd (Mrs.)
Will.	Inglish
Will.	Shields
Will.	Stoplear
John	Clifton
Benj.	Stokes
Jos. & Will.	Wall (Kinsale)

1744-8.

Joseph	Taafe (died 1753)
Andrew	Goodwin
Robt.	Holmes
Will.	Townsend
Grey	Townsend
Robt.	Calderwood
Isaac	D'Olier
James	St. Maurice
John	Gumley
Samuel	Walker

1744-8.

Thos.	Walker
Francis	Williamson
Will.	Williamson
Vere	Forster
John	Wilme
Christopher	Skinner
John	Moore
Thos.	Shepperd
Barth.	Mosse
John	Hamilton
Anthony	Kavanagh
Edward	Kavanagh
Robt.	Hopkins
Robt.	Hunter
Will.	Wilson
Thomas	Sutton
Thos.	Parsons
Will.	Walsh
Edward	Walsh
Alexr.	Richards
Chas.	Leslie
Thos.	Delmare
Thos.	Heyford
Roger	Finch
Benj.	Stokes
Arthur	Weldon
John	Wilme
Noah	Vialas
George	Murphy
John	Christie
Michael	Smith
Matthias	Browne

1745.

John	Kidd
David	Bomes
Robt.	Glanville
Edward	Raper
Hercules	Morgan (Clonmel)
John	Hamilton
Chas.	Boucher
Will.	Sinclare
John	Laughlin
Will	Wilson
James	Whithorn (for the country)
George	Beere
—?	Melaghlin
Daniel	Onge
Francis	Gore
Charles	Leslie.
———?	Gumly (Mrs.)
John	McCormuck or Cormuck }
Robt.	Rogers
———?	Jackson
Thos.	Isaac
Thos.	Green
Jonathan	Thomas

1747.

———?	Fox (Mrs.)
Peter	Rieusset
———?	Williamson (Mrs.)

GOLDSMITHS FOR WHOM PLATE WAS ASSAYED IN DUBLIN—*Continued.*

1747.

Thomas	Miles (Waterford)
Henry	Rash
——?	Price (country)
Edward	Lord

1752-5.

Jonathan	Hutton
Will.	Byrne
Thos.	Williamson
Isaac	D'Olier
Will.	Townsend
John	Laughlin
Chas.	Laughlin
Alexr.	Richards
Thos.	Walker
Benj.	Stokes
Richard	Williams
Andrew	Goodwin
Richard	Keightley
Robt.	Glanville
Robt.	Calderwood
Matthias	Browne
Henry	Sankey
Sam.	Walker
Jas.	Douglas
John	Pittar
——?	Heyford (Mrs.)
John	Wilme, jun.
William	Walsh
John	Moore
Francis	Crookshank
Thos.	Burton
Thomas	Lee
Thos.	Green
John	Kelly
Robt.	Hopkins
——?	Fox (Mrs.)
James	Warren
Jonathan	Hutton
Owen	Cassidy
Joseph	Bridgman
Daniel	Onge
Henry	Chadwick
B. or W.	Wilson
Will.	Currie
John	McCormuck
Benj.	Slack
Michael	Fowler
Jonathan	Ruston
Edward	Mockler
Thos.	Parsons
Edward	Raper
Hercules	Morgan (Clonmel)
Christopher	Skinner
Grey	Townsend
John	Kavanagh
Chas.	Dowdall
David	Bomes
Charles	Leslie
Nicholas	Lemaitre
James	Wyer
Silvester	Ince
Charles	Darragh
Abraham	Davis
Joseph	Cullen

1753.

——?	Aston
John ?	Freeth
James	Betagh
Robt.	Potter
——?	Cathry
Thomas	Miles (Waterford)
Henry	Rash
——?	Gillois
Francis	Smith
Jonathan	Pasley
John	Seawell, or Sewell

1754.

Noah	Vialas
——?	Benson
——?	Cherry (country)
Will.	Homer
Henry	Moliere
——?	Gaynor
Henry	Waldron
Edward	Lord
——?	Hothart (country)
——?	Hill
Benj.	Wilson
——?	Singleton
Vere	Forster
Robt.	Billing
Thos.	Green, jun.
Joseph	John (Limerick)
Jas.	Champion
——?	Nash (country)
Will.	Hector

1758.

Richard	Williams, sen.
Thos.	Green
Grey	Townsend
Richard	Williams, jun.
Barth.	Popkins
Robt.	Glanville
John	Pittar
Andrew	Goodwin
James ?	Holmes
Christopher	Skinner
John	Laughlin
Will. or B.	Wilson
Robt.	Hopkins
John	Moore
John	Sherwin
Thos.	Shepherd
Jno. or Sam.	Teare
Peter	Rousset
Sam.	Walker
Thos.	,,
James	Vidouze
James	Warren
Septimus	Cecill
Alexr.	Richards
James	Wyer
Benj.	Stokes
W. or B.	Wilson
John	Harrison
Will.	Currie
Joseph	Bridgman

1758.

Hugh	Caddell
Chas.	Leslie
Isaac	D'Olier
David	Bomes
John	Locker
Charles	Darragh
Edward	Mockler
Owen	Cassidy
Christr.	Skinner
Richard	Finnemoor
Thos.	Burton
Jonathan	Pasley
John	West
George	Beere
Thos.	Green
Mark	Meares
Edward	Roper
John	Catherwood
Richard	Tudor
Will.	Williamson
John	Kavanagh
John	Calderwood
Will.	Homer.

1787-8.

Henry	Nicholson
John	Daly
Michael	Keating
Walter	Harley
Michael	Homer
Thos.	Hill
Ambrose	Nicklin
John	Nicklin
John	Stoyte
George	Connor
John	Pittar
Alexr.	Tickell
James	Kennedy
Christr.	Haines
Jacob or Matt.	} West
Joseph	Jackson
Will.	Bond
James	Jones
Will.	Osborne
Joseph	Daffron
James	Kenzie
Benj.	Taitt
John	Kavanagh
Will.	Law
——?	Law & Co.
Owen	Cassidy
Robt.	Breading
Eneas	Ryan
Denis	Fray
John	Teare
——?	Cooley
John	Bolland
Richard or Robt.	} Williams
Will.	Bridgman
John	Beauchamp
Will.	Ward
——?	Cock (buckles)
Arthur	O'Neill (watchcases)

GOLDSMITHS FOR WHOM PLATE WAS ASSAYED IN DUBLIN—*Continued.*

1787-8.

Thos.	Greene
———?	Peter & Co.
George	Nangle
Ambrose	Boxwell
Jerome	Alley
Samuel	Close

1788.

John	Broom
James	Hamill
Benj.	Henfrey
Richard	Harrison (watchcases)
Thos.	Hart
Robt.	Eccleston
Gore	Sherwin
———?	Gopell (buckles)

1790.

Thos.	Nixon
Will.	Bridgman
Thomas	Bridgman
George	Nangle
Christr.	Nangle
Jas.	Jones
Thos.	Jones
Will.	Ward
Lewis?	Williamson
Richard	Harrison
John	Stoyte

1791.

John	Teare
Samuel	Teare
Patrick	Walsh
Frederick	Buck
Thomas	Green
James	England
Thomas	Mealy (Marly ?)
Thomas	Adams
Gustavus	Byrne
Michael	Smith

1791.

Christopher	Donovan
Henry	Morgan
John	Rigby
Will. or Barth.	} Delandre
John	Hart
Thomas	Sly

1793.

George	West
Thomas	Fowler
Will.	Osborne
George	Matthews

1794.

———?	Lowry
James	Anderson
John	Coleman
———?	Clayton
Richard	Singleton

1795.

Michael	Keating
James	Keating
James	McCoy
Will.	Doyle
———?	McCormick

1796.

———?	Jones & Co.
Will.	Thompson
Samuel	Neville
Thomas	Bayley

1797.

Richard	Sawyers
Thomas	Townsend
George	Wheatley
Thomas	Tudor
Joseph	Johnston

1798-9.

Roger	Carson
Sam	Teare, jun.

1809.

Sam.	Neville
Michael	Murphy
Richard	Whitford
John	Sherwin
James	Le Bass
Richard	Archbold
Francis	Hull
George	Nangle
J.	Buckton
C.	Harris
Daniel	Egan
Will.	Doyle (Belfast)
John	Seymour (Cork)
Samuel	Green (Cork)
W. D.	Stubs
Jane	Williams (Cork)
John	Teare
Richard	Garde (Cork)
Kean	Mahony (Cork)
Will.	Hamey
———?	Robinson
Will.	Heyland (Cork)
Æneas	Ryan
———?	Egan

1810.

Patrick	McNamara (Belfast)
J.	Francis
Laurence	Martin (Kilkenny)
Clarke &	West

1811.

———?	Bermingham
R.	Williams
R.	Breading
Lawrence	Martin (Kilkenny), spoons
F.	Hull, } watch-
Arthur	O'Neil & } cases
J.	Bridgman } only

OTHER ENTRIES REFERRING TO ASSAYS AND TOUCH MONEY.*

The manufacture of gold wares appears to have been mainly confined to rings and other personal ornaments. There is one minute, dated 1726, in the goldsmiths' books, which records that Thomas Sutton had a gold cup assayed, weighing 3 lb. 5 oz., but that is almost the only reference to any assay of gold vessels, except freedom boxes.

Received in the period—

			£	s.	d.
Feb. 13, 1694	to	May 8, 1695 ...	88	0	0
Oct. 28, 1696	,,	June 4, 1697 ...	55	0	7
June 8, 1697	,,	Nov. 30, 1697 ...	66	13	3
Nov. 30, 1697	,,	Mar. 2, 1698 ...	35	3	0
Mar. 4, 1698	,,	Jan. 31, 1698 ...	79	19	7½
Feb. 3, 1698	,,	May 9, 1699 ...	46	12	5
May 9, 1699	,,	Nov. 8, 1699 ...	99	0	8
Nov. 9, 1699	,,	Feb. 9, 1700 ...	51	9	6
Oct. 28, 1704	,,	Oct. 29, 1705 ...	164	17	0

1694 (Feb. 9th)—Thomas Bolton, Assay Master, to charge 1d. per oz., and to be charged ½d. per oz. for assaying his own plate.

1694　Mustard pot stamped for Vincent Kidder.
　,,　　Colledg. pot stamped for Joseph Walker.
　,,　　2 Chafing dishes, 1 lb. 4 oz., for James Weldon.

			£	s.	d
Feb. 1, 1707	to	July 31, 1707 ...	87	3	0
		Oct. 30, ,, ...	52	2	10
		Apr. 29, 1708 ...	95	8	1
		Oct. 29, ,, ...	42	17	2
		Feb. 1, 1709 ...	40	19	10
		May 2, ,, ...	39	19	1

(From 1705 to 1713 the rate was 1d. per oz. for silver, and 6d. to 7d. per oz. for gold.)

			£	s.	d.
Jan. 31, 1718	to	Oct. 31, 1718 ...	163	5	1½
May 7, 1725	,,	July 30, 1725 ...	75	11	4
Aug. 3, ,,	,,	Oct. 29, ,, ...	72	15	5
Nov. ,,	,,	Feb. 1, 1726 ...	80	10	3
Feb. 1726	,,	Apr. ,, ...	63	7	0
		July ,, ...	78	10	9
		Oct. ,, ...	67	14	7
		Jan. 1727 ...	64	15	3
		Apr. ,, ...	55	2	1
		July ,, ...	57	12	2
		Oct. ,, ...	46	4	8
		Jan. 1728 ...	66	13	3
		Apr. ,, ...	67	6	3
		July ,, ...	69	16	11
		Oct. ,, ...	53	8	1
Apr. 1729	to	July 1729 ...	61	14	9
		Oct. ,, ...	51	1	1
Oct. 1729	to	Jan. 1730 ...	79	9	6
Jan. 1730	to	Apr. ,, ...	121	11	1
Apr. ,,	,,	July ,, ...	42	6	11
July ,,	,,	Oct. ,, ...	33	9	8
Oct. ,,	,,	Jan. 1731 ...	31	19	1
Jan. 1731	,,	Apr. ,, ...	30	19	10
Apr. ,,	,,	July ,, ...	40	10	0
July ,,	,,	Oct. ,, ...	36	2	10
Oct. ,,	,,	Feb. 1, 1732 ...	50	15	3

In 1736, by a resolution (passed with a view to restraining the assay master from carrying on trade), it was ordered " that the assay master, if a shopkeeper, shall not buy nor sell any manner of plate or silver during his continuance in said office, nor shall after a limited time, which will be granted him by the corporation, keep open shop, nor work up, nor cause to be wrought up, any manner of gold or silver plate ".

			£	s.	d.
Nov. 1759	to	Nov. 1760 ...	218	12	2½
,, 1760	,,	,, 1761 ...	218	18	9
,, 1761	,,	,, 1762 ...	226	19	7
,, 1762	,,	,, 1763 ...	249	8	10½
,, 1763	,,	,, 1764 ...	265	6	1½
,, 1764	,,	,, 1765 ...	325	6	5½
		Year ending in 1777 ...	322	14	6

From 1777 to 1781 sums varying from £270 to £306 were received each year as " touch " money for the assaying of silver and gold.

A minute of 1785 with reference to "touch" money provided that for silver, Free Brothers were to pay 2d. per oz. and Quarter Brothers 4d. per oz., and for gold one shilling per oz.

Amount stamped for one year, ending October, 1787, lbs.6891, of which lbs.225 were below standard and broken.

Amount of plate stamped for one year, ending October 31st, 1788, lbs.7108, of which lbs.471 were below standard and broken.

Dish rings assayed in 1787 from February to end of year.

Thomas Jones ...	7	...	(one 9 oz.)
Christopher Haines	3	...	
Joseph Jackson ...	9	...	
Matthew West ...	5	...	
Michael Homer ...	1	...	(9 oz.)
Robert Breading ...	1	...	(8 oz.)
Total ...	26		

Dish rings assayed in 1788.

Robert Breading ...	2	...	
Joseph Jackson ...	8	...	(one 9 oz.)
Thomas Jones ...	2	...	(one 9 oz.)
Richard Williams ...	1	...	
William Bond ...	2	...	
Total ...	15		

Dish stands, 1787.

Christopher Haines	1	...
Thomas Jones ...	1	...

Dish stands, 1788.

Joseph Jackson ...	5	...	(one 7 oz.)
Richard Williams	1	...	

1788　Robt. Breading, 2 "stake" dishes, 5 lb.
　,,　　Michael Homer, 1 "stake" dish and cover, 3 lb. 2 oz.
　,,　　Richard Williams, 1 "stake" dish and stand, 3 lb. 9 oz.

* Touch money, or "touch penny"—the fee of one penny per ounce charged for assaying plate. For gold the fee was sixpence per ounce.

ENTRIES REFERRING TO PLATE ASSAYED IN DUBLIN—*Continued.*

Other articles assayed in 1787 and 1788.

Will. Osborne ...2 fecques
Joseph Jackson...1 argyle
Do. do. ...frippery stand
Do. do. ...spoon tray
Robert Breading 4 cassaroles & covers (189 oz.)
Christr. Haines...1 bushiea
Do. do. ...1 orange strainer
Denis Fray ...1 tea kitchen
B. Taitt ... ...salad spoon
M. Keating ...beef scoop
W. Osborn ...salad fork
R. Williams ...punch jug (28 oz.)
C. Haines ...asparagus shovel
D. Fray ...2 salad dishes (65 oz.)

In 1787-8 Matthew West made 496 cups averaging 12 oz. each.
„ „ Benjn. Taitt made many asparagus tongs.

An entry showing the connection between the Goldsmiths of Dublin and provincial towns of Ireland, records that " Robt. Cuffe was apprenticed to Hercules Beer, in Clonmel, in 1705 ".

Plate was assayed in Dublin for Goldsmiths and Silversmiths of Cork, Waterford, Clonmel, Kinsale, and Limerick, from 1710 to about 1755.

The following entries give details of Plate assayed in Dublin for Irish provincial goldsmiths.

		lb.	oz.	dwt.
1725	George Cartwright, for Cork	15	1	0
„	Richard Barry, for the country	4	6	0
„	George Cartwright, for Cork	13	8	0
„	Noah Vialas, for Clonmel ...	7	4	0
1726	Matt. Walker, for Limerick	10	6	0
„	Noah Vialas, for Waterford	1	2	c
„	Matt. Walker, do. ...	1	6	c
„	Do. do. do. ...	0	1	6
„	John Hamilton, for Limerick	4	3	0
„	George Cartwright, for Cork	27	10	0
„	Do. do. do.	1	7	16
„	Thos. Walker, for Cork ...	2	2	0
„	Will. Clarke, in Cork ...	20	2	0
„	Noah Vialas, for Clonmel ...	12	0	0
„	Will. Clarke, in Cork ...	12	10	13
„	Matt. Walker, for Limerick	11	3	0
„	George Cartwright, for Cork	15	8	0
1727	Will. Clarke, in Cork ...	23	8	0
„	Matt. Walker, for Limerick	13	10	0
„	— Hill, do.	3	2	0
1728	Noah Vialas, for Waterford	10	2	0
„	Matt. Walker, for Limerick	17	0	0
„	Caleb Colbeck, Limerick ...	12	9	0
„	Will. Clarke, in Cork ...	20	6	0
1730	Peter Tonnery, for the country	0	1	6

		lb.	oz.	dwt.
1730	Jonathan Buck, of Limerick	0	0	4
„	Will Clarke, of Cork ...	1	2	5
1731	Do. do.	6	7	10
1733	Do. do.	10	5	15
1758	Thos. Burton, do.	6	0	0

From Oct., 1726, to Oct., 1728, W. Clarke, Cork, had 1830 oz. assayed in Dublin.

Bright-cut teapot from Jeremiah John, Dublin, 1791, 14 oz. 1 dwt. at 15s. per oz., £10 11s. 4d.

There are other similar entries for these years, but for no other places.

Lawrence Martin, of High Street, Kilkenny, had assayed in Dublin, September, 1808, 60 tea-spoons, 12 buckles, 2 pixes, 14 hooks and eyes.

Will. Heyland, of Cork, had assayed in 1808 6 sugar tongs and 4½ doz. tea-spoons, 31 oz.

John Whelpley, of Cork, February 7th, 1808, 2 doz. table-spoons, 9 doz. tea-spoons, 1 gravy spoon.

Samuel Reily, Cork, 1808, 2 fish knives, 24 salt spoons, 12 table-spoons, 72 tea-spoons, 12 sugar tongs, 9 sugar bowls, 6 cream ewers.

Jane Williams, Grand Parade, Cork, September 1st, 1808, 2 double wine funnels, 24 forks, 10 table-spoons, 14 sauce ladles, 2 tureen ladles, 2 gravy spoons, 6 funnel plates, 22 tea-spoons, 5 sugar tongs, 1 teapot : all unfinished : 175 oz. Also November 22nd, 1808, 6 cream ewers, 1 bread basket, 48 salt spoons, 8 sugar tongs, 62 tea-spoons, 4 sauce ladles, 6 gravy spoons, 6 bottle labels, 3 butter knives : all unfinished.

Will Doyle, of 177 North Street, Belfast, had assayed in Dublin August 23rd, 1809, 1 teapot, 1 doz. buttons, 1 pair buckles.

Plate was assayed in Dublin for Irish provincial goldsmiths as under :—

		lb.	oz.	dwt.
In 1809	John Seymour, Cork ...	17	0	0
„	Jane Williams, Cork ...	—		
„	Samuel Green, Cork ...	10	11	0
„	W. or J. Heyland, Cork	2	0	0
In 1826	Richard Garde, Cork ...	13	0	0
„	Kean Mahony, Cork ...	—		

In 1811 Lawrence Martin, Kilkenny, sugar, tea and egg spoons.
In 1812-13 Nathaniel Freeman, Enniscorthy, spoons.
In 1820 W. Teulon, Cork, 68 spoons, 2 forks.

There are other entries referring to plate assayed in 1810 and 1811 for the same persons.

NAMES OF IRISH PROVINCIAL GOLDSMITHS, SILVERSMITHS, JEWELLERS, AND WATCHMAKERS,

REGISTERED IN THE BOOKS OF THE COMPANY, FROM 1784 TO 1827, IN COMPLIANCE WITH THE ACT 23 & 24 GEO. III. c. 23. (IRELAND.)

Co. ANTRIM.

Will.	Harper	...	Antrim	1784
Alex.	Mitchell	...	Ballymena	,,
John	Edmiston	...	,,	1806
Will.	Lowry	...	Ballymoney	1793
Alex.	Armstrong	...	Belfast	1784
John	Murdock	...	,,	,,
John	Knox	...	,,	,,
John	Ingram	...	,,	,,
John	Milford	...	,,	,,
James	Wilson	...	,,	,,
Alex.	McIlwrath	...	,,	,,
Thos.	Lyle	...	,,	,,
Hugh	McCulloch	...	,,	,,
Thos.	Mullen	...	,,	,,
Thos.	M'Cabe	...	,,	,,
Patrick	McKenny	...	,,	,,
Will.	Hutton	...	,,	,,
John	McClean	...	,,	1785
Thos.	Anderson	...	,,	,,
Job	Stewart	...	,,	,,
Hugh	McCulloch	...	,,	,,
Robt.	Patterson & ⎫	...	,,	1789
James	Whittle ⎭			
Matthew	Bellew	...	,,	1792
John	Williamson	...	,,	1798
George	Lepper, W.M.	...	,,	1800
Francis	Lepper, W.M.	...	,,	,,
Job	Ryder	...	,,	1802
Will.	Neilson, W.M.	...	,,	,,
James	Campbell	...	,,	1804
James	Russell	...	,,	,,
Robt.	Neil, W.M.	...	,,	,,
John	Holmes	...	,,	,,
Pat.	McNamara	...	,,	1817
James	Carruthers, W.M.		,,	1821
Thos.	Ward	...	Lisburn	1784
John	Heron	...	,,	1785
James	Ballantine	...	,,	1804
David	Moore	...	Randalstown	1784

Co. ARMAGH.

Michael	Scully	...	Armagh	1784
Thos.	Simpson	...	,,	,,
James	Scott	...	,,	1787
John	Williamson	...	,,	1796
Thos.	Malcomson	...	Lurgan	1800
Matthew	Wells	...	,,	1827

Co. CARLOW.

George	Sikes	...	Carlow	1784
Mark	Rudkin	...	,,	,,
Henry	Dyer	...	,,	1827
Will.	Callaghan	...	Tullow	1784

Co. CAVAN.

Thos.	Parr	...	Cavan	1784
Henry	Parr	...	,,	1790
John	Murphy	...	,,	1827
George	Dunbar	...	Cootehill	1805
Pat.	Quigly	...	Kilgolough	1813

Co. CLARE.

James	McLaughlin	...	Ennis	1784
Hugh	McLaughlin	...	,,	,,

Co. CORK.

Dennis	Leary	...	Kinsale	1784
Robt.	Barry	...	,,	,,
Michael	Hartnett	...	Cove	,,
James	Dwyer	...	,,	,,
John	Barry	...	Bandon	,,
Thomas	Campbell	...	Cork	,,
Robert	Stevelly	...	,,	1785
Christr.	Garde	...	,,	1821
Robt.	English	...	Mallow	1784
R. W.	Dartnell	...	Youghal	1785

Co. DONEGAL.

John	Mooney	...	Ballyshannon	1784
Sam.	Bird	...	,,	,,
Hugh	Kerr	...	Raphoe	1787
Nicholas	Davis	...	Ballybafoy	,,
Joseph	Lipsett	...	Ballyshannon	1789
Joseph	Frame	...	Raphoe	,,

Co. DOWN.

Edward	Creek	...	Newry	1784
James	Doyle	...	,,	,,
Archibald	Campbell	...	,,	,,
Adam	Liddle	...	,,	,,
Joseph	White	...	,,	1785
Hugh	Boyd	...	,,	,,
Will	M'Cabe	...	,,	,,
Hugh	O'Hanlon	...	,,	,,
Will.	White	...	,,	,,
Will. & ⎫	White	...	,,	1787
Joseph ⎭				
Hugh	Rice	...	,,	1789
Richard	Liddy	...	,,	1816
George	Blackham	...	,,	1821
Trumble	& Kane	...	,,	,,
Robt.	Whitehead	...	,,	1827
George	Frazer	...	,,	,,
Robt.	Clarke	...	Downpatrick	1800

Co. FERMANAGH.

Chas.	McCalvey	...	Enniskillen	1784
Will.	Brown	...	,,	1810

Co. GALWAY.

George	Robinson	...	Galway	1784
Austin	French	...	,,	,,
Martin	Lain	...	,,	,,
Laurence	Coleman	...	,,	,,
Francis	Dowling	...	,,	1785
Michael	O'Mara	...	,,	,,
Will.	Leathem	...	,,	1786
James	Kelly	...	,,	1799

Co. GALWAY.

Nicholas	Burdge, W.M.	...	Galway	1817
John	Clarke	...	Eyrecourt	1784
Ann	Nolan	...	Loughrea	,,
John	Melton	...	,,	,,
Thos.	Naghten	...	Athlone	,,
Timothy	Egan	...	Loughrea	,,
Patrick	Haggerty	...	Tuam	,,
Will.	Morgan	...	Ballinasloe	,,
Francis	Gannon	...	Tuam	,,
Francis	Naughton	...	,,	,,
John	Glyn	...	Ballinasloe	,,
Thos.	M'Nally	...	Headford	1785
Peter	Furey	...	Castlebar	1786
Bernard	Berne	...	,,	1787
Thos.	Waldron	...	Ballinasloe	,,
P. A.	Murphy	...	,,	,,
Will.	Hosty	...	Tuam	1800
Bernard	Kelly	...	Athlone	1804

Co. KERRY.

Dan.	Syna	...	Tralee	1784
John	Egan	...	,,	,,

Co. KILDARE.

Pat.	Diven	...	Athy	1784

Co. KILKENNY.

John	Martin	...	Kilkenny (City)	1784
Hannah	Reily	...	,,	,,
Denis	Kehoe	...	,,	,,
Francis	Walsh	...	,,	1785
Jerome	Alley	...	,,	1792
Denis	Madden	...	,,	1802
Laurence	Martin, S.S.	...	,,	1807
William	Foley	...	,,	1827

KING'S Co.

Pat.	Reynolds	...	Birr	1784
James	Donolan	...	Philippstown	,,
Joseph	Manley	...	Tullamore	,,
Joseph	Marshall	...	Birr	1785
Thos.	Tailford	...	Edenderry	1793
Michael	Cody	...	Frankford	1804

Co. LIMERICK.

Patrick	Connell	...	Limerick (City)	1784
Maurice	Fitzgerald	...	,,	,,
John	Hawley	...	,,	,,
Thos.	Burke (d. 1800)	...	,,	,,
John	Cullen	...	,,	,,
Phillip	Walsh	...	,,	,,
George	Halloran	...	,,	,,
John	Strit	...	,,	,,
Sam	Johns	...	,,	,,
John	Hackett	...	,,	,,
Matthew	Walsh	...	,,	,,
George	Moore	...	,,	,,
James	Lynch	...	,,	,,
Robert	Lynch	...	,,	,,
Arthur	Lynch	...	,,	,,
Daniel	Lysaght	...	,,	1786
Matthew	Stritch	...	,,	1788
Will.	Ward	...	,,	1798

Co. LIMERICK.

Will.	Fitzgerald	...	Limerick (City)	1800
Robert	O'Shaughnessy	...	,,	1802
Will.	Carroll	...	,,	1805
Thos.	Walsh	...	,,	1806
H.	Smith &	} ...	,,	1830
R.	Wallace			
Edward	Dartnell	...	Rathkeale	1786

Co. LONDONDERRY.

Pat.	McConegall	...	Derry	1784
John	Franks	...	,,	,,
John	Atcheson	...	,,	,,
Alex	Begley	...	Coleraine	1785
James	Preston	...	Derry	1788
Joseph	McClurg	...	Coleraine	1795
Dennis	Dogherty	...	Derry	1811
James	Coulhoun	...	,,	1814

Co. LOUTH.

George	Potter	...	Drogheda	1784
Thos.	Flood	...	,,	,,
Nicholas	Drumgoole	...	,,	,,
James	Warren	...	,,	,,
Will.	Lahy	...	,,	,,
Thos.	Anderson	...	,,	1785
James	Comerford	...	,,	1804
David	Campbell	...	,,	,,
Philip	Fineghan	...	,,	1827

Co. MAYO.

Will.	Jennings	...	Castlebar	1812

Co. MEATH.

Farrell	Lynch	...	Oldcastle	1784
Matthew	Codd	...	Navan	1786

Co. MONAGHAN.

Edward	Carolan		Carrickmacross	1784
Owen	M'Mahon	...	,,	,,
James	Kelly	...	Monaghan	,,
George	Kerr	...	,,	,,
James	M'Entee	...	,,	1788
James	Brown	...	,,	1786
David	Horner	...	,,	1809
John	Horner	...	Ballybea	1802

QUEEN'S Co.

Laurence	Crawley	...	Portarlington	1784
Will.	Myham	...	Maryborough	,,
Robert	Whelan	...	,,	1785

Co. ROSCOMMON.

Sylvester	Nolan	...	Athlone	1784
Owen	Quigley	...	,,	,,
Thomas	Payne	...	Roscommon	,,
John	Purcell	...	,,	1785
Michael	Power	...	Boyle	1788

Co. SLIGO.

John	M'Donald	...	Sligo	1784
Philip	Reilly	...	,,	,,
Andrew	Cullidon	...	,,	,,
Martin	Scully	...	,,	1785
Peter	Coan	...	,,	1795
James	Kelly	...	,,	1809

Co. TIPPERARY.

John	Quin	...	Clonmel	1784
Garrett	Russell	Carrick-on-Suir		,,
Dan.	M'Grath	...	Nenagh	,,
Will.	Thompson	...	Clonmel	,,
John	Beauchamp	...	,,	,,
Nicholas	Reynolds	...	Roscrea	,,
Will.	Cusack	...	Cashel	,,
Cavan	Ryan	...	Clonmel	,,
Daniel	Dutton	...	Cashel	,,
John	Prosser	...	,,	,,
John	Finnegan	Carrick-on-Suir		,,
Robert	Cooke	...	Clonmel	,,
Stephen	Egan	...	Roscrea	,,
Morty	Quin	...	Thurles	1792
James	Shee	...	Clonmel	1800
Dennis	Madden	...	,,	1808
Theo.	Harvey	...	,,	1815

Co. TYRONE.

Hugh	Montgomery	...	Omagh	1784
Patrick	Fleming	...	Strabane	,,
Andrew	Carshore	...	,,	1787
James	McClenaghan	...	,,	1788
John	Campbell	...	Dungannon	1789

Co. WATERFORD.

Ann	Fleming	Waterford (City)	1784
Francis	Walsh*	,,	,,
Joseph	Dillon	,,	,,
Will.	Maddock	,,	,,
Anthony	Welsh	,,	,,
Robert	Tegart &	} ,,	,,
John	O'Neill		
George	Power	,,	,,
Will.	M'Cannon	,,	,,
Thomas	Pearson	,,	1785
Ignatius	Fleming	,,	1802
Will.	O'Brien	,,	1807
Josias	Jacob	,,	1809
Stephen	Bohan	,,	1811
Richard	Cutler	Dungarvan	1784
Will.	Geary	Tullagh	,,
Edmund	Byrne	Dungarvan	1785

Co. WEST MEATH.

Hugh	Colan	...	Ballymore	1784
Thos.	Coffie	...	Kilbeggan	,,
George	Mathews	...	Mullingar	,,
Thos.	Curran	...	,,	,,
Bryan	Kieran	...	,,	,,
Peter	Calcot, W.M.	...	Athlone	1792
Bernard	Kelly	...	,,	1804

Co. WEXFORD.

Luke	Maddock	...	Ross	1784
Will.	Hughes	...	Wexford	,,
John	Roe	...	Gorey	,,
Will.	Gurly	...	Wexford	1795
Nathaniel	Freeman	...	Enniscorthy	1811
James	Ellis	...	,,	1814
Joseph	Higginbottom	...	Wexford	1827
Will.	Simpson	...	,,	,,
Andrew	Whitney	...	New Ross	,,

* Francis Walsh returned to Dublin in 1786.

CHAPTER XXV

THE IRISH PROVINCIAL GOLDSMITHS
AND THEIR MARKS

Although Dublin has been for many centuries the principal seat of the goldsmith's art in Ireland, it does not appear to have been so in more remote ages. The beautiful examples of pre-historic and early-Christian goldsmiths' work, preserved in the National Museum in Dublin, prove that the native Irish attained to great skill as goldsmiths long before the Norman Invasion and the subjugation of the Irish Kings ; and from the gold ornaments, the crucible ladles and other implements and utensils used in the refining of gold, which were discovered in a bog on the borders of Limerick and Tipperary, it appears that gold wares were manufactured in that vicinity at a very remote period.

Though goldsmiths' marks, in the modern sense, were not used—and we have no account of any system of guarantee of standard, such as hall-marks ensure—we find that some of the Irish artificers in gold and silver recorded their names on their work ; as for example, on the beautiful processional Cross of Cong, and on the shrine of the bell of St. Patrick, both of which are, in the modern sense, provincial work—for when they were wrought, Dublin had not attained the pre-eminence it afterwards acquired. But neither the marks on these objects nor the goldsmiths who wrought them are within the scope of this work. These subjects will be found fully discussed and also illustrated in the Author's *History of English Plate*.

There are no means of locating and identifying the goldsmiths who wrought the few examples of Irish mediæval plate which have survived to our own time, but we are able to trace numerous examples of Irish plate of the 17th and 18th centuries, as having emanated from the workshops of goldsmiths who exercised their craft in Cork, Youghal, Galway and Limerick, and to distinguish their respective marks.

[marginal note:] Pre-historic and early-Christian goldsmiths.

[marginal note:] Irish provincial goldsmiths of the 17th and 18th centuries.

The Records of the Dublin Goldsmiths' Company also prove that in the 18th century, from Belfast in the North to Cork in the South, goldsmiths were actively engaged in carrying on their business in almost every provincial town of any importance in Ireland.* The goldsmiths of Cork, Limerick, Waterford, Clonmel, Kilkenny, Kinsale and other places, then sent plate to Dublin to be assayed.

The tables of marks, as well as the lists of goldsmiths' names and other information appearing in the following pages, are the results of the collaboration of the Author with the late Mr. Robert Day, F.S.A. ;† the late Mr. J. R. Garstin, F.S.A., P.R.S.A.I. ; Mr. Dudley Westropp, M.R.I.A., and the late Mr. Cecil C. Woods, F.R.S.A.I., who devoted himself with unflagging zeal to the task of bringing to light every record which could be found concerning the goldsmiths of Cork.

THE GOLDSMITHS OF CORK.

References to Cork goldsmiths of the 15th and 16th centuries traced.

There is good reason for believing that fine goldsmiths' work was executed in the city of Cork, and in Youghal—a town in the same county, in the Middle Ages. Mr. Woods traced references to goldsmiths in Cork Records of the 15th and 16th centuries, and to this period some of the exquisite chalices and patens preserved in the county have been confidently ascribed. Very little, however, is known of the early history of the goldsmiths of Cork ; the records of the guild, in which they were associated with members of other trades, date no farther back than the year 1656.

Records of the Cork Guild commenced in 1656.

The first Earl of Cork (Richard Boyle, known as "the Great Earl of Cork") worked silver mines of considerable value at Minehead, a place to the eastward of Youghal. In 1631 he leased them to Captain Burgh (probably a member of the de Burgo or Burke family). The rent, payable in kind to the Earl, was, in his own language, "a fair bason and ewer, four dozen of silver plates, and eight great silver candlesticks, all to be of plain London touch, with my arms engraved on them, for the providing whereof (of the arms) I wrote to my goldsmith, Mr. Nathaniel Stoughton ".‡

By a Charter of Charles I., dated 7 April, 1631, the Mayor and Corporation of Cork were granted the *same privileges as those enjoyed by*

---

* See pages 674-5-6 for the names of Provincial Goldsmiths registered in Dublin.

† The Author is also greatly indebted to the Cork Historical and Archæological Association for permission to make extracts from their journals.

‡ Nathaniel Stoughton was by the charter of 1637 appointed one of the first members of the Incorporated Company of Goldsmiths of Dublin ; see page 566, *ante.*

No assay office at Cork. Efforts to obtain authority to establish one failed.

*Youghal,** which included the power to appoint a Clerk of Assay (or Assize), whose duties comprised the testing of weights and measures, not the assaying of the precious metals. It is certain that there was no assay master or assay office in Cork at any time subsequent to the date of the Charter. Efforts were on several occasions made by the goldsmiths of Cork, through their city council, to obtain authority for the establishment of an assay office in Cork, but their efforts were not attended with success. With reference to this subject the following minute occurs in the Council Book under date 4 January, $171\frac{3}{4}$:—

"Whereas the Company of Goldsmiths of this City are very desirous to have an Assay Master within this City as conceiving it will tend very much to the advantage, not only of those of the trade, but to all the inhabitants who have occasion to buy or make up any plate, which being a new thing, there never having been any such person in this city, ordered that Mr. Thomas Browne do write to Dublin to some friend to inquire the nature of such an officer, as to his commission, who constitutes and empowers him, and as to his fees what he receives, and report to this board."

No satisfactory result followed those inquiries, and after the lapse of nearly three quarters of a century another resolution on the same subject was recorded as follows :—

"6th February, 1786. Ordered that the Bill formerly presented to Parliament for building a bridge over the North branch of the River Lee, &c., be forthwith proceeded on . . . . It., that a clause for establishing an assay office for assaying plate in this city, be added to the above Law."

The addition of the above clause, to the Bill for building the bridge, was successfully opposed by the Dublin Goldsmiths' Company, and the establishment of an assay office was not granted. The next application was by the goldsmiths themselves. In October, 1807, they presented a memorial to the Rt. Hon. John Foster, Chancellor of the Irish Exchequer, praying for the grant of an assay office in Cork. The memorial was signed by Carden Terry, John Toleken, Isaac Solomon, Jas. Conway, Sam. Reily, John Nicolson, Nicholas Nicolson, Jas. Heyland, Thos. Montjoy, Joseph Gibson, John Whelpley and Will. Byrom. The Dublin goldsmiths opposed this application also, and it was refused. On 2 December, 1808, another memorial signed by Will. Heyland, Dan. Corbett and others (as in 1807) was forwarded to Colonel Longfield, M.P., and by him presented to the Right Hon. John Foster, repeating the application of the previous year, with a similarly unsuccessful result. The Cork goldsmiths appear to have made other applications, in the last

* See page 701, *infra*.

of which they stated that they had for twenty years been endeavouring to get an assay office established in Cork, and that they manufactured 15,000 ounces of plate there annually, but a letter dated 11 February, 1813, addressed to the Chancellor from the Dublin Goldsmiths' Company stating that there would be a loss to the Government if an assay office were established in Cork, finally disposed of the application.

Parcels of Cork plate occasionally sent to Dublin to be assayed in the 18th and 19th centuries.

There having been no regular assay at Cork, it is not known what means were adopted for testing the quality of plate manufactured there in the 17th and early part of the 18th century. Mr. Cecil Woods suggested that the goldsmiths probably assayed each other's wares. It seems equally probable that the only test used was that of the touchstone, and that when an assay by cupel was required the plate was sent to Dublin to be there assayed, as happened occasionally in the 18th century and more frequently in the early part of the 19th century, but in the 17th century the difficulties and dangers attendant upon sending plate such a distance must have been a bar to the adoption of that course.

The Cork goldsmiths incorporated with members of other trades as a Society of Goldsmiths in the year 1656.

The goldsmiths of Cork had no separate existence as a guild distinct from other crafts. They were on the 31 May, 1656, incorporated with the braziers, pewterers, founders, plumbers, white-plate workers, glaziers, saddlers and upholsterers of the city, by the name of " The Master Wardens and Company of the Society of Goldsmiths of the City of Cork "; and John Sharpe, goldsmith ; Robert Goble, brazier ; Edward Goble, brazier ; John Hawkins, saddler ; Thomas Holms, saddler ; and Robert Phillips, saddler, were appointed trustees of the Company. From 1656 to about 1820 the guild had an active existence and its proceedings were, it seemed, regularly recorded, but in the disastrous fire which occurred at the Cork Courthouse on the 27 March, 1891, almost all the ancient city muniments were destroyed and with them the books of the Goldsmiths' Corporation, so that the only records pertaining to the company which now exist are such as had been copied from the original entries by the late Dr. Caulfield, Mr. Cecil Woods, and other Cork antiquaries. After 1820 much less goldsmiths' work was wrought, and the guild lost much of its former vigour. It, however,

The guild became extinct in 1850.

lingered on till about 1840, but by 1850 it had become extinct ; railway communication with Dublin and its assay office having been established, the competition of the Dublin goldsmiths probably prevented the resuscitation of the trade in Cork.*

---

* Plate has been wrought at Cork between the years 1911 and 1921, and stamped with a mark resembling that of the ship and two castles (in one stamp), accompanied by the Dublin hall marks and the mark of W. Egan the maker.

In the 17th and 18th centuries very large quantities of plate were manufactured in Cork, and the business of the goldsmith was so remunerative that many of the leading county families in the South of Ireland were pleased to apprentice their sons to members of the craft in the city. The trade and those who followed it, were held in high esteem, as well by reason of the artistic skill displayed in the plate which was wrought in their workshops, as for the reputation for honour and integrity which its individual members enjoyed, from amongst whom were chosen many of the chief magistrates of the city. Flourishing state of the goldsmiths' craft in Cork in the 17th and 18th centuries.

The situation of Cork, with its natural harbour extending in a direct line with the Spanish peninsula and the West of France, afforded unparalleled advantages for intercourse with those countries, whence the city received not only supplies of silver but immigrant craftsmen who brought with them their knowledge of designing as practised by the goldsmiths of the continent of Europe. Much of the Cork-made plate of the 17th and 18th centuries was wrought from imported Spanish dollars, and it was no uncommon thing for a Cork goldsmith to stamp his plate with the mark "DOLLAR" to indicate the quality of the silver of which it was wrought. The continental origin of many of the Cork goldsmiths is displayed in names, such as Pantaine, Semirot, Begheagle,* Billon, Foucauld, Codier, Montjoy, and Garde, which are to be found in the list of craftsmen who worked in Cork from the 17th to the 19th century. The influence of those immigrants upon the design and execution of the goldsmiths' work which was wrought in the city, may be seen in the numerous examples of the art still preserved, which resemble the contemporary styles prevailing on the continent much more closely than English work of the same period. In contrast with this extensive foreign element it may be remarked how little the native Irish—once famous as workers in the precious metals—figure amongst the Cork goldsmiths. With two or three exceptions the O's and Mac's are absent from the list, and none of them appear to have been celebrated as craftsmen. The Continental element amongst the goldsmiths of Cork. Its influence on the "craft" there.

In his monograph on the goldsmiths of Cork, Mr. Cecil Woods said in 1895 :—

" It is no less true than strange, that, for many years previous to 1878, the city of Cork had forgotten its ancient goldsmiths—men whose labours had enriched it, and done it honour—and that none amongst the many persons who possessed fine pieces of plate stamped with the initials of those who were, in

---

* This name is also found as Bekegle.

Robert Goble,
the best known
of the Cork
goldsmiths of
the 17th century. every sense, masters of the goldsmith's art, knew the names of the makers. Fortunately, in that year, the O'Donovan tankard, marked with RG and two castles (in three stamps), was seen by Mr. Robert Day, F.S.A., who at once formed the opinion that it had been made in the latter half of the seventeenth century, in the city of Cork. Going immediately to Dr. Caulfield, F.S.A. (who, for many years before his death, was *the* authority upon all matters touching the history of Cork), he put the query : 'Who was RG who made silver plate in this city about two hundred years ago?' The reply soon came : 'Robert Goble, master of the goldsmiths' guild in 1694.'"*

This Robert Goble was the son of Edward Goble, brass founder, who was master of the guild in 1659 and four later years. Robert Goble was one of the most celebrated of all the Cork goldsmiths. He wrought many fine pieces of plate in the last quarter of the 17th century, his best known work being "The Mace of the Cork Guilds," made in 1696 for the associated guilds of which he had been master.

The Cork mace has been described in the *Journal of the Royal Historical and Archæological Association of Ireland* † by Mr. Day, and

The Mace of the
Cork Guilds. illustrated with plates from drawings by Mr. Geo. M. Atkinson, by whose permission ‡ the illustrations on pages 683 and 684 have been reproduced.

The head is octagonal, each face bearing the arms of a craft in the following order :—

(1) The goldsmiths ; (2) the pewterers ; (3) the founders ; (4) the saddlers ; (5) the glaziers and glass painters ; (6) the merchant taylors (probably) ; (7) the tin-plate workers ; and (8) the tobacco pipe makers. The stem is spirally fluted, its centre knop being spherical and ornamented with four figures in bas relief representing the Cardinal virtues : Temperance, Justice, Fortitude and Prudence. The terminal knop is pear-shaped, with a curved-sided frustrum of a cone at its extremity ; the disc at its base has the arms of Cork chased on it, to which a resemblance may be seen in the town-mark of the Cork goldsmiths of the period. On the top of the head the Royal arms of England, as borne by William and Mary, are embossed, surmounted by the Royal Crown, the work of which is inferior in quality to that of the mace itself. In fact the crown and its arches have never been finished. The cresting, formed of fleur-de-lis ornamentation, has been left as it was taken from the sand mould in which it was cast, no chasing whatever having been done upon it. This is in marked contrast to the work upon the other parts of the mace, all of which, excepting the acanthus ornamentation on the lower knop, is most excellently chased. This extraordinary contrast of fine finish and rough work appears to suggest some such explanation as that Chas. Bekegle, a Dutch immigrant, who executed some fine work in Cork, had been engaged in chasing the mace for Robert Goble, and that he fell ill before the work was completed. The fact that Bekegle died at Cork in 1697, that the finished work on the mace resembles work of the Dutch school of the period,

---

* *Proceedings of the Royal Historical and Archæological Association of Ireland* (1895).
† 1886, p. 334, and 1890, p. 300. See also Mr. Garstin's account of *Maces, &c., of Irish Corporations* (1898).
‡ And by permission of the Royal Society of Antiquaries of Ireland.

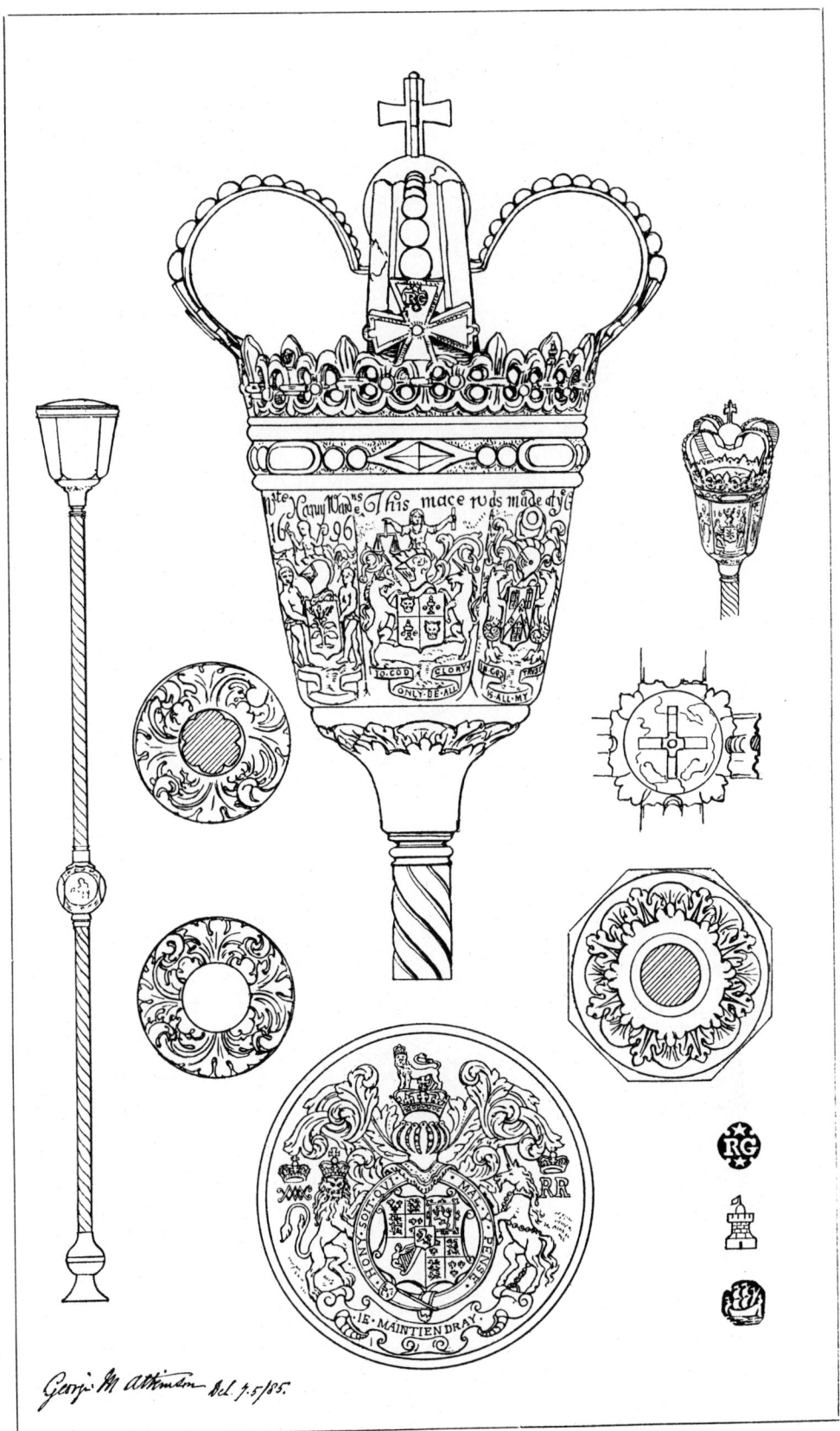

THE MACE OF THE CORK GUILDS.

THE MACE OF THE CORK GUILDS.

similar to work known to have been wrought by him ; that all Goble's other known work is much less ornate, and that Goble's mark is stamped only on the unfinished crown of the mace ; all point to the probability of the explanation being as suggested.

This mace was for some time in the possession of a family named Martin, whose ancestor was at one time erroneously credited with its manufacture. It passed into the hands of Mr. Mayne, and was afterwards redeemed for £5 by the Rev. Dr. Nelligan, who sold it at Sotheby's, where it was bought by a dealer for £30. The Science and Art Department purchased it for £73 10s., in 1869, for the South Kensington Museum, where it has ever since rested.

Charles Begheagle, the Flemish immigrant, who was warden of the Cork Guild in 1693, was certainly no less skilful than Goble ; if judged by their respective works—apart from the mace of the Cork Guilds— Bekegle would probably be ranked as the greater artist. Although no earlier mention of his name has been found, he must have been settled in Cork some years before 1693 to warrant his election to office in that year. A fine example of his work is here illustrated.

Charles Begheagle a highly-skilled immigrant goldsmith, warden of the guild in 1693. An example of his work here illustrated.

TWO-HANDLED CUP BY CHARLES BEGHEAGLE IN THE AUTHOR'S COLLECTION.
(Scale ½ Linear.)

It is a two-handled cup, the body ornamented in bold relief with an eagle (in allusion to the maker's name), melons, pomegranates, and other fruit, foliage and flowers. The handles are of the harp shape very commonly found on Irish cups of the end of the 17th century.

THE CORK GOLDSMITHS' MARKS.

THE TOWN MARK.

The earliest Cork town mark was a ship duplicated, or a ship between two castles. Often the castle, stamped twice, is found without a ship.

The earliest known examples of the Cork town mark consist of a ship duplicated, or a ship between two castles, adopted from the arms of the city. Often the ship is found in a separate stamp, between two castles struck separately by the same stamp; sometimes, however, one castle only occurs. Occasionally the ship between two castles is found all in one stamp, exactly as the charge appears in the arms of the town, and sometimes the castle is found stamped alternately with the maker's mark without a ship.

The ship mark is not at all like the amorphous thing sometimes represented as the Cork ship, but is always well-formed, considering the size of the stamp, generally with sails set on the main and fore masts, and furled on the mizzen mast, and sometimes (as in Robert Goble's ship mark) with a curious sail extending from over the figurehead to the bobstay below the bowsprit.

There were nearly as many forms of the town mark as there were goldsmiths, from which it would appear that each goldsmith had his own town-mark stamp, and that his stamp as maker was the warranty of the quality of the plate of which his wares were made.

Two or three examples of Cork plate of the 17th century have been found with makers' marks only, no town mark appearing on them, but instances of the kind are rare.

Early in the 18th century, for some reason not at present known, the use of the ship and castles mark was discontinued. The ship disappeared some time before the castles, which were used occasionally for about twenty years after the ship had been discarded.

THE STERLING MARK.

The STER-LING mark, its various forms.

Between 1710 and 1719 the word STERLING was adopted as a mark for Cork plate. The STERLING mark was used in various forms; sometimes in one long narrow stamp, occasionally in a shorter and broader stamp, the word being in two lines thus: $^{STER}_{LING}$. Sometimes the word was abbreviated to STERG or STER. The orthography of the word also varied, STARLING, STIRLING, STERLIN and STARLIN being found. The letters used were generally Roman capitals raised in a sunk field, but incuse letters are often found. Sometimes, too, the word DOLLAR is found, indicative of the plate having been wrought from

Spanish dollars (of which large quantities were imported into Cork for the use of its goldsmiths), just as the "STERLING" stamp indicated that the silver was as good as the Sterling standard, that is to say 11 oz. 2 dwts. fine. This "Sterling" mark was in no sense a town mark—we have seen that it was used in Chester and other places—but when the town mark proper was discontinued by the Cork goldsmiths, the "Sterling" mark was adopted, and in that respect it took the place of a town mark. On a rat-tail spoon of early Hanoverian pattern, bearing the mark of Reuben Millard, *c.* 1720-37, the old form of town mark—the castle struck twice—appears, at a time when "STERLING" had become the recognised standard mark of the Cork Goldsmiths. In reality the "Sterling" mark was a guarantee of quality, and a goldsmith who had sold base metal marked "STERLING" would have been liable in an action at common law, and might have been subjected to a criminal indictment for obtaining money by a false pretence.

The STER-LING mark a guarantee of quality.

In the 18th century some Cork-made plate was sent to Dublin to be assayed and marked ; the first parcel appears, from the books of the Dublin Goldsmiths' Company, to have been sent in December, 1710, by William Clarke, who occasionally had plate "touched" in Dublin afterwards. Possibly this was connected in some way with the change in the Cork marks at about that time.

THE MAKER'S MARK.

In the 17th and the early part of the 18th centuries, makers' marks on Cork plate were composed of the initials of the maker in conjunction with some heraldic device such as a crown (James Ridge), a mullet (Caleb Webb and Robert Goble), a fleur-de-lys (Caleb Rotheram), a lion rampant (George Brumley), and sometimes unaccompanied by either town mark or "STERLING," but after about 1730 these devices appear to have been seldom used. Possibly an order of the Dublin goldsmiths of 1 November, 1731, prohibiting the use of any such "ornaments" may account for this change, as the Dublin Goldsmiths' Company was empowered to regulate the craft throughout Ireland. Cork-made plate of about 1770 or later is very rarely seen without the "STERLING" mark.*

Makers' marks and devices.

* It has been suggested that the "STERLING" mark of Cork may be mistaken for a similar word stamped on plate made in the United States of America—in New York and in Providence, R.I. But as the "Sterling" mark was not adopted in America until about 1857, and the American mark is composed of light text lettering, quite unlike any "Sterling" mark ever used in the United Kingdom, and the American plate so stamped is of a style easily distinguishable, it is difficult to imagine how a mistake could be made.

From 1807, the Dublin Hall-marks and the duty mark were some
times added to the maker's mark, and the "STERLING" mark was
sometimes omitted.   Probably by reason of the Act of 1807 requiring the
King's head mark to be stamped on all plate made in Ireland, the Cork
goldsmiths were required to send their plate to Dublin, as in no other
town in Ireland was there an assay master entrusted with Government
punches ; but even after 1809, *all* Cork-made plate was not sent to
Dublin to be stamped.

NO CORK DATE-LETTER.

No date-letter
on Cork plate.
No date-letter was ever struck on Cork plate except what was
"touched" at Dublin, so that the exact year when any article was made
cannot be ascertained, but the form and decoration enable one to fix the
period, and by the mark of the maker one is able to approximate the
date as a rule within about twenty years even in the absence of any
inscribed date.   While this leaves more room for the skill derived from a
knowledge of the technique of the goldsmith, and of the various styles in
vogue at different periods, the uncertainty as to actual date, consequent
upon the absence of date-letters, proves their value where they have
been used.

All the marks which have been found on Cork plate in the course
of researches extending over a great number of years, will be found
represented in the following tables.   Since the publication of the first
edition of this work, a large number of additional marks have been traced
(largely through the researches of Mr. Dudley Westropp) ; these will be
found illustrated in the Cork tables.   The marks, however, added in
Dublin on Cork-made plate are not represented, as they are to be found
in the Dublin tables.

Marks illustrated
in tables
reproduced from
authentic
examples of
plate.
As no date-letters were used in Cork, the annexed tables of marks
cannot be divided into cycles corresponding with alphabets as in the
case of London, Dublin, &c., but for convenience of reference it has been
deemed advisable to arrange them in eight portions, each occupying a
page.   These, however, occasionally overlap, as the dates to which the
marks are respectively assigned are (within the working life of a goldsmith) of necessity almost entirely conjectural.   The marks have for the
most part been reproduced in the table exactly as found, but as stamped
in the silver they are not arranged quite so regularly as they appear in
print.   In some cases, however, the maker's mark and the " Sterling "
mark have been transposed, and to avoid the *facsimile* repetition of the
mark itself, the repeated mark has been indicated lby double commas.

The early marks are in all cases of large size and ranged in a line nearly straight, as shown in the tables. The later marks are smaller, and though generally arranged in a line are sometimes grouped in the manner of marks in Table II.

A feature which cannot escape observation is the remarkable variety in the marks of some of the Cork goldsmiths ; Robert Goble used marks of six or seven different sorts, and Stephen Walsh used five varieties, whilst some others, at different times, used nearly as many. **Variety of marks used by Cork goldsmiths.**

Following the tables will be found a list of the names of Cork goldsmiths, which was, as to the greater part, carefully and laboriously compiled by the late Mr. Cecil Woods. Mr. Woods' list has in a few instances been made more exact as regards dates by the aid of recently discovered facts, and Mr. Dudley Westropp has amplified it by the addition of many names found in old Cork directories and other records. The list has in this way been made as complete as possible.

REPRODUCTIONS IN *FACSIMILE* OF CORK GOLDSMITHS' BILLS.

Below are reproduced two receipted accounts of Michael McDermott (dated 1763) and Carden Terry (dated 1772) respectively; the originals were lent to the Author by the late Mr. Cecil Woods. These accounts are of interest in connection with the goldsmiths whose marks appear in the following tables.

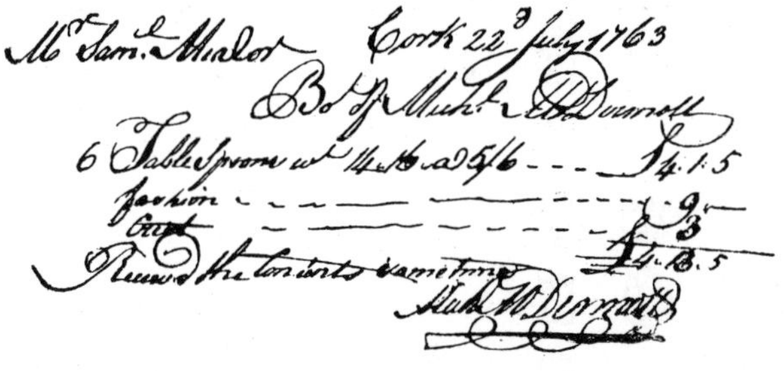

Mr. Saml. Atkalor Cork 22d July 1763
Bo.t of Mich.l McDermott
6 Table Spoons wt 14oz 16 a 5/6 --- £4.1.5
fashion --- 9
Crest --- 3
£4.13.5
Recd the contents same time
Mich.l McDermott

Mr. Kinselagh —— Cork 29th Jan 1772
Bought of Carden Terry
GOLDSMITH & JEWELLER,
at the Golden Cup, near Broad Lane
Six Gravy Spoons —— oz 7.3¼ – 6/10 £2 8 11
Cresting &c — 1: —
£2:9:11
Received the contents Cork 1 July 1772
for Carden Terry
Herbert Gillman

MARKS ON CORK PLATE.

TABLE I.—FROM ABOUT 1662 TO ABOUT 1709.

The dates are approximate, except where the articles are known to be contemporaneously dated, the extent of variation being limited by the length of the working life of the goldsmith, which to some extent may be ascertained from the list of goldsmiths' names which follows these tables.

DATE.	MARKS.	MAKER'S NAME.	ARTICLES AND OWNERS.
1662		James Ridge.	Chalice of the White Knight of co. Cork: Dublin Museum.
1663		(*Not identified*).	Communion cup and paten, dated 1663: Lismore Cathedral.
1670		Walter Burnett.	Do. do., dated 1670 and 1671: Carrigaline, co. Cork.
1673		James Ridge.	Tankard: Captain Newenham, Maryboro' House, Cork.
1679		Richard Smart.	Communion cup, dated 1679: Castlemagner. Do. do. do. 1688: St. Mary's, Shandon. Loving cup: Lord Carbery.
1680		Samuel Pantaine.	Spoon, flat stem: Mr. R. L. Pike, Kilnock, co. Carlow.
,,		Walter Burnett.	Salver on foot: Noted by Mr. Dudley Westropp.
,,		(Both marks repeated).	Tankard, flat top: The Earl of Wilton.
,,		John Hawkins.	Com. cup, dated 1680: Tracton Abbey, co. Cork.
1691		Do. do.	Chalice, dated 1691: Castlelyons, Cork.
1683		Robert Goble.	Com. cup, dated 1683: Lord Swaythling. Do. do. do. and paten: The Author's Coll'n.
1686		Do. do.	Large paten, on foot: St. Finn Barre's Cathedral, Cork.
1690		Do. do.	Do. do. do.: Carrigaline. Two casters and two bowls: Captain Sarsfield.
1692		Caleb Webb.	Two-handled cup: Dublin Museum.
,,		Robert Goble.	Communion cup, dated 1692: Inishannon. Do. do. and paten: Midleton.
1696		Do. do.	Mace of the Cork Guilds made 1696: South Kensington Museum.
,,		Walter Burnett.	Salver on foot: The Day Collection.
,,		Robert Goble.	Tankard: The late Mr. Cecil C. Woods. Two salvers: Rev. John Penrose.
,,		Do. do.	Tankard: The O'Donovan, Lisard, Skibbereen.
1697		Charles Bekegle.	Two-handled cup (see illustration): The Author's Collection.
1700		Robert Goble.	Polygonal saucer-shaped dish: Noted by Mr. Dudley Westropp.
,,		Anthony Semirot.	Salver: The Day Collection.
1705		Robert Goble.	Tea-spoons, flat stems, wavy ends: The Author's Collection.
1709		William Clarke.	Communion plate, dated 1709: Kilshanig.

MARKS ON CORK PLATE.

TABLE II.—FROM ABOUT 1709 TO ABOUT 1730.

The dates are approximate. See note at head of Table I.

DATE.	MARKS.	MAKER'S NAME.	ARTICLES AND OWNERS.
1709		Adam Billon.	Salver, dated 1709: Mr. Woods. Paten, dated 1714, and alms dish, dated 1719: St. Peter's, Cork. Paten, dated 1717: Kilcredon.
1702-29		George Brumley.	Pair of small salvers: The Author's Collection. Small oval tray, with " STARLIN " mark also: Sir Thornley Stoker.
1709		John Wigmore.(?)*	Spirally fluted porringer: Mr. Baldwin, Bandon. Cover of two-handled cup: The Author's Coll'n.
1710		Wm. Clarke.	Basting spoon: Mr. Dudley Westropp.
,,		Robert Goble.	Flagon: Christchurch, Cork.
1710-20		John Rickotts.	Coffee-pot: Noted by Mr. Dudley Westropp.
1712		Robert Goble.	Paten, dated 1712: St. Finn Barre's Cathedral. Flagons: St. Peter's, Cork.
1715-25		Robert Goble, Junr.	Plain cup: Mr. Joseph Dixon.
,,	,, IM	... ...	Coffee-pot and salver: The Day Collection.
,,		William Clarke.	Com. flagon: Carrigaline, Cork. Hanoverian spoons: Mr. Dudley Westropp.
,,		,, ,, †	Circular fruit dish: The Day Collection.
1719		Caleb Rotheram.	Table-spoons: The Rev. John Penrose. Com. cup, dated 1719: St. Peter's, Cork.
,,		William Clarke. ‡	Two patens, dated 1719: St. Peter's, Cork.
1720		,, ,,	(Also Dublin hall-marks of 1720). Gravy-spoon: Mr. Dudley Westropp.
,,		Bernald Baldwin.	Rat-tail spoons: Messrs. Crichton.
,,		... ...	Pair of candlesticks: Mr. Dudley Westropp.
1720-30		}	Mug: Messrs. Christie.
,,		} Wm. Newenham.	Hanoverian spoon: Mr. Dudley Westropp.
,,		Edward Dunsterfield.	Table-spoon, flat stem: Col. H. Malet.
1720-34		William Newenham.	Plain bowl: The Day Collection.
,,		,, ,,	Rat-tail spoon: The Rev. John Penrose.
,,		(Not identified—perhaps not Cork).	Silver oar of Castle Haven: The Day Collection.
1722		... ...	Chalice and paten, dated 1722: Rathcormac, Cork.

* This mark is extremely like that ascribed to Joseph Walker, Dublin ; see Dublin Table III., 1696.
† This mark is found on Dublin-assayed plate of 1717-8: see Dublin Table V.
‡ The *Sterling* mark on these patens is engraved, not stamped.

MARKS ON CORK PLATE.

TABLE III.—FROM ABOUT 1724 TO ABOUT 1770.

The dates are approximate.   See note at head of Table I.

DATE.	MARKS.	MAKER'S NAME.	ARTICLES AND OWNERS.
1724	THO·LILLY STERLING	} Thomas Lilly.	Cup (also with Dublin hall marks of 1724): Messrs. Crichton.
1725-6	R M STERLING	Reuben Millard.	Slop bowl (also Dublin marks of 1725-6): Noted by Mr. Dudley Westropp.
1730	WN STERLING	Wm. Newenham.	Noted by the Author.
,,	WN STERLING	,, ,,	Two-handled cup: Messrs. Crichton.
1730-40	W★B STERLING	William Bennett.	Slop bowl: Noted by Mr. Dudley Westropp.
,,	I H STERLING I H	John Harding ?	Three-pronged fork: Mr. Dudley Westropp.
,,	CR STERLING CR	Caleb Rotheram.	Plain circular bowl: Mr. J. F. Fuller.
,,	STERLING I·H	John Harding ?	Two-handled cup: Mr. H. D. Ellis.
,,	R·G	Robt. Goble, jr. ?	Small saucepan: The Day Collection.
,,	CP CP CP	Christr. Parker.	Salver: Noted by Do. Do.
1720-37	W·MARTIN	William Martin.	Plain salver on foot: Mr. D. H. Lane.
,,	W·MARTIN	Do. do.	Circular fruit-dish: The Day Collection.
,,	W·M	Do. do.	{ A pair of plain salvers: Do. Cork maces, repaired 1738 by Wm. Martin: Cork City Corporation.
,,	R*M	Reuben Millard.	Rat-tail table-spoon: Mr. J. H. Walter.
1730-40	WB STERLING WB	William Bennett or Wm. Bentley.	Table-spoons (Hanoverian pattern): Mr. D. Westropp.
1731	T.BULL	Thomas Bull.	Snuff-box, dated 1731: Do. Do.
1740	G·H STERLING	George Hodder.	Teapot: Dublin Museum.
,,	G·H ✚ G·H	Do. do.	Hanoverian spoon: Mr. Dudley Westropp.
,,	WB WB	William Bennett or Wm. Bentley.	Do. Do.: Do. Do.
1740-50	R A	... ...	Flagons, dated 1749: Kinsale.
,,	AS STERLING	} Anthony Semirot.	Salver on foot: Noted by Mr. Dudley Westropp.
1745-70	STARLING G★H	George Hodder.	Two-handled cup: Mr. Arthur Irwin Dasent.
,,	GH STERLING GH	Do. do.	{ Race cup "won 1749": Captain Perry, Kinsale. Tankard "re-made 1749": Mr. George Hodder.
,,	STARLING GH	} Do. do.	Two-handled cup: Mrs. Lindsay, Cork.
,,	G★H GH GH G‡H	*Do. do.	Articles noted by Mr. Dudley Westropp.

*Each of these marks of George Hodder is accompanied with the "STERLING" stamp.

MARKS ON CORK PLATE.

TABLE IV.—FROM ABOUT 1750 TO ABOUT 1780.

The dates are approximate.   See note at head of Table I.

DATE.	MARKS.	MAKER'S NAME.	ARTICLES AND OWNERS.
c. 1750	STERLING SB	Stephen Broughton.	Small plain tankard : Mr. Dudley Westropp.
1750-70	R·P STERLING	Robt. Potter.	Sauce-boat on three legs : Do. do.
,,	II I.IRISH II	John Irish.	Two-handled cup : The late Sir J. G. Nutting, Bart. Also with II crowned, on tea-spoon : Mr. Dudley Westropp.
,,	II STERLING	Do. do. (?)	Band of reliquary : Mr. H. S. Guinness.
1757-80	MD DERMOTT	Michael McDermott.	Table-spoons : The late Mr. Cecil C. Woods.
,,	MD STER	Do. do.	Dessert-spoons : Cork Exhibition, 1902.
,,	MD STERLING MD	Do. do.	{ Table-spoons : Mr. Woods. { Two-handled cup : Colonel Longfield.
,,	WR ,,	William Reynolds.	{ Freedom-box and sauce-boat : The Day Collec- tion. { Wine funnel : Mr. Dudley Westropp.
,,	WR ,,	Do. do.	Fish slice : The Day Collection.
,,	WR	Do. do.	Freedom box presented to Lord Shelbourne, 23 May, 1764.
,,	WR STERLING	Do. do.	Soup ladle : Mr. Dudley Westropp.
,,	,, STERLING	Do. do.	Bright cut table-spoon : Mr. Dudley Westropp.
,,	WR	Do. do.	Freedom box presented to Sir George McCarthy, 3 Nov., 1769.
,,	WR WR	Do. do.	The first mark stamped twice on a spoon, the second on a sauce-boat : Mr. D. Westropp.
,,	WR WR	Do. do.	Dessert-spoons and soup ladle : Mr. Dudley Westropp.
,,	McD STERLING	Michael McDermott.	Bright cut table-spoons : Mr. Dudley Westropp.
,,	MD ,,	Do. do.	Do. do. do. : Noted by the Author.
1760	L★R STARLING L★R	... ...	Soup ladle Noted by Mr. Dudley Westropp.
,,	IA STERLING IA	... ...	Hanoverian table-spoon : Do. do.
1760-80	WALSH SW STERLING	Stephen Walsh.	Helmet-shaped cream-jug on three legs : Mr. W. Boore.
,,	C·B STERLING	Croker Barrington.	Plain mug : Noted by Mr. Dudley Westropp.
,,	SW WALSH STERLING	Stephen Walsh.	Soup ladle : Do. do. do.
,,	SW STERLING	Do. do.	Two-handled cup : Colonel Longfield.
,,	WALSH STERLING	} Do. do.	Circular dish and cover : Mr. Dudley Westropp.
,,	SW WALSH STERLING	Do. do.	Entrée dish : Do. do.
,,	SW ,,	Do. do.	Sauce-boat on three legs : Do. do.
,,	SM ,,	Stephen Mackrill.	Cream-jug : Mr. D. H. Lane.

MARKS ON CORK PLATE.

TABLE V.—From about 1760 to about 1780.

The dates are approximate.   See note at head of Table I.

DATE.	MARKS.	MAKER'S NAME.		ARTICLES AND OWNERS.
1760-80	STERLING DMC	} Daniel	McCarthy ?	Two-handled cup: Elysium, Waterford.
,,	DMC STER	Do.	do.	Sugar bowl on three legs: Mr. J. H. Fitzhenry. Sauce-boat on three legs: Mr. Dudley Westropp.
,,	STARLING C*B	Croker	Barrington.	Two-handled cup; Messrs. Welby & Son.
,,	C·B DOLLAR	Do.	do.	Punch ladle: Mr. Dudley Westropp.
1760-85	IH STERLING	John	Hillery.*	Sugar bowl and soup ladle: The Day Collection.
1765-95	CT ,, CT	Carden	Terry.	Asparagus tongs: Mr. Dudley Westropp.
1770	IRH STER	John	Irish.	Table Forks: Mr. H. Lawson.
,,	TA STERLING TA	...	...	...	Marrow scoop: Mr. Dudley Westropp.
,,	McD *Sterling*	Michael	McDermott.	Noted by Do. do.
,,	MD STERLING	Do.	do.	Do. Do. do.
1770-88	STER JWS STER	} John	Whitney (free 1775).	Oval snuffers tray on three feet: Mr. Dudley Westropp.
1770-99	IN STERLING	John	Nicolson.	Tea-spoons: Mr. Dudley Westropp.
,,	IN STERLING	Do.	do.	Small mace: St. Finn Barre's Cathedral, Cork.
,,	JN ,,	Do.	do.	A dozen bright-cut table spoons: The Day Collection.
,,	,, NICOLSON	Do.	do.	Sugar bowl on three legs: The late Mr. Cecil C. Woods.
1777 1820	P.W STERLING	Peter	Wills.	Two plain gravy spoons: Mr. Dudley Westropp.
1780	C·T STERLING	Carden	Terry.	Plain sauce ladle: Mr. Dudley Westropp.
,,	IH STERLING IH	John	Humphreys.†	Table-spoon: Do. do.
,,	I·H ,,	Do.	do.	Table-spoon: Messrs. Debenham & Storr.
,,	JK STERLING	Joseph	Kinselagh.	Do. : The late Mr. Cecil C. Woods.
,,	I·H STERLING	John	Hillery.*	Meat skewer: Mr. Dudley Westropp.
,,	CT STERLING	Carden	Terry.	Sauce-boat on three legs: Dublin Museum.
,,	SC STERLING	(*Not identified.*)		Table-spoons: Mr. Dudley Westropp.
,,	SR ,,	Samuel	Reily.	Oval teapot stand: Do. do.
,,	JSN ,,	Jno. & Sam.	Nicolson.	Half-a-doz. bright cut tea-spoons: Mr. D. Westropp.
,,	TC STIRLING	} Thomas	Cumming.	Pair of shoe buckles: Dublin Museum.

* Or John Humphreys   † Or John Hillery.

MARKS ON CORK PLATE.

TABLE VI.—FROM ABOUT 1770 TO ABOUT 1795.

The dates are approximate.   See note at head of Table I.

DATE.	MARKS.	MAKER'S NAME.	ARTICLES AND OWNERS.
1770-80	W·M STER^c	W. Morrisey.	Circular sugar bowl on three legs: Mr. Dudley Westropp.
1770-99	NICOLSON STERLING	John Nicolson.	Bright cut table-spoons: The Author.
1777 / 1810	S.R STERLING	Samuel Reily.	Punch ladle : Mr. Dudley Westropp.
,,	S·R STERLING	Do. do.	Plain table-spoons: Do. do.
,,	SR STERL^c	Do. do.	Bright cut tea-spoons: Noted by Mr. Dudley Westropp.
,,	REILY STERLING	Do. do.	Tea-spoons: The late Mr. Cecil Woods.
1783-95	W·ROE STERLING	} William Roe.	Sugar bowl: Noted by Mr. Dudley Westropp.
,,	TG STERLING TG	... ...	Bright cut sugar tongs : Do. do.
1786-95	TH STERLING	Thos. Harman.	Do. dessert-spoons: Do. do.
1787-95	TC STERL^G TC	Tim. Conway.	Do. table-spoons : Do. do.
1787	TD STERLING	Thomas Donnallan.	Tea-spoon and two table-spoons: Mr. Dudley Westropp.
1787-95	JS ,,	John Sheehan.	Fluted and engraved sugar bowl: The Day Collection.
,,	IG STERLING	Joseph Gibson.	Bright cut tea-spoons: Mr. Dudley Westropp.
1787-99	R·S STERLING	Richard Stevens.	Teapot: Miss Hungerford, Dunowen.
,,	R-S STERLING	Do. do.	Snuff-box: Noted by Mr. Dudley Westropp.
,,	I·S ,, I·S	John Sheehan.	Plain table-spoon, turned-up end: Mr. Dudley Westropp.
,,	STERLING SHEEHAN	Do. do.	Bright-cut gravy spoon: Mr. Dudley Westropp.
,,	SHEEHAN STER^G	Do. do.	Plain table-spoons, pointed ends: Mr. Dudley Westropp.
,,	SHEEHAN STERLING	} Do. do.	Marks noted by Mr. Dudley Westropp.
,,	R·S STERLING	} Richard Stevens.	Table-spoons : Do. do.
1790 / 1800	JM^{c}N STERLING	} (Not identified.)	Bright cut spoons: Do. do.
,,	RI STERLING	} Do. do.	Do. do. : Do. do.
1795	WT STERL^c	Wm. Teulon.	Noted by the Author.
,,	W.T STERLIN^c	Do. do.	Plain sauce-boat : Noted by Mr. Dudley Westropp.
,,	WT STERLING	Do. do.	Bright cut sauce ladle : Do. do.
,,	,, STERL^c	Do. do.	Table-spoons : Messrs. Crichton.

MARKS ON CORK PLATE.

TABLE VII.—FROM ABOUT 1795 TO ABOUT 1820

The dates are approximate.   See note at head of Table I.

DATE.	MARKS.	MAKER'S NAME.	ARTICLES AND OWNERS.
1795		John Supple.	Stamped twice on shoe buckle: Mr. Dudley Westropp.
,,	WT STERLING	William Teulon.	Plain tea-spoons : Mr. Dudley Westropp.
,,	WT STERLING	Do. do.	Do. do. : Mr. Wood.
,,	HSM STERLING	(*Not identified.*)	Small repoussé sauce-boat on three legs : Noted by Mr. Dudley Westropp.
,,	WT ,,	William Teulon.	Meat skewers : Lord Carbery.
,,	TJB STERLING	(*Not identified.*)	Bright cut tea-spoons : Miss Hungerford.
1791	IW ,,	John Warner.*	{ Communion cup dated 1791 : Lislee. { A pair of two-handled cups : The Day Collection.
1780-99	,, STIRLING	Do. do.	Plain table-spoon : Mr. Dudley Westropp.
1795	IW STERLING	John Williams.*	Do. do. : Do. do.
,,	I·W STER	James Warner.*	Plain sugar tongs : Do. do.
,,	I·W STERLING	Do. do. *	Half-a-dozen tea-spoons : Do. do.
,,	I·W STERLᴳ	Do. do. *	Tall helmet-shaped cream-jug : Mr. Dudley Westropp.
,,	{ STERLING { TOLLAND { STERLING	——— Tolland.	Flat-bottomed fluted cream jug : Mr. Dudley Westropp.
1796	I·H STERLING	James Heyland.	Breastplate : R. Cork Volunteers, Do.
,,	RD STERLING	... ...	Table-spoon : Mr. Dudley Westropp.
,,	HEYLAND 👑 STERLING	} James Heyland.	Plain egg-spoons : Do. do.
,,	JK STERLING	Jos. Kinselagh.	Bright cut sugar tongs : Do. do.
,,	JMᵈ	... ...	O.E. pattern spoons : Do. do.
1800	IT TOLEKEN	John Toleken.	Wine labels : Mr. C. Deane Oliver.
,,	TWM STERLING	(*Not identified.*)	Old English pattern dessert-spoons : Mr. Dudley Westropp.
1800-20	{ GIBSON STERLING { GIBSON	Joseph Gibson.	Spirit flask : Mr. Dudley Westropp.
,,	WHELPLEY STERLING	John Whelpley.	Table-spoons : The Author.
,,	,, WHELPLY	Do. do.	Punch-ladle : Mr. Dudley Westropp.
,,	𝒦 ,, WHELPLY	Do. do. †	Mustard-spoons : Mr. Woods.

* John Warner, John Williams, and James Warner were all working in Cork at about the end of the 18th century, and, marks not being registered, it may be that the mark ascribed to John Williams was used by one of the Warners and *vice versa*. In view of the date, the Lislee cup was very probably made by John Warner.   John Williams was, at a very early period in his career, taken into partnership by his father-in-law, Carden Terry, and could not have been working separately for more than a very few years before that event.   Having regard to all the circumstances, the above ascription of the respective marks is probably correct.

† The italic K (the mark of Joseph Kinselagh) was probably struck by him when employed by John Whelply.

MARKS ON CORK PLATE.

TABLE VIII.—FROM ABOUT 1800 TO ABOUT 1838.

The dates are approximate.   See note at head of Table I.

DATE.	MARKS.	MAKER'S NAME.	ARTICLES AND OWNERS.
1800-20	GIBSON STERLING	Joseph Gibson.	Table-spoons : The Cork Club.
,,	HEYLAND ,,	William Heyland.	Do. : Do. do.
,,	,, TOLEKEN	John Toleken.	Sugar-bowl : Mr. Dudley Westropp.
1795 / 1807	T & W ,,	{ Carden Terry & / John Williams. }	Cream ewer : The late Mr. Cecil Woods.
1805	SG STIRLING	Samuel Green.	Tea-spoons : The Cork Club.
1805-14	SG / STERLING / SG	} Do. do.	Flat-bottomed cream-jug : Mr. Dudley Westropp.
,,	C·T I·W STERLING	Terry & Williams.	Dessert-spoons : Mr. Woods.
,,	T.MONTJOY ,,	Thomas Montjoy.	Table-spoons : Noted by Mr. Dudley West-ropp.
,,	IN NN	John & / Nicholas } Nicolson.	{ Sugar tongs : Mr. C. Deane Oliver. / Tea-spoons : Mr. Dudley Westropp.
1807-21	CT IW STERLING	{ Carden Terry & / Jane Williams.	{ Forks and knife-handles : Rev. Samuel Hobart Dorman. / Various other articles with Dublin marks 1807-21.
1808-20	·CORBETT· STERLING	Daniel Corbett.	Tea-spoons : Mr. Dudley Westropp.
1809-30	JS STERLING	James Salter.	Fluted and engraved sugar bowl : The Day Collection.
,,	R·G ,,	Richard Garde.	Table-spoons : Mr. M. Falk.
1810	T·MONTJOY STERLING	Thos. Montjoy.	Bright cut sugar tongs : Mr. Dudley West-ropp.
,,	CONWAY / STERLING	} James Conway.	Table-spoons : Mr. Dudley Westropp.
,,	IE STERLING	John Egan.	Plain O.E. spoons : Do. do.
,,	P.W STERLING	Peter Wills.	Fiddle-pattern tea-spoons : Mr. D. Westropp.
1810-20	WS STERLING	—— Steele ?	Do. do. : Do. do.
,,	I SOLOMON STERLING	Isaac Solomon.	Do. dessert-spoons : Do. do.
,,	IS STERLING	John Seymour.	Do. tea-spoons : Do. do.
,,	I·SOLOMON ,,	Isaac Solomon.	Do. do. : Mr. Woods.
,,	F·S ,,	(Not identified.)	Flat-bottomed cream-jug : Noted by Mr. Dudley Westropp.
,,	PG STERLING	Phineas Garde.	Fiddle-pattern tea-spoons : Mr. D. Westropp
1810-40	IS ,,	{ Isaac Solomon, or / John Seymour.	Do. do. : Do. do.
1812	GARDE STERLING	Phineas Garde.	O.E. pattern gravy spoon : Do. do.
1820	SEYMOUR STERLING	John Seymour.	Plain sugar-tongs ; Do. do.
1820-40	KM ,,	Kean Mahony.	Communion cup : Killanully.
,,	EH ,,	Edward Hawkesworth.	Tea-spoons · Mr. Woods.
1824	O.BRIEN STERLING	Francis O'Brien	Fiddle-pattern table-spoons : Noted by Mr. Dudley Westropp.
,,	MAHONY / STERLING	} Kean Mahony.	Plain mug : Noted by Mr. Dudley Westropp.
1838	M&B STERLING	(Not identified.)	Large finger ring : Do. do.

LIST OF CORK GOLDSMITHS

(FROM 1601 TO 1852, ARRANGED CHRONOLOGICALLY).

Compiled from the Records of the Cork Guild, the Court d'Oyer Hundred Book, and the Cork Corporation Records, supplemented by names found in Directories and Parish Registers.

G.S. = Goldsmith; S.S. = Silversmith; J. = Jeweller; W.M. = Watchmaker; C.M. = Clockmaker; B.F. = Brassfounder and Brazier; ? = Query—it being uncertain whether these were pewterers, founders, or some other craftsmen, and not goldsmiths, although associated with them, and masters of the Company in the years stated; d. = died.

In many instances the craftsmen mentioned in the records, although described as jewellers, watchmakers, &c., also carried on the trades of goldsmiths and silversmiths. On the other hand, a number of plumbers, glaziers, saddlers, and upholsterers were members of the "guild of goldsmiths," and some of them were masters and wardens of the guild at different times, but their names have been excluded from the following list because they were in no way connected with the goldsmith's art. It has been suggested that Edward Goble, the brass-founder, also cast silver work, which his son, Robert Goble, the goldsmith, afterwards wrought and chased.

It is probable that many of the goldsmiths worked for some years before the earliest and after the latest known mention of their names.

NAME.	Earliest Mention.	Remarks.	Latest Date or Death.	NAME.	Earliest Mention.	Remarks.	Latest Date or Death.
Morice Leyles G.S.	1601		1617	Henry Russell G.S.	1699		
Richard Gould ,,	1618		1656	William Freke ,,	Warden, 1700		
John Huethson ,, (Hewitson)	1624		,,	Caleb Rotheram S.S.	1701	Warden, 1702 Master 1707	d. 1746
James Rowe ,,	1626		1630				
James Piersey ,,	1643		1656				
John Sharpe ,,	1656	Master 1659, '65, '72, '83, & '90	,,	George Brumley G.S.		Warden, 1702	1729
Edward Goble B.F.				Roger Pinkney ?	1702		
John Hawkins	1657 Warden, 1680		1702	John Harding ,,	Warden, 1706	Master 1710	,,
Nichs. Gamble G.S.	1667	Master 1667, '71, & '5		Robert Goble ,, jr.	Warden, 1706		d. 1737
Wm. Harris ?		1669		George Farrington ,,	1710		d. 1728
Robert Goble ,,	Warden, 1672	1677, '94-5	1719	Wm. Clarke ,,	Warden, 1709-10	Master 1714	1733
Thos. Withers ?		1674		Randal Philpot ,,	1710	Warden, 1713	1715
James Ridge	1673		1700	John Mawman ,, (Pewterer)	Mentd. 1710	1716	1729
*Richd. Smart ,,	Warden. 1674	Master 1676 & '91	1691				
John Webb ?	1675	1680	1687	J'miah Burchfield ?		Master 1711	
Samuel Pantin G.S. & J.	Warden, 1678	Master 1679 & '86	1686	Christr. Hawkins ?		Master 1717	
Arthur Eason ?		1682		Bernard Baldwin ,,	1712		,,
Francis Whitcroft ?		1684		James Foulkes ,,	1712	Warden, 1718	,,
John Wall G.S.	1682			Philip Syng § ,,	,,		d. 1739
†Antny. Semirot ,, (Semiroe)	1685 Warden, 1710	Master 1712	d. 1743	Joseph Wright S.S.	,,		d. 1728
Caleb Webb ,,	1688 Warden, 1692	Master 1697		James Foucauld J.	Free 1714		d. 1729
George Robinson ,,	1690		1729	Christr. Parker G.S.	,,	Master 1721	
John James ?	1691	1692	,,	John Biss ?	1715	1719	,,
Daniel Harris ?		1693		William Martin ,,	1716	Master 1720 & '7 Warden, 1725	d. 1739
Charles Morgan G.S.	Warden, 1692	Master 1697	1701				
‡Charles Begheagle ,,	Warden, 1693		d. 1697	William Newenham ,,	Warden, 1721	Master 1726	,,
Walter Burnett ,,	Warden, 1694	Master 1700	1729	Thomas Lilly ,,	,,		
Jerome Burchill ?	1697			Reuben Millard S.S.	1721	Free 1722 Warden, 1723	d. 1737
Adam Billon G.S.	1699		1719				
John Agherne ,,			d. 1699				

* Mark occurs on money weights 1679.

† "Anthony Semirot, goldsmith," a French refugee, admitted a freeman in 1685.

‡ Charles Begheagle, a Flemish immigrant; probably worked in Cork for some years before he was elected warden in 1693, but no earlier recorded mention of his name has been found. See pages 682 and 685.

§ Emigrated to America in 1714.

LIST OF CORK GOLDSMITHS—*Continued.*

Name.	Earliest Mention.	Remarks.	Latest Date or Death.
William Thompson G.S.		Warden, 1721	1723
William Bennett G.S.	{1722	Warden, 1728	d. 1758
Edward Dunsterfield G.S.		Warden, 1722	
Simon P. Codier J.		Free 1725	1759
John Ricketts S.S.		Free 1725	d. 1738
Thomas Garry G.S.		Warden, 1726	
Daniel Crone S.S.		Free 1726	1759
Thomas Smarley		Mentd. 1726	
Jemmy Lilly ,,	1731		,,
Thomas Bull ,,		Mentd. 1732	d. 1771
William Halluran ,,	1735		
Peter Lane ,,		Free 1737	1759
George Hodder G.S.	{1738	Free 1746 / Mayor 1754	d. 1771
Wm. Bentley S.S.	1740		
*Jnthn. Buck ,,	{1740	Mentd. 1754	d. 1762
John Brunton G.S. & J.	1741		
Michael Coldwell S.S.	Mentd. 1742		d. 1752
Stephen Mackerill J.	Mentd. 1743		d. 1763
Samuel Whelpley S.S. Buckle-maker	Mentd. 1745		1781
Stephen Broughton G.S. & J.	Mentd. 1746		
Caleb Hamond S.S. & J.	Mentd. 1747		1758
John Irish S.S.	1748		1775
Croker Barrington ,,	1750		1777
Michael McDermott S.S. & G.S.	,,		d. 1784
Robert Potter G.S.	,,		
Joseph Kinselagh J. ss.	{1750	Free 1780	d. 1783
Thomas Knox S.S.		Free 1752	d. ,,
Stephen Walsh G.S. & J.	,,		1780
—— Michael S.S.	Mentd. 1752		
John Hopkins ,,	,,		
Adonijah Budd G.S. & J.	1754		1759
James Verdaile J.	,,		
James Kirk bucklemaker	,,		
John Nicolson	1756		1805
John Hillery G.S.	,,		d. 1780
James Grant	1758		

Name.	Earliest Mention.	Remarks.	Latest Date or Death.
William Reynolds S.S.		Free 1758	1790
George Duglas ,,	Free 1758		
William Whitcroft ,,	Mentd. 1759		
Gregory Philpot J.	,,		
Francis Taylor S.S.		Free 1761	1783
John Armour J.	1761		
George Lee S.S.		Free 1761	1789
Peter Baker		Free 1761	1783
Richard Harvey ,,		Free 1761	
John Platt bucklemaker	1764		
John Foley G.S. & J.	,,		1795
William Squibble S.S.	,,		1768
John Haughton ,,	,,		
Francis Gore ,,	,,		
James Dennison ,,	1765		
William Connell J.	,,		1775
Carden Terry J. & G.S.	{1766	Free 1785	d. 1821
Richard Walsh S.S.	1768		1783
William Brettridge G.S.	,,		
Alexr. Douglas ,,	1770		,,
Jnthn. Buck chaser	,,		1787
Fredk. Buck S.S.	1771		
John Christian G.S. & S.S.	1772		
Patrick Ryan ,,			d. 1792
John Egan J. & plater	1773		1795
John Humphreys S.S. & G.S.	,,		1787
John McGrath ,,			
William Wiley S.S.	1774		
Bligh Harrison J.	1775		1789
John Warner G.S.		Free 1775	1810
John Whitney ,,			
John & Saml. Nicolson S.S.	Partners, c. 1775		c. 1780
Peter Wills J.	1777		1820
Samuel Reily G.S.	,,		1812
Daniel McCarthy ,,			d. 1782
William Armour	,,		
John Long S.S.	1778		1812
William Morrissey G.S.	,,		
Thomas Cumming S.S.	1779		
Burton Wright ,,	,,		
Herbert Gillman ,,	,,		1783
James M'Mahon ,,	,,		
Kean Mahoney W.M. & working S.S.	,,		1850
John Sheehan S.S. & cutler	,,		1795
Joseph Kinselagh, jr.	{1780	Ment. 1783	
Joseph Cope S.S.	1780		

* At first in Limerick to c. 1740. List of freemen 1731.

LIST OF CORK GOLDSMITHS—*Continued.*

NAME.	Earliest Mention.	Remarks.	Latest Date or Death.	NAME.	Earliest Mention.	Remarks.	Latest Date or Death.
Joseph Nicholson G.S., J.& sword cutler	1780		1795	Isaac Soloman S.S.	1801	Free 1805	d. 1845
Joseph Taylor s.s.	,,			John Nicolson ,,	{1802		d. 1824
Edward Johnstone ,,	,,			Nicholas Bagley	1802		
Samuel Green ,,			1811	William Bagley	c. 1810	,,	
William Roe G.S. & J.	1781		1795	J. & N. Nicholson ,,	1807		c. 1820
Joseph Beauchamp s.s.	,,			* Jane Williams ,,	,,		
John Whelpley ,,			1824	James Heyland G.S.	,,		
Alexr. McDaniel ,,	1782			Thos. Montjoy		1810	d. 1824
John Rogers J.	1783			George Stotesbury w.M.		,,	
Charles Purcell ,,	,,		1787	Wm. Greaves ,,	1807	,,	
Michael James Brown ,,	,,			James Conway w.M.	1808	,,	
John Humphreys s.s.	Ment. 1783			Daniel Corbett J.J.		,,	
Thomas Campbell ,,		1784		William Heyland G.S. & s.s.	1809		,,
Mary Hillery ,,				John Seymour s.s.	,,		1827
Thomas Donallan ,,	1784		1795	Richard Garde ,,			1828
Joseph Gibson G.S., J. & w.M.	,,		d. 1820	Thos. Brooks w.M.		,,	
Thomas Harman s.s.	1785			John Carroll ,,		,,	
Robt. Stevelly & Son ,,	,,			J. Eaterby ,,	1811	,,	
George Seymour pewterer		Master 1787	1799	S. Green s.s.	1812		1812
George Aicken w.M.	1787	In Cork Directories.	1795	Phineas Garde ,,	,,		1845
Timothy Conway	,,			George Wyburd ,,	,,		1824
Michael Hartnett s.s.		1787	d. 1803	Joseph Steed J.			
Rd. Williams w.M.		,,		John Loughlin ,,	1818		
Joseph Craven ,,	,,	1787-95	1795	—— Steele s.s.	1820		
Matt. Bagnell ,,	,,	,,	,,	† James Salter ,,	1821		
John Elliott ,,	,,	,,	,,	Christr. Garde ,,			
Wm. Uppington ,,	,,	,,	,,	John Armstrong G.S.	1824		d. 1828
John Montjoy w. & c.M.	,,	,,	,,	James Hackett J.	,,		d. 1850
Henry Wherland c.M.	,,	,,	,,	Edward Hawksworth ,,	,,		1852
Jnthn. Wheeler w.M.	,,	,,	,,	Wm. Egan J. s.s.			1850
Richd. Bagley ,,	,,	,,	1824	Joseph Barry w.M.		1824	
Wm. Ross ,,	,,	,,	1810	Wm. Carroll ,,		,,	
Wm. Byron ,,	,,	,,	1824	John Callaghan J.		,,	
Richd. Stevens s.s.		Free 1788	1830	Daniel Danahy c.M.		,,	
Richd. Cullum J.	1789			Henry Obree G.S.		,,	
George Evans s.s. & ,,	,,		1796	Francis O'Brien w.M.		,,	
Michael Cooper ,,	,,		1795	Mark O'Shaughnessy w.M.		,,	
R. I.			c. 1790	James Mangan ,,		,,	
R. D.			c. ,,	Samuel Haynes ,,		,,	
William Reynolds s.s.	1790		1795	Robert Milliken ,,		,,	
—— Tolland ,,	c. ,,		c. 1800	John D. Montjoy ,,		,,	
William Tuelon ,,	1791		1844	John Murphy ,,	1826	,,	
John Williams ,,	,,		d. 1807	Thos. Garde s.s.	1828		1830
Carden Terry &	} partners, 1795			Peter Donavan J.	,,		
John Williams ,,			1806	Will. Hackett	1833		
Samuel Fryer s.s.	{1792	Free 1795	d. 1830	Thomas Oakshott s.s.	,,		
Thomas Austen w.M.	1795	1795 & 1810 In Cork Directories.	1810	Jeremiah Mack ,,	1835		
Wm. Harman ,,		1795		William Jackson s.s.&J.	1836	Directory.	1845
James Uppington		,,		Robt. Cave s.s. & J.	1840		
Richd. Montjoy c.M.	,,	,,		R. & W. Bradford s.s. & Cutlers	1843		1857
Ann. Ryan s.s.	,,	,,	,,	E. Kelly J.	,,		
James Heyland ,,	Mentd. 1795		1812	Thomas Seymour s.s.	1844	,,	1845
John Toleken ,,	,,		1836	George Cooke s.s. & J.	,,		
John Supple bucklemaker	Mentd. 1796			Patrick Mahoney G.S. & J.	,,		1852
Nicholas Nicolson s.s. & w.M.	1797		1830	Waterhouse & Co. s.s., J. & w.M.	,,		
James Warner s.s.		Free 1799	,,	Patrick McNamara s.s.	1845		,,
				S. & E.C.A. Teulon, s.s., J. & w.M.	1852		
				John Herlihy s.s.& J.	,,		
				J. Mason s.s. & c.M.	,,		

* Widow of John Williams and daughter of Carden Terry ; carried on business under the style of "Terry & Williams".

† James Salter with his family emigrated for New Zealand in 1840 in the "Sophia Pate" which was wrecked on the voyage, and all save one boy were lost.

YOUGHAL.

By a Charter of James I., dated 9 March, 1608, the Corporation of Youghal was empowered to arrange the various craftsmen of the town in appropriate guilds.

It is probable that by virtue of this Charter, the goldsmiths were associated with other hammer-wielding crafts in a common guild, but there is no evidence of the existence of a distinct guild of Youghal goldsmiths.* The number of master goldsmiths working in the town at any one time was, as far as can be gathered from records, probably never more than half a dozen. It is, however, certain that several goldsmiths practised their art in the town in the 17th and 18th centuries, and that they used in common, as their town mark (in allusion to the name of their town), the representation of a small single-masted sailing boat (similar to that found on Youghal pewter tokens of the year 1646) known heraldically as a *lymphad*, but commonly called a *yawl*. The mark was first identified by the late Mr. R. Day on the communion cup of Ightermurrough.

In the town records, Morrish Lawless and John Sharpe, goldsmiths, are mentioned in the year 1620; John Green, goldsmith, is mentioned 1652; and Edward Gillett, goldsmith, was admitted to the freedom of Youghal in 1711, elected a common councilman in 1712, and was mayor in 1721. The marks of each of these, reproduced from authentic examples, together with the marks of other goldsmiths, are illustrated in the following table, the dates which appear in the first column being, of course, approximate.

The Youghal town mark a lymphad or yawl in allusion to the name of the town.

MARKS ON YOUGHAL PLATE.

DATE (ABOUT).	MARKS.	MAKER'S NAME.	ARTICLES AND OWNERS.
1620		Morrish Lawless.	Apostle spoon : Messrs. Christie, 1902.
,,		John Sharpe.	Communion cup : St. Mary's, Youghal.
1644		John Green.	Chalice, dated 1644 : Noted at Cork in 1903, and afterwards sold at Messrs. Christie's.
1650		Do. do.	Chalice : Noted by the late Mr. R. Day, F.S.A.
1683		Bartholomew Fallon of Galway.	The Macnamara chalice, dated 1683 : Dublin Museum.
1702		(*Not identified*, but possibly Bartholomew Fallon as above.)	{Chalice inscribed *"The parish of Cloyne-priest † Apr. 4, 1702"* : Cloyne. {Paten : Killeagh.
1712		Edward Gillett.	{Communion cup inscribed *" The legacy of Mrs. Mary Brelsford, who died ye 3rd of Feby., 1712, to the Church of Ightermurrough"* : now at Corkbeg. {Paten, dated 1716 : Youghal Parish Church.
1720	,,	Austin Beere.	Communion cup and paten : Castle Martyr, co. Cork.

* A Company of Hammermen, comprising goldsmiths, blacksmiths, pewterers, and others, was incorporated in Youghal on 15 September, 1657.
† Now Clonpriest.

The following names of goldsmiths occur in the Youghal council books at the dates mentioned. It will be observed that there is a long interval—1652 to 1705—in which no goldsmith is mentioned, and as the Cloyne chalice is of that period, the list cannot be considered complete, because the name of the goldsmith whose mark occurs on that vessel cannot be filled in.

NAMES OF YOUGHAL GOLDSMITHS.

G.S. = Goldsmith ; S.S. = Silversmith ; W.M. = Watchmaker ; C.M. = Clockmaker.

Date.	Name and Designation.			Date.	Name and Designation.		
1620	Morrish	Lawless	G.S.	Free 1705 ⎫	Edward	Gillett	G.S.
1625	James	Lawless	,,	Mayor 1721 ⎭			
1628	Edward	Adams	C.M.	Free 1730	John	Gillett	S.S.
1632	Daniel	Wright	G.S.	c. 1730	Austin	Beere	,,
,,	Daniel	McRory	,,	1784	William	Huxtable	S.S.
,,	John	Sharpe	,,	1785	William	Patterson	
1638	John	Smith	,,	,,	R. W.	Dartnell	W.M.
1652	John	Green	,,	1787	Richard	Cutler	,,
				1795	Patrick	Twomy	,,

GALWAY.

The Galway town mark—an anchor.

Galway, like Youghal, is one of the old walled towns of Ireland where, in former times, there were goldsmiths who wrought plate. The Galway mark—an anchor, generally found in a shaped stamp—was first identified by the late Mr. Robert Day, F.S.A., who had noticed several examples of plate of the 17th and 18th centuries stamped with that mark. The first of such examples, a chalice (now in the Author's collection) marked with an anchor and the initials R I, both in stamps of irregular shape, was brought to Mr. Day's notice in Dublin in the year 1875. From the inscription on its foot, which records the fact that it had been procured by Mary Gabriel Skerrett for her nephew fʳ Mark Skerrett in 1732, Mr. Day surmised that the chalice had emanated from Galway, of which town the Skerretts were one of the thirteen tribal clans. A few months after he had noticed the chalice, Mr. Day, while visiting the Rev. Charles Laurence, of Lisreahan, Laurencetown, co. Galway, observed amongst the family plate of his host a cruet frame * of the George I. period with an anchor mark resembling that on the Skerrett chalice. This led to the identification of the marks on the chalice and on the cruet frame as those of Galway goldsmiths.

On the side of the cruet frame, in contemporary engraving, is a coat

* The cruet frame is now in the possession of Mr. Arthur Irwin Dasent.

of arms : *argent, a chevron between three sheldrakes* (for Kirwan) impaling, *argent, a fret* (for Blake), surmounted by the crest of Blake—*a sheldrake beaked and legged.* On the bottom of the frame, also in contemporary engraving, are the letters ${}^{K}_{P.M}$ which stand for ${}^{Kirwan,}_{Patrick\ \&\ Mary}$: Patrick Kirwan of Cregg having married Mary, daughter of Richard Martyn, on the 23 March, 1703.

The town of Galway, which is also a county—its full description being "the town and county of the town of Galway"—had within its boundaries in the 17th century thirteen leading families, their names being: Athy, Blake, Bodkin, Browne, D'Arcy, Ffort, Fallon, Joyes,* Kirwan, Lynch, Martyn, Morris and Skerrett. These families were known as "the thirteen tribes of Galway". The appellation was first used with regard to them by Cromwell's soldiers as a term of reproach, because of their extraordinary attachment to each other during the time of their troubles and persecutions. It was afterwards adopted by the families themselves as a mark of distinction, indicative of the honour pertaining to being a member of one of the tribes. The facts that the Kirwan and Blake, whose arms are impaled as above described, as well as Richard Martyn, whose daughter married Patrick Kirwan, were members of Galway tribal families, connected the cruet frame with the town of Galway. The identity of the maker of the Skerrett chalice whose initials were R I, and the identity of the maker of the cruet frame whose initials were M F, were both subsequently traced to members of two other Galway tribal families—Joyes * and Fallon—as will presently be explained.

[margin note: Galway tribal families of the 17th and 18th centuries.]

The name of Donell O'Vollaghan, Jun., G.S., Galway, has been found recorded in the year 1500, and on a quaint memorial stone, dated 1579, in the Franciscan Abbey, Galway, the names of Walter Davin, Margaret his wife, and Thomas Davin are inscribed. The goldsmiths' arms and an archaic ship—the ship being the principal charge in the arms of Galway—are also carved on the stone. This record apparently indicates that Walter or Thomas Davin (or both) were goldsmiths. From 1579 no other names of Galway goldsmiths have been traced until towards the end of the 17th century.

In Hardiman's *History of the Town and County of the Town of Galway*, reference is made to "Bye Law A.D. 1585" which states "that the new statute made by the goldsmiths concerning their own

* Or Joyce.

faculty or art is commendable so that they shall observe the same and mend their former faults". A goldsmith named Joyes or Joyce—the name is spelled in both ways—a member of one of the thirteen tribes, is mentioned in a footnote to p. 15. In his youth, Joyes, when on a voyage to the West Indies, was (Hardiman relates) captured by an Algerian pirate, taken to Algiers and there sold as a slave to a Moorish goldsmith. He remained with the Moor for a period of fourteen years, working at the goldsmith's art, and he appears to have been regarded as a highly skilled craftsman. On the accession of King William III. to the English throne, one of his first acts was the sending of an ambassador to Algiers to demand the immediate release of every British subject held there in slavery. This demand was reluctantly complied with by the Dey, and thus Joyes regained his liberty. The Moor, however, on being ordered to release Joyes, offered his only daughter to him in marriage, together with half his property, as an inducement for him to remain, but Joyes refused the offer and returned to Galway, where he carried on the business of a goldsmith with considerable success. Having no son, Joyce bequeathed his property to his daughters, one of whom was married to Andrew Ffrench, also a member of one of the Galway tribes. There was one Mark Fallon (a brother of Bartholomew Fallon) who appears to have been taken into partnership by Joyes, and who, after the death of Joyes, continued the business.

Joyes, a Galway goldsmith taken captive by an Algerian pirate. His detention in Algiers.

Although no goldsmith's name has been found between 1579 and about 1690, a goldsmith's mark occurs on a chalice made in the year 1648 for a convent near the Murresk mountains, to the West of Galway, as the contemporary inscription engraved on the foot of the chalice (set out in the following table) testifies. The only mark it bears is that of the maker—R I in a square depression. The chalice now belongs to the Augustinian Church, Thomas Street, Dublin. The maker could hardly have been Richard Joyes who is mentioned above, but might very well have been an ancestor.

From 1784 to 1817 the names of nine Galway goldsmiths are found to have been entered in the books of the Dublin Goldsmiths' Company in pursuance of the provisions of the Act of 1783, which required that all Irish goldsmiths should register their names at the Dublin Assay Office, where all Irish plate, from 1784, ought to have been assayed. Plate made by any Galway goldsmith from 1784 onwards would probably be stamped with the Dublin marks. No plate bearing the Galway mark has been found of later date than about 1730, and none earlier than about 1650.

The following table contains representations in *facsimile* of the several marks which have been found on Galway-made plate.

MARKS ON GALWAY PLATE.

The dates in the first column of the table are merely approximate and are derived mainly from dates inscribed on the articles named.

DATE (ABOUT).	MARKS.	MAKER'S NAME.	ARTICLES AND OWNERS.
1648	RI	R. Joyes, sen. (?)	Chalice inscribed "*Joannes de Burgo Aug.* me fieri fecit pro Conventu Murskensis Anno 1648*": Augustinian Church, Dublin.
1666-1684		... ...	Puritan spoon, dated 1666: Dublin Museum. Trifid spoons, dated 1673 and 1684: Dublin Museum. Do. do. : Mr. J. H. Walter and Mr. Dudley Westropp.
1695	RI ⚓ RI	Richard Joyes.	The "Skerrett" chalice†: The Author's Colln.
1700	RI ⚓ RI	Do. do.	Foot of chalice: R.C. Church, Galway.‡
,,	E G	... ...	Reliquary box: Noted by Mr. Dudley Westropp.
,,	T·P	... ...	Stamped twice on chalice: Do. do. do.
1720	I·L	... ...	Stamped twice on Galway chalice, dated 1720: Noted by Mr. Dudley Westropp.
1725	RI ⚓ RI	Richard Joyes.	The "Prendergas" chalice, inscribed "*Pray for Patk Prendergas and his wife Mary Ann, who orderd ys to be made 1725*": St. Patrick's College, Thurles.
1730	MF ⚓	Mark Fallon.	Bowl of chalice, attached to the foot mentioned above: R.C. Church, Galway.‡
,,	⚓ MF ⚓	Do. do.	The "Kirwan" cruet frame: Mr. Arthur I. Dasent.
1743-5	PI	... ...	On wedding-ring, dated 1743, and Freedom box on which is engraved "Given with freedom of Galway to Captains of East India Fleet, 1745"; arms of Galway engraved on lid.

* Joannes de Burgo, an Augustinian. Members of the de Burgo family (now called Burke) have from time to time in past generations caused other chalices to be made for the celebration of Mass. Lord Swaythling possesses one such, of the latter part of the 15th century.

† On the front facet of the spreading octagonal foot of this chalice a representation of the crucifixion is beautifully engraved, the lines, however, towards the angles present slight indications of wear. The work is evidently of about the end of the 17th century, and as the chalice is divisible into three parts, it was probably made easily portable for the celebration of Mass in remote places when the penal laws were in force. On the projecting torus moulding of the lower part of the foot (by a different hand from that which engraved the crucifixion, and obviously coarser and later work) is inscribed :— "*Pray for ye good Intention of Mary Gabriel Skerrett, who procured ys Chalice & A vestment for ye Use of her Nephew fr Mark Skerrett: 1732*". This inscription does not record that Mary Gabriel Skerrett caused the chalice to be made, but that she procured it (probably some time after it had been made and possibly at second hand). The Skerrett family was one of the thirteen tribes of Galway, as mentioned on pages 702-3 *supra*.

‡ The foot of this chalice, which bears the stamp of R. Joyes, appears to be earlier work than the bowl, which has the mark of M. Fallon; the bowl was probably broken or lost and replaced by a new one in 1730, and the date 1730 then inscribed on the foot.

In the Dublin Museum there are also three chalices dated 1717, 1718 and 1721 respectively, each of which bears the initials of R. Joyes, as illustrated in the fourth line of marks in the above table, but without the anchor mark; another chalice similarly marked was repaired by Messrs. Egan of Cork, in 1902.

MARKS ON CLADDAGH RINGS.

Plain gold wedding rings used in the Claddagh district of Galway and a few other districts in Ireland. Each ring is impressed with the mark of its maker, and also bears a representation of two hands holding a heart surmounted by a crown.

From the latter part of the 17th to the early part of the 18th century.	Mark	
	AR	Andrew Robinson, Galway.
	F	Austin French, ,,
	GR	Geo. Robinson, ,,
	JD	Dillon, Galway and Waterford.
	NB	Nicholas Burdge, Galway.
	RD	Dillon, Galway and Waterford.
	RI	Richard Joyce, Galway.
	RS	?
	TH	?
	WD	Dillon of Galway.

In the following list, the dates prior to 1784 are the years when the goldsmiths appear to have worked. From 1784 onwards the names and dates have been transcribed from the books of the Dublin Goldsmiths' Company.

NAMES OF SOME GALWAY GOLDSMITHS.

Walter	Davin (?)	1578 (?)	John	Shadwell	mentd. 1757	Francis	Dowling	1785
Thomas	Davin (?)	,, (?)	T. Fitz. F.	Lynch	d. 1771	Michael	O'Mara	,,
R.	Ioyes	1648	George	Robinson	1784	Will.	Leathem	1786
Richard	Joyes	1690 to 1720	Austin	French	,,	James	Kelly	1799
Mark	Fallon	1696 ,, 1730	Martin	Lain	,,	Nicholas	Burdge, w.m.	1817
Bartholomew	Fallon*	d. 1722	Laurence	Coleman	,,			

* See marks on Youghal plate, page 701 *ante.*

LIMERICK.

It is impossible now to determine the date when plate was first made in Limerick or to name its earliest goldsmiths. There can, however, be very little doubt, having regard to the importance of the town in the 17th century, that goldsmiths were engaged there in the exercise of their craft at that period and probably earlier. The war troubles of 1689 and subsequent years account for the suspension of the manufacture of plate until peace was restored in 1691-2, and for the disappearance in the melting pot of much, if not all, that had been previously wrought there.

Early in the 18th century, plate wrought in Limerick was sent to Dublin for the purpose of being assayed and marked, as is proved by entries in the books of the Dublin Goldsmiths' Company. In pursuance of the Act of 1783,* which required all Irish goldsmiths to register their names and places of abode with the Company of Goldsmiths in Dublin, the names of a number of Limerick goldsmiths are found to have been entered in the books of the Dublin Goldsmiths' Company in 1784 and later years. *(margin: Limerick plate sent to Dublin to be assayed in the 18th century.)*

The Limerick marks closely resemble those of Cork. The earliest known example of Limerick plate is a communion flagon at Churchtown, Buttevant, co. Cork. Its marks are, a triple-towered castle and the maker's initials (I B), each mark being duplicated alternately. For a long time these marks remained unlocated, but the discovery by Mr. Dudley Westropp of an old Limerick toll-stamp of the early part of the 18th century bearing a castle of similar form, led to their identification. The toll-stamp bears the inscription "THOLSEL COURT LIMERICK," as represented below. "Tholsel Court" was the old toll-court where the market dues were collected. *(margin: Resemblance of the marks of Limerick and Cork.)* *(margin: An old Limerick toll-stamp.)*

(Scale ½ Linear.)

* 23 and 24 George III., c. 23. See page 586 *supra*.

Table plate from about the second quarter to about the end of the 18th century, found in and around Limerick in recent years, stamped with the "STERLING" mark, was for some time believed to have been made in Cork, but names of Limerick goldsmiths having been found in the books of the Dublin Goldsmiths' Company of the period in question, that discovery led to the identification of the makers' marks as those of goldsmiths who worked and resided in Limerick, and to the establishment of the fact that the "STERLING" mark was used by the goldsmiths of Limerick, as well as by those of Cork, as a warranty that their silver was of sterling quality. On spoons made between 1780 and 1820 an additional mark bearing a rude resemblance to a fleur-de-lys or a trefoil is found. Mr. Westropp has observed at the end of the stem of nearly every bright cut Limerick spoon which has come under his notice an ornament resembling a plume of three feathers which may possibly have some connection with this trefoil-like stamped mark.

No records have been found to prove the existence of a regular guild of goldsmiths in Limerick, but workers of gold and silver were probably in past centuries associated there, as in other places, for the purpose of mutual protection. The names of ascertained members of the craft and such marks as have been found on plate made by them, are set forth in the following tables, which, although they cannot be regarded as complete, may lead to the identification of the marks of other goldsmiths who practised their art in the south-west of Ireland. It will probably be ascertained that many marks formerly believed to be those of Cork goldsmiths, but unidentifiable with any names to be found in Cork records, are really marks of Limerick craftsmen.

MARKS ON LIMERICK PLATE.

TABLE I.—FROM ABOUT 1710 TO 1784.

The dates in the first column of the table are approximate.

DATE. (ABOUT).	MARKS.	MAKER'S NAME.	ARTICLES AND OWNERS.
1710		J. Buck, senr. (?)	Com. flagon, " Presented by Sir John Pecival to Browhenny Church " (now Churchtown), Buttevant, co. Cork.
1718		Adam Buck.	Chalice, dated 1718.
1730-40		Jonathan Buck. (free 1731)	Patchbox: Mrs. Lanyon.
,,		Do. do.	Sauce-boat on three legs : Mr. Dudley Westropp.
1730-62		Do. do.	Hanoverian spoon : Mr. D. Westropp.
,,		Do. do.	Small cup : The Rev. John Penrose.
,,		Do. do.	Sauce-boat, dated 1764 : Noted by the Author. Also I·B on the seal of Killmallock 1738 : Mr. C. D. Oliver.
,,		Do. do.	Small repoussé box : Mr. Dudley Westropp.
1730-75		Joseph Johns.	Two-handled cup : Mr. Dudley Westropp. Soup ladle : Miss O'Grady. Tumbler : The Earl of Ilchester.
,,		Do. do.	Marrow spoon : Mr. C. D. Oliver.
,,		Do. do.	Freedom box : The Day Collection.
1749-50		? Joseph Johns.	Gold wedding ring engraved " R Mᶜ ᵉE, Feby. 1, 1749 " and another engraved " D ᴴ₊ M August 16, 1750 ". Also single-drop table spoons, c. 1750.
1750		Samuel Johns.	Hanoverian spoons : Mr. Dudley Westropp.
1760-85		George Moore.	Marrow scoop : Do. Do.
,,		Do. do.	Table-spoon (crook handle) : Mr. Dudley Westropp.
1768-80		Garret Fitzgerald.	Pair of ladles : Mr. Dudley Westropp.
1770		George Moore.	Noted by the Author.
1780		(*Not identified.*)	Bright-cut tea spoons : Mr. Dudley Westropp.
,,		Do. do.	Plain cream-jug on three legs : Mr. Dudley Westropp.
1784		Patrick Connell.	Bright-cut table spoon : Mr. Dudley Westropp.
,,		Do. do.	Plain table-spoon : Do. do.

MARKS ON LIMERICK PLATE.

TABLE II.—FROM ABOUT 1784 TO ABOUT 1813.

DATE (ABOUT).	MARKS.	MAKER'S NAME.	ARTICLES AND OWNERS.
1784	P·C STER P·C	Patrick Connell.	Bright cut sugar sifter: Lord Carbery.
,,	,, STERLING ,,	* Do. do.	Do. table-spoons: Mr. D. Westropp.
,,	MFG ,, MFG	Maurice Fitzgerald.	Do. do. : Do.
,,	MFG MFG MFG	Do. do.	Do. do.: The Day Collection.
,,	MFG STERLING	Do. do.	Plain spoon: Mr. Dudley Westropp.
,,	STER TB STER	Thomas Burke.	Bright cut sugar tongs: Do.
,,	TB STERLING TB	Do. do.	Noted by the Author.
,,	TB STER TB	Do. do.	Plain table-spoons: Mr. C. D. Oliver.
,,	TB STERLING	Do. do.	Bright cut tea-spoons: Mr. D. H. Lane.
,,	TB STERLING	Do. do.	Do. sugar tongs: Mr. D. Westropp.
,,	MW STERLING	Matt. Walsh.	Do. table-spoons: Do.
,,	MW STERLING	Do. do.	Sugar-tongs : Do.
1786	DL STERLING DL	Daniel Lysaght.	Plain table-spoon : Do.
,,	DL STERLING	Do. do.	Bright cut do. : Do.
,,	DL ,,	Do. do.	Do. do. : Do.
1798	WW STER WW	Wm. Ward.	Do. do. : Do.
1800	WFG STERLING WFG	Wm. Fitzgerald.	Do. dessert spoons: Mr. John R. Lloyd.
,,	WFG STERLING	Do. do.	Do. table-spoons: Mr. D. Westropp.
,,	R°S R°S	Robt. O'Shaughnessy.	Do. tea-spoons: Do.
,,	RS STERLG	Do. do.	Fiddle-pattern tea-spoons: Do.
,,	WW WW	Will. Ward.	Bright cut do. : Do.
,,	WW STERLING	Do. do.	Do. do. : Do.
,,	M C	... ...	Sauce-boats and O.E. spoons: Mrs. Dickson.
1810-20	S★P STERLING	Samuel Purdon.	Fiddle-pattern tea-spoons: Mr. Dudley Westropp.
,,	,,	Do. do.	Bright-cut tea-spoons: Do.
1800-13	IP	John Purcell.	Fiddle-pattern table-spoons: Do.

* Connell's initials on these spoons are in plain block letters thus :—**P.C** (not P·C as in the line above).   The late Mr. Robert Day, F.S.A., had spoons made by Patrick Connell with the "Sterling" mark contracted thus :—STERG.

LIST OF LIMERICK GOLDSMITHS

Compiled from the Books of the Dublin Goldsmiths' Company and from other sources.

G.S. = Goldsmith; S.S. = Silversmith; W.M. = Watchmaker; ? = Query—it being uncertain whether a pewterer, founder, or some other craftsman, and not a goldsmith, although associated with the goldsmiths.

In many instances the craftsmen mentioned in the records, although described as jewellers, watchmakers, etc., also carried on the trades of goldsmiths and silversmiths.

It is probable that many of the goldsmiths mentioned in this list worked for some years before the earliest and after the latest known mention of their names.

Name.	Earliest Mention.	Remarks.	Latest Date or Death.	Name.	Earliest Mention.	Remarks.	Latest Date or Death.
Thomas O'Carryd	1418			Philip Walsh G.S.	1777		1784
Donald Mecgyllysaghta G.S.	1559			Philip Burbridge (Bucklemaker)			d. 1780
Gilladuffe O'Cowltayn ,,	,,			John Hawley S.S.	1784		
George Buck ?	1672			Maurice Fitzgerald ,, (app. 1752.)	,,		
Robert Smith G.S.	1674	1687		John Stret	,,		
		Free 1680		Matthew Walsh	,,		
James Robinson ,,		Mayor 1698		Robert Lynch G.S.	,,		
				Arthur Lynch	,,		
Caleb Colbeck S.S.	1720	1730		James Lynch ,,	,,		
Adam Buck			d. 1725	Patrick Connell S.S.	,,		
Jonathan Buck ,,	1725	Free 1731	d. 1762	Thomas Burke G.S. & J.	,,		d. 1800
—— Hill ,,	1727			Daniel Lysaght S.S.	1786		1788
John Robinson ,,	1730	1739		Henry Downes			d. 1788
Edward Parker G.S.		Free 1731	d. 1782	Francis Phipps J.	1788		
		Free 1731		Matthew Stritch	,,		
		Sheriff 1755		William Ward G.S.	1798		
Joseph Johns ,,		Mayor 1774	1780	Samuel Purdon (Spoonmaker)	c. 1800		1846
				William Fitzgerald S.S.	1800		
George Robinson S.S.	1750	1768		Robert O'Shaughnessy S.S.	1802		d 1842
Robert Latch W.M.	,,	1766		William Carroll	1805		
John Cullen S.S.	1751		d. 1788	Thomas Walsh	1806		1846
John Gloster G.S.	1755			John Purcell W.M.			d. 1813
Garret Fitzgerald ,,	1760		d. 1780	William Fitzgerald & Son S.S.	1820		
Samuel Johns ,,	1765		d. 1795	H. Smith & }	1830		1846
George Halloran S.S.	1766		d. 1804	R. Wallace }			
Joseph Robinson ,,			d. 1767	George Hurst S.S.			d. 1842
George Moore G.S.	1768		1784	George Martin J. & S.S.	1846		
Collins Brehon ,,			d. 1768	Thomas Walsh ,,	,,		
Robert Bradford S.S.	1770			John Laing ,,	,,		
John Hackett ,,	,,		1784	Cornelius Wood ,,	,,		
James Watson G.S. & S.S.	1774			John Walsh ,,	,,		

BELFAST.

The marks illustrated below are believed to be those of Belfast goldsmiths of about the end of the 18th and beginning of the 19th centuries. The articles of plate on which the marks appear came from the neighbourhood of Belfast. The third mark, composed of the initials M B, have been suggested to be those of Matthew Bellew,* whose name appears as a Belfast goldsmith in the year 1792. The mark of a hand erect may have been intended for the Ulster hand.

MARKS ON PLATE WHICH MAY BE OF BELFAST MAKE.

APPROXIMATE DATE.	MARKS.	MAKER'S NAME.	ARTICLES AND OWNERS.
1780		... ...	Tea vase : Mr. A. D. George.
„		... ...	Sugar-tongs : Noted by Mr. Dudley Westropp.
1790		*Matthew Bellew ?	Snuff-box : The Day Collection.
1800		... ...	Table forks (4 prongs) : Do.
„		... ...	Mug with reeded bands : Dublin Museum.

NAMES OF SOME BELFAST GOLDSMITHS.

The following names of Belfast goldsmiths have been found in 17th and 18th century records :—

Andrew	McCullough	1660	Joshua	Hutton	1753, d. 1777
Will.	Barnett	1671	Ross	Sanderman, J.	1783
Thos.	McCune	1679	Hugh	McCulloch	1784-88
Will.	Mankin	1730	Matthew	Bellew	1790
Whitney	Swarbridge	1752	(apprenticed, Dublin, 1778)		
(apprenticed, Dublin, 1741)					

Names of other Belfast goldsmiths registered in the books of the Dublin Goldsmiths' Company from 1784 to 1821 inclusive will be found on page 674 *ante*. The greater part of these were probably dealers rather than manufacturers, as very little plate appears to have been wrought in Belfast during that period. It is, however, recorded that plate was assayed in Dublin in 1809 for Will. Doyle of Belfast, and in 1819 for H. Gardener of Belfast.

* Matthew Bellew, son of Rebecca Bellew of Londonderry, was apprenticed to Patrick Walsh, jeweller, Dublin, in 1778.

KINSALE.

The name of " William Walsh " occurs in Kinsale records as having, on " March 19th 1687," been " sworn Master of the Company of Black-smiths, Goldsmiths, Silversmiths, Cutlers, Glaziers, Braziers, and other Hammermen that work by fire ".   It is also recorded that in "1689 Thomas Meade, goldsmith, was admitted to the freedom of the borough," and in 1733 the names of Joseph and William Wall of Kinsale * occur in the records of the Dublin Goldsmiths' Company with reference to plate sent by them to Dublin to be assayed.   The names of Dennis Leary and Robt. Barry, of Kinsale, are found in the same records for 1784. The reader is referred to marks probably attributable to Joseph Wall or William Wall (or both) illustrated at 1700 and 1710 respectively in the table of Irish unascribed marks on page 716 *infra*.   It appears, therefore, that Kinsale was not without its craft of goldsmiths in the 17th and 18th centuries, but no plate stamped with marks which can with certainty be identified with the town having come to the Author's knowledge, it is not practicable to illustrate any example.

OTHER IRISH PROVINCIAL TOWNS.

There is very little doubt that plate was manufactured in many of the walled towns of the pale in the 16th, 17th and 18th centuries.   It was impracticable, for reasons already explained, to send plate from distant places to Dublin to be assayed, and it seems probable that provincial goldsmiths adopted marks of their own (possibly one or more of the charges from their corporate arms, as in the case of Cork), which in con-junction with the maker's mark served as a warranty of the quality of their wares.

DERRY (or Londonderry) was a city of great importance in the 16th and 17th centuries, and three goldsmiths of that city were registered in the books of the Dublin Goldsmiths' Company in 1784, one in 1811 and another in 1814, but the only known example of Londonderry work appears to be a silver breast plate bearing the mark L.DERRY P.McC., noted by Mr. Dudley Westropp as that of Patrick McConigal.

A chalice of about 1660 in Cloyne Cathedral, co. Cork, has inscribed on it : " *John Moore de Bandon fecit*," which seems to indicate that a

---

* Joseph Wall mentioned 1712, died 1734.   William Wall mentioned 1721, died 1736.

small town like Bandon, in the southern part of the county of Cork, was not without its goldsmith in the 17th century.

It is recorded in the books of the Dublin Goldsmiths' Company that a "pretended goldsmith" in KILKENNY was prosecuted for selling worthless plate in 1687, and it can scarcely be supposed that a city of such importance as Kilkenny had no *real* goldsmiths in the 17th century. What may be the mark of Mark Kelly of Kilkenny is given at 1690 in the table of Irish unascribed marks on page 716 *infra*. Five Kilkenny goldsmiths registered their names in Dublin in the 18th century, and three others registered there in the early part of the 19th century, but the Author has not been able to glean any information concerning the work of any of them. The last remark is also applicable to the goldsmiths of WATERFORD, of whom eight registered their names in Dublin in 1784, and five others registered between that year and 1812.

A chalice at Fethard, co. Tipperary, of about the middle of the 17th century, bears the marks here illustrated :—

A similar castle to that stamped on this chalice is found on Kilkenny tokens of *c*. 1657, and as a goldsmith named Edward Rothe is said to have lived in Kilkenny, 1609-24 (*Collectania de Diebus Hibernia*), this chalice may have been wrought by a goldsmith of that name.

In DROGHEDA and NEWRY there appears to have been a number of goldsmiths in the 18th century. Of the former town five were registered in 1784, and of the latter town nine were registered in 1784-5.

The names of the provincial goldsmiths referred to, and of a large number of others entered in the books of the Dublin Goldsmiths' Company in the period 1784-1827, in compliance with the provisions of the Act of 1783, are set forth in connection with the Company's records on pages 674-6, but as dealers as well as makers of gold and silver wares throughout Ireland were obliged by that Act to register their names and places of abode with the company of goldsmiths in Dublin, and as the category to which they belong is not registered, it may be that many of them were mere dealers and not goldsmiths or plate workers.

NEW GENEVA (co. Waterford).

In 1783 a number of Continental protestant immigrants who had been subjected to persecution in their own country found a refuge in Ireland. Many of them were Swiss watch-makers and working gold-smiths and jewellers from Geneva. They settled at a place which they called New Geneva, near Waterford, about a mile and a half lower down the Suir than Passage East. For their assistance and encouragement the Irish Parliament passed an Act (23 & 24 George III., c. 23) which came into operation on 1 June, 1784. These immigrants were granted an assay office and an assayer, and the following marks were prescribed for being stamped on their wares :—

FOR GOLD.

22 CARATS.	20 CARATS.	18 CARATS.
Harp crowned, and *erased*, *i.e.*, with a bar across its strings.	A plume of two feathers.	A unicorn's head, *gorged*, *i.e.*, with a collar round its neck.

This is the only instance of a statutory assay office having been set up in any part of Ireland other than Dublin. An expenditure of about £30,000 was contemplated for the establishment of these people in their settlement, and for a short time an attempt appears to have been made to carry on the manufacture of watches and jewelry. Plate does not appear to have been wrought by them. Very soon after their arrival they showed signs of discontent, their success not having been equal to their expectations, and they complained that the Government proposed to impose a tax on gold workmanship with respect to their tenements, and shortly after they returned to their own country.* The buildings which had been erected for their use were during the "rising" of 1798 converted into military barracks.

* It appears that from first to last, work was not carried on at New Geneva, and there seems to be no evidence obtainable as to any plate having been wrought there.

UNASCRIBED IRISH PROVINCIAL MARKS.

The marks illustrated below have been found on plate (apparently of Irish manufacture), in various parts of Ireland, but their origin has not in most cases been traced.

The dates are merely approximate and are derived mainly from dates inscribed on the articles named.

DATE (ABOUT).	MARKS.	ARTICLES AND OWNERS.
1611		Communion cup and cover, dated 1611: St. Nicholas-without-the-walls, Dublin.
1650		Stamped twice on tankard: Noted by Mr. Dudley Westropp.
1652		Chalice, dated 1652: The late Mr. R. Day, F.S.A.
1666		(Probably mark of Abel Ram, Dublin.) Alms dish, inscribed "*ex dono Nehemiæ Donelan*, 1666": Trinity College, Dublin.
1673		Broth basin and cover, inscribed "*ex dono J. B.*, 1673": The Author's Collection.
1680		Trifid spoon (pricked "1680"): Mr. Dudley Westropp. See Cork, 1680, and Dublin, 1696.
,,		Communion paten, on foot: St. Anne's, Belfast.
1682		Surgeon's bleeding bowl: Mr. Jas. Magee.
,,		Plain bowl, dated 1682: Noted by Mr. Dudley Westropp in Westmeath.
1690		Mark of Mark Kelly of Kilkenny (?) On chalice: Noted by Mr. Dudley Westropp.
1700		(Probably mark of J. or W. Wall, Kinsale.) The punch ladle of Kinsale: Captain Cramer.
1705		Three-pronged forks with wavy ends: Noted by Mr. Dudley Westropp.
1710		Stamped thrice on plate: Noted by Mr. Dudley Westropp.
,,		Do. do. on spoons with wavy ends: Do. do. do. See W at 1700 above.
1720		Salver on foot: Mrs. French.
1720-40		(? mark of Michael Coldwell of Cork.) Harp-handled cup: Noted by Mr. Dudley Westropp.
1726		Mark of Anthony Walsh (?) On chalice, dated 1726, when given to the Chapel of St. John, Waterford.
,,		Mark of Charles Morgan, on cup: Castleton Roche.
1750		Stamped thrice on mug: Noted by Mr. Dudley Westropp.
1756		Mark of John St. John, Dublin: Do. do. do.
1760		Stamped thrice on sauce-boat: Do. do. do.
,,		Mounts of shell snuff-box: Do. do. do.
1780		Stamped thrice on sauce-boat: Do. do. do.
,,		Stamped four times on lemon strainer: Do. do. do.
,,		On table-spoon: Do. do. do.

UNASCRIBED MARKS

WHICH CANNOT BE ALLOCATED DEFINITELY TO AN ENGLISH, SCOTCH OR IRISH MAKER OR PLACE OF ORIGIN.

DATE (ABOUT).	MARKS.	ARTICLES AND OWNERS.
1574		Cup and paten cover: Mr. H. D. Ellis. Also on communion cup at Eglwys Cymmyn, Carm., and on a number of communion cups in Cardiganshire and Pembrokeshire.
1590	COK *	On foot of chalice, characteristic of massing chalice of Roman Catholic Church: The Day Collection.
1660		Struck thrice on apostle spoon: Mr. H. D. Ellis.
1680		Rat-tail spoon: Mr. Llewellyn Davies.
,,		Mug, embossed and chased: Messrs. Jay Richard Attenborough & Co.
1700		Cylindrical box for holding nutmeg and grater: Mr. Harry Alston.
,,		Flat-stemmed spoon, pricked 1701: Mr. A. Gillman.
1730		Cream ewer: Mr. E. Assheton Bennett.
1740-50		Tripod salt: Mr. G. W. Rudkin.
,,		On four candlesticks of baluster form: Mr. Louis Wine.†
1770		Stamped twice on pierced mustard pot: Noted by Mr. Dudley Westropp.
1780	T·B·BROWN	Bright cut spoons: Noted by Mr. Dudley Westropp.
1800	H·FOSTER	Fiddle pattern spoons: Noted by Mr. Dudley Westropp.

* See James Cok, Edinburgh, 1563, pp. 498 and 510 *ante*.

† See mark of Coline Allan of Aberdeen, whose mark (illustrated on p. 533 *ante*) this resembles. The luce or pike's head may perhaps be connected with the fish mark of Banff, see p. 540 *ante*. *Three lucies haurient argent* for Lucy, are borne in the shield of Henry, Earl of Northumberland.

ADDENDA.

The following illustrations represent marks found since the preceding pages were printed :—

LONDON MARKS.

1664-5		Maker's mark of John Wasson (accompanied by the London hall marks of 1664-5), on covered tankard: Mr. J. I. Jefferson.
1714-5		Maker's mark of Richard Williams (accompanied by the London hall marks of 1714-5), on caster: Dr. Wilfred Harris.
,,		Marks found on five small table forks: Mr. A. S. Marsden Smedley. The maker's mark is probably that of John Wisdom.
1722-3		Maker's mark of Christopher Canner (probably), on octagonal tea-pot: Mr. W. H. Willson.

YORK MARKS.

1681-2		York marks of 1681-2, and the maker's mark of Joshua Geldart, stamped on a beaker belonging to Dr. Wilfred Harris.

CHESTER MARKS.

c. 1692		These marks occur on a paten, dated 1692, at Gnosall, Staffs, and should be compared with those in Table I. of the Chester marks, page 387 *ante*.
c. 1695		On standing cup: noted by the Author.

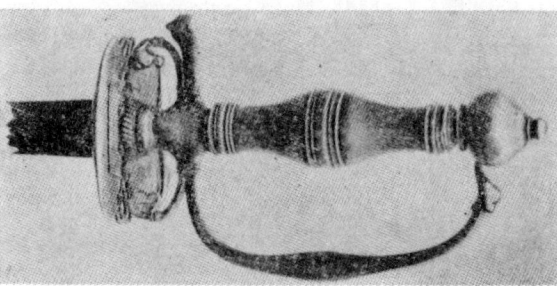

The illustration here given represents a 17th century silver sword-hilt stamped with a maker's mark only, namely **IG** The name of the maker has not been traced, and there being no other accompanying mark, it can only be stated that the sword-hilt is believed to be the work of an English provincial goldsmith.

The maker's mark is somewhat similar to that on a mace given 1685 to the Wilton Corporation, as noted on page 484 *ante*.

The sword has its original leather scabbard, and is in the collection of Mr. A. S. Marsden Smedley.

INDEX.

Marks comprising two or more letters are indexed under the first letter of the pair or group. Marks composed of intertwined letters are indexed under each letter appearing in the monogram. Devices where accompanied by initials are indexed under the first initial letter.

Marks consisting of devices difficult to identify by a short description, will be found in *facsimile* at the end of the index.

Every maker's mark contained in this book is indexed alphabetically. By referring to the indicated page the mark will be found illustrated in *facsimile*. In every ascertained case the name of the maker is connected with his mark, and where marks consist of or comprise initials the names to which they pertain are, by means of their initials, indexed also. Those goldsmiths' names which are printed in chronological order under their respective local headings, and occupy over a hundred pages of the book, are not repeated in this index, because the repetition of those surnames in alphabetical order would—except for the very short period when the Britannia standard was enforced in England— afford no help either to the plate collector or the dealer. As explained on page 236 *ante*, the manner in which the names are printed in the lists—the initials being in line vertically, with a clear space before the first letter of the surname—facilitates the finding of any particular name. The increase in the bulk of the book, which would have been caused by the repetition of about twelve thousand names has therefore been avoided.

The lists of goldsmiths' names will be found indexed under the names of the towns to which they respectively pertain.

[See next page for facsimiles.

THE FOLLOWING MARKS, WHICH CONSIST MAINLY OF DEVICES, ARE INDEXED *IN FACSIMILE*, BECAUSE THEY MAY IN THIS WAY BE MORE EASILY IDENTIFIED THAN BY THE DESCRIPTIONS UNDER WHICH THEY ARE ALREADY INDEXED.

THE END.

NEWCASTLE UPON TYNE
REFERENCE LIBRARY

267012